Paul Robert Magocsi is a Research
Fellow at the Harvard Ukrainian
Research Institute.

The Shaping of a
National Identity

Subcarpathian Rus',
1848-1948

Harvard Ukrainian Series
Published under the sponsorship of
The Harvard Ukrainian Research Institute

The Shaping of a National Identity

Subcarpathian Rus',
1848-1948

Paul Robert Magocsi

Harvard University Press
Cambridge, Massachusetts
London, England
1978

Copyright © 1978 by the President and Fellows of Harvard College
All rights reserved
Printed in the United States of America

Library of Congress Cataloging in Publication Data
Magocsi, Paul R
    The shaping of a national identity.
    (Harvard Ukrainian series)
    Bibliography: p.
    Includes index.
    1. Zakarpatskaya oblast'—History. I. Title.
II. Series.
DK511.Z3M345   301.5'92   77-5476
ISBN 0-674-80579-8

For Maria

Preface

This is the first of several monographs now in preparation, each of which deals with national movements among certain ethnic groups. In choosing groups for analysis, I have tried to select those located in border areas and under the influence of several cultures, as well as those for which the scholarly literature is either limited or nonexistent. Future studies will treat national movements among the Galician Ukrainians, the Macedonians, and the Luxembourgers. It is hoped that the methodological and organizational principles used in this work on Subcarpathian Rusyns will be applicable to those studies still in preparation.

While still a graduate student, I remember reading the introductions to several studies, all of which almost mechanically had a section with acknowledgments. At the time I thought this practice hackneyed and vowed not to do it myself. However, after undertaking a work such as this, I have been sufficiently humbled and now realize that it could not have been done without the invaluable help of numerous individuals and institutions. To these I feel greatly indebted and wish to mention here those who contributed more than they might realize.

I was one of the last of a generation that was generously supported by funds stemming from the boom in area-studies programs during the 1960s. As a result, I was able to experience the excellent individual-oriented graduate program at Princeton University, and I received grants for archival research in Czechoslovakia (1969-1970) from the International Research and Exchanges Board and for two summers of language study in Hungary (1974 and 1975) from the American Council of Learned Societies. Unencumbered postgraduate time was provided by Harvard University, first through the Committee on Ukrainian Studies and then for three years in the gracious (and sumptuous) atmosphere of the Society of Fellows.

My research would have been much less productive without the cooperation and assistance of the staffs at the Slovanská Knihovna (Slavonic Library), Universitní Knihovna (University Library), Národní Museum (National Museum), and the now abolished Historický Ústav ČSAV (Historical

Institute of the Czechoslovak Academy of Sciences), all in Prague; the Knižnica Univerzity Komenského (Comenius University Library) and Štátný Slovenský Ústredný Archív (Slovak State Central Archive) in Bratislava; the Okresna Knižnica (Regional Library), Okresný Archív (Regional Archive), and the Doslidnyi Kabinet Ukraïnistyky (Ukrainian Research Center) of the P. J. Šafárik University in Prešov; and the Muzei Ukraïns'koho Kul'tury (Museum of Ukrainian Culture) in Svidník. Materials from these institutions were generally made available without restriction. This was largely possible because the favorable atmosphere of the Prague Spring was still operative. But as I was frequently reminded, after 1970 it would have been impossible to work in Czechoslovakia on such a "taboo" subject as Subcarpathian Rus'.

Other major research centers in which I was privileged to work were the Országos Széchényi Könyvtár (Széchényi National Library) and Magyar Tudományos Akadémia Történettudományi Intézete (Institute of Historical Research of the Hungarian Academy of Sciences) in Budapest; the Kossuth Lajos Tudományegyetem Egyetemi Könyvtár (Lajos Kossuth University Library) in Debrecen; the Matica Slovenská (Slovak National Society) in Martin; Widener Library and the International Law Library at Harvard University; the New York Public Library; and the University of Illinois Library. Particular appreciation is extended to Zdeněk David, then of the Princeton University Library, Jan Stěpan, Harvard Law School Library, and especially my good friend Edward Kasinec, research bibliographer and librarian at the Harvard Ukrainian Research Institute.

I was fortunate to have had several specialists review all or part of the text and to have received substantial conceptual and factual criticism. At the initial dissertation stage the readers included Cyril E. Black, Zdeněk David, Karl W. Deutsch, John Fizer, George Florovsky, Orest Pelech, Omeljan Pritsak, Roman Szporluk, and Charles F. Townsend. The completely revised and expanded present version was read in whole or in part by István Deák, Joshua Fishman, Robert A. Kann, Edward Kasinec, Béla Kiraly, Horace G. Lunt, Victor S. Mamatey, Vojtech Mastny, Athanasius B. Pekar, Ivan L. Rudnytsky, Avhustyn Shtefan, and Bohdan Strumins'kyj. I am particularly grateful to Omeljan Pritsak, editor-in-chief of the Harvard Series in Ukrainian Studies, who spent numerous hours discussing all aspects of the problem and continually encouraged me to complete the book. By the same token, special appreciation is extended to Edward Kasinec, who not only helped to conceptualize the bibliography but also made financial support for the volume possible. Each of these distinguished scholars has with good will tried to improve the book, and whatever faults remain must be credited solely to myself.

Parts of Chapter 4 were previously published in the *East European Quarterly* (vol. 10, no. 3, pp. 347-365 [1976]) and the *Slavic Review* (vol. 34, no.

2, pp. 360-381 [June 1975]). Appreciation is extended to the editors for permission to reprint materials from those journals.

The quality of a work such as this also depends largely on the technical expertise of several persons. Among these I must salute Eliza McClennan, who drew the excellent maps, Michael K. Bourke and Olga K. Mayo, who assisted in the completion of the bibliography, Pál Morvay, Josef Staša, and Bohdan Strumins'kyj, who proofread the notes and bibliography, and Dorothea Donker, my indefatigable and almost superhumanly precise Dutch-Indonesian typist. This study was very long in the making, but it was fascinating at every turn. In times of less intense work, the subject's appeal was reinforced by many conversations with the historical figures Vasyl' Grendzha-Dons'kyi, Iuliian Revai, and Avhustyn Shtefan. Finally, deepest respect must be paid to the person who lived with this work more than one would imagine, my dearest wife, Maria Čuvanová Magocsi.

P. R. M.

Contents

Part 2. The Cultural Setting

Part 3. The Political Environment

Maps

The Shaping of a
National Identity

Introduction

This book is a study of nationalism. More specifically, it analyzes how one ethnic group was exposed to nationalism and how its leaders accepted and then presented this new ideology to the people they represented. The Subcarpathian Rusyns[1] are the people in question and during the century 1848-1948 they went through the process of national consolidation. Because the Subcarpathian region is a border area between many cultures, Rusyn national development was particularly complex. Subcarpathian Rusyn society was continually being influenced by neighboring cultures that proved attractive to various factions of the local intelligentsia. During the process of national consolidation, Subcarpathian leaders were not only concerned with fostering a national consciousness among a particular ethnic group, they were also engaged in a struggle over which national orientation to accept. Such a twofold process in national development is quite typical of many ethnic groups in border areas or zones of transitional cultures. For instance, Luxembourgers, Alsatians, Belorussians, and Macedonians, to name but a few, have undergone similar experiences.

Although much has been written about nationalism, the exact nature of the subject has not been defined. Several definitions, some complimentary, others contradictory, have been offered; one writer even concluded that "nationalism may mean whatever a given people, on the basis of their own historical experience, decide it to mean."[2] Nor has there been any agreement on when the movement began—whether in the late Middle Ages, or in the seventeenth or early nineteenth centuries. The disagreement may be due to differences in the stage of development of particular societies and the degree to which national awareness has been adopted by certain classes, whether the nobility, bourgeoisie, or the working masses. Frequently, the period following the French Revolution is viewed as the era when nationalism really came into its own, for only then did the necessary political and social changes take place, allowing all segments and classes of society to be receptive to a new ideology. Of course, such a trend had begun in the Netherlands and England as early as the sixteenth and seventeenth centuries.[3]

1

Although this study will not address itself to the kind of definitional problems that continue to plague historians and social scientists, nonetheless, certain terms must be defined: ethnographic group, ethnic group, nationality, national group, people, national consciousness, nation, nationalism, and patriotism.

The first five terms are closely related. An ethnic group is a population that in most cases possesses a distinct territory, common traditions, and related dialects. Ethnographers frequently distinguish specific characteristics and further divide ethnic groups into ethnographic groups encompassing a cluster of villages or larger area clearly distinguishable by certain characteristics of language or material culture.[4] Hence, the Subcarpathian Rusyn ethnic group may be divided into Lemkian, Boikian, and Hutsul ethnographic groups—the distinguishing features being primarily linguistic.

A nationality, people, or national group—terms used interchangeably here—usually possess the same characteristics as an ethnic group. There is, however, one crucial difference. Members of a given nationality are clearly aware of the interrelationship between themselves and their co-nationals, and they know or think that they constitute a social group distinct from all others. This awareness may be labeled national consciousness, and it is the possession of this quality, or state of mind, that allows for the transformation of an ethnic group into a nationality.

The term nation is frequently confused with nationality, particularly in working with Slavic peoples, because the term *narod* (people, nationality) is often rendered as nation. In English, however, the term nation suggests loyalty to a state or country, which may be inhabited by many nationalities. In our study, then, nationality, people, or national group on the one hand will be distinguished from nation, state, or country on the other.[5] To illustrate, France is a nation or state composed of the French, Breton, Flemish, and Basque nationalities. It is not clear whether Alsatians and Occitans should be considered ethnic groups or nationalities, for this depends on the extent of their national consciousness. Similarly, the pre-1918 Hungarian Kingdom was a nation or state that included Magyar, Rumanian, German, Croat, and Serbian nationalities, as well as Slovaks and Rusyns, ethnic groups trying to develop into nationalities. It may be mentioned that those nationalities living in multinational states are often referred to as national minorities.

Nationalism and patriotism are less difficult to define. Nationalism is an ideology, professing that humanity is divided into nationalities, that national self-government is the only form of government, and that political sovereignty or some form of independence is the primary goal. Patriotism, which is frequently confused with the more complex nationalism, is viewed here as simply an expression of love for one's own native land or immediate surroundings.[6]

The view that one is *not* born with a nationality is an assumption that underlies this study. An individual may be born into a definable ethnic group, but the attainment of a national consciousness and hence member-ship in a nationality is a process that has to be achieved through ideological and social indoctrination.[7] Hence, it is possible that individuals raised in border areas, which are surrounded by or include many ethnic groups, may in the course of a lifetime have the opportunity of being associated with one or more nationalities. Awareness of this premise is crucial for the proper understanding of ethnic groups in the developmental stage of national con-solidation.

National movements may be divided into two broad types: (1) those in which an already existing state, working through common political institu-tions, forms a nationality; or (2) those in which the leaders of an ethnic group (sometimes a minority in a multinational state) transform their con-stituencies into a nationality that then strives, and in many cases achieves, political sovereignty or independence. To the first group belong countries like France, Britain, Spain, the United States, and, in recent times, the emerging African nations. To the second group belong the former East European national minorities like the Czechs, Rumanians, and Bulgarians, as well as the Subcarpathian Rusyns.[8]

There is no doubt that the intelligentsia usually plays a leading role in national movements, particularly in multinational states where ruling governments do not foster and may even hinder developments among their minorities. It is the role of the intelligentsia to record the history and tradi-tions of a given ethnic group, codify its dialects into a literary language, and transform an individual's awareness of his relationship to a neighboring villager, valley-dweller, or co-religionist into a consciousness of unity on a wider, "national" level. Hence, any study of national development must focus on the intelligentsia and analyze the means it uses to propagate the national idea.[9]

The period in which the intelligentsia undertakes the "national awaken-ing" may be called the embryonic stage of national development. This crucial stage is usually one of internal struggle, when the leadership attempts to define acceptable linguistic, educational, literary, and religious guidelines so that the national movement may be unified when it enters the political struggle. Indeed, this embryonic stage has occurred at different times for different peoples; the Czechs and Germans developed an acceptable na-tional ideology before 1848, the Slovaks and Ukrainians did so during the second third of the nineteenth century, the Macedonians in the mid-twentieth century, and several African and Asian peoples are still doing so today.

The Subcarpathian Rusyns have been a relative latecomer in the process of national consolidation. Their intelligentsia seriously began the national awakening around 1848, and it was not until a century later that the process of national consolidation could be considered complete. During these hundred years the leaders tried to formulate an acceptable national ideology, although in the course of this struggle they were in conflict as much with themselves as with the powers that ruled them. The task of making individuals in the Rusyn ethnic group aware of their national identity was complicated by the fact that the intelligentsia itself remained for the longest time undecided as to what that identity should actually be. At first, many felt that Subcarpathian Rusyns should become Hungarians. When affiliation with a Slavic national identity became the preferred choice, there resulted a debate as to whether a Russian, Ukrainian, or independent Rusyn identity should be adopted.

This study will analyze in detail how the intelligentsia formulated a national ideology and how it was implemented. The most important period in this embryonic stage was the last thirty years, roughly from 1918 to 1948. This does not mean that a national awakening and subsequent debate had not occurred before. They had. However, the greatly restricted opportunities for education and the increase in state-supported Hungarian assimilationist efforts before 1918 did not permit an unhampered, broad-based national movement, which only took place under the Czechoslovak regime. Consequently, the years after 1918 will be the focus of attention.

After an introductory discussion describing the physical environment of the Subcarpathian Rusyns, two chapters will trace cultural and national developments before 1918. A separate chapter will view the crucial 1918-1919 period and analyze how Subcarpathian Rus' became a part of Czechoslovakia. Then I will turn to the heart of the matter—the national ideology worked out by the intelligentsia. Separate chapters will deal with the classic elements associated with nationalism: history, language, literary and cultural developments, education, and religion. The ideological basis of the national movement having been provided, three chapters will place these developments in the actual environment in order to see how local, national, and international politics influenced the success or failure of the conflicting national ideologies.

As for technical matters, I have tried to make the best of a complex linguistic situation. The Library of Congress transliteration system (without diacritical marks) is used for materials published in Russian and Ukrainian. For works that appear in Rusyn dialect and in the Subcarpathian recension of Russian (the *iazychie*), the Ukrainian pattern is employed with the following additions: ô = ô, ы = ŷ, ѣ = î. Because of the ideological significance of the traditional orthography (etymological alphabet), all titles and other references have been rendered in the original. Final hard signs (ъ) have been omitted.

Place names have been given according to the official form used in the country where they are presently located. Thus, Prešov is rendered in Slovak, Uzhhorod in Ukrainian. The first time a Subcarpathian town or village is mentioned in the text, the former Magyar name is given in parentheses. Historical geopolitical units are given in the predominant language used for most of the time that they existed. This pertains in particular to the pre-1918 Hungarian counties, which are given in Magyar.

Personal names appearing in the text have been transliterated in accordance with an individual's national orientation. Thus, the Ukrainian form Voloshyn, not Voloshin or Vološin; the Russian Fentsik, not Fentsyk or Fencik; and the Rusyn dialectal Stryps'kyi, not Sztripszky, or Stripskii. In most cases, the Ukrainian and Rusyn transliterated forms are synonymous. For those figures active before 1848, the Rusyn form of their name is given. When citing works in the footnotes, however, the form used is determined by the printed text. Materials written in Russian or Rusyn dialect but employing the Latin alphabet are cited as in the original (*karpatorusskoje, sojedinenije,* for example). This includes Rusyn immigrant activists in the United States, whose names are given in the Latin script. Where available, the dates of birth and death are included the first time a Subcarpathian activist is mentioned. More complete biographical information on leaders active during the twentieth century appears in Appendix 2. Names of bishops are followed by dates indicating birth, death, and date of consecration. Names of rulers (kings, emperors) are followed by the dates of their reigns.

With regard to terminology, Russophile refers to a native of Subcarpathian Rus' who favors the Russian national orientation. Similarly, Ukrainophile suggests allegiance to the Ukrainian orientation and Rusynophile to the Rusyn. The term *narodovets'* is rendered as populist-Ukrainophile, *russkii* (with double *s*) as Russian, *rus'kyi* as Rusyn. The phrase "traditional orthography" denotes the so-called etymological Cyrillic alphabet, which retained symbols like the *iat* (ѣ), *iery* (ы), and hard sign (ъ). Modern orthography denotes the more phonetic alphabet adopted by Subcarpathian Ukrainophiles at various times, but never by Russophiles.

Part
One | **Background**

1 | *The Geographic, Ethnographic, and Socioeconomic Setting*

Geographic Location

At first glance, the name Subcarpathian Rus' may seem rather esoteric and suggest to the reader some exotic land located far away from the centers of European civilization. However, if we look at a map of the European continent as it stretches from the Irish and Portuguese coasts in the west to the Ural Mountains in the east and from the Cape of Norway in the north to Crete in the south, we see that Subcarpathian Rus' falls practically in the very middle.

Since the sixth century, the ancestors of the Subcarpathian Rusyns have inhabited the southern slopes and adjacent valleys of the Carpathian Mountains. Until 1919, their homeland was an integral part of the multinational Hungarian Kingdom, a political entity that was itself divided into sixty-three counties (*megye, comitat*). It was in the northeastern part of that Kingdom, primarily in thirteen counties, that Rusyn villages were to be found. In none of these counties did Rusyns form a majority of the population, and only in seven of them did they represent even a substantial portion of the total number of inhabitants. Moving from west to east, the counties most heavily populated by Rusyns (according to the last Hungarian census of 1910) were: Szepes (7.1 percent), Sáros (22 percent), Zemplén (11.4 percent), Ung (38.1 percent), Bereg (42.6 percent), Ugocsa (37.5 percent), and Máramaros (44.6 percent).[1]

Because of the shortcomings of statistical information, especially for national minorities, it is difficult to determine the exact number of Rusyns. During the nineteenth century, the estimates varied greatly. As is evident from Tables 1 and 2 (see Appendix 4), there are great discrepancies between the various unofficial estimates and official census reports. This was particularly the case during the nineteenth century, with some writers suggesting as many as 800,000 Subcarpathian Rusyns, others as few as 342,000. The most recent figure, which is relatively reliable, indicates that in 1970 there were 850,277 Rusyns living within the borders of two states: the Trans-

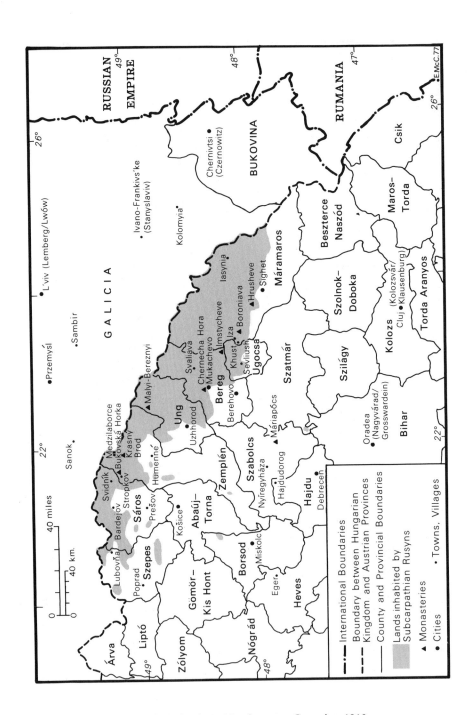

Hungarian Kingdom, Northeastern Counties, 1910

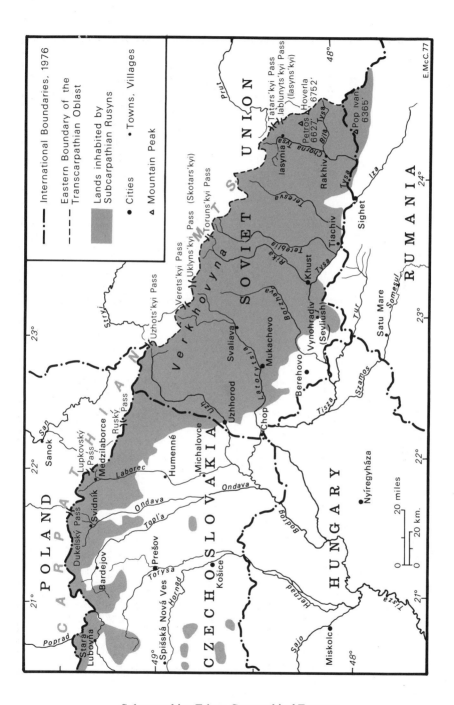

Subcarpathian Ethno-Geographical Features

carpathian Oblast' of the Soviet Ukrainian Socialist Republic and the Slovak Socialist Republic.

In terms of settlement patterns, Rusyn villages are generally located in mountainous regions, so that the geographical boundary between mountain and plain coincides in large measure with the ethnographic boundary between Rusyns to the north and Magyars or Slovaks to the south. Rusyn-inhabited territory covers about 8,820 square miles (14,700 square kilometers) and in 1938 the average population density was only 49 persons per square kilometer. Almost half the territory had a population density of less than 25, since most Rusyns lived along the lower slopes and valleys near the ethno-geographic boundary, where their density was recorded at 85 persons per square kilometer.[2]

The pattern for natural, and later man-made, transportational systems was determined by the fact that the Subcarpathian region is part of the Danubian Basin. Although there are a few passes that allow for some contact with the north, for the most part the high crests of the Carpathian Mountains separate the Subcarpathians from their Rusyn/Ukrainian brethren in southern Galicia. Moreover, isolation from the north was reinforced when these same mountain crests formed the political boundary of the Hungarian Kingdom whose government, especially during the nineteenth century, became adamant about restricting contacts between the Subcarpathians and their Galician brethren. The rivers, paths, and, later, the roads and railroads adapted to the physical setting and were laid out primarily in a north-south direction. As a result, the Subcarpathian villager was effectively cut off from his neighbor in an adjacent valley, and in several instances found it easier to travel southward along the tributaries of the Tisa River toward the lowland plain region than to move west or east. Hence, contact among Rusyns was severely limited and frequently achieved only in a Magyar or Slovak environment. Such geographical factors limited the possibility for communication between Rusyns and consequently contributed to a retardation of the development of a national consciousness.[3]

Ethno-Cultural Setting

The Subcarpathian Rusyns inhabit an ethnographic border region and as a result have been influenced by peoples in surrounding territories. Most important among these are the Galician Rusyns or Ukrainians north of the Carpathian Mountains, the Slovaks immediately to the west and southwest, and the Magyars on the lowland plains to the south. There have also been several other groups living within Rusyn ethnographic territories: Jews were once a major portion of the urban and a smaller part of the rural population, Gypsies have traditionally lived on the outskirts of most Rusyn villages, Germans have inhabited a few villages near Mukachevo (Munkács) and Svaliava (Szolyva), and Rumanians have lived along the farthest southeastern portion of Rusyn territory. Added to these have been the civil servants and government officials who have come with new regimes that ruled the area: Magyars, Czechs, Russians.

More specifically, let us look at the figures from the comprehensive census of 1930. Out of a total of 725,357 people living in Subcarpathian Rus', there were 446,916 (63 percent) Rusyns; 109,472 (15.4 percent) Magyars; 91,255 (12.8 percent) Jews; 20,719 (2.9 percent) Czechs; 13,249 (1.8 percent) Germans; 13,242 (1.8 percent) Slovaks; 12,641 (1.7 percent) Rumanians; 1,357 (0.9 percent) Gypsies; and the remainder, Poles, Serbo-Croats, and other foreigners. As of 1970, the only substantial change in this ethnic mix was the virtual elimination of the Jews (due to forcible deportation in 1944) and Czechs (due to departing civil servants), the latter being replaced by Russians who numbered 35,189 (3.3 percent) of the population.[4] The presence of these various groups has inevitably had an influence on Rusyn life-style and culture.

The Subcarpathian Rusyns have traditionally been divided into ethnographic subunits. Some writers have used a linguistic criterion to distinguish the following dialectal groups: (1) the Lemkians or *Lemaky* in the west (Szepes, Sáros, and Zemplén counties), who are most heavily influenced by the neighboring Slovaks; (2) the Boikians in the central mountainous and lowland region (Ung, Bereg, and Ugocsa counties), where Hungarian influences are pronounced; and (3) the Hutsuls in the east (Máramaros county), who are part of a distinct ethnographic group that stretches into southeastern Galicia and northern Bukovina. It should be noted that this pattern of classification parallels that given for ethnographic groups living north of the Carpathians.[5] South of the mountains, however, neither the Lemkians nor Boikians use these names to describe themselves; rather they prefer the terms Rusnak, Rusyn, or *Verkhovynets'* (Highlander).[6] Subcarpathian Rusyns have also been divided by geographical criteria into (1) *Verkhovyntsi,* or Highlanders, those who inhabit the upper mountainous regions; and (2) *Dolyshniany,* or Lowlanders, those who live in the regions closer to the plains. Some writers have combined both the linguistic and geographical patterns in describing Subcarpathian ethnographic groups.[7]

On the whole, Subcarpathian Rusyns have been equally influenced by, and in turn have influenced, neighboring Galician-Ukrainian, Slovak, and Magyar cultures.[8] Indeed, at various times, Hungarian, Slovak, Russian, and Ukrainian nationalist writers have argued that in ethnic terms (and, they subsequently conclude, in national terms also) Subcarpathian Rusyns, either one ethnographic branch or all of them, should be considered as Hungarians, Slovaks, Russians, or Ukrainians, respectively. Such arguments, however, have not usually been based on the specific conditions of the Subcarpathian environment; rather, they have reflected the chauvinist hopes of nationalist propagandists who wanted to categorize neatly a complex situation that defies oversimplification.

To be sure, Subcarpathian Rusyns speak a range of dialects that are closely related to those spoken in eastern Galicia. The Subcarpathian varieties have been classified by linguists as belonging to the Ukrainian language, even if they diverge substantially from the Ukrainian literary norm. More important, however, is the fact that language *cannot* simply be equated with nationality. Language may or may not be an important element in distinguishing national groups. From the standpoint of material culture, Subcarpathian Rusyns have also shared elements with neighboring cultures. The wooden churches frequently associated with their culture are also found in the mountainous regions of Galician Ukrainian, Slovak, Moravian Czech, and Rumanian ethnic areas. Subcarpathian Rusyn folk dress is perhaps more similar to that of the eastern Slovaks and northeastern Magyars than to that of the Galician Ukrainians. On the other hand, the religious customs which Subcarpathians inherited from the latter were transferred to Slovaks and Magyars. And at the pervasive popular level, the *csardas* is as much the national dance of Subcarpathian Rusyns as of Slovaks and Magyars.

The point is that it is dangerous to presume simply on the basis of certain ethnographic characteristics that groups living in border regions must belong to one or another of the adjacent nationalities. The material culture of an ethnic group may be recorded, described, and associated with other national groups, but such work does not necessarily cause the subjects under consideration to be aware of a larger national identity. This is an ideological process in the course of which several possibilities are open to the ethnic group.

The choices, of course, are not limitless. It is not likely that local ideologists would be successful in convincing Subcarpathian Rusyns that they are or should be Frenchmen, Irishmen, or Chinese. Yet several other serious options have been open to them. In essence, as an ethnic group, Subcarpathian Rusyns could have been consolidated into an independent nationality or they could have associated and become a part of the Magyar, Slovak, Ukrainian, or Russian nationalities. The purpose of this study is to see which of these alternatives was eventually accepted and why one succeeded and the others failed.

Socioeconomic Status

Historically, Subcarpathian Rusyns have lived in small villages and have worked on the land or in the forest. Neither the "liberation" from serfdom in 1848, the "liberation" from Hungarian rule in 1918, the "liberation" from Czechoslovakia in 1939, nor even the "liberation" from fascism and bourgeois-capitalism in 1945, changed the situation.

In 1910, 70 percent of the Rusyn population lived in villages with less than 2,000 inhabitants, while another 23 percent lived in settlements with 2,000 to 3,000 inhabitants.[9] In 1910, 89.6 percent of Rusyns were either farmers, shepherds, or woodcutters, and that percentage decreased only slightly in subsequent years: to 83.1 percent in 1930 and 70 percent in 1956. By the same token, the urban proletarian element has remained small: only 3.4 percent of Rusyns worked in mining or industry in 1910, 5.8 percent in 1930, and 9 percent in 1956.[10] The Rusyn petit-bourgeoisie or professional class has always been miniscule in size; in 1910, less than 1 percent and in 1930 only 2.6 percent of Rusyns were postal or railroad workers, barbers, shoemakers, bakers, or other small tradesmen. Similarly, in 1910 less than 1 percent, and in 1930 only 2.5 percent, served as teachers, notaries, lawyers, priests, journalists or in the military. (See Table 3.)

The urban statistics for the two cities bordering on Rusyn ethnographic territory—Uzhhorod (Ungvár) and Mukachevo—confirm further the rural nature of the Subcarpathian Rusyn population. In Uzhhorod, the main cultural and administrative center, Rusyns made up only 4 percent of the inhabitants before 1918, and by 1930 they had increased to only one-quarter of the total population. The situation in Mukachevo was more or less similar. Although Prešov (Eperjes) was an important Rusyn cultural center, especially in the nineteenth century, it is within Slovak ethnic territory and has never had more than a small fraction of Rusyn inhabitants. As for Berehovo (Beregszász), it is well within Magyar ethnic territory and thus the number of Rusyns there also has always been small. (See Table 4.)

The largest groups in the urban areas—and those that made up the petty bourgeoisie and civil and administrative services—were Jews, Magyars, and, in the twentieth century, Czechs and later Russians. The Jews were generally the tradesmen,[11] the other groups the administrators. Before the deportation of the Jewish community in 1944, almost half of Mukachevo's population was Jewish, while in Uzhhorod Jews were slightly less than one-third of the population. Magyar officials and, to a lesser degree, Magyar tradesmen, formed a significant portion of Uzhhorod's population both before and after the change of regime in 1919, although after this date their number dropped by almost two-thirds in Mukachevo, Prešov, and Uzhhorod. During the 1920's, many Czechs arrived in Uzhhorod to administer the new province (their political and social influence greatly exceeded their actual numbers), and by 1930 they represented 17 percent of the population. In 1939, Czech administrators were forced to leave and were replaced by Hungarians, while after 1945 the latter were largely replaced by Russians.[12] (See Table 4)

The Rusyns not only remained in small villages, they remained poor and illiterate. In 1910, only 22 percent of Rusyns over the age of six could read and write in their own language. This was at a time when the average literary rate was 45 percent in the Hungarian Kingdom; the rate was 67 percent among Magyars and 70 percent among Germans, and the lowest rate after the Rusyns, that of the Rumanians, was 28 percent.[13] Although we have been forced to employ data that is not exactly comparable, it is still useful to note that in 1930 only 58 percent of Rusyns older than ten years of age could read and write in their own language. Thus, even after a decade of extensive educational reforms by the Czechoslovak government, almost half the Rusyn populace was still illiterate.[14]

In essence, what do these statistics reveal and how did such conditions effect nationality developments? First, it is clear that throughout most of the period under analysis, the Subcarpathian Rusyn population was composed mainly of small agriculturalists who were born and who remained in small rural villages. Before the First World War, Rusyns lacked social mobility and failed to develop a bourgeois class out of which a national intelligentsia could have developed. This situation changed somewhat after 1918, but even then the social structure was balanced against the holding of any effective social or administrative power by Rusyns. As we shall see, the cultural and educational apparatus that did develop was staffed as much by Magyars and Czechs as by local Rusyns. Finally, poverty and illiteracy fostered economic, social, and intellectual immobility, a situation that made it even more difficult for the intelligentsia to develop a national movement and to create a national consciousness in the minds of the rural masses.

The Intelligentsia and Its Constituency

The intelligentsia and the peasant masses were the two most important groups in Subcarpathian Rus'. Their experiences differed greatly, as is evident from the composite portraits presented here, based in part on the biographies of leaders in Appendix 2. If we concentrate on those leaders active between 1918 and 1948, it is necessary to distinguish two generations among them: (1) those born before 1905, whose *Weltanschauung,* or state of mind, was formed during the Hungarian administration before the end of the First World War, and (2) those born after 1905, who developed in the considerably changed political atmosphere after 1918.

In the decades before 1918, a young Rusyn who wanted to pursue a career other than farming would most likely have entered the Greek Catholic Seminary in either Uzhhorod or Prešov, to become eventually a priest, teacher, or both. Those who entered the seminary were often the sons or grandsons of priests. Even for those young Rusyns who had already learned Magyar in the elementary schools of their native villages, it was still a shock to enter the completely Hungarian cultural and social environment of Uzhhorod and Prešov. Whereas Rusyn dialect and culture dominated the villages, the young student would find that Magyar was spoken in the dormitories, classrooms, on the streets and in the shops of the two towns. To survive in these new surroundings, one had to be proficient in the Magyar language; but in order to be truly successful, one had to accept both the internal (linguistic) and external (life style) forms of Hungarian civilization. Thus, education was likely to alienate a Rusyn from his own society; if a talented young man wanted to be anything in life, he would have to adopt the dominant Magyar culture and deemphasize, if not scorn, the Rusyn dialects and traditions of his younger years.

Nonetheless, out of this atmosphere came several individuals who could be described as Rusyn patriots, if not nationalists. Some of the better seminarians were sent each year to the Central Seminary in Budapest, and there they frequently discovered that their fellow students—Serbs, Croats, or Slovaks—were proud of their national cultures. Training in the Church-Slavonic liturgy, and the inevitable necessity to speak the "dialect" in the confessional or in the classroom, later forced some priests to function at least minimally within a Rusyn context. Moreover, contacts with Rusyns in Galicia and especially with returning immigrants from America had an enormous influence on the development of national consciousness. Publications from Galicia or from the United States made some Rusyns aware that not all cultural phenomena had to be Hungarian. Finally, the First World War, when some Rusyns served, and were even captured, on the Russian front, fostered a greater awareness and even pride in the Slavic nature of Rusyn culture.

Basically, however, that generation of the Rusyn intelligentsia educated before the First World War was the product of a religious environment in which Hungarian culture was the goal most worthy of achievement.

The generation of leaders brought up after 1918 entered a society that, in terms of Rusyn nationalism, was radically changed. First of all, in the new Czechoslovak state, a Rusyn no longer had to strive to be Hungarian. Slavic culture and Slavic brotherhood became the accepted ideals, even if it was not always clear what particular form would be adopted. The cultural shocks were less pronounced, for now Rusyn children could attend elementary and secondary schools where the local dialects or a related language were the media of instruction. The Greek Catholic Church lost its corner on the career-market and future Rusyn leaders tended to become teachers, lawyers, and civil servants, rather than priests. Prague, and to a lesser degree Bratislava, not Budapest, attracted university applicants, so that Slavic identity was further reinforced.

As a significant portion of this study will show, the Rusyn intelligentsia become convinced of its Slavic identity but was undecided whether its culture and nationality should be considered Russian, Ukrainian, or something unique. The point to be stressed here is that, unlike members of the pre-1918 intelligentsia, who at best might become local patriots, the new generation was transformed by education and by impinging political and social circumstances into becoming nationalists. Moreover, this nationalism carried within it a characteristic typical of many traditionalist societies—a heritage of religious attitudes, among which was the belief in absolutes. Hence, in most cases, members of the local intelligentsia became avid and often intolerant defenders of one point of view. Those Subcarpathians who became Ukrainophiles considered Ukrainianism as the only resolution to the problem of national identity. Similar staunch attitudes were adopted by local Russophiles and Rusynophiles.

The intellectual frame of reference for Subcarpathian leaders was limited both geographically and, in a real sense, genetically. Most spent the greater portion of their lives in Uzhhorod, Mukachevo, or Prešov, with perhaps short stays for educational or governmental purposes in Budapest, Prague, or Bratislava. As a result, they usually did not have the intellectual breadth to view their own national problem in a wider historical context. They carried a "cultural baggage" that included, among other things, a search for absolutes (perhaps the inevitable psychological state of all nationalists), and they strove to find a simple explanation for an otherwise extremely complicated ethnic and cultural problem. Many of the Subcarpathian nationalist leaders were related through blood or marriage. For instance, among the relatives of the nineteenth-century Russophile Evgenii Fentsik were, in the post-1918 generation, the avid Ukrainophile Avhustyn Shtefan and the Russophile Stefan Fentsik. Another relative was the pro-Hungarian proponent of a separate Rusyn nationality, Hiiador Stryps'kyi. These familial relations were more typical than exceptional, and, in addition, these supporters of conflicting and often antagonistic national orientations inevitably met on a frequent basis in the public places of towns whose populations were never more than 27,000. Consequently, the national movement among Subcarpathian Rusyns became to a large extent an internal struggle between a small number of intelligentsia trying to convince the rural masses, and especially each other, of the rightness (and righteousness) of their own explanation.

One final point concerning the Subcarpathian intelligentsia seems in order. Several writers, especially Marxist and non-Marxist Ukrainian scholars, have attempted to use socioeconomic factors to explain why individuals favored different national orientations.[15] In this regard, developments in twentieth-century Subcarpathian Rus' are viewed simply as a repetition of what happened in nineteenth-century Galicia. Briefly, this scenario states that Russophiles were of the older generation, politically conservative or "reactionary," and were sons of priests or rich landowners. Rusynophiles are usually described in the same terms. On the other hand, Ukrainophiles are said to be radical "progressives" whose parents were either from the working class (the peasantry) or from the "democratically-minded" intelligentsia (teachers).

This Russophile-Rusynophile versus Ukrainophile dichotomy has never been proved for Galicia, let alone Subcarpathian Rus', by any hard statistical data. Our modest analysis in Appendix 2 has revealed that there is no simple one-to-one relationship between age or social and economic status on the one hand and acquired national orientation on the other. In general, there is no great difference between the Russophiles and Ukrainophiles. Both were primarily sons of priests or peasants and became teachers, lawyers, or journalists. Here we do find that Rusynophiles follow a somewhat different pattern, since 40 percent of those surveyed were sons of priests who remained in the same calling as their fathers. As for differences in age, the Rusynophiles again stand out. Whereas among the older generation (born before 1905) there was an equal number representing each orientation, among the smaller sample from the second-generation, Russophiles and Ukrainophiles were equal and out-numbered Rusynophiles four to one. From this it might be concluded that only Rusynophiles fit the description given by Ukrainian writers. Of course, this would presume that priests are always conservative and peasants democratic revolutionaries, highly tenuous presumptions to say the least. The point is that socioeconomic status or age are not adequate to explain why individuals from the same region, and frequently from the same family, would join differing national orientations. The explanation for this phenomenon must be sought elsewhere, and some tentative answers will be provided in this study.

The distinction that might be drawn between two generations of the intelligentsia was not present among the rural peasantry. Peasant life, except for some details, was not significantly different before or after 1918. A careful review of several village church records reveals that more than 90 percent of males, and an even higher percentage of females, would die in their native or neighboring village, and would marry someone of the same religion. The men might get to see a bit more of the world while harvesting as day laborers on the Hungarian plains or shepherding on the upper slopes of the Carpathians in the summer. Many would even spend one or more years as immigrant laborers in the United States.

Each village was a self-contained unit and, at best, had frequent contact only with similar villages in the same or adjacent valleys. The dominant culture and exclusive language was Rusyn and there was no real equivalent to the superior-Hungarian (and later Czech) versus inferior-Rusyn syndrome that the budding intelligentsia encountered in urban areas. The social center was the village tavern (*korchma*) and store (*sklep*), both likely to be owned by Jews. The Rusyn peasant turned to the Jew for credit to sustain himself physically and for alcohol to soothe himself psychologically.

The other figures in this close-knit social setting were (1) the visiting or resident Greek Catholic priest—the only figure able to perform baptisms, weddings, funerals, and other rituals so crucially important to this traditionalist society; (2) his assistant, the cantor, who sometimes doubled as local elementary school teacher; (3) the resident Hungarian, and later Czechoslovak, gendarme officer whose task it was to preserve order; and (4) the band of Gypsies who, while living apart on the outskirts of the village, served as indispensable components of the social fabric, particularly in providing music at various celebrations. This latter function was no mean task since the calendar was filled annually with numerous official religious holidays as well as weddings, baptisms, and funerals. The sense of the collective was very strong in the Rusyn village and all residents participated jointly in these affairs.[16] Weddings, for instance, were not celebrated exclusively for the parents and relatives of the betrothed, but for the whole village.

Barring the yearly exodus in search of work, the only external elements in this self-centered society were the priest, the gendarme officer, and perhaps a returning immigrant from America. The First World War, however, did alter the situation somewhat. Many young Rusyns were drafted into the army and as a result they met with the empire's other Slavic nationalities: Czechs, Serbs, Croats, and Poles. These groups, who had a more developed sense of national consciousness, displayed their patriotism by proudly speaking and singing in their own languages. This affected the self-image of the Rusyn recruit, who had previously believed that his own language was not worthy for any kind of public demonstration. Rusyn soldiers who witnessed the revolutionary events in the Russian Empire were struck by how much radical social change could be brought about in a short time. Thus, those who survived the artillery and disease they encountered on the Italian and Russian fronts probably returned home with a greater sense of national pride and an even more intense desire for social change.

After 1918, external influences upon the village were increased by the presence of an elementary school teacher, who might also head the local library or reading room set up by the various cultural societies to propagate national culture. In general, however, village life in Subcarpathian Rus' remained close-knit, inward looking, and controlled by its own social system. It was the task of the national intelligentsia to break into this self-contained world and to suggest as an attractive psychological alternative identity with a larger, though less immediately tangible, national group.

2 | *Cultural Activity Prior to 1848*

Although the national movement among Subcarpathian Rusyns did not really begin until the revolutionary years of 1848-1849, it is nevertheless essential to review the state of Subcarpathian culture on the eve of those momentous events. The leaders who led the national renaissance during the second half of the nineteenth century did not arise in a vacuum, but were products of a long historical and cultural tradition. In this process the role of the Subcarpathian church and the widespread reforms undertaken by the Hapsburg rulers in the eighteenth century were of crucial significance. Both these developments set the stage for the formation of Subcarpathia's first group of leaders who came into their own during the first half of the nineteenth century.

The Role of the Church

Religion has always been closely associated with national movements in Eastern Europe. In fact, until recent times, most individuals did not identify themselves by nationality but rather by religious affiliation. This was particularly true of the Eastern Slavic peoples who since the Middle Ages had identified themselves, their language, and the land where they lived as Rus'. Since Rus' referred to membership in an Eastern-rite Christian church, any expression of "Rus'ian patriotism . . . had an exclusively ecclesiastical-religious character."[1] This congruence of religious and national identities predominated among the Subcarpathian masses until well into the twentieth century. In fact, one of the most challenging tasks of the local intelligentsia was to convince the populace to think in national and not in religious terms.

Subcarpathian Rusyns first accepted Christianity according to the Byzantine rite. Hence, their earliest religious centers—the St. Michael's Monastery in Hrusheve (Körtvelyes, Máramaros county) and the St. Nicholas Monastery on Chernecha Hora near Mukachevo—were under the Orthodox jurisdiction of Constantinople and Kiev. Although no documents exist before 1391, it is generally assumed that the church in Subcarpathian Rus' had its own diocesan seat at Mukachevo as early as the eleventh century.

21

While the Subcarpathian Rusyns were Orthodox, the rulers of the Hungarian Kingdom were Roman Catholic. Initially, this caused no problem since the first Hungarian dynasty, the Árpáds, not only tolerated but were even influenced by the precepts and traditions of the Orthodox Church. A portent of change came in the fourteenth century, when rulers from the new House of Anjou began to use the Catholic Church to buttress their own political position. The result was a series of restrictions placed especially on the Orthodox monasteries in the eastern part of the kingdom. These moves set a new stage in the history of the Subcarpathian church. From then on it would have to struggle continually in order to maintain jurisdictional and liturgical independence from the ruling Roman Catholic hierarchy. In a sense, it was this struggle that provided a platform for those local leaders who strove to uphold the distinctiveness of Rusyn religious and national culture. This was to be of no mean impact for later national developments.[2]

The next turning point came in the mid-seventeenth century. At this time the Hungarian Kingdom was divided between three warring powers. The majority of the country was still under the Ottoman Turks who had destroyed the Hungarian army at Mohács in 1526, while the northwestern territories were held by the Hapsburg rulers and eastern Transylvania by semi-independent Hungarian Protestant princes. In this triangular struggle, it is important to note that the Roman Catholic Hapsburgs and Protestant Transylvanian princes were concerned as much with their own fight over the right to the Hungarian throne as with their efforts to drive out the "heathen" Turks. To a large extent, Subcarpathian Rus' became the borderland battleground for the Hapsburg and Transylvanian rivals.

In an attempt to consolidate their own power, the Hapsburg rulers were susceptible to the demands of the Roman Catholic hierarchy in Hungary, which together with the local Jesuits wanted to incorporate the Subcarpathian diocese of Mukachevo under its own jurisdiction. The Turkish occupation had reduced substantially the size (and income) of territories belonging to dioceses like that of Eger, and such losses had to be made up somewhere—what could be more convenient than the nearby Orthodox diocese of Mukachevo? The arguments of the Jesuits also influenced the Hapsburgs, who as a leading Roman Catholic power in the era of the Counter Reformation would stop at nothing in the struggle against the "heretics." In such a context, it seemed inappropriate to have Orthodox "schismatics" living within eastern lands of the Hapsburg realm.

A similar situation had existed in the neighboring Polish-Lithuanian Commonwealth, whose eastern territories (Galicia, the Ukraine, and Belorussia) were also inhabited by an Orthodox Ukrainian and Belorussian population. The Poles did not resolve the problem by direct conversion, but instead created a new body, the Greek Catholic or Uniate Church, in 1596. With this precedent in mind, the Hapsburgs, the Hungarian Catholic hierarchy, and their Vatican supporters turned to the Rusyn population in their own country.

After several unsuccessful attempts, a meeting of sixty-three Subcarpathian Orthodox priests took place at Uzhhorod on April 24, 1646. Through the Hungarian Bishop at Eger, they swore allegiance to Rome, an act that came to be known as the Union of Uzhhorod. As a result of this union, the diocese of Mukachevo was made a part of the Greek Catholic Church and incorporated into the Roman Catholic hierarchical structure, which in practice meant subordination to the Hungarian diocese at Eger. In return, the new church was permitted to retain its own rites and traditions, including use of the Slavonic liturgy, adherance to the Julian calendar, and a married priesthood.[3]

The neighboring Protestant princes in Transylvania, however, were not about to allow these Hapsburg and Roman Catholic "intrigues" to go unchecked. Quite naturally, Protestant missionaries were active in Subcarpathian Rus', although their successes were limited to the temporary conversion of a few Rusyn villages.[4] More important was the fact that the Transylvanian rulers occupied the diocesan seat at Mukachevo, installed there an Orthodox bishop, and fostered through him and local polemicists (like the priest Mykhail Andrella of Orosvyhiv, 1637-1710) the preservation of Orthodoxy—the "old faith" (*stara vira*). Their efforts proved successful, because even after Transylvanian independence ended in 1711 Orthodoxy survived for a few decades, especially in the eastern county of Máramaros.[5]

During the first century of its existence, the Subcarpathian Greek Catholic Church had to struggle not only to eradicate the remnants of Orthodoxy but also to maintain its own autonomy in the face of encroachments by the Roman Catholic bishop of Eger. We have seen why the Eger bishops were anxious to achieve the Union of Uzhhorod. Their efforts in this development were rewarded by the Roman Catholic hierarchs in both Vienna and Rome, who after 1716 considered the bishops of Mukachevo merely as titular vicars subordinate to the bishop of Eger. Thus, beginning with the dynamic Mykhail Ol'shavs'kyi (1700-1769, consecrated 1743), all bishops of Mukachevo were required to swear an oath of obedience to their superior at Eger.

Indeed, the Subcarpathian Greek Catholic Church did reap important advantages from the union. For instance, in an attempt to attract more recalcitrant Orthodox priests, Emperor Leopold I (1657-1705) issued a decree in 1692 granting to the Greek Catholic clergy all the immunities and privileges (including the right to a tithe from the peasantry) then enjoyed by the Roman Catholic priesthood.[6] Further, young Greek Catholic seminarians were offered stipendia from a special endowed fund that was established for them at the Jesuit-administered Roman Catholic seminaries in Trnava (after 1704) and Eger (after 1733).[7] It was also at this time that the first books for

Subcarpathian Rusyns were printed: the *Katekhysys dlia naouky Ouhro-ruskym liudem* ("Catechism for the Instruction of the Uhro-Rusyn People," 1698) by Bishop Josef de Camillis (1641-1706, consecrated 1690), the *Bukvar iazŷka Slaven'ska* ("Primer of the Slavonic Language," 1699), the *Kratkoe prypadkov moral'nŷkh yly nravnykh sobranïe* ("A Brief Collection of Moral Precepts," 1727) by Bishop Iurii Bizantii (1656-1733, consecrated 1716), and the *Elementa puerilis institutionis in lingua latina* (1764) by Bishop Mykhail Ol'shavs'kyi. According to Bishop de Camillis, the *Catechism* was purposefully "written in simple dialect in order to be understood by the people," who needed to be exposed to "all the articles of faith" of the recently established Greek Catholic Church.[8] It is ironic that these "new" Subcarpathian Catholics were using the educative tools of the Protestant Reformation to eliminate competition from their own Orthodox rivals. By exposure to these publications, the Greek Catholic clergy in Subcarpathian Rus' was brought into the intellectual fold of the Vatican.

But these advantages could not fully offset the repeated complaints made by Subcarpathian priests that the spirit of the Union of Uzhhorod was being violated and that the bishop of Eger was trying to destroy the last vestiges of the autonomy once held by the diocese of Mukachevo. At a diocesan synod held in Mukachevo in February 1749, the Greek Catholic clergy, led by Bishop Ol'shavs'kyi, demanded the restoration of their former rights and the legal reestablishment of a fully independent diocese. In response, the Eger bishops argued that the Mukachevo diocese had no legal rights since: (1) there was no written proof concerning the establishment of a diocese at Mukachevo; (2) there were no existing documents from the 1649 Union of Uzhhorod; and (3) the 1649 agreement was made with a Hungarian bishopric, not with the Papal See in Rome.[9]

This period of claims and counterclaims came to be known in Subcarpathian ecclesiastical historiography as the "struggle against the influence of Eger," but the significance of these debates went beyond purely church affairs. As one historian recently remarked: "in its struggle with the 'Latin' (Catholics), the Uniate 'Rusyn' clergy had to argue not only on religious but also on historical grounds, . . . [and] in the end this led to an organized conception concerning the past of Hungarian Rusyns, i.e., to the collection of material and to the writing of the first histories."[10] Thus, what began as an attempt on the part of some Subcarpathian clergy to justify in historico-legal terms its demands for reestablishment of the diocese of Mukachevo, resulted in the creation of Subcarpathia's first "national" histories.

The first of these, by a Slovak, Adam F. Kollár (1718-1783), was entitled *Humillium promemoria de ortu, progressu et in Hungaria incolatu gentis Ruthenicae* (1749). Although this work focused primarily on the Mukachevo diocese, it did nonetheless establish the basic precepts of Subcarpathian historical development. Kollár argued: (1) that Rusyns lived in the

Danubian Basin in the first century A.D.; (2) that the Mukachevo diocese was established in the sixth century; (3) that Rusyns were Christianized before Cyril and Methodius; (4) that an independent "Rusyn princedom" existed in the early ninth century; and (5) that many Rusyn colonists came later, among whom was Prince Koriatovych of Podillia (Podolia), founder of the Mukachevo monastery on Chernecha Hora in 1360. On the basis of these statements, it was concluded that both the Rusyns and their Mukachevo diocese preceded the coming of the Magyars (896) into the Danubian Basin.[11]

The theories of Kollár were later repeated by Subcarpathia's first native historian, Ioanniky Bazilovych (1742-1821)—the Herodotus of Carpatho-Rusyn historiography.[12] As abbot of the Mukachevo monastery, Bazilovych felt obliged to prove the authenticity of the founding decree, supposedly drawn up in 1360 by Prince Koriatovych. When in 1785 a work appeared in Hungary claiming that the so-called "document of 1360" was a forgery, Bazilovych wrote a three-volume study to refute that contention.[13] His *Brevis Notitia Fundationis Theodori Koriathovits, olim Ducis de Munkacs, pro Religiosis Ruthenis Ordinis Sancti Basilii Magni, in Monte Csernek ad Munkacs, Anno MCCCLX Factae* (1799-1805), with its claims for the legal and historical rights of precedence of the Subcarpathian Rusyns, was to become the standard interpretation advanced by local writers for the next century. To this period also belong the unpublished histories of Daniel Babila, *Historia Diocesana,* and Ioann Pastelii (1741-1799), *Historia Diocesis Munkatsiensis* and *De origine Ruthenorum.*[14]

The value of these histories is that they codified for the first time the historical development of the Subcarpathian Rusyns, and in particular their church. Yet it was political reality, not intellectual disputations, that led to the reestablishment of the diocese at Mukachevo. Beginning in the 1740s, a series of revolts took place in which both Rusyn peasants and their Greek Catholic priests took part. Besides social grievances connected with increased taxes and worsening economic conditions, many Rusyn clergy and peasants took this opportunity to return to the fold of the Orthodox Church. During the 1760s, more disturbances occurred, in part stimulated by the proselytizing activity of the Serbian Orthodox Church. This Church, with its seat in Karlovci, sent a delegate who, together with a wandering monk named Sophronius, urged the Greek Catholic population of Szatmár county, among whom were some Rusyns, to return to the "old faith." If they did this, they were told, their religious and national freedom would supposedly be restored and they would be liberated from the socioeconomic impositions made by their Roman Catholic landlords.[15] A similar incident occurred in 1765 at Hajdudorog (southern Zemplén county), where local Rusyn and Magyar Greek Catholics were being influenced by Orthodox Russians living in the area. The Empress Maria Theresa (1740-1780) reacted to these events as the latest example of tsarist "intrigues" in the internal affairs of the Hapsburg Empire, and she tried to satisfy the discontented elements in the Rusyn population by setting up an independent diocese.[16]

Thus, the Empress disregarded the adamant protests of the bishop of Eger and issued a decree establishing the diocese of Mukachevo, an act approved by the Pope in September 1771. The former "apostolic vicar," Ivan Bradach (1732-1772, consecrated 1771), became Bishop, and although he died within two years, he was succeeded by Andrei Bachyns'kyi (1732-1809, consecrated 1773), who was to lay the financial, educational, and ideological groundwork for the new diocese. The existence of the diocese of Mukachevo made it possible to maintain a separate religious (and hence national) identity for the Rusyn population in Hungary.[17]

The Era of Reforms

The second half of the eighteenth century was an age of reform in the Hapsburg Empire. By the beginning of the century, the Turks had been driven out of the empire and the peasant revolts in Hungary, led usually by Transylvanian princes, were quelled. With these major threats aside, Empress Maria Theresa and Joseph II (1780-1790) turned their attention to reorganizing the internal structure of the realm. The reforms of these two rulers reached into every corner of life: governmental, military, administrative, religious, social, and educational. We have seen how such reforms touched upon Subcarpathian life when the diocese of Mukachevo was brought into being. The indirect results of this development were unexpected, because although the move was prompted by Vienna's concern with the maintenance of internal stability, it was in fact to result in the preservation of a separate Rusyn identity through the façade of religion. The reforms of the late eighteenth century, especially those in education, were also of great significance for the future of Rusyn national development.

Indeed, schools had existed on the territory of Subcarpathian Rus' long before the reform era. On the basis of indirect evidence, some scholars have surmised that a school existed in Uzhhorod as early as 1400. It is certain that the small village of Porač (Vereshegy, Szepes county) already had an elementary school in 1593.[18] By the eighteenth century, schools were in existence at the monasteries of Krasný Brod, Mukachevo, Máriapócs, Buková Hôrka, Malyi-Bereznyi, Imstycheve, and Boroniava. At the Krasný Brod monastery, a more advanced philosophical and theological school was set up, and in 1744 the school at the Mukachevo monastery was transformed by Bishop Ol'shavs'kyi into a theological school (*bohoslovs'ka shkola*). During its first academic year, two hundred students enrolled, and while it was never officially recognized as a seminary, the theological school nonetheless functioned until 1778 and provided training for several generations of Rusyn priests.[19] There is no doubt that throughout this period the Greek Catholic Church was concerned with improving the standard of education, especially among the families of clergymen. In January 1762, the vicar general Bradach required "that the sons of each priest and cantor be sent as soon as possible to the Mukachevo school," and that a monthly fine of one German gold piece be imposed on those parents who failed to comply. At the same time Bradach requested that village cantors form schools in order to provide daily instruction for the children in the Christian faith. Again, failure to do this was to result in heavy fines.[20]

But these efforts, as well meaning as they may have been, were limited to only a small portion of the population. It remained for the central government in Vienna to put forward a more elaborate scheme for public education. In 1777, Maria Theresa published the *Ratio educationis,* a decree to implement universal education. Hungary was divided into nine educational districts, one of which had its center in Uzhhorod. Five types of schools were suggested. At the elementary level the local national tongue was to be the medium of instruction, while Latin, Magyar, or both would be introduced into the more advanced schools. The *Ratio educationis* also proposed the establishment in Uzhhorod of a four-class "normal school" to train teachers. But these grandiose plans were aborted. No funds from Vienna were forthcoming, and the responsibility for organizing schools remained in the hands of the Greek Catholic Church, which especially during the years of Bishop Bachyns'kyi did a commendable job in creating a network of elementary and secondary schools.[21]

Under Bachyns'kyi's direction, the administrative seat of the diocese was in 1777 transferred from Mukachevo to Uzhhorod, and with it came the theological school, which was transformed the following year into a four-year seminary for the training of priests. A gymnasium was also opened in Uzhhorod and a network of elementary schools was established, so that by 1806 more than 300 schools were found in Rusyn villages. Teachers were trained largely by the monastery schools (especially at Máriapócs and Krasný Brod), and after 1794 by a teacher's college set up in Uzhhorod. The local dialect was used for instruction in elementary schools, while texts, if they were available at all, were usually in Church-Slavonic. In the gymnasium, teacher's college, and theological seminary, Latin, and for a short time German (1785-1790), were the languages of instruction.[22]

The rather rapid growth of schools exacerbated an already existing problem—the lack of suitable textbooks. The earlier books of Bishops de Camillis, Bizantii, and Ol'shavs'kyi were outmoded and could not respond to the needs of the expanded school system. In an attempt to rectify this problem, Rev. Arsenii Kotsak (1737-1800), a language instructor at the Imstycheve and other Subcarpathian monasteries, composed several texts, the most famous being his *Grammatika . . . iazyka slavenskago ili russkago* ("Slaveno-Rusyn Grammar," 1788). This was based on the well-known seventeenth century grammar of Meletii Smotryts'kyi. Kotsak wanted to compose a book specifically for Subcarpathian Rusyns, and his introduction in verse

not only justified his purpose but became an early example of local patriotism. After recalling how the other peoples of Europe had their own grammars, Kotsak stated that he wrote this book "so that our miserable Rusnaks
will not always be fated to remain simpletons."[23] It should be mentioned
that the term Slaveno-Rusyn as used by Kotsak (and for that matter many
of his contemporaries) did not refer to a new national language, but rather
was what may be called the Subcarpathian recension of Church Slavonic,
that is, Church Slavonic interspersed in varying degree with local
dialectisms. (See Appendix 3, pt. 1.)

Few texts were available to Rusyns because there were no printing facilities either in or near Subcarpathian territory.[24] Since the late seventeenth
century, Mukachevo's Greek Catholic bishops had several times requested
permission from the government to establish their own printshop, but their
requests were denied. Some Cyrillic publications came from the Rumanians
and Serbs, but these peoples also suffered from shortages. Thus, the only
effective source was Russia and the Ukraine, and during the seventeenth
and eighteenth centuries hundreds of Bibles, catechisms, hymnals, and
grammars found their way into the Carpathians. However, both the Greek
Catholic diocese of Mukachevo and the Viennese government viewed the
importation of these Orthodox or "schismatic" writings as an ideological
danger, and as early as 1727 an imperial decree made it illegal to possess un-
censored publications.[25] Nonetheless, permission was still not granted to set
up a Cyrillic printshop in either Prešov, Uzhhorod, or Mukachevo. Instead,
in 1770, Maria Theresa gave Joseph Kurzbeck, a Viennese printer, the right
to publish all Cyrillic publications for use in the Hapsburg Empire. To protect this closely supervised monopoly, a decree was issued the same year forbidding the further importation of Cyrillic books from beyond the borders
of the realm. Indeed, the Kurzbeck enterprise, known as the Illyrian printshop, was directed primarily to the needs of the empire's Serbs, who until
then were sending "great sums of money to Russia for religious books."[26]
In fact, only three of the fifty Cyrillic script publications prepared by Kurzbeck were for the Subcarpathian Rusyns.[27] In such a situation, books continued to be smuggled from Russia and the Ukraine.[28]

Another of Maria Theresa's and Joseph's educational and ecclesiastical
reforms, one of great importance to all Rusyns living in the Hapsburg Empire, was the establishment of centralized educational institutions for the
Greek Catholic clergy in Vienna and L'viv. These projects were a direct out-
growth of the empire's newest territorial acquisitions. In 1772, Austria,
Russia, and Prussia carried out the first partition of Poland. At that time the
Hapsburgs received the province of Galicia; three years later, neighboring
Bukovina followed. As a result, the number of Rusyns living within the borders of the empire increased substantially, so that in their wide-ranging reform program, Maria Theresa and her son, Joseph, felt obliged to pay particular attention to their newest subjects.

If Joseph II is remembered as an antagonist of the Roman Catholic Church because he limited the degree of influence exercised by the Vatican in the Austrian Empire, he at the same time came to play a very positive role in the development of Greek Catholicism. He believed that the three Catholic rites (Latin, Greek, Armenian) were equals—as "three daughters of one mother" (*drei Töchter einer Mutter*)—and that no one rite should be preferred over the others. This attitude, held also by Maria Theresa, came as a disturbing shock to some entrenched Roman Catholic prelates like the bishops of the Hungarian diocese of Eger, but it was greeted with joy by the Subcarpathian Greek Catholic clergy. They were to receive an independent and well-subsidized diocese, their own seminary, and general equality with their Roman Catholic brethren.[29]

To improve the educational level of prospective Greek Catholic priests, a Royal Greek Catholic General Seminary was set up at the Church of St. Barbara in Vienna. This institution came to be known as the *Barbareum* and functioned from 1775 to 1784. Forty-six places were made available, and of these, eleven were reserved for seminarians from the diocese of Mukachevo.[30] Despite its brief existence, the *Barbareum* was to be of great significance for the national life of Subcarpathian Rusyns. In Vienna, young Subcarpathians were exposed to the early beginnings of a Slavic revival. There they not only met fellow Rusyns from Galicia and Bukovina but also other Slavic leaders who gravitated toward the imperial capital. It was here that the seeds of Pan-Slavism were being planted, and since this ideology was not yet viewed as a political danger, it was allowed to grow. In such an environment, Rusyns attended lectures at the University of Vienna by professors like the renowned Czech scholar and proponent of Slavic culture Josef Dobrovský. Even after the seminary was discontinued, the parish of St. Barbara still remained a center where, for instance the influential Slovene philologist Bartolémy Kopitar could conduct informal discussion groups on Slavic culture. Vienna, then, became a catalyst for the promotion of a Slavic consciousness; among the Subcarpathian seminarians who experienced this environment were the grammarians and scholars Ivan Fogarashii-Berezhanyn and Mykhail Luchkai, the educator Mykhail Shchavnyts'kyi, and the bishops Hryhorii Tarkovych, and Aleksei Povchii.[31]

In 1783, Joseph II disbanded the *Barbareum* and replaced it with a system of centralized seminaries. Rusyns from Subcarpathia were expected to attend the Hungarian seminary at Eger, while those from Galicia and Bukovina were to go to L'viv. As a corollary, smaller seminaries attached to individual dioceses were to be phased out. While this in fact happened to some Galician Greek Catholic institutions, Bishop Bachyns'kyi succeeded in preserving the Uzhhorod seminary and in allowing Subcarpathian students to be transferred to the L'viv seminary, where their countryman and former *Barbareum* student, Mykhail Shchavnyts'kyi (1754-1819), became prefect. Shchavnyts'kyi was also instrumental in organizing at the University of

L'viv the first secular Rusyn institution of higher learning, the *Studium Ruthenum* (1787-1809). It now seemed as if the focus of higher education for all Rusyns in the Hapsburg Empire was being redirected from Vienna to L'viv.[32]

The result of these developments was a pronounced increase in contacts between Subcarpathian Rusyns and their brethren north of the Carpathians. At one point serious consideration was being given in Vienna to the idea of creating a single metropolinate for all Greek Catholics living in the Hapsburg Empire. The primary candidate for the position was the Subcarpathian Bishop Bachyns'kyi, but from the beginning the Hungarian government and Roman Catholic hierarchy were opposed and all such plans were dropped after 1796.[33] Indeed, several Subcarpathian students, professors, and administrators continued to study and work at L'viv's General Seminary and at the *Studium Ruthenum,* but the jealous prerogatives of the individual dioceses,[34] together with the negative attitude of the Hungarian authorities, worked against any long-term fusion of the educational, cultural, and religious institutions of Rusyns living in Galicia with those of Subcarpathians Rus'.

Nevertheless, the era of reforms undertaken by the enlightened Hapsburg rulers in the eighteenth century was to have a positive effect on developments in Subcarpathian Rus'. An independent diocese for Subcarpathian Greek Catholic Rusyns was reestablished, a network of elementary schools was brought into being, and provisions were made for higher education in Vienna and L'viv. This last development exposed Subcarpathians to Slavic peoples from other parts of the Empire and to fellow Rusyns from Galicia, and it awakened in them both an awareness of the larger world around them and a sense of their own distinct cultural identity. The effect of the groundwork laid in the era of reforms can be seen in the achievements made by the Subcarpathian intelligentsia during the first half of the nineteenth century.

The Early Nineteenth Century

Subcarpathian cultural life during the first decades of the nineteenth century was marked by three factors: (1) the exodus of talent in search of employment abroad; (2) the development of relations with neighboring Slavic peoples, in particular with Russia; and (3) the unheralded cultural achievements of a few patriotic leaders who remained and worked in the homeland. Among the latter, the earliest and most influential was Bishop Andrei Bachyns'kyi. We have already seen how this Greek Catholic priest, who enjoyed the confidence of Maria Theresa, was instrumental in having Mukachevo recognized as the seat of an independent diocese. Similarly, he was one of the key figures behind the establishment of the *Barbareum,* and when plans of ecclesiastical unity for Galicia and Subcarpathian Rus' were in the making he was a candidate for metropolitan.

It was as bishop of the Mukachevo diocese from 1773 to 1809, however, that Bachyns'kyi had the greatest impact on Subcarpathian cultural life. His first task was to create a solid base for the diocese. He did this by transferring its seat to Uzhhorod (1775) and by establishing there a chancellery (1777), seminary (1778), and episcopal residence and cathedral (1780).[35] Having achieved these material prerequisites, Bachyns'kyi created an ideological environment that would assure a Slavic and Eastern-rite religious context for Subcarpathian Rusyn culture. In a real sense, Bachyns'kyi could be considered the region's first national leader. At the Uzhhorod seminary and gymnasium, and in the numerous elementary schools founded during his tenure, he required that students know Church Slavonic and be well versed in the traditions of the Eastern rite. He remembered the local Rusyn language as well. In a pastoral letter dated September 4, 1798 he stressed that "at the seminary . . . knowledge of Rusyn [*ruskiia naukŷ*] is necessary . . . and that students trained in foreign languages will not be sent as clergy [to administer parishes] until they are trained in and accustomed to elementary Rusyn."[36] In another statement, this time directed at his parishioners and so reminiscent of Herder, Bachyns'kyi declared: "For the preservation of any people, there is no greater or stronger unifying force than the maintenance of its natural maternal language, literature and religion." And for the people of the Uhro-Rusyn (*Uhro-russkaia*) Mukachevo diocese, that was the Slaveno-Rusyn (*slaveno-ruskyi*) language or Subcarpathian recension of Church Slavonic, handed down by Saints Cyril and Methodius.[37]

To guarantee the preservation of the Subcarpathian cultural heritage, Bachyns'kyi organized an episcopal archive and requested that all old charters and documents be sent to Uzhhorod. Also during his lifetime, the episcopal library, which inherited 1,858 volumes from the former Jesuit proprietors, was expanded to include 9,000 volumes. Finally, in 1804, he published a translation of the Bible into Church-Slavonic.[38]

But Bachyns'kyi was an exception among his generation, for at the turn of the eighteenth and nineteenth centuries, the majority of talented Subcarpathian Rusyns lived and worked far beyond the borders of the homeland. Some were at the newly founded Greek Catholic educational institutions in Vienna and L'viv, among them Mykhail Shchavnyts'kyi, the vice-rector of the *Barbareum,* examiner at Vienna University, and rector of the *Studium Ruthenum* in L'viv. Four other professors from Subcarpathian Rus'— Mykhail Dudyns'kyi (d. 1789), Petro Lodii (1764-1829), Andrei Pavlovych (d. 1809), and Ivan Zemanchyk (d. 1822)—also taught at Rusyn and Polish educational institutions in Galicia.[39]

But it was in the Russian Empire that Subcarpathians reached the highest positions in education and governmental administration. The tradition of going east was already established in the early eighteenth century, when Tsar Peter the Great (1682-1725) invited a native of Subcarpathian Rus', Ivan Zeikan (d. 1742), to educate his grandson, the future Tsar Peter II (1715-1730).[40] The presence of a Subcarpathian intelligentsia in Russia was especially evident in the early nineteenth century, a time when the school system in tsarist lands was being reorganized. Between 1802 and 1820, four new lycées (in Tsarskoe Selo, Odessa, Kremenets', and Nizhyn) and five universities (in Derpt, Vilna, Kazan, Kharkiv, and St. Petersburg) were founded. However, the tsarist empire had no tradition of higher secular education, so there was a decided lack of teachers (and students) at all levels. In order to resolve this problem, an old established Russian practice was repeated: importation of talent from abroad. A ready-made source was the Hapsburg Empire, in particular the Serbs and Subcarpathian Rusyns living there.[41] In 1805, Kharkiv University sent one of its chancellors to Hungary in search of professors; he brought back nine, three of whom were Subcarpathians: Konstantyn P. Pavlovych (1782-186?), Andrei I. Dudrovych (1782-1830), and Mykhail V. Bilevych.[42] This Russian interest in Carpatho-Rusyns (from both Galicia and Subcarpathian Rus') was best summed-up by Prince A. M. Golitsyn, then tsarist minister of religious affairs and education. Responding to the demand made by Kazan University in 1820 for professors, he wrote: "One people from whom we can request scholars is the Carpatho-Russian (*karpato-rosy*), who speak the same language as us and who have preserved the faith of our fathers."[43] Such a recommendation was based on satisfaction with the work of Ivan S. Orlai (1771-1829), Petro Lodii, Vasyl' H. Kukol'nyk (1765-1821), and particularly Mykhail A. Baludians'kyi (1769-1847), Subcarpathians who had already carved out successful careers in Russia.

Orlai was the first of his generation to go east. Trained in philology and medicine, he served as director of the Bezborod'ko gymnasium in Nizhyn and the Richelieu lycée in Odessa. He was also active in organizing the medical profession in Russia and was a member of numerous German scientific societies.[44] In 1803, Orlai submitted a project to the Ministry of Education in St. Petersburg suggesting that seven of his countrymen be invited to work in Russia. In 1803-1804, three of them, Kukol'nyk, Lodii, and Baludians'kyi, did come.[45]

Kukol'nyk was named professor of experimental physics at the St. Petersburg Pedagogical Institute and later professor of Roman and Russian law at St. Petersburg University. In 1820, he preceded Orlai as the first director of the Nizhyn gymnasium. As for Lodii, he had served as dean of the philosophical faculty at L'viv University and professor of logic, ethics, and metaphysics at Cracow University before coming to Russia. In his new country, Lodii taught at the St. Petersburg Pedagogical Institute, and in 1819, when this institution was transformed into a university, he became dean of the faculty of jurisprudence. But the most impressive career in the field of law was that of M. Baludians'kyi. Simultaneous with Kukol'nyk and Lodii, he began teaching political economy at the St. Petersburg Pedagogical Institute, then in 1819 became the first rector of St. Petersburg University. Soon after his arrival, he was appointed to numerous governmental commissions and ministries concerned with financial matters and served as one of the key assistants to M. Speranskii in the new codification of Russian law, which appeared in 1830.[46]

No survey of the Subcarpathian intellectual emigration would be complete without mentioning Iurii I. Venelin (1802-1839). He came to Russia in 1823 and first worked as a teacher in Bessarabia. It was there that he became interested in the Bulgarian people, a small group of whom were living in Bessarabia. Despite his love of philology and history, he entered the medical faculty at Moscow University and in 1829 received his degree. That same year he published the first edition of his study on Bulgaria, a work that brought him lasting fame as one of the founders of the Bulgarian national renaissance. The rest of his short life was spent in teaching and publishing studies about Bulgaria and the neighboring Slavic peoples.[47]

But what effect, if any, did the activity of these emigrants have on Subcarpathian national life? First, they provided the leading governmental and scholarly circles in the tsarist empire with first-hand knowledge of what they described as the "Russians" of Hungary. It happened that their opinions could only be gratifying to the Russians. In essence, the Subcarpathian writers saw their people as part of one Russian civilization (including Great Russians, Belorussians, and Ukrainians), and their view of the supposed linguistic and ethnic affinities between the Subcarpathian Rusyns and the Russians was accepted not only by Russian writers, but by other Slavic scholars and by Rusyn leaders at home as well.

Orlai was the first to publicize his native land. In his *Istoriia o Karpato-Rossakh* ("History of the Carpatho-Russians," 1804), he called on scholars in Russia to develop an interest in their brethren living south of the Carpathians.[48] Elsewhere, he concluded that the Subcarpathian Rusyns are related to other "Russians," especially those living in *Malorossia* (Ukraine), and that despite centuries of Hungarian rule, the Rusyn language (*iazyk Ruskii*) in *Uhors'ka Rus'* is "much purer than that of contemporary Kiev."[49] Orlai was one of the few emigrants who maintained steady contact with the homeland, and during several trips he took many books there, especially to the Greek Catholic Eparchial Library in Prešov.[50] Venelin also spread knowledge about Subcarpathian Rus'. In several manuscripts, he argued that *Ugro-Rus'* is similar to Kievan, Volhynian, and Galician Rus', and that these territories are inseparable from northern Rus' (Muscovy, Novgorod, St. Petersburg). He regretted the division of the "Russian" peoples, and to preserve cultural unity he urged the adoption of one common Russian (*obshcherusskii*) literary language for all the Rus' lands.[51]

The writings of these Subcarpathian emigrants were complemented by a renewed interest among Russian and Ukrainian scholars in southern Rus', especially in the folklore and old manuscripts from medieval Kiev. This led to a concern with the Carpathian region as seen in the writings of Petr I. Keppen, Nikolai I. Nadezhdin, Izmail I. Sreznevs'kyi, and especially Mi-

khail M. Pogodin. The first half of the nineteenth century witnessed the development of Pan-Slavism, and at a time when ideas of reciprocity were
being fostered by all the Slavic peoples, Russian and Ukrainian scholars
traveled through Galicia and Subcarpathian Rus', met with local leaders,
and distributed publications.[52] Pogodin was perhaps the best known and
most effective proselytizer of these ideas. He urged the tsarist government
to finance scholarly publications and to foster contacts with "Russians beyond our borders." His reasoning was clear: "These Rusyns [rusiny], inhabitants of Galicia and northeastern Hungary—our ancient and illustrious
Galician princedom—are pure Russians [chistye russkie], just like the Russians we see in Poltava or Chernihiv; [they are] our brothers who carry our
name, speak our language, profess our faith, have one history with us;
[they] long for us from under the four-fold yoke of Germans, Poles, Jews,
and Catholicism, and bitterly complain of our lack of concern."[53] Pogodin
was the first to make Pan-Slavism an acceptable ideology in the Russian
Empire, and through his numerous publications he succeeded in creating
within Russian scholarly and political circles a continuing interest in the fate
of Galicia and Subcarpathian Rus'.[54]

In turn, within Subcarpathian Rus' there was a positive awareness of
Russia on the part of both the intelligentsia and masses. There were, of
course, some direct contacts. We have already seen how during the 1760s the
Russian "colony" in Hajdudorog, together with some Serbian proselytizers, urged local Rusyns to return to Orthodoxy. Later, the brief presence of
Russian troops in the Carpathians during the Napoleonic wars (in 1799 and
again in 1813-1814) made a positive impression on the local populace. Finally, the tsar himself, Alexander I (1801-1825), arrived at the spa near
Bardejov (Bártfa, Sáros county) in May and June, 1821. He visited the local
Rusyn population, and as an expression of sympathy awarded a large sum
of money for the construction of an Eastern-rite church.[55]

It is no wonder, then, that the works of Rusyn authors from this period
reveal a pronounced love of Russia. In one of the earliest examples of Subcarpathian poetry, Hryhorii Tarkovych (1754-1841) published an ode in
1805 dedicated to the popular Palatine of Hungary, Archduke Joseph, and
to the active leader of the Hungarian national revival, Ferenc Széchényi.
As a "Uhro-Russian," the author felt it appropriate at the same time to
lavish praise upon what he called the "Nymph of the Neva River," and
upon the poet Alexander P. Sumarokov, who, with Mikhail V. Lomonosov,
had worked to codify literary Russian.[56] In the same work, the Uhro-Russians (Ougrorossy) were described as inhabiting the Carpathian Mountains,
"the true fatherland of the Slavs, even though the sons of Russians don't
yet know this."[57] Tarkovych's ode was well known in Russia, because the
popular historian Nikolai N. Karamzin published the first forty-three verses
in the initial volume of his History of the Russian State (1817).[58] It is interesting that Tarkovych's praise of the Russians was apparently not viewed

askance by the Hapsburg authorities, since when he wrote the work he held the influential position of censor of Slavic books in Budapest,[59] and from 1818 until his death in 1841 served as the first bishop of the newly established Greek Catholic diocese at Prešov. One of his important achievements in the latter post was the establishment of an episcopal library, and through his contacts with Orlai in St. Petersburg he acquired many Russian publications for Prešov.[60]

To this period also belong the first poems by the future "national awakener" of the Subcarpathian Rusyns, Aleksander Dukhnovych (1803-1865). In 1829, he wrote two odes, one commemorating the victory of Tsar Nicholas I in the Russo-Turkish War, the other praising the Russian capture of the city of Varna. Both works express great respect for the power of Russia, and like the odes of Tarkovych, they were written in Slaveno-Rusyn, the Subcarpathian recension of Church Slavonic, which both authors assumed would be understood by Russians.[61] These same years also saw the first theatrical work in Subcarpathian literature, the anonymous "Rozprava rusnaka z poliakom" (A Conversation between Rusyn and a Pole), completed in 1834 but never published. Again, the unity of Subcarpathian Rus' with Russia was stressed. The play is a dialogue comparing Rusyn culture favorably to Hungarian culture (here for political reasons called Polish). Towards the end, the protagonist argues that the Rusnak will never be a lord and that the leading cadres in society are all Poles (that is, Hungarians). In reply, the Subcarpathian repeats what became a typical refrain of praise for the East:

> Why, Polak, do you lie like a dog
> And say that the Rusnak can never be a lord?
> You know that everyone calls Muscovy a Rusyn [*ruskii*] land,
> There Rusnaks have Tsar Nicholas;
> Muscovy is a great land; there are ministers there,
> But not the kind you have in Poland.[62]

In the development of a national consciousness, personal contacts are of immense importance. Besides the visits by Russian and Ukrainian scholars from the Russian Empire and their correspondence with Subcarpathian leaders, there is on record the case of Konstantin Matezonskii (1794-1858), a former Decembrist who was forced to leave Russia after the abortive revolt in 1829. Matezonskii settled in Uzhhorod in 1833, where he founded the first choir. Besides his musical activity, he also spread knowledge of Russia among the local populace.[63] Thus, by the first half of the nineteenth century a tradition of affinity toward Russia was well established among significant segments of Subcarpathian Rusyn society.

But Subcarpathian contacts were not limited to the Russian Empire. Other Slavic cultural activists also developed an interest in the Rusyns of

northeastern Hungary. This was largely the result of the Pan-Slavic movement, which had begun with the Slovak writers Jan Kollár and Pavel J. Šafárik. These two figures, reared in the tradition of German romanticism, led
a group of sympathizers in their own and neighboring countries who sought
out and discovered, almost with a sense of childish wonderment, all the
Slavic peoples, large and small, that lived under the yoke of foreign rule.
These "western" Slavs, in what was considered an unfavorable political
situation, concluded that the salvation of their race and its only hope for the
future was to be found in mighty Russia. Then, while exploring the lands
closest to them, they discovered to their surprise that in northeastern Hungary, literally on their own doorstep, there lived one segment of the "Russian" people, in the land of Subcarpathian Rus'.

We have already seen how Josef Dobrovský, the Czech scholar and patron saint of Pan-Slavism, influenced Subcarpathian seminarians studying
in Vienna during the late eighteenth century. He later met and corresponded
with Bishop Bachyns'kyi, and in 1814 engaged in a polemic with a Viennese
journal that claimed the Subcarpathians were not the same as those Rusyns
living in Galicia.[64] In response, Dobrovský aruged that not only were Subcarpathian Rusyns related to the inhabitants of eastern Galicia, but they
were in fact the same people as in all of Russia. He then called for further
scholarly study of Subcarpathian Rus'. The Slovene Bartholémy Kopitar
and another Czech, Ján Hromadko, also joined the polemic. Agreeing with
Dobrovský, both emphasized that the linguistic relation between Subcarpathian Rusyn and Russian was analogous to that between Moravian and
Bohemian Czech ("wie etwa das mährische zum böhmische").[65] Although
these assertions did not correspond to linguistic reality, they were, as we will
see, accepted by contemporary Subcarpathian writers.

Polish scholarly circles were informed of Subcarpathian Rus' through the
writings of Andrzej Kucharski, who met in Uzhhorod in 1828 with the Subcarpathian scholar Mykhail Luchkai and praised him for his ethnographic
work.[66] Similarly, the southern Slavs were acquainted with the Subcarpathian Rusyns, since their writings were published during the 1830s in the
first Serbian cultural journal.[67] Of great significance in these inter-Slavic relations was the activity of Iakiv Holovats'kyi, a member of the so-called
Rusyn Triad (Rus'ka triitsa) that led the national revival among Rusyns in
Galicia. He traveled to the Subcarpathian region in 1834, in 1835, and again
in 1839, and published in Prague an extensive travelogue that was widely
read in Slavic circles.[68] He met several times with Luchkai and his first-hand
acquaintance with the area was later to result in many publications on Galician and Subcarpathian Rusyn history and ethnography as well as the initia-
tion of a fruitful correspondence and exchange of publications with the
Subcarpathian national leader A. Dukhnovych.[69]

Perhaps the most extensive contacts were carried out between Subcarpathian Rusyns and their closest neighbors, the Slovaks. Works on Subcar-

pathian Rus' by Slovak authors date from the early eighteenth century, when Matej Bel included descriptions of the Subcarpathian region in his multivolume *Notitia Hungariae novae historico-geografica* (1735-1742). This was followed a century later by studies on several northeastern counties, especially Zemplén, by Anton Szirmay (a native of Prešov), and by general works on the Hungarian Kingdom by Jan Čaplovič.[70] Paval Šafárik also discussed the Rusyn problem. In his *History of the Slavic Languages and Dialects* (1826) he lamented the fact that "the Rusnaks of eastern Galicia, Bukovina, and northern Hungary are from the linguistic and historical standpoint still a *terra incognita.*"[71] He tried to rectify this situation by publishing a detailed ethnographic study of the Boikians in Galicia.[72] After extensive linguistic research, Šafárik concluded that the "Rusnak dialect *(russniakische Mundart)* in eastern Galicia and northeastern Hungary is but a variety of Little Russian," which in turn he described as one of the "three dialects of the Russian language."[73]

Like Šafárik, another Slovak, Bohuš Nosák-Nezabudov, considered Subcarpathian Rus' an unknown land. In a series of letters published in 1845 in *Orel tatranský,* the literary supplement of the first Slovak newspaper, *Slovenskije národňje novini,* Nosák called for understanding between Rusyns and Slovaks and urged Rusyns to form their own cultural organizations or to join those of the Slovaks.[74] The most influential Slovak leader, L'udovít Štúr, seconding the call of Nosák, engaged in a polemic with Magyar newspapers in a defense of the Rusyns, and, to some of his own countrymen who suggested that Slovak might be adopted as the literary language for Rusyns, he replied: "Who asks here that Rusyns should accept the Slovak language as their own. Why, they have their own beautiful Rusyn (*rusínsky*) language!"[75]

The 1820s and 1830s were years marked by the growth of the Slovak national movement led by Štúr, which was to have a decided impact on Rusyn development. The student movement in eastern Slovakia and the establishment of numerous Slovak schools in Szepes county were important factors. Moreover, during the 1830s, Dukhnovych was in close contact with the Slovak nationalist Jan Andraščik. A supporter of Štúr, Andraščik worked in the city of Bardejov where he tried to improve the cultural standard of local Slovaks and Rusyns. He published popular plays in the eastern Slovak dialect, and this undoubtedly influenced his friend Dukhnovych, who in 1847 published his *Knyzhnytsia chytalnaia dlia nachynaiushchykh* ("Reader for Beginners"), the first Rusyn text based on the popular speech.[76] Thus, despite Šafárik's and Nosák's lament that Subcarpathian Rus' was a *terra incognita,* by the mid-nineteenth century the Rusyns of northern Hungary were known to Slavic circles in both the Russian and Hapsburg Empires.

Among the local leaders in the Subcarpathian Rus' during the first half of the nineteenth century, the national movement, if that is what it could be called, was limited to the scholarly activity of a handful of individuals, the most important being Vasyl' Dovhovych, Ivan Fogarashii-Berezhanyn, and Mykhail Luchkai. Vasyl' Dovhovych (1783-1849) was a Greek Catholic priest who wrote some lyric poetry in his native Subcarpathian dialect. This was his only contribution to Rusyn affairs, however, since he spent most of his time composing Latin treatises on the philosophies of Kant, Descartes, and Newton, and as a result was elected a corresponding member of the Hungarian Academy of Sciences.[77] Dovhovych at least published his writings, even if they did not contribute directly to national developments. It was more typical in this period for authors, even with a nationalist bent, to leave their works unpublished. Among these was Ivan Iuhasevych (1741-1814), who left behind thirty hand-written volumes, including three almanacs (1806-1808), three anthologies of Rusyn folk songs, and a volume of Rusyn proverbs and tales.[78]

More nationally minded than Dovhovych, and somewhat more successful in publishing his writings than Iuhasevych, was Ivan Fogarashii-Berezhanyn (1786-1834). Clearly, his education and long residence in Vienna had a decisive influence on his attitude toward his native land. He studied at the *Barbareum,* then returned home to serve a few years as a parish priest and later rector of the Uzhhorod Theological Seminary. In 1818, he went back to Vienna and remained until his death as the priest of the Church of St. Barbara.[79] After reading his countryman Orlai's history of Subcarpathian Rus', and under the immediate influence of Kopitar's Slavic circle in Vienna, Fogarashii decided to write a study on the dialects of his homeland. The result was an extended essay entitled, "On the General Distinction between Slavonic Dialects, especially the Little and Carpathian or Uhro-Russian." He completed the manuscript in 1827 and sent it to Orlai in St. Petersburg, where it remained unpublished until the beginning of the twentieth century. Like his contemporaries, Fogarashii emphasized the linguistic unity of his people with the Rusyns of Galicia and of the Ukraine, and by implication with the Great Russians. "The Carpathian or Uhro-Russians (*Karpato ili ugro-rossiane*) are by their origin Little Russians," he wrote, and their language derives from that source.[80] Nonetheless, in "Little [Russia] as well as in Uhro-Russia, educated and cultured individuals—the clergy, gentry, cantors and teachers—write and speak a pure Old Slavonic or Rusyn language [*chistym starinnym slavianskim ili rus'kim iazykom*] as accurately and purely as the Great Russians themselves [*kak i samyi veliko-rossiane*]."[81] He called on all Slavic peoples to use this Old Slavonic language, not their own dialects, in writing. This use of Slaveno-Rusyn, or the Subcarpathian recension of Church Slavonic, is revealed in Fogarashii's *Rus'ko uhorska ili malorus'ka grammatika* ("Hungarian Rusyn or Little Rusyn Grammar," 1833) and in his other writings.[82]

Like Fogarashii, Mykhail I. Luchkai (1789-1843) was educated at the *Barbareum.* After living for a while in Italy, he returned to Uzhhorod in 1831 and remained there until his death.[83] Also like Fogarashii, Luchkai called for the use of Old Slavonic as the literary language for all Slavic peoples. In the introduction to his *Grammatica Slavo-Ruthena* (1830), he posited the theory that spoken and literary languages were different mediums and that the two should never be confused. Since Latin is the language of literature and science among the French, Germans, and Italians, he felt it only natural that Church Slavonic should be the literary medium among the Slavs. As a Pan-Slavist, Luchkai feared that the necessary drive toward Slavic linguistic unity would be undermined if separate "foreign languages" were developed from the various Slavic "dialects." With regard to the Subcarpathian dialects, he stressed that these were related to the other Little Russian dialects and as such were clearly "different from Polish, Russian, and Czech."[84] Nonetheless, he rejected the popular language *(lingua communis* or *karpato-ruskaia)* of his people as unworthy for literary expression, and composed instead a grammar in a Subcarpathian recension of Church Slavonic.[85] The tendency to write in Church Slavonic, not the vernacular, was common among most Slavic peoples at various stages in their development, and this tradition was still being maintained in the first half of the nineteenth century, by Serbian as well as by Subcarpathian Rusyn authors.

With regard to incipient Subcarpathian Rusyn nationalism, Luchkai's greatest achievement was his six-volume *Historia Carpato-Ruthenorum.* Although never published, the manuscript was used by generations of Subcarpathian writers in their own work. Following the precedent set by A. Kollár and I. Bazilovych, Luchkai concentrated primarily on the history of the Mukachevo diocese. He also accepted the theories that the Rusyns were the indigenous population and that they were converted to Christianity by Cyril and Methodius. The true value of Luchkai's work, however, stemmed from the fact that he included numerous archival documents, some of which have subsequently been lost.[86] Luchkai was known throughout the Slavic world. He met with scholars from Russia and the Ukraine who visited Uzhhorod, and for his efforts on behalf of his people he was mentioned alongside Obradović, Dobrovský, Nejedlý, and Vuk Karadžić as one of the pantheon of Slavic leaders listed in Jan Kollár's renowned epic the *Daughter of Slavia* (1832).[87]

Despite the widespread contacts with other Slavic peoples and the activity of a handful of cultural leaders, the propagation of a Rusyn national identity was clearly waning during the first half of the nineteenth century. The reasons for this are many. Although the government issued a new *Ratio educationis* in 1806 requiring that teaching in elementary schools be carried out in the mother tongue, no funds were allotted and the school system set up by Bishop Bachyns'kyi began to decline. Moreover, at the secondary level, instruction in Slaveno-Rusyn, the Subcarpathian variety of Church Slavonic, was virtually non-existent. The gymnasium and teacher's college in Uzhhorod taught in Latin, and after the death of Bishop Bachyns'kyi in

1809 the theological seminary followed suit. Knowledge of Church Slavonic and the Rusyn dialect was so poor that in 1825 Bishop Aleksei Povchii (1753-1831, consecrated 1816) felt obliged to require that it be reinstated, at least in pastoral theology and pedagogy.[88] Active in the effort to foster the teaching of Rusyn at this time were Ioann I. Churhovych (1791-1862), who served as director of the Uzhhorod gymnasium and later of the teacher's college, and Bishop Vasylii Popovych (1796-1864, consecrated 1837), who in 1840 issued an episcopal letter requiring every parish to have a school and every local cantor to teach reading and writing as well as religion.[89] Bishop Popovych, who personally supported Dukhnovych in his younger years, was regarded by other Slavic observers (I. Sreznevs'kyi, B. Nosák-Nezabudov, J. M. Hurban) as an outstanding Rusyn patriot who called for new textbooks, tried to establish an educational fund, and maintained close contact with Subcarpathian figures in the Russian Empire. However, a generally unfavorable political situation prevented Popovych from fulfilling most of his goals.[90]

During the second quarter of the nineteenth century, while the Slavic peoples of the Hapsburg Empire were becoming aware of their strength and identity, Hungarian nationalism was also on the rise. This movement, which came to equate Magyar language and culture with the Hungarian state, was directly opposed to the national strivings of the Serbs, Croats, Slovaks, Rumanians, and other minorities within the kingdom. Symbolic evidence of the equation between the Magyar nationality and the Hungarian state was the increasing importance attached to the Magyar language. Historically, Latin had been the official language, but in 1792 Magyar was introduced into secondary schools. In 1830, it became the language of internal administration, and in 1844 the sole language of administration and commerce.[91] The Subcarpathian Rusyns were, of course, directly affected by these developments. Moreover, as a result of (1) the peasant rebellion of 1831, in which Slovaks and Rusyns were the leading participants, and (2) the demands of some Rusyn priests for use of Slaveno-Rusyn in their parish schools, the Magyar press, especially the *Pesti hírlap,* edited by the fiery and intransigent Hungarian patriot Lajos Kossuth, began to publish articles accusing Rusyn leaders of pro-Russian attitudes that were a great danger to the Hungarian state.[92]

However, unlike the intelligentsia of the other minorities, Rusyn leaders in general did not defend their national identity; rather, they rushed to accommodate themselves to the new Magyar-dominated environment. Indeed, for some, Hungarian culture was legitimately attractive. Describing his school years during the 1820s, Dukhnovych recalled believing "that besides the Magyar, there is nobody on earth" and that "Extra Hungarium non est vita" (There is no life but in Hungary).[93] Armed with these beliefs, many priests voluntarily introduced the Magyar language into Rusyn schools and into the official church records *(metrikas).* At the same time, nationally minded leaders were viewed with scorn: Luchkai was removed from the episcopal chancery, Dovhovych and Dukhnovych were limited in their cultural work, and Bishop Popovych was attacked for his Slavic inclinations by the Magyarized Rusyn clergy and seminarians, who even composed insulting songs about him. Thus the cultural and national situation among Rusyns looked rather bleak on the eve of 1848.[94]

One must agree with the historian L. Haraksim that before 1848 a Rusyn national movement did not exist.[95] Although patriotic leaders like the Bishops Bachyns'kyi and Popovych supported the national heritage through the Greek Catholic Church and its subsidiary school system, they had no support from above. The government in Vienna devised laudable plans for education in the national tongue but never delivered the funds. Then, after 1825, the formerly tolerant central and local Hungarian administrations steadily adopted the views of rising Hungarian nationalism. In this situation, Subcarpathian Rus' was left with a few individuals, like Luchkai, Fogarashii, and Dukhnovych, who tried to preserve the culture of their people, but they functioned in a vacuum and were for all intents and purposes isolated. Moreover, a suitable intellectual context never developed since potential leaders like Baludians'kyi, Orlai, Venelin, and Kukol'nyk left their homeland to serve the cause of other peoples. In a real sense, the Russian Empire, ever willing to accept talented individuals from abroad, became a kind of safety-valve defusing any concentration of intellectual strength, thus aborting an incipient national movement in Subcarpathian Rus'.

This did not, however, mean that the Subcarpathian Rusyn question was ignored. On the contrary, representatives of most Slavic peoples, especially Russians and Ukrainians in the tsarist empire and Galician Rusyns and Slovaks in the Hapsburg Empire, traveled, corresponded, and wrote about their Subcarpathian brethren. As a result, this period witnessed the flowering of two trends that were to mark the future of Subcarpathian Rusyn national development: (1) a deep sympathy for Russian culture, and (2) close cooperation with Galician Rusyn, and especially Slovak, leaders.

However, unlike their Slavic neighbors, the Subcarpathian Rusyns had not achieved any of the initial steps so necessary to national consolidation. In 1848, they still had no newspapers, no scholarly journals, no national museums, and no cultural societies. Most crucial, they had not even decided what language to use. Some claimed that Slaveno-Rusyn (Church Slavonic mixed with local dialect) should be the medium, some favored the vernacular. In the end, the most important writings appeared in Latin.[96] As a result, the Subcarpathian Rusyns had no unified cultural base from which to operate and remained unprepared for the tumultuous events of 1848 and 1849.

3 | *From Embryonic Nationalism to National Assimilation*

The seventy-year period 1848 to 1918 began and ended with political and social upheavals that were to have a profound effect on the course of Subcarpathian national life. As a result of the revolution of 1848, and in particular the counterrevolutionary events that followed, the Rusyns were for the first time to enter the stage of history as a distinct political and cultural entity.

In 1848 a series of revolutionary crises spread throughout Europe and across the multinational Hapsburg Empire. Leaders representing the Czechs, Slovaks, Poles, Galician Ukrainians, Rumanians, Croats, Serbs, and other nationalities demanded political, social, and cultural autonomy for their respective peoples. The Magyars revolted en masse against Hapsburg rule, although their struggle for independence was crushed on the battlefield in 1849.

The defeat of the Magyar cause came precisely at a time when the national minorities were making their own advances—and this was to be of fateful significance for the Subcarpathian Rusyns and other national groups in the Hungarian Kingdom. In essence, for almost two decades following the Magyar defeat, centralist forces in Vienna fostered in varying degrees the interests of the minorities, while politicians in Budapest were forced to bow to the will of the Hapsburg state. The unequal balance of political influence between Vienna and Budapest was altered, however, after the conclusion of a compromise in 1867. From that time, the Magyars were left to manage their own affairs as they saw fit, and the government in Budapest soon embarked on a policy of national assimilation that put an end to the few cultural and political advances made by the national minorities. The Subcarpathian Rusyns, the last group to organize at a national level, were the most susceptible to assimilation, so that by the eve of the First World War their national life was at a new low point. This process was not reversed until the break-up of the Hapsburg Empire and the revolutionary upheavals of late 1918 and early 1919. The present chapter will trace the first stirrings of an organized national life after 1848 and then analyze the process whereby the Subcarpathian intelligentsia was largely assimilated into the dominant Hungarian civilization.

The Revolution of 1848 and Its Aftermath

Within the Hapsburg Empire the revolutionary period lasted basically from March 1848 to August 1849. Its initial phase was marked by the fall of former rulers—the resignation of Prince Metternich in March as well as the abdication of Emperor Ferdinand in December 1848—and the implementation of numerous reforms, the most significant and lasting being the abolition of serfdom. The various nationalities also put forth demands at this time. In particular, the Magyars posed the greatest threat to the Empire, and already in the spring of 1848 they were waging an armed conflict that was to result later in a drive for complete independence. But by early 1849, the reconsolidation of Hapsburg authority was well underway, and the second or military phase of the revolutionary process was soon to end with the surrender of the Hungarian revolutionary army at Világos on August 13, 1849.[1]

It was the Hungarian aspect of the revolutionary period that most directly affected the Subcarpathian Rusyns. News of the events in Budapest reached Subcarpathian Rus' as early as March 18-19, 1848, when the text of Petőfi's Twelve Points was publicly displayed on the streets of Uzhhorod and Mukachevo. This revolutionary statement, which represented the basic program of the Hungarian reformers, was received favorably by the local Rusyn intelligentsia, and in response to two of its provisos many students at the seminary in Uzhhorod rushed to join the National Guard, while some of the clergy prepared to enter the lists in the proposed election to a national diet.[2] It is characteristic that the local aristocracy, fearing a loss of its own political influence, began to spread rumors reviving the old accusations that Rusyns were Pan-Slavists and hence a danger to the state.[3]

Actually, the Rusyn response was one of unequivocal loyalty to Hungary. In a long article published in June 1848 in a Budapest newspaper, the Prešov canon Viktor I. Dobrianskii (1816-1860) argued that historically, Rusyns had always fought alongside Magyars for freedom and never revealed the slightest degree of treachery. Though in the Magyar language Rusyns are designated as *orosz,* a synonym for Russian, this was no reason to deduce that they harbored any pro-Russian sympathies. Accordingly, V. Dobrianskii argued, one should not equate Rusyns with Muscovites, nor believe that Orthodoxy is an ideology that appeals to them. Summing up his arguments, he concluded that for Rusyns "Hungarian freedom is dearer than Russian autocracy, and the pleasant atmosphere of Hungary is more attractive than the winters of Siberia."[4]

Loyalty to Hungary was again emphasized by the fact that no Rusyn delegate was present at the Slav Congress held in Prague June 2-10, 1848. That Congress, which attracted Slavic delegates both from within and beyond the borders of the Hapsburg Empire, provided an opportunity for many peoples, like the Slovaks and Galician Rusyns, to express their national goals for the first time at an international public forum.[5] Although the Subcarpathian Rusyns did not have a representative at the congress, they were not forgotten.[6] On June 7, Ivan Borysykevych, vice-chairman of the Supreme Rusyn Council (Holovna Rus'ka Rada) in L'viv, proposed that the Slovaks also look after the Hungarian Rusyns.[7] That same day, the Slovak leader, Jozef M. Hurban, issued a seven-point memorandum in the name of the Slovaks and Rusyns of Hungary. Among the demands were: (1) that the "Hungarian Slovaks and Rusyns be recognized as nationalities by the Magyars," and (2) that they receive their own elementary, secondary, and technical schools and even a university.[8] This desire for cooperation was later reiterated in a call to our Rusyn brothers *(Bratia Russyny!)* issued in Vienna by the Slovak National Council on September 10, 1848.[9]

However, the political activity of the Slovaks influenced neither the majority of Subcarpathian Rusyn leaders, who remained loyal to Hungary, nor the small circle of activists who began to formulate their own program. The latter group gravitated around Adol'f Dobrianskii (1817-1901), a figure who for all practical purposes was to dominate Subcarpathian Rusyn political life for the next several decades. Dobrianskii was born in the village of Rudlov (Érezfalva, Zemplén county). During the 1830s, he completed studies at the philosophical faculty in Košice (Kassa), the juridical faculty in Eger, and finally the mining and forestry academy in Banská Štiavnica (Selmeczbánya).[10] Later he received further specialized training in Vienna and then worked in the mining industry until 1848, when he was elected deputy to the Hungarian Parliament from the Slovak district of Banská Štiavnica. However, he was not accepted as a candidate, because the Hungarian government already considered him a Pan-Slavic agitator and a danger to the state.

Dobrianskii than settled in Prešov, where in cooperation with local Rusyn leaders he began to formulate a political program. On January 29, 1849, he led a delegation of Rusyns to Vienna. There the delegation met the new emperor, Franz Joseph, and presented to him the main proviso of Dobrianskii's political program—unity of the Subcarpathian Rusyns with their brethren in Galicia.[11] Dobrianskii then travelled to L'viv to meet with local Rusyn leaders there. He was received with great enthusiasm, and as a result the Supreme Rusyn Council, on April 20, sent a memorandum to the emperor through the governor of Galicia, Count Agenor Gołuchowski, calling for union with the Subcarpathian Rusyns. That same month the Galician Rusyn journal, *Zoria Halyts'ka,* reported favorably on the request of the Subcarpathians and published a long article by Aleksander Dukhnovych entitled: "On the situation of the Rusyns in Hungary." After tracing the historical fate of his people and their miserable conditions under the Magyars, Dukhnovych argued that the "Hungarian Rusyns were long ago united with

Galicia, and in Hungary itself [they were] recognized as an independent people." Moreover, "their national life would be completely lost in a short time if his Imperial Majesty [Franz Joseph] would not permit soon the desired union of all Austrian Rusyns into one province."[12]

It should be stressed that the activity of the Dobrianskii circle was not at all a widespread political phenomenon. Rather, it was limited to a small group of activists centered in Prešov, who were in fact disavowed by the larger and more influential pro-Magyar Rusyn clerical circles in Uzhhorod. Even the Hungarian government, so sensitive to the slightest Pan-Slavic inclinations, did not yet know of the political machinations of Dobrianskii and his group.[13]

Nonetheless, the Hungarian government's worst fears concerning Dobrianskii were confirmed. In April 1849, Dobrianskii returned to Vienna to determine the fate of his earlier petition. At that time, the Austrian government was in a state of panic, since a series of victories by the Hungarian revolutionaries had opened the way for their advance on the imperial capital. In this critical situation, Franz Joseph called on Tsar Nicholas I to send Russian troops to crush the Hungarian forces. While in Vienna, Dobrianskii met with Minister Bach, who on April 19 appointed him civil commissar to the advancing Russian army.[14] Thus, the Subcarpathian leader was to play an important role in helping those forces that were to destroy the Hungarian revolution.

The main Russian army of Prince Paskevich crossed into Hungary in June 1849 via Carpathian mountain passes that led through Subcarpathian Rusyn territory. One eyewitness later recalled how the Rusyns joyfully met the invading forces. "Our peasants continually carried baggage, while smiling children brought to the [army] camp apples, plums, nuts, etc . . ."[15] The Rusyns, whose only external contact had been with a Magyar world, were awestruck by the fact that "they freely conversed with the *Moskaly* (Russians) and without difficulty understood their language."[16] In turn, the tsarist troops recorded how the "Rusnaks greeted us with trust," and although they did not at all expect to find Slavs in Hungary—least of all "Rusnaks"—it seems from all sources that relations were very cordial.[17]

The majority of the Subcarpathian leaders, including the Greek Catholic clergy, were in a dilemma. Their traditional Magyar sympathies had initially led them to favor the revolution, but their generally conservative outlook eventually made them reject the politically extreme independence program of Hungary's Lajos Kossuth and to support instead the legitimacy of the government of Vienna.[18] For the nationally aware intelligentsia, however, the choices were clear cut. Perhaps Dukhnovych best summed up their attitude: "One thing really gave me joy in life and that was in 1849 when I first saw the glorious Russian army . . . I can't describe the feeling of gladness at seeing the first Cossack on the streets of Prešov. I danced and cried with delight . . . it was truly the first, perhaps the last, joy of my life."[19]

In the long run, it was extremely unfortunate that the first political successes experienced by Subcarpathian Rusyns coincided precisely with the period in history when the dominant Hungarian society under which they lived suffered one of its greatest defeats. Faced with overwhelming odds, the Hungarian revolutionaries were finally forced to surrender to the Austrian and Russian armies at Világos on August 19, 1849. Hungary's first prime minister and thirteen generals were shot or hanged, many more were executed or imprisoned, and for more than a decade the last vestiges of Hungarian self-rule were abolished and the country saddled with an administration controlled directly from Vienna. In such circumstances, the Subcarpathian Rusyns, under the leadership of Dobrianskii, reaped a few meager advantages from their former master's defeat.

With military and political power reconsolidated in the hands of Vienna, Dobrianskii left for the capital on October 1, 1849, in order once again to place the Rusyn question directly before the Emperor. He led a delegation that included his brother Viktor, Iosyf Sholtes, and Aleksander Ianyts'kyi. Upon their arrival, they were met by two other Rusyns, Dr. Vikentii Aleksovych and Dr. Mykhail Vysianyk, head of the general hospital in Vienna. The Subcarpathian delegation first consulted with Slovak and Galician leaders in the capital and then met with the highest government officials: the Imperial Commissar for Hungary, Baron Karl Geringer; Minister of Interior, Alexander von Bach; Minister of Justice, Anton von Schmerling; Minister of Finance, Philipp Krauss; and Minister President Felix von Schwarzenberg.[20] After receiving favorable assurances from these officials, the Rusyn delegation received an audience on October 19 with Franz Joseph. They submitted to the Emperor a twelve-point petition containing demands for implementation of the March 4, 1849 constitution, recognition of the Rusyn (*Ruski*) nationality in Hungary, establishment of a Rusyn territory, introduction of Rusyn language into schools and administration, appointment of Rusyn officials, publication of a Rusyn newspaper, and guarantees for Rusyn minorities in other parts of the kingdom. Noticeably absent was the previously stated ideal of unity with Galicia. The reason for this was simple: it was well known that Vienna opposed this goal, so the Galician Rusyn representatives urged Dobrianskii not to push the issue at this time. Nonetheless, the request for publication of a government-sponsored newspaper for all Rusyns and for guarantees that Subcarpathians could attend L'viv University were clear indications that some kind of relations with Rusyns north of the Carpathians were desired.[21]

Initially, it seemed that Dobrianskii's pro-Austrian policy would pay off. In October 1849, the government in Vienna reorganized Hungary, separating Croatia-Slavonia and Transylvania, and dividing the rest of the kingdom into five military districts, each of which was further subdivided into civil districts. The northeastern sector of the country became part of the Košice military district, made up of three civil districts. One of these, the

Uzhhorod district, including Ung, Bereg, Ugocsa, and Máramaros counties, was nominally administered by Ignác von Villetz, but practically by his advisor and deputy, Adol'f Dobrianskii. Dobrianskii viewed the Uzhhorod district as the basis for a Rusyn District in which he could implement his policies for national autonomy. Thus, when he arrived in Uzhhorod in November 1849, his first public addresses were given in Rusyn as well as in Magyar. Also, many of the officials appointed at the local level were of Rusyn nationality, Rusyn was introduced into the secondary schools, and public signs were posted in Rusyn alongside German and Magyar.[22] However, the experiment of a Rusyn District was short-lived. On March 28, 1850, the district was dissolved and Dobrianskii was transferred to Košice. Despite its brief existence, the few months of the Rusyn District did allow Rusyns some public recognition as a distinct group, and if the few political advances were overturned, the cultural innovations lasted much longer.

It is also interesting to note that Rusyns living in counties immediately to the west (Zemplén, Sáros, Szepes) made demands at this time for unification with the Rusyn District.[23] This desire was to reassert itself at various times during the next century. Another recurring theme was the paradoxical attitude of the Greek Catholic Church toward Rusyn national aspirations. While individual clergymen were in the forefront of the national movement, the hierarchy generally continued its pro-Magyar or pro-Austrian stance. Hence, a figure like Dobrianskii proved to be a great embarrassment to the clergy, and during the existence of the Rusyn District the Mukachevo eparchy argued that the appointment of Rusyn officials might alienate Slovak and Magyar members of the Greek Catholic Church.[24] Despite such local opposition, Dobrianskii did succeed in gaining some political advantages. It was in the cultural realm, however, that a more solid basis for a Rusyn national revival was laid.

If Rusyn political life was almost exclusively associated with A. Dobrianskii, Rusyn cultural activity was dominated by Aleksander Dukhnovych (1803-1865).[25] Dukhnovych was born in Topol'a (Kistopolya, Zemplén county) and educated at the gymnasium and Greek Catholic seminary in Uzhhorod. The young cleric served first in the episcopal administrations of the Prešov and Mukachevo dioceses, and after he clashed with his superiors,[26] he was relegated to the position of a parish priest. Unlike Dobrianskii, Dukhnovych spent almost all his life in the Subcarpathian region, where he exhibited many characteristics associated with activists in the early stages of nation building. He devoted himself to problems of Rusyn history,[27] ethnography, literary language, and popular education, and he worked to formulate a national literature and to organize national societies.

Dukhnovych was particularly concerned with raising the educational level of his people. Calling on Rusyn parents, he admonished that "a people without an education cannot call itself a people."[28] His 1847 elementary primer *(Knyzhytsia)* was the first text written solely in the local speech. He personally financed and distributed further editions of this work (1850, 1852), then published the *Sokraschennaia grammatika pys'mennago ruskago iazyka* ("A Short Grammar of the Rusyn Language," 1853).[29] In order to propagate these and other publications, Dukhnovych felt the need for a national organization, and in 1850 he founded the Prešov Literary Institution (Lyteraturnoe Zavedenie Priashevskoe). This was the first Rusyn cultural society, and although it did not have a legal charter, it functioned out of Dukhnovych's home for three years, sponsoring twelve publications and including among its active members Rusyns as well as local Czech and Slovak sympathizers.[30] Among its influential publications was the first published play in Subcarpathian literature, Dukhovych's "Dobrodîtel' prevyshaet bohatstvo" ("Virtue Is more Important than Riches," 1850), and the first Rusyn calendars and literary almanacs, entitled *Pozdravlenie Rusynov* ("Greetings for the Rusyns").[31] It was in the almanac for 1851 that Dukhnovych's poem "Vruchanie" ("Dedication") first appeared. This work, which became the national credo of Subcarpathian Rusyns, began with the famous words:

> I was, am, and will be a Rusyn,
> I will not forget my honorable lineage,
> And will remain its son.[32]

These publications were complemented by the appearance of the first periodicals intended for Rusyns. In 1850, the government decided to issue in Vienna a bulletin in all languages of the monarchy,[33] as well as a journal devoted specially to the Rusyns, *Vîstnyk . . . posviashchennoie . . . Rusynov avstriiskoî derzhavŷ* (1850-1866). The *Vîstnyk,* edited by the Galicians Ivan F. Holovats'kyi, Iulii Vyslobots'kyi, and Bogdan A. Deditskii, also included Subcarpathian contributors like A. Dukhnovych, A. Dobrianskii, V. Dobrianskii, Ioann Rakovskii (1815-1885), and Nikolai Nod' (1819-1862). Rakovskii later published in Budapest two newspapers for Greek Catholics in Subcarpathian Rus' and Galicia: *Tserkovnaia gazeta* (1856-1858) and *Tserkovnyi viestnik dlia Rusinov avstriiskoi derzhavy* (1858).[34]

The strong ties between the Subcarpathian Rusyns and their neighbor Slovaks continued during these years. Dobrianskii was married to a Slovak and was himself a member of the Hungarian Parliament from a Slovak district. His political activity in the name of Rusyns was always coordinated with Slovak developments. In the realm of culture, many Slovaks were members of the Prešov Literary Institution and worked closely with Dukhnovych. Recently, archival documents have surfaced revealing that during the 1850s plans were made to establish two separate Slovak-Rusyn cultural societies. The first of these was to be called Tatrín, based on Štúr's organization of the previous decade; the second was named the Society of Slavic Peoples in Hungary (Matica slovanských narodov v Uhorsku) and was to include Serbs as well as Rusyns and Slovaks. Although these societies never came into existence, the Slovak interest in Rusyns was again revealed in a memorandum issued by the Matica Slovenská (1863-1875), which called upon the "Russian people in Galicia and in Hungary" for "help and co-operation."[35] It is significant that Slovaks communicated with Rusyns in the Russian language, and throughout the nineteenth century they considered their Subcarpathian neighbors to be of Russian nationality.[36]

Relations between Subcarpathian and Galician Rusyns also increased. In an 1850 issue of the Viennese *Vîstnyk,* Rakovskii wrote: "Only a short time has passed since we began to be acquainted with our Galician brethen, and the more this continues the clearer we see that the same national spirit and aspirations move all of us."[37] In a similar vein, Dukhnovych dedicated a poem entitled "Holos radosty" (A Voice of Gladness) to Hryhorii Iakhymovych upon his appointment in 1860 as Metropolitan of the Greek Catholic Church in L'viv:

> Your people beyond the mountains are not foreign,
> Rus' is one, a single idea in all our spirits.
>   . . . . .
> Similarly we are happy if among you,
> Galicians, there are joyous times.
> And so now confidently I turn to you
> Because the Carpathians cannot separate us forever.[38]

Personal contacts continued to occur between Galician and Subcarpathian leaders and Greek Catholic seminarians in Vienna, while many Galician students came to study in the German language gymnasia of northeastern Hungary after 1849. Finally, Subcarpathian authors had their books and articles published in L'viv and Przemyśl. In particular, Dukhnovych and the Galician activist Iakiv Holovats'kyi, expanded their correspondence and exchange of books.[39]

This sudden increase in publishing activity did bring to the fore a serious problem, that of a standard or literary language. During the first half of the nineteenth century, the few members of the Subcarpathian intelligentsia wrote either in Latin or in Slaveno-Rusyn. Slaveno-Rusyn was not a codified language, but a Subcarpathian recension of Church Slavonic (mixed with Rusyn dialectisms) that varied from author to author. After 1848, when the possibilities for publishing were greater than ever before, the question of what language to use became a problem.

Because Dukhnovych dominated the cultural scene, his opinion on the language question is of importance. Basically, he employed two styles: a "low style," or Subcarpathian Rusyn vernacular, and a "high style," or Slaveno-Rusyn. On the one hand, Dukhnovych maintained the tradition of his early nineteenth century predecessors, Tarkovych, Fogarashii, and

Luchkai, by using Slaveno-Rusyn for his laudatory odes, essays, histories, and ecclesiastical writings. At the same time, he wanted to educate the masses, and realized that this could best be achieved by using the vernacular, which he subsequently employed in his poetry, satirical plays, and elementary-school books.[40] Throughout his writings, Dukhnovych tried not to mix the two styles, remaining skeptical about the vernacular, so that when Subcarpathian publications began to use too many dialectal elements, he asked critically: "Which German, Frenchman, or Englishman writes as the average person speaks? None! . . . We must liberate ourselves from the mistakes of peasant vulgarisms and not fall into the mire of peasant phraseology . . . We conclude that the problem has arisen because no differentiation is made between higher learning and books for the simple peasants."[41] It is ironic that the national awakener of the Subcarpathian Rusyns, who wrote the national anthem, numerous popular poems, and the first grammars in the local language, could frown so deeply upon the speech of his own people.

Indeed, Dukhnovych was not alone in this attitude, but it now became a question of what the "higher written style" should be. Ioann Rakovskii, an influential Subcarpathian editor in Vienna, at first maintained the Slaveno-Rusyn tradition, because Church Slavonic was a language with *dignitas,* "a 'Biblical' language," which was moreover "understandable to everyone."[42] In fact, Rusyn villagers were quite familiar with the language: it was actively used in liturgies and sermons, and even more important, Subcarpathian spoken dialects retained many of the archaic structural and lexical elements of Church Slavonic. However, the political activist A. Dobrianskii argued that for contemporary problems a more modern language should be chosen. According to him, this should be Church Slavonic's modern descendant, Great Russian, a language having dignity because it was the medium used by the government of a powerful state.[43] Eventually, Rakovskii also came around to this position, and in response to those readers—especially the clergy from Galicia—who wanted a more dialectal language, he stated that this would not be possible since the "number of dialects we have is enormous." The only solution was to "adopt the Great Russian language [*Velikorossiiskii iazyk*] for the diffusion of popular enlightenment."[44] Notwithstanding what they thought they were doing (writing in Russian), Rusyn authors began to write in a Subcarpathian recension of Russian, a medium that included varying elements of Church Slavonic, local dialect, and standard Russian—an uncodified language, difficult to understand and ironically described by some as the *iazychie,* or "macaronic jargon."[45]

Along with these linguistic controversies came the first signs of dissension between the Subcarpathian and Galician Rusyns. By the 1860s, eastern Galicia was experiencing the birth pangs of its own national renaissance. The Galician Rusyn intelligentsia was undecided as to its own national identity. Basically, two factions existed: (1) the "Old Rusyns," or Russophiles, led by Bogdan Deditskii, Ioann Naumovich, and Iakiv Holovats'kyi (now Golovatskii), who argued that Rusyns in the Hapsburg Empire were part of one unitary Russian nation that stretched from the Carpathians to the Pacific; and (2) the "Populists" or Ukrainophiles, led by Danylo Taniachkevych, Volodymyr Barvins'kyi, and Oleksander Barvins'kyi, who stressed that the Rusyns of Austro-Hungary and those in southern Russia (the Ukraine) were one people and that together they formed a distinct Ukrainian nationality. The Galician Polonophiles, led by Ivan Vahylevych, although agreeing with the Ukrainophile national position, felt that their political future should be in close alliance with the Poles.[46]

Among these conflicting groups, the Ukrainophiles were to become the most dynamic. In this period, however, they were still striving to raise the local Galician Rusyn dialects to the level of a viable literary medium, and in opposition to the Russophiles they rejected both Church Slavonic and Great Russian. But this was precisely the issue that upset Rusyn leaders in Subcarpathia. Dukhnovych summed up the general attitude of his own countrymen when, towards the end of his life, he bluntly criticized the linguistic orientation of the Galician Ukrainophiles:

Excuse me, brothers, if I am insulting someone but I must state that truly your writings are not in good taste. Your contemporary *belles-lettres* are suitable for use only in the tavern, for Hryts' and for Ivan, so that they can smile and laugh but not learn . . . I don't understand for what reason you could suddenly change the pure Rusyn language to Ukrainian [*chysta ruskaia mova na Oukraynskuiu*]—as if Galicia were in the Ukraine. In Galicia, so far as I know, there is another dialect . . . Your task should be to awaken the Ukraine so that it would adopt the original script and learn Rusyn grammar . . . I say that I don't understand what attractive force draws Galicia to the Ukraine.[47]

Indeed, Dukhnovych and other Subcarpathians continued to maintain close relations with the Russophile centers in L'viv, such as the Russian National Home (Russkii Narodnyi Dom), the Stavropigian Institute (Stavropigiiskii Institut), and the Galician-Russian Society (Galitsko-Russka Matitsa), and they published frequently in the Russophile organs *Slovo* (1861-1887), *Naukovyi sbornik* (1865-1869), and *Literaturnyi sbornik* (1869-1886).[48] After the 1880s, however, it was the Ukrainophiles, led by "radical" populists like Ivan Franko, Mykhailo Pavlyk, and Ostap Terlets'kyi, who clearly dominated the struggle to capture the allegiance of the Rusyn population in Galicia. As a result, the Russophile and Magyarone intelligentsia in Subcarpathian Rus' became even further alienated from their brethren to the north.

Despite what might seem like feverish activity in the years after 1848, in retrospect it is evident that this early stage of the Subcarpathian Rusyn national movement did not have any deep roots. For all intents and purposes it was limited to a very small group associated with the Dobrianskii-Dukhno-vych circle. Yet there were some solid achievements. Until 1867, Rusyn schools were fortunate to have their own inspector in the person of Viktor Dobrianskii, and between 1862 and 1869 individual professorships in Rusyn language and Rusyn history functioned at the Uzhhorod gymnasium. After 1849, the Rusyn language was also introduced by Dukhnovych at the Prešov gymnasium and two years later it was taught at the Košice Academy.[49]

As a counterbalance to these modest advances, however, there continued the traditional pro-Hungarian policies of the Greek Catholic hierarchy. Its generally antinationalist stance was revealed in various ways. For instance, the Mukachevo diocese, suspicious of Dukhnovych and others from Prešov, refused in 1851 to purchase any of the Rusyn literary almanacs published by the Prešov Literary Institution.[50] Then, in an attempt to accommodate itself to what it believed was Vienna's less positive attitude toward the national minorities, the diocese replaced Rusyn with Latin for administrative use. Another symbolic instance of its reticent position came in 1860, when, according to Vienna's October Diploma, the empire was to be restructured on a federalist basis. This move stimulated the various nationalities to act, and the Serbs and Slovaks sent petitions to Budapest. But the Uzhhorod Greek Catholic chancellery, fearing it might alienate the Magyars, only submitted an address to the local landowners asking, if possible, that it be included along with their own plea before the Hungarian Parliament.[51]

Though the Magyar politicians were for more than a decade secondary to the will of Vienna, by the 1860s their position had begun to improve. For instance, the imperial government was losing interest in playing off the national minorities against the Magyars, and the repercussions of this change in policy were soon evident. Although three Rusyns (A. Dobrianskii, Iurii Markush, and Aleksander Sherehel') were elected to the Budapest parliament in 1861, Dobrianskii's mandate was rejected by the Hungarian government. He nonetheless published his proposed parliamentary speech, which called for dividing Hungary into five national districts: German-Magyar, Serbian, Rumanian, Russian, and Slovak.[52] Dobrianskii was elected again in 1865 and served until 1868, when his parliamentary career was brought to an untimely end by government pressure.[53]

As the political position of Hungary began to improve during the 1860s, it seemed to some Rusyn patriots that the majority of their leaders exhibited an increasing desire to assimilate with Magyar culture. This phenomenon was graphically satirized in a popular play entitled, "Semeinoe prazdenstvo" ("The Family Celebration," 1867), by Ivan Danylovych-Korytnians'-kyi (1834-1895). This is the story of a young Rusyn who wants at all costs to become a Magyar, until he falls in love with a beautiful as well as patriotic girl who makes him return to the tradition of his "poor motherland, . . .

Uhors'ka Rus'."[54] The almost uncontrollable urge of Rusyns to Magyarize themselves forced Dukhnovych to write in 1863:

Those servile Rusyns in Hungarian national dress attach themselves to the aristocracy. They don't know Rusyn and don't want to know it. And tell the truth, haven't our own Rusyn demagogues betrayed our nationality more than the Magyars? Who protested against the just election of A. Dobrianskii to Parliament? Wasn't it Rusyns themselves?—moreover, priests, fathers, and defenders of the Rusyn people (as they like to call themselves)! So brothers, don't blame the Magyars for our oppression, but blame ourselves! We complain that others are oppressing us, but we don't do anything. We are always of such small character, and to tell the truth we don't want to raise ourselves up![55]

In an attempt to reverse the trend toward Magyarization, Rusyn leaders began to organize national societies. The first was the Society of St. John the Baptist (Obshchestvo sv. Ioanna Krestitelia), founded in Prešov in September 1862 by A. Dukhnovych and A. Dobrianskii. Its primary goal was the "education of Russian [Rusyn] youth for the future advantage of a national movement and renaissance."[56] The society soon included four hundred members (many of whom were Slovak national leaders in the Prešov Region), and it founded a student dormitory in Prešov (the Alumneum), organized local student circles, and served for a brief period as a platform for Dobrianskii's political programs. This activity was short-lived, however, because, after the death of Dukhnovych in 1865, the society functioned effectively only as an administrator for the Alumneum.[57]

Of even greater long-term significance for the future of Rusyn nationalism was the establishment in Uzhhorod in 1863 of the first Cyrillic-language printshop.[58] Since the end of the seventeenth century, Subcarpathian leaders had asked for their own printing facilities, but their requests went unheeded. Writings by native authors had to be sent for publication to Trnava, Vienna, Budapest, L'viv, or other Galician towns. Now, finally, they would have close access to a printing press, an instrument of crucial importance to national movements.

About the same time, plans were being made for the establishment of a new Rusyn national society. With the death of Dukhnovych, the focus of national life moved from Prešov, the site of the first two national societies, to Uzhhorod. There at the theological seminary a so-called Theological Society (Hittani Társulat) was set up in 1864. From members of this group came a request for government approval of a statute to establish an organization tentatively called the Literary Society of Subcarpathian Sons of the Eastern Catholic Church. This request was granted, although the organization did not really begin functioning until 1866, and then under a new name, the Society of St. Basil the Great (Obshchestvo sv. Vasiliia Velikago).

Initially, the St. Basil Society was headed by a group of local priests, but, beginning in October 1866, its chairmanship came into the hands of the political activist A. Dobrianskii. The founding membership numbered 350, and by 1870 the society had 700 members. The society's goals were primarily cultural: to provide Russian- and Magyar-language school texts for the Mukachevo and Prešov dioceses, and to publish newpapers and religious writings that would respond to the spiritual needs of the Greek Catholic Church.[59] Toward this end, the society revived the annual almanac *Mîsiatsoslov* in 1866, and the following year published *Svît* (1867-1871), the first Rusyn newspaper to appear in the homeland. By the last year of its existence *Svît* had as many as five hundred subscribers. Following the lead of Dobrianskii, the society's cultural and linguistic orientation was Russophile. Thus, the publications that were sponsored, such as those of Ioann Mondok (1824-1886) and Viktor Kimak (1840-1900), were in a Sub-carpathian recension of Russian, or, in the case of the grammars by Kirill Sabov (1838-19??) and Ioann Rakovskii, in standard Russian.[60] To the same period also belongs the government-sponsored *Ouchytel'* (1867-1868), the first newspaper for Rusyn teachers, edited by Andrei Ripai (1829-189?).[61] Thus, despite the laments of Dukhnovych that "in Hungary the Rusyn nationality no longer exists,"[62] a number of Subcarpathian patriots were nonetheless propagating national interests.

The twenty years from 1848 to 1868 have rightly been described as the era of a Subcarpathian Rusyn national renaissance.[63] The revolutionary events of 1848-1849 provided a convenient opportunity for an energetic political leader, Adol'f Dobrianskii, to formulate publicly for the first time the idea of a Rusyn nationality. Even if political successes were limited to a few months of tenuous autonomy, they nonetheless made an impression and re-mained in the collective consciousness of educated Rusyn society. More important, though, were the cultural achievements of Aleksander Dukhno-vych. The first readers, literary almanacs, literary and cultural societies, and national anthem were created by him during this period, while through him and several of his countrymen closer relations were established with the more nationally advanced Slovaks and Galician Rusyns. Hence, despite Duknovych's claims that a trend toward Magyarization had already per-meated Rusyn society, the 1860s were to witness the foundation of the first national organizations and the first locally published Subcarpathian news-paper.

However, in another sense, Dukhnovych's fears were justified. The Sub-carpathian national awakening had no depth. Unlike other nationalities, Rusyns were thrust into the post-1848 political arena completely unpre-pared. They had not yet established a clear sense of their own identity, nor did they have even the rudiments of a cultural base. Thus, the Rusyn national renaissance remained the work of a few individuals, who in the short period of twenty years were not able to affect the illiterate masses in any significant way.

How then, one might ask, did these leaders achieve the successes they did between 1848 and 1868? The answer is simple. They entered public life at a time when their Hungarian rulers were completely subordinated to Vienna, when the imperial government felt it advantageous from time to time to give token support and encouragement to the Rusyns and other minorities. However, this fortunate combination of events was to change after 1867, a year that ushered in a new era in the history of Hungary.

The Policy of Magyarization

Vienna's policy of centralization and direct rule over the Hungarian Kingdom proved in the end to be a failure. After Hungary's defeat in 1849, some leaders, like Prime Minister Batthyány, were executed, while others, like President Kossuth, were in exile. Those who remained or returned home, like Ferenc Deák, Baron József Eötvös and Count Gyula Andrássy, were for the time being without power, but not yet completely deprived of political influence. Magyar society, as depicted in the popular novels of Mór Jókai, was awaiting the chance to reverse its unfortunate political situation. The future improvement in Hungary's internal political life came about as a result of Austria's failure in the realm of foreign affairs.

A portent was the Austro-French-Sardinian War of 1859, when the Hapsburg Empire was forced to relinquish the rich province of Lombardy. During this conflict, there was serious talk of revolt in Hungary, and at the front the Magyar troops proved to be unreliable. A more serious threat to the empire came in 1866, when Austria's last hopes to influence the course of German politics were dashed by Prussian military might on the Bohemian fields of Sadová, near Hradec Králové (Königgrätz). Again, the Hungarians were reluctant participants in the struggle. Vienna was forced to realize, however, that its interests could no longer lie in a German Central Europe, now dominated by Prussia, but that internal consolidation of her own lands and political compromise with the intransigent Hungarians had to be the order of the day. Actually, negotiations between the Viennese court and Hungary's adept negotiator Ferenc Deák had been going on intermittently since 1865, without much success. It was Austria's defeat at the hands of Prussia that broke the political stalemate.[64]

The result was an *Ausgleich* or "compromise," negotiated in 1867 and implemented during the following year. According to this agreement, the dual monarchy of Austria-Hungary came into existence. Basically, the conduct and financing of foreign affairs and defense were recognized as the "common subjects" of both halves of the monarchy, while all other administrative affairs were to be handled on the one hand by the emperor and the parliament in Vienna for the seventeen Austrian crownlands, and on the other by the emperor (as king of Hungary) together with the parliament in Budapest for the Hungarian Kingdom. Despite dissatisfaction in some Magyar political circles, the Compromise of 1867 must be viewed as a sucess for Hungary, since it renewed the laws of 1722-1723 and 1790, by which the country was to be ruled exclusively by its own laws. Within the first few years of the *Ausgleich* the Hungarian parliament consolidated its centralist policy, effectively abolishing the separate status of Transylvania and other autonomous units and transforming the kingdom into "one and the same state complex."[65] Only Croatia-Slavonia was allowed to retain its own diet (*Sabor*) and a degree of internal autonomy.

As for the national minorities, the parliament refused to allow them any corporate recognition. According to "Law XLIV of 1868 on the equality of rights of the nationalities," it was proclaimed that "all citizens of Hungary constitute a single nation, the indivisible, unitary Magyar nation [*Magyar nemzet*], of which every citizen, to whatever nationality [*nemzetiség*] he belongs, is equally a member . . ."[66] Despite liberal guarantees protecting the use of national languages in official and religious affairs, the provisions of the 1868 law were never really implemented. While members of national minorities had the right to become Magyars, they could not propagate their own cultures in any organized way. All national societies were automatically considered illegal, since according to the law of 1868, there was only one nation, the Magyar nation. Thus, the reorganization of the Hapsburg empire brought about by the *Ausgleich* of 1867 may have guaranteed in theory the rights of the nationalities in both halves of the monarchy, but in practice those minorities living within the Hungarian Kingdom were to be left to the whims of the Magyar ruling classes.[67]

The implications of Hungarian Law XLIV of 1868 were soon felt among the Subcarpathian Rusyns. In 1869, a decree was passed forbidding the teaching of history in Rusyn at the Uzhhorod gymnasium, and within a few years the Rusyn language was dropped as a required subject.[68] A more serious threat to national development was the policy of István Pankovics (1820-1874) who served as bishop of the Mukachevo diocese from 1867 to 1874. Pankovics, perhaps more than any of his contemporaries, best embodied the Magyarone state of mind, which now more than ever was supported by the Hungarian government. In a heated discussion with Ivan Sil'vai (1838-1904), one of his more nationally minded priests, the bishop openly admitted: "If now we live under the rule of the Magyars, then we should become Magyars."[69]

In line with this thinking, Pankovics directed his wrath against the St. Basil Society. In an episcopal decree sent out in December 1870, he attacked the society's newspaper, *Svît,* for its "dangerous tendencies" and forbade his clergy to maintain any ties with the publication.[70] The following September he forced A. Dobrianskii and I. Rakovskii out of the society and replaced them by more Magyarone-minded priests. Simultaneously, *Svît* was discontinued and succeeded by *Novŷi svît* (1871-1872) edited by Viktor Gebei (1838-1896), but even this organ proved to be too "nationalist" and was soon replaced by *Karpat* (1872-1886). Under the editorship of Nikolai Gomichkov (1833-1886), this new paper limited itself to government news, and in its last years published half of each issue in Magyar as well as in the Subcarpathian recension of Russian.[71]

Continuing his efforts to undermine the Subcarpathian "Russophile nationalists," Pankovics had certain influential teachers and editors removed from their posts. Kirill Sabov was sent to southern Hungary and Iurii Ignatkov to Budapest. Disgusted by this unfortunate turn of events, Viktor Kimak, Mikhail Molchan (b. 1832), and Irinei Bachinskii continued the Subcarpathian tradition of going east, and left to pursue their careers in Russia.[72] In 1873, Pankovics ended the program that sent young Rusyn seminarians to study in Vienna, because he feared that in the Hapsburg capital they would be susceptible to "Muscovite" influence. That same year, a new vicariate was established at Hajdudorog to serve the Greek Catholics in what is now northeastern Hungary. There local priests strove to Magyarize the liturgy, and despite the disapproval of Rome, the Magyar language was introduced into some parts of the mass.[73] Finally, Pankovics put an end to the fund for the establishment of a Rusyn National Home (Narodnyi Dom), which was begun in May 1870 under the auspices of the St. Basil Society. By early 1871, 5,500 guldens had been collected, enough to purchase temporary quarters on episcopal property, but Pankovics had the building sold and at the seventh congress of the society in 1872 the fund was liquidated and the remaining monies given to the Society's general budget. At the eighth congress of the society in 1873, a call was made to change its name and publish more books in Magyar. Although this was not done, from then on the St. Basil Society, for all practical purposes, was no longer productive.[74]

How did the nationally minded intelligentsia react to these machinations? Initially, there were public attacks on the "Pankovics camp" in a short-lived satirical journal *Sova* (1871), edited by Emanuel Grabar (d. 1910), V. Kimak, and K. Sabov, but after six issues this newspaper was forced to disband and its editors made to leave their homeland.[75] The intransigent Dobrianskii also put up a fight, but his own position was severely undermined. In 1869 his parliamentary immunity was taken away and he returned to his estate in the village of Čertižné (Nagyesertész, Zemplén county). Two years later he published a political program for "Austrian Rus'," renewing his 1849 call for unification of Galicia, Bukovina, and Subcarpathian Rus'.[76] His days in Hungary, however, were numbered. In 1871, an attempt was made on his life, which resulted instead in the death of his son. Finally, in 1875, he emigrated to St. Petersburg. Six years later he returned to Austria and settled in L'viv, where he was promptly put on trial (with his daughter Olga Grabar and several leading Galician Russophiles) for treason, the chief prosecutor being none other than Kálmán Tisza, minister-president of Hungary. Dobrianskii was acquitted, and he retired to Vienna and then Innsbruck until his death in 1903. During his last years, he maintained close contact with political and scholarly circles in the Russian Empire and with Russophile leaders in Galicia. His writings in this period stressed the need for a federal restructuring of the Hapsburg Empire on the basis of nationalities, and he continued to defend the idea of uniting his own "Carpatho-Russian" people with one unified Russian civilization and to reject the development of the Ukrainian "separatist" movement in Galicia.[77] For all intents and purposes, however, Dobrianskii, like other active Rusyn nationalists, was, during the 1870s, removed from a direct role in Subcarpathian cultural affairs.

With the passing from the scene of Dukhnovych, Dobrianskii, Rakovskii, and Pankovics, Rusyn national life came to be dominated by two groups during the 1880s: (1) a small group of patriots who attempted to preserve some kind of Slavic national identity; and (2) a large group of Magyarones who favored complete assimilation with Magyar culture. One young Subcarpathian writer, Iulii Stavrovskii-Popradov (1850-1899), feared that the growing struggle between the Russophiles and Magyarones would decimate the incipient national movement and hoped that: "At least the young people among us should not belong to any party nor participate in the controversies of the older people. The duty of young people is only to love their own nation and within their capabilities contribute to its well-being . . . Arise, then, brothers and friends, to this holy task, to the defense and preservation of the nationality."[78]

A small group of nationally conscious Rusyns did heed Stavrovskii-Popradov's call, but their effectiveness was limited partly because of unfavorable political conditions and partly because of their own internal divisions. Their differences were usually articulated in debates over language, a question that still had not been resolved. Basically there were two factions within the nationalist intelligentsia: (1) the Rusynophiles or populists, who wanted to raise the cultural level of the masses by writing in a dialectal-based language; and (2) the Russophiles, who maintained that literary Russian (perceived to be the legitimate modern descendant of Church Slavonic) was the only sophisticated means of communication. Until the 1890s the populists were in the minority, even though they were favored by the Hungarian government, which had continually frowned on using a "foreign" language—Russian—for Subcarpathian publications. It was the government's displeasure with Russian that forced the discontinuation of Rakovskii's *Tserkovnaia gazeta* and *Tserkovnyi viestnik* in 1858 and led to the demise of *Svît,* which according to Bishop Pankovics was using a "language from a foreign country."[79] To the degree that the Hungarian government favored any publications for Rusyns, it looked to those authors who used a language based on the Subcarpathian dialects. This was the case with the *Zemskii pravytel'stvennŷi vîstnyk dlia korolevstva Uhorshchynŷ* (1850-1859), with the *Hazeta dlia narodnykh uchytelei* (1868-1874), which like its predecessor, *Ouchytel',* was first published in Russian, but after 1872 was issued in Rusyn dialect, and with the first government-sponsored elementary school texts, which were in the Subcarpathian recension of Russian. The tolerance toward the newspaper *Karpat* can also be explained by the fact that its editor, N. Gomichkov, "wanted to write in such a language, which possibly all could understand."[80] As might be expected, these first attempts at writing in a vernacular based language resulted in an uncodified mixture of Rusyn dialect combined with Magyar, Russian, and Church Slavonic elements.[81]

In an attempt to improve this situation, Teodor Zlots'kyi (1846-1926) completed in 1883 the first grammar based solely on Subcarpathian dialects, *A karpátalji orosznyelv oknyomozó grammatikája* ("A Practical Grammar of the Carpatho-Russian Language"), but even though a subscription to purchase the work was announced, it was never published.[82] Vasylii Chopei (1856-1934), a native of Subcarpathian Rus' and gymnasium professor in Budapest, was to have more success. Following the Ministry of Education's desire to have introductory texts in Rusyn (*rutén nyelv*), he published in 1881 a grammar and reader for elementary classes.[83] This was followed two years later by the first Rusyn-Magyar dictionary, which was awarded a prize by the Hungarian Academy of Sciences. In the introduction, Chopei pointed out that the Subcarpathian dialects are related to other Rusyn dialects north of the Carpathians and that by all means this "Rusyn language [*rus'kyi iazyk*] is independent and cannot be considered a dialect of Russian [*narîchyem rossyiskoho*]."[84] The language of Chopei was based on the Rusyn dialects of the lowland regions of Bereg, Ugocsa, and Máramaros counties, so that there were inevitably many Magyar loanwords. This aspect was particularly odious to Russophile authors, who viewed Chopei's language as a subversion of the "Russian" tradition in Subcarpathian Rus' and yet another step along the road of Magyarization.[85] We have seen how local authors may have thought they were writing in Russian, while in fact their language was a Subcarpathian recension of Russian—a combination of Church Slavonic, Russian, and dialectisms. That the actual linguistic capabilities of Subcarpathian writers were severely limited is revealed in the candid admission of Ivan Sil'vai (1838-1904): "At the beginning of the 1860s my knowledge of the Russian language was still insufficient. It was restricted to the speech of the common people . . . If I wanted to write something in Russian, I would first have to compose it in Magyar and then translate it into Russian; but this translation was extremely awkward, heavy, and filled with Magyarisms."[86]

By the end of the 1860s, however, at least some Subcarpathian authors had become proficient in Russian. For instance, the series of grammars, readers, and textbooks in literature, geography, and arithmetic by I. Rakovskii, K. Sabov, and V. Kimak, published by the St. Basil Society, were written in standard Russian, and these were the texts used in those few Subcarpa-

thian secondary schools offering instruction in "Russian" during the late
nineteenth century.[87] A high point in the Russophile orientation during
these years came in the work of Aleksander Mitrak (1839-1913). This prolific linguist, ethnographer, and historian completed in 1871 a massive
Russian-Magyar dictionary, which he was forced to publish at his own cost,
since the St. Basil Society rejected it "for political reasons" and the Hungarian Academy of Sciences "on scholarly grounds." The work, which
finally appeared a decade later, was a dictionary of standard Russian (with
some local dialectisms of Slavic origin) and became a useful tool for other
Subcarpathian authors.[88] Among these were Anatolii F. Kralitskii (1835-
1894), Ivan Sil'vai (Uriil Meteor), Iulii Stavrovskii-Popradov, and Ioann
Dulishkovich (1815-1883), who wrote a three-volume history of the Subcarpathian Rusyns.[89] Each of these authors strove with varying degrees of success to write in standard Russian, and even Aleksander Pavlovych (1819-
1900), a prolific poet who wrote almost exclusively in the dialect of his native Makovytsa region near Svidník (Sáros county), argued for the adoption of Russian for Subcarpathian cultural life.[90] In the face of increased
government pressure and the pervading tendency to assimilate with Magyar
society, this faction of the Subcarpathian nationalist intelligentsia held up
Lomonosov and Derzhavin as ideals and considered association with Russian culture as the only defense against complete national disintegration.
Their attitude was poignantly expressed in an article on the "Russian people" by Mitrak, in which he showed pride in the unity of Subcarpathians
with Russians: "It is comforting to know that besides us there still lives in
this world a people who speak as we do, pray to God in the same churches
as we, and whose bravery, richness and . . . cultural level place them among
the leading peoples."[91]

   This need, among Subcarpathian leaders, to turn toward Russia was best
summed up by the contemporary Ukrainian publicist, Mykhailo Drahomanov: "Uhro-Rusyn nationalism must take on Muscovite forms precisely because it is 'purely nationalistic', without any social implications. Such a
nationalism always depends on the state and not on the people—and since a
Ukrainian-Rusyn state does not exist, but a Muscovite-Petersburg one does,
it is only natural that Uhro-Rusyn nationalists incline their thoughts toward
this state."[92] As a result, the Subcarpathian Russophiles scorned not only
their countrymen like Chopei, who tried to raise the Rusyn dialects to the
level of a literary language, but also the Ukrainophiles in Galicia who were
successfully creating a Ukrainian literary language. They turned a deaf ear
toward Ivan Franko, Volodymyr Hnatiuk, and other Galician Ukrainians
who wanted to spread their ideology southward, and replied, in the tradition of Dukhnovych: "On this side of the Carpathians there is not one educated Russian [russkii] person who could be fascinated by your independent
script [the Ukrainian phonetic alphabet] and independent dreams . . . Between us there cannot be any general cooperation, so leave me in peace."[93]

The Further Decline in National Life and the Impact of the First World War

The 1890s inaugurated a new period in Subcarpathian national life in the sense that the Russophile faction of the intelligentsia was to give way to a group of younger writers, the "populists," who favored writing in a language based on local dialects. Nonetheless, it should be remembered that both factions of the nationalist intelligentsia, Russophile and Populist Rusynophile, were to remain in the minority, since the Magyarone trend toward national assimilation was to dominate Subcarpathian life right through the years of the First World War.

One of the last of the influential Russophile writers was Evgenii Fentsik (1844-1903).[94] Fentsik wrote poetry, drama, short stories, and historical essays, and, when the newspaper *Karpat* began to publish many of its articles in Magyar, he submitted his writings instead to the Galician Russophile journal *Slovo*. Finally, he decided to start a new journal, *Listok* (1885-1903), and to return to the language and cultural orientation of *Svît,* which in Fentsik's mind was the "generally accepted Russian literary language, formed on the basis of Church Slavonic."[95] But in a society where the schools did not teach Russian and where the intelligentsia used Magyar, or at best a "mixture of various [Slavic] jargons," the new journal could not count on a large readership. In an attempt to attract more subscribers, a supplement in Rusyn dialect was added, but even this did not help and at Fentsik's death *Listok* had only twenty-five subscribers.[96]

Clearly, by the turn of the twentieth century the tide had turned against the Russophiles, who were being replaced by younger writers like Evmenii Sabov (1859-1934), Iurii Zhatkovych (1855-1920), Avhustyn Voloshyn (1874-1925), Hiiador Stryps'kyi (1875-1949), and Mykhail Vrabel' (1866-1923).[97] Although they differed in approach, they all basically moved away from the association with Russian culture that was characteristic of their predecessors, and instead emphasized the history, folklore, and especially language of their own people. In a sense, they continued the Rusynophile populist orientation established by V. Chopei in the 1880s, although they lacked for the most part the official backing of the Hungarian government.

The fate and direction of Rusyn national life was now in the hands of these few writers, and their activity reveals to what degree the nationalist movement was still viable. While not the oldest in the group, E. Sabov was nonetheless a kind of transitional figure between the older Russophiles and the younger populist Rusynophiles. Sabov defended what he was fond of calling "the traditional Subcarpathian literary language," which he illustrated in the first parallel Rusyn-Magyar grammar, published in 1890 for students interested in "studying the Ugro-Russian literary language." Instead of Great Russian literary examples, he chose Rusyn folk tales and poems by local authors like Dukhnovych, Mitrak, and Fentsik. Moreover, his language was not standard Russian, but rather another variant of the Subcarpathian recension of Russian (distinguished by a heavy dependence on local Rusyn dialect).[98] To stress even further the achievements and unique development of Subcarpathian culture, Sabov published in 1893 the first anthology and literary history of his native land.[99] As Sabov's career developed, he continually stressed the distinctiveness of his own people and remained circumspect about associating Subcarpathian Rusyns with either Russians or Ukrainians.

From this period came also two popular textbooks: the *Bukvar'* ("Primer," 1898) of M. Vrabel', written in Rusyn popular speech, and the first edition of A. Voloshyn's *Metodicheskaia grammatika ugro-russkago literaturnago iazyka* ("Methodological Grammar of the Ugro-Russian Literary Language," 1899), written in a very strongly dialectally based Subcarpathian recension of Russian.[100] This greater concern with the local language and tradition led naturally to a concrete realization of the linguistic and cultural similarities found in neighboring Galicia. In essence, the populists were the first generation of Subcarpathians to show some sympathy toward the Ukrainophile movement north of the mountains. H. Stryps'kyi and Iu. Zhatkovych, for instance, were associated with the influential Shevchenko Scientific Society and both published in L'viv. Moreover, it was probably Stryps'kyi who, while studying in L'viv, provided the idea of establishing in 1897 the first Subcarpathian reading room (Greko-katolyts'ka chytal'nia) in the border village of Skotars'ki (Kis-szolyva, Bereg county), which then received books from the Prosvita Society in Galicia.[101]

For their part, the Galician Ukrainophiles devoted much attention to the Subcarpathian region. This was largely the result of a trip made through Subcarpathian Rus', in 1875-1876, by the distinguished exiled scholar from the Russian Ukraine, Mykhailo Drahomanov. Drahomanov was deeply moved by what he saw as the unfortunate lack of national consciousness among the Subcarpathian Rusyns and he wrote many essays about their plight. Toward the end of his life, in 1894, he was honored in Galicia with a jubilee ceremony, and it is interesting to note that in the response he sent from exile in Bulgaria, Drahomanov devoted one-third of his remarks to Uhors'ka Rus', which like a "wounded brother I can never forget." He had sworn to improve the situation there, and when this was no longer possible, he "placed this oath on the consciousness" of those many Galician countrymen who were honoring him.[102] Indeed, his students, like I. Franko, V. Hnatiuk, and others, did try, through scholarly research and publicistic work, to fulfill the directive of their mentor.

But this does not necessarily mean that the Subcarpathian populists were willing to accept for their own people the national ideals of their Galician Ukrainophile brethren. They were not yet ready to go so far. Thus, Voloshyn warned clearly against "those terrible diseases of Ukrainianism [*vikrainizma*] and radicalism that have recently spread in Galicia, have brought about continual strife, and have alienated the Rusyn from his church, his language, and even from his name Rusyn."[103] At this stage, Subcarpathian

Rusynophiles could argue only that a cultural and linguistic orientation based on the language and traditions of their own homeland was valid. They were convinced that their culture had its own vibrant and rich historical past and that it was related most closely to that of Galicia and not to Russia.[104]

Besides new publications, Subcarpathian society also witnessed a revival of organizational activity toward the end of the century. After more than two decades of inactivity, the St. Basil Society was revitalized in 1895, although it is characteristic that the deliberations were held in Magyar. The renewed organization tried to put aside its Russophile past. Instead it praised the contemporary social order and put forth claims for the existence of an independent Rusyn nation.[105] In 1902, the St. Basil Society was dissolved and succeeded by the Unio Publishing Company (Unió Könyvnyomda Részvény Társaság), whose primary purpose was the production of Rusyn-language periodicals and books. Among the more influential was the newspaper *Nauka* (1897-1914, 1918-1922), with the supplement *Selo* (1911-1912), edited by A. Voloshyn. There also appeared a second Rusyn language weekly in Budapest, *Nedîlia* (1898-1918), published by the Hungarian Ministry of Agriculture. *Nedîlia's* editor, M. Vrabel', commented that many want us to publish "in a grammatical language, but the simple peasants do not understand the grammatical language [presumably the medium of Fentsik and other Russophiles]; they are only able to understand the simple popular style [*prostonarodnyi styl'*] . . . We write in such a way so that the peasants understand us, even though this approach is not appreciated by many of our intelligentsia."[106] Unlike previous Subcarpathian periodicals, *Nauka* and *Nedîlia* were filled almost exclusively with news items and literary works by local authors whose subject matter was drawn from the Subcarpathian region. In effect, these two organs came to symbolize the last expression of Rusyn national life during the final years of Hungarian rule.[107]

Since the early 1870s, however, the nationalist intelligentsia, whether Russophile or populist in orientation, had represented only a small minority of educated Subcarpathians. By far, the largest majority anxiously strove to assimilate with Magyar culture. Why was Magyar culture so attractive?

After the signing of the 1867 Compromise with Vienna, the Hungarian government found itself in the most politically advantageous situation it had known since the Middle Ages. None of the parties involved, however, considered the compromise to be an ideal solution, and actually the Magyars viewed it only as a starting point from which to bargain for even greater autonomy within the Dual Monarchy. Moreover, they were operating with fresh memories of a defeated revolution, political executions, and imprisonments, as well as with a deep mistrust of the Viennese government, on the one hand, and of its own national minorities, on the other. To make matters worse, the Magyars were forced to accept the fact that they were a minority in their own country, outnumbered by the other national-ities.[108] These factors determined the policies of Hungary's influential Minister-President Kálmán Tisza, who dominated Hungarian politics from 1874 to 1890.

Before the balance of power with Vienna could be redressed in favor of Budapest, the Hungarian government had first to ensure political consolida-tion at home. Tisza "believed that a sufficiently energetic and systematic policy of assimilation would Magyarize a sufficient number of the Nationalities to tilt the national balance in Hungary decisively in favor of the Magyars."[109] Thus, Budapest's traditional opposition to centralized Hapsburg authority, and the almost pathological fear that the Magyars were a minority in their own country, resulted in an increasingly restrictive policy toward the national minorities.

Moreover, the uncomfortable feeling of being a non-Indo-European peo-ple surrounded by Slavs, Germans, and Rumanians on all sides was ever present in the Magyar consciousness. The earlier prediction of Herder that the Magyars would eventually disappear through absorption by their more populous neighbors seemed to be confirmed by contemporary census re-ports.[110] Magyar society's response to this situation was to develop a cult of illusion, a self-indulging sense of superiority in the mission and role of their unique culture and language, a national trait that Magyars called *délibáb* and which one recent critic perceptively translated as "a gift for wish-fulfillment."[111] The complete Magyarization of all aspects of life in the Hungarian Kingdom came to be the vehicle for *délibáb,* and a host of writ-ers like Mór Jókai, painters like Victor Madarász, Bertalan Székely, Gyula Benzúr, and Mihály Munkácsy, and composers like Ferenc Erkel and Mi-hály Mosonyi depicted in a late romantic spirit the glories of Hungary's past and the brightness of its future.[112] The culmination of all these develop-ments came in 1896 when a series of government-sponsored building and monument projects was realized and massive demonstrations were organ-ized to celebrate the achievements of Hungarian civilization in the thou-sandth year since the arrival of the Magyars in the Carpathian basin.[113] To participate fully in late nineteenth-century Hungarian society, one had to be a Magyar, and for many Rusyns, Slovaks, Germans, Jews, and to a lesser extent Croats and Serbs, the act of national assimilation seemed well worth the effort.[114]

To be sure, members of the national minorities were aided in this task by the Hungarian government. A number of organizations were established whose names clearly indicated their purpose: The Highlands Hungarian Public Education Society (Felvidéki Magyar Közművelődési Egyesület), the Greek Catholic Society of Faithful Magyars (A Hű Magyarok Görögkato-likus Egyesülete), and the various circles for the Magyarization of family and place names. Of particular importance in the assimilation process was the school system, which by steady progression became almost completely Magyarized. Starting at the highest level, the nationality law of 1871 made Magyar the official language of Budapest University, so that fluency in that language became a prerequisite for anyone wanting to enter the professions or civil service. The teacher's college at Uzhhorod already taught in Magyar, and when a new one was opened by the Greek Catholic Church in Presov in 1895 only Magyar was used. At the gymnasium level, with the exception of a course taught by E. Sabov in Rusyn during the 1880s at Uzhhorod, everything was in Magyar. Only in the elementary schools, traditionally run by the Greek Catholic Church, was Rusyn still the medium of instruction. But this too was to change. Beginning in the 1870s, the state began to establish many elementary schools in which Magyar was the exclusive language. Then, in 1897, a new school-law required the introduction of a Magyar study plan and proficiency in the Magyar language by the fourth class.[115]

The culmination of this process came in 1907 with the education acts of Count Albert Apponyi. Emphasis was on the teachers, all of whom were made state employees, even those who taught in church schools. They were forced to take a special oath of loyalty to the state and were legally "bound to encourage and strengthen in the soul of the children the spirit of attachment to the Hungarian fatherland and the consciousness of membership in the Hungarian nation."[116] It is interesting to note that even the nationally conscious A. Voloshyn could write in 1910 that "with this law Count Albert Apponyi has gained the deep appreciation of the whole country, and by his erudition, oratorical talent, piety, and love of people he has gained respect before the whole civilized world."[117] Statistics, of course, most graphically reveal the decline in the Rusyn educational system. In 1874, there were 479 Rusyn-language elementary schools; by 1896 the number had declined to 189, by 1906 to 23, and after that to zero. In 1896, there were also 255 Rusyn-Magyar bilingual schools, but by 1913 there were only 34 left. Hence, on the eve of the First World War only 34 elementary schools offered Rusyn children any instruction in their native tongue.[118]

Yet in the end, despite the Hungarian government's many efforts to assimilate the national minorities, the Subcarpathian Rusyns, at least, were not as well assimilated as the writings of Slavic authors and their sympathizers would lead one to believe. For instance, while between 1890 and 1900 the percentages of all the other minorities in Hungary declined, the percentage of Subcarpathian Rusyns increased slightly (2.21 percent to 2.24 percent). The official Hungarian census of 1900 recorded 410,283 Rusyns; this number did not differ substantially from the estimate of 422,070 given by the Galician-Ukrainian scholar Stepan Tomashivs'kyi, who perhaps more than any other contemporary writer investigated the census records in depth.[119]

This is not to suggest that Hungarian officials did not, willingly or unwillingly, falsify their statistical reports. They did. The point to stress here, however, is that, while most of the Subcarpathian intelligentsia became Magyarized, the mass of the population remained unaffected.[120] Only the implementation of an effective universal-education system, combined with an increase in social and economic mobility, could have provided the groundwork for the desired large-scale assimilation of Rusyns. But during the late nineteenth and early twentieth centuries Hungary was still a pre-industrial, underdeveloped society that was unable to provide the kind of totalitarian prerequisites that are necessary to change the thought processes and national sentiments of a people.

Perhaps because it was unsuccessful in its efforts to assimilate the relatively stable number of Rusyns, the Hungarian government felt obliged to apply pressure on Subcarpathian society. These forms of pressure ranged from electoral discrimination, police surveillance of suspected Pan-Slavs, limitation of contacts with Galicia, and polemical attacks on the revived St. Basil Society,[121] to trials for treason against peasants who converted to Orthodoxy. The return to Orthodoxy in Subcarpathian Rus', which began in the late nineteenth century, was stimulated by monetary and ideological support from both the United States and the Russian Empire.

In the 1880s the first waves of Rusyn, Slovak, and Magyar emigrants left Hungary. The poverty of Carpathian villages had worsened following a dislocation in the Hungarian economy. In essence, while agricultural productivity rose as a result of modernization in farming techniques, there was a concomitant decrease in the need for agrarian labor, which in turn could not be readily absorbed into urban areas because of the relatively slower rate of industrialization. Thus, although the peasants, whether of Rusyn, Slovak, or Magyar nationality, were legally liberated from serfdom in 1848, they still remained economically and socially immobilized and in debt to the large landholders or, more often than not, to the local Jews. One source of relief was to flee to America, and by the eve of the First World War almost 150,000 Rusyns, mostly from Szepes, Sáros, Zemplén, and Ung counties, had done so.[122]

It was in the New World that Rusyn industrial workers and their clerical intelligentsia became exposed to various national and religious ideologies. Besides close contacts with Slovak immigrants, the Subcarpathian Rusyns were initially united in fraternal and cultural organizations with Russophile and Ukrainophile immigrants from Galicia. The Hungarian government was particularly wary of these relations, because they feared that Russian and, worse yet, Ukrainian nationalism might be spread in the homeland by returning immigrants.[123] Even more crucial was the exposure to Orthodoxy. When the hierarchy of the Roman Catholic Church in the United States proved unwilling to accept Greek Catholic priests into their jurisdictions, many Rusyns protested and turned instead to the Russian Orthodox Church, which, supported by tsarist funds, was only too eager to accept the new converts.[124] Returning immigrants brought American dollars and Orthodox ideology back to the homeland, where small Orthodox communities were established in the early twentieth century in Iza (Máramaros county), Becherov (Biharó, Sáros county), and Velyki Luchky (Nagylucska, Bereg county).[125] By 1913, approximately 1,500 persons had converted to Orthodoxy. The Rusyns were anxious to convert, since the itinerant Orthodox priests did not demand the hated tithes that the Greek Catholic Church required. Thus, the Orthodox movement was prompted as much by discontent with social conditions as by religious fervor.[126]

These few Orthodox communities may have been a bit troublesome for the local Greek Catholic hierarchy, but they probably would not have bothered the Hungarian government had the Russians not entered the picture. During the late nineteenth and early twentieth centuries, both scholarly and political circles in Russia showed a great interest in the so-called "Russian" population living within the Hapsburg Empire, which included eastern Galicia, Bukovina, and Subcarpathian Rus'—that "one extremity indivisible from all the rest of Rus' [i.e., Russia]."[127] Vladimir Lamanskii, an outstanding scholar of Slavic history and civilization, influenced a whole generation of students to study the "Russian" population living beyond the borders of the tsarist empire. Among these was Aleksei L. Petrov (1859-1932), who began to study in depth the problem of Subcarpathian Rus'. Beginning in 1884, Petrov made several trips to the region and produced a monumental series of documentary, statistical, historical, and ethnographic studies. Petrov's interest in the Carpathian region was complemented by that of other scholars living in Russia and in Galicia, such as Konstantin L. Kustodiev, Vladimir A. Frantsev, Ilarion Svientsyts'kyi, Evhenii Perfets'kyi, Ivan P. Filevich, Grigorii Devollan, Iul'ian A. Iavorskii, and especially Fedor F. Aristov. Aristov wrote several works (mostly unpublished) on literary and historical developments in "Carpathian Russia" (Galicia, Bukovina, and Subcarpathian Rus'). Then, in 1907, he founded a Carpatho-Russian Museum in Moscow, which functioned for ten years and became an invaluable source for materials on the Carpathian region.[128]

But it was the Russian Foreign Office and the more politically-oriented organizations set up in the tsarist empire that really worried the Hungarian government. For instance, the powerful Konstantin P. Pobedonostsev, who was a member of the tsarist Council of Ministers and Director-General of the Russian Holy Synod, "had the most intense interest" in seeing one day that Russia annex Subcarpathian Rus' and Galicia. Pobedonostsev met on several occasions with Dobrianskii and gave his blessing to the Subcarpathian emigré's political activity and support of the Russophile orientation in the homeland.[129] After Pobedonostsev fell from power in 1905, Russian interest in Subcarpathian Rus' was taken up by a member of the Russian Duma, Count Vladimir Bobrinskii. In 1907, Bobrinskii founded the Galician-Russian Benevolent Society (Galitsko-russkoe Blagotvoritel'noe Obshchestvo), and the following year he visited Galicia and then participated in the Slav Congress in Prague, where he spoke about the unfavorable plight of the "Russians" living under Hapsburg rule. In 1913, he also helped to set up in St. Petersburg a Committee for Aid to the Starving in Galicia (Komitet dlia pomoshchi golodaiushchim v Chervonnoi Rusi). It was through these organizations that the Russian government and Russian Orthodox Church sent books, priests, agitators, and money to support Orthodoxy and Russophilism on both sides of the Carpathians.[130] Among the recipients of funds were the Russophile newspapers *Slavianskii viek* (1900-1905) in Vienna; *Chervonaia Rus'* (1888-1891), *Russkoe slovo* (1890-1893), and *Galichanin* (1893-1894) in L'viv; and *Russkaia pravda* (1910-1913) and *Pravoslavnaia Bukovina* (1913) in Chernivtsi. As a result, the return to Orthodoxy, which was financed by American immigrant dollars and Russian "rolling" rubles, was viewed by the government in Budapest not simply as a schismatic religious movement but as a blatant form of political infiltration that was a great danger to the Hungarian state.[131]

As a result, Magyar apprehension about Rusyn relations with Russia was transformed into a pathological fear, and between 1904 and 1906 three trials were held in Sighet (Máramarossziget), Debrecen, and Budapest against the recent converts to Orthodoxy. The most infamous of these was the trial held in Sighet from December 29, 1913, to March 3, 1914. Ninety-four Rusyns, including three women, were accused of "high treason against the Hungarian state" because they had converted to Orthodoxy. The Sighet trial became a cause-célèbre, drawing observers and witnesses (including a passionate appearance by Count Bobrinskii) from the Slavic world both within and beyond the borders of the Hapsburg Empire. Despite unfavorable publicity, the court nonetheless sentenced thirty-two persons to fines and to prison terms ranging from several months to four-and-a-half years.[132]

Considering the internal and external factors impinging on Subcarpathian society, it is not surprising that in the several decades before the First World War the majority of educated Rusyns, both in the homeland and in Budapest, became Magyarized. This was possible because, in one sense, Hungary was a very tolerant society. In keeping with the nationalities law of 1871, each citizen, despite his ethnic or religious origins, was free to become a Magyar. There was no discrimination if one accepted the Magyar identity whole-heartedly, and it is no surprise that a considerable number of Rusyns, Slovaks, Croats, Germans, and especially Jews became respectable Magyars. By the turn of the century this process had gone so far that one Hungarian publicist who traveled through Subcarpathian Rus' could write in 1901 that: "Among them I did not even discover a trace of particularism. *Actually I found there only Rusyn-speaking Magyars. Their intelligentsia is composed of priests and teachers. These are pure Magyars. Their social and domestic language is only Magyar.* They completed Magyar schools and married intelligent Magyar women. In short, they are Magyars from head to toe . . . *Today we must thank this intelligentsia that the Rusyn people feel themselves Magyar.*"[133] Of course, continued the author, it would be in the best interests of the country to liquidate any remnants of Rusyn national feeling. "At this time we cannot have any more important task than to liberate this Magyar-feeling people from the claws of destructive forces [Pan-Slav influences], *and regarding their language, to fuse it with Magyar.* Don't forget that the Rusyn wants to become a Hungarian . . . *We will in a short time Magyarize the four hundred thousand souls in this land.*"[134]

Literary and scholarly circles in Subcarpathian Rus' turned more and more toward Magyar as a means of expression, as revealed in the first completely Magyar-language newspaper for Rusyns, *Kelet* (1888-1901), and the first Rusyn scholarly journal, *Felvidéki sion* (1889-1891). These publications, edited by Gyula Drohobeczky (Drohobets'kyi, 1853-192?) and Sándor Mikita (Mykyta, 1855-19??), respectively, included political, social, and religious commentary as well as historical articles by authors like Iu. Zhatkovych. But the most widely read organ of the local Rusyn intelligentsia was the *Görögkatholikus szemle* (1899-1918), edited by Viktor Kaminskii (1854-1929). This weekly, published first by the St. Basil Society and later by Unio, became the most influential periodical for Rusyns. As might be expected, all these papers supported the policies of the Hungarian government and the Greek Catholic Church, and propagated implicitly and sometimes explicitly the idea of national assimilation.[135]

The circle of Rusyn professionals in Budapest revealed even more than their brethren in the homeland a desire to become Magyar. As is characteristic of recent converts, they became the most extreme proponents of the new ideology—in this case Magyarism. The leading figures in this group were the parliamentary members Jenő Szabó (1843-1921) and Endre Rabár, the lawyers Jenő Pásztély and Miklós Kutkafalvy (1882-19??), the physician Emil Demjanovics, the painter Ignác Roskovics (1854-1915), and the pedagogues Kálmán Demkó (1852-1918) and Ödön Kecskóczy. Their ideological goals were straightforward: to disassociate themselves and their people from the idea of a Rusyn nationality and to define themselves instead as Magyars of the Greek Catholic faith.[136]

To achieve their goals, they established: (1) the National Committee for Magyars of the Greek Catholic Rite (Görög Szertatású Katholikus Magyarok Országos Bizottságát) in 1898, headed by Jenő Szabó; (2) the Union of Magyar Greek Catholics in 1902; (3) several university student clubs; and (4) the Budapest weekly *Görög katholikus hírlap* (1903-1905), edited by Kálmán Demkó and János Pirodán. While in theory these organizations were to represent Hungarian Greek Catholics of all national backgrounds, in reality ethnic Rusyns made up most of the leadership and more than seventy percent of the membership. The Budapest Rusyns wanted to replace Church Slavonic with Magyar in the Greek Catholic liturgy, and in March 1900 they organized a pilgrimage of 461 persons to Rome to try to achieve their goal. The Vatican rejected their demand, but they nevertheless went ahead and introduced Magyar into the liturgy of the first Greek Catholic Church in Budapest upon its foundation in 1904.[137] An important concession did come in 1912, however, when the Vatican agreed to transform the vicariate of Hajdudorog into an independent diocese. Within the 160 Greek Catholic parishes located in Rusyn and Rusyn-Magyar villages in the Hajdudorog diocese, Church Slavonic was officially replaced by classical Greek, although in practice Latin and Magyar became the medium of expression.[138]

Beside the out-and-out assimilationists, there were also some Budapest Rusyns who, while they accepted Magyarization, still devoted a good portion of their lives to productive scholarship about their native land. The most outstanding of these was Antal Hodinka (1864-1946), a historian and member of the Hungarian Academy of Sciences, and Sándor Bonkáló (1880-1959), a linguist and university professor. Hodinka published several studies on the history of the Greek Catholic diocese of Mukachevo and on Rusyn socioeconomic history, while Bonkáló wrote on Rusyn language and culture, arguing that "the Carpatho-Rusyns [*kárpátalji rutének*] certainly form to a degree a separate national body."[139] To this group must also be counted Hiiador Stryps'kyi, a curator in the ethnographic section of the National Museum in Budapest, whose many publications included linguistic, historical, and ethnographic works about his own people, and Oreszt Szabó (1867-194?), an official in the Ministry of Interior who published a general survey on Hungary's Rusyns.[140] Finally, there were also Magyars who exhibited great interest in the Rusyns. Among these were Károly Mészáros (1821-1890), who wrote a history of the Rusyns and was instrumental in having the first permanent printshop set up in Uzhhorod in 1861.[141] Of even more significance to Rusyn cultural life was Tivadar Lehoczky (1830-1915), a native of Fiume who lived in Mukachevo from 1855 until his death. During these years he published the first Magyar translations of Rusyn folk songs and proverbs, wrote several histories on Bereg county and on his adopted city, and in 1911 established a museum that for several decades was the only repository for archeological materials from the Subcarpathian region.[142]

In the late nineteenth century, the Subcarpathian Rusyns were considered, if briefly, as a factor in the Hungarian political scene. Although as a group they were represented neither in the parliament nor at the Nationalities Congress of 1895,[143] they were nonetheless courted by the oppositional Catholic People's party of Count Nándor Zichy. This party promised to improve economic and cultural conditions among the minorities, and in 1895 it set up branches in Uzhhorod, Mukachevo, and Sevliush (Nagyszőllős, Ugocsa county). Later it gave a large subvention to set up the Magyar-language newspaper *Kelet* and gained the support of some of the Greek

Catholic clergy, who hoped to regain some of the prerogatives lost by their church.[144]

Fearing that the Catholic party might acquire a base of support in Rusyn areas that would undermine the strength of the ruling party, government officials met in Budapest, in March 1896, with Bishop Iulii Firtsak (1836-1912) of Mukachevo. The bishop, who was returning from a trip to Rome, took this opportunity to inform the government of the dire economic state of his people. He presented Minister-President Bánffy with a memorandum stating, among other things, that "in the mountainous regions inhabited by the Rusyn people in Máramaros, Bereg, Ung, and Zemplén [counties] it is necessary to create adequate living conditions before the emigration to America can stop."[145] Anxious to obtain Firtsak's political support, the government proposed to him a secret five-point compromise that included: (1) and (2) more financial aid for the Greek Catholic Church; (3) election of a priest to the parliament; (4) economic aid to Rusyn areas; and (5) appointment of a county lord lieutenant (föispan), other representatives, a school inspector, and judges from among the Greek Catholic population. The first three points were fulfilled rather quickly, the fifth one was ignored completely, while the fourth, economic aid, received attention only after the bishop acted a second time.[146]

Early in 1897, Firtsak issued a "Memorandum for the Advancement and Improvement of the Spiritual and Material Conditions among the People of Rusyn Language Living in the Northeastern Carpathians and in Ruthenia." In response to this move, the Ministry of Agriculture appointed a well-known economic administrator, Ede Egán (1851-1901) to reorganize on an economically rational basis the agricultural system in Bereg county. This was the beginning of the so-called Highlands Action (Hegyvidéki akció), which lasted until Egán's death. The program was designed to stem the tide of emigration as well as to undermine the ability of the Catholic People's Party to play upon national and socioeconomic issues. Egán also called for publication of books in Rusyn, promised Iu. Zhatkovych to support him in the preparation of a Rusyn ethnographic encyclopedia, and did in fact subsidize the publication in Budapest of the Rusyn-language newspaper Nedî-lia. Although these goals were apparently favorable to Rusyn nationalism, Egán's underlying motives were expressed in a report to the Hungarian Ministry of Agriculture: "I believe it is necessary to make use of this favorable situation in order to win over once and for all this nationality and to completely Magyarize it."[147]

Hence, threatened briefly by a potential rival party, the Hungarian government called on Bishop Firtsak, who, as Magyar writers like to say, acted as all true Rusyns (the gens fidelissima) should, and remained loyal to the state. But the advantages derived from Firtsak's compromise were short lived. In 1901, Egán was found mysteriously murdered and the Highlands

Action died with him. Crippling poverty, a continued increase in emigration and national assimilation were to remain the order of the day as long as Rusyns lived within the Hungarian Kingdom.[148]

The outbreak of the First World War in August 1914, and the four years of hostilities that followed, intensified the poverty and continuing assimilation of the Subcarpathian Rusyns. The only variant was in emigration. Because of the war, Rusyns, like other potential immigrants, were cut off from the ports that led to America and instead were funneled into the military trenches, where more than half died from wounds or disease. Nonetheless, Rusyns marched off without protest to the Italian and Russian fronts, and many hoped to be chosen for the highest honor, service in the Hungarian National Army, the *Honvéds*.[149]

At home, the trend toward Magyarization continued. In the summer of 1915, the Ministry of Cults in Budapest organized a Central Commission of Greek Catholics for the purpose of revising liturgical books, introducing the Gregorian calendar, and abolishing the use of the Cyrillic alphabet.[150] Although this effort failed, the intensely Magyarone Bishop István Novak (1879-1920, consecrated 1913) took it upon himself to introduce these measures in the Prešov diocese, and in the fall of 1915 Cyrillic was replaced by the Magyar script in school and in liturgical texts, and the Gregorian calendar was put into force. Support for these changes and expressions of love for Greek Catholicism and Hungary were the dominant themes of the new diocesan weekly *Nase otecsesctvo* (1916-1919). On the basis of a "decision in Parliament," the Magyarone Bishop Antal Papp (1867-1924) followed his Prešov colleague, and in September 1916 the same measures were introduced into the Mukachevo diocese.[151]

These acts seemed to be the final steps in the process of full Magyarization —and there was no protest at all among the Rusyns.[152] The intelligentsia, of course, was for the most part assimilated. Even nationally conscious populists like A. Voloshyn, Iu. Zhatkovych, M. Vrabel', and E. Sabov were loyal to Hungary. An indication of this love of the fatherland at the grass-roots level came at a national council held in the village of Verets'ky (Alsóvereczke, Bereg county) during the spring of 1915. There, several priests addressed a petition to the government declaring: "We propose and request that the use of the old names 'Rusyn' and 'Maloros' be finally discontinued and that we be called Hungarians or Catholics of the Eastern Rite, so that in this way we will be liberated from the repugnant and loathsome accusations of 'anti-patriotism' . . . [If this is done] the insinuations that we are related and that we are one in spirit with our enemies, the Russians, would cease."[153]

Such a declaration emphasized how eager the Subcarpathian intelligentsia was to convince the Hungarian government that it need not be so suspicious of the seemingly natural Rusyn inclination toward Russia. There was good reason for such suspicions, however. Of the many letters sent from Subcarpathian families to their sons and husbands at the front (communications that were intercepted by Austrian censors), the following phrases occurred repeatedly: "I and the whole village pray to God that the Russians are victorious"; and "It will be good if the Russians come, they will take the land from the landlords and give it to the poor."[154] At the same time, tsarist Russia had done its best to encourage such developments. Besides the various organizations set up by Count V. Bobrinskii, a group of Galician Russophiles led by the scholar Iul'ian Iavorskii and the editor Semen Labenskii emigrated to Russia, where in 1913 they set up a Carpatho-Russian Committee for Liberation (Karpato-Russkii Osvoboditel'nyi Komitet) in Kiev. Its goal was to prepare the groundwork for the future incorporation of Hapsburg Carpatho-Russian territories into Russia. Besides the publications of the Kiev-based committee, numerous other publicists churned out pamphlets about "Rus' beyond our borders."[155] This whole movement was approved by the Russian Ministry of Foreign Affairs and after the outbreak of the war received official blessing from the highest circles in the tsarist court. In August 1914, a proclamation over the signature of Grand Duke Nicholas, the supreme commander of the Russian army, was issued to the "Russians of Austria-Hungary." They were called upon to "stand up to greet the Russian warrior," so that they will be able to find their places "in a great undivided Russia"—"in the bosom of Mother Russia."[156] By late August, tsarist troops had crossed into Galicia, and during the winter months of 1914-1915 about 7,000 reached the Carpathians, where many officers expressed joy at finding "Russians" in Hungary. In turn, they were warmly greeted by the Subcarpathian population, and it was reported that 238 Rusyns voluntarily joined the Russian army.[157]

At the same time, in neighboring Galicia, the occupying Russian forces set up a civil adminstration headed by Count Iurii Bobrinskii, the brother of the tsarist propagandist Count V. Bobrinskii, while in Bukovina the local Russophile agitator Aleksei Gerovskii (1883-1972) was given broad authority to liquidate rival Ukrainophile organizations. In this way, the Russian army hoped to gain the support of the local population, all of whom they wrongly suspected to be Russophile.[158]

The Austro-Hungarian authorities were aware of these machinations and when the Russian army retreated they took widescale reprisals against the Rusyn population. While some retaliatory measures were reported in Subcarpathian Rus', these were especially fierce in Galicia, where the so-called Talerhof massacres took place. The result was the execution of many innocent peasants for no other reason than that they called themselves *rus'-kyi*.[159]

It is interesting to note that Hungarian troops operating in Galicia were the most sadistic in this regard. Moreover, the government in Budapest, which was literally infected by a paranoia of anything Russian, tried to re-

duce Russian influence by supporting Ukrainian nationalism. One indication of this was the establishment in Budapest of a new journal, *Ukránia*
(1916-1917), which attempted to foster sympathy in Hungarian society for
the cause of Ukrainian statehood.[160] It was such an attitude that allowed the
Ukrainian Sich Riflemen, a volunteer unit of the Austro-Hungarian Army,
to be stationed in Subcarpathian Rus' as early as 1914 in order to fight off
the Russian advance. The presence of this Ukrainian force could not have
helped but influence the local intelligentsia.[161] Yet, as one might expect,
most of these pro-Ukrainian developments occurred without the knowledge
of the Rusyn masses, who continued to lose men in the war, to experience
physical destruction in the villages at home, and to suffer from a famine because of worsening economic conditions.[162] Thus, despite some exposure to
their nationally conscious Russian and Ukrainian brethren during the war
years, Dr. Agoston Stefan (1877-1944), a Subcarpathian lawyer and later a
leading politican, could still confidently declare: "In ten years Rusyn youth
will be Magyar not only in spirit but in language also. Fruitless will be the
attempt of other Slavic peoples . . . who strive to free their [Rusyn] relatives. In the Carpathians there will be no relatives because here only Magyars will be everywhere!!"[163]

Nonetheless, precisely at a time when Subcarpathian Rusyns seemed fated
to disappear as a distinct ethnic group, the seeds of a new national revival
were being sown. Within the ranks of the Austro-Hungarian army, Rusyn
draftees met for the first time with Czechs, Serbs, Croats, and other Slavic
peoples, who, having a stronger national consciousness, were proud to
speak and sing in their own languages. The younger Rusyn soldiers soon
thought that perhaps they, too, should not be ashamed of their native "dialect." Then, as the war progressed, many Rusyns were captured on the eastern front. Some waited out the hostilities in relatively comfortable circumstances, others joined both the White and Red Russian armies, as well as the
Czechoslovak Legion, which had a special Carpatho-Russian division made
up of volunteers from Galicia and Subcarpathian Rus'.[164] In this Russian
environment, Rusyns renewed their sense of national awareness, and after
the revolutionary upheavals of 1917-1918 they became cognizant of how
social change might be brought about by armed revolution. In essence,
these Rusyns were no longer isolated in a Magyar world, and this was to
have a critical impact on their thought and on their actions in the fluid political and social situation that existed in their homeland after the war.

During the seventy years from 1848 to 1918, Subcarpathian Rusyn national development ran full circle. Before 1848, the majority of the Subcarpathian intelligentsia had not yet become nationally aware and only a few
individuals could be described as Rusyn patriots, primarily because they exhibited an antiquarian interest in their homeland. In 1918, the majority of
the Subcarpathian intelligentsia identified itself as Hungarian, while again
only a handful of conscious patriots identified with a Slavic heritage.

The intervening years did witness a national renaissance, with energetic leaders like the politician Dobrianskii and the writer Dukhnovych codifying the initial political and ideological orientations of the national movement. To them goes much of the credit for the first Rusyn newspapers and cultural organizations, and for the establishment of extensive contacts with the neighboring Slovaks and Galician Rusyns. Even if many aspects of the national ideology, especially the problem of language, remained to be worked out, the first steps at national consolidation had been made. However, the Rusyn movement was not given the time it needed, for after 1867, when Hungary was left to its own devices, a policy of Magyarization was begun in earnest. By the time of the First World War, the majority of Rusyn and, for that matter, Slovak leaders had become assimilated to Hungarian culture, so that some contemporary observers felt both groups would be destined for complete assimilation within a matter of a few years.[165]

Yet, in the absence of a deep-rooted educational system, the official policy of Magyarization never struck deep roots. Most of the population was left to its own devices and stuck to its traditional identity. When the experience of the First World War proved too taxing for the Austro-Hungarian monarchy, it collapsed in late 1918, giving way to an entirely different political order that allowed the Subcarpathian Rusyns a new lease on life. In effect, the years between 1918 and 1945 proved to be a true renaissance for Subcarpathian Rus', a time when the details for a Rusyn national ideology could be worked out. Before we focus on these developments, however, it is necessary to review how the political events of 1918-1919 shaped the course of the decades that were to follow.

4 | The Incorporation of Subcarpathian Rus' into Czechoslovakia

During the last months of 1918 profound political and social changes shook the Austro-Hungarian Empire. In late October, as Hapsburg administrative authority began to dissolve, Poles, Ukrainians, Czechs, Slovaks, Serbs, Croats, and Rumanians organized national councils to determine their political futures. From November 1918 to May 1919, Rusyns living in the northeastern counties of Hungary also formed many councils, which proposed various political alternatives: autonomy within Hungary, complete independence, or union with Russia, the Ukraine, or the new state of Czechoslovakia. Although these choices reflected the traditional political and cultural allegiances of Rusyn leaders, the international situation in 1919 proved favorable to only one—union with Czechoslovakia.

During the years 1918 and 1919, the Subcarpathian Rusyn problem went through three phases: the American phase, during which Rusyn immigrants in the United States discussed the fate of their homeland; the Subcarpathian phase, when local leaders set up national councils to consider the immediate future of the territory; and the Parisian phase, where the question was raised and decided upon at the peace conference. In the course of each phase, the leaders involved were constantly forced to keep in mind two aspects of the problem: the national desires of the local population and the political demands of the leading world powers. The combination of these two factors resulted in unification with Czechoslovakia.

Political Activity among Rusyn Immigrants in the United States
During the last months of the First World War, many immigrant groups in the United States became actively concerned about the fate of their respective homelands. Already in early 1918 it was evident that the map of Europe would be remade after the war, and immigrant leaders hoped to influence the course of those future changes. The potential economic and political strength of the American immigration was also recognized by statesmen in eastern and southern Europe. National spokesmen like Tomáš G. Masaryk and Ignacy Paderewski, for instance, spent several months in the

76

United States, where they solicited support among their overseas brethren for the idea of Czechoslovak and Polish statehood.[1] It was also at this time that Rusyn-American immigrants began seriously to consider organizational efforts on behalf of their native land. In comparison with other immigrant groups, Rusyns entered the political arena quite late, but they ultimately achieved their goals.[2]

Like most immigrants from eastern and southern Europe, Rusyns came to the United States to improve their economic status. and bv 1914 about 100,000 had settled in the New World. These former woodcutters, shepherds, and farmers were transformed into industrial workers who found employment in the mining and manufacturing centers of Pennsylvania, New York, New Jersey, and Ohio. Most Rusyns did not intend to remain in America, but wished only to earn enough dollars so that they could return to the "old country" and pay off a mortgage or buy a new homestead and more land. Despite the "temporary" nature of their stay, they did establish several organizations, especially in the vicinity of Pittsburgh, Pennsylvania.

The largest of these was the Greek Catholic Union of Rusyn Brotherhoods (Sojedinenije Greko-Kaftoličeskich Russkich Bratstv), founded in Wilkes-Barre, Pennsylvania, in 1892. This was basically an insurance organization concerned with the physical welfare of its members, though it also strove to preserve the integrity of the Greek Catholic Church in the United States. The union published an influential newspaper, the *Amierykanskii russkii vîstnyk* (1892-1952), and by 1918 counted over 90,000 members in both regular and youth lodges. A smaller group was the United Societies of the Greek Catholic Religion (Sobranije Greko-Katholičeskich Cerkovnych Bratstv) which was also an insurance organization, but was administered directly by the hierarchy of the Greek Catholic Church. The United Societies published the organ *Prosvîta* (1917 to the present) and had about 9,000 members in regular, Sokol (gymnastic), and youth chapters.[3]

The ideological policies of these and other Rusyn immigrant organizations reflected traditions brought from Europe. Initially, the ecclesiastical organizations, and to a lesser degree the lay organizations, tried to include Rusyn immigrants from Galicia, Bukovina, and Subcarpathian Rus', as well as Slovaks and Magyars of the Greek Catholic rite. To avoid controversy, these organizations referred to their members with noncontroversial names, such as Rusyn or the ethnically nonspecific "Slavish." The influential Greek Catholic Union was subtitled with the catch-all "A Fraternal and Benefit Society Comprised of Catholics of Greek and Roman Rite and of Slavonic Extraction or Descent," while the Greek Catholic Church, with its Galician-Ukrainian, Slovak, Magyar, and Croatian, as well as Carpatho-Rusyn, adherents, tried not to favor any one ethnic group over the others.

However, the tendency toward separation, in particular between Rusyn immigrants from Subcarpathian Rus' and those from Galicia, was already evident in 1894. In that year, a Rusyn (later renamed Ukrainian) National

Union was set up to accommodate nationally conscious Ukrainian immigrants from Galicia. This new organization began to compete for members with the older Greek Catholic Union, and any attempts toward cooperation between the two groups broke down completely after 1907, when a Galician Ukrainophile priest, Soter Ortyns'kyi (1866-1916, consecrated 1907), was appointed bishop for Greek Catholics in the United States.[4] Backed by the Greek Catholic Union, a group of immigrant priests from Subcarpathian Rus' opposed Ortyns'kyi—especially his "policy of making the diocese Ukrainian"—and they strove "to protect the Uhro-[Subcarpathian] Rusyns and segments of the Galicians against Ukrainian propaganda."[5] The continual disagreements between the Galician Ukrainophile clergy on the one hand, and priests from Subcarpathian Rus' (strongly supported by the Greek Catholic Union) on the other, finally led to a papal decree of April 1918, which divided the Greek Catholic Church in the United States into a Subcarpathian and Galician branch, each to be headed by its own administrator.[6]

The Rusyn-American community was not only rent by regional Subcarpathian-Galician conflicts, but also by large-scale conversions to Orthodoxy. The American Catholic hierarchy refused to recognize married Greek Catholic priests and this resulted in the defection to Orthodoxy of more than 29,000 Rusyns between the years 1891 and 1909.[7] These Orthodox Rusyn immigrants soon became staunch advocates of a Russian national orientation.

The relationship of the Subcarpathians to the Slovak immigrants in this early period was more positive. For instance, the Greek Catholic Union's newspaper was initially printed and to a degree influenced by Peter V. Rovnianek, the founder of the National Slovak Society. This organization, which included immigrants from "Slovakia" of all religious beliefs, as well as the Pennsylvania Slovak Roman and Greek Catholic Union, attracted many Rusyns. Political cooperation between Slovak and Rusyn immigrants was also evident, and as early as 1904 representatives of both groups at the world congress of Slavic journalists in St. Louis addressed a petition to the Hungarian government protesting the fate of their brethren at home.[8]

In turn, the Hungarian government tried, through the Trans-Atlantic Trust Company in New York and through the Austro-Hungarian consulates in Cleveland, Pittsburgh, and Wilkes-Barre, to combat the "pernicious" effect of Subcarpathian contact with Slovaks, Galician Ukrainophiles, and Russophiles, and to assure a favorable attitude on the part of the Greek Catholic Union and Greek Catholic hierarchy. The union successfully resisted such infiltration, but the Church remained staffed with Magyarone priests.[9] Such a situation fostered frequent controversy between the Rusyn clergy and the lay leadership of the Greek Catholic Union, and this was the predominant feature of Rusyn immigrant life in the early years of this century.

Political concerns did not take precedence among Subcarpathian immigrants until the last years of the First World War, when Allied military victories and Wilsonian rhetoric seemed to forecast imminent changes in the structure of eastern Europe. Reflecting on the fate of their homeland, Rusyn immigrant leaders considered the following alternatives: union of Subcarpathian Rus' with Russia, union with the Ukraine, full independence, autonomy within Hungary, or autonomy within Czechoslovakia.

The first public demonstration of Rusyn political attitudes came at the Russian Congress, held in New York City on July 13, 1917. Organized by the Galician Russophile Petr P. Hatalak, this congress was composed of Rusyn immigrants from "Carpathian Russia"—Galicia, Bukovina, and Subcarpathian Rus'.[10] Most of the participants were delegates from Russophile organizations set up by immigrants from Galicia and Bukovina. The Subcarpathians were represented by the chairman of the Greek Catholic Union, the editor of the Union newspaper, and by Nicholas Pačuta, chairman of a "Carpatho-Russian" political organization—the American Russian National Defense (Amerikansko-Russkaia 'Narodnaia Obrana'). Although the Orthodox hierarchy was well represented, Galician Ukrainophile leaders and Subcarpathian clergy from the Greek Catholic Church were noticeably absent. The latter had only recently issued a resolution stating "that the most advantageous thing for those sons of our people who are citizens of Hungary would be to remain within Hungary after the war with full guarantees of autonomy."[11]

The congress issued a memorandum that traced the unfortunate history of "Carpathian Russia" and then declared: "The whole Carpatho-Russian people steadfastly demand the liberation of Carpathian Rus' [*Prikarpatskaia Rus'*] from foreign domination, and with the broadest autonomy the unification of all Carpathian Rus', according to its ethnographic boundaries, with its sister—a great, democratic Russia."[12] This memorandum was presented to the Russian and other Allied embassies as well as to the State Department in Washington. However, the British ambassador's opposition to the idea of union with Russia, along with the Bolshevik *coup d'état* in November, made the Russian solution unfeasible. The chairman of the Russian Congress later recalled: "Towards the end of 1917 it was already clear to all Uhro-Rusyn leaders in America that Uhro-Rus' cannot be united with Russia . . . because . . . in Russia the Bolsheviks already controlled the government."[13]

The proclamation of Ukrainian independence at Kiev in January 1918, and the ratification in March of the Treaty of Brest-Litovsk, which recognized an independent Ukraine, may have stimulated a few Subcarpathians to favor union with the Ukraine. An organization called the Ukrainian Federation of the United States claimed to represent "more than 700,000 Ruthenians and Ukrainians" and submitted a memorandum to President Wilson on June 29, 1918, asking that he "endorse the endeavors of their mother countries for national unity and constitutional freedom" from the "unjust and incompetent rule of the Romanoff and Hapsburg dynasties."[14]

But the most influential faction among Rusyn immigrants was that represented by the Greek Catholic Union. At the beginning of 1918, the Union's newspaper called upon its readers to think in political terms and to consider four possible "alternatives" for the homeland: Hungary, Czechoslovakia, the Ukraine, or Russia.[15] By the end of the year, Rusyn immigrants had accepted the Czechoslovak "alternative," and they did so primarily because of two men: Tomáš G. Masaryk, the future first president of Czechoslovakia, and Gregory I. Zsatkovich (1886-1967), the future first governor of Subcarpathian Rus'.

The change in United States policy toward the Austro-Hungarian Empire was also of crucial importance for budding immigrant politicians. Wilson's famous Fourteen Points had stated the general principle of self-determination for all nations, but it was a declaration by Secretary of State Lansing that really raised immigrant hopes. Although the United States did not specifically call for the dismemberment of Austria-Hungary, Lansing stressed, on June 28, 1918, that "all branches of the Slav race should be completely freed from German and Austrian rule."[16] Statements like these provided favorable propaganda for the efforts of leaders like Masaryk, who arrived in the United States on May 1 in order to gather support for Czechoslovak independence among American Czechs and Slovaks.

It was in the course of negotiations with Slovak immigrants in Pittsburgh at the end of May that Masaryk first met a Rusyn representative, in the person of Nicholas Pačuta. Although Czech and especially Slovak leaders might have considered annexing some Rusyn-inhabited territory, they did not originally plan to incorporate the entire Subcarpathian Rusyn region into their new nation. On the other hand, Czech leaders hoped to be allied in some way with Russia, whether through a dynastic union as proposed by Karel Kramář, or through close political and economic cooperation, as envisaged by Masaryk and Beneš. Since one of Russia's war aims was the acquisition of Galicia, a Czech-ruled Subcarpathian Rus' would assure direct access between the Czechs and Russians. That Russian politicians thought the area might become a proverbial bridge between East and West is attested to by Ivan Marković, a Slovak exile who worked for the Czechoslovak cause in Russia during the war. He later recalled that the "Russian Pan-Slavists set their sights as far as the Poprad River and perhaps even farther westward, and I remember well that in 1916 we had some difficulties because on a map of [future] Czechoslovakia, Slovakia was outlined as far as Uzhhorod." Masaryk first raised the issue of Subcarpathian Rus' during his stay in Kiev in 1917, where he discussed the problem with Ukrainian leaders who at the time were demanding autonomy within the Russian Empire. Massaryk later recalled that "it was only a pious wish, but I had to consider a plan in Russia and especially in the Ukraine, because Ukrainian leaders discussed with me many times the future of all Little Russian [Ukrainian] lands outside of Russia. They had no objection to the unification of Subcarpathian Rus' with us.''[17]

In the United States, Masaryk found that most Slavic groups were aware of the struggle being waged on behalf of Czechoslovak independence. Following the path of Czech and Slovak immigrants, many Rusyns had already volunteered for service in the Czechoslovak regiment that was fighting alongside the Allies in France. The Czechoslovak orientation was in particular being fostered by N. Pačuta, a recent convert to Orthodoxy who was not only chairman of the American Russian National Defense, but until early 1918 also an editor of the Greek Catholic Union's newspaper.[18] Pačuta was formerly an advocate of Subcarpathia's incorporation into Russia, but now he realized the futility of such a plan, negotiated with Slovak leaders, and drew up a memorandum proposing union instead with Czechoslovakia. He delivered this document to Secretary of State Lansing in April and to Masaryk on May 30.[19] The Czech statesman accepted the memorandum, though he rightly surmised that Pačuta was acting more or less on his own and did not represent the wishes of the larger and more influential Greek Catholic Rusyn community.[20]

By May 1918, however, Rusyn leaders had still not formulated any political program. A few individuals in the Greek Catholic Union may have talked of the Ukraine or Czechoslovakia, but on the whole, most immigrants were either disinterested in politics or satisfied to follow their priests, who were convinced that "the most responsible solution for the Rusyns of Hungary is to remain further under the Hungarian crown."[21] The official organ of the Greek Catholic administration disavowed the suggestion "that Hungarian Rusyns *(uhorski rusiny)* be united with the Galician Ukrainians,"[22] since the clergy was reluctant "to mix in the affairs of foreign countries."[23] One group of priests met in McKeesport, Pennsylvania, in March 1918, and "unanimously expressed their policy, which was that we remain loyal to Hungary."[24] Differences over the "political" questions further exacerbated relations between the Greek Catholic Union and the Church.

These problems were finally resolved when Rusyn clerical and lay leaders joined together at the fifteenth convention of the Greek Catholic Union, held in Cleveland, Ohio, and Braddock, Pennsylvania, June 9-22, 1918. After a heated debate, N. Pačuta, the former Russophile and now advocate of cooperation with the Czechs and Slovaks, was branded an Orthodox renegade and expelled from the union; a new chairman, Julij Gardoš, was elected. At the instigation of the clergy, the convention decided thenceforth to use only the terms "Uhro-Rusyn" or "Rusyn" when referring to its members, so as to distinguish them clearly from their Galician Ukrainian and Russian brethren. Most important, a policy of political activism was decided upon, and at the last session a nine-man commission was formed (later to be joined by nine priests) in order "to continue intensive action with the aim to liberate *Uhorska* [Hungarian] Rus'."[25]

To fulfill the task of "liberation," and to work out common political aims, lay and ecclesiastical leaders met at Homestead, Pennsylvania, on July 23, 1918. First, the Greek Catholic Union (Sojedinenije) joined with the smaller United Societies (Sobranije) to form an American National Council of Uhro-Rusyns (Amerikanska Narodna Rada Uhro-Rusinov).[26] Reverend Nikolaj Chopey was elected chairman and Julij Gardoš, A. Koval, A. Koscelnik, and A. Petach vice-chairman. The council then proclaimed itself the sole legal representative for Uhro-Rusyn immigrants and adopted the Homestead Resolution:

> If the pre-War boundaries remain, Rusyns, as the most loyal people— *gens fidelissima*—deserve that Hungary provide her with autonomy.
>
> If new boundaries are made, they should be made according to nationality; thus, Uhro-Rusyns can belong nowhere else than to their nearest brothers by blood, language, and faith, to the Galician and Bukovinian Rusyns.
>
> But if we are divided by foreign aspirations from Ukrainians and Old-Russians [Galician Russophiles], the National Council demands in this case autonomy for Uhro-Rusyns so that they can preserve their national character.[27]

The resolution, reflecting the attitudes of the pro-Hungarian clergy and pro-Galician lay readers, made no mention of the Czechoslovak solution. From August until November, Rusyn leaders continued to debate the relative advantages and disadvantages of the various alternatives, though in general, the Hungarian proposal lost ground to the idea of union with the Galicians and Bukovinians.[28]

As for the Czechoslovak movement, the Rusyn press was very unfavorable, directing its wrath especially at Slovak immigrants, because they claimed certain Rusyn-inhabited territories as part of a future Slovakia and because they continued "to associate with our fallen down '*bolsheviki*' [Pačuta] mob leaders."[29] Stiff polemics were exchanged in the Slovak and Rusyn press over the question of to whom the nationally-mixed counties of Sáros, Szepes, Abaúj, Borsod, Zemplén, and Ung should belong.[30] The Rusyn message was unequivocal: "Hold your horses, [Slovak] brethren, and be satisfied with your boundaries made a year or two ago when you thought that the Uhro-Rusyns were dead . . . We want liberty and independence . . . and as Rusyns we are trying to make unity with other Rusyns, left out from Russia and Ukrainia [sic] . . . in Galicia and Bukovina, and to create for our fathers and brethren a free Carpathian Republic, instead of being the gain of anybody."[31]

The so-called Ukrainian solution, or desire for a free Carpathian Republic, requires some explanation. As was obvious from the ecclesiastical controversies, the majority of Rusyn immigrants from Subcarpathian Rus' felt themselves to be distinct from Ukrainians. In effect, the proposed Carpathian Republic was to include three separate districts (*kantony*): in Subcarpathia would be *Uhorska* (Hungarian) Rus', and in Galicia a Ukrainian district and Carpatho-Russian Lemkian district—a kind of federation "after the example of Switzerland!"[32] This artificial territorial division of eastern Galicia was supposed to respond to the needs of the two national orientations there: the Ukrainophile, which considered the population to be Ukrainian, and the Russophile, which considered it to be "Russian," or, in local terminology, "Lemkian." Most often, Subcarpathian immigrant leaders called for union only with the Carpatho-Russian Lemkians. Thus, it would be incorrect to assume, as many Ukrainian writers do, that Uhro-Rusyn immigrant proposals to unite with Galicia and Bukovina were an indication of Ukrainian national consciousness.

Even though Greek Catholic immigrant organizations continued to criticize the Czechoslovak alternative, that solution was finally accepted. The explanation for this can be found by examining the activity of the young Pittsburgh lawyer Gregory I. Zsatkovich.[33] Though a native of Subcarpathian Rus', Gregory was brought to the United States at the age of four, educated in American schools, and became a successful lawyer. His father Pavel was a co-founder of the Greek Catholic Union and an activist in the struggle to oppose Hungarian infiltration into that organization, but Gregory seems not to have been directly involved in Rusyn affairs until the late summer of 1918. As is evident from his proposals, he advocated the idea that the Subcarpathian- or Uhro-Rusyns were a distinct nationality. This fact justified their demand for separate political as well as national rights.[34]

Because of Zsatkovich's ability to operate within the American system, the National Council of Uhro-Rusyns called upon him in October 1918, to prepare a memorandum for President Wilson. Having drawn up the document, he arranged (with the help of Congressman Guy E. Campbell, Democrat of Pennsylvania) a meeting with the President on October 21.[35] Zsatkovich's memorandum differed considerably from the Homestead Resolution. The first demand was "that our Uhro-Rusyn people be recognized as a separate people, and if possible as completely independent." If this were not possible, the peace conference might propose unification, with full autonomy, with neighboring Slavic peoples. Finally, if Hungary's borders remain intact, then full autonomy should be sought there. Significantly, nothing specific about unification with Galicia and Bukovina was included and no mention at all was made of Czechoslovakia.[36]

Presumably, Wilson recommended seeking autonomy within some larger state and also advised Zsatkovich and his colleagues to enter the Mid-European Democratic Union—a group of Eastern European politicians representing eleven nationalities who organized a meeting on October 23-26 at Independence Hall in Philadelphia. At Zsatkovich's request, a nationally separate Uhro-Rusyn delegation was accorded membership in the union. In Philadelphia, Zsatkovich met with Masaryk to discuss the possibility of uniting Subcarpathian Rus' with the new Czechoslovak state. Zsatkovich later claimed that Masaryk told him: "If the Rusyns decide to join the Czechoslovak Republic, they shall constitute a fully autonomous state."[37] However, Reverend Valentine Gorzo (1869-1943), another member of the Rusyn delegation, asked Masaryk skeptically: "How can we agree with our brother Slovaks if, as your map shows, you have taken half of our population and our Rusyn land. We demand a Rusyn territory from the Poprad to the Tisa Rivers."[38] On this critical question, the future president was credited with saying: "The frontiers will be so determined that the Rusyns will be satisfied."[39]

Whether or not Masaryk made these oral promises to Zsatkovich in Philadelphia, it is certain that no written agreement was concluded between the two men, either on October 25 or on the next day, when they joined other Eastern European leaders to sign the "Declaration of Common Aims of the Independent Mid-European Nations."[40] On the other hand, Masaryk was presented with a memorandum from Nicholas Pačuta of the American Russian National Defense. Like Pačuta's first memorandum delivered to the Czech statesman in May, the new one called for "the union of all the Carpathian Russians on an autonomic (sic) basis with the Czechoslovak State."[41]

On October 29, Zsatkovich reported the results of his meetings with Wilson and Masaryk to the American National Council of Uhro-Rusyns. However, he still did not publicly support the idea of joining Subcarpathian Rus' to Czechoslovakia.[42] The next few weeks were marked by further negotiations, and Rusyn newspapers were filled with discussions of whether to unite with Czechoslovakia or the Ukraine.[43]

It was not until November 12, at a meeting of the National Council held in Scranton, Pennsylvania, that the Czechoslovak solution was finally adopted. Zsatkovich succeeded in having the following resolution accepted: "That Uhro-Rusyns with the broadest autonomous rights as a state, on a federative basis, be united with the Czechoslovak Democratic Republic, with these conditions, that to our country must belong all the original Uhro-Rusyn counties: Szepes, Sáros, Zemplén, Abaúj, Borsod, Ung, Ugocsa, Bereg and Máramaros".[44] The territorial clause was to be the source of future difficulty since Slovaks were already claiming as their own the first six counties. Zsatkovich also proposed at the Scranton meeting that a plebiscite be placed before all Rusyns in the United States in order to determine "where Uhro-Rusyns in the old country should belong, as an autonomous state in a Czechoslovak or Ukrainian federation."[45]

On November 13, Zsatkovich met with Masaryk, who "expressed great pleasure" with the Scranton resolution and stressed the need for a plebiscite so that the decision to join Czechoslovakia should not be viewed "only as a decision of members of the National Council which could be objected to at the Peace Conference in Paris."[46] The next day Zsatkovich reported the recent developments in a telegram to President Wilson, who responded with congratulations "on the progress made toward satisfactory relations."[47]

Finally, the organs representing Greek Catholic Rusyn organizations came out in support of the Czechoslovak alternative. Throughout the summer, the idea of union with Galicia had been proposed, and the only objection was a fear that the more "progressive" Ukrainian language and grammatical principles would replace our "dear Uhro-Rusyn language."[48] However, the practical reality of an existing Czechoslovak state, as opposed to a still unrecognized Ukrainian government in Galicia, forced American Rusyns to link their destiny with Prague.[49] It should be mentioned that several Greek Catholic priests met in Pittsburgh on November 19 to protest the Scranton resolution,[50] but their discontent was to have only limited effect on the Rusyn-American public.

The American phase came to an end in December 1918, when a plebiscite was held in the various lodges of the Greek Catholic Union (Sojedinenije), the United Societies of the Greek Catholic Religion (Sobranije), and in Uhro-Rusyn Greek Catholic parishes. According to Zsatkovich's suggestion, made in Scranton, each lodge and parish was alotted one vote for every fifty members.[51] This indirect balloting was actually conducted in less than half of the existing lodges and parishes. For example, as of May 31, 1918, there was a total of 874 lodges in the Greek Catholic Union, but only 372 returned a vote in the plebiscite. Similarly, of the 158 chapters in the United Societies, only 46 responded.

Nevertheless, Zsatkovich received the desired result: out of 1102 votes submitted, 732 (67 percent) were for union with Czechoslovakia and 310 (28 percent) for union with the Ukraine. Although not among the suggested choices, 27 votes were cast for total independence, 10 votes for union with Russia, 9 for Hungary.[52] Zsatkovich immediately informed Czechoslovak authorities in both Prague and Paris, as well as the State Department in Washington, of the results. The plebiscite gave greater credence to the decision of the American National Council of Uhro-Rusyns, since it seemed to be an expression of popular will and not just the desire of a few energetic leaders. Despite the subsequent fluctuations of political fortune that were to occur in the homeland, the decision made at Scranton, Pennsylvania, and elaborated in the plebiscite was of crucial importance and would influence the diplomats in Paris who were to redraw the map of Europe.[53]

The Revolutionary Period in Subcarpathian Rus', 1918-1919

The dissolution of Hapsburg rule in late October 1918, and the ensuing social and economic dislocations accompanying the last weeks of the First World War, led to a series of national and social revolutions that found expression in the convocation of national *radas*, or councils, among the minority groups within the Hungarian Kingdom. During the last days of October, the Slovaks, Rumanians, and Croats, respectively, met in councils that supported separation from Hungary. At the same time, Hungarian politicians under the leadership of Count Mihály Károlyi formed a revolutionary government in Budapest on October 31, and then two weeks later called into existence a Hungarian republic. This new government included a Ministry for Nationalities, headed by Oszkár Jászi, whose task it was to develop a program of autonomy for the various nationalities and thus preserve the territorial integrity of Hungary.[54] But the many centuries of Hungarian rule, which had culminated in an extensive policy of Magyarization and in a lost war, virtually doomed from the start any enlightened minority policy that the new Hungarian leaders might have proposed. National independence, closely allied with desires for social liberation, made the governments in Prague, Bucharest, and Belgrade seem more attractive than Budapest.

The Rusyns also expressed a desire for national and social liberation, especially after soldiers returning home told of the revolutions taking place in the former Russian Empire. At secret meetings held in Uzhhorod in September 1918, two former Subcarpathian prisoners of war informed Rusyn leaders of the recent events in Russia and the Ukraine, and then discussed the feasibility of greater autonomy within Hungary or perhaps union with their brethren beyond the Carpathians. To explore the latter possibility, it was decided to send the young gymnasium professor Avhustyn Shtefan (b. 1893)[55] to Vienna to meet with parliamentary representatives from Galicia. The latter suggested that in accord with Wilson's principle of self-determination the best course of action would be to form national councils throughout the Subcarpathian region.[56]

Following this recommendation, the Rusyn intelligentsia (primarily priests, lawyers, and teachers) organized around four centers: Prešov, Uzhhorod, Khust (Huszt), and Iasynia (Kőrösmező). The geographical location of these towns coincided with their proposed political aims. Prešov, to the west, eventually became the center of the pro-Czechoslovak movement; Uzhhorod and later Mukachevo, on the central lowlands, represented the pro-Hungarian solution; Khust, farther east, declared for union with the Ukraine; and Iasynia, in a remote sector of the Carpathians, became the center of a short-lived, independent political entity.

The first national council (Russka Narodnia Rada) met on November 8, 1918, in Lubovňa (Ólubló), a small town located in the westernmost portion of Rusyn ethnographic territory, in what is now Czechoslovakia. Delegates from the surrounding counties of Sáros and Szepes gathered under the leadership of a local priest, Emyliian Nevyts'kyi (1878-1939), and drew up a manifesto stating that those present were "imbued with the democratic spirit of the times" and "in protest against any force from foreign powers over our Rusyn [rus'kii] land."[57] Nevyts'kyi also wanted to gauge the attitude of the local population, and during the month of November he sent out two questionnaires. The explanations accompanying both of these contained clear evidence that the Lubovňa Council was oriented toward union with the Rusyns living north of the Carpathians: "We are Rusyns! Because we live in the Carpathians, we are called Carpathian Rusyns. But we know that Rusyns similar to us live beyond the Carpathians. Their speech, customs, and faith are the same as ours, as [they] are our brothers. With them we ethnographically form one great multi-million people."[58] The questionnaires included questions that formulated the issue of Rusyn political fate as a choice between "remaining with Hungary" or "uniting with Rus' (Ukraine)." The available evidence reveals that Rusyns in the region around Lubovňa were generally opposed to Hungary, but not necessarily united behind any one political solution: some favored union with Rus' (Ukraine), some complete independence, others union with Czechoslovakia.[59]

An attempt to secure autonomy in Hungary was also initiated in early November by the Greek Catholic priests Petro Gebei (1864-1931), Avhustyn Voloshyn, and Simeon Sabov (1863-1929). On November 9, more than one hundred persons gathered in Uzhhorod to form a national council. Referring to the "errors" of "Rusyns in many places who want to unite with the Ukraine," Reverend Sabov declared: "This movement, the *Rada uhrorus'-koho naroda* [Council of Uhro-Rusyn People] is not separatist; on the contrary, it wants in fact to serve the territorial integrity of Hungary."[60] The resolution issued by the Uzhhorod Council stated that the "Uhro-Rusyn people adhere to their ancestral fatherland Hungary . . . and protest against all attempts to separate" them from the homeland. This was followed by demands for special autonomy for the Greek Catholic Church; for agricultural, social, and industrial reforms; and for other privileges for national minorities, as proposed by the Károlyi government. The council claimed itself the sole legal representative for the Rusyn people and began to negotiate with Hungarian officials in Budapest, who suggested a reorganization of the country on the model of Switzerland; a separate "Ruthene canton" would be established. Magyarone Rusyns in both Máramaros and Ugocsa counties met during the following weeks to proclaim their loyalty to Hungary and their support for the council in Uzhhorod.[61]

On December 10, 1918, thirty-six members of the Uzhhorod Council were invited to Budapest by Dr. Oreszt Szabó (1867-194?), a native of Subcarpathia and an official in the Ministry of Interior, who was appointed adviser to the government on Rusyn affairs. Among those present at the meeting were representatives of a Budapest-based Uhro-Rusyn political party (formed on December 8) who promised "to stand or fall on the side of Hungary," and a few skeptical leaders like Stepan Klochurak (b. 1895) and Dr. Mykhailo Brashchaiko (1883-1973) who stated that "Carpatho-Rusyns were gravitating toward the Ukraine" and that no decisions should be made without first consulting the population at home. As a result of the meeting, a memorandum was addressed to Prime Minister Károlyi expressing "the hope and faith that in its decisions the Peace Conference would devote special attention" to the Rusyns of Hungary.[62] Until such time, demands were made for national and internal administrative autonomy, and protests lodged "against the taking of territory by Czechs, Slovaks, Rumanians, and other nations."[63]

In an attempt to satisfy Rusyn demands, the Károlyi regime adopted an autonomy project, Law No. 10, of December 21, 1918, which called into existence the autonomous province of Rus'ka Kraina. However, this province comprised only those Rusyns living in the counties of Máramaros, Bereg, Ugocsa, and Ung; the inclusion of other Rusyn areas (parts of Zemplén, Sáros, Abaúj-Torna, and Szepes counties) would be postponed "until the time for the conclusion of a general peace."[64] The law further provided for full autonomy in internal matters (education, religion, national language), to be clarified after the establishment of a Rusyn National Assembly (Rus'kii Narodnii Sobor). Executive organs for Rus'ka Kraina were placed in a ministry (*ruszin miniszterium*) with headquarters in Budapest and a governor in Mukachevo.[65]

The activity of the pro-Hungarian Uzhhorod Council and its initial success in negotiations with the Budapest government were met by opposition from various parts of Subcarpathian Rus'.[66] On November 19, the Lubovňa Council reconvened in Prešov. About two hundred peasants and forty priests gathered under the leadership of the Beskid family, in particular Dr. Antonii Beskid (1855-1933), who replaced E. Nevtys'kyi as chairman. Dr. Beskid was in close contact with Russophile leaders from Galicia (Andrei Gagatko, Dmitrii Vislotskii, and others) who originally wanted the Rusyn-inhabited lands both north and south of the Carpathians to be united with Russia. The Prešov Council issued a manifesto that included general demands for "self-determination" and "national freedom," and called for a delegate to be present at the future "international peace conference"; however, it did not mention unification with any particular state.[67]

The following weeks witnessed a struggle between the Nevyts'kyi and Beskid factions in the Prešov Council. Nevyts'kyi still maintained the hope, expressed at smaller meetings in Bardejov (November 27), Svidník (November 29), Stropkov (November 30), Medzilaborce (December 2), and Humenné (December 3), that union with Rus' (Ukraine) should be brought about.[68] Beskid, on the other hand, pushed for a more practical solution—association with the new Czechoslovak state. To secure this goal, he met in Martin (Túrócszentmárton) with the Slovak National Council. On November 30, that body called upon "our brother Rusyns": "With the greatest love, we beg you as a free people to come closer to us, to unite with us."[69]

Beskid was supported in his efforts by the Galician Russophiles, who realized that Russia was a lost cause and thus hoped that Czechoslovakia would save Rusyn lands north of the Carpathians from future Polish control. On December 21, members of the so-called Russian (Galician) Council of Lemkians joined with the Beskid faction to form a Carpatho-Russian National Council (Karpato-Russkaia Narodnaia Rada). From the beginning, this group favored unification with Prague; moreover, the continuing political and military instability in both Galicia and the Russian Ukraine made the Czechoslovak solution seem more feasible than ever. Nevyts'kyi's protests went unheeded and by the end of December the arrival of Czechoslovak Legionnaires in eastern Slovakia further advanced the aims of Beskid, so that in early January the Prešov Council could declare openly for union with Czechoslovakia.[70]

Opposition to the pro-Hungarian Uzhhorod Council was also substantial in the eastern county of Máramaros, where sentiment for the Ukraine was, widespread. At a series of three meetings held at Khust on November 3, 7, and 10, the few Hungarian supporters present were overwhelmed by the rhetoric of a Rusyn lawyer, Dr. Iulii Brashchaiko (1879-1946), who called for union with the Ukraine.[71] Similarly, on December 8, 1918, a Carpatho-Rusyn National Council (Karpats'ka-Rus'ka Narodna Rada) was formed at Svaliava. Those present rejected the Uzhhorod Council because "it is Magyar" and decided to address a memorandum to the peace conference, which in turn should send an armed force "so that the Rusyn people could free themselves from the 1000 year old [Hungarian] yoke and unite with the Greater Ukraine where Rusyns live also."[72]

Continued anti-Hungarian sentiment was evident at a meeting in Marmarosh Sighet arranged by the Budapest government on December 18, 1918. In an attempt to engender support for the Hungarian cause, the first speaker proclaimed that "the Rusyn . . . people can find happiness only as a part of Hungary," but this speech was continually interrupted by cries of "we don't need anything from the Magyars, long live the Ukraine, let us go to the Ukraine."[73] Consequently, a Marmarosh Rusyn National Council (Maramorosh'ka Rus'ka Narodnia Rada) was formed under the chairmanship of Dr. Mykhailo Brashchaiko, and a manifesto was adopted calling for union with the Ukraine and the convocation of a new national council to be held at Khust on January 21.

Among the signatories to the Marmarosh manifesto was Dr. Agoston Stefan, a leading member of the Uzhhorod Council who had just returned from negotiations with Hungarian leaders in Budapest. Stefan, soon to become governor of the autonomous Rus'ka Kraina, was a well-known Magyarone, yet at the same time he signed a resolution calling for union with the Ukraine. In fact, many Rusyn leaders were participants in councils that professed antithetical political ends. Such a phenomenon was indicative not only of a certain degree of opportunism on the part of these individuals, but also of the unstable and rapidly changing conditions in Subcarpathian Rus' after the war.

The Subcarpathian leaders who called for unification with the Ukraine generally held the traditional view that the Ukraine was a Rus' land similar to their own. Because the relations they had with Galicia were usually with the Russophile intelligentsia, the Subcarpathians were either unsympathetic toward or unaware of actual Ukrainian national and political goals. They might favor unification of all Ukrainian lands, but not separation from Russia or the use of Ukrainian instead of Russian as a literary language. Hence the head of the Lubovňa Council, E. Nevyts'kyi, could formulate a manifesto calling for union with Rus' (Ukraine) as well as sign a Galician memorandum claiming that all Rusyns were part of the Great Russian nation and that Ukrainianism was a dangerous separatist movement created by Austro-German propaganda.[74] On the other hand, Dr. Iulii Brashchaiko and his brother Mykhailo were pronounced Ukrainophiles who thought clearly in terms of union with an independent Ukrainian state when they put forth their demands at the meetings in Khust and Marmarosh Sighet.

Ukrainian developments proceeded beyond Subcarpathian expectations. Ukrainophile parliamentarians from Galicia organized a national council in late October, and on November 1, 1918, they met in L'viv where they called into being an independent West Ukrainian Republic.[75] The new republic claimed jurisdiction over "the Ukrainian parts" of Galicia, Bukovina, and Subcarpathian Rus', but its authority was immediately challenged by Polish forces who, by the end of the month, had pushed the Ukrainians out of the city. Until April 1919, the beleaguered national council of the West Ukrainian Republic met in Stanyslaviv. The situation in the former Russian Ukraine was not much better. There, the Directorate of the Ukrainian National Republic (originally based in Kiev) was from December 1918 fighting for survival against the forces of the Soviet and White Russian armies. On January 22, 1919, in the midst of a critical military situation, a delegation from the West Ukrainian Republic went to Kiev in order "to unify the century-long separated parts of one Ukraine . . . Galicia, Bukovina, Uhors'ka Rus' [Subcarpathia] with the Great Ukraine beyond the Dnieper."[76] Actual territorial unification, however, was not to be achieved.

While there was an undeniable sense of kinship felt by Subcarpathian Rusyns for those peoples in Galicia and Bukovina who spoke a similar language and worshiped in the same church, it was the social issue that especially provoked interest in the lands beyond the Carpathians. Returning soldiers and other refugees, who were Bolshevik "in sentiment, if not by conviction,"[77] spread tales of how the lords had been driven away and the land given to the people. Thus, the Svaliava Council manifesto called for union "with the councils in the Ukraine because these councils give the peasants the gentry and state lands."[78] Likewise, "in the area around Khust . . . the movement for emigration to the Ukraine has been strengthened. The landless hope to get there good, fertile land."[79] A petition from one small mountain village summed up Subcarpathian national and social desires: "We are Rusyns who live in the Carpathians near the Galician border, we want to unite with the Russian Ukraine where we will use state lands and forests so that everything will be for the common citizens; here we are very poor people because the landlords have pressured us so much that one cannot even survive."[80]

Another indication of Rusyn opposition to Hungary took place in the far eastern village of Iasynia. In the early morning of January 7, 1919, a group of demobilized Rusyn soldiers led by Dmytro (18??-1973) and Vasyl' Klempush, Stepan Klochurak, and Dmytro Nimchuk (1897-1944), in cooperation with troops sent by the West Ukrainian Republic, drove out the garrison of 250 Hungarian national guardsmen. The new force occupied Marmarosh Sighet for a while, but was soon forced back home by the Rumanian army. The local leaders favored unification with an independent Ukraine, but since this was not yet feasible they established instead on February 5 their own "Hutsul Republic," which came to control the territory surrounding Iasynia (representing about 20,000 inhabitants). This "miniature state," administered by a forty-two member elected council and a four-man government, existed until June 11, 1919, when Rumanian troops occupied the area.[81]

Thus, by the beginning of 1919, the Subcarpathian Rusyns had responded to the political crisis by creating a series of national councils, which proposed four possible solutions: federation with Czechoslovakia (Prešov), autonomy within Hungary (Uzhhorod), union with the Ukraine (Marmarosh Sighet), or independence (Iasynia). The first months of the new year were to witness a struggle between these four orientations, but it was not until the spring that the outcome became clear.

During the month of January the Czechoslovak and Ukrainian solutions gained support. On January 7, 1919, Dr. A. Beskid invited local leaders and Galician Russophiles (the Lemkian Council) to Prešov, where they declared for union with Czechoslovakia.[82] A few days later Beskid conveyed this decision to Czech politicians in Prague, who immediately sent him as the Rusyn delegate to the peace conference in Paris. The Czechoslovak solution was put in writing on January 31 at another meeting of the Prešov Carpatho-Russian National Council. After stating that the Rusyns were members of the Great Russian people, the manifesto regretted that unfavorable political conditions made union with a united Russia impossible; thus "we desire to live for better or worse with our Czechoslovak brethren."[83]

The situation in Uzhhorod was not yet clear. While many Rusyn leaders had accepted an autonomous status for their land within Hungary and had already set up political parties and cultural organizations,[84] the procrastination of the Budapest government led to increased disillusionment, summed up later by a leading figure in the Uzhhorod Council, A. Voloshyn: "When it became clear that Magyar autonomy for Rus'ka Kraina was not a serious thing, we met already on January 1, 1919, with Milan Hodža, chief representative of the Czechoslovak Republic in Budapest, and asked whether the Republic would occupy all of Subcarpathian Rus'."[85]

Since November 1918, Milan Hodža had been in Budapest, where he was negotiating with the Károlyi government for the evacuation of Hungarian troops from Slovakia. The Czechoslovak representative was approached by several Rusyn leaders. The first of these was a twenty-two member delegation, led by Mykhailo Komarnyts'kyi of the Svaliava Council, who "demanded the separation [of Subcarpathian Rus'] from the Hungarian state and union (preferably) with the Ukraine, or if that were not possible, with the Czechoslovak state."[86] The Svaliava delegation also gave Hodža a memorandum stating:

> The Rusyn people desire autonomy on the territory of the counties of Ung, Bereg, Ugocsa, and Máramaros; as an autonomous body, they request to be attached either to a Ukrainian state or for reasons of an economic and geographic nature, preferably to the Czecho-Slovak Republic.
> The delegation submits at the same time a request that the High Command of the Allied armies order the occupation of Rusyn territory in Hungary by a Ukrainian or Czechoslovak army so that the population can freely decide its fate.[87]

These requests fit in well with Hodža's desire that Czech troops occupy territory at least as far east as the city of Uzhhorod.

The Czechoslovak representative was less well disposed toward Voloshyn and Petr Legeza, whom he met in Budapest on January 1, 1919. Hodža considered these Uzhhorod Council members to be "opportunists," basically satisfied with the concept of autonomy (of Rus'ka Kraina) within Hungary, but afraid that the Károlyi government would renege on its promises. Although Voloshyn asked for help from the Prague government, he refused to make a written request until Czech troops had occupied Uzhhorod.[88]

Two days later, Hodža met again with Komarnyts'kyi, whose Svaliava Council he considered to be more representative of the popular will than the pro-Hungarian Uzhhorod Council. Komarnyts'kyi reiterated the request for Czech troops, and according to Hodža the Rusyn leader "completely agreed today to the union of Uhors'ka [Hungarian] Rus' to us [Czechoslovakia]."[89] Later, in Paris, the negotiations between Hodža and Komarnyts'kyi were to be used as one of the justifications for the incorporation of Subcarpathian Rus' into Czechoslovakia.

The arrival of the Czechoslovak legionnaires in Uzhhorod on January 15 put the city definitely within the new country's sphere of influence, and two weeks later came the news of the pro-Czechoslovak decision reached by Rusyn immigrants in the United States. "Only at the end of January," wrote Voloshyn, "did we find out from two Czech captains (Písecký and Vaka), sent to us in Uzhhorod by President Masaryk, that you, [our]

American brothers, already decided that we be united to the Czechoslovak Republic.''[90] Voloshyn and other members of the Uzhhorod Council continued to maintain relations with the Hungarian government, but the presence of Czechoslovak troops in the city, together with knowledge of the Rusyn immigrant decision, helped persuade many Subcarpathian leaders that their interests could best be safeguarded by reaching an accord with Prague.[91]

The Ukrainian orientation received its strongest and, as it turned out, last impetus during the first weeks of 1919. At the Council of the West Ukrainian Republic, held on January 3 in Stanyslaviv, two Subcarpathian representatives proclaimed: "Our hearts long for the Ukraine. Help us. Give us your fraternal hand. Long live one unified Ukraine."[92] Despite its own precarious situation in the face of the Poles, the West Ukrainian Republic announced to the Hungarian government that in accord with the "right of self-determination, its military forces would occupy those parts of Hungary where more than half the inhabitants are Rusyns."[93] Accordingly, a few Ukrainian military units crossed the Carpathians and arrived in Iasynia on January 12 to help the Hutsuls, and then pushed on to reach Mukachevo and Sighet on January 14-16. They remained in the area until driven out by the Hungarians and Rumanians during the following week.[94]

The most important expression of pro-Ukrainian sentiment in Subcarpathian Rus' was made by the General Council of Hungarian Rusyn-Ukrainians (Vsenarodni Zbory Uhors'kykh Rusyniv-Ukraïntsiv), which met in Khust on January 21. Arranged by Drs. Iu. and M. Brashchaiko, the dominant figures at previous meetings in Khust and Marmarosh Sighet, the General Council was made up of 420 delegates chosen by 175 smaller councils from Máramaros, Bereg, Ugocsa, and Ung counties. The estimated 1200 Rusyns present made Khust the most representative of the many national councils to date.[95] Its resolution expressed a desire to belong to a United Ukraine (*Soborna Ukraïna*), requested that Ukrainian armed forces (presumably from the West Ukrainian Republic) occupy their land, and, claiming to represent all Rusyns south of the Carpathians, rejected the Hungarian Law No. 10 and an autonomous Rus'ka Kraina.[96] Plans were also made to send a delegation to Stanyslaviv and even to Kiev, but the Polish occupation of eastern Galicia and the unstable political situation in the Dnieper Ukraine soon caused a decline in enthusiasm for the Ukrainian solution.

Meanwhile, the Károlyi regime in Budapest, concerned about the widespread pro-Ukrainian sentiment expressed at the Khust Council, made an effort to organize as soon as possible an administration for Rus'ka Kraina; the administration had been centered in Mukachevo. On February 5, 1919, temporary authority was invested in a council composed of forty-two members drawn from four Rusyn counties, presided over by Minister Oreszt Szabó and Governor Dr. Agoston Stefan.[97] Elections to a thirty-six member

Soim (Diet) were held on March 4 and a week later the first session was held, but the representatives adjourned the body until the Hungarian government defined clearly the borders of the province. In fact, the government was also under pressure from conservative factions in Budapest who felt that Károlyi "gave the Rusyns more than they desired . . . and that this 'more' was detrimental to Hungary."[98] As for the borders, the Minister of Interior declared that "not even a small part of the Magyar population . . . can ever be left under the authority of an uncultured and economically backward Rusyn people."[99] Such an opinion did not augur well for any kind of Rusyn autonomy in Hungary.

Before the Soim was to meet again, Bolshevik elements under Béla Kun replaced the Károlyi regime on March 21. A Soviet Rus'ka Kraina was proclaimed, but this had little effect on the governing personnel; the noncommunist Dr. Stefan was reappointed, this time with the title of commissar. The Kun government hoped that local national councils would administer the area, and elections to such bodies were held on April 6 and 7. As a result, Hungarian-Soviet Rus'ka Kraina, which maintained real authority only in the county of Bereg, had two legislative bodies: the recently elected national councils and the Soim chosen under the Károlyi government. The Soim did meet on April 17, but after a brief session it again refused to conduct further business unless the Hungarian government, within a period of eight days, specified the boundaries of the province.[100]

During its few weeks of existence, Rus'ka Kraina was provided with a constitution "that recognized the independence of the Rusyn people" within the Hungarian Soviet Republic. With regard to the troublesome question of boundaries, the constitution avoided the issue by stating that "now the establishment of borders for Rus'ka Kraina is not necessary because the Soviet Republic does not recognize legally established state borders."[101] Cultural autonomy seemed guaranteed, Rusyn was declared the official language, a few school texts were published, and a Rusyn language department was established at the University of Budapest.[102] Under the influence of a generally far-left political atmosphere, various decrees were promulgated that called for nationalization of mines, industry, and transportation, and for requisition of property from landlords and the church. A Rusyn Red Guard (Rusyns'ka Chervona Gvardiia) was also formed as part of the Hungarian Soviet army and death penalties imposed on "counter-revolutionaries" and "speculators" who withheld foodstuffs.[103]

The decrees passed in Rus'ka Kraina during the month of April had only limited effect in the region surrounding the cities of Mukachevo and Berehovo (Beregszász). Czechoslovak troops were slowly moving eastward from Uzhhorod, while the Hutsul Republic had control over most of Máramaros county. But despite its tenuous existence, the nominally autonomous province of Rus'ka Kraina was to be important in future ideological disputes. Indeed, Marxist historians have overestimated the importance of the

"Soviet rule" that began in late March. They see the period as an unsuccessful though important precedent for the dictatorship of the proletariat established in 1944.[104] In 1919, however, Soviet rule had not established deep roots in the area, and even some Marxists have had to admit that "many [in fact, most—PRM] of the decrees of the Soviet government were not implemented."[105] Of more immediate significance for the subsequent history of Subcarpathian Rus' was the fact that in Rus'ka Kraina Rusyns legally had their own autonomous province and Soim. During its twenty years of administration in the province, the Czechoslovak regime was to be continually reproached with the argument: "Our land as Rus'ka Kraina already received autonomy from the Magyars at the end of 1918 . . . In the framework of *Rus'ka Avtonomna Kraina* the leaders of our people saw a guarantee of our national liberty."[106]

Fearing the growth of Bolshevik power in East Central Europe, Czechoslovak legionnaires under the French General Edmond Hennocque were given orders in mid-April to attack Hungarian Soviet troops. Moreover, Soviet rule in the area was at the same time being undermined by a series of "counterrevolutionary" uprisings that were supported by the Rus'ka Kraina commissar himself, Dr. A. Stefan. In conjunction with the Czechoslovak military action, a Rumanian army moved in from the southeast, and by the end of the month all governing remnants in Rus'ka Kraina were dissolved.[107] The Hungarian orientation in Subcarpathian Rus' was doomed.

International Diplomacy and Unification with Czechoslovakia

Meanwhile, the Czechoslovak cause was scoring important successes on the international diplomatic front. During the Parisian phase of the incorporation process, there was never much doubt that the Czechoslovak solution to the problem of Subcarpathian Rus' would be accepted by the peacemakers. Neighboring Poland and Rumania were not serious obstacles. Although Poland was quite adamant in demanding all of Galicia, including ethnically solid Ukrainian lands, Polish diplomats did not make any claims to Rusyn-inhabited territory south of the Carpathians, with the exception of a small area near Lubovňa.[108] Rumania originally expected Russia to annex Subcarpathian Rus', and in the secret treaty signed with the Allies in 1916 the Tisa River was set as the future boundary between the two states. When Russia was no longer a contender for the territory, Prime Minister Brătianu claimed for Rumania all of Máramaros county so as to extend its common frontier with Polish-occupied Galicia, but the Council of Foreign Ministers at the peace conference rejected his request and the Rumanians only received those parts of Máramaros county south of the Tisa.[109]

To be sure, delegations from the Ukrainian governments in Stanyslaviv and Kiev and from the Hungarian government presented their grievances in Paris, but the Allied statesmen were not convinced that the Ukraine could last as a viable political entity and looked upon Hungary as a defeated power whose claims should not be taken seriously.[110] The peace conference was also the recipient of memoranda from representatives of the anti-Bolshevik Russian Political Conference[111] and Russophile National Council of L'viv, which stressed that the "Russian people of former Austria-Hungary [meaning Rusyn-Ukrainians in Galicia, Bukovina and Subcarpathia] . . . declare their wish to realize a simple union, autonomous and federative, with a democratic Russian state."[112] The continuance of Bolshevik rule and the undetermined outcome of the civil war, however, eliminated in Allied minds any possibility for Russian rule in Subcarpathian Rus'. In such circumstances, the Czechoslovak delegates, Prime Minister Karel Kramář and Minister of Foreign Affairs Edvard Beneš, could be almost certain of success.

Because they were anxious to show western diplomats that Czechoslovakia had the support of Subcarpathian Rusyns, Beneš and Kramář welcomed the presence of A. Beskid, chairman of the pro-Czechoslovak Prešov Council, who had been in Paris since late January, and G. Zsatkovich and J. Gardoš, delegates from the American National Council of Uhro-Rusyns, who arrived in the French capital on February 13 armed with the decisions embodied in the Scranton resolution and plebiscite. Initially, the Council of Ten (headed by Wilson, Clemenceau, Lloyd George, and Orlando) began to hear orally the territorial claims of the new states, but this procedure was so time consuming that separate commissions were created to decide first on feasible borders and then make appropriate recommendations. The Commission on Czechoslovak Affairs, composed of representatives from the United States, Great Britain, France, and Italy, held sessions during the month of February. This Commission was chaired by Jules Cambon, the French ambassador, who consistently propounded his country's desire that Czechoslovakia, like Poland, should include as many strategic territories as possible so that in the future it might be part of a *cordon sanitaire,* an effective counterweight to Germany on the one hand and to Bolshevik Russia on the other.[113]

The Commission on Czechoslovak Affairs began its work by considering the territorial claims of eleven *Mémoires* drawn up by Beneš and Kramář. *Mémoire No. 6* dealt with the "Ruthenians of Hungary" and it proposed "as the most acceptable solution . . . to include these people in the Czechoslovak Republic as an autonomous province."[114] This proposal was a departure from the original plans of Czech leaders. Masaryk's first sketch (1915) for an independent Czechoslovak state did not include Rusyn-inhabited territory from either Subcarpathian Rus' or from what later became eastern Slovakia. But in his last plan before the end of the war, the proposed eastern boundary was moved to the Uzh River and thus a Rusyn minority of about 90,000 was included within a future Czechoslovakia, although concrete demands for all the Rusyn-inhabited lands were not really formulated until the Paris Peace Conference.[115]

In *Mémoire No. 6,* Beneš and Kramář recognized that "the Ruthenians of Hungary never belonged to the Czechoslovak regions," yet the other alternatives—uniting with Galicia (to be controlled perhaps by Russia, Ukraine, or Poland) or remaining in Hungary—were not acceptable. Union with Galicia was favored by a few, "but the majority of the population remained indifferent."[116] Furthermore, the Poles "have always categorically stated that they do not want the Ruthenians of Hungary attached to their country."[117] As for allowing the Ruthenians "to remain under Hungarian domination," "this would be contrary to all the principles of justice and democracy in the name of which the present war was conducted."[118]

Despite such moral indignation, the most convincing argument was that the inclusion of Rusyn territory would allow Czechoslovakia to have a common boundary with Rumania—a point of "great importance to the two countries in view of the continued Hungarian menace."[119] Finally, without mentioning any specific country, it was argued that "certain circles in the Allied countries" would not wish the future ruler of Galicia (Russia was still considered a possibility by some) to have a foothold on the southern side of the Carpathians. The *Mémoire* concluded by stating that "certain representatives of the Rusyns of Hungary" had already expressed the wish to unite with Czechoslovakia, and the statement from the Svaliava Council (December 18), delivered to Hodža in Budapest, as well as the protocol of the Prešov National Council (January 7, 1919), were attached as proof of these desires.[120]

One issue was not at all made clear in *Mémoire No. 6*—the question of Rusyn borders. The statistical information that was included referred to the fact that Rusyns inhabited the former Hungarian counties of Sáros, Szepes, Zemplén, Ung, Bereg, Ugocsa, and Máramaros. However, the first four were specifically designated in the accompanying *Mémoire No. 5* as part of Slovakia. Not only Czech, but also Slovak, leaders claimed rights to these counties,[121] and by early 1919 all four of them (with the exception of eastern Ung County) were occupied by Czech troops and placed under the jurisdiction of the minister of Slovak affairs, in Bratislava. The Slovak leaders were later reluctant to give up any of their claims and this issue became a basis for discord between Rusyn politicians and the Czechoslovak government.

The territorial question not even mentioned in the text of *Mémoire No. 6* concerned those Rusyns (Lemkians as they were called) living north of the Carpathian Mountains. The Galician Russophiles, who united with A. Beskid in January, 1919 to form the Prešov (Carpatho-Russian) Council, had in mind the express purpose of uniting "all the Carpatho-Russians" as one autonomous unit in Czechoslovakia.[122] In Paris, Beskid pressed this issue in conversations with Prime Minister Kramář, a well-known friend of Russia and supporter of a territorially large Czechoslovak state.[123] Kramář encouraged Beskid in his efforts on behalf of the Galicians, and Beskid submitted a memorandum to the Prague government[124] on March 12 and sent another one on April 20 directly to the peace conference; both memoranda included the demand that the Galician "Carpatho-Russians . . . not be torn away from its Russo-Hungarian stock, but also be joined to the Czechoslovak Republic."[125] But the more sober Beneš, backed by the Rusyn-American leader Zsatkovich, was opposed to any territorial expansion beyond the Carpathians.[126]

With regard to the Ruthenian territories south of the Carpathians, the Commission on Czechoslovak Affairs accepted the Czechoslovak solution and on March 12 stated its recommendations in a report that was approved by the Central Territorial Commission two weeks later.[127] The only remaining task was to work out acceptable language that could be incorporated into the final treaty. Thus, the initial discussions in Paris proved that the Allied powers would actively support the incorporation of Subcarpathian Rus' into Czechoslovakia.

Assured that the peace conference was inclined toward the Czechoslovak solution, Zsatkovich left for the homeland. He arrived in Uzhhorod on March 10 and began to solicit the support of local leaders organized in a Rusyn Club (Rus'kii Klub) headed by A. Voloshyn, the former leader of the pro-Hungarian Uzhhorod Council, who now openly favored Prague. The atmosphere in the city was tense because nearby Mukachevo, only twenty-five miles farther east and still under Hungarian control, was by the end of the month to become the center of Soviet Rus'ka Kraina. Uzhhorod expected any day a military invasion, and to calm such apprehensions Zsatkovich left for Prague on April 20 to request the dispatch of Czech troops for the region.[128] The unstable military situation and the Bolshevik presence in Rus'ka Kraina delayed the formal implementation of the pro-Czechoslovak cause until early May, when it was finally considered safe enough to call a general meeting made up of Rusyn representatives from the former Prešov, Uzhhorod, and Khust councils.[129]

On May 8, 1919, some two-hundred delegates from these councils gathered in Uzhhorod to form a Central Russian National Council (Tsentral'na Russka Narodna Rada). The proceedings where chaired by A. Voloshyn, and about 1,200 people were present. After reviewing the varied decisions of the previous national councils, the following resolution was unanimously accepted: "The Central Russian National Council publicly declares that in the name of the whole nation it completely endorses the decision of the American Uhro-Rusyn Council to unite with the Czecho-Slovak nation on the basis of full national autonomy."[130] Before adjourning, A. Beskid was elected (in absentia) chairman, and A. Voloshyn, Miron Stripskii, and Dr. M. Brashchaiko, vice-chairmen.[131]

In five subsequent sessions of the Central Russian National Council, between May 9 and 16, the Rusyn leaders worked out details of the future relationship between the "Russian State" (Russkii Shtat)—as Subcarpathian Rus' was called—and Czechoslovakia. The concept of statehood was undoubtedly devised by Zsatkovich, who thought the territory should be internally self-governing, that is, analogous to a state of the United States. Already on the first day of debate, the Galician Russophiles (well represented on the Uzhhorod Central Council) reiterated "that our task is to free and unite all Carpatho-Rusyns, including the [Galician] Lemkians."[132] Both Voloshyn and Zsatkovich agreed in principle, but they thought it unwise to deal with Galicia until the problem of Subcarpathian Rus' was satisfactorily solved. Nevertheless, the Galicians did manage to have a motion passed to request school textbooks from the Russophile Kachkovskii Society in L'viv. The Uzhhorod Central Council also decided to recommend Gregory Zsatkovich "as Minister with full power for our state."[133]

The last session made clear the Rusyn view of Subcarpathia's future political status. The council decided to accept a fourteen-point plan (drawn up by Zsatkovich) as the basis for unification with Czechoslovakia. Point one stated that "the Rusyns will form an independent state in the Czecho-Slovako-Russian-Republic [Chesko-slovensko-russka respublika]." Great stress was put on the fact that "in all administrative and internal matters the Ugro-Russian state will be independent" (Point 4). The boundaries of this state would eventually be decided upon by a joint Ugro-Russian-Czechoslovak Commission (Point 2). Until such time, the "Russian State" should include not only Rusyn territories east of the Uzh River, but also the northern portions of Szepes, Sáros, and Zemplén counties (Point 13)—at that time under Slovak administration. The plan's last point reserved the right of the "Russian State" to appeal to the projected court of a League of Nations, which would decide on disputes that might arise with the Czechoslovak government.[134]

On May 23 a delegation of 112 members from the Central Russian National Council arrived in Prague to meet with President Masaryk and to express its desire for union. As Reverend Voloshyn later recalled, great faith was placed in "our Czech brothers": "Golden Prague solemnly greeted [and] sincerely cared for the Rusyns, and we returned home with hope for a better future."[135] Nevertheless, the question of internal autonomy, the resolution of the Slovak-Subcarpathian boundary, and the cultural policy to be adopted for the province—issues already raised at several sessions of the Central Russian National Council—developed into serious problems that were to plague relations with the central government for the next two decades.

While Rusyns were meeting in Uzhhorod to demand union with Prague, the Czechoslovak claim to Subcarpathian Rus' was being strengthened on the diplomatic and military fronts. On May 8, the Council of Foreign Ministers asked for the recommendations of the Commission on Czechoslovak Affairs, which in turn requested Beneš to submit proposals on the form of autonomy to be granted to the Rusyns. Beneš delivered a six-point project that provided for a special diet with "legislative power in all linguistic,

scholastic and ecclesiastical questions" and the appointment of a Governor
who "shall represent the final authority . . . in all matters affecting internal
administration (political matters)."[136] Provision was also made for the
nomination of a native Rusyn minister-without-portfolio in the Czechoslovak government. This project was unanimously recommended to the
Council of Foreign Ministers, which at its meeting of May 23 also proposed
the inclusion of a clause allowing Rusyns to appeal, if necessary, to the
League of Nations.

When the Committee on New States considered the Rusyn problem, however, it deleted many of the original provisions for autonomy proposed by
Beneš. Arguing that "it was neither necessary nor desirable to bind the
Czecho-Slovak State in a treaty too close as to details,"[137] the Committee
on New States submitted four revised articles, which were approved on June
16, accepted by the Council of Foreign Ministers on August 6, and formally
validated in the Minorities Treaty signed with Czechoslovakia on September
10, 1919, at Saint Germain-en-Laye.[138] That document endowed "the Ruthene territory south of the Carpathians" with "the fullest degree of self-
government compatible with the unity of the Czecho-Slovak state" (Article
10); provided for a special diet and governor responsible for linguistic, educational, and religious matters (Article 11); promised to choose officials as
far as possible from the local population (Article 12); and guaranteed the
territory "equitable representation in the legislative assembly of the
Czecho-Slovak Republic" (Article 13).[139] These provisions were later incorporated into the constitutional charter of the Czechoslovak republic on
February 29, 1920.[140]

Having secured a legal right to occupy Subcarpathian Rus', the Czechoslovak government responded to calls from leaders in the region for protection against "a revival of Bolshevism" and "a renewed assault of Magyar chauvinism."[141] To meet the offensive undertaken in May by Béla
Kun's Soviet Hungarian army, Czechoslovak legionnaires were ordered to
advance south and west from Uzhhorod, and they eventually reached the
Hungarian border town of Berehovo in early August. Rumanian troops had
previously dispersed the leaders of the Iasynia "Hutsul Republic" and occupied Subcarpathian territory east of Mukachevo.[142]

During the summer months, both Zsatkovich and A. Beskid communicated frequently with Czech and Slovak officials in Paris, Prague, and
Bratislava, and a temporary compromise was reached concerning the controversial issues of autonomy and the western border of the new province.
A provisional frontier was set along the Uzh River, and as a result about
90,000 Rusyns in the Prešov region were left under Slovak administration.[143] With these developments, the Subcarpathian and Parisian phases
came to a close and all Rusyn territory south of the Carpathians was securely in the hands of Czechoslovak and Rumanian troops.

We have seen how the future of Subcarpathian Rus' was influenced first by the activity of Rusyn immigrants in the United States and later by many national councils in the homeland. In both cases, the possibility for autonomous development within Hungary was challenged at first by an eastward orientation that looked for salvation in Russia or the Ukraine and then by acceptance of the more feasible westward solution and union with Czechoslovakia. Indeed, these choices reflected Subcarpathian developments during the decades after 1848, when Rusyn leaders were, in varying ways, attracted to Hungarian, Russian, Slovak, Galician Rusyn (Ukrainian), and Czech cultures. Thus, it was quite natural for these alternatives to be the focus of attention during the revolutionary events of late 1918 and early 1919.

Political reality, however, helped narrow the field of options. The possibility of Russian rule in the area was eliminated by the Bolshevik Revolution of 1917 and by the ensuing civil war in that country. Hungary's claims were invalidated because the Budapest government had been on the losing side in the recent war and then ruled by a Soviet regime—two black marks in the eyes of victorious Allied powers. Neither neighboring Poland nor Rumania were prepared to challenge Prague's authority in the territory, and as for union with an independent Ukraine, this proved impossible after the Ukrainian governments in L'viv and in Kiev were driven out by Polish armies on the one hand and by White and Red Russian armies on the other. Hence, Czechoslovakia remained the only feasible alternative, and if at the beginning of the First World War "few people would have guessed that this territory, situated so far from Prague and hence very little known there, was to become part of the new state,"[144] by the spring of 1919 it was obvious that Subcarpathian Rus' was to become part of the new republic. Moreover, this solution responded to the Subcarpathian tradition of cooperation with Slovaks and Czechs, actively maintained by one faction of the Rusyn intelligentsia in 1918-1919, and most importantly it fulfilled the desires of the influential French delegation to the peace conference, which hoped for the creation of a large Czechoslovak state that, via Subcarpathian Rus', would have a common border with a future ally, Rumania. In such circumstances, the first Czechoslovak minister of foreign affairs, Edvard Beneš, could haughtily declare in his first report to the National Assembly that "the problem of the Uhro-Rusyns was resolved at the Peace Conference quite easily and without much difficulty."[145]

During the critical period from November, 1918 to May, 1919, various problems arose whose resolution was to be the subject of debate and conflict in Subcarpathian Rus' for the next twenty years. These issues were political (unity with what country and under what conditions), cultural and national (problems of language and national identity), and socioeconomic (land reform and cancellation of church dues).

At a time of such great political stress and fluctuation, the details of the national issue could not be explored beyond the general acceptance by most Rusyn leaders of the Slavic character of their people. However, more serious problems appeared at the beginning of the 1919-1920 school year. According to the *Generální Statut,* the first temporary Czechoslovak law for Subcarpathian Rus', the language for official and educational purposes was to be the "místní," or local language.[146] But just what was this local language? Almost as many answers were suggested as there were teachers.

This was only one of the many problems that came to the surface in a situation where Hungarian authoritarianism was being replaced by Czechoslovak liberal democracy. For the first time, the Rusyn intelligentsia could work out in a relatively unrestricted atmosphere the thorny issue of national identity, and the manner in which they resolved questions of interpreting the historical past, and of language, literature, education, and religion will be the subject of the following chapters.

Part Two | The Cultural Setting

5 | *The Use of History*

A nationality has been defined as "a community of people who feel that they belong together in the double sense that they share deeply significant elements of a common heritage and that they have a common destiny for the future."[1] The basis of a nationality's common heritage is its history, and it is the task of the nationalist intelligentsia, first, to devise, or in the words of Bernard Lewis, to "invent" a suitable history containing a sufficient amount of glory to attract potential adherents, and, second, to convince individuals within a given group that they in fact do have a common past.[2]

That historians, nationalist or otherwise, have tended to embellish the facts is nothing new. Ernest Renan went so far as to suggest: "To forget—I will venture to say—to get one's history wrong are essential factors in the making of a nation."[3] Hence, it is not uncommon for nationalist writers to devise pedigree histories that would reveal the ancient lineage or autochthonous nature of their people. Many simply restate the antiquated genealogical approach to history. In this vein, Britain's development was traced back to the giant Albion and to Brutus of Troy or to Brut, the grandson of Aeneus. Similarly, Russia's beginnings were found in a Slavic tribe that settled on the Adriatic Sea before the fall of Troy, while Lithuania's ancestors were to have derived from the ruins of that ancient city. During the height of romanticism, one Hungarian historian, István Horvát, convinced a large segment of his countrymen that the Pyramids were built by Hungarians, that Homer's epics really dealt with Hungarian history, and that the Romans had Hungarian blood in their veins.[4] And today, Kemal Atatürk's spurious theory that "the Turks were a white, Aryan people, originating in Central Asia, the cradle of modern civilization," has been accepted as official doctrine and continues to be taught in all schools in Turkey.[5]

Indeed, one should not consider the propagators of these legends as conscious falsifiers. While several tales were in fact the pure figments of the imaginations of nineteenth-century nationalists, many others had been handed down by word of mouth, or preserved by medieval chroniclers in

105

numerous redactions of manuscripts, and then readily accepted by less discerning writers, who usually cared less for the facts than for making their countrymen proud of their past. To complete the "double sense" of community alluded to above, history was "to be consulted . . . closely to yield the glories of the . . . past which may be taken as a warranty for a glorious future."[6]

The various factions of the intelligentsia in Subcarpathian Rus' also made use of history to foster their respective ideologies. As a result, there developed Rusynophile, Magyarone, Russophile, and Ukrainophile histories of the Subcarpathian Rusyns.[7] These histories were sometimes based on the work of first-rate scholars, sometimes on the superficial theories of polemical journalists or romantic belletrists.

The Rusyn Historical Interpretation

The first histories of Subcarpathian Rus' were written during the early nineteenth century. These works were motivated largely by the need for Greek Catholic clergymen to justify, on the basis of historical documents and traditions, the legal status and property holdings of the church. (See pp. 24-25.) This motivation was soon reinforced by the wave of Romanticism and by the Herderian emphasis on the *Volk,* which stimulated a greater interest in the past and in national histories.

As a result, Subcarpathian writers like Ioanniky Bazilovych, Ivan Orlai, Iurii Venelin, and Mykhail Luchkai compiled the first extensive histories. Although concerned primarily with ecclesiastical developments, these studies nonetheless provided a conceptual framework for the early history of the Subcarpathian Rusyns that was to be accepted for generations to come. This framework was based on five premises: (1) the Rusyns were autochthonous, that is, they inhabited their land before the coming of the Magyars in 896; (2) they had an independent state, Marchia Ruthenorum or Rus'ka Kraina, ruled at times by Rusyn princes, including Emerich, *Dux Rusinorum,* the son of the famous Hungarian King, Stephen I; (3) they were converted to Christianity in the wake of the mission of Methodius, and their eastern tradition was later to have a decisive influence on Hungarian ecclesiastical developments; (4) their struggle to maintain independence was marked by uprisings like that of Petro Petrovych in the early fourteenth century; and (5) in 1360 their last independent ruler, Prince Fedor Koriatovych, arrived in Mukachevo with 40,000 Rusyns and founded a monastery there, which was to become the spiritual and cultural center of Subcarpathian life.[8]

From the Subcarpathian point of view, the most important premises were that the Rusyns were autochthonous and that they possessed their own medieval state, Rus'ka Kraina. Such arguments were part of a response to those legal theorists who proposed that the state created by the Hungarian kings was the first political entity to be established on the territory of the

Hungarian Kingdom. In the face of the Hungarian states-rights ideology, Rusyn writers stressed the idea of *Rus'ka Kraina* to justify their own historico-judicial legitimacy.

The five basic premises of Rusyn historical development were repeated with slight variations by different writers. For instance, Venelin stated that the first Rusyns came from the Ukraine along with the Magyars in the late ninth century, and that the two peoples divided the new land beyond the Carpathians. The Rusyns received the northern portion of Pannonia (including Slovakia, which bordered on Great Moravia), and as a result received Christianity directly from Methodius.[9] The political leader A. Dobrianskii also argued that the Rusyns were the indigenous population, but he was more anxious to prove that Szepes county had belonged to Kievan Rus' during the tenth and eleventh centuries.[10] In his *Istinnaia istoriia Karpato-Rossov* ("True History of the Carpatho-Rusyns," 1853), Dukhnovych stated unequivocally that while many Rusyns did come with the Magyars, they found other Rusyns living in the region already. Moreover, he argued that Rusyns had had a great influence on Magyar culture and language, and that even the name Ugriia stemmed from Igor, the ninth-century prince of Kiev.[11]

It is actually the influential, though unreliable, twelfth-century chronicle by "Anonymous," *Gesta Hungarorum,* that is the source for the theory that Rusyns were in the region well before the Magyars.[12] The chronicler also speaks of a so-called Rusyn Prince Laborets' of Uzhhorod who defended his lands until killed by the invaders. This incident was elaborated upon in nineteenth-century romantic tales by the Slovak Bohuš Nosák-Nezabudov and the Rusyn Anatolii Kralitskii.[13] Whereas the somewhat mythical Laborets' was shrouded in legend, it was Fedor Koriatovych who, as "Prince of Mukachevo" *(Ducis de Munkach),* received much attention in the historical writings of Iurii Zhatkovych and in a long ode by Evgenii Fentsik.[14] The Greek Catholic Church and its importance in the history of the Subcarpathian Rusyns was also a popular subject, as revealed through the biographies of leading clergymen and in several histories of the eparchies and monasteries.[15]

Despite these addenda, nothing much was changed regarding the five basic premises of early Rusyn history. These were adopted by Hermann Bidermann, the Austrian author of the first scholarly history of the region, and by Ioann Dulishkovich, the local writer who in the 1870s compiled a dry three-volume history of his people.[16] With an increase in cultural activity after the incorporation of the territory into Czechoslovakia, Rusyn authors continued to elaborate and in many cases to glorify the history of their ancestors. Nikolai A. Beskid (1883-1947) wrote two long monographs showing that Rusyns inhabited Pannonia well before the arrival of the Magyars, and that, as part of Kievan Rus', Subcarpathians lived in lands as far west as a line running southward from Cracow along the Hron River in western Slovakia to the bend in the Danube just north of Budapest.[17] The prolific church historian Vasylii Hadzhega (1864-1938) also accepted the nineteenth-century five-point framework for early Rusyn history and in particular emphasized the importance of the national hero Prince Fedor Koriatovych, who "holds first place in the history of our Subcarpathian Rusyn people."[18] Similarly, Irynei Kontratovych (1878-1957) claimed that the ancestors of the modern Rusyns were already in the Carpathians in the sixth century.[19] In his popular textbook *Ystoriia Podkarpatskoî Rusy dlia naroda* ("History of Subcarpathian Rus' for the People," 1924), Kontratovych stressed the role of Prince Laborets' and more specifically of Prince Koriatovych, who established the Saint Basil Monastery near Mukachevo—"the foundation of our spiritual, ecclesiastical, and secular culture."[20] The widely used textbook by Vira I. Fedelesh (1879-1967) and the writings of A. Voloshyn also stressed the autochthonous nature of the Rusyn population, their relations with Kievan Rus', and the significance of princes Laborets' and Koriatovych.[21]

As might be expected, the Rusyn historical interpretation was attacked from many quarters, in particular by distraught postwar Magyar polemicists, who on the basis of supposed historical and legal precedent argued for the reconstitution of the Hungarian Kingdom according to the prewar boundaries. In an attempt to refute such arguments, Iulii Gadzhega (1879-1945) published a pamphlet in 1928 that reviewed the existing literature concerning the settlement of the Carpathian Basin and the Christianization of its inhabitants. He reemphasized the two basic premises of the Rusyn interpretation and concluded that "the Russians [Subcarpathian Rusyns] are the indigenous population of former Hungary" and that the "beginning of Christianity in Hungary is tied directly to the activity of the eastern church, first of all with the Russian-Slavonic rite and secondly with the Greek."[22] As for the controversial *Gesta Hungarorum*, which first declared that Rusyns already inhabited the Carpathians when the Magyars arrived, Petr Sova (b. 1894) stated in his history of Uzhhorod: "It [the chronicle] contains nothing fantastic. On the contrary, everything in it is clear, logical and moreover probably true."[23] Accepting these arguments at face value, it was possible for a Rusyn children's journal to sum up the early history of Subcarpathian Rus' in the following way: "More than a thousand years ago the Rusyns settled in the Carpathians and beyond the Tisa up to the Danube. They were a free, independent people."[24]

As with many national minorities wanting to justify their legal status, Rusyn writers concentrated for the most part on the origins and early history of their people. For instance, Orlai, Venelin, and Dobrianskii only brought their surveys down to the fifteenth century, Bazilovych and Dulishkovich, respectively, to the beginning and end of the seventeenth century, and Luchkai to the early nineteenth century. Even Vasylii Hadzhega, whose several histories of the church included developments in the twentieth century, concentrated most of his discussion on the earlier periods. A few Subcarpathian writers published short studies in Russia that dealt with events during the late nineteenth century, but for the most part these were polemical tracts intended on the one hand to praise the activity of the local Russophile intelligentsia and on the other to castigate the treacherous acts of the "infamous" Magyarizer Bishop Pankovics.[25] These years also witnessed the appearance of the first cultural history, written by Evmenii Sabov. He viewed Subcarpathian Rusyn literature more or less as a distinct entity not dependent on or related to developments in either Russia or the Ukraine.[26]

For the most part, it was a few popular textbooks and other short studies that provided an attractive history of the more modern periods. The galaxy of events and heroes included: (1) the Union of Uzhhorod in 1646, which created the Greek Catholic Church, whose monasteries and schools "supported and preserved Russian [Subcarpathian Rusyn] culture and language";[27] (2) the Rusyn people who fought for Prince Ferenc Rákóczi II, " 'their own good lord' whom every Rusyn loved and respected greatly";[28] (3) Bishop Andrei Bachyns'kyi, who "re-established" the "ancient Eparchy of Mukachevo"; and (4) Adol'f Dobrianskii and Aleksander Dukhnovych, who achieved great political and cultural successes for Subcarpathian Rusyns in the decades after the revolution of 1848.[29]

Other personalities that proved worthy of praise included Ivan Orlai, Iurii Venelin, Mykhail Baludians'kyi, and several others who in the early nineteenth century emigrated to Russia and made very successful public careers but never forgot their homeland. By setting up these and other Rusyn "success stories" as models for the nation, Iulii Gadzhega tried to dispel the accusations of some that Rusyns were a "lazy and stupid people."[30]

There was, of course, another source from which the intelligentsia might have created a heroic past. Traditionally, the Carpathian Mountains served as a refuge for brigands who fled social oppression and then lived as Robin Hoods, robbing the rich and giving to the poor. In this vein, figures like Jánošík among the Slovaks and Dovbush among Galician Rusyns became national symbols. Even though Subcarpathian Rusyn folklore was filled with tales of Carpathian brigands, nationalist leaders did not feel they were worth writing about.[31] One exception was the belletrist Vasyl' Grendzha-Dons'kyi. He wrote a moving short story about the outlawed Il'ko Lypei, who fought against the Czech gendarmerie in the 1930s.[32] But it was a Czech author, Ivan Olbracht, who was to immortalize Subcarpathian brigands through a powerful novel about Mykola Shuhai and his wife Erzhika (who in the early 1970s was still alive in her native village).[33] In a more parochial manner, Antonii Bobul'skii (1877-194?) created the Rusyn everyman and anti-hero David Shrapnel', who like his more famous Czech counterpart in Hašek's *Good Soldier Schweik,* undermined the operations of the Austro-Hungarian army by his ironic and seemingly innocent stupidity.[34]

But brigands and dumb soldiers were not the stuff from which "true" heroes were made. Rather these had to have some dignity and be princes, soldiers, statesmen, or cultural and religious leaders.[35] It was perhaps too much to expect of an intelligentsia, most of whom had only recently raised themselves from the peasantry to the more sophisticated provincial "city life" of Uzhhorod, Mukachevo, and Prešov, that they should make heroes from a rural context they preferred to forget. This might seem like a contradiction when remembering that one characteristic of the nationalist intelligentsia was the need to praise the "pure and unspoiled *Volk*." To be sure, the *Volk* were all important, as long as one could write or talk about them from the comfort of an urban seminary, editorial office, and local or national parliament. Thus, local writers tried to provide the Rusyn masses with a historical consciousness that was filled with glory-laden events and ideal heroes drawn exclusively from the Subcarpathian past.

The Hungarian Historical Interpretation

Older Hungarian writers tended to accept the historical authenticity of the Rusyn population. The first Hungarian histories of the Subcarpathian Rusyns, written by Antal Décsy and Károly Mészáros, stated that Rusyns already inhabited the Danubian basin when the Magyars arrived, and that although the latter accepted Christianity in allegiance to Rome, the Hungarian church used Old Slavonic in its liturgy and was greatly influenced by eastern Orthodoxy up until the early twelfth century.[36] Tivadar Lehoczky also argued that upon their arrival the Magyars found Rusyn sheepherders in the Carpathians, while other Rusyns who came with Árpád remained in the region as border guards and formed the basis for an autonomous territory ruled by its own princes and known as *Kraina.*[37]

Beginning in the late nineteenth century this traditional interpretation was fully revised. Initially, there was a "positivist" period in Hungarian historiography, when medieval chronicles and other documents were systematically collected and critically analyzed. Several controversial passages in the *Gesta Hungarorum* that were unfavorable to Magyar nationalism could now be disregarded, and authors like János Karácsonyi could revise Hungarian historiography and justify with less difficulty "the historical right of the Magyar nation to the territory of our fatherland from the Carpathians to the Adriatic Sea."[38] According to Karácsonyi, when the Magyars came to the banks of the Tisa and upper Danube in 896, their "settlement was not injurious to any other nation, there being no other organized state on the territory in question, which was uninhabited and uncultivated."[39] Revisionist historiography reached its culmination in the school of intellectual history and ideas (*szellemtörténet*), represented by the extremely popular eight-volume synthesis of Hungarian history by Bálint Hóman and Gyula Szekfű.[40] Published after the First World War, when Hungary was deprived of two-thirds of the historic lands of St. Stephen, this work attempted to discover the "essence" of history and to reveal the underlying spiritual forces that unified and fostered the Hungarian nation since its origin. At the same time it also complemented the government's foreign policy, which demanded international boundary revision and the legally and morally justified reunification of the lands of the Crown of St. Stephen. More specifically, the Magyars were viewed as the only politically active and creative people of the former kingdom, and even if other peoples inhabited the area before their arrival, these "minorities" had no influence whatsoever on the development of the state and only in later centuries did, they have an impact on the ethnic composition of the country. The Magyars inhabited the area before the Serbs and Rumanians, and the Slovaks and Rusyns did not have numerical significance until the thirteenth to fifteenth centuries. Thus, the maintenance of Hungary for so many centuries was the handiwork of the Magyar people, while the minorities entered the political scene only infrequently, as during the nineteenth century, when the Hapsburgs in Vienna used them in an attempt to decrease the political power of Budapest.[41]

These theories of Hungarian precedence were adapted to the history of Subcarpathian Rus' by the Magyarized Rusyns Antal Hodinka, Sándor Bonkáló, and Hiiador Stryps'kyi. With regard to the original population of Subcarpathian Rus', Hodinka pointed out that "it was only much later, i.e., toward the middle of the thirteenth century, that the process of settlement started, and very slowly in the beginning."[42] Moreover, the settlement of Rusyns was organized by the Hungarian government, which, concerned for the defense of its unprotected northern border, called upon large landowners, like the Berzeviczy, Görgey, and Drugeth families, who in turn hired immigrant agents (*kenéz* or *soltész*) to invite colonists (*hospites*) to the uninhabited region. From the fourteenth to seventeenth centuries various waves of Rusyn immigrants from Galicia arrived. Although the national hero Koriatovych did exist, he did not arrive with 40,000 immigrants and was not responsible for any settlements.[43] The new colonists received tax-exempt privileges and were especially favored by the benevolent King Mátyás Corvinus (1458-1490).[44] To document his case, Hodinka listed property and livestock holdings to show that until the late sixteenth century, Rusyns were economically prosperous. Then things began to change, because Vienna found out about this tax-exempt population and tried to remove its privileges. Later, the countryside was ravaged by imperial troops in the course of a series of revolts against Hapsburg rule during the late seventeenth and early eighteenth centuries.[45] It was during the greatest of these revolts, led by Prince Ferenc Rákóczi II, that Rusyns joined en masse the army of "their master." The Rusyns were victims of Viennese attempts at centralization and, "remembering 'the more happy days of the past'," fought in an attempt to regain their lost freedom.[46] Hodinka explains that "this is how the Rusyn people became the *gens fidelissima* of Prince Ferenc Rákóczi, and why this people still cherishes the memory of their former master while glancing with regret on the economic situation they once had."[47] The revolt was put down by the Hapsburg forces and the plight of the Rusyns continued to worsen in the eighteenth century, especially after the failure of the reforms of Maria Theresa. A more liberal Hungarian government headed by Lajos Kossuth[48] liberated the serfs in 1848, but according to Hodinka this measure was soon rendered ineffective by the political machinations of Vienna. Only after 1867, when "a certain degree of independence" was obtained, could the "Hungarian nation and its governments . . . undertake the most meritorious efforts to assuage the miserable conditions of the Rusyns living at the foot of the Carpathians."[49]

The Hungarian interpretation of Rusyn history was that the Rusyns came as guests, invited by the Magyars to settle in Subcarpathian Rus', where they lived in very favorable circumstances until the Hapsburg government in Vienna imposed its centralized rule. This development not only limited the political prerogatives of the Magyars, but also caused a marked decline in the living standard of the Rusyns.

Other writings supported the Hungarian viewpoint. In his exhaustive history of the Mukachevo Greek Catholic diocese, Hodinka accepted the thesis of the Hungarian ecclesiastical historian János Karácsonyi that initially western Christianity played a decisive role in Hungary and only later did the Eastern Church—in its Greek not Slavonic form—have any influence.[50] The cultural, national, and linguistic development of the Subcarpathian Rusyns was outlined in several short studies by S. Bonkáló. This Magyarized Rusyn occupied the first chair of Rusyn studies at the University of Budapest (1919-1921) and from that post he began to inform the Hungarian public about one of the country's "temporarily" lost territories.

Bonkáló agreed with Hodinka concerning the later settlement of the region and rejected any theories suggesting that the Rusyns may have had their own political history.[51] With regard to national identity they had to be considered a distinct Slavic people: "Their civilization, language and *Weltanschauung* deviate in one way or another from their nearest social brethren, from the Ukrainian civilization, language, and *Weltanschauung.*"[52] And as for the Russians, Rusyns are "as far away from them as from the Serbs and Bulgars."[53] This theory was buttressed by linguistic evidence presented in his own writings and those of Hiiador Stryps'kyi, then a curator in the National Museum in Budapest. Both argued that the oldest Rusyns, the *Dolyshniany,* who settled on the lower mountain slopes and immediate plain, had come from Volhynia and Podillia, through Moldavia and Transylvania, before settling in Subcarpathian Rus'. Living for so many centuries in close contact with Magyars and in physical isolation from their ancestors, they had developed a distinct culture, one that differed significantly from that of the Hutsuls and other Rusyns who came much later from Galicia and settled in the immediately adjacent *Verkhovyna,* or upper mountainous slopes, near their former homeland.[54] It was the *Dolyshniany* who formed the kernel of a Rusyn civilization, which had even developed its own literature—based on a language close to the spoken dialects—in the late seventeenth and eighteenth centuries.[55] Of course, the crucial determinant in these developments, argued Bonkáló, was not the East, but rather the West, which brought the Reformation and the church union. Rusyns accepted from Protestantism, which was securely entrenched in northeastern Hungary and Transylvania, the idea of preaching and publishing religious works in a language understandable to the people.[56]

These favorable beginnings of Subcarpathian Rusyn culture were shattered by the "Slavic idea" of the nineteenth century, which, in the writings of the first pan-Slavist, Jan Kollár, proposed the concept of one eastern Slavic people, the Russian, into which Belorussians, Ukrainians, and Subcarpathian Rusyns were merged. Consequently, the Hungarian interpretation is very critical of men like Dobrianskii and Dukhnovych, who suppposedly rejected Subcarpathian tradition and looked to the East. This "Carpatho-Rusyn intelligentsia was not bothered by the fact that they wanted to transplant to Subcarpathia a foreign language and a foreign-minded literature which neither they nor the common man understood. This gulf, which opened wide between the intelligentsia and the people, was made greater by Russophilism."[57] This "artifical" Russophilism received a further stimulus through the guise of "schismatic" Orthodoxy, brought to Subcarpathian Rus' at the end of the century by immigrants returning from the United States and by propagandists in the pay of tsarist Russia. To make matters worse, some Rusyns were infected by the Ukrainian national ideology, especially after the First World War. Then in 1918-1919, the Czechoslovak regime illegally occupied the territory and for the next two decades they denied Rusyns their internationally recognized right to autonomy and fostered cultural and national chaos so that a Subcarpathian Rusyn literature and culture were never allowed to develop.[58]

The Hungarian historical interpretation was used actively for the last time during the years 1938 and 1944 when the Budapest regime attempted to justify its occupation of Subcarpathian Rus'. Publicists emphasized the existence of a separate Uhro-Rusyn people who historically had every reason to remember the benefits of living under the Crown of St. Stephen—the eternal symbol of the historic pre-1918 Hungarian Kingdom.[59] Scholars also set to work to stress the indelible bonds between Rusyn and Magyar civilization,[60] as well as the value of "Uhro-Rusyn" literature and culture as it flourished in the seventeenth and eighteenth centuries and then again for a short time during the last years of Hungarian rule before the First World

War.[61] As expected, the Czechoslovak regime was strongly criticized for its illegal seizure of the territory in 1919 and for its refusal to grant autonomy to the Rusyns, which the Hungarians had supposedly done in 1919 and promised to do again in 1939.[62]

Under the new regime, Irynei Kontratovych, now a Magyarone, readily contradicted his earlier writings and declared that: "We, Subcarpathian Rusyns, unfortunately cannot compliment ourselves with some kind of glorious independent national history . . .We were a poor people of serfs."[63] Thus, it was necessary to create a new pantheon of heroes, which included Prince Ferenc Rákóczi II, his mother Helena Zrinyi, the nineteenth-century reformer István Széchényi and the revolutionary Lajos Kossuth, and the contemporary defender of St. Stephen's Crown, the Regent Miklós Horthy.[64] Local pro-Hungarian Rusyn activists were on the one hand quick to attack the tradition of Slavophilism and the spread of Ukrainianism during the Czechoslovak regime, while on the other ready to praise the tradition of autonomy the Rusyns had realized briefly within Hungary (Rus'ka Kraina) in 1918-1919.[65] As for the question of cultural traditions and national identity, Stryps'kyi summed up the problem quite clearly: "You know, we Rusyns are westerners. We are related to the West geographically and historically, related economically and religiously, related politically and linguistically . . . We don't want to have anything to do with the Russian-Tatar culture of eastern Moscow . . . because that Russian culture is foreign to us."[66] And to those who stressed the area's relation to Ukrainian civilization, Stryps'kyi adamantly retorted: "The Rusyn has his own separate language, separate culture, and separate literature."[67]

The Russian Historical Interpretation

In order to understand the Russophile and Ukrainophile opinions of Subcarpathian Rus', it is necessary first to survey briefly the Russian and Ukrainian interpretations concerning the general historical development of Eastern Europe. The conflict between Russian and Ukrainian ideologists was based in large part on differing interpretations of the history of Kievan Rus', a loosely structured political entity centered on the Dnieper River from the late ninth to the thirteenth centuries. Russian historians frequently referred to Kiev as the "mother of Russian cities," whose culture represented the first stage of an eastern Slavic civilization that was later to have its center in Moscow and St. Petersburg.

Kievan Rus' reached a critical turning point during the twelfth century, when, following the death of Prince Vladimir Monomakh in 1125, some of his offspring established themselves in Kiev, while others went north, notably his last son, Iurii Dolgorukii, who became Prince of Suzdal (1149-1157). Conflict between Kiev and the North was especially marked during the reign of Iurii's son, Andrei Bogoliubskii, Prince of Vladimir (1157-1174). Subsequently, it was the line of princes established in

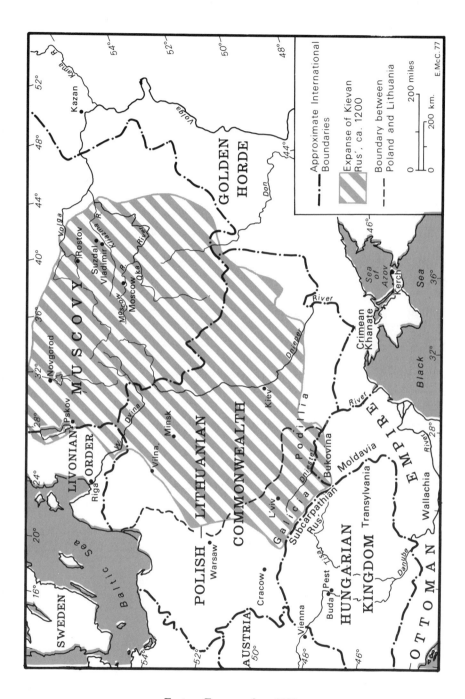

Eastern Europe, circa 1550

Vladimir-Suzdal, and later Muscovy, who were to play the most important role in maintaining political continuity and independence in the northern portion of Kievan Rus'. Among these was Ivan III (1462-1506), who emphasized that he was sovereign of all Rus'—"Gosudar Vseia Rusi." The importance of the rulers in the North was further enhanced by the transfer in 1328 of the Orthodox metropolitanate from Kiev to Muscovy. Later, four factors added to the increasing prestige of the northern princes: (1) Filofei's concept of Muscovy as the "Third Rome" and thus the only "Orthodox" successor to Constantinople; (2) Metropolitan Makarii's association of the Muscovite state with the whole Orthodox world; (3) the legend of the Muscovite inheritance of the Kievan crown of Vladimir Monomakh; and (4) Ivan III's marriage to a Byzantine princess.[68]

Hence, Russian historiography came to be dominated by the so-called linear theory of political centers: Kiev, Suzdal, Vladimir, Moscow, and finally St. Petersburg. The first influential formulation of this theory was set forth in Nikolai Karamzin's twelve-volume *Istoriia gosudarstva rossiiskago* ("History of the Russian State," 1816-1826), in which the history of eastern Slavdom was identified exclusively with the development of the Muscovite-Russian state.[69] Following Karamzin, Russian authors showed that not only political power, but even the Church and other aspects of Kievan civilization were transferred to the north. Finally, Mikhail Pogodin concluded that the population had even moved away from Kiev. Basing his statements primarily on linguistic evidence, Pogodin argued that after the Tatar invasion in the thirteenth century, the "Great Russian" inhabitants of Kiev and its surroundings fled to the North, and that only during the following century were the depopulated southern areas resettled by a new people from the Carpathians—the ancestors of the present-day Ukrainians.[70]

The linear theory was further elaborated in the writings of the two most influential nineteenth-century Russian historians, Sergei Solov'ev and Vasilii Kliuchevskii. Both emphasized the unity of Russian history as expressed in the development of the Russian national state with its center in Moscow, and later St. Petersburg. Summing up this interpretation, Solov'ev wrote: "At the end of the twelfth century [Kiev] . . . revealed its incapacity to develop any solid foundations for a single state. Following a definite path from the beginning, all the best elements of the land poured out of the southwest toward the northeast. Settlement moved in the same direction, and with it the course of history."[71]

The geographic transfer of political power centers and the idea of the unity of one eastern Slavic, or Russian, people was challenged from the beginning by Ukrainian writers. The Cossack chroniclers of the late seventeenth and eighteenth centuries discussed in a rather independent fashion the historical development of the Zaporozhian Cossack Hetmanate and stressed the elements of continuity with medieval Kievan Rus'.[72] Similar ideas were incorporated into the *Istoriia Rusov* ("History of Rus'," 1846), written sometime during the late eighteenth century. This work, which stressed the superiority of Ukrainian culture over Muscovite, was to have a great influence on the subsequent development of Ukrainian nationalism.[73] Other Ukrainian historians expressed their opposition to the Russian interpretation. Mykola Kostomarov emphasized the psychological and political differences between Ukrainians and Russians, while Volodymyr Antonovych challenged Pogodin's theory of population transfers.[74]

These studies laid the groundwork for Mykhailo Hrushevs'kyi's broad synthesis in his monumental ten-volume *Istoriia Ukraïny-Rusy* ("History of Ukraine-Rus'," 1904-1936.)[75] Hrushevs'kyi's fundamental theories were first expounded in an article published in 1904: "The Traditional Scheme of 'Russian' History and the Problem of a Rational Organization of the History of the Eastern Slavs."[76] Challenging the irrationalities of the Russian linear scheme, Hrushevs'kyi offered an alternative conceptualization. Since Kiev and Vladimir-Muscovy were politically, culturally, and nationally different, it was "irrational" to link the two cultures together. In essence, the heritage of Kievan civilization did not pass to the north, but shifted its focus only slightly to the west, to Galicia-Volhynia, during the thirteenth century.[77] His new history of the Ukraine continued with the Lithuanian-Polish era of the fourteenth to sixteenth centuries, the Zaporozhian Cossack Hetmanate during the seventeenth and eighteenth centuries, and finally the brief period of Ukrainian statehood 1917-1918. Hrushevs'kyi was opposed to the Russian emphasis on the history of state institutions, and he continued to underline the independent development of the Ukrainian lands from the time of Kievan Rus' to the establishment of the modern Ukrainian state.[78] Moreover, he steadfastly refused to accept the unified development of all the eastern Slavs: "There is no common Russian [*obshcherusskaia*] history or common Russian [*obshcherusskii*] people."[79]

The extensive research of Hrushevs'kyi could not be disregarded, and his work influenced an entire generation of younger Russian scholars. Aleksandr Presniakov realized the need to separate the histories of northern and southern Rus', and in a study of the formation of the Great Russian state he traced the origin of Russian political development not to Kiev, but to the Rostov region, northeast of Muscovy, in the twelfth and thirteenth centuries.[80] Furthermore Presniakov, together with the Belorussian historian Matvei Liubavskii, undermined Pogodin's theories on population movement. Liubavskii pointed out that the inhabitants of Muscovy came primarily from the Novgorod region and the lands just to the west of the Volga-Oka triangle, and that only later did some people arrive from the Kiev region.[81] Similarly, the Ukrainian writings prompted Russian historians to reevaluate the contributions of the "West Russian" lands to the political and cultural history of Eastern Europe. George Vernadsky was particularly concerned with these developments; however, while he emphasized the significance of "West Russian" civilization, he still considered the area part of one unitary Russian society and culture.[82] Although Vernadsky corrected the simplistic view that "Russian [*rossiiskaia*] statehood, Russian culture . . . in no way can be called Great Russian statehood or Great Russian culture,"[83] he nonetheless made "clear that Ukrainians and White Russians are branches of the Russian nation [*russkii narod*]."[84]

Russian scholars and publicists who emigrated to Czechoslovakia after the Bolshevik Revolution and Civil War contributed further to the Russian-Ukrainian polemic. One author argued that "the Ukraine has played its role in the history of humanity as a part of Russia. Russian culture, Russian statehood is in large part the work of Ukrainians," and for that reason the "Ukrainian people can be proud of all those values that adorn the common Russian culture."[85] Nonetheless, "they wish to create a new people" and do have a "potential" that has to develop.[86] Such an opinion recognized the dynamics of historical development, but the tolerance with which it was expressed was rare in writings on the subject.

For the most part, Russian émigré authors were quick to renew the charge that Ukrainianism was simply an invention of the Austrian and German foreign offices, which strove to undermine the Russian Empire. In 1919, a pamphlet written by one émigré warned the Czech public to beware: "There is no Ukrainian people nor Ukrainian language! Both names are only the fruit of Polish-German politics."[87] According to this view, the proclamation of Ukrainian independence in Kiev (January 1918) was just another negative result of German and Austrian interference in Russian affairs, while the concept of a separate Ukrainian culture was an unfortunate by-product of Polish imperialism.[88] Similarly, with the establishment of the Ukrainian Soviet Republic in 1923, Ukrainianism was considered by many Russian émigrés to be nothing more than an artificial ideology forcibly imposed from above by the apparatus of a Soviet police state.[89]

The Russian and Ukrainian interpretations of Eastern European history were almost entirely incompatible. The Russian linear and unitary theories saw the heritage of Kievan Rus' as being maintained and expanded after the transfer of political power to Muscovy in the north. In contrast, the Ukrainian interpretation stressed the independent development of the territories in the south from those in the north and suggested that the vestiges of state institutions and culture in Kievan Rus' formed the basis of the modern Ukrainian civilization—quite distinct from Russian society centered in Muscovy or St. Petersburg. Let us see how writers from these two schools adapted their theories to the history of Subcarpathian Rus'.

Initially, writers who adopted the Russian interpretation (Russians from the tsarist empire and Russophiles from Galicia) accepted most of the five basic premises that made up the Rusyn historical intrepretation discussed earlier in this chapter. The most important of these was that Rusyns were the autochthonous inhabitants of the Carpathians. As early as 1842, Nikolai I. Nadezhdin argued on historical, ethnographic, topographic, and even linguistic grounds that the "Russian element stretched to the South-West, on both sides of the Carpathians, right up to the Danube, long before the arrival of the Magyars in Pannonia; and that the Magyars did not bring Russians [*Russy*] with them, but found them already there, then settled down and lived among them."[90] Moreover, for Nadezhdin the Carpathians became the original source for all eastern Slavic civilization. After visiting the area, he declared that the "beginnings of our history, the origin and meaning of our ancient chronicles, the spread of the beneficial rays of Christianity in our Fatherland, the coming to us of the Church-Slavonic language which had such an important influence on our spiritual and literary formation—all these items which had been more or less mysterious and unclear to me, suddenly became understandable."[91]

These theories were maintained until the late nineteenth century by Ivan Filevich, a professor at Warsaw University, who argued that the "Carpathians belong to the Russian people and have belonged to them for all time, as long as history can recall."[92] Moreover, not only was the region a part of Kievan Rus', it was the source from which that civilization sprang.[93] Other writers also emphasized that Subcarpathian Rus' received Christianity from Cyril and Methodius, that before the coming of the Magyars it was ruled by Prince Laborets', who was allied with Chervona Rus' (Galicia and Bukovina) and Kievan Rus', and that Prince Koriatovych did indeed play an important role as a colonizer and symbol of the Rusyn's autonomous existence.[94]

However, almost simultaneous with Nadezhdin, another Russian, Arist A. Kunik, rejected the idea that Rusyns were the indigenous population of the Carpathians. In 1844, Kunik argued that Rus' was a concept denoting religion, not national affiliation, and that Rusyns could not have been in Pannonia before the Magyars.[95] This view was also supported in the linguistic studies of Aleksei I. Sobolevskii.[96] Thus, one school of Russian historiography had put forth the idea of the later settlement of Rusyns well before Hungarian revisionist and Magyarone scholars like Hodinka and Bonkáló were to make this the basis of their own views. In 1859, Vladimir I. Lamanskii, the influential professor of comparative Slavic history at St. Petersburg University, questioned in a rather obtuse manner the conclusions of Kunik and accepted the pre-Magyar settlement of Rusyns "as long as it is not positively proven [that they] . . . did not appear in Hungary until the thirteenth and fourteenth centuries."[97] But it was one of Lamanskii's students, Aleksei L. Petrov, who was to disregard the hesitations of his mentor and to develop most fully a complete revision (and rejection) of all the premises that Subcarpathian historiography had so cherished.

Petrov was one of a group of Russian and Galician Russophile émigré scholars, including Vladimir Frantsev, Aleksander A. Kizevetter, Antonii

Florovskii, Iul'ian Iavorskii, Dmitrii Vergun, George Vernadsky, and I. Lappo, who settled in Prague and were grouped around the Russian Free University (Russkii Narodnyi, later Svobodnyi Universitet), the Russian Historical Archive (Russkii Zagranichnyi Istoricheskii Arkhiv), and the Slavonic Library, all of which flourished under the patronage of the Czechoslovak government during the inter-war period. These writers had either previously or while in Prague written about the westernmost branch of the "Russian" people living in Subcarpathian Rus', but it was Petrov who devoted most of his energies to this subject. His ideas were best summed up in a critical introduction to one of his last works, where he made clear his aim to destroy the mythology upon which he felt Rusyn historiography was based. Discounting the *Gesta Hungarorum,* the chronicle by "Anonymous," as worthless, Petrov said that in early times the Carpathians were covered by an "impenetrable forest" so that Rusyns did not begin to settle there until the late twelfth century.[98] He also concluded that geographical conditions unfavorable to travel precluded any Subcarpathian relations with Greater Moravia in the ninth century—and thus any conversion to Christianity by Methodius. Moreover, there were never any princely Rusyn leaders, and the concept of Marchia Ruthenorum was a fiction of uninformed medieval German chroniclers, one that was accepted at face value and later put forward under the name of Rus'ka Kraina in the history of Bidermann.[99]

Petrov's most devastating blow to the premises of early Rusyn historiography was his refusal to accept the "legends" about Petro Petrovych and Fedor Koriatovych. Petrovych was not a Rusyn prince protecting the Orthodox faith from the inroads of Catholicism, but rather an independent warlord jealous of the Hungarian king's growing power. Moreover, Petrovych was not a Rusyn, but a Magyar; not Orthodox, but Roman Catholic.[100] As for Koriatovych, the so-called Document of 1360 was a forgery, and although he was ruler of Podillia, he did not arrive in Mukachevo until the end of the fourteenth century, and certainly not with 40,000 Rusyns but only with his personal retinue. Furthermore, the Monastery of St. Basil was already in existence, and if Koriatovych did contribute some aid to the ecclesiastics, he was completely forgotten after his death in 1414, until his "rise from the dust of centuries" in 1690.[101] In short, according to Petrov, "the political history of the Carpatho-Russians [*Karpatorussov*] is only an illusion, only a mirage."[102] He felt that the propagation of myths about a supposed historical past could not guarantee Rusyn political autonomy at that time (1930) nor in the future, and that tales about fictitious leaders from the past only served to camouflage the true hero of Subcarpathian Rus', "the Carpatho-Russian people."[103] The opinions of Petrov were accepted in a general survey of Subcarpathian Rus' written for the Czech public by Kirill Kokhannyi-Goral'chuk (1888-1974), a Russophile émigré who worked for the Czechoslovak Ministry of Culture in Uzhhorod during the 1920s.[104]

Besides the medieval period, Russian historiography also concentrated on developments in the nineteenth century and on the cultural and literary history of Subcarpathian Rus'. Several studies focused on the post-1848 national revival and especially on the activities of Dobrianskii, Dukhnovych, and other local Russophiles who stimulated the Subcarpathian intelligentsia to identify itself with Russian civilization.[105] Much less positive were descriptions of the Greek Catholic Church, and in particular its hierarchy, which was portrayed as having betrayed the "true" (Orthodox) faith since the seventeenth century, succumbing to the pressures first of Latinization, then of Magyarization, both to the detriment of Rusyn national development.[106] As might be expected, all these studies lamented the widespread poverty in the region and greatly criticized the Magyarization policy of the Budapest government, in particular Magyarone leaders like Bishop Pankovics who were responsible for the increase in national assimilation among the Rusyn populace.[107] The only positive aspect of these years was the fact that the propaganda of the separatist and radical Ukrainophile movement could find no supporters among the nationally conscious Subcarpathians.[108] In such an unfavorable political situation, however, one Russian author could still write confidently in 1878 that "there will come a time when Hungarian Rus' will find help in our literary circles. Books, texts and newspapers from the Russian people will appear in large numbers, and only then can Hungarian Rus' look with self-confidence upon the five million strong Magyar nation and say: 'Leave me along, behind me is all of Russia'."[109] By the time of the First World War, Russian writers were promising salvation for Subcarpathian Rus' through liberation by the tsar's armies.[110]

The decline of Russian influence at the international level, followed by the country's Bolshevization, forced émigré writers to reevaluate the importance of their former homeland for political development in Subcarpathian Rus'. In such a situation Czechoslovakia was viewed as the best guarantee for the national survival of the Subcarpathian Rusyns.[111] Although the Prague regime was sometimes criticized for following a pro-Ukrainian policy, Russian émigré writers both in Prague and in Subcarpathian Rus' praised the economic achievements under Czechoslovak rule and pointed out that the region was the only "Russian" land enjoying a free existence at that time.[112]

Émigré literary scholars working in Prague, Uzhhorod, and Mukachevo also wrote several surveys and individual biographies that attempted to prove that "Carpatho-Russian literature makes up a part of Russian literature."[113] At the first international meeting of Slavic philologists, held in Prague in 1929, a Russophile émigré from Galicia, Iul'ian Iavorskii, presented a detailed methodological study on the "Significance and Place of Transcarpathia in the General Scheme of Russian Literature." He divided Subcarpathian literary developments into four periods, which had to be considered both within the context of common Russian (*obshcherusskaia*) and common Little Russian (*obshchemalorusskaia*) literary history, although at the same time Subcarpathian literature was to be recognized as a distinct entity. Ukrainian literature was recognized as only one aspect, and a very recent one, of Little Russian literature, which was considered to be an integral part of the common Russian literary development. In this framework, it was the fourth and most recent period, "the renaissance," which was the most important, because it included the late nineteenth-century writers Dukhnovych, Mitrak, Sil'vai, Stavrovskii-Popradov, and especially Fentsik, all of whom associated themselves with Russian culture and succeeded in writing in literary Russian. Although the twentieth century had seen the rise of the "Ukrainophile" school in Subcarpathian Rus', a historically justified Russian tradition was still being maintained by local writers like Andrei Karabelesh and Mikhail Popovich.[114]

This conceptual framework formed the basis for the writings of Evgenii Nedziel'skii (1894-195?), a Russian émigré activist in Uzhhorod, who published what is still the most comprehensive history of Subcarpathian Rusyn literature, and Georgii Gerovskii (1886-1959), who contributed the article on Rusyn language to the standard Czechoslovak encyclopedia.[115] The Russian interpretation was also supplemented in several surveys and biographies of Subcarpathian authors by Dmitrii Vergun and Aleksander V. Popov, and by the local Russophile Pavel Fedor (1884-194?).[116]

The scholarly literature propounding the Russian historical interpretation provided the source from which Russophile publicists in Subcarpathian Rus' could argue their case against the Rusynophiles and Ukrainophiles in their struggle to gain the allegiance of the Subcarpathian populace. One local politician of the Russophile orientation summed up his position thus: "Russian culture was created and perfected by all the branches of the Russian tribe, Great Russians as well as Little Russians and Belorussians. Both mighty Russia, and within its limits Galicia and Subcarpathian Rus', participated in this work."[117] Unified Russia (*edinaia Rossiia*), inhabited by one Russian people (*russkii narod*), "stretched from Uzhhorod to Vladivostok and from Murman to the borders of China and India,"[118] and most often the slogan "from Poprad to the Pacific" was used when delineating the territory of this one Russian nation.[119]

To be sure, the propagators of the Russophile interpretation recognized that within this "unified Russia" there existed "many local peculiarities, customs, and dialects"[120] (in particular Great Russian, Belorussian, and Little Russian), but these were considered subordinate to the larger whole. The inhabitants of Subcarpathian Rus' might belong to the Little Russian branch, but this was always historically part of one Russian civilization; hence, the "Carpatho-Russian people are a direct branch of one Russian people."[121] The argument continued: Subcarpathian Rus' was part of Russia in Kievan times, and although it was forcibly torn away by the Magyars, the Slavic inhabitants maintained an allegiance to the East, especially in their defense of Orthodoxy, which withstood the inroads of western Catholic culture until the eighteenth century.[122] With the beginnings of a national awakening in the late nineteenth century, Subcarpathian Rus' "aspired to revive the almost completely lost ties with Russian [obshcherusskii] culture."[123] All the important local intellectual leaders—Dobrianskii, Fentsik, Pavlovych, Stavrovskii-Popradov, Sil'vai—"understood that the one road to cultural progress and national rebirth is to join the Russian culture."[124] The greatest figure in the national revival, Aleksander Dukhnovych, was described as "a blood brother of the whole Russian people [who] was not enticed by some kind of frauds of the recent Populists [narodovtsy] and Ukrainians."[125]

Supporters of the Russophile interpretation categorically denied the existence of a separate nationality variously called Little Russian, southern Russian, Ukrainian, or Rusyn. Even the famed Ukrainian poet, Taras Shevchenko was considered nothing more than a "Little Russian" provincial author whose works in that dialect (as opposed to writings in the artifical Ukrainian "jargon" of Galicia) were read and understood by all Russians.[126] The idea of an independent Ukrainian or Rusyn nation was seen as a superficial product of Western political machinations, either Austrian, German, Polish, or Hungarian in origin, and it had to be resisted. In short, "the Rusyn nation like the Ukrainian nation never existed."[127] As for the potential confusion in terminology, the Russophile National Catechism for Subcarpathian Rus' stated that "Russian and Rusyn mean the same thing."[128]

The Ukrainian Historical Interpretation

Some of the earliest Ukrainian writings about Subcarpathian Rus' came from scholars like Mykhailo Drahomanov, Volodymyr Hnatiuk, Mykhailo Hrushevs'kyi, Ivan Franko, and Stepan Tomashivs'kyi, who were associated with Ukrainian cultural institutions in L'viv during the late nineteenth and early twentieth centuries. Another group included Ukrainians from both Galicia and the Russian Empire who after the First World War settled in Czechoslovakia, a country that tolerated and supported not only Russian but Ukrainian émigré cultural activity as well. Among those who wrote on Subcarpathian problems were Ivan Pan'kevych, Volodymyr Birchak, and Vasyl'Pachovs'kyi, who staffed the school administration in Uzhhorod, Evhenii Perfets'kyi, professor at the Comenius University in Bratislava, Oleksandr Mytsiuk at the Ukrainian Economic Academy (Ukraïns'ka Hospodars'ka Akadmiia, established 1922) in Poděbrady, and Dmytro Doroshenko at the Ukrainian Free University (Ukraïns'kyi Vilnyi Universytet, established 1921) in Prague.[129]

Ukrainian interpretations of early developments in Subcarpathian Rus' contained, like Russian writings, two schools of thought, one glorifying the distant past of the Rusyns and another more skeptical of those historical facts that seemed to be based on legend. To the first school belonged Hnatiuk, Hrushevs'kyi, and Mytsiuk, who accepted the evidence in the *Gesta Hungarorum* and the Kievan *Povest vremmenykh let* as proof that the direct ancestors of the Subcarpathian Rusyns were the so-called White Croatians who had inhabited the region in the seventh and eighth centuries, well before the arrival of the Magyars.[130] Moreover, Subcarpathian Rus' was at that time within the cultural sphere of Greater Moravia, from which Christianity was received, and even after the arrival of the Magyars the Rusyns had their own princes and maintained an autonomous existence in Marchia Ruthenorum. The last of their rulers was the fourteenth-century Koriatovych, considered particularly important as a great colonizer.[131] This favorable view of early Subcarpathian history was accepted by the poet and playwright Vasyl' Pachovs'kyi, who wrote the first popular textbook of Rusyn history published in Czechoslovakia. This work emphasized the integral relationship between the Subcarpathian region and Kievan Rus'; hence, in his preface the author called out: "Carpatho-Rusyns, Rusyn children! Lift up proudly your heads, stand up straight, look around you and recognize that you are the sons of the oldest, most ancient people in eastern Europe! Your people have lived on this land for 1,500 years! Your people numbering forty million has settled from the Poprad River to the Caucasus Mountains on a black, rich land which is two times larger than old Hungary."[132]

Two decades later, when Subcarpathian Rus' had received its autonomy, the Ukrainian public, especially in Galicia, riveted its attention on events among their brethren. This renewed interest prompted young scholars like Omeljan Pritsak and Mykola Andrusiak to write histories that reiterated, on linguistic and archeological grounds, the autochtonous nature of the population and the existence of autonomous Subcarpathian rulers in the Middle Ages.[133]

The second school of Ukrainian writers included Izmail Sreznevs'kyi, Dmytro Bahalii, and especially Evhenii Perfets'kyi who argued that Rusyns did not reach the Subcarpathian region until after the Magyars, that is, during the eleventh to thirteenth centuries. Furthermore, Perfets'kyi was convinced that Koriatovych did not arrive with 40,000 Rusyn colonists and that this, like other tales about this leader, so dear to local writers, was based on "pure legend."[134]

As for the later periods, the economic historian O. Mytsiuk agreed with the Hungarian interpretation of Hodinka, that the decline in economic conditions among Rusyns began with the seventeenth-century revolts, and that the subsequent centralization imposed by the Viennese government, especially under Maria Theresa, only made matters worse. There is no mention, however, of Rusyns as *gens fidelissima*; rather, Ferenc Rákóczi II is seen as having exploited the misery and discontent of the peasant population for his own political goals.[135]

The existence of ties between Subcarpathian Rus' and Galicia and the importance of the Greek Catholic Church as an institution preserving Rusyn nationality were two themes that dominated the Ukrainian interpretation. Ecclesiastics like Bishop Andrei Bachyns'kyi were praised, since he tried to improve the educational level of the local populace and to unify Greek Catholics on both sides of the Carpathians.[136] The Subcarpathian national awakener of the late nineteenth century, Aleksander Dukhnovych, was idealized, especially for his belief that "those on the other side of the mountains are not foreign to us."[137] Some writers overlooked the fact that Subcarpathian contacts were exclusively with Russophile elements in Galicia and they even disregarded the explicitly anti-Ukrainian statements of Dukhnovych and other members of the Subcarpathian intelligentsia. M. Andrusiak went so far as to claim that the pronounced Russophile A. Dobrianskii called for the creation of Ukrainian schools and Ukrainian publications in Subcarpathian Rus'. Dobrianskii was viewed as the first Subcarpathian political leader in the modern period, although his "Muscophile" political and cultural policies alienated the Austrian and Hungarian governments as well as the local population, so that the result was denationalization and Magyarization.[138] In short, "Muscophilism, which began in Hungary at the moment of the Rusyn awakening in 1848, demoralized the intelligentsia and destroyed all desire to work for the people."[139] Nonetheless, as Drahomanov points out, the Subcarpathian masses continued to maintain contact with Galicia, and their natural desire to unite with their Ukrainian brethren was shown again in 1918-1919. Unfortunately, these legitimate goals were undermined, first by Czechoslovak politicians in Prague, who in cooperation with Rusyn immigrants in the United States annexed the province, refused to grant autonomy, and supported the local Russophiles at the expense of Ukrainianism.[140]

Ukrainian writers also had their own interpretation of the cultural history of Subcarpathian Rus'. The Galician literary scholars Ivan Franko and Mykhailo Vozniak had analyzed Subcarpathian writings, especially from the seventeenth and eighteenth centuries,[141] but it was their younger countryman Volodymyr Birchak who was to provide a general survey of Subcarpathian literature. Drawing on his predecessors, Birchak argued that the seventeenth and eighteenth centuries buttressed the creation of a Subcarpathian literature written in a language based on local dialects, a notion adopted again by authors like V. Chopei, Iu. Zhatkovych, M. Vrabel', and A. Voloshyn in the late nineteenth century, and by V. Grendzha-Dons'kyi and Iu. Borshosh-Kum'iats'kyi in the twentieth century. The last two, together with their younger colleagues, had in fact adopted standard Ukrainian and hence reiterated Subcarpathia's cultural association with other Ukrainian lands. The only anomaly in this development came in the nineteenth century, when Subcarpathian authors wrote first in Latin, and then, under the influence of a "cold, chilling wind from the North which froze our young literature," in Russian.[142] As a result, the importance of a figure like Dukhnovych lay in those of his works written in a language close to the local dialect, although his greatest potential was undermined by his unsuccessful effort to write in Russian.

Thus, the Ukrainian interpretation was virtually the reverse of that proposed by Nedziel'skii and local Russophiles. One group's cultural heroes became the other's enemies. On the other hand, the Ukrainian Birchak was somewhat closer to the Hungarian view as outlined by Bonkáló and Stryps'-kyi. But whereas the Magyarones frowned on the increasing tendency of some Subcarpathian writers to use standard Ukrainian rather than developing a separate Rusyn literature, Ukrainian scholars saw this trend as a healthy return to the language of the people, which was identified as a dialect of Ukrainian.

During the 1920s and 1930s, the ideological struggle among various national factions of the Subcarpathian intelligentsia sharpened, and each orientation argued for the rightness (and righteousness) of its historical interpretation. By associating national identity with language, Ukrainophiles reminded the Russophiles that their language was not a dialect of Russian and that even the respectable St. Petersburg Academy of Sciences had proclaimed in 1905 "that the Little Russian people must have the same right as the Great Russian to speak publicly and to publish in their own national tongue."[143] Since the various dialects of Subcarpathian Rus' were closely related to the Little Russian or Ukrainian language as spoken in Galicia, the population had to be considered Ukrainian. Similarly, Magyarone writers defended the idea of a separate Uhro-Rusyn language distinct from either Russian or Ukrainian.

Like the local Russophiles, the Ukrainophiles responded to all Rusyno-philes—whether pro-Hungarian, pro-Czechoslovak, or independent—in the same negative way. First of all, the name Rusyn was widespread among people on both the northern and southern slopes of the Carpathians, and in fact it was considered to be an archaic term fully synonymous with the more modern designation Ukrainian. Secondly, since the Ukrainophiles stressed the unity of Subcarpathian Rus' with Galicia, and by extension its unity with all Ukrainian lands, any suggestion that those Rusyns who lived south of the Carpathians comprised a separate nation was dimissed as the fictitious invention of Hungarian, and later Czech, ruling circles. "Very foolish are those who want to make of our Rusyns a separate people, and from their speech a separate language."[144] As Russophile ideologists rejected the idea of an independent Ukrainian nation, so together with local Ukrainophiles they denied that an independent Rusyn nationality south of the Carpathians could ever exist. Such an attitude reminds one of the German historian Heinrich von Treitschke and his opinion about the Alsatians, an ethnic group, like the Subcarpathian Rusyns, with a distinct language and culture: "We Germans, who know both Germany and France, know better what is for the good of the Alsatians than do those unhappy people themselves, who in the perverse conditions of a French life, have been denied any true knowledge of modern Germany. We desire, even against their will, to restore them to themselves."[145]

It was from the standpoint of insecurity or inferiority that local Russophile and Ukrainophile writers attacked the concept of a separate Rusyn nationality. They felt that in cultural terms "there cannot be a literature for a people numbering less than half a million souls."[146] "One would have to be blind to think that a small people numbering half a million and living amidst a sea of nations great in number could survive or could create some kind of separate culture or literature."[147] And in the words of A. Voloshyn, why try to create an independent nationality or culture when "we can draw from the rich Little Russian and still richer Great Russian cultures."[148]

This kind of criticism was put before those few who felt that, while the Subcarpathian Rusyn people were related to Russians and Ukrainians, they were nonetheless quite distinct. Although local authors had well-developed theories concerning the early history of Subcarpathian Rus', these did not necessarily clash with either the Russian or Ukrainian conceptualizations. Subcarpathian Rus' could easily be considered a provincial component of a larger Russian or Ukrainian world. According to such thinking, the concept of Rusynism would be only the lowest stage in a hierarchy of group loyalties that were not opposed to a Russian or Ukrainian higher stage.[149] In essence, one could be simultaneously a resident of a certain village in Subcarpathian Rus', and, by self-description, a Rusyn, a citizen of Czechoslovakia, a Ukrainian, or Russian. None of these identities was mutually exclusive.

The problem of self-identification is well illustrated by the following conversation. Attempting to discover the nationality of a local villager, the inquirer began:

You are Slavs?
Certainly.
Poles, perhaps?
No. . .
Russians?
No.
Slovaks?
We are their neighbors. But that's all.
Ukrainians?
Not exactly.

The interviewer then suggested:

Nevertheless, you recognize that your language is very close to Ukrainian. You speak Ukrainian with several dialectal variations. If a Ukrainian comes here, you understand him without difficulty. Your villages are laid out in the manner of those in Galicia or the Greater Ukraine: the same way to build houses, same external characteristics of habits, culture, same beds, same dress, same embroidery, same traditions, same superstitions. Don't your Hutsuls belong to the purest type of Ukrainian?

Yes, all this is true in detail. But we are not any less Rusyn.[150]

In such a context, the most popular national figure, Aleksander Dukhnovych, could be viewed as any one or all of the following: a symbol of a common Russian (*obshcherusskii*) unity, a close ally of Galician Ukrainians, or a true representative of the Rusyns, "a people . . . [who] want to become among the Slavic peoples an equal independent brother."[151] Subsequently Dukhnovych's famous line "I was, am, and will be a Rusyn" was hailed by all three national orientations, because the poet's Rusyn could be considered a Russian, a Ukrainian, or a symbolic representative of an independent nationality.

Nevertheless, for some Rusyns there was an underlying if undefinable feeling that they were different from their brethren to the north and east. Although viewed by Russophile publicists as the leader of their movement, Evmenii Sabov, when speaking about his Rusyn people and their language declared: "We have neither Ukrainian nor Russian statehood; there is not even the thought of forcing on [our] villages the Ukrainian or Muscovite pronunciation."[152] This emphasis on localism, or what otherwise may be described as embryonic Rusyn nationalism, received clearer formulation with the appearance in 1935 of the newspaper *Nedîlia*. The first issue summarized the Rusyn position: "We highly praise the cultural strength of both the Great Russian and Ukrainian peoples, with honor we support their just national aims and aspirations, but nonetheless we should not harm ourselves. We also have our own history, our own traditions, our own problems, aims and aspirations, our own cultural and political needs, and these we must put first."[153]

But if the Rusynophile historical interpretation could easily be incorporated into the Russian or Ukrainian schemes, and if literary monuments and cultural leaders like Dukhnovych could be transformed into supporters of the Ukrainian or Russian viewpoints, what particular heritage remained to the Rusyns? Aleksei Petrov, the same scholar who undermined so many of the myths of local Rusyn historiography, had already provided the answer —"the Carpatho-Russian people" themselves. Neither a supposed Rusyn state nor princely rulers, but rather the simple Rusyn people, should be praised. They had their heroes—the Robin Hoods like Shuhai and Lypei who robbed the rich and gave to the poor. Moreover, they had an abundant tradition of folklore—proverbs, poetry, music, art, and architecture—from which to develop a distinct culture. However, as pointed out earlier, Rusynophile historians were reluctant to give up their legendary princely heroes for more mundane ones. Also, no local author ever pressed the idea of a distinct Rusyn historical heritage; rather, they tended to see Subcarpathian Rus' as either part of, or compatible with, the Hungarian (Hodinka, Stryps'-kyi, Bonkáló), Russian (Iu. Gadzhega, N. Beskid), or Ukrainian (V. Had-zhega) past. In short, there never existed a significant number of leaders committed to the idea of creating all the cultural forms necessary to provide a solid basis for a separate Subcarpathian Rusyn national ideology.

6 | *The Problem of Language*

Language has long been emphasized as a key factor in national movements. An important advocate of this idea was the eighteenth-century German writer Johann Gottfried von Herder: "Has a people anything dearer than the speech of its fathers? In its speech resides its whole thought domain, its tradition, history, religion, and basis of life, all its heart and soul. To deprive a people of its speech is to deprive it of its eternal good."[1] This precept of Herder was taken up wholeheartedly by nationalist writers in the nineteenth century, especially those in East-Central Europe, where most nationalities did not have their own state or political structure. As a result, ideological elements, such as historical tradition and especially languages, served to justify the existence of nationalities. In the words of Oszkár Jászi, the perceptive critic of the Hapsburg Empire, "the mother tongue became almost sacred, the mysterious vehicle of all the national endeavors."[2] While nationalist writers were providing attractive histories for their peoples, language came to be the direct link between the present-day inhabitants of a territory and its supposed glorious past. If, by the twentieth century, language was no longer the predominant factor in those nationalist movements that had achieved political independence, it nonetheless retained its importance for those minorities who had still not achieved statehood and for whom linguistic identity continued to equal national identity.[3]

Subcarpathian Rus' was such an area, and throughout its embryonic stage of national development language remained preeminent in the minds of local national ideologists, who valued it as a "most precious treasure."[4] Several popular pamphlets referred to language as the "alpha and omega of national consciousness,"[5] and called upon Rusyns "never to forget the words which Herder spoke—'He who does not love his mother tongue . . . does not deserve to be called a man'."[6] Moreover, in the absence of a well-developed literature or system of cultural and educational institutions, the Subcarpathian Rusyn problem remained "so closely related to the language question" that the concept of nationality came to be directly "identified with language."[7]

Among the various peoples of Europe, the embryonic stage of national development was a time when the respective nationalist intelligentsias engaged in theoretical battles in an effort to find an acceptable form of language. In general, theorists either wanted: (1) to revive a traditional language as found in religious texts; (2) to create a new standard based on a fusion of closely related dialects; or (3) to adopt an already established language used by neighboring or related peoples.[8] The Subcarpathian Rusyn intelligentsia tried each of these alternatives, although in the years between 1919 and 1945 it was the second and more especially the third option that proved to be most attractive. It should be remembered that in the course of these debates, language was never viewed in isolation—political-qua-national issues always had a great influence on linguistic decisions.

While the language question was worked out by most nationalities during the nineteenth century, among Subcarpathian Rusyns the problem was never really resolved and was still being debated in earnest during the period 1918 to 1945. One perceptive satirist recalled those years in the following way. "The time when the 'language question' [*iazykovyi vopros*] prevailed was the most romantic in the history of Transcarpathia. Just imagine, everywhere in the cities and villages, in the reading rooms, theaters, government offices and cafés, everywhere, no matter where there were people, they talked continually about the 'language question'. Oh, what times those were! When, for instance, the weather did not change for a long time and the people did not have anything to talk about—there was for them a good topic:—'the language question'."[9]

Language Theories

Like other ethnic groups, the Subcarpathian Rusyns spoke a series of distinct but related dialects. Despite the fact that they inhabited an ethnographic transitional zone and as such were influenced by neighboring peoples, they were unquestionably neither Magyar nor Rumanian, but Slavic. At the same time, their speech differed from that of their Slavic neighbors to the west and northwest, the Slovaks and Poles. In essence, the Subcarpathian varieties of speech—classified by modern linguists as part of the Lemkian, Boikian, Transcarpathian, and Hutsul dialectal groups of the Ukrainian language[10]—were obviously very close to the dialects spoken by neighboring Slavs in eastern Galicia. These were the southwesternmost forms of East Slavic, and linguists have not hesitated to treat them as dialects of Ukrainian.

The difficulty arose regarding the position of Ukrainian, which remained unclear until recent times. Was Ukrainian a dialect of Russian, as most Russian linguists claimed, or was it a separate Slavic language? Basically, three viewpoints developed that were not substantially different from one another. However, when the separate languages were given separate names, they were also assigned a position in a hierarchy, which in part reflected their degrees of linguistic development.

Traditional linguists who grew up in the Russian Empire considered the Russian language to be identical with East Slavic, which in turn included two major dialectal subdivisions, Belorussian and Ukrainian. In this scheme, the Subcarpathian Rusyn dialects were relegated to a very minor status as a branch within a branch. On the other hand, Ukrainian scholars held that within the abstract unity of East Slavic there existed three languages of *equal* status: Russian, Belorussian, and Ukrainian. This scheme afforded more dignity to the local dialects in the southwest, including the Subcarpathian ones. To carry the argument to its ultimate, it could be argued that Subcarpathian Rusyn is sufficiently different from other Ukrainian dialects to be considered a separate language.

At the heart of the matter was the problem of dignity, and this raised a series of questions. What medium of communication—loyal Rusyn dialects, standard Ukrainian, or standard Russian—would Subcarpathian leaders feel most comfortable with?[11] Which of these forms could be accepted for formal communication and at the same time be dignified enough to express Subcarpathian Rusyn civilization? In trying to answer these questions, several linguistic orientations were to develop.[12]

In his analysis of the Subcarpathian language question, the noted Ukrainian linguist Ivan Zilyns'kyi correctly recognized the political implications of the problem and divided the disputants into four groups. First, there were the *Karpatorossy,* who considered themselves members of "one indivisible Russian people" and who described the Ukrainian language as nothing more than an artificial jargon. Second, there were the "stubborn Carpathian 'Rusyns', conservative and regional patriots" who also did not recognize Ukrainian, but rather spoke and wrote in a "noble" local Carpatho-Russian language—the Subcarpathian recension of Russian used by writers during the late nineteenth century. Third, there were the Rusyn-populists (*rusyny-narodovtsi*), who were basically Ukrainian in outlook but still in the process of transition from Subcarpathian Rusyn dialectal archaisms and traditional orthography to the standard Ukrainian language. Fourth were nationally conscious Ukrainians who wrote in standard Ukrainian and who used the modern orthography.[13] A fifth orientation, not mentioned by Professor Zilyns'kyi, was the Rusyn trend, which foresaw the possibility of formulating a literary language based solely on local dialects.

The position of the *Karpatorossy,* or Russophiles, regarding the language of Subcarpathian Rus' was most competently outlined by Georgii Gerovskii. He recognized the existence of only one Russian language containing three dialectal groups: the northeastern or Great Russian, the south Russian or Little Russian, and the western or Belorussian.[14] The Subcarpathian dialects, in turn, belonged to the Little Russian group, but unlike many scholars who underlined the close relationship between the dialects north and south of the Carpathian Mountains, Gerovskii concluded "that next to the other dialects which make up the South Russian group, Subcarpathian dialects occupy a completely independent position . . . and must be considered as a dialect independent of the others in the group."[15]

Local Russophile polemicists stressed that in Subcarpathian Rus' there had never been any language question in the past nor was there one at present.[16] Supposedly, the local intelligentsia always expressed a desire to write in the so-called common Russian (*obshcherusskii*) literary language. Theoretically, this *obshcherusskii* language was considered to be a fusion of the Great Russian, Little Russian, and Belorussian languages, although in practice it was basically literary Great Russian with many local dialectal elements. The first standardization of the *obshcherusskii* language for use in Subcarpathian Rus' appeared in Aleksander Mitrak's *Russko-mad'iarskii slovar'* ("Russian-Magyar Dictionary," 1881). According to Russophile theorists, Mitrak's language represented the ideal toward which Subcarpathian authors must strive, while that of his contemporary, Vasylii Chopei, who compiled a more dialectally based dictionary, *Rus'ko-madiarskii slovar'* ("Rusyn-Magyar Dictionary," 1883), was branded an "opportunist" and "typical nationalist renegade."[17]

But why was Mitrak praised? Because his dictionary used the language of Pushkin, Gogol, Turgenev, and Tolstoy—"the literary language of the Carpatho-Russians."[18] Furthermore, in answer to those critics who argued that the *obshcherusskii* language was foreign to the local population, one polemicist cited a passage from Tolstoy and then concluded: "This excerpt of the 'Muscovite' [*obshcherusskii*] language contains about 80 words, and we are convinced that here [in Subcarpathian Rus'] you will find no one, not even an illiterate peasant, who would say that he did not understand all but 3 percent of these words."[19]

The second category, referred to as conservative and regional "Carpatho-Russian patriots," was best represented by Evmenii Sabov. In his few short and not very clear pronouncements on the subject, Sabov recognized the validity of the *obshcherusskii* language for Subcarpathian Rus'.[20] However, he did not stress Pushkin, Tolstoy, or other Great Russian authors as the best guides, but rather "our excellent writers"—Sil'vai, Popradov, and Fentsik—whose works were based on the principles developed in the grammars of Dukhnovych and the dictionary of Mitrak. Sabov himself was opposed to what he considered outside influence, in particular the Ukrainian movement in Galicia. Accepting the political realities of the present, he stressed that "the Carpathians separate us" from the East and "our task in the future is to support the political unity of the Czechoslovak Republic as well as to bring closer together the Russian [i.e. Carpatho-Russian] and Czech cultures."[21] "There is no place here for Muscophilism, and still less for Ukrainianism . . . we need neither the Russian nor Ukrainian languages"[22] but rather "our own pre-War literary language" used by Rusyn authors "from Dukhnovych to Popradov."[23]

The third and fourth groups considered by Zilyns'kyi were the local

Rusyn populists and nationally conscious Ukrainians from Galicia who settled in Subcarpathian Rus'. They always emphasized that Ukrainian was a language independent from Russian. Accordingly, not only did the dialects of Subcarpathian Rus' belong to the Ukrainian language, but the Carpathian Mountains were not a linguistic barrier because dialects spoken on the northern Galician side were closely related to those spoken on the southern slopes.[24] To be sure, Subcarpathian Rusyn dialects were "corrupted" by many Magyar and Slovak words; thus, the Verkhovyna dialects, spoken in the northernmost mountainous regions, were considered by Ukrainian theorists as the purest.[25] Ukrainophiles welcomed the Czechoslovak policy calling for use of the native language, which, of course, they considered a dialectal form of Ukrainian.[26]

Like the Russophile polemicists, Ukrainophiles justified their linguistic arguments through their interpretation of Subcarpathian literary history. The literary models to be followed were dialectally based works from the seventeenth and early eighteenth centuries, which were revived again as ideals by Subcarpathian writers at the turn of the twentieth century. At the same time, the use of Russian (or attempts to write in Russian) lasted for a few decades after 1848 and were to be considered as "only an episode in our history."[27] Of much greater importance during the "Russophile" late nineteenth century was the appearance of Vasylii Chopei's dialectally based dictionary. While Russophiles branded this work as a product of Magyarization, Ukrainophiles hailed it as an important milestone in the process of language development: "This dictionary of Chopei was the first precious return to the national tongue."[28]

The Ukrainians argued further that recent developments in Subcarpathian Rus' revealed an increasing tendency to write in a language based on popular speech patterns instead of the "artificial" Subcarpathian recension of Russian. Such a positive trend, they thought, should be continued, and standard Ukrainian, written in the simplified modern orthography, should eventually be adopted. As a precedent, Ukrainophiles pointed to the example of late nineteenth-century Galicia, where the Galician recension of Russian (the *iazychiie*) was replaced by popular dialectal writings and later by standard Ukrainian. It was most natural, then, that a similar process be repeated in Subcarpathian Rus' so that the "national living language, i.e. Ukrainian, reign in the place that it deserves."[29]

A fifth group, not included in Zilyns'kyi's classification, was the Rusyn orientation, which called for the creation of an independent Slavic, Subcarpathian Rusyn language based exclusively on one or more of the local dialects. Initially, this trend was the least defined, and in many cases it simply represented the frustrated reactions of unsophisticated critics who were fed up with what they considered superfluous language disputes. One amateur linguist wrote: "Many times I realized the fact that the language of the people in Subcarpathia is neither Russian nor Ukrainian,"[30] while another more adamant rebuttal to the Russian-Ukrainian controversy began: "No gentlemen! In Subcarpathian Rus' lives only one Rusyn [*rus'-kii*) people: Rusyns—Subcarpathian Rusyns [*podkarpatskî rusynŷ*), who neither are afraid nor ashamed that they are Rusyns. These Rusyns want to live in their own manner [*po-svoemu*], to write and to speak in their own language."[31]

Ivan Pan'kevych (1887-1958), the Galician-Ukrainian linguist who worked for the School Administration in Uzhhorod, tried to approach the problem in a systematic manner. In 1920, he drew up a standard form for codifying linguistic material, and he "requested the help of all teachers, intelligentsia and priests who live among the people . . . to diligently [collect and] forward material according to the questionnaire."[32] However, despite frequent reminders, there was little interest among the local intelligentsia in serious research, and "after ten years there was still no dictionary . . . because during those ten years only eight colleagues cooperated with us."[33] Pan'kevych's efforts reflected his own scholarly interest in Subcarpathian dialects and not any attempt to create a separate Rusyn literary language. Thus, during the Czechoslovak regime the desire of some to "raise our own dialect to the level of a literary language" was to remain the unfulfilled hope of a few isolated individuals.[34]

A serious interest in creating a separate Subcarpathian Rusyn language was also expressed by the pro-Hungarian scholar Hiiador Stryps'kyi. We have seen how, on the basis of the "Hungarian" interpretation of Subcarpathian literary history, Stryps'kyi had formulated this goal as early as 1907, and, during the brief existence of Rus'ka Kraina in early 1919, both he and Sándor Bonkáló had prepared some Rusyn dialectal texts and made plans to publish a dictionary.[35] Political events led to the postponement of these efforts, although in Budapest Stryps'kyi still maintained his interest in formulating a standard Rusyn literary language. He emphasized that there was "a great difference" between those Rusyns, the *Verkhovyntsi*, who lived in the highlands, and those, the *Dolyshniany*, who inhabited the lower slopes and plains. The latter were the oldest and thus "the purest Rusyns of all Subcarpathian Rus'."[36] Therefore, the dialect of the *Dolyshniany*, even if heavily influenced by Magyar, should serve as the basis for a Rusyn literary language. After careful analysis of old documents and the local speech, Stryps'kyi concluded that Rusyn dialects contained rich enough material to form a literary language. Moreover, it was "not in harmony" for Rusyns to use either Russian or Ukrainian.[37] When, during the Second World War, Subcarpathian Rus' was made a part of Hungary, theories and plans were again put forward "to develop into a literary language the spoken popular language [*hovorenŷi narodnŷi iazyk*] of the Subcarpathian territory."[38] Once more Stryps'kyi revived the plea for a Rusyn dictionary, and some contributions in this direction were made.[39]

The Initial Policy of the Czechoslovak Government

From the first days of the Czechoslovak regime in Subcarpathian Rus' the question of language was intimately associated with political issues and the problem of national identity (see Chapter 4). Legally, any final decision concerning language was reserved for a proposed Soim (Diet), as outlined in Article 11 of the Treaty of St. Germain (September 1919) and later reiterated in the *Generální Statut,* the temporary administrative law for Subcarpathian Rus' issued on November 18, 1919. This stipulation was then legalized on February 29, 1920, in paragraph 6 of Czechoslovak Law No. 122, which stated: "to the Soim that will be established for Subcarpathian Rus' belongs the right to normalize the language for this territory in such a manner so as not to disrupt the unity of the Czechoslovak Republic."[40]

But the promised Soim did not come into existence until 1938, when an autonomous legislative body was established. Meanwhile, some decision had to be made concerning the specific language to be used for official and educational purposes in Subcarpathian Rus'. The Prague government had not yet worked out the details of this matter, and its task was further complicated by imprecise information from local Czech officials about the language question: "The name of the local population is not fixed: they call themselves Rusnaks, Rusyns, Subcarpathian Rusyns; they call their language Russian [*ruská řeč*]. The language is Little Russian [Ukrainian], that is a particular local dialect, and the people themselves are ethnographically Little Russians."[41] To be sure, the above guidelines were not very precise. Was the language of the population Russian, Little Russian (Ukrainian), or a particular local dialect?

To answer this question, the civil administration in Subcarpathian Rus' requested the aid of the Ministry of Culture. The result was a meeting of fifteen Czech academicians and linguists in Prague on December 4, 1919. Two weeks later the scholars returned a report on the literary language for the province, the most important conclusion being that "a decision on the literary language of any people or branch belongs first of all to its own members."[42] The report opposed the creation of an "artificial, new, literary, Slavic language for the population of Carpathian Rus'." Moreover, because the *Generální Statut* had already called for the use of the "local" dialect in educational and official matters, and since the scholars were agreed that the speech of the inhabitants in Subcarpathian Rus' was "indisputably a Little Russian dialect," it was "necessary to recognize as the literary language of the population, the Little Russian literary language, used by their closest neighbors and fellow countrymen, i.e., the Galician Ukrainian language." Instead of the modern orthography, "unpopular among the Carpathian Rusyn population," it was suggested that the traditional orthography be used. The academicians also favored the importation of books and teachers from Galicia and considered "unjustified" any fears that such a policy would lead to "Ukrainian irredentism" in Subcarpathian Rus'. Although the report supported the introduction of the Ukrainian language, the population of the area was not to forget that they simultaneously belonged to the Great Russian nation— "jako Ukrajinci jsou příslušníky velikého národa ruského."[43] Consequently, the introduction of Russian was recommended as a required subject in secondary schools.

Thus, during the first years of Czechoslovak administration in Subcarpathian Rus', official policy regarding language favored the use of the "místní" (local) language in elementary schools. Because this local language was considered a variant of the Ukrainian spoken in Galicia, it was considered advantageous to import both grammars and teachers from that province.

Although these guidelines were met with great displeasure from many segments of the local intelligentsia, they were nonetheless introduced into the local school system. Josef Pešek, the first Superintendent of Schools in Subcarpathian Rus', declared that the *Generální Statut* had "resolved the language question" when it called for the use of the local language.[44] Moreover, continued Pešek, the Czech Academy confirmed that "the Subcarpathian Rusyn [*podkarpatoruský*] language is Little Russian and consequently it is necessary to use the Ukrainian language in Subcarpathian Rus'."[45]

In response to these administrative decrees, some Rusyn leaders replied that only the proposed Soim could legally decide the language question.[46] Because the Czechoslovak government initially favored the Ukrainian orientation, local Russophiles were adamantly opposed to official policy. According to them, "the arguments and public disputes on language matters in Subcarpathian Rus' began only after November 18, 1919, i.e., after the proclamation in Uzhhorod of the *'Generální Statut'* for the organization of Subcarpathian Rus' . . . Prague created the language mess in Carpathian Rus'."[47] Eventually, the Russophiles were joined by the Ukrainophiles and Rusynophiles in blaming the Czechoslovak government for having created the problem of language. They all stated that Prague welcomed refugees from Galicia who brought with them the Russian-Ukrainian language dispute, which caused among the formerly united Subcarpathian Rusyn intelligentsia divisiveness along linguistic as well as political lines.[48]

This interpretation by the discontented Rusyn leaders was clearly oversimplified. True, Czech policy did favor the importation of textbooks and teachers from Galicia, but this was not the cause of the language dispute in Subcarpathian Rus'. The seeds of controversy had been sown during the second half of the nineteenth century, when a split developed between those national leaders who favored the use of the Russian literary language and those who were inclined to use a more popularly based dialectal form.[49] In

essence, prior to 1918, only the increase in Magyarization kept these embry-
onic linguistic disputes below the surface. During the democratic Czecho-
slovak administration, however, these repressed problems came to the fore.
Consequently, it would be unjust to blame either the Czech government or
Galician immigrants for having created a language dispute in Subcarpathian
Rus' during the 1920s.

Language Programs and Textbooks

During the 1919-1920 school year, the lack of grammars and textbooks
was one of the most pressing problems facing the new Czechoslovak school
administration in Subcarpathian Rus'. As a temporary solution, teachers
made use of A. Voloshyn's elementary-school grammar, first published in
1899 and reprinted in a slightly revised version in 1919.[50] Voloshyn's original
text was in the Subcarpathian recension of Russian, with many dialectisms,
and in the revised edition even more local dialectal usages appeared. "In so
far as he did not know any literary language well, in his [Voloshyn's] hands,
the grammar turned out to be a 'Carpatho-Rusyn conglomerate' [the true
iazychiie]."[51] The 1919 edition was recommended for use in elementary
schools at the first teacher's congress held in Uzhhorod on April 16-17,
1920. Voloshyn's subsequent textbooks all employed the traditional orthography, included many dialectal elements, and replaced Russian grammatical principles by patterns similar to those used in Galician Ukrainian grammars.[52] This transformation was not difficult, since Voloshyn always
favored the Verkhovyna dialects, which were closest to the Ukrainian language as spoken in Galicia.

Grammars were also needed for the higher grades. The head of the school
administration, Josef Pešek, tried to resolve the problem by inviting the
Galician-Ukrainian linguist, Ivan Pan'kevych, to come to Uzhhorod in
December 1919. Pan'kevych was given the responsibility "to regulate the
language of instruction and official language" for Subcarpathian Rus'.[53]
To fulfill this task, he outlined a plan for the publication of a dialectal dic-
tionary, and in 1922 he published the first edition of his controversial
Hramatyka rus'koho iazŷka ("Grammar of the Rusyn Language").[54]

The Pan'kevych grammar attempted to fulfill the principles of official
Czechoslovak policy, that is, to use the "local language" (which was related
to Galician Ukrainian) written in the traditional orthography.[55] The latter
script was in and of itself not without psychological importance to the
Rusyn masses. In contrast to their immediate neighbors and the Czechoslovak administration, who all used the Latin alphabet, the Cyrillic
alphabet's traditional orthography, with the decorative *iat'* (ѣ), *iery* (ы) and
hard sign (ъ), had become a distinct symbol of Rusyn culture. Thus, to
tamper in any way with the old orthography was considered a threat to
sacred tradition.[56]

In March 1923, another teacher's congress was called, at which School Superintendent Pešek pushed through his proposal to employ the Pan'-kevych grammar in the Subcarpathian school system. But Pešek's policy was met with fierce opposition in many quarters, most especially among the local Russophiles. The Czech school superintendent was accused of wanting to create a separate "Rusyn" people and Pan'kevych an artificial "Rusyn" language.[57] In reality, Pan'kevych was a conscious Ukrainian and hopeful that someday standard literary Ukrainian would be used throughout Subcarpathian Rus'. He rightly realized, however, that literary Ukrainian could not be introduced immediately, and so he tried to create a kind of "compromise" language, with a Galician Ukrainian grammatical base overlaid with local Subcarpathian dialectisms.[58] Like Voloshyn, Pan'kevych favored the Verkhovyna dialect, the one closely related to Ukrainian as spoken in Galicia. In two revised editions of his grammar (1927 and 1936), Pan'-kevych retained the traditional orthography but moved steadily in the direction of literary Ukrainian by eliminating many local dialectisms.

In response to official policy, which only recognized the Pan'kevych grammar in Subcarpathian schools, the Russophile intelligentsia called for the introduction of a Russian grammar published by the Dukhnovych Society.[59] Although a Galician Russophile, Aleksander Grigor'iev, actually wrote the grammar, it was published under the name of the well-known local patriot Evmenii Sabov.[60] It was clear from the opening sentence that this grammar was not concerned with the local language spoken in Subcarpathian Rus': "The present grammar contains the Russian literary language in its written and not its spoken form."[61] Only in "exceptional cases" was the "particular oral speech of Subcarpathian Rus' " considered, the aim being to eliminate these exceptions so as to make easier the study of local Carpatho-Russian authors (Sil'vai, Stavrovskii-Popradov, Fentsik) and the works of "Pushkin, Gogol, Lermontov and other classics of Russian literature."[62] The modern orthographic reforms that were introduced throughout the Soviet Union were deliberately shunned and the traditional alphabet was employed throughout the text.

The Sabov grammar became the rallying point for Russian leaders opposed to the government's educational policy. During its first session, the Russophile Dukhnovych Society proposed that 10,000 copies of the grammar be published.[63] In subsequent years, continued demands were made that in all Subcarpathian schools the Russian literary language be used exclusively and in conformity with the Sabov text—the latest in a long line of grammars from Dukhnovych (1853) to Voloshyn (1919) that were in the "true Carpatho-Russian tradition."[64]

The Czechoslovak school administration in Uzhhorod consulted with the Ministry of Culture in Prague, which in turn asked a distinguished Czech Slavist, Professor Jiří Polívka, and A. Voloshyn for their opinions of the

Sabov grammar. Voloshyn rejected the grammar for use in any Subcarpathian school.[65] Polívka, on the other hand, stated that even though the work was *not* based on the dialects of the region, but was rather "a text of literary Russian," it nevertheless might be used in secondary schools where "Russian is taught as a separate subject."[66]

The government delayed action on this matter and it was not until October 1, 1936, that the Sabov grammar was finally recommended for use in schools.[67] This move caused Ukrainian sympathizers to conclude that the Prague administration was trying to play one national orientation off against the other. However, one might also view the central government's decision as a latent concession to Russophile requests. As early as February 1920, Prague received the first of many petitions decrying the presence in Subcarpathian Rus' of "Ukrainian separatists from Galicia [who were] trying to create a new 'Rusyn language'."[68] The basic demand, then as later, was that "our children be taught Russian."[69]

Moreover, it must be admitted that the majority of teachers in Subcarpathian Rus' were long opposed to the local school administration's textbook policy. At a teacher's congress held at Berehovo in 1923, Pan'kevych's grammar was rejected and Voloshyn's 1919 text was favored by a vote of 544 to 2. A memorandum was dispatched to Prague, which stated that the signers would "adhere to the Voloshyn grammar [1919] and the Mitrak dictionary until the final decision of the Soim. The grammars of Pan'kevych and Birchak are rejected because they do not conform to the character of the Carpatho-Russian language."[70]

Then the Teacher's Society (Uchitel'ske Tovarishchestvo) commissioned M. I. Vasilenkov to prepare a new grammar. At a congress of the society, held at Mukachevo in January 1925, Vasilenkov's text was recommended for use in the "lower classes of elementary schools" because it was "based on our dialects" and "in essence does not differ from the Voloshyn grammar of 1919."[71] In fact, the Vasilenkov text followed primarily Russian grammatical patterns. In June 1926 this same Congress rejected any suggestions for creating a separate Rusyn language, and in May 1929 reiterated that the concept "national language according to tradition" meant the use of the 1919 Voloshyn grammar in the schools.[72] Thus it can be argued that the acceptance by the Czechoslovak administration of the Sabov grammar in 1936 was an attempt to alleviate discontent and to fulfill the many requests for the introduction of the Russian language into the school system of Subcarpathian Rus'.

During the 1930s the division between the Russian and Ukrainian orientations was clear. The Russophiles favored the 1919 Voloshyn grammar for elementary schools and the Sabov grammar for the higher grades. To help the generally Magyarized intelligentsia struggling to write in literary Russian, several Magyar-Russian dictionaries were published, including the massive second part of Mitrak's work.[73] On the other hand, the populist

Ukrainophile orientation at first supported the "compromise" language of Pan'kevych, as revealed in the many elementary grammars and readers by Aleksander Markush (1891-1971) and Iuliian Revai (b. 1899) which were accepted for use in local schools by the Ministry of Education.[74] This same tendency to use the local dialect to learn standard Ukrainian was seen in the *Magyar-ruszin szótár* ("Magyar-Rusyn Dictionary," 1928), by E. Bokshai, Iu. Revai, and M. Brashchaiko, who gave local dialectal words first and then their literary Ukrainian equivalents.[75] The trend toward Ukrainian became more pronounced in the later editions of Pan'kevych's grammar and especially in five secondary school readers prepared by Volodymyr Birchak (1881-1945).[76] Finally, in 1936, Frants Ahii (b. 1899) published the first Ukrainian elementary textbook in Subcarpathian Rus' that used modern orthography and only a few dialectisms. This was followed by Iaroslav Nevrli's two-part grammar for secondary schools, written in standard literary Ukrainian and adopted for use by the government of Carpatho-Ukraine during the autonomous period of 1938-1939.[77]

The relative success or failure of the competing linguistic orientations was revealed in the development of the periodical press during the Czechoslovak administration. The few secular Rusyn dialectal publications (*Rusyn,* 1920-1921; *Rusyn,* 1938; *Zorja,* 1920-1930), even one in Latin script (*Novoje vremja,* 1925-1933), did not find widespread support. The Russophile orientation was represented by political newspapers that tried to write in Russian, but which in fact were in the Subcarpathian recension of Russian (*Karpato-russkii vîstnyk, Karpatorusskii golos, Russkaia zemlia, Zemlediel'skaia politika, Narodnaia gazeta*), and by literary and scholarly periodicals (*Karpatskii krai, Karpatskii sviet, Russkii narodnyi golos*) that appeared in literary Russian. The populist-Ukrainophile orientation was initially represented by publications in dialect, which later adopted modern orthography and the standard literary language.[78] The first newspaper to make this change was the Communist *Pravda,* later *Karpats'ka pravda,* in 1925, followed by the Social-Democratic *Narod,* later *Vpered,* in 1926, and the Christian-Nationalist *Svoboda* in 1930. Somewhat slower in linguistic reform were the children's magazines, *Pchôlka* and *Nash rodnŷi krai,* later *Nash ridnyi krai,* and the scholarly journals, *Podkarpatska Rus'* of the Pedagogical Society and *Naukovŷi zbôrnyk,* later *Naukovyi zbirnyk,* of the Prosvita Society. On the other hand, some publications—*Nasha zemlia, Uchytel's'kyi holos,* and *Ukraïns'ke slovo*—appeared in standard Ukrainian from the very beginning.

The highpoint of Ukrainian language periodicals came during the autonomous regime of late 1938 to early 1939. Subcarpathian Russian language publications could only appear in Prešov or Prague, and beginning with the third issue, the official journal of the autonomous government, *Uriadovyi vistnyk,* appeared only in Ukrainian. This was complemented by Ukrainian language political organs (*Nova svoboda, Nastup*), popular, literary, and theatrical magazines (*Karpats'ka Ukraïna, Hoverlia, Nova stsena*), and a few issues of the Greek Catholic monthly *Blahovistnyk,* edited by the Ukrainophile monk, Sevastiian Sabol (b. 1909).[79]

These developments reveal that before 1939 there were no serious attempts to formulate a separate Rusyn literary language based on one or more of the Subcarpathian dialects. Indeed, there had even been a few writers (all Greek Catholic priests) who published in their own version of Subcarpathian Rusyn. One was the historian Vasylii Hadzhega, whose prolific writing always appeared (despite the displeasure of certain editors) in Rusyn. Because of his stubbornness, he was described by one critic as a "completely isolated representative of the local tradition for a Subcarpathian Rusyn literary language."[80] Others included Ivan Muranii (1881-1945), who composed several plays, and Emyliian Bokshai (1889-1976), author of catechisms, prayer books, and church histories for use in church and state schools.[81] Generally, the Greek Catholic Church issued its official diocesan publications in Rusyn, and the unofficial organs of the Prešov diocese, *Russkoe slovo,*[82] and of the Mukachevo diocese, *Nedîlia,* were published partially or completely in dialect. Edited by Emyliian Bokshai, *Nedîlia* prided itself on the idea that the newspaper could be understood by any Rusyn.[83] In fact, the language was never codified and *Nedîlia*'s only goal was to adopt a "middle-of-the-road" policy and avoid the Russian-Ukrainian controversy. Notwithstanding some demands that "our language—the Subcarpathian Rusyn language—must become the language of instruction in all our schools,"[84] the editors explicitly stated that "our newspaper in the pure popular language [*na chysto narodnom iazŷtsî*]" is not going to solve the language question nor provide a new grammar.[85] Thus, during the Czechoslovak regime, no serious effort was made to create a separate Rusyn literary language, so the field was left open to the Russophile and Ukrainophile orientations.

The situation changed drastically after the incorporation of Subcarpathian Rus' into Hungary in March 1939. Recalling the opposition of the Ukrainophile autonomous government to Hungarian political designs, Budapest made every effort to eliminate any Ukrainianist sympathies in its newly obtained province. A law was passed in 1939 declaring that Magyar and "Magyar-Russian" (*magyar és magyar-orosz*) were the official languages.[86] "Magyar-Russian" actually reflected the Hungarian concept of a separate Uhro-Rusyn nationality, and this idea was fostered by concerted efforts in the realm of language. The ministerial council in Budapest "considered it necessary to have a suitable Rusyn grammar," which, in the words of Commissioner Kozma, would help to promote "a patriotic Rusyn orientation" and convince this people that they were *not* Ukrainian, but Rusyn.[87] Finally, the literary and linguistic theories of Stryps'kyi and Bonkáló could be put into practice. The first attempt in this direction came with the appointment of a twelve-member commission in Uzhhorod, which published in 1940 a grammar of the Uhro-Rusyn language for secondary schools. According to the introduction by Julius Marina (b. 1901), a Greek Catholic canon and advisor to the office of education in Uzhhorod, this text was: (1) to return to the principles laid down in the Voloshyn grammars of 1907 and 1919; (2) to avoid common Russian (*obshcherusskii*) and Galician-Ukrainian forms; and (3) to ensure the "natural right of the people to use its own language and thus apply the most important pedagogic principle: to teach the people in its native language."[88] The language was dialectal (with some Russianisms), based on the vernacular used by Rusyns in the central lowlands (the *Dolyshniany*), and it used the traditional orthography with the addition of the *feta* (ɵ).

One year later the newly formed Subcarpathian Academy of Sciences (Podkarpatskoe Obshchestvo Nauk) published a new Uhro-Rusyn grammar by Ivan Haraida (18??-1945). As in the 1940 text by the language commission, Haraida hoped to end the domination of the Russian, and most especially the Ukrainian, language in Subcarpathian schools "so that young people could be liberated from language influences brought here from abroad and with this book learn to love their own mother tongue [*materynskyi iazŷk*]."[89] The chief characteristics of Haraida's grammar were the use of many dialectal words and of the traditional orthography, "because our cultural life is still closely related to our Church and our [eastern] rite, and our Church books traditionally used these letters and still do today."[90] The grammars by the commission and by Haraida were complemented by a series of five readers designed for use in the first seven classes of elementary school.[91]

The main publications propagating the Rusyn language were the weeklies *Karpatska nedîlia,* later *Nedîlia* (1939-1944), and *Lyteraturna nedîlia* (1941-1944), which attempted "to develop and raise . . . our mother tongue to the level of a literary language."[92] *Karpatska nedîlia,* subtitled "an organ of Magyar-Rusyn brotherhood," claimed to be the successor of *Nedîlia,* the Greek Catholic weekly edited by E. Bokshai during the Czechoslovak regime. *Lyteraturna nedîlia* included works written in dialect by Subcarpathian authors of all national orientations: Ukrainophiles like Iulii Borshosh-Kum'iats'kyi, Aleksander Markush, Marko Barabolia (1910-1945), Luka Dem'ian (1894-1968), and Fedir Potushniak (1910-1960), Russophiles like Emel'ian Baletskii (b. 1919) and Dmytro Vakarov (1920-1945), and Magyar-one-Rusynophiles like Irynei Kontratovych, Hiiador Stryps'kyi, and Ivan Muranii. The Subcarpathian Academy of Sciences also fostered use of Rusyn through its scholarly journal *Zoria—Hajnal* (Uzhhorod, 1941-1943), and through publications for the broader public that drew upon Subcarpathian folklore and also translations from the works of Shakespeare and Jókai.[93]

These government-supported efforts to create a separate Uhro-Rusyn language were opposed by several leaders of the Subcarpathian intelligentsia. Since the Ukrainophiles were either in exile or silenced, the protest was led by Russophiles, both pro- and anti-Hungarian, who had remained at home. After the 1940 commission grammar appeared, Georgii Gerovskii published a study that criticized and rejected all attempts to reverse the historically based tendency of Subcarpathian writers to create literary works in Russian.[94] Haraida's grammar was also attacked several times in the Russophile political newspaper *Karpatorusskii golos* (1939-1942), which, like *Russkoe slovo* (1940-1943), continued the practice of pretending to publish in Russian when it actually used the Subcarpathian recension of Russian.

Thus, in 1944, after more than a quarter of a century, the language question was not yet resolved in Subcarpathian Rus'. At the beginning of the Czechoslovak administration, official policy favored the use of a dialectally based language closely related to the Ukrainian employed in Galicia. This populist trend first used dialectal forms with traditional orthography and later moved steadily in the direction of standard Ukrainian. Meanwhile, the more conservative intelligentsia, who expressed themselves at the teacher's congresses, preferred the so-called traditional "Carpatho-Russian language" as represented in the 1919 Voloshyn grammar and the 1924 Sabov grammar.

By the 1930s, it seemed that no serious attempt would be made to create a separate Subcarpathian Rusyn literary language and that only Russian or Ukrainian had credence. The latter was especially popular among teachers of the younger generation, many of whom were members of the Teacher's Assembly (Uchytel's'ka Hromada). This organization was clearly Ukrainian in orientation, used only the modern orthography in its publications, and favored the use of Galician Ukrainian grammars.[95] The greater acceptance of a standard Ukrainian language led impartial Czech observers to conclude "that compared with Russian, Ukrainian is today [1937] more dynamic in Subcarpathian Rus'."[96]

Yet, it would be incorrect to assume that in 1938 the Ukrainian language was favored by the majority of either the local intelligentsia or the public.[97] The Russian language was still very much alive in Subcarpathian Rus' and continued to thrive during the years of the Hungarian occupation, when Ukrainianism was banned and, for the last time, support was being given to the idea of a separate Uhro-Rusyn language. On the other hand, the creation of a viable independent Rusyn literary language would have required at least one of two prerequisites: (1) the existence for several decades of a political system that favored such a development; or (2) the existence of some charismatic literary figures, through whose works Subcarpathian Rusyn could be raised to a level of prestige that would prove attractive to a large readership. Neither of these criteria was ever fulfilled. Hence, in 1945, the Subcarpathian intelligentsia was no closer to resolving the language question than it had been in 1919.

7 | Literary and Cultural Developments

Literature and Nationalism

The idea of a common heritage is basic to a national identity. This heritage is expressed not only through historical writings, but also through literature. In fact, it is more often via belles-lettres, and not through the more esoteric realm of historical writing, that the common national traditions are articulated and passed on directly to the people. Both young and old are likely to associate their national heritage with some famous stanzas of patriotic poetry or verses from a play that have become embedded in the collective mind. Poetic lines of national anthems often become the best known symbols of national identity.

Literature is so integral a part of nationalism that the success of some movements has been closely dependent on the creation of a vibrant literary corpus attractive to contemporary and future generations. One has only to think of writers like Mickiewicz for the Poles, Petőfi for the Magyars, and Shevchenko for the Ukrainians to realize the importance of literature in stimulating and maintaining a national consciousness.

Subcarpathian authors also tried to create a literature that would foster the cause of national solidarity, and we have seen how the first stirrings of a national awakening in the decades after 1848 were in large measure due to the influential writings of figures like Aleksander Dukhnovych. His works were to remain the symbol of Subcarpathian Rusyn national existence until well into the twentieth century. During the years 1919 to 1945, a host of younger Subcarpathian writers tried to maintain the nationalist tradition begun by Dukhnovych and his successors. Under the relatively tolerant atmosphere of the Czechoslovak regime, these authors published numerous works in all genres, and this burst of literary activity led historians to refer to the period as a "revival" or "renaissance" of Subcarpathian Rusyn literature.[1]

However, as in other aspects of national life, the literary situation in Subcarpathian Rus' was characterized by rivalry and conflict between the Russophile, Ukrainophile, and Rusynophile national orientations. Initially,

145

the first two orientations prevailed, so that literary developments came to be governed by what may be called the "dialectical (language dualism)—national principle."[2] Unfortunately, at a time when the young literary life required a concentration of all productive energies, this dualism proved to be counterproductive, because "both currents operated alongside each other without contacts and did not permit any advantageous organization and centralization of cultural forces and educational work."[3]

Subcarpathian authors had not moved beyond the romantic and realist idioms that had dominated the European literary scene in the nineteenth century. It is not surprising, then, that nationalism and social concerns continued to be the predominant themes, and authors of all three orientations dealt with these issues. Nationalism was expressed in eulogies about the homeland or the mother tongue, in laudatory historical epics, or in declarations of allegiance to the Ukrainian or Russian nations. The social issue was revealed through realistic descriptions of the miserable conditions of the Rusyn peasants.[4]

Local patriotism was an important element in many of the early poems by the Ukrainophile author Iulii Borshosh-Kum'iats'kyi. His first volume of poetry, *Vesnianì kvîtŷ* ("Spring Flowers," 1928), contained songs of praise addressed to "our mother tongue" (*Liuby rôdnu movu*) and "our dear homeland" (*Liubît' rôdnyi krai*).[5] Love of one's birthplace and language was also a theme in many poems by another Ukrainophile, Vasyl' Grendzha-Dons'kyi and by the Russophile authors Andrei Karabelesh (1906-1964) and Mikhail Popovich (1908-1955).[6] The simple, almost naive, expression of passion for the homeland was summed up best by Borshosh-Kum'iats'kyi:

> I love you, native land,
> As my own mother
> In you I want to live for centuries,
> In you I want to die![7]

According to one historian of nationalism, "loyalty to familiar places is relatively natural, [but] . . . it requires artificial effort . . . to render man loyal to the sum total of places . . . in an entire country inhabited by his nationality."[8] This transformation from "natural" patriotism to conscious nationalism in Subcarpathian literature was best represented in the writings of Vasyl' Grendzha-Dons'kyi,[9] who drew much material from his native Máramaros, the far eastern county inhabited by the freedom-loving and proud Hutsuls. Typical of this genre was the poem "Princess of the Hutsuls," set in the distant past, and the play "Sotnia Mocharenka," which dealt with the revolutionary events of 1918-1919, when the Hutsuls set up an independent republic.[10] More sophisticated attempts at fostering national pride by idealizing the past were made in *Chervona skala* ("The Red Cliff,"

1930-1931), an epic poem about the legendary thirteenth-century ruler of Khust, Prince Bohdan, and the play "The Last Battle," which described the heroic defense of Khust during the seventeenth-century Turkish invasions. [11]

Grendzha-Dons'kyi was continually preoccupied with the national consciousness of his people. "More than anything," he stated in 1935, "I wish to bring forth heroes from our wretched Transcarpathian history and present them in epic poetry." [12] His best effort was the historical tale *Petro Petrovych* (1937). Supposedly based on local folk tales and "historical scholarship," the poem transforms Petrovych into the patriotic leader of a grandiose revolution against the Hungarian king during the early fourteenth century. [13] From the outset, the poet encourages national pride and praises the so-called Marchia Ruthenorum—an independent Rusyn state that supposedly existed before the 896 Magyar invasion. When Petrovych becomes worried about the advances of the Hungarian king, he seeks advice from his father who tells him: "Don't forget, my sons, that the Land of the Rusyns [*Kraina Rusyniv*), or as it was called in Latin: 'Marchia Ruthenorum' is a principate, a state within a state. This was already so among our ancestors." [14] The message was explicit—not only did Rusyns have much to be proud of, but the revisionists in Budapest must know that they had neither legal nor historical rights to Subcarpathian Rus'.

The question of national allegiance was also an important theme, and local authors composed short plays intended to stimulate national pride in Rusyn audiences. A typical scenario usually included a young girl, untainted by "false" national ideologies, who acted as the defender of the Rusyn people against the local Magyarone, Muscophile, and Czechophile *panove*. [15] An example was Borys Martinovych's "At Dawn," which described conditions shortly after the First World War, a time when the Magyar influence was still strong in Subcarpathian Rus'. Unlike her own parents, who were proud that they spoke Magyar, the young heroine, Marta, followed the example of her grandfather, who did not feel obliged to speak Magyar and who "openly identified himself as a Rusyn." [16] When a Russian officer came to the province and asked Marta to teach him Hungarian, the young patriotic girl retorted: "I'm telling you to leave me alone! I am a Rusyn! A Hutsul, and not a Magyar! I don't even want to hear Magyar! Enough already!" [17]

Avhustyn Voloshyn also employed a young female patriot who adamantly opposed the older generation of national traitors. In his play "Marusia Verkhovynka," the setting is a little village where national and language questions are a topic of debate. Already in the first act a peasant proclaims: "I just don't understand: before the War to become a *pan* it was necessary to learn Magyar, now—Russian [*po-moskovs'komu*] or something . . . And when will it be *po-nashomu?* [literally: in our language]." [18] Unlike the peasant, whose unanswered questions left him sighing in despair, Marusia took her local adversaries to task. To the village notary, Werner, she replied: "Before the War they say you loyally served your former *panove,* forgetting that you were a German and wanting to make us into Magyars . . . Now you want to make us into Muscovites by bringing here a *pan* school . . . And tomorrow, or later, what are you going to make out of us —Poles, or Germans? Excuse me if I say that this reminds me of a gypsy who was asked: What is your religion? He answered: so which one do you need?"[19] Combining the national and social issues, Marusia turned to the Jewish innkeeper: "Listen, Pan Davidovych . . . I know that you would want to have your children taught in other schools so that it would be easier to do business and suck the blood from the poor Rusyns. But we are not businessmen and we don't need them: We are Rusyns, sons of a great nation, and forever we will be with them, even if you put up ten Magyar, Muscophile or other schools!"[20]

But what was this "great nation" to which Marusia referred? Initially, Ukrainophile authors adopted a kind of Rusynophile position; they wrote in local dialect and restricted their horizons to their native land. For instance, in his early poetry Borshosh-Kum'iats'kyi proclaimed "I am a Rusyn" and his homeland was "the green highlands [Verkhovyna] of Subcarpathia [*Pôdkarpatia*]."[21] Similarly, Grendzha-Dons'kyi's first cycle of poems *Kvity z tern'om* ("Flowers with Thorns," 1923), referred only to the Rusyns of "dear Verkhovyna."[22] However, by the late 1920s, the extension of national allegiance to include the whole Ukraine became an important principle, as in the writings of Grendzha-Dons'kyi and other contributors to his journal, *Nasha zemlia.*[23]

First of all, to avoid any terminological confusion, Grendzha-Dons'kyi made it clear that "Our name is Ukrainian/ And not Rusnak-Rusyn."[24] Moreover, the Carpathian Mountains were no barrier to national unity:

> We already know, dear brothers,
> Whose children we are . . .
> The Beskyds do not divide us
> From our brother.
> My blood brother from beyond the Carpathians
> Is not a foreigner to me,
> I will tell the whole world
> That I am a Ukrainian.[25]

This identification with the Ukraine was most graphically depicted in a poem, "Be Ready," by the Basilian monk Sevastiian Sabol (pseudonym Zoreslav). He saw the "Prophet" and the "Messiah" in the East, where Kiev was calling with songs of hosanna, and in a passionate finale proclaimed:

> In the glory of the sun
> In a rage of song

> Will arise from ruins,
> Will finally come forth
> Adorned in freedom—
> The magnificent, sacred halo
> of the Ukraine.[26]

If Ukrainophile authors preferred to describe Subcarpathian Rus' as a Ukrainian land, local Russophiles continually stressed that their fatherland should only be called Rus'.[27] Proud of his "glorious Verkhovina," Popovich proclaimed: "You were and will be/ a Russian land."[28] Similarly, the works of the two best-known Russian-language authors, Andrei Karabelesh and Mikhail Popovich, were filled with references to Subcarpathia's relations with the "Russian" East.[29] It should be emphasized, however, that these authors did not consider their people to be Great Russians (Muscovites), but rather a branch of one Russian nation:

> We are not alone! From the Tisa and Poprad
> To the far, golden, Siberian mountains,
> To the Pacific waters live one galaxy;
> Everywhere one people throughout the whole expanse.[30]

And in the absence of political unity, it was language that united all the Russian peoples: from the Carpathians and Beskids to the Urals, Caucasus, and Altai, everywhere was heard the "resonant, mighty, grandiose [Russian] language!"[31] In a sense, the Subcarpathian Russophiles continued the nineteenth-century Pan-Slavic tradition, which longed for the unity of all the Slavic peoples under the leadership of "a holy, renewed Russia."[32]

> Don't forget these prophetic words,
> My brothers, my friends:
> Only great Moscow
> Holds us in its embrace.
> . . . .
> All these fields and mountains,
> From Uzhhorod to the Kremlin—
> This is the Russian expanse,
> This is the Russian land![33]

It has been asserted that unlike their Ukrainian-oriented brethren, Russophile authors in Subcarpathian Rus' "ignored local themes" because they were afraid of becoming provincial in outlook.[34] Yet it would be a mistake to assume that regional, patriotic subjects were absent from their work. We have mentioned above the love of Subcarpathian nature that pervaded much of the Russian-language poetry. Moreover, local historical figures from Dukhnovych and Evmenii Sabov to Masaryk, G. Zsatkovich, and A.

Beskid were frequently praised in eulogies by Karabelesh and Popovich.[35] Thus, Russophile authors did stress the particular qualities of their Carpathian homeland, although they never forgot that it must continue to be "drenched in a flowered aroma" and "enlightened by the ruddy East."[36]

The enduring poverty of the Rusyn peasants, especially in the Verkhovyna, and the increase in unemployment caused by the economic crisis during the 1930s were underlying themes in much of the literature that appeared in Subcarpathian Rus'. Both Russophile and Ukrainophile authors lamented the sad fate of their people: "I hear the weeping of my homeland/ Its inaudible weeping/ Fate's executioner has alloted/ Eternal want and poverty."[37] Suffering reigned supreme throughout the land, whether in the countryside, where "Over the villages loom/ Bellfries and crosses,/Under them silently weep the people—/Victims of the darkness";[38] or in the cities: "On the streets the unemployed/ Speak about bread/ For their hungry children at home/ And about a cold tombstone."[39] Grendzha-Dons'kyi summed up his observations in the introduction and conclusion to a poem entitled, "This is my Native Land!"

> Landlords . . . Prison . . .
> Sorrow . . . Affliction . . .
> Chains . . . Police . . .
> This is my native land![40]

Poets reacted to the widespread poverty in two ways: with a passive acceptance of the situation as the inevitable fate of mankind, or with a spirited call for the awakening and liberation of the homeland. Andrei Karabelesh best represented the former outlook.[41] Many of his poems were addressed to the "Almighty One" and his verses clearly implied that the sins of the Rusyns were the cause of their suffering.[42] Much in Karabelesh's work revealed outright pessimism and despair: "O God, my God, for what/ Were we born into this world?"[43]

But Karabelesh's negative pessimism and passivity were more than matched by the appearance of many verses which looked forward to a bright future. His Russophile colleague Mikhail Popovich proclaimed:

> Brothers, stand together in a body
> Against the darkness which is oppressing us! . . .
> Stand together in thought—
> And the blessed time will come![44]

By the 1930s, this wishful expectation was transformed into a proletarian call for poets to take immediate action in order to relieve the economic plight of the Rusyn masses:

In the twentieth century
You can't while away your time on trifles.
Look—the working generation
Is doomed to destruction by capitalists.
. . . .
Join the struggle for the solidarity of
all the oppressed,
And toward this unifying, grandiose idea
Lead the working class.
Poets, now!
Let your voice be heard in the leading ranks,
And write choruses about hunger and oppression![45]

The call was heeded by younger Russian language authors like Vasilii Dobosh (b. 1917), Emel'ian Baletskii, and Andrei Patrus-Karpatskii (b. 1917), whose verses were filled with themes about social liberation and the expectation of inevitable change.[46]

However, it was the Ukrainophile Vasyl' Grendzha-Dons'kyi who most fully stressed the problem of social and psychological injustice. In his short novel *Il'ko Lypei: A Carpathian Brigand,* which was based on the experiences of a real-life childhood friend, the author had a chance to develop one of his favorite themes: the demoralizing effect of wealth and the desire for freedom. Disowned by his wealthy father for having married a poor girl, Il'ko turns to drink and is sentenced to prison for brawling. He soon escapes and discovers that his wife only married him because he was to inherit riches. Emotionally distraught, Il'ko refuses to return to prison and characteristically declares: "I will not give up my freedom so soon, I will preserve it in life and death."[47] Thus, like his real-life and literary predecessor, Mykola Shuhai, Il'ko Lypei spends his last days as a Robin Hood bandit in the Carpathians—robbing from the rich and giving to the poor. Through Lypei, Grendzha-Dons'kyi epitomized the fate of the Subcarpathian Rusyn people, a national group that continued to remain culturally, socially, and economically downtrodden.

In both linguistic and literary developments, we have seen that, of the three orientations, the Rusynophile trend never evolved in a serious way. There was a dramatic literature based on village themes, which because it was intended for the masses, was written in dialect or in a Subcarpathian recension of Russian. The most prolific authors in this genre were the Galician Russophile Antonii Bobul'skii (1877-194?), the local Russophiles Sion I. Sil'vai (1876-1932), Pavel S. Fedor, Dmitrii Antalovskii, the Ukrainophiles Grendzha-Dons'kyi and Iryna Nevyts'ka (1886-1965), and the Rusynophile Ivan Muranii.[48] However, no author ever pressed the idea of formulating a separate literature written in Rusyn dialect. Although poets like Grendzha-Dons'kyi and Borshosh-Kum'iats'kyi, for instance, did write in dialect in their early works, in a short time they became fully Ukrainophile, from both the linguistic and national standpoints. Even the popular prose writers Luka Dem'ian, Aleksander Markush, and Iryna Nevyts'ka, whose works were primarily in Rusyn dialect, became allied with the Ukrainophiles.[49] Recognizing the increased popularity of the Ukrainian movement, critics writing in the early 1930s claimed that the Russian orientation was doomed to eventual dissolution.[50]

Such negative opinions regarding the survival of the Russian literary orientation in Subcarpathian Rus' were based on an unreliable analogy with the situation in Galicia during the nineteenth century. On both sides of the Carpathians, the Russian (*obshcherusskii*) movement was described as representing the aristocratic and conservative elements in society, while the populist or Ukrainian movement was seen as a democratic and socially liberating force.[51] Russian literature in Subcarpathian Rus', "turning away from the people and from local soil, found itself between heaven and earth, without any roots in the living populace." It was "a literature for the intelligentsia, a completely exceptional phenomenon in this democratic age"; so wrote the competent Czech critic, Antonín Hartl, in 1930.[52]

Indeed, Russian literary production in the province during the 1920s was in large part the work of émigrés like Aleksander V. Popov (1893-19?), Dmitrii N. Vergun (1871-1951), Vasilii R. Vavrik (1889-1970) and Lev N. Tyblevich,[53] who instilled in their Subcarpathian followers a love of Russia, but at the same time lamented that their former homeland was being destroyed by a Soviet regime. Some, like Tyblevich, even went so far as to claim that, thanks to the Czechoslovak regime, Subcarpathian Rus' had become the last Russian land:

> Only here in the Carpathian country
> Has Russian blood remained.
> Where our Czech brethren protect us
> From the packs of our enemies.[54]

Such anti-Soviet attitudes also entered the few collections of poetry by Karabelesh, Popovich, and Pavel S. Fedor, who represented the local contributors to Russian-language literature.

The following decade, however, did not witness a decline of Russian literature in Subcarpathian Rus'. On the contrary, there was an increase in the number, and marked improvement in the quality, of Russian-language writers. Educated in local Russian gymnasia, especially in Mukachevo, a new generation of young Subcarpathians like V. Dobosh, E. Baletskii, A. Patrus-Karpatskii, and Fedor Ivanchov (b.1916) entered the literary scene.[55] Their works first appeared in the gymnasium student journal *Nashi stremleniia* (1935-1937), in the newspaper *Russkii narodnyi golos* (1934-1938), and in the series of the Sodruzhestvo Society, edited by the émigré critic Evgenii Nedziel'skii. Unlike the émigré authors of the previous decade, these young Russophiles could not be accused of being either conservative or reactionary.[56] Their writings were filled with a concern for social justice and equality, so that the Russophiles could consider their literature contemporary and responsive to issues that were "a matter of life and death for the Carpatho-Russian people."[57]

To be sure, it was not easy, if even possible, for the semiliterate masses of Subcarpathian Rus' to understand literary Russian, and there was much truth in the statement of one critic that Karabelesh was "a foreigner at home" with "no public, no readers."[58] Nevertheless, Russian was still a subject of instruction in all gymnasia, so that new cadres of readers and writers were constantly in the making. Hence, by the end of the second decade of Czechoslovak rule, the Ukrainian literary movement was well established and growing in importance. Still, literature written in Russian was being produced, and even if its tempo was not as dynamic as that of its rival, it was nonetheless far from becoming a nonexistent cultural force.

Some Subcarpathian authors, especially of the Ukrainophile orientation, placed their literary talents in the service of the autonomous regime that lasted for a few months from late 1938 to early 1939. V. Grendzha-Dons'kyi and S. Sabol became editors of government and religious journals and, as we have seen, they changed the language of these publications to standard Ukrainian. One young writer, Mykola Rishko (b. 1907) expressed in verse joy at spending his first Christmas in an autonomous Carpatho-Ukraine:

> For centuries we awaited this festive day . . .
> While suffering under enemies in our own homes.
>> Rejoice my great, invincible people
>> Join in shining ranks
>> To greet a holy Christmas in unity
>> From the Tisa to the Don, and beyond the Caucasus.[59]

Even the Russophile Andrei Patrus-Karpatskii hailed the existence of the new autonomous government and attempted some verses in Ukrainian:

> We are all one, one, one
> In Carpatho-Ukraine,
> In Kiev, in Bukovina,
> In the Prešov region, in Galicia
>> No one can break us
>> In these threatening times.[60]

But the favorable development for Ukrainophiles was ended by the Hungarian occupation of Subcarpathian Rus' beginning in March 1939. Until the arrival of the Red Army in late 1944 all Ukrainian language publications were banned. Several authors (V. Grendzha-Dons'kyi, A. Karabelesh, A. Patrus-Karpatskii) fled from the homeland, while those that remained were allowed to publish only if they wrote in Russian or in dialect, which was officially described at the time as the Uhro-Rusyn language. In fact, many Ukrainophiles like Iu. Borshosh-Kum'iats'kyi, A. Markush, L. Dem'ian, and F. Potushniak did write in, or had their works edited into, the accepted Uhro-Rusyn norm. More prolific were a group of young Russophiles who formed "literary schools" at the Uzhhorod, Mukachevo, and Khust gymnasia and published six literary almanacs.[61] Writers like E. Baletskii and the émigré E. Nedziel'skii (who used the pseudonyms Iurii Vir and I. Goverla) were joined by Ivan Kercha (pseud. Tania Verkhovinka, 1914-1951), Georgii Goida (pseud. Karpatskii, 1919-1955), Kirill Golos (pseud. Krasin, Vershan, b. 1921), Vasilii Sochka (pseud. Borzhavin, b. 1922), Mikhail Shpitser (pseuds. Vershinskii, Bezprizornyi, 1921-1944), Dmytro Vakarov (1920-1945), and others who wrote in Russian.[62]

This literature was similar to that produced during the Czechoslovak regime, that is, short stories based on rural life, lyric poems expressing love for the beauties of the homeland, and moving descriptions of the sad fate of its suffering inhabitants.[63] With regard to the national issue, the expression of Ukrainian sympathies in print was out of the question, and despite official approval there was no praise for the idea of a separate Uhro-Rusyn nationality. On the other hand, the idea of unity with Russia was expressed both implicitly and explicitly, with traditional praise for cultural unity with Rus' and the expectation of eventual liberation from the East. Given contemporary political reality, Subcarpathian authors filled their works with symbolic references (Sun, Star, Light, Day, North, East) to their brothers in the East who would one day bring them salvation. E. Baletskii reminded his fellow poets.: "You do all believe that after the days of suffering/ A new age will dawn?"[64] It was evident that any change must come from "the eastern star" and that "Soon the day will come/when borders will disappear/and between brothers there will be no/boundary to the north."[65]

The desire for unity with brethren beyond the Carpathians was complemented by a call for internal unity. Open scorn was addressed to those Subcarpathian politicans who in the name of Uhro-Rusynism or some other ideology cooperated with the Hungarian regime. In a poem subtitled "the hero of our time," Ivan Kercha surely had pro-Hungarian Rusyn leaders in mind when he wrote:

> With leftists—he's a left-winger,
> And with rightists—a right winger

He's a blasphemer
As well as a true believer
He's honest as an angel
Cunning as a demon;
Without shame, insincere
A malicious hypocrite.[66]

This continued division along national lines between the Russophiles and
Uhro-Rusynophiles and the tendency of many Subcarpathian leaders to
cooperate with the Hungarian government was also viewed as detrimental
for the national cause.

I believe, I believe in greater days,
And I believe, friends, in a time
When evil will leave people
And agreement will unite us together.
When the quarrelsome, destructive,
                    naive, and haughty,
"I and you," will disappear.
When such prophets will be
Who will unite us simply as "we."[67]

In 1945, after almost three decades of publication activity, Subcarpathian
authors had still not succeeded in creating a unified literature. As ever, they
remained divided along linguistic and national lines. Only one thing was
clear: despite the existence of works in dialect, no authors ever seriously
thought of forming a separate Subcarpathian Rusyn literature, even though
such a goal was not opposed by the Czechoslovak government and was actually favored by the Hungarian regime during the Second World War. Moreover, even among the Ukrainophiles and Russophiles there was never any
local author who was sufficiently talented to attract a large following. For
this reason, the Subcarpathian intelligentsia was forced to rely on the
"greats" of Russian or Ukrainian literature—Pushkin, Tolstoy, Shevchenko, Franko—who were considered as their own. Finally, no Subcarpathian writer during the years 1918 to 1945 was ever popular enough to be
known among any large segment of the population. If a Subcarpathian
Rusyn was asked to name an author or literary work that he considered his
own, he would most likely have named Dukhnovych and recited one of the
national hymns written in the nineteenth century. To conclude, it must be
recognized that the proliferation of national themes in belles-lettres may
have helped consolidate attitudes among certain factions of the intelligentsia, but that no one author gained the stature needed to make literature a
crucial factor in determining the national affiliation of the populace.

Cultural Organizations

Cultural organizations have historically played a crucial role in national movements, especially among peoples who did not have a state apparatus and who in general lacked control over their own political destiny. Among Slavic peoples, such societies were called *maticas*. They became the primary vehicle for propagating national ideals among East European ethnic groups, and between 1826 and 1882 several were established by the Serbs, Czechs (and Moravians separately), Croats, Lusatian Sorbs, Galician Rusyns, Slovaks, Slovenes, and Poles. We have seen how the Subcarpathian Rusyns set up similar societies in 1850 and again in 1867, although both these efforts proved to be short-lived.[68]

Under the Czechoslovak regime, Rusyn organizational efforts began again in earnest, and in the spring of 1920 the first attempts were made to establish a cultural organization for Subcarpathian Rus'. On April 29, a general council of local leaders met in Uzhhorod under the leadership of Dr. Iulii Brashchaiko. As an indication of support from the Prague government, Dr. Jan Brejcha, the provincial administrator, and Josef Pešek, superintendent of the school administration, attended the meeting. Nothing positive resulted, however, because the Rusyns present remained divided along political lines established the previous autumn and fought among themselves regarding the national and linguistic orientation of the proposed cultural organization.[69] The Russophiles Andrei Gagatko (1884-1944), Ilarion Tsurkanovich (1878-194?), and Dr. Antonii Beskid vigorously opposed the proposals of the populist-Ukrainophile organizers Brashchaiko and A. Voloshyn. The result was a complete disruption of the proceedings—a symbolic indication of the deep rift between Rusyn leaders that was to be a standard feature of Subcarpathian political and cultural life for the next two decades.

Subsequently, on May 9, 1920, Dr. Iu. Brashchaiko called another meeting, inviting only populist Ukrainophiles and Rusynophiles; this meeting led to the establishment of the Tovarystvo Prosvîta Pôdkarpatskoî Rusy (Prosvita Society). Iu. Brashchaiko was elected Chairman and among those included on the central committee were A. Voloshyn, Dr. Mykola Dolynai, Dr. I. Pan'kevych, A. Shtefan, Dr. V. Hadzhega, Dr. H. Stryps'kyi and S. Klochurak.[70] The aim of the Prosvita Society was the "cultural and economic uplifting of the Rusyn people [*rus'kyi narod*] living within the borders of the Czechoslovak Republic,"[71] a task to be carried out by the publication of popular and scholarly books "written in the national tongue and accessible to every Subcarpathian Rusyn."[72] In addition, the original constitution intended to set up agricultural cooperatives, to help farmers obtain tools and machines, to organize musical, gymnastic, theatrical, and educational circles, and to establish libraries, national homes, and a "Central National Museum for all Subcarpathian Rus'."[73]

The Prosvita Society was divided into publishing, literary-scientific, organizational, library, theatrical, museum, and economic sections, and the example to be followed was that of Galicia. The name Prosvita, which means enlightenment, was copied from the Prosvita Society established in L'viv in 1868. Moreover, many Galician Ukrainians, like Ivan Pan'kevych, Volodymyr Birchak, and Vasyl' Pachovs'kyi, who had emigrated to Subcarpathian Rus' during the early 1920s, brought the valuable experience they had gained in working to improve the national and educational conditions of the Rusyns in Galicia. Welcomed by the Czechoslovak government, the Galician Ukrainians received positions in many governmental, educational, and cultural institutions, and it is not an exaggeration to say that "of all the Ukrainian lands where . . . Ukrainian emigrants worked, their efforts had the greatest importance in Transcarpathia."[74]

The Galician experience, which had transformed Rusyns into nationally conscious Ukrainians, had to be repeated, according to these leaders, in Subcarpathian Rus'. In the words of V. Pachovs'kyi, "'Prosvita' set for itself one task: in Galicia there should not be one illiterate Rusyn . . . And should not Subcarpathian Rusyns take up the example of their brothers? Subcarpathian Rusyns must also uplift the education of the people and make each Rusyn aware of his rights and obligations towards his people."[75] The catalyst for this national transformation was to be the reading room, where Subcarpathian villagers could obtain newspapers and books and hear lectures. A minimum of ten members was required to set up a local affiliate of Prosvita. The aim of these grass-roots cultural organizations was clear: "In the reading rooms our peasants must first of all be taught that they are Rusyns . . . The reading room must teach our peasants to love their mother tongue—everything that is Rusyn."[76]

Many of the reading rooms contained libraries, and the Prosvita Society set up a broad publishing program to make material available for all segments of the population. Initially, most of the publications were written in a dialectally based language in the traditional orthography, but by 1930 the gradual approach toward literary Ukrainian was augmented, and the modern orthography employed. Of importance was a popular series including about sixty different titles that were primarily agricultural, literary, and historical in content;[77] a children's journal, *Pchôlka* (1922-1932); eighteen short studies dealing with the language, literature, and history of the province;[78] and the erudite fourteen-volume *Naukovŷi zbornyk Tovarystva 'Prosvîta'* (1922-1938), edited by I. Pan'kevych, V. Birchak, V. Hadzhega, and A. Voloshyn.

As a focal point for the Prosvita reading-room network, plans were made to construct a *Narodnyi Dom* (National Center). Czechoslovak President Tomáš Masaryk donated 100,000 crowns toward this goal, which was achieved in October 1928 when the society celebrated the opening of a modern center in Uzhhorod that included a museum, library, reading room, and movie theater.[79] Although the impact of the economic depression and the cutback in government support during the 1930s diminished Prosvita's publishing and theatrical program, the Society nevertheless continued to be an important feature in the cultural life of the province.

The Russophile faction of the local intelligentsia boycotted the Prosvita Society and called 148 cultural leaders to Uzhhorod on March 23, 1923, to set up a rival organization, the Russkoe Kul'turno-Prosvietitel'noe Obshchestvo imeni Aleksandra Dukhnovicha (Dukhnovych Society). Evmenii Sabov, a long-time defender of the so-called "Carpatho-Rusyn tradition," was chosen to be chairman, although the organizer and guiding spirit was the younger Russophile activist Dr. Stepan Fentsik (1892-1945). Among those elected to the society's central committee were Dr. Iosif Kaminskii (1878-1944), Bishop Petro Gebei, Dr. Simeon Sabov, Konstantin Nevitskii, Nikolai Dragula, Dr. Petr Petrigalla, Dr. Nikolai Beskid, Dr. Aleksander Beskid, and Dr. Iulii Gadzhega.[80]

The Dukhnovych Society attracted those in the Subcarpathian intelligentsia who for various reasons were dissatisfied with the increasingly Ukrainian-oriented Prosvita. The aim of the new organization was to foster the "cultural development of the Russian [russkii] people living within Czechoslovakia, and most important to educate them in a moral, patriotic and Russian spirit, exclusive of all political activity."[81] In subsequent years, the Russian character and anti-Ukrainian attitude of the organization were to be continually emphasized: "In the course of its one-thousand-year history, our people always called themselves Russian. They always considered their language, their lineage, their customs, their church, and other institutions as Russian."[82]

Even flags, the symbolic trappings of national sovereignty, were employed. While the Prosvita Society displayed the blue and yellow trident that was used by the independent Ukrainian republic in Kiev and by the Western Ukrainian government in L'viv (1918-1919), the Dukhnovych Society chose the "Russian [obshcherusskii], tricolored, national flag [as] . . . a symbol, an external mark that we are Russian and . . . a part of the great Russian nation [velikaia russkaia natsiia]."[83] Similarly, as the local Prosvita Society maintained close relations with the Shevchenko and Prosvita societies in L'viv, so did the Dukhnovych Society stress its affinity with the Russophile Kachkovskii Society in Galicia and with Russian émigré organizations in Prague, Sofia, Belgrade, Paris, and the United States.[84] Nevertheless, despite these external signs of allegiance to a nation abroad, the Prosvita and the Dukhnovych societies always stressed their loyalty to the Czechoslovak republic.[85]

The Dukhnovych Society was divided into twelve sections: organizational and educational, scientific-literary, publications, theatrical, musical, choral, sports, Russian Scouts, National Center, National Archives, Russian women, and sanitary-hygienic. Among the society's activities were the erection of monuments to Subcarpathian national leaders[86] and the celebration of an annual Russian Day Festival (*Russkii Den'*), which in effect was a folk festival where speeches, parades, folk dancing, and singing were the order of the day. Another important achievement was the Russian National Center (Russkii Narodnyi Dom) established in Uzhhorod in December 1932.

The publication section sponsored the journals *Karpatskii krai* (1923-1924) and later *Karpatskii sviet* (1928-1933), containing articles of a literary, scholarly, and polemical nature whose purpose was "to strive for an awakening of Carpathian Rus', which could then feel more deeply its profound internal relation to Russian culture and Russian literature."[87] Contributors included Russian émigrés living in Prague and Subcarpathian Rus' and local authors like A. Karabelesh and M. Popovich. The Dukhnovych Society also published 115 pamphlets (the *Izdanie* series, 1924-1937), which included reprints of articles from *Karpatskii sviet* as well as original plays, collections of poetry, and almanacs. However, unlike the Prosvita Society, which published many pamphlets of practical use for Rusyn peasants (written in a dialectally based language), the material of the Dukhnovych Society was usually limited to the esoteric realms of literature and cultural history. Moreover, since the Russian literary language was employed, the Subcarpathian reader could understand the text only with great difficulty.

The Dukhnovych Society was most proud of its work in the establishment of reading rooms throughout the province. As in the Prosvita Society, a minimum of ten members was required to set up a village reading room, which then served as a local center for educational, theatrical, musical, and scouting activities.[88] A larger number of reading rooms supposedly represented superior cultural activity and thus justified a claim to more government funds. Unfortunately, no two sources agree on the number of reading rooms existing in any given year.[89] The discrepancies could be due to fabricated statistics or to the fluctuating relationship between a local reading room and its professed national orientation. Most often the affiliation of the reading room was dependent on the attitude of the local teacher. The arrival of a new teacher might have prompted a different affiliation. Furthermore, the Czechoslovak Ministry of Education and Culture supplied funds for the establishment of state reading rooms and libraries that were not dependent on either the Dukhnovych or Prosvita Societies, although the latter frequently claimed them in their statistics.

At best we can only offer, in Table 5, a representative sample of the number of reading rooms based on data compiled in 1929 by the Russophile Subcarpathian-Russian Popular Education Association (Podkarpatorusskii Narodoprosvietitel'nyi Soiuz). These were the only detailed statistics available, and according to this source, the Dukhnovych Society had 202 reading rooms while Prosvita had only 83. Most interesting was their geographical layout. The Dukhnovych Society was unquestionably strongest in central Bereg county, particularly in the areas around Mukachevo, Svaliava, and Nyzhni Verets'ky. In western Ung county, the proportion was roughly two to one in favor of Dukhnovych, while in eastern Máramaros, a stronghold of Ukrainianism, the proportion was reversed in favor of Prosvita.[90] The last available statistics showed that the Prosvita Society had increased its total number to 253 in 1937, while the Dukhnovych Society, with 297 rooms in 1936, continued its leadership in reading-room activity.[91] The Dukhnovych Society claimed 21,000 members, Prosvita, 15,000.[92]

Notwithstanding these figures, the Dukhnovych Society was the less dynamic of the two cultural organizations during the 1930s. For instance, its publication program was severely curtailed. To be sure, the decrease in governmental support that affected the Dukhnovych Society also struck the Prosvita Society. More important, however, were the attitudes of leaders in each organization. Whereas Prosvita was headed by individuals like Avhustyn Voloshyn, Volodymyr Birchak, and Ivan Pan'kevych—teachers and scholars continually in close contact with Subcarpathian cultural life— the Dukhnovych Society was under the influence of Stepan Fentsik and Iosif Kaminskii, men who were more interested in local politics and personal advancement than in serious, sustained cultural work among the masses. This was underlined after 1934, when Evmenii Sabov, the nominal head of the Dukhnovych Society, died. Soon the society became a platform for the propagation of Stepan Fentsik's political views. A brief attempt to depoliticize the organization came with the election of Senator Edmund Bachinskii (1880-1947) as chairman in June, 1936, but he resigned three months later in protest against Secretary Fentsik's continued use of the society for political purposes.[93] By 1937, Fentsik's relations with Polish and Hungarian revisionists had become common knowledge, and the Dukhnovych Society was discredited in the eyes of many inhabitants throughout the province.[94]

Indication of the growing popularity of the Ukrainian orientation, and simultaneous decrease of the Russian orientation, can be observed in the degrees of success registered by the Prosvita and Dukhnovych societies in organizing manifestations during the late 1930s. Prosvita convoked a series of congresses that met in Svaliava, Rakhiv, Perechyn, and other villages throughout Subcarpathian Rus'. Although aimed at stimulating Ukrainian national pride, these gatherings were frequently political, and especially antigovernmental, in nature. Prosvita's dominance in garnering popular support was indisputable after the General Prosvita Congress that took place in Uzhhorod on October 17, 1937. Upwards of 30,000 persons gathered in one of the largest manifestations ever organized in Uzhhorod. The pro-Ukrainian and antigovernmental character of the congress was made explicit by the speakers, among whom were Social-Democratic, Communist, and extreme nationalist delegates.[95]

The Dukhnovych Society could hardly match the massive support of its

Ukrainian rival. In the last months of the Czechoslovak regime, Fentsik announced the celebration of another annual Russian Day Festival, to be held on September 12, 1938 in Mukachevo, the center of Russophile strength. But despite the call to members of the society, to Dukhnovych Scouts, and to local students, only 190 people participated.[96] The poor showing was not only a reaction to Fentsik's foreign political ventures, but it also revealed that in the struggle between the two cultural societies for the allegiance of the local population, by the 1930s Prosvita had proved to be the most successful.

Besides the Prosvita and Dukhnovych Societies, there were many other social and cultural organizations established in Subcarpathian Rus' during the Czechoslovak regime, such as the Provincial Museum Society (Zemská Musejní Společnost), and the Educational Benevolent Fund (Shkol'naia Pomoshch'), which from 1920 operated a library and four student dormitories, various choral groups, and a short-lived opera group headed by Z. G. Ashkinazi under the patronage of Russophile leaders in Mukachevo.[97]

However, of greatest importance for crystalizing a feeling of national consciousness, especially among young people, were the scouting organizations. Besides conducting traditional activities, the scout camps in Subcarpathian Rus' also became centers for the propagation of nationalism. This was particularly true of the Ukrainophile Plast organization, first begun in 1921. Long-time scoutmaster Leonyd Bachyns'kyi (b. 1896), an émigré from Galicia, stressed the integral relationship between scouting and the national movement: "To love the fatherland, its customs, traditions and language, to learn how to help and show the way to his nation so that it can become great and powerful, to defend the nation with tenacity and character from any harm, to raise the culture of the homeland —these are the primary and basic tasks of the Plast scout."[98] To further these goals, Plast published the monthly, *Plastun* (1923-1935), and a series of pamphlets (adventure stories, playlets, and moral tracts) in which a gradual trend from the dialect to standard Ukrainian was characteristic.[99] By the 1930s Plast was fully associated with the Ukrainian movement and its more than three-thousand scouts (1935) formed an important component in pro-Ukrainian manifestations throughout the province.

Following the lead of the Ukrainophiles, the Dukhnovych Society created a section for scouts in order to endow young Subcarpathians with a sense of belonging to the Russian nationality. The Russian scout movement was not begun until 1929 and never achieved the organizational basis that Plast had, although it counted five-hundred members in 29 affiliates during its first year of operation.[100]

With the return of the Hungarian regime to Subcarpathian Rus' in late 1938 and early 1939 the situation changed radically for existing cultural organizations. Because of its Ukrainophile orientation, the Prosvita Society was closed and the property in its National Home in Uzhhorod and in its village affiliates was confiscated. Similarly, the Plast scouting camps were dissolved. The Russophile Dukhnovych Society continued to exist on paper, although its leader, S. Fentsik, was engaged full time in political activity, and for all intents and purposes the organization ceased to function.[101]

This vacuum was filled on January 26, 1941, when at the initiative of a few local leaders and with the support of the Hungarian government the Subcarpathian Scientific Society (Podkarpatskoe Obshchestvo Nauk—Kárpátaljai Tudományos Társásag) was established in Uzhhorod. The goals of the new organization were outlined in the opening address by the Hungarian administrator for Subcarpathia, Commissar Miklós Kozma. "The Society must work to create an independent Rusyn national consciousness," because "this people does not want to be anything else than it is in reality, that is, Rusyn, whose distinct, independent national culture intends to develop within the context of the legal and moral framework of the Crown of St. Stephen."[102] Indeed, this was the first cultural organization to adopt a Rusynophile position and one of its most important goals was the codification of a distinct literary language.

To achieve this goal, a broad publishing program was initiated by the director of the society, Ivan Haraida. He had already written a grammar of the Uhro-Rusyn language and now had an opportunity to use this medium for several categories of material. First among these was the monthly *Lyteraturna nedîlia* (1941-1944), which included original literary works by local authors, translations from world literature (Cervantes, K. Hamsun, Conan Doyle, M. Jókai, Maupassant, Poe, Shakespeare, Strindberg), and scholarly studies on Subcarpathian history and culture. Haraida also edited a popular series of short stories and histories (*Narodna Byblioteka,* 29 titles); children's books (*Dîtocha Byblioteka,* 8 titles); agricultural almanacs (1942 and 1943); and a monthly "journal for Subcarpathian youth," *Rus'ka molodezh* (1942-1944). Finally, a scholarly review, *Zoria-Hajnal,* appeared in three large illustrated volumes (1941-1943), as well as a literary-scientific series (30 titles) that included both reprints from *Zoria-Hajnal* and new monographs. A few articles in *Zoria-Hajnal,* separate monographs, and translations from contemporary Rusyn literature also appeared in Magyar, "because the goal of the Society is not only to develop the Subcarpathian Rusyn language, but also to allow the educated Magyar public to be acquainted with the cultural achievements of Subcarpathia and with love and responsibility follow the cultural work of the Rusyn people."[103]

From the organizational standpoint, the Subcarpathian Scientific Society consisted of three sections: (1) scientific; (2) artistic and ethnographic; (3) Rusyn language and literature. However, unlike the Prosvita and Dukhnovych Societies, which were open to massive membership, the new organization was designed as a center for the intelligentsia and hence limited to thirty-five members. The retired professor from Budapest Antal Hodinka was elected chairman and the local Greek Catholic historian Irynei Kontratovych vice-director, although the actual functioning of the society was conducted by Haraida. Individuals of all national orientations were accepted as long as they, in the words of Kontratovych, followed the traditions of their ancestors, who did not "look to the North or East, but rather, even in their misery, always turned to the South, to Budapest, because the apostolic crown of St. Stephen was for them a symbol which united in magnificent harmony true patriotism: Magyar St. Stephen and Rusyn nationalism."[104] These ideas formed the basis of works written by Hodinka and his countrymen from Budapest, Bonkáló and Stryps'kyi, who published frequently in the society's publications. Other members included the local Rusynophiles Emyliian Bokshai, Aleksander Il'nyts'kyi (1889-1956), and Ivan Muranii, the Ukrainophile Aleksander Markush, and the Russophiles Petr Sova (b. 1894) and Konstantin Stripskii. The society planned to set up local reading rooms, but this plan never came to fruition.[105]

There were also other organizations set up during the Hungarian regime. Among them were the Bercsényi Union of Subcarpathian Fighters (Kárpátaljai Batársak Bercsényi-Szövetsége), the Ivan Kurtiak Cultural Society (Kurtyák Iván Kulturális Egyesület), the Association of Fighters in the East, Association for the Protection of the Magyar Race (Fajvedő), the Union of Subcarpathian Rusyns in Budapest, and the Rákóczi Carpathian Cultural Society (Kárpátaljai Rákóczi Kultúrszövetség). Each was designed to bring Rusyns closer to Magyar civilization, even at the expense of assimilation, so that from the standpoint of Rusyn national development they made no positive contribution.[106]

Theater and Art

It was early recognized that theatrical performances would be an important stimulus to national allegiance and pride among the Rusyn population, and the constitutions of both the Prosvita and Dukhnovych societies expressed an intent to organize theatrical circles throughout the region. The psychological effect of seeing heroic and patriotic deeds performed on the stage in the national language could not be overestimated. Undoubtedly, the type of repertoire and choice of language were crucial questions that had to be faced by both amateur and professional theaters.

The first theatrical organization was an amateur circle set up by Prosvita; from July to September, 1920, it gave seven performances of the patriotic Ukrainian play "Natalka Poltavka," and interest was so great that it was decided to establish a permanent theater. The presence of many professional Ukrainian émigré actors in Czechoslovakia made available much talent and led to the creation on January 1, 1921, of the Rusyn Theater of the Prosvita Society (Rus'kii Teatr Tovarystva Prosvîta). The following summer Uzhhorod's Rusyn Theater received a subsidy of 250,000 crowns from President Masaryk and was reorganized by the renowned Ukrainian director Mykola Sadovs'kyi (1856-1933).

Despite subsequent financial difficulties, the Rusyn Theater played ten seasons (1921-1929), averaging 133 performances a year. Most popular among these were the Ukrainian patriotic operas and dramas: "Zaporozhets' za Dunaiem," "Taras Bul'ba," "Bohdan Khmel'nyts'kyi," "Natalka Poltavka," and "Oi, ne khody, Hrytsiu." All performances were given in the Ukrainian language, and the theater's frequent tours throughout Subcarpathian Rus' helped to create a lively interest and feeling of allegiance towards the Ukraine.[107]

Unlike Prosvita, the Dukhnovych Society never had a professional theater. In fact, the only productions in Russian by a professional group were the few performances given in Uzhhorod by the Moscow Art Theater (Moskovskii Khudozhestvennyi Teatr) of Prague. The existence of local theatrical circles, however, was of great importance, and in this realm the Dukhnovych Society was most active. In 1936, the Dukhnovych reading rooms had 214 theatrical circles, 144 of which had their own stages, while Prosvita had 143 circles with 64 stages. The total number of performances in 1931 was listed as 574, while in 1936 there were 1,000.[108] The Czechoslovak government, in turn, was generous in its support of local theatrical activity, contributing thirty to ninety thousand crowns annually. One historian described the situation thus: "Even with the lack of leadership, theatrical activity grew, and for this small land and people took on fantastic proportions! Regarding the number of performances, the village began to overtake the city."[109]

In the individual reading room and theatrical circle, the local teacher played a crucial role. It was he who urged the villagers to participate as actors or spectators, he who chose the repertoire, he who stimulated an appreciation for the theater among the Rusyn masses. In response to necessity, these amateur productions were performed in local dialect, and, as for material, Subcarpathian dramatists like Dmitrii Antalovskii, A. Bobul'skii, V. Grendzha-Dons'kyi, I. Nevyts'ka, S. Sil'vai, and P. S. Fedor wrote a series of simple plays that could easily be adapted to amateur productions.[110]

Despite Prosvita's dissociation from the Rusyn Theater in late 1929, and the virtual end to government funding, the company still played for a few more seasons. Under the direction of another Ukrainian immigrant, M. Arkas, the Rusyn Theater gave 230 performances during the 1931-32 season, but without further subsidies it was impossible for it to continue, and in the 1935-36 season only one drama was performed.[111]

The widespread interest in theater expressed by the Subcarpathian population prompted a provincial government decision in September 1931 to organize and subsidize a professional company. These plans, however, were not realized until the summers of 1934 and 1935, when courses were organized to develop talent. Both Russian and Ukrainian immigrants were employed as instructors. Finally in April 1936, the Subcarpathian National Theater (Zemskii Podkarpatorus'kii Narodnŷi Teatr) was established. The ruling board included Subcarpathia's Rusynophile Governor Konstantyn

Hrabar (1877-1938), the Uzhhorod Superintendent of Schools Viktor Klíma, the Ukrainophile A. Voloshyn, and the Russophile I. Kaminskii. Policy was determined, however, by Klíma and his successor František Galvatý—both Czechs. In theory, the Subcarpathian National Theater was to perform all of its plays in Rusyn and to draw especially on the repertoire of local dramatists. In practice, works written in Russian were translated into dialect, while Ukrainian plays were performed in the original. If in Prague and other Czech cities the Subcarpathian National Theater was lauded with praise, at home it was harshly criticized by both Russophiles and Ukrainophiles for its use of an "artificial" Rusyn language. The steady barrage of criticism contributed to a leadership crisis during the 1937-38 season, when, despite a large annual government subsidy of 450,000 crowns, the National Theater gave only seventy-two performances.[112]

One reason for the crisis was the rivalry of the New Theater (Nova Stsena), a Ukrainian company founded in Khust by the brothers Iurii and Evhen Sherehii in February 1934. Two years later, the New Theater became an affiliate of Khust's Prosvita Society, and in April 1938, a self-supporting corporation under the direction of Ivan Hryts'-Duda (b. 1911). In the tradition of the Rusyn Theater, the New Theater performed a repertoire of classical Ukrainian plays and operettas. After unsuccessful plans in 1938 to unite the Subcarpathian National Theater with the New Theater, many members of the former company resigned and went to Khust. Despite only a minimum subsidy from the state (10,000 crowns in 1938), the New Theater nonetheless managed to give 236 performances.[113]

If plays in Rusyn dialect written by Subcarpathian authors dominated the repertoire of local amateur theatrical circles, at the professional level the Ukrainian orientation was by far the superior. In the 1920s, the presence of Ukrainian immigrants in Czechoslovakia provided a strong cadre of professional performers who had a decisive influence in the formation of younger talent that was to come to the fore during the following decade.[114] Another explanation for the success of the Ukrainian theater may be found in the repertoire itself. While Russian dramatic and operatic literature was characterized by the grand and heroic, the Ukrainian tradition found its strength in rural themes and folk motifs. The enormous popularity throughout the region of Ukrainian works like "Zaporozhets' za Dunaiem" or "Oi ne khody, Hrytsiu" could not be matched by any Russian works.[115] Thus, while the amateur theaters propagated local themes found in the Subcarpathian Rusyn dramatic repertoire, the professional Ukrainian-language theaters, centered in the larger cities, fostered among the intelligentsia, and especially students, a sympathy and love for the culture and traditions of the Ukraine.

After the return of the Hungarian regime, both the Subcarpathian National Theater and the New Theater were dissolved. Organized theatrical activity was not revived until January 1942, when a Rusyn National Theater

(Rus'kyi Narodnŷi Teatr) was reorganized in Uzhhorod under the leadership of Mykhail Lugosh (19??-1968). The new company included personnel from both the Subcarpathian National Theater and the New Theater, and in keeping with the official nationality policy it performed mostly plays written by local authors in Rusyn dialect.[116]

Other arts also played a role during the embryonic stage of national development. During the nineteenth century, many painters, sculptors, and composers who were under the influence of romanticism created works based on themes that were intended to stimulate national pride. One has only to recall the paintings and musical scores of the Poles Matejko and Moniuszko, the Czechs Mánes, Myslbek, Smetana, and Dvořák, the Magyars Székely, Benczúr, and Erkel, and the Russians Surikov, Repin, Borodin, and Mussorgsky to realize the integral relationship between art and nationalism.

Although Subcarpathian Rus' never produced a composer who wrote symphonic works incorporating nationalist motifs,[117] the region did produce several painters. Until the end of the First World War, however, there was no Subcarpathian school of painting. Subcarpathian-born artists like József (Zmii) Miklóssy (1792-1841) and Ignác Roskovics (1859-1915), the sculptor Ödön Szamovolszky (1878-1914), and Hungary's famed painter Mihály Munkácsy (born Leo M. Lieb in Mukachevo) were totally absorbed in the artistic milieu of Hungary, even if Miklóssy and Roskovics did paint works for many Subcarpathian churches. Similarly, another artist of Rusyn origin, the impressionist and art historian Igor E. Grabar (1871-1960), made his career in Russia and had no real influence on his homeland.[118]

The situation changed after Subcarpathian Rus' became a part of Czechoslovakia. Two young Rusyn painters, Iosyf Bokshai (1891-1975) and Adal'bert Erdeli (Erdélyi) (1891-1955), felt that if their homeland was to receive autonomy Subcarpathian artists should have that same privilege. Hence, they set up a school of painting known as the Subcarpathian Barbizon, named after the little French village where the realists Rousseau, Corot, and Millet lived during the mid-nineteenth century. Actually, only Bokshai and Emilian Hrabovs'kyi (1892-1955) maintained the style of the French Barbizon and of the later impressionists; Erdeli and his younger followers, Fedir Manailo (b. 1910), Ernest Kontratovych (b. 1912), Andrii Kotska (b. 1911) and others, produced works that recalled the expressionist, cubist, and surrealist styles of contemporary Western Europe.[119]

In 1921 Bokshai and Erdeli organized the first exposition of Subcarpathian artists in Mukachevo; during the next two decades several joint and individual shows were held throughout Subcarpathian Rus', as well as in Prague, Brno, Bratislava, Košice and other Czechoslovak cities. To train a younger generation of artists, Bokshai and Erdeli founded a public art school in 1927 and then united Subcarpathian artists in the Society of

Fine Arts in Subcarpathian Rus' (Tovarystvo diiachiv obrazotvorchykh mystetstv na Pidkarpats'kii Rusi), set up in Uzhhorod in 1931. The society was headed by Erdeli and included resident artists of all national backgrounds, among the more active being Ladislav Kaigl, Josef Tomášek, Milada Benešová-Špalová, Zoltán Soltesz, and the sculptors Jaromír Cupal and Nikolai Ostashkin. The Czechoslovak government was generous in offering official commissions and in providing stipends for study tours. After the Hungarian regime returned, a new Union of Subcarpathian Artists (Soiuz Podkarpatskŷkh Khudozhnykiv) was formed, which held its initial show in 1940 and founded a permanent exhibition in 1942.[120]

It should be emphasized that the Subcarpathian Barbizon painters were not interested in national problems per se, but rather were concerned with the problems of artistic creation—art for art's sake. However, as one critic pointed out, Bokshai and Erdeli had ceased their travels to the art centers of western Europe by the end of the 1920s, because, like Paul Gauguin, they had found their isle of Tahiti, their primitive inspirational source, right at home in Subcarpathian Rus'.[121] The result was a prolific school of Subcarpathian artists whose styles may have been influenced by the West, but whose subject matter was almost exclusively drawn from the region. While the Rusyn sculptor Olena Mondych (b. 1902) created a series of busts and statues of national leaders (Dukhnovych, E. Fentsik, A. Dobrianskii, A. Mitrak), which still decorate many public places,[122] no Subcarpathian painter felt the urge to create the kind of vast canvases based on historical themes that were so typical among romantic painters of the nineteenth century. Nevertheless, the landscapes of Bokshai, the portraits of Erdeli, and the moving expressionist depictions of the hard life of Rusyn villagers in the paintings of Manailo and Kontratovych did much to foster a clear sense of Subcarpathian identity that viewers from both within and beyond the province could easily recognize.

Between 1919 and 1945 the Subcarpathian intelligentsia tried through various cultural media to instill a national consciousness in the population. In literature, drama, cultural organizations, theater, even indirectly art, each of the three national orientations was represented, and although at times one trend may have been dominant—such as the Ukrainian in literature—at the end of the period in question, the Russophile, Ukrainophile, Rusynophile, and by force of circumstance the Magyarone currents all seemed to be as well entrenched as ever.

8 | *Educational Developments*

The educational system is one of the most crucial factors in creating a national consciousness. The continued success of national movements depends largely on the degree to which they can attract young people, so that a proper "nationalist" education in the classroom is of utmost significance. The degree of national consciousness within a given population is directly proportional to its level of literacy.

Children are not born with any inherent notion, or love, of their supposed nationality, and until eight or nine they do not know what the homeland is. Some parents may instill national awareness in their offspring at an early age, but often the school system carries out this task.[1] Politicians and educators in both Europe and America have long been aware of the importance of education, and a nineteenth-century U. S. Senator once concluded: "So the American school must be the great nourisher of the nation! The school for the nation! All education for the nation! Everything for the nation!"[2]

From the beginning, the Subcarpathian intelligentsia also realized the significance of education. We have seen how, in the second half of the nineteenth century, the first great national leader, A. Dukhnovych, devoted most of his life to writing primers, grammars, and other pedagogical works. Similarly, A. Markush was to argue in the 1920s that "The future of our land and our people lies in the state of our culture, which in turn is dependent upon our schools . . . Our future is in our schools."[3] Of course, the successful inculcation of a national ideology in young students presumes that those who control the educational system have a clear idea of what those ideals should be. In Subcarpathian Rus' between 1919 and 1945 this was not the case, and as we shall see neither the Czechoslovak or Hungarian governments, nor the various factions of the local intelligentsia, were ever willing or able to overcome the divisions that characterized Subcarpathian life.

The Establishment of the Czechoslovak Educational System

While the Czechoslovak regime has been criticized for its cultural, economic, religious, and political policies in Subcarpathian Rus', there is almost unanimous praise for its achievements in education.[4] The former Hungarian regime was not noted for its concern with the education of the country's rural population, least of all in those areas that contained national minorities. Thus, before 1918, illiteracy among the Rusyns was somewhere between 70 and 90 percent, and many villages, especially in eastern Máramaros county, did not contain one inhabitant who could read or write.[5]

Schools did exist in Subcarpathian Rus' under the Hungarian administration. In 1913-1914, there were 634 elementary schools, although the First World War lowered that number to 517. These figures, however, require some clarification. The number of children attending Subcarpathian elementary schools in 1913-1914 was estimated at 130,000. With 634 schools this would be an average of approximately 200 children per school. By far the majority of elementary schools contained only one classroom, and since there was a total of only 980 teachers, each instructor would have had up to 150 students. Such unfavorable pedagogical conditions were aggravated by the fact that, by 1914, Magyar was the exclusive language of instruction in all but 34 elementary schools. And even in those where some lessons were taught in the mother tongue, Magyar was still the main medium of instruction.[6]

The Czechoslovak regime was very concerned with rectifying the abominable state of education in the province. As Table 6 reveals, in 1920 there were 475 elementary schools, 321 of which were designated as "Rusyn."[7] Eighteen years later the number of elementary schools had risen to 803. Two important trends were in evidence at the lower educational levels: a steady decrease in the number of ecclesiastical schools and a rapid increase in Czech-language schools. For instance, in 1920 there were 249 elementary-church schools, and in 1938 there were only 84. On the other hand, although in 1920 there were but 22 Czech schools, by 1938 that number had increased to 188.[8] As a result of these trends, the influence of religion in the formation of young minds was tempered by civic and national concerns. The enormous increase in schools using the Czech language was particularly unpopular among local Rusyn leaders, because the number of schools provided for Czech children (primarily sons and daughters of the newly arrived bureaucracy in Subcarpathian Rus') far outweighed their percentage in the total population.[9]

Advances were also made in secondary education. In 1917-1918 there were three gymnasia, three teacher's colleges, and three technical schools— all with instruction only in Magyar. At the end of two decades the Czechoslovak school administration had increased these figures to eight gymnasia, five teacher's colleges, and five technical schools.

These figures only barely suggest the enormous financial, cultural, and psychological problems encountered and overcome by the Czechoslovak province. The lack of school buildings and the need to repair those damaged during the First World War required large sums of money. Thus, in the first decade the Prague government invested more than forty-one million crowns, which provided for repairs, extensions, and fifty-two new schools.[10] An even greater problem was the absence of teaching personnel. Many teachers who had served during the Hungarian administration were opposed to the new regime and 428 of them were released—a figure that represented almost half the teaching force in 1919.[11] And where were replacements to be found? The lack of trained local cadres compelled the school administration to call on external aid.

Coincidentally, the social and political upheavals of the post-War period throughout Europe provided a fund of educated Russian and Ukrainian emigrants and Czech legionnaires.[12] Within a decade the teaching force in Subcarpathian Rus' more than doubled—from about 1,000 in 1920 to 2,362 in 1931—while the number of teachers in Rusyn schools rose from 496 to 1,277, many of whom were either Russians from the former tsarist empire or Russophiles and Ukrainophiles from Galicia.[13] One source for the year 1922 listed 106 immigrant teachers, 79 of Ukrainian nationality and only 27 Russian.[14] These immigrants played an important role in the linguistic and cultural developments of the province; similarly, they were to have a great influence in the Subcarpathian classroom, where they could propagate national and social ideals they could not do in their homelands.

Of course, the existence of a physical plant does not automatically guarantee the presence of students, and one enormous difficulty encountered by the Czech regime was the resistance of the local population to education. Typical of peasant societies, the population in Subcarpathian Rus' was tradition-bound and apt to be wary of any change. If peasants were urged to send even one of their children to school, the response was given: "He's not going to be a notary or a priest, so why should he know how to read and write?" Furthermore, "Grandfather could not read nor write and he still went on living." The stubbornness of Rusyn parents, particularly in the rural areas, was not easily surmounted, yet in the course of a few years the school administration could claim a great psychological victory. While in 1919-1920 only 25-30 percent of the children attended school, by 1933 up to 90 percent did.[15] Looked at in another way, there were 80,630 Rusyn students enrolled in schools in 1931, a figure that represented 20 percent of the total Rusyn population of the province.[16]

The school administration was also concerned with the uneducated adult segment of the population, and special courses for illiterates were established. Between 1919 and 1930, 1,473 courses were organized, with

64,700 participants.[17] Nineteen local reading rooms and 291 libraries, similar in format to those of the Prosvita and Dukhnovych societies, were also established.[18] Finally, the school administration sponsored a series of publications, including the children's journal *Vînochok* (1919-1924), *Uchytel'* (1920-1936), and *Uriadovŷi vîstnyk* (1921-1938), which included articles on pedagogy and reports concerning official educational policy.[19] Associated with the school administration was the Pedagogical Society (Pedagogychne Tovarystvo), which published the children's journal *Nash rodnŷi krai* (1923-1938) and the more scholarly *Podkarpatska Rus'* (1923-1936), which was designed to provide information dealing with all aspects of the homeland—in short, "to serve primarily instructors as an aid to teaching."[20] The Pedagogical Society also issued a series of forty-five textbooks for use in Subcarpathian schools, which, in the words of A. Voloshyn, were "written in the simple, national, literary language," that is a dialectal variation of Ukrainian in the traditional orthography.[21]

The Role of the Teacher in the Development of a National Consciousness

Leaders in Subcarpathian Rus' were quick to recognize the relationship between nationalism and the school system. In the words of one comtemporary commentator: "One of the most important tasks of education in elementary schools is the development of the national spirit . . . The school must give to the children and future citizens the feeling of nationality so that they know what they are and who they are. The future of our people depends on our national, that is on our educational upbringing."[22]

The role of the local teacher, then, was to be crucial. If he was a Russophile, then the students would study literary Russian and learn to idealize Pushkin, Turgenev, and Tolstoy; if a Ukrainophile, then Taras Shevchenko, the "melodious" Ukrainian language, and tales of Bohdan Khmel'nyts'kyi and the Zaporozhian Cossacks would be venerated; if a Rusynophile, as there were many who were educated and who taught in Hungarian schools before the First World War, then Magyar cultural and political heroes would be replaced by local historical figures and instruction given in a personal variant of what was claimed to be the "Carpatho-Rusyn language." Finally, for those Rusyn children who might have been enrolled in one of the many Czech language schools, national identity would be emphasized in terms of Czechoslovak citizenship, and in some cases a Czech national consciousness might result.

The influence of the teacher was, of course, largely dependent on how he was viewed in the village. In fact, respect for teachers was very great among the peasantry. Of all the so-called influential village *panove* (priests, notaries, shopkeepers), the teacher was the one most trusted by the people. "During the revolution [1918-1919] the teacher was the only *pan* in the village who did not have to flee, who was not maltreated, driven away, or beaten by the people, because the simple people considered him their own.''[23] Herein lies the reason for the domination of his influence not only in the schools, but also in reading rooms, theatrical circles, and other rural sociocultural activities.

The national orientation of the village teacher was in large part dependent upon the superintendent of schools in Uzhhorod (who was always of Czech nationality) and his subordinates, the fourteen district school inspectors. The first superintendent, Josef Pešek (1919-1924), favored Galician immigrants of Ukrainophile orientation, whereas his successor, Josef Šimek (1924-1929), was inclined to hire former Czech legionnaires. Add to these categories Russian immigrants and local Carpatho-Rusyn instructors and the reader may get some idea of the variety of influences to which children in Subcarpathian Rus' were exposed. Unfortunately, this combination was pedagogically unsound, as it was not uncommon for students to receive instruction in Russian, in some Carpatho-Rusyn dialect, and in Ukrainian. At the secondary level, students might be obliged to respond in Russian to one teacher, in Ukrainian to a second, and in some Rusyn dialect to a third.[24]

As we have seen, the Czech school superintendents had no choice but to rely largely on émigrés to fill teaching posts during the 1920s. Besides the departure of almost half the teaching force in 1919, those Hungarian-trained Rusyn teachers who did remain were poorly qualified to provide instruction in the mother tongue. For example, of the 976 elementary and municipal school teachers in 1920, only 43 had completed secondary school.[25] This situation changed somewhat during the 1930s when graduates of Subcarpathia's three teachers' institutes began to fill positions throughout the province. Between 1919 and 1932, 916 Rusyns received teaching certificates.[26] The national orientations of these teachers were determined by which institute they attended: if an alumnus of the Greek Catholic male or female institutes in Uzhhorod (headed by A. Voloshyn, Viktor Zheltvai, and Vasyl' Lar), then they were likely to be Ukrainophile; if they had attended the state institute in Mukachevo (headed by O. Khromiak), then they were usually partisans of the Russophile orientation. Based on the number of students in these institutes—346 in Uzhhorod (male and female) and 151 in Mukachevo (1931-32)—one would assume that in the future the Ukrainophile orientation was likely to be the dominant one among teachers (and hence students) in Subcarpathian Rus'.[27] An analysis of the various teacher and student organizations supports this premise.

The first organization that temporarily united the teaching force was the Teacher's Society of Subcarpathian Rus' (Uchitel'ske Tovarishchestvo Podkarpatskoi Rusy), established in 1920 under the leadership of Vasilii Shpenik. Although the Teacher's Society planned to provide a broad program of cultural and social aid to students and to its own members, in practice it ''spent much time and money on conferences, at which much was said but little done."[28] Debate at these conferences centered on the question of language, and the lack of any clear orientation was indicative of the broad range of opinion that existed among Subcarpathian teachers. In later years, however, the organization and its journal, *Narodna shkola* (1921-1938), became a platform for the Russophile orientation.[29]

Adherents of the populist-Ukrainophile orientation were first concentrated in the Pedagogical Society (Pedagogychne Tovarystvo), founded by a hundred delegates in 1924.[30] As an affiliate of the Uzhhorod school administration, the Pedagogical Society avoided active participation in the language and national controversies. "To care for our youth, to care about its education—this is the most important aim of our society."[31] Such a goal was carried out by the publication of textbooks for use in Subcarpathian schools. Later, under the leadership of Ukrainophiles like A. Voloshyn, A. Shtefan and Iu. Revai, the trend towards the populist-Ukrainophile orientation was inevitable, and at its 1928 congress the society "accepted the scientific principle that Subcarpathian Rusyns are a Little Russian [Ukrainian] people."[32]

A critical turning point in the fortunes of the populist-Ukrainophile movement was the 1929 congress of the Teacher's Society. Having failed to reach agreement on the language question, a few Ukrainophile teachers broke away and founded a new organization, the Populist Teacher's Society (Narodovets'ke Uchytel's'ke Tovarystvo). Led by Avhustyn Shtefan and Aleksander Polians'kyi, the new association was uncompromising on the language and national issues. "The people themselves speak their own language, Ukrainian, and so the language question is solved."[33] The new society was especially opposed to the use of textbooks in any language other than Ukrainian in Subcarpathian schools "because our people are Ukrainian, its children Ukrainian."[34] The rapid increase in membership of the Populist Teacher's Society, later renamed the Teacher's Assembly (Uchytel's'ka Hromada), was indicative of the Ukrainian movement's growing strength during the 1930s. While only a few years previous the Russophile Teacher's Society had contained the majority of teachers, by 1934 the Teacher's Assembly claimed 1,211 of the 1,874 "Rusyn" teachers throughout Subcarpathian Rus'.[35] Moreover, the assembly professed a clear-cut program of Ukrainianization, while the rival Teacher's Society continued to call for the use of an undefined language "that conforms to our tradition and our past."[36]

The Ukrainophile-Russophile dichotomy was also evident in student life. Most Subcarpathian students attended university in Prague or Bratislava, and it was in Prague in 1920 that the first student organization, the Renaissance Association (Vozrozhdenie), was founded. Only temporarily, however, could the Renaissance unite all Rusyn students, and in 1922 a populist-Ukrainophile group set up the rival Circle for Aid to Subcarpathian Students (Kruzhok Sotsial'noï Pomoshchy Pidkarpatskykh Studentiv), later renamed the Union of Subcarpathian Students (Soiuz Pidkarpatskykh Rus'kykh Studentiv).[37]

The Renaissance Association founded a chorus and a balalaika orchestra, and later published in Prague the monthly *Molodaia Rus'* (1930-1931) and two literary collections, *Al'manakh Vozrozhdentsev* (1933 and 1936), which clearly defined the association's Russophile orientation.[38] In 1927, an attempt was made to unite both groups in a Central Union of Carpatho-Russian Students (Tsentral'nyi Soiuz Karpatorusskykh Studentiv), but disputes over the national issue caused the secession of the Ukrainophile Soiuz. Other associations of Subcarpathian students, which were set up in Mukachevo (1929), Chynadieve (1930), Prague (1931), Bratislava, Khust, Svaliava, and Prešov (1933), also failed to unite the opposing factions and were either Russophile or Ukrainophile in orientation.[39]

Developments during the 1930s revealed some basic differences in attitudes between the rival factions. In general, Russophile students were primarily occupied with cultural and pedagogical activities not directly related to contemporary problems. Typical was the Self-Education Circle (Samoobrazovatel'nyi Kruzhok), formed at the Mukachevo gymnasium in 1932 to propagate classical and Soviet Russian literature.[40] Russophile students also provided most of the membership of the Circle for the Study of Subcarpathian Rus' (Kruzhok po istorii Podkarpatskoi Rusi), founded in September 1931 at the initiative of the rector of the Russian National University in Prague. Headed by the Russian émigré scholars Iul'ian A. Iavorskii, Ivan Panas, M.M. Novikov, and Vsevolod V. Sakhanov, this circle sponsored a series of public lectures in Prague, a seminar at the Russian University, and a lecture tour in Subcarpathian Rus', all dealing with various aspects of Rusyn culture.[41] It is interesting to note that the Ukrainian émigré community in Prague did not sponsor similar scholarly projects on the Subcarpathian region.

On the other hand, Ukrainophile students from Subcarpathian Rus', imbued with national conviction, became social and political activists. Simultaneous with the founding in 1929 of the Populist Teacher's Society, there was organized in Uzhhorod the first Congress of Populist Youth (Z'ïzd Narodovets'koï Molodi), which identified itself and the people of Subcarpathian Rus' as Ukrainian. At the Second Congress (1934), held in Mukachevo in honour of the medieval national hero Fedor Koriatovych, more than 9,650 students from eighty-four villages participated. By the late 1930s, then, the Ukrainophile student movement was the more active and certainly the more vociferous of the two factions. In fact, it was "this nationally conscious Ukrainian youth [which] served later as the most important cadre in the formation of the Carpathian Sich," the military force that was to engage in battle with the Czechoslovak and Hungarian armies in an effort to gain independence for the province of Carpatho-Ukraine in late 1938 and early 1939.[42]

The success of the Ukrainian movement was due in large part to the energetic leadership of confident and uncompromising leaders like Stepan Rosokha (b. 1908), a Subcarpathian student and the co-editor of the Prague journal *Proboiem* (1933-1944). The radically nationalist, and in some cases demagogic, nature of the Ukrainophile student movement was indicated by the tenor of many articles that appeared during the late 1930s. Opposed to the government's indecisive nationality policy in the province, Rosokha declared that "the nationality and language of Subcarpathia is Ukrainian . . . Likewise we are, were, and will remain Ukrainian."[43] Another young nationalist expressed his frustration with the attitude that "the struggle between the nationalities can be solved 'reasonably, democratically, [and] justly.' "[44] This same author concluded that soon the Ukrainophile orientation would have to dominate, even if force had to be used. In fact, suggestions of this sort reflected the atmosphere of increased national tension that caused not only ideological but also physical clashes between the opposing factions.[45]

The extremist position of some Subcarpathian student nationalists was graphically illustrated by their reaction to the movement led by Ivan V. Andrashko. Raised a Dukhnovych Boy Scout and later a member of the Russophile Renaissance Association, Andrashko set up a study circle in Prague in the early 1930s and soon after published a journal, *Zhivaia mysl'* (1932-1936). Basically, Andrashko regretted that "our one Carpatho-Russian people" was divided into "two enemy camps,"[46] and instead of prolonging this destructive tendency, he argued for the equal propagation of the "Russian and Ukrainian cultures [that] are both native, dear, and valuable to us."[47] Although he preferred to use the term Rusyn, he did not argue for the existence of a separate nationality.[48] For his efforts at bringing Subcarpathian Ukrainophiles and Russophiles together, he was praised by some (the traditionalist E. Sabov, and the Czech critic A. Hartl), but for the most part attacked from both sides. A trial for his removal from the Russophile Renaissance Association on charges of national treason seemed to epitomize the intense degree of friction that existed in student circles.[49]

The educational, cultural, and political circumstances in Subcarpathian Rus' created a situation where it was not uncommon to find many families that included a "Russian" child, a "Ukrainian" child, and a "Rusyn" child. The antagonisms of the nationalist intelligentsia were carried on by young people, and, without political change, it is likely that these controversies would have continued for generations to come.

The Educational Policy of the Autonomous Government and the Hungarian Regime

Indeed, political changes were forthcoming, but the regimes that governed Subcarpathian Rus' between late 1938 and 1944 were not in power long enough to make any significant alteration in the mentality of the young people who passed through the school system. The first of these was the autonomous government of A. Voloshyn, which ruled from late October 1938 to mid-March 1939. Although the projected Diet (Soim) was to be given the final say regarding the language to be taught in schools, it was soon clear that in educational and cultural matters the new administration was distinctly Ukrainian. While Voloshyn was theoretically responsible for education and culture, he actually delegated these affairs to Avhustyn Shtefan, the ardent Ukrainophile who had headed the Commercial Academy in Mukachevo. Having lost the chief cities of Uzhhorod, Mukachevo, and Berehovo in November 1938, the various gymnasia, professional schools, and teacher's colleges were relocated in small towns in the north and east of the truncated province of Carpatho-Ukraine. Ukrainophiles clearly dominated the school administration, and by a decree passed on November 25, all teachers, directors and inspectors were required to use the Ukrainian language. The closing of most Czech schools, begun the previous month, was completed, and plans were made to transfer the Ukrainian Free University from Prague to the provincial capital of Khust.[50]

The work of the Ukrainophile administration in Khust was brought to an untimely end after the Hungarian occupation of the whole region in March 1939. With regard to education, the Hungarian government set for itself one task: to transform the Ukrainophile-dominated school administration into a bulwark of pro-Hungarian Uhro-Rusyn nationalism. The young Greek Catholic priest Julius Marina was appointed head of the Department of Religion and Culture in Uzhhorod, and other Rusynophile or Magyarone individuals (usually Greek Catholic priests) were appointed as directors of the various schools. The first step was to release all teachers who served during the Voloshyn regime and require the newly employed to be competent in the Magyar language. The latter proviso was particularly important since five out of seven gymnasia, and sixteen of eighteen municipal schools, were required to give instruction in Magyar. Plans were also made as early as 1939 to introduce the Magyar language into the kindergartens.[51] For the time being, most of the elementary schools were allowed to employ the Rusyn language as defined in the Haraida grammar and supplementary texts. Eventually, however, 320 of the 430 elementary schools gave instruction in Magyar.[52]

The change in administration had a drastic effect on the educational system, as indicated by the sharp decline in the number of students. For instance, before the return of the Hungarians, there were 1,500 students in the Mukachevo gymnasium, while in 1939-40 there were only 785. The total number of Rusyn students in all gymnasia also declined from 2,407 in 1939-40 to 1,743 in 1941-42. Yet despite these decreases, the Hungarian Ministry of Interior still felt that there were "too many Rusyn students in the gymnasia and municipal schools."[53] At the university level, there were about 600 Rusyn students, although most of them continued their studies in now German-controlled Prague. The Hungarian regime allotted 150 places for Rusyns at Debrecen and Budapest Universities, although by 1940-41 only 72 were in attendance.[54] As for student organizations, the various Ukrainophile and Russophile groups were disbanded and were replaced by the Levente Society for students between the ages of 12 and 23. Actually, this organization was run by the Hungarian military and filled with informers who supplied the government with details about the widespread pro-Ukrainian and pro-Soviet sentiment that existed among the youth of the province.[55] Among teachers, the Ukrainophile Teacher's Assembly (Hromada) and the Czechoslovak-sponsored Pedagogical Society were outlawed, and only the Russophile-Rusynophile Teacher's Society (Uchitel'ske Tovarishchestvo) was permitted. This society continued publishing its monthly *Narodna shkola* (1939-1944), which argued in vain for the introduction of complete cultural autonomy for Rusyns.[56]

Under such conditions, it is not surprising that the Hungarian regime did not succeed in creating a generation of conscious Subcarpathian Uhro-Rusyns. First of all, five years is too short a time to achieve such a transformation. Secondly, local Russophiles were still left at their posts and they frequently voiced their anti-Rusynophile opinions both within and beyond the classroom. (See pp. 143-144.) The prevalence of Russian-language literature written by gymnasium and university students trained during the Czechoslovak regime further attested to the continuing strength of the Russophile orientation. Finally, Uhro-Rusynism came to take on an odious flavor, since for some local Hungarian officials it was still considered the first step to assimilation with the Magyar nationality, while for many young people it was an ideology being propagated by a regime that was engaged in a war for its own survival and not adverse to police surveillance and brutality in order to maintain conformity and at least outward loyalty on the home front. Hence, Uhro-Rusyn patriotism came to be closely associated with collaboration.

Between the years 1919 and 1944 there was never a single nationality policy established and implemented over a long term by the educational administrations of the governments that ruled Subcarpathian Rus'. The Czechoslovak government allowed the Russophile, Ukrainophile, and Rusynophile orientations to be propagated; the brief autonomous regime permitted only the Ukrainophile; while the Hungarians favored a Rusynophile and tolerated a Russophile trend. The result was as one might expect. In the absence of any consistent educational policy concerning national orientation, there developed three generations of conscious and sometimes intolerant Subcarpathian Russians, Ukrainians, and Rusyns, with a few Czechoslovaks and Hungarians thrown in for good measure. Subcarpathian society had to wait until 1945, this time under a Soviet regime, before any clearly defined nationality policy would be introduced in the schools.

9 | *The Religious Factor*

The local Greek Catholic Church was for many centuries the carrier of Rusyn nationalism, and most of the national leaders during late eighteenth and nineteenth centuries were priests. On the other hand, this same church also produced figures, especially among the hierarchy, who were in the forefront of the movement for assimilation with Magyar culture. The Orthodox revival in Subcarpathian Rus' at the beginning of the twentieth century was in part a reaction to these assimilationist tendencies within the Greek Catholic Church.

In the years after 1918, religion was still an important factor in the lives of Subcarpathian Rusyns. However, it no longer had unlimited and unchallenged sway over the minds of the people. State-sponsored schools and a young, secular intelligentsia provided national and social ideologies that sometimes complemented but often rivaled the goals of organized religion. This chapter will review the positions of the Subcarpathian Greek Catholic and Orthodox churches regarding the complicated nationality issue.

The Orthodox Movement

The early years of the Czechoslovak regime were marked by the phenomenally rapid growth of the Orthodox church. Times were changing, and Subcarpathian villagers surmised that if the Hungarian gendarme and landlord had been driven away successfully, so too should another "exploiter," the Greek Catholic priest, be made to leave. Whereas before the war, Hungarian officialdom had clamped down hard on the conversion-to-Orthodoxy movement, the Czechoslovak regime either kept its hands off, and, in a "democratic" manner, allowed the question of religious affiliation to be decided by the people, or in some instances encouraged the Orthodox movement, which was viewed as a counterbalance to the many Magyarone Greek Catholic priests. Prague's policy was also prompted by the general anti-Catholic attitude held by many leading figures in the Czechoslovak republic, beginning with President Masaryk, and expressed poignantly in the popular slogan of the time: "Away from Rome."[1]

178

In the words of one polemicist, Orthodoxy was attractive because "the Carpatho-Russian people were able . . . to find in it a solution to their socioeconomic and national aspirations.[2] Traditional sources of displeasure were the so-called *koblina* and *rokovina*, feudal duties the peasants owed to the local Greek Catholic clergy. The *koblina* was payable in agricultural produce or money, while the *rokovina* demanded physical labor. Whenever the Orthodox took over a parish, these duties, at least in the initial months, were canceled. Thus, for the Rusyn peasant, acceptance of Orthodoxy meant simply that "it is not necessary to pay."[3] Orthodox propagandists were quick to capitalize on this social issue: "Converting to Orthodoxy, the community got the chance to rid from its midst the exploiting, parasitical Uniate priest."[4]

Russian émigrés and some local Russophiles then proceeded to present Orthodoxy as the essence of Russianness, which in turn was hailed as the indissoluble spiritual bond that linked Subcarpathians with their brethren to the East. In a pamphlet addressed to the "Russian people in Slovakia," Senator Iurko Lazho wrote:

During the War, the Muscovites were here. The Magyars told us that they were a terrible race, who cut up people, who did not believe in God, and other such stupidities. These Muscovites came here, but did not eat anyone nor cut up anyone, and their priests served in the church like ours and even better, because they preserved the Russian rite in its purest [form] without any varied or Roman [Catholic] admixtures. [Our] people saw that the Muscovites were the same Russian nation as us.[5]

Inevitably, the socioeconomic and national issues were joined. After the Bolshevik Revolution, news filtered into Hungary via returning soldiers that in Russia the peasants were beginning to take the land from their former oppressors. As a consequence, the call—"We want the same as in Russia"—signified a feeling of social as well as national affiliation with the East.[6]

It was during the early 1920s that the growth of Orthodoxy was most rapid in Subcarpathian Rus'. In 1910 there were only 577 Orthodox adherents among Rusyns, but that number increased rapidly to 60,986 in 1921 and 112,034 in 1930.[7] The conversion of a local village and the subsequent transfer of church property were hardly ever achieved by peaceful means. The result was a spread of anarchic conditions and a situation that, at the time, was compared to a religious war. A typical case went something like this:

The agitation usually began in the tavern, where the agitator met with the loudest brawlers of the village. After a short conversation, encouraged by noisy arguments and vodka, a villager began to cry out against his parish priest. In two or three days a "committee" was organized by the "adversaries" of the priest. This committee did not at once convert to Orthodoxy, but showered the bishop with complaints and deputations against the parish priest, demanding an investigation against him or his direct removal. Then came various malevolences, demonstrations, threats against the priest, terrorization of the church curators, etc. From the committee letters came to the parish priest in which he was ordered to leave the village. The committee each time demanded more resolutely that the priest get out, because "otherwise it will be bad!" Meanwhile, members of the committee convinced the peasants that it is not necessary to pay the priests *koblina,* nor perform *rokovina* [duties], and promised to divide the church land among the people. Thus, the parish priest was left without help or necessary income.

When in such circumstances a priest still remained at his post, the threats intensified: his windows were broken or shot up, [his] well poisoned, grain or stable and in some cases even the parish residence set afire, the priest himself assaulted and beaten, etc. In the face of this, the government remained indifferent, saying: "Freedom of conscience! Freedom of religion!"[8]

The preceding account was confirmed by many newspaper articles and police reports which were filled with descriptions of attacks against Greek Catholic priests and the forcible occupation of church property.[9]

The Czechoslovak government was blamed by Greek Catholics for its support of Orthodoxy and general anti-Catholic policies, and was accused by Orthodox sympathizers of "police repression" and interference in jurisdictional matters.[10] Indeed, there were many anti-Catholic officials in Prague as well as in Subcarpathian Rus' who welcomed the spread of Orthodoxy. They were aware that a large percentage of the Greek Catholic priests were still Magyarone in sentiment, and so they praised the "Slavic," anti-Magyar, and "democratic character of the Orthodox priests."[11] The Vice-governor of Subcarpathian Rus', Antonín Rozsypal, declared that the local administration "should not oppose the spontaneous change of Greek Catholics to the Orthodox faith."[12] Prague soon became concerned, however, with the continued pattern of lawless anarchy and disorganized character of the Orthodox movement. As a result, many members of the Czechoslovak government began to be receptive to claims that Orthodoxy in Subcarpathian Rus' was associated with Bolshevism, anarchism, or even Russian monarchical irredentism.[13]

Subsequent government policy was decisively influenced by opinions expressed in the reports of local officials. Typical was the following report from eastern Slovakia:

The slogan for the whole movement is: "Away with Rome, since our mother is Russian, our land Russian, our faith Russian-Orthodox." Its behavior is irresponsible and terroristic . . . It is clear to everyone who knows the local conditions that soon will come the inevitable time when Orthodoxy will mean [an attempt] for unification with Russia, it will be a source of Russian irredentism. As for the internal political importance of Orthodoxy and its agressive methods: occupation of property, attacks against the opposition, disregard for public authorities, use of the masses, etc.—[these] are the practical methods of Bolshevism.

The report concluded: "Disregard of legal norms by the Orthodox Church means . . . anarchy, which today can still be resisted by an increase in the number of gendarmes, but the future spread of Orthodoxy can only be kept in line by using the Army."[14] Obviously, it was in the best interest of the government to halt the disorder and violence associated with the spread of Orthodoxy and to establish social order in its eastern province.

In principle, the Prague government was obliged to leave internal religious matters to the jurisdiction of a proposed local Diet (Soim), but until such a body was formed, it was necessary to put an end to the Greek Catholic-Orthodox "religious war."[15] Toward this end, the provincial administration in Uzhhorod officially liquidated on May 7, 1920, the *koblina* and *rokovina* duties, even though some priests, for lack of other income, still requested payment.[16] The government also desired a responsible organizational basis for the Orthodox movement: the first attempts were made during the summer of 1921 at the first Orthodox congress, which created a temporary Carpatho-Russian Eastern Orthodox Church.

The following decade witnessed a struggle among Orthodox parishioners in Subcarpathian Rus', in particular between some who recognized the superiority of the Serbian patriarch in Belgrade, and others the patriarch in Istanbul. Prague, however, only recognized the Serbian jurisdiction, which was given sole authority over the Orthodox Mukachevo-Prešov eparchy, created in 1931.[17] The disputes over jurisdictions, combined with the removal of feudal duties and renewed activity of the Greek Catholic Church, caused a decline in the expansion of the Orthodox movement. The period of "religious war" was over, and many Orthodox parishes returned to the fold of the Greek Catholic Church.[18]

As an organized body, the Orthodox Church in Subcarpathian Rus' was headed by a bishop who resided in Mukachevo, while missionary activity was entrusted to five monasteries. The monastery at Ladomirová (eastern Slovakia) was responsible for publishing and issued the annual *Pravoslavnyi russkii kalendar'* (1925-1941), the bi-weekly newspaper *Pravoslavnaia Rus'* (1928-1943)—with a children's supplement, *Dietstvo vo Khristie*—and the official journal of the diocese, *Pravoslavnyi karpatorusskii viestnik* (1935-1938). These publications tried to use the literary Russian language, and their content was filled with praise for Orthodoxy and the Russian (*obshcherusskii*) orientation as the only valid religious and national choices for the population of Subcarpathian Rus'.[19]

The Greek Catholic Church

Despite the rapid growth of the Orthodox movement, the Greek Catholic Church still continued to be the dominant religious force among Subcarpathian Rusyns. The 1930 census listed 359,166 Greek Catholics in the province, the majority of Rusyn nationality.[20] But if the Orthodox movement was primarily Russian in orientation, the Greek Catholic Church contained partisans of all national orientations. For example, Russophile leaders such as Evmenii Sabov, Stepan Fentsik, and Iulii Gadzhega; the Ukrainophiles such as Avhustyn Voloshyn, Viktor Zheltvai (1890-1974), and Sevastiian Sabol; and proponents of a separate Rusyn nationality such as Aleksander Il'nyts'kyi, governor Konstantyn Hrabar, and Emyliian Bokshai, were all Greek Catholic priests. Nonetheless, this Slavic character was only one aspect of Greek Catholicism. Trained in Hungarian schools and products of pre-1918 Hungarian society, the Greek Catholic clergy remained largely Magyarone in outlook during most of the Czechoslovak regime.

Magyarones filled the upper echelons of the Greek Catholic hierarchy. Characteristic were the bishops of the Prešov and Mukachevo dioceses, István Novak (1879-1932) and Antal Papp (1867-1945), who, like many other former Hungarian officials, refused to swear the oath of allegiance to the new Czechoslovak republic. Since becoming bishop of the Prešov diocese in 1914, Novak had avidly supported the government policy of Magyarization, and in protest against the new Czechoslovak administration he left his diocese in October 1918 to settle in Budapest. Bishop Papp remained for a few more years in Uzhhorod and did swear the Czechoslovak oath in 1923, but he was under constant suspicion for his pro-Magyar sympathies and the following year he, too, left for Hungary.[21]

The presence of these Magyarones, the cancellation of the *koblina* and *rokovina*, and the uncontrolled spread of Orthodoxy made initial relations between the Greek Catholic Church and the Czechoslovak government extremely difficult. Only gradually were tensions removed. Of course, it was in the interest of the Greek Catholic hierarchy to support the government, which alone had the power to end the requisition of church property by Orthodox converts.[22] A first step was taken in September 1921, when a delegation of Greek Catholic priests declared allegiance to the Czechoslovak regime. Finally, after various requests by the church, a law was passed in June 1926, which assured each priest an annual income of 9,000 crowns, compensation for religious instruction in state schools, and a guaranteed government pension. At the same time, the church gave up its right to demand payment of the *koblina* and *rokovina*. As a result of this act, the basic causes for misunderstanding between the Greek Catholic clergy and the government were eliminated.[23]

In 1924, Petro Gebei was appointed bishop of the Mukachevo diocese and for the next seven years the Slavic character of the Greek Catholic Church was reinforced. Gebei ordered that all internal church correspondence and sermons be conducted in the national language. He also promoted the diffusion of bibles, prayer books, and other publications in a language that would be understandable to the people; among these were *Blahovîstnyk* (1921-1942)—a monthly "spiritual journal for Subcarpathian Rusyns," and *Dushpastŷr'* (1921-1941)—the official organ of the Mukachevo and Prešov dioceses. Both these publications as well as the prosletyzing *Myssiinŷi vîstnyk* (1931-1938) were edited by Aleksander Il'nyts'kyi and written in a dialectally based language in traditional orthography.[24] Parish priests were called on to reject not only the Magyar but also the Russian (*obshcherusskii*) language and were urged "as true populists to follow the path of the populist orientation, the path of scientific truth."[25]

In opposition to the Russian-oriented Orthodox Church, some observers began to identify the Greek Catholic Church as Ukrainian in national orientation.[26] This dichotomy was certainly valid for Galicia, where since the late nineteenth century, the Greek Catholic Church had been an active propagator of Ukrainianism while the Orthodox Church had defended Russophilism. But in Subcarpathian Rus', these divisions were not so easily distinguishable. Indeed, some prelates, like A. Voloshyn, emphasized the Greek Catholic relationship to the populist-Ukrainian cultural movement: "When we, with deep love, turn to our Little Russian [Ukrainian] nationality and mother tongue . . . [this] only means a natural order to love (*ordinem charitatis*) . . . [and] devotion to our Greek Catholic culture."[27] Moreover, the activity of the Redemptist and Basilian monastic orders was to have a significant influence on the development of Ukrainianism in the region.[28]

Although in 1917 Subcarpathian Basilians adopted an invitation to carry out monastic reform on the model of the Magyar Jesuits, the revolutionary events of the following years made this impossible. When the issue was finally resolved in late 1920, it was decided to have the reform led instead by Basilians from Galicia, the majority of whom were conscious Ukrainians.[29] Initially, the Galicians were accused of "Ukrainian chauvinism" and "separatist politics" by the Magyarone Bishop Papp, of "Ukrainian irredentist" and "anti-Czech tendencies" by the Czechoslovak authorities, and of anti-Russian propaganda by local Russophiles, but after Bishop Gebei was installed they were left alone to carry out their work.[30]

Besides the internal reform of the order, the Basilian fathers, led by monks from Galicia, helped to spread the Ukrainian cultural orientation through publications and missionary and educational activities. Between 1925 and 1935, the order's own printing plant in Uzhhorod issued upwards of 375,000 religious pamphlets, almanacs, prayer books, and other works.[31] The Basilians also had an effective educational system that included a school at the St. Nicholas Monastery in Malyi-Bereznyi, founded in 1926, and a gymnasium for future seminarians and laity in Uzhhorod, opened in 1937. These institutions were led by the Galicians Stephen Reshetylo, Hlib

Kinakh, Polykarp Bulyk, and Iosyp Martynets', whose teachings fostered a new generation of Subcarpathian Ukrainophile clergy, among whom were the poet Sevastiian Sabol-Zoreslav and the future émigré historians Athanasius Pekar (b. 1922) and Alexander Baran (b. 1926).[32]

Notwithstanding these developments, one would be hard pressed to describe the Greek Catholic Church as a center of Ukrainianism. To be sure, many Magyarone priests had, by force of the changed political circumstances, recognized the value of the Subcarpathian Rusyn national culture. Yet even if most of the Greek Catholic priests eventually accepted the populist cultural movement, they did not identify themselves in name or in spirit as Ukrainian. Gebei considered himself, and was described by others as a good Rusyn (*chystyi Rusyn*), that is, one who stressed his individual national character even though he participated in Russophile and Ukrainophile cultural endeavors. In none of Gebei's addresses, nor in any of the Greek Catholic Church's publications, were the people of Subcarpathian Rus' referred to as other than Rusyn.

The local parish priest was urged to drop his aristocratic Magyarone pretentions and "become the leading patriot of his people . . . The priest of the Rusyn people must be a Rusyn patriot."[33] Whereas Rusyn patriotism and populist-Ukrainianism were indistinguishable during the 1920s, this situation changed in the next decade. The populist interest in raising the cultural level of the local Rusyn population was transformed into a Ukrainian nationalism that was not concerned with Subcarpathian Rus' and its people as an end in itself but only as one part of a larger and more important whole —the Ukrainian nation beyond the Carpathians.[34] Most Greek Catholic priests, and especially the church's hierarchy, never went this far, and in response they attempted to formulate more clearly a Rusyn national ideology. Such a trend was particularly evident after 1932 when Aleksander Stoika (1890-1941, consecrated 1933) succeeded Gebei as bishop.

Bishop Stoika favored the Rusynophile national explanation for Subcarpathian Rus', and his views met with favor among Prague officials who welcomed any opportunity to neutralize the Russian and Ukrainian movements. Since the 1920s Stoika had supported the Autonomist Agricultural Union (secretly financed by Hungary) and other organizations that had as their goals separate cultural and national autonomy for the Rusyns.[35] As part of his Rusynophile national policy, Bishop Stoika sponsored the publication of the newspaper *Nedîlia* (1935-1938). Edited by the Greek Catholic priest Emyliian Bokshai, *Nedîlia* was opposed to what it called Ukrainian irredentism and Russian pan-Slavism. "We do not need . . . Ukrainian political ideology . . . because we prefer to be a small fragment in a non-Rusyn [*neruska,* or Czechoslovak] state, than a nothing in your Ukrainian."[36] Moreover, "we do not have to depend on Slavophilism, nor on Russia, which did not save us when it had the chance."[37] Under the circumstances, Czechoslovakia was considered the only "safeguard of our national life," and "what happens in Russia, in Galicia, in America, or in Hungary should not be important for us."[38] The inhabitants of Subcarpathian Rus' should have been proud that they were Rusyns and aware that "historical, legal, and cultural conditions" had created out of them a distinct national entity.[39]

During the 1930s, then, certain leading elements within the Greek Catholic hierarchy supported the concept that the Subcarpathian Rusyns formed a separate Slavic nationality, whose culture was intimately associated with the Greek Catholic Church and whose political existence was dependent on the goodwill of the Czechoslovak Republic. Subsequently, the Church tried to organize a Rusynophile cultural organization, so as to offset the antagonism between the Russophile Dukhnovych Society and the Ukrainophile Prosvita Society. A Cultural Home for Greek Catholic Rusyns was opened in November 1935, and the following summer the first Greek Catholic Day was held in Velykyi Bychkiv. Local priests were requested to set up Greek Catholic reading rooms.[40] Nevertheless, these belated efforts did not succeed in providing an effective organizational basis for an independent Rusyn national movement.

The Churches during the Autonomous and Hungarian Regimes

During the few months of late 1938 and early 1939, when Subcarpathian Rus' received its long-awaited autonomy, the Greek Catholic Church was split between those who favored remaining within a federated Czechoslovakia and those who wished to return to Hungary. After November 2, the Ukrainophile government, headed by Monsignor A. Voloshyn, was deprived of the southern lowlands in Subcarpathian Rus', and as a result the Greek Catholic Diocese of Mukachevo was split in two. To administer the 280 parishes that remained in the rump territory of Carpatho-Ukraine, Rome appointed, on November 15, Bishop Dionysii Niaradii (1874-1940) as apostolic administrator in Khust.[41] The appointment of Niaradii, a known Ukrainophile, was a clear indication that the Vatican recognized the U-krainian orientation in the autonomous region. During his brief administration, Niaradii depended heavily on the Ukrainophile Basilian order: S. Reshetylo was appointed secretary to the bishop, S. Sabol became editor of the popular journal *Blahovistnyk,* and monks and nuns who were forced to leave Hungarian-occupied territory were given positions in the Ukrainophile-dominated school administration.[42]

The Orthodox bishop, with jurisdiction over 140 parishes and five monasteries, also eventually came out in support of the Voloshyn regime.[43] This does not mean, however, that the majority of the Orthodox population—indoctrinated by their love of all things Russian—accepted the Ukrainian ideology of the Khust government. During these months there was opposition from Orthodox communities, most especially from Iza, the Russophile center near Khust.[44]

While Greek Catholic Ukrainophiles were giving their support to the autonomous Carpatho-Ukraine, Bishop Stoika and the rest of the episcopal curia remained in Uzhhorod and came out in support of the Hungarian regime. We have seen how the young canon Julius Marina served as advisor to the local Hungarian commissar and to the Ministry of Education responsible for creating an Uhro-Rusyn language and a pro-Hungarian Rusyn national consciousness. Similarly, A. Il'nyts'kyi remained advisor to the commissar until 1944, was appointed to the Hungarian parliament in 1940, and elected chairman of the Subcarpathian Academy of Sciences in June 1942. He also revived the Greek Catholic Rusynophile newspaper *Karpatska nedîlia* and edited it from 1939 to 1941. Finally, another Greek Catholic priest, Irynei Kontratovych, was, with the layman Ivan Haraida, responsible for formulating a Rusyn national ideology, so that for all intents and purposes the returning Hugarian regime implemented the Rusynophile orientation almost exclusively through the local Greek Catholic clergy.[45]

Although the Hungarian government toyed with the idea of removing Bishop Stoika, they accepted him in the end. The bishop's appreciation was expressed in a radio speech made in March 1939, when the Hungarians re-united all of Subcarpathian Rus'. Stoika called upon his "Rusyn people" to pray for our Regent Horthy, "who with the warmest fatherly love opened his heart . . . and united all of us with Hungary, which for a thousand years was the homeland of our fathers and forefathers."[46] The official Rusyn nationality policy propagated by Hungary was in keeping with Stoika's own views, and he especially praised the publications of the Subcarpathian Academy "as religious, patriotic and scholarly in content, written by respected authors in the national tongue."[47] As for the Ukrainophile elements in the Greek Catholic Church, activists like A. Voloshyn and many of the Basilians were forced to flee. Those Basilian monks who were not natives of the region, for instance, were ordered to leave in 1939 and most settled in the Diocese of Prešov which was still under the control of the Slovak government.[48]

The situation for the Russophile Orthodox Church was much worse. The last Orthodox Bishop for Subcarpathian Rus', Vladimir Raich, was ordered to return to his native Yugoslavia in March 1939, and two years later he died in a Hungarian concentration camp. Left without a bishop, the Orthodox Church in Subcarpathian Rus' was accused of association with Communism and things Russian, and various forms of pressure were employed in an effort to have Orthodox Rusyns return to the Greek Catholic Church.[49]

The traditional dominance of the church in Subcarpathian culture had been decidedly challenged after 1918 when a new generation of lawyers, politicians, editors, writers and other laymen not directly dependent on the

Greek Catholic Church or the newly established Orthodox Church took over the direction of national life. Nonetheless, religion continued to be the psychological mainstay of the population, and all national manifestations, programs, and organizations were certain to include representatives of the Greek Catholic as well as Orthodox churches. Moreover, the churches themselves took an active part in national developments via participation in the political, educational, and cultural life of the province.

While the Orthodox Church became a stronghold for the Russophile orientation, the larger Greek Catholic Church included Russophile, U-krainophile, Rusynophile, and Magyarone supporters. In a sense, both churches would have preferred to avoid the nationality issue altogether, but certain adamant clergymen were determined to press their own national ideology through religious publications, speeches, and other activities. To be sure, the Greek Catholic Church had a strong faction of Ukrainophiles, concentrated especially in the Basilian order. Yet for the most part, the hierarchy and other leading members remained either Magyarone in sympathy, or, if Slavic in orientation, favored some degree of Subcarpathian Rusyn separateness. These two trends most successfully complemented each other during the years 1939 to 1944, when, under the Hungarian regime, Rusynism was allowed its last chance to survive as a national ideology. In a sense, the existence of a distinct Rusynophile orientation depended in large part on the support of the Greek Catholic Church, and the church's generally passive stance toward the potentially rival ideology of nationalism goes far in explaining the failure of the incipient Rusynophile movement.

Part Three | The Political Environment

10 | *The Political Consolidation of Subcarpathian Rus', 1919-1929*

The preceding five chapters have analyzed the means by which the intelligentsia tried to formulate and implement a national ideology for Subcarpathian Rusyns between the years 1919 and 1945. The following three chapters will view this same period from the standpoint of political development. Two aspects will be stressed: first, the attempts of Rusyn leaders to gain political autonomy for their homeland; and second, the impact of local, national, and international politics on the formulation and development of the various national ideologies.

The eventual goal of nationalist movements is political independence or, at least, autonomy. In fact, the doctrine of nationalism "holds that humanity is naturally divided into nations, that nations are known by certain characteristics, and that the only legitimate government is national self-government."[1] The Subcarpathian Rusyns both in 1849-1850 and in 1918-1919 strove for, and to a degree were successful in attaining, a degree of cultural and even political autonomy; this struggle was continued in the decades after 1919.

No society exists in isolation, least of all a national minority that lives in a political system dominated by another nationality. The strengths and weaknesses of the varying national orientations among Rusyns were to a significant degree influenced by local politics (the administrations in Subcarpathian Rus' and eastern Slovakia), by national politics (the Czechoslovak government in Prague), and by the international situation (the foreign policies of Hungary, Germany, Poland, and the Soviet Union). It is the interrelationship between politics and the various national orientations that is of concern here.

The First Administrations

The first decade of Czechoslovak rule in Subcarpathian Rus' was marked by frequent disagreement and misunderstanding between Rusyn political leaders and the Prague government. Nevertheless, the period ended as it began—with a generally optimistic attitude among Rusyns that the political,

191

economic, and sociocultural problems of their homeland could best be solved within the framework of the Czechoslovak republic. The prevailing attitude during these years was best summed up by A. Voloshyn: "In the interest of our people, I consider it necessary to cooperate with [our] Czech brothers, to cooperate with the government . . . With the help of the government we can achieve all our rights."[2]

After the dissolution of the Hungarian administered Rus'ka Kraina in April 1919, the western portion of Subcarpathian Rus' came under the control of Czech legionnaires, the remainder (east of Mukachevo) was occupied by the Rumanian army. Until the establishment of a representative government, as stipulated in the Treaty of St. Germain, the Czechoslovak-controlled area was administered by the local military commander, General Hennocque, who proclaimed on November 18, 1919, the *"Generální Statut* for the Organization and Administration of Subcarpathian Rus'." This statute defined the River Uzh as the temporary demarcation line between Slovakia and the so-called "Autonomous Russian Territory."[3] Moreover, until the convocation of a local Soim (Diet), the territory was given the "historical name Subcarpathian Rus' " (*Podkarpatskaia Rus'*) and the Rusyn *(rusinskii)* language was legalized for use in schools and other official activities. Finally, "in order to establish order in the territory," it was decided to appoint an administrator and a Directorate—the latter intended as an "advisory board for the legislation and administration" of the province.[4]

The Ministry of Interior in Prague appointed in August 1919 a Czech administrator, Dr. Jan Brejcha, and a five-member Directorate. The latter was headed by Gregory Zsatkovich, the American immigrant leader who favored the Czechoslovak solution, and eventually included the local leaders Iulii Brashchaiko, Avhustyn Voloshyn, Iulii Gadzhega, Emylii Torons'kyi, and Ievhen Puza (1880-1922).[5] From the very beginning Rusyn politicians were opposed to the Czechoslovak "military dictatorship," which was considered at variance with the provisions of the Treaty of Saint Germain. In particular, Rusyn plaints focused on demands for autonomy, which meant elections to a local Soim and appointment of a governor with responsible power. The border with Slovakia could not be recognized as final because the Saint Germain treaty referred to all "Russian Territory south of the Carpathians." Accordingly, "we demand the Lubovňa district in Szepes County and all of Sáros, Zemplén and Ung Counties, because in these areas the majority of inhabitants are Rusyn."[6] The autonomy and border questions were to plague Rusyn-Czechoslovak relations for two decades.

Indeed, it was in the interest of the republic to find dependable Rusyn leaders with whom cooperation would be possible. President Masaryk hoped to work with Zsatkovich. However, this young lawyer from Pittsburgh, who was used to the American milieu, clashed with Prague officials over the exact legal and political status of Subcarpathian Rus'. Dissatisfied with the local Czech administrator and with the limited advisory function of the Directorate, Zsatkovich resigned in February 1920. Prague's response was to abolish the position of administrator and to appoint Zsatkovich first governor of the province. He accepted the post and immediately initiated a policy designed to prepare for elections to a Soim before March 1921, to give Subcarpathian Rus' "autonomy in the widest sense of the word," and to expand the province's territory farther west.[7]

Governor Zsatkovich compared the relationship between Subcarpathian Rus' and the Czechoslovak republic to the political system in the United States, where each state was endowed with "full self-government in its internal affairs."[8] Consequently, in paragraph 2, section 4, of the Czechoslovak constitution, the term "místní správa" (literally, local administration) was interpreted by Zsatkovich as internal affairs and thus state self-government in the American style.[9] In his official reports, Zsatkovich often referred to himself as president of Rusinia, which "according to the decision of the Peace Conference .... will be an autonomous state in the Czechoslovak Republic and will have self-government in the broadest sense of the term."[10] In the end, Zsatkovich did not convince the Prague government, did not achieve his stated aims, and resigned on March 16, 1921. For the next two years, the administration remained in the hands of the Czech vice-governor, Petr Ehrenfeld.

Despite the constant friction between Zsatkovich and the Czechoslovak government, his brief tenure in office revealed that at least some persons in the province were willing to cooperate with Prague. There were as many, however, who were antagonistic to the new regime, and Subcarpathian political life came to be characterized by a rivalry between local progovernment and antigovernment factions. The united front presented by Rusyn leaders at the Central Russian National Council in Uzhhorod (May 8-16, 1919) did not last long.[11] Not everyone could be appointed to the few leading positions offered to Rusyns by the Czechoslovak government. Those left out became avid opponents of official policy, decried the refusal to implement autonomy, and adopted a "national" interpretation different from that accepted by Prague and its Rusyn supporters.

The Central Russian National Council continued to meet a few times during the summer of 1919, but at a meeting on October 9, internal conflicts split the group into two factions. Former Vice-Chairman A. Voloshyn was removed while Chairman Antonii Beskid and the Galician Russophile Andrei Gagatko remained in control. Voloshyn, a member of the Directorate, supported Zsatkovich, while Beskid, who coveted the governorship for himself, attacked both the Czechs and his former Rusyn colleagues for their administration of the province. Moreover, Beskid's council claimed itself to be the sole legal representative of the Rusyn people.[12]

The outcome of the October 9 meeting was typical of Subcarpathian political affairs. Personal feuds, not political or national issues, were the real
cause of alienation between the conflicting groups. Zsatkovich and the
Directorate were also opposed to Prague's administration of the province—
and for the same reasons as Beskid's faction—the lack of autonomy
and the "unjust" Slovak-Rusyn border. Without any real political differences between Rusyn leaders, the national issue became an outlet to express
personal rivalries.

In practice, Zsatkovich, Voloshyn, and other members of the Directorate
supported the Czechoslovak administration, which favored the populist
Rusyn-Ukrainophile orientation in cultural and educational matters.[13] In
opposition to this, Beskid, Gagatko, and other Russophiles attacked Zsatkovich for his "rusinstvo" and for having created the language and
national disputes.[14] They proclaimed the Russophile (obshcherusskii) orientation as the only valid one, and it became fashionable for them to criticize
Prague's support of the "Ukrainian separatists" and to describe "the Carpatho-Russians [Karpatorossy] as a small part of the multitudinous and
mighty Russian people . . . from the Poprad [River] to Kamchatka."[15]

By early 1920 it was clear that Rusyn political leaders could not remain
united in the Russophile Central National Council headed by Beskid.[16]
Consequently, the province became fertile ground for the establishment of
political parties that were to prepare for future elections. Although the
government opposed the formation of local independent parties and
favored the creation of provincial affiliates of Czech political parties, which
could then be controlled from Prague, in fact, both national affiliates and
local groups were formed. These first Subcarpathian parties were usually
classified according to their pro- or anti-government stance. Without
exception, they proclaimed a desire to improve the economic status of the
Rusyn peasants and to fight for the realization of autonomy. On the national
issue, most progovernment parties favored the populist-Ukrainophile position, while opposition groups were Russophile in orientation.[17]

Subcarpathian affiliates of the Agrarian (Republican) and Social
Democratic parties were established in 1920. At first, the Agrarian party
took a neutral stand on the national issue, but it later became Russophile
and basically maintained this stance even after a Ukrainian branch was set
up in 1934.[18] Like the Agrarian, the Social Democratic party recognized
that the most important issue in the province was the economic question.
"The people of Subcarpathian Rus' demand . . . bread, work, pasturage
and land."[19] Although the Social Democrats clashed with Prague over the
question of autonomy, they favored the government's support of the
populist-Ukrainian orientation in cultural affairs.[20]

Other progovernment parties were organized by two former members of
the Directorate, Iulii Brashchaiko and Avhustyn Voloshyn. The first of
these was the Rusyn-Agriculturist (Rus'ko-Khliborobska) party, which was

established in August 1920. Again lip service was paid to the economic question: "The goal of our party is that Rusyns become lords of their own land."[21] Demands also included unification of "all Rusyns from the Poprad to the Tisa" rivers, guarantees for "the widest possible autonomy," and "diffusion of our mother Rusyn language" (*maternŷi rus'kii iazŷk*), which was identified as a dialectal form of Ukrainian.[22] The Rusyn-Agriculturalist party was closely associated with the Greek Catholic Church, and in 1925 was transformed into the clerical Christian-National (Khrystiians'ka-Narodn'a) party, a branch of the Prague-based Populist (Lidová) party. Loyalty to the Czechoslovak government was especially stressed, and despite the recognition of Subcarpathia's ethnographic allegiance with the Ukraine, "geographical, economic, and cultural reasons have drawn us to Prague and not to L'viv or Kiev."[23]

As for the opposition, the largest and most influential political organization was the Communist party, first set up in March 1920 under the name of the International Socialist Party of Subcarpathian Rus'. This group was dominated by local Magyars and Jews like Dr. József Gáti (1885-1944), Armin Dezse (1883-1944), Moszes Simon, Erne Seidler (1886-1940), Béla Illés (b. 1895), Pál Török (1896-1936), Ene Hamburger, and Hermann Feier (1892-1953), who had participated in or were sympathetic to the short-lived Hungarian Soviet regime of April 1919.[24] Under the leadership of Ivan Mondok (1893-1941), the International Socialists joined with other Czechoslovak leaders in May, 1921 to form a Subcarpathian affiliate of the Czechoslovak Communist party. Local party leaders attacked the "comedy of 'voluntary' union . . . with Czechoslovakia that took place against the will of the broad masses of the population" and reiterated that "we [Rusyns] are slaves, an eastern colony of Czech imperialism . . . and [thus] want to join with our brothers in the Union of Soviet Republics."[25]

The Communists were opposed in principle to the "bourgeois" governmental system of the Czechoslovak republic, and thus called for immediate social revolution. In the first address given to the Czechoslovak Chamber of Deputies by a Subcarpathian representative, Dr. József Gáti declared: "It is known that the only solution to the problem and question of existence in Subcarpathian Rus' is the immediate expropriation of the great landlords' property and the conclusion of the closest political and economic union with Soviet Russia."[26] "Only a victorious proletarian revolution can guarantee the self-determination of nations."[27] Obviously such goals had both larger political and national implications, and in his speech as delegate to the meeting of the Fifth Comintern held in Moscow in June 1924, Subcarpathian Deputy Ivan Mondok argued that: "We want the framework of the USSR to be filled out. We want that the [Soviet] Union include the Carpathians and ask of the Party leaders that they, without any kind of diplomatic subterfuge, speak out on this question."[28] To these calls for union, the Comintern could only respond that it "recognized the necessity for the Communist Parties of Poland, Czechoslovakia, and Rumania to proclaim slogans for unification with the Soviet worker-peasant Republic of Ukrainian territories severed into parts by imperialism."[29]

Despite their unequivocal sympathies with a Soviet-style system, the Subcarpathian Communists were not above such "bourgeois" concerns as elections to an autonomous Soim or the problem of the Slovak-Rusyn border. On more than one occasion, Communist deputies called for implementation of the St. Germain treaty, and although these demands were frequently qualified with revolutionary jargon, Deputy Mondok could still admit: "We in Subcarpathian Rus' will struggle to the end for autonomy, even if this autonomy is not the kind we need."[30]

The initial attitude of Subcarpathian Communists toward the national issue varied from vagueness to contradiction. Before 1926, the party organs *Pravda* (1920-1922) and *Karpats'ka pravda* (1922-1933; 1935-1938) were written in a mixture of local dialect and Russian, although when referring to the inhabitants, only the terms "Rusyn people" and "Rusyn language" were employed.[31] Similarly, either Magyar, Slovak, or Rusyn (mixed with some Russian) were used by Subcarpathian parliamentarians in Prague. Yet notwithstanding this rather lukewarm Rusynophile orientation, Deputy József Gáti could still conclude that "Subcarpathian Rus' is the most southern extremity of the Russian [*ruský*] nation."[32] As we shall see, Communist policy on the nationality issue was to change abruptly in 1926.[33]

In spite of the continued existence of Beskid's Russophile Central National Council, the leaders of that organization also formed independent political parties. Antonii, together with his relatives Konstantin and Nikolai Beskid, founded in May 1921 the Russian National (Russkaia Narodnaia) party. This party, based in Prešov, eastern Slovakia, was particularly concerned with rectifying the "temporary" demarcation line between Slovakia and Subcarpathian Rus'.[34] Accordingly, the more than 85,000 Rusyns living under a Slovak administration would eventually have been united with their eastern brethren, and until that time been guaranteed full cultural autonomy. In the words of Iurko Lazho, the first Rusyn senator elected to the National Parliament: "We demand that our Russian villages be united with Subcarpathian Rus', and while we are still in the Košice župa [eastern Slovak administrative district] the Vice-župan must be Russian and all the local officials, judges and notaries know Russian."[35]

The Russian National Party was complemented in Subcarpathian Rus' by the Labor (Trudovaia) party, which propounded the slogan that "no man should be allowed to live and become rich from the work of another man."[36] Led by the Galician and Bukovinian Russophiles Andrei Gagatko and Ilarion Tsurkanovich, this group was especially critical of the Czechoslovak government, which was accused of dividing "the Carpatho-Russian population into two parts: the western and the eastern."[37] The Labor party demanded that the border question be favorably settled and that the Czechoslovak government immediately cease its anti-Orthodox, anti-Russian, and pro-Ukrainian policies. Furthermore, "the Russian book language" (*russkii knizhnii iazyk*) was to be introduced in all Subcarpathian schools, because "our Carpatho-Russians . . . are part of the Russian people."[38]

The last of the anti-government parties was the Subcarpathian (Podkarpatskii), later renamed the Autonomist, Agricultural Union (Avtonomnyi Zemlediel'skii Soiuz), founded in 1920 by Ivan Kurtiak (1888-1933) and Iosif Kaminskii (1878-1944). The Union stated its intention to protect the economic, cultural, and political interests of the peasantry, "to establish the borders of Subcarpathian Rus' from the Poprad to the White Tisa Rivers so that all Rusyns in the republic will be united," and to guarantee an early convocation of the Soim.[39] "As for the language question, we demand the institution of the *status quo ante* [that is, before 1919] and demand the end to all kinds of foreign influences in our cultural affairs."[40] "We need neither Russia, nor the Ukraine, nor Hungary . . . we need our free land with our own rights, traditions and with our language and sons born from our people."[41] This was, of course, a direct rebuttal to Prague's initial support of Zsatkovich and the populist Rusyn-Ukrainophile orientation. Although the party claimed independence from outside elements, its leaders were in fact paid by the Hungarian government. They soon began to hail the autonomy given the Rusyns in 1919 by the Hungarian government as preferable to the present Czechoslovak administration, and in an interview Kurtiak stated bluntly: "A thousand years we were friendly [with Hungary] and in the future we will also remain good friends."[42]

It would be wrong to overemphasize the role of political parties in Subcarpathian Rus', either in this early period or during the 1930s, because the majority of the population was simply not used to a democratic political system. In practice, that organization which propounded the most convincing promises (and which provided the most food and liquor at party meetings) would stand the best chance of success among the electorate. An apt description was given by one long time visitor to the province.

Formerly the Ruthene would leave politics alone. He had no chance of hearing a political address until the candidate appeared for the election. Then it was a time of alcohol for everyone and cash and promises. But now the people have become politically minded and in the Republic we have 25 or 30 parties. I know someone here [in S.R.] who is a member of about a dozen and he goes to meetings every other night. I dare say it will do him no more harm than going to a dozen night clubs if he had them.[43]

Furthermore, neither politics, cultural affairs, nor national identity were of great importance to the Rusyn peasants: rather, bread and land—in short, physical survival.

Even if the local parties had only marginal influence on the development of individual national consciousness, it was useful to survey briefly their platforms, because the Prague government was concerned with the attitudes that these various political groups maintained toward the Czechoslovak administration. As a result, the government's policy for Subcarpathian Rus', especially its attitude toward the nationality question, was determined to a large extent by the pro- or anti-Czechoslovak stance of the local leaders.[44]

The anti-Czechoslovak pronouncements of the Russophile leaders were most evident in a series of memoranda and resolutions addressed to President Masaryk, the government in Prague, and the League of Nations in Geneva. The first of these was sent by Antonii G. Beskid, chairman of the Russophile Central National Council, to Vlastimil Tusar, the new Social-Democratic prime minister. The subject of complaint was the situation of the Rusyns in eastern Slovakia, and Tusar was asked "in these difficult hours to protect and defend us against the attacks from our western Slovak brethren."[45] The initial problem was the reluctance of the Slovak administration to introduce the Russian language in village schools where Rusyns lived. Several memoranda followed with various criticisms that were summed up in a fourteen-point declaration of the Russophile Central National Council, sent to President Masaryk on January 18, 1920.[46] This document requested the Czechoslovak government to guarantee in writing Subcarpathia's right to legislative and administrative autonomy and to resolve the Slovak-Rusyn border question. With the exception of foreign, military, financial, and communications affairs, all other matters were to be resolved by the Rusyns themselves.[47] A resolution attached to this declaration was even more stringent in tone. The Paris Peace Conference was declared invalid, and it was demanded that "the autonomy granted by the Czechoslovak republic will not be less than that guaranteed by the Hungarians in Law Ten of 1918." In conclusion: "We Rusyns consider the present system illegal, inhuman and unsupportable."[48]

The January declaration and resolution were followed by a memorandum "from a peasant deputation in Autonomous Carpathian Rus'," which recognized the Russophile Central National Council as the only legal representative of the Rusyn people. The deputation included the "demand that we be recognized as Russians and that our children be taught the Russian language."[49] The desires for autonomy, a new Slovak border, and the use of Russian were repeated in subsequent memoranda issued by the Central National Council and the Russian National Party.[50] In April 1922, members of the latter party addressed a memorandum to the League of Nations requesting aid in order: (1) to unite the Rusyns of eastern Slovakia with Subcarpathian Rus'; (2) to introduce elections to a Soim and to the National Parliament; and (3) to secure autonomy for the province. The memorandum criticized the government in strong terms: "Three years [our] people have been living under a military dictatorship . . . We will state the truth clearly and openly . . . Resting on the power which they have in their hands, the Czechoslovaks want to destroy us."[51]

In response to these protests, the Czechoslovak government stated that Subcarpathian Rus' was not yet mature enough for autonomy. In legal terms, "elections to an autonomous Diet for Subcarpathian Rus' necessarily presuppose the definite fixation of borders"; yet "without the definite fixation of borders for Subcarpathian Rus', it is impossible to proceed with elections to the Diet and to promulgate the law relative to the autonomy of this territory."[52] Such circular arguments could not hide the fact that the Czechoslovak government was reluctant to implement autonomy until it could be assured of internal consolidation within the province and the loyalty of Rusyn leaders. In essence, the Czech attitude was governed by the following premise: "Democracy and freedom are ideals exquisite for a cultured nation; for a backward people in primitive condition these [ideals] must be used with reserve and caution."[53]

Czechoslovak Policy in Subcarpathian Rus'

During the first years of the Czechoslovak regime, the Prague government did not have any definite policy for Subcarpathian Rus', because it knew little if anything at all about the area. "That land and its people were a *terra incognita.*"[54] "In short, before the [First World] War we perhaps never even heard of Carpathian Rus'."[55] Although, during the nineteenth century, Czech and Slovak leaders did know about the Subcarpathian Rusyns, nonetheless Prague newspaper editors either pretended to be, or actually were, unaware of these people, and accordingly their columns reflected the wildest speculations regarding the eastern province. In one interview, the Czech vice-governor, P. Ehrenfeld, bluntly admitted: "Prague knows nothing about Carpatho-Russia. They have a vague idea that bears run around the streets . . . Before one continues to propagate such ideas, I must emphasize that on the streets of the capital, Uzhhorod, there are, to be sure, chickens and geese where soldiers, young girls, Jews, and officials walk, [but] never bears."[56] Such colorful and ironic descriptions were also found in the first Czech pamphlets about the area. Recalling Austria's fateful decision of 1908, Subcarpathian Rus' was compared to a new Bosnia.[57] Moreover, for the Czechoslovak republic, the eastern province could only be considered a "difficult task," "a brake rather than an advantage," "a sick body . . . which needs the careful and soft hands of a doctor."[58]

The Hungarian government was duly condemned as the cause of Subcarpathia's sad state, and it became standard practice to begin both official and unofficial reports with attacks on the former regime: "The injuries which the former Hungarian state apparatus committed against its national minorities has left perhaps the most drastic example of lawlessness in the land of Subcarpathian Rusyns. For centuries [they] were . . . defiled both culturally and economically."[59] "Subcarpathian Rus' lived in true material and cultural misery . . . The Hungarian regime did not care in the least."[60] "There was probably no other people in all of Europe so destitute and culturally deprived as the Rusyns of former Hungary."[61] Kirill Kokhannyi-Goral'chuk, head of the Ministry of National Culture in Uzhhorod, turned to the scriptures for an analogy: "In Subcarpathian Rus' it was like before the Biblical creation of the world: above nothing, below nothing: darkness."[62] In the same vein, the influential Czech parliamentarian Václav Klofáč declared before the Senate in obviously exaggerated terms: Subcarpathian Rus' "never had any schools, nor education, nor anything. I never in the world saw such a black Africa as in the highlands of Subcarpathian Rus'."[63] These views were further propagated through the re-publication in Czech translation of eyewitness reports written by Hungarian authors before the First World War.[64] Finally, the Czech masses were imbued with the following impression of the former regime through the words of Jaroslav Hašek in his enormously popular contemporary novel, *The Good Soldier Schweik:*

> When later at about lunchtime they reached Humenné, where the station showed the same traces of fighting, preparations were made for lunch and the men in the transport could in the meantime catch a glimpse of a public secret, and observe how after the departure of the Russians the authorities treated the local population, who were related to the Russian armies in speech and confession.
>
> On the platform surrounded by Hungarian gendarmes stood a group of arrested Ruthenians from Hungary. It included priests, teachers and peasants from far and wide in the region. All of them had their hands tied behind their backs with cord and were fastened to each other in pairs. Most of them had broken noses and bumps on their heads, since immediately after their arrest they had been beaten up by the gendarmes.
>
> A little further away a Hungarian gendarme was amusing himself with a priest. He had tied his left foot with a cord, held the cord in his hand and forced him with his rifle but to dance a czardas. Then he tugged at the cord so that the priest fell on his nose, and as the priest had his arms tied behind his back he could not get up but made desperate attempts to turn on his back, perhaps to be able to raise himself from the ground. The gendarme laughed so heartily at this that tears ran from his eyes, and when the priest tried to get up he gave another tug at the cord and the priest was on his nose again.
>
> At last a gendarmerie officer put an end to this and ordered the prisoners to be taken away to an empty barn behind the station until the train had passed. There they were to be beaten and pounded without anyone being able to see it.[65]

Considering such conditions, it seemed understandable that Rusyns would want to rid themselves of the "devastating" Hungarian regime and decide voluntarily on May 8, 1919, to unite with the Czechoslovak republic. This was the interpretation that appeared over and over again in the writings of the country's two foreign ministers, Edvard Beneš and Kamil Krofta,[66] in numerous popular pamphlets about the area, and in the widely read saga of the establishment of the republic by the journalist Ferdinand Peroutka.[67]

The underlying message was clear. Despite the fact that Rusyns took it upon themselves to make such a "revolutionary" decision as unification with Czechoslovakia, they were nevertheless not yet mature enough to govern themselves. Indeed, some promises were broken and certain stipulations of the international treaties calling for autonomy were not fulfilled, but the Prague government was making this up through cultural, and to a lesser degree economic, aid to the stricken area.[68] Rusyns would just have to experience several years of Czech tutelage before they could be ready for autonomy.

Armed with these beliefs, and convinced of the rightness (and righteousness) of their own benevolent mission among their eastern brethren—such an attitude applied to Slovaks as well as Rusyns—the government in Prague was easily influenced by those reports which emphasized the "primitive conditions" in the area. In the words of one official:

> We were convinced of the lowest level of the people there [in S.R.] by the following incident. Returning from one inspection tour we met a woman who was carrying two pigs under her arms. Not far from us the woman sat down alongside the road and suckled the pigs—from her own breasts. We were taken aback and asked a man walking nearby why the woman was doing such a thing and how would she be able to suckle her own children later. He replied quite nonchalantly that the pigs might have died of hunger on the trip and that would cost money, while children aren't worth anything.[69]

Whether or not this incident was true, descriptions of such discomforting circumstances dominated reports sent to Prague. And how could such "uncivilized," "un-Czech" conditions be rectified? This same report had a response: if some of "our people" (Czechs) were transferred to the area, it would become a paradise.

In fact, the administration, bureaucracy, and gendarmery in Subcarpathian Rus' were soon staffed largely by Czechs.[70] Prague claimed that, as among Slovaks, so among Rusyns, there was a definite insufficiency of qualified local personnel. Thus, "many years must pass before Subcarpathian Rus' would be somewhat economically and culturally improved" so as to receive autonomy.[71] One might understand why Czechs felt the way they did. Their own national development took a century before statehood was realized. With this frame of reference, how could Rusyns expect the same within a few years?

A special five-member parliamentary commission was appointed to work out policy for Subcarpathian Rus', but in the end Rusyn demands for the appointment of a responsible governor, elections to a local Soim, and institution of the broadest autonomy were not to be fulfilled.[72] Instead, the government's priorities were directed at the economy: "the question of Subcarpathian Rus' [must] become less political, and economic matters [must] be placed in the forefront."[73] Even the recommendation for elections to the Prague Parliament was met by one official with the following suggestion:

As already mentioned earlier, the population is politically *immature and completely dependent on the Jews.* [italics in the original] If elections were introduced in Subcarpathian Rus', *only Jews and Magyars* would be chosen and [this] would surely not fulfill our intentions. Thus, it would be best to hold elections according to the *Hungarian method,* that is *dictate individuals* who are to be elected, or do not hold elections at all until conditions improve."[74]

The refusal by the Czechoslovak government to fulfill the political demands of Rusyn leaders led to the series of protests analyzed at the beginning of this chapter. Prague's interpretation of these protests decisively influenced the government's attitude toward the Russian, populist-Ukrainian, and Rusyn national orientations. In short, local circumstances and the international political situation during the 1920s caused the Czechoslovak government to favor the populist-Ukrainophile point of view.

By the fall of 1919, Czechoslovak opinion was opposed to the Russophile leaders in Subcarpathian Rus', and the Russophile Central National Council, as reorganized by A. Beskid and his supporters, was viewed as a "threat to our state."[75] The Russophiles' only consistent friend in Prague was Karel Kramář, the republic's first prime minister, who originally hoped the country would be ruled by a Romanov prince; when that proved impossible, he still continued to work for the overthrow of the Bolshevik regime in Russia. However, as early as June 1919, Kramář's leading role was undermined as a result of the first communal elections, and the Subcarpathian Russophiles lost an important link to the ruling circles in Prague.[76] Even *České slovo,* the organ of the National Socialist Party (led by Václav Klofáč), which usually supported the Subcarpathian Russophiles, was critical of "the Great Russian movement headed by Dr. Beskid and conservative Rusyns from Galicia and Bukovina" (Gagatko and Tsurkanovich) as a danger to the new republic.[77]

Czech newspapers were filled with articles depicting the unfavorable activity of tsarist officers and Russian Communist infiltrators in Subcarpathian Rus'.[78] Moreover, local Russophiles were identified as opponents of the Czechoslovak Republic, and this description was not without substance. The Subcarpathian Labor Party newspaper, *Russkaia zemlia,* stated: "it was bad under the Hungarian regime, now it is still worse"; while party leader A. Gagatko concluded that "the reciprocal trust between the Carpatho-Russian people and the administration does not exist anymore."[79] A. Beskid and his relatives in eastern Slovakia were also closely watched by the authorities for their "anti-Czech," "radical" activity.[80]

The Czechoslovak government became convinced that the Russophile movement was "in the end working for the detachment of Subcarpathian Rus' from the Czechoslovak republic."[81] In contrast to the local populist-Ukrainophiles, "love and devotion toward the Czechoslovak republic can only rarely be found among supporters of the Great Russian orientation."[82] The memoranda, resolutions, and statements of the local Russophile leaders were interpreted as convincing proof of that orientation's anti-Czechoslovak stance.[83]

If the Prague government feared the Russophile movement because of statements by local leaders, it was even more concerned with the so-called Rusynophile orientation. One of the first Czech-language newspapers in the region summed up the perceived danger: "Under the veil of 'Rusynism', the 'Uhro-Rusyns' are in the hands of Magyar irredentists."[84] According to Budapest, both Slovakia and Subcarpathian Rus' were illegally under Czechoslovak occupation, and these areas had to be returned to Hungary.

The Hungarian government found ready allies in a group of Magyarone Rusyns living in Budapest and in those discontented Rusyns and Magyars who left the region after the establishment of the Czechoslovak regime. Pro-Hungarian propagandists included the university professors József Illés-Illjásevics (1871-19??), László Balogh-Beéry, Antal Hodinka, and more especially the former Lord Lieutenant of Bereg, Miklós Kutkafalvy. In August 1919, Kutkafalvy founded a Uhro-Rusyn political party in Budapest, which claimed to represent the "true" voice of the Rusyn people.[85] A long memorandum outlining several reasons why Rusyns should remain within Hungary was immediately sent to the Paris Peace Conference.[86] This was followed by a more detailed criticism of Czechoslovak shortcomings in the area in a petition addressed to the League of Nations in 1922.[87]

Kutkafalvy also worked closely with other discontented leaders from what was already Czechoslovakia, and, together with the Slovaks Viktor Dvorčák and Dr. František Jehlička, he headed the Union of Magyar Friends of the National Minorities in Budapest. Indeed, the Hungarian government was quite willing to finance these activities, as well as a Ministry of Minorities, in which Kutkafalvy served as secretary until 1921, and a chair of Rusyn Studies at the University of Budapest, occupied by Sándor Bonkáló until 1922.[88] While all this was taking place, another anti-Czech Rusyn, the former Magyarone governor of Rus'ka Kraina, Dr. Agoston Stefan, was campaigning in Poland against the Prague regime and for the return of Subcarpathian Rus' to Hungary.[89]

The Czech press followed closely these revisionist machinations and in

1920 reported that Hungary and Poland "were preparing an attack on Subcarpathian Rus'."[90] Also, the Prague government distrusted the local Rusyn intelligentsia, especially the many Magyarone Greek Catholic priests, who were considered "far more dangerous to our republic than true Hungarians."[91] Rusynism, then, was associated with Magyar revisionism and as such was fully discredited in Czech ruling circles.

As a result, the populist-Ukrainophile orientation was the only remaining option that could be supported. Despite the traditional Russophile sentiment within Czech society, Jaromír Nečas (1898-1944), who was to become a Social Democratic parliamentary deputy from Subcarpathian Rus', led a group of fellow Czechs who wrote several pamplets and articles in praise of Ukrainians. "We are surrounded all about by enemies. Until now only the Ukrainians are friendly to us and write about us with sympathy."[92] Furthermore, "our [Czech] national leaders like Čelakovský, Havlíček, Palacký, Rieger and others" recognized the independent national identity of the Ukrainians. It was argued that since the Slavic population of Subcarpathian Rus' was Ukrainian, a pro-Ukrainian policy would be in the best Czech tradition.[93]

The new government of the Social Democratic prime minister Vlastimil Tusar, which came to power in July 1919, was favorable to the populist-Ukrainophile orientation. Minister of Education Gustav Habrman appointed Josef Pešek as superintendent of schools in Uzhhorod, and in official circles the language and nationality of the local inhabitants was considered to be Little Russian or Ukrainian. (See also pp. 136-138.) This policy complemented political developments in the province, since the so-called "local movement" was associated with Zsatkovich and Voloshyn. "This movement contains the intelligentsia which is not Magyarized—priests, teachers and people who speak Rusyn and who want to develop within the framework of the Czechoslovak republic."[94] After the resignation of Zsatkovich, the Czech vice-governor, Petr Ehrenfeld, continued to support the populist-Ukrainophile Prosvita Society and its theater. As for local political organizations a progovernment bloc was created by cooperation between the Rusyn-Agriculturalist, Social Democratic, and Agrarian parties.[95]

Thus, the Czechoslovak policy regarding the nationality question in Subcarpathian Rus' was determined by both internal and external factors. The antigovernment memoranda of the Beskid-Gagatko faction and the threats of Hungarian revisionists debased the Russophile and Rusynophile orientations in the eyes of Prague. Of the three, the populist-Ukrainophile trend came to be considered not only the most culturally viable but also the most politically reliable.

The Normalization of Political Life

Not until 1923 were the first steps taken by the Czechoslovak government to introduce representative institutions in Subcarpathian Rus'. Although

Prime Minister Antonín Švehla was still wary of the "primitive conditions" in the area,[96] in August a new governor was installed and in October elections took place at the local level. The following March, elections were held to the National Assembly in Prague.[97]

Czechoslovak leaders were concerned with recruiting a group of local leaders who could garner enough progovernment votes in the coming elections. The reliable Agriculturist-Social-Democrat-Agrarian bloc proved insufficient, and further support would have to be found among the Russophile politicans. Consequently, in its attempt to secure political consolidation within the province, Prague's policy underwent certain changes that were to affect the government's attitude toward the nationality question.

The first great concession to the Russophiles came in August 1923, when Antonii Beskid was appointed governor of Subcarpathian Rus'. In return, Prague found an ally in the chairman of the opposition Russophile Central National Council and Russian National party. The ambitious Beskid had achieved his one goal—the coveted governorship—and he was more than willing to revise his statements to accord with the Agrarian party, which by 1922 had succeeded the Social Democratic party as the dominant force in Czechoslovak politics. "My program of activity in Subcarpathian Rus'," he declared, "agrees closest with that of the Carpatho-Russian Agrarian party."[98] After 1923, protests by the Russophile Central National Council (Beskid-Gagatko faction) regarding the Rusyns in eastern Slovakia diminished and the language question became the primary issue of complaint.[99]

Of greater significance was the simultaneous appointment of the Czech Agrarian leader Antonín Rozsypal (1866-1937) as vice-governor. This position represented Prague's control in Subcarpathian politics,[100] and since the passive Beskid was satisfied with his figurehead position, the situation was left de facto in the hands of Rozsypal. In short, the populist-Ukrainophile Zsatkovich and Ehrenfeld administrations were replaced by the pro-Russophile Beskid-Rozsypal administration.

As mouthpiece for the new regime, Beskid made clear his position on the nationality issue. Soon after taking office he expressed the "opinion that the language of instruction in Subcarpathian Rus' can only be Russian,"[101] and in subsequent years reiterated: "We demand to be educated in the Russian spirit because we are Russian. We demand the flowering of the Russian literary language which must be in our schools.[102] To be sure, the populist-Ukrainophile educational policy of the first years of Czechoslovak rule could not be immediately altered. Nevertheless, Beskid pledged that "immigrants from the East, especially from Galicia [that is, nationally conscious Ukrainians], who in the first days after the revolution occupied without any rights the best places in the administrative apparatus, will be removed."[103] Certain Galician Ukrainians, like the advisor for language to the school administration Ivan Pan'kevych, were under pressure to leave, but despite this the school administration still maintained its populist-Ukrainophile orientation. However, with the establishment of the rival

Russophile Dukhnovych Society in 1923, the Ukrainophile Prosvita Society lost the support of the leading figures in the local administration.[104]

The policies of Beskid and especially Rozsypal raised a storm of protest among progovernment populist-Ukrainophile leaders. A. Voloshyn expressed the dilemma that existed in the minds of many Ukrainophiles who still had faith in their Czech brothers:

> We can freely designate the cultural and nationality policy espoused by the administration as anti-Rusyn [*protirusinský*] denationalization . . . During the first years we felt here and there the help of fraternal hands . . . However, the arrival of the present regime has acted like a cloud over a young blooming plant. The governor himself [Beskid] announced a struggle against the populist movement, which the Hungarian and Magyarone press attempted to discredit before Prague as Ukrainian irredentism, while it was actually this handful of Rusyn patriots who were the initiators of the union of Subcarpathian Rus' with Czechoslovakia—and this during a time of the existence of the Ukraine . . . The new regime has introduced a destructive policy against all that was achieved during the first years.[105]

The first seeds of distrust toward Prague were sown and they were to bloom during the next decade in the form of Ukrainian nationalism.

Prague's attempt to broaden its base of political support in Subcarpathian Rus' did not succeed, because, with the exception of Beskid, the leaders of the Russophile parties (Gagatko-Kaminskii) joined, after 1925, the oppositional Magyarone Rusynophile (Kurtiak), Communist, and local Magyar (Korláth, Egry) parties. As a test, elections to the two houses of the National Assembly were held in 1924 and 1925. Of the 254,200 votes cast in 1924, the progovernment bloc gained only 40 percent. At the head of the opposition was the Communist party, which received 39.4 percent of the votes. The following year found a 54 to 46 percent ratio, once again in favor of the opposition. The Communists still received the most votes, though their percentage declined to 30.8 percent of the total.[106] The most successful of the progovernment parties was the Agrarian, which rose from a meager 6.4 percent in 1924 to 14.2 percent in 1925. Thus, in the 1924-1925 and 1925-1929 National Assemblies, respectively, 10 out of 13 and 9 out of 13 Subcarpathian deputies and senators were decidedly opposed to the Prague regime.

As a result of these elections, and especially the strength of the Communist party, it was clear that a considerable degree of dissatisfaction with the Czechoslovak regime existed in Subcarpathian Rus'. Thus, at a time when Prague was working to satisfy the demands of its German and Slovak minorities in the other parts of the republic, and when elements in many European capitals were actively calling for an alteration of Czechoslovakia's borders, it was imperative that the economic and political situation be stabilized in the far eastern province. As for Rusyn demands regarding an autonomous Soim, it became even more evident after the elections that Prague would not allow the establishment of such a body until it could be assured of a progovernment majority.

To rectify the unfavorable political situation in the province, Prime Minister Švehla decided to bolster the local Agrarian party organization. He was extremely dissatisfied with the 1924-1925 elections and attributed the antigovernment showing to poor leadership in political campaigning, to insufficient attention regarding economic problems, and to a "simple lack of knowledge of the given situation by the apparatus of the [Agrarian] party."[107] Švehla decided to place in Subcarpathian Rus' "completely new people, young, responsible, serious, experienced and most important his own confidants trained in his school."[108] Among those dispatched to invigorate the Agrarian party were two Czechs, Jan Brandejs and Josef Zajíc (1892-19??). It was also decided to remove Governor Beskid, who had lost the confidence of Agrarian party leaders as early as 1926.[109]

The government continued its program of land reform and planned to integrate Subcarpathian Rus' further into the structure of the Czechoslovak republic by making it a fourth province, similar to Bohemia, Moravia-Silesia, and Slovakia. This effort toward further centralization met with vigorous opposition from Rusyn politicians of all orientations, who demanded that their homeland receive an autonomous Soim and not be made a Prague-administered province. On February 8, 1927, massive protests were held in Uzhhorod, where all shops were closed and a work boycott staged. One Czech newspaper reported that: "Since the union of Subcarpathian Rus' with Czechoslovakia, the population of that land has not expressed such disturbance and dissatisfaction as today."[110] The next day even the rival politicians cooperated briefly in a joint session of the Russophile (Gagatko-Kaminskii) and Populist-Ukrainophile (Voloshyn) Central National Councils. They addressed a petition to the government demanding: (1) the formation of a parliamentary commission to prepare for elections; (2) the convocation of a soim "in the nearest future"; and (3) the establishment of a definitive Slovak-Rusyn frontier to be determined only after conducting a national plebiscite in eastern Slovakia.[111]

However, the protests were ignored and Administrative Reform Act No. 125, which affected the republic as a whole, was passed on July 14, 1927. When it became effective one year later, Subcarpathian Rus', or the Subcarpathian Russian Land (Země Podkarpatoruská), became the fourth province of the Czechoslovak Republic; the disputed "demarcation line" with Slovakia was recognized, with some slight changes, as the legal border. The former three districts or *župy* (established in 1921 with seats in Uzhhorod, Mukachevo, and Sevliush) had already been replaced, in July 1926, by one unified district with its center in Mukachevo. Now, the province was

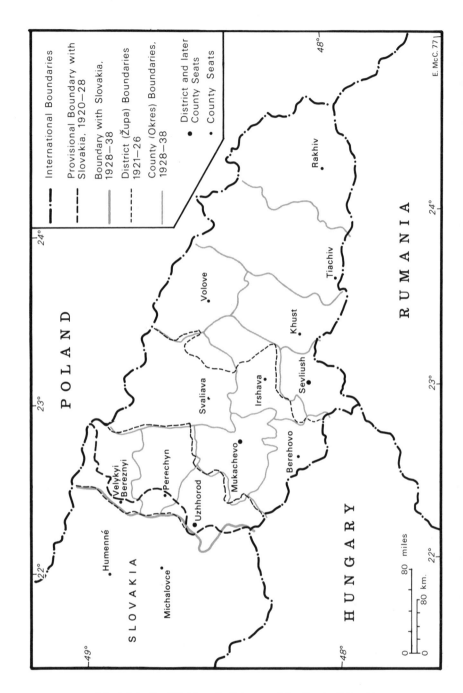

Administrative Divisions in Subcarpathian Rus', 1920-1938

divided into twelve counties (*okresy*), each with its own assembly and coun-cil. In Uzhhorod, a provincial assembly was created, made up of twenty-four members, two-thirds of whom were elected, the remaining third appointed. The vice-governor simultaneously became president of the province, a position which made him chairman of the provincial assembly and gave him responsibility for appointing the heads (*okresní hejtman*) of the counties. Since the provincial president was responsible directly to Prague, real power was not concentrated in the hands of the Subcarpathian governor, but in Rozsypal, or any other Czech who became vice-gover-nor.[112]

Despite the wide-spread opposition to the Administrative Reform Act, as expressed by Subcarpathian politicians in speeches in the National Assembly and in protests to the League of Nations,[113] Prague's efforts at political con-solidation met with success, as revealed by the results of the 1929 elections. For the first (and last) time, the integrating, progovernment parties gained a majority of 54 percent of the votes in the elections to the National Assem-bly. In the four years since the last election, the Agrarian party managed to increase its total from 34,916 to 77,519 votes (14 to 29 percent), while the Communists declined from 75,669 to 40,538 votes (30.8 to 15.2 percent).[114] Even still, just seven of the thirteen Subcarpathian representatives spoke out in favor of the government.

The Czechoslovak government was primarily concerned with securing the loyalty of the province, and the results of the 1929 elections represented a degree of success in that direction. Prague's support of the Agrarian party, however, was interpreted by many populist-Ukrainophiles as unfavorable from the national point of view. By the late 1920s, most leaders in the Agrarian party expressed themselves as Russophile in orientation. For in-stance, Senator Edmund Bachinskii presented an "Agrarian party resolu-tion which stated that it [the Party] will from now on support the Russian majority and strive to introduce in our schools the Russian literary lan-guage."[115] Moreover, both Governor Beskid (who remained in office until 1933) and Vice-Governor Rozsypal became pronounced adversaries of the Ukrainophiles.[116] Add to this the fact that the opposition Communist party supported Ukrainianism after 1926, and it could be argued that Prague's political needs would eventually lead to a completely anti-Ukrainian stance. But in the following chapter, we will see that the need for political consoli-dation forced the Czechoslovak government to renounce exclusive support for either the Russophile or Ukrainophile orientations.

The first decade of Czechoslovak rule in Subcarpathian Rus' began in an atmosphere of mutual trust and confidence. Rusyn leaders were filled with optimistic hopes when they arrived in Prague on May 20, 1919, to express their desire to join the new republic. An active participant of that first dele-gation later recalled: "Golden Prague solemnly greeted [and] sincerely cared for the Rusyns, and we returned home with hope for a better future."[117] Even the noted Ukrainophile author V. Grendzha-Dons'kyi, an otherwise acerbic critic of the Prague regime, wrote during the first years: "We are not flatterers, but here the facts speak that our true friends are the Czechs."[118]

The Czechoslovak administration, however, soon made many enemies among Rusyn political and cultural leaders. The failure to implement the promised autonomy, to convoke a local Soim, and to rectify the Rusyn-Slovak border were causes of constant friction. The dispatch of Czech officials and the unnecessary "interference" in educational and ecclesiastical affairs only intensified Rusyn dissatisfaction. Finally, in its attempt to secure political consolidation in the province, Prague tried to curry the favor of Russophile leaders and consequently alienated many of its loyal populist-Ukrainophile supporters.

Nevertheless, the elections of 1929 revealed to the government that among Rusyns there was still a substantial degree of confidence in the Czechoslovak republic. After ten years, Subcarpathian authors proudly re-iterated that before 1919 their "enemies exploited us in the Carpathians; now freedom is everywhere in our midst."[119] Borshosh-Kumiats'kyi ad-mitted: "I know that conditions here [in S.R.] are exceptionally difficult, but I am convinced that with the help of your [Czech] people, there . . . 'will come a better day'."[120]

After ten years, most Rusyns continued to feel that the future of their homeland lay in a close association with the Czechoslovak republic. Indeed, Prague was soon to be in need of the loyalty of all its citizens. The second decade, however, revealed that the consolidation of political life, as re-vealed by the 1929 elections, was only a temporary phenomenon, and that antigovernment forces were soon to dominate Subcarpathian Rus'.

11 | *The Decline in Subcarpathian-Czechoslovak Relations, 1930-1937*

A Legacy of Discontent

If the first decade of Czech rule in Subcarpathian Rus' ended on a relatively positive note, the situation was quite different at the end of the 1930s.

> The Subcarpathian milieu [in 1932], where one worked so creatively and with pleasure before, changed its external and internal character so that the law of might and power began to assert itself. 'Macht geht vor Recht'.[1]

> In seventeen years [1936] Subcarpathian Rus' has made great progress . . . Its economic situation, however, is today very, very bad; the anti-state opposition has more importance than representatives of an active pro-state policy . . . [who] are by many even hated.[2]

Prague's refusal to institute the promised autonomy alienated an ever greater number of Rusyn leaders. The central government continued to be directly involved in the educational and cultural problems that plagued the area, and this "interference" increased the dissatisfaction among Subcarpathian leaders. Unfortunately, this same decade was marked by a world-wide economic crisis and an increase in political tension throughout Europe —developments that had a negative impact on Czechoslovak-Subcarpathian relations. It was a period of growing intolerance, which did not bode well for any future cooperation between the Rusyns and the Prague government. The prevailing atmosphere was perhaps best described in the opening words of a new journal edited by the school administrator and future parliamentary deputy Iuliian Revai: "Conditions [in Europe] are right now so strained that one shot could serve as a reason for the outbreak of a new world war. No discussions, consultations, meetings or conferences can help. The material order of things is such now that like man without bread, one cannot live without war."[3]

The 1930s witnessed an increase in friction between the Russophile and Ukrainophile orientations, and Prague tried to balance off these conflicting forces by supporting the Rusynophile current. As a result, some alienated Russophiles looked abroad and were drawn closer to Polish and Hungarian political revisionists, while the non-Communist Ukrainophiles, especially of the younger generation, eschewed foreign intrigues and became proponents of a radical, anti-Czechoslovak nationalism. By 1938, it was clear that Prague's half-hearted responses to Subcarpathia's demands for autonomy would no longer be tolerated by local leaders, and a basic change in the province's political status was viewed as the only solution. The Munich crisis made such a change possible.

Political, national, and economic questions continued to be the central features of Subcarpathian discontent. Rusyn leaders reiterated that the Czechoslovak government had an international legal obligation to grant autonomy—in particular, to convoke a local Soim and to give the local governor responsible authority. Prague, in turn, responded that Subcarpathian Rus' was still not mature enough for self-rule. Rusyns also refused to recognize their western border, which left more than 90,000 of their brethren in the Prešov Region of eastern Slovakia; but to demands for a plebiscite in that area and possible boundary rectifications, the central government responded that nothing could be accomplished without Slovak cooperation. Since Prague had its hands full with Slovakia, especially with the growing autonomist movement led by Andrej Hlinka, it was not likely to risk alienating Slovaks any more by asking them to give up some of their territory. In such a situation, the demands by Subcarpathian parliamentarians for border rectifications were laughed at by the leading Prague newspapers and flatly rejected by Slovak polemicists.[4]

Another sore point was the new provincial administration, which began to function in 1928. Instead of an autonomous Soim, Subcarpathian Rus' received a provincial assembly, which was viewed by Rusyn leaders as a direct hindrance to their strivings for autonomy. Finally, the influx of Czech officials, who occupied all the leading positions in the provincial bureaucracy, remained a sore point. Very few Rusyns held offices with decision-making authority. Furthermore, the Czech newcomers demanded schools for their children, and between 1920 and 1938 the number of Czech language schools rose disproportionately from 22 to 188. This trend was viewed by nationally conscious Rusyns as a threat to their own national existence.[5]

The nationality issue was closely allied with the language question, and the Czechoslovak government became inextricably involved in this problem, As long as there was no local Soim, language, educational, and other cultural matters had to be decided by administrative decree. Thus, the central Ministry of Education in Prague attempted by itself to resolve the language chaos. In 1931, Minister Ivan Dérer called a series of meetings of representatives from the opposing factions to try to evolve some common policy.[6] Populist-Ukrainophile leaders pointed out that a decision to use the local language was already stated in the *Generální Statut* of 1919. Of course, the term "local language" was never explicitly defined and this resulted in great variations among the different grammars, dictionaries, and textbooks used in Subcarpathian schools.[7] On the other hand, Russophile leaders considered the language issue a political one: "not the Prague Parliament, but a Russian autonomous provincial Soim . . . will decide on the governmental official language."[8] In fact, Dérer upheld the principles of the *Generální Statut* and called for a "unified development on the basis of the local language of the people,"[9] but this policy never really extricated the government from the impasse, and both Ukrainophiles and Russophiles concluded that Prague's interference was another instance of deliberate denationalization.

In addition to the political and cultural problems, by 1932 an economic crisis had struck hard throughout Czechoslovakia. The positive effect of the land reform and the rise in Subcarpathian living standards during the 1920s were wiped out by the depression. Unemployment figures in the province rose tremendously: from 7,057 persons in 1930 to 19,451 in 1933 and 16,528 in 1936.[10] Strikes, mortgage foreclosures, grain shortages, and starvation became common phenomena,[11] and despite the projects to build roads, bridges, and other public works, the government failed to relieve substantially the poverty of the peasantry. While the capital, Uzhhorod, was beautified by the construction of the impressive government sector (Galago), "the Czechoslovak state administration left the Rusyn people in the Carpathians in a condition which can be described by one word: poverty." "We constantly have the impression that the population on the whole in Subcarpathian Rus' is not economically better off than before the revolution [1918-1919]."[12] Notwithstanding plans to undertake further public projects that might help to alleviate unemployment, even the Agrarian party admitted that the government could not fulfill Subcarpathia's economic needs.[13] The resultant widespread poverty, combined with political and national frustrations, provided an ever-increasing number of discontented individuals who were to become supporters of various anti-government movements.

Hungarian Revisionism and the Rise of Autonomist Parties

One indication of the growing friction between the Czechoslovak government and its eastern province was the increase in activity among the autonomist parties. Among these, the most important was the Autonomist Agricultural Union (Avtonomnyi Zemlediel'skii Soiuz, or AZS), already active during the 1920s under the leadership of Ivan Kurtiak, Andrei Brodii (1895-1945), Julius Földesi (1875-1947), and Mykhail Demko (1894-1946).[14] A second organization claiming to be autonomist was the Russian National Autonomist party (Russkaia Natsional'no-Avtonomnaia Partiia, or RNAP), established upon the initiative of Stepan A. Fentsik in 1935. Although other locally based parties existed briefly, only these two managed to survive.[15] The reason was that, even though they received no support from national organizations based in Prague, they drew on the resources of foreign governments. In fact, Brodii's AZS and Fentsik's RNAP became instruments of Hungarian and Polish foreign policies, respectively.

Hungarian foreign policy throughout the interwar period was aimed at rectifying what Budapest considered the unjust results of the 1920 Treaty of Trianon. Hungary had been obliged to recognize the loss of the Burgenland to Austria, of Croatia and the Bačka (Vojvodina) to Yugoslavia, of Transylvania to Rumania, and of Slovakia and Subcarpathian Rus' to Czechoslovakia. Less than one-third of the pre-1918 Hungarian Kingdom remained. What was formerly northern or highland Hungary (Felvidék) was considered the area most likely to be "returned to the homeland," and after almost a decade of futile protests to the League of Nations, one polemicist writing on the problem of Subcarpathian Rus' and Hungarian integrity was forced to agree with the example of Bismarck: only *mit Blut und Eisen* (with blood and iron) could this lost territory be regained.[16] Moreover, success in this direction would fulfill another "important aim of Hungarian foreign policy—the attainment of a common Polish-Hungarian border."[17] To fulfill these goals and to regain Subcarpathian Rus', Hungarian policy focused on four activities: (1) the establishment of a series of organizations within Hungary itself to convince the populace of the positive value of a revisionist policy; (2) the subsidizing of Hungarian parties in Subcarpathian Rus' so as to immunize the local Magyar minority there from Czechoslovak influence; (3) the support of Rusyn parties in the province that were opposed to Czechoslovak policy; (4) the creation of a propaganda network to convince the West (especially Great Britain, France, Italy, and the League of Nations) of the validity of Hungary's territorial claims.[18]

It was in conjunction with the third aspect of Hungarian foreign policy that Budapest began to increase its contributions to Brodii's AZS. Ostensibly, the AZS claimed to defend Rusyn interests by struggling for "an autonomous Subcarpathian Rus' from the Poprad to the Tisa Rivers."[19] While party leaders pledged loyalty to the Czechoslovak republic, their actions were in fact determined by the example of Deputy Kurtiak, who as early as 1926 declared: "It is necessary to look abroad for justice where these unpleasant circumstances [in Subcarpathian Rus'] will be cancelled by the decree of stronger states."[20] Later, Deputy Brodii went so far as to claim that "if today such a situation arose in which the Chinese would help Rusyns, then over ninety percent of our people would be ready to go to the Chinese."[21]

From the national standpoint, the AZS was clear on one thing, its opposition to anything associated with Ukrainianism.[22] If, during the 1920s, Kurtiak seemed to adopt a Rusynophile position, under the leadership of Brodii no support was ever given to the idea of an independent Rusyn nationality or language. Rather, the AZS demanded "Russian schools for our

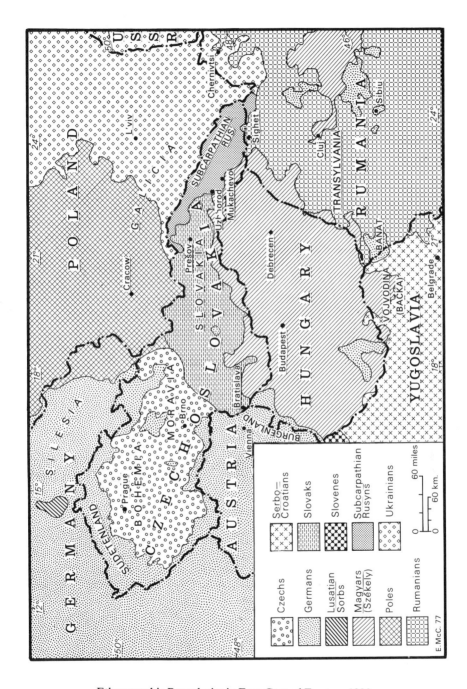

Ethnographic Boundaries in East-Central Europe, 1930

children,"[23] courted the Russophile Dukhnovych Society, and expressed special sympathy for the sufferings and "denationalization" of the "Russian people" in eastern Slovakia.[24] Despite this concern, the AZS nonetheless found it possible to join the ticket of Hlinka's Slovak Autonomist Populist Party, whose ideology was largely devised by another Hungarian paid agent, Béla Tuka. Even if the AZS endorsement of the Russophile orientation was superficial, the foreign machinations of the party's leaders still did much to discredit Russophilism in the opinion of both the Czechoslovak government and the local populace.

Indeed, Prague was soon aware of the AZS's affiliation with the Hungarian government. Police reports from both Subcarpathian Rus' and eastern Slovakia were filled with detailed information on party leaders and the means by which they received Hungarian funds. These reports made clear that Kurtiak and Brodii were in the service of Budapest and that the "AZS movement was unfriendly and destructive for Czechoslovakia."[25]

While the AZS received funds from Hungary, Fentsik's RNAP catered to Poland's anti-Czechoslovak interests.[26] Fentsik was ambitious and wished to play some leading role in Subcarpathian life. He first became opposed to the Czechoslovak government when it began to support the populist-Ukrainophile orientation. Not content with leadership in the Dukhnovych Society, this errant Greek Catholic priest sought appointment as bishop of the Mukachevo diocese in 1930. Having failed in this endeavor, he turned to politics. In opposition to Brodii and Kaminskii, Fentsik befriended the Polish consul in Uzhhorod, and as early as 1931 received funds from him to publish a weekly newspaper, *Karpatorusskii golos*. In 1934-1935, he traveled to the United States, where he collected from Rusyn-American immigrants money that was used to establish the Russian Nationalist Autonomist party (RNAP) in March 1935.[27] Too small to survive alone, the RNAP united with the National Union (Národní Sjednocení) led by the conservative and Russophile Czech leader Karel Kramář.

The RNAP demanded "full autonomy and the fixation of borders from the Poprad to the Tisa Rivers."[28] With these aims in mind, Fentsik and his cohorts actively campaigned among the Rusyns of eastern Slovakia. Like many other party platforms, the RNAP included the standard promise to give more land to the peasants. The antigovernmental stance of the party was evident in its demands for the "immediate" institution of complete autonomy and the elimination of all Czech elementary schools in Subcarpathian Rus'. Regarding the national issue, Fentsik's party was not only "national" and "Autonomous" but "Russian." "These three words best characterized the essence of our party and its aims," among which was "the immediate introduction of the Russian literary language in all types of schools and finally the approval by the Subcarpathian governor of Russian textbooks."[29]

To the dismay of many of its members, the Russophile Dukhnovych

Society was used by Fentsik for propaganda purposes. This "enfant terrible" of Subcarpathian life even declared at a public meeting of his party that in political relations the examples of Hitler and Mussolini should be followed.[30] As a result of his escapades, Fentsik came under the close scrutiny of the Czechoslovak police; not only his connections with Polish officials, but also his contacts with Rusyn-American immigrants were viewed as a threat to the security of the republic.

At the beginning of this study, we stressed the role played by Rusyn immigrants in the movement to unite Subcarpathia with Czechoslovakia. After 1919, the importance of the immigration shifted somewhat from the political to the economic sphere, and American dollars sent to the family in "the old country" made up a substantial part of the province's income. Most leaders at home were well aware that "the relations of our Subcarpathian Rusyn people to our brothers in America is a very important matter . . . and thus we want to enter into systematic contact with our brothers beyond the sea."[31] The immigrants continued to be concerned with political questions, although their attitude toward Czechoslovakia altered radically when Prague failed to institute the autonomy promised for Subcarpathian Rus'. The return of Zsatkovich to the United States was a signal for the anti-Czechoslovak trend, which picked up momentum with the creation of the Rusin Council for National Defense at Pittsburgh on November 28, 1922. Headed by Michael Yuhasz, Sr., this new organization sent appeals to Prague and to the League of Nations protesting against the "iron-heeled tyranny" of "the Czech yoke" placed on their brethren in the homeland. Lack of autonomy, the Slovak border question, widespread poverty, persecution of the Greek Catholic Church, and "the forced Ukrainization of the schools and language of the Rusins" were the prime areas of complaint.[32] Though frequently based on hearsay evidence, these protests were a source of embarrassment to the Czechoslovak government, which considered the charges important enough to require official responses.[33]

While the Yuhasz group was made up primarily of Greek Catholics, a new organization, the Carpatho-Russian Union, was established at Pittsburgh in June 1933.[34] This Union, which included Orthodox as well as Greek Catholic members, soon became the mouthpiece for all Rusyn-Americans, and it began to furnish Fentsik with money to further his anti-Czechoslovak propaganda.[35]

A third organization to which Czechoslovak consular representatives in the United States paid particular attention was the Lemko Association, founded in 1929 by immigrants (Lemkians) from Galicia and including many from eastern Slovakia.[36] At a time of increased economic hardship in Subcarpathian Rus', Prague officials became worried about the Lemko Association's unlimited praise for the Soviet Union—"proletarian Russia" —and the diffusion of anti-Czechoslovak propaganda that was printed in the United States and brought to eastern Slovakia via the neighboring Lemkian populace in Poland.[37] Local police reports stressed that the area "was deluged with irredentist publications," the content of which clearly threatened the integrity of Czechoslovakia.[38]

By the 1930s, the Hungarian and Polish governments as well as Rusyn immigrant groups (of Greek Catholic, Orthodox, and Bolshevik persuasion) were actively supplying funds for propaganda directed against the Czechoslovak administration in Subcarpathian Rus'. But how were these developments coordinated so as to provide a real threat to the Prague government? And how was this to affect the nationality question in the province?

After the conclusion of the Czechoslovak-Soviet pact in 1935, the trend toward closer Hungarian-Polish relations was stepped up. Hungarian Premier Gömbös visited Marshal Piłsudski, who emphasized that Poland "would never follow a policy that might be detrimental to Hungary."[39] Soon Poland was to support Budapest's territorial claims for the return of Subcarpathian Rus'. To reach this common goal, both governments were interested in reducing the personal rivalry between their respective Rusyn agents, Brodii and Fentsik, an endeavor that was not achieved until 1938. In the meantime, Hungarian theoreticians prepared an autonomous program for Brodii's AZS, while the Polish Embassy in Prague worked closely with Fentsik to help prepare his visit to the United States during the winter of 1934-35.[40]

Budapest's support of the Subcarpathian autonomous parties was only one aspect of its revisionist foreign policy, whose basic "principle . . . was to create the maximum number of problems and difficulties for the Czechoslovak government."[41] Hungary had never really recognized the Treaty of Trianon. On November 20, 1920, the day it was submitted to the Hungarian Parliament, the speaker recited aloud the following creed:

> I believe in one God
> I believe in one Fatherland
> I believe in one divine eternal Truth
> I believe in the resurrection of Hungary.
>   Amen.[42]

During the years that followed, Hungarian school children were required to recite aloud this "Magyar Creed" twice every day, while the phrase, "Nem, nem soha" ("No, No, never!"), repudiating the hated Trianon Treaty, was found on signs in all public places throughout the country.

It was in such an atmosphere that no less than nineteen organizations were founded to propagate the "righteousness" of the nation's foreign policy. Among these were the Hungarian Frontier Readjustment League

(Magyar Revizios Liga), the League for the Integrity of Hungary (Terült-védő), the Highland Organization (Felvidéki Egyesülitek Szövetség), and the most influential irredentist group—the National Union (Magyar Nem-zeti Szövetség) under the leadership of Baron Zsigmond Perényi, a former landlord in Subcarpathian Rus'.[43]

Hungarian diplomats and publicists were also active throughout Europe, attempting to convince Western statesmen of their revisionist point of view. In London, Hungarian revisionism was defended by the parliamentarians Lord Viscount Rothermere, Sir Robert Donald, and Sir Robert Gower. In 1927, Donald visited the Magyar minority in Czechoslovakia, and in 1933 Rothermere arranged for a lecture tour in England for the former Hungarian prime minister Count Stephen Bethlen. Bethlen demanded "the creation of a Ruthenian national autonomy . . . in order that they [Rusyns] may be at absolute liberty to choose of their own accord the country of their adop-tion."[44] The English statesmen backed Bethlen's views through their own writings, which called for border revisions in favor of Hungary.[45] In Paris, the plight of Hungary was defended by a lawyer, Georges Desbons, who argued that "it is necessary to change the map of Czechoslovakia [and] the sooner the better, because she has created the formidable danger of Subcar-pathian Rus', or if you prefer Hungarian Ruthenia."[46]

Perhaps the least successful of Budapest's anti-Czechoslovak efforts was the attempt to transform the Hungarian minority in Subcarpathian Rus' into a solid antigovernmental force. The oppositional Magyar National and Magyar Christian Socialist parties in the province averaged about 11 percent of the vote in each parliamentary election, and their representatives (Dr. Endre Korláth and Károly Hokky) kept up a steady barrage of harsh criti-cism against the Czechoslovak regime.[47] Nonetheless, Prague seemed fairly convinced that the Hungarians were "on the whole, especially in the villages, loyal citizens; and even if constantly and systematically barraged with irre-dentist propaganda, they are happy within our state."[48]

Considering these factors, the Czechoslovak government rightly associ-ated the autonomist political movement in Subcarpathian Rus' with Hun-garian-Polish revisionism. Moreover, Brodii and Fentsik's nominal associ-ation with the Russophile national orientation made that trend seem once again less favorable to Czech policy-makers. At the same time, the Ukrain-ian movement was also, because of its rapid growth and influence, viewed critically by the Czechoslovak government, which would have preferred a more neutral force in Subcarpathian politics. This situation led Prague to support a policy of Rusynism.

The Reaction of the Czechoslovak Government

Prague kept a close watch on Budapest's revisionist activity, and, espe-cially at the League of Nations in Geneva, both countries directly exchanged propaganda blasts.[49] Hungary, however, was only one of the many unfriendly forces surrounding Czechoslovakia. After Hitler came to power, he soon made obvious his support for the claims of the more than 3 million Germans in Bohemia. Moreover, the conclusion of a nonaggression pact between Germany and Poland in January 1934, accompanied by anti-Czechoslovak statements from Polish leaders, were developments Prague followed with increasing anxiety. With this realignment of European powers, Czechoslavakia became ever more dependent on French foreign policy and, along with France, signed a pact with the Soviet Union in May 1935. However, of most immediate concern to Czechoslovak leaders was the need to strengthen ties within the so-called Little Entente.[50]

The Little Entente came into existence in 1920-1921 when Yugoslavia, Rumania, and Czechoslovakia were drawn together because of their opposition to Hungary. Each of the three countries contained substantial territory that, before 1918, was part of the Hungarian Kingdom; each was strongly opposed to Budapest's revisionist claims. While Hungarians were calling for changes in the map of Europe and meeting for that purpose with leaders of Italy and Poland, Czechoslovak officials were busily trying to reinforce the Little Entente. Indeed, the only territorial link in the entente was the common border between Subcarpathian Rus' and Rumania, so that Prague's concern with its eastern province was greater than ever. Edvard Beneš, then Czechoslovak minister of foreign affairs, underlined this fact in 1933: "Without Slovakia and Subcarpathian Rus', the Little Entente would be purely and simply impossible . . . Never will we abandon Subcarpathian Rus', because it is precisely on Slovakia and Subcarpathian Rus' that we are building our policy of the Little Entente, our policy for all of Central Europe. . . . We will therefore never allow our territorial link with Rumania to be cut."[51] Beneš, of course, was trying to impress upon the outside world the supposed internal unity of the Czechoslovak republic. Thus, after meeting with the Rumanian Foreign Minister, Titulescu, in the eastern Slovak city of Košice (November 1933), Beneš returned to visit Slovakia in December and Subcarpathian Rus' during the following Spring.

While in Uzhhorod (May 3-6, 1934), Minister Beneš delivered a long speech tracing in detail the developments that led to the unification of Subcarpathian Rus' with Czechoslovkia in 1919. Although autonomy was not yet introduced, he pointed to the achievements in education, public works, and land reform as an indication of Prague's good will and concern for the Rusyn people.[52] More important, Beneš' remarks signaled a basic change in the government's attitude toward its eastern province.

Initially, many Czech politicians argued that Subcarpathian Rus' was to be part of Czechoslovakia only until the Russian question was settled, and one contemporary writer urged his countrymen to realize that "we [Czechs] are only holders of a foreign deposit which we will have to give up some day."[53] It was even rumored that, as late as 1930, Masaryk was prepared to negotiate with Hungary for the return of all regions that had more than 50 percent Magyar population—and this included the whole southern flank of Subcarpathian Rus'.[54] Beneš, however, was categorically opposed to any such plans: "Subcarpathian Rus' is definitely within the Czechoslovak republic and its political allegiance has been decided for the next century."[55] This quite optimistic forecast was followed by a direct rebuttal to Hungarian and any other revisionist programs: "We will defend Subcarpathia to the last drop of blood."[56]

The international political situation in Europe during the 1930s caused Prague to modify its attitude toward Subcarpathian Rus', and this was also to affect the government's influence on the nationality issue within the eastern province. Whereas the populist-Ukrainophile, and later Russophile, movements were favored during the 1920s, by the mid-1930s Czechoslovak policy makers came to feel that in the interest of the republic the third, or neutral, Rusynophile current would be the most reliable. There was no longer any real danger from the Magyarone priests, since many had accepted the Czechoslovak regime; moreover, Budapest now gave its greatest support to the Russophile autonomist parties. On the other hand, the Ukrainian movement seemed to be too influential, and talk about the unity of a united (*Soborna*) Ukraine or a united Soviet Ukraine among some leaders awakened in Czechs fears of Ukrainian irredentism. Consequently, the safest choice seemed to be support for a loyal and dependable Rusynophile orientation.

Indeed, many Czech publicists and scholars who worked on this problem, including President Masaryk, Florian Zapletal, František Tichý, and František Hlaváček, argued that the Rusyns of Subcarpathia were a branch of one Little Russian or Ukrainian people.[57] This view was especially emphasized by Czech Communist sympathizers like Ivan Olbracht, Stanislav K. Neumann, and Zdeněk Nejedlý in their writings about the eastern province.[58] Yet, at the same time, neither these nor other Czech and Slovak writers could deny certain distinctive features of Subcarpathian Rusyn civilization. "The Subcarpathian Rusyns are not and do not want to be Russians nor Ukrainians, but Rusyns," admitted the pro-Ukrainian F. Tichý.[59] In 1936, the prolific specialist on Rusyn literature Antonín Hartl explained the problem in these terms: "The Rusyns are a part of the Ukrainian nation, but they lack one essential characteristic, the realization of this belonging. This is not a question for linguistic specialists, because language alone does not create national consciousness; the Rusyns still lack precisely that trait which . . . is expressed by the German term, *Volkswille.*"[60] Although by the mid-1930s a large portion of Subcarpathia's intelligentsia and student population was aware of a Ukrainian national identity, there is no doubt that the majority of the uneducated or semieducated masses considered themselves simply as Rusyns. It was in the best Czechoslovak interest, then, to transform this lack of "Ukrainian national will" into a conscious "Rusynism," a concept that they hoped would make evident the interrelationship between Rusyn, Czech, and Slovak cultures, and at the same time serve as a loyal, pro-Czechoslovak integrating force. Perhaps Ivan Olbracht best summed up this potential when he wrote in 1931: "There is no doubt that this [Subcarpathian Rusynophile] orientation, which would like to create in Subcarpathia a new, little Slavic nation whose life would develop only within the borders of the republic and which would not be threatened by either Russian or Ukrainian irredentism, would be the most sympathetic to the Prague government. It is also certain that it [Rusynophile orientation] would find the greatest support in the villages which do not have any understanding of the Ukrainian-Russian struggle and which slightly derogatorily refer to Ukrainians as Poles and Russians as Muscovites."[61]

The potential development of a separate pro-Czechoslovak Rusyn nationality was aided by the fact that, according to international treaty (St. Germain) and the Czechoslovak constitution, a distinct, self-governing (*samosprávné*) territory called Subcarpathian Rus' did exist. And even though the promised autonomy was never really implemented by Prague, there were nonetheless many tangible elements that continually reinforced the distinctiveness of the region. For instance, Rusyns were not considered a minority (except in eastern Slovakia), and hence, along with Czechs and Slovaks (officially "Czechoslovaks"), they were one of the dominant nationalities in the republic. As a result, the Rusyn language (never clearly defined, but in Cyrillic traditional orthography) appeared alongside Czech (and sometimes Magyar) on all village, town, and street signs, as well as on official documents and on the ubiquitous seals that cropped up wherever a bureaucrat could lay his hands.[62] This same language was printed on some denominations of Czechoslovak paper money.

Subcarpathian Rus' also had its own symbol—a profile of a standing red bear facing, to the left, a field of blue and yellow horizontal bars—which was found on regional flags and on the "intermediate" and "great" symbols of the Czechoslovak republic. Rusyns had their own national hymn (with words by Dukhnovych and music by S. Fentsik), which was always performed alongside the Czechoslovak hymn at official functions in both Subcarpathian Rus' and the Prešov Region in eastern Slovakia.[63] Finally, the province was quite similar to many larger countries surrounding it; it had: (1) a Rusyn population living beyond its borders—in eastern Slovakia; and (2) a large proportion of its own inhabitants (37 percent) who were not Rusyn. Despite the fact that the region had a high percentage of minority populations, official and unofficial circles throughout Czechoslovakia generally perceived Subcarpathian Rus' to be a Rusyn land, as indicated in its new name, received in 1928, the Subcarpathian Rusyn Land (*Země Podkarpatoruská*). All of these factors might have been used effectively to help foster the idea of a separate Rusyn nationality.

To stress their affinity and sympathy with the province, many Czech writers and officials were fond of remarking that they could understand and be easily understood by Rusyns when visiting Subcarpathian villages.[64] There were even several attempts to publish Rusyn-language newspapers in Latin script,[65] and sometimes in Prague newspapers this led to suggestions that the "only answer" to the Russian-Ukrainian language struggle was the "introduction of the Czech language into Rusyn schools."[66]

Despite such opinions, however, the Czechoslovak government never seriously entertained the idea of introducing Czech as the basic medium of instruction in Rusyn schools. On the other hand, no formal attempts were ever made to create a separate Rusyn literary language. In fact, Prague's policy of "Rusynism" was not a well-developed program aimed at solving the cultural and national problems within the province. Rather, in response to the increasing political tension both in Subcarpathian Rus' and throughout Europe in general, "Rusynism" became a compromise that at best might have helped to inspire the population of the province with confidence and respect toward the Czechoslovak state.

With this in mind, Czechoslovak officials and some publicists welcomed Bishop Stoika's publication of the pro-Czechoslovak, Rusyn-dialectal newspaper *Nedîlia*, as well as the attempt by the Greek Catholic Church to set up a cultural society that might neutralize the Prosvita-Dukhnovych rivalry.[67] Prague's turn toward Rusynism was further reflected in the establishment between 1935 and 1936 of the National Economic Union for Subcarpathian Rus' (Národohospodářský Svaz pro Podkarpatskou Rus) and the Subcarpathian Rusyn Matica (Matice Podkarpatoruská) in Prague, and the Association for the Friends of Subcarpathian Rus' (Klub přátel Podkarpatské Rusi) in Bratislava.[68] The Association, headed by Jaroslav Zatloukal, sponsored the publication in Czech of a collection of Rusyn literature, a comprehensive anthology about the province (*Podkarpatská Rus,* 1936), and a monthly journal, *Podkarpatoruská revue* (1936-1938), designed "to inform the Czechoslovak public about all conditions in Subcarpathian Rus'."[69] Another Czech-Language journal, *Most mezi východem a západem* ("The Bridge between East and West," 1936-1938) was established in Khust to fulfill the same goal. The Czech public also received impressions about Subcarpathian Rus' through the works of Karel Čapek, Vladislav Vančura, Ivan Olbracht, and other writers,[70] and through trips made by tourists and boy scouts who returned to Bohemia and Moravia with vivid memories of the "exotic" eastern land within the borders of their own country.[71]

Within the province itself, special radio programs were broadcast, beginning in 1934, and the government provided funds to establish a Subcarpathian National Theater, which in 1936 began to give performances in Rusyn dialect.[72] All these efforts were expected to result one day in the creation of a strong Rusyn national consciousness. One ethnographer made the following prediction: "More and more the Carpatho-Russians [*karpatorusové*] are developing into an independent branch and national unit . . . which already has many individual attributes of an independent people." The author concluded that after twenty or thirty years of development, Subcarpathian Rus' "would surely overcome the chaos of the divisive cultural, linguistic and political orientations and crystallize into an independent, individual nationality—into a Carpatho-Russian [*karpatoruský*] people."[73]

Czechoslovak policy makers were also concerned with the vacant Subcarpathian governorship. In his Uzhhorod speech, Minister Beneš stated that the "government has not nor will it ever forget its responsibilities . . . Autonomy will be introduced in the near future." The first step in that direction was to come in 1935 with the appointment of a new governor.[74] The Russophile Antonii Beskid had died in 1933, and since that time the province had been in the hands of a Czech, the aging Vice-Governor Antonín Rozsypal. Rozsypal had become extremely unpopular because of his Russophile tendencies, his reluctance to introduce any kind of autonomy, and his opposition to the appointment of a new governor. The ruling Agrarian party leaders decided a governor had to be found and Rozsypal had to go.[75]

In conjunction with Prague's policies of consolidation in the political sphere and of "Rusynism" in the cultural, it was essential to choose a Rusynophile candidate. The choice was Konstantyn Hrabar, who was appointed on March 20, 1935. Hrabar proved to be most acceptable to Czech leaders because he was "a convinced proponent of Czechoslovak-Rusyn national rapprochment and unity, . . . [and] a representative of the local [Rusyn] language orientation"—that is, "a good Rusyn who speaks at home with his family in Rusyn."[76] In any case, it was the opinion of one Czech advisor that the governor in Subcarpathian Rus' "was never needed for critical, but only tactical issues . . . [and] his chief task would be to appease the friction caused by the language struggle."[77] Hrabar was not opposed to such a role and thus was the most reliable person willing to support Prague's policy of Rusynism.

Czechoslovak plans regarding autonomy in Subcarpathian Rus' were decisively influenced by the results of the parliamentary elections held in May 1935. They were an enormous setback for the government, 63 percent of the vote being cast for parties definitely opposed to the Prague administration. Just one year after Beneš pledged to defend Subcarpathian Rus' "to the last drop of blood," the population clearly revealed its underlying discontent. The effects of the depression and widespread poverty played into the hands of the Communist party, which tallied 78,334 votes (24.4 percent), almost double the number it received in the previous parliamentary election. Fentsik's RNAP, in alliance with the National Union, received 28,954 votes (8.9

percent), while Brodii's AZS garnered 44,982 (13.9 percent).[78] The ruling Agrarian party received 60,747 votes (19 percent), 10 percent less than in 1919. In fact, the only noticeable gain made by a progovernment party was that of the pro-Ukrainian Social Democratic party, which got 29,749 votes (9.2 percent). Nevertheless, the 63 percent majority for the opposition was a definite indication of the Rusyn population's lack of confidence in the Czechoslovak government.[79]

Prague hoped to rectify this disaster by making concrete plans to introduce the long-awaited autonomy, and the appointment of the Slovak centralist Milan Hodža as Prime Minister in November 1935 was a step in this direction. Hodža wanted to placate the autonomous desires of the Slovaks as well as the Rusyns, whom he had known first hand since before the war, and for whom he had great sympathy. Actually, before he succeeded Masaryk in 1935, Beneš had already set the guidelines for negotiation when he urged that "Russophiles, Ukrainophiles, and Rusynophiles must at all costs reach agreement with Czechoslovaks for a common future policy . . . so that in such a way the [Rusyn] population can take into their hands the goal of autonomy."[80] The initiative to begin talks came from the constitutional committee in Parliament as early as November 1935, although Hodža met first with the Slovaks and did not turn to the Subcarpathian problem until one year later.[81]

In fact, two proposals had previously been submitted by members of the AZS, in the form of a published memorandum by Iosif Kaminskii in January 1931 and a parliamentary bill by Ivan Kurtiak in November 1931 (signed by members of the Magyar and German opposition).[82] Now, in response to Hodža, Stepan Fentsik submitted another parliamentary bill (signed by members of the Slovak opposition) in June 1936. Then, in a rare show of unity, both Russophiles and Ukrainophiles met in August 1936 to revive the Central National Council and draw up a proposal for autonomy, which was submitted on November 28.[83] Most of the proposals called for implementation of the broadest autonomy, as stated in the Treaty of St. Germain, as well as unification of Rusyn territory in eastern Slovakia. As a result, Hodža virtually ignored these demands and dealt solely with six members of the parliamentary government coalition, headed by Senator Edmund Bachinskii and Deputy Iuliian Revai who worked out a proposal for autonomy in November 1936. Expectations rose in Subcarpathian Rus' during that year because it seemed as if Prague was finally acting seriously on the issue of autonomy.[84]

But the government delayed once again, rejected the proposals of the parliamentary coalition (especially because of the demands for Rusyn territory in Slovakia and for broad powers to the Subcarpathian governor), and finally passed its own "temporary" Law No. 172, which took effect in October, 1937. Dubbed the first stage of autonomy, this law increased slightly the responsibility of the governor: he received the right to name certain functionaries and to offer an opinion on language and religious matters, and he was appointed chairman of the provincial assembly. Instead of the elected Soim Rusyn leaders demanded, a gubernatorial council of twenty-four appointed members was created. Although Law No. 172 was a far cry from the kind of political autonomy envisioned by many Rusyns, it was nonetheless accepted by Governor Hrabar and by members of the progovernment parliamentary coalition as a positive first step in the building of a secure, Czechoslovak-oriented Subcarpathian Rus'.[85]

In essence, "the promised autonomy was to remain on paper; the governor continued to lack any authority and was without power."[86] Nonetheless, the administration began to praise itself for the economic progress it had achieved during the past few years and, as in the 1920s, claimed once again that the economic situation in the province would have to be improved before full autonomy could be realized.[87] In the meantime, the critical language question, and other national matters, were not to be resolved by a local Soim, but once again by the Prague administration.

The worst interference of this kind was the language questionnaire of 1937.[88] In a decree issued by the Ministry of Education on September 14, a plebiscite was to be held among Rusyn parents to find out if they preferred the *Rus'ka* grammar of Pan'kevych or the *Russka* grammar of Sabov. This was an esoteric question, far from the realm of a half-literate parent's competence. Yet the vote was held, Pan'kevych's text being billed as *malorus'-kyi (ukraïns'kyi)* and Sabov's as *russkii.* Since the questionnaire was formulated in this way, a parent would think that the choice was between a Ukrainian text, on the one hand, and a Russian (*russkii,* which is phonologically similar to *rus'kyi,* or Rusyn) text on the other. The result was a decisive victory for Sabov's Great Russian grammar—313 to 114 schools preferring it. The irony was that Pan'kevych's text was far closer to the Rusyn (*rus'kyi*) dialects spoken by the populace.[89] The Russophile leaders, particularly Fentsik, gloated over the vote, which was considered an indication of "the final defeat of Ukrainianism," while the Ukrainophile Revai declared in Parliament that such a plebiscite was both antischolarly and illegal.[90] Nonetheless, the Czechoslovak government was satisfied that it had solved the issue in a "democratic" manner!

Actually, it was the rapidly expanding Ukrainian movement that could find no satisfaction in any aspect of Prague's recent policy of Rusynism. Besides resentment toward the presence of Czech officials and the steady increase in Czech elementary schools, there was added disillusionment because of the administration's deliberate vacillation on the autonomy issue. Such developments were frankly viewed as an attempt to denationalize (to make Czech) the population of Subcarpathian Rus'. Finally, the language questionnaire of 1937 was for many Ukrainophiles convincing proof of the government's lack of sincerity.

The recent Czechoslovak policy, which catered to the Russophile orientation on the one hand and gave half-hearted support to the Rusynophile current on the other, seemed to reflect certain proposals made by one Czech official at the end of 1933:

> Since Subcarpathian Rus' is from the economic standpoint a very backward land, from the political standpoint an unenlightened land, from the religious standpoint a bigoted land where all possible beliefs run rampant, it would be most expedient to encourage the natural assimilation of the Rusyns with Slovaks and Czechs and to support and cultivate in them not a foreign [Russian or Ukrainian] orientation, but rather to awaken in them . . . and to foster a pro-state orientation.
>
> This is even more necessary since we [Czechs] are a minority and every increase in the population of Czechoslovak nationality would mean a reinforcement and strengthening of the state. Since Rusyns do not have their own culture, do not have their own literature, do not have even one language, it would be from the standpoint of the state advantageous if this almost half-million Slavic people would become assimilated with the two Czech and Slovak branches, out of which . . . would result an amalgamation into one branch.[91]

As stated above, this attitude may have been believed by some individuals, but it was not the goal of the government. The policy of Rusynism was intended to consolidate the internal political situation in Czechoslovakia; it was not a means toward national assimilation. Many Ukrainophiles, however, did equate the two, and the result was a qualitative change in the attitude of many activists within the Ukrainian movement.

The Radicalization of the Ukrainian Movement
As we have seen, the policy of Rusynism adopted about 1935 by the Czechoslovak government resulted in greater friction between Prague and Ukrainophile leaders in Subcarpathian Rus'. At a time when the Ukrainian movement was becoming ever more influential throughout the province, Prague seemed to be reversing the pro-Ukrainian policy it followed during the early 1920s. What were the reasons for such a change and how did Ukrainophiles react to this modification of official policy?

Perhaps the best explanation for Czechoslovak policy can be found in what may be called the law of survival. Every nation is concerned primarily with its own perpetuation as an existing body, and with threats by Germany, Poland, and Hungary coming from all sides, Czechoslovak leaders became extremely sensitive to criticism even in the mildest form. Since its claim to Subcarpathian Rus' was recognized in 1919 by international treaty, Prague reacted strongly to any ideologies suggesting that Rusyn interests might lie beyond the borders of Czecoslovakia. On this basis, Czechoslovak official circles became especially wary of any movements tinged by Ukrainian irredentism. In fact, by the late 1930s, almost any manifestation of

Ukrainian national feeling by Subcarpathian Rusyns was interpreted as a desire to break away from Czechoslovakia in order to unite with some future united Ukrainian state.

Prague's apprehensiveness toward the Ukrainian movement, however, was not a recent phenomenon. During the 1920s, when the Czechoslovak Academy of Science and Uzhhorod school administration supported the Little Russian (or Ukrainian) cultural orientation, local police were carefully searching for any indications of Ukrainian irredentism. They were particularly suspicious of the Basilian monks, then arriving in large numbers from Galicia. For instance, an investigation of the Basilian printing office in Uzhhorod turned up leaflets which read, "Out with the Czechs, long live the Ukraine and Ukrainian revolutionary organization, long live terror."[92] Arrests were made and the authorities concluded that even if most of the propaganda was directed at the Polish administration in Galicia, "interrogations of those apprehended revealed that they wanted 'to free' not only the Ukraine belonging to Poland, but also Subcarpathian Rus'."[93]

Similarly, a pamphlet entitled *Subcarpathia's Struggle for Statehood* was found to be widespread among the religious order. This work analyzed the events leading to Czechoslovakia's "imperialist" annexation of Subcarpathian Rus' in 1918-1919 and declared the provisions of the treaty of St. Germain, as well as the Czechoslovak Constitution, to be illegal, since they were opposed "to the will of the Ukrainian [i.e., Subcarpathian Rusyn] people."[94] In conclusion, the author made his anti-Czechoslovak stance clear: "All the enslaved masses of Subcarpathian Ukraine long for union with the Ukrainian masses of the whole Ukraine, seeing in this [union], liberation from age-long servitude. The Ukrainian masses of Subcarpathia are condemned to hard slavery by the Czechoslovak government and to a long struggle for their liberation and unification with the working masses of the whole Ukraine. Nonetheless, this struggle will end by their victory."[95] Language such as this forced the Czechoslovak authorities to keep an eye on all Ukrainian and Ukrainophile groups located within and beyond its borders. Of course, Prague's democratic regime not only tolerated but continued to encourage cultural development among Ukrainians, Russians, and other Slavic immigrants living in Czechoslovakia.[96] At the same time, however, such a policy permitted the spread of various ideologies, some directly opposed to Czechoslovakia's presence in Subcarpathian Rus'.

Police reports were filled with statements describing the activity of the Galician-based Ukrainian Military Organization (UVO) and the Organization of Ukrainian Nationalists (OUN), both of which had affiliates in Subcarpathian Rus' that were "working for the forcible detachment of the province from Czechoslovakia and for its incorporation into a Greater Ukraine."[97] Similarly, a Berlin-based Ukrainian monarchist movement, headed by Hetman Pavlo Skoropads'kyi, was credited with having agreed that Subcarpathian Rus' would be returned to Hungary after the "resurrection" of Ukrainian statehood.[98] Even if these groups were not yet considered dangerous in 1930, it was felt that they might, in the near future, prove to be a magnet for the youth of the province. In fact, Czech observers felt that the younger generation was "the greatest danger," because it "was educated by Ukrainian teachers, . . . spoke Ukrainian, [and was] politically oriented toward a Great Ukraine in which they saw salvation for the Rusyn people."[99]

While Hungarian, Polish, and German authorities were increasing their propaganda barrage against Czechoslovakia, Prague officials became suspicious of all autonomist, or potentially autonomist, movements. For example, in an effort to limit the spread of Ukrainianism, the Ministry of Interior declared in 1933 that it was illegal to use the name Ukrainian when referring to the population or territory of Subcarpathian Rus'. This decree was upheld three years later by a Prague administrative tribunal.[100] An attempt was also made to have all Ukrainian immigrant organizations guarantee support for Czechoslovakia's retention of the province.[101] Even local fire-companies in Subcarpathian Rus' came under criticism for being infested with members of the *Sich*, nominally a cultural organization, but suspected of being a paramilitary one.[102]

But the government was most concerned about Ukrainianism, because it had become the nationality policy of the Communist party, one of the strongest political forces in the province. Before 1926, the local Communist organization (dominated by Magyars) was undecided on the nationality issue. Later, Ivan Mondok recalled at the Fifth Congress of the Czechoslovak Communist Party (1924) that "We did not know what we actually were." "Were we *Rusy*, Rusyns, or *rus'kii* with a soft 's'; in short we didn't know what we were."[103] In December 1925, however, Subcarpathian delegates to the Ninth Congress of the Communist Party of the Soviet Ukraine accepted the decision that their people were to be considered Ukrainian and nothing else. The 1920s marked a high point in the revival of Ukrainian culture, even under Soviet auspices,[104] and territories like Galicia, Bukovina, and Subcarpathian Rus', which belonged to Poland, Rumania, and Czechoslovakia, respectively, were considered Ukrainian lands that one day must be liberated and united with the Soviet Ukraine. It was in this context that a Ukrainian policy seemed most feasible, and at the Seventh Congress of the Subcarpathian Communist Party, held in December 1926, it was finally announced that the nationality and "language question no longer exist." "It is obvious to us that we are a part of the Ukrainian people . . . and finally we will end . . . all 'language questions' [and dispense] with the names 'Rusyn', 'rus'kyi or 'russkii'."[105] After February 1926, *Karpats'ka pravda* was printed only in literary Ukrainian, and by the end of the year the homeland was referred to only as Transcarpathian Ukraine (*Zakarpats'ka Ukraïna*). Moreover, the "population inhabiting the territory officially [known as] Subcarpathian Rus' and the Prešov Region is a part of the Ukrainian nation."[106] Russophilism and Rusynism were considered ideologies that would aid Prague in its goal of Czechization,[107] and in preparation for the 1930 census, the party campaigned with the slogan: "Show that you belong to the great 40 million strong Ukrainian people, which in the Soviet land has already liberated itself from foreigners and from the bourgeoisie and is building socialism."[108] To stave off criticisms of disloyalty to the Czechoslovak republic, Deputy Gáti argued in a self-contradictory manner: "we are not irredentists as the bourgeois press interprets [this term]; we only want to free and to unite all Ukrainians."[109]

The Communists, like the Orthodox proselytizers before them, gave the language and nationality question a socioeconomic twist. According to Marxist theory, in the nineteenth century the Subcarpathian bourgeoisie either sold themselves to the "reactionary" Russophile movement or became pro-Hungarian Magyarones. In recent years, a trend to join the Czechoslovak ruling class was evident. Only the Subcarpathian peasants and workers preserved their original "Ukrainian" speech pattern and national character. Subsequently, it was the role of the Communist party to maintain in the future the Ukrainian national identity of the population.[110]

In various ways, the Soviet Ukraine provided support for the Communist organization of Subcarpathian Rus'. Since January 1926, the offices of the Communist Party of the Western Ukraine (a Galician organization in exile in Kharkiv) included a special section for Subcarpathian affairs, headed by an exile from Uzhhorod, Dr. Oleksandr Badan (1895-1933).[111] Kharkiv also became a center for many Rusyns like Ivan Petrushchak (1902-1961), Ivan Turianytsia (1901-1955), and Oleksa Borkaniuk (1901-1942)—each important during or after the Second World War—who were sent to study at the party school, as well as the home of political refugees like Ivan Mondok, a former Communist deputy forced to leave Czechoslovakia. The Soviet Ukrainian party boss, Mykola Skrypnyk, guaranteed a fixed number of subscriptions that would fund the publication in Uzhhorod of a politico-literary monthly, *Nasha zemlia* (1927-1929). Edited by the popular local Ukrainophile writer Vasyl' Grendzha-Dons'kyi, this was the first Subcarpathian periodical to describe systematically the progress achieved by "our Ukrainian brethren in the Soviet Union."[112] Grendzha-Dons'kyi and Badan were also given the opportunity to publish their works in the Soviet Ukraine.[113] Finally, the Soviet model was used in local Communist youth organizations, which propagated Marxism and, unwittingly, Ukrainian nationalism among their members.[114]

As for political policy, an important tactical change took place sometime after 1935. In May of that year an alliance treaty was signed between the Soviet Union and Czechoslovakia, and the order came from Moscow that the local communist parties must lead the "popular front of all anti-fascist forces" and aid Prague in its struggle against totalitarian Germany.[115] Consequently, the Subcarpathian Communists toned down their demands for unity with the Soviet Ukraine, and even if they continued to warn Rusyns not to "be deceived by Czech [bourgeois] autonomy"[116] or by "those slogans which deceive the working masses in the interests of foreign [German, Hungarian, Polish] and domestic [Fentsik and Brodii] fascism," they nonetheless renewed their pledge "to open their hands to all workers and all organizations which honestly want to struggle for the fulfillment of autonomous rights."[117] The 1937 program of the Subcarpathian party organization called for "the full realization of autonomous rights guaranteed by the Constitution, especially the drawing up of candidate-lists for a [local] Soim."[118] Such an attitude implied the acceptance of Czechoslovak rule in Subcarpathian Rus', and the Communists even recommended that their own members join other "progressive" elements and enter the Prosvita Society, which had previously been considered an unfavorable "bourgeois-nationalist organization."[119] Party cooperation with the growing Ukrainian movement was also evident at the massive Prosvita Congress held in Uzhhorod on October 17, 1937, when Communist Parliamentary Deputy Oleksa Borkaniuk delivered one of the main addresses.[120]

Despite these tactical moves, however, the Communist party remained strongly opposed to the Prague regime. As a result, conservative elements in Czechoslovak and Subcarpathian societies associated one part of the Ukrainian movement with Communism, which in turn was viewed as a constant revolutionary threat to governmental stability. Indeed, Prague did change its attitude toward the Ukrainophile orientation, because simultaneously there was a qualitative transformation in the attitude of the movement's leaders. Within less than two decades, many Rusyns of the populist-Ukrainophile cultural orientation became fully aware and confident of a Ukrainian national identity. Not every Rusyn went through this transformation, however, and those who did not were pejoratively labeled as *Nedîliashnyky,* after the newspaper *Nedîlia* (1935-1938), which served as the organ of the Rusynophile orientation. Usually of the older generation, the *Nedîliashnyky* were afraid that by becoming Ukrainian they would lose something of their local Subcarpathian heritage. In the words of Emyliian Bokshai, former editor of *Nedîlia*: "At first the Ukrainophiles used a popular language like ours and even called themselves Rusyns. Unfortunately, they later began to use a new script [modern orthography], claim that they were Ukrainians, and scorn things Rusyn. They changed!"[121]

Other Subcarpathians, however, were proud that their Rusyn people were part of the Ukrainian nation. The writers V. Grendzha-Dons'kyi and Iu. Borshosh-Kumiats'kyi, and politico-cultural leaders A. Voloshyn and Iu. Revai, initially considered themselves Rusyn, but eventually professed a Ukrainian identity. "We, Subcarpathian Rusyns," declared Revai, "are a small fragment of the great Ukrainian people that lives beyond the Carpathians."[122] On the other hand, the *Nedîliashnyky* and intransigent Ru-

syns like Governor Hrabar and Greek Catholic Bishop Stoika were considered to be both nationally unenlightened and as dangerous as Russophiles.[123]

As we have seen, more and more authors, editors, and teachers dispensed
with dialectal forms and adopted literary Ukrainian, written in the modern
orthography. In the political realm, the Russophile domination of the leading pro-government Agrarian party was tempered after December 1935,
when a group of younger members formed a Ukrainophile section, represented by the newspaper, *Zemlia i volia* (1934-1938). Their aim was to defend "the Ukrainian people of Subcarpathia, their language and their culture. In this way we want to transform the ignorant Rusyn into a conscious
member of the Ukrainian people."[124] By the late 1930s, Ukrainophiles not
only dominated the Communist party but also composed an important faction within the pro-Czechoslovak Agrarian party.

To be sure, enemies of the movement were apt to describe all Ukrainophiles as irredentists who wanted to detach Subcarpathian Rus' from
Czechoslovakia and unite it to a future, independent and free Ukrainian
state.[125] The Ukrainophiles were aware of these attacks and anxious to
make known their loyalty to the state. A poster announcing the October
1937 Prosvita Congress, which appeared in many places throughout Subcarpathia, declared: "We voluntarily joined the Czechoslovak Republic and
we are loyal citizens of our democratic state."[126] At the same time, it was
stressed that state loyalty and national loyalty might be two different things,
so that "in language and cultural matters we were and will be a part of the
great 50 million strong Ukrainian nation, and this, our national and cultural
unity, we will never in any way renounce."[127] Accepting this premise, it was
further argued that "we Subcarpathian Ukrainians have the right to call on
our people abroad."[128]

In every group, there are extremists, and the Ukrainian movement in
Subcarpathian Rus' was no exception. As the police reports suggested, it
was among youth that the most radical anti-Czechoslovak attitudes were
expressed. Reflecting the general trend toward fascism during the 1930s,
one young Ukrainophile from Subcarpathian Rus' did not hide his disgust
with "the 'holy' ideas of Slavism, humanism, democracy, brotherhood."
The allusion to Masaryk's teachings was obvious. The author continued:
"These concepts are beautiful dreams. They are destructive illusions which
weaken us . . . In relationships between peoples, where the law of strength
prevails, Ukrainians [of Subcarpathian Rus'] have no other help than one:
to become the strongest."[129] While the Prague administration was conducting its "democratic" language questionnaire, the Prosvita Society in Uzhhorod staged a massive demonstration on October 17, 1937. Pride in U-
krainianism was the order of the day, and the radical nationalist Dr. Stepan
Rosokha categorically ruled out all cooperation with the government.
"Until now we fought for the autonomy of Transcarpathia, but now we

don't want autonomy from the Czechs any more, because we want an Independent and United Ukrainian State, for which we will struggle to the last drop of blood."[130]

Yet it would be wrong to describe the Ukrainian movement in Subcarpathian Rus' as being irredentist or opposed to the integrity of the state. With the exception of some immigrant groups (more dangerous in police reports than in reality), and the rash statements of a few leaders, most Ukrainophiles (eventually even the Communists) favored the continued existence of Czechoslovakia. While the Russophile autonomists were actively courting Warsaw and Budapest, Ukrainophiles were primarily interested in cultural independence and autonomy—but both *within* the Czechoslovak republic. While it was still possible, the renowned Ukrainophile, A. Voloshyn emphasized in public his deep appreciation to the Prague regime for its "policy of genuine democracy and Slavonic brotherhood," and, as late as the spring of 1938, Iu. Revai proclaimed that even in these "hardest of times . . . the flowering of Subcarpathian Rus' is closely tied to the fate of the Czechoslovak Republic."[131]

Perhaps by granting a greater degree of autonomy than was offered in the "temporary" law of 1937 and by interfering less in the cultural—especially linguistic—affairs of the province, the Czechoslovak administration would have maintained the support of the Ukrainophile faction. But "Czech politicians and Czech bureaucrats in Prague and in Uzhhorod . . . accepted the position that autonomy in Subcarpathian Rus' would be possible only after 25 or 50 years."[132] The policy of Rusynism, and especially the language questionnaire, only forced many leaders—Ukrainophles included—into the opposing camp.

The result was that with the exception of Governor Hrabar, Bishop Stoika, and the Czech bureaucracy, Prague entered the critical year of 1938 with hardly any support among Subcarpathian leaders. During the previous seventeen years, the government had favored at various times the populist-Ukrainophile, Russophile, and Rusynophile national orientations. None of the three, however, was allowed to dominate, and such a policy resulted in a situation similar to that which existed when the Czechoslovaks first entered the province, that is, the existence of three national currents. The only difference was that the general faith expressed by Rusyns in their "Czech brethren" in 1919 was, in less than two decades, transformed at best into distrust and at worst into support of antagonistic foreign governments.

12 | The Period of International Crises, 1938-1944

The year 1938 was fateful for the Czechoslovak republic. The German threat, which began in earnest after the rise to power of Hitler, reached fruition in September with the signing of the Munich Pact. This agreement marked the first stage in the destruction of Czechoslovakia. Consequently, the nationality problem and political developments in Subcarpathian Rus' were profoundly influenced by external events. During the next seven years the international situation largely determined the nationality policies that the local intelligentsia was permitted to follow.

During the first months of 1938, Subcarpathian leaders created a common front for negotiations with the Prague government. Eventually, this policy proved successful, because after the Munich Crisis, when Czechoslovakia was transformed into a federal state, Subcarpathian Rus' received its long-sought autonomy. As for the nationality issue, the Ukrainophile orientation came to dominate the situation after the break-up in late October of the Russophile-Ukrainophile alliance. The Ukrainophile ascendence lasted until the Hungarians occupied the province in March 1939.

The new Hungarian administration attempted to liquidate entirely the Ukrainophile orientation and to replace it with a policy of Rusynism, which the Czechoslovak government had grudgingly favored in recent years. A pro-Hungarian or Uhro-Rusyn orientation came to be the only one permitted during the years of the Second World War. International developments, however, were to influence the nationality question once again. By October 1944, Soviet armies had driven out the Hungarians, and soon various local councils were established that demanded incorporation into the Soviet Union. In June 1945, the province became legally a part of the Soviet Ukraine and the nationality issue was thenceforth beyond discussion—the local populace was declared Ukrainian and any arguments favoring a Russophile or Rusynophile orientation were dismissed outright.

Political Developments before the Munich Pact
The incorporation of Austria into Germany in March 1938 was a definite sign that Czechoslovakia would soon be subjected to increasing pressure

from her western neighbor. Moreover, within Czechoslovakia itself the Sudeten-German minority, under Konrad Henlein and the Slovak autonomists led by Msgr. Jozef Tiso, had become ever more adamant and uncompromising in their demands. Subcarpathian leaders, too, realized that their situation might be improved if they were united in their dealings with Prague. Unity of the various Subcarpathian political factions became the essential prerequisite for success, and local leaders were stimulated to cooperate after the government's consistent refusal to implement the first stage (1937) of the autonomy law.

A common front arose first among Subcarpathia's parliamentary representatives. The Russophile Bachinskii and the Ukrainophile Revai had already cooperated in drawing up an autonomy proposal the year before, and in early 1938 they agreed to continue to work together for Subcarpathian autonomy. Similarly, the Russophile autonomist leaders Brodii and Fentsik agreed to put aside their disputes, and in April they formed a Carpatho-Russian autonomist bloc. Soon they were willing to collaborate with Bachinskii. Thus, by the spring of 1938 national antagonisms had been temporarily superseded by political expediency, and Subcarpathian politics came to be dominated by four of the province's parliamentarians—Bachinskii, Revai, Brodii, and Fentsik.[1]

The drive toward Subcarpathian unity was further influenced by the arrival of a delegation from the American Carpatho-Russian Union, including its chairman, Joann Popp, financial secretary, Rev. Joann Vanchishin, and general secretary, Dr. Aleksei Gerovskii (1883-1972). Gerovskii was a native of Galicia who had come to Subcarpathian Rus' during the 1920s and worked to propagate Orthodoxy and the Russophile orientation. Ordered to leave Czechoslovakia in 1927, he eventually settled in the United States, where he helped to found the Carpatho-Russian Union, a group of Orthodox and Greek Catholic Rusyn immigrants who were opposed to Czechoslovakia's administration of the homeland.[2] Although his proposed visit was opposed by many Prague officials, Prime Minister Hodža decided that at such a critical moment in the country's international relations, it was necessary to get Gerovskii on the side of the republic "at all costs."[3] The immigrant delegation was permitted to enter Czechoslovakia in May, meetings were held with Hodža, and comprehensive tours of both eastern Slovakia and Subcarpathian Rus' took place. As a result of Gerovskii's presence, many Subcarpathian parliamentarians joined to form a Russian Bloc in June, and even local Russophiles and Ukrainophiles cooperated for a while.[4]

A concrete example of unity came at a joint session of the First Russian-Ukrainian Central National Council (hereafter R-UCNC), which met in Uzhhorod on May 29, 1938. Presided over by Brodii, Revai, and Gerovskii, the R-UCNC issued a resolution which made clear that it "firmly supported the position of the unity of Subcarpathian Rus' with the Czechoslovak Republic and the inviolability of its borders."[5] Nevertheless, the old demands were rephrased again: "to introduce in the shortest possible time elections to a Subcarpathian autonomous Soim and to unite with Subcarpathian Rus' that territory in eastern Slovakia inhabited by Rusyn-Ukrainians."[6] In the meantime, the council requested that the government immediately fulfill six requests, among which were the establishment of a Subcarpathian ministry in Prague, the removal from Uzhhorod of the Czech superintendents for education and national culture, and the subordination of the provincial administration to the governor.

Although the Czechoslovak government did not fulfill any of these demands, Prime Minister Hodža did arrange a series of meetings with Subcarpathian leaders during the month of July. After conferring on separate occasions with Governor Hrabar, Deputy Revai, and Senator Bachinskii, the prime minister declared that the government did not oppose holding elections to a Soim before the end of the year.[7] At the same time, Bachinskii and other Agrarian leaders presented the government with a new project for autonomy, one which was also supported by the Ukrainophile A. Voloshyn.[8] Prague, however, could not yet concentrate fully on Subcarpathian Rus', because the more pressing problem of the Sudeten Germans had reached a point of insoluble crisis.[9]

While Subcarpathian leaders were negotiating in Prague, events in the province made the local populace aware of imminent political changes. In particular, the Ukrainian orientation became more politicized. A series of Prosvita congresses were held during the summer months in centers of Ukrainian strength like Khust, Velyka Kopania, and Rakhiv. Speakers stressed that the local populace had a duty to become not only nationally conscious but politically active in the struggle for self-rule. Young nationalists in particular emphasized that: "the old Rusyn type—a slave—was being transformed into a new kind of conscious Rusyn-Ukrainian, aware of his own national unity and strength. The Rusyn must learn to see, to want, to live, and to think."[10] By September, recent university graduates like Stepan Rosokha, Ivan Rohach (1913-1942), and Vasyl' Ivanovchyk had decided to respond to Polish and Hungarian border threats by forming a paramilitary organization, the Ukrainian National Defense (Ukraïns'ka Natsional'na Oborona).[11]

While the Czechoslovak government and public focused its attention on the Sudeten German crisis, members of the R-UCNC called a general meeting in Uzhhorod on September 4. The 1,100 participants accepted the previous resolution drawn up by the council's leaders at the May 29 meeting, and a delegation headed by A. Voloshyn and Iu. Revai was dispatched to meet with Prime Minister Hodža in Prague. Despite a renewed pledge that the government would arrange for elections before the end of the year, Subcarpathian leaders were not convinced by Czech promises and the R-UCNC "decided not to undertake further discussions . . . until the government presents a responsible and concretely formulated project for autonomy."[12] More formal resolutions followed. Through the initiative of Gerovskii, members of the Russian Bloc in Parliament met with German, Hungarian, Polish, and Italian diplomats in Prague, and on September 13 they submitted memoranda to Lord Runciman, the English delegate sent to Czechoslovakia, in an attempt to mediate the crisis between the Czechs and Germans in Bohemia.[13] One week later, the Russian Bloc, joined now by Fentsik and Revai (but not the Communists), signed a declaration in Prague demanding that self-government for the province be instituted immediately.[14] This was the state of Subcarpathian-Czechoslovak relations on the eve of the Munich crisis.

The Establishment of Subcarpathian Autonomy and the Carpatho-Ukraine

Hitler's claim to the Sudetenland—the border areas in Bohemia and Moravia inhabited by three million Germans—was recognized after a series of meetings that culminated in the Munich Pact of September 30, 1938. On that day, President Beneš of Czechoslovakia was forced to accept the decisions reached by the leaders of Great Britain, France, Italy, and Germany—Chamberlain, Daladier, Mussolini, and Hitler. As a result of the Munich Pact, Czechoslovakia lost large tracts of territory from its western provinces.[15]

Governmental changes in Prague were imminent, and after Munich negotiations were renewed with Subcarpathian leaders. During the first days of October, a delegation of Ukrainophiles and Russophiles headed by Revai, Bachinskii, and Brodii met with the new prime minister, General Jan Syrový. In the reorganization of his cabinet on October 4, Syrový appointed Dr. Ivan Parkanyi (b. 1896), the secretary to the Czechoslovak president for Rusyn affairs, as minister for Subcarpathian Rus'. During the next few days, the situation in Czechoslovakia continued to change rapidly. President Beneš resigned on October 5, and the next day Slovak leaders met in Žilina to demand the immediate implementation of autonomy for their province. This request was fulfilled, and on October 7, Prime Minister Syrový appointed Jozef Tiso premier of an autonomous Slovakia.[16]

Subcarpathian leaders who participated as observers at Žilina were quick to follow the lead of the Slovaks. At a joint meeting of the R-UCNC in Uzhhorod on October 8, it was "unanimously decided to demand the same rights for Subcarpathian Rus' as have been or will be granted to Slovakia.[17] It was also proposed that in the autonomous government Andrei Brodii should be appointed premier and Dr. Edmund Bachinskii, Dr. Ivan P'eshchak, Iuliian Revai, Avhustyn Voloshyn, and Dr. Stepan Fentsik as ministers. After two days of negotiations, Prime Minister Syrový accepted the proposed candidates, and on October 11 appointed the first autonomous government of Subcarpathian Rus'.[18] Governor Hrabar had already resigned, the office of vice-governor was abolished, and Parkanyi was relieved as minister in the Prague cabinet.[19] With these changes in Slovakia and Subcarpathian Rus', the former unitary republic was transformed into the federal state of Czecho-Slovakia.

It should be emphasized that from the beginning (May 29, 1938), the union of local Ukrainophile and Russophile leaders was extremely tenuous. In practice, members of the Ukrainophile and Russophile National Councils met more often in separate sessions than in the joint R-UCNC. The latter primarily functioned in negotiations with the Czechoslovak government; as soon as autonomy was attained, however, the R-UCNC ceased to exist. During the month of October, the Russophile faction seemed to have the upper hand, with four out of six members in Brodii's cabinet, but their hegemony was to dissipate in a few weeks.

The Brodii cabinet functioned from October 11 to 26, 1938. During that time, the premier reiterated his position on the nationality question and attacked the Czechoslovak administration, which in his view had conducted, for almost two decades a pro-Ukrainian, "anti-Russian educational and cultural policy."[20] Incensed at the number of Czech schools, Russophile leaders called for the liquidation of those located in places "where there was an insufficient number of Czech children."[21] An intensive campaign was also undertaken to unite Rusyn-inhabited territory in eastern Slovakia with Subcarpathian Rus'. Brodii declared in his initial speech as premier, "that the first government of Carpathian Rus' will undertake all measures . . . in order to unite all the Russian [russkaia] territories in the Carpathians (from the Poprad to the Tisa Rivers) in one unitary, free state."[22] Ministers Fentsik and P'eshchak were sent to the area and their call for union was met with widespread support among Rusyns living there.[23]

But Brodii and Fentsik were most concerned about conducting a plebiscite to decide the political future of the province. Both leaders favored the return of Hungarian rule and felt that if a plebiscite were held among the local inhabitants, a clear majority would oppose Czecho-Slovakia and perhaps favor Hungary. To popularize such an improbable goal, Fentsik used his young followers, the so-called Black Shirts (Chornorubashniki), in a series of demonstrations calling for a general plebiscite.[24] Thus, Hungarian and Polish foreign policy aims for a common border were being worked out, and these two Rusyn "autonomists" were fulfilling the orders of Budapest and Warsaw. Indeed, other Russophiles, like Bachinskii and some Agrarian party leaders, opposed the return of the province to Hungary, but Brodii called a closed meeting of the Russophile Central National Council, which accepted the idea of a plebiscite.[25]

The Czechoslovak government was aware of these developments, and on October 26 Syrový met with the Subcarpathian ministers in Prague. Brodii was accused of treason and arrested; Fentsik escaped successfully to the nearby Polish Embassy. Prime Minister Syrový then appointed a new Subcarpathian government with Avhustyn Voloshyn as prime minister and

Iuliian Revai and Edmund Bachinskii as ministers.[26] This began the domination by the Ukrainophile orientation of the political life of the province.

After less than a week in office the Voloshyn cabinet underwent its first crisis. Since September, the Hungarians had been pressing for border revision, and technically the four-power guarantees provided in the Munich Pact were to become operative only after Polish and Hungarian claims were satisfied. The Hungarian government demanded all of Subcarpathian Rus' as well as the southern fringe of Slovakia, which was inhabited by Magyars. During October, while officials from Budapest were negotiating with Slovak and Rusyn delegates at the border town of Komárno, plans were also being worked out with Poland to coordinate terrorist attacks on Subcarpathian Rus'. Former Minister of Interior Miklós Kozma (who was later appointed Hungarian commissar of Subcarpathia), organized the Rongyos Gárda or voluntary legions *(szabadcsapatok)* to attack the southern border regions, while Polish irregulars did the same in the north.[27] These actions were undertaken to increase tension, and when negotiations at Komárno did prove unsuccessful, Germany and Italy were called in to arbitrate. At a meeting in Vienna on November 2, Hungary was awarded the Magyar-inhabited territories along the southern border of Slovakia and Subcarpathian Rus', including the province's capital, Uzhhorod, and the other leading cities of Mukachevo and Berehovo. Czechoslovak authorities and Voloshyn's government were given a week to evacuate, and the capital of the truncated autonomous province was transferred eastward to the town of Khust.[28]

Pro-Hungarian members of the Russophile Central National Council and of Brodii's AZS, among them Dr. Iosif Kaminskii, Mykhail Demko, Dr. Vladimir Gomichkov, Senator Julius Földesi, and Aleksei I. Il'kovich, remained in Uzhhorod to greet the Hungarian army and to plan for the autonomy they expected to receive from Budapest.[29] Similarly, the supporters of Fentsik formed a Russian National Council (Russkii Natsional'nyi Soviet), and immediately began a campaign to gain for Hungary the remaining portion of Subcarpathian Rus' and the Rusyn-inhabited territories in eastern Slovakia. Fentsik was appointed a member of the Hungarian Parliament in Budapest and then made his way to Uzhhorod, where in each issue of his party organ, large letters "saluted the one and undivided Carpathian Rus' from the Poprad to the Tisa, autonomous within the borders of the Hungarian Kingdom."[30] As we have seen, Bishop Aleksander Stoika and other influential prelates also remained in Uzhhorod and eventually came out in support of the Hungarian regime. (See p. 186.)

After its transfer to Khust, the Voloshyn government began to consolidate itself and to take on the characteristics of an autonomous state. In order to protect the province against future incursions by Hungarian terrorists, the recently established Ukrainian National Defense was transformed

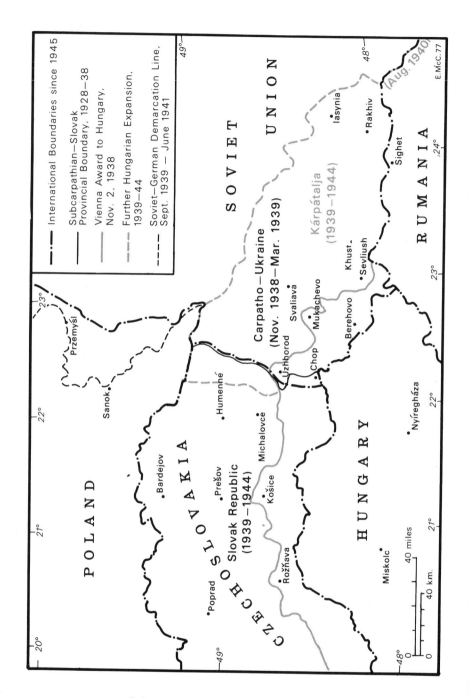

Subcarpathian Border Changes, 1938-1945

into a military force, the Carpathian Sich, led by Dmytro Klempush (18??-1973) and other avid Ukrainian nationalists, like Ivan Roman, Ivan Rohach (1913-1942), and Stepan Rosokha.[31] The Sich was recognized by the Czecho-Slovak government and authorized to carry weapons and to wear uniforms. To facilitate relations with Prague, a Subcarpathian governmental mission was set up in the Czecho-Slovak capital.[32] On November 22, 1938, the autonomous province was given legal status when the Parliament passed a constitutional act. By this act, the former administrative apparatus was dismantled and all competence placed in the hands of a three-man Subcarpathian ministry. Most important, a provision was included which called for elections to a Soim within five months. The Soim was to decide on the question of the official name and language of the province.[33] Even before the Soim had met, the Voloshyn regime went ahead and Ukrainianized the school system as well as the numerous official and unofficial publications that appeared. (See pp. 141-142 and 176.)

The autonomous province even made its mark, if briefly, in the international arena. In neighboring Polish Galicia, Ukrainians, led by the influential Greek Catholic Metropolitan of L'viv, Andrii Sheptyts'kyi, looked with great hope upon Subcarpathian Rus'. The Galician Ukrainians continued their traditional concern with Subcarpathian Rus', a concern that had begun with the nineteenth-century scholars Drahomanov, Franko, and Hnatiuk, and they followed very closely developments among their brethren to the south. They considered the region to be the first "Ukrainian" land to gain its freedom, and to protect this achievement many Galician volunteers crossed the mountains to join the Carpathian Sich.[34] It must be admitted that their enthusiasm was not always appreciated by the Subcarpathian leadership and general populace. For one thing, these newcomers reacted to the Czechoslovak government as if it were synonomous with the Polish regime in Galicia, and at the same time they viewed all Subcarpathian Russophiles and Rusynophiles (many of whom were respected local patriots) as traitors who must be liquidated or at least removed from any position of influence. For its part, the leadership in Khust resented the interference of the Galicians, and in response began to advocate that Subcarpathian "Ukrainians" were, after twenty years of Czechoslovak rule, more mature than their Galician brethren, and, having the only "Ukrainian" government in Europe, they would serve as a beacon for the other Ukrainian lands. Minister Revai was quoted at the time: "Usually they say the sun rises from the East, but this time it's coming from us!"[35]

Voloshyn also turned for aid to immigrants in the United States, where a Special Committee for the Defense of Carpatho-Ukraine was established in New York City in October 1938. This committee was made up for the most part of Ukrainian immigrants from Galicia.[36] On the other hand, the Subcarpathian immigrant community, led by the Greek Catholic Union and Gerovskii's Carpatho-Russian Union, sent "protests against the establishment of Ukraine on an immemorial Russian land as ordered by Premier Voloshyn.''[37] They saw their homeland being transformed into a center of pro-Nazi Ukrainian nationalism.

There was, in fact, some basis for such accusations. Hitler was interested in the general Ukrainian problem to the degree that it could be used for his own purposes, that is, to weaken Soviet Russia. Thus, for a while Berlin viewed Subcarpathian Rus' in the context of the larger Ukrainian question, and at the Vienna Arbitration in November, Foreign Minister von Ribbentrop assured Voloshyn that Germany would support his homeland both politically and economically. Speculation mounted that perhaps this small Carpathian province could be used as a "piedmont" for the creation of a unified Ukraine under Hitler's domination. Some steps were taken in this direction: Berlin set up a consulate in Khust, and in December 1938 two economic agreements were signed in Berlin providing for trade and German exploitation of Subcarpathia's mineral resources.[38] In the end, the province did not become a stepping stone to a free, united Ukraine, although the belief circulating in late 1938 that "Germany will build an independent Carpatho-Ukraine" did help to boost the self-confidence and pride of the local leaders.[39]

Despite the domination of the Ukrainophile orientation, the Russophiles were not entirely inactive. The pro-Hungarian activities of Fentsik and Brodii did discredit further the Russophile national orientation, but most Russophiles nonetheless remained loyal subjects and supported the concept of a federated Czecho-Slovak state. To replace the influential Agrarian party and the autonomist parties of Fentsik and Brodii, some Russophiles founded a Russian Populist National Party (Russkaia Vsenarodnaia (Natsional'naia Partiia).[40] In Khust, a group of twenty-five Russophiles and Rusynophiles met on November 14 to establish a Central Russian National Council. Their aim was to defend "Russian" interests in the autonomist province, and they sent a memorandum to Prague demanding that the Voloshyn government be replaced by a cabinet headed by Minister Edmund Bachinskii and including Deputy Pavel Kossei (1896-194?) and former Governor of Rus'ka Kraina Dr. Agoston Stefan.[41]

The Central Russian National Council was led by Vasilii Karaman (1897-1959), Petr P. Sova, and Pavel S. Fedor, all of whom had served in the school administration in the pre-Munich Czechoslovak regime.[42] They protested against the dismissal of Russophiles from the school administration and complained of the general "Ukrainian terror" and the excesses of the Carpathian Sich, which maintained "concentration camps exclusively for Katsapy [pejorative term for local Russophiles] and Moskaly.''[43] In Prague, Russophile Subcarpathian university students protested against the use of the name Carpatho-Ukraine, while Minister Bachinskii and Deputy Kossei complained to the central government about the forced Ukrainianization being perpetrated by the Khust regime.[44]

Meanwhile, the Voloshyn cabinet was having increasing difficulties with the central government, especially after November 30, when Parliament choose Dr. Emil Hácha as the new president of Czecho-Slovakia. Despite Hácha's record of anti-Ukrainianism in Subcarpathian affairs,[45] he reappointed Voloshyn and Revai as ministers and dropped the only Russophile, Bachinskii; the government announced that the latter's vacant post would be filled at a later date. When, on January 16, 1939, Hácha appointed General Lev Prchala as third minister, a wave of protest swept Carpatho-Ukraine. Prchala was formerly the commander of the Czechoslovak army stationed within the province, and though himself a Czech, he was a known supporter of the Russophiles. Such qualifications made him entirely unacceptable to Khust governmental circles.[46]

Another cause for friction between Prague and Khust was the abolition of the former Subcarpathian provincial administration on January 1, 1939. Since many "former Czechoslovak" officials were not reemployed by the Voloshyn government—including 820 school teachers from the liquidated Czech schools—their fate became the responsibility of the central government. Moreover, Voloshyn also had difficulties with the Slovak government, since the Ukrainophile government continued the policy of the Brodii cabinet and demanded the union of the Rusyns in eastern Slovakia with Carpatho-Ukraine. Aggressive nationalists in Khust went so far as to proclaim "that the Ukrainian flag will fly over the Tatras."[47] The Tiso administration was angered by this issue, although in the strongly Russophile Prešov region of eastern Slovakia, the desire to unite with Carpatho-Ukraine virtually disappeared when it was realized that the Voloshyn government was Ukrainophile in orientation.[48]

Notwithstanding enormous difficulties faced by the Khust administration, preparations were made to fulfill one of the oldest political demands of Subcarpathian leaders, elections to an autonomous Soim. On January 12, 1939, Voloshyn decreed that elections would be held exactly one month later. To clarify the internal political changes since the establishment of autonomy, all political parties were declared invalid[49] and new parties called on to submit candidates by January 22. A new party, the Ukrainian National Union (Ukraïns'ke Natsional'ne Ob'iednannia), was created on January 13 under the leadership of Fedir Revai (1893-194?), the brother of Deputy Iuliian Revai. The Union presented a list of thirty-two candidates, many of whom were prominent local members in various pre-Munich political parties, but now united under one dominant force—"the Idea of Ukrainian nationalism."[50] For various reasons, the lists of the Russophile "Group of Subcarpathian Rusyns" and Orthodox candidates from the village of Iza were not accepted by the electoral commission. Thus, the populace was presented with only the list of the Ukrainian National Union.[51]

While the newspapers published by Fentsik and Brodii in occupied Uzhhorod called for the union of Carpatho-Ukraine with Hungary, the

Voloshyn government suggested that Soim elections would be a kind of plebiscite that would reveal the political attitudes of the people. The party newspaper, *Nova svoboda,* stated that by voting for the Ukrainian ballot, one favored the present government of Carpatho-Ukraine as well as the federative alliance with Czechs and Slovaks.[52] In this frame of reference, the results of the February 12 election turned out overwhelmingly positive for the Ukrainophiles. A substantial majority of 244,922 persons accepted the Ukrainian ballot, while only 17,752 were opposed.[53] It was generally accepted that "the elections were held in an atmosphere of calm and respect, without terror or corruption."[54]

The success registered by the Khust government was short lived, since the government survived only four more weeks. By February 1939, it had finally become evident to many political observers in Western Europe that Hitler was only waiting for the right moment to dismantle the remainder of Czecho-Slovakia and to give Hungary the signal to occupy all of Carpatho-Ukraine. Along the Hungarian and Polish borders terrorists renewed their attacks, while internally the remaining weeks of the Voloshyn administration were marked by increased friction with the Prague government.

The refusal of Ukrainians to accept the Czech General Prchala as minister in the autonomous government, and the extreme anti-Czechoslovak position of some Carpathian Sich members, gave Prague the impression that Voloshyn could no longer rule the province.[55] In fact, there was increasing internal conflict between, on the one hand, the older Ukrainophiles like Voloshyn and the Brashchaiko brothers and, on the other, the younger anti-Czechoslovak extremists like state secretaries S. Rosokha and I. Rohach. The latter were backed by the Sich, which by that time had come to be dominated by fanatic Ukrainian nationalists who had only recently come from Galicia.[56] President Hácha's delay in convening the Soim only aggravated matters. Furthermore, reports from various sources accused the Ukrainophile regime of continued terrorism against the local Russophiles, perpetrated especially by extremists in the Sich military organization. In such a situation, President Hácha decided to reorganize the Khust government, and on March 6 reappointed Voloshyn but dropped Iuliian Revai, who, with his brother Fedir, was viewed in Prague as an anti-Czecho-Slovak Ukrainian nationalist.[57] Stepan Klochurak (b. 1896) took Revai's place and General Prchala was named minister once again. A few days later Voloshyn's cabinet was expanded, but the tension between Czech and Subcarpathian leaders continued to increase until local Czechoslovak troops, commanded by General Prchala, fought a pitched battle with the Carpathian Sich on March 14.[58]

That same day, on Hitler's orders, chief minister Tiso announced the independence of Slovakia, and the Hungarian army began to march on Carpatho-Ukraine. While fighting was taking place between Carpathian Sich units and Hungarian troops, Voloshyn convened the Soim on the afternoon of March 15. In six sessions conducted until early evening, the twenty-two elected representative who were present passed a decree establishing the Republic of Carpatho-Ukraine. Avhustyn Voloshyn was chosen president and Iuliian Revai (in absentia) prime minister and minister for foreign affairs.[59]

This declaration of independence was more symbolic than real. The region was abandoned by the Prague regime (which itself ceased to exist) as well as by Hitler, whose revised plans for the Ukraine did not require the participation of this now insignificant Carpathian territory. In their hopeless situation, the members of the Carpatho-Ukrainian government were, in the face of the Hungarian invasion, forced to flee the country just a few hours after their symbolic declaration. On orders from Prague, Czechoslovak army units did not put up any resistance, and the defending Carpathian Sich was overwhelmed after stiff resistance by the advancing Hungarians. By March 16, the Hungarian army had control of Khust and in the next few days occupied all of Carpatho-Ukraine.[60]

The events in Europe during 1938 had a direct effect on the political and national status of Czechoslovakia's eastern territories. As a result of the Munich Crisis, Subcarpathian Rus' finally received its long-awaited autonomy. For a few months, Subcarpathians had their own government, their own military force, and their own elected diet, even if all this occurred during a time of economic hardship, strained relations with the Prague regime, loss of territory to the Hungarians, and the constant threat of military attack by Budapest and Warsaw. Indeed, the crucial goal of all nationalist movements was attained—self-government.

However, in terms of national identity, the autonomous regime, especially after November, did not view itself as representing a separate nationality, but rather as part of the Ukrainian nation. Symbolically, Dukhnovych's "Ia Rusyn bŷl, esm' y budu" ("I was, am, and will remain a Rusyn") was replaced by "Shche ne vmerla Ukraïna" ("The Ukraine Will Never Die") as the province's national hymn.

But this did not mean, as many Ukrainophile writers assert, that the local populace rejected the Russophile or Rusynophile national orientations. The February 1939 elections, for instance, were as much, if not more, a vote of confidence in the continued existence of a federated Czecho-Slovakia than an indication of Ukrainian national consciousness. In essence, a defense of the given political situation and rejection of Hungarian revisionist propaganda was not necessarily an indication of conscious Ukrainianism on the part of the local population.[61] There were still many Russophile leaders who were anti-Hungarian, and their exclusion from participation in the Carpatho-Ukrainian government did not mean that the Russophile or even Rusynophile national orientations were dead.

Still, it must be admitted that the Ukrainophile orientation did increase its influence and prestige among large segments of the local population during the stormy months of autonomy. At a time when Russophiles like Brodii and Fentsik, and Rusynophile Greek Catholic clerics like Bishop Stoika and Monsignor Aleksander Il'nyts'kyi opted for Hungary, the Ukrainophiles basically remained loyal subjects of Czecho-Slovakia and opposed all Hungarian and Polish intrigues against the homeland. Because of its pronounced anti-Hungarian stance, the Ukrainophile orientation spread rapidly, especially among the younger generation. The return of the Hungarians, however, put a temporary end to these developments, and the new administration was to make every effort to stamp out anything that related the province or its people with Ukrainianism.

The Return of Hungarian Rule

The incorporation of Subcarpathian Rus' into Hungary, completed in March 1939, was an important second stage in Budapest's revisionist policy. Once more Hungary reached the crest of the Carpathians, and for a few months, at least, gained the coveted common border with Poland.[62] The region was renamed Subcarpathia *(Kárpátalja)* and was ruled directly from Budapest. However, since revisionist propagandists had been promising that, under the Crown of St. Stephen, Subcarpathian Rus' would receive autonomy, local collaborators believed that "in the Hungarian state the Carpatho-Rusyns will receive the kind of self-government that they could not achieve during the last twenty years."[63] Hence, at least initially, Budapest felt obliged to formulate plans for self-rule.

As early as March 17, 1939, Hungarian Prime Minister Pál Teleki announced at a meeting of the ministerial council that the government intended to introduce autonomy in the newly acquired territory.[64] Teleki was himself a distinguished geographer and sympathetic to minority problems. He wanted the proposed Subcarpathian autonomy to be a model for other "lost Hungarian lands" that would in the future be regained for the fatherland. Teleki was supported in his endeavors by Brodii and Fentsik, who demanded immediate elections to a Subcarpathian national assembly. This would be the first step toward an eventual broad autonomy to be patterned on Law Ten of December 1918, by which the Károlyi regime called into being the political entity Rus'ka Kraina.[65]

For almost two decades Budapest had criticized the nationality policy of the Czechoslovak government, and in an attempt to avoid Prague's mistakes it established a minority institute at Pécs University, where legal experts were called upon to analyze, among other problems, the question of Subcarpathian autonomy. Various propagandistic pamphlets appeared that put forward supposedly feasible projects for a future autonomous Hungarian Carpathia.[66] Finally, after nine different proposals, the head of the minority institute, Professor István Egyed, submitted a project to Teleki that was accepted as being "true to the idea of the Crown of St. Stephan."[67] The proposed Subcarpathian Territory *(Kárpátalja vajdaság)* was to be ruled by a governor (who had to be a member of the Hungarian gentry) and a forty-member diet. Within the territory, the Rusyn language [*rutén nyelv*] was to be equal with the state language, although in all Rusyn schools Magyar would be a required subject.[68]

On July 23, 1940, the autonomy bill was introduced in the Hungarian Parliament, but this was the first and last time any serious attempt was made to legalize Subcarpathian self-rule. The press in Budapest had, from the beginning, expressed reservations, and the military was opposed because it feared that even the slightest semblance of autonomy would be a potential danger to the security of the country. Such an attitude seemed doubly convincing after September 1939, when the Soviet Union occupied eastern Poland and thus acquired a common border with Hungary. Great opposition was also expressed by the so-called "wild" Hungarians—local Magyars who refused to live in a Rusyn province—and by conservative public opinion, which was unfavorably reminded of the 1918 Jászi plan for a federated Hungary.[69] Finally, in the autumn of 1940 József Bölöny published a detailed criticism of the bill and concluded that autonomy for Carpathia would not be feasible because it would "strike a rift in the unity of the Hungarian state."[70] In subsequent years, some Social Democratic and Agricultural party deputies in the Hungarian Parliament mentioned the Subcarpathian autonomy issue, but it was never again seriously considered by the government. As a result, the loyal Brodii, whom the Hungarians so long trusted, became "dissatisfied" with Budapest policy and after 1941 was convinced that self-government would never be offered by the regime.[71]

The Subcarpathian Territory was ruled by the military until June 1939, but after that time a civil administration, headed by a commissioner, was appointed by the regent of Hungary, Miklós Horthy. During the six years of Hungarian rule, the territory had four commissioners: Baron Zsigmond Perényi (1939-1940), Miklós Kozma (1940-1941), Vilmos Tomcsányi (1941-1944), and General András Vincze (1944).[72] To aid the commissioners, Aleksander Il'nyts'kyi was appointed as counsellor, and a twelve-member advisory board was formed. Although the commissioner's headquarters was in Uzhhorod, that city and all other territory acquired at the Vienna Award of November 2, 1938, were considered integral parts of Hungary. Thus, the Subcarpathian Territory had the same boundaries as Voloshyn's Carpatho-Ukraine, and was divided for administrative purposes into three regions.[73]

In May 1939, parliamentary elections were held, but not in those territories acquired by Hungary during the previous year, which thus excluded Subcarpathia. Instead, Regent Horthy appointed in June twelve delegates to represent the Subcarpathian Territory: S. Fentsik, A. Il'nyts'kyi, and I. Kaminskii were appointed to the upper house,[74] while A. Brodii headed a group of nine deputies in the lower house, including former AZS members Iurii Bentse, Ivan Bokshai, and Ivan Shpak, former activists in the Russophile Central National Council Aleksander Chuga, Petr Gaevich, Vladimir Gomichkov, and Ödön Zsegora, and former Magyar party deputy and senator in the Czechoslovak Parliament Károly Hokky (1883-196?). Later Adal'bert Rishko, Julius Földesi, Mykhail Demko, and Stefan Budai were added.[75] All of these men had, for two decades, represented the pro-Hungarian faction of the Russophile and Rusynophile orientations, and they were avid opponents of the Czechoslovak regime. Now, in the Budapest Parliament, five of them joined Brodii to form a Uhro-Rusyn Club whose purpose was to press for the realization of autonomy. Despite the lack of any local elections, Brodii's AZS and Fentsik's RNAP continued to exist, and in 1940 they merged on paper with Endre Korláth's local Magyar party to form "a united bloc." In subsequent years, Commissioner Kozma called for the creation of a Rusyn-Magyar party (1941) and Brodii tried to establish a National Union of Subcarpathian Rusyns (1944).[76] All these developments were without significance, however, since in fact the Subcarpathian Territory continued to be administered by Budapest, first through the local commissioner and his advisors, and then, toward the end of the war, directly by the Hungarian military.

If the Hungarian government did not allow self-government, it did permit Rusyns to handle some cultural and educational matters within the territory. Certain guidelines, of course, had to be followed. Among these, the most important was a total rejection of the Ukrainophile orientation, which resulted in the closing of the Prosvita Society and liquidation of all Ukrainian-language publications.[77] Although the faithful Brodii and Fentsik continued, in their party newspapers, to support the Russophile current,[78] it was the Rusynophile, or rather Uhro-Rusyn, national orientation that the Hungarian administration favored. While the Czechoslovak regime had, since about 1935, half-heartedly supported a Rusynophile orientation, the new Hungarian administration made an all-out effort to convince the local population that they constituted a separate Uhro-Rusyn nationality whose past history and culture were intimately related with Hungarian civilization.

The Uhro-Rusyn theory was applied to Subcarpathian history, language, and literature and it was implemented through the school system, cultural organizations, and the Church. (See Chapters 5-9). Clearly, the Hungarian administration that returned to Subcarpathian Rus' in 1939 did not have exactly the same attitude as those pre-1918 Budapest leaders who refused even to recognize that the local inhabitants were anything other than "Greek Catholic Magyars."

In fact, large segments of the Hungarian public felt sincerely that after twenty years of "occupation and chaos" this lost territory inhabited by both Magyars and brother Rusyns was being rightly reunited with the homeland.[79] Guidebooks and even Magyar-Rusyn phrasebooks (both Russophile and Rusynophile) were published so that the Subcarpathian Territory would be better known.[80] Two decades of Czechoslovak administration, with advances in education, forced Hungary to revise its approach.

Rusyn culture could no longer be dismissed outright, and certain concessions had to be made. Nonetheless, within a few years, supporters of an assimilationist policy, especially in education, dominated the local administration.[81] And, as for promises of autonomy, no serious efforts were ever undertaken.

In the end, during almost six years of rule, the Hungarian regime did not succeed in gaining the confidence of the local population. True, in the beginning the occupying forces brought foodstuffs, and the peasants' status improved slightly,[82] but the government's policy of repealing the land reforms of the Czechoslovak administration, combined with the increasing pressures of the Second World War, made the economic situation in Subcarpathian Rus' worse than ever.[83]

Finally, the planned terror and concerted effort to liquidate all remaining Ukrainophile elements alienated large segments of the local population. Since many "mixed" families contained at least one Ukrainophile member, fear and hatred were instilled in parents and relatives who might not otherwise have considered themselves Ukrainian. As a result, many Subcarpathians hid in the inaccessible mountainous areas and then fled across the Carpathians into Soviet-controlled Galicia. In 1939-1940, for instance, it has been variously estimated that between 15,000 and 50,000 people left. After 1941, when this route was closed off by Hitler's invasion of the Soviet Union, the Hungarian police arrested 10,805 Rusyns—in particular young people who were suspected of Ukrainian or pro-Soviet sentiments.[84] Spying, arrests, and political trials became the rule, and the situation reached its worst in 1944 when, under German pressure, the Hungarian government deported the large Jewish community to concentration camps.[85] A regime that practiced terror on the one hand and national assimilation on the other could not expect to convince the local citizens that they were members of a unique independent Uhro-Rusyn nationality, destined to live on lands belonging to and protected by the Hungarian Crown of St. Stephen.

The controversies concerning national identity that existed in Subcarpathian Rus' during the Czechoslovak regime continued under Hungarian rule. While the Ukrainophile orientation could not express itself openly, the Russophile faction, especially the demagogic Fentsik, continued to attack Rusynophiles like Haraida for "debasing" the Russian literary tradition.[86] Furthermore, many Ukrainophile writers continued to function by having their works published in the traditional orthography. Thus, as late as 1944 the national question was no closer to being resolved. What nationality lives in Subcarpathian Rus'? Rusyn, Ukrainian, or Russian? For the majority of the population, and even for many of the intelligentsia, "this question was not clarified . . . until the Soviet period."[87]

13 | *The Soviet Period*

Efforts to Liberate the Homeland during the Second World War

The struggle for the liberation of Subcarpathian Rus' was actually part of the general movement carried on by Czechoslovak leaders during the Second World War, President Edvard Beneš, who was forced to leave his homeland in October 1938, went to Paris and then to London, where, in July 1940, he set up a Czechoslovak provisional government. This government-in-exile was recognized by the Allied Powers—the United States, Soviet Union, Great Britain, France. Most important, none of the Allied governments recognized the Munich Pact or any other international treaties that truncated the territory of Czechoslovakia in late 1938.[1] Thus, Beneš succeeded in having the pre-Munich borders of Czechoslovakia recognized as a postwar goal of the Allies; this, of course, included the eastern province, Subcarpathian Rus'.

Subcarpathian leaders from the Ukrainophile autonomous government, like Voloshyn, Revai, Klochurak, and Grendzha-Dons'kyi, settled in Prague or Bratislava after the Hungarian invasion. During the war years, these men issued secret memoranda calling for the unification of their homeland with a Soviet, or future independent, Ukrainian state.[2] This was in direct conflict with the goals of the Czechoslovak government-in-exile, which although not having any Subcarpathian ministers, nonetheless did appoint Dr. Pavel Tsibere (b.192?), in October 1940, to the state council, a body intended to be an advisory board for President Beneš. From the standpoint of the nationality problem, the appointment of Tsibere, a little-known Russophile, suggested that Czechoslovak officials were not prepared to concede that Subcarpathian Rus' was a Ukrainian land as proclaimed by the autonomous Voloshyn government. In fact, a decree by Beneš nullified all acts passed on the territory of Czechoslovakia after September 29, 1938.[3] This meant that Subcarpathia's long-sought autonomy, as guaranteed by a Czechoslovak constitutional law of November 1938, was declared invalid. When referring to its former eastern province, Czechoslovak leaders still used the terms Subcarpathian Rus' (*Podkarpatská Rus*) for the territory

250

and Carpatho-Russian or Rusyn for the population. Later, a Subcarpathian Ukrainophile, Ivan Petrushchak, was appointed to the state council, but he too repudiated Voloshyn's autonomous regime and called for the creation of a "new republic of free and equal Slavic peoples."[4]

Like Masaryk during the First World War, Beneš was anxious to gain the support of Rusyns living in the United States. After the resignation of Governor Zsatkovich in 1921, American-Rusyn groups had, for almost two decades, criticized the Prague government for its administration of their homeland. The excesses of the Hungarian regime, however, convinced most of these same immigrants that Subcarpathian Rus' should be reunited after the war to a restored Czechoslovakia. Temporarily putting aside their sectarian differences, the American Carpathian-Russian Council of Pittsburgh, representing for the most part Greek Catholics, and headed by Gregory Zsatkovich, joined with the Orthodox Carpathian-Russian Unity of Gary, Indiana, headed by Rev. Ivan Ladižinsky (b.1905), in March 1942, to form an American Carpathian-Russian Central Conference. The new organization was led by Zsatkovich, and speakers at the first meeting included Jan Masaryk and Jan Papanek, respectively vice-prime minister and minister plenipotentiary of the Czechoslovak government-in-exile.[5] The conference issued a joint declaration calling for the "liberation of Carpathian-Russia from the brutal enforced occupation of the Hungarians (Magyars), and its re-union as an autonomous self-governing state under the terms of the St. Germain-en-Lay Treaty with Czechoslovakia."[6] However, President Beneš made no promises and went no further than to state that "Subcarpathian Russia has never ceased legally to be part of the Czechoslovak Republic" and that he looked "forward to an early restoration of the full life of the pre-Munich Czechoslovak Republic and of a new stage of thriving and prosperity of her people."[7] Despite the lack of any concrete guarantees, the publications of the American Carpathian-Russian Council (*The Carpathian*, 1941-1943) and the Carpathian-Russian Unity (*Jedinstvo-Unity* 1942-1943) nonetheless joined with that of the Czechoslovak Government Information Service in New York (*Karpatorusskije novosti*, 1944-1945) in the call for a restoration of a Czechoslovak state according to the pre-Munich boundaries.[8]

Not only American immigrants, but also Rusyn leaders in London raised the question of Subcarpathia's status in a renewed Czechoslovakia. Beneš promised that "there was no question about state decentralization," but again he was not at all specific about autonomy and could only state that any changes in the constitution of Subcarpathian Rus' would have to be undertaken "with the consent of the people."[9] As for the nationality question, the central government "would not create any obstacle for the Ukrainian or Russian orientations in regard to national culture."[10] However, when Tsibere proposed a more concrete program, in the form of guarantees for autonomy and the use of the Russian language in the province, he was removed as head of the Subcarpathian bureau and in late 1943 left the state council.[11] Only after the Slovak Uprising in August 1944 did the London government-in-exile finally accept the principle that "the new republic must be . . . a fraternal republic of three equal nations: Czechs, Slovaks, and Carpatho-Ukrainians."[12]

The most decisive action taken by Czechoslovak leaders in regard to the problem of Subcarpathian Rus' was to improve the status of Rusyns then in the Soviet Union. The more than twenty-thousand refugees from the Hungarian-controlled province who in 1939-1940 sought freedom by fleeing to Galicia were arrested on charges of having illegally crossed into Soviet territory. Tried by military courts, they were convicted of espionage, given sentences ranging from three to eight years, and deported to labor camps. Within the next few years, approximately sixty percent perished.[13]

The Czechoslovak govenment-in-exile became concerned about the fate of these imprisoned Rusyns and wanted them freed so that they could join the new Czechoslovak Army Corps, under General Ludvík Svoboda, organized in July 1941 on Soviet territory. Finally, in early 1943, about 2,700 Rusyns were freed from the labor camps and allowed to join the Corps. As a result, the Czechoslovak armed forces attached to the Red Army took on a distinctly Rusyn character, with more than sixty-six percent of the Corps being from Subcarpathian Rus'.[14]

As for the national orientation of the Rusyn soldiers, most of them "had not participated in the arguments between the Russophiles and Ukrainophiles [and] considered themselves to be Rusyn."[15] At first, there were many nationally active men, especially Ukrainophiles, but the experience in the labor camps dampened any enthusiasm for things Ukrainian or Russian. Czechoslovak authorities made the most of the situation and began to stress in Corps publications that: "in its history, Subcarpathian Rus' developed its own particular economic and political conditions completely different from those on the other side of the Carpathians. We have our own particular national character . . . We have our own particular interests, for which we have fought through the centuries."[16]

Thus, it seemed that the postwar plans the Czechoslovak authorities had for Subcarpathian Rus' would not be much different from the policy followed prior to 1938. The autonomous period and Ukrainian ascendence was forgotten, and Prague, it appeared, would strongly favor a pro-Czechoslovak Rusyn national orientation.

The Incorporation of Subcarpathian Rus' into the Soviet Ukraine

But neither the plans of Beneš to re-create a Czechoslovakia according to its pre-Munich borders, nor the hopes of Rusyn soldiers to liberate their Subcarpathian homeland were to be fulfilled. By mid-August 1944, the Czechoslovak Corps was ready to approach the Uzhok Pass and proceed southward to Uzhhorod, but at the last moment it was suddenly transferred

by the Soviet High Command (without the approval of the London government-in-exile) to the armies of the First Ukrainian Front, which were to
engage in a bloody struggle for the Dukla Pass in northeastern Slovakia.
Only the Red Army under the command of General Ivan Petrov was to enter
Subcarpathian Rus' in October 1944.[17] Within ten days, virtually the whole
province was under the control of Soviet troops. The Red Army was greeted
favorably by the local population and soon Czechoslovak and Soviet flags
were flying in most villages.[18]

Indeed, Subcarpathian Rus' was still legally considered part of Czechoslovakia, and since 1943 President Beneš had been convinced that "we are
in agreement with Soviet Russia that . . . Subcarpathian Rus' will again be
in the Czechoslovak Republic."[19] In December of that year Beneš and
Stalin concluded a pact, which was later supplemented by an agreement on
May 8, 1944, giving the "delegate of the Czechoslovak Government on the
scene . . . complete power to reconstitute civil and military authority
throughout the country."[20] Armed with such an understanding, a Czechoslovak delegation for the liberated territories arrived in Khust on October
27, 1944. Led by František Němec, the twenty-member delegation included
two generals whose aim was to recruit local Rusyns into the Czechoslovak
army. There was also one native of Subcarpathian Rus' in the delegation,
the Communist leader Ivan Turianytsia. The delegation's task was to make
contact with local committees and to attempt to set up a Czechoslovak
administration in the province, but Němec and his associates did not succeed.[21]

Real power was in the hands of the Red Army and the local national
committees that were organized in almost every village. Made up of leaders
of varying political backgrounds, these committees at first favored the re-
establishment of the Czechoslovak regime. By early November, however,
local Communists and other pro-Soviet elements clearly dominated the
committees and a movement for union with the Soviet Ukraine was under
way.[22]

Of great importance during these weeks was the activity of the
reorganized Subcarpathian Communist party, which held its first conference
in Mukachevo on November 19,1944. Claiming that the people of Subcarpathian Rus' "belong to the Ukrainian nation," the conference adopted a
resolution which "demanded that historical injustice be removed and that
the Transcarpathian Ukraine be re-united with the Soviet Ukraine."[23] In a
speech by the Czechoslovak representative, Ivan Turianytsia, a call was
made to prepare for a national council that would be representative of the
whole population.[24]

Such a council was organized in Mukachevo on November 25-26, 1944.
Six-hundred delegates chosen by the local national councils unanimously
adopted a "Manifesto . . . for the Reunification of Transcarpathian Ukraine
with the Soviet Ukraine."[25] The Mukachevo Manifesto decided "to reunite

the Transcarpathian Ukraine with its great mother, the Soviet Ukraine, and to leave the framework of Czechoslovakia."[26] It also asked for entry into the Soviet Union and announced the election of a national council, which alone had the power to represent "the will of the people."[27] A seventeen-member Mukachevo National Council was chosen, with Ivan Turianytsia as chairman and Petr Sova and Petro Lintur (1909-1969) as vice-chairmen. On December 5, the council informed the Czechoslovak leaders in London of its decisions, suggested that Němec and his delegation leave "within three days," and instructed the local national committees throughout the province to heed only its commands.[28]

In, practice, the Czechoslovak delegation never established any effective control over the province, and on February 2, 1945, Němec and his group left for Slovakia. This move was latent recognition of the fact that Transcarpathian Ukraine was really being administered by the Mukachevo National Council. The council began to make all the necessary internal changes to facilitate entry into the Soviet Union. Symbolically, Uzhhorod had already been put on "Moscow time" (two hours later) on November 5, 1944, and the following January the Soviet national anthem was adopted.[29] During the first months of its rule, the Mukachevo Council nationalized the banks and some industries, and began to distribute land to the peasantry.[30] The organs of justice were also put under the council's control, following a decree authorizing the establishment of a "special court" to judge those who collaborated with the Hungarian government.[31] As for religious affairs, the Orthodox Church was transferred in December from the jurisdiction of the partiarch of Belgrade to that of Moscow.

That Beneš and his government-in-exile did not oppose these developments is quite understandable. German and Hungarian forces had still not been driven from Czechoslovak territory, and only the Soviet armies could achieve this. Furthermore, several Czechoslovak leaders feared that any dispute with Moscow might lead to the loss of Slovakia.[32] In fact, one branch of the illegal Slovak Communist party had, since 1940, called for Slovakia's incorporation into the Soviet Union. Such ideas were still in the air even after the Slovak National Uprising of August-September 1944, when the Slovak National Council declared that the new republic would consist of three equal peoples: Czechs, Slovaks, and Transcarpathian U-krainians. As late as March 1945, the newly formed Ukrainian National Council in Prešov demanded that Rusyns in eastern Slovakia be united with the Soviet Union—only later did they accept the principles of the Slovak National Council and continued unity with a renewed Czechoslovak state.[33] Ever conscious of these broader issues, Zdeněk Fierlinger, Czechoslovak minister in Moscow, probably best summed up the feeling of Beneš and his government during the winter months of 1944-45: "Between the Soviet and Czechoslovak governments there was a quiet but clear understanding that no conflict should be allowed to occur over Subcarpathian Rus'."[34] As a result, Czechoslovak leaders began to convince themselves that Subcarpathian Rus' was not of central importance to their cause and that the territory had been accepted in 1919 only on a temporary basis until the Ukrainian problem was settled. Now that neighboring Galicia and northern Bukovina were part of a united Soviet Ukraine, it seemed only natural that Subcarpathian Rus' should follow suit.

For his part, Stalin informed Beneš in January, 1945 that the "Soviet government has not forbidden nor could it forbid the population of the Transcarpathian Ukraine from expressing its national will . . . although the issue can only be settled by [signing] a treaty . . . just before or after the end of the war with Germany."[35] In this way the Mukachevo Council's demands for unification with the Soviet Ukraine were fulfilled, and on June 29, 1945, a treaty was signed by Prague and Moscow recognizing the cession of the Transcarpathian Ukraine (Subcarpathian Rus') to the Ukrainian Soviet Socialist Republic.[36] In November, the treaty was unanimously ratified by the Czechoslovak National Assembly in Prague and the Presidium of the Supreme Council of the Soviet Union in Moscow. The new Soviet-Czechoslovak border was to follow, with a few exceptions, the Slovak-Subcarpathian boundary of 1938, and citizens of "Ukrainian or Russian nationality living . . . in Slovakia" (the Rusyn minority in the Prešov Region) were given the right to opt for Soviet citizenship and to resettle in the Soviet Union.[37]

The Soviet acquisition of Subcarpathian Rus' had internal propagandistic value. At a time when the Ukrainian Soviet Socialist Republic was denied the right to maintain diplomatic relations with foreign countries (a privilege one would have expected after the Ukrainian SSR's entry into the United Nations in 1945), the incorporation of the Transcarpathian region served as a kind of compensation to Ukrainian patriots who could at the least be satisfied that all the Ukrainian lands were now united in one country.

The National and Cultural Policy of the New Regime

With the conclusion of the treaty with Czechoslovakia, the Soviet Union gained international recognition for its last territorial acquisition (to date)[38] and finally secured a foothold south of the strategic Carpathian Mountains, a goal of tsarist governments since the time of Peter the Great. In this process, the nationality question was of crucial importance, since the presumed desire of the local population, influenced by their supposed national affinity, was given as the primary reason for the new territorial acquisition.

Unlike all the previous governments that had ruled Subcarpathian Rus', the Soviet regime had a clear-cut policy regarding national identity. The policy of the Soviet Ukrainian Communist party, ratified in 1926, was applied: the local Slavic inhabitants, notwithstanding what they called themselves, were to be considered Ukrainian. In the first census in 1945, all persons who said their nationality was Rusyn (*rus'kyi*), Carpatho-Russian (*karpatoross*), or any other variant, were listed in documents and identity papers as Ukrainian.[39] Such official action did not suddenly transform all Subcarpathian Rusyns into conscious Ukrainians; however, in the three decades since 1945 the Soviet regime seems to have achieved remarkable success where others had failed so often before. Let us see how this was accomplished.

The writings of historians were used by various national leaders and government officials to support their own ideologies and programs. (See Chapter 5.) History was given even greater attention in the Soviet state, for it was considered a "powerful weapon of communist education [which] must wholly serve the cause of the struggle for communism."[40] The past, or more precisely an acceptable version of the past, must serve as the justification for the present. In Subcarpathian Rus', the local populace was to be taught that the long history of their homeland had followed a stormy but inevitable route—one which led finally to unification with the Soviet Union in 1945.

Although the details of this process still had to be worked out, the broad outlines were stated on June 30, 1945, the day after the conclusion of the treaty with Czechoslovakia. In a long historical article that appeared in Moscow's *Pravda,* the author emphasized that Slavic peoples had inhabited Subcarpathian Rus' as early as the sixth century and had maintained close contacts with their brethren to the East until the ninth century, when "wild Hungarian tribes . . . thrust themselves into the Tisa valley," and "after a bloody struggle with the Transcarpathian Slavs, occupied their land." During the long centuries that followed, Subcarpathians tried several times, as in the revolution against the Hapsburgs in the early eighteenth century and again in 1918-1919, to fulfill "their eternal dream"—"re-unification with the great Ukrainian and Russian peoples."[41]

A host of writers from within and beyond the region were called upon to prepare popular and scholarly studies emphasizing this interpretation. For the most part, Marxist scholarship had to start from scratch, because Soviet Ukrainian publications during the 1920s and 1930s had paid virtually no attention to the region, and the only existing Marxist history of Subcarpathian Rus' was banned because its author, Oleksandr Badan, was declared to be an ideological revisionist.[42]

A new roster of writers was invited to create a revised history for Subcarpathian Rus'. Among the first of these was the renowned Marxist scholar and Czechoslovak minister of education Zdeněk Nejedlý, whose study of Subcarpathian medieval history appeared in a Moscow scholarly journal in 1945. By arguing that the region was not part of Greater Moravia during the ninth century, he helped to undermine the view of "bourgeois" Czech historiography, which continually stressed the long-standing ties between Subcarpathian Rus' and the western Slavs.[43] It was also necessary to erase any positive memories that Rusyns had toward Masaryk's Czechoslovakia.

This was begun in two lengthy articles by Irina N. Mel'nikova. According to her, Subcarpathian Rus' was forcibly incorporated into Czechoslovakia "against the will of the people," and despite strikes and other forms of protest the "dictatorship of the Czech imperialist bourgeoisie" was imposed upon the "eastern colony" in the early 1920s.[44]

Soviet Russian scholarship on Subcarpathian Rus' reached its high point in the writings of Ivan G. Kolomiets, who might rightly be called the Pokrovsky of Subcarpathian historiography. In four extensive volumes, he disregarded the conclusions of all previous "bourgeois" writings and attempted to "explain through Marxist-Leninist principles" the basic stages in the development of Subcarpathian Rus' from the ninth to the early twentieth centuries. In his exposé he drew a historical canvas of white and black, good and bad, "ours" and "the foreign." Into the first category were placed the people, the Subcarpathian masses, and their cultural representative, the Orthodox Church. Into the second category fell the Hungarian feudal regime with its landlords and Magyarized Rusyn bourgeoisie, in particular the Uniate Church and its leaders, who, as "lackeys" of the Vatican, exploited materially and spiritually the local population.[45] Kolomiets was subsequently criticized for his simplistic notions and strait jacket characterizations of Subcarpathian developments. But most especially he was guilty of treating the region in isolation and not as an integral part of general Ukrainian developments. This was a most serious shortcoming, because Soviet historians were expected to support the international argument for acquiring the province, an argument based on the people's acceptance of their Ukrainianness. In the words of one critic: "We need regional history, but it is necessary to write it so that while reading it, every Transcarpathian or Galician, wherever he may be, should first of all feel himself to be a Ukrainian and not a Rusyn, Lemkian, Hutsul, Boikian, etc.; he should feel himself to be a son of his native Ukrainian nation, be loyal to it, and praise the native customs, language, and history.[46]

To correct the dangers of provincialism, which might lead to separatism, and to prove that things were never as good as in the socialist present, a historical apparatus was set up in Uzhhorod in association with the university and state archives. Since 1947, the Uzhhorod University has published a scholarly journal, *Naukovi zapysky,* and has sponsored several conferences devoted to Subcarpathian history. Also, many monographs and documentary collections have been published by the local state publishing house, and the region has been the focus of attention in the programs of publishers in L'viv and Kiev. Clearly, the Soviet government has provided significant sums of money to ensure the writing of acceptable histories, whose style, presentation, and *tirage* would make them attractive and available to a "wide circle of readers, teachers, propagandists, and all those who are interested in the history of Transcarpathia."[47]

In the first decades, specialized studies were the rule, and only in very recent years have Soviet scholars prepared general histories of Subcarpathian Rus' that reflect the conclusions of Marxist-Leninist scholarship.[48] The Marxists have basically accepted the Rusyn interpretation of early Subcarpathian history, with its emphasis on a glorious past represented by local heroes like the princes Laborets', Petrovych, and Koriatovych. (See pp. 106-110.) The settlement of the region by ancestors of the Rusyns at the time of Christ, and other undocumented events, have been treated as historical facts, supported by archeology and folklore.[49] As might be expected, relations with the East are continually emphasized, whether it be the tenth and eleventh centuries, when Subcarpathia is considered to have been a "part" of Kievan Rus'; the mid-seventeenth century, when some Rusyns participated in the Khmel'nyts'kyi revolution; the seventeenth and eighteenth centuries, when trade and cultural relations (especially the arrival of books) with Russia and the Ukraine were pronounced; or the years 1918-1919, when, under the influence of Lenin and the Bolshevik Revolution in Russia, the largest Subcarpathian national councils called for union with the Ukraine and then established a Soviet government lasting forty days, albeit under the aegis of Hungary.[50]

Of course, the Soviet historical view is still filled with "enemies of the people." The greatest of these is the Greek Catholic or Uniate Church, which, during its 300 years of existence (1649-1949), was an instrument of Latinization, Magyarization, and economic exploitation.[51] The feudal pre-1918 Hungarian regime and the bourgeois-democratic state of Masaryk's Czechoslovakia (with its local "imperialist stooges," Governors Zsatkovich, Beskid, and Hrabar) are also denigrated.[52] Finally, the worst epithets are reserved for the "fascist turncoats" in the service of Hitlerian Germany (Voloshyn, Revai), who set up a "marionette" autonomous government in 1938-1939, and of Horthyite Hungary (Fentsik, Brodii), who supported the "brutal and reactionary regime" during the Second World War.[53] With the exception of those "forty Soviet days in 1919" and the subsequent establishment of the Communist party, whose activities have been profusely documented,[54] Marxist writers give the impression that nothing good occurred politically until 1945.

In the cultural sphere, Marxist writers have recognized some bright spots. The Orthodox Church and its struggle for survival is seen as a healthy reaction to the Greek Catholic "exploiters," and among praiseworthy figures is the seventeenth-century Orthodox priest Mykhail Andrella of Orosvyhiv, who has received much attention for his polemics against the idea of union.[55] Nineteenth-century national leaders like Dukhnovych were initially underrated. It was argued that Subcarpathian literature was not part of the general development of Ukrainian literature and generally not worthy of study. Moreover, the majority of writers were Greek Catholic priests who were not concerned with social problems and who identified themselves with Muscophilism and tsarist Russia. This short-sighted view has been revised substantially by scholars like Vasyl' L. Mykytas', so that the whole nineteenth century has been rehabilitated and accepted as a postive era in Subcarpathian cultural history.[56] From this period, only Dobrianskii, the leader of the "clerical-bourgeois" intelligentsia with no concern for "social problems," is still viewed as a reactionary. Similarly, in the twentieth century, Russophile writers like Karabelesh and Tyblevich, and Ukrainophiles like Voloshyn, are black-listed because of their ideological stance or political activity.[57]

To summarize, the accepted Soviet view of Subcarpathian history sees the region's development as a part of eastern Slavic and Ukrainian history. A revised pantheon of heroes has been created that includes supporters of Orthodoxy, peasant revolutionaries against the feudal regime, intellectual leaders who praised the East, and members of the Communist party who protected the interests of the suffering masses after 1919. Add to this the writings of Marx and Lenin, the exploits of the Red Army, and unending tracts about the social, economic, and cultural achievements since 1945,[58] and the "correct" historical interpretation for Subcarpathian Rus' is complete.

The problem of language, which plagued the Subcarpathian intelligentsia, was resolved under the Soviet regime without any particular difficulties. We have seen how, as early as 1926, on orders from Moscow and Kiev, the Subcarpathian Communist party accepted the principle that the local Slavic population spoke dialects of Ukrainian and hence the literary form of that language was the only one acceptable. (See pp. 229-230.) As a result, when the party stated, in November 1944, that schools must offer "free instruction for all children in their native tongue,"[59] literary Ukrainian was the form adopted. Old textbooks, notwithstanding their linguistic orientation, were rejected, and Soviet Ukrainian books were sent from Kiev. As a result, the alphabet was finally standardized, and former orthographic experiments that included letters like "ô", "г", "ы", "ъ" were done away with for good. Standard literary Ukrainian was declared to be the only acceptable form for publications, radio, television, and for some public signs.

Of course, the acceptance of Ukrainian did not mean the end of the Russian language in the region. On the contrary, where Czech and Magyar were used before for official purposes, Russian has now taken their place. After all, Subcarpathian Rus' is a part of the Soviet Union, where Russian is de facto, if not de jure, the official language. Hence, most official announcements, identity cards, and the main daily newspaper, *Zakarpats'ka pravda,* appear in both Russian and Ukrainian editions. On the other hand, official papers, place names, and restaurant menus are only in Russian. Furthermore, Russian is taught in all schools beginning at the elementary level. The textbooks and other publications are, of course, Soviet and adopt the modern orthography, thus ending the debates over the use of "ѣ" and the hard sign "ъ," which were argued about so often in the past by the local Russophile intelligentsia. In a sense, the Russian language, which has always found favor among one segment of the Subcarpathian population, is better off than ever before.[60]

In fact, it is only the Rusyn dialect—whether in Cyrillic or Latin script—which no longer appears in publications. Even those writers who use dialectisms for local color are sometimes criticized for not adopting literary Ukrainian forms.[61] This does not mean, however, that the study of the Subcarpathian dialects is neglected. On the contrary, since 1945 the dialects have been analyzed systematically and in depth at Uzhhorod State University's Department of Ukrainian Language, by talented linguists like Iosyf Dzendzelivs'kyi, Pavlo M. Lyzanets', Vasyl' Dobosh and others, who have expanded considerably the pioneering work of Pan'kevych. Two anthologies of studies on the dialect (*Dialektolohichnyi zbirnyk,* 1955-1957) and two volumes of a monumental dialectal atlas (I. O. Dzendzelivs'kyi, *Linhvistychnyi atlas ukraïns'kykh narodnykh hovoriv Zakarpats'koï oblasti,* 1958-1960) have already appeared. Moreover, M. A. Hrytsak is preparing a dialectal dictionary, which already includes more than one million entries, and a special four-man group is also working on such a dictionary.[62] A glance at any bibliography of linguistic research in the U-krainian SSR will reveal that at least two-fifths of the published materials in dialectology are based on the dialects of the Subcarpathian region.[63]

In short, the Soviet regime has declared the language problem to be a nonproblem. Ukrainian is considered to be the mother tongue of the Slavic population and, along with Russian, is used in education, official matters, and the rest of public life. The dialects are respected and systematically researched for their scholarly value, but in no way has there been any attempt to use them as the basis for the creation of a separate literary language.

As in language use, so in literature, writers of Ukrainian and Russian work side by side. The most famous writers from the older generation, the Ukrainophile Grendzha-Dons'kyi and the Russophile Karabelesh, emigrated during the Second World War to Czechoslovakia, and stayed, but many others remained behind to continue literary careers in the service of the new regime. These included A. Markush, Iu. Borshosh-Kum'iats'kyi, L. Dem'ian, F. Potushniak, and Mykhailo Tomchanii (1914-1975), who republished former or new works in standard Ukrainian, and the Russian-language writers M. Popovich, G. Goida, and A. Patrus-Karpatskii (who now writes in Ukrainian).[64]

The linguistic change from dialect or Russian to standard Ukrainian was sometimes difficult for older writers, but still it was only a technical difficulty. More complex was the mental transformation writers had to undergo, for in a Soviet state they had to place themselves fully in the service of society and create works that could be easily understood and could serve as positive and inspiring examples of Communist idealism. Literature of this kind was dubbed in official parlance as socialist realism. However, since Subcarpathian authors came from a local literary tradition that was often marked by pessimism and despair, they first had to make a profound psychological about-face before they could become effective socialist-realists.

Nationalist themes in previous writings, whether they were expressed in lyrical praise for the homeland or in declarations of spiritual unity with a Ukrainian or Russian East, no longer had relevance. Since questions of political allegiance and national identity were resolved, the "national question in the context of Soviet reality took on a different meaning." In essence, it meant (1) transforming the underdeveloped Subcarpathian region into a society of modern industry and cooperative agriculture; (2) doing away with privileges and creating equality for all nationalities in the social and political sphere; and (3) developing a culture that would reject "bourgeois-nationalist ideology" for "communist ideals of equality, friendship and brotherhood of all peoples," that is, a culture "socialist in content and national in form."[65] The hierarchy of moral values had to be revised; the supreme object of one's life was no longer to follow the rules of Christ in order to assure a favorable afterlife, but rather to fulfill the precepts of Lenin to guarantee paradise on this earth in a Soviet state. Thus, a person was to consider himself first and foremost as a Soviet citizen, a productive holder of a particular socially productive occupation, and only secondarily as a member of a given national group which may speak a language other than the dominant "Soviet" language, Russian.

This was the context in which Subcarpathian writers were expected to write. Literary themes like the historical past, previously used to propagate national pride and self-respect, were now used only to stress the positive present and glorious future. In the words of one critic: "The reader needs monumental historical works about our heroic forbears . . . in order that youth, seeing the awful past, will love the present even more." At the same time, "we need books about the positive hero of our time who through his life, his conduct, and his activity will ignite a desire [in others] to follow his example."[66] To be sure, certain Subcarpathian historical figures served as subject matter for writers, but it was Lenin, the revered father of history's first socialist state, who became the true "hero of our time."[67]

With such goals clearly established, Soviet Subcarpathian authors have provided in an almost mechanical way the necessary literary material. Historical themes are most frequently encountered in short stories and novels, which have replaced poetry as the predominant literary form. Every historical period has been duly castigated, whether it be the full sweep of several decades from the Austro-Hungarian to Soviet regimes (F. Potushniak's novel, *Povin'* ["The Flood," 1959] and M. Tomchanii's trilogy: *Zhmeniaky* ["The Zhmeniak Family," 1961-1964], *Tykhe mistechko* [The

Quiet Hamlet," 1969], and *Braty* ["Brothers," 1972]); or more limited time spans such as the revolutionary years of 1918-1919 (Semen Pan'ko's *Pid synimy Beskydamy* ["Under the Blue Beskyd Mountains," 1962]), "capitalist-bourgeois" Czechoslovakia (M. Tomchanii's *Skrypka-ioho molodist'* ["The Violin—His Youth," 1968] and Ivan Chendei's *Teren tsvite* ["The Blooming Bramble Bush," 1958]), the 1938-1939 months of fascist-inspired autonomy (Iurii Meigesh's *Verkhovyntsi* ["The Verkhovynians," 1961] and V. Ladyzhets's *Perekhrestia* ["The Crossroad," 1967]), and the brutal occupation during the Second World War (Ivan Dolhosh's *Synevyr,* 1968). Perhaps the classic work of Subcarpathian socialist realism is the novel *Svet ty nash, Verkhovine* ("Verkhovyna, Our Land so Dear," 1954), by the Russian author Matvei Tevel'ev (1908-1962) from Leningrad, who lived in the region after the war. In this 550-page historical novel, a poor Rusyn boy who becomes an agronomist (and Communist) is juxtaposed to a whole gallery of "villains": Zsatkovich of General Motors, Rusyn "lackeys" of the Czech government, Masaryk, Beneš, Voloshyn, the Czech shoe industrialist Bat'a—they are all there. Probably because of this, Tevel'ev's novel was endorsed for wide distribution through translations into English, French, German, and Czech.

Indeed, Subcarpathian socialist-realist literature reminds one of the writings of Marxist historians. It is a good-guy versus bad-guy literature, the former invariably being the poorest peasants, workers, Communist revolutionaries, and deprived students, the latter being the landlords, priests, Hungarian or Czechoslovak gendarmes, fascist military officers, bourgeois (usually Ukrainian) nationalists, and, finally, kulaks, who in theory are rich peasants but in fact are any peasants who want to hold on to their private landholdings.[68]

Subcarpathian artists also joined the belletrists in the change to socialist realism. The leading painters of the older generation, I. Bokshai, A. Erdeli, E. Kontratovych, and F. Manailo, were complemented by the younger painters Anton Kashshai (b. 1921), Andrii Kotska (b.1911), and Havrylo Hliuk (b. 1912), and the sculptor Vasyl' Svyda (b. 1913). Generously supported by the state—Bokshai, for instance, has been made a National Artist of the Soviet Union—these artists have turned out many works that graphically illustrate and supposedly inspire a positive attitude toward the new society. Most representative are Erdeli's "The Betrothed Young Collective Farmers" (1954), Manailo's "The Carrier [Gas Line] of Friendship" (1961), Hliuk's "Lumber Jacks" (1954), Kotska's "Ivan Kobal, a Kolkhoz Team Leader" (1960), and Svyda's wooden group-statues "I'm Going to Join the Partisans" (1948) and "Carpathian Woodcutters Signing the Stockholm Manifest" (1951). Thus, since 1945 Subcarpathian artists have avoided strictly nationalist themes and have instead produced descriptive (and usually banal) works that can be easily understood by the masses and that serve as ideal models or goals to be followed by all respectable citizens in a communist society.[69]

Cultural organizations have been completely reorganized. Gone are the rival Ukrainophile Prosvita and Russophile Dukhnovych societies, as well as the Magyarone Subcarpathian Academy of Sciences which propagated the idea of a separate Uhro-Rusyn nationality. In their stead, the Soviet government has invested considerable sums of money to established a complex network of accessible cultural centers, and by 1971 there were 818 libraries, 746 clubs, 703 movie houses, 3 museums, and 1 theater in operation.[70]

Uzhhorod has remained Subcarpathia's cultural center, and during 1946 several professional institutions were established. The first of these was the Transcarpathian Philharmonic Orchestra (Zakarpats'ka Filharmoniia) in February, followed by the Transcarpathian State Song and Dance Ensemble (Zakarpats'kyi Narodnyi Khor URSR) in June, and the Transcarpathian State Ukrainian Theater (Zakarpats'kyi Oblasnyi Derzhavnyi Ukraïns'kyi Muzychnodramatychnyi Teatr) in November. The following year a Russian-language theater was founded in Mukachevo. All these institutions were designed to propagate the cultural achievements of the broader Soviet society as well as the specific contributions of the Subcarpathian homeland. It is more than symbolic that the Song and Dance Ensemble—the active preservers of the local folk culture—began their inaugural and subsequent concerts by singing the Soviet national anthem and songs about the party.[71]

In 1948, the first professional museum in Subcarpathian Rus' was established in the restored medieval castle of Uzhhorod. The Transcarpathian Regional Museum (Zakarpats'kyi Kraieznavchyi Muzei) has gathered over 40,000 artifacts and 2,000 works of art, many of which are displayed in a permanent exhibition of the history of the region and in an art gallery. The main thrust of the display is to contrast the poverty and suffering of the past to the social, economic, and cultural achievements made under the Soviet regime. This contrast was further enhanced in 1970 when the first outdoor museum on the territory of the Soviet Ukraine was opened. The Transcarpathian Museum of Folk Architecture (Zakarpats'kyi Muzei Narodnoï Arkhitektury i Pobutu) was set up next to the castle in Uzhhorod and includes genuine examples of wooden architecture from all corners of the province. As one writer remarked: "the past is in direct contrast to the achievements of the Soviet period which are revealed in the main [inner] portion of the museum."[72]

The Soviet way of life and the offical view regarding the Ukrainian identity of the Subcarpathian population have been propagated through books and periodicals as well as cinema, radio, and television. It is also important to note that the writings of scholars and belletrists have been allowed the greatest distribution. Under the new regime, all former private and institutional publishers were abolished and replaced in 1946 by a single

Regional Book and Journal Publishing House in Uzhhorod. Later expanded and reorganized under the name Karpaty, this state-run enterprise has produced a remarkable number of books—in twenty-five years, 1,400 titles have been issued with an average printing of 13,604. In one year alone, 1971, Karpaty printed 2,059,000 books, making the Transcarpathian Oblast' the fourth largest producer of books in the Ukrainian SSR.[73] Moreover, the main newspaper, *Zakarpats'ka pravda* (1944-) had a circulation in 1970 of 130,000 copies daily.[74] The government has obviously made every effort to assure that publications reach the widest audiences.

Lenin's dictum that the cinema is the most far-reaching means for educating the masses has also been put into practice. By 1971, 703 facilities for showing films were in existence with an average of 93 seats per facility. Each year 222,000 showings take place in the region, with 40,000-45,000 persons seeing films each day; this averages out to 15 films per person each year. The total number of admissions to films reached an incredible 15,900,000 in 1971, about half of these in facilities located in villages. Ten films and several documentaries have been made about Subcarpathian Rus' —one about the Transcarpathian Song and Dance Ensemble, entitled *Verkhovyno, maty moia,* being the most popular both within and beyond the borders of the region.[75] Thus, Subcarpathians have been effectively exposed to those ideologies presented in motion picture films.

Besides seeing motion pictures, Subcarpathians are reached in their homes and places of work by radio and more recently by television. Again, Lenin recognized from the beginning that radio was "for us an absolute necessity, both from the standpoint of propaganda and agitation, especially for the illiterate masses of the population, and for the transmission of lectures."[76] In the past, Rusyns had only one program available under the Czechoslovak regime (1934-1938) and then but a few minutes daily under the Hungarians during the Second World War. Since 1946, however, Uzhhorod has had its own radio station with full daily programming in Ukrainian and Russian. Beginning in 1964, the city also obtained its own television studio with receivers and transmitters for stations in L'viv, Kiev, and Moscow. Of course, the effectiveness of radio and television is dependent to a significant degree on the number of receivers that are available: in 1971 the province had 227,100 radios (one for every four people) and 121,900 television sets (one for every eight people). Added to these are 122,600 loudspeakers located inside factories, along village streets, and in other public places.[77]

The importance of the cinema, radio, and television cannot be overestimated. Through these facilities of modern communication, the Soviet government is able to reach into every corner of Subcarparthian life. As a result, all segments of the population have been exposed and influenced by standard Ukrainian and Russian speech and have been constantly reminded of their own Ukrainian national identity as well as the precepts of a Soviet way of life.

In order to create a new Soviet society and to integrate the Rusyn population into the larger Ukrainian national community, the government has found it necessary to undermine certain key elements in traditional Subcarpathian life. The first bulwark of tradition to be attacked was the deep attachment of the Subcarpathian peasant to the land—his own land. At first, the new regime made itself popular by confiscating landholdings of the church and other large proprietors and by redistributing 52,700 hectares of land to 54,500 small-landholding and landless peasants. As part of this process, "thousands of poor people" from the highlands were transferred to the more fertile lands in the south. Such population transfers uprooted people from their immediate native surroundings, made them dependent if not sympathetic to their new benefactor, and rendered them more pliable and susceptible to the psychological and ideological changes the government was implementing. Almost as soon as the land distribution was completed, these same peasants were urged to join collective farms. The process began slowly in early 1946, picked up momentum in late 1948, and by 1950, 94.4 percent of all cultivable land was in collective and state (*kolkhoz*) farms.[78]

Almost simultaneous with this process was the dismantling of another bulwark of Subcarpathian tradition, the Greek Catholic Church. That church had been outlawed in Galicia in early 1946 and it was not long before it was outlawed in the Transcarpathian Oblast'. The symbolic confiscation in March 1947 of the national religious shrine at the monastery on Chernecha Hora near Mukachevo was followed by the premature death of Bishop Romzha on November 1. Finally, on August 28, 1949, the Greek Catholic Church was officially liquidated. Led by Rev. Irynei Kontratovych, the local historian who was active in cultural affairs under the Hungarian regime, the three-hundred-year union with Rome was renounced and all the remaining property and jurisdictional authority of the Greek Catholic Church were placed under the hegemony of the Orthodox patriarchate in Moscow.[79] The liturgy was not affected to any substantial degree by this change, although under the new regime church marriages and funerals were discouraged and religious holidays and popular processions were either reduced in number or abolished altogether. May 1, the international workers day, and November 7, the anniversary of the Bolshevik revolution, replaced Christmas and Easter as the main official holidays of the yearly calendar.[80]

The Greek Catholic Church and its seminary in Uzhhorod had been the last bastions of the Rusynophile orientation. Priests like A. Il'nyts'kyi, J. Marina, E. Bokshai, and Vasylii Shereghii had helped to propagate the idea of a separate Rusyn nationality through their publications and teaching. Now they were in prison or had fled westward. Local church publications were discontinued and the few still available came from the Orthodox patriarchate in Moscow and were usually in Russian. Finally, the church was allowed only limited possibilities for gaining new parishioners, since there were no longer any church-administered schools, and church attendance among the younger people declined enormously.

But it is through the school system that the government has its best opportunity for replacing tradition-bound individuals with new generations of Soviet men. In a decree passed on April 20, 1945, by the National Council of the Transcarpathian Oblast', it was declared that: "The instruction and education of the youth on the territory of the Transcarpathian Ukraine is the task of the government, to whom the complete control of all education, instruction, and surveillance belongs."[81] A committee of five-hundred teachers had already met in December 1944 to call for union with the Soviet Ukraine and the adoption of Soviet principles of education in local schools. Responding to the words of Lenin, the Subcarpathian school was to become the "tool of the dictatorship of the proletariat."

The first step was to increase the size of the physical plant. Despite the solid network of schools set up during the Czechoslovak regime, Soviet writers claimed that by late 1944 there were only 445 schools left in operation: 420 elementary, 18 municipal, and 7 gymnasia.[82] The table below shows how these numbers have changed:

Type of school	1950/51	1960/61	1971/72
Elementary	475	365	244
Municipal	318	331	332
Gymnasia	54	130	157
Total	852	835	743

The absolute number of students has also risen substantially—from 139,212 in 1950/51 to 203,875 in 1971/72. To this must be added the 544 nurseries, day-care centers, and kindergartens, which had a total of 27,646 children enrolled in 1971/72.[83] Hence, through its all-embracing school system the state has from the earliest age direct access to one-quarter of the total population of the region.

From the point of view of national orientation, one source indicates the following distribution of schools for the year 1957/58:[84]

Type of school	Ukrainian	Russian	Magyar	Moldavian
Elementary	331	7	35	2
Municipal	254	3	52	9
Gymnasium	96	11	13	1
Total	681	21	100	12

More recent statistics for the school year 1969/70 reveal that there has been a consolidation in the total number of schools, but that the ratio with regard to nationality has remained the same: 614 Ukrainian schools (with over 163,000 students), 15 Russian schools (11,500 students), 70 Magyar schools (21,500 students), 12 Moldavian schools (4,300 students), and 32 mixed schools.[85] Following the principle that children should be taught in their native language, standard Ukrainian is the medium of instruction for the Rusyn population, with Russian schools for children of the armed forces (who are stationed in great numbers in the region), and Magyar and Moldavian (Rumanian) schools for these two minorities.

The first institution of higher learning in the history of Subcarpathian Rus' was founded under Soviet rule. Uzhhorod State University opened its doors in 1945 with 168 students enrolled in four faculties: history, biology, philology, and medicine. By 1971/72, the number of faculties had increased to twelve, with 10,857 students enrolled. From the beginning, the languages of instruction were Ukrainian and Russian. The existing public and church-run teacher's colleges were abolished and replaced in 1946 with a Teacher's Institute, which a few years later was incorporated into the university.[86]

As for youth organizations, the formerly influential and frequently nationalist Ukrainophile Plast Scouts and Russophile Dukhnovych Scouts, together with the many local student-societies and university groups in Prague and Bratislava, were not revived after the war. Since then, Subcarpathian students have usually attended Uzhhorod University or schools in L'viv, Kiev, and Moscow. To enable them to show loyalty to the new regime a Subcarpathian Student Union (Soiuz Molodi) was convened in December 1944 to demand unification with the Soviet Union. About the same time 21,000 young people joined the Red Army. At the present, Subcarpathian students are members of the all-union Komsomol, with their own newspaper *Molod' Zakarpattia* (in a Ukrainian edition only).[87]

From the standpoint of national identity, what has been the result of these substantial social and educational changes implemented by the Soviet regime since 1945? To answer this question, I have personally observed, even if superficially, the situation in Uzhhorod; but, more importantly, I have conducted extensive interviews: (1) with people who were born and educated in Soviet Transcarpathia and who are now living in Eastern Europe; (2) with people from other parts of the Soviet Union who have worked as teachers in the area; and (3) with Soviet and non-Soviet visitors to the region.

Without exception, members of the younger generation identify themselves as being of the Ukrainian nationality and as part of one Ukrainian people. They realize that in the past (as witnessed by their own parents, grandparents, and relatives) Subcarpathians may have identified themselves as Rusyn, Carpatho-Russian, Czech, or Austro-Hungarian, for example. Some of the older people may still make such "mistakes," but the youngsters feel they know better and have become conscious Ukrainians. Even locally born children who attend Russian-language schools are taught that they are of the *ukrainskaia narodnost'* ("Ukrainian nationality"). Through adult education courses and through books, newspapers, radio, and television, large segments of the older generation have also come to accept this view, so that it is only a matter of time before the last "non-Ukrainian" Subcarpathians pass from the scene. Recent census data confirm this trend. There has been both an absolute and relative increase in the number of Ukrainians living in the Transcarpathian Oblast': from 686,464 (74.7 percent of the total) in 1959 to 808,131 (76.5 percent) in 1970.[88]

Thus, the Soviet regime's consistent policy with regard to national identity seems to have been successful. Moreover, even older Russophiles survive well in the new situation (for example, the writer-politician P. Sova, the folklorist P. Lintur, the poet M. Popovich), since, considering the realities of the Soviet state, using the Russian language is as feasible, if not more advantageous, than using Ukrainian. Thus, only the Rusynophile orientation has no place in the new society.

The situation in Soviet Transcarpathia can be usefully compared with the recent development of nationalism among two other groups of Subcarpathian Rusyns not living under Soviet rule. These are the approximately 135,000 Rusyns living in the Prešov Region of northeastern Czechoslovakia and the 25,000 Rusyns in the Vojvodina region of Yugoslavia.

The Rusyns in the present-day Prešov Region were historically inseparable from those in the Transcarpathian Oblast'. The first incidence of separation came in 1818, when a Greek Catholic diocese was established with a seat in Prešov. But this did not affect contact between the Prešov diocese and the older Mukachevo diocese, and in fact the greatest nineteenth-century Subcarpathian national leaders—Dukhnovych, Dobrianskii, Pavlovych, Kralitskii, and Stravrovskii-Popradov—were natives of the Prešov Region, and they functioned as well in one Rusyn diocese as another. This was possible before 1918, because all lived in the Hungarian Kingdom. The first real legal and administrative division came under the Czechoslovak regime, when Rusyns of the Prešov Region were placed under Slovak administration and, in 1919, divided from their eastern brethren by a provisional boundary that became permanent in 1928. Although free movement between the two areas was allowed, the Prešov Region Rusyns were a minority in Slovakia and, as such, had much less control over their own affairs than did their brethren in Subcarpathian Rus'. Beginning in 1939, the Prešov Region became part of a semi-independent Slovak state that was separated by a heavily guarded military border from the

Hungarian-controlled Subcarpathian territory. This division was further strengthened after 1946, when the Soviet government constructed a boundary of barbed-wire, watch towers, and land mines, which effectively cut off Rusyns in Czechoslovakia from those in the Soviet Union.

With regard to the nationality issue, Rusyns in the Prešov Region also witnessed conflicts among the local intelligentsia, who argued over an acceptable orientation. However, while Ukrainianism had scored successes in Subcarpathian Rus' during the interwar period, it was virtually absent in the Prešov Region. For instance, there were several Russian and Rusyn newspapers and thirty-seven affiliates of the Russophile Dukhnovych Society, but only one short-lived Ukrainian newspaper and one affiliate of the Prosvita Society. The region's parliamentary representatives (Lazho, Zhidovskii, and P'eshchak) were all Russophiles, and the Prešov diocese contained for the most part Russophile or Rusynophile priests. In 1927, a Russian Home (*Russkii Dom*) was founded in Prešov, and in 1936 a Russian-language gymnasium opened its doors. We have already seen how Prešov Region Rusyns rejected association with the autonomous Subcarpathian Rus' when they discovered it to be dominated by Ukrainophiles, and how during the Second World War the Russophile orientation, through its organ *Novoe vremia* (1939-1943), managed to survive in the face of pressure from Slovak nationalists.[89]

This was the tradition that Rusyns in the Prešov Region carried into the postwar era. The first variation came in March 1945, when, under the influence of local Communist party members, a new self-styled governing body was established in Prešov under the name Ukrainian National Council (Ukraïns'ka Narodna Rada). Such a title was chosen because the Council initially followed the lead of their brethren in Mukachevo and demanded unification with the Soviet Union. However, even when Czechoslovakia won back the Prešov council's allegiance, the name Ukrainian was maintained in the newly established National Theater (Ukraïns'kyi Narodnyi Teatr) and office for Ukrainian schools (Referat Ukraïns'kykh Shkil). But these entities were Ukrainian in name only, since the National Council published its newspaper, *Priashevshchina* (1945-1951), in Russian, the theater put on plays in Russian, and the local schools taught younger children in literary Russian! This situation prevailed for more than five years until, in the early 1950s, the already Communist-controlled government decided to end the confusion and declared by fiat that the Rusyns of the Prešov region—notwithstanding what they called themselves or what they felt themselves to be—must be considered henceforth only as Ukrainian. As the local inhabitants later recalled, they became Ukrainians overnight.[90]

New "Ukrainian" organizations were founded. Ukrainian periodicals replaced Russian ones, and local writers were called upon to re-explain in historical terms the correctness of the new interpretation.[91] In order to remain active, Russophile leaders had to become Ukrainophiles. Indeed, some did just this, but the vast majority of the Rusyn population resented these machinations, and rebelled in the only way they knew how. If Russian (which they considered synonymous with Rusyn) could not be taught in local schools, and if they could not be legally recognized as Russians or Rusyns, then they would prefer to have Slovak-language schools and to identify themselves with the Slovak nationality. Their rationalization? If Russian/Rusyn (rus'kyi) identity had to be given up, then it would be better to become Slovak than Ukrainian.[92] The government, especially the Slovak administration in Bratislava, felt it appropriate to bow to the will of the people and permitted the liquidation of Russian schools.[93]

A few figures will graphically illustrate the process. In 1948, when Russian was still the language of instruction, there were 275 elementary schools, 41 municipal schools, and 4 gymnasia in operation. After the adoption of the Ukrainian language, these numbers declined rapidly so that by 1966 there were only 68 elementary schools, 3 municipal schools, and one gymnasium. By 1970, there were only 30 elementary schools left where Ukrainian was even partially the language of instruction.[94] Even more drastic were the results of the postwar censuses. One author has calculated that on the basis of the 1930 census, when 91,079 persons in the Prešov Region declared themselves to be Rusyn, there should have been 135,000 Rusyns in 1970. However, official statistics show only 42,146 persons who were willing to identify themselves by one of the three accepted designations—Ukrainian, Russian, or Rusyn.[95]

Where have the rest gone? Nowhere! They have assimilated actively or passively into the Slovak nationality. The point is that neither the government in Czechoslovakia (which has liberally poured in large sums of money to support a Ukrainian museum, publications, research institute, cultural societies, and folk groups) nor the local Rusyn intelligentsia have fostered a consistent national policy since 1945. First Russian, then Ukrainian, and during the Prague Spring of 1968, even a Rusyn orientation came into vogue. This confusion had especially negative results on a minority population living in a land where Slovak is the official language and the one heard daily in administrative offices, on radio, and on television. The result of this inconsistency has been national assimilation, which for all intents and purposes has reduced by more than two-thirds the number of Rusyns in the region.

The situation in Yugoslavia followed yet another course. Unlike the fluctuation in Czechoslovakia and the government-imposed, consistent policy in the Soviet Union, the Rusyns of the Vojvodina have been left to work out their own national ideology. Unlike their co-nationals in the Prešov Region, however, the Vojvodinian intelligentsia has for the most part agreed to propagate one clearly defined orientation.

These people first migrated to the Bačka Region, as the Vojvodina was then called, during the reign of Maria Theresa, who was concerned with settling frontier areas that had only recently been won back from the Ottoman

Turks. The colonists originally came from the westernmost Rusyn areas, near Bardejov and Trebišov, which were adjacent to, or within, Slovak ethnographic territory.[96] Many linguists even consider their speech to be an eastern Slovak rather than a Rusyn dialect.[97] Despite their problematic linguistic affiliation, they brought their own Greek Catholic faith, their names Rus' and Rusnak, and, when their first publications appeared in the early twentieth century, Cyrillic script was used.

But what identity and what language was to be adopted: the local dialect or some more-developed linguistic form like Russian, Ukrainian, or Slovak? This problem was largely resolved by Havryil Kostel'nyk (1886-1948), a popular writer and national leader who chose to raise the Vojvodinian Rusyn dialect to the level of a literary language. He published the first literary work (Z moioho valala ["From My Village," 1904]) and the first grammar (Hramatyka bachvan'sko ruskei beshedi, 1923) for the new fledgling language.[98] These works became models for the local intelligentsia, and even if during the interwar period there were Russophiles and a small faction of Ukrainophiles among the Vojvodinian Rusyns, the main newspapers, almanacs, and other publications continued to appear in Bačka Rusyn.

The greatest impetus for the development of a separate language and nationality came after 1945, under the tolerant regime of Tito's Yugoslavia. In the face of continued Croatian and Serbian conflicts, the Yugoslav government tried to satisfy at least the smallest minorities and allowed the Rusyns free reign in their national affairs. The local intelligentsia decided to maintain the tradition of Kostel'nyk and set about to further develop and standardize their language so that it could be used in a modern technological society. Through numerous grammars, dictionaries, textbooks, periodicals, and other publications they have created a sociologically complete language—in the words of one Soviet scholar, "the newest Slavic language."[99] The corollary to this has been a strong sense of national pride and identity among the Vojvodinian Rusyns, who have resisted successfully the temptation to assimilate with the dominant Serbian or other neighboring nationalities.[100]

Thus, the past thirty years have provided three considerably different cases of Subcarpathian Rusyn national development. In a sense, all three traditional orientations have been tried: the Ukrainophile orientation was successfully implemented among the majority of Rusyns in Soviet Transcarpathia; the Russophile and later Ukrainophile orientations were applied inconsistently, and consequently succumbed to Slovak assimilation, in the Prešov Region; while the Rusynophile orientation has reached the stage of an accepted separate nationality in Yugoslavia. It is evident that each of the three orientations was in theory feasible, and the success of any one depended on the degree to which the ruling government and local intelligentsia could agree to work out and implement a consistent nationality policy.

14 | *Conclusion*

The embryonic stage of national development in Subcarpathian Rus' began in 1848 and lasted for approximately one-hundred years. During this time the local intelligentsia attempted to work out a national ideology and identity that could be implemented and accepted by the masses of the population. Quite naturally, the Subcarpathian intelligentsia did not function in isolation and had to be responsive to the needs and demands of those political regimes that ruled the homeland.

In a sense, the century-long embryonic stage in Subcarpathian national development did not end with the majority of the population having a clear-cut understanding of their national identity. The Russian, Ukrainian, and Rusyn orientations each had enough adherents to prevent any one of them from becoming dominant. As we have seen, this balance was broken after 1945 by the Soviet regime, which gave exclusive support to one orientation, the Ukrainian.

It would be an oversimplification, however, to say that the success of one orientation was due simply to the intervention of a political regime that imposed its will on the population. The relative success or failure of the contending national orientations can only be determined by viewing them simultaneously from both internal and external perspectives. That is to say, the existence of internal factors, such as historical writing, language, literature, cultural organizations, the educational system, and the church, has to be analyzed in the context of local, national, and international political developments. Only by taking into consideration the dynamic relationship of influences and responses between these internal and external factors can we hope to discern why one orientation was successful in a given situation and why others failed.

Chapter 1 showed that, besides its own distinctive characteristics, Subcarpathian Rusyn society, as a borderland civilization, was strongly influenced by several cultures, in particular the Galician-Ukrainian, Slovak, Hungarian, and Russian. As a result, when national identity became a relevent issue, Subcarpathian leaders naturally gravitated toward these four cultures, and some began to identify themselves and their people as belonging to one or another of them. Various factors encouraged or hampered each of the competing ideologies.

The first to drop out of the running were the Slovak and Hungarian orientations. The Slovaks had experienced the same political and socioeconomic development as the Rusyns prior to 1918. Furthermore, the eastern Slovak dialects and western Rusyn dialects were closely related, and the whole region of what is now eastern Slovakia had, over the centuries, developed a culture that was the common patrimony of both the Slovaks and Rusyns living there. However, despite these similarities, there was one crucial difference—religious affiliation. Slovak civilization was always predominantly Roman Catholic, and although the Greek Catholic Church included people who were, or who became, nationally Slovak, the Rusyn clerical intelligentsia, which set the foundations of a national movement in the late nineteenth century, looked, from the very beginning, to the East as the source of their own spiritual and cultural inheritance. The use of the Latin alphabet by Slovaks, and Cyrillic by Rusyns, was only the most external manifestation of these profoundly felt differences. As a result, during the embryonic stage of Rusyn national development there was never any serious suggestion, even under the Czechoslovak regime, that Subcarpathian Rusyns should identify with the Slovak nationality. Although such a tendency does exist, it has come about only since the 1950s, and it is limited to those Rusyns who remained within Slovakia after the Second World War.

The Hungarian or Magyarone orientation had a much better chance of winning over the Rusyn intelligentsia. First of all, the Rusyns were ruled by Hungary until 1918 and then again briefly from 1939 to 1944. Between 1868 and 1918 the Hungarian government tried forcibly to Magyarize the minority groups under its control, and they might have been successful had not the international political situation turned against their country in 1918-1919. The Magyar language was completely foreign to the Rusyn population, but given the political situation at the beginning of the twentieth century, neither the local Rusyn dialects, nor Russian, nor Ukrainian could be considered viable alternatives. Moreover, Rusyns, especially those who left their villages, Magyarized rapidly and felt themselves quite comfortable in a Hungarian environment. Subcarpathian Rus' was integrated within Hungarian society, which in turn was tolerant enough to absorb fully individuals of any background who accepted the Magyar nature of the state they lived in. Given a few more decades, during which several generations of Rusyn youngsters would have been educated only in Magyar language schools, then the Hungarian orientation might very well have eliminated all the others. However, the incorporation of the region into Czechoslovakia in 1919 fostered a Slavic rebirth, resulting in the effective elimination of the Magyar orientation, which even five years of partial revival during the Second World War could not restore.

As a result, after 1918, when the Subcarpathian national movement really got off the ground, only the Rusyn, Russian, and Ukrainian orientations had any chance of being accepted. Of these three, the separatist, or Rusyn, national orientation was the weakest, basically because of the attitudes of the local intelligentsia. No leader was ever willing to fashion a Rusyn literary language on the basis of any of the regional dialects. As a result, no writer was able to use a language that could be called standard literary Rusyn. Even Dukhnovych, whose writings in dialect included some of the best known literary phrases to enter the collective national psyche, did not hesitate to scorn openly the language of the peasants and to try to compose his "serious" writings in Slaveno-Rusyn, the Subcarpathian recension of Church Slavonic. For whatever reason, the sense of inferiority so prevalent in minorities or just plain disinterest, the Subcarpathian intelligentsia preferred to adopt already developed languages and literatures and to associate themselves with "higher" cultures rather than to develop their own.

In such circumstances, even government efforts to foster a separate Rusyn identity failed. The Czechoslovak government tried during the late 1930s and the Hungarian regime during the Second World War. But the general indecisiveness and contradictory policies of Prague, and the short-termed and only partial support of Budapest, made success unlikely. This does not mean that Subcarpathian civilization did not possess the potential to be transformed into a separate nationality. It did. What the Rusyn orientation lacked, however, was purposeful leadership. That the potential existed was revealed by the miniscule group of Rusyns in Yugoslavia, where a determined intelligentsia and favorable political circumstances combined to allow the creation of a separate Rusyn nationality.

While the Rusyn orientation generally lacked dynamic leaders, the Russian and Ukrainian orientations did have strong partisans among Subcarpathian leaders as well as among the many Russian and Ukrainian émigrés who settled in the region and promoted their own national views. Between 1919 and 1939 both orientations had well-developed cultural organizations and a continuous influx of younger people who received Russian or Ukrainian language training, or both, and national indoctrination in the schools and youth organizations. Both orientations also produced talented writers who developed a Subcarpathian literary corpus in the Russian and Ukrainian languages.

Despite this seeming equality, the Ukrainian orientation had made more converts in Subcarpathian Rus' by the end of the 1930s. Russophiles were more interested in playing politics than in undertaking sustained cultural work, especially at the grassroots level, as many Ukrainophiles were doing. Perhaps more important was the fact that when Subcarpathians were systematically exposed to the Russian and Ukrainian literary languages, and when they learned about the cultural heritages of Russia and Ukraine, they felt instinctively closer to the latter.

Although history could be interpreted to make the region seem part of a larger Russian entity, Subcarpathian Rusyns still spoke a series of dialects that were closely related to the Ukrainian dialects of Galicia. Ancestral migrational patterns revealed that the majority of Subcarpathian settlers had come from Galicia. The dominant Greek Catholic Church and all the attendant customs and rites were essentially similar to those in Galicia. Finally, the Subcarpathians had the same development as the Ukrainians. After all, Ukrainians were for centuries downtrodden by the Russians, Poles, and Turkic peoples of the steppes, and this unenviable position, which was sometimes interspersed with glory-filled Cossack rebellions, may have seemed more familiar to Subcarpathians than powerful, imperial Russia did. In essence, Russian aristocratic culture was probably intrinsically less congenial to Subcarpathian Rusyns than was Ukrainian peasant culture.

Having said this, it must also be admitted that association with things Russian was still an ineffable quality of Subcarpathian life. One crucial factor was the name Rus'. For Subcarpathian Rusyns, Rus' was the symbol of one's self, one's family, one's village, one's homeland. The concept of the Ukraine, however, was viewed as something completely foreign. As a result, despite geographical and linguistic differences, Russia seemed closer to Subcarpathians, precisely because in one way or another that civilization actively maintained the idea of Rus'. Finally, Ukrainian nationalism, in the aggressive, even fanatic form in which it came from Galicia during the 1930s, proved to be entirely alien to many Subcarpathians, even some who were otherwise favorably inclined to Ukrainianism.

Thus, despite the seeming advantages of Ukrainianism, as late as 1945 the Russian and Rusyn orientations were still very much alive. Actually, the Soviets could probably have chosen any one of the three and could have, through the facilities of mass education and modern communications, made Subcarpathians into Russians, Ukrainians, or a separate Rusyn nationality. They felt obliged, however, to accept the Ukrainian option so as to be consistent with the ideology of the local Communist party, as well as with the arguments put forward on the international forum to justify their new territorial acquisition. Having made that decision, the new regime consistently applied one national interpretation, and after three decades it has been successful in transforming the majority of younger, and many older, Subcarpathian Rusyns into conscious Ukrainians.

The Subcarpathian Rusyns were a small people living at the crossroads of several cultures. During their century of embryonic national development, between 1848 and 1948, the local intelligentsia was favorably disposed toward several national affiliations, but during the crucial last three decades of this era only the Russian, Ukrainian, and Rusyn orientations proved to be feasible. Although any one of the three might have been implemented, because of the specific culture of the region and the demands of political reality, only the Ukrainian orientation proved to be enduring.

Appendix 1

The Problem of Nomenclature

The Name of the People

Ethnic terms should be used in the
form in which they become crystallized
in their environment, and not in the
version given them in far-away lands.[1]

In this study, the terms Rusyn or Subcarpathian Rusyn are used for the people under consideration and Subcarpathian Rus' for the territory they inhabit. The name Rusyn was chosen because it is the name used by the inhabitants and by most of their leaders.

Until the twentieth century, the people who described themselves as Rusyns did so because they were expressing allegiance to the Eastern Christian (Greek Catholic or Orthodox) Rus' Church. Thus, for several centuries the term Rusyn had primarily a religious, not national, connotation. This being the case, it was also possible for ethnic Slovaks or Magyars of the Greek Catholic faith to call themselves Rusyns. The resultant confusion over the religious and the ethnic qua national sense of the word Rusyn led to great inconsistencies and later to political controversies when census takers attempted to record precisely the make-up of villages along the Magyar-Rusyn, and more especially the Slovak-Rusyn, ethnic boundary.[2]

In order to distinguish the population under consideration, it is necessary to apply the adjective Subcarpathian. The reasons for this are twofold: (1) Rusyn is a generic name used since the Middle Ages to describe all eastern Slavs; and (2) even after the names Russian, Belorussian, and Ukrainian came into general use among those peoples, the term Rusyn continued to be used by Ukrainians in the mountainous regions north and east of the Carpathian crests, that is, in southern Galicia and northern Bukovina. Thus, "Subcarpathian" more clearly defines the Rusyns in question as those who live south of the Carpathians in areas that, before 1918, belonged to the Hungarian Kingdom.

As might be expected, before attaining national consciousness, Subcarpathian Rusyns described themselves by a variety of names that reflected either geographic or ethnographic characteristics. Among the names using geographic criteria, the most popular way to define oneself was simply as a person "from here." In this same vein, Rusyns who lived in the lowlands might use the names *Dolyshniany, Dolyniany,* or *Nyzhniany* (lowland dwellers) in contrast to the *Verkhovyntsi, Horniany,* or *Horyshniany* (highland dwellers) who lived on the upper slopes of the mountains.[3] It was also common to name oneself after a particular village or town, such as *Uzhhorodchan* (person from Uzhhorod) or more often after the old Hungarian counties, such as *Sharyshan* (person from Sáros county) or *Zemplynchan* (person from Zemplén county). Finally, *Krainiak* or *Krainian* (border dweller) was used among Rusyns in Zemplén and Ung counties.[4]

Smaller Rusyn ethnographic subgroups have also had their own names. Among those most frequently seen in the literature are *Lemky* (Lemkians), *Boiky* (Boikians), and *Hutsuly* (Hutsuls). These names are based on linguistic and ethnographic criteria and refer to the three basic dialectal groups, moving from west to east through Rusyn ethnographic territory on both sides of the Carpathians. However, in Subcarpathian Rus' only Hutsuls describe themselves as such. Subcarpathians in the Boikian region use the names Rusyn or *Dolyshnianyn*, those in the Lemkian region the name Rusnak.[5] Several other names, based on either mode of speech, dress, or activity have also been recorded, such as *Bliakhy* (probably from Vlach), *Lemaky* (Sáros, Zemplén, and Ung counties), *Lopatky* (Ung county), *Lyshaky* (Máramaros county), and *Sotatsi* (from northeast of Humenné).[6]

Despite this maze of regional names, the most common denominator has been Rusyn, sometimes with the prefixes Uhro- (Hungarian-, reflecting location according to state) or Subcarpathian (reflecting geographical location). These names are attested from earliest times. For instance, the first printed book intended for Subcarpathian Rusyns was entitled *Katekhysys dlia naouky Ouhroruskym liudem* ("Catechism for the Instruction of the Uhro-Rusyn People," 1698), while the earliest poem in which a national name appears is the eighteenth-century "Pîsn o Rusnakakh" (Song of the Rusnaks), which uses the terms Rusyn and Rusnak.[7] With the beginnings of the national awakening after 1848, the names Rusyn and Subcarpathian Rusyn became fixed. These were the terms chosen by the "national awakener," Aleksander Dukhnovych, who wrote both the national anthem, "Podkarpats'kii rusynŷ/Ostav'te hlubokii son!" ("Subcarpathian Rusyns/ Arise from your deep slumber!") and the most popular national poem which began with the lines: "Ia Rusyn bŷl, esm' y budu" ("I was, am, and will remain a Rusyn").[8]

During the nineteenth century, several other names were used to describe the population: *karpatoross* (Carpatho-Ross), *ugro-ross* (Hungarian Ross) and *karpatorusskii* (Carpatho-Russian) or simply *russkii* (Russian).[9] The last two forms were maintained by Subcarpathian Russophiles in the twentieth century. For the most part, local Ukrainophiles used the name Rusyn (which they considered an archaic form for Ukrainian) until the 1930s. Thus, in the early writings of Vasyl' Grendzha-Dons'kyi and Iulii Borshosh-Kum'iats'kyi, only the name Rusyn is found. Similarly, the important political and cultural leader Avhustyn Voloshyn called his people Rusyn, and did not use the name Ukrainian in public until pressured to do so in the Prague Parliament by Communist delegates during the late 1920s. Ukrainian was adopted by the local Communist party in 1926 and by other Ukrainophile political parties in the years that followed. (See Chapter 11.) These developments did not affect the Prešov Region, however, where the local intelligentsia did not adopt the name Ukrainian until 1945.

Despite their tendency to adopt the names Ukrainian or Russian, both local Ukrainophiles and Russophiles argued that their respective preferences were only modern forms of the name Rusyn. Furthermore, both groups agreed that the people themselves preferred the name Rusyn.[10] Considering these factors, one can only agree with the decision made in 1920 by the editors of *Rusyn,* the first daily newspaper for Subcarpathian Rus': "The fact is that for us, for our people, the only correct name is 'Rusyn'. This name is used by all our people, this name was used by all our national writers."[11]

In a sense, it is in writings originating from beyond the region that we find the greatest terminological confusion. The oldest sources in this regard are the Latin documents of the Vatican, the Hungarian Catholic Church, and the Hungarian government. Here we find *Ruteni* and *Rutheni*, which were the names given by writers of late antiquity to all the eastern Slavs.[12]

Publications in Magyar most often use the name *orosz* and in some cases *kisorosz.* But these terms mean, respectively, Russian and Little Russian (Ukrainian); thus, in order to describe the Subcarpathian population more precisely the names *magyarorosz* (Magyar-Russian), *uhrorusz* (Uhro-Rusyn), *ruszin* (Rusyn), or *rutén/ruthén* (Rusyn) might be used.[13]

Russian writers use the adjective Carpatho-Russian (*karpatorusskii*), but this does not distinguish Subcarpathians from their immediate brethren in southern Galicia and northern Bukovina, while Ukrainian writers prefer Carpatho-Ukrainian (*karpatoukraïns'kyi*) or Transcarpathian Ukrainian (*zakarpatoukraïns'kyi*). The Czechoslovak government adopted the name *rusín* (Rusyn) and the corresponding adjectives *rusínský* (Rusyn) or *podkarpatorusky* (Subcarpathian Rusyn).[14] Actually, the last name could also mean Subcarpathian Russian, and whenever Czech publications use the term *rusky* (as many recent official publications do), it is sometimes not possible to know whether reference is made to Subcarpathian Rusyns or to Russians.[15]

Publications in major western languages basically use names derived from the Latin *rutheni:* in German, *Karpato-Ruthenen;* French, *ruthènes* or *ruthènes subcarpathiques;* and in English, Ruthenians or Carpatho-Ruthenians. However, some writings in these languages do not distinguish between Rusyn and Russian; hence, one also finds *Karpatorussen, russes subcarpathiques,* and Carpatho-Russians. English-language publications by Rusyn-American immigrants have used either Rusin, Carpatho-Rusin, or Carpatho-Russian to describe themselves.[16]

The Name of the Territory
Some of the earliest names given to Subcarpathian Rus' suggested that the region was a border territory inhabited by Rusyns. In the eleventh century, Western European sources referred to the area as Marchia Ruthe-

norum (Ruthenian borderland), Marchia being derived from the German *Mark* (borderland). In 1031, this land was awarded by the Hungarian king to his son Emerich, who appropriately received the title *Dux Ruizorum* (Duke of the Ruthenian land).[17] Two sixteenth-century Polish sources used the terms *ukraina węgierska* (Hungarian Ukraine or borderland—1619) and *Ukraina Mukacsiensis* (Mukachevo Ukraine or borderland—1662).[18] Historically, Hungarian sources reflected the structure of the kingdom, so that references to Rusyn-inhabited territory per se did not exist. One can only find references to: (1) individual counties (such as Sáros, Zemplén, Máramaros) that were partially inhabited by Rusyns; (2) *Felvidék* (the Highland), which included the mountainous areas where both Slovaks and Rusyns lived; and (3) to the Mukachevo (*Munkács*) and later Prešov (*Eperjes*) dioceses, which had jurisdiction over all Greek Catholics (ethnic Slovaks and Magyars as well as Rusyns) in the northeastern part of the kingdom. When, in the late nineteenth century, Hungarian writers took cognizance of the ethnic complexity of their country, Rusyn territory was sometimes called *Ruténföld* (Ruthenian land). In late 1918, the name *Ruszka Krajna* (Rusyn land) was given by Budapest to its short-lived autonomous province, while in reference to the Czechoslovak-ruled region, *Ruszinskó* (Rusinia) was used.[19]

The Czech name for Rusyn-inhabited lands was established after 1918. *Rusínsko* (Rusinia) was used for awhile, but *Podkarpatská Rus'* (Subcarpathian Rus') predominated, since it was the official name given to the republic's easternmost province. This name, of course, did not comprise the Rusyns living under Slovak administration.

During the late nineteenth and early twentieth centuries, when writings about Subcarpathian Rus' increased, Russian-language works referred to the region as *Ugorskaia Rus'* (Hungarian Rus'), *Karpatskaia Rus'* (Carpathian Rus'), and less frequently as *Prikarpatskaia Rus'* (Rus' near the Carpathians). Carpathian Rus' was probably used most often, but this in effect meant all the lands in the Carpathian Mountains (southeastern Galicia and northern Bukovina, as well as Subcarpathian Rus') where "Russians" lived.[20]

Ukrainian authors first used *Uhors'ka Rus'* (Hungarian Rus'), *Karpats'ka Rus'* (Carpathian Rus'), and sometimes *Uhors'ka Ukraïna* (Hungarian Ukraine) or *Prykarpats'ka Ukraïna* (Ukraine near the Carpathians) to describe the region.[21] By the 1930s *Karpats'ka Ukraïna* (Carpatho-Ukraine) and *Zakarpats'ka Ukraïna* (Transcarpathian Ukraine) predominated[22]—the former being the official name of the autonomous government in 1938-1939, the latter being used alongside *Zakarpats'ka oblast'* (Transcarpathian oblast') as the official name under post-1945 Soviet rule. These Ukrainian names may be appropriately used when dealing with recent developments, but not for the period before 1945, because with the exception of a few months (November 1938 to March 1939) when the terms Carpatho-

Ukraine and Carpatho-Ukrainian were adopted, neither was used either by the inhabitants or by the governments that ruled the area. In rejecting the more recent Ukrainian terminology, the following principle is upheld: "It is essential that a terminology of ethnical and geographical names contemporary to the epoch be applied; it is most confusing and even misleading to transfer present-day concepts to times when these concepts were not in existence or implied a content other than the modern one."[23]

Western-language writers have also been inconsistent in describing the region. All usually begin with Rus' and render this term, in their respective language, either as Ruthenia or, incorrectly, as Russia. To this proper noun, an adjectival variant of Carpathian is added. Hence, there is the French *Ruthénie subcarpathique* or *Russie subcarpathique,* the Italian *Russia subcarpatica* or *Ruthenia subcarpatica,* the German *Karpatorussland,* and the English Ruthenia, Carpatho-Ruthenia or Subcarpathian Ruthenia, Carpatho-Russia or Subcarpathian Russia, and Carpatho-Ukraine or Transcarpathian Ukraine. Following the lead of the American-born Governor Zsatkovich, some Rusyn immigrant publications during the 1920s and 1930s used the name Rusinia.[24]

One final word on the name of the territory inhabited by Rusyns in present-day northeastern Czechoslovakia: this area has come to be known as the Prešov Region (Russian *Priashevshchina;* Ukrainian *Priashivshchyna*). The name is derived from the city of Prešov, which, although itself is not within Rusyn ethnic territory, has nonetheless been the seat of a Greek Catholic diocese since 1818 and a traditional cultural and political center for local Rusyns. Some writers have also called this area as a whole *Priashevskaia Rus'* (Prešov Rus'), *Skhidna Slovachchina* (Eastern Slovakia), and *Pidduklians'kyi krai* (The land under the Dukla Pass), while the territory north of Bardejov and Svidník is called *Makovytsa,* as in the writings of the popular nineteenth-century writer Aleksander Pavlovych.[25]

To summarize, in this study Subcarpathian Rus' is used to describe all the territory that Subcarpathian Rusyns inhabit. This name has been chosen for two reasons: (1) the adjective Subcarpathian clearly suggests that the territory in question lies south of the Carpathians, and (2) Rus' is the most accurate rendition of *Русь,* a concept suggesting both the religious and national affiliation of the inhabitants. For the years after 1918, Subcarpathian Rus' will generally be used when referring to the easternmost province of Czechoslovakia (*Podkarpatská Rus*), which after 1939 was under Hungarian rule (*Kárpátaljai vajdaság*) and after 1945 under Soviet rule (*Zakarpats'ka oblast'*). The region inhabited by Subcarpathian Rusyns, that has been under Slovak administration since 1918 will be referred to as the Prešov Region.

Appendix 2

Comparative Biographies

The eighty-one individuals whose biographies are given here were some of the most prominent national leaders in Subcarpathian Rus' in the post-1918 period. A larger sample would have been preferable, but it is extremely difficult to find adequate information for every rubric. Even for the figures discussed here, certain rubrics remain unanswered.

The numbers given in the biographical entries refer to the following:

(1) Dates of birth and death.
(2) Place of birth: town, *okres* (smaller territorial division under the Czechoslovak and Soviet governments), and county (larger division under Hungarian regime before 1918 and the Czechoslovak regime during the 1920s).
(3) Profession of father.
(4) Own profession.
(5) Place of education: elementary, middle, gymnasium, university, and professional.
(6) National orientation.
(7) Political orientation.
(8) Activity.
(9) Major publications dealing with Subcarpathian Rusyns.

Under rubrics 3 and 4, "professions," the classification "teacher" means elementary or middle school teacher, the classification "professor" refers to employment at a gymnasium, theological seminary, commercial academy, or university. The classification "priest/professor" suggests a person was trained for both professions; many of these persons were primarily active as professors. The classification "minor civil servant" refers to positions such as bank clerk, railroad conductor, or postal clerk.

There may be several classifications under rubrics 6 and 7, "national orientation" and "political orientation," because some individuals changed their loyalties in response to altering internal and external conditions. It should be noted that national and political orientations are separate categories; thus, if, for instance, a Russophile or Rusynophile was at the same time a Magyarone or a Czechophile, this would be indicated as pro-Hungarian or pro-Czechoslovak under the rubric "political orientation."

The statistical summary of the information included within the eighty-one biographical entries is broken down according to the three basic national orientations: Russophile, Ukrainophile, and Rusynophile. Since complete information was not available for each individual, no one category will have a total of eighty-one, the original sample.

Under the categories of "profession of father" and "own profession," if more than one profession appears in either, the first is chosen for entry in the statistics. For "education," all places of secondary education are entered, even if there is more than one for some persons. The category "activity" reveals the manner in which the person contributed most to national life.

Statistical Summary

County of birth	Russophile	Ukrainophile	Rusynophile	Total
Szepes	1	0	0	1
Sáros	4	2	1	7
Zemplén	2	2	3	7
Ung	0	3	4	7
Bereg	4	3	7	14
Ugocsa	2	1	3	6
Máramaros	1	10	9	20
Elsewhere in Hungarian Kingdom	3	0	1	4
Galicia	3	7	0	10
Bukovina	1	0	0	1
Russian Empire (Ukraine)	2	1	0	3
Other	1	0	0	1

Profession of father				
Peasant	7	12	7	26
Priest	6	7	13	26
Priest/professor	1	0	0	1
Professor	0	0	0	0
Teacher	2	4	5	11
Lawyer	0	0	0	0
Journalist	0	0	1	1
Minor civil servant	1	3	1	5
Professional artisan	0	0	0	0
Businessman	0	2	0	2
Other	1	1	0	2

Own Profession				
Peasant	0	1	0	1
Priest	2	1	4	7

	Russophile	Ukrainophile	Rusynophile	Total
Priest/professor	3	3	7	13
Professor	2	7	3	12
Teacher	3	3	2	8
Lawyer	5	3	5	13
Journalist	6	6	1	13
Minor civil servant	0	2	0	2
Professional artisan	0	0	2	2
Businessman	2	1	2	5
Other	1	2	2	5

Education

Gymnasia				
Uzhhorod	3	3	11	17
Mukachevo	3	1	4	8
Prešov	4	0	2	6
Berehovo	1	2	1	4
Sighet	0	3	2	5
Khust	0	1	1	2
Other	5	3	6	14
Commercial academies				
Mukachevo	0	2	0	2
Other	0	1	1	2
Teacher's colleges				
Uzhhorod	1	2	3	6
Prešov	2	1	0	3
Sighet	0	1	0	1
Budapest	0	1	0	1
Theological seminaries				
Uzhhorod	3	2	7	12
Prešov	1	2	1	4
Budapest	2	2	5	9
Other	1	2	2	5
Universities				
Budapest	2	3	7	12
Vienna	1	4	1	6
L'viv	0	4	1	5
Chernivtsi	2	1	0	3
Prague (Charles)	6	1	0	7
Bratislava (Comenius)	1	1	0	2
Cluj	1	1	2	4

	Russophile	Ukrainophile	Rusynophile	Total
Kharkiv (Communist party schools)	0	3	0	3
Other	4	5	4	13
Activity				
Priest/ecclesiastical administrator	0	1	4	5
Professor/educational administrator	5	9	3	17
Government official	4	1	7	12
Writer/scholar	6	8	7	21
Politician/editor	9	8	4	21
Professional artisan	0	1	2	3
Other	0	1	1	2

Alys'kevych, Andrii

(1) 1870-1949   (2) Zaluvka; Stanyslaviv; Galicia
(3) priest   (4) professor
(5) gymnasium, Zolochov; university, Vienna and L'viv
(6) Ukrainophile   (7) pro-Czechoslovak
(8) Alys'kevych was a teacher and leading educational administrator. He began teaching at the Brodii (1896-1900) and L'viv (1900-1910) gymnasia in his native Galicia, and held his first administrative posts as director of the Ukrainian Female Teacher's College in L'viv (1909-1910), and the Ukrainian gymnasia in Przemyśl (1910-1917) and Drohobych (1918-1919). He was also active in educational organizations as treasurer of the Pedagogical Society (from 1902), co-founder of the Teacher's Aid Cooperative (1905) in L'viv, and as chairman of the School Aid Society (1910-1917) in Przemyśl. In May, 1919, Alys'kevych was sent by the Western Ukrainian government to Vienna and Prague to obtain school textbooks. In the fall of 1919 he was appointed, at the suggestion of Voloshyn, director of the gymnasium in Berehovo, where the following year he established a Rusyn section. In 1922, he was appointed director of the gymnasium in Uzhhorod. He was also active in the Ukrainophile Plast scouting movement and since 1925 was treasurer and member of the presidium of the Pedagogical Society in Uzhhorod. Alys'kevych was a Germanist by training, and between 1898 and 1911 he published several textbooks on German literature and a study of German dialects; he was also editor of the children's journal in L'viv, *Dzvinok* (1904, 1906-1908).

Bachinskii, Edmund Stepanovich, LL.D.

(1) 1880-1947   (2) Kalyny; Tiachiv; Máramaros
(3) priest   (4) lawyer, judge
(5) university, Budapest
(6) Russophile   (7) pro-Hungarian, pro-
                                                 Czechoslovak
(8) Before and during the First World War, Bachinskii was an official in Debrecen and other towns. He did not return to his homeland until 1921, then he served as mayor of Uzhhorod (1923) and as a member of the provincial government. He was also chief counselor to the regional court in Košice and chairman of the Provincial Union of Cooperatives. From 1929 to 1938 he served as senator in the Prague Parliament for the Republican party. Bachinskii was a member of the Russophile Dukhnovych Society from 1927 until 1936, when he briefly served as its chairman. He was also a member of the Russophile branch of the Central National Council. During the autonomous period he served as Minister of Interior in the first Subcarpathian government, which he represented at the border negotiations with Hungary. Bachinskii's brother-in-law was the Rusynophile governor K. Hrabar. In 1945, Bachinskii was arrested by the Soviet secret police and convicted of anti-Soviet activity. He died in prison.
(9) "Kooperatsiia na Podkarpatskoi Rusi" (1936)

Badan, Oleksandr, LL.D.

(1) 1895-1933   (2) Galicia
(3) —   (4) lawyer, judge
(5) —
(6) Ukrainophile   (7) pro-Czechoslovak, pro-Soviet
(8) Badan arrived in Czechoslovakia in 1919 and first served as a jurist in eastern Slovakia. From 1923 he was a lawyer in Khust and Berehovo. In March 1920, he was one of the two organizers of the Social Democratic party and soon after became active in local Communist party activity. In December 1925, he was a delegate to the Ninth Ukrainian Communist Party Congress in Kharkiv. Forced to leave Czechoslovakia in 1928, he emigrated to Kharkiv where, until his untimely death, he served the Ukrainian Communist party boss, M. Skrypnyk, as advisor on Subcarpathian Rus'. He was also a member of the Institute for National Questions at the Ukrainian Institute for Marxism.
(9) *Istoriia sotsial'noho rukha* (1923); "Popivs'ka zhandarmeriia na Zakarpatti" (1926); *Zakarpats'ka Ukraïna* (1929); see also Bibliography.

Barabolia, Marko (pseudonym for Ivan Rozniichuk)

(1) 1910-1944?   (2) Trebushany (Dilove); Rakhiv;
                                      Máramaros
(3) peasant   (4) teacher
(5) middle school, Khust; commercial academy, Mukachevo
(6) Ukrainophile   (7) pro-Czechoslovak
(8) Little is known about this enigmatic figure other than that he worked
for Unio publishers in Uzhhorod for a while during the 1930s and then
taught in elementary schools near and in Iasynia and Rakhiv. After the
Hungarian take-over, Barabolia attended a teacher's qualifier course in
Debrecen in 1940. In 1944 he was drafted into the Hungarian Army. He was
Subcarpathia's only real satirist and published his first work in 1928.
(9) *Z-pid ïdkoho pera* (1941)

Beskid, Anton Grigorievich, LL.D.

(1) 1855-1933   (2) Hanigovce; Sabinov; Sáros
(3) priest   (4) lawyer
(5) gymnasium, Uzhhorod; university, Budapest
(6) Russophile   (7) pro-Czechoslovak
(8) Beskid was already politically active in his native Prešov region during
the Hungarian regime. He practiced law in Budapest (1883-1885), Kež-
marok (1885-1906), and Prešov (1906-1910), where he also served as legal
counsel to the Prešov Greek Catholic Diocese. He then represented the
Lubovňa district (Szepes county) for the oppositional People's party in the
Budapest Parliament (1910-1918). After the war, he was one of the first
leaders to favor unification of Rusyns with Czechoslovakia and worked toward this goal as chairman of the Prešov National Council in November
1918, as representative to the Paris Peace Conference from January 1919,
and as chairman (in absentia) of the Uzhhorod Central National Council of
May, 1919. In October 1919, he became head of the Russophile faction of
the Central National Council which opposed the new government. In 1920
he founded the Russian National Bank in Uzhhorod, which, shortly after,
merged with the Subcarpathian Bank. Finally, in 1923, he was appointed
governor of the province, although he remained relatively inactive in this
post until his death. Throughout he was an outspoken supporter of the
Dukhnovych Society and protagonist of the local Ukrainophiles and populists.

Beskid, Mikhail Grigorievich

(1) 1858-1928   (2) Jastrabie; Sabinov; Sáros
(3) priest   (4) priest
(5) gymnasium, Prešov; theological seminary, Uzhhorod and Prešov
(6) Russophile   (7) pro-Czechoslovak
(8) Beskid was part of a family that was politically active in the Prešov Region, especially in support of the Russophile orientation. Mikhail had already developed a strong national awareness as a young boy, since his father's home in Legnava (Szepes) was a meeting place for the local intelligentsia. He was ordained a Greek Catholic priest and served in parishes at Jarabina (Szepes), Medvedzie (Sáros), and, from the late 1880s until his death, in Lukov (Sáros). Before the First World War he opposed vocally the Magyarization policies of Bishop Novak in Prešov, and in late 1918-early 1919 was an active participant in all sessions of the Prešov Russian National Council, where he spoke out in favor of unity with Czechoslovakia. He was subsequently chosen to serve in the župa administration in Košice.

Beskid, Nikolai Aleksandrovich, Ph.D.

(1) 1883-1947   (2) Boldogkőváralja; Abaúj
(3) priest   (4) priest
(5) elementary, Santova; gymnasium, Prešov; theological seminary,
     Budapest
(6) Russophile   (7) pro-Czechoslovak
(8) Beskid was ordained a Greek Catholic priest in 1906 and began his career in the chancery of the Prešov diocese, first as clerk (1906), then as secretary (1908) to the bishop. In 1912 he was appointed to the diocesan legal council. About this time he was sent as a parish priest to Legnava, a village near Stará Lubovňa. As a cousin of A. G. Beskid, Rev. N. Beskid became involved in politics after the war as publisher of the Russophile *Golos russkago naroda* in Prešov and as vice-chairman of the Russian National party. After his cousin became governor, N. Beskid devoted the rest of his life to parish work and writing several histories of his people, some of which, because of their anti-Czechoslovak nature, were published by Rusyn immigrants in the United States. He was also a member of the Dukhnovych Society and chairman of its publications section.
(9) *Karpatska Rus'* (1920); *Karpatorusskaia drevnost'* (1928); *Karpatorusskaja pravda* (1933); *Dukhnovichi* (1934); see also Bibliography.

Birchak, Volodymyr, Ph.D.

(1) 1881-1945   (2) Liubintse; Strii; Galicia
(3) priest   (4) professor
(5) gymnasium, L'viv; university, L'viv and Cracow
(6) Ukrainophile   (7) pro-Czechoslovak
(8) Birchak began his professional and literary career in Galicia. From 1905 to 1919 he was a professor in L'viv and Drohobych and member of an art for art's sake literary group, Moloda Muza (1906-1909). In 1919 Birchak emigrated to Uzhhorod, where he was appointed a member of the Subcarpathian school administration and professor at the gymnasium (1921-38). He published several language textbooks, several studies of Subcarpathian literature, and was an editor of the Prosvita Society's scholarly journal, *Naukovŷi zbornyk*. He was a leading member of Plast, the Ukrainophile scouting organization in Subcarpathia, and of the Shevchenko Scientific Society in L'viv. He also authored several works of prose during these years. Although a Ukrainian nationalist, Birchak became alienated from the local autonomous government in late 1938 because he was from Galicia. After the Hungarian occupation, he emigrated to Prague where he was later arrested by the Soviet secret police in 1945.
(9) *Literaturna stremlinnia Pidkarpats'koï Rusi* (1921, 1937); *Zolota skrypka* (1937); *Karpats'ka Ukraïna* (1940); see also Bibliography.

Bobul'skii, Antonii (pseudonyms: Nemchuk, Dido Mikula, David Shrapnel', Ivan Pevchuk)

(1) 1877-194?   (2) Cracow; Galicia
(3) police inspector   (4) printer, editor
(5) elementary, Cracow (Polish) and Przemyśl (Russian); trade school
(6) Russophile   (7) pro-Czechoslovak
(8) Bobul'skii arrived in Uzhhorod in 1896 and worked in the print shop of Bartolémy Jäger. He remained there after the establishment was taken over by Julius Földesi and by 1920 was appointed director of the company's publishing program. Bobul'skii founded the short-lived *Karpatorusskii vîstnyk* in 1918 and then revived it in 1920 as the organ of the Autonomous Agricultural Union. He was the most prolific playwright in the region, composing in the Subcarpathian recension of Russian many short plays that were performed by amateur groups. Besides plays, he sponsored a series of inexpensive brochures, the Desheva Biblioteka (1909-1925), and wrote a satirical novel about a Rusyn named David Shrapnel' and his adventures in war.
(9) *Uiko yz Ameryky: p'esa* (1922); *Kandydat: vesela yhra* (1923); *Voiennyia sobîtiia Davyda Shrapnelia y Yvana Pîvchuka* (1924); *Nîmaia nevîsta: veselaia yhra* (1926, 1932)

Bokshai, Emyliian

(1) 1889-1976   (2) Kobylets'ka Poliana; Rakhiv;
                                               Máramaros
(3) priest   (4) priest/professor
(5) elementary, Lalove; gymnasium, Mukachevo (1889-1907); theological
    seminary, Budapest (1907-1911)
(6) Rusynophile   (7) pro-Czechoslovak
(8) Like his father, Bokshai was ordained a Greek Catholic priest. He
served as a chaplain in Mukachevo during the First World War and in early
1919 was secretary of the Rus'kii Klub. From 1918 to 1944 he was a professor of religion at the Uzhhorod gymnasium. During the 1930s Bokshai became the chief spokesman for the Rusynophile orientation, primarily
through the paper he edited, *Nedîlia* (1935-1938). He was also the author of
numerous religious manuals and a history of the church written in dialect,
which were used in Subcarpathian secondary schools. After 1945 he resided
in Košice.
(9) *Nauka o vîrî* (1924); *Ystoriia Staroho Zavîta* (1925); co-author, *Madiars'ko-rus'kyi slovar'* (1928)

Bokshai, Iosyf Iosyfovych

(1) 1891-1975   (2) Kobylets'ka Poliana; Rakhiv;
                                               Máramaros
(3) priest   (4) artist, professor
(5) gymnasium, Mukachevo; art academy, pedagogical section, Budapest
    (completed 1919)
(6) Rusynophile   (7) pro-Czechoslovak, pro-
                                               Hungarian, pro-Soviet
(8) Just after completing his art studies, Bokshai was drafted into the Austro-Hungarian army in September 1914. In March 1915 he was captured on
the eastern front; for the rest of the war he was in Russian camps in Turke-
stan and then spent time on a farm near Dnipropetrovs'k. After 1919 he was
an art instructor at the Uzhhorod gymnasium. Together with A. Erdeli, Bokshai founded a distinct school of Subcarpathian painting. He participated in
the first exposition of Subcarpathian artists (1921) and was a founding
member of the Circle of Artists in Subcarpathian Rus' (1922). He remained
active during the Hungarian regime and under the Soviets has been hailed as
the most outstanding painter from the region. His honors include National
Artist of the USSR and corresponding member of the Soviet Academy of
Arts.
(9) "Marlířství na Podkarpatské Rusi" (1936)

Bonkáló, Sándor, Ph.D. (pseudonym: O. Rakhovskii)

(1) 1880-1959   (2) Rakhiv; Rakhiv; Máramaros
(3) teacher   (4) university professor
(5) elementary, Rakhiv; gymnasium, Uzhhorod; theological seminary,
    Uzhhorod; university, Budapest (completed 1917), Leipzig, and
    Petrograd
(6) Rusynophile   (7) pro-Hungarian
(8) Bonkáló received a firm grounding in Slavic linguistics in Budapest and
Petrograd, having studied with professors Asboth, Shakhmatov, and
Baudouin de Courtenay. While still a student in Budapest, he became a
member of the Union of Hungarian Greek Catholics (1902), which favored
the assimilation of Rusyns. He began a teaching career at the Magyar gymnasia in Szeged, Gyöngyös, and Zalaegerszeg (1906-1916). In 1914 he was
awarded a prize by the Russian Academy in St. Petersburg for a study
(never published) of the relationship of Rusyn to Magyar. In 1919 he was
appointed professor of the newly created chair of Rusyn and Russian languages and literatures at Budapest University. He also prepared at this time
dialectal texts (never used) for Rusyn schools. In 1924 he was retired after
the position he held was abolished; during the following years he published
several popular and scholarly studies on the Subcarpathian Rusyn, Russian,
and Ukrainian languages and on Slavic languages and culture in general. In
1945 Bonkáló was appointed to the renewed chair of Russian studies at
Budapest University and held this position until retired for a second time in
1948.
(9) *A ráhoi kisorosz nyelvjárás leíro hangtana* (1910); "Die ungarländischen Ruthenen" (1922); *A kárpátalji rutén irodalom és művelődés* (1935);
A Ruthének (Ruszinok) (1940); see also Bibliography

Borkaniuk, Oleksa Oleksiivych (pseudonym: Karavan)

(1) 1901-1942   (2) Iasynia; Rakhiv; Máramaros
(3) peasant, lumberjack   (4) journalist
(5) elementary, Iasynia; commercial academy, Mukachevo; university,
    Kharkiv (1926-1929)
(6) Ukrainophile   (7) pro-Soviet
(8) Borkaniuk was one of the most popular Communist leaders. In 1925 he
entered the youth branch (Komsomol) of the Subcarpathian Communist
party. After studying three years in the Soviet Ukraine, he returned to his
homeland in 1929 to serve as first secretary of the regional Komsomol. He
was subsequently active in journalism as editor of the Communist organs
Karpats'ka pravda (1929-1933) and *Pratsiuiucha molod'* (1930-1936). In

1934 he was elected secretary of the Subcarpathian Communist party and from 1935 to 1938 served as deputy to the Prague Parliament. He maintained continual contact with the Soviets, returning there in the summer of 1935 as a delegate to the seventh Communist International and then again in 1939 seeking refuge after the Hungarian occupation. In December 1941, Borkaniuk led a detachment of partisan parachutists who descended on Subcarpathian Rus'. He was captured by the Hungarian police in March 1942 and executed the following October.

Borshosh-Kum'iats'kyi, Iulii Vasyl'ovych

(1) b. 1905   (2) Velyki Kom'iaty; Sevliush;
                                                       Ugocsa
(3) peasant   (4) teacher
(5) teacher's college, Uzhhorod (completed 1925)
(6) Ukrainophile   (7) pro-Czechoslovak, pro-Soviet
(8) Borshosh-Kum'iats'kyi was an elementary school teacher who taught in several Subcarpathian villages. His literary career began with the publication of a collection of poems in 1928. He was one of the first local writers to use literary Ukrainian and by the 1930s had become a fervent advocate of that orientation. He continued to publish in literary journals under the Hungarian regime. Borshosh-Kum'iats'kyi welcomed the Soviet regime in his writings and was elected a member of the Union of Writers in the Ukraine. After 1945 he continued his pedagogical career in Uzhhorod's school for the deaf and dumb.
(9) *Vesnianî kvîtŷ* (1928); *Z moho kraiu* (1929); *Kraïna dyv* (1934); *Z nakazu naroda* (1938); *Krov klyche* (1938); *Hrai trembito* (1958)

Brashchaiko (Bajor), Iulii, LL.D.

(1) 1879-1946   (2) Hluboka; Uzhhorod; Ung
(3) peasant   (4) lawyer, editor
(5) gymnasium, Sighet and Uzhhorod; university, Budapest
(6) Ukrainophile   (7) pro-Ukrainian
                                                       pro-Czechoslovak
(8) Brashchaiko was a lawyer in Khust and Uzhhorod until the end of Hungarian rule in 1919. Late in that year he became the leading figure (along with his younger brother Mykhailo) of the faction that called for union of Subcarpathian Rus' with an independent Ukrainian state. Brashchaiko tried to achieve this goal by convening three national councils in Khust (November 1918), and then leading a group that refused to accept the pro-Hungarian orientation of the government-sponsored Rusyn Congress in Budapest (December). During the following spring, he realized the futility of the

Ukrainian solution and agreed to serve as vice-chairman of the Central National Council in Uzhhorod, which in May 1919 called for union with Czechoslovakia. As a result, he was subsequently appointed to serve on the Directorate (1919-1920), where he was responsible for trade.

From 1920 to 1939 he maintained a law practice in Uzhhorod, and at the same time was an active Ukrainophile political organizer. In 1920 he organized the Rusyn-Agriculturalist party and after 1923 he served as a member of the presidium in the Christian-National party. In 1920 he helped to organize the Podkarpatskii Bank and that same year was elected first president of the Prosvita Society. He served as founding editor (1932-1938) of the newspaper *Ukraïns'ke slovo* and was chairman of the Union of Lawyers in Subcarpathian Rus' and the Nadiia Society, and a member of the central committee of the People's party. Brashchaiko was an active participant during the autonomous period: he was appointed head of the boundary commission (November 1938), was elected to the Diet (February 1939), and was appointed Minister of Finance, Industry, and Commerce in the last Carpatho-Ukrainian government (March 14, 1939). After the Hungarian occupation, he led a two-man delegation to Budapest seeking to reach a modus vivendi for the Ukrainophiles. The mission failed and his subsequent activity is unknown.

Brashchaiko, Mykhailo, LL.D.

(1) 1883-1973   (2) Blazhiieve; Berehovo; Bereg
(3) peasant   (4) lawyer, editor
(5) gymnasium, Uzhhorod and Sighet; law faculty, university, Cluj and
    Vienna
(6) Ukrainophile   (7) pro-Ukrainian,
                                     pro-Czechoslovak
(8) Mykhailo Brashchaiko worked with his older brother Iulii to promote the Ukrainian orientation in their homeland. Mykhailo did this first as chairman of the national councils at Sighet (December 1918) and at Khust (January 1919). He was sent in early 1919 as a delegate from the Khust Council to pledge unity with the government of the Western Ukrainian Republic, located in Stanyslaviv, Galicia. He helped organize the Agriculturalist Party, serving as the editor (1920-1924) of its newspaper, *Rus'ka nyva,* as well as the Christian National party, of which he was vice-president (1923-1938). Mykhailo later was chief editor (1932-1938) of his brother's newspaper, *Ukraïns'ke slovo*. During the 1920s, he was chairman of the Rusyn Theater and a member of the Uzhhorod city council. He was also chairman of the Shkôl'na Matka Rusynôv and a member of the Prosvita Society and of the Ukrainophile faction of the Central National Council. He

was active during the autonomous period as member of the executive committee of the Ukrainian National Union (January 1939) and of the Diet
(February 1939). It was Mykhailo Brashchaiko who introduced the bill on
March 15, 1939, proclaiming independence for Carpatho-Ukraine.
(9) *Ches'ko-rus'ki vzaemynŷ* (1923); co-author of *Madiars'ko-rus'kyi slovar'* (1928)

Brodii, Andrei

(1) 1895-1946   (2) Kyv'iazhd'; Irshava; Bereg
(3) church cantor, peasant   (4) teacher
(5) teacher's college, Uzhhorod
(6) Rusynophile   (7) pro-Hungarian
(8) Brodii began his career before 1914 as a village teacher in Velykyi Bychkiv. He was wounded in service during the First World War, and after the
armistice favored the maintenance of Hungarian rule in the homeland. Under the Czechoslovak regime, Brodii was a leader of the autonomist political movement that eventually favored unity with Hungary. In 1920 he was a
founding member of the Subcarpathian, later renamed Autonomous, Agricultural Union (AZS), and served as its chairman from 1933 to 1944. After
the death of Ivan Kurtiak in late 1932, Brodii held the party's seat in the
Prague Parliament until 1938. He was a member of the presidium of the
Dukhnovych Society, editor of the short-lived satirical journal *Tyukodi
pajtás* (1920) and of *Kárpáti futár* (1921-1924), and publisher of the AZS
organ *Russkii vîstnyk* (1923-1939). In 1938, Brodii was chief negotiator for
the joint Central National Council in September and was appointed by
Prague as premier-minister of Subcarpathia's first autonomous government
in October. Arrested in November for pro-Hungarian activity, he fled first
to Budapest, then later returned to Uzhhorod after it was occupied by Hungary in November. In May 1939 Brodii was appointed to the lower house of
the Hungarian Parliament, where until 1944 he led a group of Rusyns who
tried to gain some autonomy for their homeland. He emphasized this program in his newspapers, *Russkaia pravda* (1939-1940) and *Russkoe slovo*
(1940-1944). Realizing that Hungary was to lose the war, he tried to contact
Soviet agents through the Slovak National Uprising, in August 1944. These
efforts were rejected. Brodii was apprehended in 1945, and the following
year put on trial and condemned to death for collaboration with the Hungarian regime.
(9) *Hroshy iak d'iavol: p'esa* (1922); *Spekulianty: p'esa* (1934); "Das Karpathenland im St. Stefansreich" (1939); "Der Panslawismus und die Russinen des Karpatenlandes" (1943)

Dem'ian, Luka Vasyl'ovych

(1) 1894-1968   (2) Verkhni Vorota; Svaliava; Bereg
(3) peasant   (4) railroad conductor, peasant
(5) elementary, Verkhni Vorota
(6) Ukrainophile   (7) pro-Czechoslovak, pro-Soviet
(8) Dem'ian was one of the first Subcarpathian prose writers to use exclusively dialect in his works. Although a peasant with only an elementary education, he began his interest in literature by collecting with his brother about a thousand Rusyn folktales, many of which were published in the pre-1918 newspapers *Nauka* and *Nedîlia*. Dem'ian published his first collection of short stories in 1920 and continued to publish under all regimes that ruled the area. After 1945 he became a member of the Union of Writers in the Ukraine. In 1928, Dem'ian left his farm and worked on the Czechoslovak railways, eventually becoming a conductor. He was also a member of the Agriculturalist party.
(9) *Chort na vesîliu* (1920); *Vîd'ma* (1924); *Yz sela* (1943); *Vesillia bez zhenikha* (1956); *Zustrich* (1960)

Demko, Mykhail

(1) 1894-1946   (2) Ujlak (Bodzásújlak); Sečovce;
                                           Zemplén
(3) peasant   (4) journalist, teacher
(5) teacher's college, Uzhhorod (completed 1913)
(6) Rusynophile   (7) pro-Hungarian
(8) Demko was part of that group of Rusyns who were active in autonomous parties under Czechoslovakia and who eventually sought union with Hungary. After completing his studies in 1913, he began teaching in Pistrialove (Bereg), but the following year was drafted into the army, serving throughout the war as a member of the Honvéds. After the hostilities ended, he refused to swear the oath of allegiance to Czechoslovakia and thus had to leave teaching. He became a journalist and edited *Kárpáti futár* and *Russkii vîstnyk*. He was a founding member, in 1920, of the Subcarpathian, later Autonomous, Agricultural Union, of which he became first secretary. He was a staunch critic of Prague's policies in the region and participated in "Russian" minority congresses in Riga, Warsaw, and Belgrade, as well as the European minority congresses in Geneva. At home, he organized the Karpatorusskii Orel and after 1938 became an active leader in the local theater. Demko welcomed the return of Hungarian rule and in 1939 was appointed both advisor to the Uzhhorod administration on economic

matters and deputy to the Lower House of Parliament. He was apprehended by local authorities in 1945, convicted the following year of collaboration with the wartime Hungarian regime, and was executed.
(9) editor, *Pis'ma A. Dukhnovicha k Ia. Golovatskomu* (1927); editor, *Zemledîl'skii kalendar'* (1934-1942)

Erdeli (Hryts'), Adal'bert Mykhailovych

(1) 1891-1955 (2) Zahattia; Irshava; Bereg
(3) teacher (4) artist, professor
(5) gymnasium, Mukachevo (completed 1911); art academy, Budapest (1911-1916)
(6) Rusynophile (7) pro-Hungarian, pro-Czecho-slovak, pro-Soviet
(8) Together with I. Bokshai, Erdeli was one of the leading painters and organizers of artistic activity in Subcarpathian Rus'. In 1917 he founded the first Club of Artists in Uzhhorod. Together with Bokshai he participated in the first exposition of Subcarpathian art (1921) and was elected first chairman of the Society of Artists of Subcarpathian Rus' (1931). He taught art in the Mukachevo gymnasium and Uzhhorod Teacher's College (1917-1922), then alternated between working and having expositions in western Europe (Munich, 1922-1926 and Paris, 1929-1931) and in Czechoslovakia (Brno, 1928 and Prague, 1929). He also travelled to Austria, Switzerland, and Italy during these years and acquired stylistic influences from the most modern artistic currents. At home, he worked with Bokshai to train a new generation of Rusyn artists. Erdeli avoided all political activity and found it possible to work under all regimes that ruled in his homeland, in the last instance serving as chairman of the Soviet Transcarpathian Union of Artists (1945-1955).

Fedinec, Ladislav

(1) b. 1890 (2) Malyi Rakovets'; Sevliush; Ugocsa
(3) peasant (4) banker
(5) elementary, Khust; commercial academy, Fiume
(6) Rusynophile (7) pro-Czechoslovak
(8) Fedinec was drafted into military service soon after finishing school in 1913. He served in the Austro-Hungarian army throughout the First World War and was discharged with the rank of lieutenant. He did not participate in the revolutionary events of 1918-1919. Beginning in 1920 he became active in Uzhhorod's Podkarpatskii Bank, as first clerk responsible for administration and organization (1920-1925), then as vice-chairman (1926) and chairman (1927-1930). In 1928, he was appointed a member of the

Czechoslovak Banking Control Organization. The Podkarpatskii Bank was important because it was an attempt (although unsuccessful) to gain, with the help of Rusyn-American immigrant monetary support, "economic autonomy" for Subcarpathian Rus'. In 1930, Fedinec left Uzhhorod and for almost two decades managed his family's farm in Streda nad Bodrokom in eastern Slovakia. After the Second World War, Fedinec was viewed by some as a potential leader for a Rusyn national orientation that was not tainted by association with Hungary. The Soviets were not interested, however, and he emigrated from Czechoslovakia in 1949, arriving the following year in Canada, where he organized the anti-Communist Council of Free Podkarpatsky Rusins. He opposed the incorporation of his homeland into the Soviet Union, joined anti-Communist Czechoslovak groups after emigrating to New York City in 1955, and published the *Rusin Bulletin* (1953-1960) to propagate his Rusynophile and pro-Czechoslovak orientation.
(9) "Podkarpatskij Bank v Užgorodje" (1932)

Fedor, Pavel Stepanovich

(1) 1884-194?   (2) Nové Město; Košice; Abaúj
(3) —   (4) teacher, writer
(5) elementary, Humenné; middle, Humenné; teacher's seminary, Prešov
    (1899-1903)
(6) Russophile   (7) pro-Czechoslovak
(8) Fedor began an elementary school teaching career in the Prešov Region villages of Habura (1903-07) and Pčoline (1914-18). As soon as the Czechoslovaks arrived in December 1918, they appointed him a school commissioner, secretary to the Prešov Region school inspector (1922), and after 1923 an official in the school administration and later school inspector. Fedor was an active Russophile, serving as member of the presidium and vice-secretary of the Dukhnovych Society and as vice-chairman of the Teacher's Society. He was first a member of the Agrarian party and then helped to found (1935) the Russian National Autonomous party. He remained in this group until late 1938, when he signed a petition with other Russophiles denouncing Fentsik's Hungarian machinations and pledging loyalty to Czechoslovakia. Fedor was a prolific author of cultural histories, poetry and plays, many of which were performed in local theaters. During the Hungarian regime, he served as chief editor of *Narodna shkola* (1939-1944).
(9) *A.I. Dobrianskii* (1927); *Ocherki karpatorusskoi literatury so vtoroi pol. XIX stolietiia* (1929); *Pravda pobiezhdaiet: p'esa* (1929); *Mysli: poèziia* (1929)

Fentsik, Stefan Andreevich, Ph.D. (pseudonym: Pishta)

(1) 1892-1945   (2) Velyki Luchky; Mukachevo;
                                           Bereg
(3) priest   (4) priest/professor, editor
(5) gymnasium, Uzhhorod and Berehovo; theological seminary, Budapest
    (1910-1914) and Vienna (1914-1918); Charles University, Prague (1922);
    Sárospatak, juridicial studies (1918-1922)
(6) Russophile   (7) pro-Polish, pro-Hungarian
(8) Fentsik was one of the most ambitious figures in the region. Nephew of
the great nineteenth-century national leader Evgenii Fentsik, Stefan wanted
at all costs to play a leading role in the affairs of his homeland, whether as
bishop, Russophile nationalist, or politician in the service of Poland or
Hungary. In the early 1920s he was a professor at the Uzhhorod seminary,
during which time he directed the chorus "Harmonia" and the Uzhhorod
amateur symphony orchestra. At that time he wrote the music for Subcarpathia's national anthem. In 1931, he made a bid to be appointed bishop.
This failed, and for his "unpriestly" activity he was suspended from the
priesthood in 1934.

Fentsik was secretary and actual administrator of the Duknovych Society
from its establishment in 1923. By the 1930s he had entered politics full
time, publishing the "autonomist" organs *Karpatorusskii golos* (1932-
1934), *Nash put'* (1935-1938), and *Molodaia Rus'* (1938). In 1935 he
founded the Russian National Autonomous party and for the next three
years was its deputy in the Prague Parliament, where he spoke out frequently demanding autonomy and Russian schools. He received money for
these ventures from Rusyn-American immigrants (among whom he garnered great popularity during a trip in 1934-1935) and from the Polish government.

By 1938, he had agreed to work with the Hungarian-supported Brodii and
was appointed minister plenipotentiary in the region's first autonomous
government (October). In early November he fled to Budapest, where he
was appointed to Parliament, and then returned to Uzhhorod, where he
organized a fascist-type youth group (the Black Shirts) to insist that all Subcarpathian Rus' be returned to Hungary. In the summer of 1939, Fentsik
was appointed to the Upper House of the Hungarian Parliament and continued to publish *Karpatorusskii golos* (1938-1942). In 1945, he was apprehended and hung by local vigilantes who accused him of treason against the
people.

Throughout, Fentsik remained a Russophile and attacked through his
numerous publications what he considered the Ukrainophile policy of the
Czechoslovak government and the Uhro-Rusyn policy of his patrons, the
Hungarian government.

(9) *Chitanka dlia naroda* (1933); editor, *Russkii narodnyi kalendar' OIAD 1928-1934; Kárpátoroszok multja és jelene* (1939); see also the Bibliography.

Földesi (Fedorenko), Julius

(1) 1875-1947 (2) Sobrance; Sobrance; Ung
(3) — (4) publisher
(5) gymnasium, Uzhhorod
(6) Rusynophile (7) pro-Hungarian
(8) Földesi began his long career in printing as an apprentice to the Bartholémy Jäger printshop in Uzhhorod. He also was the head of the printshop of the St. Basil the Great Society (1899) and its successor Unio (1902). In 1907, he bought out Jäger and operated the Földesi Printshop until it was nationalized in early 1945. Under the Czechoslovak regime he joined Kurtiak and Brodii as a member of the Autonomous Agricultural Union and published its organ *Karpatorusskii vîstnyk*. Between 1935 and 1938 he served that party as senator in the Prague Parliament. His long-time pro-Hungarian stance led to an appointment as deputy to the Hungarian Parliament and advisor to the Commissioner of the Carpathian Territory (1939-1944). After the arrival of the Soviet forces, Földesi was arrested and died in prison in Sambov.
(9) *Az autonom kárpátoroszország államjogi vázlata* (1927); "Üzenet és felhívás as észak-amerikai Kárpátoroszokhoz" (1939); "Természeti kincseink Kárpátaljan" (1939)

Gadzhega, Iulii N., D.D. (pseudonym: Iulii Rusak)

(1) 1879-1945 (2) Kyv'iazhd'; Irshava; Bereg
(3) teacher (4) priest/professor
(5) —
(6) Russophile (7) pro-Czechoslovak
(8) Gadzhega was one of the leading Russophile writers. He was ordained a Greek Catholic priest and served from 1910 as professor of Biblical studies and prefect of the Greek Catholic Seminary in Uzhhorod. He favored unity with Czechoslovakia at the Uzhhorod National Council (May 1919) and was then appointed to the governing Directorate and made responsible for church affairs. At this time he was also editor of *Karpat* (1919). From its establishment (1923) Gadzhega was a member of the presidium of the Dukhnovych Society and chairman of its literary-scientific section. During the late 1930s he was imprisoned on a morals charge and suspended from the priesthood. His numerous writings dealt primarily with theological questions and the history of the church in Subcarpathian Rus'.

(9) *Stat'i po voprosam 'pravoslaviia', narodnosti i katolichestva* (1921); *Istoriia obshchestva sv. Vasiliia Velikago* (1925); *Dva istoricheskikh voprosa* (1928); *Vospominaniia* (1938); see also the Bibliography.

Gagatko, Andrei Mikhailovich, LL.D.

(1) 1884-1944   (2) Andrusovtse; Galicia
(3)   —   (4) editor
(5)   —
(6) Russophile   (7) pro-Czechoslovak
(8) Gagatko was one of those Russophiles from Galicia who came to Sub-carpathian Rus' in early 1919 and hoped that at least the Lemkian region north of the Carpathians would be annexed to Czechoslovakia. He stated these aims while secretary of the Uzhhorod National Council (May 1919), which pledged unity with Czechoslovakia. Gagatko stayed on in Uzhhorod, where he founded the Carpatho-Russian Labor party, which was allied with the Czech National Socialist party in Prague. From 1924 to 1929, Gagatko served his party as deputy in the Prague Parliament. He was also chairman of the Shkol'naia Pomoshch', which set up several dormitories in the region and provided scholarships for needy students.
(9) *Po sluchaiu iubileinykh torzhestv v Podkarpatskoi Rusi* (1924)

Gebei, Petro Mikhailovych

(1) 1864-1931   (2) Kal'nyk; Mukachevo; Bereg
(3) priest   (4) priest/professor
(5) gymnasium, Uzhhorod; theological seminary, Budapest (completed
    1889)
(6) Rusynophile   (7) pro-Czechoslovak
(8) Gebei was one of the leading administrators in the Greek Catholic Church (Mukachevo diocese). Among his many posts in Uzhhorod before the First World War were: professor of canon law and prefect of discipline at the theological seminary (1889), spiritual director of the female middle school (1892), professor of religion at the gymnasium (1906), director of the Alumneum (1907), and rector of the cathedral (1912). He was also active in Rusyn cultural life, serving as treasurer of the St. Basil Society (1895-1902), founding member and later director of Unio (1902), and editor of *Nauka* and the annual calendars, *Mîsiatsoslov*. As a member of the Central Commission of the Greek Catholic Church in August 1915, he opposed the Magyarization policy of the government. Nonetheless, like many priests, he hoped to reach an accommodation with Hungary and in 1918 worked to organize the pro-Hungarian Uzhhorod National Council (November) and participated in the Rusyn Congress in Budapest (December). By May 1919 he favored Czechoslovakia and was a member of the Central National Council in Uzhhorod.

Under Czechoslovak rule, Gebei maintained his high administrative positions as general vicar (1922-1924) and then as bishop of the Mukachevo diocese (1924-1931). During his bishopric Gebei successfully contained the spread of Orthodoxy and regularized relations with the Czechoslovak government. In national matters, he followed a "middle-of-the-road" Rusyn orientation, tried to avoid disputes, and was a member of both the Ukrainophile Prosvita and Russophile Dukhnovych societies.

Gerovskii, Aleksei Iul'ianovich, LL.D.

(1) 1883-1972   (2) L'viv; Galicia
(3)   —   (4) editor
(5) elementary, Innsbruck; gymnasium, Innsbruck and Chernivtsi; university, Chernivtsi
(6) Russophile   (7) pro-Russian
(8) Gerovskii came from a long line of Russophiles whose aim was to see the whole Carpatho-Rusyn region become part of Russia. He was raised in the Russophile atmosphere that dominated the home of his maternal grandfather, Adol'f Dobrianskii, the Subcarpathian leader who lived the last decades of the nineteenth century in Innsbruck, Austria. His own father was head of the Stavropigian Institute in L'viv and a member of the Austrian Parliament.

The young Gerovskii began his public career as publisher of the Russophile newspaper *Russkaia pravda* (1910-1913) in Chernivtsi, Bukovina. He was present at the Marmarosh-Sighet trial (1913-1914), then was arrested by the Hungarian, and later the Austrian, government for anti-state activity. In 1914 he escaped and fled to Russia. Between 1915 and 1918 he worked in the tsarist Foreign Office as an advisor on Austria-Hungary's "Russian" affairs. As a monarchist, he was attached to Denikin's Volunteer Army and published in Ekaterinodar the short-lived newspaper *Edinaia Rus'* (1918).

After the war Gerovskii arrived in Subcarpathian Rus' to propagate his Russophile ideas. He did this through promotion of the Orthodox movement and of local Russophile leaders. He was a participant in the minority congresses in Geneva, and for his general anti-Czechoslovak statements was forced to leave Subcarpathian Rus' in 1927. He went first to Yugoslavia, where he organized a Carpatho-Russian Committee (1927-1929), and then to the United States, where he became general secretary of the Carpatho-Russian Union (1935-1938). Through his leadership, American immigrant money was channeled to Subcarpathia's anti-Czechoslovak Russophile politicians. In the summer of 1938 Gerovskii led a Rusyn-American delegation to Prague and the homeland, where he acted as intermediary between Russophile and Ukrainophile leaders. He also went to Budapest in September 1938 to discuss with officials there maintenance of the Russophile orientation if the territory was returned to Hungary. Back in the United States during the Second World War, Gerovskii spoke out against the effort to have Subcarpathia returned to Czechoslovakia and after 1945 polemicized against the Ukrainian policies of the Soviet regime.

(9) "Jak upravl'ali mad'ary v Karpatskoj Rusi" (1945); "Iza i Sigotskii protsess" (1961); see also the Bibliography.

Gerovskii, Georgii Iul'ianovich, Ph.D.

(1) 1886-1959   (2)   —
(3)   —   (4) professor
(5) elementary, Innsbruck; university, Leipzig and Saratov
(6) Russophile   (7) pro-Czechoslovak
(8) Like his older brother Aleksei (see above), Georgii Gerovskii had a Russophile upbringing, but he became a scholar not a politician. He was a librarian at Saratov University before the First World War and then came to the Subcarpathian region in 1922. He was trained as a linguist and wrote several studies of Subcarpathian Rusyn dialects—including a major entry for the Czechoslovak encyclopedia (1934)—trying to prove that they were related to Great Russian not Ukrainian. After the Second World War he worked in Prague, and until 1959 he was professor of Russian language and literature at the P.J. Šafárik University in Prešov.
(9) "Russkii iazyk v tserkovno-slaviansko-russkoi grammatikie Mikhaila Popa-Luchkaia" (1930); "Jazyk Podkarpatské Rusi" (1934); *Istoriia ugrorusskoi literatury v izobrazhenii V. Birchaka* (1943); "Istoricheskoe proshloe, narodnaia rech', i narodnaia kul'tura Priashevshchiny" (1948); see also Bibliography.

Goidich, Pavel (Petro) Stepanovych

(1) 1888-1960   (2) Ruské Pekl'any; Prešov; Sáros
(3) priest   (4) priest/professor
(5) gymnasium, Prešov; theological seminary, Prešov and Budapest (completed 1911)
(6) Rusynophile   (7) pro-Czechoslovak
(8) Goidich was ordained a Greek Catholic priest in 1911 and at first assisted his father in a small parish in the Prešov Region. From 1912 to 1917 he served as prefect of the boarding school, Alumneum, in Prešov, and taught religion in that city's secondary schools. He also began to work in the episcopal offices of the Prešov diocese, first as secretary to Bishop Novak (1914-1918), then as director of the chancery (1918-1922). In 1922 he entered the Basilian Monastery of Chernecha Hora near Mukachevo. Two years later he was ordained a monk in the Order of St. Basil the Great, then made assistant superior to the Basilian monastery in Uzhhorod and prefect of the Greek Catholic gymnasium there. In 1926, Goidich returned to Prešov as apostolic administrator of the diocese and in February 1927

was appointed bishop. During the 1930s he steered a middle-of-the-road Rusyn nationality policy, trying to balance off the local Russophiles on the one hand and Slovakophiles on the other. He again defended Rusyn national interests, during less favorable circumstances, under the Slovak state (1939-1944). When the communist government decided to dismantle the Greek Catholic Church, Goidich was arrested in 1950 and the following year imprisoned for life on trumped-up charges of subversion against the state, including supposedly giving aid (1946-1947) to Ukrainian nationalists. He died in Leopoldov prison, near Bratislava.

Grendzha-Dons'kyi, Vasyl' Stepanovych (pseudonym: Stepan Berezenko)

(1) 1897-1974   (2) Volove; Volove; Máramaros
(3) peasant   (4) bank clerk
(5) elementary, Volove; commercial academy, Budapest; art academy, Budapest
(6) Ukrainophile   (7) pro-Ukrainian
(8) Grendzha-Dons'kyi was a leading Ukrainophile and one of the most prolific Subcarpathian writers in the twentieth century. After a brief elementary education he worked as a postman. In 1915, he entered the Hungarian Honvéds and was soon wounded on the Russian front. Sent back to Budapest to recuperate, he entered a commercial school and art academy there. In 1918, he was mobilized again on the Rumanian and Italian fronts, then he returned to Budapest in October. He was arrested briefly for participation in Communist manifestations and then served in the Hungarian Soviet Army against the Rumanians. Throughout this period, Grendzha-Dons'kyi was a loyal Hungarian. He did not desert, as many of his countrymen did, on the Russian front. Moreover, his first poetry was in Magyar and his first wife a devoted Magyar patriot. In 1920, he was employed in an insurance company in Budapest.

It was not until the summer of 1921 that he returned illegally to his homeland, where he was employed as a clerk in the Podkarpatskii Bank in Uzhhorod. By 1923, he had ended his Hungarian sympathies and begun to take an active role in Rusyn cultural life, supporting the populist-Ukrainophile orientation. In that year, he edited the daily newspaper *Rusyn,* published two collections of poetry, and was elected to the executive committee of the Prosvita Society. His subsequent national activity included the publication of several works of poetry, prose, and drama, many translations, and the editorship of the pro-Soviet journal *Nasha zemlia* (1927-1929). During the 1920s, Grendzha-Dons'kyi achieved many firsts in Subcarpathian Rus', among these being the first independently published collection of poetry (1923), the first work in literary Ukrainian (1924), and the first work published in the Soviet Union (1928). In the next decades, he joined the Ukrainophile nationalists as frequent contributor to *Ukraïns'ke slovo* (1932-1938) and assistant editor of *Nova svoboda,* the leading daily during the autonomist period. He was also a member of the executive board of the Ukrainophile faction of the Central National Council (1938) and of the Ukrainian National Union (January 1939).

For his pro-Ukrainian stance, he was arrested by the Hungarians in March 1939 and sent to a concentration camp, where he was believed to have been killed. (The Slovak poet, Janko Kral', published a eulogistic poem about him soon after.) However, Grendzha-Dons'kyi was released, returned briefly to Khust and then to Bratislava in August 1939, where he remained until his death. During the war years he was an announcer for the Ukrainian-language program on Slovak radio. He was also connected with anti-Hungarian Ukrainophile leaders from the homeland. He worked in the film studio Tatra (1939-1964), joined the Czechoslovak Communist Party (1945), and after difficulties in the 1950s was lauded by the Communist regime as the leading Ukrainian writer in Czechoslovakia. He was a member of the Ukrainian Writers Union of Czechoslovakia, continued to publish until his death, and was awarded an official title for outstanding service to art.

(9) *Kvîtŷ z tern'om* (1923); *Zolotî kliuchî* (1923); *Shliakhom ternovym* (1924); *Il'ko Lypei—karpats'kyi rozbiinyk* (1936); *Petro Petrovych* (1937); *Chervona skala* (1930-1931, 1938); see also the Bibliography.

Hadzhega, Vasylii Nikolaievych, S.T.D.

(1) 1864-1938   (2) Poliana; Rakhiv; Máramaros
(3) priest   (4) priest/professor
(5) gymnasium, Uzhhorod and Levoča; theological seminary, Uzhhorod
     (1881-1883) and Budapest (1883); university, Vienna (1883-1887)
(6) Rusynophile   (7) pro-Czechoslovak
(8) Hadzhega was one of the most prolific native-born historians. After being ordained a Greek Catholic priest, he served before the First World War as a parish priest and then was raised to the office of archdeacon for Ung County. Also at this time he began his teaching career at the Uzhhorod Theological Seminary. His national activity included chairmanship of the Rus'kii Klub (1919), membership in the presidium of the Prosvita Society and editorship of its scholarly journal, *Naukovŷi zbôrnyk*. He was also honorary member of the Shevchenko Scientific Society in L'viv. Although sympathetic to the Ukrainophiles, he did not associate completely with them, never accepting, for instance, literary Ukrainian as the language of his own writings. Hadzhega wrote primarily on the history of the church in the region. He was also a canon and papal prelate for the diocese of Mukachevo.

(9) "Dodatky k istoriî Rusynov y rus'kykh tserkvei" (1922-1937); "Ivan Fogarashii" (1927); "Mykhail Luchkai: zhytiepys y tvorŷ" (1929); see also the Bibliography.

Haraida, Ivan

(1) 18??-1945   (2) Nyzhni Remety; Berehovo;
                                           Bereg
(3) peasant   (4) professor
(5) university, Cracow
(6) Rusynophile   (7) pro-Hungarian
(8) Haraida was a native of Subcarpathian Rus', but did not play any role
in its development until the years of the Hungarian regime (1939-1944). At
that time, however, he was responsible, almost single-handedly, for creating
a cultural program that would propagate the idea of a separate Uhro-Rusyn
nationality. To do this he wrote a Rusyn grammar and edited the scholarly
and literary journals *Zoria-Hajnal* (1941-1943) and *Lyteraturna nedîlia*
(1941-1944). He was also actual director of the Subcarpathian Scientific Society (1940-1944) and author of many linguistic and historical studies. In
1945 he was arrested by the Soviet regime and executed for treason.
(9) *Hrammatyka uhrorusskoho iazŷka* (1940); ''Halyts'ka polytyka uhorskykh korolëv Beilŷ III-ho y Andriia II-ho'' (1943); co-editor, *Zahal'na
bibliohrafiia Podkarpatia* (1944)

Hodinka, Antal, Ph.D.

(1) 1864-1946   (2) Ladomirov; Snina; Zemplén
(3) priest   (4) university professor
(5) elementary, Sighet (1871-1873); gymnasium, Uzhhorod (1873-1882);
      theological seminary, Budapest (1882-1886); university, Budapest
      (completed 1891).
(6) Rusynophile   (7) pro-Hungarian
(8) Hodinka was one of the few scholars native to Subcarpathia who
achieved international repute in the twentieth century. He worked exclusively in a Hungarian environment, but nonetheless devoted much of his
scholarship, and even some political and cultural activity, to his native land.
Hodinka began his professional career well before the First World War and
held the following positions: staff member of the National Museum in
Budapest (1888), fellow at the Institute for Austrian Historical Research in
Vienna (1889-1891), archivist and librarian for the Royal Commission in
Vienna (1892-1906), and professor of Hungarian cultural history at the Law
Academy in Bratislava (1906-1918). He was also elected corresponding
(1910) and full member (1933) of the Hungarian Academy of Sciences. He
continued his professional career in post-Trianon Hungary at the University
of Pécs (1918-1935), where he also served as dean of the faculty and president (1932-1933).
   Hodinka's scholarly interests ranged from Hungarian cultural history
and relations with the South Slavs and Russians to the political and religious
history of his homeland. He was also active in the Hungarian-Ruthenian

political party as author of its manifestos to the Paris Peace Conference demanding the return of Subcarpathian Rus' to Hungary. He believed the Rusyn fate was best served by being linked with Hungary, and when this was achieved again, during the Second World War, he agreed to serve as the chairman of the Subcarpathian Academy of Sciences in Uzhhorod. This was in fact only an honorary position since his advanced age forced him to remain in Budapest.

(9) *A munkácsi görög katholikus püspökség története* (1909); *A munkácsi görög szertartású püspökség okmánytara* (1911); *Gens fidelissima* (1915, 1937); "L'habitat, l'économie, et le passé du peuple ruthène" (1924); see also the Bibliography.

Hrabar, Konstantyn Leontynovych

(1) 1877-1938   (2) Uzhhorod; Ung
(3) priest   (4) priest
(5) elementary, Uzhhorod; gymnasium, Uzhhorod (comp. 1895); theological seminary, Esztergom (1895-1901)
(6) Rusynophile   (7) pro-Czechoslovak
(8) Hrabar was ordained a Greek Catholic priest and served in parishes in Velyki Luchky (1901-1907) and Dubrivka (1908-1921). He began his civil and political career in February 1919, when he was elected to the Diet of the Hungarian-organized autonomous Rus'ka Kraina. It was Hrabar who called for the dissolution of that body unless Budapest defined (and it never did) the borders of the province. In May 1919 he was a member of the pro-Czechoslovak Uzhhorod Council and of the delegation that went to Prague to pledge allegiance to the new republic. Hrabar left his parish duties for good after 1921, serving as director of the Podkarpatskii Bank (1921-1928), member of the city council (1923) and mayor of Uzhhorod (1933-1935), and vice-chairman of the Chamber of Commerce and Industry in Košice. He was also a member of the Rusyn-Agriculturalist and Christian-National parties (1920-1925) and then of the ruling Republican-Agrarian party (1925-1938). The latter party felt he was the most reliable candidate and succeeded in having him appointed governor of Subcarpathian Rus' in 1935, a post he held until the establishment of autonomy in October 1938. Hrabar avoided the growing Russophile-Ukrainophile conflicts and favored the adoption of a pro-Czechoslovak Rusyn orientation. He died less than two months after he was relieved of the governorship.

Il'nyts'kyi, Aleksander

(1) 1889-1947   (2) Chornyi Ardiv; Sevliush;
Ugocsa
(3) priest   (4) priest, editor
(5) gymnasium, Satu Mare and Uzhhorod; theological seminary, Uzhhorod
(6) Rusynophile   (7) pro-Hungarian
(8) Il'nyts'kyi, a leading dignitary of the Greek Catholic Mukachevo diocese, supported a pro-Hungarian Rusynophile national orientation. After his ordination (1914) he served as a parish priest in the villages of Il'nytsia and Velyki Luchky. He soon entered the ecclesiastical administration as notary (1916) and advisor (1921) to the chancery. He was later appointed a canon (1930) and was active in the struggle against Orthodoxy as chairman of the Central Office for Defense of the Church (1925) and chairman of the Missionary Society (1928). He also served as editor of the official Greek Catholic publications: *Dushpastŷr'* (1924-1938), *Myssiinŷi vîstnyk* (1931-1938), and *Dobrŷi pastŷr'* (1932-1942).

Il'nyts'kyi welcomed the returning Hungarian regime in 1939 and was rewarded through appointments as advisor to the commissioner for Subcarpathia (1939-1944) and as lord in the Upper House of the Hungarian Parliament (1939-1944). He supported the idea of a separate Uhro-Rusyn nationality as editor of *Karpatska nedîlia* (1939-1941) and chairman of the Subcarpathian Academy of Sciences (1942-1944). After the death of Bishop Stoika (1943), he administered the Mukachevo diocese for seven months. Because of his strong pro-Hungarian views, he was arrested by the Soviet police in 1945, tried, and found guilty of treason. He died in prison.
(9) "Ruszinok és magyarok" (1939); co-author, *Za narod Podkarpatia* (1940); "Madiarskoe pravytel'stvo y narodnŷi iazŷk Podkarpatskykh Rusynov" (1943)

Kaminskii, Iosif Viktorovich, LL.D.

(1) 1878-1944   (2) Rakovec nad Ondavou; Michalovce; Zemplén
(3) priest/professor   (4) editor, lawyer
(5) gymnasium, Uzhhorod; university, Budapest and Cluj
(6) Russophile   (7) pro-Hungarian
(8) Kaminskii was a political opportunist willing to work with any regime or faction that would guarantee him some role in the local administration. He was the son of Viktor Kaminskii, the director of the teacher's college in Uzhhorod and editor of the *Görög katholikus szemle*. Iosif, a reserve

officer, was recalled into the Hungarian army in 1915 and was soon after captured on the Russian front. After a short prison sentence he led a relatively comfortable life as a tutor to an aristocratic family living in Siberia (1917-1918). During this time he developed Russophile affinities and even published short articles in the local *Ural'skaia zhizn'*. Nonetheless, he did not shed his Hungarian loyalties and after returning home became personal secretary to Rus'ka Kraina's Minister Oreszt Szabó (1918-1919).

Under the Czechoslovak regime, Kaminskii served for a while as treasurer of the Ukrainophile Prosvita Society, then became head of the Russophile faction of the Central National Council and joined Ivan Kurtiak to form the oppositional Subcarpathian, later Autonomous, Agricultural Union (1920-1923). By 1923, Kaminskii had decided to join the pro-government Agrarian party, which chose him as deputy to the Prague Parliament (1924-1925). He fell out with the Czechoslovak regime and by 1927 had rejoined the Autonomous Agricultural Union; however, he continued to have personal disagreements with other similar-thinking pro-Hungarian Russophiles and published his own organ, *Karapatorusskii golos* (1932-1934). During these years Kaminskii also served as chairman of the Union of Cooperatives and editor of its journal, *Druzhestvennyi viestnik* (1926-1927), chairman of the Union of Subcarpathian Journalists, member of the Uzhhorod City Council, and member of the board of the Subcarpathian National Theater (1936-1938). He also published several short studies on local history and edited some calendars for the Dukhnovych Society. In late 1938, he welcomed the return of the Hungarians, and in June 1939 he was appointed to the Upper House of the Hungarian Parliament, a post he held until his death.

(9) "Nasha avtonomiia: samouprava" (1922); *Natsional'noe samosoznanie nashego naroda* (1925); *Istoriia Tsentral'noi Russkoi Narodnoi Rady* (1927)

Karabelesh, Andrei Vasil'evich

(1) 1906-1964   (2) Tybava; Svaliava; Bereg
(3) forester   (4) teacher, professor
(5) elementary, Tybava; gymnasium, Miskolc (1919-1920) and Mukachevo (1918-1919, 1920); theological seminary, Uzhhorod; Charles University, Prague; academy of art, Prague (completed 1934)
(6) Russophile   (7) pro-Czechoslovak
(8) Karabelesh was the most talented Russian-language poet in the region and the pride of such organizations as the Dukhnovych Society. While still a student he published two large collections of poetry (1928 and 1929), which were filled with mystic and pessimistic views of the homeland as well as with praise for Russian culture. Reflective of this attitude was his conversion to Orthodoxy in 1932. After completing his studies he taught in elementary schools (1934-1937) and then at the Mukachevo gymnasium (1937-1938). He also was an editor of the student literary journal, *Nashi stremleniia*

(1935). Karabelesh emigrated to Litomyšl, Bohemia (1940), and then was imprisoned in a concentration camp (1941-1945). After the Second World War he went to Prešov, where he was a professor at the Šafárik University. He was elected to the Ukrainian Writers Union of Czechoslovakia and continued to publish in Russian, but after being removed from that organization (1957) he returned to Bohemia.

(9) *Izbrannyia stikhotvoreniia* (1928); *V luchakh razsvieta* (1929); *Na smertel'nom rubezhe* (1953); *V Karpatakh* (1955)

Klempush, Dmytro

(1) 18??-1973   (2) Iasynia; Rakhiv; Máramaros
(3) peasant   (4) lumber business
(5) elementary, Iasynia
(6) Ukrainophile   (7) pro-Ukrainian
(8) Dmytro Klempush, together with his older brother, Vasyl', played an important role in the military life of the region. As a young man he joined the uprising that, in January 1919, drove the Hungarian gendarmes out of his native mountainous town of Iasynia, where a "Hutsul Republic" was soon established. For the next two decades he was occupied with his lumber business until November 1938, when he was appointed Supreme Commander of the Carpathian Sich, the military arm of the autonomous province. In March 1939 Klempush led his force in skirmishes with Czechoslovak troops and then in three days of fighting against the invading Hungarian army.

Klochurak, Stepan

(1) b. 1895   (2) Iasynia; Rakhiv; Máramaros
(3) lumber business   (4) editor
(5) gymnasium, Sighet; juridical academy, Sighet; Comenius University,
    Bratislava
(6) Ukrainophile   (7) pro-Czechoslovak
(8) Klochurak was a leading Ukrainophile politician. He was among the small group who protested against Hungarian policy at the Rusyn Congress in Budapest (December 1918). He returned to his native village to lead a force of Hutsuls that drove the Hungarians out of the region (January 1919), and during the following month, when a "Hutsul Republic" was established, he was chosen chairman of the national council, commander of the army, and head of war and external affairs. After the miniature state was occupied by Rumanian troops (June 1919), Klochurak was imprisoned in Rumania for several months.

Under the Czechoslovak regime, he was a founding member and secretary of the Subcarpathian Social Democratic party and editor of its organs,

Narod (1920-1921) and *Vpered*. During the 1930s he joined the Ukrainian branch of the pro-government Agrarian party and was editor of its local Ukrainian organ, *Zemlia i volia* (1934-1938). He was also a member of the presidium of the Prosvita Society from its establishment (1920) and general secretary of the Union of Tobacco Growers in Subcarpathian Rus'. He also served on the delegation of the Russian-Ukrainian National Council that negotiated with Prague in September 1938.

During the autonomous period, Klochurak was secretary to Premier Minister Voloshyn, delegate at the Vienna Arbitration (November 1938), member of the Presidium of the Ukrainian National Union (January, 1919), deputy to the Diet (February), minister of Health, Public Works, and Economic Affairs (March 7), and minister of Defense and Agriculture (March 15). After the Hungarian occupation, he fled to Prague where he remained until arrested by the Soviet police in 1945. He was imprisoned (1945-1956) in the Soviet Union on trumped-up charges of working for the union of Subcarpathian Rus' with Slovakia during the Second World War. Since his release he has resided in Prague.

Kokhannyi-Goral'chuk, Kirill V.

(1) 1888-1974

(2) Khotin; Bessarabia; Russian Empire (Ukraine)

(3) peasant

(4) journalist

(5) elementary, Khotin; gymnasium, Feodosa (Crimea)

(6) Russophile

(7) pro-Czechoslovak

(8) Kokhannyi-Goral'chuk was active as an educational administrator during the first decade of Czechoslovak rule in Subcarpathian Rus'. His early years were typical of many Russian émigrés at the beginning of the century. After teaching in elementary schools in the Ukraine, he was suspected of revolutionary activity and sent by the tsarist government to Siberia (1905-1906). In 1911, he fled to western Europe, meeting the writers Gorky in Italy (Capri) and Hašek in Switzerland. Hašek invited Kokhannyi to Prague (1912), where he taught Russian in the Tolstoy Circle until his arrest by the Austrian authorities. In 1919, he entered the Czechoslovak Ministry of Education, which sent him the following year to Uzhhorod to serve as head of the Department of National Culture (1920-1930). During these years he published several studies on Subcarpathian Rus' and edited the Latin-script Rusyn-language newspaper *Zorja* (1920-1930). After returning to Prague, he remained in the Ministry of Education (1930-1948), responsible for student affairs.

(9) *O Podkarpatské Rusi* (1929); *Podkarpatská Rus v minulosti a přitomnosti* (1931); see also the Bibliography.

Kontratovych, Irynei

(1) 1878-1957   (2) Dubrynych; Perechyn; Ung
(3) priest   (4) priest
(5) theological seminary, Uzhhorod
(6) Rusynophile   (7) pro-Hungarian, pro-Soviet
(8) Kontratovych was perhaps the only leader who functioned in relatively high positions under all the regimes that ruled Subcarpathian Rus' in the twentieth century. He was ordained a Greek Catholic priest before the First World War and served in several parishes. He was a self-trained historian who wrote several studies on the homeland, the most popular being a history text for secondary schools that went through three editions. During the Hungarian regime of the Second World War he served as vice-president of the Subcarpathian Academy of Sciences (1941-1944), while under the Soviets he agreed to convert to Orthodoxy (1949) and to lead the campaign to liquidate the Greek Catholic Church. He served for a time as administrator of the Mukachevo Orthodox Eparchy.
(9) *Ystoriia Podkarpatskoî Rusy* (1924, 1925, 1930); *K istorii starodavniago Uzhgoroda i Podk. Rusi do XIV vieka* (1928); *Ocherki iz istorii Mukachevskoi eparkhii* (1931); see also the Bibliography.

Kurtiak, Ivan

(1) 1888-1933   (2) Khust; Máramaros
(3) peasant, church curator   (4) teacher
(5) gymnasium, Uzhhorod
(6) Rusynophile   (7) pro-Hungarian
(8) Kurtiak was the first important leader of the pro-Hungarian autonomists. After his early death he was hailed as a martyr in the struggle against the Prague regime for local self-government. He was a cantor and elementary-school teacher before the First World War and during the revolutionary period was appointed by the Hungarian regime as school inspector for Khust (November 1918). He refused to take the civil servant's oath of allegiance to Czechoslovakia and entered politics full time. He was founder and chairman of the Subcarpathian Agricultural Union (1920-1923) and its successor the Autonomous Agricultural Union (1924-1933), and served the party as deputy to the Prague Parliament from 1924 until his death. Kurtiak was extremely popular among the Magyarone Greek Catholic hierarchy.

Kutkafalvy [Kutka], Miklós, LL.D.

(1) 1882-19??   (2) Vel'ký Ruskov; Sečovce;
                                                Zemplén
(3) priest   (4) lawyer
(5) university, Budapest
(6) Rusynophile   (7) pro-Hungarian
(8) Kutkafalvy was an active leader among those Rusyns who felt that complete assimilation with Hungarian culture was the best alternative. He expressed these views in 1905 as editor of the *Görögkatholikus hírlap* (1905)
and as chairman of the Pál Vasári Union of Greek Catholic University students in Budapest. He began his law practice in 1908, then served as a reserve officer in the Austro-Hungarian army during the First World War. In
December 1918, he was appointed as the new Hungarian government's
representative to Bereg County. He tried to maintain the region for Hungary and organized a military force to fight against both the Czechoslovak
and Rumanian armies. He was present at most of the Rusyn national councils (1918-1919) and spoke in favor of union with Hungary. He also established, and was chairman of, the Rusyn-Hungarian political party in Budapest. After the region became part of Czechoslovakia, Kutkafalvy lead the
irredentist movement from Budapest as under-state secretary in the Ministry
for Minorities (1919-21) and later as deputy in the Hungarian Parliament.
He played no role in the region when it was ruled by Budapest after 1939.
(9) *Brátyá Ruszinö* (1920); *Uj proklamáció a magyarországi ruthén néphez*
(1920); *A Génuai Konferenciához* (1922)

Marina, Julius, J.C.D. (pseudonym: Julius Madarász)

(1) b. 1901   (2) Luh; Rakhiv; Máramaros
(3) teacher   (4) priest/professor
(5) elementary, Uzhhorod (completed 1910); gymnasium, Sighet, Piarist
     Fathers (completed 1920); theological seminary, Uzhhorod (1920-1924);
     Pontificia Universitas Gregoriana, Rome (1927-1929)
(6) Rusynophile   (7) pro-Hungarian
(8) Marina was one of the leading figures who helped the Hungarian regime
administer Subcarpathian Rus' between 1939 and 1944. He was ordained a
Greek Catholic priest (1926) and began his career as professor of canon law
and church history (1930-1939) and vice-rector (1926, 1930-1939) at the
Uzhhorod Theological Seminary. Already during these years he supported
anti-Czechoslovak political movements as a member of the directorate of
Fentsik's Russian National Autonomist party (1935-1938). When the Hungarian military arrived in Uzhhorod on March 15, 1939, Marina was appointed an advisor to the new regime. He held this post until September,
when he was appointed head of the Subcarpathian section of the Hungarian
Ministry of Education and National Enlightenment. In this position, he was

responsible for approving textbooks and choosing teachers and other local cultural administrators who favored Hungarian rule and who believed in the Uhro-Rusyn national orientation. He fled from Uzhhorod (October 1944) before the advancing Soviet army and eventually made his way to the United States where he served as a parish priest (1949-1971).
(9) *Memoirs* (1975-1977)

Markush, Aleksander Ivanovych

(1) 1891-1971   (2) Khust; Khust; Máramaros
(3) railroad guard   (4) teacher
(5) middle school, Khust; teacher's college, Sighet (completed 1910)
(6) Ukrainophile   (7) pro-Czechoslovak, pro-Soviet
(8) Markush was an influential pedagogue and prose writer. He was an elementary-school teacher in Tiachiv for almost thirty-five years (1910-1944) as well as school inspector for that region (1923-1938). He was also the founding editor and publisher of the children's journal *Nash rodnŷi krai* (1923-1939), which was published in Rusyn, and vice-chairman of the Pedagogical Society (1924-1938). Under the auspices of that society he authored and coauthored several readers and geography texts that were authorized for use in Subcarpathian schools. His literary works consisted primarily of short stories about rural life (in dialect and later in Ukrainian), which he was able to have published under the Czechoslovak, Hungarian, and Soviet regimes.
(9) *Vŷmîrialy zemliu y ynshŷ opovîdania* (1925); *Iulyna* (1942); *Korovku hnaly ta ynshî opovîdania* (1943); *Maramoros'ki opovidannia* (1956)

Mondok, Ivan (pseudonym: Ivan Il'kov)
(1) 1893-1941   (2) Ruský Hrabovec; Snina;
                                                      Zemplén
(3) cantor, teacher   (4) journalist
(5) elementary, Ruský Hrabovec; middle, Uzhhorod; teacher's college,
    Uzhhorod (1910-1913); Institute of History, Kharkiv
(6) Rusynophile, Ukrainophile   (7) pro-Soviet
(8) Mondok was an important Communist politician. As a student in Uzhhorod, he became exposed to local Social-Democratic politics and was expelled from school for a brief period because of this. He began his career as a teacher and notary in the village of Ublja (1913-1915). In December 1915 he was inducted into a Hungarian Honvéd unit and the following June was captured on the Russian front. Transferred to a prisoner camp in Astrakhan, he was further exposed to Social-Democratic propaganda and in 1917 joined the local SD (Bolshevik) party. He subsequently attended the First All-Russian Council of Revolutionary Communists in Moscow (April 1918), where he met with the Hungarian Communist leader Béla Kun. He

also became a Soviet citizen and fought for the Bolsheviks in the Russian Civil War during the summer of 1918. He was earmarked, however, for revolutionary work in Hungary, first attending the Moscow school for Hungarian propagandists (September 1918), then returning to Budapest in the entourage of Kun (November). The same month he was sent to Uzhhorod to organize a Communist party there. He later returned to Budapest (April 1919) to organize a newspaper for Communist Rus'ka Kraina. After the fall of the Kun regime he sought refuge along with other Hungarian Communists in Vienna.

Mondok was instructed by the party to return to Uzhhorod where he immediately founded the Rusyn Communist organ *Pravda* (April 1920). He remained editor of that newspaper, of its annual almanacs, and *Holos zhyttia* (1929-1930). Mondok was the party's choice to serve as deputy in the Prague Parliament (1924-1929) as well as delegate to the ninth Congress of the Communist Party of the Ukraine (December 1925). He also led the first group of Subcarpathian Communists to study in the Soviet Union (June 1927). He was arrested (March 1930) by Czechoslovak authorities for anti-state activities (mostly strikes), and although released in a few months, he was ordered by the party to emigrate to the Soviet Union (July) where he remained until his death. He became a graduate student at the Institute of History in Kharkiv and was a delegate to the fifth and sixth Cominterns in Moscow.

(9) editor, *Kalendar' Karpats'ka pravda*

Muranii, Ivan
(1) 1881-1945   (2) Tur'i Remety; Perechyn; Ung
(3) postmaster   (4) priest/professor
(5) gymnasium, Miskolc; theological seminary, Uzhhorod (completed
      1905)
(6) Rusynophile   (7) pro-Czechoslovak
(8) Muranii came from a family of Subcarpathian patriots, his mother being a daughter of A. Dukhnovych, his wife a daughter of I. Sil'vai. Muranii was ordained a Greek Catholic priest (1905) and served as administrator in Neresnytsia (1907-1910) and as parish priest in Berezovo (1910-1919). He then entered a long teaching career as professor of Rusyn language at the Uzhhorod gymnasium (1919-1933) and Teacher's College (1933-1945), where he propagated the use of a local dialectal language and cultural orientation for the region. He revealed this trend in his plays, short stories, and translations into Rusyn of the works of Shakespeare, Dickens, and Poe. He was also a founding member of the Dukhnovych Society, but did not associate with the Russophile tendencies of some of its members.
(9) *Tarasovych: ystorychna p'esa* (1936); *Opovîdania y baiky* (1941); *Davnî diaky ta ynshî opovîdania* (1943)

Nedziel'skii, Evgenii, Ph.D. (pseudonyms: Aleksander Izvorin, Iurii Bir, V. Turii, I. Goverla)

(1) 1894-195?   (2) Sumy; Kharkiv; Russian Empire (Ukraine)

(3) —   (4) editor

(5) Moscow University; Charles University, Prague

(6) Russophile   (7) pro-Czechoslovak

(8) Nedziel'skii was a Russophile scholar from the northeastern part of the Ukraine who settled in the Subcarpathian region during the 1920s. For the next two decades he published a score of studies dealing in particular with the literary and cultural history of Subcarpathian Rus'. His history of literature (1932) is still the standard in the field. He was also editor-in-chief of the culturally oriented organ *Russkii narodnyi golos* (1934-1938) and author of several poems that appeared in literary almanacs during the Hungarian regime. After the Second World War he lived in Czechoslovakia and was active in cultural affairs in the Prešov Region.

(9) *Ocherk karpatorusskoi literatury* (1932); *Ugro-russkii teatr* (1941); "Suchasnî rus'kî khudozhnyky" (1942-1943); "I.A. Sil'vai" (1957); see also the Bibliography.

Nevyts'ka, Iryna (pseudonyms: Anna Novak, Anna Horiak)

(1) 1886-1965   (2) Zbudska Bela; Medzilaborce; Zemplén

(3) teacher, agronomist   (4) journalist

(5) elementary, Sabinov (German); teacher's college, Prešov

(6) Ukrainophile   (7) pro-Czechoslovak

(8) Iryna Nevyts'ka (née Buryk) was the only leading female national activist in Subcarpathian Rus'. In 1903, while still a student at the Prešov Teacher's College, she married Professor Emyliian Nevyts'kyi, who was later ordained a Greek Catholic priest. The young couple went to live in the village of Ujak (Szepes county). Iryna helped her husband to organize the first post war national council, which took place at Stará Lubovňa in November 1918. In 1921, after her husband was forced to go to America, she moved to Prešov, where she organized the first Rusyn women's society—the Union of Rusyn Women in the Prešov Region (1922)—the first exhibition of Rusyn culture in Prešov (1927), and the first populist-Ukrainophile newspaper for the region, *Slovo naroda* (1931-1932). She was also instrumental in organizing dramatic productions, both of her own works and of the classical Ukrainian repertoire. In 1929, Nevyts'ka moved to Uzhhorod where she continued political and cultural work as organizer of the first congress of women in Subcarpathian Rus' (1934), as founder and chairman of the Ukrainian Agricultural Worker's party, and as editor of its organ, *Narodnia syla* (1936-1938). She was also a member of the executive board of the

Ukrainophile faction of the Central National Council (1938). Throughout these two decades, Nevyts'ka published many children's poems and tales, short stories, plays, and the first novel by a Subcarpathian author (1924). After the Hungarian forces arrived in 1939, Nevyts'ka returned to Prešov where she remained until her death.

(9) *Pravda pobîdyla* (1924); *Darunok* (1929); *Pryhody Matiia Kukolky* (1929-1930, 1968)

Nevyts'kyi, Emyliian

(1) 1878-1939	(2) Jedl'ová; Stropkov; Sáros
(3) priest	(4) priest/professor

(5) university, Budapest; theological seminary, Prešov and Budapest

(6) Ukrainophile   (7) pro-Czechoslovak

(8) Nevyts'kyi was a professor at the Prešov Teacher's College. After ordination as a Greek Catholic priest, he was placed in a parish at Ujak (Szepes county). In November 1918, he organized (with his wife Iryna), in the nearby town of Stará Lubovňa, the first national council, which called for union with Galicia. He was an adamant opponent of Hungarian rule and organized a plebiscite in the Prešov Region calling on local Rusyns to vote on their political future. Before the end of the year the focus of political activity changed to Prešov, and Nevyts'kyi's leading position was taken over by A. G. Beskid and his relatives, who favored unification with Czechoslovakia. Nevyts'kyi befriended the first governor of Subcarpathian Rus', Gregory Zsatkovich, who sent the national activist to the United States (1920) in order to solicit funds from Rusyn-American immigrants. He returned the same year, but after being watched closely by Czechoslovak authorities he decided to emigrate (1921) permanently to the United States, where he became a priest in the Pittsburgh Ruthenian Exarchy. In 1938-1939 he organized the Committee for the Defense of Carpatho-Ukraine, which tried (in vain) to convince Rusyn immigrants to give their support to the Voloshyn regime.

Ostapchuk, Iatsko

(1) 1873-1959	(2) Galicia
(3) peasant	(4) large farmer
(5) —	

(6) Ukrainophile   (7) pro-Czechoslovak

(8) Ostapchuk was already a political activist in Galicia, first a member of the Ukrainian Radical party, then, after 1897 of the Ukrainian Social Democratic party, which chose him to serve in the Vienna Parliament (1907-1911). In 1912, he emigrated to Subcarpathian Rus' and operated a large farm near Strabichovo Goronda. During the First World War, he was a member of the Union for Liberation of the Ukraine and worked among

Ukrainian prisoners-of-war in Freistadt. In 1920, he organized the Social-Democratic party for Subcarpathian Rus' and remained active in that organization, sometimes as its chairman, until 1938. He was a supporter of the Prosvita Society and for some years its vice-chairman. He did not play any role in the autonomous government and after the Hungarians came he emigrated to Bohemia.

(9) "Uhors'ka Ukraïna, ïï stan i zavdannia ches'koï polityky" (1920)

Pachovs'kyi, Vasyl', Ph.D.

(1) 1878-1942   (2) Zhulych; Zolochiv; Galicia
(3) priest   (4) professor
(5) —
(6) Ukrainophile   (7) pro-Czechoslovak
(8) Pachovs'kyi taught in the Stanyslaviv and L'viv gymnasia before the First World War and also belonged to the L'viv literary group Moloda Muza (1906-1909). At that time he had already published several collections of poetry. From 1915 to 1918 he worked in Austrian camps with Ukrainian prisoners-of-war and in 1920 emigrated to Subcarpathian Rus'. He was a professor of history at the Berehovo gymnasium (1920-1929), and took an active role in the Ukrainophile movement, especially as a supporter of the Prosvita Society in Uzhhorod, which published his popular history of the region. Pachovs'kyi also wrote the libretto for "Korjatovič" (1921), the first Czech film about Subcarpathian Rus'. In 1930, he returned to Galicia, taught at the gymnasium in Przemyśl, and continued to publish literary works.
(9) *Chto to Prosvîta* (1920); *Istoriia Podkarpatskoî Rusy* (1921, 1946); *Sribna zemlia* (1938)

Pan'kevych, Ivan Artemovych, Ph.D.

(1) 1887-1958   (2) Tseperov; Galicia
(3) peasant   (4) professor
(5) elementary, Tseperov; gymnasium, L'viv (1899-1907); university, L'viv
    (1907-1910) and Vienna (1910-1912)
(6) Ukrainophile   (7) pro-Czechoslovak
(8) Pan'kevych was the leading Ukrainophile scholar and pedagogue in Subcarpathian Rus'. He had begun doing national work among the people in his native Galicia, where before the First World War he established many Prosvita libraries and served as secretary of the Prosvita Society in L'viv. During the war years he was professor of Russian language at the Theresian Academy in Vienna (1915-1919), then, in November 1919, he registered as an external student in Prague's Charles University. The following year, the Czechoslovak government appointed him to the school administration in Uzhhorod as supervisor (*referent*) responsible for language in the schools of

Subcarpathian Rus'. It was in this capacity, and as professor at the Uzhhorod gymnasium (1920-1938), that he wrote his controversial grammar for municipal schools, which went through three editions. He was a cofounder of the Pedagogical and Prosvita societies and almost singlehandedly edited the latter's scholarly journal, *Naukovŷi zbornyk* (1922-1938). He was also the first editor of the children's journal *Vînochok* and pedagogical journal *Uchytel'*. Pan'kevych tried, through these publications, to introduce literary Ukrainian as the official language for the region, and for this reason he was the focus of attack among the anti-Ukrainophiles. He studied linguistics in Prague (1923-1927) and for his scholarly achievements was elected to the Shevchenko Scientific Society in L'viv (1924) and the Slavic Institute in Prague (1927). His later years were devoted to numerous writings on language and folklore, including an authoritative analysis of Subcarpathian dialects (1938), and to teaching, as director of the Ukrainian gymnasium in Perechyn (November 1938 – March 1939), at the Ukrainian Free University in Prague (1939-1945), and at Charles University in Prague (1945-1950).
(9) *Hramatyka rus'koho iazyka dlia molodshykh klas shkil serednikh i horozhans'kykh* (1922, 1927, 1936); "Khto buv Ivan Berezhanyn" (1931); *Ukraïns'ki hovory Pidkarpats'koï Rusy i sumezhnykh oblastei* (1938); *Narysy istoriï ukraïns'kykh zakarpatskykh hovoriv* (1958); see also the Bibliography.

Parkanyi, Ivan, LL.D.

(1) b. 1896   (2) Teresova; Tiachiv; Máramaros
(3) teacher   (4) lawyer
(5) elementary, Kalyny; gymnasium, Berehovo; university, Budapest
(6) Rusynophile   (7) pro-Czechoslovak
(8) While still a student in Budapest, Parkanyi was the editor and administrative director of the newspaper *Budai újsag*. Immediately after the war, he returned home and served in the new Czechoslovak administration at the county level, first in Khust (1918-1920) and later Mukachevo (1920-1921). In 1921 he served briefly as chief county administrator in Dovhe, then became county deputy chief of protocol (1921-1924). In 1924, he was summoned to Prague to serve in the president's office as advisor to the central government for Subcarpathian affairs. He held this post until 1939, having also become governor of Subcarpathian Rus' for two days (October 9-11, 1938) before autonomy was granted. From 1948 to 1952, he served in the central government and since his retirement has lived in Prague.

Patrus-Karpatskii, Andrei M. (pseudonym: Mykola Karpats'kyi)

(1) b. 1917   (2) Tereblia; Tiachiv; Máramaros
(3) peasant   (4) editor
(5) gymnasium, Khust (1931-1935) and Mukachevo (1935-1937)
(6) Russophile, Ukrainophile   (7) pro-Czechoslovak, pro-Soviet
(8) Patrus was one of several Russophile writers who began publishing in
the 1930s in Russian, but under the impact of later events changed to
Ukrainian. He began publishing poetry while still a gymnasium student and
contributed to *Nashi stremlinnia* and to Rusyn-American Russophile publications. He was also a member of the Russophile Self-Education Circle at
the Mukachevo gymnasium. His first writings in Ukrainian appeared during
the autonomous period (1938-1939). After the Hungarians took over, he
fled to the Soviet Union (1939) and later joined the Czechoslovak army
corps (1942). In 1945, he returned to his native land, has continued to publish, and is a member of the Union of Writers in the Ukraine.
(9) *Pletia po sovesti* (1937); *Batkivshchyna klyche do boiu* (1943); *Odnoï
materi my dity* (1946); *Beskyde, vidrado moia* (1961)

P'eshchak, Ivan, LL.D.

(1) 1904-1972   (2) Vel'ký Lipník; Stará Lubovňa;
                                         Szepes
(3) peasant   (4) lawyer
(5) middle, Prešov; teachers' college, Prešov; law faculty, Charles Univer-
    sity, Prague (1930-1931)
(6) Russophile   (7) pro-Czechoslovak, pro-Soviet
(8) P'eshchak began his career as an elementary school teacher in L'ucin
(1924-1930) and Vel'ká Driečna (1930-1933). He also served as editor of the
Prešov youth journal *Russkaia shkola* (1926-1932). After completing his
law studies, he worked as a lawyer's apprentice in Uzhhorod (1933-1934),
and then was chosen by the Autonomous Agricultural Union to represent
his native Prešov Region as a deputy in the Prague Parliament (1935-1938).
From this platform he criticized the Prague government and Slovak administration for their assimilationist policies toward the Rusyn population in the
Prešov Region. He was later made a state secretary in the first autonomous
government for Subcarpathian Rus', headed by A. Brodii (October 1938).
After the dissolution of that government, he returned to the Prešov Region
where during the Second World War he operated a law office in Medzilaborce. In 1943, he joined the Carpatho-Russian liberation movement in
Prešov, and in 1945 was one of the founders of the Prešov National Council. In the late 1940's he was supervisor (*referent*) for Ukrainian schools in
the Prešov Region, and during the 1950's served as legal advisor to the state
construction firm in Prešov.

Polivka, Ivan Andreevich

(1) 1866-1930   (2) Brežnička; Stropkov; Zemplén
(3) teacher   (4) teacher
(5) elementary, Bukovce and Máriapócs; gymnasium, Prešov; teacher's
college, Uzhhorod (completed 1884)
(6) Russophile   (7) pro-Hungarian,
                                               pro-Czechoslovak
(8) Polivka was an elementary-school teacher in the Prešov Region villages
of Sedliska (1884-1887) and Svidník (1889-1919). Before the First World
War, he had already founded a Youth Union, a cooperative organization,
Spolok, and written a six-part textbook (1896) in Russian for use in local
schools. He also collected many folk songs that were published in the collection of M. Vrabel' (1890). In November 1918 he became the chairman of the
national council in Svidník, which eventually favored union with Czechoslovakia. The new authorities designated him briefly (late 1918) as commissioner of Makovytsa (the region around Svidník and Bardejov) and later as
school inspector in Uzhhorod (1919-1923). He was also a member of the
presidium of the Dukhnovych Society.
(9) *Uchebnaia kniga real'nykh nauk* (1896); *Vînets stykhovtvorenii Aleksandra Iv. Pavlovycha* (1920)

Popovich, Mikhail Vasil'evich (pseudonym: Ivan Rusnak)

(1) 1908-1955   (2) Velyki Kom'iaty; Sevliush;
                                               Ugocsa
(3) peasant   (4) lawyer
(5) gymnasium, Mukachevo; Charles University, Prague
(6) Russophile   (7) pro-Czechoslovak, pro-Soviet
(8) Popovich was a Russophile poet who stressed his homeland's cultural
affinities with Russian civilization. His law practice ended under the Hungarian regime, which arrested him (1943) for contact with local partisans.
Released from a concentration camp in 1945, he was appointed by the
Soviet regime as head of the Transcarpathian branch of the Kiev publishing
house Radians'ka Shkola. He later joined the Soviet Communist party
(1947) and was awarded numerous medals for service to his homeland.
(9) *Rannie stikhi* (1928); *Khata* (1937); *Dumy o Verkhovine* (1959)

Prykhod'ko, Oleksa K.

(1) b. 1887   (2) Kn'iazhpol; Podillia; Russian
                                         Empire (Ukraine)
(3) —   (4) professor
(5) seminary, Kam'ianets' Podil'sk (1900-1908); University of Warsaw,
Music Institute (1908-1915)
(6) Ukrainophile   (7) pro-Czechoslovak
(8) Prykhod'ko was a key figure in the musical and theatrical life of Subcarpathian Rus'. In 1917 he established the Ukrainian National Chorus in
Kiev, where he also held a position as gymnasium professor and member of
the musical section of the Ukrainian Ministry of Culture. In 1920, he arrived
in Uzhhorod with eighteen singers and that same year he established the
Kobzar Ensemble. He then established and directed the National Chorus
(1921-1928), the orchestra and chorus of the Rusyn Theater of the Prosvita
Society (1921-1929), and the Teacher's Chorus of Subcarpathian Rus' (1928-
1938). He tried, through music, to instill Ukrainianism in the local population. Prykhod'ko also taught Ukrainian language and literature at the Uzhhorod Seminary (1922-1923, 1925-1938) and at the Commercial Academy
(1923-1925) when it was in Uzhhorod. Because of the Hungarian occupation, he emigrated (1940) to Prague.
(9) *Probudylas' Rus'* (1968)

Revai, Iuliian Ivanovych

(1) b. 1899   (2) Mircha; Velykyi Bereznyi; Ung
(3) teacher   (4) educational administrator
(5) elementary, Mircha and Kosil'ieva Pastil'; gymnasium, Uzhhorod
(6) Ukrainophile   (7) pro-Czechoslovak
(8) Revai was one of the most popular native-born Ukrainophile leaders in
Subcarpathian Rus'. He was an organizer of the Social Democratic party in
Mukachevo (1920), then went to Uzhhorod (1923) where he was appointed
supervisor of the economic and administrative section of the Ministry of
Education in Uzhhorod. He was also secretary (1924) of the Pedagogical
Society, for which he wrote many textbooks, editor of *Uchytel'*, and a
school inspector. His Ukrainophile sympathies led him to membership in
the Prosvita Society, the Teacher's Assembly (Hromada), and the scouting
organization Plast. By the 1930s, Revai had become directly active in
politics, first as member of the presidium of the Social-Democratic party,
then as its deputy to the Prague Parliament (1935-1938). There he was a
member of the parliamentary group that negotiated for autonomy with the
Czechoslovak government (1938). His views were further propagated as
editor of the political journal *Do peremohy* (1935-1936) and as vice-chairman of the Ukrainian section of the Russian-Ukrainian Central National
Council (1938).

During the months of autonomy, Revai was appointed Minister of Commerce and Public Works in the Brodii and first Voloshyn cabinets (October 1938). He authored the bill for Subcarpathian autonomy accepted by the Prague government (November), represented the autonomous province in negotiations for economic agreements with Germany (December), was elected deputy to the Diet (February 1939), and was appointed premier minister and minister of foreign affairs (in absentia) in the last government (March 15, 1939). Revai spent the years of the Second World War in Bratislava, then emigrated to Germany (1945) and the United States (1948) where he has been director of the credit association Samopomich (1948-), director of the office of the Ukrainian Congress Committee of America (1949-1957), and director of the Ukrainian Institute and the Carpathian Research Center in New York.
(9) co-author, *Rus'ko-madiarska terminologiia* (1923); co-author, *Madiars'ko-rus'kyi slovar'* (1928); "Dovkola avtonomiï Podkarpats'koï Rusy" (1936); see also the Bibliography.

Rosokha, Stefan, LL.D.

(1) b. 1908   (2) Drahovo; Khust; Máramaros
(3) peasant   (4) editor
(5) elementary, Drahovo; gymnasium, Berehovo (1922-1930); Charles
    University, Prague (1930-1934); Ukrainian Free University (1934-1936)
(6) Ukrainophile   (7) pro-Ukrainian
(8) Rosokha was an avid Ukrainophile who began his national career as a student leader in Prague. There he was head of the Union of Subcarpathian University Students (1933-1937), Union of Greek Catholic Youth (1931-1934), and the local branch of the Prosvita Society (1931-1943). He made his anti-Czechoslovak views known as editor of *Proboiem* (1933-1944), which later became the platform of the Organization of Ukrainian Nationalists.
    During the months of autonomy he was a member of the supreme command of the Carpathian Sich (November 1938), was on the executive committee of the Ukrainian National Union (January 1939), was elected to the Diet (February 1939), and elected vice-president of the Diet's presidium (March 15, 1939). After the Hungarian occupation, he went to Prague, where he continued to publish *Proboiem* and *Nastup* (1938-1944). He was arrested by the Gestapo in January 1944 and released from the Theresian concentration camp in May 1945. He immediately emigrated to Regensburg, West Germany, then to Canada (1949), where he publishes the newspaper, *Vil'ne slovo* (1960-).
(9) *Soim Karpats'koï Ukraïny* (1949)

Sabol, Sevastiian Stefan, S.T.D. (pseudonyms: Zoreslav, Iurii Borzhava)

(1) b. 1909   (2) Prešov; Prešov; Sáros
(3) state prison warden   (4) priest
(5) elementary, Prešov (1914-1918); Basilian College, Dobromyl' (1926-
    1931); Pontifica Universitas Gregoriana, Rome (1931-1936, 1949-1950)
(6) Ukrainophile   (7) pro-Czechoslovak
(8) After being ordained a Greek Catholic monk in the Order of St. Basil
the Great, Sabol went to Uzhhorod. There he was prefect for students at the
Theological Seminary (1936-1938) as well as editor of the diocesan publications *Blahovîstnyk* (1936-1939) and *Missionar* (1937-1938). He also published, under the pseudonym Zoreslav, two collections of poetry (1933,
1936) that revealed an intense love and devotion to all things Ukrainian. He
again revealed this attitude during the months of autonomy while serving as
chaplain to the Carpathian Sich. Because of his Ukrainophile sympathies,
Sabol was arrested by the Hungarians (April 1939) and expelled to Slovakia.
There he was appointed provincial superior of the Order of St. Basil until
forced to flee to Austria (1948). The Czechoslovak Communist authorities
sentenced him, in absentia, to life imprisonment (December 1948) on
charges of having engaged in anti-state activity, such as aiding Ukrainian
nationalists from Galicia. After receiving his doctorate in Rome (1950), he
emigrated to the United States, where he served in various pastoral capaci-
ties and is now superior of the Carpathian branch of the Basilian order.
(9) *Zi sertsem u rukakh: poeziï* (1933); *Sontse i blakyt':poeziï* (1936); *Vid
Uhors'koï Rusy do Karpats'koï Ukraïny* (1956)

Sabov, Evmenii Ivanovych (pseudonym: E. Ivanov)

(1) 1859-1934   (2) Verb'iazh; Svaliava; Bereg
(3) priest   (4) priest/professor
(5) elementary, Verb'iazh; gymnasium, Uzhhorod, Mukachevo, Prešov,
    and Levoča; theological seminary, Uzhhorod (1877-1881)
(6) Rusynophile   (7) pro-Hungarian,
                                                    pro-Czechoslovak
(8) Sabov came from a family of Rusyn patriots (his uncle was the gram-
marian Kirill Sabov, his godfather Ioann Dulishkovich). He should not be
confused with his contemporary Jenó Szabó (1843-1921), who led the group
of Budapest Rusyns favoring national assimilation. After ordination as
a Greek Catholic priest (1885), Sabov began a career teaching Rusyn at the
Uzhhorod gymnasium (1887-1898). He was active in national affairs, being
a leading member of the St. Basil the Great Society and its successor Unio, a
co-founder of the newspaper *Nauka,* and the author of a widely used grammar (in the Subcarpathian recension of Russian) and the first anthology of

Subcarpathian Rusyn literature (1892). In 1898 he went to Sevliush as a parish priest and was eventually appointed archdeacon (1917) for the county of Ugocsa.

Under the Czechoslovak regime he became the honorary chairman of the Dukhnovych Society (1923-1934), although in his own writings he disavowed Russophilism in favor of a "traditional Carpatho-Rusyn" cultural orientation.

(9) *Russkaia hrammatyka y chytanka k yzucheniiu lyteraturnaho iazŷka uhro-russkykh* (1890); *Khristomatiia tserkovno-slavianskikh i ugro-russkikh literaturnikh pamiatnikov* (1893); see also the Bibliography.

Sabov, Simeon Andreevich, S.T.D.

(1) 1863-1929   (2) Velykyi Rakovets'; Sevliush;
                                                           Ugocsa
(3) priest   (4) priest/professor
(5) elementary, Uzhhorod; gymnasium, Uzhhorod; theological seminary, Uzhhorod (completed 1885); Avgustin Seminary, Vienna (completed 1894)
(6) Russophile   (7) pro-Hungarian,
                                                           pro-Czechoslovak
(8) Sabov was ordained a Greek Catholic priest (1887) and served a parish in Horinchove (Máramaros) for a few years. After the death of his wife he went to Vienna to complete his education. He was appointed professor of religion at the Sighet gymnasium (1894-1896), then was sent to the United States as a parish priest in Cleveland (1896-1899). While in the New World he petitioned Rome to appoint a Greek Catholic bishop for Rusyn-Americans. Back home he served a parish in Stanov (Bereg) and in 1907 was appointed professor of dogma and philosophy and vice-rector of the Uzhhorod Theological Seminary. In 1914 he was made a canon of the Mukachevo diocese. Sabov was appointed to the central committee for Magyarization of Greek Catholic parishes (September 1915), although he opposed this action.

In November 1918 he was the principal founder and first speaker at the Rusyn National Council in Uzhhorod, which pledged loyalty to Hungary. By the following spring he had participated in the joint Central National Council in Uzhhorod, which pledged loyalty to Czechoslovakia. Sabov was chosen honorary member of the Dukhnovych Society (1923), to which he donated 40,000 crowns (1926) in order to establish a fund to award prizes to authors of the best works written about the "Russian" aspects of Subcarpathian Rus'. He was the author of many theological studies.

Shtefan, Avhustyn Emyliiovych

(1) b. 1893   (2) Poroshkovo; Perechyn; Ung
(3) priest   (4) professor, editor
(5) gymnasium, Berehovo; theological seminary, Uzhhorod; university, Budapest (completed 1918)
(6) Ukrainophile   (7) pro-Czechoslovak
(8) Shtefan was a leading educator and propagator of Ukrainianism in Subearpathian Rus'. His father was a Greek Catholic priest who founded the first Ukrainophile-affiliated Prosvita Society (1896) in the region, while his maternal grandfather was Evgenii Fentsik, the leading nineteenth-century Russophile. The young Shtefan was thrust into public life in October 1918, when he was sent by Voloshyn to discuss the current Subcarpathian political situation with Galician parliamentary representatives in Vienna. He returned home to participate in the pro-Ukrainian Khust National Council (January 1919) and the pro-Czechoslovak Uzhhorod (May 1919) National Council. He was also active in journalism as associate editor of the first Subcarpathian daily, *Rusyn* (1920-1922), and as associate editor of the Ukrainophile teacher's organ *Uchytel's'kyi holos* (1929-1938).

Shtefan began his pedagogical career at the Uzhhorod Teacher's College (1918-1919), then was professor at the Uzhhorod gymnasium (1920-1922) and the director of the State Commercial Academy in Uzhhorod and later in Mukachevo (1922-1938). Under his influence, a new generation of consciously Ukrainian Subcarpathians was formed. At the same time, he participated in politics as a member of the advisory board to the cities of Uzhhorod (1922) and Mukachevo (1933-1937) and as a leading member of the pro-Czechoslovak Agrarian party (1929-1938). He was especially active during the autonomous period as actual administrator of educational and religious affairs in the Voloshyn cabinets (November 1938 to March 1939), member of the Ukrainian National Union's executive board (January 1939), member (February 1939) and president (March 1939) of the Diet, and Minister of Education and Religious Affairs (March 1939).

After the Hungarians arrived, he fled to Yugoslavia, then Bratislava, where he was director of the Ukrainian Academy of Commerce (1939-1940). He later served as director of the Ukrainian gymnasium in Prague (1940-1945) and in Augsburg, West Germany (1945-1949). In 1949, he emigrated to the United States and taught at a Ukrainian Catholic high school for girls in Stamford, Connecticut (1949-1969). While in this country he published many short works about his homeland.

(9) co-author, *Hramatyka ukraïns'koï movy* (1931); *From Carpatho-Ruthenia to Carpatho-Ukraine* (1954); *Za pravdu i voliu: spomyny* (1973); see also the Bibliography.

Sova, Petr Petrovich

(1) b. 1894   (2) Nové Zamky; Nové Zamky;
                                                     Komárom
(3) —   (4) professor
(5) law academy, Prešov
(6) Russophile   (7) pro-Czechoslovak, pro-
                                                     Hungarian, pro-Soviet
(8) Sova was a Russophile active in Subcarpathian political and cultural
life. During the Czechoslovak regime he served first as a department head in
the Uzhhorod section of the Ministry of Education and then as cultural
attaché to the governor's office. He later became vice-mayor (1924-1927)
and then member of the city council of Uzhhorod. As a supporter of the
drive for autonomy, he served as secretary to the Russophile faction of the
Central National Council, founding member of the Russian National Autonomist Party (1935), and author of a proposal for Subcarpathian autonomy
(1938). In cultural affairs he was a supporter of the Dukhnovych Society,
acting as librarian and member of its presidium. He was also chairman of
the educational-benevolent fund Shkol'naia Pomoshch' (1935-1938). During
these years he published the first of several studies on the history of Uzhhorod.
   Sova was opposed to the Ukrainophile administration of Voloshyn and
became vice-chairman of the Central Russian National Council in Khust
(November 1938), which called on the Prague government to give some
power to the local Russophiles. Under the Hungarians he was appointed to
the Regent's Commisariat and to the Uzhhorod city council, posts he held
until the arrival of the Soviet troops. He again adapted to the new political
situation and led the drive for unity with the Soviet Union in his capacity as
vice-chairman of the Mukachevo National Council (November 1944) in
charge of the local economy. Since 1945 he has contributed to Soviet guidebooks on the region.
(9) "Podkarpatskaia Rus' i russkii iazyk" (1936); *Proshloe Uzhgoroda*
(1937); "Ungvár multja" (1943); *Arkhitekturnye pamiatniki Zakarpat'ia*
(1961); see also the Bibliography.

Stefan, Agoston, LL.D.

(1) 1877-1944   (2) Batar; Szatmár
(3) teacher   (4) lawyer
(5) gymnasium, Sighet and Satu Mare; university, Budapest and Cluj
(6) Rusynophile   (7) pro-Hungarian,
                                                     pro-Czechoslovak
(8) Stefan was one of the few pre-1918 Magyarones who became a Rusynophile supporter of the Czechoslovak regime. He began a law practice in

Rakhiv (1905) and was active in public life as editor of *Tiszavölgy* (1903) and chairman of the local branch of the oppositional Independent party. He was called to Budapest by Károlyi to join his revolutionary government in November 1918, and the following month he was appointed governor of the newly created Rus'ka Kraina, a post he held even after the Communists took over the region (March-April, 1919). He was instrumental in leading a local force against the Communists, but was in turn driven out by Czechoslovak troops. He subsequently fled to Poland and for the next five years (1919-1924) he led a campaign to have his homeland reunited with Hungary.

Then, Stefan reached an accord with Prague, returned to Subcarpathian Rus', and was promptly chosen by the ruling Agrarian party as a deputy to the Prague Parliament (1925-1929). But in 1929 he returned to his law practice in Rakhiv and subsequently particpated in public life only briefly, as a member of the anti-Ukrainian Central Russian National Council in Khust (November 1938).

(9) *Ruszka-Krajna népbiztosának előterjesztése a magyarországi tanácsok országos gyülésének Budapesten* (1919)

Stoika, Aleksander

(1) 1890-1943   (2) Karachyn; Sevliush; Ugocsa
(3) peasant   (4) priest
(5) gymnasium, Uzhhorod (completed 1910); theological seminary, Uzhhorod (1910-1912) and Budapest (1912-1915)
(6) Rusynophile   (7) pro-Czechoslovak,
                                           pro-Hungarian
(8) Stoika was a leading Greek Catholic prelate who favored a Rusynophile orientation in national affairs. After ordination, he began his ecclesiastical career in administration, first as archivist in the episcopal office of the Mukachevo diocese (1915), then as secretary to the Magyarone Bishop Papp. It was probably at this time that his Hungarian sympathies were confirmed. He continued to rise in the hierarchy, being appointed canon and head of the episcopal chancery (1930), vicar of the eparchy (1931), and then bishop (1932). In this last post he instituted a program to aid the poor of his diocese. He also favored all attempts, such as that of the newspaper *Nedîlia,* at avoiding the Russophile-Ukrainophile controversy, and he was sympathetic to pro-Hungarian local politicians. When the Vienna Award gave Uzhhorod to Hungary (November 1938), Stoika remained as bišhop in Uzhhorod until he regained jurisdiction over the whole of the Mukachevo diocese in March 1939. He became, ex officio, a member of the Upper House of the Parliament in Budapest (June 1939), although he soon became distraught with the Hungarian refusal to grant autonomy.

(9) "K uporiadkovaniu sviashchenycheskykh derzhavnŷkh zhalovanii" (1927); "Derzhavnoe zhalovanie dukhovenstva" (1928)

Stryps'kyi, Hiiador Nikolaievych, Ph.D. (pseudonyms: Iador, Bilenkii, S. Novyk, Stotozhenko, Mikesh, Beloň Rusinský, Ruskotsi, Th. Beregiensis)

(1) 1875-1949   (2) Shelestove; Mukachevo; Bereg
(3) priest   (4) cultural administrator
(5) elementary, Fridieshovo; gymnasium, Uzhhorod (completed 1893);
    university, Budapest (1893-1896), L'viv (1896-1898), and Cluj (1898)
(6) Rusynophile   (7) pro-Hungarian
(8) Stryps'kyi was the scholar who most consistently propagated the idea of a separate cultural policy for the Subcarpathian Rusyns. He spent most of his life as a librarian, first at the Transylvanian Museum in Cluj (Kolozsvár) (1888-1908) then, after 1908, as vice-curator of the ethnographic section of the National Museum in Budapest. While in Cluj he lectured at the university on Subcarpathian culture and published several studies, including a seminal analysis of early Rusyn literature (1907). His first contact with the political world came during the First World War when the government asked him to publish the journal *Ukránia* (1916-1917), which was intended to foster Hungarian interest in the Ukraine. Although sympathetic to Ukrainians (he studied in L'viv with Ivan Franko), Stryps'kyi was always careful to point out that Subcarpathian Rusyns should not be confused with their related, but distinctly different, brethren to the north and east. In late 1918 he was appointed section chief for Rusyn affairs in the Ministry of Cults and Education and advisor to the Ministry of National Minorities. In this position, he made plans to create a Rusyn literary language and for this purpose organized in Budapest, in early 1919, the publishing house Chas, a chair of Rusyn studies at Budapest University, and the newspaper *Rus'ka Krayna*.

After Subcarpathian Rus' became part of Czechoslovakia it was not clear whether Stryps'kyi would return to his homeland (he was a member of the Prosvita Society's presidium) or remain in Budapest (he was still an advisor to the irredentist Hungarian Ministry of National Minorities). He could not reach an accord with the Prague regime and thus remained at Budapest's National Museum. He published many scholarly works, among which were studies on Rusyn language, literature, folklore, and history. For his achievements he was elected a member of the Hungarian Academy of Sciences, the Shevchenko Scientific Society in L'viv, and the Subcarpathian Academy of Sciences.

(9) *Starsha rus'ka pys'mennost' na Uhorshchyni* (1907); *Chytanka dlia doroslykh* (1919); *Hdî dokumenty starshoi ystorii Podkarpatskoi Rusy* (1924); see also the Bibliography.

Szabó, Oreszt, LL.D.

(1) 1867-194?   (2) Drahove; Khust; Máramaros
(3) priest   (4) lawyer
(5) —
(6) Rusynophile   (7) pro-Hungarian
(8) Szabó was one of those Rusyn-born leaders who made a successful career in Hungarian public service. By the turn of this century he was a judge for the Jaád district in Besztercze-Naszód county and after 1913 he was a ministerial secretary in the Ministry of the Interior. During the First World War he was government representative to the general headquarters of the army. For his services he was honored with the Jubilee Award for Civil and State Service.

Szabó maintained contact with Rusyn affairs as a member of the assimilationist Union of Hungarian Greek Catholics (1902) and as author of a major work on his people (1913). Then, in December 1918, he was appointed government minister to the newly established Rus'ka Kraina. The same month he organized the Rusyn Congress in Budapest and strove to keep the territory within Hungary. When the Communist regime came to power (March 1919), he refused to continue his post in Rus'ka Kraina. After this period, Szabó played no active role in Rusyn affairs.
(9) *A magyar oroszokról (ruthének)* (1913); "A Ruszinföld autónomiájáról" (1939)

Tsibere, Pavel P.

(1) —   (2) Zaluzh; Mukachevo; Bereg
(3) peasant   (4) student
(5) gymnasium, Mukachevo; Charles University, Prague
(6) Russophile   (7) pro-Czechoslovak
(8) Tsibere was a young Russophile who played a brief role in political affairs during the Second World War. As a university student during the 1930s he was a member of the Renaissance Society, chairman of the Society of Greek Catholic Students in Prague, and an editor of the journal *Zaria* (1938). In the summer of 1938 he was sent by Bishop Stoika as a delegate to the world peace conference of Catholic students. During the period of autonomy, he was a member of the Russian National Council in Khust (November 1938), which opposed the local Ukrainophile regime. After the Hungarians took over, he fled to France, then to England, where, despite the fact that he was relatively unknown, he was appointed by Beneš as Subcarpathian representative to the State Council of the Czechoslovak govern-

ment-in-exile in London. In August 1944, he went to Moscow in this capacity, and in early 1945 he returned to his homeland. Tsibere was subsequently arrested by Soviet authorities, and served several years in prison for alleged contacts with the West. In recent years, he has been teaching English in a village near Chop.

Tsurkanovich, Ilarion

(1) 1878-19??   (2) Davidovitse, Bukovina
(3) peasant, cantor   (4) editor
(5) gymnasium, Chernivtsi and Rădăuti; university, Chernivtsi
(6) Russophile   (7) pro-Czechoslovak
(8) Tsurkanovich was a member of that group of Russophiles from Galicia and Bukovina who came to Subcarpathian Rus' at the close of the First World War and who became pro-Czechoslovak political leaders. Before the war, in Chernivtsi, he was a member of the student organization Karpat and an editor of Gerovskii's Russophile organ *Russkaia pravda,* and he was active for the defense at the Marmarosh-Sighet trial (1913-1914). He was suspected by the Austrian government for his Russian sympathies and imprisoned from late 1914 until July 1918. He was sentenced to death in 1917, but the sentence was commuted. In early 1919 he joined the Czechoslovak army, and later that year he settled in Uzhhorod and founded the Carpatho-Russian Labor party. He edited the party's organ *Russkaia zemlia* (1923, 1925-1938) and was its senator in the Prague Parliament (1929-1935). He was also briefly editor of *Russkii narodnyi golos,* and director of the print-shop of the Educational-Benevolent Fund—Shkol'naia Pomoshch'.

Turianytsia, Ivan Ivanovych

(1) 1901-1955   (2) Riapid; Mukachevo; Bereg
(3) railroad worker   (4) chimney sweep, construction
                                               worker
(5) Institute of Journalism, Kharkiv (1930-1933)
(6) Ukrainophile   (7) pro-Soviet
(8) Turianytsia was a prominent Subcarpathian leader during the Soviet period. He was inducted into the Austro-Hungarian army (October 1917), and after the end of the war he joined the Rusyn Red Guard (March 1919), which fought with the Hungarian army in Rus'ka Kraina and Slovakia. He returned home at the end of 1919, then went to Budapest (1921) where he worked as a chimney sweep. By 1925 he was back in Mukachevo, employed in a construction firm, and then he joined the Subcarpathian Communist party. He served as Mukachevo party secretary (1928-1929), then went to study journalism in Kharkiv (1930-1933). After returning home, he was appointed secretary of the Communist union movement (1933-1938). When the Hungarians took over, Turianytsia went back again to the Soviet Union

(March 1939), working first with his wife in a factory in Voroshilovgrad (1940-1941), then joining the Czechoslovak Army Corps (January 1942). He was also elected both Subcarpathian delegate (1941) and member of the plenum (1943) of the Pan-Slavic Anti-Fascist Committee in Moscow.

In October 1944 he returned home as a member of the Czechoslovak delegation and initially favored reunion with Prague. But soon he called for union with the Soviet Ukraine and propagated this goal as chairman of the Mukachevo National Council (November, 1944). Turianytsia was to hold leading positions in the new government: chairman of the Transcarpathian Communist party (1946-1948), deputy in the Supreme Council of the USSR (1946), deputy in the Supreme Council of the Ukrainian SSR (1947), member of the central committee of the Communist party of the Ukraine (1946-1954), and chairman of the Transcarpathian Council of Workers Deputies (1946-48). For his services to the cause of unity with the USSR, Turianytsia was the only civilian buried in the Red Army cemetery in Uzhhorod.

Vakarov, Dmytro Onufriiovych (pseudonym: Dyma, D.V.)

(1) 1920-1945   (2) Iza; Khust; Máramaros
(3) peasant   (4) student
(5) gymnasium, Prague (Russian) and Khust; university, Budapest
(6) Rusynophile   (7) pro-Soviet
(8) Vakarov was a young poet who began publishing in the several literary almanacs that appeared during the Second World War. His works were filled with expectation of liberation from the East. He was a member of the anti-fascist underground movement and was arrested by the Hungarians in 1944. He died in a concentration camp the following year. During the Soviet period several collections of his unpublished works have appeared and he has subsequently been hailed as a martyr who symbolically died in the struggle for liberation of the homeland.
(9) *Izbrannye stikhi* (1955); *Vybrani poeziï* (1957); *Izbrannoe* (1963)

Voloshyn, Avhustyn Ivanovych (pseudonym: A. Verkhovyns'kyi)

(1) 1874-1945   (2) Kelechyn; Volove; Máramaros
(3) priest   (4) priest/professor, editor
(5) elementary, Kelechyn; gymnasium, Uzhhorod (1883-1892); theological
    seminary, Uzhhorod (1892-1896) and Budapest
(6) Rusynophile, Ukrainophile   (7) pro-Czechoslovak
(8) Voloshyn was clearly the most active and prolific Rusyn national leader of the twentieth century. There were not many aspects of Subcarpathian cultural life in which he did not play some role. His national allegiance developed in a pattern typical for many of his countrymen; that is, he started out as a Rusynophile, then by the 1920s began to express openly the belief that Subcarpathian Rusyns were part of one Little Russian or Ukrainian nationality.

Voloshyn was a leading educator. He began as a professor (1900) and later became director of the Uzhhorod Teacher's College (1917-1938). He also authored numerous grammars and readers in dialect for elementary schools as well as textbooks in arithmetic, physics, pedagogy, and logic. He founded and served as chairman of the Pedagogical Society (1924) and Teacher's Assembly (1929).

Besides schoolbooks, Voloshyn wrote several plays and served as editor of *Nauka* (1903-1914), the annual *Mîsiatsoslov* (1901-1921), and *Svoboda* (1922-1938). He was also instrumental in founding the Greek Catholic journal *Blahovîstnyk* (1922) and in reviving the daily newspaper *Rusyn* (1923).

Voloshyn was continually concerned with Rusyn political and national affairs. He played a leading role in the Unio Society before the First World War and was appointed a member of the Central Commission of the Greek Catholic Eparchy, which strove to Magyarize Rusyn parishes (1915). He stood opposed to these efforts. In November 1918, he was the guiding spirit of the pro-Hungarian Uzhhorod National Council, then came to favor Czechoslovakia, working for unity with that country in his capacity as chairman of the Rus'kii Klub (March 1919), vice-chairman of the Central National Council in Uzhhorod (May 1919), and member of the delegation that went to Prague to pledge Rusyn allegiance. He was then appointed to the Directorate (1919-1920) responsible for educational and cultural matters. Subsequently, Voloshyn was chairman of the Christian-National party (1923-1939) and was chosen by the People's party as its deputy to the Prague Parliament (1925-1929). He was always interested in economic matters and was instrumental in organizing the Podkarpatskii Bank and the Cooperative Union. He was for a time vice-chairman of the Prosvita Society and soon was considered the nominal head of the Ukrainophile orientation.

It was inevitable that during the autonomous period he would play an active role, first as state secretary in the Brodii Cabinet (October 1938), then as premier-minister of the remaining cabinets (October 26, 1938 - March 14, 1939). The Czechoslovak government had been throughout convinced of his loyalty. He was symbolically elected president of Carpatho-Ukraine on March 15, 1939. Forced to flee after the Hungarian invasion, Voloshyn eventually settled in Prague (1940) where he taught at the Ukrainian Free University until his arrest by the Soviet secret police in 1945. He never made it to trial, but died in a Soviet prison. Voloshyn has subsequently become a national hero and martyr among Ukrainophiles in the West and has been accused of anti-national fascist and Nazi collaboration by his Marxist detractors at home.

(9) *Metodycheskaia hrammatyka uhrorusskoho literaturnoho iazŷka dlia narodnŷkh shkol,* 6 rev. eds. (1899-1930); *O pys'mennom iazŷtsî podkarpatskykh rusynov* (1921); *Spomynŷ* (1923, 1959); *Marusia Verkhovynka: p'esa* (1931); see also the Bibliography.

Zaklyns'kyi, Kornylo Romanovych

(1) 1889-1966   (2) L'viv, Galicia
(3) teacher   (4) professor
(5) university, Vienna, L'viv, and Chernivtsi
(6) Ukrainophile   (7) pro-Czechoslovak
(8) Zaklyns'kyi was the son of a leading Ukrainian pedagogue and national leader in Galicia. Kornylo came to Subcarpathian Rus' after the First World War and became a professor at the gymnasium in Berehovo (1920-1938). He passed on his Ukrainophile views to a younger generation through his courses and membership in the Plast scouting organization and the Prosvita Society. In 1939, he was arrested and imprisoned briefly by the Hungarians, then spent the rest of the war in Prague as a teacher in the Ukrainian gymnasium and as director of the Ukrainian Museum. He retired in 1947 and spent the remaining years of his life publishing on Subcarpathian folklore and literature in various scholarly journals in Czechoslovakia.
(9) *Narodni opovidannia pro davnynu* (1925); "Narys istoriï Krasnobrids'koho monastyria" (1965); "Deshcho pro Mykhaila Vrabelia" (1967)

Zheltvai, Viktor Iuliievych

(1) 1890-1974   (2) Crăciuneşti (Krachunovo);
                                           Máramaros
(3) priest   (4) priest/professor
(5) theological seminary, Uzhhorod; Budapest Pedagogical Academy
(6) Ukrainophile   (7) pro-Czechoslovak
(8) Zheltvai was a leading Ukrainophile pedagogue. After ordination as a Greek Catholic priest he taught at the Uzhhorod Teacher's Seminary for Women, of which he was director until 1934. He was an active journalist, serving as editor of *Nauka* (1919-1923) and its successor *Svoboda* (1923-1938), which was the organ of the Christian-National Party. Zheltvai was a close associate of Voloshyn and other Ukrainophiles, first as a member of the Rus'kii Klub (1919) and later as a member of the Prosvita Society's presidium.
(9) *Zhyvot sviatŷkh* (1913); *Rozdumai to dobre!* (1921)

Zhidovskii, Ivan Il'ich, LL.D. (pseudonym: Iastreb Karpatskii)

(1) b. 1897   (2) Šarišské Jastrabie;
                                           Sábinov; Sáros
(3) peasant   (4) editor
(5) elementary, Šarišské Jastrabie; gymnasium, Piarist, Sabinov (1909-1915) and Prešov (1919); Comenius University, Bratislava (1924)
(6) Russophile   (7) pro-Czechoslovak, pro-Soviet
(8) Ivan Zhidovskii was a leading Russophile publicist from the Prešov Region. While serving in the Austro-Hungarian army, he was captured on

the Russian front (1916). After the Russian Revolution, he served in the Red Army (1918-1919) as a political commissar for the 216th international regiment. In 1919, he returned to Czechoslovakia to continue his education. During the 1920s, he served as a tax assessor in Uzhhorod, and during the 1930s as director of the Podkarpatskii Bank in Prešov and as a lawyer in Uzhhorod. As publisher of the *Narodnaia gazeta* (1924-1936) and the *Russkaia narodnaia gazeta* (1937-1938), he called for the introduction of the Russian language into schools in the Prešov Region and criticized the policies of the Slovak administration. He was a member of the Russian National party, the Russophile branch of the Central National Council, the Dukhnovych Society, and the Druzhina Society.

During the existence of the Slovak state (1939-1944), he operated a law practice in Giraltovce and joined the underground Carpatho-Russian national liberation movement that was formed in Prešov in the fall of 1943. After the war, he served as editor to the Czechoslovak State Council in Košice (1945) and to the Ministry of Information in Prague (1945-1947). He then returned to Prešov and worked as a notary (1947-1953), and since his retirement in 1955 has served as legal counsel to various state-owned enterprises.

Zhidovskii, Petr Il'ich

(1) 1890-1947   (2) Šarišské Jastrabie;
                                                 Sabinov; Sáros
(3) peasant   (4) tavern keeper
(5) no formal education
(6) Russophile   (7) pro-Czechoslovak
(8) Like his younger brother Ivan, Petr Zhidovskii was a Russophile publicist active in the Prešov Region. As a fifteen-year-old uneducated youth, he emigrated to the United States (1905), returning home five years later as a self-educated activist who attempted to raise the national consciousness of his fellow Rusyns. He was drafted into the Austro-Hungarian army in 1914, but deserted; he was later arrested and imprisoned.

During the Czechoslovak regime, he operated a tavern in his native village and became interested in politics. He was chosen by the Agrarian party to represent his people as deputy in the Prague Parliament (1935-1938). There he spoke out against the poor economic conditions and encroaching Slovakization in his homeland. In September 1938, he joined his parliamentary colleague from the Prešov Region, I. P'eshchak, in submitting a memorandum to the English representative in Prague, Lord Runciman, and demanding help from him for unification of their homeland with Subcarpathian Rus'. After the establishment of the Slovak state (March 1939), he initially agreed with the Agrarian party's decision to support the regime, but after promises for the Rusyn minority were unfulfilled, Zhidovskii began to agitate against the regime and was arrested briefly for anti-state activity. Upon his release, he became a member of the underground Carpatho-Russian national liberation movement based in Prešov (1943). After Soviet troops came to the region, Zhidovskii became the vice-chairman of the Prešov National Council (March 1945), the self-styled representative body for Rusyns in the Prešov Region, and director of the publishing house Slavknyha.

Zsatkovich, Gregory Ignatius, LL.D.

(1) 1886-1967   (2) Holubyne; Svaliava; Bereg
(3) journalist   (4) lawyer
(5) elementary, New York City; middle, De Witt Clinton High School, New York City; St. Vincent College, New York City; College of the Holy Ghost, Pittsburgh; University of Pennsylvania, Philadelphia
(6). Rusynophile   (7) pro-Czechoslovak,
                                           pro-Rusyn independence
(8) Zsatkovich was the American immigrant leader most responsible for having his homeland united with Czechoslovakia. He favored the Rusynophile orientation and was the only one to put forth serious claims for Subcarpathian political independence as well. He was brought to the United States at the age of five and grew up in Pittsburgh, Pennsylvania. His father, Pavel, was an influential immigrant spokesman and editor of the Greek Catholic Union's influential newspaper, the *Amerikansky russky viestnik*. After completing his education, Gregory worked as a lawyer for General Motors Corporation and did not really participate in Rusyn-American affairs until the summer of 1918, when he was asked by the American Council of Uhro-Rusyns to serve as their spokesman. In the following months he met with President Wilson, with Tomáš Masaryk, the future Czechoslovak president, and headed the Uhro-Rusyn delegation to the Mid-European Union in Philadelphia (November 1918). Zsatkovich succeeded in having the Subcarpathian Rusyns recognized as a separate people, but was urged to seek unity with another state. His choice was Czechoslovakia, and he gained the support of the immigrants through the Scranton Resolution (November) and a plebiscite (December). He then led an American delegation to the homeland (February 1919) and helped to organize the Rus'kii Klub in Uzhhorod (March). His political demands for broad autonomy were adopted by the Uzhhorod Central National Council (May). He spent the summer of 1919 negotiating with Czechoslovak officials in Prague and Paris, and for his efforts he was appointed chairman of the governing body, the Directorate (August), and first governor of Subcarpathian Rus' (April 1920). During his tenure in these offices he allied with the local populist-Ukrainophiles, although he himself stressed Subcarpathian Rusyn national distinctness, as revealed in the daily newspaper *Rusyn,* published by his brother, Theophil.
    Zsatkovich's claims for implementation of autonomy, elections to the

Prague Parliament, and unification with the Prešov Region were rebuffed by the Czechoslovak government and he resigned in protest (March 1921). Upon his return to the United States he published several anti-Czechoslovak tracts, then concentrated primarily on his own law practice. He also served as city solicitor for Pittsburgh, legal counsel to the Pittsburgh Greek Catholic Eparchy, and founded the Slav Congress. By the 1930s he had dropped his separatist position and accepted the view that Subcarpathian Rusyns were part of one Russian civilization.

During the Second World War he reversed his anti-Czechoslovak stand and became chairman of the American Carpatho-Russian Central Conference, which favored the reunification of the homeland with Czechoslovakia. He expressed these new goals as editor of the journal, *The Carpathian* (1941-1943).

(9) *Otkrytie-Exposé byvšoho gubernatora Podkarpatskoj Rusi* (1921)

Appendix 3
Varieties of Written Language

1. Slaveno-Rusyn (Subcarpathian Recension of Church Slavonic)

Съ болѣзнію сердца вижду, же многихъ родителей сынове по больше рокахъ изъ латинскихъ школъ, сѣмо на ексаменъ приходящіи и до сану клирическаго вступити желающіи, въ своей руской науцѣ такъ барзъ занезбаліи и глупіи невѣжды приходятъ, же ани читати, ани самое еще имя свое написати, изъ напѣву же, или изъ уставу церковнаго ани уста растворити отнюдъ не знаютъ. Зане еще шесторочніи нѣкіи руское свое набоженство оставиша, безъ которыя однакожъ науки — аки нуждныя нуждою средствія — до сана клирическаго вступити не могутъ, отсюду же бываетъ : яко таковіи невѣжды потребуютъ въ семинаріи отъ початку рускія науки съ кривдою богословской науки и фундаціи зачинатися учити.

> »Окружнее письмо Епископа Андрея Бачинскаго, 4.IX.1798«, ч. 496. Cited in František Tichý, *Vývoj současného spisovného jazyka na Podkarpatské Rusi* (Prague, 1938), p. 72.

Вѣмъ : Палласъ при Невѣ престолъ положила, — Неблагодарна! Оужокъ, Латюркѹ лишила. Карпатъ Славлновъ есть истый Отецъ, Мати, Но разсѣлнны дѣти то не ищѹтъ знати.

    .   .   .   .   .

Рѹсскїл Мѹзы! Съ карпатскихъ снидите гѹр ; До Оуга, во мой став'тесл Владычій дворъ. Внѹшите : Ѿ Песта вѣсть радостнѹ прїлхъ, Что Праздникъ строитсл на Дѹнайскихъ стрѹлхъ.

> Г. Тарковичъ, *Тезоименитству Его Царскаго Высочества, Пресвѣтлѣйшаго Государя Іосифа,... его превосходителствомъ г. графомъ Францішкомъ Сечени и прочая во соборѣ Музъ...* (Buda, 1805). Cited in Tichý, *Vývoj*, pp. 157-158.

Рок҂ во Пряшовской Греко-Каѳолїческой Дїецезїи и Градѣ обсчее кнїгохранїлїсче ради того благосклонно ѹчреждити изволїл, да бы и межд҂ сїм простым҃ и ѹбогїм но еднакож законным своим повелѣтелем и любезном҂ Отечеств҂ пріемным и вѣрным҃ Ѹгро-Р҂скїм народом, iак҃ н҂жное просвѣсченїе и благонравїе, так҃ искраїнныя бесѣды и словесности познанїе легчае и скорѣе распространїтїся возмогло.

> И. Фогороссы, *Русько-угорска ілі малоруска грамматіка* (Vienna, 1833). Cited in E. Sabov, *Khristomatiia tserkovno-slavianskikh i ugro-russkikh literaturnykh pamiatnikov* (Uzhhorod, 1893), p. 57.

2. The Language of Aleksander Dukhnovych.

"LOW" STYLE

Мамко, мамко к҂п҃ ми книшк҂,
Тинт҂, папїрь, и табличк҂,
Бо iа пойд҂ до школы,
Оучитися по воли.
Бо iа быся рад҃ оучити,
Iакбы Бог҂ посл҂жити,
Iакбы людей оучтити,
И iак҃ спасенным҃ быти.

> *Книжиця читалная для начинающихъ* (Budapest, 1847). Cited in O. Dukhnovych, *Tvory*, vol. 1 (Prešov and Bratislava, 1968), p. 200.

Чмуль. Што розкажете мои люби Панове, ци паленьку, ци вино; ци пиво, вшытко маю, завчером ємь принѣс ганискову из Дуклѣ, вино из самого Токаю, а пиво из Шебеша, такоє як золото; раскажете и закусити?

Многомав. Вшытко дай жиде, годен я заплатити и вшытку твою худобу.

Чмуль. (*Иде до коморы смѣючися*). Мою худобу; — ай вай, и цѣлоє село бы вы выплатили. О вы пан кто бы ся с вами мѣряв?

> *Добродѣтель превышаетъ богатство : игра* (Przemyśl, 1850). Cited in Dukhnovych, *Tvory*, vol. 1, p. 590.

"HIGH" STYLE

О славная природо! тебе я величаю въ твоемъ велелѣпіи, — какъ ты прекрасна! Твоя чистая одежда, твой невинный уборъ изящнѣйшій, пріятнѣйшій есть, нежели всѣхъ художниковъ искуснѣйшія рукодѣланія, ты превышаешь острѣйшій умъ, и человѣкъ только подражатель есть твоего великолѣпія, — о я тутъ со всѣмъ доволенъ, ты мой на земли небесный рай!

> »Память Щавнака«, in *Поздравленіе Русиновъ на годъ 1851* (Vienna, 1851), pp. 71-72. Cited in Tichý, *Vývoj*, p. 177.

Тое Начало разныи народы разно именуютъ, мыже называемъ Его Богъ, кой понеже первый Началщикъ всего есть, отъ негоже происходятъ вся, и прото самъ собою, и въ себѣ живетъ, Премудрый, и много добрый, благій, отъ никого не пріялъ, что имѣетъ, но всѣмъ все движеніе далъ...

Богъ таже есть Начало всѣхъ существъ неистребимое, не разрушимое. Онъ создалъ вся, чрезъ него суть вся, вся живутъ, вся движутся на сильное повелѣніе Его, Онъ смотритъ на все, и прото Бога назвать должно всѣмъ, т.е. Богъ есть Все, и Вся.

> *Естественно духовная разсужденія* (Prešov, 1855). Cited in Dukhnovych, *Tvory*, vol. 2 (1967), pp. 572-574.

3. Literary Languages Between 1848 and 1918.

SLAVENO-RUSYN TRADITION

Ибо прежде мы старали смы ся писати по формамъ великорусскаго языка, нынѣ же хочемъ писати по нашему областному русскому нарѣчію. Отсюда слѣдуе, что должно быти различіе между грамматическими формами и правописаніемъ двохъ журналовъ, преемствовавшихъ другъ друга подъ редакціею нашею. Но тутъ же и представляеся намъ вопросъ : якому правописанію и якой грамматицѣ послѣдуемъ мы при употребленіи нашего областнаго русскаго нарѣчія? Пишемъ ли мы по собственной грамматицѣ, или ачей руководствуемся изданною нѣкоторою у насъ грамматикою? Не могши сказати, что мы приняли смы за руководство нѣкоторую изъ существовавшихъ у насъ грамматикъ, мы вынуждены смы объявити, что мы вознамѣрили смы писати по собственной грамматицѣ, или лучше сказавши, поелику изданной нами грамматики нѣтъ, мы рѣшили смы ся руководствовати собственными соображеніями по части употребленія нами письменнаго русскаго языка.

> Іоаннъ Раковскій, *Церковный Вѣстникъ для Русиновъ австрійской державы* (Budapest, 1858), no. 1. Cited in Tichý, *Vývoj*, p. 180.

Намъ потребно познати природу (натуру) и явленія въ ней, гдѣ все изъ якой-то причины бываетъ и дѣется : и такъ не увѣримъ легко различнымъ суевѣріямъ (бабонамъ, ворожкамъ) и безумнымъ баснямъ (приповѣдкамъ) неукихъ людей, но изъ природы увидимъ премудрость и всемогущество Сотворителя свѣта, который такъ премудро устроилъ всё для своей славы, и человѣку на пользу (хосенъ).

> From the introduction to Іоаннъ Поливка, *Учебная книга реальныхъ наукъ для подкарпатскихъ угрорусскихъ народныхъ школъ ... въ IV. частяхъ*, Pt. 1 (Prešov, 1896), p. 8.

SUBCARPATHIAN RECENSION OF RUSSIAN

Путевыя впечатлѣнія на верховинѣ

Соч. А. Митрака.

Верховиною обыкновенно называютъ у насъ тѣ гористыя части ужанскаго, бережанскаго и мараморошскаго комитатовъ, которыя — своимъ болѣе холоднымъ климатомъ, убогою, густогористою землею, особымъ говоромъ и одѣяніемъ своихъ жителей, — отличаются отъ прочихъ, хотя также гористыхъ мѣстностей нашей сѣверовосточной Угорщины. И на самомъ дѣлѣ. Верховина — отдѣльный, особый край : тамъ уже не созрѣетъ кукуруза, столь любимое растеніе нашего народа, только овесь и овесь повсюду; хижины не бѣлены, изъ смерековаго дерева; хлопы сорочки свои не на переди, но на зади связываютъ; словомъ повсюду особыя, отличительныя черты на лицѣ и человѣка и природы.

> From *Свѣтъ* (Uzhhorod, 1867), no. 13. Cited in Sabov, *Khristomatiia*, p. 122.

Языкъ и словесность

Соч. А. Кралицкаго.

Въ нашей старинной литературѣ вмѣсто слова »народъ« употребительно было слово »языкъ«, т. е. народъ и языкъ значили одно и то-же. Оттуду въ богослужебныхъ книгахъ поется : Съ нами Богъ, разумѣйте языцы (народы языч.) и пр. И дѣйствительно, значеніе этихъ словъ тѣсно связываетъ ихъ между собою. Всѣ люди, отъ природы говорящіе однимъ языкомъ, составляютъ одинъ народъ, какъ всѣ, одаренные даромъ слова, составляютъ одинъ родъ человѣческій. Безъ дара слова человѣкъ не былъ бы человѣкомъ.

> From *Листокъ*, vol 4 (Uzhhorod, 1888), p. 289. Cited
> in Sabov, *Khristomatiia*, p. 119.

Между тремя сиротами Лука былъ самый старшій. Многоразъ сжалился онъ надъ своей матерью, когда видѣлъ, что она и собственный кусникъ хлѣба раздѣляетъ съ дѣтьми. Для того, какъ скоро онъ выучилъ школы, пошелъ служити къ одному хозяину. Тамъ велъ себя хорошо. Хозяинъ очень полюбилъ его, и другаго года далъ ему большую плату.

> Иванъ Гашпаръ, *Руская книга чтенія* (Budapest,
> 1870), translated from Magyar by Evgenii Fentsik. Cited
> in Sabov, *Khristomatiia*, p. 158.

Efforts to write in the popular language

Коли вже вопросъ сякъ поставльѐнъ, по мому ачей не буде даремна праця досвѣдчити, ожъ руськый языкъ мае то̀лько права на назывъ самосто̀йного языка, якъ хотькоторый изъ славянскихъ його братовъ.

У насъ нема истого, еднакого руського языка, каждый видѣкъ указуе даякусь самосто̀йно̀сть во здоженю и выговорѣ сло̀въ; черезъ сесе можъ порозумѣти, ожъ нашъ языкъ на дакотрѣ стямки и пять сло̀въ мае. Кедь хочеме, обы нашѣ руснакы насъ порозумѣли, такъ треба писати, обы тотожнѣ слова ро̀жныхъ видѣко̀въ брали ся, а дуже частнѣ знаки пожертвовали ся на долю загальныхъ.

> From the introduction to Василій Чопей, *Русько-ма-
> дярский словарь—Rutén-magyar szótár* (Budapest, 1883),
> pp. xi, xxiii-xxiv.

Русины въ Угорщинѣ никда еще не мали такой дешевой (туньой), красной, поучительной газеты, якъ »Недѣля«.

»Недѣля« выходитъ въ дуже красной формѣ каждый тыждень, мае 16 печатанныхъ (друкованныхъ) сторонъ и уже на недѣлю достане ю каждый предплатникъ до рукъ.

> Advertisement for the monthly *Недѣля : поучительно-господарска газета для угро-русского народа* (Budapest, 1898-1918), edited by M. Vrabel'.

Ot Pozsonya do Nizsnyaho Dunaja, ot Karpat do Adriaticseszkoho morja sztoit za otecsesztvo jeden voodusevlennöj i na vszi zsertvö hotovöj narod.

> Latin (Magyar) alphabet used in the later years of *Negyilya* (Budapest, 1916), no. 8, p. 113.

Хмары еще лѣпше затемнѣли.

— Боже! Якъ може чоловѣкъ такъ глубоко упасти до грѣха! Я нынѣ могъ быти щастливый чоловѣкъ, что люде могли мнѣ завидѣти...

Задаремно хотѣвъ бы ся вернути, оковы все му коло ухъ звонять. Не мае отчизны, домовства, не е мѣста, де бы голову спокойно положивъ.

Луна червенымъ засвѣтила, а хмары еще лѣпше затемнѣли. Образъ перемѣнився, руку къ небу поднявъ : кто виненъ сему смутному состоянію. Зубы ему скрежетали! Я не виненъ... Я статочно хотѣвъ жити... И слезы потокомъ потекли изъ очей.

> From the short story »Жебракъ«, by Ириней Легеза [Иванъ Лоцуга], in *Наука* (Uzhhorod, 1913), no. 2, p. 10.

На зеленомъ поли пиля красного города попасовавъ Василь волы. — Все за ними ходивъ. — Позиравъ ихъ красно укручены рогы, а пакъ киваючый ся гребѣнь на шеѣ. — А ще коли почали зъ хвостомъ мухы обганяти, то онь цѣле му ся полюбило. Радовавъ ся, што такъ мирно пасуть зелену пашу.

Разъ попозиравъ на дерева (стромы), и што тамъ стямивъ! На едномъ деревѣ онь смѣють ся на него черешнѣ. — Не давъ ся довго панькати; лишивъ волы, бо такъ гадавъ собѣ, ожь они и безъ него годны пасти. — Вылѣзъ скоро на черешню, и почавъ ѣсти черешнѣ.

> Павелъ Генце, *Читанка для народныхъ школъ*, vol. 1 (Budapest, 1889), translated from Magyar by Vasylii Chopei. Cited in Sabov, *Khristomatiia*, p. 159.

Осталася Марька сиротою. Межъ чужими людьми тяжко было ей жити. Терпѣла она голодъ и холодъ, и не слыхала ласкаваго слова. Прийшло ей въ гадку (въ голову), якъ ей мати говорила : Молися Богу, Марько, Богъ пошле тебѣ счастье и здоровье; Богъ поможе тебѣ. И молилася Марька усердно.

> Августинъ Ив. Волошинъ, *Методическа грамматика карпаторусского языка для народныхъ школъ* (1899), pt. 2 (2nd ed.; Uzhhorod, 1919), pp. 62-63.

4. The Russian Language After 1918.

SUBCARPATHIAN RECENSION OF RUSSIAN

Василь : (Входя въ комнату). Слава Іисусу Христу! Рыбко моя дорога! Все лишь плачучей тебя нахожу. Не проливай даремно свои дорогія слезы, коли тѣмъ и такъ не поможешь нашей бѣдѣ. Твой отецъ, особенно же мати, закаменѣли въ своей коравости; они и не бзпокоются [sic!], что и ты и я загинемъ съ тоски (отъ жаля); ихъ лишь богатство Гаврилы интерсуетъ. Выгнали меня, яко пса, и обои забожилися предо мною, что доколѣ они живутъ, ихъ Маруся не пойдетъ за такого жебрака, якій я, и твердо мнѣ заказали приближатися къ тебѣ.

> Сіонъ Сильвай, *Маруся : народная пьеса*, Изданіе культурно-просвѣтительнаго общества имени Александра Духновича, no. 94 (Uzhhorod, 1930), p. 4.

STANDARD RUSSIAN

Русскій языкъ

Какъ струны на звонкой, задумчивой лирѣ,
Какъ въ битвѣ кипучей пронзающій штыкъ,
Какъ яркій свѣтильникъ въ полночной квартирѣ,
Какъ кровля средь бури, такъ важенъ ты въ мірѣ, —
О, древній, сіяющій русскій языкъ!

. . . .

Ты свѣточъ и звонъ, ты цвѣтенье народа,
Ты въ буряхъ кровавыхъ столѣтій возникъ;
Ты вѣчный источникъ славянскаго рода,
Въ тебѣ справедливость, просторъ и свобода,
О, громкій, могучій, великій языкъ!

> А.В. Карабелешъ, *Въ лучкахъ разсвѣта* (Uzhhorod, 1929), p. 15.

Настоящая грамматика является грамматикой русскаго литератур-
наго языка въ его письменномъ, а не устномъ употребленіи…. совре-
менный русскій литературный языкъ въ своемъ письменномъ употребленіи является произведеніемъ всего русскаго народа (въ особенности
его образованныхъ классовъ) и общимъ литературнымъ языкомъ для
всѣхъ вѣтвей русскаго народа.

> Евм. Ив. Сабовъ, *Грамматика русскаго языка для*
> *среднихъ учебныхъ заведеній Подкарпатской Руси,*
> Изданіе ОИАД, no. 1 (Uzhhorod, 1924), p. 1.

Нашѣ родной край

Нашъ родной край находится подъ горами Карпатами. Мы тутъ
родились, тутъ живемъ и тутъ хотимъ умерти. Тутъ родилися, жили
и умерли наши отцы и дѣды.

Мы русскій народъ. Русскими были наши отцы и дѣды, русскими
будемъ и мы.

Наша мила краина — Подкарпатская Русь, а наша держава —
Чехословакія.

> И. Добошъ и П. Федоръ, *Карпаторусскій букварь,*
> Изданіе Учительскаго товарищества Подк. Руси,
> 3rd rev. ed. (Uzhhorod, 1930), p. 90.

5. The Populist Orientation and Ukrainian Language After 1918.

Vernacular

Якась непріятельска сила розбила народ наш релігійно, вызвала
классовѣ и партійнѣ борьбы и недовѣріе к интелигенціи, сія же изовсѣм
утратила здорову оріентацію своеѣ народноѣ политики.

Особливо остро выступають стороны в языковых спорах, котрѣ
найлѣпше забаламутили умы и сердця наших людей и сіи споры суть
головнѣйшими перепонами об'единеня всѣх сил к одушевленной
просвѣтной, экономичной и политичной працѣ.

> Авг. Волошин, *О письменном языцѣ подкарпатских*
> *русинов* (Uzhhorod, 1923), p. 3.

Як можемо спôзнати наш рôдный край?

Около нашого села є бôльше сел. Мы вже были в сих селах. Сѣ села творять нашу рôдну околицю.

Нашѣ села та наша околиця наймилѣйшѣ нам на свѣтѣ. Мы любимо их понад все та добре их пôзнаємо.

Дальшѣ горы та долины, дальшѣ села и городы творять нашу рôдну краину : Пôдкарпатску Русь.

> А. Маркуш и М. Шпицер, *По родному краю : учебник геоґрафіѣ*, Выд. Педаґоґічного товариства Подк. Руси, no. 26 (Uzhhorod, 1926), p. 15.

Vernacular-standard Ukrainian intermediary

Кождому вѣдомо єсть, що язык Пôдкарпатских Русинôв єсть найдальшою полуднево-западною частею малоруського (украинського) языка. Будучи сусѣдом рôзных народов, а то Румунôв, Мадярôв и Чехословакôв, набрав ôн од них много новин, чужих для руського языка. Дальше положенє геоґрафичне, т.є. гористый край, потворив окреми языкови островы в дечôм одлични од себе. Не маючи выробленоѣ сильноѣ литературноѣ традиціѣ, письменни люде радили собѣ в письмѣ всѣляко, а найчастѣйше одбѣгали од живоѣ струѣ народнього языка. Я постановив опертися на живый народній язык и взяв пôд увагу тѣ говоры, котри суть найчистѣйши од чужих вплывôв и котри служили за основу першим галицьким писателям Н. Устіяновичови и Могильницкому, т.є. говоры верховински и мараморошськи. 3-4

> Иван Панькевич, *Граматика руського языка для молодших кляс шкôл середних и горожаньских* (Prague and Bratislava, 1922).

Руська литература Пôдкарпатскоѣ Руси выявила в минувшинѣ мало творчости. На протязѣ довгих рокôв змогла она дати лиш два збôрники-альманахи, якѣ выйшли в р. р. 1851. и 1852., один у Вѣдни, другий в Пряшевѣ при активнôй праци А. Духновича.

. . . .

Годиться зазначити, що пôдкарпатска литература од найдавнѣйших часôв живилася соками Сходу. Коли нарôд пôд економичным оглядом був зависимый од Заходу, то пôд духовым оглядом все держав звязки зо Сходом. Пôдкарпатска Русь — се та межа, де стрѣчаєся захôдна культура зо схôдною. З того погляду треба и оцѣнювати даякѣ литературнѣ явища.

»Трембѣта« : литературный Альманах, Выдавництво Товариства Просвѣты, no. 65 (Uzhhorod, 1926), p. 3.

STANDARD UKRAINIAN (GALICIAN VARIANT)

Рахів у неділю

Подивися улицями,
кільки тут красок,
хвилюється в злоті сонця
море запасок.

І гутірок в селі повно…
мовчить тепер ґрунь,
цвіте село вишивками
гуцульських красунь.

Всі улиці у Рахові —
кольоровий рух,
а в легінів блиска топір,
черес і кожух.

Ю. Боршош-Кумятський, *В Карпатах світає* (Prague, 1935), p. 19. Cited in Tichý, *Vývoj*, pp. 208-209.

До його рядів знову горнуться всі селяни. Вони втікають від панів і йдуть воювати, битись за волю рідного краю. Вони бажають злуки з рідними братами. Не хочуть служити угорським панам, не хочуть жити в спілці з гнилою Угорщиною. Геть від угрів, чим скорше, геть! Петро побачив, де сила. Шляхта пішла з ворогами — нехай іде, за Петром стоять селяне. Ті самі, яких дотепер не уважали за людей. В селян руки мозолясті, але тяжкі… З далеких осель приходили вони і просились на війну. Покидали жінок, дітей, покидали служити панам, бо воївода принесе їм волю…

В. Ґренджа-Донський, *Петро Петрович : історична повість,* Вид. Тов. українських письменників і журналістів, no. 3 (Uzhhorod, 1937), pp. 170-171.

6. Subcarpathian Rusyn Trend After 1918.

INDIVIDUAL VARIANTS

Русины! Знаєме, што голодуєте, въ великой бидѣ єсте, украли отъ васъ ваши »пріятелѣ« ваше маленькоє газдовство.

Знаєме, што хотятъ васъ чехомъ, москальомъ переставити, знаєме, што хотятъ украсти отъ васъ вашу стару вѣру, вашъ стародавный материнскій языкъ. Болитъ наше сердце за васъ и зробилисме, учинилисме вшитко; што лемъ сме могли и не перестанеме и на дале старатися о васъ.

> *Прокламація до угроруського народа* (Budapest, 1919),
> p. 3.

Ruszinö! Znájeme, sto holodujete, vo velokoj bigyi jeszte, ukráli ot vász vási "prijátelyi" váse málenykoje gázdóvsztvo.

Znájeme, sto hotyát vász csechom, mászkályom peresztáviti, znájeme, sto hotyát ukrászti od vász vásu sztáru viru, vás sztárodávnöj máterinszköj jázök. Bolit náse szerdcze zá vász, i izrobiliszme usitko, sto lem szme mohli zá vász i ne peresztáneme i ná dálse sztárátiszja zá vász.

> *Proklamacijá do uhroruszjkoho národá* (Budapest, 1919),
> p. 3.

Якій живот провадили? На се загально то можем отповѣсти, что кочуючій, но однакож занималися уже не лиш скотоводством, на что их принудила и сама земля, найперше тым, что из найбольшоѣ части за Тисою до Семигорода, и на повноч до великих лѣсов карпатских, дуже водяниста была, всяды рѣки богато заливали околицю и туй были майже сталое заводненье и постоянна повѣнь, от чого сама земля, яко сталое повѣнное мѣсто, губо-подобна сталася и найспособнѣйша скотоводству; прецѣнь занималися уже и земледѣльством, мали сѣм там и осѣдки.

> Василій Гаджега, »Додатки к исторіи Русинов и
> руських церквей в Ужанской жупѣ«, *Науковый збор-
> ник Товариства* »*Просвѣта«*, vol. 2 (Uzhhorod, 1923),
> p. 12.

Sotaci — rusnaci

Dachtore slovaci tverdza, že na Slovensku ňit rusinov. Pravda tote panove ne čitali historiu, bo keby bul'i čital'i, ta by znali, že sotaci, to su po kervi, po svojich obyčajoch, po svojej bešedze potomci ruskych predkov. Šak my dneška dobre zname, že naše braca, chtore še pred 50 rokami od nas prescahovali do Serbii ta oňi tam hutora tak isce, jak i my po sotacky, svoju reč uznavaju za rusku i vydavaju s ciriliku pisane sotacke noviny. Ta kedz jim šl'ebodno priznavac svoj jazyk za ruski i chranic svoje ruske slovo, to i my mame pravo povedac švetu, že i my sme rusine, bo sme potomci ruskich predkov a naša bešeda je ruska bešeda zmišana s pol'skimi, slovenskimi i mad'arskimi slovami.

Sotak page from *Русскій вѣстникъ*, Sept. 2, 1934.

Мы честуеме пересвѣдченье кождого чоловѣка. Мы высоко цѣниме културну силу так великорусского як и украинского народа, мы в почести держиме их оправедливѣ національнѣ цѣли и стремленья, але при том не хочеме забыти о своем. Мы маеме також свою исторію, маеме своѣ традиціѣ, своѣ властнѣ проблемы, цѣли и стремленья, своѣ културнѣ и политичнѣ потребы, а то мусиме положити на першое мѣсто.

Зато рѣшили мы сю нашу новинку выдати и писати на чисто народном языцѣ.

Editorial statement from the first issue of *Недѣля* (Uzhhorod), March 6, 1935.

ATTEMPTS TO CREATE A LITERARY NORM

Кождий народ усилуєть-ся тепер освідомити своїх ближних не тôлько в політичних ділах, але и в културних-просвітних, бо добрі знають, што с людьми неписьменними, або мало освіченими далеко пойти не мож.

.   .   .   .

Так само робити повинні єсьме и мы, Русины, а то ще и с подвôйною силою, бо другі народы мають свою просвіту вже давно, а мы зачинаєме її ширити аж тепер.

Переходячи в нову добу нашого културного житя, можеме тепер уже сміло выявляти свою *руськость*, с котрою до осени 1918 року мусілисьме таїти-ся, а тепер сміло можеме выповісти, што мы *маєме право завести у нас руські школы* сільскі, ґімназії, фахові школы, потому *руську администрацію* по урядах и руське правосудіє.

. . . .

Руська-Країна становить од Попраду ож до жерела Тисы одну неподільну власть народну.

Ядор [Stryps'kyi, Hiiador]. *Читанка для дорослих* (Mukachevo, 1919), pp. 8-9.

Написати грамматику такого языка, котрый до сихъ поръ еще не мавъ систематичной грамматики, есть легкое дѣло.... Але написати грамматику письменного языка для такого языка и для такого народа, у котрого до сихъ поръ появилося уже множество грамматикъ всякого можливого напряма и идей безъ того, чтобы хотъ одна изъ нихъ была принята цѣлою супольностью безъ противорѣчій и безъ осудительной и презрительной критики просто изза той причины, что интеллигенція того народа еще и нынѣ не вытворила в собѣ ясный поглядъ о національной принадлежности — ся задача здаеся для каждого, кто симъ вопросомъ занимався, майже нерозрѣшимою.

Наше стремленя не было иншое, якъ установити сталѣ и всѣми однако уживанѣ грамматичнѣ формы нар. языка, чтобы такимъ способомъ могли выдаватися книжки и новинки для народа найлегше понятнымъ языкомъ.

Иванъ Гарайда, *Грамматика руського языка.* Vŷd. PON, no. 1 (Uzhhorod, 1941), p. 6.

Смотрячи на то, что авторъ и члены комиссіи при составленіи настоячей грамматики только интересы угрорусского народа, мали передъ очами, что въ минувшинѣ всѣ доказали свою любовь къ угрорусскому народу, надѣюся, что ихъ щиру роботу наше учительство прійме съ найбольшимъ довѣріемъ и порозумѣніемъ. Най держитъ оно сію грамматику своею урядовою грамматикою и придержоватися еѣ най считае урядовою повинностью. Еслибы и указалися ошибки, или недостатки въ первомъ изданіи сей грамматики, они легко могутъ быти отстранени въ слѣдуючихъ изданіяхъ граматики на основаніи отповѣдныхъ научныхъ разбираній и дискуссій.

From the introduction by Юлій Марина, *Грамматика угрорусского языка для середныхъ учебныхъ заведеній* (Uzhhorod, 1940), pp. 7-8.

На початку лекціѣ гол. совѣтодатель звернув увагу на неправильность названія »угрорусский« и подчеркнув, что »руський« е правильное. Послѣ сего згадав руський націонализм, котрый не означае панславизм, але любов до родной грудки землѣ и языка и вѣрность до святостефанской отчины. Присутнѣ провадили сей прояв гол. совѣтодателя довготреваючим рукоплеском и оваціями.

Карпатска недѣля (Uzhhorod), April 14, 1940.

Рѣшеня проблемы руського литературного языка есть найнеобходимѣйшою и найтруднѣйшою задачею Подкарпатского Общества Наукъ.

Головна задача литературного языка заключаеся въ томъ, чтобы всѣ, котрѣ говорятъ по руськи, порозумѣли его. Тому не можъ у всему придержоватися до нарѣчій поодинокихъ областей, но неотмѣнно треба глядати такѣ формы и слова, котрѣ по можливости всяды ихъ розумѣютъ на территоріи Подкарпатя.

Александеръ Бонкало, »Руський литературный языкъ«, *Зоря-Hajnal*, vol. 1, nos. 1-2 (Uzhhorod, 1941), p. 54. Translated from Magyar by Ivan Haraida.

7. Literary Language of the Vojvodinian (Bačka) Rusyns.

Перше слово

Нє мог сом тоту граматику написац так кратко, як ше обично пишу граматики, призначени за народни школи. А то пре тоти причини :

1. Граматика диялекту, хтори так далєко од кнїжковей бешеди, як наша бачваньско-руска бешеда муши буц ширше написана уж прето, же би ше могло розпознац, дзе заправо спада тот диялект? яки у ньому цудзи елементи? и одкаль вони походза?

2. По моей думи тота граматика мушела буц так написана, же би отверала драгу до кнїжкового руско-україньского языка, як тиж до сербского чито горватского языка; а прето тота граматика муши и глїбше и ширше бешеду розпатрац.

Ґабор Костелник, *Граматика бачваньско-рускей бешеди* (Srpski Karlovac, 1923).

Литературни язик Руснацох Югославиї иснує уж пол вика : основни норми того язика були оформени и утвердзени у »Граматики бачванско-рускей бешеди«, друкованей 1923. р. у Ср. Карловцох, а автор тей кнїжки визначни поет, писатель и науковец Г. Костельник (1886-1948). У тедишнїм чаше створени найприкладнейши условия за розвиток и усовершованє руского литературного язика. Гоч ше зявює як язик реґионалного типу, руски язик зоз тим не меней обдарени з велькима друалтвенима функциями — то язик школи, радия, мистецкей и науковей литератури; з часци вон ше тиж хаснує у дїловодстве и у органох управяня.

Александер Д. Дуличенко, »З историї формованя руского литературного язика«, *Нова думка*, vol. 2, no. 4 (Vukovar, 1973), p. 46, translated from Russian by Vlado Kostel'nyk.

Appendix 4
Tables

TABLE 1. Population of the Subcarpathian Rusyns: Unofficial Estimates

Year	Total number of Rusyns	Source
1826	700,000	I. Orlai, "Otviet," *Trudy i zapiski Obshchestva istorii drevnosti rossiiskikh,* vol. 1 (1826)
1826	350,000	P. Šafařík, *Geschichte der slawischen Sprache und Literatur nach allen Mundarten* (1826)
1829	511,605	J. Csaplovics, *Gemalden von Ungarn* (1829)
1840	471,500	Ia. Holovats'kyi, "O halicské a uhorské Rusi," *Časopis Českého Museum,* vol. 17, no. 1 (1843)
1842	625,000	P. Šafařík, *Slovanský národopis* (1842)
1846	500,000	Karel Zap, *Všeobecný zeměpis,* Česká Matice, pt. 1 (1846)
1846	800,000	L. Štúr, *Slovenskje národňje novini* (March 6, 1846)
1846	478,310	Josef Höfler, in J. Hain, *Handbuch der Statistik des österreiches Kaiserstaates* (1852)
1849	800,000	*Vyslanstva rusynov uhorskykh v Vidny* (1849)
1849	700,000	A. Dukhnovych, "Sostoian'ie rusynôv v Uhorshchynî," *Zoria halytskaia,* no. 31
1849	625,000	Ia. Holovats'kyi, *Rozprava o iazŷtsî iuzhnoruskôm y ieho narîchiiakh* (1849)
1851	447,377	K. von Czoerning, *Ethnographie der oesterreichischen Monarchie* (1857)
1852	500,000	I. Sreznievskii, "Rus' Ugorskaia," *Viestnik Imperatorskago russkago geograficheskago obshchestva,* vol. 1, nos. 1-2 (1852)
1862	600,000	A. Dukhnovych, Letter to the Prague Slavic journal *Slovienen,*
1862	500,000	H. Bidermann, *Die ungarischen Ruthenen, ihr Wohngebiet, ihr Erwerb, und ihre Geschichte,* vol. 1 (1862)
1869	455,000	Brachelli, *Statistische Skizze der österreichischen Monarchie*
1869	448,000	F. Schmidt, *Statistik der oesterreichisch-ungarischen Kaiserstaates* (1872)
1869	596,500	V. Křížek, *Statistika císařství Rakouského* (1872); A. S. Budolovich, *Statisticheskiia tablitsy razpredieleniia Slavian* (1875)

Year	Total number of Rusyns	Source
1874	500,000	V. Terletskii, *Ugorskaia Rus' i vozrozhdenie soznaniia narodnosti mezhdu russkimi v Vengrii* (1874)
1875	500,000	N. N. [I. Sil'vai], "O sovremennom polozhenii russkikh v Ugrii," *Slavianskii sbornik,* vol. 1 (1875)
1878	463,786	Ia. Holovats'kyi, "Karpatskaia Rus'," *Narodnyia piesni galitskoi i ugorskoi Rusi,* vol. 1 (1878)
1878	520,000	M. Drahomanov, *Literatura ukraïns'ka proskrybovana riadom rossyis'kym* (1878)
1880	520,000	I. Ohonovs'kyi, *Studien auf dem Gebiete der ruthenischen Sprache* (1880)
1880	353,226	J. Jekelfalussy, *A magyar korona országainak helységnévtára* (1888)
1885	500,000	G. A. De-Vollan, *Ugro-russkiia narodnyia piesni* (1885)
1887	342,351	V. Lukych, *Uhors'ka Rus', iey rozvôi y tepereshnii stan* (1887)
1888	485,000	A. L. Petrov, "Zamietki po Ugorskoi Rusi," *Zhurnal MNP,* vol. 279, no. 2 (1892)
1889	507,973	E. Fentsik, "Chislennost' Ugrorussov," *Listok,* vol. 5, no. 9 (1889)
1890	636,000	H. Kupchanko, *Nasha rodyna* (1897)
1890	485,345	V. Frantsev, "Obzor vazhnieishikh izuchenii Ugorskoi Rusi," *Russkii filologicheskii viestnik,* vol. 45 (1901)
1896	600,000	A. P. Liprandi, "Zabytyi ugolok Russkoi zemli," *Russkaia besieda,* vol. 2, no. 4 (1896)
1900	600,000	T. Florinskii, *Zarubezhnaia Rus'* (1900)
1900	346,921	P. Balogh, *A népfajok Magyarországon* (1902)
1900	422,070	S. Tomashivs'kyi, "Uhors'ki Rusyny v s'vitli madiars'koï uriadovoï statystyky," *Zapysky NTSh, vol. 56 (1903)*
1900	500,000	S. Tomashivs'kyi, *Etnografichna karta Uhors'koï Rusy* (1910)

Note: The year in the left column represents the census upon which the given author based his estimate or the year in which the source was published.

TABLE 2. Population of the Subcarpathian Rusyns: Official Census Reports

Year of census	Total number of Rusyns	Subcarpathian Rus'	Slovakia
1840	442,903	—	—
1850	440,600	—	—
1880	344,063	—	—
1890	369,482	—	—
1900	410,283	—	—
1910	447,566	—	—
1921	458,128	372,500	85,628
1930	537,995	446,916	91,079
1959-60	721,899	686,464	35,435
1970	850,277	808,131	42,146

Sources: Alexius von Fényes, *Statistik des Königreichs Ungarn,* pt. 1 (Budapest, 1843), pp. 38-39, 54-58; *A magyar korona országaiban az 1891. év. elején végrehajtott népszámlálás eredményei,* vol. 1, *Magyar statisztikai közlemények,* új folyam, vol. 1 (Budapest, 1893) pt. 2, pp. 180-195; *Magyar statisztikai közlemények,* új sorozat, vol. 27 (Budapest, 1909), pp. 102-105, and vol. 42 (Budapest, 1912), pt. 2, pp. 35-36; *Zprávy státního úřadu statistického republiky československé,* vol. 14 (Prague, 1933), no. 170; *Štatistický lexikon obcí v republike československej* [1921 census]: vol. 3, *Slovensko* (Prague, 1927), p. 159, and [1930 census] vol. 3, *Krajina Slovenská* (Prague, 1936), p. xviii; *Československá statistika,* Nová Řada, vol. 35 (Prague, 1965), p. 322; L. O. Tkachenko, "Dynamika etnichnoho skladu naselennia Zakarpattia," *Narodna tvorchist' ta etnohrafiia,* vol. 50 no. 1 (Kiev, 1974), p. 65.

Note: The figures for the 1880 through 1910 censuses are based on identity according to native language; those for 1921 through 1970 according to nationality. The figure for the 1850 census refers to all of the Hungarian Kingdom; those for the 1840 and 1880 through 1910 censuses refer only to the thirteen counties of northeastern Hungary enumerated in the text (p. 9 and n. 1); the figures for 1921 through 1960 refer to those areas incorporated into Czechoslovakia and the Soviet Union.

TABLE 3. Occupational Status of the Subcarpathian Rusyn Population

Occupational category	1910		1930	
	Total no.	Percentage	Total no.	Percentage
1. Agriculture and forestry	401,430	89.6	447,133	83.1
2. Mining and industry	15,396	3.4	31,462	5.8
3. Commerce, credit, communications, transport	3,786	0.8	13,814	2.6
4. Civil service and other public servies	3,266	0.8	13,670	2.5
5. Domestic and day workers	18,077	4.0	1,812	0.3
6. Retired, private wealth, unknown	5,611	1.0	30,104	5.5
Total	447,566	99.6	537,995	99.8

Sources: *Magyar statisztikai közlemények,* vol. 56 (Budapest, 1915), pp. 330-433; *Československá statistika,* vol. 116 (Prague, 1935), pt. 1, p. 17; pt. 2, pp. 33-35, 51-53. The 1930 figures represent the total Rusyn population in both Subcarpathian Rus' and Slovakia.

Note: The nine-fold occupational category system of the Hungarian statistics was condensed to coincide for comparative purposes with the six-fold system used in Czechoslovak statistics. Category 3 includes small tradesmen (barbers, shoemakers, bakers) under the heading commerce; postal and railroad workers under the heading communications and transport. Category 4 includes notaries, judges, teachers, priests, doctors, journalists and artists, military under the heading civil service and other public services.

TABLE 4. Population of Cities Adjacent to or Near Subcarpathian Rusyn Ethnic Territory

	Total			Rusyns			Jews[a]			Magyars			Czechs/Slovaks[b]		
	1910	1921	1930	1910	1921	1930	1910	1921	1930	1910	1921	1930	1910	1921	1930
Berehovo	12,933	13,846	19,007	221	1,328	1,954	3,909	4,592	5,680	12,432	8,379	9,190	55	—	2,279
Mukachevo	17,275	20,865	26,102	1,394	4,936	6,476	7,675	10,012	11,313	12,686	4,864	5,561	42	—	2,284
Prešov	16,323	17,577	21,775	47	328	557	2,673	3,477	3,965	7,976	1,948	937	6,494	12,126	16,525
Uzhhorod	16,919	20,601	26,675	641	2,807	6,260	5,305	6,244	7,357	13,590	7,712	4,499	1,219	—	4,572

Sources: Publications statistiques hongroises, n.s., vol. 64 (Budapest, 1920), pp. 106-107, 128-129; Statistický lexikon obcí v republice československé [1921 census], vol. 3, Slovensko (Prague, 1927), and vol. 4, Podkarpatská Rus (Prague, 1928); Statistický lexikon v republice československé [1930 census], vol. 3: Krajina Slovenská (Prague, 1936), and vol. 4, Země Podkarpatoruská (Prague, 1937); Zprávy státního úřadu statistického republiky československé, vol. 14, no. 170 (Prague, 1933).

[a]This is a religious category and not exactly comparable to the other national categories. For instance, Czechoslovak statistics had separate entries for Jewish (židovská) nationality and Jewish or Hebrew (izraelské) religious denomination. However, not all persons listed as of Jewish religion identified themselves as Jewish nationality; in 1930 in Uzhhorod, 7,357 persons were recorded as Jewish in religion, but only 5,897 of these identified themselves as Jewish in nationality. Hence, to get a more accurate picture of the number of Jews, the number indicated above is based on religious affiliation.

[b]For Berehovo, Mukachevo, and Uzhhorod, the figures refer to Czechs (although it should be remembered that a certain number of Slovaks lived in these cities also); for Prešov, the figures refer to Slovaks.

TABLE 5. Duknovych and Prosvita Society Reading Rooms in Subcarpathian Rus', 1929

	County										
Ung			Bereg			Ugocsa			Máramaros		
School district	D	P	School district	D	P	School district	D	P	School district	D	P
Uzhhorod	24	7	Berehovo	1	2	Sevliush	20	5	Khust	6	6
Velykyi Bereznyi	14	13	Irshava	26	5				Rakhiv	7	18
			Mukachevo	17	2				Tiachiv	3	8
			Orosvyhiv (Rosvegovo)	27	0				Volove	6	14
			Svaliava	51	3						
Total	38	20	Total	122	15	Total	20	5	Total	22	46

Source: "Statistika o dieiatel'nosti kul'turnykh i prosvietitel'nykh organizatsii na Podkarpatskoi Rusi," *Karpatskii sviet*, vol. 3, nos. 5-6 (Uzhgorod, 1930), pp. 995-999.

TABLE 6. Development of Schools in Subcarpathian Rus', 1920-1938

Language of instruction	Elementary			Municipal			Gymnasia			Teacher's Seminaries			Professional and Technical		
	1920	1931	1938	1920	1931	1938	1920	1931	1938	1920	1931	1938	1920	1931	1938
Rusyn[a]	321	425	463	7[b]	16[c]	21	3	4[e]	5[f]	3	3	4	3	6[g]	5[g]
Czech	22	158	188	1	2	23			1		1	1			
Magyar	83	101	117	2			1	1	2						
Other	49	43	35												
Total	475	727	803	10	18	44[d]	4	5	8	3	4	5	3	6	5

Source: *Školství na Podkarpatské Rusi v přítomnosti* (Prague, 1932); František Stojan, ed., *Representační sborník veškerého školství na Podkarpatské Rusi při příležitosti 20 letého rvání ČSR.*

[a]Rusyn is used here as a translation for the official Czech term "podkarpatoruský" which referred to a school whose language of instruction might have been Russian, Ukrainian, or the local dialect.
[b]Five schools with Magyar classes.
[c]Twelve schools with Czechoslovak classes, four with Magyar.
[d]This number represents schools that also contain thirty Magyar classes, six German classes.
[e]Three gymnasia with Czechoslovak sections, one with Magyar.
[f]Two gymnasia with Czechoslovak sections, one with Magyar.
[g]One school with Czechoslovak section, one with Magyar.

Notes

RK   Regentskii Komyssariat, Uzhhorod.
RNG   *Russkii narodnyi golos*
SAV   Slovenská Akadémia Vied, Bratislava.
SPV   Slovats'ke Pedahohichne Vydavnytstvo, Bratislava.
SPVVUL   Slovats'ke Pedahohichne Vydavnytstvo. Viddil Ukraïns'koï litera-
            tury, Prešov.
ŠSÚA   Štátný Slovenský Ústredný Archív, Bratislava.
SVK   Štátná Vedecká Knižnica, Košice and Prešov.
SVKL   Slovenské Vydavateľstvo Krásnej Literatúry, Bratislava.
TP   Tovarystvo 'Prosvita,' Uzhhorod.
TsKKSUT   Tsentral'nyi Komitet Kul'turnoho Soiuzu Ukraïns'kykh Trudia-
            shchykh, Prešov.
UDU   Uzhhorods'kyi Derzhavnyi Universytet, Uzhhorod.
UTPR   Uchitel'skoe Tovarishchestvo Podkarpatskoi Rusi, Uzhhorod.
UVI   Ukraïns'kyi Vydavnychyi Instytut, L'viv.
ZOV   Zakarpats'ke Oblasne Vydavnytstvo, Uzhhorod.

Introduction

1. This people has also been known as Ruthenians, Carpatho-Russians, and Carpatho-Ukrainians. For a discussion of nomenclature, see Appendix 1.

2. Louis L. Snyder, *The Meaning of Nationalism* (New Brunswick, N.J., 1954), p. 11.

3. Hans Kohn, *The Idea of Nationalism: A Study in Its Origins and Background* (New York, 1958), pp. 3-4. For a survey of the theories of nationalism, see Karl W. Deutsch, *Nationalism and Social Communication: An Inquiry Into the Foundations of Nationality,* 2nd ed. (Cambridge, Mass., 1966), pp. 17-28; Boyd C. Shafer, *Faces of Nationalism: New Realities and Old Myths* (New York, 1972), pp. 3-22; and Anthony D. Smith, *Theories of Nationalism* (New York, 1972), pp. 8-40.

4. For various approaches to defining these terms, see Fredrik Barth, *Ethnic Groups and Boundaries* (Boston, 1969), esp. pp. 9-38; Wsevolod W. Isajiw, "Definitions of Ethnicity," *Ethnicity,* vol. 1 (1974), pp. 111-124; and the introduction of Nathan Glazer and Daniel P. Moynihan, in their *Ethnicity: Theory and Experience* (Cambridge, Mass., 1975), pp. 1-26.

5. This distinction between nation and nationality was clearly delineated by Carlton J. H. Hayes, *Essays on Nationalism* (New York, 1928), and later elaborated by Snyder, *The Meaning of Nationalism,* p. 59. However, many writers have made the term nation synonymous with nation-state, people, and nationality; the resultant confusion makes it difficult to distinguish between the existence on the one hand of a state, and on the other of its habitants who might belong to several different nationalities and cultures. Cf. Shafer, *Faces,* pp. 13-17; Smith, *Theories,* pp. 174-191; Rupert Emerson, *From Empire to Nation: The Rise of Self-Assertion of Asian and African Peoples* (Boston, 1960), pp. 95-139; *Nationalism: A Report by a Study Group of Members of the Royal Institute of International Affairs,* 2nd ed. (New York, 1966), pp. 3-9; Dankwart A. Rustow, *A World of Nations: Problems of Political Modernization* (Washington, D.C., 1967), pp. 20-31; Louis L. Snyder, *The New Nationalism* (Ithaca, N.Y., 1968), pp. 57-59.

6. Elie Kedourie, *Nationalism* (London, 1971), p. 9; Smith, *Theories,* p. 171; Hayes, *Essays,* p. 23; Snyder, *The Meaning of Nationalism,* p. 148.

7. This assumption has been accepted implicitly or explicitly by most theorists: Deutsch, *Nationalism*; Shafer, *Faces,* p. 13; Kohn, *Idea of Nationalism,* pp. 6ff.; Carlton J. H. Hayes, *Nationalism: A Religion* (New York, 1960), pp. 9-10; Kedourie, *Nationalism,* pp. 81-85.

8. Emerson, *From Empire to Nation,* pp. 114-131; Kohn, *Idea of Nationalism,* pp. 329 ff.; Otto Pflanze, "Characteristics of Nationalism in Europe, 1848-1871," *Review of Politics,* vol. 28, no. 2 (Notre Dame, Ind., 1966), pp. 139-143.

9. Hugh Seton-Watson, *Nationalism and Communism* (New York, 1964), pp. 12-13; R. Auty, "The Linguistic Revival Among Slavs of the Austrian Empire, 1780-1850: The Role of Individuals in the Codification and Acceptance of New Literary Languages," *The Modern Language Review,* vol. 53, no. 3 (London, 1958), pp. 392-404. For a sociological definition of the nationalist intelligentsia, see Smith, *Theories,* pp. 133-138.

1. The Geographic, Ethnographic, and Socioeconomic Setting

1. *Annuaire statistique hongrois,* n.s., vol. 19 (Budapest, 1913), pp. 13-14. The other six countries in the northeast having a Rusyn population were: Abaúj, Borsod, Gömör, Szabolcs, Szatmár, and Torna. According to the 1910 census, there were also 10,400 Rusyns living in Bács-Bodrog county (an area known as the Bačka, now the Vojvodina of Yugoslavia) and 7,950 living in Szerém, Pozsega, and Verőcze counties (which formed Slavonia and the Srem, now in the Croatian Republic of Yugoslavia), but these groups will not be considered in this study nor included in the statistics on Rusyns in the former Hungarian Kingdom. *Magyar statisztikai közlemények,* n.s., vol. 42, pp. 35-36.

2. V. Kubiiovych, "Liudnist'," in *Karpats'ka Ukraïna* (L'viv, 1939), pp. 41-45. Cf. Jiří Král, *Podkarpatská Rus* (Prague, 1924), pp. 51-54.

3. Král, *Podkarpatská Rus,* pp. 7-33; Karel Matoušek, *Podkarpatská Rus* (Prague, 1924), pp. 7-45; V. A. Anuchin, *Geografiia sovetskogo Zakarpat'ia* (Moscow, 1956), pp. 9 ff; Sándor Bonkáló, *A kárpátalji rutén irodalom és művelődés* (Pécs, 1935), pp. 7-8.

4. *Zprávy státního úřadu statistického republiky československé,* vol. 14 (Prague, 1933), no. 170; L. Tkachenko, "Dynamika etnichnoho skladu naselennia Zakarpattia," *Narodna tvorchist' ta etnohrafiia,* vol. 50, no. 1 (Kiev, 1974), p. 65.

5. Z. Kuzèla, "Tribal Division and Ethnographic Groups," in *Ukraine: A Concise Encyclopaedia,* vol. 1 (Toronto, 1963), pp. 282-284.

6. On problems of nomenclature, see Appendix 1.

7. For the different ethnic classifications of Subcarpathian Rusyns, see Iakov F. Golovatskii [Holovats'kyi], *Narodnyia piesni Galitskoi i Ugorskoi Rusi,* vol. 3, pt. 2 (Moscow, 1878), pp. 671-744; G. A. De-Vollan, *Ugro-russkiia narodnyia piesni,* Zapiski Imp. Russkago geograficheskago obshchestva po otdieleniiu ètnografii, vol. 13, pt. 1 (St. Petersburg, 1885), pp. 7-26; Aleksei L. Petrov, "Zamietki po Ugorskoi Rusi," *Zhurnal MNP,* vol. 179, no. 2 (St. Petersburg, 1892), pp. 450-453; Antal Hodinka, "Die Ruthenen," in *Die österreichisch-ungarische Monarchie in Wort und Bild: Ungarn,* vol. 5, pt. 2 (Vienna, 1900), pp. 406-416; Dmytro Doroshenko, *Uhors'ka Ukraïna* (Prague, 1919), pp. 4-5; Václav Drahný and František Drahný, *Podkarpatská Rus, její přírodní a zemědělské poměry* (Prague, 1921), pp. 24-32; Král, *Podkarpatská Rus,* pp. 61-62; Adam Fischer, *Rusini, zarys etnografji Rusi* (L'viv, 1928), pp. 7-9; Theodora Beregiensis [Hiiador Stryps'kyi], "Iak narod dîlyt' sebe," *Lyteraturna nedîlia,* vol. 2 (Uzhhorod, 1942), pp. 185-189.

8. Jan Húsek, *Národopisná hranice mezi Slováky a Karpatorusy* (Bratislava, 1925), pp. 220-342. Studies of cultural interaction in the area have been limited primarily to language. Cf. Ivan Pan'kevych, *Ukraïns'ki hovory Pidkarpats'koï Rusy i sumezhnykh oblastei* (Prague, 1938), pp. 14-31; I. O. Dzendzelivs'kyi, *Ukraïns'ko-zakhidnoslov'ians'ki leksychni paraleli* (Kiev, 1969); P. M. Lyzanets', *Magyar-ukrán nyelvi kapcsolatok* (Uzhhorod, 1970), and his three articles in *Slov'ians'ko-uhors'ki mizhmovni ta literaturni zv'iazky* (Uzhhorod, 1970), pp. 99-112, 120-131, 134-143.

9. *Statistická přiručka republiky československé,* vol. 2, pt. 2 (Prague, 1925), p. 58.

10. See Table 3. The figures for 1956 do not refer to Subcarpathian Rusyns per se, but rather to the population of the Transcarpathian Oblast'. Occupational breakdown according to the nationality of the inhabitants is not available in statistics published since 1945. The 9 percent figure includes not only workers engaged in industry and mining but also in the building trades and supporting rail and road transportation services. Anuchin, *Geografiia,* p. 136; *Narodne hospodarstvo Zakarpats'-koi oblasti: statystychnyi zbirnyk* (Uzhhorod, 1957), p. 122.

11. Unlike other areas of eastern Europe, however, in Subcarpathian Rus' trade was not the exclusive domain of Jews. According to the 1930 census, there were 91,255 Jews in Subcarpathian Rus'. Of these, 39.1 percent were engaged in commerce and credit; 24.3 percent in mining and industry; 21.4 percent in agriculture; 9.3 percent retired, private wealth, or unknown; and 5 percent civil and other public services. *Československá statistika,* vol. 116 (Prague, 1935), pp. 60-63.

12. In 1959, 29,599 persons, or 3 percent of the population of the Transcarpathian Oblast', were listed as Russian. Tkachenko, "Dynamika," p. 65.

13. *Magyar statisztikai közlemények,* n.s., vol. 64, pt. 2 (Budapest, 1920), p. 178.

14. *Annuaire statistique de la république tchécoslovaque* (Prague, 1937), p. 12.

15. See pp. 230 and 256-259.

16. P. Bogatyrev, "Ulohy etnografa na Podkarpatské Rusi a na východním Slovensku," in Jaroslav Zatloukal, ed., *Podkarpatská Rus* (Bratislava, 1936), pp. 293-294.

2. Cultural Activity Prior to 1848

1. Henryk Paszkiewicz, *The Making of the Russian Nation* (London, 1963), p. 308.

2. On the early developments of the Subcarpathian church, see E. Perfeckij, "Východní církev Podkarpatské Rusi v nejstarší době," in *Podkarpatská Rus* (Prague, 1923), pp. 94-98; and Ignác Rath, *Naboženské dějiny Podkarpatské Rusi do r. 1498* (Prague, 1933), pp. 9-17.

3. There is a substantial literature on the events resulting in the Union of Uzhhorod. For a useful discussion, see Michael Lacko, *The Union of Užhorod* (Cleveland and Rome, 1966); and Atanasii V. Pekar, *Narysy istorii tserkvy Zakarpattia* (Rome, 1967), pp. 22-32. The new church was originally known as Uniate, a name that is still used in Subcarpathian lands today. However, the local clergy protested that this designation was derogatory, so that in 1771 Empress Maria Theresa declared "Greek Catholic" to be the official name of the church.

4. The last Orthodox bishop of Máramaros, Iosyf Stoika (d. 1711) reached an agreement with the Transylvanian Protestants in 1694. This had little effect, since within a few decades most Rusyn villages became Greek Catholic. On the effect of Protestantism in the region, see A. L. Petrov, *Otzvuk reformatsii v russkom Zakarpat'e XVI v.* (Prague, 1923) and Vasylii Hadzhega, "Vplyv reformatsii na podkarpatskykh rusynov," *Zoria-Hajnal,* vol. 3, no. 1-4 (Uzhhorod, 1943), pp. 5-48.

5. The extremely complex developments regarding the role of Transylvania are described in detail by Oleksander Baran, "Tserkva na Zakarpatti v rr. 1665-1691," *Bohosloviia,* vol. 32 (Rome, 1968), pp. 77-145. Cf. Lacko, *Union,* pp. 147-155.

6. The decree is reprinted in Antal Hodinka, ed., *A munkácsi görög szertartású püspökség okmánytára* (Uzhhorod, 1911), doc. 268.

7. This fund was called the Jány-Leopoldian Foundation after Bishop F. Jány of Szerém and Emperor Leopold I, both of whom donated the money. The actual

instigator for the fund was the Hungarian counterreformation leader Cardinal Kollonits, who did much to strengthen the fledgling Greek Orthodox Church. See Vasilij Shereghy and Vasilij Pekar, *The Training of the Carpatho-Ruthenian Clergy* (Pittsburgh, 1951), pp. 81-86; and Beloň Rusínsky [Hiiador Stryp'skyi], "Trnavská univerzita v službe unionistickej idey," *Pamiatke Trnavskej univerzity* (Trnava, 1936), pp. 253-254.

8. From the introduction cited in Ievhenii Perfets'kyi, "Drukarni ta starodruky Pidkarpats'koï Rusy-Ukraïny," *Bibliolohichni visty*, no. 4 (Kiev, 1926), p. 29. Unless otherwise indicated, this and all other translations have been made by the author. These first printed books are briefly described in *ibid.*, pp. 26-34; in Hiiador Stryps'kyi, "Z starshoï pys'mennosty Uhors'koï Rusy," *Zapysky NTSh*, vol. 117-118 (L'viv, 1913), 179-195; and in Rusínský, "Trnavská univerzita," pp. 243-257. For a detailed analysis of the de Camillis *Catechism*, see Paul R. Magocsi and Bohdan Strumins'kyj, "The First Carpatho-Ruthenian Printed Book," *Harvard Library Bulletin*, vol. 25, no. 3 (Cambridge, Mass., 1977), pp. 292-309. A photofacsimile of the *Bukvar* was recently reprinted in Mykhailo Mol'nar, *Slovaky i ukraïntsi* (Bratislava and Prešov, 1965), pp. 119-158.

9. The details of the struggle against Eger are found in Koloman Žatkovič, *Jagerskoje vl'ijanije: bor'ba protiv toho v istorii Mukačevskoj grečeskoho obrjada diocezii* (Homestead, Pa., 193?). Cf. Pekar, *Narysy*, pp. 32-62; Basil Boysak, *The Fate of the Holy Union in Carpatho-Ukraine* (Toronto and New York, 1963), pp. 55-86.

10. L'udovít Haraksim, *K sociálnym a kultúrnym dejinám Ukrajincov na Slovensku do roku 1867* (Bratislava, 1961), pp. 88-89.

11. Vasylii Hadzhega, "Persha sproba istoriï hreko-katolycheskoï mukachevskoï eparkhiï," *Naukovyi zbornyk TP*, vol. 3 (Uzhhorod, 1924), pp. 1-27; Haraksim, *K sociálnym a kultúrnym dejinám*, p. 89.

12. On Bazilovych's career, see Evgenii Nedziel'skii, *Ocherk karpato-russkoi literatury* (Uzhhorod, 1932), pp. 90-91; on his historical writings, see Koloman Zsatkovics, "Magyaroroszok történetírásanak története," *Századok*, vol. 24 (Budapest, 1890), p. 645 and Evgenii Perfetskii, "Obzor ugrorusskoi istoriografii," *Izviestiia ORISIAN*, vol. 19, no. 1 (St. Petersburg, 1914), pp. 297-300.

13. The Koriatovych document was first labeled a forgery by the Transylvanian bishop Ignatius Batthyanyi, in his *Leges ecclesiasticae Regni Hungariae*, I (Alla Karolina, 1785). Bazilovych's influence was persuasive, however, and even the paleographic and historical arguments set forth by Aleksei L. Petrov and Ivan I. Kholodniak in the twentieth century failed to convince patriotic Subcarpathian writers that the document was a forgery. "O podlozhnosti gramoty kniazia Feodora Koriatovicha 1360 g.," 2nd rev. ed., in A. L. Petrov, *Drevnieishiia gramoty po istorii karpato-russkoi tserkvi i ierarkhii 1391-1498 g.* (Prague, 1930), pp. 179-215. Cf. Perfetskii, "Obzor," pp. 297-301, and Chapter 5 of this book.

14. Perfetskii, "Obzor," p. 296; Oleksa V. Myshanych, *Literatura Zakarpattia XVII-XVIII stolit': istoryko-literaturnyi narys* (Kiev, 1964), pp. 80-82.

15. Boysak, *The Fate of the Holy Union*, pp. 90-93.

16. The Russian "colony" consisted of an Orthodox priest and a few army officers sent in 1764 to supervise the Tokaj vineyards owned by the tsarist court. The Hapsburg authorities viewed the colony as a "Russian agency" of Catherine II, one which planned to foment among the local Greek Catholic populace a movement to return to the Orthodox "schism." Actually, the initiative in this case came less from St. Petersburg than from the local Orthodox priest, who incited the Serbian population living nearby to request an Orthodox priest from the diocese of Karlovac. Hermann I. Bidermann, *Russische Umtriebe in Ungarn* (Innsbruck, 1867), pp. 14-15;

Oleksander Baran, *Iepyskop Andrei Bachyns'kyi i tserkovne vidrodzhennia na Za-karpatti* (Yorkton, Saskatchewan, 1963), pp. 8-9; Aleksei L. Petrov, "K istorii 'rus-kikh intrig' v Ugrii v XVIII viekie," in *Karpatorusskii sbornik* (Uzhhorod, 1930), pp. 123-127. On earlier Russian "intrigues" in the area since the Rákóczi rebellion at the beginning of the eighteenth century, see Bidermann, *Russische Umtriebe,* pp. 1-14, and A.V. Florovsky, "Russo-Austrian Conflicts in the Early 18th Century," *The Slavonic and East European Review,* vol. 47 (London, 1969), pp. 94-114.

17. Pekar, *Narysy,* pp. 58-71; Eduard Winter, "Die Kämpfe der Ukrainer Ober-ungarn um eine nationale Hierarchie im Theresianischen Zeitalter," *Kyrios,* vol. 11 (Königsberg, 1939-40), pp. 129-141.

18. It is interesting to note that Porač was one of the few Rusyn villages that accepted Protestantism, and the establishment of a school was a direct result of the ideals of the new religion. Vasylii Hadzhega, "O pervŷkh pochatkakh narodn'oho shkôl'nytstva na Pôdkarpatskôi Rusy," *Podkarpatska Rus',* vol. 4, no. 2 (Uzh-horod, 1927), pp. 29-31; Andrii Chuma and Andrii Bondar, *Ukraïns'ka shkola na Zakarpatti ta skhidnii Slovachchyni (istorychnyi narys),* pt. 1 (Prešov, 1967), pp. 8-9; Myshanych, *Literatura Zakarpattia,* pp. 12-13.

19. Myshanych, *Literatura Zakarpattia,* pp. 14-15; Chuma and Bondar, *Ukra-ïns'ka shkola,* pp. 15-16; Shereghy and Pekar, *Training,* pp. 30-34.

20. Pastoral letter published in Vasylii Hadzhega, "Pastŷrskyi lyst Ioanna Brad-acha o nauchovaniu dîtei yz roka 1762," *Podkarpatska Rus',* vol. 4, no. 6 (Uzh-horod, 1927), pp. 136-139.

21. Chuma and Bondar, *Ukraïns'ka shkola,* pp. 28-31; Myshanych, *Literatura Zakarpattia,* pp. 18-19; Julius Kornis, *Education in Hungary* (New York, 1932), pp. 8-16.

22. Shereghy and Pekar, *Training,* pp. 35-44; Chuma and Bodnar, *Ukraïns'ka shkola,* pp. 31-39; Hadzhega, "O pervŷkh pochatkakh," vol. 4, nos. 4 and 5, pp. 82-86 and 110-114.

23. Introduction cited in Myshanych, *Literatura Zakarpattia,* p. 67, and Vasyl' Mykytas' and Olena Rudlovchak, eds., *Poety Zakarpattia: antolohiia zakarpatou-kraïns'koï poeziï (XVI st.-1945 r.)* (Bratislava and Prešov, 1965), p. 126. For an analysis of Kotsak's language, see Ivan Pan'kevych, "Slavenorus'ka hramatyka Arseniia Kotsaka druhoî polovynŷ XVIII vîka," *Naukovŷi zbornyk TP,* vol. 5 (Uzhhorod, 1927), pp. 232-259. On his career, see H. Kynakh, "Arsenii Kotsak," *Zapysky Chyna sv. Vasyliia Velykoho,* vol. 2, nos. 3-4 (Zhovkva, 1927), pp. 336-353; Nedziel'skii, *Ocherk,* pp. 78-80; on his many manuscripts, see Vasyl' L. Mykytas', *Davni rukopysy i starodruky: opys i kataloh,* pt. 2 (L'viv, 1964), pp. 13-16, 36-45.

24. In 1851, the Subcarpathian church historian Andrei Baludians'kyi (d. 1853) advanced the supposition that printing facilities existed during the mid-seventeenth century at the Hrusheve Monastery in Máramaros county. This theory was accepted and developed further by Subcarpathian and other writers (Cf. Magocsi and Stru-mins'kyj, "The First Printed Book," p. 299), but was proved to have no basis in fact by Hiador Sztripszky, "Volt-e könyvsajtó a máramarosi Körtvélyesen?," *Zoria-Hajnal,* vol. 2, nos. 1-2 (Uzhhorod, 1942), pp. 5-34.

25. Nevertheless, book imports from the East continued. For an estimate of the number, see Myshanych, *Literatura Zakarpattia,* pp. 30-38. On the Rumanian-Ser-bian connection, see Petrov, "K istorii 'russkikh intrig'," pp. 123-133.

26. From the decree of the Viennese Hofkammer, cited in Ambrozii Andro-khovych, " 'Illiriis'ka' drukarnia i knyharnia Osypa Kurtsbeka 1770-1792 r. ta ïï zviazky z uhors'koiu i halyts'koiu zemleiu," *Zapysky NTSh,* vol. 150 (L'viv, 1929), p. 111.

27. These appeared in 1770. Of the two titles written by Bishop Bradach, all

copies of his *Bukvar'* (except one) and *Sbornyk* were later destroyed by Roman Catholic prelates who opposed the drive for independence of the Mukachevo diocese and thus labelled the author and his publications "schismatic." Cf. Perfets'kyi, "Drukarni ta starodruky," p. 33; and Iador Stryps'kyi, "Vîden'skyi Bukvar' r. 1770," *Lyteraturna nedîlia,* vol. 3 (Uzhhorod, 1943), pp. 274-276. The third publication was Maria Theresa's land reform, the *Urbarium* of 1766, which was translated into Rusyn (Máramaros dialect as spoken near Rakhiv). This text was republished and analyzed by Aleksei L. Petrov, *Pervyi pechatnyi pamiatnik ugro-russkago nariechiia: Urbar i inye sviazannye s krest'ianskoi Marii Terezy reformoi dokumenty,* in *Sbornik ORISIAN,* vol. 84, no. 2 (St. Petersburg, 1908).

28. Androkhovych, " 'Illiriis'ka' drukarnia," pp. 109-120; Myshanych, *Literatura Zakarpattia,* pp. 131-136. For an idea of the kind of "imported" publications from this time that are still held in Subcarpathian libraries, see the three descriptive catalogues by Vasyl' L. Mykytas' listed in the Bibliography (refs. 0045, 0046).

29. Eduard Winter, *Byzanz und Rom im Kampf um die Ukraine 955-1939* (Leipzig, 1942), pp. 129-137. Winter concluded that: "In contrast to Poland, the Austrian government from the very beginning saw in the equality of the Uniate Church the best defense against the East.... To maintain the vitality of the Uniate Churches was the unwritten basic law of the Austrian government." Ibid., p. 137.

30. Hermann Zschokke, *Die theologischen Studien und Anstalten der katholischen in Österreich* (Vienna and Liepzig, 1894), pp. 546-550; Shereghy and Pekar, *Training,* pp. 49-52; Willibald M. Plöchl, *St. Barbara zu Wien,* vol. 1 (Vienna, 1975), pp. 40-49.

31. Jan Máchal, "Podkarpatští Rusové a slovanské obrození," in Miloš Weingart, ed., *Slovanský sborník věnovaný . . . prof. Františku Pastrnkovi* (Prague, 1923), p. 211.

32. Zschokke, *Die theologischen Studien,* pp. 982-984; Winter, *Byzanz und Rom,* pp. 123-125; Ambrozii Androkhovych, "L'vivs'ka 'Studium Ruthenum'," *Zapysky NTSh,* vol. 131 (L'viv, 1921), pp. 123-195; vol. 132 (1922), pp. 185-217; vols. 136-137 (1925), pp. 43-105.

33. Baran, *Iepyskop Andrei Bachyns'kyi,* pp. 42-47; Pekar, *Narysy,* p. 96.

34. Despite efforts at cooperation between Rusyns north and south of the Carpathians, certain provincial attitudes and petty jealousies kept them estranged from each other. As an omen for the future, it was characteristic of these relations that the Subcarpathian Shchavnyts'kyi was removed in 1787 from his post as rector of the *Studium Ruthenum* in L'viv because (1) "he did not know fluently Polish and the [Galician] Rusyn language"; (2) he did not belong to the local eparchy; and (3) because as a foreigner (!) he did not know the customs of the local people. He subsequently returned to his homeland to become vice-director of the theological seminary in Uzhhorod. Androkhovych, "L'vivs'ke 'Studium Ruthenum'," *Zapysky NTSh,* vol. 131 (1927), pp. 41-46.

35. Baran, *Iepyskop Andrei Bachyns'kyi,* pp. 27-35.

36. Cited in ibid., pp. 55-56 and in Evmenii Sabov, *Khristomatiia tserkovnoslavianskikh ugro-russkikh literaturnykh pamiatnikov* (Uzhhorod, 1893), p. 57.

37. From a pastoral letter dated January 1, 1806, cited in František Tichý, *Vývoj současného spisovného jazyka na Podkarpatské Rusi* (Prague, 1938), p. 154 and in Baran, *Iepyskop Andrei Bachyns'kyi,* pp. 56-57. For an example of Bachyns'kyi's Slaveno-Rusyn, see Appendix 3, pt. 1. For further insight into his cultural activity, see eleven of his pastoral letters (dated 1797 to 1806) published by Andrii Shlepets'kyi, "Mukachivs'kyi iepyskop Andrii Fedorovych Bachyns'kyi ta ioho poslannia," *Naukovyi zbirnyk MUKS,* vol. 3 (Bratislava and Prešov, 1967), pp. 226-241.

38. Baran, *Iepyskop Andrei Bachyns'kyi,* pp. 54-55. An extensive excerpt from

Bachyns'kyi's translation is found in Sabov, *Khristomatiia,* pp. 17-48. For Bachyns'kyi's comments on problems of publication, see K. Kustodiev, "Tserkov' ugorskikh russkikh i serbov v ikh vzaimootnoshenii," *Pravoslavnoe obozrienie,* no. 6 (Moscow, 1873), pp. 1017-1021.

39. Androkhovych, "L'vivs'ke 'Studium Ruthenum'," *Zapysky NTSh,* vol. 131 (1927), pp. 41-46, 86-92; Chuma and Bondar, *Ukraïns'ka shkola,* pp. 41-43; Myshanych, *Literatura Zakarpattia,* pp. 16-17; Volodymyr Birchak, *Literaturni stremlinnia Pidkarpats'koï Rusy,* 2nd ed. (Uzhhorod, 1937), pp. 61-62.

40. Anton V. Florovskii, "Karpatoross I. Zeikan—nastavnik imperatora Petra II-go," in *Karpatorusskii sbornik,* pp. 112-122, and "I. A. Zeikan—pedagog iz Zakarpat'ia: stranitsa iz istorii russko-zakarpatskikh kul'turnykh sviazei pri Petre Velikom," in *Russkaia literatura XVIII veka i slavianskie literatury* (Moscow, 1963), pp. 105-122. See also Ia. I. Shternberh, "Novi materialy pro Ivana Zeikania," *Tezy dopovidei ta povidomlennia,* Seriia istorychna, vol. 3 (Uzhhorod, 1959), pp. 49-54.

41. Tamara Baitsura, *Zakarpatoukrainskaia intelligentsiia v Rossii v pervoi polovine XIX veka* (Bratislava and Prešov, 1971), pp. 20-22.

42. Ilarion S. Svientsitskii, "Obzor snoshenii Karpatskoi Rusi s Rossiei v l-uiu pol. XIX v.," *Izviestiia ORISIAN,* vol. 11, no. 3 (St. Petersburg, 1906), pp. 286-288.

43. Cited in ibid., p. 289.

44. Baitsura, *Zakarpatoukrainskaia intelligentsiia,* pp. 150-166; Nedziel'skii, *Ocherk,* pp. 110-113.

45. "Memorandum of the Court Surgeon Orlai on several Carpatho-Russian professors," reprinted in Baitsura, *Zakarpatoukrainskaia intelligentsiia,* pp. 26-28.

46. Ibid., pp. 55-101; Nedziel'skii, *Ocherk,* pp. 113-117; Chuma and Bondar, *Ukraïns'ka shkola,* pp. 44-48; A.N. Fatieev, *Akademicheskaia i gosudarstvennaia dieiatel'nost' M.I. Baludianskago v Rossii,* Izd. OIAD, no. 76 (Uzhhorod, 1931).

47. Nedziel'skii, *Ocherk,* pp. 118-123; Baitsura, *Zakarpatoukrainskaia intelligentsiia,* pp. 166-184. See also Tamara Baitsura, *Iurii Ivanovych Venelin* (Bratislava and Prešov, 1968).

48. Orlai's *Istoriia o Karpato-Rossakh, ili o pereselenii Rossiian v Karpatskiia gory i o prikliucheniiakh s nimi sluchivshikhsia* was first published in *Sievernyi viestnik,* pts. 1 and 3 (St. Petersburg, 1804), and later reprinted in full by Ilarion S. Svientsitskii, *Materialy po istorii vozrozhdeniia Karpatskoi Rusi,* vol. 1 (L'viv, 1905), pp. 56-83.

49. Letter of Orlai to the St. Petersburg's Society for Russian History and Antiquities, read in 1824 and published in their *Trudy i zapiski,* vol. 1 (1826), pp. 220-228. Quotation cited from Svientsitskii, *Materialy,* vol. 1, p. 46.

50. Svientsitskii, "Obzor snoshenii," p. 297.

51. See the articles of Venelin reprinted in Svientsitskii, *Materialy,* vol. 1, pp. 86-120.

52. Svientsitskii, "Obzor snoshenii," pp. 303-329. For the correspondence of Keppen, Pogodin, and Sreznevs'kyi with Galician-Rusyn and other Slavic leaders, see Svientsitskii, *Materialy,* vol. 1, pp. 121-194. Cf. Vladimir Frantsev, "Obzor vazhnieishikh izuchenii Ugorskoi Rusi," *Russkii filologicheskii viestnik,* vol. 45 (Warsaw, 1901), pp. 154-156; Ivan Žeguc, *Die nationalpolitischen Bestrebungen der Karpato-Ruthenen 1848-1914* (Wiesbaden, 1965), pp. 35-38. See also Chapter 5.

53. M.P. Pogodin, "Letter to the Ministry of Culture upon return from a trip to Europe in 1839," in his *Istoriko-politicheskiia pis'ma i zapiski vprodolzhenii Krymskoi voiny* (Moscow, 1874), pp. 27-28.

54. Michael Boro Petrovich, *The Emergence of Russian Panslavism, 1856-1870* (New York, 1956), pp. 25-61. The Russian government also fostered several plans at

this time to expand into "Carpatho-Russia." Svientsitskii, "Obzor snoshenii," pp. 279-281; N. A. Beskid, *Karpato-russkaja pravda* (Homestead, Pa., 1933), pp. 6-7; Haraksim, *K sociálnym a kultúrnym dejinám,* pp. 103-104.

55. Bidermann, *Russische Umtriebe,* pp. 16-17, 54-55; Svientsitskii, "Obzor snoshenii," pp. 271-273.

56. Several authors—Ivan Franko, *Zhytie i slovo,* vol. 3 (L'viv, 1895), pp. 461-465; Nedziel'skii, *Ocherk,* p. 89; Myshanych, *Literatura Zakarpattia,* p. 72; Vasyl' Mykytas', *Haluzka mohutn'oho dereva: literaturnyi narys* (Uzhhorod, 1971), p. 25 —consider the allusion to the Nymph of the Neva to be Tsarina Catherine II, but Svientsitskii, *Materialy,* vol. 2 (L'viv, 1909), p. 8, n. 1, and Tichý, *Vývoj,* p. 29, have argued that this reference is to the Palatine Joseph's Russian wife, Princess Aleksandra Pavlovna, whose death in 1801 provoked expressions of grief among all the Slavic peoples of Hungary. It is interesting to note that Sumarokov claimed his knowledge of Russian was due to the efforts of his father and the latter's teacher, a native of Subcarpathian Rus', Ivan A. Zeikan. See Vasyl' L. Mykytas', *Davnia literatura Zakarpattia* (L'viv, 1968), p. 129.

57. Cited from the complete ode, "Tezoymenytstvu Eho Tsarskaho Vŷsochestva, Presvîtlîishaho Hospodaria Iosyfa . . ." reprinted in Tichý, *Vývoj,* pp. 157-159; and in Mykytas' and Rudlovchak, *Poety Zakarpattia,* pp. 134-136. See also Appendix 3, pt. 1.

58. N. M. Karamzin, *Istoriia gosudarstva Rossiiskago,* 4th ed., vol. 1 (St. Petersburg, 1892) pt. 2, p. 79, n. 302. In this extensive footnote, Karamzin comments on the unfortunate plight of the "Russians [*Rossiiane*] living in . . . Hungary," and then cites Orlai's work, but he does not mention Tarkovych as author of the ode.

59. Actually Buda. Budapest did not come into existence until 1872, when Obuda, Buda, and Pest were united. To simplify matters, Budapest will appear in the text even when referring to events before 1872.

60. On Tarkovych's life see Athanasius B. Pekar, *Historic Background of the Eparchy of Prjashev* (Pittsburgh, 1968), pp. 11-14.

61. "Triumf Nykolaia Pavlovycha samoderzh . . ." and "Oda na vzatie Varnŷ . . ." are reprinted in Oleksandr Dukhnovych, *Tvory,* vol. 1 (Bratislava and Prešov, 1968), pp. 171-176.

62. Cited in Mykytas', *Haluzka,* p. 174. For further discussion of this work, see ibid., pp. 172-176.

63. It was through Matezonskii that Dukhnovych received first-hand knowledge of Russia. Olena Rudlovchak, "Oleksandr Dukhnovych: zhyttia i diial'nist'," in Dukhnovych, *Tvory,* vol. 1, p. 60. On Matezonskii, see Vasylii Hadzhega, "Konstantyn Matezonskyi, pershyi khordyrygent hr.-kat. tserkvy v Uzhhorodî," *Podkarpatska Rus',* vol. 6, nos. 1 and 2 (Uzhhorod, 1929), pp. 1-7, 29-36; and Volodymyr Hoshovs'kyi, "Pochatky khorovoho spivu na Zakarpatti," *Naukovyi zbirnyk MUKS,* vol. 6, pt. 1 (Bratislava and Prešov, 1972), pp. 97-104.

64. The article that provoked the polemic was entitled "Russniaken in der Marmarosch," *Vaterländische Blätter,* no. 45 (Vienna, 1812). It was cryptically signed E. R.

65. The Dobrovský and Kopitar-Hromadko responses appeared respectively in *Slovanka* (Prague, 1814), pp. 104-110, and in the *Wiener allgemeine Literaturzeitung,* vols. 2 and 3 (Vienna, 1814-15). The whole problem is discussed by František Tichý, "Josef Dobrovský a Podkarpatská Rus," in *Josef Dobrovský: sborník statí k stému výročí smrti* (Prague, 1929), pp. 332-343, and A. Rot, "Pro kul'turni zv'-iazky chekhiv i slovakiv iz zakarpats'kymy ukraïntsiamy," in *Z istoriï chekhoslovats'ko-ukraïns'kykh zv'iazkiv* (Bratislava, 1959), pp. 320-324. For the attitude of

other Czech national leaders toward the Rusyn problems, especially in Galicia, see Florian Zapletal, *Rusíni a naši buditelé* (Prague, 1921), pp. 3-23.

66. A. Kucharský, letter dated March 19, 1828, *Časopis společnosti wlastenského Musea,* vol. 2, pt. 2 (Prague, 1828), pp. 127-131. See also Frantsev, "Obzor," p. 157, and Helena Rudlovčaková, "K otázkam vzájomnych kultúrnych stykov Slovákov a zakarpatských Ukrajincov v polovici minulého storočia," *Sbornik Ševčenkovský FFUPJŠ,* vol. 5 (Bratislava, 1965), pp. 149-150.

67. Information on I. Venelin and M. Luchkai, and a folk song in Rusyn, (*narechiem rusniachkim*) are found respectively in the *Letopis Matice Serbske,* pt. 21 (Buda, 1830), pp. 124-125; pt. 30 (1832), pp. 148-152; and pt. 48 (1839), pp. 86-88. For Rusyn-Serbian contacts in the earlier part of the century, see Kustodiev, "Tserkov' ugorskikh russkikh i serbov," pp. 1012-1034.

68. See the Bibliography (ref. 0647).

69. A detailed biography and bibliography of Holovats'kyi's works are given by Fedor F. Aristov, *Karpato-russkie pisateli: izsliedovanie po neizdannym istochnikam,* vol. 1 (Moscow, 1916), pp. 76-128. Cf. Rudlovčaková, "K otázkam vzájomnych kultúrnych stykov," pp. 150-152, and her "Na podorozhakh z Ia. Holovats'kym," *Duklia,* vol. 12, no. 4 (Prešov, 1964), pp. 79-83.

70. A. L. Petrov, "M. Bél: 'Tractatus de re rustica Hungarorum' a 'Notitia Hungariae novae'," *Věstník Kralovské české společnosti nauk,* vol. 40 (Prague, 1925), and his *K. Fejérvary, 'De moribus et ritibus Ruthenorum' i analogichnyia sviedieniia M. Belia i A. Sirmai,* Biblioteka Zapysok Chynu Sv. Vasyliia Velykoho, no. 6 (Zhovkva, 1929); Perfetskii, "Obzor," pp. 301-304; Mol'nar, *Slovaky,* pp. 20-25, and his "Štúrovci a Zakarpatská Ukrajina," in *L'udovit Štúr, život a dielo, 1815-1856* (Bratislava, 1956), p. 490; Aleksei L. Petrov, *Prediely ugrorusskoi riechi v 1773 g. po offitsial'nym dannym* (St. Petersburg, 1911), pp. 29-32; Perfetskii, "Obzor," pp. 301-304.

71. *Geschichte der slawischen Sprache und Literatur nach allen Mundarten,* 2nd ed. (Prague, 1869), pp. 141-142, n. 2.

72. P.J. Šafařik, "O zemi gmenowané Bojky," *Časopis Českého Museum,* vol. 11, no. 1 (Prague, 1837), pp. 23-36.

73. Šafařik, *Geschichte,* p. 141. On his writings about Rusyns, see Rot, "Pro kul'turni zv'iazky," pp. 324-325; and Mol'nar, *Slovaky,* pp. 27-33.

74. Nosák's "Listy z neznámej zeme k L." and other writings on Subcarpathian Rusyns are reprinted in Mol'nar, *Slovaky,* pp. 159-219. For a discussion of their importance, see ibid., pp. 44-58; František Tichý, "Bohuš Nosák a Podkarpatské Rusíni," *Sborník Matice Slovenskej,* vol. 5, nos. 1 and 2 (Turčiansky Sv. Martin, 1927), pp. 1-11; and Rudlovčaková, "K otázkam vzájomnych kultúrnych stykov," pp. 152-165.

75. *Slovenskje národňje novini,* March 6, 1846, reprinted in Mol'nar, *Slovaky,* pp. 220-223. In this article, Štúr particularly criticized the use of the name Rusnak (*Rusznyak*) and claimed the only valid form was Rusyn (*Rusín*).

76. Rudlovchak, "Oleksandr Dukhnovych," pp. 36, 47-48. A photo-reproduction of the 116-page grammar is found in Dukhnovych, *Tvory,* vol. 2 (1967).

77. Some of Dovhovych's Rusyn poems have been reprinted in Tichý, *Vývoj,* pp. 159-164, and in Mykytas' and Rudlovchak, *Poety Zakarpattia,* pp. 150-158. On his life, see Evgenii Fentsik, "Ocherk ugro-russkoi pis'mennosti," *Listok,* vol. 8 (Uzhhorod, 1892), pp. 76-78; Sabov, *Khristomatiia,* pp. 192-193; Nedziel'skii, *Ocherk,* pp. 92-94; Birchak, *Literaturni stremlinnia,* pp. 73-75; and Mykytas', *Haluzka,* pp. 36-43; on his manuscripts and publications, see Mykytas', *Davni rukopysy,* pt. 2, pp. 16-18, 46-48.

78. Mykytas', *Haluzka,* pp. 27-28. Other little-known authors from this period

who left several unpublished works were: Andrei Val'kovs'kyi, Ivan Ripa (1764-1851), and Mykhail Bystran. See ibid., pp. 19-23, 29-36; and Myshanych, *Literatura Zakarpattia*, pp. 73-77. For texts of some of their works, see Mykytas' and Rudlovchak, *Poety Zakarpattia*, pp. 137-149.

79. On his life and work, see Nedziel'skii, *Ocherk*, pp. 101-106; Birchak, *Literaturni stremlinnia*, pp. 68-73; Tichý, *Vývoj*, pp. 41-44; Plöchl, *St. Barbara zu Wien*, pp. 174-183; and especially Vasylii Hadzhega, "Ioan Fogarashii," *Podkarpatska Rus'*, vol. 5, no. 10 (Uzhhorod, 1928), pp. 207-224, and Ivan Pan'kevych, "Khto buv Ivan Berezhanyn—Mykhailo Luchkai chy Ivan Fogarashii?," *Naukovŷi zbornyk TP*, vols. 7-8 (Uzhhorod, 1931), pp. 168-188.

80. "'V obshche o razlichii Slavianskikh nariechii, sobstvenno zhe o malo i karpato ili Ugrorusskikh," in Svientsitskii, *Materialy*, vol. 1, p. 48.

81. Ibid., p. 54.

82. The introduction to the grammar is reprinted in Sabov, *Khristomatiia*, pp. 72-73. See also Appendix 3, pt. 1.

83. The most extensive biography of Luchkai is by Vasylii Hadzhega, "Mykhayl Luchkai, zhytiepys y tvorŷ," *Naukovŷi zbornyk TP*, vol. 6 (Uzhhorod, 1929), pp. 1-128. See also František Tichý, "Michail Lučkaj," in Weingart, *Slovanský sborník*, pp. 215-220; Fentsik, "Ocherk," pp. 87-88; Nedziel'skii, *Ocherk*, pp. 97-101; and Birchak, *Literaturni stremlinnia*, pp. 80-85.

84. *Grammatica Slavo-Ruthena: seu Vetero-Slavicae et actu in montibus Carpathicis Parvo-Russicae, seu dialecti vigentis linguae* (Buda, 1830), pp. vi ff.

85. Of several analyses made of Luchkai's grammar, the most extensive are by Vasyl' Simovych and Georgii I. Gerovskii. See the Bibliography (refs. 1388, 2060).

86. Luchkai's *Historia* was to be published in Košice (1842) or Buda (1843) but has remained in manuscript form in the University (formerly Episcopal) Library in Uzhhorod. A brief analysis is given in Mykytas', *Davni rukopysy*, pt. 2, pp. 58-60; Perfetskii, "Obzor," pp. 304-306; and in Svientsitskii, *Materialy*, vol. 2, pp. 110-113. The latter reference also includes textual excerpts from the *Historia*, cf. pp. 113-117.

87. *Slávy dcera*, 4th ed. (Prague, 1868), song 4, sonnet 65, p. 249.

88. Rudlovchak, "Oleksandr Dukhnovych," p. 30. Cf. Iulii Gadzhega, *Istoriia Uzhgorodskoi Bogoslovskoi Seminarii v eia glavnykh chertakh*, Izd. OIAD, no. 35 (Uzhhorod, 1928), p. 31.

89. Nedziel'skii, *Ocherk*, pp. 94-96; Chuma and Bondar, *Ukraïns'ka shkola*, pp. 40-52; Ev. I. Sabov, *Russkii literaturnyi iazyk Podkarpatskoi Rusi*, Izd. OIAD, no. 7 (Mukachevo, 1925), pp. 5-8; and Hadzhega, "Mykhayl Luchkai," p. 94.

90. I. P. Rusak, "Mukachevskaia eparkhiia i eia bor'ba za prava russkago iazyka i narodnosti vo vremia episkopa Vasiliia Popovicha," in *Karpatorusskii sbornik*, pp. 50-68.

91. Daniel Rapant, *Ilegálna mad'arizácia, 1790-1840*, Spisy historického odboru Matice Slovenskej, no. 9 (Turčiansky Sv. Martin, 1947), pp. 3-51; Julius Kornis, *Ungarische Kulturideale 1777-1848* (Leipzig, 1930), pp. 49-209.

92. Haraksim, *K sociálnym a kultúrnym dejinám*, pp. 111-114. On the 1831 rebellion, which was touched off by a severe outbreak of cholera, see Daniel Rapant, *Sedliacké povstanie na východnom Slovensku roku 1831*, vol. 1 (Bratislava, 1953).

93. "Kratkaia biohrafyia Aleksandra Dukhnovycha, kanonyka Priashevskaho, ym samŷm napysannaia," *Duklia*, vol. 11, no. 3 (Prešov, 1963), p. 84. For an analysis of the Hungarian intellectual atmosphere of the time, see Andor Tarnai, *Extra Hungarium non est vita . . .*, Modern Filológiai Füzetek, no. 6 (Budapest, 1966).

94. Hadzhega, "Mykhayl Luchkai," pp. 100-118; Rudlovchak, "Oleksandr Dukhnovych," p. 56.

95. Haraksim, *K sociálnym a kultúrnym dejinám,* p. 102.

96. Indeed, fierce linguistic battles were still being waged among factions within the Slovak, Serbian, and Croatian intelligentsias in the 1840s, but early in the next decade, one literary standard was accepted by each of these peoples. On the other hand, these three groups, and especially the Czechs, already had well-established schools, publications, and cultural societies. R. Auty, "The Linguistic Revival Among Slavs of the Austrian Empire, 1780-1850," *Modern Language Review,* vol. 53, no. 3 (London, 1958), pp. 392-404.

3. From Embryonic Nationalism to National Assimilation

1. For a general survey of the revolutionary events, see C. A. Macartney, *The Hapsburg Empire 1790-1918* (New York, 1969), pp. 322-426.

2. I. N. Mel'nikova, *Zakarpatskaia Ukraina v revoliutsii 1848 goda* (Prešov, 1952), pp. 34-38; I.G. Kolomiets, *Ocherki po istorii Zakarpat'ia,* pt. 2 (Tomsk, 1959), pp. 116-118. See also the memoirs of a contemporary observer, Ivan Sil'vai, "Avtobiografiia" (1898), in his *Izbrannye proizvedeniia* (Bratislava, 1957), pp. 96-101.

3. L'udovit Haraksim, *K sociálnym a kultúrnym dejinám Ukrajincov na Slovensku do roku 1867* (Bratislava, 1961), pp. 121-122.

4. Cited in ibid., p. 123. For V. Dobrianskii's biography, see Ivan Matsyns'kyi, ed., "Slovnyk istorychnoho zhyttia zakarpats'kykh ukraïntsiv," *Duklia,* vol. 15, no. 4 (Prešov, 1967), pp. 76-77.

5. For detailed accounts of the Slovak and Galician participation at the Congress, see Daniel Rapant, *Slovenské povstanie roku 1848-49,* vol. 2, pt. 1 (Turčiansky Svätý Martin, 1950), pp. 1-28; Ivan Bryk, "Slavians'kyi zïzd u Prazi 1848 r. i ukraïns'ka sprava," *Zapysky NTSh,* vol. 129 (L'viv, 1920); Florian Zapletal, *Rusíni a naši buditelé* (Prague, 1921), pp. 23-32; and Martha Bohachevsky-Chomiak, *The Spring of a Nation: The Ukrainians in Eastern Galicia in 1848* (Philadelphia, 1967), pp. 34-41.

6. They were first mentioned at a meeting of the Polish-Galician Rusyn section on June 3, when Karel Zap, the Moravian Czech scholar, stated that the "Rusyns were not fully represented and regrets that there are no delegates from Hungary." From the protocol reprinted in Václav Žáček, ed., *Slovanský sjezd v Praze 1848: sbírka dokumentů* (Prague, 1958), p. 266.

7. Cited from the protocol of the general council of the Congress. Ibid., p. 319.

8. Memorandum reprinted in Rapant, *Slovenské povstanie,* vol. 2, pt. 2, p. 51, and in Mykhailo Mol'nar, *Slovaky i ukraïntsi* (Bratislava and Prešov, 1965), pp. 227-228.

9. Memorandum reprinted in ibid., pp. 229-230, and in Rapant, *Slovenské povstanie,* vol. 2, pt. 2, pp. 158-159. See also the discussion of Ivan Žeguc, *Die nationalpolitischen Bestrebungen der Karpato-Ruthenen 1848-1914* (Wiesbaden, 1965), pp. 19-22, 32-35.

10. On Dobrianskii's career, see F. F. Aristov, *Karpato-russkie pisateli,* vol. 1 (Moscow, 1916), pp. 145-233; Evgenii Nedziel'skii, *Ocherk karpatorusskoi literatury* (Uzhhorod, 1932), pp. 132-145; Stepan Dobosh, *Adol'f Ivanovich Dobrianskii: ocherk zhizni i deiatel'nosti* (Bratislava, 1956); Matsyns'kyi, "Slovnyk," vol. 15, no. 3, pp. 75-79; Kolomiets, *Ocherki,* pp. 140-179, and *Sotsial'no-èkonomicheskie otnosheniia i obshchestvennoe dvizhenie v Zakarpat'e vo vtoroi polovine XIX stoletiia,* vol. 2 (Tomsk, 1962), pp. 428-462. For other specialized studies, see the works of F.F. Aristov, P.S. Fedor, A.V. Popov, S.P. and F. Zapletal in the Bibliography (refs. 0913, 0914, 0945, 1039, 1052, 2256).

11. Mel'nikova, *Zakarpatskaia Ukraina,* pp. 94-95; Haraksim, *K sociálnym a kultúrnym dejinám,* p. 103.

12. "Sostoian'e Rusynôv v Uhorshchynî," *Zoria Halyts'ka,* no. 31 (L'viv, 1849), cited in Iurii Bacha, *Literaturnyi rukh na Zakarpatti seredyny XIX stolittia* (Bratislava and Prešov, 1961), p. 48.

13. The brief arrest of Dukhnovych on April 27, 1849, was not a result of his political goals or his relations with Galicia, but because he published books in Rusyn. That the Hungarian government was not aware of Dukhnovych's contacts with L'viv is evidenced by the fact that after his release he was chosen on May 9 to serve as a member of the county commission for Sáros. Haraksim, *K sociálnym a kultúrnym dejinám,* pp. 134-135; Mikhal Danylak, *Halyts'ki, bukovyns'ki, zakarpats'ki ukraïntsi v revoliutsiï 1848-1849 rokiv* (Bratislava and Prešov, 1972), pp. 174-175.

14. For his services to Russia, Dobrianskii was to be awarded the Order of St. Vladimir from Prince Paskevich, the Order of St. Anne from General Ridiger, and two letters of commendation in 1849, as well as an order from Emperor Franz Joseph to wear these Russian medals together with the inscription: "For the pacification of Hungary and Transylvania." Aristov, *Karpato-russkie pisateli,* pp. 148-149.

15. Sil'vai, "Avtobiografiia," p. 103.

16. Ibid.

17. The quote is taken from the published notes of an officer, M. D. Likhutin, cited in I. O. Panas, "Karpatorusskie otzvuki russkago pokhoda v Vengrii 1849 goda," in *Karpatorusskii sbornik* (Uzhhorod, 1930), p. 224. Panas also discusses the positive attitude and writings of other contemporaries. Cf. Kolomiets, *Ocherki,* pp. 128-137; Mel'nikova, *Zakarpatskaia Ukraina,* pp. 107-128; Žeguc, *Die nationalpolitischen Bestrebungen,* pp. 39-42; and Georgii Vernadskii, "Ugorskaia Rus' i eia vozrozhdenie v seredinie XIX vieka," *Golos minuvshago,* vol. 3, no. 3 (Moscow, 1915), pp. 5-17.

18. Haraksim, *K sociálnym a kultúrnym dejinám,* pp. 138-140.

19. "Kratkaia byohrafyia Aleksandra Dukhnovycha, kanonyka priashevskaho ym samŷm napysannaia," reprinted in *Duklia,* vol. 11, no. 3 (Prešov, 1963), p. 85.

20. Haraksim, *K sociálnym a kultúrnym dejinám,* pp. 153-157; Danylak, *Halyts'ki, bukovyns'ki, zakarpats'ki ukraïntsi,* pp. 180-183; Kolomiets, *Ocherki,* pp. 144-149; Mel'nikova, *Zakarpatskaia Ukraina,* pp. 128-134; Žeguc, *Die nationalpolitischen Bestrebungen,* pp. 43-47; I. Pereni, *Iz istorii zakarpatskikh ukraintsev* (Budapest, 1957), pp. 43-45.

21. The text of the Memorandum of the Hungarian Rusyns (*Pam'iatnyk Rusynôv Uhorskykh*) was first printed (in part) in *Zoria Halyts'ka,* nos. 90 and 91 (L'viv, 1849), pp. 537-538, 540-543, and later in Ilarion S. Svientsitskii, ed., *Materialy po istorii vozrozhdeniia Karpatskoi Rusi,* vol. 2 (L'viv, 1909), pp. 129-148. Recently, the complete text, from the handwritten copy of Aleksander Ianyts'kyi, was published by Mykola Rusynko, "Vyslanstva Rusyniv Uhors'kykh u Vidni 1849 r.," *Naukovyi zbirnyk MUKS,* vol. 6, pt. 1 (Svidník, Bratislava, and Prešov, 1972), pp. 63-86.

22. Among the Rusyn officials were Aleksander Nehrebets'kyi, secretary to the Lord Lieutenant (*főispán*), and Ivan Liakhovych, Iosyf Lelovych, Ivan Vaida, Liudvik Chers'kyi, Iurii Nevyts'kyi, Ivan Pasteli, Rudol'f Dobrians'kyi, Vasylii Il'nyts'kyi, Ivan Gorzo, and Ivan Popovych, all heads of districts. On the various aspects of the Rusyn District, see Kolomiets, *Ocherki,* pp. 145-149; Pereni, *Iz istorii,* pp. 45-47; Dobosh, *A. I. Dobrianskii,* pp. 49-52; Žeguc, *Die nationalpolitischen Bestrebungen,* pp. 47-50; Danylak, *Halyts'ki, bukovyns'ki, zakarpats'ki ukraïntsi,* pp. 183-184; and Haraksim, *K sociálnym a kultúrnym dejinám,* pp. 157-159.

23. Ibid., pp. 167-168.

24. Ibid., pp. 162-163; Kolomiets, *Ocherki,* pp. 119-120; Pereni, *Iz istorii,* pp. 47-48.

25. The best biography is by Olena Rudlovchak, "Oleksandr Dukhnovych: zhyttia i diial'nist'," in Oleksandr Dukhnovych, *Tvory,* vol. 1 (Bratislava-Prešov, 1968), pp. 15-168. Cf. Aristov, *Karpato-russkie pisateli,* pp. 49-61; Kolomiets, *Ocherki,* pp. 179-201, and *Sotsial'no,* vol. 2, pp. 462-476; Bacha, *Literaturnyi rukh,* pp. 130-154. See also the entries under F. F. Aristov, N. A. Beskid, V. Mykytas', A. V. Popov, and M. Rychalka in the Bibliography (refs. 0915, 0916, 1011, 1040, 1051, 1167, 1168).

26. Dukhnovych suffered as a result of personality conflict with his superior, Hryhorii Tarkovych, the first bishop of the Prešov diocese, who served from 1818 to 1841. Cf. Rudlovchak, "O. Dukhnovych," pp. 33ff.

27. His theories are discussed in Chapter 5; his major works are listed in the Bibliography (refs. 1278-1280).

28. Aleksander Dukhnovych, *Narodnaia pedagogiia v pol'zu uchylyshch y uchytelei sel'skykh* (L'viv, 1857), p. 89. Dukhnovych has been hailed as the person who wrote the first study in Ukrainian pedagogy. For analyses of his theoretical and practical pedagogical work, see Mykhailo Rychalka, *O. V. Dukhnovych: pedahoh i osvitnii diiach* (Bratislava, 1959), pp. 103 ff.; and the articles by M. F. Koval', M. I. Rychalka, A. D. Bondar, F. I. Naumenko, A. A. Chuma, and O. P. Mazurkevych, in *Oleksandr Dukhnovych: zbirnyk materialiv naukovoï konferentsiï, prysviachenoï 100-richchiu z dnia smerti* (Prešov, 1965), pp. 213-310.

29. A polemic has arisen around the language of the *Sokrashchennaia grammatika.* Vladimir Terletskii, *Ugors'kaia Rus' i vozrozhdenie soznaniia narodnosti mezhdu russkimi v Vengrii* (Kiev, 1874), p. 27, first pointed out that Dukhnovych's original text in Slaveno-Rusyn was changed without the author's knowledge, and initially, to his dismay, Russianized for publication by a fellow Subcarpathian, Ioann Rakovskii. Actually, the changes were made by Rakovskii and his mentor, Vasilii Voitkovskii, a Russian Orthodox priest living near Budapest. Cf. František Tichý, *Vývoj současneho spisovného jazyka na Podkarpatské Rusi* (Prague, 1938), pp. 67-68; Sandór Bonkáló, *A kárpátalji rutén irodalom és művelődés* (Pécs, 1935), p. 50; Bacha, *Literaturnyi rukh,* pp. 135-136; Dukhnovych, *Tvory,* vol. 2, pp. 615-616. Russophile authors claim that Dukhnovych was pleased with the final text since it coincided with his own desire to write in standard Russian. Nedziel'skii, *Ocherk,* pp. 152-153; N. A. Beskid, *A. V. Dukhnovich i ego poèziia,* Izdanie OIAD, no. 74 (Uzhhorod, 1930), pp. 18-30; A. V. Popov, *A. V. Dukhnovich* (Mukachevo, 1929), pp. 5-12, 22-30. For a linguistic analysis of Dukhnovych's grammars, see M. M. Shtets', "Mova 'Bukvaria' ta inshykh posibnykiv O. V. Dukhnovycha," in *Oleksandr Dukhnovych: zbirnyk,* pp. 189-191.

30. Among the Rusyn members were Adol'f and Viktor Dobrianskii, Antonii Rubii, Aleksander Pavlovych, Andrei Popovych, Andrei Baludians'kyi, and Nikolai Nod'. The Czech participants were drawn mostly from those civil servants sent to Hungary during the Bach regime. Nedziel'skii, *Ocherk,* p. 131. Among the Slovak members were the well-known national leaders Bohuš Nosák-Nezabudov, Bohumil Nosák, Peter Kellner-Hostinský, and Jan Andraščik. Mol'nar, *Slovaky,* p. 70. For further details on the Literary Institution, see František Tichý, "Dejiny podkarpatsko-ruského literárneho spolku prešovského," *Slovenské pohl'ady,* vol. 40 (Turčiansky Sv. Martin, 1924), pp. 468-471; Rudlovchak, "Oleksandr Dukhnovych," pp. 110ff., and her "Priashivs'ka literaturna spilka Dukhnovycha i literaturni problemy," *Duklia,* vol. 13, nos. 1-4 (Prešov, 1965), pp. 88-93, 56-66, 79-88, 76-87.

31. The play was actually published in Galicia (Przemyśl). It was recently reprinted in Dukhnovych, *Tvory,* vol. 1, pp. 585-625. Its dialectal language has been analyzed by Iosyf O. Dzendzelivs'kyi, "Do kharakterystyky leksychnoho skladu dramy O. Dukhnovycha 'Dobrodîtel' prevyshaet bohatstvo'," in *Oleksandr Dukhnovych: zbirnyk,* pp. 151-169.

The literary almanacs prepared by Dukhnovych are listed in the Bibliography (refs. 0422, 0423, 0431, 0839, 0840). Only those for 1851 and 1852 were sponsored by the Prešov Literary Institution; its other publications included Dukhnovych's *Kratkii zemlepys dlia molodykh Rusynov* (Przemyśl, 1851), reprinted in Dukhnovych, *Tvory*, vol. 2, pp. 273-304, and his popular *Khlîb dushy yly nabozhnŷia molytvŷ y pîsny dlia vostochnŷia tserkvy pravoslavnŷkh khristian* (Vienna, 1851). On the calendars and almanacs, see the discussion by O. Rudlovchak, in *Politychni ta kul'turni iuvileĭ 1975* (Prešov, 1974), pp. 203-205.

32. Reprinted in various versions, with commentary, in Dukhnovych, *Tvory*, vol. 1, pp. 248-253, 685-688. For a literary analysis of his poetry and prose, see the general negative appraisal of Ivan Sozans'kyi, "Poetychna tvorchist' Oleksandra Dukhnovycha," *Zapysky NTSh*, vol. 86 (L'viv, 1908), pp. 1-123; and the more favorable views of Beskid, *A. V. Dukhnovich;* Volodymyr Birchak, *Literaturni stremlinnia Pidkarpats'koï Rusy*, 2nd rev. ed., (Uzhhorod, 1937), pp. 94-102; Bacha, *Literaturnyi rukh*, pp. 137-236; Olena Rudlovchak, "Tvorchyi shliakh Dukhnovycha," in *Oleksandr Dukhnovych: zbirnyk*, pp. 115-150; and Vasyl' L. Mykytas', *Haluzka mohutn'oho dereva: literaturnyi narys* (Uzhhorod, 1971), pp. 43-65, 125-130.

33. The version for the Scarpathian Rusyns was edited by Ivan Rakovskii: *Zemskii pravytel'stvennyi vîstnyk dlia Korolevstva Ouhorshchynŷ* (Vienna, 1850-1859).

34. György Böőr, *A magyarországi ruszin időszaki sajtó a XIX. században* (Cluj, 1943). For biographical information on Rakovskii, see Aristov, *Karpato-russkie pisateli*, pp. 129-144; Nedziel'skii, *Ocherk*, pp. 158-166; and Matsyns'kyi, "Slovnyk," vol. 15, no. 6, pp. 90-92. On Nod', who was parish priest at the St. Barbara Church in Vienna, see Willibald M. Plöchl, *St. Barbara zu Wien*, vol. 1 (Vienna, 1975), pp. 201-204.

35. For a discussion of Slovak-Rusyn relations and texts of mutually laudatory poetry, founding protocols, and memoranda, see Mol'nar, *Slovaky*, pp. 70-89, 231-265, 300-307; and B. Polla, "Návrhy stanov slovenskorusínskeho Tatrína a Matice slovanských národov v Uhorsku," *Historické štúdie*, vol. 6 (Bratislava, 1960), pp. 321-335. Cf. Helena Rudlovčakova, "K otázkam vzájomných kultúrnych stykov Slovákov a zakarpatských Ukrajincov v polovici minulého storočia," *Sborník Ševčenkovský FFUPJŠ*, vol. 5 (Bratislava, 1965), pp. 156-165.

36. In 1906, the influential Slovak leader Svetozár Hurban Vajanský wrote how "every book written 'in Rusyn' [Ukrainian] was a blow against Slavism because the variegated script and dialects pasted into literature weakens the Slavic spirit and can easily become prey to Germanization . . . The only vibrant language is Russian. Who will read the unsystematic 'language' of all those Frankos; who in the wide world will read the weak products of the unknown 'Ukrainian' giants? Absolutely nobody!" Cited in Mol'nar, *Slovaky*, pp. 96-97.

37. Cited in Tichý, *Vývoj*, p. 47.

38. Poem first appeared in 1860 and is reprinted with commentary in Dukhnovych, *Tvory*, vol. 1, pp. 337-338, 700-702.

39. Kyrylo Studyns'kyi, "Aleksander Dukhnovych i Halychyna," *Naukovŷi zbornyk TP*, vol. 3 (Uzhhorod, 1924), pp. 32-36, 66-103; Tivadar Bacsinszky, *Orosz-ruszin kapcsolatok a XIX. század közepén* (Uzhhorod, 1942), pp. 21-74; Mikhail Demko, ed., *Pis'ma A. Dukhnovicha k Ia. Golovats'komu* (Mukachevo, 1927); Bacha, *Literaturnyi rukh*, pp. 47-64. It was from Dukhnovych that Holovats'kyi recieved many of the folk songs included in his monumental *Narodnyia piesni Galitskoi i Ugorskoi Rusi*, 3 vols. (Moscow, 1878).

40. For sample texts, see Appendix 3, pt. 2 There exists a controversy on the exact nature of Dukhnovych's language. One scholar has classified his writings chronologically: (1) Slaveno-Rusyn until the late 1840s; (2) Rusyn (*beskydo-rus'ka*)

dialect during the late 1840s and early 1850s; and (3) the Subcarpathian recension of Russian (the *iazychie*) from the mid-1850s until his death. See Rudlovchak, "Oleksandr Dukhnovych," pp. 105-106, 152-159. Cf. Nedziel'skii, *Ocherk,* pp. 156-158; Birchak, *Literaturni stremlinnia,* pp. 102-105; Iurii Bacha, "Uchast' zakarpats'kykh ukraïntsiv u dyskusiï pro shliakhy rozvytku literatury v zakhidnykh zemliakh Ukraïny v kintsi 40-kh i na pochatku 50-kh rr. XIX stolittia," *Sbornik FFUPJŠ,* vol. 1 (Bratislava, 1960), pp. 48-64, and *Literaturnyi rukh,* pp. 79-96, 117-129.

For purely linguistic analyses, see Tichý, *Vývoj,* pp. 50-60; Dzendzelivs'kyi and Shtets' in *Oleksandr Dukhnovych: zbirnyk,* pp. 151-169, 189-191; and Petro P. Bunhanych, "Movni riznovydy virshovanoï tvorchosti O. Dukhnovycha ta suchasni iomu zasoby movnoho spilkuvannia," in ibid., pp. 170-183.

41. Letters from Prešov, in *Zoria Halyts'ka,* no. 50 (L'viv, 1852), p. 498.

42. *Vistnyk,* no. 38 (Vienna, 1850), cited in Haraksim, *K sociálnym a kultúrnym dejinám,* p. 173.

43. "Vzgliad A.I. Dobrianskago na vopros ob obshcheslavianskom iazykie" (1888), discussed in Nedziel'skii, *Ocherk,* pp. 141-142. See also Tichý, *Vývoj,* pp. 63-64; Kolomiets, *Ocherki,* pp. 164 ff.; Bacha, *Literaturnyi rukh,* pp. 106-109.

44. *Vîstnyk* (Vienna, 1858), p. 48, cited in Tichý, *Vývoj,* pp. 65-66. For a detailed discussion of Rakovskii's views on language, see ibid., pp. 65-68; Bacha, *Literaturnyi rukh,* pp. 97-100, 109-116; and V.A. Frantsev, "Iz istorii bor'by za russkii literaturnyi iazyk v Podkarpatskoi Rusi v polovinie XIX st.," in *Karpatorusskii sbornik,* pp. 1-49.

45. For examples, see the texts in Appendix 3, pt. 3.

46. Volodymyr Hnatiuk, *Natsional'ne vidrodzhennie avstro-uhors'kykh u-kraïntsiv* (Vienna, 1916), pp. 24-46; Ostap Terlets'kyi, *Halyts'ko-rus'ke pys'menstvo 1848-1865 rr.* (L'viv, 1903); V. Malkin, *Russkaia literatura v Galitsii* (L'viv, 1957), pp. 46 ff.; Ivan L. Rudnytsky, "The Ukrainians in Galicia under Austrian Rule," *Austrian History Yearbook,* vol. 3, pt. 2 (Houston, Texas, 1967), pp. 408-416; Peter Brock, "Ivan Vahylevych (1811-1866) and the Ukrainian National Identity," *Canadian Slavic Papers,* vol. 14, no. 2 (Ottawa, 1972), pp. 153-189.

47. *Vîstnyk,* no. 11 (Vienna, 1863), cited in Studyns'kyi, "Dukhnovych i Halychyna," p. 92. Dukhnovych seems to be arguing that the literary language for Subcarpathian Rusyns, the so-called *ruskaia mova,* is the same (if not even more original) than that used by Great Russian writers, and that Galician Ukrainophiles have broken away from this tradition and instead use local dialect. For this reason, Dukhnovych considers them "anti-Rusyn."

48. As an example of his close ties with the Galician Russophiles, Dukhnovych gave his personal archives to the Russian National Home in L'viv. On later developments, see Haraksim, *K sociálnym a kultúrnym dejinám,* pp. 176-177; Michal Danilák, "Styky haličských a zakarpatských Ukrajincov v 2. polovici XIX. storočia," in *Zhovten' i ukraïns'ka/kul'tura* (Prešov, 1968), esp. pp. 42-47.

49. Andrii Chuma and Andrii Bondar, *Ukraïns'ka shkola na Zakarpatti ta Skhidnii Slovachchyni,* pt. 1 (Prešov, 1967), pp. 56-68, 77-78.

50. Vasylii Popovych, the nationally conscious Rusyn bishop of Uzhhorod, remained in office until his death in 1864. Although an active supporter of Dukhnovych before 1848, he became cautious and more reluctant to support Rusyn national endeavors after the Hungarian Revolution. In fact, Popovych was instrumental in blocking many of the plans Dukhnovych and other national leaders put forward. Rudlovchak, "Oleksandr Dukhnovych," p. 83. A more favorable view of Popovych's activity after 1848 is given by Iu. P. Rusak [Iulii Gadzhega], "Mukachevskaia eparkhiia i eia bor'ba za prava russkago iazyka i narodnosti vo vremia episkopstva Vasiliia Popovicha," in *Karpatorusskii sbornik,* pp. 50-67.

51. Haraksim, *K sociálnym a kultúrnym dejinám,* pp. 179-189. Macartney,

Habsburg Empire, pp. 527-528, erroneously states that the Rusyns followed the lead of the Serbs and Slovaks in submitting petitions to Budapest. It is ironic that Dobrianskii was instrumental in formulating the 1861 petition of the Slovaks, but that he was prevented from doing the same for his own people.

52. *Rede des ungarischen Landtags-Abgeordneten Adolf Ritter von Dobrzansky in der Adres-Angelegenheit* (Vienna, 1861).

53. Aristov, *Karpato-russkie pisateli,* pp. 150-161; Dobosh, *A. I. Dobrianskii,* pp. 63-90, 101-110; Kolomiets, *Ocherki,* pp. 152-158; Pereni, *Iz istorii,* pp. 58-72; Kolomiets, *Sotsial'no,* vol. 2, pp. 440-445; Žeguc, *Die nationalpolitischen Bestrebungen,* pp. 54-61, 68-71. For a detailed discussion of Dobrianskii's political thought during the 1860's and the activity of other Rusyn representatives to Parliament, see L'udovit Haraksim, "Die Russinen und der Ausgleich," *Der österreichisch-ungarische Ausgleich 1867* (Bratislava, 1971), pp. 746-763; Mária Mayer, "A Ruszinok (Kárpátukránok) és az 1865. évi képviselőválasztás," *Századok,* vol. 108, nos. 4-5 (Budapest, 1974), pp. 1142-1175.

54. The play, published in Kolomyia, Galicia, is analyzed by Mykytas', *Haluzka,* pp. 186-195, and Nedziel'skii, *Ocherk,* pp. 192-194. His biography is in Evgenii Fentsik, "Ocherk ugro-russkoi pis'mennosti," *Listok,* vol. 12, 1 (Uzhhorod, 1896), pp. 15-18.

55. *Vîstnyk,* no. 6 (Vienna, 1863), pp. 22-23, cited in Rudlovchak, "Oleksandr Dukhnovych," p. 161.

56. Cited in Rudlovchak, "Oleksandr Dukhnovych," p. 140.

57. Ibid, pp. 139-147; Dobosh, *A. I. Dobrianskii,* pp. 93-94. For more details on the Society, see Andrii Dutsar, "Iz istorii priashivs'kykh ukraïns'kykh (rusyns'kykh) serednikh shkil ta hurtozhytkiv," *Duklia,* vol. 13, no. 3 (Prešov, 1965), pp. 100-104.

58. Actually, a printshop already functioned in Uzhhorod between 1845 and 1849, and in nearby Berehovo between 1846 and 1881. But they could only print works in Magyar and Latin. After many demands by the Rusyn intelligentsia (especially by Dukhnovych and Ioann Churhovych), Károly Jäger reopened the Uzhhorod printshop in 1861 (this shop had, besides Magyar and Latin, Hebrew type), and finally two years later he received Cyrillic (*grazhdanka*) type. Iador Stryps'kyi, "Pochatky drukarstva na Podkarpatiu," *Zoria-Hajnal,* vol. 2, nos. 3-4 (Uzhhorod, 1942), pp. 262-287.

59. Aleksander Fedorovich, "Korrespondentsiia iz Uzhgoroda (ob otkrytii literaturnogo Obshchestva sv. Vasiliia V.), *Naukovyi sbornik . . . Galitsko-russkoi Matitsy,* vol. 2, nos. 1-4 (L'viv, 1866), pp. 360-362; Sil'vai, *Izbrannye,* pp. 126-129, 357-359; Iulii Gadzhega, *Istoriia 'Obshchestva sv. Vasiliia Velikago' i riech' ko dniu 60 lietiia ot ego uchrezhdeniia,* Izdanie OIAD, no. 15 (Uzhhorod, 1925), pp. 6-23. For the attitude of Ioann Rakovskii and other leaders on the role of the society, see their letters to Bishop Pankovych, reprinted in Iulii Rusak [Iulii Gadzhega], *Vospominaniia* (Uzhhorod, 1938), pp. 99-104.

60. For biographies of these authors, see Fentsik, "Ocherk," vol. 9 (1893), pp. 17-18, 101, 221-222, 259; and vol. 10 (1894), pp. 247-248; Nedziel'skii, *Ocherk,* pp. 185-189; O. Rudlovchak, "Viktor Kymak," in *Politychni,* pp. 211-213. For reference to the grammars, see the Bibliography. On the language of Sabov's text, see Tichý, *Vývoj,* pp. 69-70. Sabov also prepared a reader for upper classes, *Kratkii sbornik izbrannykh sochinenii v prozie i stikhakh dlia uprazhneniia v russkom iazykie* (Uzhhorod, 1868) with forty-four excerpts exclusively from Great Russian authors like Karamzin, Lermontov, Pushkin, and Turgenev. A content analysis is given in Ivan Em. Levyts'kyi, *Halytsko-ruskaia bybliohrafiia XIX-ho stolîtiia 1801-1886,* vol. 2 (L'viv, 1895), pp. 109-110.

61. Nedziel'skii, *Ocherk,* pp. 194-195; Q. Rudlovchak, "Pershyi pedahohichnyi

chasopys: do stolittia vykhodu u svit hazety 'Uchytel'," *Shkola i zhyttia*, vol. 3, no. 10 (Prešov, 1966-67), pp. 2-3. For Ripai's biography, see Fentsik, "Ocherk," vol. 10 (1894), pp. 5-7, 259-261.
62. Cited in Studyns'kyi, "Dukhnovych i Halychyna," p. 91.
63. Nedziel'skii, *Ocherk,* p. 125, refers to the period as the "kul'turno-natsional'noe vozrozhdenie"; Tichý, *Vývoj,* p. 44, and Georgij Gerovskij, "Jazyk Podkarpatské Rusi," in *Československá vlastivěda,* vol. 3, *Jazyk* (Prague, 1934), p. 496, as the "národní obrození"; Haraksim, *K kultúrnym a sociálnym dejinám,* p. 171, as the "doba buditel'ská."
64. Macartney, *The Habsburg Empire,* pp. 489-494, 537-551.
65. Ibid., pp. 551-560.
66. Cited in ibid., p. 560. An English translation of the law is found in Scotus Viator [R. W. Seton-Watson], *Racial Problems in Hungary* (London, 1908), pp. 429-433.
67. On the failure to implement the nationalities law, see ibid., pp. 135 ff.; and Oscar Jaszi, *The Dissolution of the Habsburg Monarchy,* 2nd ed. (Chicago, 1960), pp. 314-337.
68. It should be mentioned that in 1867 Rusyns represented less than half the student body in the Uzhhorod gymnasium. Chuma and Bondar, *Ukraïns'ka shkola,* p. 82.
69. Sil'vai, *Izbrannye,* p. 144.
70. The decree is cited in Uriil Meteor [Ivan Sil'vai], "Polozhenie ugorskikh russkikh pod upravleniem Stefana Pankovicha, Episkopa Mukachevskago" (1874), reprinted in his *Izbrannye,* pp. 378-380.
71. Ibid., pp. 363-384; Gadzhega, *Istoriia Obshchestva,* pp. 23-26; Dobosh, *A. I. Dobrianskii,* pp. 94-98; Kolomiets, *Sotsial'no,* vol. 2, pp. 244-263; Žeguc, *Die nationalpolitischen Bestrebungen,* pp. 74-76; Avhustyn Voloshyn, *Spomynŷ* (Uzhhorod, 1923), pp. 45-53; Böőr, *A magyarországi ruszin időszaki sajtó,* pp. 30-54. For the biographies of Gebei and Gomichkov, see Fentsik, "Ocherk," vol. 9 (1893), pp. 91-92 and vol. 10 (1894), p. 7; and Nedziel'skii, *Ocherk,* pp. 237-239.
72. Ibid., p. 187; Chuma and Bondar, *Ukraïns'ka shkola,* p. 82; Olena Rudlovchak, "Do istoriï hazety 'Sova'," *Duklia,* vol. 18, no. 1 (Prešov, 1970), pp. 74-75.
73. Iulii Gadzhega, *Istoriia Uzhgorodskoi Bogoslovskoi Seminarii v eia glavnykh chertakh,* Izdanie OIAD, no. 35 (Uzhhorod, 1928), p. 17; Atanasii Pekar, *Narysy istoriï tserkvy Zakarpattia* (Rome, 1967), pp. 102-104.
74. Sil'vai, *Izbrannye,* pp. 129-138, 386-387; Gadzhega, *Istoriia Obshchestva,* pp. 29-30, 42-43; Kolomiets, *Sotsial'no,* vol. 2, pp. 263-264; Mykytas', *Haluzka,* pp. 10-12; Rudlovchak, "Do istoriï 'Sova'," pp. 69-75. See also Gabor G. Kemény, ed., *Iratok a nemzetiségi kérdés történetéhez Magyarországon a dualizmus korában,* vol. 1, *1867-1892* (Budapest, 1952), doc. 113, pp. 405-408.
75. For the satirical illustrations in this journal, see Sil'vai, *Izbrannye,* pp. 353-387. E. Grabar, who was married to A. Dobrianskii's daughter, Ol'ga, was elected from Máramaros county to the Hungarian Parliament in 1869. He drew the illustrations for *Sova* in Budapest, where he stayed until pressured to leave the country in the late 1870s. He finally reached Russia, where he remained until his death. His son Igor, who spent his youth on the Dobrianskii estate in Čertižne, was to become the renowned painter, critic, art historian, member of the Soviet Academy of Sciences, and director of the Institute of Art History of the USSR. See Chapter 7.
76. *Proekt politicheskoi programmy dlia Rusi avstriiskoi* (L'viv, 1871).
77. On this period in Dobrianskii's life as well as analyses of his various projects, see Aristov, *Karpato-russkie pisateli,* pp. 161-229; Nedziel'skii, *Ocherk,* pp.

135-145; Dobosh, *A. I. Dobrianskii*, pp. 101-156; Kolomiets, *Ocherki*, pp. 156-179 and his *Sotsial'no*, vol. 2, pp. 445-462.

78. Cited in Nedziel'skii, *Ocherk*, p. 220.

79. On the closing of Rakovskii's newspapers, see his own statement in Stepan V. Dobosh, "Do znaidenoho dokumentu Rakovs'koho," *Duklia*, vol. 13, no. 3 (Prešov, 1965), pp. 97-100; the government decree reprinted in Frantsev, "Iz istorii bor'by," pp. 22-26; and the discussion in Kolomiets, *Ocherki*, pp. 201-205. On *Svît*, see Pankovics's decree reprinted in Sil'vai, *Izbrannye*, pp. 378-381.

80. Cited in Tichý, *Vývoj*, p. 95. On the problem of language in Subcarpathian newspapers and especially criticism of *Karpat*, see ibid., pp. 68-69; Nedziel'skii, *Ocherk*, pp. 238-239; Gadzhega, *Istoriia Obshchestva*, pp. 30-32; Birchak, *Literaturni stremlinnia*, pp. 110-120; Avh. Voloshyn, *O pys'mennom iazŷtsî podkarpatskykh rusynov* (Uzhhorod, 1921), pp. 24-27.

81. For sample texts, see Appendix 3, pt. 3. For references to the early school books, see the Bibliography. (refs. 0794, 0814)

82. Nedziel'skii, *Ocherk*, pp. 195-197; Tichý, *Vývoj*, p. 105. For a discussion of Zlots'kyi's other writings, see Nykolai Lelekach, "Podkarpatskoe pys'menstvo na pochatku XX vîka," *Zoria-Hajnal*, vol. 3, nos. 1-4 (Uzhhorod, 1943), pp. 239-242.

83. *Rus'ka azbuka y pervonachal'na chytanka dlia pervoho kliasa naròdnŷkh shkòl* (Budapest, 1881); *Chytanka dlia narodnŷkh shkol*, vol. 1, from the Magyar text of Pál Genczy, adopted to the Bereg, Ugocsa, and Máramaros dialects (Budapest, 1889).

84. Laslov Chopei, *Rus'ko madiarskyi slovar'* (Budapest, 1883), pp. xxii-xxv. On Chopei's language, see the texts in Appendix 3, pt. 3 and the discussion in Tichý, *Vývoj*, pp. 106-109; and Kolomiets, *Sotsial'no*, vol. 2, pp. 215-218. On his career, see József Szinnyei, *Magyar írók, élete és munkái*, vol. 2 (Budapest, 1893), pp. 424-425. Both Chopei and the linguistic-cultural orientation he represented deserve more attention than they have been accorded.

85. A polemic concerning Chopei's language arose soon after the appearance of his dictionary. For the contemporary negative viewpoint of the Russophiles, see "Natsional'noe dvizhenie v Ugorskoi Rusi," *Galitsko-russkii viestnik*, vol. 1, no. 1 (St. Petersburg, 1894), pp. 60-61; L. Vasilevskii (Plokhotskii), "Vengerskie 'rusnaki' i ikh sud'ba," *Russkoe bogatstvo*, no. 3 (St. Petersburg, 1914), pp. 378-379. For praise by the populists, see Vasyl' Lukych, *Uhors'ka Rus', iei rozvôi y teperishnŷi stan* (L'viv, 1887), pp. 26-27; Hnatiuk, *Natsional'ne vidrodzhennie*, p. 35. In the twentieth century, the debate over Chopei was continued by Subcarpathian Russophiles and Ukrainophiles; see Chapter 6.

86. Sil'vai, "Avtobiografiia," pp. 118-119.

87. On the Society's publishing activity, see Evmenii Sabov, *Khristomatiia tserkovno-slavianskykh i ugro-russkikh literaturnykh pamiatnikov* (Uzhhorod, 1893), pp. 201-208; Hadzhega, *Istoriia Obshchestva*, pp. 36-41; Nedziel'skii, *Ocherk*, p. 182.

88. *Russko-mad'iarskii slovar'* (Uzhhorod, 1881). The Magyar-Russian part was completed soon after, but not published until 1921. For a detailed lexical analysis of the 834-page Russian-Magyar dictionary, see Tichý, *Vývoj*, pp. 71-94. On Mitrak's life and other writings, see Nedziel'skii, *Ocherk*, pp. 205-210; Kolomiets, *Ocherki*, pp. 219-226, and *Sotsial'no*, vol. 2, pp. 490-495; Mykytas', *Haluzka*, pp. 91-98.

89. On Dulishkovich's historical writings, see Chapter 6. For biographical information on these authors, Fentsik, "Ocherk," vol. 9 (1893), pp. 18-19, 54-55, 258-259; Nedziel'skii, *Ocherk*, pp. 197-205, 210-225, and "Ivan Antonovich Sil'vai," in

Sil'vai, *Izbrannye,* pp. 13-76; Birchak, *Literaturni stremlinnia,* pp. 122-140; Kolomiets, *Ocherki,* pp. 208-211, 226-231, and *Sotsial'no,* vol. 2, pp. 480-483, 487-490; Mykytas', *Haluzka,* pp. 98-111, 131-160; and the individual studies by F. F. Aristov, N. A. Beskid, S. Dobosh, A. Pekar, A. V. Popov, and F. Tichý in the Bibliography (refs. 0917, 0924, 0925, 0934, 1030, 1041, 1044, 1067).

90. Nedziel'skii, *Ocherk,* pp. 169-175; Mykytas', *Haluzka,* pp. 66-91. The most complete work on this author is Andrei Shlepetskii, "Tvorcheskoe nasledie Aleksandra Pavlovicha," *Sborník FFUPJŠ,* vol. 4, no. 2 (Bratislava, 1965), pp. 41-96.

91. A. Mitrak, "Russkii narod," *Mîsiatsoslov na hod 1866 dlia russkykh uhorskiia kraynŷ* (Uzhhorod, 1865), pp. 50-54, cited in *Oleksandr Dukhnovych: zbirnyk,* p. 60. On the influence of Russian literature in Subcarpathian Rus', see P. V. Lintur, "Traditsii russkogo klassitsizma v literature Zakarpat'ia XIX v.," in *Russkaia literatura XVIII veka i slavianskie literatury* (Moscow and Leningrad, 1963), pp. 123-136.

In a report on the recollections of Subcarpathians to the Russian invasion of 1849, one correspondent from Russia recalled the words of a Rusyn he interviewed: "We know who we are; we know what is the truth and what is falsehood . . . We know that the Muscovites are not some kind of Mongol wild men, but rather Russian people like us; that we are the same exact Muscovites as they, and they are the same Rusyns as we are." "Mnenie karpato-russa o posledstviiakh russko-vengerskoi voiny 1849 goda," *Slavianskie izvestiia,* no. 6 ([St. Petersburg] 1890), pp. 106-107.

92. M. Drahomanov, *Spravy Uhorskoi Rusy* (L'viv, 1895), pp. 6-7.

93. Letter of Ivan Sil'vai to V. Hnatiuk, dated November 7, 1897, cited in V. Hnatiuk, "Prychynok do istoriï znosyn halyts'kykh i uhors'kykh rusyniv," *Literaturno-naukovyi vistnyk,* vol. 7, no. 10 (L'viv, 1899), p. 170. For similar negative replies to Galician Ukrainians by S. Sabov, Iu. Stavrovskii-Popradov, and others, see Nedziel'skii, *Ocherk,* pp. 256-258; D. Doroshenko, *Uhors'ka Ukraïna* (Prague, 1919), pp. 24-25; and Pereni, *Iz istorii,* pp. 101-103.

On the other hand, these and other Subcarpathians did supply the Galicians like Franko, Hnatiuk, Stepan Tomashivs'kyi, and Ivan Verkhrats'kyi with literary, ethnographic, and linguistic materials for the studies they composed about Rusyns living south of the mountains. On these relations, see Birchak, *Literaturni stremlinnia,* pp. 148-149; Žeguc, *Die natsionalpolitischen Bestrebungen,* pp. 85-91; I. O. Dzendzelivs'kyi, "Spivrobitnytstvo V. Hnatiuka z Iu. Stavrovs'kym u 1896-1899 rr.," *Zapysky Naukovoho tovarystva KSUT,* vol. 1, no. 1 (Prešov, 1972), pp. 43-64; Pavlo Lisovyi, *Cherez Beskydy: literaturna besida* (Uzhhorod, 1972).

94. On Fentsik's life and work, see Dimitrii N. Vergun, *A. E. Fentsik i ego miesto v russkoi literature,* Izdanie OIAD, no. 22 (Uzhhorod, 1926); Nedziel'skii, *Ocherk,* pp. 226-234; Birchak, *Literaturni stremlinnia,* pp. 140-147; Kolomiets, *Ocherki,* pp. 211-219, and *Sotsial'no,* vol. 2, pp. 483-487; Mykytas', *Haluzka,* pp. 111-123, 160-170, 195-201.

95. Cited in Tichý, *Vývoj,* p. 95.

96. On Listok, see ibid., pp. 95-98; Voloshyn, *Spomynŷ,* pp. 54-55; and O. Rudlovchak, "Lystok," in *Politychni ta kul'turni,* pp. 150-152.

97. On the life and work of these individuals, see Appendix 2; Nedziel'skii, *Ocherk,* pp. 245-248, 252-263, 266-270; Antonín Hartl, *Literární obrození podkarpatských rusínů v letech 1920-1930* (Prague, 1930), pp. 54-59; Birchak, *Literaturni stremlinnia,* pp. 150-155; Lelekach, "Podkarpatskoe pys'menstvo," pp. 235-238, 246-250. See also the memoirs of A. Voloshyn and E. Sabov and the individual studies of V. Birchak, V. Hnatiuk, A. V. Popov, D. Papharhai, and K. Zaklyns'kyi in the Bibliography (refs. 0675, 0676, 0679, 0680, 0705, 0927, 0939, 0940, 0961, 1029, 1042, 1082).

98. Eumén Szabó, *Orosz nyelvtan és olvasókönyv—Russkaia hrammatyka y chytanka* (Uzhhorod, 1890). On the language of this work, see Tichý, *Vývoj,* pp. 114-

117 and especially the analyses of E. Baleczky: "Iazyk hrammatyky E. Sabova z 1890-ho roku," *Zoria-Hajnal,* vol. 2, nos. 3-4 (Uzhhorod, 1942), pp. 336-350 and his *Szabó Eumen orosz nyelvtanának hangtana,* Irodalmi és tudományos könyvtár, no. 28 (Budapest, 1943).

99. On his *Khristomatiia,* see Chapter 5, p. 109.

100. Vrabel's *Bukvar'* was published in 15,000 copies. For some of the many grammars of Voloshyn, see the Bibliography (refs. 0824-0831). For textual samples, see Appendix 3, pt. 3. Voloshyn's linguistic development from the "traditional Carpatho-Rusyn language" to a more dialectally based language has caused much polemical argumentation. Cf. Nedziel'skii, *Ocherk,* pp. 245-247; Birchak, *Literaturni stremlinnia,* pp. 154-155; Gerovskij, "Jazyk," pp. 508-509.

101. Avhustyn Shtefan, *Za pravdu i voliu: spomyny i deshcho z istoriï Karpats'-koï Ukraïny* (New York, 1973), pp. 213-215.

102. "Vidpovid' M. Drahomanova na iubileini pryvitannia 16.XII.1894," reprinted in M.P. Drahomanov, *Vybrani tvory,* vol. 1 (Prague, 1937), pp. 91-92. For other works by Drahomanov on the region, see the Bibliography (refs. 0625, 0626).

103. *Mîsiatsoslov tserkovnŷi na 1909* (Uzhhorod, 1908), cited in Nedziel'skii, *Ocherk,* p. 247, n. 2.

104. The existence of a rich literary tradition in Subcarpathian Rus', especially in the seventeenth and eighteenth centuries, was made known by H. Stryps'kyi (under the pseudonym Bilen'kyi), who attacked the attempt of Subcarpathian authors to write in Great Russian and concluded that "250 years ago they [Subcarpathian Rusyns] wrote better and clearer than now," that is, in a dialectally based popular language. *Starsha rus'ka pys'mennost' na Uhorschynî* (Uzhhorod, 1907). See also Chapter 5, p. 113.

105. Gadzhega, *Istoriia Obshchestva,* pp. 34-35; M. Mayer, "Beiträge zur Geschichte der Ruthenen (Karpatoukrainer) um die Jahrhundertwende," *Acta Historica Academiae Scientarium Hungaricae,* vol. 19, nos. 1-2 (Budapest, 1973), pp. 119-124.

106. Cited in Lelekach, "Podkarptskoe pys'menstvo," p. 233.

107. On these journals, see ibid., pp. 229-234; Gadzhega, *Istoriia Obshchestva,* pp. 34-35; Voloshyn, *Spomynŷ,* pp. 55-63.

108. The first modern census was compiled by Elek Fényes in the 1830s, and the disturbing result was that only 40 percent of the population gave Magyar as their mother tongue. It was not until 1900 that a majority did so—51.4 percent—and in the last census, 1910, Magyar speakers were recorded at 54.9 percent. Macartney, *Habsburg Empire,* p. 725; Jászi, *Dissolution,* pp. 274 ff.

109. Macartney, *Habsburg Empire,* p. 693. It should be stressed that this chauvinist policy, expressed poignantly by the revolutionary Kossuth's proposition "that there were many nationalities in Hungary but only one nation, the Magyar," was characteristic of Hungary only in the late nineteenth and early twentieth centuries. Jászi, *Dissolution,* pp. 298-313.

110. "Now they [the Magyars] are among the Slavs, Germans, Vlachs, and other peoples the smaller part of the territory's population, and after a century perhaps one will hardly hear their language any more." Johann Gottfried Herder, *Ideen zur Philosophie der Geschichte der Menschheit* (1791), cited in Peter F. Sugar and Ivo J. Lederer, eds., *Nationalism in Eastern Europe* (Seattle, Wash., 1969), p. 264, n. 15. Herder's later more positive comments on the development of the Magyar language and literature were disregarded in Hungary.

111. For a brilliant discussion of the cult of illusion in late nineteenth century Hungary, see William M. Johnston, *The Austrian Mind: An Intellectual and Social History* (Berkeley, Calif., 1972), pp. 344-356. Cf. L.G. Cigány, "Hungarianness: The Origin of a Pseudo-Linguistic Concept," *The Slavonic and East European Review,* vol. 52, no. 128 (London, 1974), pp. 325-328. The extreme lengths to which chau-

vinistic attitudes could be carried were revealed by one "enthusiastic Magyar scholar [who] 'demonstrated' that, properly speaking, Adam, the first man, was a Magyar." Jászi, *Dissolution*, p. 264.

112. Of Jókai's nearly one-hundred novels, the most sympathetic to Hungary's past and present plight were: *Erdély arany kora* ("The Golden Age of Transylvania," 1852), *Török világ Magyarországon* ("The Turks in Hungary," 1853), *Kárpáthy Zoltán* (1854), *Szomorú napok* ("Day of Wrath," 1856), *Az új földesúr* ("The New Landowner," 1863), *A kőszívű ember fiai* ("The Baron's Sons," 1869), *A jövő század regénye* ("The Novel of the Coming Century," 1872-1874).

Among the many large historical canvases that contributed to the spirit of the times were: Madarász's "Lamentation over László Hunyadi" (1859) and "Zrínyi and Frangepán in the Prison of Wienerneustadt" (1864); Székely's "Finding the Body of Louis II on the Battlefield of Mohács" (1860), "The Women of Eger" (1867), and "Thököly's Farewell"; Benzúr's "László Hunyadi Bids Farewell to His Friends" (1866) and "The Recapture of Buda Castle in 1686" (1896); and Munkácsy's "The Magyar Conquest" (1896).

At the same time, the National Theater in Budapest was filled with stirring patriotic melodies of Erkel's operas, *László Hunyadi* (1844) and *Bán Bánk* (1861), from which the passionately stirring "Hazám, hazám, te mindenem" ("My Country, Country, My All"), derives.

113. The memory of this event was preserved for future generations in the massive Millennium Memorial on Heroes' Square in Budapest, constructed by the sculptor György Zala between 1896 to 1929. The complex includes Árpád and the leaders of the other original tribes seated on horseback under the central pediment, which is framed in the background by a massive semicircular colonnade with statues of fourteen of Hungary's greatest heroes. Joseph de Jekelfalussy, *The Millennium of Hungary and Its People* (Budapest, 1897).

114. Two of the nineteenth-century's greatest Magyars were of Slovak origin: the revolutionary leader Lajos Kossuth, whose uncle was a Slovak poet, and the renowned writer Sándor Petőfi (born Petrovič). See Scotus Viator, *Racial Problems*, p. 49. Among the many other outstanding assimilated Magyars who came from among the national and religious minorities were: the historian Vilmos Fraknói (born Frankl), the sociologist and radical politician Oszkár Jászi, the Marxian critic Georg Lukács (born Löwinger), the historian Henrik Marczali (born Morgenstern), the painter Mihály Munkácsy (born Lieb), the literary historian Ferenc Toldy (born Schedel), and the Orientalist Ármin Vámbéry (born Wamberger). On the achievements of Magyar Jews, especially in the natural sciences, see William McCagg, *Jewish Nobles and Geniuses in Modern Hungary* (Boulder, Colo., 1972), and George Barany, " 'Magyar Jew or: Jewish Magyar'? (To the Question of Jewish Assimilation in Hungary)," *Canadian-American Slavic Studies,* vol. 7, no. 1 (Pittsburgh, 1974), pp. 1-44.

115. Chuma and Bondar, *Ukrains'ka shkola*, pp. 88-98; Macartney, *Habsburg Empire*, pp. 723-725; Kolomiets, *Sotsial'no,* vol. 2, pp. 181-195 passim, 220-244; Žeguc, *Die nationalpolitischen Bestrebungen*, pp. 116-119.

116. The law further provided that Magyar be used for most subjects and that no book of "patriotic content" may be used without the approval of the minister of education. External forms and symbols were given great importance. All school signs were in Magyar, the coat of arms of Hungary was prominently displayed inside and outside the school, and pictures of Hungarian historical events were placed in the classroom. Portraits of church dignitaries were allowed, but any direct or symbolic references to SS. Cyril, Methodius, or Basil, the patron saints of Rusyn as well as Slavic culture in general, were to be regarded as treasonable. For a fuller discus-

sion, see Scotus Viator, *Racial Problems,* pp. 227-233; and I. Dolmanyos, "Kritik der Lex Apponyi," in *Die nationale Frage in der Osterreichisch-Ungarischen Monarchie 1900-1918* (Budapest, 1966), pp. 233-304.

117. *Kalendar' na hod 1910* (Uzhhorod, 1909), p. 24.

118. Statistical table in Chuma and Bondar, *Ukraïns'ka shkola,* pp. 108-109. Kolomiets, *Sotsial'no,* vol. 2, pp. 195-202, provides statistics that differ substantially from Chuma and Bondar.

119. S. Tomashivs'kyi, "Uhors'ki Rusyny v s'vitlï madiars'koï uriadovoï statystyky," *Zapysky NTSh,* vol. 5-6 (L'viv, 1903), pp. 45-46. Later Tomashivs'kyi revised his estimate upward to 500,000: "Etnohrafichna karta Uhors'koï Rusy," in V.I. Lamanskii, ed., *Stat'i po slavianoviedieniiu,* vol. 3 (St. Petersburg, 1910), p. 221. For an attempt by a Hungarian writer to show that in terms of numbers the minorities actually fared better in the nineteenth century than in previous centuries, see Étienne Szabó, "L'assimilation ethnique dans le bassin des Carpathes avant 1918," *Revue d'histoire comparée: études hongroises,* n.s., vol. 21 (Paris, 1943), pp. 279-330. For a comparison of official statistics and estimates by varying authors, see Appendix 4, Tables 1 and 2.

120. Indeed, before the census taker, the Rusyn peasant did not really understand what national identity meant. He could only think in terms of religious or regional (village, river valley) affiliation. Such confusion was especially prevalent along the Slovak-Rusyn ethnographic border where in one census a village's inhabitants might declare themselves Slovak, in another census Rusyn. Much ink has flowed in arguments concerning this problem. An objective discussion is provided by Jan Húsek, *Národopisná hranice mezi Slováky a Karpatorusy* (Bratislava, 1925), pp. 343-498.

121. Local Magyar-language newspapers published in Uzhhorod: *Ungvári közlöny, Ung,* and especially *Kárpáti lapok,* edited from 1895 to 1903 by the adamant anti-Rusyn Aladár Románecz, attacked the St. Basil Society for supposedly exhibiting lack of faith in the fatherland and for still being under the influence of the agitator Dobrianskii. Gadzhega, *Istoriia Obshchestva,* p. 34; Mayer, "Beiträge," p. 121. As for the Galicians, the Hungarian government was particularly incensed by the publication of a protest petition authored by the Ukrainian leaders Ivan Franko and Volodymyr Hnatiuk, "I my v Ievropi: protest halyts'kykh rusyniv proty madiars'koho tysiacholittia," *Zhytie i slovo,* vol. 5, no. 1 (L'viv, 1896), pp. 1-9.

122. On the basis of official statistics, one historian concluded that only 60,000 Rusyns emigrated in the period 1871-1914, but this figure does not reflect the numerous illegal departures. Oleksander Mytsiuk, "Z emihratsiï uhro-rusyniv pered svitovoiu viinoiu," *Naukovyi zbirnyk TP,* vols. 13-14 (Uzhhorod, 1937-38), pp. 21-32. For more realistic estimates, see Pereni, *Iz istorii,* pp. 124-125; Kolomiets, *Sotsial'no,* vol. 1, pp. 332-363; V. Taitak, "Pereselennia ukraïntsiv Skhidnoï Slovachchyny do 1913 r.," *Duklia,* vol. 9, no. 4 (Prešov, 1961), pp. 97-103; Mariia Maier, "Zakarpats'ki ukraïntsi na perelomi stolit'," in *Zhovten' i ukraïns'ka kul'tura* (Prešov, 1968), pp. 49-73; P.K. Smiian, *Revoliutsiinyi ta natsional'no-vyzvol'nyi rukh na Zakarpatti kintsia XIX-pochatku XX st.* (L'viv, 1968), pp. 74-79; and V. Il'ko, *Zakarpats'ke selo na pochatku XX st. (1900-1919 rr.)* (L'viv, 1973), pp. 129-133.

123. See the Budapest archival documents on the activity of Soter Ortyns'kyi, the first Greek Catholic Bishop in the United States (a Ukrainian from Galicia) in Kemény, *Iratok,* vol. 5, *1906-1913* (Budapest, 1971), pp. 391-397. Cf. Chapter 4.

124. The first large conversion to Orthodoxy was the community led by Father Alexis Toth of Minneapolis, Minnesota. Cf. Walter C. Warzeski, *Byzantine Rite Rusins in Carpatho-Ruthenia and America* (Pittsburgh, 1971), pp. 105-110; Keith S. Russin, "Father Alexis G. Toth and the Wilkes-Barre Litigations," *St. Vladimir's Theological Quarterly,* vol. 16, no. 3 (Crestwood, N.Y., 1972), pp. 128-149.

125. Among the most influential publications were Toth's brochure, *Kde treba iskati pravdu?* (New York, 1890), which became the "Bible of Orthodox peasants in Transcarpathia," and *Bratskii priviet brat'iam i sestram karpatorussam, zhivushchim v predielakh karpatskikh gor i v Amerikie* (St. Petersburg, 1893), written by Mykhail Sarych, a native of Sáros county. Although the latter was published in Russia, many copies reached Subcarpathian Rus' via the United States. Maier, "Zakarpats'ki ukraïntsi," p. 67; Pereni, *Iz istorii,* pp. 94-95.

126. It is no coincidence that the influential Russophile leader Ioann Rakovskii served as parish priest in Iza from 1871 to 1885. During these years he fostered in his parishioners a love for Russia and its traditions. Estimates of the number of Orthodox Rusyns before the War vary greatly, from 577 in 1910 in the Hungarian census to 30,000 in 1912 in Il'ko, *Zakarpats'ke selo,* pp. 150-151. Cf. Ilija Kačur, *Stručný prehl'ad histórie pravoslávnej cirkvi v bývalom Uhorsku a v Československu* (Prešov, n.d.), pp. 102-106; Pekar, *Narysy,* pp. 113-116; József Rédei, "A ruténék vallásos tömegmozgalmai," *Huszadik század,* vol. 30 (Budapest, 1914), pp. 470-473; Pereni, *Iz istorii,* pp. 125-134; Kolomiets, *Sotsial'no,* vol. 2, pp. 409-411; Žeguc, *Die nationalpolitischen Bestrebungen,* pp. 107-112; Smiian, *Revoliutsiinyi . . . rukh,* pp. 109-114. Mayer, "Beiträge," pp. 136-139, has suggested that another important source of Orthodox ideology for Subcarpathian Rus' was the neighboring Rumanian population.

127. A. P. Liprandi, "Zabytyi ugolok Russkoi zemli," *Russkaia besieda,* vol. 2, no. 4 (St. Petersburg, 1896), p. 74. For a discussion of the many articles published in Russia about Subcarpathian Rus' at this time, see Vladimir Frantsev, "Obzor vazhnieishikh izuchenii Ugorskoi Rusi," *Russkii filologicheskii viestnik,* vol. 45, nos. 1-2 (Warsaw, 1901), pp. 190-197; Evgenii Perfetskii, "Obzor ugrorusskoi istoriografii," *Izviestiia ORISIAN,* vol. 19, no. 1 (St. Petersburg, 1914), pp. 336-339; K. Ia. Grot, "Karpato-dunaiskiia zemlia v sud'bakh slavianstva i v russkikh istoricheskikh izucheniiakh," in *Novyi sbornik statei po slavianoviedeniiu* (St. Petersburg, 1905), esp. pp. 128-140; and Kolomiets, *Sotsial'no,* vol. 2, pp. 538-541, 544-546.

128. Unfortunately, the holdings of the museum were moved in 1917 and subsequently lost. On Petrov and Frantsev, see Iu.A. Iavorskii, *Iz istorii nauchnago izsliedovaniia Zakarpatskoi Rusi* (Prague, 1928); on Kustodiiev, see Olena Rudlovchak, "Za zavisoiu mynuloho: materialy do vzaiemyn Zakarpattia z Rosiieiu," *Duklia,* vol. 18, no. 4 (Prešov, 1970), pp. 59-68. See also the biographic accounts by T.F. Aristova, P.S. Fedor, I. Kondratovych and I. Pan'kevych in the Bibliography, (refs. 0918, 0919, 0944, 0980, 1028), and see Chapter 5.

129. Robert F. Byrnes, *Pobedonostsev: His Life and Thought* (Bloomington, Ind., 1968), pp. 221-225.

130. V. A. Bobrinskii, *Prazhskii s''iezd: Chekhiia i Prikarpatskaia Rus'* (St. Petersburg, 1909); "Bobrinskij gróf és magyarországi ruthének," *Huszadik század,* vol. 30 (Budapest, 1914), pp. 98-100; Bedwin Sands, *The Russians in Galicia* (New York, 1916), pp. 7-10. For details on organizational activity, see *Otchet o dieiatel'-nosti Galitsko-russkago blagotvoritel'nago obshchestva za 1912 god* (St. Petersburg, 1913) and *za 1913-1914 god* (St. Petersburg, 1914).

131. It is interesting to note that *Russkaia pravda* was run by the nephews of A. Dobrianskii, Aleksei and Georgii Gerovskii, who settled in the Subcarpathian region after the war. Another Russophile editor from Bukovina, Ilarion Tsurkanovich, was later to be elected a senator in the Prague Parliament from Subcarpathian Rus'. On these figures, see Chapters 6 and 10 and Appendix 2.

For details on the prewar influence of Russia in the Carpathians, see A. Gerovskii, "Russkie rubli dlia Karpatskoi Rusi," *Svobodnoe slovo Karpatskoi Rusi,* vol. 4, nos. 1-2 (Newark, N.J., 1962), pp. 9-10; Rédei, "A ruténék," pp. 473-476; Bohdan Svitlynskii, "Avstro-Uhorshchyna i Talerhof," in *Voennye prestupleniia Gabsburgskoi Monarkhii 1914-1917 gg.* (Trumbull, Conn., 1964), esp. pp. 23-38; René Martel, "La politique slave de la Russie d'avant-guerre," *Affaires étrangères,* vol. 6, no. 10 (Paris, 1936), pp. 625-631, and vol. 7, no. 1 (1937), pp. 58-59; Z.A.B. Zeman, *The Break-Up of the Habsburg Empire, 1914-1918* (London, 1961), pp. 5-13; Károly Gulya, *A magyarországi rutén kérdés 1910-1914 között,* Acta Historica, vol. 31 (Szeged, 1968), pp. 6-10.

132. The principal accused was a woodcutter from Iasynia, Aleksei Kabaliuk, who under the influence of the Gerovskii brothers left to enter a Russian monastery. With the help of the Gerovskii's and Count Bobrinskii, Kabaliuk returned to the Subcarpathian village of Iza in 1911 to propagate Orthodoxy in the region. *Otchet . . . za 1913-1914 god,* pp. 23-31; Pekar, *Narysy,* pp. 117-119; Kačur, *Stručny prehl'ad,* pp. 106-114; Martel, "La politique slave," pp. 623 ff.; Pereni, *Iz istorii,* pp. 146-152; Kolomiets, *Sotsial'no,* vol. 2, pp. 410-420; Smiian, *Revoliutsiinyi . . . rukh,* pp. 149-154. See also the individual studies on the trial by K. Beskid, A. Gerovskii, M. Hrabets', and A. Štefánek in the Bibliography (refs. 1166, 1371, 1498, 2109). Among the correspondents present at the trial were prominent Slovak leaders: the writer Josef Gregor-Tajovský, "Listy z Marmarošsky Sihoti" [1913-14], in *Dielo,* vol. 6 (Bratislava, 1958), pp. 489-538; and the future Premier Minister of Czechoslovakia, Milan Hodža, "U karpatských Rusov" [articles from *Slovenské listy,* 1898-1914], in his *Članky, reči, štúdie,* vol. 3 (Prague, 1931), pp. 291-322.

133. M. Bartha, *Kazár földön* (Cluj, 1901), cited from the Czech translation: *V zemi Chazarů* (Mukachevo, 1927), p. 96. Italics in the original.

134. Ibid., pp. 98-100.

135. Voloshyn, *Spomynŷ,* pp. 69-70; Lelekach, "Podkarpatskoe pys'menstvo," Kolomiets, *Sotsial'no,* vol. 2, pp. 318-342 passim; Mayer, "Beiträge," p. 120; Smiian, *Revoliutsiinyi . . . rukh,* pp. 68-69. On the careers of these editors, see Nedziel'skii, *Ocherk,* p. 275; and Szinnyei, *Magyar írók,* vol. 2, p. 1088 and vol. 8 (1902), pp. 1316-1317.

136. Mayer, "Beiträge," pp. 139-140; Vladimir Gomichkov, "Nashi v Budapeshtie," *Zemlediel'skii kalendar' na vysokonosnyi god 1936* (Uzhhorod, 1935), pp. 106-109. On the careers of Demko and J. Szabó, see Szinnyei, *Magyar irók,* vol. 2, pp. 777-779, and vol. 13 (1909), pp. 218-219. On Kutkafalvy, see Appendix 2.

137. Mayer, "Beiträge," pp. 140-147; Rusak, *Vospominaniia,* pp. 6-11; Pekar, *Narysy,* pp. 104-105. On the Rusyn pilgrimage to Rome, see the memorial book *Emlékkönyv a görög katholikus magyarok római zarándoklatáról* (Budapest, 1901).

138. The Vatican argued against the use of Magyar because it was not a "liturgical language," but although plans were made to train the clergy in classical Greek, this never really worked out. Pekar, *Narysy,* pp. 105-107; Gulya, *A magyarországi ruthén kérdés,* pp. 15-19. For a contemporary panegyric of these developments, see Jenő Szabó, *A görög-katholikus Magyarország utolsó kálvária útja* (Budapest, 1913). For a later account which tries to prove that the Greek Catholics in this region were originally ethnically Magyar, see János Karácsonyi, *A görögkatholikus magyarok eredete* (Budapest, 1924).

139. Sándor Bonkáló, *A kárpátalji rutén irodalom és művelődes* (Pécs, 1935), p. 10. On the writings of these two figures, see Chapter 5 and the references in the Bibliography (refs. 0498, 0838, 1197-1202, 1466-1477). On their careers, see Hartl, *Literární obrození,* pp. 56-57; Nedziel'skii, *Ocherk,* pp. 265-266; Appendix 2; and the biographies by J. Perényi and B. Vardy in the Bibliography (refs. 1033, 1075).

140. On the careers of these figures, see Appendix 2; on their writings, see Chapter 5 and the Bibliography (refs. 0073-0075, 0820, 0870, 2124-2134, 2149).

141. The need for a printshop arose when Mészáros moved his weekly, *Kárpáti*

hirnök, from Sárospatak to Uzhhorod. Stryps'kyi, "Pochatky drukarstva," pp. 277-278. On his writings, see Chapter 5 and the Bibliography (refs. 1774, 1775). On his career, Szinnyei, *Magyar írók,* vol. 8 (1902), pp. 1163-1168.

142. His ethnographic works included: *Magyar-orosz népdalok* (Sárospatak, 1864), and *A magyar-orosz nép közmondásai és példabeszédei,* Kisfaludy társaság, vol. 12 (1877). On his historical writings, see Chapter 5 and the Bibliography (refs. 1698-1703). On his career, see Szinnyei, *Magyar írók,* vol. 7 (1900), pp. 977-985. Cf. József Jankovich, "A munkácsi Lehoczky-múzeum régészeti ásatásai a cseh megszállás alatt," *Zoria-Hajnal,* vol. 2, nos. 3-4 (Uzhhorod, 1942), pp. 290-302; and János Váradi-Sternberg, *Utak, találkozások, emberek: írások az orosz-magyar és ukrán-magyar kapcsolatokról* (Uzhhorod, 1974), pp. 168-169.

143. At this meeting in Budapest, Serbian, Rumanian, and Slovak leaders agreed on a joint program to present before the government. Paragraph 3 stated that a League was being formed to protect the "nationalities in all legal ways, and hope that the Germans and Ruthenes will join them." Program reprinted in Scotus Viator, *Racial Problems,* pp. 476-477. Yet in spite of several calls for cooperation, Rusyn leaders refused to form a national platform in conjunction with the other minorities. *Dejiny Slovenska,* vol. 2 (Bratislava, 1968), pp. 485-497; Jan Podešt', "Styky podkarpatorusko-rumunské," in Jaroslav Zatloukal, ed., *Podkarpatská Rus* (Bratislava, 1936), p. 101.

144. In 1894-95, after a long political struggle, the Hungarian Parliament finally succeeded in passing five bills which took away many prerogatives of the Catholic Church. Among the new provisions were that: (1) civil marriages were compulsory; (2) births, deaths and marriages must be registered by the state; (3) individuals had the right to declare themselves of no confession; and (4) Judaism was made an established religion. Macartney, *Habsburg Empire,* pp. 678-699.

145. Cited in Maier, "Zakarpats'ki ukraïntsi," pp. 56-57.

146. Mayer, "Beiträge," pp. 123-126.

147. Cited in Maier, "Zakarpats'ki ukraïntsi," p. 60.

148. Pereni, *Iz istorii,* pp. 134-142; Kolomiets, *Sotsial'no,* vol. 1, pp. 363-382; Maier, "Zakarpats'ki ukraïntsi," pp. 57-64; Mayer, "Beiträge," pp. 126-130; Smiian, *Revoliutsiinyi . . . rukh,* pp. 20-46. On Egán's career, see Szinnyei, vol. 2, pp. 1214-1216. There has been much speculation that the Highlands Action was anti-Semitic in character, since it aimed at undercutting the economic dominance of Jews over Rusyns. Moreover, legend has it that Egán was killed by Jews precisely for that reason. For further details, see Egán's brochure, *Ekonomichne polozhenie rus'-kykh selian v Uhorshchyni* (L'viv, 1901); Frigyes Paris, *Tájékoztató a ruthén actiónál való működésem felől* (Budapest, 1904), pp. 525-536, 846-874.

149. For example, Vasyl' Grendzha-Dons'kyi, the avid Ukrainophile and Subcarpathian patriot during the 1920s and 1930s (see Chapter 7) began his literary career with verses in Magyar and proudly served the Hungarian fatherland during the war as a member of the *Honvéds.*

150. The Uzhhorod Diocese was represented on the Commission by Bishop Antal Papp and by the clerical professors Petro Gebei, Simeon Sabov, Iurii Shuba, and Avhustyn Voloshyn. All protested that no reforms were necessary. For details, see Rusak, *Vospominaniia,* pp. 11-23; Voloshyn, *Spomynŷ,* pp. 76-86 and his "Oborona kyrylyky: iak oboronialysia pidkarp. rusyny proty ostann'oho ataku madiaryzatsiï pered perevorotom?," *Naukovyi zbirnyk TP,* vol. 12 (Uzhhorod, 1937), pp. 86-94; Pekar, *Narysy,* pp. 108-110. The Marxist writer, Smiian, *Revoliutsiinyi . . . rukh,* pp. 69-72, claims incorrectly that all the clergy present favored the government's policy.

151. Voloshyn, "Oborona," pp. 94-99; Pekar, *Narysy,* p. 110; Žeguc, *Die*

nationalpolitischen Bestrebungen, pp. 119-122. On the attitude of the Rusyn press, especially *Nase otecsesztvo*, see Olena Rudlovchak, "Do pytan' zhurnalistyky v ukraïntsiv Skhidnoï Slovachchyny," *Duklia*, vol. 10, no. 3 (Prešov, 1963), pp. 66-67.

152. Voloshyn, *Spomynŷ*, p. 86, later recalled: "How far our national consciousness declined during [the First World] War is clearly shown by the fact that the people did not show any opposition at all to the removal of the Cyrillic alphabet from the schools."

153. *Görögkatholikus szemle*, no. 20 (1915), cited in Iosif Kaminskii, "Vospominaniia," *Karpatorusskii golos*, no. 9 (Uzhhorod, 1933).

154. Cited with many other examples in M. Maier, "Stanovyshche trudiashchykh Zakarpattia v roky pershoï svitovoï viiny," *Ukraïns'ko-uhors'ki istorychni zv'iazky* (Kiev, 1964), p. 220.

155. The Kiev Carpatho-Russian Committee prepared maps and brochures about Galicia specially for Russian Army officers and supplied them with a list of Galician villages where known Russophiles lived. M. Lozyns'kyi, *Halychyna v zhyttiu Ukraïny* (Vienna, 1916), pp. 39-42. For examples of other titles (sometimes politically provocative) published in Russia at this time, see the entries under N. N. Bakhtin, T. D. Florinskii, I. I. Gumetskii, P. E. Kazanskii, V. P. Ponomarev, Ia. Spanovskii, S. Troitskii, A. F. Vasil'ev, L. Vasil'evskii, and G. A. Voskresenskii in the Bibliography (refs. 1132, 1327, 1403, 1576, 1940, 2090, 2184, 2215, 2242).

156. From the proclamation, reprinted in *Viestnik Evropy*, vol. 49, no. 9 (Petrograd, 1914), pp. 346-347. On the propaganda from Russia, see Z. A. B. Zeman, *The Break-Up of the Habsburg Empire, 1914-1918: A Study in National and Social Revolution* (London, 1961), pp. 52-54; C. Jay Smith, *The Russian Struggle for Power, 1914-1917* (New York, 1956), pp. 8-13.

157. For the positive feeling among Cossack officers, see Gregory P. Tschebotarioff, *Russia, My Native Land* (New York, 1964), p. 47. On the favorable reaction of the Rusyns, see Alois Hora, *Podkarpatská Rus* (Prague, 1919), pp. 17-18; V. I. Netochaiev, "Zakarpattia v roky pershoï svitovoï imperialistychnoï viiny (1914-1917 rr.)," *Dopovidi ta povidomlennia*, Seriia istoryko-filolohichna, vol. 1 (Uzhhorod, 1957), pp. 26-29; Iurii Kachii, "Zv'iazky naselennia Zakarpattia z rosiis'kym viis'kom v roky pershoï svitovoï viiny," *Arkhivy Ukraïny*, no. 6 (Kiev, 1965), pp. 41-47; Smiian, *Revoliutsiinyi . . . rukh*, pp. 158-170; Shtefan, *Za voliu i pravdu*, pp. 302-304; *Zakarpats'ke selo*, pp. 152-154.

158. Sands, *The Russians in Galicia*, pp. 10-22; Dmytro Doroshenko, *Moï spomyny pro nedavnie mynule* (1914-1920), 2nd ed. (Munich, 1969), pp. 24-28, 67-75, 105-151; Smith, *Russian Struggle*, pp. 89-90.

159. Dimitri A. Markoff, *Belgium of the East* (Wilkes-Barre, Pa., 1920), pp. 7-16; and the detailed *Talergofskii al'manakh: propamiatnaia kniga avstriiskikh zhestokostei, izuvierstv i nasilii nad karpato-russkim narodom vo vremia vsemirnoi voiny 1914-1917 gg.*, 4 vols. (L'viv, 1924-1932)—reprinted in *Voennye prestupleniia*. Il'ko, *Zakarpats'ke selo*, p. 154, claims that in October 1914 alone, eight-hundred Subcarpathian Rusyns were arrested. On trials and retaliations in Subcarpathian Rus', see Hora, *Podkarpatská Rus*, p. 18; Smiian, *Revoliutsiinyi . . . rukh*, pp. 165-168, 171-178; Shtefan, *Za voliu i pravdu*, pp. 304-305.

160. The journal, whose establishment coincided with the interest of the Central Powers in creating an independent Ukrainian state, was edited by the Subcarpathian Rusyn, Hiiador Stryps'kyi, who was careful to stress that the Ukrainian problem had no relation to Subcarpathian Rus'. Dmytro Doroshenko, *Uhors'ka Ukraïna* (Prague, 1919), pp. 26-27. Nonetheless, one leaflet did appear, *Egy emlékirat* (Sopron, 1915), suggesting that the Subcarpathian Rusyns be called Ukrainians.

161. In April 1915, the Sich forces organized a public celebration in Mukachevo to commemorate the Ukrainian poet Taras Shevchenko, which, according to one Subcarpathian eye-witness "made a deep impression on those present." Shtefan, *Za voliu i pravdu,* pp. 293-300. Cf. Smiian, *Revoliutsiinyi . . . rukh,* pp. 155-159; and Stepan Ripets'kyi, *Ukrains'ke Sichove Striletstvo* (New York, 1956), pp. 80-91.

162. As a result of drought, 1917 was a particularly unproductive year in agriculture. Maier, "Stanovyshche," pp. 221-227.

163. S.A., *Görög katholikus szemle,* no. 19 (1916). For similar appraisals, see the contemporary accounts of Ivan Nimchuk, in *Vistnyk Soiuzu vyzvolennia Ukraïny* (Vienna), October 31, 1915—cited in Shtefan, *Za voliu i pravdu,* pp. 265-266; Doroshenko, *Moï spomyny,* pp. 451-453; L. Vasilevskii (Plokhotskii), "Vengerskie 'rusnaki' i ikh sud'ba," *Russkoe bogatstvo,* no. 3 (St. Petersburg, 1914), pp. 362-368.

164. For instance, Iosif Kaminskii, later a leading Russophile in Subcarpathian Rus', spent most of the war years in a comfortable situation with a Russian aristocratic family in Siberia. On Rusyn military participation, see V. R. Vavrik, *Karpatorossy v Kornilovskom pokhodie i Dobrovol'cheskoi Armii* (L'viv, 1923); František Šip, "Naše finanční pomoc při vzniku karpatoruských vojsk na Sibiři," *Naše revoluce,* vol. 3 (Prague, 1925-26), pp. 388-391.

One study, B. Spivak and M. Troian, *40 nezabutnikh dniv* (Uzhhorod, 1967), p. 24, suggests that 8,000 Subcarpathians returned from Russia after the war. Among these were Ivan Mondok, Ivan Lokota, Erne Seidler, and Béla Illés, all of whom were to become prominent leaders in the Subcarpathian Communist Party. *Dobrovol'tsi* (Uzhhorod, 1971), pp. 87-92; and *Narysy istoriï zakarpats'koï oblasnoï partiinoï orhanizatsiï,* vol. 1 *(1918-1945 rr.)* (Uzhhorod, 1968), p. 11.

165. R.W. Seton-Watson, *A History of the Czechs and Slovaks,* 2nd ed. (Hamden, Conn., 1965), p. 283, later argued that if Hungary had continued to exist unimpaired the Slovaks would have had at best ten more years of existence.

4. The Incorporation of Subcarpathian Rus' into Czechoslovakia

1. On the activity of Czechs, Poles, and other eastern and western European immigrant groups, see the individual chapters in Joseph P. O'Grady, ed., *The Immigrants' Influence on Wilson's Peace Policies* (Lexington, Ky., 1967).

2. The activity of Rusyn-American immigrants in this period has been discussed by various authors. For a survey of the literature on this problem, see Paul R. Magocsi, "The Political Activity of Rusyn-American Immigrants in 1918," *East European Quarterly,* vol. 10, no. 3 (Boulder, Colo., 1976), pp. 347, 359-360.

3. For the early history of Rusyn immigrant development, see Walter C. Warzeski, *Byzantine Rite Rusins in Carpatho-Ruthenia and America* (Pittsburgh, 1971), pp. 95-128 and Petr Kokhanik, *Nachalo istorii Amerikanskoi Rusi,* 2nd ed. (Trumbull, Conn., 1970), pp. 479-514.

4. On this controversial figure, see Bohdan P. Procko, "Soter Ortynsky: First Ruthenian Bishop in the United States, 1907-1916," *Catholic Historical Review,* vol. 58, no. 4 (Washington, D.C., 1973), pp. 513-533.

5. Program of the Rusyn Civilian Church Council, May 14, 1908, cited in Warzeski, *Byzantine Rite Rusyns,* p. 120. Ortyns'kyi's unpopularity also increased because he was responsible for having to administer a Papal decree, the "Ea Semper" of July 18, 1907, which revoked several practices of the eastern rite, among them the acceptance of married priests. The more unpopular provisions of the "Ea Semper" were later revoked ("Cum Episcopo Graeco-Rutheno," August 17, 1914). Stephen C. Gulovich, "The Rusin Exarchate in the United States," *The Eastern Churches Quarterly,* vol. 6 (London, 1946), pp. 477-479.

6. Gabriel Martyak was chosen the Subcarpathian administrator, Peter Ponia-tyshyn, the Ukrainian. Warzeski, *Byzantine Rite Rusyns,* pp. 114-124; Atanasii V. Pekar, *Narysy istoriï tserkvy Zakarpattia* (Rome, 1967), pp. 183-187.

7. See pp. 66-67.

8. "Podkarpatští Rusíni v Americe před válkou a za války," *Naše revoluce,* vol. 4 (Prague, 1926-27), pp. 270-271. The petition was signed by Michael Yuhasz, Chairman of the Greek Catholic Union, and by Pavel J. Zsatkovich, editor of the *Amierykanskii russkii vîstnyk.*

9. The first Apostolic Visitor for Greek Catholics in the United States, Andrei Hodobai (1902-06), was an important agent for the Budapest authorities. Ibid.; Mariia Maier, "Zakarpats'ki ukraïntsi na perelomi stolit'," in *Zhovten' i ukraïns'ka kul'tura* (Prešov, 1968), pp. 65-70.

10. Petr Hatalák, *Jak vznikla myšlenka přípojiti Podkarpatskou Rus k Česko-slovensku* (Uzhhorod, 1935), pp. 11-21; Victor S. Mamatey, "The Slovaks and Carpatho-Ruthenians," in O'Grady, *Immigrants' Influence,* pp. 240-241; Joseph Danko, "Plebiscite of Carpatho-Ruthenians in the United States Recommending Union of Carpatho-Ruthenia with the Czechoslovak Republic," *Annals of the Ukrainian Academy of Arts and Sciences,* vol. 11, nos. 1-2 (New York, 1964-1968), pp. 185-186.

11. Cited from a resolution by thirty-two Subcarpathian Rusyn priests who met in New York on June 28, 1917. *Prosvîta,* July 12, 1917; *Svoboda* (Jersey City, N.J.), July 17, 1917.

12. "Memorandum Russkago Kongressa v Amerikie, sozvannago 'Soiuzom osvobozhdeniia Prikarpatskoi Rusi' posviashchaemyi svobodnomu russkomu narodu v Rossii, russkomu uchreditel'nomu sobraniiu, russkomu pravitel'stvu," cited from the Russian text reprinted in Zdeněk Peška and Josef Markov, "Pří-spěvek k ústavním dějinám Podkarpatské Rusi," *Bratislava,* vol. 5 (Bratislava, 1931), pp. 517-518.

13. Hatalák, *Jak vznikla myšlenka,* p. 19.

14. Cited from United States State Department document 763.72119/1775, supplied to me by Professor V. Mamatey. There is no indication that immigrants from Subcarpathian Rus' were members of the Ukrainian Federation. The mem-orandum was signed by Miroslav Sichinsky, who later represented the Ukrainians at the Mid-European Union in Philadelphia, where Subcarpathian Rusyns were recog-nized as a separate national group.

15. Michael J. Hanchin, "Alternatyvŷ," *Amierykanskii russkii vîstnyk* (Home-stead, Pa.), January 3, 1918. This, and all other references, are from the "Russian" edition of the newspaper printed in Cyrillic alphabet.

16. *Papers Relating to the Foreign Relations of the United States,* Supplement 1, *The World War 1918,* vol. 1 (Washington, D.C., 1933), p. 816.

17. Markovič quotation from I. Markovič, *Slováci v zahraničnej revolúcii* (Prague, 1923), p. 36. On Russian war aims, which did include the Subcarpathian region, see above, Chapter 3. Masaryk quotation from Tomáš G. Masaryk, *Světová revoluce za války a ve valce 1914-1918* (Prague, 1938), p. 290. Masaryk is the only source regarding the Ukrainian point of view. None of the Ukrainian lead-ers (D. Doroshenko, P. Khrystiuk, A. Margolin, I. Mazepa, V. Petriv, V. Vynny-chenko) mentions in his memoirs any conversation with Masaryk about the Subcar-pathian problem. Nor does O. I. Bochkovs'kyi, in his informative account of Ma-saryk in Kiev—*T. G. Masaryk: Natsional'na problema ta ukraïns'ka pytannia* (Podě-brady, 1930), pp. 135-153—say anything about discussions regarding Subcarpathian Rus'. The silence on this matter is intriguing since in late 1918 the West Ukrainian

and Ukrainian National Republics claimed sovereignty over all "Ukrainians" living south of the Carpathians. On the other hand, it is possible that initially Ukrainian politicians in Kiev were not opposed to Masaryk's designs on Subcarpathian Rus', because in the summer of 1917 they were desperately trying to obtain military support from the Czech Legion then stationed in the Ukraine.

18. Nikolai Pachuta, "Cheshsko-slovenska armada," *Amierykanskïi russkïi vîstnyk,* January 17, 1918.

19. The text of these memoranda were not available to the author, although in his memoirs Masaryk mentioned the one given to him: *Světová revoluce,* p. 291. For a discussion of the contents of both memoranda, see Hatalák, *Jak vznikla myšlenka,* pp. 20-31; and "Carpathian Russians and the Czechoslovaks" in *The Bohemian Review,* vol. 2, no. 5 (Chicago, 1918), pp. 70-72; and Karel Pichlík, *Zahraniční odboj 1914-1918 bez legend* (Prague, 1968), p. 466, note.

20. Masaryk, *Světová revoluce,* pp. 290-291.

21. *Prosvîta,* March 14, 1918.

22. Ibid., January 24, 1918.

23. Ibid., January 17, 1918.

24. Cited in "Podkarpatští Rusíni v Americe," p. 276.

25. *Prosvîta,* June 20 and July 4, 1918; *Svoboda,* July 2, 1918; *Amierykanskïi russkïi vîstnyk,* July 11, 1918. The protocols of the Cleveland-Braddock Convention appear in each issue of *Amierykanskïi russkïi vîstnyk* from July 4, 1918, to January 23, 1919, and the Convention is summarized in "Istorija Greko-Kaft. Sojedinenija," *Zoloto-Jubilejnyj Kalendar' Greko Kaft. Sojedinenija v S.Š.A.* (Munhall, Pa., 1942), pp. 53-55.

26. *Prosvîta,* July 25, 1918; *Amierykanskïi russkïi vîstnyk,* August 1, 1918.

27. The original text of the Homestead Resolution appears under the heading "Do vsîkh Uhro-Rusynov zhiiushchykh v Soed. Derzhavakh Amerykî," in *Amierykanskïi russkïi vîstnyk,* August 8, 1918, and *Prosvîta,* August 8, 1918. This text differs substantially from the one which appears in most other studies, whose authors have based their versions on the account given by G. Zsatkovich in his *Otkrytie-Exposé byvšeho gubernatora Podkarpatskoj Rusi, o Podkarpatskoj Rusi,* 2nd ed. (Homestead, Pa., 1921), p. 3. The Rusyn-American leader was not present at the Homestead deliberations, and for his own political reasons claimed that the first demand was "complete independence" and the last simply "autonomy." Zsatkovich clearly misrepresented the Homestead Resolution by deleting the demand for autonomy specifically within Hungary. For a discussion of the conflicting interpretations of this problem, see Magocsi, "Political Activity," p. 363, n. 36.

28. *Amierykanskïi russkïi vîstnyk,* August 29, 1918, and September 5, 1918.

29. Editorial in English, "Answer to our 'Bolsheviki'," ibid., August 22, 1918. See also ibid., September 12, 1918.

30. The Rusyn immigrants, most of whom came from these disputed areas, were incensed at those Slovaks who refused to consider Rusyns as anything else but "Slovak Greek Catholics": ibid., August 15, 1918. See also articles in *Prosvîta,* September 19 and October 3, 1918.

31. "Answer to our 'Bolsheviki'," *Amierykanskïi russkïi vîstnyk,* August 29 and September 5, 1918.

32. Ibid., November 21, 1918.

33. On Zsatkovich and other Subcarpathian leaders mentioned in this chapter, see below, Appendix 2.

34. Zsatkovich wrote extensive editorials in late 1918 stressing the independent nature of Subcarpathian Rusyns. See his "Kraj Uhro-Rusinov—Uhro-Rusinija," *Prosvîta,* October 31, 1918.

35. At the meeting with Zsatkovich were Julij Gardoš—acting head of the

American Council of Uhro-Rusyns, Rev. Nikolaj Chopey, Rev. Valentine Gorzo, Andrej Petach, Georgij Komloš, and Michael J. Hanchin.

36. The memorandum appears in *Amierykanskïi russkïi vîstnyk,* October 24, 1918, and *Prosvîta,* October 31, 1918.

37. Žatkovič [Zsatkovich], *Otkrytie-Exposé,* p. 5.

38. *Prosvîta,* February 21, 1926.

39. Žatkovič, *Otkrytie-Exposé,* p. 5.

40. Both Danko, "Plebiscite," p. 189, n. 12 and Mamatey, "Slovaks and Carpatho-Ruthenians," p. 244, n. 38, have correctly refuted the erroneous suggestion that a so-called "Philadelphia Agreement," signed by Zsatkovich and Masaryk, pledged the union of Subcarpathian Rus' to Czechoslovakia. For the origin of the "Philadelphia Agreement" theory, see C. A. Macartney, *Hungary and Her Successors* (London, 1937), p. 215; and the earlier Vojta Beneš, *Masarykovo dílo v Americe* (Prague, 1925), p. 73. A facsimile of the Declaration of Common Aims is reproduced in Walter K. Hanak, *The Subcarpathian Ruthenian Question: 1918-1945* (Munhall, Pa., 1962), p. 10, while a good discussion of the work of the Mid-European Union is found in Arthur J. May, "The Mid-European Union," in O'Grady, *Immigrant's Influence,* pp. 250-271.

41. Memorandum of the American-Russian National Defense, Dedicated to Professor T. G. Masaryk, the Illustrious and Tireless Worker for the Emancipation of the Slavic Nations" (Pittsburgh, 1918)—citation taken from the reprint in Peška, "Příspěvek," vol. 5, p. 130. This memorandum was also signed by G. Kondor, president of the Supreme Tribunal, and I. Drimak, supreme recorder of the Greek Catholic Union.

42. "Protokol yz zasîdaniia Tsentral'noho Vŷbora Amierykanskoi Narodnoi Radŷ Uhro-Rusynov" (Homestead, Pa., October 29, 1918), *Amierykanskïi russkïi vîstnyk,* November 7, 1918.

43. Ibid.

44. "Protokol iz Zasîdaniia Amerykanskoi Narodnoi Rady Uhro-Rusynov poderzhanoho dnia 12-ho Noiabria, 1918, v Skrenton, Pa.," ibid., November 14, 1918.

45. Ibid. Protocol also reprinted in *Prosvîta,* November 28, 1918.

46. Žatkovič, *Otkrytie-Exposé,* pp. 5-6; Masaryk, *Světová revoluce,* p. 292.

47. Correspondence between Zsatkovich and Wilson is reprinted in Danko, "Plebiscite," pp. 203-205.

48. The grammatical principle most feared was the modern phonetic orthography adopted by Ukrainophiles in Galicia. The Uhro-Rusyn commentator felt that if the Carpathian Mountains remained as a border, they "will defend us so that the phonetic fish will not eat our more miserable yet to us dear Uhro-Rusyn language." *Amierykanskïi russkïi vîstnyk,* November 14, 1918.

49. An interesting Rusyn commentary on the neighboring Slovaks: "As for language, speech, literature, there is no such fear before Slovaks as Ukrainians. Slovaks don't have a literature. Ukrainians have one. Thus, we would sooner lose our Uhro-Rusyn character with Ukrainians than with the Czecho-Slovaks." Ibid., November 21, 1918. See also *Prosvîta,* November 21, 1918.

50. Among those who signed the protest were A. Holosnyay, J. Szabo, and N. Szabados, all of whom had served in the clerical representation that signed the Homestead Resolution in July. *Prosvîta,* November 28, 1918. See also the recollections of Rev. N. Szabados in the *Amerikai magyar népszava,* November 8, 1924.

51. This meant that if a given lodge or parish had, for instance, fifty members—twenty-six voting for Czechoslovakia, twenty-four for the Ukraine or Hungary—that one alloted vote would be cast for Czechoslovakia.

52. The results of the plebiscite appeared in *Prosvîta,* January 2, 1919, and

Amierykanskii russkii vîstnyk, January 5, 1919. They have been subsequently reprinted in Danko, "Plebiscite," pp. 191-202.

53. Reflecting on these developments, one historian concluded that "The Ruthenian immigrants in America did determine the fate of their compatriots at home—a unique case, it appears, of the influence of an immigrant group in America on the political history in Europe." Mamatey, "Slovaks and Carpatho-Ruthenians," p. 249.

54. Oszkar Jászi, *Revolution and Counter-Revolution in Hungary* (London, 1924), p. 38.

55. Avhustyn Shtefan, a Subcarpathian Ukrainophile, should not be confused with Dr. Agoston Stefan, the local Magyarone who served as governor of Rus'ka Kraina in 1919. On both figures, see below, Appendix 2.

56. Petro Stercho, *Karpato-ukraïns'ka derzhava* (Toronto, 1965), pp. 112-114; Avhustyn Shtefan, *Za pravdu i voliu: spomyny i deshcho z istoriï Karpats'koï U-kraïny,* vol. 1 (Toronto, 1973), pp. 315-338.

57. Cited in Ortoskop [Mykhailo Tvorydlo], *Derzhavni zmahannia Prykarpatskoï Ukraïny* (Vienna, 1924), pp. 9-10. For the text of another Lubovňa declaration, see Petr K. Smiian, *Zhovtneva revoliutsiia i Zakarpattia: 1917-1919 rr.* (L'viv, 1972), p. 31.

58. Reprinted in Peška and Markov, "Příspěvek," pp. 526-527.

59. M. Tvorydlo analyzed fifty-five completed questionnaires he had in hand. As for remaining with Hungary, fifty-one were opposed, two for, two abstained. In response to whether union with Rus' (Ukraine) was desired, twenty-eight were favorable, twenty wanted complete independence, two were for Hungary, five were for the Ukraine, but, if that was not possible, for Czechoslovakia. These figures are only a sample, since it is not known how many questionnaires were completed and returned to Nevyts'kyi. Ortoskop, *Derzhavni zmahannia,* pp. 11-12.

60. Speech quoted in I.V. Kaminskii, "Vospominaniia," *Karpatorusskii golos,* no. 26 (Uzhhorod, 1933) and in Smiian, *Zhovtneva revoliutsiia,* p. 40.

61. The resolution is reprinted in Ortoskop, *Derzhavni zmahanniia,* p. 22; Kaminskii, "Vospominaniia," no. 27; Iulii Rusak [Iulii Gadzhega], *Vospominaniia* (Uzhhorod, 1938), p. 33. The Uzhhorod Council chose Simeon Sabov chairman, Aleksei Kossei vice-chairman, A. Voloshyn secretary, Feodor Hulovych, Iulii Grigashii, and Iosif Kaminskii members. For further details, see ibid., pp. 30-36; Avhustyn Voloshyn, *Spomynŷ* (Uzhhorod, 1923), pp. 89-90; Kaminskii, "Vospominaniia," nos. 26-27; Alois Raušer, "Připojení Podkarpatské Rusi k československé republice," in J. Zatloukal, ed., *Podkarpatská Rus* (Bratislava, 1936), pp. 66-67; Gábor Darás, *A Ruténföld elszakításának elözményei, 1890-1920* (Budapest, 1936), pp. 98-99; I.N. Mel'nikova, "Kak byla vkliuchena Zakarpatskaia Ukraina v sostav Chekhoslovakii v 1919 g.," *Uchenye zapiski Instituta slavianovedeniia,* vol. 3 (Moscow, 1951), pp. 111-112; Stercho, *Karpato-ukraïns'ka derzhava,* pp. 114-115; Smiian, *Zhovtneva revoliutsiia,* pp. 40-41.

62. The memorandum is reprinted in Kaminskii, "Vospominaniia," no. 30. The program of the Uhro-Rusyn political party appears in *Proklamatsiia do uhrorus'koho naroda* (Budapest, 1919), pp. 25-26. See also *Karpato-rus'kii vîstnyk* (Uzhhorod), December 23, 1918; Kaminskii, "Vospominaniia," nos. 27-28; Darás, *A Ruténföld,* pp. 99-103; Rusak, *Vospominaniia,* pp. 36-37.

63. Kaminskii, "Vospominaniia," no. 30; Rusak, *Vospominaniia,* p. 37.

64. Leaders in Uzhhorod demanded that "the whole Rusyn people from the Poprad to Tisa Rivers be united" and that protests be sent to the Entente regarding the "illegal occupation" of the Prešov Region (in eastern Slovakia) by the Czechoslovaks. Evmenii Sabov, "Do rus'koho naroda," *Rus'ka Kraina* (Uzhhorod), January 1, 1919.

65. "Narodnŷi zakon chysla 10 pro samoupravu rus'koho narodu zhyvushcho-ho na Uhorshchynî," reprinted in Ortoskop, *Derzhavni zmahannia,* pp. 32-33. An English translation is available in Peter G. Stercho, *Diplomacy of Double Morality: Europe's Crossroads in Carpatho-Ukraine, 1919-1939* (New York, 1971), pp. 399-400.

66. The occurrence of anti-Hungarian activity prompted Antal Papp, the pro-government bishop of Uzhhorod, to send to all his priests a circular requesting that they aid in controlling "the secret agitation for union with the Ukraine or Czechoslovakia" as well as the "anti-Christian Social-Democratic radical agitation." The appeal was dated Uzhhorod, November 28, 1918, and is reprinted in Ortoskop, *Derzhavni zmahannia,* pp. 22-23 and in an edited version in *Taiemne staie iavnym (Dokumenty pro antynarodnu diial'nist' tserkovnykiv na Zakarpatti v period okupatsïi)* (Uzhhorod, 1965), doc. 51.

67. Manifesto reprinted in Peska and Markov, "Příspěvek," pp. 524-526.

68. Ortoskop, *Derzhavni zmahannia,* pp. 13-14; Mykola Andrusiak, "Istoriia Karpats'koï Ukraïny" in *Karpats'ka Ukraïna* (L'viv, 1939), p. 98; Krzysztof Lewandowski, *Sprawa ukraïnska w polityce zagranicznej Czechosłowacji w latach 1918-1932* (Wrocław and Warsaw, 1974), pp. 86-87. Unfortunately, the resolutions of these smaller councils have never been published or summarized in any of the existing literature.

69. The Slovaks also promised "full autonomy" in ecclesiastical and educational affairs as well as the establishment of a university in the near future. "Proclamation of the Slovak National Council, Turčiansky Sv. Martin, November 30, 1918," reprinted in Peška and Markov, "Příspěvek," pp. 527-528. See also Karol A. Medvecký, *Slovenský prevrat,* vol. 1 (Trnava, 1930), pp. 60-61. The failure to fulfill these promises was to be a source of constant friction between Rusyn leaders and the Czechoslovak government.

70. Ortoskop, *Derzhavni zmahannia,* pp. 13-17. Ladislav Tajtak, *Národodemokratická revolúcia na východnom Slovensku v roku 1918* (Bratislava, 1972), pp. 97-103.

71. Raušer, "Připojení," p. 66; Smiian, *Zhovtneva revoliutsiia,* pp. 34-35; Darás, *A Ruténföld,* p. 103.

72. "Protokol Narodn'oho Zibrannia v Svaliavi, December 8, 1918," reprinted in Ortoskop, *Derzhavni zmahannia,* pp. 18-19. See also Augustin Stefan, *From Carpatho-Ruthenia to Carpatho-Ukraine* (New York, 1954), p. 20 and Smiian, *Zhovtneva revoliutsiia,* pp. 35-36.

73. "Maramarosh-Sihotskii sbor," *Karpato-rus'kii vîstnyk,* December 23, 1918; "Protokol Maramarosh'koi Rus'koi (Ukrains'koi) Narodnoi Radŷ, December 18, 1918," reprinted in Ortoskop, *Derzhavni zmahannia,* pp. 20-21.

74. "Memorandum Narodnago Sovieta Russkago Prikarpat'ia," Sanok, December 13, 1918, reprinted in Peška and Markov, "Příspěvek," pp. 528-531. Ukrainian writers have confused the geographic term Rus' (Ukraine) with U-krainian nationalism and have erroneously considered Nevyts'kyi and the Lubovňa Council to be Ukrainophile. See Iatsko Ostapchuk, "Uhors'ka Ukraïna, ïï stan i zavdannia ches'koï polityky," *Kalendar' 'Vperedu'* (L'viv, 1920), p. 121; Ortoskop, *Derzhavni zmahannia,* pp. 8-17; Stefan, *From Carpatho-Ruthenia,* pp. 19-20; Stercho, *Karpato-ukraïns'ka derzhava,* p. 117; Vasyl' Hryvna, "Vplyv Zhovtnia na natsional'no-vyzvol'nyi rukh ukraïntsiv Chekhoslovachchyny," in *Zhovten' i ukraïns'ka kul'tura* (Prešov, 1968), pp. 127-130; Smiian, *Zhovtneva revoliutsiia,* pp. 30-34.

75. Ukrainian leaders claim that at the October 19 meeting of the National Council in L'viv a letter from Subcarpathian leaders (unnamed) was read; it concluded with the request: "You, our brethren, must stand behind us and unite with

us. Our people demand such salvation so that finally we can be liberated from the yoke of another people.'' Cited in a work by the chairman of the L'viv National Council, Kost Levyts'kyi, *Velykyi zryv: do istorii ukraïns'koï derzhavnosty vid bereznia do lystopada 1918 r. na pidstavi spomyniv ta dokumentiv* (Lviv, 1931), p. 118. See also Mykhailo Lozyns'kyi, *Halychyna v rr. 1918-1920* (Vienna, 1922), p. 29. No work by a Subcarpathian author, however, has mentioned the sending of a letter to L'viv as early as October 1918.

76. The Kiev universal is cited in Lozyns'kyi, *Halychyna*, pp. 68-69. For the complicated circumstances under which this so-called Fourth Universal was issued, see John S. Reshetar, *The Ukrainian Revolution* (Princeton, 1952), pp. 110-113.

77. Jászi, *Revolution*, p. 37. "Young soldiers returning from Russia have in particular brought the irresistable Bolshevik propaganda. They are causing an uproar against priests." From an article entitled "Bolsevizmus Máramarosban," *Görög-katholikus szemle* (Uzhhorod), December 15, 1918. On the impact of soldiers returning from the Russian front, see also *Shliakhom Zhovtnia: zbirnyk dokumentiv,* vol. 1 (Uzhhorod, 1957), docs. 17, 19, 20, 22, 26, 28, 29; and V.I. Netochaiev, "Vplyv Velykoï Zhovtnevoï sotsialistychnoï revoliutsiï na Zakarpattia i rozhortannia borot'by trudiashchykh za vozz'iednannia z usim ukraïns'kym narodom v 1918-1919 rr.," *Naukovi zapysky,* vol. 30 (Uzhhorod, 1957), pp. 46-48.

78. Cited in Stefan, *From Carpatho-Ruthenia,* p. 20; Smiian, *Zhovtneva revoliutsiia,* p. 36; Netochaiev, "Vplyv," p. 53.

79. *Görög-katholikus szemle,* November 24, 1918. For examples of village petitions that called for union with the Ukraine in late 1918, see Netochaiev, "Vplyv," pp. 52-53, and *Shliakhom Zhovtnia,* vol. 1, docs. 38-41, 49-51.

80. Cited in Fedor Vico, "Ohlas mad'arskej republiky Rád v ukrajinských obciach Zakarpatska," *Nové obzory,* vol. 1 (Prešov, 1959), p. 48.

81. Despite aid from the West Ukrainian Republic, leaders like Vasyl' Klempush emphasized that the *"Hutsuls* [term used by the local Rusyns] themselves created the uprising and not the Galicians. Our *Hutsul* National Council decided to break away from Hungary and unite with the Ukraine." Avhustyn Shtefan, *Ukraïns'ke viis'ko v Zakarpatti* (Toronto and New York, 1969), pp. 11-21; Smiian, *Zhovtneva revoliutsiia,* pp. 55-59; "Hutsulska Republyka," *Nedîlia Rusyna,* vol. 1 (Uzhhorod, 1923), pp. 54-55, 59-60.

82. The protocol of the Prešov meeting is included as an annex to the Czechoslovak Delegation's *Mémoire No. 6,* reprinted in *La Paix de Versailles,* vol. 9, *Questions territoriales,* pt. 1 (Paris, 1939), pp. 99-100 and in Stercho, *Diplomacy,* pp. 404-405.

83. Manifesto reprinted in Peška and Markov, "Příspěvek," pp. 531-532. The anti-Ukrainianism of Beskid and his Galician allies was emphasized: "We consider the separatism of Ukrainian politicians a temporary phenomenon—anti-Slavic, anti-cultural, anti-social—a product of Austro-German imperialism." The decision of the Prešov Council was opposed by former chairman Emyliian Nevyts'kyi, who issued proclamations the same day calling for union with the Ukraine. Reprinted in Ortoskop, *Derzhavni zmahannia,* pp. 14-16. Despite Nevyts'kyi's rhetoric calling for the Ukraine, his discontent was not motivated by displeasure with the Russophile attitude of the Prešov Manifesto, but rather with the usurpation of the Council's leadership by Beskid and his supporters.

84. In December and January a Rusyn Democratic Party (*Ruszin demokrata párt*), Rusyn National Party (*Ruszin néppárt*), and Dukhnovych Literary Society were founded. Rusak, *Vospominaniia,* pp. 37-47. The thirty-one paragraph protocol establishing the Dukhnovych Society, dated January 10 and signed by A. Voloshyn, is reprinted in *Rus'ka Kraina,* January 15, 1919.

85. Voloshyn, *Spomynŷ,* p. 92, and his *Dvî polytychnî rozmovŷ* (Uzhhorod, 1923), pp. 6-7.
86. Report of Hodža to the Ministry of Foreign Affairs in Prague, December 19, 1918: *Slovenský rozchod s Mad'armi roku 1918: dokumentárny výklad o jednaniach dra Milana Hodžu ako čsl. plnomocnika s Károlyiho mad'arskou vládu v listopade a prosince 1918* (Bratislava, 1929), pp. 68-69.
87. Annexe No. 1, dated December 18, 1918, attached to *Mémoire No. 6*—reprinted in *La Paix de Versailles,* pp. 98-99, and in Stercho, *Diplomacy,* pp. 403-404.
88. Report of Dr. Milan Hodža, representative of the Czechoslovak Republic in Budapest, to the Ministry of Foreign Affairs in Prague, January 3, 1919, in A. Kocman et al., eds., *Boj o směr vývoje československého státu,* vol. 1 (Prague, 1965), doc. 28. Voloshyn's first account of the meeting was given in "Rus'ka Krayna y chekhy," *Rus'ka Kraina,* January 15, 1919.
89. Kocman, *Boj,* vol. 1, doc. 28. According to Ortoskop, *Derzhavni zmahannia,* p. 9 and Kaminskii, "Vospominaniia," no. 49, Komarnyts'kyi never signed any memorandum requesting union with Czechoslovakia. Nevertheless, the latter did sign the December 18, 1918, *procès verbale* and later, the May 8, 1919 formal declaration of union with Czechoslovakia.
90. Voloshyn, *Dvî polytychnî,* p. 7 and his "Interv'iu" in *Rusyn* (Uzhhorod), March 21-23, 1923. The Czech officers met on February 1 in Uzhhorod with S. Sabov, A. Voloshyn, P. Gebei, and Iu. Gadzhega. Rusak, *Vospominaniia,* pp. 56-57.
91. A survey of the weekly newspaper *Rus'ka Krayna,* edited by A. Voloshyn, Viktor Zheltvai, and Emyliian Bokshai, reveals the change of mind among Uzhhorod's intelligentsia. Initially, praise was lauded on the new autonomy and attacks directed against the Czechoslovaks and Ukrainians: "Rus'ka Krayna," Evmenii Sabov, "Do rus'koho naroda," "Stavaime do Ukraynŷ," January 1, 1919; and O. Szabo, "Bratia ruskî!," January 8, 1919. By the middle of the month, their attitude changed to calls for union with the Ukrainians, but realization that the latter were weak and thus the Czechoslovaks were the best choice: "Rus'ka Krayna y chekhy," January 15, 1919. Letter from reader and commentary, A. Voloshyn, "Chto bude s namy?," January 22, 1919; "Nash tserkovnyi vopros," and "Mîrkuime, ne pyluime!," January 29, 1919.
Nevertheless, as late as February 9-10, 1919, the Uzhhorod Council, under S. Sabov and A. Voloshyn, submitted a memorandum to Rus'ka Kraina's Minister O. Szabó demanding implementation of Law Ten, and on February 13 expressed its complete faith in Minister Szabó. Kaminskii, "Vospominaniia," No. 42; Rusak, *Vospominaniia,* pp. 50-54.
92. Lozyns'kyi, *Halychyna,* p. 60. The letter of invitation to Brashchaiko, dated December 25, 1918, is reprinted in *Shliakhom Zhovtnia,* vol. 1, p. 496, n. 34. The Subcarpathian delegates to the Stanyslaviv meeting were the Hutsul leaders S. Klochurak and D. Klempush. Shtefan, *Nashe viis'ko,* p. 9; I. Nahayewsky, *History of the Modern Ukrainian State, 1917-1923* (Munich, 1966), p. 135.
93. "Spysok Ukraynŷ do Uhorshchyny," *Rus'ka Kraina,* January 22, 1919.
94. For details on these operations, see Shtefan, *Nashe viis'ko,* pp. 13-19.
95. *Rus'ka Kraina,* January 29, 1919; Kaminskii, "Vospominaniia, no. 35; Rusak, *Vospominaniia,* pp. 47-48. See also Raušer, "Připojení," p. 66; Stefan, *From Carpatho-Ruthenia,* p. 21; Netochaiev, "Vplyv," pp. 56-61; Smiian, *Zhovtneva revoliutsiia,* pp. 61-70.
96. The resolution is reprinted in Stercho, *Diplomacy,* p. 401, and partially in Ortoskop, *Derzhavni zmahannia,* pp. 21-22.
97. "Ukaz pravytel'stva Uhorskî Narodnî Republyky chysla 928/1919 v dîlî

orhanyzatsiĭ Rus'koho Pravytel'stvennoho Sovĭtu" (dated Budapest, February 5, 1919), *Karpato-rus'kii vĭstnyk,* February 3, 1919.

98. *Budapesti hírlap,* January 6, 1919 — cited in Smiian, *Zhovtneva revoliutsiia,* p. 47.

99. *Budapesti hírlap,* February 2, 1919 — cited in Smiian, *Zhovtneva revoliutsiia,* p. 51.

100. See the laudatory article on commissar Stefan and his revolutionary, anti-bourgeois speech, reprinted in *Rus'ka pravda* (Mukachevo), April 12, 1919. Mel'-nikova, "Kak byla vkliuchena," pp. 123-124. For further details, see V. V. Usenko, *Vplyv Velykoï Zhovtnevoï sotsialistychnoï revoliutsiï na rozvytok revoliutsiinoho rukhu v Zakarpatti v 1917-1919 rr.* (Kiev, 1955), pp. 131-135; Kaminskii, "Vospo-minaniia," no. 33; Eva S. Balogh, "Nationality Problems of the Hungarian Soviet Republic," in I. Völgyes, ed., *Hungary in Revolution, 1918-19* (Lincoln, Nebraska, 1971), pp. 101-103; Mykhailo Troian, *Uhors'ka komuna 1919 r.* (L'viv, 1970), pp. 129-131; Smiian, *Zhovtneva revoliutsiia,* pp. 95-109.

101. "Konstytutsiia Rus'koi Kraini," *Rus'ka pravda,* April 12, 1919. Also reprinted in *Shliakhom Zhovtnia,* vol. 1, doc. 125.

102. Usenko, *Vplyv,* pp. 150-151; Troian, *Uhors'ka komuna,* pp. 136-138; Balogh, "Nationality problems," pp. 103-104; Iul'ian A. Iavorskii, "Literaturnye otgoloski 'rus'ko-krainskago' perioda v Zakarpatskoi Rusi 1919 goda," in *Karpatorusskii sbornik* (Uzhhorod, 1930), pp. 79-87.

103. Usenko, *Vplyv,* pp. 136-154; Troian, *Uhors'ka komuna,* pp. 131-135; *Shliakhom Zhovtnia,* vol. 1, docs. 78-153. The Red Guard was established on April 9 and continued to fight against the Czech and Rumanian armies until as late as July. B. I. Spivak, "Do pytannia pro uchast' trudiashchykh Zakarpattia u zakhysti Uhors'koï Radians'koï Respubliky u 1919 rotsi," *Dopovidy ta povidomlennia,* Seriia istorychna, no. 4 (Uzhhorod, 1960), pp. 60-77; V. I. Netochaiev, "Z istoriï borot'by trudiashchykh Zakarpattia proty nastupu interventiv u kvitni 1919 roku," ibid., pp. 77-85.

104. "Despite the relatively short period of existence of Soviet rule in the Mukachevo area . . . its importance was very great . . . [Soviet rule] was an important and moral and political victory for Bolshevik ideas . . . The age-long struggle of the workers of Transcarpathia against the internal exploiters and external counterrevo-lutionaries came to a close in late October 1944, with the liberation of Transcarpa-thia from fascist occupation by the heroic Red Army and the union with the Soviet Ukraine." M. V. Troian, "Borot'ba trudiashchykh Mukachivshchyny za Radians'ku vladu v 1918-1919 rr.," *Naukovi zapysky,* vol. 30 (Uzhhorod, 1957), pp. 83-84.

105. Ibid., p. 76. There is no indication in Soviet or other sources that the decrees were greeted with favor by the local populace, and it is quite likely that the forced acquisition of foodstuffs (*Shliakhom Zhovtnia,* vol. 1, Docs. 89-91, 109, 112, 128) were met with dissatisfaction and opposition by the peasantry.

106. I. V. Kaminskii, quoted in "Postupova abo konservativna polytyka?," *Rusyn,* February 6, 1923. See also his "Nasha avtonomiia (samouprava)," *Russkii zemledĭl'skii kalendar'* (Uzhhorod, 1922), pp. 69-70.

107. Usenko, *Vplyv,* pp. 159-177; Balogh, "Nationality Problems," pp. 104-105.

108. Commission polonaişe des travaux préparatoires au congrès de la paix, *Mémoire sur la Galicie* (Paris, 1919); *Le Spisz, l'Orawa et le district de Czaca* (War-saw, 1919); *Territoires polonais en Hongrie septentrionale* (Paris, 1919).

109. Sherman D. Spector, *Rumania at the Paris Peace Conference: A Study of the Diplomacy of Ioan I.C. Brătianu* (New York, 1962), pp. 127-128.

110. The representative of the Kievan Ukrainian National Republic in Paris, G. Sydorenko, submitted a statement, dated May 5, 1919, which opposed the Czechoslovak solution and declared "that the Ukrainian people will never admit the separation of this part of territory from the Ukrainian Republic." The territory indicated comprised the former Hungarian counties of Máramaros, Ugocsa, Bereg, Ung, Zemplén, Sáros, and part of Szepes. *La Paix de Versailles*, pp. 271-272. See also the more developed claims with accompanying map in the 125-page *Mémoire sur l'indépendence de l'Ukraine presénté à la Conférence de la Paix par la délégation de la République ukrainiènne* (Paris, 1919).

The Uhro-Rusyn political party in Budapest, headed by Dr. Miklós Kutkafalvy-Kutka, submitted a memorandum dated August 5, 1919, to the Entente protesting the Czechoslovak "occupation" of Subcarpathian Rus'. The Rusyn language text appeared in *Proklamatsiia*, pp. 35-51; the French translation, *Aide-mémoire adressé aux puissances alliées et associées* (Vienna, 1919), is reprinted in *The Hungarian Peace Negotiations*, vol. 1 (Budapest, 1921), pp. 483-489.

111. The Russian Political Conference was composed of former members of the Provisional Government in Petrograd who tried to have a non-Bolshevik Russia represented at the Peace Conference. On May 10, 1919, they submitted a memorandum including demands for eastern Galicia, Bukovina, and Carpatho-Russia. John M. Thompson, *Russia, Bolshevism and the Versailles Peace* (Princeton, N.J., 1966), p. 399.

112. Dmitrij Markoff, *Mémoire sur les aspirations nationales des Petits-Russiens de l'ancien empire austro-hongrois* (Paris, 1919). Markoff, a former representative from L'viv in the Viennese Parliament, was a Russophile in close contact with Beskid and the Galician members of the Prešov Council. Unlike the latter, however, who favored unification with Czechoslovakia, Markoff still hoped for the resurrection of a "democratic Russia"; the *Mémoire* states that he conveyed these goals to President Masaryk, who "amiably received" the Russophile leader in Prague on December 24, 1918.

113. D. Perman, *The Shaping of the Czechoslovak State* (Leiden, 1962), pp. 121-133.

114. *Mémoire No. 6*, in *La Paix de Versailles*, p. 97.

115. Perman, *The Shaping*, pp. 14-27. Masaryk's 1915 sketch is reproduced at the end of Perman's study.

116. *Mémoire No. 6*, p. 97.

117. Ibid.

118. Ibid., p. 98.

119. Ibid.

120. Ibid., p. 85. See also *Mémoire No. 2: Les revendications territoriales de la République Tchécoslovaque*, in *La Paix de Versailles*, pp. 34-39.

121. Vavro Šrobár, *Osvobozené Slovensko: pamäti z rokov 1918-1920* (Prague, 1928), pp. 303-304; *Slovenský rozchod*, pp. 59, 65-66.

122. This goal was stated in the protocol of the Carpatho-Russian National Council, Prešov, January 7, 1919 (attached to *Mémoire No. 6*) and also in a memoir by the same Council, dated Prešov, January 31, 1919 — reprinted in Peška and Markov, "Příspěvek," vol. 5, pp. 531-532.

123. In 1914, Kramář had conceived the creation of a Czechoslovakia that would include Lusatian and German territory (almost as far north as Berlin), Silesia, a corridor to Yugoslavia, Slovakia (with a southern boundary along the Danube), and Subcarpathian Rus'. Such a state was planned as a crownland in a future east European federation to be dominated by tsarist Russia. A map of the 1914 project is

found in Fedor Houdek, *Vznik hránic Slovenska,* Knižnica 'Prúdov', no. 4 (Bratislava, 1931), p. 92.

124. This document, presented to Minister Václav Klofáč, a close collaborator of Kramář, also included an annex which outlined the advantages to be gained from petroleum deposits if Czechoslovakia annexed the Lemkian region. Memorandum reprinted in Kocman, *Boj,* vol. 1, doc. 54.

125. Anthony Beskid and Dimitry Sobin, *The Origin of the Lems, Slavs of Danubian Provenance: Memorandum to the Peace Conference concerning their national claims* (n.p., n.d.), p. 23. On an enclosed map, the territory of the "Russes des Carpathes (Lemki)" was marked to include an area along the northern crest of the Carpathians stretching roughly from Lubovňa in the west to Uzhhorod in the east. The northernmost extent included the Galician towns of Dukla and Sanok. On May 1, 1919, the Prešov Council also addressed a memorandum to President Wilson to protest the separation of Lemkian lands from Czechoslovakia and their occupation by Polish troops. Reprinted in Peška and Markov, "Příspěvek," vol. 5, pp. 531-534.

126. On April 28, Beneš admitted to Zsatkovich his reluctance even to press Marshal Foch for the occupation of Subcarpathian Rus', because he feared such a request would be interpreted as imperialistic. "Polnoe spravozdanie h-na H.Y. Zhatkovycha," *Amierykanskii russkii vistnyk,* June 5, 1919.

127. The delegate from Italy was the sole member of the commission who opposed Czechoslovakia's annexion of Subcarpathian Rus'. Italy favored a viable Hungary to serve as a balance to Yugoslavia, and if deprived of Subcarpathian Rus' the Budapest government would lose direct contact with its only other potential ally—Poland. Perman, *The Shaping,* pp. 148-149.

128. On April 28, Zsatkovich prepared for Foreign Minister Beneš a memorandum whose subtitle clearly indicated its content: "Memorandum, korotkaia ystoriia o polozhenii mezhdu Uhro-Rusynamy y prychynŷ iak naiskorshoi okupatsii toi chasty Uhro-Russkoi Terrytorii, kotora est esche pod pravleniem teperîshnoho Sovietskoho Mad'iarskoho Pravytel'stva," reprinted in *Amierykanskii russkii vistnyk,* June 5, 1919.

129. Iaroslav Kmitsikevych, "1919-i rik na Zakarpatti (spohad)," *Naukovyi zbirnyk MUKS,* vol. 4, pt. 1 (Bratislava-Prešov, 1969), pp. 381-384; G.I. Žatkovič, *Otkrytie-Exposé,* pp. 10-15 and his "Polnoe spravozdanie"; Kaminskii, "Vospominaniia," no. 64; Rusak, *Vospominaniia,* pp. 59-64.

130. *Protokoly obshchago sobraniia podkarpatskikh russkikh rad i . . . Tsentral'noi Russkoi Narodnoi Rady* — reprinted in *Karpatorusskije novosti* (New York), May 15, 1944.

131. Kmitsikevych claims that Beskid was present on May 8, but this is not borne out by the protocols or by another participant, G. Zsatkovich, who reported that Beskid remained in Prešov waiting (in vain) to be called by the government to Prague. "Uriadovŷi report Amerykanskoi Komyssii Rusynov," *Amierykanskii russkii vistnyk,* July 3, 1919.

132. Protocol of May 8 in *Karpatorusskije novosti,* May 15, 1944.

133. Protocols of May 14 and 15, *Karpatorusskije novosti,* May 15, 1944; *Amierykanskii russkii vistnyk,* July 3, 1919; N. A. Beskid, *Karpatskaia Rus'* (Prešov, 1920), pp. 105-106.

134. Protocol of May 16 in *Karpatorusskije novosti,* May 15, 1944.

135. Voloshyn, *Spomynŷ,* p. 94.

136. Beneš' memorandum of May 17 is reprinted in Francis Deák, *Hungary at the Paris Peace Conference: The Diplomatic History of the Treaty of Trianon* (New York, 1942), pp. 449-450.

137. Report of June 15, cited in Stercho, *Diplomacy*, pp. 36-37. For Beneš' account of the negotiations, see his *Promova pro pidkarpatorus'kyi problem i ioho vidnoshennia do chekhoslovats'koï respubliky* (Uzhhorod and Prague, 1934), pp. 25-34.

138. The primary source for the above account is Miller's *Diary*, especially vol. 13, which is the basis for all later accounts. For a discussion of the Subcarpathian question at Paris, see Stercho, *Diplomacy*, pp. 29-38.

139. *Traité entre les Principales Puissances Alliées et Associées et la Tchécoslovaquie* (Paris, 1919), pp. 26-27.

140. "Ústavní listina Československé republiky," Chapter 1, paragraph 3 in *Sbírka zákonů a nařízení státu československého*, pt. 26 (Prague, March 6, 1920), p. 256.

141. Letter of Antonii Beskid to Karel Kramář, Czechoslovak Minister in Paris, dated Prague, June 20, 1919 (Archiv Národního Musea, Fond Kramář, personal correspondence). For the atmosphere in Uzhhorod and fear of local leaders even after May 1919, see Augustin Vološin, "Napady madarsjkych komunistiv v 1919," in Jozef Zimák, ed., *Vpad mad'arských bol'ševikov na Slovensko v roku 1919* (Bratislava, 1938), pp. 237-240.

142. "T.G. Masaryk ministru národní obrany . . . nutné provedení vojenské okupace Podk. Rusi, 8.VIII.1919," in Kocman, vol 2, p. 78; Raušer, "Připojení," pp. 69-70. The Rumanians did not leave the province until July 1920, and despite friendly relations with Czechoslovakia, some Rumanian propagandists tried to inflame an irrendentist movement in Máramaros county. Spector, *Rumania*, p. 222.

143. The dispatches of the Rusyn leaders are reprinted in Žatkovič, *Otkrytie-Exposé*, pp. 9-17, and Beskid, *Karpatskaia Rus'*, pp. 67-91.

144. Kamil Krofta, "Ruthenes, Czechs and Slovaks," *The Slavonic and East European Review*, vol. 13 (London, 1934-35), p. 626.

145. Edvard Beneš and Karel Kramář, *Československá zahraniční politika: dvě řeči pronesené v Národním shromáždění dne 30 září 1919* (Prague, 1919), p. 18.

146. The "Generální statut pro organisaci a administraci Podkarpatské Rusi" was issued in Uzhhorod on November 18, 1919 and ratified on April 26, 1920 by law 356, *Sbírka zákonů a nařízení státu československého*, pt. 49, May 22, 1920, pp. 413-914.

5. The Use of History

1. Rupert Emerson, *From Empire to Nation: The Rise to Self-Assertion of Asian and African Peoples* (Boston, 1960), p. 95.

2. Boyd C. Shafer, *Faces of Nationalism* (New York, 1972), pp. 333-334. After language, Carlton Hayes placed historical traditions "a close second . . . in importance in constituting a nationality and distinguishing it from others." *Nationalism: A Religion* (New York, 1960) p. 4.

3. Ernest Renan, "Qu'est-ce qu'une nation?" (1882), *Oeuvres complètes*, vol. 1 (Paris, 1947), p. 891.

4. Bernard Lewis, *History—Remembered, Recovered, Invented* (Princeton, N.J., 1975), esp. pp. 53-69; Shafer, *Faces of Nationalism*, pp. 199-206, 335-336; Dankwart A. Rustow, *A World of Nations: Problems of Political Modernization* (Washington, D.C., 1967), pp. 40-47; Louis J. Lekai, "Historiography in Hungary, 1790-1848," *Journal of Central European Affairs*, vol. 14, no. 1 (Boulder, Colo., 1954), pp. 3-18.

5. Bernard Lewis, *The Emergence of Modern Turkey* (London, 1961), p. 353.

6. Gustave E. von Grunebaum, *Modern Islam* (New York, 1964), p. 35. Cf. Joshua A. Fishman, *Language and Nationalism* (Rowley, Mass., 1972), pp. 15-17.

7. There is also an abundant historical literature on Subcarpathian Rus' written by Czech and Soviet authors, but these historiographic "schools" did not really begin until after Czechoslovakia and the Soviet Union obtained political control of the area. The Czech interpretation is discussed in Chapter 10, the Soviet in Chapter 13.

8. For a content analysis of the early histories of the area, see Kálmán Zsatkovics, "A magyaroroszági oroszok történetirásának története," *Századok*, vol. 24 (Budapest, 1890), pp. 568-573, 644-660; E. Perfetskii, "Obzor Ugrorusskoi istoriografii," *Izviestiia ORISIAN*, vol. 19, no. 1 (St. Petersburg, 1914), pp. 291-306; Joseph A. Rácz, "Le développement de la litterature historique carpatho-ukrainienne," *Revue d'histoire comparée*, vol. 22 (Paris, 1944), pp. 172-175.

9. Iurii I. Venelin, "Nieskol'ko slov o Rossiianakh Vengerskikh, i takzhe odno slovtso Istoricheskoe o Pravoslavnoi Greko-Vostochnoi Tserkvi v Vengrii" (1822), in I.S. Svientsitskii, *Materialy po istorii vozrozhdeniia Karpatskoi Rusi*, vol. 1 (L'viv, 1905), pp. 93-96; Ivan Orlai, "Istoriia o Karpato-Rossakh ili o pereselenii Rossiian v Karpatskiia gory i o prikliucheniiakh s nimi sluchivshikhsia" (1804), in ibid., pp. 61-64.

10. A. I. D. [Adol'f I. Dobrianskii], "O zapadnykh granitsakh Podkarpatskoi Rusi, so vremen sv. Vladimira," *Zhurnal MNP*, vol. 208 (St. Petersburg, 1880), pp. 134-159.

11. Aleksander Dukhnovich, "Istinnaia istoriia Karpato Rossov ili Ugorskikh Rusinov" (1853), trans. into Russian by F. Aristov and first published in *Russkii arkhiv*, vol. 52, nos. 4-5 (Moscow, 1914), pp. 529-559, reprinted in O.V. Dukhnovych, *Tvory*, vol. 2 (Bratislava-Prešov, 1967), pp. 531-566. On Dukhnovych's historical writings, see F.F. Aristov, "'Istinnaia Istoriia Karpato-Rossov' A.V. Dukhnovicha: znachenie A.V. Dukhnovicha, kak ugro-russkago istorika," *Russkii arkhiv*, vol. 52, no. 5 (Moscow, 1914), pp. 143-155; I.G. Kolomiets, *Sotsial'no-èkonomicheskie otnosheniia i obshchestvennoe dvizhenie v Zakarpat'e vo vtoroi polovine XIX stoletiia*, vol. 2 (Tomsk, 1962), pp. 533-535.

12. One critical observer described this chronicle as "the most famous, the most obscure, the most exasperating, and most misleading of all the early Hungarian texts." C. A. Macartney, *The Medieval Hungarian Historians: A Critical and Analytical Guide* (Cambridge, 1953), p. 59.

13. B. Nosák-Nezabudov, "Laborec: povest' rusínska," *Orol tatránski*, vol. 1 nos. 28-30 (Bratislava, 1845-46), reprinted in Mykhailo Mol'nar, *Slovaky i ukraïnsti* (Bratislava and Prešov, 1965), pp. 207-219, and in Ukrainian translation by Kornii Zaklyns'kyi (Bratislava and Prešov, 1966); Anatolii Kralitskii, "Kniaz Laborets: istoricheskaia poviest' iz IX vieka," *Galichanin*, vol. 1, no. 1, pts. 3-4 (L'viv, 1863), pp. 73-85, reprinted in *Vŷd*. TP, no. 53 (Uzhhorod, 1925), and in Iu. A. Bacha and O. M. Rudlovchak, eds., *Khrestomatiia novoï zakarpats' koï ukraïns'koï literatury: druha polovyna XIX storichchia* (Bratislava, 1964), pp. 113-123.

14. For the many works of Zhatkovych on Koriatovych, see Perfetskii, "Obzor," pp. 316-320 and the list in Nykolai Lelekach and Yvan Haraida, *Zahal'na bybliohrafiia Podkarpatia* (Uzhhorod, 1944), pp. 137-139. Vladimir [Evgenii Fentsik], "Kor'iatovich," *Mîsiatsoslov na hod 1870* (Uzhhorod, 1869), pp. 35-42, reprinted in Vasyl' Mykytas' and Olena Rudlovchak, eds., *Poety Zakarpattia: antolohiia zakarpatoukraïns'koï poeziï (XVI st.-1945 r.)* (Bratislava and Prešov, 1965), pp. 287-294.

15. See the histories of dioceses and monasteries and the biographies of church leaders in the Bibliography (refs. 0951, 0970, 0972-0974, 0977, 0988, 0999, 1036, 1080, 1084-1087, 1646-1651, 1785, 2268, 2269).

16. Bidermann argued that the Rusyns did not precede but came with the Magyars, and that Koriatovych did bring 40,000 followers with him. In this same work Bidermann propounded for the first time the idea of Rus'ka Kraina —

Marchia Ruthenorum, proved supposedly by the existence of a document dated 1127. *Die ungarischen Ruthenen, ihr Wohngebiet, ihr Erwerb und ihre Geschichte,* 2 vols. (Innsbruck, 1862-67), esp. vol. 1, pp. 5-13 and vol. 2, pp. 39 ff. Ioann Dulishkovich, *Istoricheskiia cherty Ugro-Russkikh,* 3 vols. (Uzhhorod, 1874-77), esp. vol. 1 and vol. 2, pp. 3-15.

17. Nikolai A. Beskid, *Karpatorusskaia drevnost',* Izdanie OIAD, no. 43 (Uzhhorod, 1928) and *Karpatorusskaja pravda* (Homestead, Pa., 1933), pp. 70-176. See also his *Karpatskaia Rus'* (Prešov, 1920), pp. 119-152.

18. V. Hadzhega, "O pereseleniu kniazia Fedora Koriatovycha do Madiarshchyny," *Podkarpatska Rus',* vol. 6, no. 7 (Uzhhorod, 1929), p. 153. See also his "Kniaz Fedor Koriatovych i Maramarosh," ibid., vol. 7 (1930), pp. 68-75, 99-113, and vol. 8 (1931), pp. 141-148, 169-175; and especially his "Dodatky k ystoriî rusynôv y rus'kykh tserkvei v buv. zhupî Zemplynskôi," *Naukovŷi zbôrnyk TP,* vols. 7-8 (Uzhhorod, 1931), pp. 18-89, and vol. 9 (1932), pp. 1-67. For a list of other works by this prolific historian, see the Bibliography (refs. 0957-0959, 1405-1417).

19. Ir. M. Kontratovych, *K istorii starodavniago Uzhgoroda i Podkarpatskoi Rusi do XIV vieka,* Izdanie OIAD, no. 39 (Uzhhorod, 1928), pp. 4-5.

20. Irynei M. Kondratovych, *Ystoriia Podkarpatskoî Rusy dlia naroda,* Vŷd. TP, nos. 35-37 (Uzhhorod, 1924), pp. 38-39.

21. Vîra I. Fedelesh, *Uchebnyk ystoriy Podkarpatskoi Rusy ot naidavnîishykh chasov do dneshnykh dnei y Chekhoslovakiy do XIV vîka,* 2nd rev. ed. (Uzhhorod, 1924), pp. 5-30. Augustin Volosin, "Carpathian Ruthenia," *The Slavonic and East European Review,* vol. 13, no. 38 (London, 1935), p. 373, and his "Řecko-katolická církev v Podkarpatské Rusi," in Josef Chmelař et al., eds., *Podkarpatská Rus* (Prague, 1923), p. 99. On Fedelesh, see the obituary by Ivan Shlepetskii in *Svobodnoe slovo Karpatskoi Rusi,* vol. 9, nos. 3-4 (Newark, N.J., 1967), p. 18.

22. Iulii Gadzhega, *Dva istoricheskikh voprosa: starozhili-li karpatorossy i o nachalakh khristianskoi religii na Podkarpatskoi Rusi,* Izdanie OIAD, no. 42 (Uzhhorod, 1928), pp. 26, 45.

23. P. Sova, *Proshloe Uzhgoroda* (Uzhhorod, 1937), p. 20.

24. Ivan Makarenko, "Z zhytia narodôv y velykykh liudei," *Pchôlka,* vol. 3, nos. 7-8 (Uzhhorod, 1925), p. 118.

25. Vladimir Terletskii, *Ugorskaia Rus' i vozrozhdenie soznaniia narodnosti mezhdu russkimi v Vengrii* (Kiev, 1874), pp. 12-52; N. N. [Ivan Sil'vai], "O sovremennom polozhenii russkikh v Ugrii" and "Polozhenie ugorskikh russkikh pod upravleniem Stefana Pankovicha, Episkopa Mukachevskago," *Slavianskii sbornik,* vol. 1 (St. Petersburg, 1875), reprinted in I. A. Sil'vai, *Izbrannye proizvedeniia* (Bratislava, 1957), pp. 343-389.

26. Evmenii Sabov, "Ocherk literaturnoi dieiatel'nosti i obrazovaniia Ugro-russkikh," in his *Khristomatiia tserkovno-slavianskikh i ugro-russkikh literaturnikh pamiatnikov* (Uzhhorod, 1893), pp. 183-210—reprinted in Izdanie OIAD, vol. 8 (Uzhhorod, 1925).

27. Fedelesh, *Uchebnyk,* p. 34.

28. Kondratovych, *Istoriia,* p. 74.

29. Fedelesh, *Uchebnyk,* pp. 33-44; Kondratovych, *Ystoriia,* pp. 48-103. N. Beskid, P. S. Fedor, and D. Zubritskii also wrote biographies of Dobrianskii and of Dukhnovych. See the Bibliography (nos. 0945, 1092, 1167, 1168).

30. Iulii Rusak [Iulii Gadzhega], *Ocherki kul'turnoi istorii Podkarpatskoi Rusi* (Uzhhorod, 1927). Perhaps the most graphic illustrations of Rusyn national hagiography are found in the immigrant publications of Joseph Hanulya, *Rusin Literature* (Cleveland, 1941) and Michael Roman, *Short Biographies of Famous Carpatho-Russians* (Munhall, Pa. 1962).

31. For texts of folk-tales (transcribed in the 1960s), see *Lehendy Karpat* (Uzh-

horod, 1968), pp. 13-61. See also the discussion by V. Mel'nyk, *Istoriia Zakarpattia v usnykh narodnykh perekazakh ta istorychnykh pisniakh* (L'viv, 1970), pp. 52-108, 158-172.

32. V. Grendzha-Dons'kyi, *Il'ko Lypei, karpats'kyi rozbiinyk: povist',* Ukraïns'ka biblioteka, no. 48 (L'viv, 1936), reprinted in his *Shliakhom ternovym: vybrani tvory* (Bratislava and Prešov, 1964), pp. 260-339. See also Chapter 7.

33. Ivan Olbracht [Kamil Zeman], *Nikola Šuhaj loupežník* (Prague, 1933). Since its first appearance, this novel has become one of the most widely read in Czechoslovakia and has been translated into French, German, English, and Russian. For a recently transcribed folk tale about Shuhai, see *Lehendy Karpat,* pp. 71-72. Cf. Mel'nyk, *Istoriia Zakarpattia,* pp. 158-161 and a general discussion of the phenomenon of the Robin Hood hero in Subcarpathian Rus' in the essay by Ivan Olbracht, "Loupežníci," in his *Hory a staletí: kniha reportáží z Podkarpatska,* 2nd ed. (Prague, 1935), pp. 89-131.

34. Antonii Bobul'skyi, *Voennŷe sobŷtyia Davyda Shrapnelia y Ivana Pevchuka,* illus. Josyf Bokshai (Uzhhorod, 1924).

35. There is evidence that through Rusyn folklore the common people preserved legends about their national heroes Prince Laborets' and Prince Koriatovych. It is difficult, however, to know if these legends actually originated with the folk masses, or if they were handed down from the intelligentsia and subsequently "folklorized." Cf. K. Zaklyns'kyi, "Perekaz pro kniazia Labortsia," *Podkarpatska Rus',* vol. 1, no. 1 (Uzhhorod, 1923), pp. 17-18; I. Pan'kevych, "Kniaz' Fedor Koriiatovych v usnôi narodnôi tradytsii," ibid., vol. 7, no. 3 (1930), pp. 47-52; K. Zaklyns'kyi, *Narodni opovidannia pro davnynu* (Košice, 1925), pp. 4-6; Josef Dušánek and František Gabriel, *Pověsti ze Zakarpatské Ukrajiny* (Prague, 1946), pp. 17-28, 93-100; Mykola Mushynka, *Z hlybyny vikiv* (Bratislava and Prešov, 1967), p. 341; Mel'nyk, *Istoriia Zakarpattia,* pp. 22-26, 37-40.

36. Antal Décsy, *Az magyar oroszokrúl való igen rövid elmélkedés* (Košice, 1797), pp. ii-iv, 1-32; Károly Mészáros, *A Magyarországi oroszok története* (Budapest, 1850). See also the discussion in Gadzhega, *Dva istoricheskikh voprosa,* pp. 9-13.

37. Tivadar Lehoczky, *Beregvármegye monographiája,* vol. 1 (Uzhhorod, 1881), pp. 116-117.

38. From his book, *A magyar nemzet történeti joga hazánk területéhez a Kárpátoktól le az Adriáig* (Nagyvárad [Oradea], 1916).

39. John de Karácsonyi, *The Formation of the Nationalities in Hungary* (Berne, 1919), p. 3. This apologetic extract from the author's book (see note 38) was reprinted in three more editions in English and French in 1919 and 1920.

40. *Magyar történet,* 8 vols. (Budapest, 1928-1934), followed by seven more editions in five volumes, the last one in 1941-1943.

41. For a discussion of Hungarian historiography, see Josef Macůrek, *Dějepisectví evropského východu* (Prague, 1946), pp. 279-286; Stephen Borsody, "Modern Hungarian History," *Journal of Modern History,* vol. 24, no. 4 (Chicago, 1952), pp. 398-405; the comprehensive survey by Tibor Baráth, "L'histoire en Hongrie, 1867-1935," *Revue historique,* vol. 177 (Paris, 1936), pp. 84-144, 595-644; vol. 178 (1936), pp. 25-74; and Steven Bela Vardy, *Hungarian Historiography and the Geistesgeschichte School* (Cleveland, 1974), pp. 62-68.

42. Antal Hodinka, "L'habitat, l'économie et le passé du peuple ruthène au sud des Carpathes," *Revue des études hongroises et finno-ougriènnes,* vol. 2 (Paris, 1924), p. 253. This study is an abridged version of the author's *Uttsiuznyna, gazdustvo y proshlost' iuzhno-karpats'kykh rusynuv,* published in Rusyn (Ubl'a-Uzhhorod dialect) with no indication of the place or date under the pseudonym Eden

Sokŷrnyts'kŷi Syrokhman. The work was addressed to "My good brothers" in the Carpathians and attempted to reveal to them that historical truth cannot be destroyed by Czech and Slovak anti-Hungarian propaganda.

The theory of the later settlement of Rusyns was first put forward by Hodinka in his *A munkácsi görög-katholikus püspökség története* (Budapest, 1910), pp. 58-89.

43. Hodinka, "L'habitat," pp. 253-262; [Hodinka], *Uttsiuznyna,* pp. 24-55.

44. On Corvinus' popularity, as expressed in Rusyn folk tales, see Eugen Perfeckij, "Podkarpatské a haličskoruské tradice o králi Matyášovi Corvinovi," *Sborník filosofické fakulty university Komenského,* vol. 4, no. 42 (Bratislava, 1926), pp. 219-278. Cf. Mushynka, *Z hlybyny vikiv,* pp. 315-316; *Lehendy Karpat,* pp. 118-123, 221-224.

45. [Hodinka], *Uttsiuznyna,* pp. 15-24, 55-93; Antal Hodinka, *A kárpátalji rutének lakóhelye gazdasaguk es multjuk* (Budapest, 1923); Hodinka, "L'habitat," pp. 262-271.

46. Ibid., p. 271. For praise of Rákóczi in Rusyn folklore, see Dušánek and Gabriel, pp. 133-141; *Lehendy Karpat,* p. 224. Cf. Mel'nyk, *Istoriia Zakarpattia,* pp. 67-77.

47. Hodinka, "L'habitat," p. 271. Hodinka elaborated upon the loyalty of Rusyns in Hungary in *Gens fidelissima: II Rákóczi F. beregmegyei rutén jobbágyai az 1704-1711-i szabadságharczban* (Uzhhorod, 1915) and *Gens Fidelissima* (Budapest, 1937).

48. Kossuth was also described favorably in some Rusyn folk-tales and songs. Oreszt Szabó, *A magyar oroszokról (Ruthének)* (Budapest, 1913), pp. 101-109; Ivan Franko, "Koshut i koshuts'ka viina," *Zhytie i slovo,* vol. 1, no. 3; vol. 2, no. 6 (L'viv, 1894), pp. 461-477, 346-348; Mel'nyk, *Istoriia Zakarpattia,* pp. 117-118.

49. Hodinka, "L'habitat," p. 272. Cf. Szabó, *A magyar oroszokról,* pp. 267-272.

50. Hodinka, *A munkácsi,* pp. 58-59. Stryps'kyi adopted a similar position in his *Jegyzetek a görög kultúra Árpádkori nyomairól* (Budapest, 1913). Among the influential works of Karácsonyi on this subject are: *Magyarország egyháztörténete főbb vonásaiban 970-től-1900-ig* and *A görögkatholikus magyarok eredete* (Budapest, 1924). For a discussion of this problem, see Hodinka, *A munkácsi,* pp. 35-57 and Gadzhega, *Dva istoricheskikh voprosa,* pp. 26-46.

51. Sándor Bonkáló, *A magyar rutének* (Budapest, 1920), pp. 5-22; and his "Die ungarländischen Ruthenen," *Ungarische Jahrbücher,* vol. 1 (Berlin, 1922), pp. 215-226.

52. Sándor Bonkáló, *A kárpátalji rutén irodalom és művelődés* (Pécs, 1935), p. 10.

53. Ibid.

54. Bonkáló also pointed out that some Rusyns still live in eastern Transylvania and that they have markedly influenced the speech of the local Szekler population. Bonkáló, *A magyar rutének,* pp. 22-31; Bonkáló, "Die ungarländischen Ruthenen," pp. 226-232; Iador Strypskii, *Hdî dokumentŷ starshei ystorii Podkarpatskoi Rusy?: O mezhevŷkh nazvaniiakh* (Uzhhorod, 1924), pp. 30-32.

55. Stryps'kyi first stressed the importance of this early literature in his seminal work: *Starsha rus'ka pys'mennost' na Uhorshchynî* (Uzhhorod, 1907). Cf. Bonkáló, "Die ungarländischen Ruthenen," pp. 316-318; Bonkáló, *A kárpátalji rutén,* pp. 16-38. This period received exclusive attention in the few publications prepared under the auspices of the Hungarian-oriented Rus'ka Kraina (1918-1919). See Chapter 6 and the Bibliography (ref. 0838).

56. Ibid., p. 16.

57. Ibid., p. 46. For the generally negative view of nineteenth-century

developments, see ibid., pp. 42-61 and Tivadar Bascinszky, *Orosz-ruszin kapcsolatok a XIX. század közepén* (Uzhhorod, 1942).

58. Szabo, *A magyar oroszokról,* pp. 225-260; Gábor Darás, *A Ruténföld elszakításának előzményei 1890-1920* (Budapest, 1936); Bonkáló, *A kárpátalji rutén,* pp. 61-77; József Rácz, "A legújabb ruszin irodalom," *Kisebbségi körlevél,* vol. 7, no. 4 (Pécs, 1943), pp. 219-234.

59. For examples of this literature, see the essays by L. Balogh-Beéry, G. Darás, J. Illés, and G. Kemény in the Bibliography (refs. 1141-1147, 1250-1255, 1521-1523, 1577-1580). As for terminology, pro-Hungarian authors argued that *Rusyny* and *Uhrorusy* were the names used by the people and hence all other national designations should be eliminated. S. Bonkáló, "Kárpátorusz, nagyorosz, orosz, ruszin, rutén, uhrorusz, ukrán," *Láthatár,* vol. 7, no. 7 (Budapest, 1939), pp. 292-295; Ivan Iatsko, "Tempora mutantus," *Lyteraturna nedîlia,* vol. 1, no. 2 (Uzhhorod, 1941), p. 14.

60. Sándor Bonkáló, *A Rutének* (Budapest, 1940). See also the articles by Tivadar Baczinszky on Rusyn national consciousness, János Gáspár on racial features, in *Zoria-Hajnal,* vol. 3, nos. 1-4 (Uzhhorod, 1943), pp. 177-200, 360-514; József Rácz on ecclesiastical art, Petro Myloslavskyi on folk songs, László Balogh-Beéry on familial ties, and Vilmos Balás on geography, in ibid., vol. 2, nos. 1-2 (1942), pp. 43-129; and Gabór Kemény, "Ungarn und die ruthenische Kulturgeschichte," *Donaueuropa,* vol. 3 (Budapest, 1943), pp. 597-610.

61. *Istoriia podkarpatskoî lyteraturŷ* (Uzhhorod, 1942); Nykolai Lelekach, "Podkarpatskoe pys'menstvo na pochatku XX vîka," *Zoria-Hajnal,* vol. 3, nos. 1-4 (Uzhhorod, 1943), pp. 229-257.

62. Tivadar Ortutay, *Cseh világ a Kárpátokban* (Uzhhorod, 1941). For a discussion of Hungarian writings on Subcarpathian Rus' during the Second World War, see Kolomiets, *Sotsial'no,* pp. 562-564.

63. Irynei Kontratovych, "Novî puty podkarpatskoi ystoriohrafiî," *Zoria-Hajnal,* vol. 1, nos. 1-2 (Uzhhorod, 1941), p. 44.

64. I. Kontratovych, *Grof Stefan Seichenii,* Narodna bybliotechka PON, no. 5 (Uzhhorod, 1941); Antonii Lukovych, *Vytiaz Nykolai Hortii v Nad'banî,* Narodna byblioteka PON, no. 8 (Uzhhorod, 1941).

65. Andreas Brodi, "Der Panslawismus und die Russinen des Karpatenlandes," *Südostdeutsche Rundschau,* vol. 2, no. 6 (Budapest, 1943), pp. 443-451; A.S.I. [A. Il'nyts'kyi], "Razvitie ukrainskoi ideologii na Podk. Rusi," *Zemlediel'skii kalendar' na god 1939* (Uzhhorod, 1938), pp. 90-92; Antonii Topol'skii, "Ukrainizm—cheshka politika," ibid., pp. 66-67; Iosif Kaminskii, "Avtonomiia karpatorusskago naroda v Mad'iarii," ibid., pp. 43-47; István Fenczik, *A kárpátaljai autonómia és a kisebbségi kérdés* (Kecskémet, 1941).

66. Iador Strypskyi, "Zabludîlym sŷnam Podkarpatia," *Lyteraturna nedîlia,* vol. 1, no. 14 (Uzhhorod, 1941), pp. 117.

67. Ibid., p. 118.

68. Michael T. Florinsky, *Russia: A History and an Interpretation,* vol. 1 (New York, 1964), pp. 13-175; Natalia Polońska-Vasylenko, *Two Conceptions of the History of Ukraine and Russia* (London, 1968), pp. 9-28.

69. See the discussions in Macůrek, *Dějepisectví,* pp. 217-218 and Polońska-Vasylenko, *Two Conceptions,* pp. 29-30.

70. M.P. Pogodin, "Izsliedovaniia, zamiechaniia i lektsii o russkoi istorii," *Izviestiia Akademii Nauk,* vol. 7 (St. Petersburg, 1856), pp. 410-422. Cf. Polońska-Vasylenko, *Two Conceptions,* pp. 30-31.

71. S.M. Solov'ev, *Istoriia Rossii s drevnieishikh vremen',* vol. 4, no. 1 (St. Petersburg, 1894), p. 1343. See also V.O. Kliuchevskii, *Kurs russkoi istorii,* vol. 1 (Moscow, 1904), pp. 344-356, 388-393. Cf. Macůrek, *Dějepisectví,* pp. 220-222;

Polońska-Vasylenko, *Two Conceptions,* pp. 31-38; Florinsky, *Russia,* pp. 44-48, 73-79.

72. Dmytro Doroshenko, "A Survey of Ukrainian Historiography," *Annals of the Ukrainian Academy of Arts and Sciences,* vols. 5-6 (New York, 1957), pp. 38-59.

73. This work was translated into modern Ukrainian with a critical introduction by Oleksandr Ohloblyn (New York, 1956). Cf. Doroshenko, "Survey," pp. 76-90; Polońska-Vasylenko, *Two Conceptions,* pp. 49-54.

74. M.I. Kostomarov, "Dve russkiia narodnosti" and "Cherty narodnoi iuzhno-russkoi istorii," *Osnova,* vol. 3 (St. Petersburg, 1861); V. Antonovych, "Kiev, ego sud'ba i znachenie s XIV po XVI stolietie (1362-1569)," *Kievskaia starina,* vol. 1 (Kiev, 1882), pp. 1-48. Cf. Macůrek, *Dějepisectví,* pp. 225-226; Polońska-Vasylenko, *Two Conceptions,* pp. 54-58; Doroshenko, "Survey," pp. 132-145, 176-187.

75. On Hrushevs'kyi's writings, see Macůrek, *Dějepisectví,* pp. 226-228; Polońska-Vasylenko, *Two Conceptions,* pp. 58-60; Doroshenko, "Survey," pp. 262-275.

76. "Zvychaina skhema 'russkoï' istorii i sprava ratsional'noho ukladu istorii Skhidn'oho Slovianstva," in V. I. Lamanskii, ed., *Stat'i po slavianoviedieniiu,* vol. 1 (St. Petersburg, 1904), pp. 298-304. Translated and reprinted in the *Annals of the Ukrainian Academy of Arts and Sciences,* vol. 2, no. 4 (New York, 1952), pp. 355-364.

77. Ibid., pp. 356-357.

78. Michel Hruchevsky, *Abrégé de l'histoire de l'Ukraine* (Paris and Prague, 1920). See also the discussion held at the Ukrainian Historical-Philological Society in Prague (1930): *Otkoudu iest' posh'la Ruskaia Zemlia . . .* (Prague, 1931), pp. 1-30.

79. "Zvychaina skhema," p. 363.

80. A. E. Priesniakov, *Obrazovanie velikorusskago gosudarstva: ocherki po istorii XII-XIV stolietii* (St. Petersburg, 1918), pp. 26-47. On his writings, see the introduction by Alfred Rieber to the translation, A. E. Presniakov, *The Formation of the Great Russian State* (Chicago, 1970), pp. xxviii-xlii. Cf. Polońska-Vasylenko, *Two Conceptions,* 38-40.

81. M. K. Liubavskii, *Obrazovanie osnovnoi gosudarstvennoi territorii veliko-russkoi narodnosti: zaselenie i ob"edinenie tsentra* (Leningrad, 1929), pp. 4-30.

82. George Vernadsky, *A History of Russia,* especially vol. 4, *Russia at the Dawn of the Modern Age,* and vol. 5, *The Tsardom of Moscow, 1547-1682* (New Haven, 1959-69). Cf. Polońska-Vasylenko, *Two Conceptions,* pp. 41-44.

83. G. V. Vernadskii, *Nachertanie russkoi istorii,* pt. 1 (Prague, 1927), p. 230.

84. Ibid., p. 229.

85. P. M. Bitsilli, *Problema russko-ukrainskikh otnoshenii v svietie istorii* (Prague, 1930), p. 17.

86. Ibid., p. 13.

87. K. Koržinský, *Původ a vývoj hnutí ukrajinského* (Moravská Ostrava, 1919), p. 4.

88. Vernadskii, *Nachertanie,* p. 22, n. 3; I. Lappo, *Proiskhozhdenie ukrainskoi ideologii novieishago vremeni,* Izdanie OIAD, no. 28 (Uzhhorod, 1926), p. 13.

89. Ibid., p. 23. This view was even accepted by the relatively more objective Bitsilli, *Problema,* p. 38.

90. N. Nadezhdin, "Zapiska o puteshestvii po iuzhno-slavianskim stranam," *Zhurnal MNP,* vol. 34 (St. Petersburg, 1842), p. 103.

91. Ibid., p. 104.

92. I. Filevich, "Ocherk karpatskoi territorii i naseleniia," ibid., vol. 197, no. 4 (1895), pp. 364-365.

93. "Only in the Carpathians can Russian historical science find solid ground

for explaining the beginnings of the Kievan state." I. Filevich, "Ugorskaia Rus' i sviazannye s neiu voprosy i zadachi russkoi istoricheskoi nauki," *Varshavskie universitetskie izvestiia,* vol. 5 (Warsaw, 1894), p. 28.

94. Arsenii, "Russkie v Vengrii," *Zhurnal MNP,* vol. 138 (St. Petersburg, 1868), esp. pp. 699-704; Grigorii Devollan, "Ugorskaia Rus'," *Russkii arkhiv,* vol. 16, no. 1 (Moscow, 1878), pp. 236-238; Ia. F. Golovatskii, "Karpatskaia Rus'," in his *Narodnyia piesni Galitskoi i Ugorskoi Rusi,* vol. 3, pt. 2 (Moscow, 1878), pp. 607, 687-691; Anonymous, "Golos iz Ugorskoi Rusi," *Russkaia mysl',* vol. 1, no. 3 (Moscow, 1880), pp. 1-13; Hryhorii Kupchanko, *Nasha rodyna* (Vienna, 1897), pp. 174-181.

95. E. Kunik, *Die Berufung der schwedischen Rodsen durch die Finnen und Slawen* (St. Petersburg, 1844), p. 169. Cf. Filevich, "Ugorskaia Rus'," pp. 5-8. A Subcarpathian Rusyn scholar living in Russia also suggested that his people did not arrive in their homeland until the twelfth century. A. Deshko, "O Karpatskoi Rusi," *Kievlianin,* vol. 3 (Moscow, 1850), p. 19.

96. A Sobolevskii, "Kak davno Russkie zhivut v Karpatakh i za Karpatami," *Zhivaia starina,* vol. 4 (St. Petersburg, 1894), pp. 524-526.

97. V. I. Lamanskii, *O Slavianakh v Maloi Azii, v Afrikie i v Ispanii,* pt. 2, *Istoricheskiia zamiechaniia* (St. Petersburg, 1859), p. 62.

98. A. L. Petrov, *Drevnieishiia gramoty po istorii karpatorusskoi tserkvi i ierarkhii 1391-1498 g.* (Prague, 1930), pp. 7-8. On Petrov, see Chapter 3, for his writings see the Bibliography (refs. 0059-0061, 0120-0124, 0509, 0510, 0668, 0669, 1921-1932).

99. Ibid., pp. 20-51.

100. Ibid., pp. 52-55.

101. In that year the so-called Document of Koriatovych came to light and was soon used by local administrators to gain rights to a village and other income that had previously belonged to the Rákóczi family. Ibid., pp. 55-60, 179-203.

102. "Zadachi karpatorusskoi istoriografii," reprinted in ibid., p. xi.

103. Ibid.

104. K. Kochannyj-Goralčuk, *Podkarpatská Rus v minulosti a přítomnosti* (Prague, 1931), pp. 9-18, 32-55.

105. Devollan, "Ugorskaia Rus'," pp. 243-247; O. Matisov, "Dvizhenie narodnoi zhizni v Ugorskoi Rusi," *Besieda,* vol. 1, nos. 6-7 (Moscow, 1871), pp. 225-248, and Petr Feerchak, *Ocherk literaturnago dvizhenia ugorskikh russkikh* (Odessa, 1888), pp. 25-38; "Natsional'noe dvizhenie v Ugorskoi Rusi," *Galitsko-russkii viestnik,* vol. 1, no. 1 (St. Petersburg, 1894), pp. 49-62; L. Vasilevskii (Plokhotskii), "Vengerskie 'rusnaki' i ikh sud'ba," *Russkoe bogatstvo,* vol. 23, no. 3 (St. Petersburg, 1914), pp. 368-376. See also the Galician Russophile viewpoint in Filipp I. Svistun, *Prikarpatskaia Rus' pod vladieniem Avstrii,* 2 vols. (1896-97) (2nd ed.; Trumbull, Conn., 1970), pp. 177-179; and Kupchanko, *Nasha rodyna,* pp. 193-205.

106. Devollan, "Ugorskaia Rus'," pp. 247-250; Arsenii, "Russkie," esp. pp. 707-716; Kupchanko, *Nasha rodyna,* pp. 181-191; K. L. Kustodiev, "Kongress katolikov Vengrii i Ugorskie-Russkie," *Pravoslavnoe obozrienie,* nos. 3-5, 10, 12 (Moscow, 1871); "Otchet o vtorom periodie zasiedanii kongressa dlia organizatsii avtonomii katolicheskoi tserkvi Vengrii . . . ," ibid., nos. 3-4 (1872), pp. 450-476, 642-650; Ugroruss, "Latinizatsiia i mad'iarizatsiia russkikh v Vengrii," *Russkoe obozrienie,* vol. 4 (Moscow, 1893), pp. 634-656.

107. Anonymous, "Golos," pp. 15-24; Feerchak, *Ocherk,* pp. 38-42; Matisov, "Dvizhenie," vol. 7, pp. 229 ff.; Putnik [Vladimir Frantsev], "Sovremennoe sostoianie Ugorskoi Rusi," *Russkii viestnik,* vol. 265 (Moscow, 1900), pp. 629-655; Zh. Z. I. [Aleksei L. Petrov], "Iz Koshits' (Ugriia)," *Slavianskoe obozrenie,* vol. 1, no. 2

(St. Petersburg, 1892), pp. 160-172; Svistun, *Prikarpatskaia Rus'*, pp. 289-292; Kochannyj-Goralčuk, *Podkarpatská Rus*, pp. 86 ff. See also the entries for Bakhtin and Liprandi in the Bibliography (refs. 1132 and 1717).

108. Feerchak, *Ocherk*, p. 23; Putnik, "Sovremennoe sostoianie," pp. 642-645.

109. Devollan, "Ugorskaia Rus'," p. 250.

110. See Chapter 3, p. 73.

111. Viktor Dvorský, "Země Podkarpatská Rus," in D. Vergun, ed., *Osm přednášek o Podkarpatské Rusi* (Prague, 1925), pp. 5-10.

112. Kochannyi-Goralčuk, *Podkarpatská Rus*, pp. 79-158; A.V. Popov, ed., *Karpatorusskiia dostizheniia* (Mukachevo, 1930).

113. D. Vergun, "Karpatoruská literatura: stručný přehled," in Vergun, *Osm přednášek*, p. 46.

114. Iu. A. Iavorskii, "Znachenie i miesto Zakarpat'ia v obshchei skhemie russkoi pis'mennosti: nieskol'ko metodologicheskikh spravok i viekh," *Sborník prací I. sjezdu slovanských filologů v Praze 1929*, vol. 2 (Prague, 1931), pp. 74-89. See also Chapter 7, pp. 149-153.

115. Evgenii Nedziel'skii, *Ocherk karpatorusskoi literatury* (Uzhhorod, 1932), esp. pp. 5-18; Georgij Gerovskij, "Jazyk Podkarpatské Rusi," in *Československá vlastivěda*, vol. 3 (Prague, 1934), pp. 480-515; see also his criticism of the Ukrainian interpretation: *Istoriia ugro-russkoi literatury v izobrazhenii Volodimira Birchaka* (Mukachevo, 1943). See the entries for Nedziel'skii in the Bibliography (refs. 1816-1824).

116. See the Bibliography (refs. 0945, 1039-1044, 1076, 1303, 2221).

117. Speech by Iosif Kaminskii, in "Protokol iubileinago torzhestva . . . Arkhidiakona Evmeniia Ivanovicha Sabova . . . i 7-ogo Obshchago Sobraniia OIAD, 2.VI.1929," *Karpatskii sviet*, vol. 3, nos. 5-6 (Uzhhorod, 1930), p. 977.

118. Antonii Lukovich, "Natsional'naia i iazykovaia prinadlezhnost' russkago naseleniia Podk. Rusi," ibid., vol. 2, no. 1 (1929), p. 399.

119. Poprad is the name of a town and river at the foot of the Tatra Mountains in north-central Slovakia. This area is traditionally considered the farthest western extent of the Rusyn population.

120. Lukovich, "Natsional'naia . . . prinadlezhnost'," p. 399.

121. Stephen Fentsik, "Doklad sekretardieloproizvoditelia OIAD, 2.VI.1929," *Karpatskii sviet*, vol. 2, nos. 5-6 (Uzhhorod, 1929), p. 632. See also Iosif Kaminskii, *Natsional'noe samosoznanie nashego naroda*, Izdanie OIAD, vol. 13 (Uzhhorod, 1925), p. 3; Lukovich, "Natsional'naia prinadlezhnost'," p. 401; Petro Kryvda-Sokolenko, " 'Ukraynyzatsiia' Podkarpatskoi Rusy," *Karpatorusskii kalendar' 'Lemko' 1923* (Uzhhorod, 1922), pp. 109-123; and the pronouncements of the Russian émigrés: Professor A. A. Kizevetter and Senator Ilarion Tsurkanovich, in "Protokol 8-ogo Obshchago Sobraniia OIAD, 1.VI.1930," *Karpatskii sviet*, vol. 4, nos. 3-4 (Uzhhorod, 1930), pp. 1159, 1163; and Lappo, *Proiskhozhdenie*, p. 23.

122. N. Pavlovich, *Russkaia kul'tura i Podkarpatskaia Rus'*, Izdanie OIAD, vol. 23 (Uzhhorod, 1926).

123. Ibid., p. 11.

124. Ibid., p. 12.

125. Speech of Evmenii Sabov, in "Protokol iubileinago torzhestva . . . Sabova . . . i 7-ago Obshchago Sobraniia OIAD, 2.VI.1929," *Karpatskii sviet*, vol. 3, nos. 5-6 (Uzhhorod, 1930), p. 976.

126. A. M. Volkonskii, "V chem glavnaia opasnost'?—Maloross ili ukrainets?," ibid., vol. 2, no. 4 (1929), pp. 496-497; Lappo, *Proiskhozhdenie*, pp. 8-9.

127. Stepan Fentsik, ed., *Chitanka dlia naroda*, Izdanie OIAD, vol. 3 (Uzhhorod, 1933), pp. 35-36. On Ukrainianism as an artificial creation, see Konstantin

Stripskii, "Iazyk literaturnoe traditsii Podkarpatskoi Rusi," *Karpatskii sviet,* vol. 3, nos. 9-10 (Uzhhorod, 1930), p. 1031 and "Protokol 8-ago Obshchago Sobraniia OIAD, 1.VI.1930," ibid., vol. 4, nos. 3-4 (1931), p. 1153.
   128. *Narodnyi katikhiz,* Izdanie OIAD, vol. 19 (Uzhhorod, 1926), p. 2. On the problem of nomenclature, see Appendix 1.
   129. Other scholarly institutions of importance in Prague were the Ukrainian Historical-Philological Society (est. 1923), the Museum of the Liberation (est. 1925), and the Historical Cabinet (est. 1930) in the Ukrainian Sociological Institute. On the achievements of the Ukrainian scholarly community in Prague and Poděbrady, see Doroshenko, pp. 395 ff.; Symon Narizhnyi, *Ukraïns'ka emigratsiia: kul'turna pratsia ukraïns'koï emigratsiï mizh dvoma svitovymy viinamy,* pt. 1 (Prague, 1942), pp. 119-209; Arkadii Zhyvotko, *Desiat' rokiv ukraïns'koho istorychnoho kabinetu (1930-1940),* Inventáře Archivu Ministerstva vnitra v Praze, Series C, vol. 1 (Prague, 1940), pp. 3-16.
   130. Mykhailo Hrushevs'kyi, *Istoriia Ukraïny-Rusy,* vol. 1 (3rd ed.; Kiev, 1913), p. 223, and vol. 2 (L'viv, 1905), p. 487. In volume 2 the author gives the seventh and eighth centuries as the time of arrival; in the revised edition of volume 1, he says the sixth and seventh centuries. Volodymyr Hnatiuk, "Chy zakarpats'ki ukraïntsi avtokhtony?," *Literaturno-naukovyi vistnyk,* vol. 76, no. 3 (L'viv, 1922), pp. 269-276; Oleksander Mytsiuk, *Narysy z sotsial'no-hospodars'koï istoriï b. uhors'koï, nyni Pidkarpats'koï Rusy,* vol. 1 (Uzhhorod, 1936), pp. 62-63. Mytsiuk argues that though descendents of Rusyns were in the region before the Magyars, the names Rus' and Rusyn did not actually reach Subcarpathia until the twelfth and thirteenth centuries. Ibid., pp. 14-16. Dmytro Doroshenko, *Uhors'ka Ukraïna* (Prague, 1919), p. 12, states that although we have no certain information, "Ukrainians" did not settle in Subcarpathian Rus' after the Magyars.
   131. Hrushevs'kyi, *Istoriia,* vol. 2, p. 488 and Vol. 4 (Kiev, 1907), pp. 171-172. Mytsiuk, *Narysy,* vol. 1, pp. 14, 63-65, argues that Koriatovych may have arrived with as many as 60,000 colonists and he calculates that this included approximately 7,000 to 8,000 families. Cf. Doroshenko, *Uhors'ka Ukraïna,* p. 12.
   132. Vasyl' Pachovs'kii, *Istoriia Pôdkarpatskoî Rusy* (Uzhhorod, 1920), p. 3. According to this author, Rusyns (1) received Christianity from Methodius in Greater Moravia; (2) influenced the Hungarian Christian church which was initially of eastern rite; and (3) had their own princes in Subcarpathia (list of names given). Furthermore, Petro Petrovych was depicted as having fought for the liberation of Rusyns, while Koriatovych's greatest service was the settlement of 40,000 Rusyns in the region. Pachovs'kii, *Istoriia,* pp. 23-40, 75-86, 98-104.
   133. Omelian Pritsak, "Khto taki avtokhtony Karpats'koï Ukraïny?," *Nova zoria,* no. 1 (L'viv, 1939), pp. 15-16; M. Andrusiak, "Istoriia Karpats'koï Ukraïny," in *Karpats'ka Ukraïna* (L'viv, 1939), pp. 88-92.
   134. I. I. Sreznevskii, "Rus' Ugorskaia: otryvok iz opyta geografii russkago iazyka," *Viestnik Imperatorskago russkago geograficheskago obshchestva,* vol. 1, nos. 1-2 (St. Petersburg, 1852), pp. 1-28; D. I. Bagaliei, *Ocherki iz russkoi istorii,* vol. 1 (Kharkiv, 1911), p. 127; Eugen Perfeckij, *Sociálně-hospodářské poměry Podkarpatské Rusi ve století XIII-XV* (Bratislava, 1924), pp. 7 ff., and his "Dvě stati k dějinám Podkarpatské Rusi: 2. Kníže Fedor Koriatovič Mukačevský," *Sborník filozofickej fakúlty university Komenského,* vol. 1, no. 6 (Bratislava, 1922), pp. 126-132.
   135. Mytsiuk, *Narysy,* vol. 2 (Prague, 1938), pp. 19-37, 139-163.
   136. Doroshenko, *Uhors'ka Ukraïna,* pp. 13-15; Andrusiak, "Istoriia," pp. 92-93. Mytsiuk recognizes the positive achievement of some hierarchs like Bachyns'kyi,

but he tends to agree with those writers who equate acceptance of the Union with a decline in Rusyn nationalism. See his *Narysy,* vol. 2, esp. pp. 101-103.

137. Kyrylo Studyns'kyi, "Aleksander Dukhnovych i Halychyna: studiia," *Naukovŷi zbornyk TP,* vol. 3 (Uzhhorod, 1924), pp. 28-103.

138. Andrusiak, "Istoriia," pp. 93-96; Doroshenko, *Uhors'ka Ukraïna,* pp. 15-26, does recognize that Subcarpathians generally scorned the Ukrainianism of the Galician intelligentsia. See also the earlier Vasyl' Lukych, *Uhors'ka Rus', iey rozvôi y teperîshnii stan* (L'viv, 1887), p. 8-30.

139. Lukych, *Uhors'ka Rus',* p. 23. M. Drahomanov takes a much less critical view of Muscophilism, recognizing that it at least represented some kind of national consciousness which, he argues, will eventually lead its adherents to Ukrainianism. *Spravi Uhorskoï Rusy* (L'viv, 1895), pp. 9-15.

140. Ibid., p. 4; Doroshenko, *Uhors'ka Ukraïna,* pp. 27-32; Andrusiak, "Istoriia," pp. 96-100.

141. Ivan Franko, "Karpato-rus'ke pys'menstvo XVII-XVIII vv.," *Zapysky NTSh,* vols. 37-38 (L'viv, 1900), pp. 1-162; Mykhailo Vozniak, *Istoriia ukraïns'koï literatury,* vol. 3, pt. 2 (L'viv, 1924), pp. 108-122.

142. Volodymyr Birchak, *Literaturni stremlinnia Pidkarpats'koï Rusy* (1st ed., Uzhhorod, 1921; 2nd rev. ed., Uzhhorod, 1937), p. 94. See also Ie. Iu. Pelens'kyi, "Pys'menstvo," in *Karpats'ka Ukraïna,* pp. 108-121.

143. Cited from *Za ridne slovo: polemika z rusofilamy* (Mukachevo, 1937), pp. 20-21.

144. Ibid., p. 59.

145. Heinrich von Treitschke, *Zehn Jahre deutscher Kämpfe,* 3rd ed., vol. 1 (Berlin, 1897), p. 326, cited in Hans Kohn, *The Idea of Nationalism* (New York, 1958), p. 582, n. 13.

146. Pavlovich, *Russkaia kul'tura,* p. 17.

147. P. Lyshak, *Rishenyi iazykovoho voprosu* (Tiachiv-Uzhhorod, 1935), p. 3.

148. Interview with Avhustyn Voloshyn, in *Rusyn* (Uzhhorod), February 18, 1923.

149. On the simultaneity of group loyalties, see David M. Potter, "The Historian's Use of Nationalism and Vice-Versa," *The American Historical Review,* vol. 67, no. 4 (New York, 1962), pp. 931-932.

150. René Martel, *La Ruthénie subcarpathique* (Paris, 1935), pp. 132-133.

151. *V pamiat' Aleksandra Dukhnovycha 1803-1923* (Uzhhorod, 1923), p. 7.

152. "Protokol 9-ago godichnago obshchago sobraniia OIAD, 7.VII.1931," *Karpatskii sviet,* vol. 5, no. 6 (Uzhhorod, 1932), p. 1320. Russophile ideologists were forced to admit: "True, Sabov in his patriotism sometimes seemed local, his national horizon being limited to the high Carpathians." A.V. Popov, "Evmenii Ivanovich Sabov: kritiko-biograficheskii orcherk," ibid., vol. 2, no. 5 (1929), p. 556.

153. *Nedîlia* (Uzhhorod), October 6, 1935. For a further discussion of Rusynism, see Chapter 11.

6. The Problem of Language

1. *Briefe zu Beförderung der Humanität* (1783), cited in Carlton J. H. Hayes, *Essays on Nationalism* (New York, 1928), p. 13.

2. Oscar Jaszi, *The Dissolution of the Habsburg Monarchy* (Chicago, 1929), p. 262.

3. Joshua Fishman, *Language and Nationalism* (Rowley, Mass., 1972), pp. 40-55. As recently as 1960, one student of nationalism could write: "The test, then,

by which a nation is known to exist is that of language." Elie Kedourie, *Nationalism* (London, 1960), p. 68. For criticism of the nationalist precept that language is an absolute criterion for national identity, see Frederick Hertz, *Nationality in History and Politics* (London, 1950), pp. 78-97; Dankward A. Rustow, *A World of Nations: Problems of Political Modernization* (Washington, D.C., 1967), pp. 47-58, and Boyd C. Shafer, *Faces of Nationalism* (New York, 1972), pp. 331-333.

4. Interview with Avhustyn Voloshyn in *Rusyn,* February 18, 1923.

5. Stepan A. Fentsik, *Aloiz Irasek: pamiatnaia knizhka,* Izdanie PNS, vol. 3 (Uzhhorod, 1930), p. 3.

6. M. Vozniak, *Nash rodnŷi iazŷk,* Knyzhky Rusyna, no. 15 (Uzhhorod, 1923), p. 28.

7. Antonŷi Hartl, *Osnovŷ rus'koî narodnoî y kul'turnoî polytyky,* Knyzhky Rusyna, no. 5 (Uzhhorod, 1923), p. 20.

8. R. Auty, "The Linguistic Revival Among Slavs of the Austrian Empire, 1780-1850: The Role of Individuals in the Codification and Acceptance of New Literary Languages," *The Modern Language Review,* vol. 53, no. 3 (London, 1958), pp. 392-404; Einar Haugen, *Language Conflict and Language Planning: the Case of Modern Norwegian* (Cambridge, Mass., 1966), pp. 3-26; Fishman, *Language and Nationalism,* pp. 55 ff.

9. Marko Barabolia, "Oi stelysia ty, barvinku, na ioho mohyli (Trahediia ne v diiakh, ale diiet'sia v 1999 rotsi)" (1929), in *Tuteshniats'ka Guberniia: satyry* (Bratislava and Prešov, 1970), pp. 42-43.

10. F. T. Zhylko, *Narysy z dialektolohii ukraïns'koï movy* (Kiev, 1955), pp. 89-155; Ivan Pan'kevych, *Ukraïns'ki hovory Pidkarpats'koï Rusy i sumezhnykh oblastei* (Prague, 1938). For the borders of these dialectal areas as they cross Subcarpathian territory, see Map 2. This three-fold classification applies to regions both north and south of the Carpathians. On the other hand, the Russophile scholar, Georgii Gerovskii treated the Subcarpathian region in isolation. He deleted the Hutsul dialects and for the remaining territory distinguished seven basic dialects and seven more subgroups. See his "Jazyk Podkarpatské Rusi," in *Ceskoslovenská vlastivěda,* vol. 3 (Prague, 1934), pp. 460-480 with map.

11. We have seen above (Chapters 2 and 3) that Church Slavonic, Magyar and to a degree Latin were also options put forward during the nineteenth century.

12. The author is grateful to Horace G. Lunt and Omeljan Pritsak, Harvard University, for many of the ideas presented above.

13. Ivan Zilyns'kyi, *Mova zakarpats'kykh ukraïntsiv* (L'viv, 1939), p. 4.

14. Gerovskij, "Jazyk," p. 461.

15. Ibid., pp. 466-467.

16. Iulii Gadzhega in the preface to V.A. Frantsev, *K voprosu o literaturnom iazykie Podkarpatskoi Rusi,* Izdanie OIAD, vol. 2 (Uzhhorod, 1924), p. 2.

17. Chopei was attacked not only for his use of dialectal words but especially for the inclusion of Magyar words which were widespread in the Rusyn language. Evgenii Nedziel'skii, *Ocherk karpatorusskoi literatury* (Uzhhorod, 1932), p. 239. The Mitrak-Chopei dichotomy was further stressed by Russophile leaders who praised Mitrak. See Shtefan A. Fentsik, "Pochemu my otkryvaem pamiatnik A.A. Mitraku?," *Karpatskii sviet,* vol. 4, nos. 5-7 (Uzhhorod, 1931), pp. 1194 ff. and Konstantin Stripskii, "Iazyk literaturnoi traditsii Podkarpatskoi Rusi," *Karpatskii sviet,* vol. 3, nos. 9-10 (Uzhhorod, 1930), p. 1090. For the nineteenth century context, see Chapter 3.

18. Igor Iv. Gus'nai, *Iazykovyi vopros v Podkarpatskoi Rusi* (Prešov, 1920), p. 3. See also Iulii Gadzhega, *Istoriia Obshchestva sv. Vasiliia Velikago i riech' ko dniu 60-lietiia ot ego uchrezhdeniia,* Izdanie OIAD, vol. 16 (Uzhhorod, 1925), p. 60; Antonii Lukovich, "Natsional'naia i iazykovaia prinadlezhnost' russkago naseleniia

Podk. Rusi," *Karpatskii sviet,* vol. 2, no. 1 (Uzhhorod, 1929), p. 399; K. Stripskii, "Iazyk," p. 1093.

19. Gus'nai, *Iazykovyi vopros,* pp. 29-30.

20. Evmenii Sabov, *Russkii literaturnyi iazyk Podkarpatskoi Rusi i novaia grammatika russkago iazyka,* Izdanie OIAD, vol. 7 (Uzhhorod, 1925), p. 8. On Sabov's career see Appendix 2.

21. Evmenii Sabov, "Riech' arkhidiakona vtorichno izbrannago predsiedatelia karpatorusskago obshchestva im. A. Dukhnovicha," *Karpatskii krai,* vol. 1, nos. 3-4 (Uzhhorod, 1923-24), p. 45.

22. Evmenii Sabov, "Literární jazyk Podkarpatské Rusi," in Jos. Chmelař et al., eds., *Podkarpatská Rus* (Prague, 1923), p. 127.

23. Sabov, "Riech' arkhidiakona," p. 46.

24. Pan'kevych, *Ukraïns'ki hovory,* p. 395; *Za ridne slovo: polemika z ruso-filamy* (Mukachevo, 1937), p. 24. Other linguists, both Ukrainian and non-Ukrainian, have classified Carpathian dialects not with neighboring Galicia, but with those of the northern Ukraine. For a discussion of the literature on this problem, see Pan'kevych, *Ukraïns'ki hovory,* pp. 356-372.

25. Avhustyn Voloshyn, *O pys'mennom iazŷtsî Podkarpatskykh Rusynov* (Uzhhorod, 1921), p. 37; his *Praktychna hramatyka rus'koho iazŷka,* 2nd ed. (Uzhhorod, 1928), pp. 3-4; and Ïzhak, *Ukraïnets' chy russkii? Lektsiï dlia naroda* (Mukachevo, 1938), p. 68.

26. "The Subcarpathian Rusyns, as part of the 40 million Little Russian people, can develop their own culture only in their own national language." Discussion with A. Voloshyn, "Predstaviteli dvukh protivnykh stran o likvidatsii iazykovogo spora," *Podkarpatskaia Rus'* (Mukachevo), August 8, 1926.

27. *Za ridne slovo,* p. 25. See also Chapter 5.

28. *Za ridne slovo,* p. 29. Cf. Voloshyn, *O pys'mennom iazŷtsî,* p. 28.

29. *V borot'bi za pravdu: promova Iuliiana Revaia na Vseprosvitians'komu zïzdi v Uzhhorodi, dnia 17.X.1937* (Uzhhorod, 1938), p. 25.

30. "Jazyk lidu v Podkarpatsku: řeč velkoruská či ukrajinská," *České slovo* (Prague), May 3, 1924.

31. *Nedîlia,* April 26, 1936.

32. "Kvestionar dlia zbirannia narodopisnykh (etnolohichnykh materialov v Pôdkarpatskôi Rusi dlia slovaria nashoho iazyka," *Uchytel',* vol. 1, no. 3 (Uzhhorod, 1920), p. 15. Also Ivan Pan'kevych, "Podkarpato-rus'kii diialektologichnŷi (oblastnŷi) slovar'," *Podkarpatska Rus',* vol. 1, no. 1 (Uzhhorod, 1923), pp. 24-30.

33. Ivan Pan'kevych, "Diialektychnŷi podkarpatorus'kyi slovar'," ibid., vol. 10 (1933), p. 56. See also Iosyp Dzendzelivs'kyi, "Ivan Pan'kevych iak dialektoloh," *Naukovyi zbirnyk MUKS,* vol. 4, pt. 1 (Bratislava and Prešov, 1969), pp. 194-206.

34. "Panrusyzm i rusynyzm," *Nedîlia,* October 25, 1936.

35. See the Bibliography (nos. 0820, 0838). For sample texts, see Appendix 3, pt. 6. For a full context analysis of these extremely rare publications, see Iu. A. Iavorskii, "Literaturnye otgoloski 'rus'ko-krainskago' perioda v Zakarpatskoi Rusi 1919 goda," in *Karpatorusskii sbornik* (Uzhhorod, 1930), pp. 79-87.

36. Iador H. Strypskii, *Hdî dokumentŷ starshei ystoriy Podkarpatskoi Rusy? O mezhevŷkh nazvaniiakh* (Uzhhorod, 1924), p. 30. On the *Dolishniany* as the purest Rusyn group, see also Petr Feerchak, *Ocherk literaturnago dvizhenie ugorskikh russkikh* (Odessa, 1888), p. 11; and Dmytro Doroshenko, *Uhors'ka Ukraïna* (Prague, 1919), pp. 3-4.

37. Strypskii, *Hdî dokumentŷ,* p. 41.

38. Antal Hodinka in the introduction to Ivan Haraida, *Hrammatyka rus'koho iazŷka,* Vŷdania PON, no. 1 (Uzhhorod, 1941), p. 3.

39. Ia. Bîlen'kyi [Hiiador Stryps'kyi], "Kto bŷ menî pomahav v pomnozheniu

slovaria" and "Tsy iazŷk naroda bîdnyî?," *Karpatska nedîlia* (1940); Petro Myhovk-Snizhnyk, "Prychynky do slovaria narodnoho iazŷka," *Lyteraturna nedîlia,* vol. 1, nos. 7-8 (Uzhhorod, 1941), pp. 55-56, 62-63.

40. "General'nyi statut avtonomnoi Podkarpatskoi Rusi" (MUKS); *Sbírka zákonů a nařízení státu československého* (Prague, 1920), p. 269.

41. "Memorandum o Podkarpatské Rusi" (ANM, Fond Dr. Starý, carton 1), p. 3.

42. Ministerstvo školství a národní osvěty, "Spisovný jazyk pro Podkarpatskou Rus" (ANM, Fond Dr. Starý, carton 1).

43. Ibid.

44. Josef Pešek, "Kulturní otázky Podkarpatské Rusi, *Lidové noviny* (Prague), July 29, 1923.

45. Ibid.

46. Ivan Zhidovskii, *Iazykovyia prava avtonomnoi Podkarpatskoi Rusi* (Prešov, 1930), p. 11.

47. N. Zorkii, *Spor o iazykie v Podkarpatskoi Rusi i cheshskaia Akademiia Nauk* (Uzhhorod, 1926), pp. 7, 31. Cf. Stripskii, "Iazyk," p. 1093; Iosif Kaminskii, *Natsional'noe samosoznanie nashego naroda,* Izdanie OIAD, vol. 13 (Uzhhorod, 1925), p. 10; "Deklaratsiia kul'turnykh i natsional'nykh prav karpatorusskago naroda," *Karpatskii sviet,* vol. 4, nos. 5-7 (1931), pp. 1207-1212.

48. P.P. Sova, "Podkarpatskaia Rus' i russkii iazyk," *Russkii narodnyi kalendar' na god 1937,* Izdanie OIAD, vol. 115 (Uzhhorod, 1936), p. 81; Voloshyn, *O pys'mennom iazŷtsî,* pp. 3-4; First editorial in *Nedîlia* (Uzhhorod), October 6, 1935. For the reasons behind the political divisions, see Chapter 10.

49. See Chapter 3, pp. 58 ff.

50. *Metodicheskaia grammatika ugro-russkago literaturnago iazyka dlia narodnykh shkol* (Uzhhorod, 1899); *Metodycheska hrammatyka karpato-russkoho iazyka dlia narodnykh shkol,* 2 pts. (Uzhhorod, 1919). For a sample text, see Appendix 3, pt. 3.

51. Mykola Shtets', *Literaturna mova ukraïntsiv Zakarpattia ta Skhidnoï Slovachchyny,* Pedahohichnyi zbirnyk, no. 1 (Bratislava and Prešov, 1969), p. 41. Voloshyn himself declared: "Understandably, not having completed study in a Rusyn (*rus'ki*) gymnasium and university, I could not at once formulate a clear orientation of the grammatical arguments regarding the Little Russian [Ukrainian] language." Avhustyn Voloshyn, "Panu Hahatkovi," *Rusyn* (Uzhhorod), March 10, 1923.

52. Voloshyn's first dialectally based text that followed Ukrainian (Little Russian) grammatical principles was published in Hungarian: *Gyakorlati kisorosz (rutén) nyelvtan* (Uzhhorod, 1907; reprinted Uzhhorod, 1920). A revised edition was later prepared and authorized in 1930 for use in Subcarpathian elementary schools: *Praktychna hramatyka rus'koho iazŷka,* 2nd ed. (Uzhhorod, 1928). For a discussion of the changes in Voloshyn's language, see Shtets', *Literaturna mova,* pp. 41 ff; Gerovskij, "Jazyk," pp. 508-510; Nedziel'skii, *Ocherk,* pp. 245-248; G. I. Gerovskii and V. Iv. Krainianitsy, eds., *Razbor grammatiki ugrorusskogo iazyka* (Uzhhorod, 1941), pp. 16-19.

53. Ivan Pan'kevych, "Mii zhyttiepys," *Naukovyi zbirnyk MUKS,* vol. 4, pt. 1 (Bratislava and Prešov, 1969), p. 33.

54. For sample text, see Appendix 3, pt. 5.

55. The Pan'kevych grammars also included the letter "ô" which could be pronounced according to the desire of the reader as [o], [u], [ü], or [i]. The traditional orthography and the letter "ô" (also used in the Voloshyn and other Galician grammars) were much criticized. In mockery of those editors who refused to use the modern orthography, the satirist M. Barabolia quipped: "Then follow the grammar of

Pan'kevych (only please don't forget to place, where necessary, the circumflexes, because since it is winter rain may fall and drench the poor 'o')." Marko Barabolia, "Pershii lyst do redaktsiï 'Pchîlky' v Uzhhorodi," *Pchôlka,* vol. 7 (Uzhhorod, 1929).

56. An important goal of the populist Ukrainian orientation was the eventual replacement of the traditional orthography by a modern, more phonetic orthography in which each letter represented a specific sound. See Mykola Shtets', "Rozvytok ukraïns'koho pravopysu na Zakarpatti i v Skhidnii Slovachchyni," *Naukovyi zbirnyk MUKS,* vol. 4, pt. 1 (Bratislava and Prešov, 1969), pp. 279-290. It is interesting that one Russophile critic lamented the cost of using the hard sign (ъ) in some publications. It was estimated that more than 24,000 crowns per year could be saved in printing costs if this symbol were dropped! "Gdie tverdyi znak?," *Zhivaia mysl',* vols. 2-3 (Prague, 1933), p. 25.

57. The same article in a pro-Russophile Czech daily described Pešek as a "traitor," "lover of Franz Josef," and "Austrian bureaucrat." "Ještě o jazykové otázce v Karpatské Rusi," *České slovo,* February 27, 1921. Anti-Pan'kevych commentary is found in Evmenii Sabov, *Russkii literaturnyi iazyk;* Zorkii, *Spor o iazykie;* Georgij Gerovskij, "'Mluvnice ruského jazyka' Ivana Paňkeviče," *Slavia,* vol. 6 (Prague, 1927), pp. 133-142; *Grammatika Pan'kevicha: razbor eia, na osnovanii dannykh nauki o iazykie, po retsenzii Professor Georgiia Gerovskago* (Uzhhorod, 1930).

58. Pan'kevych, "Mii zhyttiepys," p. 38. The term "compromise language" is borrowed from Shtets', *Literaturna mova,* pp. 41-43, in his analysis of Pan'kevych's grammar.

59. Evmenii I. Sabov, *Grammatika russkago iazyka dlia srednikh uchebnykh zavedenii Podkarpatskoi Rusi,* Izdanie OIAD, vol. 1 (Uzhhorod, 1924).

60. The use of Sabov's name as well as those of eight other local leaders who were labeled "editors" was a tactical ploy to remove suspicion that Galician immigrants played any role in the Russophile orientation. The Galician Ukrainophile I. Pan'kevych would have also preferred to have the second edition of his grammar published under the name of the local Ukrainophile A. Voloshyn. Letter of Pan'kevych to V. Hnatiuk, Uzhhorod, October 19, 1924, in *Naukovyi zbirnyk MUKS,* vol. 4, pt. 1 (Bratislava and Prešov, 1969), p. 84.

61. Sabov, *Grammatika,* p. 1. For a sample text, see Appendix 3, pt. 4.

62. Ibid., p. 5.

63. "Protokol sostavlennyi 27.XII.1923 v Uzhgorodie na pervom ocherednom sobranii OIAD," *Karpatskii krai,* vol. 1, nos. 3-4 (Mukachevo, 1923-24), pp. 35-39.

64. Stepan Fentsik, "Doklad sekretaria-dieloproizvoditelia OIAD na iubileinom kongressie v Uzhgorodie, 2.VI.1929 goda," *Karpatskii sviet,* vol. 2, nos. 5-6 (Uzhhorod, 1929), p. 632; Gerovskij, "Jazyk," pp. 511-512.

65. Augustin Vološin, "Posudek o knize 'Gramatika ruského jazyka . . .'," Uzhhorod, February 5, 1925 (ANM Fond Dr. Starý, carton 1, folder 5).

66. "Ministerstvo školství a národní osvěty v Praze," letter of Professor Polívka, Prague, April 21, 1925, ibid.

67. Shtets', *Literaturna mova,* p. 27.

68. "Memorandum podané deputací selského stavu Autonomní Karpatské Rusi," in *Memorandum o Podkarpatské Rusi* (ANM, Fond Dr. Starý, carton 1), p. 22.

69. Ibid. As governor of Subcarpathian Rus', A. Beskid declared: "We demand the development of the Russian literary language which should also be in our schools." "Protokol 7-ogo obshchago sobraniia OIAD, 2.VI.1929," *Karpatskii sviet,* vol. 3, nos. 5-6 (Uzhhorod, 1930), p. 981.

70. "Memorandum učitelstva z Podkarpatské Rusi," *Národní listy* (Prague), August 3, 1923. The decision at this Congress was depicted as a victory for the Russian *(ruský)* orientation even though Voloshyn's 1919 text was actually more dialectally oriented than other texts in the Subcarpathian recension of Russian.

71. M. Iv. Vasilenkov, *Nasha riech': metodicheskaia grammatika dlia russkikh narodnykh shkol Podk. Rusi*, pt. 1, *dlia II i III shkolnykh godov* (Mukachevo, 1925).

72. Shtets', *Literaturna mova*, pp. 22-23.

73. See the Bibliography (refs. 0769, 0772, 0774, 0777).

74. Between 1923 and 1937 they prepared twelve primers and readers for grades one through eight, and four readers in geography and civics. The books were published by the State Publishing House in Prague or the Pedagogical Society in Uzhhorod. For references, see the *Bibliografický katalog* (Prague, 1922-1946) and the supplement "Chytanky y ynshî shkol'nî podruchnyky" to Nykolai Lelekach and Ivan Haraida, *Zahal'na bybliohrafiia Podkarpatia*, in *Lyteraturna nedîlia*, vol. 4, nos. 9-11 (Uzhhorod, 1944).

75. Emyliian Bokshai, Iuliian Revai, and Mykhailo Brashchaiko, *Magyar-ruszin szótár-Madiars'ko-rus'kyi slovar'*, Vŷdania PTPR, no. 32 (Uzhhorod, 1928). See also the earlier dictionaries by Markush-Fotul-Revai and E. Toronskii in the Bibliography (refs. 0776, 0779).

76. Pan'kevych's *Hramatyka*, 2nd rev. ed. (Prague, 1927) and 3rd rev. ed. (Prague, 1936) did retain the etymological script with the letter "ô". The traditional script was also retained in Birchak's *Rus'ka chytanka dlia I. kliasy hymnaziinoî y horozhanskykh shkôl* (Prague, 1922); *II* (1922); *III* (1923), *IV. Vzorŷ poeziî y prozŷ* (1924; 2nd ed., 1928); and *Vesna: Rus'ka chytanka dlia I. klasŷ hymnaziinoî* (Prague, 1925).

77. See the Bibliography (refs. 0780, 0809).

78. For sample texts, see Appendix 3, pt. 5. The literary almanacs of the populist writers also revealed a distinct trend towards Ukrainianism. The first almanac, *Trembîta: lyteraturnŷi al'manakh*, Vŷd. TP, No. 65 (Uzhhorod, 1926), used the traditional orthography and referred to "our Rusyn language" and "podkarpatska lyteratura." The next almanac, *Al'manakh pidkarpats'kykh ukraïns'kykh pys'-mennykiv* (Sevlush, 1936), used the modern orthography and referred to "Subcarpathian writers of the Ukrainian orientation as Ukrainian authors." František Tichý, *Vývoj současného spisovného jazyka na Podkarpatské Rusi* (Prague, 1938), pp. 125-127.

79. On the press, see A. V. Popov, "Kul'turnyia dostizheniia za 10 liet na P. Rusi," in *Karpatorusskiia dostizheniia* (Mukachevo, 1930), pp. 70-71; Iosif Kaminskii, "Karpatorusskaia zhurnalistika poslie 1919 goda," in *Podkarpatskaia Rus' za gody 1919-1936* (Uzhhorod, 1936), pp. 137-139; Arkadii Zhyvotko, *Istoriia ukraïns'koï presy*, Ukraïns'kyi tekhnichno-hospodars'kyi instytut, course no. 62 (Regensburg, 1946), pp. 184-187; Shtets', *Literaturna mova*, pp. 44-45; and the bibliographies: Arkadii Zhyvotko, *Presa Karpats'koï Ukraïny* (Prague, 1940); and Lelekach and Haraida, *Bybliohrafiia*, pp. 39-51.

80. Tichý, *Vývoj*, p. 120. For a sample text, see Appendix 3, pt. 6.

81. Ivan Muranii *Tarasovych: istorychna p'esa* and his *Testament: komediia* (Uzhhorod, 1936). Bokshai's school texts included: *Nauka o vîrî* (Uzhhorod, 1924), *Istoriia tserkvy Khristovoie* and *Istoriia Staroho zavîta* (Uzhhorod, 1925); *Liturhyka dlia narodnŷkh y horozhanskykh shkol* (Uzhhorod, 1935).

82. The Prešov diocese was suspicious of "Ukrainian" elements in the Uzhhorod diocese and from the very beginning prepared its own school texts. These included Ioann Kyzak's *Bukvar' dlia narodnykh shkol Eparkhiy Priashevskoi* (Prešov, 1919) and *Chytanka dlia narodnŷkh shkol* (Prešov, 1920), which, like the newspaper *Russkoe slovo*, included Rusyn dialectal texts and efforts at writing in

literary Russian, and the more clearly Russian text of Aleksander Sedlak, *Grammatika russkago iazyka dlia narodnykh shkol eparkhii Priashevskoi* (Prešov, 1920). See the analysis in Shtets', *Literaturna mova,* pp. 101-129.

83. Frequently, letters like the following were printed: "I was used to the fact that when I took in hand some Rusyn [reference here to Russian language] journal, every third, fourth word I did not understand. For there were many aristocratic [*panskî*] words . . . which were in no way understandable. But when I read *Nedîlia* each word is clear to me because it is written as we Rusyns speak [*iak my rusynŷ hovoryme*]." Letter of Ivan Fedak, *Nedîlia,* October 20, 1935.

84. *Nedîlia,* November 15, 1936.

85. *Ibid.,* October 6, 1935. For sample text, see Appendix 3, pt. 6.

86. Law 6200/1939 is reprinted in Imre Miko, *Nemzetiségi jog és nemzetiségi politika* (Cluj [Kolozsvár], 1944), pp. 356-357.

87. "Minutes of the Ministerial Council meeting," October 11, 1940, and a "Report of the Commissioners Office," August, 1941, *Shliakhom Zhovtnia,* vol. 5 (Uzhhorod, 1967), docs. 103, 138.

88. *Hrammatyka uhrorusskoho iazŷka dlia serednykh uchebnykh zavedenii* (Uzhhorod, 1940), pp. 3-8. The commission included the Rusynophiles: E. Bokshai, I. Muranii and the Russophiles Vasilii Shpenik, Vasilii Popovich, Konstantin Stripskii, and Pavel Fedor. For sample text, see Appendix 3, pt. 6.

89. Ivan Haraida, *Hrammatyka rus'koho iazŷka,* Vŷdania PON, no. 1 (Uzhhorod, 1941), p. 3.

90. Ibid. A new letter "е" = "йо" or "ьо" was also added.

91. These texts were entitled *Tsvît dîtskoi mudrosty* and were all published by the Regent's Commissariat in Uzhhorod in 1939 (*Pervŷi tsvît* was issued in a second edition in 1940).

92. "Ot redaktsii," *Lyteraturno-naukova pryloha Karpatskoi nedîli,* vol. 1, no. 1 (Uzhhorod, 1941), p. 1. The first of these weeklies was edited by A. Il'nyts'kyi and A. Nemet, the second by I. Haraida. For sample text, see Appendix 3, pt. 6.

93. *Podkarpatskî narodnî kazky,* 2 vols., Narodna Bybliotechka PON, nos. 4 and 13 (Uzhhorod, 1941-42); Vasyl' Pipash, ed., *Zbornychok hutsulskykh narodnŷkh pîsen' kolomŷiok* (Tiachiv, 1941); Petr Lyntur, *Uhrorusskiia koliadky,* Bybliyoteka sovremennŷkh uhrorusskykh pysatelei (Uzhhorod, 1942); V. Shekspir, *Zhyvot y smert' Korolia Rycharda III-ëho,* trans. I. Muranii, Lyteraturno-Naukova Bybliyoteka PON, no. 8 (Uzhhorod, 1942); Mavrykii Iokai, *Dvî otdanytsî,* Narodna Bybliyoteka PON, no. 12 (Uzhhorod, 1942).

94. Gerovskii and Krainianitsy, *Razbor.*

95. Shtets', *Literaturna mova,* pp. 67-72.

96. Tichý, *Vývoj,* p. 134. In 1931, the perceptive Czech writer Ivan Olbracht wrote: "Ukrainian will dominate the country. And even if today they are equal, Russian will steadily decrease." "Země bez jména," in *Hory a staletí* (Prague, 1950), p. 79.

97. Even Mykola Shtets', who constantly stresses the importance of Ukrainian, can at best conclude that "at the end of the 1930s in Transcarpathia, the idea of 'for one [given] people one literary language . . . one script' found deep roots." Shtets', *Literaturna mova,* p. 86.

7. Literary and Cultural Developments

1. Antonín Hartl, *Literární obrození Podkarpatských Rusínů v letech 1920-1930* (Prague, 1930) and his *Die literarische Renaissance der Karpathoruthenen* (Prague, 1932).

2. Evmenii Nedziel'skii, "Sovremennaia karpatorusskaia literatura," *Tsentral'naia Evropa,* vol. 4, no. 4 (Prague, 1931), p. 203.

3. Hartl, *Literární obrození,* p. 4.

4. Vladimir Birčak, "Dnešní stav podkarpatské literatury," in J. Zatloukal, ed., *Podkarpatská Rus* (Bratislava, 1936), p. 194; Iurii Baleha, *Literatura Zakarpattia 20-kh-30-kh rokiv XX stolittia* (Kiev, 1962), p. 82.

5. Iulii Borshosh-Kumiats'kyi, *Vesnianî kvîtŷ: poeziî*, Byblioteka novynky 'Nash rodnyi krai', no. 17 (Uzhhorod, 1928). For an analysis of his work, see Hartl, *Literární obrození*, pp. 18-21; Volodymyr Birchak, *Literaturni stremlinnia Pidkarpats'koï Rusy*, Vyd. PTPR, no. 45, 2nd ed., (Uzhhorod, 1937), pp. 162-165; Baleha, *Literatura Zakarpattia*, pp. 88-115. Unless otherwise indicated, the biographies of authors mentioned in this chapter are found in Appendix 2.

6. V. Grendzha-Dons'kii, "Liuby rôdnu movu," "Bezdol'na maty," in *Kvîtŷ z tern'om* (Uzhhorod, 1923); A. Karabelesh published more than 70 poems praising Subcarpathia in the sections "S prirodoiu naedinie," "Strana vospominanii," and "V rodnom kraiu," in *V luchakh razsvieta* (Uzhhorod, 1929); see M. Popovich, "O sen," "Rodimyi krai," in his *Pervye stikhi* (Prague, 1928), and "Vesna," "Lish my . . . ," in his *Khata*, Iz. OIAD, no. 100 (Uzhhorod, 1937).

7. "Liubliu tebe, rôdnŷi kraiu," in Borshosh-Kumiats'kyi, *Vesnianî kvîtŷ* p. 16.

8. Carlton J. H. Hayes, *Nationalism: A Religion* (New York, 1960), p. 9.

9. On Grendzha-Dons'kyi's works, see Hartl, *Literární obrození*, pp. 11-18; Birchak, *Literaturni stremlinnia*, pp. 157-162; Baleha, *Literatura Zakarpattia*, pp. 115-128, 221-231; and especially Mykhailo Mol'nar, "Dolia spivtsia polonyn," in Vasyl' Grendzha-Dons'kyi, *Shliakhom ternovym (Vybrani tvory)* (Bratislava and Prešov, 1964), pp. 3-52.

10. "Kniazivna Hutsulii," in *Zolotî kliuchi*, Vŷd. TP, no. 33 (Uzhhorod, 1923), p. 10; "Sotnia Mocharenka," in *Ukraïns'ke slovo* (Uzhhorod, 1932), Nos. 14-17. See also Grendzha-Dons'kyi's "Bii pid Syhotom," in *Shliakhom ternovym* (Uzhhorod, 1924), p. 9. "The heroic period of 1918-1919 is my favorite theme," wrote Grendzha-Dons'kyi (quoted in Mol'nar, "Dolia," p. 27): see also his *Nazustrich voli: zbirka opovidan' z chasiv revoliutsiï 1918/19 ta inshi* (Uzhhorod, 1930).

11. *The Red Cliff* was first published in *Pchôlka*, vol. 9, nos. 1-10 (Uzhhorod, 1930-31), and later revised in *Chervona skala (Kniaz Bohdan): epos pro khusts'kyi zamok z XIII v.*, Knyhozbirnia tov. ukraïns'kykh pys'mennykiv, no. 4 (Uzhhorod, 1938); "Ostannîi bôi," in *Pchôlka*, vol. 10, nos. 3-4 (Uzhhorod, 1931-32), pp. 78-80, 99-101, 134-138.

12. Interview with Grendzha-Dons'kyi in *Novyi chas* (L'viv), October 6, 1935.

13. *Petro Petrovych: istorychna povist'*, Knyhozbirnia tov. ukraïns'kykh pys'mennykiv, no. 3 (Uzhhorod, 1937). Grendzha-Dons'kyi was aware of, but nonetheless ignored completely the research of A. L. Petrov, which had discounted the Petrovych legend (see Chapter 5) and was criticized by contemporary critics for this. See the discussion in Mol'nar, "Dolia," pp. 43-46.

14. *Petro Petrovych*, p. 8. Within *Marchia Ruthenorum*, Grendzha-Dons'kyi included territory as far south as Debrecen in Hungary and Oradea (Nagyvárad) and Cluj (Koloszvár) in present-day Rumania.

15. *Panove* is the plural form of the Czech and Ukrainian word *pan*, which variously means "gentleman," "sir," "lord," "master." The word appears most often in Subcarpathian literature with a negative connotation and as a synonym for the ruling classes—the Hungarian, and later the Czechoslovak, administrators, large landowners, and bourgeoisie.

16. Borys Martinovych, *Na svîtaniu: p'esa na 4 dîi z doby perevorotu na Podkarpats'kôi Rusy*, Vŷd. PTPR, no. 38 (Uzhhorod, 1930), p. 7.

17. Ibid., pp. 7-8.

18. Andrii Verkhovyns'kyi [Avhustyn Voloshyn], *Marusia Verkhovynka: piesa na try dîi* (Uzhhorod, 1931), p. 11.

19. Ibid., p. 19.

20. Ibid.

21. "Ia Rusyn," in Borshosh-Kumiats'kyi, *Vesnianî kvîtŷ,* pp. 11-12.

22. V. Grendzha-Dons'kyi, "Bludnomu synkovi," in *Kvîtŷ z tern'om* (Uzhhorod, 1923), p. 23.

23. V. Grendzha-Dons'kyi, "Vstavaimo," in *Trembîta: lyteraturnŷi al'manakh,* Vŷd. TP, no. 65 (Uzhhorod, 1926), pp. 19-30 and his "Shchyre pryvitannia shliut hruni stepam," *Nasha zemlia,* vol. 1, no. 4 (Uzhhorod, 1927), p. 5; Marusia Tysians'ka [Mariia Kabaliuk], "Oi, khto zh tebe . . . ," ibid.; K. Chuha [Mykola Chyrs'kyi], "Stohin Zakarpattia," ibid., vol. 2, no. 7 (1928), p. 13.

24. "My ukraïntsi," ibid., vol. 1, no. 1 (1927), p. 3.

25. Havrylo Bokshai, "Nas Beskydy ne rozluchat'," ibid., vol. 1, no. 3 (1928), p. 13.

26. Zoreslav [Sevastiian Sabol], "Hotovi," in *Sontse i blakyt'* (Uzhhorod, 1936), pp. 69-70. On his writings, see Birchak, *Literaturni stremlinnia,* pp. 165-169.

27. "O Rus', moi krai, strana rodnaia," from Vasilii Dobosh, "Liubov' k rodine," in *Sviataia zloba,* Biblioteka Sodruzhestvo, no. 1 (Uzhhorod, 1936), p. 11; "Otchizna! Rus'! Strana rodnaia," from Andrei Patrus, "Otchizne," in *Plet'iu soviesti,* Biblioteka Sodruzhestvo, no. 4 (Uzhhorod, 1937), p. 17.

28. M. Popovich, "Verkhovina," in *Khata,* p. 8.

29. On the writings of these authors, see Hartl, *Literární obrození,* pp. 23-30; Pavel Fedor, *Ocherki karpatorusskoi literatury so vtoroi poloviny XIX stolietiia,* Izdanie OIAD, no. 56 (Uzhhorod, 1929), pp. 70-76; Birchak, *Literaturni stremlinnia,* pp. 174-176; Baleha, *Literatura Zakarpattia,* pp. 137-148, 154-167.

30. A. Karabelesh, "Liubi svoi krai," in his *V luchakh razsvieta,* p. 312.

31. A. Karabelesh, "Russkii iazyk," in *Karpatskii krai,* vol. 1, nos. 11-12 (Mukachevo, 1924), p. 25; and in his *V luchakh razsvieta,* pp. 15-16.

32. "V luchakh razsvieta," in Karabelesh, ibid., p. 330. Also: "In order to understand our Russian people/ Both at home and in hard exile/ We are all of one indivisible family,/ We are all native Slavs," in "Moia molitva," ibid., p. 309.

33. M. Popovich, "Ne zabud'te," in *Al'manakh Vozrozhdentsev* (Prague, 1933), p. 22. See also his "Pora, pora by nam sozdat' " and "Slavianskaia lipa," in *Pervye stikhi* (Prague, 1928), pp. 9, 16.

34. Birčak, "Dnešní stav," p. 194; Hartl, *Die literarische Renaissance,* p. 14.

35. A. Karabelesh, "Dukhnovichu," in *Karpatskii sviet,* vol. 1, no. 4 (Uzhhorod, 1928), p. 49, "Na smert' russkago bortsa"—dedicated to Simeon Sabov—ibid., vol. 2, nos. 2-3 (1929), p. 446 and "E.I. Sabovu," ibid., vol. 2, nos. 5-6 (1929), p. 595; M. Popovich "Zaviety nashikh predkov," "Chernetskii monastyr'," in *Pervye stikhi,* pp. 11, 34, and "Geroi," in *Khata,* p. 5. See also Dmitrii N. Vergun, "Karpatskii Rusnak"—dedicated to Governor A. G. Beskid—in *Karpatskii krai,* vol. 1, no. 1 (Mukachevo, 1923), pp. 13-14.

36. "Ubiezhdenie," in Karabelesh, *V luchakh razsvieta,* p. 44.

37. A. Karabelesh, "Pod shum osenniago dozhdia," in *Izbrannyia stikhotvoreniia,* Izdanie OIAD, no. 36 (Uzhhorod, 1928), p. 52.

38. Mikhailo Popovich, "U nas . . . " (c. 1935), reprinted in *Dumy o Verkhovine* (Uzhhorod, 1959).

39. Iulii Borshosh-Kum'iats'kyi, "Na vulytsi," in *Kraïna dyv* (Uzhhorod, 1934), p. 28.

40. "Otse mii ridnyi krai," censored from *Nasha zemlia,* vol. 2, no. 4 (Uzhhorod, 1928), p. 16; first published in *Duklia,* vol. 10, no. 2 (Prešov, 1962), p. 26.

41. "Zviezdy" and "Plach Karpat," in *Izbrannyia stikhotvoreniia,* pp. 13, 96.

42. "Molitva," "Psalom I," "Psalom XII," "Khristos Voskres," "Moguchaia Sila," ibid., pp. 3, 22-24, 30.

43. "Dlia chego my zhivem?," ibid., p. 26. See also his "Uviadanie" and "Pessimizm," pp. 34, 36, and his "Gde schast'e?"—"Wherever we look or go/ We do not find happiness in strength/ It is hidden in an eternal dream/ It is in the lifeless tomb," in *V luchakh razsvieta*, p. 79.

44. "Vstan'te, brat'ia," in *Pervye stikhi*, p. 8. Also his "Synam karpatskim"—"Arise to a new life, brothers/ . . . The time has begun to struggle with darkness/ Our fatherland is calling us/ To a free, a new life!," ibid., p. 4.

45. Andrei Patrus-Karpats'kyi, "Poetam," cited in Birchak, *Literaturni stremlinnia*, p. 178.

46. See, for instance, Vasilii Dobosh, "Moi put'," "Iskusstvo zhit'," in *Sviataia zloba* (Uzhhorod, 1936), pp. 23, 29-30; Lev Bezdomnyi-Mansvetov, "K literature," cited in Oleg Grabar, *Poèziia Zakarpat'ia, 1939-1944* (Bratislava, 1957), p. 25. For a discussion of works by these authors, see Baleha, *Literatura Zakarpattia*, pp. 148-153, 231 ff.

47. *Il'ko Lypei, karpats'kyi rozbiinyk: povist'* (L'viv, 1936), p. 89. This work was reprinted in his *Shliakhom ternovym (Vybrani tvory)*, pp. 260-339.

48. On the writings of these authors, see Hartl, *Literární obrození*, pp. 30-31, 34-37, 40-47.

49. On the writings of these authors see Hartl, *Literární obrození*, pp. 31-38; Baleha, *Literatura Zakarpattia*, pp. 175-213.

50. Even the Russian émigré, E. Nedziel'skii, suggested that "in belles-lettres the Ukrainian tendency has recently taken first place." "Literatura i izdatel'skaia dieiatel'nost' na Podk. Rusi poslie perevorota," in *Podkarpatskaia Rus' za gody 1919-1936* (Uzhhorod, 1936), p. 133.

51. Avhustyn Voloshyn, *O pys'mennom iazŷtsî Podkarpatskykh Rusynov*, Vŷd. TP, no. 1 (Uzhhorod, 1921), pp. 15-16; Hartl, *Literární obrození*, p. 4. On the social origins of the local intelligentsia, see Chapter 1 and the statistical analysis in Appendix 2.

52. Hartl, *Literární obrození*, p. 24. As early as 1923 this same author considered "the Great Russian [*velkoruská*] orientation an anachronism," in "Jazyk a pisemnictví na Podk. Rusi," *Nové Čechy*, vol. 6, no. 2 (Prague, 1923), p. 69.

53. Popov was editor of *Karpatskii krai* and active leader of the Russophile movement in Subcarpathian Rus'. Vavrik and Vergun were Galician Russophiles who lived in Prague where they publicized the fate of the "Russian" people in Czechoslovakia's far eastern province. On these writers, see Hartl, *Literární obrození*, pp. 52-53; Baleha *Literatura Zakarpattia*, pp. 167-169; V. R. Vavrik, *Krest'iane-poèty* (Louvain, 1973), pp. 7-9; and *Československé práce o jazyce, dějinách a kultuře slovanských národů od r. 1760* (Prague, 1972), p. 498.

54. Lev Tyblevich, "Russkaia sud'ba," *Rifmy* (Mukachevo, 1932), p. 6. Cf. V. R. Vavrik, *Piesni. Rus'. Trembita* (Uzhhorod, 1921).

55. After the Second World War, Ivanchov has lived in Czechoslovakia and published in Ukrainian. On his life and work, see Il'ia Voloshchuk, *Sovremennaia ukrainskaia literatura v Chekhoslovakii* (Bratislava, 1957), pp. 123-132; Fedir Kovach, *Deiaki problemy rozvytku ukrains'koï literatury v Chekhoslovachchyni (pisliavoiennyi period)* (Prešov, 1973), pp. 20-23 and passim.

56. Eugen Nedziel'skij, "Karpatoruská literatúra po prevrate," *Slovenské pohl'ady*, vol. 53, no. 10 (Turčianský Sv. Martin, 1937), pp. 534-536, 538-541; Grabar, *Poèziia*, pp. 23-27. Baleha, *Literatura Zakarpattia*, pp. 62, 231-237, has rightly pointed out that "progressive" tendencies existed in works of Russophile as well as Ukrainophile authors. See also Ivan Vyshnevs'kyi, *Tradytsiï ta suchasnist'* (L'viv, 1963), pp. 119 ff.

57. "Vozzvaniia karpatorusskikh pisatelei k obshchestvennosti," *Russkii narodnyi golos* (Uzhhorod), October 27, 1937.

58. František Tichý, *Vývoj současného spisovného jazyka na Podkarpatské Rusi* (Prague, 1938), p. 125.
59. Cited in Petro Stercho, *Karpato-ukraïns'ka derzhava* (Toronto, 1965), p. 91.
60. Cited in ibid.
61. Among these were: *12: sbornik molodykh ugrorusskikh poètov* (Uzhhorod, 1940); *Zhivaia struia* (Mukachevo, 1941); *Shagi* (Mukachevo, 1941); *Budet den'* (Khust, 1941); *Nakanunie* (Uzhhorod, 1941); *Literaturnyi al'manakh* (Uzhhorod, 1943). For a content analysis of these and individual collections by G. Goida, V. Sochka, and I. Kercha, see Grabar, *Poèziia,* pp. 53-144.
62. Brief biographical descriptions of these authors are found in Vasyl' Mykytas' and Olena Rudlovchak, eds., *Poety Zakarpattia: antolohiia zakarpatoukraïns'-koï poeziï XVI st.-1945 r.* (Bratislava and Prešov, 1965), pp. 634-642. On literary developments during these years, see ibid., pp. 57-67; Grabar, *Poèziia,* pp. 29-52; Iurii Baleha, *Khudozhni vidkryttia chy pravda faktu?* (Uzhhorod, 1969), pp. 42-48, and the studies by Iu. Baleha, M. Iasko, P. Lisovyi, and V. Pop in the Bibliography (refs. 1136, 1512, 1720, 1943).
63. For instance: "Gory i dolia," "Na Verkhovine," and "Vzdokhi po rodine," by Vasilii Sochka; "V Karpatach" and "Rodina" by Iurii Kachii (b. 1925); and the many lyric poems by Dmitrii Vakarov. Reprinted in Mykytas' and Rudlovchak, *Poeziia Zakarpattia,* pp. 560 ff.
64. "Mukachevo," in *Zhivaia struia* (Mukachevo, 1940), pp. 7-8, reprinted in *Poeziia Zakarpattia,* pp. 502-503.
65. Mikhail Shpitser, "Zaria s vostoka," in *Budet den'* (Khust, 1941), p. 32; Dmytro Vakarov, "Sentiabr' 1939 goda," both poems reprinted in Mykytas' and Rudlovchak, *Poeziia Zakarpattia,* pp. 566, 545.
66. "Tip (Geroi nashego vremeni)," in *Literaturnyi al'manakh* (Uzhhorod, 1943), p. 25, reprinted in Mykytas' and Rudlovchak, *Poety Zakarpattia,* p. 543.
67. Iosip Arkhii (b. 1920), "V otvet priiatelevi," reprinted in Grabar, *Poeziia,* p. 102.
68. For an interesting comparative study of the *matica* phenomenon, see Stanley B. Kimball, *The Austro-Slav Revival: A Study of Nineteenth-Century Literary Foundations,* Transactions of the American Philosophical Society, n.s., vol. 63, pt. 4 (Philadelphia, 1973). On the early Subcarpathian organizations, see Chapter 3.
69. For political developments at this time, see Chapter 10.
70. Pavlo Iatsko, "Spomyny pro pershi zbory 'Prosvity,'" in *Z nahody desiat'-litn'oho iuvileiu istnovannia tovarystva Prosvita na Pidkarpats'kii Rusy: 29.IV.1920 - 29.VI.1930,* Vŷd. TP, no. 152 (Uzhhorod, 1930), pp. 3-8; Avhustyn Voloshyn, "Zaisnovannia i rozvytok t-va Prosvita," *Kalendar' Prosvita* (Uzhhorod, 1938), pp. 70-72.
71. *Statut Tovarystva 'Prosvîta' v Uzhorodî* (Uzhhorod, 1924), p. 3. The original constitution (1920) referred only to the Rusyns of Subcarpathian Rus'.
72. *Statut tovarystva 'Prosvîta' Pôdkarpatskoî Rusy* (Uzhhorod, 1920), p. 6.
73. Ibid., pp. 6-7.
74. Symon Narizhnyi, *Ukraïns'ka emigratsiia: kul'turna pratsia ukraïns'koï emigratsiï mizh dvoma svitovymy viinamy,* Studiï Muzeiu vyzvol'noï borot'by Ukraïny, vol. 1 (Prague, 1942), p. 321.
75. Vasyl' Pachovs'kii, *Chto to Prosvîta?,* Vŷd. TP, no. 1 (Uzhhorod, 1920), pp. 8-9.
76. "Iak zakladaty y vesty chyt. 'Prosvita'?" (n.p., n.d.), p. 2.
77. Vŷdavnytstvo tovarystva 'Prosvîta' v Uzhorodî (1920-1930). Included in the series were works by local authors like L. Dem'ian, V. Grendzha-Dons'kyi, and M. Pidhorianka, and Ukrainian classics of I. Franko and M. Kotsiubins'kyi.
78. Vŷdavnytstvo Tovarystva 'Prosvîta', lyterarno-naukovŷi oddîl (1921-1927).

79. "K slavnostnímu otevření 'Národního domu' v Užhorodě," *Lidové listy* (Prague), October 20, 1928; Iurko Sokolovych, "Narodnŷi Dôm-kul'turna palata Rusynôv," *Kalendar' 'Prosvîty' 1929* (Uzhhorod, 1928), pp. 66-69.

80. "Protokol sostavlennyi 27. XII. 1923 . . . na pervom ocherednom sobranii OIAD," *Karpatskii krai,* vol. 1, nos. 3-4 (Mukachevo, 1923-24), pp. 35-39.

81. *Ustav Russkago kul'turno-prosvietitel'nago obshchestva imeni Aleksandra Dukhnovicha* (Uzhhorod, 1923), p. 3.

82. "Rezoliutsiia 8-ogo obshchago sobraniia OIAD, 1.VI.1930," *Karpatskii sviet,* vol. 3, nos. 5-6 (Uzhhorod, 1930), p. 1003. Of the many anti-Ukrainian statements made by the Dukhnovych Society, see especially "Protokol 9-ago godichnago obshchago sobraniia OIAD, 7.VI.1931," ibid., vol. 5, no. 6 (1932), pp. 1315-1347.

83. S. Fentsik, *Nash natsional'nyi gimn,* Izdanie OIAD, no. 26 (Uzhhorod, 1926), pp. 4-5. Of great importance to the society was the use of the name Dukhnovych, the nineteenth-century leader still so popular among the inhabitants of Subcarpathian Rus'. In an interview (February 1970), the influential Ukrainophile leader Iuliian Revai stated that it was a great mistake for Prosvita to choose a name which for all practical purposes was alien to the local population.

84. Besides the émigré representatives at the Dukhnovych Russian Day celebrations, local leaders also traveled abroad. See Stepan A. Fentsik, "Moia poiezdka v Bolgariiu na V s"iezd russkikh uchenykh, 14-28.IX.1930," *Karpatskii sviet,* vol. 3, nos. 7-8 (1930), pp. 1036-1051, and his *Uzhgorod-Amerika: putevyia zamietki, 1934-1935* (Uzhhorod, 1935).

85. "Above all I [want to] stress that in cultural-national matters our attitude towards the Czechoslovak government must remain loyal." Speech by Fentsik at the eighth congress (June 1, 1930) of the Dukhnovych Society in "Dieiatel'nost' OIAD v 1929/30 godu," *Karpatskii sviet,* vol. 3, nos. 5-6 (1930), p. 1001. For subsequent activity that contradicted the above statement, see Chapter 11.

86. Statues were erected to A. Dukhnovych in Sevliush (1925), Uzhhorod (1929), Khust (1931) and Prešov (1933); to Ev. Fentsik in Uzhhorod (1926); to A. Mitrak in Mukachevo (1931); and to A. Pushkin in Chynadiievo (1937).

87. "Nasha programma i nasha tsiel'," *Karpatskii krai,* vol. 1, no. 1 (Mukachevo, 1923), p. 3. *Krai* was edited by the Russian émigré A. Popov; *Sviet* was nominally edited by Evmenii Sabov, but practically by S. Fentsik.

88. Stepan A. Fentsik, "Rukovodstvo k organizatsii Russkikh Narodnykh chitalen' im. A. V. Duknovicha . . . ," *Karpatskii sviet,* vol. 2 no. 10 (1929), pp. 743-753.

89. For 1931, two Russophile sources—*Podkarpatskaia Rus' za gody 1919-1936* (Uzhhorod, 1936), p. 115, and Georgij Gerovskij, in *Československá vlastivěda,* vol. 3 (Prague, 1934), p. 514—listed Dukhnovych affiliates at 274 and Prosvita at 111, while a third source—"Deklaratsiia kul'turnykh i natsional'nykh prav Karpatorusskago naroda," *Karpatskii sviet,* vol. 4, nos. 5-7 (1931), p. 1208—listed, respectively, only 230 and 70 affiliates for the two societies.

90. The geographical layout suggested by Table 5 is confirmed by an analysis of the membership (1934) in the Ukrainophile Teacher's Assembly. While only 355 (49 percent) of the teachers in Bereg county belonged to the Teacher's Assembly, 186 (60 percent) were members in Ung county and 486 (75 percent) in Máramaros. *Uchytel's'kyi holos,* vol. 5, no. 6 (Mukachevo, 1934), p. 109.

91. *Karpats'ka molod,* vol. 1, nos. 6-7 (Velyka Kopania, 1937), p. 15; *Podkarpatskaia Rus',* p. 115. In eastern Slovakia, the Dukhnovych Society (37 reading rooms) was by far the superior: Ivan I. Zhidovskii, "Priashevskaia Rus' v bor'bie za svoi prava," ibid., pp. 89-91.

92. Evmenij Nedzielskij, "Spolek Alexandra V. Duchnoviče," and Ivan

Paňkevič, "Spolek 'Prosvita' v Užhorodě," in Zatloukal, *Podkarpatská Rus,* pp. 298-299.

93. *Nedîlia* (Uzhhorod), June 14 and September 27, 1936.

94. A letter by one villager (from Rostok) to the editor of an anti-Fentsik Russophile newspaper concluded: "And since Fentsik carried on his politics even in the Dukhnovych reading room, we decided to establish a Prosvita instead of a Dukhnovych reading room." "Komu èto nuzhno?," *Russkii vîstnyk* (Uzhhorod), January 26, 1936. On Fentsik's political activity, see Chapter 11.

95. Stercho, *Karpato-ukraïns'ka derzhava,* pp. 40-42.

96. *Nova svoboda* (Uzhhorod), September 15, 1938.

97. *Školstvi na Podkarpatské Rusi v přítomnosti* (Prague, 1933), p. 48; Iurii Borzhava, *Vid Uhors'koï Rusy do Karpats'koï Ukraïny* (Philadelphia, 1956), pp. 31-35; "Osnovania Rus'koho Natsional'noho Muzeia v Uzhhorodî," *Podkarpatska Rus',* vol. 7, no. 6 (Uzhhorod, 1930), pp. 123-124; Petr Sova, "Spolek 'Školnaja pomošč v Užhorodě," in Zatloukal, *Podkarpatská Rus,* p. 300; *'Kolomŷika':* *Zbôrnyk prysviachenŷi I. zîzdu Rus'kykh Natsional'nŷkh Khorov Podkarpatskoî Rusy* (Uzhhorod, 1926); B. Martynovych, "Spîv y natsional'nî khorŷ na Pôdkarpatskôi Rusy," *Kaliendar 'Prosvîtŷ' 1929* (Uzhhorod, 1928), pp. 137-144. Lev Bezruchko, *Z pisneiu po svitakh i ridnykh zakutkakh* (New York, 1951), pp. 99-118.

98. L. Bachyns'kyi, "Plast y relygiia," *Podkarpatska Rus',* vol. 5, no. 3 (Uzhhorod, 1928), p. 34. See also Mykola Vaida, "Pered vidznachenniam 50-richchia Plastu na Zakarpatti (1921-1951)," *Visnyk Karpats'koho Soiuzu,* vol. 2, nos. 2-3 (New York, 1971), pp. 10-11.

99. The series Plastova Byblioteka, 24 vols. (Uzhhorod, 1925-1929), was edited by L. Bachyns'kyi.

100. Stepan A. Fentsik, "Russkoe kul'turno-prosvietitel'noe OIAD v Uzhgorodie na Podkarpatskoi Rusi," in A. Popov, ed., *Karpatorusskaia dostizheniia* (Mukachevo, 1930), pp. 90-116; "My preodolieli krizis," *Karpatskii sviet,* vol. 6, nos. 1-2 (1933), p. 1353.

101. Grabar, *Poèziia,* pp. 30-31; Loránt Tilkovszky, *Revízió és nemzetiségpolitika Magyarországon* (Budapest, 1967), pp. 232-233.

102. "Rîch' rehentskoho komyssaria vytiazia Nykolaia Kozma z Leveldu dnia 26-ho ianuara 1941 roka z nahodŷ zaosnovania Podkarpatskoho Obshchestva Nauk," *Zoria-Hajnal,* vol. 1, nos. 1-2 (Uzhhorod, 1941), p. 12.

103. Ibid., p. 10. To further this aim, Haraida also prepared an anthology of Rusyn short stories in translation: *Ruszin elbeszélők,* Szláv irók, no. 1 (Uzhhorod, 1943).

104. "Protokol napysanŷi v Ungvarî 26-ho ianuara 1941 hoda na zakladaiuchom sobranii Podkarpatskoho Obshchestva Nauk," *Zoria-Hajnal,* vol. 1, nos. 1-2, p. 183.

105. Ibid., pp. 180-184; "Protokol napysanŷi . . . dnia 25-ho maia 1941 r. na sviatochnom sobraniy PON," ibid., pp. 184-186; V. Sherehii, "Odyn rok uspishnoi pratsi Podkarp. Obshchestva Nauk," *Lyteraturna nedîlia,* vol. 3 (Uzhhorod, 1943), pp. 142-144; Nicolas Harcsár, "La Société savante de Subcarpathie de Ungvár," *Revue d'histoire comparée: études hongroises,* vol. 21 (Paris, 1943), pp. 624-626.

106. Tilkovszky, *Revizió* pp. 232-233, 250.

107. F. Bazylevych, "Vôsîm lît pratsî rus'koho teatru T-va 'Prosvîta'," *Kaliendar 'Prosvity' 1929* (Uzhhorod, 1928), pp. 127-133; Iurii Sherehii, "P'iatdesiatyrichchia ukraïns'koho teatru na Zakarpatti," *Nove zhyttia* (Prešov), January 16 and 29, 1971, and February 5, 1971; Bezruchko, *Z pisneiu,* pp. 112-115. Sadovs'kyi himself was much less enthusiastic about the Rusyn Theater. In a letter written during the 1920s he complained about the primitive conditions he was forced to

work in and the local "audiences made up of magyarized Rusyns who scarcely know the Ukrainian language." Cited in V. Vasyl'ko, *Mykola Sadovs'kyi ta ioho teatr* (Kiev, 1962), p. 170.

108. Evgenii Nedziel'skii, *Ugro-russkii teatr* (Uzhhorod, 1941), p. 7.

109. Ibid., p. 54.

110. The most popular of these was Sion Sil'vai's, *Marusia*, Izdanie OIAD, no. 94 (Uzhhorod, 1930), which included all the favorite elements of Rusyn village life. The parents of Marusia refused to give their daughter to poor Vasylii who "did not know that poverty in the eyes of people is a great sin" (p. 18). After working two years in America, Vasylii returned as a rich 'pan', and only then was he considered worthy to marry Marusia. Written in a Subcarpathian recension of Russian, this play is filled with social themes but no references to national identity, nor to nationality issues. A list of the local dramatic repertoire is attached to the work of Nedziel'skii, *Ugro-russkii teatr*. Cf. the first part of this chapter.

111. Iu. Sherehii, "P'iatdesiatyrichchia," February 12, 1971.

112. Nedziel'skii, *Ugro-russkii teatr,* pp. 63-74; Iu. Sherehii, "P'iatdesiatyrich-chia," February 19, 1971; František Gabriel, "Otázka zemského divadla podkarpatoruského," *Podkarpatoruská revue,* vol. 1, no. 2 (Bratislava, 1936), pp. 6-8.

113. Iu. Sherehii, "P'iatdesiatyrichchia," February 19, 1971.

114. Writing about the theater during the 1920s, one author rightly concluded that "these theatrical undertakings existed exclusively thanks to the forces of the Ukrainian and Russian immigrants." Stepan S. Fedor, "Teatral'noe dielo na podk. Rusi," in *Podkarpatskaia Rus',* p. 142.

115. The author is thankful here for the opinions expressed in interviews (June 1971) with Ivan Hryts'-Duda.

116. *Lyteraturna nedîlia,* vol. 2, no. 4 (Uzhhorod, 1942), p. 32; Tilkovszky, *Revízío,* p. 250.

117. There was, however, a rich tradition of distinct folk and religious liturgical music from the region. The Slovak composer, Eugen Suchoň, did write a moving piece for chorus and orchestra entitled "Žalm Země Podkarpatskej" (Psalm of the Carpathian Region — 1937-38), based on a collection of poetry by Jaroslav Zatloukal, and which lamented the sad plight of the Rusyns.

118. Osyp Bokšaj, "Malířství na Podkarpatské Rusi," in Zatloukal, *Podkarpatská Rus,* pp. 214-215; A. Izoryn, "Suchasnî rus'kî khudozhnyky," *Zoria-Hajnal,* vol. 2, nos. 3-4 (Uzhhorod, 1942), pp. 390-395; Hryhorii Ostrovs'kyi, *Obrazotvorche mystetstvo Zakarpattia* (Kiev, 1974), pp. 14-34.

119. For a discussion of the work of these and other artists before 1945, see Izoryn, "Suchasnî rus'kî khudozhnyky," pp. 410-415 and *Zoria-Hajnal,* vol. 3, nos. 1-4 (Uzhhorod, 1943), pp. 258-282; Ostrovs'kyi, *Obrazotvorche mystetstvo,* pp. 37-103.

120. Bokšaj, pp. 215-217; Izoryn, "Suchasnî rus'kî khudozhnyky," vol. 2, nos. 3-4, pp. 395-400; Stepan Hapak, "Ukraïns'ke obrazotvorche mystetstvo v pershii Chekhoslovachchyni," *Zhovten' i ukraïns'ka kul'tura* (Prešov, 1968), pp. 566-591.

121. Izoryn, "Suchasnî rus'kî khudozhnyky," vol. 2, nos. 3-4, p. 406.

122. On this artist, who spent most of her creative life in Prague, see Ostrovs'kyi, *Obrazotvorche mystetstvo,* pp. 80-81.

8. Educational Developments

1. Boyd C. Shafer, *Faces of Nationalism* (New York, 1972), pp. 194-199.

2. Words of Senator Albert J. Beveridge (Republican, Indiana) in an address at a midwestern college. Cited in ibid., p. 196.

3. Aleksander Markush, *Shkolny voprosŷ* (Uzhhorod, 1922), p. 42.

4. A Ukrainian émigré in Vienna wrote as early as 1923 that "from the point of view of schools, Subcarpathian Ukraine [Rus'] is one of the most fortunate Ukrainian territories." Antin Krushel'nyts'kyi, "Natsional'ne pytannia v shkil'nytsvi na Prykarpatti," *Nova hromada,* nos. 3-4 (Vienna, 1923), p. 59. Cf. the opinions of the Russian émigré A.V. Popov, "Shkol'noe dielo na Podk. Rusi v 1919-1929 godakh," in *Karpatorusskiia dostizheniia* (Mukachevo, 1930), pp. 41-53; the local Ukrainophile, A. Stefan, "Education and Schools: Transcarpathia 1919-29," in *Ukraine: A Concise Encyclopedia,* vol. 2 (Toronto, 1971), pp. 381-383; and the Marxist A. M. Ihnat, "Stan osvity na Zakarpatti v 20-30kh rr. XX st.," in *Velykyi Zhovten' i rozkvit vozz'iednanoho Zakarpattia* (Uzhhorod, 1970), pp. 212-221.
5. The Hungarian statistics for 1910 indicated that 79 percent of Rusyns could not read or write in their native tongue; the figure for Máramaros county was 89 percent. *Magyar statisztikai közlemények,* n.s., vol. 61:*1910. évi népszámlálása,* pt. 5 (Budapest, 1916), pp. 586-589. Cf. Josef Pešek, "Školství v Podkarpatské Rusi," in J. Chmelař et al., *Podkarpatská Rus* (Prague, 1923), p. 161.
6. Krushel'nyts'kyi, "Natsional'ne pytannia," pp. 51-52; Pešek, "Školství," p. 161; Josef Pešina, "Národní školství na Podkarpatské Rusi," in Jaroslav Zatloukal, ed., *Podkarpatská Rus* (Bratislava, 1936), pp. 259-262; see also Chapter 3.
7. "Rusyn" is used here as the equivalent of "podkarpatoruská," a term employed in the official statistics to describe schools in Subcarpathian Rus' which may have had the Russian, Ukrainian, or Rusyn language as the medium of instruction.
8. The decrease in Greek Catholic Church schools was especially marked—from 164 to 19 between 1920 and 1938; the decrease in the number of Roman Catholic (20 to 17) and Evangelical (44 to 31) schools was less. František Stojan, ed., *Representační sborník veškerého školstvi na Podkarpatské Rusi* (Uzhhorod, 1938).
9. Pešina, "Školství," pp. 263-264.
10. Pavel St. Fedor, "Krátký nástin školství na Podkarpatské Rusi," in *Publikace pro zem Podkarpatská Rus 1919-1932* (Uzhhorod, 1932), pp. 65-69; *Školství na Podkarpatské Rusi v přítomnosti* (Prague, 1933), pp. 25-26.
11. The situation was particularly critical in secondary schools: "Of the 80 professors teaching during the 1918-1919 school year, only 6 were willing to serve the Czechoslovak regime after the revolution." Ibid., p. 32.
12. In the new Czechoslovak republic, the legionnaires were lauded as heroes and given many of the highest positions in the country's economic and military life. Some legionnaires of lower rank who may have had some knowledge of Russian from their military days were given positions as teachers in Subcarpathian Rus'. In "Rusyn" elementary schools there were thirty-seven teachers of Czechoslovak nationality (probably legionnaires) in 1920 and forty-nine in 1931. Ibid., pp. 14-15.
13. Ibid., pp. 14-36.
14. ANM, Fond Dr. Stary, carton 1, folder 2.
15. Pešek, "Školství," p. 169; René Martel, *La Ruthénie subcarpathique* (Paris, 1935). p. 106.
16. *Školství na Podkarpatské Rusi,* pp. 14-45.
17. Ibid., p. 48; Cyril Kochannyj, *O Podkarpatské Rusi* (Prague, 1929), p.33.
18. "Statistika o dieiatel'nosti kul'turnykh i prosvietitel'nykh organizatsii," *Karpatskii sviet,* vol. 3, nos. 5-6 (Uzhhorod, 1930), p. 999. Again, there is no agreement among the sources; Kochannyj, *O Podkarpatské Rusi,* p. 33, claimed that by 1927 there were 140 state reading rooms and 179 libraries in operation.
19. *Vînochok* was edited by I. Pan'kevych, Iar. Rozvoda, and, as part of *Nash rodnŷi krai* (1924), by A. Markush; *Uchytel'* was edited by I. Pan'kevych, Iu. Revai, and S. Bochek.
20. *Nash rodnŷi krai,* 21 vols., was edited by Aleksander Markush. This journal

also published the series "Byblioteka novynky 'Nash rodnŷi krai', " 17 vols., which included translations and original literary works (Borshosh-Kum'iats'kyi, Zlots'kyi, for example). *Podkarpatska Rus'*, 13 vols., was edited by A. Shtefan and Pavel Iats'ko.

21. "Besîda predsîdatelia Pedagogychnoho T-stva na II. zahal'nom z'îzdî, 8.V.1926," *Podkarpatska Rus'*, vol. 3, no. 6 (Uzhhorod, 1926), p. 132. The language used was based on the Pan'kevych grammar, although after 1935 literary Ukrainian with modern orthography was employed.

22. V. Hasynets', "O rozvyvaniu narodnoho dukha," *Uchytel'*, vol. 12, nos. 1-2 (Uzhhorod, 1931), p. 14.

23. Markush, *Shkolny voprosŷ*, p. 23.

24. A. D. Bondar, "Iz istorii shkoly v Zakarpatskoi Ukraine do vossoedineniia ee s Sovetskoi Ukrainoi," *Sovetskaia pedagogika,* vol. 18, no. 3 (Moscow, 1954), p. 102.

25. *Školství na Podk. Rusi,* p. 19. In the introduction to a guide for school administrators, a local teacher trained in Hungarian schools requested that his colleagues forgive his ungrammatical language: "I wrote only as I knew how." Ivan Lizak, *Rukovodstvo dlia uchytel'stva narodnykh shkol na Podk. Rusi* (Uzhhorod, 1933).

26. *Školství na Podkarpatské Rusi,* p. 38.

27. Ibid., p. 36; Mykola Shtets', *Literaturna mova ukraïntsiv Zakarpattia i Skhidnoï Slovachchyny pislia 1918* (Bratislava, 1969), p. 23.

28. Pešek, "Školství," p. 167. See also *Statut 'Uchytel'skago Tovarystva Podkarpatskoi Rusy'* (Uzhhorod, 1920).

29. Shtets', *Literaturna mova,* pp. 37, 98-99; also Chapter 6. *Narodna shkola* was edited by Vasilii Antalovskii and Miron Petrigalla.

30. "Spravozdania o diial'nosti Pedagogychnoho T-va Podk. Rusy do kontsia ianuara 1926," *Podkarpatska Rus'*, vol. 3, no. 2 (Uzhhorod, 1926), p. 39.

31. Iu. Revai and A. Voloshyn, "Vpyshuitesia v chlenŷ Pedagogychnoho Tovarystva," ibid., vol. 2, no. 1 (1925), p. 16.

32. "Rezolutsiî predlozhenî na zahal'nôm z'îzdî Pedagogychnoho Tov. dnia 6 okt. 1928," ibid., vol. 5, nos. 8-9 (1928), p. 176.

33. *Uchytel's'kyi holos,* vol. 3, no. 1 (Mukachevo, 1932), p. 2.

34. Ibid., vol. 3, no. 2 (1932), p. 1. See also "Iz zvychainykh zahal'nykh zboriv Kruzhka Narodovets'koho Uchytel's'koho T-va v Uzhhorodi," *Ukraïns'ke slovo* (Uzhhorod), May 1, 1932.

35. *Uchytel's'kyi holos,* vol. 5, no. 6 (Mukachevo, 1934), p. 109. In 1935, 1,650 members belonged to the Teacher's Assembly, according to Vasyl' Markush, "Zakarpattia," in *Entsyklopediia ukraïnoznavstva: slovnykova chastyna,* vol. 2 (Paris-New York, 1955-1957), p. 721; two years later the Teacher's Assembly included 1,555 of the 2,222 teachers in Subcarpathia—St. Merekht, "Uchytel's'ka hromada— nasha hordist'," *Nash prapor* (L'viv), October 15, 1937.

36. Shtets', *Literaturna mova,* pp. 65-72; also Chapter 6.

37. S. Antalovskij, "Karpatoruské studentstvo," in Zatloukal, *Podkarpatská Rus,* pp. 102-104.

38. See especially the anti-Ukrainian articles by Aleksiei A. Farinich: "Kto vrag narodnoi kul'tury," *Molodaia Rus',* vols. 3-4 (Prague, 1930), pp. 24-25; "Iz sviataia sviatykh ukrainskoi kul'tury" and "Ukrainskii vopros," *Al'manakh Vozrozhdentsev* (Prague, 1933), pp. 86-88, 98.

39. Ivan S. Shlepetskii, "Vozrozhdenie karpatorusskago studenchestva," ibid. (1936), pp. 71-75; L. K. Gumetskii, "Kratkaia istoriia o-va karpatorusskikh studentov 'Vozrozhdenie' i ego dieiatel'nost' v nastoiashchee vremia," in *Karpatorus-*

skiia dostizheniia, pp. 145-158; P. F. Komanitskii, "OKS 'Vozrozhdenie' i studencheskie organizatsii," in Ivan S. Shlepetskii, ed., *Priashevshchina* (Prague, 1948), pp. 301-307.

40. Oleg Grabar, *Poèziia Zakarpat'ia 1939-1944* (Bratislava, 1957), p. 23.

41. "Kruzhok po izucheniu Podkarpatskoi Rusi pri Russkom Narodnom Universitetie v Pragie v 1931-32 uch. godu," *Zhivaia mysl'*, nos. 2-3 (Prague, 1933), pp. 22-25. I know of no information indicating whether the circle continued to function after 1932. On the contributions of these scholars to Subcarpathian studies, see *Československé práce o jazyce, dějinách a kultuře slovanských národů od r. 1760* (Prague, 1972), pp. 193-194, 416.

42. Simon Narizhnyi, *Ukraïns'ka emigratsiia*, vol. 1 (Prague, 1942), p. 329. Cf. Petro Stercho, *Karpato-ukraïns'ka derzhava* (Toronto, 1965), pp. 40-41.

43. S. Rosokha, " 'Protypravne' chy polityka?," *Proboiem*, vol. 3, no. 3 (Prague, 1936), pp. 39-40.

44. V. H., "Baika pro lis, toporyshche ta klyn (abo chomu biemo peredovsim ukraïntsiv)," ibid., p. 35. For details on government policy and the Ukrainophile response during the 1930s, see Chapter 11.

45. In 1929, a Ukrainian student from the Uzhhorod Teacher's College attempted to assassinate the head of the Dukhnovych Society, Evmenii Sabov. *Dielo o pokushenii na E.I. Sabova*, Izdanie OIAD, no. 99 (Uzhhorod, 1930).

46. I. V. Andrashko, "Pievets krest'ianskago goria," *Zhivaia mysl'*, no. 1 (Prague, 1932), p. 9.

47. Ivan Andrashko, "Ne razbivaite naroda," ibid., no. 4 (1934), p. 15.

48. Andrashko's rather obtuse reasoning led to misunderstanding in the mind of his critics. Cf. the Ukrainophile, Ivan Siryi, "Bil'she svitla!," ibid., no. 6 (1934), pp. 7-9 and the Russophile, Ukrainoross, "Prezhde vsego nuzhno poniat'," ibid., pp. 9-13. He later clarified his position, criticized the idea of a separate nationality as "odious Rusynism," and called for the existence of one Subcarpathian culture using both Russian and Ukrainian language and literature. See his follow-up discussion "Ne razbivaite naroda," ibid., nos. 7-8 (1935), pp. 9-21 and his "Nashchupyvanie orientatsii," ibid., nos. 14-15 (1936), pp. 19-22.

49. "Riech' zashchitnika v protsessie O.K.S. Vozrozhdenie protiv studenta kollegi I. V. Andrashko," ibid., no. 6 (Prague, 1934), endpapers.

50. "Zakryite ches'ki shkoly po selakh," *Nova svoboda*, November 25, 1938; Volodymyr Birchak, *Karpats'ka Ukraïna: spomyny i perezhyvannia* (Prague, 1940), pp. 26-27; Iurii Borzhava [Sevastiian Sabol], *Vid Uhors'koï Rusy do Karpats'koï Ukraïny* (Philadelphia, 1956), pp. 42-43.

51. *Shliakhom Zhovtnia: zbirnyk dokumentiv*, vol. 5 (Uzhhorod, 1967), docs. 105, 148, 163; B. I. Spivak, *Narysy istoriï revoliutsiinoï borot'by trudiashchykh Zakarpattia v 1930-1945 rokakh* (L'viv, 1963), p. 295; Loránt Tilkovszky, *Revizió és nemzetiségpolitika Magyarországon (1938-1941)* (Budapest, 1967), pp. 247-248.

52. K. O. Kutsenko, "Zakarpattia v roky fashysts'koï okupatsii ta vyzvolennia ioho Radians'koiu Armiieiu," *Naukovi zapysky UDU*, vol. 30 (Uzhhorod, 1957), p. 126. On language use in text books at this time, see Chapter 6.

53. "Report by Ministry of the Interior to the Ministerial Council," January 30, 1942, *Shliakhom Zhovtnia*, doc. 148.

54. *Magyar statisztikai évkönyv*, n.s., vol. 49: *1941* (Budapest, 1943), p. 184. In 1940, Premier Teleki proposed a chair of Rusyn studies at Debrecen University where such matters could supposedly be dealt with in the correct manner by a Hungarian professor. Nothing came of these plans. Tilkovszky, *Revizió*, p. 248.

55. *Shliakhom Zhovtnia*, docs. 67, 70, 105.

56. Ibid.; Spivak, *Narysy*, p. 292; Kutsenko, "Zakarpattia," pp. 126-127. Later

the Royal Ministry of Religion and Culture published in Rusyn a bi-monthly *Vistn̂yk narodnŷkh uchytelev* (Budapest, 1942-1944).

9. The Religious Factor

1. Masaryk considered that the Czech contribution to world history was epitomized by the Hussite Reformation of the fifteenth century, whose moral and political ideas (including an anti-Vatican stance) he hoped would be implemented by the new republic. See Masaryk's pre-1914 essays: *Los von Rom* (Boston, 1902), and "Jan Hus and the Czech Reformation" (1910), in his *The Meaning of Czech History* (Chapel Hill, N. C., 1974), pp. 3-14. Cf. Ludvík Němec, *Church and State in Czechoslovakia* (New York, 1955), pp. 96-145.

2. Z.G. Ashkinazi, *Pravoslavnoe dvizhenie v Podkarpatskoi Rusi* (Uzhhorod, 1926), p. 3.

3. "Schvalovanie sriadenia a stanov pravoslavných naboženských obci na Slovensku," GKB, Prezidiálne spisy, carton 9, folder 63.

4. Ashkinazi, *Pravoslavnoe dvizhenie*, p. 25.

5. Iurko Lazho, *Russkomu narodu na Slovensku* (Vyšný Svidník, 1924), p. 30. See also the citations from contemporary pro-Orthodox publications in Iulii Gadzhega, *Stat'i po voprosam 'pravoslaviia', narodnosti i katolichestva* (Uzhhorod, 1921), pp. 28-39.

6. Ashkinazi, *Pravoslavnoe dvizhenie*, p. 26. See also Jan Húsek, *Národopisná hranice mezi Slováky a Karpatorusy* (Bratislava, 1925), pp. 78-86.

7. *Zprávy státního úřadu statistického republiky československé*, vol. 14, no. 170 (Prague, 1933); "Přehled o šíření se pravoslavného vyznání na Podk. Rusi" (ANM, Fond Dr. Starý, carton 1, folder 5).

8. A. Voloshyn, "Relihiini vidnosyny na Pidk. Rusy," in *Acta Conventus Pragensis pro Studiis Orientalibus a. 1929 celebrati* (Olomouc, 1930), pp. 218-219.

9. "Pravoslávne hnutie" (ŠSÚA, Fond MPS, carton 143, folder 6789/1924). For instance, twenty-four villagers were wounded in a clash between Orthodox and Greek Catholic adherents in Barbovo. *Podkarpatskaia Rus'* (Mukachevo), September 5, 1926. See also "Pravoslavný teror na Podkarpatskej Rusi," *Slovenský východ* (Košice), April 5, 1923.

10. See the discussions in Atanasii V. Pekar, *Narysy istoriï tserkvy Zakarpattia* (Rome, 1967), pp. 128-130; Ashkinazi, *Pravoslavnoe dvizhenie*, pp. 30-34.

11. Josef Pešek (Subcarpathian Superintendent of Schools and Culture), "Kulturní otázky Podkarpatské Rusi," *Lidové noviny* (Prague), July 29, 1923.

12. A. Rozsypal, "Opis," Uzhhorod, June 4, 1924 (ŠSÚA, Fond MPS, carton 143, folder 6789/1924).

13. "Orthodox propaganda in those territories [Subcarpathian Rus' and eastern Slovakia] is in essence nothing other than Bolshevik Russophilism." Letter of the Ministerstvo školství a národní osvěty, Prague, May 23, 1924 (ŠSÚA, Fond MPS, carton 143, folder 6789); "The Orthodox movement in Subcarpathian Rus' is controlled by very reactionary people, blind followers of Russian monarchism." *České slovo* (Prague), March 28, 1923. See also the Czech and Slovak press reports: "Pravoslavný teror na Podkarpatskej Rusi," *Slovenský východ*, April 5, 1923, and "Komunismus a pravoslaví," *28 říjen* (Prague), April 1, 1924.

14. "Pravoslavné hnutie," pp. 8-11.

15. "Důvodová zpráva" (ANM, Fond Dr. Starý, carton 1, folder 5).

16. In a meeting with Greek Catholic leaders in Uzhhorod, Minister Milan Hodža declared: "The Greek Catholic Church still today imposes on its faithful labor and natural duties, thus such devices which are nothing other than unfortunate remainders from serfdom and which in no way can be associated with the legal standing of a free citizen." "Stát a řeckokatolická církev," *Čech* (Prague), March 14, 1920.

17. The Prague government considered the Serbian jurisdiction in Subcarpathian Rus' a temporary solution until the establishment of an autocephalous Orthodox Church for Czechoslovakia. "Opis Ministerstva školství a národní osvěty," Prague, July 16, 1928 (ŠSÚA, Fond KÚ, carton 638, folder 31240/28).

18. Pekar, *Narysy,* pp. 123-127; Ilija Kačur, *Stručný prehl'ad histórie pravoslávnej cirkvi v byválom Uhorsku a v Československu* (Prešov, 196?), pp. 122-148.

19. Inok Aleksei, "Pravoslavie na Podk. Rusi" in *Podkarpatskaia Rus' za gody 1919-1936* (Uzhhorod, 1936), pp. 97-100; P. Popradov, "Podkarpatoruské pravoslaví," in Jaroslav Zatloukal, ed., *Podkarpatská Rus* (Bratislava, 1936), pp. 282-283.

20. A small percentage of Greek Catholics were of Magyar nationality. *Zprávy.* There were also a few minor sects like the Adventists, Baptists, and Bible study groups whose doctrines were spread among Rusyns by immigrants who returned from the United States. "Sekty na Mukačevsku," *Lidové noviny* (Prague), July 29, 1923.

21. Pekar, *Narysy,* pp. 130-131; "Biskup Papp šlubuje vernosť republike," *Slovenský východ,* August 26, 1923. See also Chapter 3.

22. "Řeckokatolická církev na Podk. Rusi stále ještě pod útiskem," *Lidové listy* (Prague), October 10, 1925.

23. "The question of the *koblina* and *rokovina* is definitely ended by the so-called *congrua* law, No. 122/1926. By this act, the *koblina-rokovina* can be considered only as a 'voluntary gift' . . . the priest does not have the right to demand its fulfillment." Bishop Gebei to the clergy of the Mukachevo diocese (GKB, Fond Prezidiálne spisy, carton 10, folder 64).

24. Other publications edited by Il'nyts'kyi included the *Dushpastŷr* supplement, *Dobrŷi pastŷr'* (1932-42)—"a practical journal of sermons for the Rusyn Greek Catholic clergy," and a series of small pamphlets on religious affairs: Knyzhky 'Dushpastŷr'ia' (1925-26).

25. *Bratskoe slovo ko vîrnŷm sŷnam greko-kat. tserkvy* (Uzhhorod, 1922), pp. 5-6.

26. František Tichý, "Náboženský a církevní problém Podkarpatské Rusi," *Kalich,* vol. 2 (Prague, 1922), p. 118.

27. Interview in *Rusyn* (Uzhhorod), February 18, 1923.

28. Pekar, *Narysy,* pp. 146-151.

29. Athanasius B. Pekar, "Basilian Reform in Transcarpathia," *Analecta OSBM,* vol. 7 (Rome, 1971), pp. 160-162.

30. Ibid., pp. 165-170; "Řád Sv. Vasila Velkého/Basiliani na Podk. Rusi—informace" (ANM, Fond Dr. Starý, carton 1, folder 5). On the response of the Czechoslovak government, see Chapter 11.

31. Pekar, *Narysy,* p. 148, n. 66.

32. Pekar, "Basilian Reform," pp. 170-174.

33. *Bratskoe,* p. 4.

34. See Chapter 11.

35. Pekar, *Narysy,* pp. 151-154, 205-206. Stoika's association with the Agricultural Autonomist Union seemed to bear out the suspicions of a 1931 Uzhhorod police report. While still a candidate for the Bishopric, many Rusyn priests opposed Stoika because he was "Hungarian in thought" and supported "by certain Hungarian circles." *Taiemne staie iavnym: dokumenty,* 2nd ed. (Uzhhorod, 1965), doc. 86.

36. *Nedîlia* (Uzhhorod), April 26, 1936.

37. From the conclusion of a ten-part series of articles authored by a Chestnyi Rusyn, "Panrusyzm i rusynyzm," *Nedîlia,* November 8, 1936.

38. "8-ho maia," *Nedîlia,* May 10, 1936; editorial, ibid., January 19, 1936.

39. *Nedîlia,* January 19, 1936.

40. *Nedîlia,* December 1, 1935, and August 2, 1936.

41. Niaradii was a native of Ruski Krstur in the Rusyn-inhabited region of the Bačka (Vojvodina), Yugoslavia. He was appointed administrator for the Greek Catholic Krževci diocese in 1914 and a year later made a bishop. Between 1922 and 1927 he also served as interim administrator for the Prešov diocese, where he became known as a Ukrainophile in national affairs. Pekar, *Narysy*, p. 209.

42. Pekar, *Narysy*, pp. 155-157; Petro Stercho, *Karpato-ukraïn'ska derzhava* (Toronto, 1965), pp. 84-85.

43. See the call, dated March 10, 1939, of Orthodox Bishop Dionisii to support the forthcoming meeting of the Carpatho-Ukrainian Soim (Diet). *Taiemne staie iavnym,* doc. 103.

44. Ibid., p. 86.

45. Pekar, *Narysy,* pp. 157-158; B. I. Spivak, *Narysy istoriï revoliutsiinoï borot'by trudiashchykh Zakarpattia v 1930-1945 rokakh* (L'viv, 1963), pp. 293-296. See also Chapters 5, 6, and 12.

46. *Taiemne staie iavnym,* doc. 104. See also other statements by Stoika, ibid., docs. 105, 106 and the praise expressed for the "re-unification" with Hungary by A. Il'nytskii, "Kartynŷ o russko-mad'iarskom bratství," *Zemledîl'skii kalendar' na hod 1939* (Uzhhorod, 1938), pp. 40-43.

47. Pastoral letter of July, 1941, cited in "Nash Preosviashchenŷi Epyskop pro vydania Podk. O-va Nauk," *Lyteraturna nedîlia,* vol. 1, no. 15 (Uzhhorod, 1941), pp. 131-132.

48. Pekar, "Basilian Reform," pp. 174-175.

49. J. J. Olas, "Pravoslavije pri Austro-Uhorščini, Čechoslovakii, i Mad'ar-ščini," *Karpatorusskije novosti* (New York), August 31, 1944; Pekar, *Narysy,* p. 161; Loránt Tilkovszky, *Revízió és nemzetiségpolitika Magyarországon (1938-1941)* (Budapest, 1967), pp. 251-253. In 1941, the Orthodox Church in Hungary received a new administrator, Mikhail Popov, a Don Cossack by origin who had lived the last twenty years in Hungary. *Taiemne staie iavnym,* docs. 108, 109, 114.

10. Political Consolidation in Subcarpathian Rus', 1919-1929

1. Elie Kedourie, *Nationalism* (London, 1960), p. 6. Cf. Anthony D. Smith, *Theories of Nationalism* (New York, 1971), p. 171 and Boyd C. Shafer, *Nationalism: Myth and Reality* (New York, 1955), pp. 196-212.

2. Interview with Avhustyn Voloshyn, *Rusyn* (Uzhhorod), February 18, 1923.

3. In 1929, a definitive boundary was set farther west so that thirty-two more villages were included within Subcarpathian Rus'. This border was never recognized as final by Subcarpathian political leaders, who still hoped to gain sovereignty over the territory in eastern Slovakia inhabited in 1930 by 91,079 Rusyns. See Map 4.

4. "General'nyi statut avtonomnoi Podkarpatskoi Rusi," *Úřední noviny* (Uzhhorod), February 18, 1920. An English translation of this document is available in Peter G. Stercho, *Diplomacy of Double Morality* (New York, 1971), pp. 41-43. See also Hans Ballreich, *Karpathenrussland: Ein Kapitel tschechishen Nationalitätenrechts und tschechische Nationalitätenpolitik* (Heidelberg, 1938), pp. 50-53; and Zdeněk Peška, "Podkarpatská Rus," *Slovník veřejného práva československého,* vol. 3 (Brno, 1934), pp. 111-112.

5. General Edmond Hennocque, "Brat'a Rusnaki!," *Pravda* (Uzhhorod), September 20, 1919. See also Zsatkovich's "Proklamatsiia Prezydenta Rusyniy k 'Tsentral'noi Rus'koi Radî y chrez niu vsîm Uhro-Rusynam," *Amierykanskii russkii vîstnyk* (Homestead, Pa.), November 4, 1919; Iulii Pusak [Iulii Gadzhega], *Vospominaniia* (Uzhhorod, 1938), pp. 74-79; I. N. Mel'nikova, "Ustanovlenie diktatury cheshskoi imperialisticheskoi burzhuazii v Zakarpatskoi Ukraine v 1919-1920 gg.," *Uchenye zapiski Instituta slavianovedeniia,* vol. 4 (Moscow, 1951), pp. 86-88.

6. Cited in "Imja D-ra Brejchi." After his appointment as head of the Direc-

torate, Zsatkovich proclaimed that these areas "will definitely belong to our state."
"Proklamacia dr. Žatkovičova," *Slovanský východ* (Košice), June 22, 1921.
    7. G. I. Žatkovič, *Exposé byvšeho gubernatora Podkarpatskoj Rusi o Podkarpatskoj Rusi* (Homestead, Pa., 1921), pp. 25-34; Mel'nikova, "Ustanovlenie," pp. 88-89.
    8. "Dr. Žatkovič o autonomii Podkarpatské Rusi, *Tribuna* (Prague), April 17, 1921. Zsatkovich was quoted in January, 1920: "I will work to introduce principles and laws [in S.R.] which have in fact made America a great and glorious state." "Zhatkovich i Podk. Rus," *Russkii narodnyi golos* (Uzhhorod), January 1, 1935.
    9. Žatkovič, *Exposé*, p. 16; "Krize ústavy nikoli guvernera Podk. Rusi?," *Tribuna*, May 10, 1921. For the official legal interpretation, see Peška, "Podkarpatská Rus," pp. 108-111.
    10. "Spravoyzdanie Predsîdatelia Dyrektoriuma Avtonomychnoi Rusyniy," *Amierykanskii russkii vîstnyk*, November 18, 1919. See also his "Uriadovŷi report Amerykanskoi Komyssiy Rusynov," ibid., July 3, 1919. It is interesting to note that Rusinia received extensive attention in a popular American book on conversation.

"Ever hear of George Zatkovich?'
. . . .
"No. Who was he?"
"He was the fellow who took the Constitution and made himself president of a European republic with it."
"And what republic was that?"
"Rusinia."
"Rusinia? There never was any such republic."
. . . .
"O, yes, there was."
. . . .
"Rusinia!" the lawyer laughs. "Sounds like the name of a country in a musical comedy."

Milton Wright, *The Art of Conversation* (New York and London, 1936), p. 191.
    11. A. Voloshyn has asserted that on the evening of May 8 a dispute arose between Zsatkovich and the Galician Russophile, A. Gagatko, who later joined the Czech administrator Brejcha in a political struggle against the future first governor. A. Voloshyn, "Ko voprosu polytychnoî konsolydatsiî," *Rusyn* (Uzhhorod), February 25, 1923.
    12. "Sjezd delegátů Karpatské Rusi," *Venkov* (Prague), October 12, 1919; Iosif Kaminskii, *Istoriia Tsentral'noi Russkoi Narodnoi Rady* (Uzhhorod, 1927); Rusak, *Vospominaniia*, pp. 86-88.
    13. See Chapter 8. It should nonetheless be noted that at two separate sessions of the Central National Council (May 9 and 14—when Voloshyn presided) proposals were accepted to use in Subcarpathian schools textbooks prepared by the Russophile Kachkovskii Society in L'viv. *Protokoly obshchago sobraniia podkarpatskikh russkikh rad i pervykh 5-ti zasiedanii Tsentral'noi Russkoi Narodnoi Rady* (Uzhhorod, 1919).
    14. Rusak, *Vospominaniia*, pp. 70-71.
    15. Speech of A.M. Gagatko in "Protokol obshchago sobraniia OIAD, 4.VI. 1928," *Karpatskii sviet*, vol. 1 (Uzhhorod, 1928), pp. 608-609. See also the earlier anti-Ukrainian statements of Antonii Beskid (1919) cited in N. A. Beskid, *Karpatskaia Rus'* (Prešov, 1920), pp. 92-95.
    16. Actually, Voloshyn's supporters also claimed that they were the only legal representatives of the Central National Council, that originated in Uzhhorod on

May 8, 1919. In practice, Voloshyn and the populist-Ukrainophiles joined political parties, many of which were pro-government, while Beskid's Russophile Central Council (later headed by Iosif Kaminskii) remained opposed to the government, met irregularly, and drew up memoranda demanding autonomy. During the 1930s, a Ukrainianophile Central National Council was revived among supporters of Voloshyn and on a few occasions joined Kaminskii's Russophile National Council in a united front against the government.

17. Jan Brandejs, "Vývoj politických poměrů na Podkarpatské Rusi v období 1918-1935" in Jan Zatloukal, ed., *Podkarpatská Rus* (Bratislava, 1936), pp. 72-75; O. Badan, "Klasy ta partiï na Zakarpats'kii Ukraïni," *Prapor marksyzmu*, vol. 2, no. 3 (Kharkiv, 1928), pp. 208-233; Stepan Rosokha, *Soim Karpats'koï Ukraïny* (Winnipeg, 1949), pp. 15-24.

18. See note 115, this chapter. The national viewpoint can be followed by the language used in the party's organs. *Selo* (1920-1924) was in dialect, *Zemlediel'skaia politika* (1927-1938) in Russian, *Zemlia i volia* (1934-38) in Ukrainian.

19. *Persha promova tov. posla inzh. Ia. Nechasa v spravakh Podkarpatskoi Rusy* (Uzhhorod, 1924), p. 8.

20. Ibid., p. 32. "Chy mozhe Rusyn obniaty uriad hubernatora sered nynìshykh obstavyn," *Vpered* (Uzhhorod), December 11, 1922. The party was headed by Evhenii Puza and Iatsko Ostapchuk, a prewar politician in Galicia who emigrated to Subcarpathian Rus' in 1912.

21. "Konhres khlîborobskoî partiï," *Rusyn*, March 1, 1923.

22. "Prohrama nashoi partii," *Rus'ka nyva*, vol. 1, nos. 1-2 (Uzhhorod, 1920).

23. Avhustyn Voloshyn, *Dvî polytychnî rozmovŷ*, Knyzhky 'Rusyna', no. 3 (Uzhhorod, 1923), p. 24. Cf. *Bratskoe slovo ko vîrnŷm sŷnam hreko-kat. tserkvy* (Uzhhorod, 1922). Voloshyn, who served as deputy from 1925 to 1929, was the party's only representative in Parliament. He clearly admitted that "the people who live in the Ukraine and call themselves Ukrainian, and our own Subcarpathian people who call themselves Rusyn are the same people." *Těsnopisecké zprávy o schůzích Poslanecké Sněmovny*, II. období, 170 schůze, October 25, 1928, p. 152.

24. B. Spivak, *U polum'i revoliutsiinykh boïv: do istoriï vynyknennia i diial'nosti pershykh komunistychnykh orhanizatsiï na Zakarpats'kii Ukraïni* (Uzhhorod, 1959), pp. 51-108; *Narysy istoriï Zakarpats'koï oblasnoï partiinoï orhanizatsiï*, vol. 1, *1918-1945 rr.* (Uzhhorod, 1968), pp. 31-65.

25. The first citation is from a speech by I. Mondok at the Sixth Comintern, Moscow, August 18, 1928; the second from a circular issued by the Central Committee of the Subcarpathian Communist Party, September 20, 1925. Reprinted in *Shliakhom Zhovtnia: zbirnyk dokumentiv*, vol. 2 (Uzhhorod, 1961), docs. 236, 87.

26. *Těsnopisecké zprávy*, I. období, 259 schůze, April 9, 1924, p. 426.

27. I. Gáti, "Proti odnětí sebeurčovacího práva podkarpatským narodům," *Rudé pravo* (Prague), June 7, 1927. For Czech police reports and other Communist statements on revolution, see also *Shliakhom Zhovtnia*, docs. 131, 302.

28. Speech of Comrade Vasil'ev [Mondok], June 26, 1924, reprinted in *Shliakhom Zhovtnia*, doc. 22.

29. From the Comintern resolution on the "Nationality Question in Central Europe and the Balkans: the Ukrainian question," reprinted in ibid., doc. 23.

30. *Těsnopisecké zprávy*, I. období, 344 schůze, June 3, 1925, p. 181. A few months later Gáti hesitatingly qualified that "the word autonomy we have always used in the sense of autonomy for the workers and we always emphasized that we are not struggling for civil autonomy but for the dictatorship of the proletariat." Ibid., 370 schůze, October 5, 1925, p. 1155. For further calls for autonomy, elections to a Soim, and rectification of the "unjust" Slovak-Rusyn border, see speeches by Gáti,

ibid., II, období, 12 schůze, March 4, 1926, pp. 537-541; Mondok, ibid., 61 schůze, January 15, 1927, pp. 1634-1635 and 110 schůze, November 30, 1927, pp. 134-141; Gáti, ibid., 149 schůze, June 27, 1928, pp. 17-22; Sedoriak, ibid., 150 schůze, June 28, 1928, pp. 99-102 and 172 schůze, November 6, 1928, pp. 43-53.

31. Pavlo Lisovyi and Mykhailo Babydorych, *Trybuna trudiashchykh* (Uzhhorod, 1970), pp. 5-36; Mykola Shtets', *Literaturna mova ukraïntsiv Zakarpattia i Skhidnoï Slovachchyny* (Bratislava, 1969), pp. 38-39. On the Party's change of language after 1926, see Chapter 11.

32. Speech of Gáti in *Těsnopisecke zprávy*, II. období, 6 schuze, December 21, 1925, p. 212.

33. See Chapter 11, pp. 229-231.

34. *Pravidlo organizovaniia, programma i ustav Russkoi Narodnoi Partii* (Prešov, 1922).

35. Iurko Lazho, *Russkomu narodu na Slovensku* (Vyšný Svidník, 1924), p. 44. For publishing this and other brochures and newspapers, Lazho was indicted by the county court in Vyšný Svidník for illegal printing, but his parliamentary immunity was upheld by the Senate. *Tisky k těsnopiseckým zprávám o schůzích Senátu,* I. období, 11 zasedání, Tisk 2244.

36. "Nasha programma," *Russkaia zemlia* (Uzhhorod), June 1919.

37. A. M. Gagatko, *Po sluchaiu iubileinykh torzhestv v Podkarpatskoi Rusi* (Uzhhorod, 1924), p. 15.

38. "Nasha programma"; Harion J. Curkanovič, "Ideové směrnice karpato-ruských politických stran," Cyklus přednášek, no. 10 (Prague, 1931), p. 11. See also the interpolation of Senator Tsurkanovich in *Tisky k těsnopiseckým zprávám,* Senát, III. období, Interpelace 232/4, June 4, 1930.

39. "Prohramma Podkarpatskoho Zemledîl'skoho Soiuza," *Russkii zemledîl'-skii kalendar' na hod 1922* (Uzhhorod, 1922), pp. 135-141; "Prohramma polytyche-skoi partii Avtonomnaho Zemledîl'skaho Soiuza," *Karpato-ruskii vîstnyk* (Uzhhorod), extra flier, February 1924.

40. Ibid.

41. "Dîiatel'nost' nashei partii," *Russkii . . . kalendar' . . . 1922*, p. 143. Cf. Kurtiak's addresses to Parliament, *Těsnopisecké zprávy,* I. období, 301 schůze, Nov. 19, 1924, pp. 383-384; 365 schůze, September 29, 1925, pp. 746-748; II. období, 12 schůze, March 4, 1926, p. 583.

42. *Nemzeti ujság,* December 25, 1924. See also his adamantly anti-Czechoslovak statements in Parliament, *Těsnopisecké zprávy,* I. období, 259 schůze, April 9, 1924. Kurtiak even went so far as to praise the former Hungarian school system whose "highest laws" guaranteed the existence of Russian (*russkii*) schools now closed under the Czechoslovak regime. Ibid., 365 schůze, Sept. 29, 1925, pp. 746-748. See also Chapter 11.

43. Rusyn informant cited in Henry Baerlein, *In Czechoslovakia's Hinterland* (London, 1938), pp. 46-47.

44. "Politické strany na Podkarpatské Rusi" (ANM, Fond Dr. Starý, folder 2). As for the nationality issue, the Ministry of Foreign Affairs gave the following appraisal: "The orientation of Dr. Beskid is Great Russian *(velkoruský)* which proclaims the people to be a part of the Great Russian nation and strives to introduce into the schools, at least the upper grades, the Great Russian literary language . . . The orientation of Dr. Zsatkovich proclaims the people as Little Russians and strives to introduce in all schools only the local (*lidový*) language." *Memorandum o Podkarpatské Rusi* (ANM, Fond Dr. Starý, folder 4), p. 6.

45. Memorandum of Ant. Gr. Beskid to Vlastimil Tusar, dated Prešov, July 24, 1919—reprinted in N. A. Beskid, *Karpatskaia Rus',* pp. 71-72.

46. For the texts of these, see ibid., pp. 73-91.
47. "Deklarace . . . Centrální Ruské Národní Rady v Užhorodě dne 18.I.1920."
in *Memorandum o Podkarpatské Rusi,* p. 8.
48. "Resoluce CRNR . . . dne 18.I.1920" in ibid., p. 10.
49. Ibid., p. 22.
50. Memorandums issued by the CRNR in July 1920 (ANM, Fond Dr. Starý,
carton I, folder 4) and by the Central Committee of the Russian National Party in
September, 1921 (ŠSÚA, Fond MPS, carton 467, folder 5650/1922) protested that
"the so-called 'autonomy' was only an empty promise."
51. "Memorandum karpato-russkago naroda, prinadlezhashchago dovremenno
k Slovakii, napravlen k vp. derzhavnym delegatam Soiuza Narodov" (ŠSÚA, Fond
MPS, carton 73, folder 1247).
52. Ministre des Affaires Étrangères, *Mémoire concernant la Russie subcarpathique: territoire ruthène au sud des Carpathes* (Prague, 1921), p. 36. On the exchange of memoranda, see Ballreich, *Karpathenrussland,* pp. 84-97, and Stercho,
Diplomacy, pp. 18-19, 96-103.
53. "Rusňacký rychtář jindy a dnes," *Na pravo,* March 6, 1926.
54. Antonín Hartl, *Podkarpatští Rusíni a my* (Prague, 1930), p. 3.
55. Lev Vojtěch, *Brána na východ (Karpatská Rus)* (Prague, 1920), p. 7. "Subcarpathian Rus' was of course unknown to Czechs, we can almost say absolutely unknown." Ferdinand Peroutka, *Budování státu,* vol. 3 (Prague, 1936), p. 1608.
56. Cited in Richard Katz, "Beim Gouverneur Zatkovich," *Prager Tageblatt*
(Prague), February 26, 1921.
57. Alois Hora, *Organisace státní správy Podkarpatské Rusi* (Prague, 1919), p.
4. "About Subcarpathian Rus', its people and life, we know very little in the historic
[Czech] lands. I would say that it is a land which we, before the War, imagined to be
like Siberia or even worse." František Šmula, "Dopis českého učitele z Podk.
Rusi," *Venkov,* May 25, 1924.
58. Karel Kadlec, *Podkarpatská Rus* (Prague, 1920), pp. 5, 27. Cf. Hora, p. 4.
59. "Podkarpatská Rus s hlediska menšinových otázek" (ANM, Fond Dr.
Starý, carton 1, folder 5). See also the chapters "The Unfortunate People" and
"The Magyar Crime" in Vojtěch, *Brána na východ,* pp. 10-21.
60. Ministre des Affaires Étrangères, *Mémoire,* p. 5.
61. Kadlec, *Podkarpatská Rus,* p. 19.
62. C. V. Kochannyj-Goralčuk, in *Pět let veřejné péči o výchovu lidu v
Československé Republice* (Prague, 1925), p. 35.
63. *Těsnopisecké zprávy,* 232 schůze Senátu, November 5, 1924, p. 106.
64. These included Edmund Egan's *Hospodářský stav rusínských venkovanů v
Uhrách* (Prague, 1922) and Mikloš Bartha's *V zemi Chazarů* (Mukachevo, 1927).
Prefaces to the new editions stressed that the situation had not appreciably changed
and that the Rusyns would have to be prepared for democracy and autonomy. See
also Chapter 3.
65. Jaroslav Hašek, *The Good Soldier Švejk* (1921-1924), trans. Cecil Parrott
(New York, 1974), pp. 573-574.
66. Edvard Benesh, *Promova pro pidkarpatorus'kyi problem i ioho vidnoshennia do chekhoslovats'koï respubliky* (Prague, 1934), pp. 11-41; Kamil Krofta, *Byli
jsme za Rakouska . . .* (Prague, 1936), esp. pp. 133-134.
67. Kadlec, *Podkarpatská Rus,* pp. 14-78; Alois Hora, *Uherská Rus za války a v
míru* (Prague, 1919); articles by Karel Kadlec and Josef Chmelař, in Jos. Chmelař et
al., *Podkarpatská Rus* (Prague, 1923), pp. 9-16, 184-189; Jan Húsek, *Národopisná
hranice mezi Slováky a Karpatorusy* (Bratislava, 1925), pp. 51-55; Jiří Král, *Podkarpatská Rus* (Prague, 1924), pp. 5-7; Karel Matoušek, *Podkarpatská Rus* (Prague,

1924), pp. 202-219; D. Richard, *Podkarpatská Rus jindy a nyní: politické a narodo-hospodářské náčrtky* (Mukachevo, 1927); K. Kochannyj-Goralčuk, *O Podkarpatské Rusi* (Prague, 1929), pp. 3-22, and *Podkarpatská Rus v minulosti a přítomnosti* (Prague, 1931), pp. 63-100; Alois Raušer, "Připojení Podkarp. Rusi k Československé republice," in J. Zatloukal, ed., *Podkarpatská Rus* (Bratislava, 1936), pp. 60-72; Otakar Skýpala, *Dnešní Podkarpatská Rus* (Prague, 1937); Peroutka, *Budování státu,* pp. 1598-1622.

68. See the speech of the pro-government Social-Democratic Deputy, Jaromír Nečas, *Těsnopisecké zprávy,* I. období, 259 schůze posl. sněmovny, April 9, 1924, pp. 435-442.

69. "Podkarpatská Rus, 1921" (ANM, Fond Dr. Starý, carton 1, folder 2), p. 3.

70. At the provincial, county, and local levels in 1920 there were 54 departmental heads, of which 21 were Czech and 20 Rusyn. Of 181 office workers, 122 were Czech and only 29 Rusyn. As for notaries, there were 104 Czech, 69 Rusyn, and 65 Hungarian. Ministre des Affaires Étrangères, *Mémoire,* pp. 9-10.

71. Karel Kadlec, "Dva roky Podkarpatské Rusi," *'Národní listy* (Prague), December 2, 1920.

72. "Parlamentní 'Pětka' pro záležitosti podkarpatoruské," *Večerní tribuna* (Prague), January 28, 1922. On subsequent activity of the parliamentary commission, see "Stanovyshche na Pidkarpatti," *Nova Ukraïna,* vol. 4, no. 1 (Prague, 1925), pp. 108-110.

73. "Zápis o poradě komise referentů ministerstev dne 16.I.1922" (ANM, Fond Dr. Starý, carton 1, folder 2).

74. "Podkarpatská Rus, 1921," p. 4.

75. "Poměry v Podkarpatském Rusínsku," *Lidové noviny,* October 19, 1919.

76. For a concise discussion of Kramář and the politics of this period, see Victor S. Mamatey and Radomír Luža, eds., *A History of the Czechoslovak Republic 1918-1948* (Princeton, N.J., 1973), pp. 64-65.

77. "Podkarpatská Rus," *České slovo,* October 14, 1919.

78. "Řádění Denikovců v Podkarpatské Rusi," *Právo lidu* (Prague), June 11, 1920; "Plukovník Jan Němeček," *Tribuna,* June 12, 1920; "Karpatoruský bolševism," *Právo lidu,* June 2, 1920; "Bolševické plány komunistické revoluce," *Venkov,* July 30, 1920.

79. *Russkaia zemlia,* no. 42 (1920); Andrej Gagatko, "Na okraj jubilejních slavností v Podkarpatské Rusi," *České slovo,* October 10, 1924.

80. Report of the *Župan* in Šaris district, Prešov, December 5, 1920. (ŠSÚA, Fond MPS, carton 52, folder 1652/1921).

81. Dr. Otakar Růžička, "Politické proudy v Přikarpatské Rusi," Prague, December 12, 1919 (ANM, Fond Dr. Starý, carton 1, folder 3).

82. Ibid.

83. From the legal standpoint, the Russophiles claimed that Subcarpathian Rus' united with the Czechoslovak Republic only at the Uzhhorod Council of May 8, 1919, and that all laws or acts of the Czechoslovak government prior to that date were to be considered invalid. In 1923, the Ministry of Foreign Affairs settled the legal controversy by decree: "Subcarpathian Rus', like Slovakia, is considered a part of the Czechoslovak Republic from October 28, 1918" (ŠSÚA, Fond MPS, carton 56, folder 5832).

84. "Náš poměr k Rusům," *Česko-ruský svaz* (Mukachevo), November 12, 1921.

85. On the goals and activity of this party, see its *Proklamatsiia do uhro-rus'-koho naroda* (Budapest, 1919), pp. 3-34. This document was written in Rusyn dia-

lect and issued simultaneously in Cyrillic and in Latin script: *Proklámacija do uhro-ruszjkoho národa.*

86. Ibid., pp. 35-51. This was signed by Dr. Miklós Kutkafalvy-Kutka (chairman), Ivan Prodan (vice-chairman), Vaszily Balogh (secretary), Dr. József Illés-Illjásevics (chairman of the commission for foreign affairs), and followed by eighty signatures.

87. [A. Hodinka and J. Illés-Illyásevics,] *Informations relatives à l'organisation du territoire des Ruthènes au sud des Carpathes, présentées par les Ruthènes emigrés, au secretariat général de la Société des Nations* (Budapest, 1922).

88. *La Russie subcarpathique au point de vue de la question des nationalités* (Prague, 1922), pp. 15-16; Férenc Boros, *Magyar-csehszlovák kapcsolatok 1918-1921-ben* (Budapest, 1970), pp. 101, 155; Mamatey and Luža, *History,* pp. 84-85.

89. "Politické pomery v Podkarpatské Rusi," *Slovenský denik* (Bratislava), April 1, 1920. Later, as a deputy in the Prague Parliament for the progovernment Agrarian Party, Stefan did admit to this activity. See his initial address, *Těsnopisecké zprávy,* 13 schůze posl. sněmovny, II. období, March 11, 1926, pp. 756-767.

90. "Die ungarische Gefahr," *Prager Tagblatt,* November 28, 1920; "Vážné nebezpečí polsko-mad'arských úkladů," *Večerní české slovo,* November 24, 1920.

91. "As everywhere there are also in Subcarpathian Rus' magyarones who are far more dangerous to our republic than true Hungarians." In "Z Podkarpatské Rusi," *Lidové noviny,* March 23, 1920.

92. Jaromír Nečas, *Uherská Rus a česká žurnalistika: neuzavírejte kruh našich nepřátel* (Uzhhorod, 1919), p. 5. See also his *Východoevropská tragedie a Ukrajina* (Prague, 1919); O. Gozdawa, *Uherská Ukrajina* (Prague and Kiev, 1919); and Richard, *Podkarpatská Rus,* pp. 59 ff.; and the discussion in Krzysztof Lewandowski, *Sprawa ukraińska w polityce zagranicznej Czechosłowacji w latach 1918-1932* (Wrocław and Warsaw, 1974), pp. 81-86.

93. Florian Zapletal, *Rusíni a naši buditelé* (Prague, 1921), pp. 3-4; Mykhailo Brashchaiko, *Ches'ko-rus'ki vzaemynŷ* (Uzhhorod, 1923). Actually, Czech authors referred to the *místní* or *lokální* orientation as Rusyn—*rusínský.* In order to avoid confusion with the magyarone Rusynophile orientation, we have decided to describe the "local" orientation as populist-Ukrainophile.

94. Růžička, "Politické proudy."

95. "Plán programu, dle nehož vláda hodlá . . . postupovati na Podk. Rusi, 1922" (ANM, Fond Dr. Starý, carton 1, folder 5); Report of Vice-governor Ehrenfeld, October, 1922 (ibid., folder 2).

96. As recently as February 1923, Švehla reiterated in an interview that "elections cannot be held in Subcarpathian Rus'." The population, used to the Hungarian feudal system, was not yet ready for Czechoslovak democracy, and must first be raised to the cultural and economic levels of the other Slavic peoples. "Minister predseda Švehla o Podkarpatskej Rusi," *Slovenský východ,* February 2, 1923.

97. Brandejs, "Vývoj," pp. 74-75.

98. Cited in "Pokoj lidem dobré vůle," *Tribuna,* November 18, 1923. For details on the Agrarian party and its competent leader Švehla, see Mamatey and Luža, *History,* pp. 61-68.

99. Kaminskii, *Istoriia.* The initial speech of Deputy Gagatko in the Prague Parliament stressed unity with Russian culture, but praised Czechoslovakia and expressed the hope that autonomy would be fulfilled. *Těsnopisecké zprávy,* 259 schůze posl. sněmovny, April 9, 1924, pp. 479-480. His following addresses resumed an anti-Czechoslovak stance and were particularly critical of "imported Ukrainianism." Ibid., 279 schůze, June 25, 1924, pp. 1097-1102; 301 schůze, November 19, 1924, pp. 374-382.

100. The vice-governor (always a Czech) was the immediate superior for referents of the departments (finance, agriculture, and education, for example) and heads of the civil administration, including the *župans* of the three administrative districts of Subcarpathian Rus'. The vice-governor also countersigned all acts of the governor, and in cases of disagreement between the two, the Prague government made the final decision. Peška, "Podkarpatská Rus," pp. 112-114; Ballreich, *Karpathenrussland,* pp. 55-56.

101. "Nová správa Podkarpatské Rusi," *Lidové noviny,* November 17, 1923.

102. Quoted in "Protokol . . . 7-ogo obshchago sobraniia OIAD, 2.VI.1929," *Karpatskii sviet,* vol. 3, nos. 5-6 (Uzhhorod, 1930), p. 981. Cf. Beskid's introductory remarks, "Podkarpatskaja Rus, kak avtonomnaja čast' Respubliki," in Gustav Bianchi, ed., *Publikace pro zem Podkarpatská Rus 1919-1932* (Uzhhorod, 1932), p. 21.

103. Cited in *Tribuna,* November 18, 1923.

104. During the 1920s, government funds for the rival cultural societies were allotted by the Ministry of National Culture, headed in Uzhhorod by a Russophile immigrant from Bukovina, Kirill Kokhannyi-Goral'chuk. In an interview with the author (January 1970), Kokhannyi stated that he liberally supported any group that was seriously interested in the promotion of culture.

105. Augustin Vološin, "Župní novela a Podkarpatská Rus," *Lidové listy,* February 16-17, 1927.

106. Agrarian Party leader Jan Brandejs analyzed the strength of the Communist appeal in Subcarpathian Rus': "Communism responds perfectly to the present low intellectual level of both the Rusyn worker and small landholder. The Rusyn villages in the Verkhovyna form, so to speak, a collective in which all the small landholders have the same tiny, low, dark, wooden houses with one room and a stable . . . all dress the same, eat the same food every day . . . have the same parcels of land, in short they all are in the same poverty . . . They are against individualism and for that reason Communism has penetrated to their blood and bones . . . And so, as long as the worst poverty continues, Communism will last . . ." Brandejs, "Vývoj," p. 84.

107. Jan Brandejs, "Spominy" (ANM, Fond Brandejsa, carton 2), p. 6.

108. Ibid.

109. Prime Minister Švehla stated: "Beskid must be removed from the governorship. In his place must be put a more understandable, serious, and active Rusyn figure." Already at this time Konstantin Hrabar was decided upon as the best candidate. Ibid., pp. 467-468.

110. "Podkarpatská Rus bouřlivě protestuje proti zemskému zřízeni," *Večerní práva lidu* (Prague), February 9, 1927.

111. "Podkarpatská Rus proti zemského zřízení," *Národní osvobození,* February 17, 1927; "Petition of the Ústřední Ruská Národní Rada, Uzhhorod, 18.II. 1927," (ANM, Fond Dr. Starý, carton 1, folder 4), signed by M. Brashchaiko and I. Kaminskii.

112. "Zákon ze dne 14.VII.1927 č. 125 o organisace politické správy," *Sbírka zákonů a nařízení státu československého* (Prague, 1927), pp. 1149-1461. For details on these administrative changes, see Peška, "Podkarpatská Rus," pp. 107-114 passim; Ballreich, *Karpathenrussland,* pp. 63-69; and Stercho, *Diplomacy,* pp. 55-60.

113. See addresses by Kurtiak (Autonomist Agricultural Union), Gagatko (Labor party), and Mondok (Communist), *Těsnopisecké zprávy,* II. období, 61 schůze posl. sněmovny, February 15, 1927, pp. 1650-1656; by Kurtiak and Gáti (Communist), ibid., 91 schůze, June 28, 1927, pp. 1956-1961; by Mondok, ibid., 92 schůze, June 30, 1927, pp. 2131-2145; and by Gagatko, ibid., 93 schůze, July 1, 1927. See also Ivan Kurtyak, *Pétition des Ruthènes en Tchécoslovaquie concernant l'autonomie de la Russie subcarpathique* (Uzhhorod, 1928).

114. Brandejs, "Vývoj," pp. 76-83.

115. "Protokol OIAD," p. 983. The first Agrarian Deputy in Parliament, Iosif Kaminskii (1924-1925), who was temporarily progovernment, set the tone for the party: "We stand on the basis of our traditions . . . We, to be sure, live far from Rus', but we nonetheless want and will support the cultural unity of our Carpatho-Russians with the rest of the Russian world." *Těsnopisecké zprávy,* I. období, 303 schůze posl. sněmovny, Nov. 21, 1924, p. 997. During the second parliament (1925-1929), Dr. Agoston Stefan called for the formulation, for official use, of a Rusyn grammar based on the local spoken language (Cf. his speech, *Těsnopisécke zprávy,* II. období, 13 schůze, March 11, 1926, p. 760), while his colleague Dr. František Králík (a Czech) called for a plebiscite among the teachers (Cf. ibid., 5 schůze, December 19, 1925, p. 153). During the third and fourth parliaments (1929-1935 and 1935-1938), Deputies Vasil Shcheretskii frequently criticized the government's supposed policy of Ukrainization (Ibid., III. období, 303 schůze, December 1, 1933, pp. 104-105); Pavel Kossei called for standardized grammars and a language decision to be decided by the Carpatho-Russian people (Ibid., IV. období, 21 schůze, December 11, 1935), while Josef Zajíc (a Czech) avoided the issue altogether. In the Senate, Edmund Bachinskii remained throughout a staunch Russophile (*Tisky k těsnopiseckým zprávám,* Senát, III. období, 6 zasedání, Tisk 859/1, June 23, 1932; 7 zasedání, Tisk 939/1, November 28, 1932 and Tisk 964/2, December 19, 1932).

116. In a letter to the Prosvita Society, Governor Beskid refused to attend its 1923 Congress "as long as [Prosvita] does not agree with Carpatho-Russian cultural life and as long as your organization serves political interests." Cited in "Nový dohled snášelivosti guvernéra Beskida," *Lidové listy,* December 21, 1923. Later Vice-governor Rozsypal refused to attend the 1923 inauguration of Prosvita's National Home because he had to attend "a horse show and also an apple fair." Ibid., October 20, 1928.

117. A. Voloshyn, *Spomyný* (Uzhhorod, 1923), p. 94.

118. *Rusyn,* February 13, 1923.

119. A. Karabelesh, "Desiat' liet," *V luchakh razsvieta* (Uzhhorod, 1929), p. 332.

120. Cited in Hartl, *Podkarpatští Rusíni,* p. 18. See also glorious praise for the Czechoslovak government by the Rusyn Agrarian Party Deputy, Vasil Shcheretskii (a peasant), in *Těsnopisecké zprávy,* III. období, 6 schůze posl. sněmovny, December 20, 1929, pp. 128-131.

11. The Decline in Subcarpathian-Czechoslovak Relations, 1930-1937

1. Jan Brandejs, "Spominy" (ANM, Fond Brandejs, carton 2), p. 581.

2. A. Raušer, "17 let od připojení Podkarpatské Rusi k ČSR," *Podkarpatoruská revue,* vol. 1, n. 4 (Bratislava, 1936), p. 7.

3. *Do peremohy,* vol. 1, no. 1 (Uzhhorod, 1935), p. 1.

4. Deputy Ivan Kurtiak demanded a plebiscite be held in the area before July 1, 1928. See his interpelation in *Tisky k těsnopiseckým zprávám,* Poslanecká sněmovna, II. období, 6 zasedání, Tisk 1569/XIV, May 16, 1928. The government responded that hopefully the newly established Slovak and Subcarpathian provincial assemblies would "reach finally an agreement on the common provincial borders." "Odpověď vlady," in ibid., Tisk 1768/VII, September 29, 1928.

For criticism by Czech journalists, see "Komedianství karpatoruských oposičníků," *Venkov* (Prague), April 16, 1927 and "Otázka hranic Podkarpatska a Slovenska," *Lidové noviny* (Prague), April 24, 1927. For the response of Slovak autonomists, see *Slovenská politika* (Bratislava), September 2, 1928; Ján Ruman, *Otázka slovensko-rusínskeho pomeru na východnom Slovensku* (Košice, 1935); Andrej Dudáš, *Rusínská otázka a jej uzadie* (Buenos Aires, 1971), pp. 211-225; and the discussion in Ivan Bajcura, *Ukrajinská otázka v ČSSR* (Košice, 1967), pp. 39-45.

5. In 1927, the Subcarpathian administration included 255 Czechs, 142 Rusyns, 56 Magyars, 17 Slovaks, and 22 others. "Seznam počtu státních zaměstnanců" (ANM, Fond Dr. Starý, carton 1, folder 5). On the provincial government and school issues see Chapter 8.

6. "Protokol iz iazykovoï konferentsiï iaka vidbulasia v Prazi 17 bereznia 1931," *Podkarpatska Rus'*, vol. 7, nos. 2-3 (Uzhhorod, 1931), pp. 56-61.

7. "Memorandum tov. Prosvîta v Uzhhorodî o iazŷkovôm sporî," ibid., vol. 8, no. 4 (1931), pp. 81-85. On the *Generální Statut's* language provisions, see Chapter 6.

8. Ivan Zhidovskii, *Iazykovyia prava avtonomnoi Podkarpatskoi Rusi* (Prešov, 1930), p. 11. See also "Khronika," in *Karpatskii sviet,* vol. 3, nos. 9-10 (1930), pp. 1103-1104.

9. From Dérer's response to the demands of Senators E. Bachinskii and I. Tsurkanovich for the introduction of Russian. *Tisky k těsnopiseckým zprávám,* Senát, III. obdobì, 3 zasedání, Tisk 303/3, October 9, 1930. See also his response to a similar demand in ibid., 8 zasedání, Tisk 1026/1, February 2, 1933.

10. These figures are given after subtracting the number of jobs found by the seven employment bureaus in Subcarpathian Rus'. Thus, for the year 1936 there was an all-time high of 27,054 unemployed, of which 10,526 found work. *Annuaire statistique de la République tchécoslovaque* (Prague, 1937), p. 222. On the general impact of the depression throughout the country, see Victor S. Mamatey and Radomír Luža, *A History of the Czechoslovak Republic 1918-1948* (Princeton, N.J., 1973), pp. 142-145.

11. For numerous reports by local officials, police and gendarmerie officers, see the documents in *Shliakhom Zhovtnia: zbirnyk dokumentiv,* vols. 2, 3, and 4, 1924-1938 (Uzhhorod, 1961-1964).

12. Ivan Židovský, *Ruská otázka v Československu: věci Podk. Rusi* (Prešov and Uzhhorod, 1933), pp. 6, 11.

13. The extent of the poverty, which continued to worsen, was the *only* issue that all parties, whether coalition or opposition, agreed upon. An Agrarian party memorandum of 1932 began with the analysis: "The general agricultural and economic crisis in Subcarpathian Rus' has reached such proportions that today it is no longer possible to speak of price or marketing crises, but rather about a complete ruination of Subcarpathian agriculture and with that the whole economic life of this land." "Memorandum republikanské strany zemědelského a malorolnického lidu pro vládu republiky československé," *Podkarpatské hlasy* (Uzhhorod), February 26, 1932.

14. See Chapter 10.

15. Some short-lived local parties were the Party of the Discontented Autochthons (Partiia Nedovolenŷkh Tuteshniakov), founded in April, 1933 and opposed to both the Czechoslovak administration and local Communists; the Front of Russian Agriculturalists and Workers (Front Russkikh Zemlediel'tsev a Robochikh), established by Konstantin Beskid in eastern Slovakia (June 1936) to oppose Fentsik's RNAP; and the Ukrainian Agricultural Workers Party (Ukraïns'ka Selians'ko-Robitnychna Partiia) founded in 1936 by socially-minded Ukrainophile leaders like Iryna Nevyts'ka, Ivan Hryts', and Vasyl' Kuz'myk. For lack of funds all these groups dissolved. *Se to! Se nam treba!! Se my khocheme!!!* (Uzhhorod, 1933); Konstantin Beskid, "Dopis do Ministerstva Rada v Praze, 14.VII.1936" (ŠSÚA, Fond Prezídium KÚ, carton 189, folder 1392/37).

16. Albert Bereghy [László Balogh-Béery], *Ruthén kérdés és az integritás* (Budapest, 1933), pp. 50-51. On Hungarian revisionism during the early 1920s, see Chapter 10.

17. Štefan Fano, "Protičeskoslovenské ostrie pol'sko-mad'arského zbližovania

v rokoch 1934-1936," *Slovanský přehled*, vol. 56, no. 5 (Prague, 1970), p. 342. The Hungarian position was most succinctly outlined in a study by the magyarone Rusyn László Balogh-Béery, *A magyar-lengyel közös határ és a ruthén terület* (Budapest, 1936). See also Jörg K. Hoensch, *Der ungarische Revisionismus und die Zerschlagung der Tschechoslowakei* (Tübingen, 1967), pp. 1-48.

18. Jan Brandejs, "Dějiny Mad'arska po roce 1918" (ANM, Fond Brandejs, carton 2), pp. 101-106.

19. This phrase was written large in each issue of the party organ, *Russkii vîstnyk,* and a special "autonomist" poem was composed by A. Brodii in the issue of April 3, 1938. "Unfortunately, we must state that the main stipulation for the union [with Czechoslovakia] of our autonomous Subcarpathian Rus' has not yet been fulfilled. Without the realization of autonomy, there can be neither political, cultural, nor economic progress here." Mikhail Demko, "Zasiedanie kraevago predstavitel'stva: deklaratsiia AZS," *Russkii narodnyi golos* (Uzhhorod), March 28, 1935.

20. Speech by Kurtiak in *Těsnopisecké zprávy,* II. období, 15 schůze posl. sněmovny, March 16, 1926, p. 932.

21. Speech by Brodii in ibid., III.období, 266 schůze, April 27, 1933.

22. See Kurtiak's speeches in ibid., I. období, 365 schůze, September 29, 1925, p. 716; III. období, 13 schůze, February 3, 1930, pp. 43-46.

23. Address delivered by AZS representative Mikhail Demko, "Protokol 8-ogo Obshchago sobraniia OIAD, June 2, 1930," *Karpatskii sviet,* vol. 4, nos. 3-4 (Uzhhorod, 1931), p. 1163. See also the parliamentary speech of Brodii in *Těsnopisecké zprávy,* IV. období, 126 schůze posl. sněmovny, December 15, 1937, esp. pp. 70-71.

24. See the speeches of Brodii in *Těsnopisecké zprávy,* III. období, 282 schůze, June 8, 1933, pp. 52-53; 347 schůze, November 8, 1934, esp. pp. 145-147; IV. období, 69 schůze, December 2, 1936, pp. 143-145.

25. Presidium policejního ředitelství, Uzhhorod, April 27, 1934, (ŠSÚA, Fond Prezídium KÚ, carton 245, folder 27276/38). Other reports described most leaders of the AZS as pro-Hungarian; see Policejní ředitel, Uzhhorod, March 21, 1935 (ŠSÚA, Fond PR, carton 251, folder Mat 75/1). At an AZS meeting in eastern Slovakia, Brodii was credited as stating that "we must stick together like the Czechs so that one day we can give them what they're giving us." Zemské četnické velitelství, Bratislava, April 27, 1934 (Ibid.).

26. Poland had a heritage of strained relations with her southern neighbor; in particular, the Těšín border dispute and Prague's refusal to allow the transportation across Czechoslovak soil of Hungarian supplies to Warsaw during the Polish-Soviet war. Poland, moreover, had difficulty with her own large Ukrainian minority in Galicia and was incensed at Prague's tolerance of Ukrainianism in Subcarpathian Rus'. Mamatey and Luža, *History,* pp. 33-35.

27. Štefan Fano, "Zakarpatská Ukrajina v politike súsedov a fašistických mocnosti 1933-39" (unpublished doctoral thesis; Bratislava, 1971), pp. 64-71; Stepan A. Fentsik, *Uzhgorod-Amerika: putevyia zamietki* (Uzhhorod, 1935). Also reports by Velitel četnické stanice, Humenné, February 22, 1935 and Prezídium Zemského Úřadu pro zemi Podk. Rus, Uzhhorod, April 25, 1935 (ŠSÚA, Fond Prezídium KÚ, carton 190, folder 24269/37).

28. Stepan A. Fentsik, Letter to the President of Czechoslovakia, May 7, 1937, (ŠSÚA, Fond Prezídium KÚ, carton 190, folder 24269/37).

29. *Programma Russkoi Natsional'no Avtonomnoi Partii* (Uzhhorod, 1935), p. 29. Like Kurtiak and Brodii, Fentsik was opposed to everything Ukrainian. See especially his parliamentary speech in *Těsnopisecké zprávy,* IV. období, 105 schůze posl. sněmovny, pp. 55-56.

30. Report of Zemské četnické velitelství, Bratislava, August 7, 1936 (ŠSÚA, Fond PR, carton 251, folder Mat 75/1). Fentsik's RNAP, and to a lesser degree Brodii's AZS, were popularly known as Subcarpathia's fascist parties.

31. Editorial in *Rusyn* (Uzhhorod), March 3, 1923.

32. Michael Yuhasz, Sr., *Wilson's Principles in Czechoslovak Practice: The Situation of the Carpatho-Russian People under the Czech Yoke* (Homestead, Pa., 1929) and his *Petition Concerning the Educational Complaints of the Autonomous Carpatho-Russian Territory South of the Carpathian Mountains . . . Presented to the League of Nations* (Homestead, Pa., 1932). See also Walter C. Warzeski, *Byzantine Rite Rusins in Carpatho-Ruthenia and America* (Pittsburgh, 1971), pp. 165-171.

33. Walter K. Hanak, *The Subcarpathian-Ruthenian Question* (Munhall, Pa., 1962), pp. 23-27. Lengthy quotations from the protests and Czech responses are found in René Martel, *La Ruthénie subcarpathique* (Paris, 1935), pp. 76-92.

34. Georgij Sabov, "Karpatorusskij Sojuz v Ameriki," *Kalendar' organizacii Svobody na hod 1936* (Perth Amboy, N.J., 1935), pp. 62-64.

35. "Our American brothers gave me 40,000 crowns so that I may dispose of this sum at my personal discretion." Stepan A. Fentsik, "Predislovie," *Karpatskii sviet*, vol. 7, no. 1 (1938), p. 1. Cf. "Amerykanskî 'pravoslavni' protestuiut' protyv Ch. S. Republyky,'" *Nedîlia* (Uzhhorod), October 27, 1935.

36. Letter from the Czechoslovak Consul, Cleveland, April 21, 1934 (ŠSÚA, Fond Prezídium KÚ, carton 55, folder Ukrajinská otázka; also cartons 490-491). On the Association, see Simeon Pysh, *A Short History of Carpatho-Russia* (1938; 2nd ed., n.p., 1973), pp. 46-48.

37. A Slovak gendarmery report contained excerpts from the 1936 *Lemko Kalendar:* "Only the Soviet system will bring us, Carpatho-Russians, autonomy . . . and social justice. Czechs and Poles cannot adopt such a system." Zemské četnické velitelství, Bratislava, May 7, 1937 (ŠSÚA, Fond Prezídium KÚ, carton 189, folder 1392/37). For further praise of the Soviets, see A. V. Shestakov, *Ystoryia sovitskoho soiuza i korotka ystoryia Karpatskoi Rusy* (New York, 1938). To be sure, the Polish government was opposed to Soviet-style propaganda, but it supported the Lemkian separatist movement in western Galicia in an attempt to weaken the U-krainian movement. Prague officials feared Poland would support the anti-Ukrainian Lemko movement in eastern Slovakia for its own use. Letters of the Czechoslovak Ambassador in Warsaw, May 28 and September 6, 1934 (ŠSÚA, Fond Prezídium KÚ, carton 55, folder Ukr. otázka).

38. Zemské četnické velitelství, Bratislava, 22.X.1937 (ŠSÚA, Fond Prezídium KÚ, carton 189, folder 1392/37). Finally, by a decree of October 14, 1937, the Czechoslovak Ministry of Interior made it illegal to import the immigrant newspaper *Lemko* (New York) or *Russky viestnik* (Pittsburgh) "via the post office or other means." Ibid.

39. Országos Levéltár—küm. res. pol. 1934/17/573: cited in Fano, "Protičeskoslovenské," p. 344. See also Maciej Kózmiński, *Polska i Węgry przed drugą wojną światową* (Warsaw, 1970), pp. 87-94.

40. Ibid., pp. 94-97; Fano, "Zakarpatská Ukrajina," pp. 65-70.

41. Martel, *La Ruthénie subcarpathique,* p. 161.

42. "Excerpts from Minutes of the National Assembly, 128th Meeting, November 13, 1920," *Papers and Documents relating to the Foreign Relations of Hungary,* vol. 1 (Budapest, 1939), p. 988.

43. *Minority Grievances in Russinsko,* Publications of the Hungarian Frontier Readjustment League, vol. 4 (Budapest, 1928); Brandejs, "Dějiny," pp. 101-102; Hoensch, *Der ungarishche Revisionismus,* pp. 9-11; Peter G. Stercho, *Diplomacy of Double Morality* (New York, 1971), pp. 162-175.

44. Count Stephen Bethlen, *The Treaty of Trianon and European Peace: Four Lectures Delivered in London in November, 1933* (London, 1934), p. 83.

45. Rothermere used his own newspaper, *The Daily Mail,* to publish the famous articles: "Hungary's Place in the Sun: Safety for Central Europe" (June 21, 1927) and "Europe's Powder Magazine [Czechoslovakia]: Gross Injustice Making for War" (August 30, 1927). Cf. Robert Donald, *The Tragedy of Trianon: Hungary's Appeal to Humanity* (London, 1928) and Robert Gower, *The Hungarian Minorities in the Succession States* (London, 1937). For a discussion of these developments, see Juraj Purgat, *Od Trianonu po Košiče: k mad'arskej otázke v Československu* (Bratislava, 1970), pp. 78-85.

46. Georges Desbons, *Les erreurs de la paix: la Hongrie après le traité de Trianon* (Paris, 1933), p. 121. Among other westerners who favored in varying degrees Budapest's point of view were the English scholar of Hungarian affairs C. A. Macartney: "in view of the economic connections of the country, the course most advantageous to the Ruthenes themselves . . . would be to return the whole district [S.R.] to Hungary . . ." in *Hungary and Her Successors* (London, 1937), p. 247; and the Swiss geographer Aldo Dami, *Les nouveaux martyrs: destin des minorités* (Paris, 1930), pp. 177-208. See also the comprehensive apologetic anthology prepared by Count Albert Apponyi for western consumption: *Justice for Hungary: A Criticism of the Effect of the Treaty of Trianon* (London, 1928). On other anti-Czechoslovak polemical literature emanating during this period from Germany, Italy, Hungary and Poland, see Paul R. Magocsi, "An Historiographical Guide to Subcarpathian Rus'," *Austrian History Yearbook,* vols. 9-10 (Houston, Texas, 1973-74), pp. 238-239.

47. See, for instance, the speeches of Korláth, *Těsnopisecké zprávy,* 369 schůze posl. sněmovny, I. období, October 2, 1925, pp. 1007-1010; 67 schůze, IV. období, November 30, 1936, pp. 15-25; and the more recent tract by Charles J. Hokky, *Ruthenia, Spearhead toward the West* (Gainesville, Fla., 1966). Cf. Purgat, *Od Trianonu po Košice,* pp. 85-98.

48. Dr. Schenk, "Podkarpatská Rus" (Prague, December, 1933), p. 4. A memorandum (c. 1925) of the Organization of Hungarian Journalists in Czechoslovakia stated that "the Hungarian people in the Czechoslovak Republic have complete freedom and more rights than their brothers living in Hungary." "Podkarpatská Rus v zrcadle pravdy" (ANM, Fond Brandejs, carton 4).

49. For details on the exchange of memorandums, see Stercho, *Diplomacy,* pp. 96-106.

50. Mamatey and Luža, *History,* pp. 216-238; C. A. Macartney and A. W. Palmer, *Independent Eastern Europe* (New York, 1966), pp. 320-333.

51. Concluding remarks of a speech given by Beneš to the Slovaks at Nové Zámky on December 7, 1933. Reprinted in *Le Monde slave,* vol. 11, no. 2 (Paris, 1934), pp. 213-214.

52. Edvard Benesh, *Promova pro pidkarpatorus'kyi problem i ioho vidnoshennia do chekhoslovats'koï respubliky* (Uzhhorod and Prague, 1934), pp. 16-55.

53. K. Kadlec, *Podkarpatská Rus* [A speech delivered at the Státovědecká společnost, Prague, April 21, 1920] (Prague, 1920), p. 26. Cf. Ferdinand Peroutka, *Budování státu,* vol. 3 (Prague, 1936), p. 1607.

54. Felix John Vondraček, "The Foreign Policy of Czechoslovakia, 1918-1935" (Ph.D. dissertation, Columbia University, New York, 1937), p. 326.

55. Benesh, *Promova,* p. 45. This view was reiterated by Beneš' successor, Dr. Kamil Krofta, who served as Minister of Foreign Affairs from 1936 to 1938. He also emphasized the area's strategic importance and concluded that: "the Czechoslovak Republic [must] most decisively reject all attempts at revision . . . and with all its

might defend this land [S.R.] . . . against anyone as a permanent and inseparable part of its state." *Podkarpatská Rus a Československo* (Prague, 1934), p. 61. See also his "Ruthenes, Czechs, and Slovaks," *Slavonic and East European Review,* vol. 13, no. 38 (London, 1935), p. 626.

56. Benesh, *Promova,* p. 33.

57. This principle had also come to dominate popular literature about the province intended for the Czech public. Jiří Král, *Podkarpatská Rus* (Prague, 1924), pp. 61-64; Karel Matoušek, *Podkarpatská Rus* (Prague, 1924), pp. 99-102.

Masaryk "approved of introducing Little Russian [Ukrainian] into the schools and public offices." See his *The Making of a State: Memories and Observations 1914-1918* (New York, 1927), p. 258.

On the work of the other figures mentioned, see the several articles by Mykola Mushynka: "Frantishek Hlavachek 90" and "Frantishek Tikhyi 80," in *Naukovyi zbirnyk MUKS,* vol. 3 (Bratislava-Prešov, 1967), pp. 28-30, 109-111; "Frantishek Tikhyi—80 richnyi," *Duklia,* vol. 14, no. 3 (Prešov, 1966), pp. 51-53; "Nevtomnyi doslidnyk zakarpatoukraïns'koï kul'tury: Frantishek Tikhyi," ibid., vol. 16, no. 4 (1968), pp. 343-344; "Doslidnyk kul'tury zakarpats'kykh ukraïntsiv" [F. Zapletal], ibid., vol. 18, no. 1 (1970), pp. 56-60.

58. Olbracht wrote a perceptive book of essays, or reportage, entitled *Hory a staletí,* 2nd ed. (Prague, 1935). On his *Nikola Šuhaj loupežník* and other novels, see Chapter 5; also Mykhailo Roman, "Iuvilei druha zakarpats'koho narodu," *Duklia,* vol. 20, no. 1 (Prešov, 1972), pp. 36-38. Neumann's writings include *Enciány s Pop Ivana* (Prague, 1933) and *Československá cesta* (Prague, 1934-35), esp. vol. 1, pp. 112-135, and vols. 2-3, pp. 9-154. On Nejedlý's many articles, see Mykhailo Mol'nar, "Ukraïnistychni zatsikavlennia Zdenieka Neiedloho," *Duklia,* vol. 21, no. 5 (Prešov, 1973), pp. 60-68. Cf. also V. Káňa, *Zakarpatsko: Reportáž ze života u-krajinského proletariátu v Československu* (Prague, 1932).

59. F. Tichý, "Podkarpatská Rus a my," *Čas* (Prague), June 16, 1921. See also the Slovak writer, Andrej Mráz, "Volanie Podkarpatskej Rusi," which appeared in a special issue devoted to Subcarpathian Rus' in the Slovak literary journal *Slovenské pohl'ady,* vol. 53, no. 10 (Turčiansky Sv. Martin, 1937), pp. 566-576; and the 26 articles by the Slovak Communist intellectual, Laco Novomeský, discussed in Mykhailo Mol'nar, "Latso Novomes'kyi pro ukraïntsiv," *Duklia,* vol. 23, no. 6 (Prešov, 1975), pp. 33-40.

60. A. Hartl, "Deux problèmes de la Russie subcarpathique," *Le Monde slave,* vol. 13, no. 2 (Paris, 1936), p. 101.

61. Olbracht, *Hory a staletí,* p. 78.

62. Cyril Horáček, "Dnešní stav národnostní a jazykové otázky u nás," in *Československá vlastivěda,* vol. 5, *Stát* (Prague, 1931), pp. 220-222; Zdeněk Peška, "Podkarpatská Rus," in *Slovník veřejného práva československého,* vol. 3 (Brno, 1934), pp. 107-115.

63. On the historical precedents for the symbol, see Avhustyn Shtefan, "Kol'ory-herby i prapory Zakarpattia," in *Al'manakh Provydinnia na rik 1971* (Philadelphia, 1970), pp. 156-161. On the hymn, see A. Dukhnovich-St. Fentsik, *Nash natsional'nyi gimn,* Izdanie OIAD, no. 26 (Uzhhorod, 1926).

64. Neumann, *Enciány,* pp. 32, 95; Dr. Otokar Růžička, "Politické proudy v Přikarpatské Rusi," Prague, November 12, 1919 (ANM, Fond Dr. Starý, carton 1, folder 3), p. 5.

65. *Pravda* (1919-1920); *Novoje vremja* (1925-1933). See also above Chapter 6.

66. Vasilij Mudraninecz, "Problémy Podkarpatské Rusi," *Venkov* (Prague), March 13, 1934.

67. Czech support, however, was limited to verbal encouragement. At a time

when the government agreed to give 30,000 crowns a year to both the Prosvita and Dukhnovych Societies, "we did not receive one crown from the state." Statement to the author in an interview (August 1971) with the former editor of *Nedîlia,* Emyliian Bokshai. In the face of blistering attacks against the "illiteracy" of *Nedîlia's* language, Czech literary scholar A. Hartl, "Deux problèmes," p. 99, praised the newspaper's Rusynism.

68. The *Matice Podkarpatoruská* was a philanthropic organization that organized benefits for Subcarpathia's starving population. "Stanovy spolku Matice Podkarpatoruské," May 11 1936 (ANM, Fond Brandejs, carton 2).

69. The literary anthology was edited by Antonín Hartl: *Pozdravení Rusinů: Výbor z literatury podkarpatoruské 1920-1935* (Bratislava, 1936). On Zatloukal, see Měčislav Krhoun, "Jaroslav Zatloukal a Zakarpatská Ukrajina," in *Zhovten' i u-kraïns'ka kul'tura* (Prešov, 1968), pp. 248-253.

70. The region provided the subject matter for Čapek's *Hordubal* (1933); Van-čura's *Poslední soud* (1930); Olbracht's *Nikola Šuhaj loupežník* (1933) and *Golet v údoli* (1937); Vančura and Olbracht's joint film scenario "Nevěrná Marijka"; Z.M. Kuděj's *Horalská republika* (1933); Jindra Zoder's *Petro* (1935); and Jaroslav Zatloukal's *Vítr s polonin* (1936) and *Zrazená země* (1938). See Roman, "Iuvilei," pp. 36-38; Krhoun, "Jaroslav Zatloukal," pp. 248-253; Antonín Hartl, "Podkar-patská Rus v české literatuře," in J. Zatloukal, ed., *Podkarpatská Rus* (Bratislava, 1936), pp. 207-209.

71. The government put out handsome travel brochures (in English) under the title "Subcarpathian Russia, Czechoslovakia." The region also received detailed coverage in the widely read *Sbírka průvodců "Orbis": Průvodce po československé republice,* 2nd ed. vol 3, *Slovensko-Podkarpatská Rus,* ed. František Gabriel, (Prague, 1937), pp. 597-735. See also Jaroslav Dostál, *Podkarpatská Rus,* Knižnice Klubu československých turistů, 2nd ed., vol. 6 (Prague, 1936) and the somewhat superficial Karel Hansa, *Stero črt a obrázků z Podkarpatské Rusi* (Prague, 1935).

72. The radio programs for Subcarpathian Rus' were broadcast from studios in Košice, Slovakia. All material dealt with the province and was presented in Rusyn dialect as well as in Russian and Ukrainian. For a sample of the programs during the first year of existence, as well as other information, see Fedir Ivanchov, ed., *Hovoryt' Priashiv . . . 30 rokiv ukraïns'koho radiomovlennia v Chekhoslovachchyni* (Prešov, 1968), pp. 14-30, 107-112. On the theater, see Chapter 7.

73. Jan Húsek, "Rodí se podkarpatoruský národ?" *Podkarpatoruská revue,* vol. 1, nos. 7-8 (Bratislava, 1936), pp. 6-8.

74. Benesh, *Promova,* p. 35. The minister argued, p. 37, that until now autonomy was not introduced for fear that the "economically, socially and politi-cally . . . superior" Hungarian and Jewish minorities would gain complete control and that "the minority would have ruled the majority."

75. This decision was made by the Agrarian party chairman, Rudolf Beran, as early as 1929, but Rozsypal managed to resist removal until December 31, 1936. Brandejs, "Spominy," pp. 546-547, 682-690. The praise for Rozsypal by Russophile leaders is evident in the article by Ivan I. Zhidovskii, "Vospominaniia o Antoninie Rozsypalie," *Russkii narodnyi golos,* May 11, 1937.

76. Schenk, "Podkarpatská Rus," p. 7.

77. Ibid., p. 15.

78. In Parliament, Brodii and Fentsik cooperated with the anti-government "Autonomist bloc," made up of the Slovak Hlinka party (twenty-two deputies), the Magyar parties (eight deputies) in Slovakia and Subcarpathian Rus', and the Sude-ten-German Henlein party (forty-four deputies). In December 1935, the intransigent Henlein called on Slovaks and Rusyns to make their demands for self-determination.

79. Jan Brandejs, "Vývoj politických poměrů na Podkarpatské Rusi v období 1918-1935," in Zatloukal, *Podkarpatská Rus,* pp. 76-83.

80. Benesh, *Promova,* p. 48.

81. On Hodža and his policies, see Mamatey and Luža, *History,* pp. 81-82, 123-124, 145 ff.

82. Kaminskii's sixty-four-paragraph proposal appeared in *Zakonoproekt ob avtonomii Podkarpatskoi Rusi* (Uzhhorod, 1931); Kurtiak's sixty-five-paragraph proposal in *Tisky k těsnopiseckým zprávám,* Poslanecká sněmovna, III. volební období, 4 zasedání, Tisk 991, November 26, 1931.

83. Fentsik's proposal included forty-two paragraphs: *Tisky k těsnopiseckým zprávám,* Poslanecká sněmovna, IV. volební období, 3 zasedání, Tisk 624, June 10, 1936. The CRNR demanded unification of those territories in eastern Slovakia that had a Rusyn majority and election within six months to a forty-five-member Soim. The fifty-four-paragraph project was signed, among others, by A. Voloshyn, Iu. and M. Brashchaiko, and S. Klochurak for the Ukrainophiles, and by I. Kaminskii and A. Brodii for the Russophiles. *Zakonoproekt Tsentral'noi Russkoi Narodnoi Rady o konstitutsii avtonomnoi Podkarpatskoi Rusi* (Uzhhorod, 1937).

84. Brandejs, "Spominy," pp. 668-676; Stercho, *Diplomacy,* pp. 60-63. Ladislav Suško, "Rokovania o autonómii Zakarpatskej Ukrajiny od roku 1936 do leta 1938," *Nové obzory,* vol. 15 (Prešov, 1973), pp. 37-44.

85. Law No. 172 and a government bill on the temporary functions of the Subcarpathian governor (*Tisky k těsnopiseckým zprávám,* Poslanecká sněmovna, IV. období, 5 zasedání, Tisk 936, June 3, 1937) were debated at length for two full days. Deputies Revai (Social Democrat), Chaim Kugel (Zionist-Social Democrat), and Zajíc (Republican), defended the measure; Borkaniuk (Communist), Brodii (AZS) and Fentsik (RNAP), joined by Kurdt (Sudeten-German), Schwarz (Czech), and Klíma (Czech-Communist) opposed the measure. *Těsnopisecké zprávy,* IV. období, 105 schůze posl. sněmovny, June 15, 1937, pp. 4-41 and 106 schůze, June 17, 1937, pp. 3-66.

For secondary literature on this question, see Zdeněk Peška, *Nové zřízení Podkarpatské Rusi* (Prague, 1938); Hans Ballreich, *Karpathenrussland: ein Kapitel tschechischen Nationalitätenrechts und tschechischer Nationalitätenpolitik* (Heidelberg, 1938), pp. 69-76. Stercho, *Diplomacy,* pp. 63-66, implies that all Subcarpathian leaders opposed the new law, but this is not borne out by the parliamentary debates referred to above.

86. Brandejs, "Spominy," p. 777.

87. In his opening speech to the seventh session of the Provincial Assembly, Subcarpathia's new Czech vice-governor, Jaroslav Merník (1937-1938), dealt only with agricultural and economic questions and stated that he had no time to deal with language or political questions. "Proslov zemského vicepresidenta dne 1.IV.1937" (ANM, Fond Brandejs, carton 2). Czechs continued to praise the regime for its accomplishments in the area during 1937-1938. Jan Brandejs, "Podkarpatské aktuality," *Brázda* (Prague), April 13, 1938.

88. Czech reasoning for introducing the questionnaire was based on the suggestions of President Beneš: "On the language and school questions, Rusyns must theoretically and practically in a democratic manner come to agreement themselves. If they cannot agree to the uniformity of language in the elementary schools, then they must accept a compromise solution, choose one language as the main one, and another which will be used in full measure alongside the main one by provision of the minority law." Cited in A. Raušer, "President dr. Edvard Beneš a Podkarpatská Rus," *Podkarpatoruská revue,* vol. 1, no. 1 (Bratislava, 1936), p. 7.

89. *Russkii narodnyi golos,* February 15, 1938; Mykola Shtets', *Literaturna*

mova ukraïntsiv Zakarpattia i skhidnoï Slovachchyny (Bratislava, 1969), pp. 29-31. For the particular characteristics of the Pan'kevych and Sabov grammars, see Chapter 6.

90. S. Fentsik, "Dieiatel'nost' Obshchestva Dukhnovicha v Uzhgorodie," *Karpatskii sviet,* vol. 7, no. 1 (1938), p. 42; "Interpelace poslance J. Revaye," *Tisky k těsnopiseckým zprávám,* Poslanecká sněmovna, IV. volební období, Tisk 1152/III, November 27, 1937. Reprinted separately, *Interpelatsiï i zapyty podani v parlamenti 27.XI.1937* (Uzhhorod, 1938). Cf. his speech in *Těsnopisecké zprávy,* IV. obdobi, 142 schůze posl. sněmovny, March 18, 1938, esp. pp. 8-14. Not all Czechs reacted favorably to the questionnaire: Fr. Trávniček, "O spisovnou mluvu Podkarpatské Rusi," *Lidové noviny,* February 16, 1938.

91. Schenk, "Podkarpatská Rus," p. 16.

92. "Řád Sv. Vasila Velkého/Basiliáni/ na Podk. Rusi—informace" (ANM, Fond Dr. Starý, carton 1, folder 5), p. 2. On the influence of Basilians in propagating Ukrainianism, see Chapter 9.

93. "Nové zatýkaní ukrajinských revolucionářů na Podkarpatsku," *Reformer* (Prague), August 26, 1926. See also "Zatčený ředitel řádové tiskárny v Užhorodě," *Lidové noviny,* August 11, 1926.

94. Ortoskop, *Derzhavni zmahaniia Prykarpats'koï Ukraïny* (Vienna, 1924), p. 35. This work was attributed to the Ukrainian immigrant Mykhailo Tvorydlo, an agronomist who worked for a while in the law offices of the Brashchaiko brothers.

95. Ibid., p. 66.

96. Prague "was the major center of the refugee Ukrainian intelligentsia," and it was also estimated that more than ten thousand Ukrainian soldiers from Galicia were in Czechoslovakia. S. Baran, "Ukrainian Political Refugees," in *Ukraine: A Concise Encyclopedia,* vol. 1 (Toronto, 1963), pp. 861 ff. On Russian and Ukrainian institutions in Czechoslovakia during this period, see Chapter 5.

97. Report of the Zemské vojenské velitelství, Košice, 21.VII.1932 (ŠSÚA, Fond Prezídium KÚ, carton 232, folder 301/38, section 3111/32). On the activity of these organizations during the 1930s, see John A. Armstrong, *Ukrainian Nationalism 1939-1945* (New York, 1955), pp. 18-25.

98. Reports from the Czechoslovak Embassy in Warsaw and from the Czechoslovak General Consul in Munich (ŠSÚA, Fond Prezídium KÚ, carton 232, folder 301/38, section 6265/33, and folder 354/37); *Lidové noviny* (Brno), August 12, 1931; "Blázni kramaři s bláznem: Dobrodruh Skoropadski prodal Mad'arům Podk. Rus," *České večerní slovo* (Prague), August 7, 1931.

99. Report of the Policejní ředitel, Košice, 23.VIII.1930 (ŠSÚA, Fond Prezídium KÚ, carton 232, folder 301/38, section 13949/30).

100. The Ministry of Interior decree was a reaction to the program of the Populist Teacher's Society, which proclaimed Ukrainian as its official language. René Martel, "Le nom d' 'ukrainien' en Russie subcarpathique," *Le Monde slave,* vol. 14, no. 1 (Paris, 1937), pp. 560-569. The use of the blue and yellow flag was also temporarily outlawed in 1934 because "blue and yellow are the colors of the Ukrainian nation." However, in December of that same year, a decree legalized the flag as the official Subcarpathian banner. Stercho, *Diplomacy,* pp. 88-90.

101. In 1935, the government summoned to Mladá Boleslav, in Bohemia, a congress of "Ukrainian Democratic organizations." Although the congress was boycotted by the majority of Ukrainian organizations, the hundred or so delegates who did attend accepted the principle that "Ukrainians in Carpatho-Ukraine are, and will remain, loyal subjects of Czechoslovakia, and that they will firmly resist all irredentism and all attempts at separation from ČSR." Nikolay Salisnjak, "The

Problem of Carpathian Ukraine," *Contemporary Russia,* vol. 2, no. 3 (London, 1938), pp. 325-326.

102. "Nový nápor Ukrajinců na totalisování země?," *Podkarpatské hlasy* (Uzhhorod), January 7, 1935.

103. "Protokol V. řádného sjezdu Komunistické strany Československa (sekce Komunistické Internacionály)," pp. 139-140—cited in Ivan Bajcura, "KSČ a ukrajinská otázka," *Z mynuloho i suchasnoho ukraïntsiv Chekhoslovachchyny* (Bratislava, 1973), p. 11.

104. On the Ukrainianization of the Soviet Ukraine during this period, see Basil Dmytryshyn, *Moscow and the Ukraine 1918-1953* (New York, 1956), pp. 57-90.

105. "Kinets' iazykovoho pytannia," *Karpats'ka pravda* (Uzhhorod), December 5, 1926. For a discussion of these developments see O. Badan, "Klasy ta partiï na Zakarpats'kii Ukraïni," *Prapor marksyzmu,* vol. 2, no. 3 (Kharkiv, 1928), pp. 223-224; Shtets', *Literaturna mova,* pp. 55-60; Ivan Bajcura, *Ukrajinská otázka v ČSSR* (Košice, 1967), pp. 54-57 and his "KSČ a ukrajinská otázka," pp. 9-13.

106. Speech of Mondok, *Těsnopisecké zprávy,* II. období, 45 schůze posl. sněmovny, October 20, 1926, p. 224.

107. Speech of Nikolai Sedoriak, ibid., 172 schůze, November 6, 1928, pp. 45-46.

108. *Holos zhyttia* (Uzhhorod), December 1, 1930.

109. Speech in *Těsnopisecké zprávy,* II. období, 51 schůze, November 23, 1926, p. 548.

110. O. Badan, "Natsional'ne pytannia na Zakarpats'kii Ukraïni," *Chervonyi shliakh,* vol. 6, no. 1 (Kharkiv, 1928), pp. 130-141.

111. It is interesting to note that the Subcarpathian section in Kharkiv bypassed the Prague-based Czechoslovak Communist Party and sent aid to local comrades in the homeland either directly or through the Soviet Embassy in Prague. Report of the Policejní ředitelství Uzhhorod, 22.IX.1932 (ŠSÚA, Fond Prezídium KÚ, carton 232, folder 301/38, section 3111/32); *Narysy istoriï Zakarpats'koï oblasnoï partiinoï orhanizatsiï,* vol. 1, *(1918-1945 rr.)* (Uzhhorod, 1968), pp. 121-123.

112. Czechoslovak authorities banned its original name, *Ukraïns'ka zemlia* (Ukrainian Land), and after the appearance of pro-Ukrainian and anti-Czechoslovak articles, the editor was forced to stop publication. Vasyl' Grendzha-Dons'-kyi, "Moï spohady" (unpublished memoirs, Bratislava, 1966), pp. 38-51; M. Mol'-nar, commentary in V. Grendzha-Dons'kyi's *Shliakhom ternovym: vybrani tvory* (Bratislava and Prešov, 1964), pp. 373-377.

113. V. Grendzha-Dons'kyi, *Ternovi kvity polonyn: poeziï* (Kharkiv, 1928). The first systematic Marxist history of the province also appeared: Oleksandr Badan, *Zakarpats'ka Ukraïna: sotsial'no-ekonomichnyi narys* (Kharkiv, 1929). See the introduction to this book by M. Skrypnyk reprinted in his *Statti i promovy,* vol. 2 (Kharkiv, 1931), pp. 144-147.

114. M. Klympotiuk, *Iunist' v borot'bi* (Uzhhorod, 1959); *Nezhasnyi iunosti vohon'* (Uzhhorod, 1968). On the education of Subcarpathian Communists in Kiev, Kharkiv, and Moscow, see ibid., p. 12 and O. Dovhanych and O. Khlanta, *Ivan Ivanovych Turianytsia* (Uzhhorod, 1972), p. 23.

115. Iu. Iu. Slyvka, *Revoliutsiino-vyzvol'na borot'ba na Zakarpatti v 1929-1937 rr.* (Kiev, 1960), pp. 113-116; Mamatey and Luža, *History,* pp. 153, 229-230.

116. "Communist Party pre-election announcement" (May 1935), *Shliakhom Zhovtnia: zbirnyk dokumentiv,* vol. 4 (Uzhhorod, 1964), doc. 55.

117. From the speech of Deputy Oleksa Borkaniuk, *Těsnopisecke zprávy,* IV. období, 11 schůze posl. sněmovny, November 7, 1935, p. 60. Cf. also his speech in ibid., 40 schůze, April 29, 1936, esp. pp. 148-149.

118. "Prohrama Zakarpats'koï kraiovoï orhanizatsiï, 29.V.1937," *Shliakhom Zhovtnia,* vol. 4, doc. 152. For other Communist demands for autonomy, see docs. 180-182, 207.

119. "Circular from the Subcarpathian Central Committee to all Party organizations, 8.V.1934," ibid., Doc. 25.

120. Ibid., doc. 169.

121. Interview with the author, August, 1971.

122. Iu. Revai, *V borot'bi za pravdu: promova . . . na Vseprosvitians'komu zïzdi v Uzhhorodi, 17.X.1937* (Uzhhorod, 1938), p. 5. V. Grendzha-Dons'kyi claims he became a Ukrainian as early as 1924 because he feared the Rusyns would become Czechified (interview with author, March 1970). See also, Chapter 7.

123. Stalenko, "Popy i Sviate Pys'mo," *Proboiem,* vol. 3, no. 3 (Prague, 1936), pp. 42-44; Ivan Bihunets', "Dukhovenstvo malo buty kerivnykom narodovets'koï pratsi," ibid., pp. 44-45.

124. "Nasha meta," *Zemlia i volia,* August 10, 1934.

125. The National Democratic party, which was Russophile, stated that "to support this other movement [Ukrainian] means to go against the interests of our state." Vladimir Sís, "Svátek Podkarpatské Rusi," *Národní listy* (Prague), May 8, 1934.

126. "Manifest do ukraïns'koho narodu Pidkarpattia" (Uzhhorod, October 17, 1937).

127. Ibid.

128. *Za ridne slovo: polemika z rusofilamy* (Mukachevo, 1937), p. 59. It is not clear whether this help was to come from abroad or from Ukrainian émigrés "from beyond the Carpathians, who living here [in Subcarpathian Rus'] are for us neither emigrants nor foreigners. They are our brothers . . ." Ïzhak, *Ukraïnets' chy russkii?* (Mukachevo, 1938), p. 74.

129. V. H., "Baika pro lis, toporyshche ta klyn (abo: chomu biemo peredovsim ukraïntsiv)," *Proboiem,* vol. 3, no. 3 (Prague, 1936), pp. 35-36.

130. Cited in Petro Stercho, *Karpato-ukraïns'ka derzhava* (Toronto, 1965), p. 42.

131. Agustin Vološin, "Carpathian Ruthenia," *The Slavonic and East European Review,* vol. 13, no. 38 (London, 1935), p. 378; Revai's address in *Těsnopisecké zprávy,* IV. obdobi, 142 schůze posl. sněmovny, March 18, 1938, p. 10. See also his speech in ibid., 40 schůze, April 29, 1936, p. 126, and "Spivpratsia koalytsiinykh partiï na Pidk. Rusy," *Do peremohy,* vol. 1, no. 1 (Uzhhorod, 1935), p. 18.

132. Brandejs, "Spominy," p. 997.

12. The Period of International Crises, 1938-1944

1. Jan Brandejs, "Spominy" (ANM, Fond Brandejs, carton 2), pp. 730 ff.; Štefan Fano, "Zakarpatská Ukrajina v politike súsedov a fašistických mocností, 1933-1939" (unpublished doctoral thesis; Bratislava: Ústav dejín europských socialistických krajín SAV, 1971), pp. 152-153; Ladislav Suško, "Rokovania o autonómii Zakarpatskej Ukrajiny od roku 1936 do leta 1938," *Nové obzory* (Prešov, 1973), pp. 47-48.

2. Suško, "Rokovania," 48-52; Andrii Kovach, "Stanovyshche zakarpats'-kykh ukraïntsiv (rusyniv) i zanepad pershoï ChSR," *Naukovyi zbirnyk MUKS,* vol. 6, pt. 1 (Svidník, Bratislava, and Prešov, 1972), pp. 12-14. On Gerovskii, see also Chapters 3 and 11 and Appendix 2.

3. Hodža arranged for an official reception upon Gerovskii's arrival in Prague and it was rumored that the prime minister provided him with 500,000 crowns. Brandejs, "Spominy," pp. 779-786. Hodža knew the American-Rusyn leader before

the First World War, when, as a Slovak member of the Budapest Parliament, he helped get Gerovskii released from a Hungarian prison. "Aleksei Iulianovich Gerovskii," *Svobodnoe slovo Karpatskoi Rusi,* vol. 7, nos. 1-10 (Newark, 1965), p. 7.

4. For Gerovskii's account of these developments, see *Karpatskaja Rus' v češskom jarmi* (n.p., 1939?), pp. 3-15. Recently, Suško, "Rokovania," pp. 52-58, has pointed out on the basis of archival evidence that Gerovskii's reputation wavered during his stay, and that in the end only Brodii and other pro-Hungarian Rusyns supported him. The Russian Bloc included the deputies Brodii (AZS), P'eshchak (AZS), Kossei (Agrarian), and Zhidovskii (Agrarian), and the senators Bachinskii (Agrarian) and Földesi (AZS). The Communists did not join, nor did deputies Revai (SD) or Fentsik (RNAP), although the latter two were to cooperate with the bloc at a later date.

5. "Rezoliutsiï ukhvaleni na zasidanni holovnoï upravy Pershoï Rus'koï (Ukraïns'koï) Tsentral'noï Rady v Uzhhorodi dnia 29.V.1938," *Nova svoboda* (Uzhhorod), June 15, 1938.

6. Ibid.

7. In an open letter to the American delegate Gerovskii, Hodža stated "that I will do all in my power so that elections to an autonomous Soim can still be introduced this year." "Pis'mo d-ra M. Hodzhi d-ru A. Iu. Gerovskomu," *Russkii narodnyi golos* (Uzhhorod), July 2, 1938. See also "Gubernator Podk. Rus u predsiedatelia pravitel'stva," ibid., July 12, 1938; and Hodža's letter to Gerovskii, July 9, 1938, reprinted in *Karpatskaja Rus',* p. 15.

8. The sixty-five-paragraph project called for a sixty member Soim elected on a proportional basis determined by national groups living in the province, that is, Rusyns, thirty-eight representatives; Magyars, nine; Jews, seven; Czechs, four; Rumanians, one; Germans, one. "Zakonoproekt respublikanskoi partii ob avtonomii peredan predsiedateliu pravitel'stva," *Russkii narodnyi golos,* July 1, 1938; Petr Sova, *Zakonoproekt ob avtonomii Podkarpatskoi Rusi* (Uzhhorod, 1938).

9. It was not until August 31 that Hodža conferred again with the Subcarpathian politicians, and in particular with the Russophiles—Brodii, Bachinskii, and Shcheretskii. Gerovskii was also present, although he was more than ever discouraged with the Czechoslovak administration and left secretly for Budapest on September 5. "Predstaviteli AZS i RZP u prem'er ministra dra Godzhi," *Russkii vîstnyk* (Uzhhorod), September 4, 1938.

10. From the speech of Ivan Rohach at Velyka Kopania on August 6, 1938. Quoted in Petro Stercho, *Karpato-ukraïns'ka derzhava,* (Toronto, 1965), p. 49.

11. Ibid., p. 51; "Proholoshennia Ukraïns'koï Natsional'noï Oborony," *Nastup* (Uzhhorod), October 23, 1938.

12. "Komunikat Pershoï Ukraïns'koï Tsentral'noï Narodnoï Rady, 14.IX. 1938," *Nova svoboda,* September 15, 1938.

13. "Predstaviteli Russkago Avtonomnago Bloka u Rensimena," *Prashevskaia Rus'* (Prešov), September 17, 1938. For the English texts of the memoranda, one on Subcarpathian Rus' and another on the Prešov Region, see *Karpatskaja Rus',* pp. 21-25. See also A. Iu. Gerovskii, "Chekhoslovatskii 'Liberalizm'," *Svobodnoe slovo Karpatskoi Rusi,* vol. 10, nos. 9-10 (Newark, 1968), pp. 3-5.

14. A photostatic copy of this declaration appears in *Karpatskaja Rus',* p. 17, and in *Svobodnoe slovo Karpatskoi Rusi,* vol. 1, nos. 7-8 (Newark, 1959), p. 8. The same day the Russian National Council submitted a resolution demanding self-government and union of all Rusyns, including those in eastern Slovakia, into one state. Resolution in *Russkii vîstnyk,* September 25, 1938.

15. Czechoslovakia ceded to Germany 28,000 square kilometers of territory with 3,615,833 inhabitants, of whom 2,806,638 were German and 719,127 were Czech.

Poland later gained 895 square kilometers of territory in the Těšín district of Silesia. Hubert Ripka, *Munich: Before and After* (London, 1939), pp. 508-509. See also Victor S. Mamatey and Radomír Luža (eds.), *A History of the Czechoslovak Republic* (Princeton, N.J., 1973), pp. 239-252.

16. On the developments in the Second Republic (October 1938-March 1939), see the article by Theodor Prochazka in Mamatey and Luža, *History,* pp. 255-270.

17. "Protokol Tsentral'noi Russkoi Narodnoi Rady i Pershoï Rus'koï Ukraïns'koï Tsentral'noï Narodnoï Rady," cited in Stercho, *Karpato-ukraïns'ka derzhava,* p. 55. The Russophiles were represented by senators Bachinskii and Földesi, deputies Brodii, Kossei, P'eshchak, Zhidovskii, and Fentsik, and Dr. Iosif Kaminskii, Dr. Vladimir Gomichkov, and Mykhail Demko. The Ukrainophiles included Deputy Revai, A. Voloshyn, and Stepan Klochurak. Observers included Minister Parkanyi and the Ukrainophiles Avhustyn Shtefan and Dr. Iulii Brashchaiko. Cf. *Karpatskaja Rus',* p. 17.

18. Minister of Agriculture Feierabend, who was present at the negotiations with Subcarpathian leaders, has asserted that the Rusyns were only interested in increasing their number in the government. Eventually, Brodii, Bachinskii, and Revai were appointed ministers, while Voloshyn and P'eshchak were made state secretaries, and Fentsik representative for discussing the Slovak-Rusyn border. Dr. Ladislav K. Feierabend, *Ve vládách Druhé republiky* (New York, 1961), pp. 48-50. Cf. Gerovskii's version in *Karpatskaja Rus',* pp. 17-20; and František Lukeš, *Podivný mír* (Prague, 1968), pp. 84-85.

19. Actually Parkanyi succeeded Hrabar on October 9 and held the post of governor for two days. Peter G. Stercho, *Diplomacy of Double Morality: Europe's Crossroads in Carpatho-Ukraine, 1919-1939* (New York, 1971), pp. 114-118; Kovach, "Stanovyshche," pp. 19-20. Cf. Volodymyr Birchak, *Karpats'ka Ukraïna: spomyny i perezhyvannia* (Prague, 1940), pp. 7-12.

20. "Cheshskaia shkol'naia politika na Podk. Rusi," *Russkii vîstnyk,* October 16, 1938.

21. "Manifest Tsentral'noi Russkoi Narodnoi Rady v Uzhgorodie, 14.X.1938," *Prashevskaia Rus',* October 29, 1938. Also "Likvidatsiia ches'kykh shkil tam, de nemaie dostatochnoho chysla ditei ches'koï narodnosti," *Nova svoboda,* October 21, 1938.

22. Speech of October 12 in Uzhhorod, cited in *Russkii vîstnyk,* October 16, 1938. The Rusyns of eastern Slovakia were always mentioned in Russophile declarations, and since 1935 Brodii's *Russkii vîstnyk* included in each issue a four-page supplement written in dialect and Latin script, the *Sotatskii russkii vîstnyk.* The Sotaks inhabited several villages northeast of Hummené that bordered Slovak ethnographic territory. Though their national allegiance was disputed, Subcarpathian leaders rejected all claims that they were Slovak. Voloshyn also considered the Sotaks to be Rusyn (that is, Ukrainian). Interview with Premier Voloshyn, January 5, reported by Prezidium Policejného riaditel'stva v Prešove (ŠSÚA, Prezídium KÚ, carton 297, folder 310/39).

23. Slovak police reports during the month of October were filled with reports of meetings, intercepted telegrams sent to Fentsik and Bachinskii, memoranda, and leaflets, all of which revealed the desire of Rusyns in eastern Slovakia to unite with Subcarpathian Rus'. Local teachers and Greek Catholic priests were particularly active. (ŠSÚA, Fond Prezídium KÚ, carton 237, folder 62212/38, and Fond Ministerstva vnutra, carton 3, folder 4/38). Another Rusyn deputy from the area, Petr Zhidovskii, was in contact with the Polish ambassador in Prague, who supported the union with Subcarpathian Rus'. Not only would a Russophile eastern Slovakia help to lessen the strength of the Ukrainian movement, but when the area was

returned to Hungary, Poland's border with her southern neighbor would be increased in length. Archiwum Akt Nowych, Ministerstvo Spraw Zagranicznych, Warsaw, PIII, fasc. 5436 and 5463, cited in Fano, "Zakarpatská Ukrajina," pp. 195-196. Cf. Kovach, "Stanovyshche," pp. 25-26.

24. B. I. Spivak, *Narysy istoriï revoliutsiinoï borot'by trudiashchykh Zakarpattia v 1930-1945 rokakh* (L'viv, 1963), pp. 258-259.

The Russian National Black-Shirt Guard (Russkaia Natsional'naia Gvardiia Chornosorochechnikov) was established in September 1938 and included primarily Russian scouts of the Dukhnovych Society. Fentsik also established a journal, *Molodaia Rus'* (edited by Ivan Fed'kovich, 1938), intended for the youth of his autonomist party, but after eleven numbers had appeared the editors resigned in protest against their leader's Polish and Hungarian intrigues.

25. Brodii was especially supported in his plebiscite drive by I. Kaminskii, V. Gomichkov, M. Demko, and Petr Gaevich—all of whom were, after the Hungarian occupation, appointed to the Budapest Parliament. Stercho, *Diplomacy,* pp. 118-120, 255-256. Cf. *Shliakhom Zhovtnia,* vol. 5 (Uzhhorod, 1967), doc. 5.

26. Feierabend, *Ve vládách,* pp. 50-51; Brandejs, "Spominy," pp. 828-829; Stercho, *Diplomacy,* pp. 122-123; Lukeš, *Podivný mír,* pp. 128-130.

27. *Shliakhom Zhovtnia,* vol. 5, doc. 7; Birchak, *Karpats'ka Ukraïna,* pp. 47-48; Stercho, *Diplomacy,* pp. 286-312 passim; M. Adam, "Zaharbannia Zakarpattia khortysts'koiu Uhorshchynoiu v 1938-1939 rr.," in *Ukraïns'ko-uhors'ki istorychni zv'iazky* (Kiev, 1964), pp. 85-87; Maciej Kózmiński, *Polska i Węgry przed drugą wojną światową (1938-1939)* (Warsaw, 1970), pp. 192-218 passim. On Hungarian negotiations with Poland to coordinate their attacks, see the diplomatic dispatches in Magda Ádám, ed., *Magyarország külpolitikája 1938-1939,* Diplomáciai iratok Magyarország külpolitikájához 1936-1945, vol. 3 (Budapest, 1970), docs. 7, 9, 12, 18, 40, 53, 55, 60, 65, 67, 84.

28. The irregular border that cut direct rail communication with Czecho-Slovakia deprived the province of 1,523 square kilometers territory and 172,233 people (based on the 1930 census), 36,735 of whom were of Rusyn nationality. For details on the border changes, see Aldo Dami, *La Ruthénie subcarpathique* (Geneva-Annemasse, 1944), pp. 296-306. On the diplomatic negotiations, see Jörg K. Hoensch, *Die ungarische Revisionismus und die Zerschlagung der Tschechoslowakei* (Tübingen, 1967), pp. 130-142 and 181-198.

29. See the articles by Mikhail Demko, "V novoi situatsii," A. Il'nytskii, "Kartiny o russko-mad'iarskom bratstvie," and Demko's radio speech in *Zemlediel'skii kalendar' na god 1939* (Uzhhorod, 1938), pp. 34-36, 40-43, 75-79.

30. *Karpatorusskii golos,* November 27 and December 15, 1938.

31. Stercho, *Diplomacy,* p. 125. The Sich also included Communist members, Spivak, *Narysy,* p. 274. Klempush was a recognized hero because of his successful leadership in establishing the independent Hutsul state in 1919. Roman, Rohach, and Rosokha were Prague university graduates known for their strong anti-Czechoslovak bias. See Chapters 4 and 11.

32. Presided over by Vikentii Shandor, the Subcarpathian Bureau included seven members. A Central State Economic Council was also set up in Prague, which included five representatives from Carpatho-Ukraine. Vikentii Shandor, "Karpats'ka Ukraïna—zfederovana derzhava," *Zapysky NTSh,* vol. 177 (New York, 1968), pp. 9-10. In January 1939, a weekly newspaper, *Karpato-ukrajinská svoboda* (edited by A. Išková) began publication in an attempt to inform the Czech public about Carpatho-Ukrainian and general Ukrainian affairs.

33. The autonomy bill was first introduced in Parliament by Deputy Iu. Revai on November 17, 1938. It was identical with the Slovak autonomous bill, except that

Revai proposed the terminology "Carpatho-Ukraine," "Carpatho-Ukrainian government," and "Ukrainian language." "Návrh poslance Juliana Révaye na vydání ústavního zákona o autonomii Karpatské Ukrajiny," *Tisky k těsnopiseckým zprávám,* Poslanecká sněmovna, IV. období, Tisk 1433. However, the text finally recommended (item 1434) used only the term Subcarpathian Rus' (*Podkarpatská Rus*). On November 30, Prague legalized the name Carpatho-Ukraine as an alternate, and Voloshyn's administration used this term whenever referring to the autonomous province. The delay in legalizing the new name was allegedly due to considerations for Polish feelings. Lukeš, *Podivný mír,* p. 189.

34. Michael Winch, *Republic for a Day: An Eye-Witness Account of the Carpatho-Ukraine Incident* (London, 1939), pp. 208-209; A. Dad, *Chotyry z tysiachi: v dvorichchia Bereznia Karpats'koï Ukraïny* (Prague, 1941); Stercho, *Diplomacy,* pp. 256-257.

35. Cited in Birchak, *Karpats'ka Ukraïna,* p. 34. See also Brandejs, "Spominy," p. 840 and Winch, *Republic,* pp. 138, 143-147.

36. For the views and activity of the Ukrainian immigrants, see Ivan Karpatskij, *Piznajte pravdu* (New York, 1939); Stercho, *Diplomacy,* pp. 257-259, 281-283; and A. Dragan, *Ukrainian National Association: Its Past and Present (1894-1964)* (Jersey City, N.J., and New York, 1964), pp. 109-113.

37. "Kabelogrammy pereslannyia Karpatorusskim Soiuzom, 6.XI.1938," reprinted in *Dnevnik,* December 15, 1938.

38. When the German consul arrived in Khust in February, 1939, Fedir Revai established a German-Ukrainian Cultural Society. For details on these developments, see Theodore Prochazka, "Some Aspects of Carpatho-Ukrainian History in Post-Munich Czechoslovakia," in *Czechoslovakia Past and Present* (The Hague, 1968), pp. 107-114; Stercho, *Diplomacy,* pp. 312-316; Roman Ilnytzkyj, *Deutschland und die Ukraine 1934-1945,* 2nd ed., vol. 1 (Munich, 1958), pp. 168-189. Marxist historiography has overemphasized these relations and incorrectly described Voloshyn and more especially the Revai brothers as German agents working toward the destruction of the Soviet Union. See Spivak, *Narysy,* pp. 275-279; Iurii Slyvka, *Pidstupy mizhnarodnoï reaktsiï na Zakarpatti v 1938-1939 rr.* (L'viv, 1966); Ivan Pop, "Zakarpats'ka Ukraïna v ievropeis'kii kryzi 1938-1939 rr.," *Duklia,* vol. 15, no. 1 (Prešov, 1967), pp. 62-66; Ladislav Suško, "Nemecká politika voči Slovensku a Zakarpatskej Ukrajine v období od septembrovej krízy 1938 do rozbitia Československa v marci 1939," *Československý časopis historický,* vol. 21, no. 2 (Prague, 1973), pp. 179-196; Štefan Fano, "Zakarpatská Ukrajina v politických kalkulaciach susedných štátov v období od Mníchova po marec 1939," *Slovanské štúdie,* vol. 11, *História* (Bratislava, 1971), pp. 61-79.

39. Birchak, *Karpats'ka Ukraïna,* p. 5.

40. I. S. Shlepetskii, "Rus' ne pogibnet," *Dnevnik* (Prague), November 30, 1938. While no Russian language newspaper was published in Subcarpathian Rus' during the Voloshyn regime, *Dnevnik*—"an organ of Carpatho-Russian youth," continued to appear in Prague and was one of the few sources of information on the Russophile movement.

41. Police telegram-report sent to the Ministry of Defense in Prague; Bratislava, November 15, 1938 (ŠSÚA, Prezídium KÚ, carton 298, folder 2695/39); *Dnevnik,* November 30, 1938.

42. Karaman was a native of eastern Slovakia and later became Chairman of the Prešov Ukrainian National Council (1944). On the others, see Appendix 2.

43. *Dnevnik,* December 15, 1938. Unquestionably, one such detention camp was set up in Dubina and there were rumors that two others existed. Operated by the Carpathian Sich—sometimes without the knowledge of Voloshyn's administration

—the camps served as a check-point for Galician Ukrainian refugees, but also interned those Russophile elements who refused to accept the Ukrainian aspect of the present regime. Winch, *Republic,* pp. 95-96; Report by V. Karaman, Prezídium policajného riaditel'stva v Prešove, December 31, 1938 (ŠSÚA, Fond Prezídium KÚ, carton 297, folder 310/1939). The pro-Hetmanate Ukrainian émigré faction also confirmed the prevalence of actions against Subcarpathian Russophiles undertaken by the Galicians. Cf. *Komunikat presovoho viddilu Het'mans'koï upravy.* Berlin, June 5, 1939.

44. "Protest Tsentral'nago Soiuza Podkarpatorusskikh Studentov," *Dnevnik,* November 30, 1938; Brandejs, "Spominy," p. 843. Khust's official newspaper frequently ran articles filled with warnings addressed to Russophile recalcitrants: " 'Russkii' tabor, chy Madiarons'kyi smitnyk?," "Rosiis'ki emigranty provokuiut," *Nova svoboda,* November 27, 1938; and in an interview, Premier Voloshyn prematurely declared: "Thank God, Russophilism is completely liquidated." *Karpato-ukrajinská svoboda* (Prague), January 20, 1939.

45. Hácha was President of the Highest Court of Appeals in Prague, which, in 1936, refused permission for the Prosvita Society to adopt the name Ukrainian. Consequently, Hácha was praised by the Russophiles. *Dnevnik,* November 30, 1938. See also Chapter 11.

46. Stercho, *Diplomacy,* pp. 127-130; Birchak, *Karpats'ka Ukraïna,* pp. 48-52.

47. *Nastup* (Khust), January 17, 1939.

48. One study—Štefan Pažur, "O vývoji narodnostných pomerov na východnom Slovensku v jesenných mesiacoch roku 1938," *Nové obzory,* vol. 10 (Prešov, 1968), pp. 13-25—has tried to prove that the desire of Rusyns in eastern Slovakia to unite with Subcarpathian Rus', openly expressed during the summer of 1938, was still evident after October. But there is overwhelming evidence in Slovak police reports (otherwise exceptionally sensitive to the slightest indication of Russophilism or Ukrainianism) that for Rusyns in eastern Slovakia "the Ukrainian orientation is alien and in the end they reject any kind of revision of borders in favor of Carpatho-Ukraine." Prezídium Policejného riaditel'stva v Prešove, January 11, 1939 (ŠSÚA, Prezídium KÚ, carton 297, folder 310/1938). See also carton 298, folder 62212/38. Also, on November 22, 1938, the Russian National Council (Russkii Narodnyi Soviet) of Prešov voted overwhelmingly against unity of Rusyns in eastern Slovakia with Subcarpathian Rus'. Andrii Kovach, "Natsional'na polityka Slovats'koï Respubliky po vidnoshenniu do rusyniv-ukraïntsiv (1939-1945 rr.)," in *Zhovten' i ukraïns'ka kul'tura* (Prešov, 1968), p. 136. Soon after, the Prešov Council decided to enter the elections to the Slovak parliament, for which two Rusyns were elected in January 1939. Kovach, "Stanovyshche," pp. 26-28.

49. Actually, Communist party activity was declared illegal as early as October 20, 1938, in a decree passed by the Czecho-Slovak government and enforced by the Uzhhorod police authorities. "Donesennia Uzhhorods'koï politseis'koï dyrektsiï . . . pro zaboronu diial'nosti komunistychnoï partiï, 2.XI.1938," *Shliakhom Zhovtnia: zbirnyk dokumentiv,* vol. 4 (Uzhhorod, 1964), doc. 216. According to Iuliian Revai (interview with author, October 1970), the Voloshyn regime promised to leave the Communist organization alone if it agreed not to organize strikes or other protests against the Khust regime. Both sides concurred and there was a remarkable lack of Communist public activity after November 1938. Cf. ibid., vol. 5 (Uzhhorod, 1967).

50. Stepan Rosokha, *Soim Karpats'koï Ukraïny* (Winnipeg, 1949), p. 29; Stercho, *Diplomacy,* pp. 147-150. The breakdown included ten previous members from Voloshyn's Christian National Party, ten Social Democrats, seven Agrarians, two representatives of Ukrainian Nationalist Youth, and one member of the German Party.

51. The Subcarpathian Rusyn group was headed by a local teacher, Mikhail Vasilenkov, but the list was not accepted on grounds that the group did not represent a political party and did not supply the necessary funds for printing a list of candidates—both provisions stipulated in the Czecho-Slovak law regulating electoral practices. N. Lemko, "Cherhovyi uspikh," *Karpato-ukrajinská svoboda*, February 3, 1939; Stercho, *Diplomacy*, pp. 150-151. According to Winch, pp. 156-158, Russophile leaders headed by Deputy Pavel Kossei and Dr. Agoston Stefan were put into jail until after the January 22 deadline for submitting the lists. Cf. *Shliakhom Zhovtnia*, vol. 4, doc. 217.

52. "Narode, nekhai bude volia Tvoia," *Nova svoboda*, February 5, 1939. Cited in Stercho, *Diplomacy*, pp. 151-152, note 36.

53. Of the 376 villages participating in the elections, only 19 returned clear majorities against the Ukrainian ticket. In Khust, the capital and largest settlement in the province, 8,330 votes were cast—6,208 for the Ukrainians, 2,122 opposed. List of election returns in Stercho, *Karpato-ukraïns'ka derzhava*, pp. 242-252.

54. Brandejs, "Spominy," p. 849. See also Birchak, *Karpats'ka Ukraïna*, pp. 58-61; Shandor, "Karpats'ka Ukraïna," p. 14; and Rosokha, *Soim*, pp. 32-51. As a direct observer of the February 12 elections, Winch, *Republic*, pp. 151-155, claims that the procedures did not provide a safe means to protest the Ukrainian list. There was obvious pressure placed on voters by the presence of armed Carpathian Sich propagandists in most villages. Even one pro-Ukrainian journalist admitted that the pre-election campaign had taken on a "fanatical character." Cited in Rosokha, *Soim*, p. 52. Moreover, voting was obligatory in Czecho-Slovakia, and boycotters could be fined.

55. The dominant attitude in Prague was that if "Khust could not provide order, it must be provided by Prague through the appointment of Prchala." Brandejs, "Spominy," p. 856. "The government in Khust is not in control of the situation." Prezídium Policéjneho riaditel'stva v Prešove, January 11, 1939. (ŚSÚA, Prezídium KÚ, carton 297, folder 310/1939). See also Feierabend, *Ve vládách*, p. 94.

56. Birchak, *Karpats'ka Ukraïna*, pp. 31-46. One observer reported the following conversation. *Sich* guard to peasant, "You are a Ukrainian." "No, I am a Rusyn." "What, you are a Ukrainian, aren't you?" "I am a Rusyn." "Come on; you—are—a—Ukrainian." "All right, I am a Ukrainian." Winch, *Republic*, p. 131. There were also reports of beatings perpetrated by *Sich* guards against Russophile teachers who refused to comply as the above peasant. *Dnevnik*, December 15, 1938.

57. Lukeš, *Podivný mír*, pp. 241-242. It has been asserted that Voloshyn himself sent Iu. Brashchaiko and S. Klochurak with a secret letter to Prague requesting the central government to relieve Revai. Brandejs, "Spominy," p. 861.

58. Among the new members appointed on March 9 to Voloshyn's Cabinet were the pro-Czecho-Slovak Dr. Iulii Brashchaiko, Dr. Mykola Dolynai, and Dr. Iurii Perevuznyk. The military clash occurred when the Sich refused Prchala's orders to disarm. Stercho, *Diplomacy*, pp. 131-137; Birchak, *Karpats'ka Ukraïna*, pp. 65-74; Feierabend, *Ve vládách*, p. 146.

59. Protocols of five sessions are reprinted in Rosokha, *Soim*, pp. 60-88. See also Stercho, *Diplomacy*, pp. 153-159.

60. According to Budapest radio, the Hungarian Army recorded 74 dead and 140 wounded. In battle, Carpathian Sich losses were about the same, but it has been estimated that upwards of 4,000 were killed after hostilities ceased. Avhustyn Shtefan, *Ukraïns'ke viis'ko v Zakarpatti* (Toronto and New York, 1969), p. 27; *Karpats'ka Ukraïna v borot'bi* (Vienna, 1939), Stercho, *Diplomacy*, pp. 374-386. On Hungary's diplomatic preparations for the invasion which began on March 3, see the dispatches in *Magyarország külpolitikája*, docs. 378-438.

61. Even large segments of the intelligentsia were far from being conscious Ukrainians. After twenty years of educational work in Subcarpathian Rus', the Galician-Ukrainian V. Birchak wrote that "after 1919 the intelligentsia began to call itself Rusyn (*rus'ka* and *rusyns'ka*), Russian, and Carpatho-Rosy, but [in 1939] it was still not nationally conscious." Birchak, *Karpats'ka Ukraïna,* p. 5.

62. Andrew Bajcsy-Zsilinszky, "Subcarpathia's re-incorporation creates a common Polish-Hungarian Frontier," *Danubian Review,* vol. 6, no. 11 (Budapest, 1939), pp. 14-16.

63. *Karpatorusskii golos,* March 28, 1939.

64. Spivak, *Narysy,* p. 285.

65. Letter of Fentsik to Teleki, July 1939 in *Shliakhom Zhovtnia,* vol. 5, doc. 45.

66. Among the publications of the Pécs Minority Institute dealing with Subcarpathian autonomy were: no. 4, László Balogh-Beéry, *A ruthén autonómia* (Pécs, 1937); no. 12, István Fenczik, *A Kárpátaljai autonómia és a kisebbségi kérdés* (Kecskemét, 1941); no. 13, Gábor Kemény, *Ez a föld Magyarország!* (Kecskemét, 1941).

67. Cited in Loránt Tilkovszky, *Revizió és nemzetiségpolitika Magyarországon 1938-1941* (Budapest, 1967), p. 218.

68. Ibid., p. 219.

69. These "wild" Hungarians also proposed the resettlement of all Rusyns somewhere in the Ukraine, and their project received the support of Henrik Werth, then Chief of the General Staff. Ibid., pp. 236-237, and *Shliakhom Zhovtnia,* vol. 5, docs, 157, 165.

70. *A Kárpátaljai Vajdaságról és annak önkormányzatáról szóló törvényjavaslat bírálata* (Budapest, 1940), p. 11.

71. *Shliakhom Zhovtnia,* vol. 5, doc. 66. "During the War, the autonomy question was set aside. We were told that in wartime there must not be any mention of autonomy." From the transcript of the 1945 trial of Brodii and others, cited in Spivak, *Narysy,* p. 286. During the late summer, 1944, Brodii even tried to make contact with the leaders of the Slovak Uprising.

72. The first two Commissioners were natives of Subcarpathian Rus', although as members of the Hungarian government they resided most of their lives in Budapest. Perényi (b. 1870) was a specialist in international law and advisor on border revisionism, Kozma (1884-1941) was former Minister of Interior and organizer of the Hungarian terrorist raids into Subcarpathian Rus' in 1938-39. Tomcsányi (b. 1880) was government advisor; Vincze a career military officer. The Commissioners were aided in the administration of the Territory by Subcarpathian politicans like Julius Földesi and Endre Korláth—both former Senators in the Czechoslovak Parliament, AZS Party activists like Adal'bert Rishko and Mykhail Demko, and Greek Catholic priests Julius Marina (head of the Department of Religion and National Culture), Demianovych, and Tivadar Ortutay. Spivak, *Narysy,* pp. 286-287.

73. In March 1939, Hungarian troops crossed into eastern Slovakia, and by a protocol of April 4, Slovakia ceded some forty villages with about forty thousand inhabitants. There were not given to the Subcarpathian Territory, but like lands gained at the first Vienna Award became an integral part of Hungary.

74. Actually, Fentsik was appointed as early as November 25, 1938, and after addressing the Hungarian Parliament in the name of "the Carpatho-Russian people" the self-styled Fascist Führer returned to Uzhhorod to the greetings of his Russian Scouts and "Russian Fascist Black Shirts." *Karpatorusskii golos,* November 25 and December 2, 1938.

75. *Nedîlia,* May 31, 1942; Tilkovszky, *Revizió,* p. 183.

76. Spivak, *Narysy,* pp. 287, 291.

77. Two former members of Voloshyn's last Cabinet (March 9-14, 1939) who re-

mained at home, Mykola Dolynai and Iulii Brashchaiko, came to Budapest and, on July 9,1939, delivered a memorandum to the Ministry of Culture asking the government to follow a Ukrainian cultural policy in the Territory. Their requests went unheeded. Tilkovszky, *Revizió*, p. 249, n. 80; *Magyarország külpolitikája,* doc. 488.

78. Fentsik's *Karpatorusskii golos,* edited by Vasilii Labanich, was published until 1942, while Brodii's *Russkoe slovo,* edited by Ivan Shpak, appeared twice a week until 1944.

79. Interview (May 1975) with Joseph Szövérffy (now professor at the State University of New York at Albany), who was a Magyar student living in Budapest during 1938-1939.

80. See the Bibliography (refs. 0752, 0753, 0775, 0795, 0803, 0808, 1252, 1254).

81. Under Commissioner Tomcsányi (1941-1944), each Subcarpathian administrative body received a Hungarian "advisor," and his decisions, not those of the local Rusyn official, were most often implemented. Interview of author with Julius Marina, April 1972.

82. The Hungarian regime made efforts to convince itself as well as the western world of its economic achievements in the newly occupied province. *Za narod Podkarpatia: chto stalosia dosy na Podkarpatiu? Odnorochna robota madiarskoho pravytelstva* (Uzhhorod, 1940); Andrew Fall, "The Economic reconstruction of Subcarpathia," *Danubian Review,* vol. 7, no. 5 (Budapest, 1939), pp. 20-24; Aldo Dami, "Ce que j'ai vu en Subcarpathie," and Jean Stark, "La Reconstruction de la Subcarpathie," *Nouvelle Revue de Hongrie* (Budapest, 1940), pp. 345-358.

83. Loránt Tilkovszky, "A csehszlovák földreform magyar revíziója az első bécsi döntéssel átcsatolt területen (1938-1945)," *Agrártörténeti szemle,* nos. 1-2 (Budapest, 1964), pp. 113-172. Cf. *Shliakhom Zhovtnia,* vol. 5, docs. 35, 41, 47.

84. For various estimates on those who fled to the Soviet Union, see Ivan Vanat, "Zakarpats'ki ukraïntsi v chekhoslovats'komu viis'ku v SRSR," in *Shliakh do voli, Naukovyi zbirnyk MUKS,* vol. 2 (Svidník, Bratislava, and Prešov, 1966), p. 186, n. 13. The first big show trial came in August 1942, when, of the 137 accused, 6 were executed and 5 received life imprisonment. The rest received prison sentences. *Nedîlia,* September 27, 1942. Later, of the 123 prisoners accused of Ukrainian activity, 114 were amnestied. See the interview with Commissioner Tomcsányi in *Nedîlia,* January 17, 1943.

85. According to the official report of the Special Commission for damages during the war years ("occupation"), dated Uzhhorod, December 1945, a total of 183,395 persons (112,500 Jews and 70,895 Rusyns) were deported between 1941 and 1944 to concentration camps, where 114,982 perished. *Shliakhom Zhovtnia,* vol. 6 (Uzhhorod, 1965), doc. 217. On the Jews, see Randolph L. Braham, "The Destruction of the Jews of Carpatho-Ruthenia," in *Hungarian Jewish Studies* (New York, 1966), pp. 223-235. Cf. *Shliakhom Zhovtnia,* vol. 5, docs. 62, 73, 102, 117, 179, 182, 183, 187, 218-220, 224-234, 237-244.

86. The author has unfortunately not had the opportunity to view *Russkoe slovo* or *Karpatorusskii golos* from this period, but polemics with these newspapers occurred frequently. For instance, see Ivan Rusnachysko, "Daskol'ko skromnykh voprosov 'nastoiashchym russkim'," *Lyteraturna nedîlia,* vol. 1, no. 3 (Uzhhorod, 1941), pp. 23-24.

87. Undated letter by the Subcarpathian author Ivan Chendei, cited in I. Vyshnevs'kyi, *Tradytsiï ta suchasnist'* (L'viv, 1963), p. 116.

13. The Soviet Period

1. Unlike Great Britain and France, the United States and Soviet Union had never recognized the Munich Pact, and by 1942 they had accepted the concept of a future Czechoslovakia with pre-Munich borders. That same year British and French

leaders also agreed that the Munich Pact was invalid. František Němec and Vladimir Moudry, *The Soviet Seizure of Subcarpathian Ruthenia* (Toronto, 1955), pp. 62-66.
2. A group headed by the writer V. Grendzha-Dons'kyi called, in 1939, for unification with the Soviet Union. "Illegal'nyi Komitet, pratsiuiuchyi za prykliuchenniam Karpats'koï Ukraïny do Soiuzu RSR v Bratislavi: Memorandum" (ŠSÚA, Prezídium KÚ, carton 298, folder 568/39); Vasyl' Grendzha-Dons'kyi, "Moï spohady" (unpublished memoirs; Bratislava, 1966), pp. 144-145. On the other hand, A. Voloshyn, Iu. Revai and A. Shtefan signed an agreement with the Organization of Ukrainian Nationalists in July 1939 that recognized Voloshyn as legal president of Carpatho-Ukraine, which in turn was to be considered an integral part of a future united Ukrainian state. Text reprinted in Ostap Chorniak, "V 30-littia derzhavnotvorchoho chynu ukraïns'koho Zakarpattia" (unpublished typescript), p. 8.
On November 30, 1939, Voloshyn supposedly addressed to Hitler and Tiso a memorandum which called for the union of Subcarpathia with Slovakia. On the basis of this act, Voloshyn, Perevuznyk, Dolynai, and Klochurak were apprehended and in Moscow (1945) sentenced to life imprisonment. The latter three were subsequently amnestied in 1962. Also, a so-called "plan" was outlined in a letter to Hitler by Voloshyn in 1941 requesting the establishment of a Ukrainian monarchy on the territory of the Soviet Ukraine. Although denied by former Minister Iu. Revai as a fabrication (interview with author), Soviet historians have accepted the "plan" as having been proposed. For the text, see Borys I. Spivak, *Narysy istoriï revoliutsiinoï borot'by trudiashchykh Zakarpattia v 1930-1945 rokakh* (L'viv, 1963), pp. 297-299. Voloshyn was reputed to have had contact during the War with Czecho-Slovakia's last Prime Minister, Rudolf Beran, but, with the exception of Iu. Revai, Shtefan, and Rosokha, who escaped to the West, all other leaders were picked up by Soviet agents in 1945 and played no subsequent role in Subcarpathian affairs. Nicola Sinevirsky, *Smersh* (New York, 1950), pp. 149-155.
3. "The Decree of the President concerning the Re-establishment of the Legal Order (August 3, 1944) stipulated that legal norms promulgated during the time of oppression were *not* part of the Czechoslovak legal system, and stated expressly that the time of oppression began on September 30, 1938." Nemec and Moudry, *Soviet Seizure,* p. 61, n. 6.
4. Ivan Petruščak, *Karpatští Ukrajinci a Slované* (London, 1944), p. 28.
5. *The Carpathian*, vol. 3, nos. 7-9 (Pittsburgh, 1943), pp. 7-10; Ivan Vanat, "K niektorým otázkam zahraničneho odboja zakarpatských Ukrajincov počas druhej svetovej vojny," in *Zhovten' i ukraïns'ka kul'tura* (Prešov, 1968), pp. 361-362; Walter C. Warzeski, *Byzantine Rite Rusins in Carpatho-Ruthenia and America* (Pittsburgh, 1971), pp. 251-257.
6. Cited in *The Carpathian,* p. 10.
7. Letter of Beneš to the American Carpathian-Russian Council, reprinted in ibid., p. 12.
8. Not all American Rusyns favored a return of Czechoslovak rule. Magyarone Greek Catholic priests like V. Gorzo and J. Thegza still favored the idea of a plebiscite, and on the occasion of its fiftieth anniversary in 1942, the influential Greek Catholic Union was proud to publish greetings from pro-Hungarian leaders at home (Bishop Stoika, Msgr. A. Il'nyts'kyi, E. Ortutay, J. Illés-Illjásevics, J. Földesi, M. Demko). Michael Roman, ed., *Zoloto-Jubilejnyj kalendar' Greko Kaft. Sojedinenija v S.Š.A.* (Munhall, Pa., 1941), pp. 305-314. Similarly, the Orthodox Russophile émigré, Dr. A. Gerovskii, claimed to be the only legal representative of Subcarpathia's first (October 1938) autonomous government — authority actually delegated to him in Budapest by Fentsik in 1939. Subsequently, Gerovskii bitterly attacked Beneš and warned of "the threat of a new Czech yoke." *Svoboda-Liberty* (New York), May 8, 1944.
9. Statement of Beneš to the State Council, London, February 3, 1944, quoted

in *Karpatoruskije novosti,* March 15, 1944.

10. Ibid.

11. Tsibere delivered a memorandum to the State Council on July 20, 1943, which requested "that still during the War the government make a declaration on autonomy for Subcarpathian Rus' . . . which will be the basis for the return of Subcarpathia to the Czechoslovak Republic." Cited in Vanat, "K niektorým otázkam," p. 365.

12. Statement of Jan Šverma at a meeting of the Slovak National Council, October 3, 1944, from the unpublished diary of M. Faltán, cited in Edo Friš, *Myšlienka a čin: úvahy o Československu, 1938-48* (Bratislava, 1968), p. 104. The London government agreed to this principle on October 10, 1944. Vanat, "K niektorým otázkam," pp. 367-368.

13. Ibid., p. 364; Ivan Vanat, "Zakarpats'ki ukraïntsi v chekhoslovats'komu viis'ku v SSSR," in *Shliakh do voli; Naukovyi zbirnyk MUKS,* vol. 2 (Bratislava-Prešov-Svidník, 1966), pp. 186-188; Vasyl Markus, *L'incorporation de l'Ukraine subcarpathique à l'Ukraine soviétique, 1944-1945* (Louvain, 1956), p. 25; Josef Reiner, *V tankové brigádě: politická práce v naší tankové jednotě v SSSR* (Prague, 1964), p. 25.

14. As of October 30, 1943, the Corps included 3,348 soldiers: 2,210 Rusyns, 563 Czechs, 543 Slovaks, and 231 other nationalities. Vanat, "Zakarpats'ki," p. 188. The delay in releasing the imprisoned Rusyns was due to the fact that it was difficult to know "how our boys would fight after such a severe experience as the work camps. It was not easy to explain why youngsters, who came to see the Soviet Union with an open heart . . . were judged as criminals." Illia Voloshchuk, "Politychni vidnosyny u chekhoslovats'komu viis'ku v SRSR," in *Shliakh do voli,* p. 214.

15. Ibid., p. 215.

16. "Odvichna borot'ba pidkarpatorus'koho narodu za svobodu," *Nashe viis'ko v SRSR,* March 25, 1943, cited in Vanat, "Zakarpats'ki," p. 192. The military newspapers appeared daily in Czech and Ukrainian. Notwithstanding the point of view of the Subcarpathian soldier-reader, literary Ukrainian was employed since the pro-Communist editors, Iurko Borolych, Marta Terpai, and Illia Voloshchuk, followed the party line on the question of national affiliation. Iu. Kundrat, "Chekhoslovats'ka viis'kova presa v SRSR," *Duklia,* vol. 23, no. 3 (Prešov, 1975), pp. 55-63; Illia Voloshchuk, "Zakarpats'ki ukraïntsi u chekhoslovats'komu viis'ku v SRSR," ibid., pp. 64-67.

17. On the last minute change of strategy, see Václav Kovařík, *Ženisté v boji* (Prague, 1962), p. 18. On the Dukla Pass operations see Ludvík Svoboda, *Z Buzuluku do Prahy* (Prague, 1961); on the operations in Subcarpathian Rus', Andrei A. Grechko, *Cherez Karpaty,* 2nd ed. (Moscow, 1972).

18. Markus, *L'incorporation,* p. 26. *Shliakhom Zhovtnia: zbirnyk dokumentiv,* vol. 6 (Uzhhorod, 1965), docs. 20-21. Despite intense Ukrainian propaganda in 1938-39 and the reputed anti-Czechoslovak attitude of the population, with one or two exceptions the blue and yellow flag flown by the Voloshyn government was not seen anywhere.

19. Speech of Beneš in Chicago, May 22, 1943, cited in *Karpatorusskije novosti,* October 1, 1943.

20. Text cited in *Svoboda-Liberty,* May 8, 1944. On Beneš in Moscow, see Němec and Moudry, *Soviet Seizure,* pp. 76-82; 173-177; Markus, *L'incorporation,* pp. 27-30.

21. Němec subsequently stated that his freedom of action was limited and as early as December 29, 1944, recommended to President Beneš that the Czechoslovak government accept the loss of Subcarpathian Rus'. Němec and Moudry, *Soviet*

Seizure, p. 83 ff., especially doc. 61. Markus, who was a participant in the Mukachevo Council, feels that "Němec and his collaborators did not show much initiative." Markus, *L'incorporation*, p. 36.

22. Ibid., pp. 33-34; Němec and Moudry, *Soviet Seizure*, pp. 102-109; Zdeněk Fierlinger, *Ve službách ČSR: paměti z druhého zahraničního odboje*, vol. 2 (Prague, 1948), pp. 386-410; I. F. Evseev, *Narodnye Komitety Zakarpatskoi Ukrainy—organy gosudarstvennoi vlasti (1944-1945)* (Moscow, 1954), Czech translation by I. F. Jevsejev, *Z dějin Zakarpatské Ukrajiny* (Prague, 1956), pp. 64-71; Josef Korbel, *The Communist Subversion of Czechoslovakia, 1938-1948* (Princeton, N.J., 1959), pp. 99-109.

23. "Rezoliutsiia 1-ï konferentsiï KPZU pro vozz'iednannia Zakarpats'koï U-kraïny z Radians'koho Ukraïnoiu," in *Shliakhom Zhovtnia*, vol. 6, doc. 41. The term "re-united" (*vozz'iednaty*) was based on the fact that the province was a part of Kievan Rus' for a short time during the thirteenth century and then "re-occupied" once again by Hungary. Moreover, the term Transcarpathian Ukraine (*Zakarpats'ka Ukraïna*) was the only one used in official and other publications after the liberation.

24. As late as October 29, 1944, Turianytsia (political advisor in the Czechoslovak Delegation) declared in a public address in Khust that liberated Subcarpathian Rus' would remain a part of Czechoslovakia, Němec and Moudry, *Soviet Seizure*, p. 92. But in his November 19 speech to the Communist Party conference he declared that "the age-long desire" of our people is to unite with the Soviet Ukraine. *Shliakhom Zhovtnia*, vol. 6, doc. 40.

25. Facsimile in Markus, *L'incorporation*, p. 115.

26. Ibid.; *Shliakhom Zhovtnia*, vol. 6, doc. 51; Němec and Moudry, *Soviet Seizure*, pp. 264-268.

27. The manifesto was signed by the 663 delegates present, and by January 1, 1945, 250,000 signatures were gathered throughout the province. Jevsejev, *Z dějin*, pp. 74-78. A member of the Council, Markus, *L'incorporation*, p. 46, has stated that the delegates were under definite pressure to accept the Manifesto and any divergent proposals (such as a suggestion for a general plebiscite) were summarily rejected. On the other hand, the Czechoslovak delegate informed President Beneš that the Mukachevo Council represented "a popular and spontaneous movement" and that the demands of the Manifesto should be accepted (Němec and Moudry, *Soviet Seizure*, doc. 61).

28. Markus, *L'incorporation*, pp. 45-52; Němec and Moudry, *Soviet Seizure*, Doc. 263; *Shliakhom Zhovtnia*, vol. 6, docs. 58 and 59; Fierlinger, *Ve službách*, pp. 425-600 passim.

29. *Shliakhom Zhovtnia*, vol. 6, docs. 25 and 94.

30. Ibid., docs. 122, 129, 188; Jevsejev, *Z dějin*, pp. 84-104; Markus, *L'incorporation*, pp. 53-58. The land was subsequently collectivized in 1948-1949.

31. *Shliakhom Zhovtnia*, Vol. 6, doc. 82, dated 18.XII.1944. Actually, the Czechoslovak delegation had, over the signature of Němec, already issued a decree, "Instructions on detaining persons, Khust, 7.XI.1944," authorizing district and local committees to arrest "those who took part in the governments and in the conduct of the public administration after September 29, 1938." This included, obviously, officials of Voloshyn's administration and Carpathian Sich guards as well as Hungarian collaborators. Němec and Moudry, *Soviet Seizure*, doc. 5. In June, 1946, the "people's trial against former collaborators" was held in Uzhhorod. The prosecutor was the former Subcarpathian student leader in Prague, Ivan Andrashko, and among the sentenced were A. Brodii and M. Demko (death), and I. Shpak, Iu. Bentse, A. Hrabar-Kricsfalusy, E. Ortutay, Ö. Zsegora, and A. Rishko

(prison terms ranging from six to fifteen years). "Protses zakarpats'kykh kvislingiv," *Radians'ka Ukraïna,* June 8, 1946.

32. Ladislav K. Feierabend, *Soumrak československé demokracie* (Washington, D.C., 1967), pp. 106-115; Němec and Moudry, *Soviet Seizure,* pp. 173-176.

33. L'ubomir Lipták, *Slovensko v 20. storočí* (Bratislava, 1968), pp. 227-255; Ivan Bajcura, *Ukrajinská otázka v ČSSR* (Košice, 1967), pp. 72-76.

34. Fierlinger, *Ve službách,* p. 452.

35. Letter of Stalin to Beneš, dated January 23, 1945, reprinted in ibid., p. 558.

36. Markus, *L'incorporation,* pp. 63-87. The treaty is reprinted in ibid., pp. 121-124; *Shliakhom Zhovtnia,* vol. 6, docs. 162-163.

37. Declarations of citizenship had to be submitted before January 1, 1946. About ten thousand Rusyns from eastern Slovakia responded and were settled in Volhynia, an area in northwestern Ukraine where a Czech minority had lived since the eighteenth century and now decided to return to Bohemia. Rusyn soldiers who served in the Czechoslovak Corps under General Svoboda were allowed, with their families, to remain in postwar Czechoslovakia. About half of them did so.

38. A few groups did protest against this act. Rusyn immigrants in the United States, even the adamant Russophiles who continued to praise the Red Army for its war efforts, protested the "illegal and forcible annexation of Podkarpatska Rus' to the Soviet Union." These groups were particularly opposed to the "Ukrainianization" of their homeland. See the 1945 *Protest* and *Memorandum in behalf of Podkarpatskaja Rus* sent to the U. S. State Department by the Pittsburgh Greek Catholic Diocese; and "Soveršilosja," in *Karpatorusskij Narodnyi Kalendar na hod 1946* (New York, 1945), pp. 36-41.

During the 1950s a Council of Free Podkarpatsky Rusins was set up in New York by Ladislav Fedinec (former president of the Podkarpatskii Bank), who published the *Rusin Bulletin.* Opposed to the Soviet "occupation" of the homeland, this group worked closely with the Council of Free Czechoslovakia. Some Czech authors also refuse to recognize the Soviet acquisition as being legal, despite the fact that the Czechoslovak Parliament unanimously ratified the treaty of cession. Korbel, *Communist Subversion,* pp. 107-108; Josef Josten, *Oh My Country* (London, 1949), pp. 40-43, 56-57.

It is interesting to note that during the Prague Spring of 1968 some voices were raised inquiring when the Soviet Union would return to Czechoslovakia its "lost" eastern province. Finally, the Soviet dissident Andrei A. Amal'rik has predicted that one day his country will be forced to return the region to Hungary. *Prosushchestvuet li Sovetskii Soiuz do 1984 goda?* (Amsterdam, 1969), p. 60. It should be stressed that none of these claims has ever been taken seriously by responsible Western powers.

39. For the most part the census was conducted by students in the presence of political officers from the Red Army. A typical encounter went something like this: Student to peasant — "What is your nationality?" Response : "I am a Rusyn [Ia rus'kyi]." Officer to peasant: "You mean you are from Russia [Rossiia]?" Response: "No, I'm from here." Officer to student: "Write Ukrainian!" Interview (November, 1971) with former Subcarpathian student and census taker, Dr. John Fizer, Rutgers University.

40. From M. A. Zinoviev, *Soviet Methods of Teaching,* cited in Cyril E. Black, ed., *Rewriting Russian History,* 2nd rev. ed. (New York, 1962), front papers. On the Soviet method of writing history see the essays in ibid.; Konstantin F. Shteppa, *Russian Historians and the Soviet State* (New Brunswick, N.J., 1962); and the poignant

comments of Bernard Lewis, *History—Remembered, Recovered, Invented* (Princeton, N.J., 1975), pp. 53 and 69.

41. *Pravda*, July 1, 1945, reprinted in Ukrainian translation in *Shliakhom Zhovtnia*, vol. 6, doc. 173.

42. On Badan's writings see Chapter 11 and the Bibliography (nos. 1123-1125). On the dearth of Soviet Ukrainian interest in Subcarpathian Rus' during these years, see the almost total lack of references in Myron Korduba, *La littérature historique soviétique-ukrainienne* (1938), Harvard Series in Ukrainian Studies, vol. 10, 2nd ed. (Munich, 1972).

43. Zdeněk Needli, "Istoriia Zakarpatskoi Rusi do XIV stoletiia," *Izvestiia Akademii nauk SSSR. Seriia istorii i filosofii,* vol. 2, no. 4 (Moscow, 1945), pp. 201-220.

44. I. N. Mel'nikova, "Kak byla vkliuchena Zakarpatskaia Ukraina v sostav Chekhoslovakii v 1919 g.," *Uchenye zapiski Instituta slavianovedeniia,* vol. 3 (Moscow, 1951), pp. 104-135; "Ustanovlenie diktatury cheshskoi imperialisticheskoi burzhuazii v Zakarpatskoi Ukraine v 1919-1920 gg.," ibid., vol. 4, pp. 84-114.

45. I.G. Kolomiets, *Ocherki po istorii Zakarpat'ia,* pts. 1 (Tomsk, 1953) and 2 (Tomsk, 1959); *Sotsial'no-èkonomicheskie otnosheniia i obshchestvennoe dvizhenie v Zakarpat'e vo vtoroi polovine XIX stoletiia,* 2 vols. (Tomsk, 1961-62).

46. Fedir Naumenko, "Ivan Havrylovych Kolomiiets'—istoryk ukraïns'koho Zakarpattia," in *Zhovten' i ukraïns'ka kul'tura* (Prešov, 1968), p. 102. On the general emphasis on relations of Transcarpathia with other Ukrainian lands in all periods, see F. P. Shevchenko, "Mistse Zakarpattia v zahal'noukraïns'komu istorychnomu protsesi," in *Velykyi Zhovten' i rozkvit vozz'iednanoho Zakarpattia* (Uzhhorod, 1970), pp. 43-54.

47. A cliché which appears in the front papers of most Soviet publications. For a discussion of Marxist historiography on the region, see Kolomiets, *Sotsial'no,* vol. 2, pp. 566-582; V. V. Pal'ok, "Deiaki pytannia istoriï Zakarpattia z naidavnishykh chasiv do kintsia XVIII st. v ukraïns'kii radians'kii istoriohrafiï," in *Kul'tura i pobut naselennia ukraïns'kykh Karpat* (Uzhhorod, 1973), pp. 105-112; N.P. Mishchenko, "Ukraïns'ka radians'ka istoriohrafiia pro rozvytok promyslovosti i robitnychoho klasu Zakarpattia za roky radians'koï vlady," in *Velykyi Zhovten' i rozkvit vozz'iednanoho Zakarpattia* (Uzhhorod, 1970), pp. 339-347.

48. These have grown progressively in size, from the encyclopedic entry "Zakarpats'ka Ukraïna," in *Ukraïns'ka radians'ka entsyklopediia,* vol. 5 (Kiev, 1961), pp. 136-138; to the extensive historical introduction in *Istoriia mist i sil Ukraïns'koï RSR: Zakarpats'ka oblast'* (Kiev, 1969), pp. 9-69; to the first individual monograph: *Shliakhom do shchastia: narysy istoriï Zakarpattia* (Uzhhorod, 1973).

49. S.I. Peniak, "Do pytannia pro chas zaselennia skhidnymy slov'ianamy Verkhn'oho Potyssia," in *Velykyi Zhovten',* pp. 73-85. For the results of archaeological research, see the works of V. Bidzilia, I.M. Hranchak, F. Potushniak, and Iu. Smishko in the Bibliography (refs. 1176a, 1501, 1953a, 2077a). The Soviets have published numerous collections of folktales (including many items that supposedly reveal the grassroots popularity of Lenin). See for instance the entries in Ia. P. Prylypko, *Ukraïns'ke radians'ke karpatoznavstvo: bibliohrafiia* (Kiev, 1972). On the use of folkloric material as historical data, see V. Mel'nyk, *Istoriia Zakarpattia v usnykh narodnykh perekazakh ta istorychnykh pisniakh* (L'viv, 1970).

50. For the major works dealing with these topics, see the studies by M. Lelekach, O. Myshanych, P.K. Smiian, B. Spivak, M. Troian, V. Usenko, and B.

Spivak in the Bibliography (refs. 1705, 1709, 1799, 2077, 2094, 2095, 2180-2183, 2194).

51. For examples of this literature, see the two volumes of documents and the anti-Greek Catholic polemic by S. Borshavs'kyi listed in the Bibliography (refs. 0495, 0521, 1205).

52. See the works of I.G. Kolomiets, V. Il'ko, I. Mel'nikova, and P.K. Smiian in the Bibliography (refs. 1520a, 1608, 1770, 1771, 2076).

53. See the work of Iu. Slyvka and P. Khalus in the Bibliography, (refs. 1585, 1586, 2073).

54. The major works include nine volumes of documents and several general histories which concentrate primarily on the party (see the Bibliography, refs. 0512, 0513, 0518, 0519, 1179, 1583, 1584, 1587-1589, 1769, 1811, 1991, 2074, 2092, 2094).

55. V. L. Mykytas', *Ukraïns'kyi pys'mennyk-polemist Mykhailo Andrella* (Uzhhorod, 1960). Andrella has also been the focus of attention in the general literary histories of Oleksa V. Myshanych, *Literatura Zakarpattia XVII-XVIII stolit'* (Kiev, 1964), pp. 46-48; and Vasyl' L. Mykytas', *Davnia literatura Zakarpattia* (L'viv, 1968), pp. 149-219.

56. The key work in this reevaluation is the well-documented monograph by Mykytas', *Haluzka mohutn'oho dereva: literaturnyi narys* (Uzhhorod, 1971). See also his biography *O. V. Dukhnovych* (Uzhhorod, 1959); the extensive list of recent Marxist scholarship, "Bibliohrafiia literatury pro zhyttia i tvorchist' O. Dukhnovycha 1945-1965," in *Oleksandr Dukhnovych: materialy naukovoï konferentsiï* (Presov, 1965), pp. 351-361; and I. Iu. Kashula, "O.V. Dukhnovych i vyvchennia ioho spadshchyny," in *Velykyi Zhovten' i rozkvit vozz'iednanoho Zakarpattia* (Uzhhorod, 1970), pp. 523-529.

57. The Uzhhorod University professor Iurii Baleha still feels it necessary to characterize Subcarpathian writers in the twentieth century as being either black or white, that is, "reactionary" (Karabelesh, Voloshyn) or "progressive" (usually Ukrainophiles like Borshosh-Kum'iats'kyi, Markush, Dem'ian, Grendzha-Dons'kyi). See his studies in the Bibliography (refs. 1134-1136).

58. A laudatory travel account describing the enormous changes in the region was translated into a "western" language as early as 1948: W. Safanow, *In der Transkarpaten-Ukraine* (Berlin, 1948). This has been followed by numerous publications intended for local consumption: *Zdobutky braterstva* (Uzhhorod, 1967); *I brat bratovi ruku podav* (Uzhhorod, 1970); *Vesna vidrodzhenoho kraiu* (Uzhhorod, 1974); H. I. Shman'ko, *Mitsna iak krytsia* (Uzhhorod, 1975); and many tourist guides and "picture books" intended for visiting Soviet citizens and foreigners: *Sovetskoe Zakarpat'e: spravochnik* (Uzhhorod, 1957); *Zakarpattia - Zakarpat'e - Transcarpathia - Transcarpathie - Transkarpathien* (Uzhhorod, 1962); *Verkhovyno, maty moia* (Uzhhorod, 1967); and *Zakarpattia* (Kiev, 1974). The latest of these is a feature article by Alexei Flerovsky, "Verkhovina - My Love!," and interview, "Transcarpathia, A Transformed Land," in *Soviet Life,* no. 7 (Moscow and Washington, D.C., 1975), pp. 2-15.

59. From a Communist party decree published in *Zakarpats'ka pravda,* November 21, 1944—cited in A. D. Bondar, "Iz istorii shkoly v Zakarpatskoi Ukraine do vossoedineniia ee s Sovetskoi Ukrainoi," *Sovetskaia pedagogika,* vol. 18, no. 3 (Moscow, 1954), p. 107.

60. Russian is also one of the primary subjects of study at the philological faculty of the Uzhhorod University. H. S. Tokar, "Rozrobka pytan' rosiis'koho movoznavstva na Zakarpatti za roky radians'koï vlady," in *Velykyi Zhovten',* pp. 558-576. Nor has the Magyar language been neglected. The equivalent to *Zakarpat'ska pravda* is *Kárpáti Igaz Szó,* and besides this there are three county news-

papers and a youth newspaper in Magyar, as well as radio and television programs and a department of language and literature at Uzhhorod University. P.M. Lyzanets', "Rozvytok uhors'koï filolohiï v Uzhhorods'komu derzhavnomu universyteti," ibid., pp. 577-582.

61. Hryhorii Udovychenko, "Styl' i mova opovidan' M. Tomchaniia," *Karpaty,* vol. 11, no. 3 (Uzhhorod, 1958), p. 67.

62. For further details see Iosyf Dzendzelivs'kyi, "Stan i problemy doslidzhennia ukraïns'kykh hovoriv Zakarpats'koï oblasti URSR ta Skhidnoï Slovachchyny," in *Zhovten' i ukraïns'ka kul'tura* (Prešov, 1968), pp. 255-282; and K. I. Halas et al., "Dosiahnennia ukraïns'koho ta slov'ians'koho movoznavstva na Zakarpatti za roky radians'koï vlady," in *Velykyi Zhovten',* esp. pp. 537-552.

63. N. Korolevych et al., *Slov'ians'ka filolohiia na Ukraïni: bibliohrafiia (1958-1962 rr.)* (Kiev, 1963), pp. 52-72, and *(1963-1967 rr.),* pt. 1 (Kiev, 1968), pp. 115-137.

64. On the works of these and other writers during the Soviet period, see I. Vyshnevs'kyi, *Tradytsiï ta suchasnist'* (L'viv, 1963); V. S. Pop, "Rozvytok novely na Zakarpatti pislia Velykoï Vitchyznianoï viiny," *Duklia,* vol. 14, no. 6 (Prešov, 1966), pp. 49-55; Iurii Baleha, *Khudozhni vidkryttia chy pravda faktu?* (Uzhhorod, 1969), esp. pp. 52-219; and the bibliography *Pys'mennyky Radians'koho Zakarpattia,* 2nd ed. (Uzhhorod, 1960).

65. N. P. Makara and I. M. Chavarha, "Osushchestvlenie Leninskoi natsional'noi politiki na Zakarpat'e," in *Kul'tura i pobut,* pp. 6-7.

66. Baleha, *Khudozhni vidkryttia,* p. 79.

67. V. S. Pop, "Obraz V.I. Lenina v tvorchosti pys'mennykiv Zakarpattia," in *Kul'tura i pobut,* pp. 10-18; *Lenina slaviat' Karpaty* (Uzhhorod, 1969).

68. Even Iurii Baleha, a determined defender of socialist realism, finds it necessary to criticize the "banal" and "superficial" plots in many recent Subcarpathian novels. Baleha, *Khudozhni vidkryttia,* p. 80..

69. Hryhorii Ostrovs'kyi, *Obrazotvorche mystetstvo Zakarpattia* (Kiev, 1974), pp. 104-195. See also the illustrations in *Zakarpats'kyi khudozhnii muzei* (Kiev, 1973) and *Izobrazitel'noe iskusstvo Zakarpat'ia* (Moscow, 1973).

70. *Narodna osvita, nauka i kul'tura v Ukraïns'kii RSR* (Kiev, 1973), pp. 14-15.

71. *Shliakhom do shchastia,* pp. 258-264; I. Hranchak and V. Pal'ok, *Misto nad Uzhem* (Uzhhorod, 1973), pp. 246-252.

72. *Shliakhom do shchastia,* p. 263. Cf. Hranchak and Pal'ok, *Misto,* pp. 252-256.

73. *Narodna osvita,* p. 286; Baleha, *Khudozhni vidkryttia,* p. 51; I.H. Shul'ha, "Rozvytok kul'tury radians'koho Zakarpattia," in *Velykyi Zhovten',* p. 477. A large proportion of Karpaty's production consists of many volumes published on contract for firms in Hungary.

74. For a content analysis of this organ and its role as a propagandizer of the Soviet regime, see Pavlo Lisovyi and Mykhailo Babydorych, *Trybuna trudiashchykh: do 50-richchia hazety 'Zakarpats'ka pravda'* (Uzhhorod, 1970), pp. 81-154.

75. *Narodna osvita,* pp. 256-268; Shul'ha, "Rozvytok kul'tury," p. 470; A. V. Popovych, "Rol' radians'koho kinomystetstva v politychnomu vykhovanni trudiashchykh Zakarpattia," in *Velykyi Zhovten',* pp. 490-494.

76. Cited in I. P. Fil', "Z istoriï radiofikatsiï zakhidnykh oblastei Ukraïns'koï RSR (1944-1950 rr.)," in *Kul'tura i pobut,* p. 47.

77. *Narodna osvita,* pp. 300-301.

78. D. Suprun, *Spokonvichna mriia zbulasia* (Kiev, 1969), pp. 115-119, 137-141; *Shliakhom do shchastia,* pp. 172-174, 215-222.

79. Michael Lacko, "The Forced Liquidation of the Union of Uzhhorod," *Slovak Studies*, I, *Historica*, vol. 1 (Rome, 1961), pp. 145-185; Vasyl' Markus', "Nyshchennia hreko-katolyts'koï tserkvy v Mukachivs'kii Ieparkhiï v 1945-50 rr.," *Zapysky NTSh*, vol. 169 (Paris and New York, 1962), pp. 385-405; Atanasii V. Pekar, *Narysy istoriï tserkvy Zakarpattia* (Rome, 1967), pp. 159-170.

80. V. M. Lohoida, "Hromadians'ki sviata radians'koho Zakarpattia i podolannia relihiinykh perezhytkiv," in *Kul'tura i pobut*, pp. 60-65. The government has not been entirely successful in eradicating the influence of religion. M. M. Boldyzhar et al., "Deiaki pytannia borot'by z relihiinymy perezhytkamy," in *Velykyi Zhovten'*, pp. 420-434.

81. Decree no. 58, cited in Bondar, "Iz istorii," p. 106.

82. Soviet statistics are inconsistent, some giving more, others less in 1944. The figures here are taken from Makara and Chavarha, "Osushchestvlenie," p. 8.

83. *Narodna osvita*, pp. 58-60, 132-143.

84. *Shliakhom do shchastia*, pp. 246-247.

85. Roman Szporluk, "The Ukraine and the Ukrainians," in Z. Katz, ed., *Handbook of the Major Soviet Nationalities* (New York and London, 1975), p. 39.

86. *Narodna osvita*, pp. 169-171; Hranchak and Pal'ok, *Misto*, pp. 227-236; Shul'ha, "Rozvytok," pp. 465-467; *Shliakhom do shchastia*, pp. 251-252.

87. Ibid., pp. 169-170; T. S. Seheda, "Spilka molodi Zakarpats'koï Ukraïny v borot'bi za vozz'iednannia Zakarpattia z Radians'koiu Ukraïnoiu (lystopad 1944—cherven' 1945 rr.)," in *Velykyi Zhovten'*, pp. 270-282; *Nezhasnyi iunosti vohon'* (Uzhhorod, 1968), pp. 33-43.

88. L.A. Tkachenko, "Dynamika etnichnoho skladu naselennia Zakarpattia," *Narodna tvorchist' ta etnohrafiia*, vol. 1, no. 1 (Kiev, 1974), p. 65.

89. On cultural developments between 1919 and 1945, see Bajcura, *Ukrajinská otázka*, pp. 36-65; Mykola Shtets', *Literaturna mova ukraïntsiv Zakarpattia i Skhidnoï Slovachchyny* (Bratislava, 1969), pp. 101-129; Ivan Vanat, "Shkil'ne pytannia na Priashivshchyni pid chas domiunkhens'koï respubliky," *Duklia*, XIV, 5 and 6 (Prešov, 1966), pp. 60-68 and 59-64; Olena Rudlovchak, "Literaturni stremlinnia ukraïntsiv Skhidnoï Slovachchyny u 20-30-kh rokakh nashoho stolittia," in *Zhovten' i ukraïns'ka kul'tura*, pp. 145-171; Andrii Kovach, "Ukraïntsi Priashivshchyny i deiaki pytannia kul'turnoï polityky Slovats'koï Respubliky," *Naukovyi zbirnyk MUKS*, IV, pt. 1 (Bratislava, Prešov, and Svidník, 1969), pp. 401-412.

90. Bajcura, *Ukrajinská otázka*, pp. 89-123 passim; Pavel Maču, "National Assimilation: The Case of the Rusyn-Ukrainians of Czechoslovakia," *East-Central Europe*, vol. II, no. 2 (Pittsburgh, 1975), pp. 106-109.

91. An interesting contrast is found between the Russophile: Ivan S. Shlepetskii (ed.), *Priashevshchina: istoriko-literaturnyi sbornik* (Prague, 1948) and the Ukrainophile: Ivan Matsyns'kyi, *Rozmova storich* (Bratislava-Prešov, 1965), esp. pp. 13-230; and Iurii Bacha, Andrii Kovach, and Mykola Shtets', *Chomu, koly i iak* (Prešov, 1967).

92. Prešov Region "anti-Ukrainianism" can be explained in part by the fact that the "reidentification" process came at a time when Ukrainianism was being associated with anti-Soviet bourgeois-nationalism, when people feared they may be deported eastward if they did not identify themselves as Slovaks, when the Greek Catholic Church was outlawed (1950), and when land was being taken away from the peasantry and collectivized (1950-52). Maču, "National Assimilation," pp. 105-114.

93. It should be remembered that Slovaks were taking out their wrath at this time against the Magyar minority along the southern border and generally against all

elements or regions that did not identify themselves as Slovak. Juraj Zvara, *Mad'arská menšina na Slovensku po roku 1945* (Bratislava, 1969), pp. 46 ff.

94. Maču, "National Assimilation," pp. 116-117.

95. Ibid., pp. 129-130.

96. General descriptions are given by Jan Auerhan, *Československá větev v Jugoslavii,* Knihovna československého ústavu zahraničního, no. 1 (Prague, 1930), pp. 80-85; Oleksa Horbach, "Ukrainians Abroad: in Yugoslavia," in *Ukraine: A Concise Encyclopedia,* vol. 2 (Toronto, 1971), pp. 1248-1253.

97. The key figures in this debate are the Galician-Ukrainian Volodymyr Hnatiuk, "Slovaky chy Rusyny?: prychynok do vyiasnenia sporu pro natsional'nist' zakhidnykh rusyniv," *Zapysky NTSh,* vol. 42, no. 4 (L'viv, 1901), pp. 1-81, and the Czech František Pastrnek, "Rusíni jazyka slovenského: odpověd' panu Vlad. Hnat-jukovi," in V. I. Lamanskii, ed., *Stat'i po slavianoviedieniiu,* vol. 2 (St. Petersburg, 1906), pp. 60-78.

98. On Kostel'nyk, see the biography by Diura Papharhai in Havryil Kostel'nyk, *Poezyia na bachvansko-srymskym ruskym lyteraturnym iazyku* (Novi Sad, 1970), pp. 7-87.

99. Aleksander D. Dulichenko, "Stanovlenie i razvitie rusinskogo literaturnogo iazyka v Iugoslavii," *Sovetskoe slavianovedenie,* vol. 8, no. 3 (Moscow, 1972), pp. 38-50, and his "Z istoriyi formuvania ruskoho lyteraturnoho iazyka," *Nova dumka,* vol. 2, no. 4 (Vukovar, 1973), pp. 46-47. See also Oleksa Horbach, "Li-teraturna mova bachvans'ko-srims'kykh ('rusyniv')," *Zapysky NTSh,* vol. 169 (New York and Paris, 1962), pp. 265-282. For sample texts, see Appendix 3, pt. 7.

100. Paul R. Magocsi, "The Rusyns of Yugoslavia," *Europa Ethnica,* vol. 34, no. 1 (Vienna, 1977), pp. 5-8; and his "Moï vrazhennia z podorozhi po Iugoslaviï," *Nova dumka,* vol. 3, no. 8 (Vukovar, 1974), pp. 116-118.

Appendix 1

1. Henryk Paszkiewicz, *The Making of the Russian Nation* (London, 1963), p. 15, n. 65.

2. On this problem, see Jan Húsek, *Národopisná hranice mezi Slováky a Kar-patorusy* (Bratislava, 1925), pp. 6-18, 398-460, and Ondrej R. Halaga, *Slovanské osídlenie Potisia a východoslovenskí greckokatolíci* (Košice, 1947), pp. 58-116. The Ukrainian ethnographer Volodymyr Hnatiuk divided Greek Catholics in the Prešov Region into: (1) "ethnically" pure Rusnaks (or Rusyns); and (2) a linguistically Slovakized group known as *Sloviaks (Slovjaks).* See his "Rusyny Priashivs'koï eparkhiï i ikh hovory," *Zapysky NTSh,* vol. 35 (L'viv, 1900), pp. 1-25. Slovak authors consider *Slovjaks,* who make up the majority of Greek Catholics in the Prešov diocese, to be ethnically Slovak.

3. A Petrov, *Stat'i ob Ugorskoi Rusi,* appended to *Zapiski istoriko-filologi-cheskago fakul'teta Imp. S.-Peterburgskago universiteta,* vol. 81 (St. Petersburg, 1906), pp. 11-12; Iador Strypskii, *Hdî dokumenty starshei istorii Podkarpatskoi Rusi? O mezhevykh nazvaniiakh* (Uzhhorod, 1924), p. 30.

4. A. Dukhnovych, "O narodakh krainianskykh yly karpatorossakh" (1848), *Karpaty,* no. 1 (Uzhhorod, 1958), pp. 121-123; Petrov, *Stat'i,* p. 12.

5. Z. Kuzela, "Tribal Division and Ethnographic Groups," in *Ukraine: A Concise Encyclopedia,* vol. 1 (Toronto, 1963), pp. 282-284. For further details, see Volodymyr Okhrymovych, "Zvidky vziala sia nazva Boiky?," *Zhytie i slovo,* vol. 3 (L'viv, 1895), pp. 143-146, and the entries "Boiky," by S. Rabii-Karpyns'ka, "Hu-tsul'shchyna," by V. Kubiiovych and V. Vintsents, and "Lemky," by V. Kubiio-vych, in *Entsyklopediia ukraïnoznavstva: slovnykova chastyna* (Paris and New York, 1955-1970), pp. 149-150, 466-470, 1275-1280.

6. A. Dukhnovych, *Istinnaia istoriia karpato rossov ili ugorskikh rusinov* (1853), reprinted in his *Tvory,* vol. 2 (Bratislava and Prešov, 1967), pp. 539-543; Petrov, *Stat'i,* pp. 14-17; "Bliakhy," *Lyteraturna nedîlia,* vol. 3 (Uzhhorod, 1943), pp. 135-136.

7. A key line in the poem, "Song of the Rusnaks," reads: "Kazhdyi rusyn dobrŷ khlop" (Every Rusyn is a good guy), cited in Vasyl' Mykytas' and Olena Rudlovchak, eds., *Poety Zakarpattia* (Bratislava and Prešov, 1965), p. 91.

8. From the poems "Vruchanie" (1851) and "Podkarpatskii Rusynŷ" (1860s), reprinted in their original form in Dukhnovych, *Tvory,* vol. 1, pp. 248, 382. The Russian scholar Aleksei L. Petrov criticized the term "podkarpatskii rusinŷ," since, according to him, the people did not live "under" the Carpathians, but "in" them. *Karpatorusskiia mezhevyia nazyvaniia iz. pol. XIX i iz nach. XX v.* (Prague, 1929), p. 18, n. 1.

9. This was the period when the Russophile orientation dominated Subcarpathian intellectual life. See, for instance, the poems "Ia russkii" by Iulii Stavrovskii-Popradov and "K Ugorskoi Rusi" and "Russkii narod" by Evgenii Fentsik in Mykytas' and Rudlovchak, *Poety Zakarpattia,* pp. 260, 280-282, 284-286. *Karpatoross* was first used in 1804 by Ivan Orlai (see the Bibliography, no. 1851).

10. "It is true that among Subcarpathian Ukrainians the name Rusyn (*rus'kyi*) with a soft 's' is still widespread." *Za ridne slovo: polemika z rusofilamy* (Mukachevo, 1937), p. 102. "The Carpatho-Russians have preserved the oldest names . . . 'Rusnak' or 'Rusyn'." P. P. Sova, "Podkarpatskaia Rus' i russkii iazyk," *Russkii narodnyi kalendar' na god 1937,* Izdanie OIAD, no. 115 (Uzhhorod, 1936), p. 69. Other propagandists claimed that "Russian (*russkii*) and Rusyn (*rus'kyi*) mean the same." *Narodnyi katekhiz,* Izdanie OIAD, no. 19 (Uzhhorod, 1926), p. 2.

11. "Mŷ Rusinŷ," *Rusyn* (Uzhhorod), August 25, 1920.

12. Boris Unbegaun, *L'origine du nom des Ruthènes,* Onomastica, no. 5 (Winnipeg, 1953); J. B. Rudnyckyj, in *Ukraine: A Concise Encyclopedia,* vol. 1, pp. 10-12.

13. S. Bonkáló, "Kárpátorosz, nagyorosz, orosz, ruszin, rutén, uhrorusz, ukrán," *Láthatár,* vol. 7, no. 7 (Budapest, 1939), pp. 292-295. Cf. the Bibliography (refs. 1104, 1105, 1197-1201, 1250-1255, 1973, 2014, 2145, 2149).

14. Russian scholars particularly object to the adjective *rusínský,* because according to them it "is an artificial term completely incorrect from a philological standpoint." A. Petrov, "Kdy vznikly ruské osady na uherské Dolní zemi a vůbec za Karpaty?," *Český časopis historický,* vol. 29 (Prague, 1923), p. 411. n. 3. See also Sova, "Podkarpatskaia Rus'," p. 70 and I. S. Svientsitskii, "Obzor snoshenii Karpatskoi Rusi s Rossiei v l-uiu polovinu XIX v.," *Izviestiia ORISIAN,* vol. 11, no. 3 (St. Petersburg, 1906), p. 257.

15. Although since 1945 the Czechoslovak government has adopted the name Ukrainian to describe the Rusyn population of the Prešov Region, official statistics still use interchangeably the terms *ukrajinský, ruský* and since 1968 *rusínský.* Pavel Maču, "National Assimilation: the Case of the Rusyn-Ukrainians of Czechoslovakia," *East-Central Europe,* vol. 2, no. 2 (Pittsburgh, 1975), pp. 102-131 passim.

16. Cf. the Bibliography, refs. 1175, 1249, 1420, 1422, 1754, 1756, 1789, 1790, 2264. It is interesting to note that at the Paris Peace Conference, official documents referred to "the country of the Ruthenes (or Ruthenians) south of the Carpathians." David Hunter Miller, *My Diary at the Peace Conference,* vol. 13 (New York, 1924), p. 245. English-language documents by the Czechoslovak delegation at Paris referred to the Ruthenians of Hungary.

17. These terms first appeared in the *Annales Hildesheimenses* and the *Vita*

Chunradi Archiepiscopi Saliburgensis (1177). H. J. Bidermann, *Die ungarischen Ruthenen, ihr Wohngebiet, ihr Erwerb, und ihre Geschichte,* vol. 2 (Innsbruck, 1867), p. 59; A. Petrov, *Drevnieishiia gramoty po istorii karpatorusskoi tserkvi i ierarkhii, 1391-1498 g.* (Prague, 1930), pp. 30-51; O. Stavrovs'kyi, *Slovats'ko-pol's'ko-ukraïns'ke prykordonnia do 18 stolittia* (Bratislava and Prešov, 1967), pp. 14-24.

18. B. Barvins'kyi, *Nazva 'Ukraïna' na Zakarpatti,* Onomastica, no. 4 (Winnipeg, 1952).

19. Cf. the Bibliography, refs. 1108, 1109, 1141, 1253, 1523, 2008. It is interesting to note that in the standard Magyar language encyclopedia, *Révai nagy lexikon,* 21 vols. (Budapest, 1911-1935), there is no entry for the territory comprising Subcarpathian Rus'. The population is discussed along with Little Russians, that is, Ukrainians (*kisoroszok*) under the entry *orosz* (Russian), and only in the supplement (vol. 21) is there a separate entry for *rutén irodalmi* (Rusyn culture).

20. Cf. the Bibliography, refs. 0615, 1099, 1219, 1262, 1337, 1483, 1484, 1931, 1932, 2096, 2154.

21. Cf. the Bibliography, refs. 0108, 0626, 1274, 1731, 2188.

22. Neither of these terms were permitted by the Czechoslovak authorities (see Chapter 9), although they were used in publications appearing in the Soviet Ukraine (Cf. the Bibliography, refs. 0077, 1123-1125, 1693, 1786). Many Ukrainian writers in the West use the term Carpatho-Ukraine based on the February, 1939 decision of the autonomous Diet (Cf. the Bibliography, refs. 1747, 1749, 1977, 1984-1987, 2023-2025, 2101, 2102, 2106, 2112-2120).

23. Paszkiewicz, *Making of the Russian Nation,* p. 304.

24. Cf. the Bibliography, refs. 1140, 1160, 1161, 1245, 1543, 1733, 1754, 1756, 1788-1790, 2020.

25. Ivan Vanat, "Do pytannia vzhyvannia terminiv 'Zakarpattia' ta 'Priashivshchyna'," in *Zhovten' i ukraïns'ka kul'tura* (Prešov, 1968), pp. 602-603; I. Shlepetskii, "Istoricheskii ocherk Makovitsy," in Aleksandr Pavlovich, *Izbrannye proizvedeniia* (Prešov, 1955), pp. 503-522.

Bibliography

This bibliography includes a comprehensive listing of various kinds of materials that can be used to analyze the nationality problem in Subcarpathian Rus'. It does not pretend to be a complete bibliography on the region; in general, items dealing with problems of the nineteenth and twentieth centuries predominate.

The entries are arranged in alphabetical order according to the author's last name or, if that is lacking, the title of the work. In some instances, materials are listed under the sponsoring organization. Since the works cited are written in several languages, a single author's name may appear in varying spellings. The main entry for any given author renders his name as it would appear in the language of his nationality. All works by that author, despite their language, are entered under this main entry; however, if the rendition of the last name for a particular work differs from the main entry, the variant form appears in brackets. Moreover, there is a system of cross references directing the reader to the main entry, for example, Sztripszky, see Stryps'kyi.

The entries provide, where possible, complete bibliographical data: author or editor, title (as it appeared in the original), series (if applicable), place of publication, and publisher; volume, number, and page numbers are given for articles in journals and collected works. With only a few exceptions, articles that appeared in newspapers are not listed; however, there is a comprehensive list of newspapers in section II, A. Annotations are kept to a minimum and appear only to describe major bibliographic tools, to provide the contents of collected works (with author cross-references), and to explain those items whose subject matter is not evident from the title.

The bibliography is organized as follows:

I. REFERENCE AIDS

A. Bibliology, bibliography, historiographical analyses

Under this rubric are included not only the traditional annotated and unannotated bibliographies and historiographical analyses, but also archival guides and histories of book publishing and printing establishments.

0001   Aristov, Fedor F. *Khronologicheskii perechen' napechatannykh sochinenii A.V. Dukhnovicha.* Izdanie OIAD, no. 45. Uzhhorod, 1929. Also in *Karpatskii sviet,* vol. 1, no. 7 (Uzhhorod, 1928), pp. 221-228. Third edition: Izdanie OIAD, no. 55. Uzhhorod, 1929.

0002   Aristov, Fedor F., and Beskid, N. A. *Khronologicheskii perechen' napechatannykh sochinenii Evgeniia Andreevicha Fentsika.* Izdanie OIAD, no. 78. Uzhhorod, 1932. Also in *Karpatskii sviet,* vol. 5, no. 4 (Uzhhorod, 1932), pp. 1282-1294.

0003   Bacha, Iurii. "O. V. Dukhnovych v doteperishnii otsintsi." *Duklia,* vol. 8, no. 4 (Prešov, 1960), pp. 122-131.

0003a Bibliografia k dejinám východneho Slovenska, 3 vols. Košice: SVK, 1962. Unannotated bibliography with sections history, dialects, literary history, and bellettres of Ukrainians in Slovakia.

0004 Bibliografický katalog. 17 vols. Prague, 1922-46. Annual publication with unannotated listings for works published in Czechoslovakia in the Subcarpathian Rusyn (podkarpatoruská), Russian, and Ukrainian languages.

0005 Bibliografický katalog časopisectva republiky československé za rok 1920. Prague: Československý ústav bibliografický, 1921.

0006 Bibliografie české historie. 4 vols. Prague: Historický klub, 1929-1951. Each of the volumes published to cover the period from 1925-1926 through 1937-1941 included a subsection of works dealing with Subcarpathian Rus'.

0007 "Bibliohrafiia literatury pro zhyttia i tvorchist' O. Dukhnovycha, 1945-1965." Oleksandr Dukhnovych: zbirnyk materialiv. Edited by M. Rychalka et al. Prešov: KSUT, 1965, pp. 351-361.

0008 Bilak, S. M. "Do pytannia krytyky burzhuazno-natsionalistychnykh istoriï Zakarpattia (1919-1944 rr.)." Kul'tura i pobut naselennia ukraïns'kykh Karpat. Edited by I. M. Hranchak et al. Uzhhorod: UDU, 1973, pp. 65-73.

0009 Böőr, György. A magyarországi ruszin időszaki sajtó a XIX században. Cluj [Koloszvár]: A Ferenc József tudományegyetem történeti intézete, 1943.

0010 "Bybliografiia: knyzhky y statî, iakî poiavylysia v poslidnôm chasî y odnosiat'sia do Podkarpatskoî Rusy." This section, with detailed annotated entries, appeared on the last pages of each issue of Podkarpatska Rus' Uzhhorod, 1924-1936).

0011 Danyliuk, D. D. "Deiaki pytannia rozvytku kapitalizmu ta formuvannia robitnychoho klasu Zakarpattia v ukraïns'kii radians'kii istoriohrafiï." Kul'tura i pobut naselennia ukraïns'kykh Karpat. Edited by I. Hranchak et al. Uzhhorod: UDU, 1973, pp. 81-84.

0012 Delehan, M. "Deiaki osoblyvosti katalohizatsiï dokumental'nykh materialiv doradians'koho periodu na Zakarpatti." Arkhivy Ukraïny, vol. 23, no. 1 (Kiev, 1969), pp. 54-57.

0013 Dzendzelivs'kyi, Iosyf O. "Stan i problemy doslidzhennia ukraïns'kykh hovoriv Zakarpats'koï oblasti URSR ta Skhidnoï Slovachchyny." Zhovten' i ukraïns'ka kul'tura. Prešov: KSUT, 1968, pp. 255-283.

0014 Fentsik, Stepan A. Spisok knig rekomendovannykh v sel'skiia biblioteki na Podkarpatskoi Rusi. Uzhhorod: PON, 1929.

0015 Filevich, Ivan P. "Ugorskaia Rus' i sviazannye s neiu voprosy i zadachi russkoi istoricheskoi nauki." Varshavskiia universitetskiia izvestiia, vol. 5, no. 3 (Warsaw, 1894), pp. 1-32.

0016 Frantsev, Vladimir. "Obzor vazhnieishikh izuchenii Ugorskoi Rusi." Russkii filologicheskii viestnik, vol. 45 (Warsaw, 1901), pp. 145-197.

0016a Halas, K. I. "O.L. Petrov i ukraïns'ka onomastyka." Voprosy russkogo i sopostavitel'nogo iazykoznaniia. Edited by G.S. Tokar' et al. Uzhhorod: UDU, 1969, pp. 55-71.

0017 Hres'ko, Mykhailo. "Zakarpattia—ochyma mandrivnykiv i vchenykh." Zhovten', vol. 18, no. 11 (L'viv, 1968), pp. 130-138.

0018 Iavorskii, Iul'ian A. Iz istorii nauchnago izsliedovaniia Zakarpatskoi Rusi,

Prague: Izd. Zhivoe slovo, 1928. Bibliography of works by Vladimir A. Frantsev and Aleksei L. Petrov.

0019 ———· *K bibliografii literatury ob A. V. Dukhnovichie.* Izdanie OIAD, no. 52. Uzhhorod, 1929. Also in *Karpatskii sviet,* vol. 2, no. 1 (Uzhhorod, 1929), pp. 404-407.

0020 Ihnatiienko, Varfolomii. *Bibliohrafiia ukraïns'koi presy, 1816-1916.* Trudy Ukraïns'koho naukovo-doslidchoho instytuta knyhoznavstva, vol. 4. Kharkiv, 1930. Reprint: State College, Pa: Wasyl O. Luciw, 1968. Includes several Subcarpathian serials with indications of years, periodicity, and editors.

0020a Ivasiuta, M. K. et al., eds. *Zakhidni oblasti Ukraïns'koi RSR u Velykii Vit-chyznianii viini Radians'koho Soiuzu 1941-1945 rr.* L'viv: ANURSR, L'vivs'ka naukova biblioteka im. V. Stefanyka, 1972, especially pp. 129-135 and 157-192. Includes works dealing with the partisan movement and Soviet military operations in Subcarpathian Rus'.

0020b *K jazykovým otázkam ukrajincov na Slovensku: bibliografické príspevky. Prešov: SVK, 1960.*

0021 Kaminskii, Iosif V. "Karpatorusskaia zhurnalistika poslie 1919 goda." *Podkarpatskaia Rus' za gody 1919-1936.* Edited by E. Bachinskii. Uzhhorod: RNG, 1936, pp. 137-139.

0022 Kertesz, Janos. "Die Bibliographie der Ruthenenfrage." *Glasul Minoritătilor,* vol. 13 (Lugoj, Rumania, 1935), pp. 123-132.

0023 Kipsová, Mária, et al. *Bibliografia slovenských a inorečových novín a časopisov z rokov 1919-1938.* Martin: Matica Slovenska, 1968.

0024 Kolomiets, Ivan G. "Istoriografiia, istochniki i literatura." *Sotsial'no-èkonomicheskie otnosheniia i obshchestvennoe dvizhenie v Zakarpat'e vo vtoroi polovine XIX stoletiia,* vol. 2. Tomsk: Izd. Tomskogo universiteta, 1962, pp. 524-615.

0025 Kontratovych, Irynei. "Noví puty podkarpatskoi ystoryohrafiï, vol. 1, nos. 1-2 (Uzhhorod, 1941), pp. 44-53.

0026 ———· "Stremlînia za rus'ku pechatniu na Podkarpatskôi Rusy y pamiatnyky staropechatnŷkh tserkovnŷkh knyh." *Podkarpatska Rus',* vol. 1, no. 4 (Uzhhorod, 1923), pp. 97-100.

0027 Král, Jiří. "Dnešní stav vědeckého výzkumu Podkarpatské Rusi a naše nejbližší úkoly do budoucna." *Sborník československe' společnosti zeměpisné,* vol. 30 (Prague, 1924), pp. 53-57. Published separately: Prague, 1924.

0028 ———· *Geografická bibliografie Podkarpatské Rusi,* pts. 1 and 2: *za rok 1923-1926.* Travaux géographiques tchèques, nos. 11 and 13. Prague: Geografický ústav Karlovy university, 1923-1928. Despite its title, this bibliography includes works on all aspects of the region; it is an unannotated list of 2,156 entries, with index.

0029 Kuz'ma, Ivan. "Vŷdavnytstvo knyzhok dlia narodnŷkh shkôl." *Podkarpatska Rus',* vol. 5, nos. 8-9 (Uzhhorod, 1928), pp. 186-189.

0030 Latak, Diura. "Lyteratura Rusnatsokh." *Književnosti narodnosti Vojvodine, 1945-1972: Lyteratura narodnostsokh Voivodyny.* Novi Sad, 1973.

0031 Lelekach, Mykola, and Haraida, Ivan. "Bybliohrafiia podkarpatskoi rus'koi ystoriî lyteraturŷ." *Zoria-Hajnal,* vol. 2, nos. 3-4 (Uzhhorod, 1942), pp. 459-467.

0032 ———· "Bybliografiia podkarpatskoi rus'koi lyteraturŷ," *Zoria-Hajnal,* vol. 3, nos. 1-4 (Uzhhorod, 1943), pp. 515-524.

0033 ———· *Zahal'na bybliografiia Podkarpatia.* Lyteraturno-naukova byblioteka, no. 30. Uzhhorod: PON, 1944. Supplemented in *Lyteraturna nedîlia,* vol. 4, nos. 9-11 (Uzhhorod, 1944). Still the most comprehensive bibliography of the region, it includes 2,799 unannotated entries with special emphasis on Hungarian-language materials.

0034 Levyts'kyi, Ivan E. *Halytsko-ruskaia bybliohrafiia XIX stolîtiia: 1801-1886.* 2 vols. L'viv, 1888-1895. Continued for the years 1887-1893 in *Materiialy do ukraïns'koï bibliografii.* 3 vols. L'viv: Bibliografichna komisiia NTSh, 1909-11. The most comprehensive bibliography, including Subcarpathian individual titles and serials with analytics, arranged according to date of publication.

0035 Lisovyi, Petro M. "Do pytannia pro pochatok zhurnalistyky na Zakarpats'kii Ukraïni." *Ukraïns'ke literaturoznavstvo,* vol. 8 (L'viv, 1970), pp. 68-75.

0036 ———· "Persha zakarpats'ka hazeta [Uchytel']." *Ukraïns'ke literaturoznavstvo,* vol. 12 (L'viv, 1971), pp. 22-26.

0037 Magocsi, Paul R. *Carpatho-Ruthenians in North America: A Bibliography.* Balch Institute Historical Reading Lists, no. 31. Philadelphia, 1976.

0038 ———· "An Historiographical Guide to Subcarpathian Rus'." *Austrian History Yearbook,* vols. 9-10 (Houston, Texas, 1973-74), pp. 201-265. Reprinted in Harvard Ukrainian Research Institute Offprint Series, no. 1. Cambridge, Mass. [1975]. Translated into Vojvodinian Rusyn by Dura Herbut: "Istoriografiini voditel' za Podkarpatsku Rus." *Nova dumka,* vol. 5, no. 12 (Vukovar, Yugoslavia, 1976), pp. 121-129.

0038a ———· "Recent Documentary Publications." *Recenzija,* vol. 2, no. 2 (Cambridge, Mass., 1972), pp. 62-86.

0039 Magocsi, Paul R., and Mayo, Olga K. *Carpatho-Ruthenica at Harvard: A Catalog of Holdings.* Englewood, N.J.: Transworld Publishers, 1977.

0040 Magocsi, Paul R., and Strumins'kyj, Bohdan. "The First Carpatho-Ruthenian Printed Book." *Harvard Library Bulletin,* vol. 25, no. 3 (Cambridge, Mass., 1977), pp. 292-309.

0041 Matsyns'kyi, Ivan. "20 lit ukraïns'koï vydavnychoï spravy na skhodi respubliky." *Duklia,* vol. 17, no. 3 (Prešov, 1969), pp. 1-11.

0042 Mishchenko, N.P. "Ukraïns'ka radians'ka istoriohrafiia pro rozvytok promyslovosti i robitnychoho klasu Zakarpattia za roku radians'koï vlady." *Velykyi Zhovten' i rozkvit vozz'iednanoho Zakarpattia.* Uzhhorod: UDU, 1970, pp. 339-347.

0043 Mushynka, Mykola. "Bibliohrafiia prats' Volodymyra Hnatiuka pro 'Uhors'ku Rus' '." *Naukovyi zbirnyk MUKS,* vol. 3 (Bratislava, Prešov, and Svidník, 1967), pp. 215-220.

0044 ———· "Bibliohrafiia prats' dots. d-ra Ivana Pan'kevycha." *Naukovyi zbirnyk MUKS*, vol. 4, pt. 1 (Bratislava, Prešov, and Svidník, 1969), pp. 148-164.

0045 Mykytas', Vasyl' L. *Davni knyhy Zakarpats'koho derzhavnoho kraieznavchoho muzeiu.* L'viv: Vyd. LU, 1964. Includes 130 entries with content analyses of rare Subcarpathian manuscripts and printed books.

0046 ———· *Davni rukopysy i starodruky: opys i kataloh.* 2 vols. Uzhhorod and L'viv: Vyd. LU, 1961-64. Includes a history of the Uzhhorod University (formerly Episcopal) Library, followed by 481 annotated entries revealing the resources available to the Subcarpathian intelligentsia.

0047 ———· "Tvorchist' O. Dukhnovycha v otsintsi doradians'koho literaturoznavstva." *Oleksandr Dukhnovych: zbirnyk materialiv.* Edited by M. Rychalka. Prešov: KSUT, 1965, pp. 93-114.

0048 Nevrlý, Mikuláš. *Bibliografia ukrajiník v slovenskej reči, 1945-1964.* Bratislava: SAV, 1965.

0049 Ohloblyn, Olexander. "Historiography of the Carpathian Ukraine." In his "Ukrainian Historiography, 1917-1956." *Annals of the Ukrainian Academy of Arts and Sciences,* vols. 5-6 (New York, 1957), pp. 391-394.

0049a Pal'ok, Vasyl' V. "Deiaki pytannia istoriï Zakarpattia z naidavnishykh chasiv do kintsia XVIII st. v ukraïns'kii radians'kii istoriohrafiï." *Kul'tura i pobut naselennia ukraïns'kykh Karpat.* Edited by I.M. Hranchak. Uzhhorod: UDU, 1973, pp. 105-112.

0049b ———· *Istoriia Zakarpattia v ukraïns'kii radians'kii istoriohrafii,* pt. 1. Uzhhorod: UDU, 1974.

0050 Pan'kevych, Ivan [Y.P.]. "Tsy môh buty drukar' Shvaipol't Fiol' v Hrushevî y tu pechataty knyhy?" *Podkarpatska Rus',* vol. 1, no. 3 (Uzhhorod, 1923), pp. 93-94.

0051 Pashaeva, N. M. "Istoricheskaia biblioteka—istoriku karpatskogo regiona." *Kul'tura i pobut naselennia ukrains'kykh Karpat.* Edited by I. M. Hranchak et. al. Uzhhorod: UDU, 1973, pp. 182-188.

0052 Pazhur, Olena. *Bibliohrafiia pro doslidzhennia ukraïns'kykh hovoriv Skhidnoï Slovachchyny.* Prešov: Derzhavna naukova biblioteka, 1972. Includes 486 unannotated entries and an index.

0053 ———· *Bibliohrafiia knyzhkovykh vydan' SVKL, ukraïns'koï redaktsiï v Priashevi (1956-1960), SPVVUL (1960-1970), vybir z ukraïns'kykh vydan' inshykh vydavnytstv.* Supplement to *Duklia,* vol. 19, no. 6 (Prešov, 1971).

0054 ———· [Pažurová, Helena]. *Ukrajinci Československa 1962-1964: Bibliografia kníh, časopiseckých a novinových článkov.* Bibliografia vychodného Slovenska 1945-1964, vol. 12, pt. 1. Prešov: Štátna vedecká knižnica, 1967.

0055 Perfets'kyi, Evhenii. "Drukarni ta starodruky Pidkarpats'koï Rusy-Ukraïny." *Bibliolohichni visti,* vol. 4, no. 4 (Kiev, 1926), pp. 26-34.

0056 ———· [Perfeckij, Eugen]. "Nejdůležitější studie o dějinách Podkarpatské Rusi." "Dvě stati k dějinám Podkarpatské Rusi." *Sborník filozofickej fakulty university Komenského,* vol. 1, no. 6 (Bratislava, 1922), pp. 115-126.

0057 ———· [Perfetskii, E.]. "Obzor Ugro-russkoi istoriografii." *Izvestiia ORISIAN,* vol. 19, no. 1 (St. Petersburg, 1914), pp. 291-341.

0058 ———· "Pechatnaia tserkovno-slavianskaia kniga Ugorskoi Rusi v XVII-XVIII viekakh." *Izvestiia ORISIAN,* vol. 20, no. 2 (St. Petersburg, 1916), pp. 277-294.

0059   Petrov, Aleksei L. "Eshche dva slova ob izuchenii Ugorskoi Rusi." *Zhivaia starina,* vol. 13, no. 3 (St. Petersburg, 1903), pp. 276-278. Reprinted as "Arkhivy i biblioteki Ugorshchiny" in Petrov's *Stat'i ob ugorskoi Rusi* (ref. 1931), pp. 19-20.

0060   ——· "Staropechatnyia tserkovnyia knigi v Mukachevie i Ungvarie." *Zhurnal MNP,* vol. 275, no. 5 (St. Petersburg, 1891), pp. 209-215. Reprinted in *Listok,* vol. 10, nos. 13, 14, 15 (Uzhhorod, 1894), pp. 148-149, 160-162, 171-173; and in Petrov, *Stat'i ob ugorskoi Rusi* (ref. 1931), pp. 65-71.

0061   ——· *Zadachi karpatorusskoi istoriografii.* Prague, 1930. Also in Petrov's *Drevnieishiia gramoty* (ref. 1921), pp. v-xix.

0062   Prylypko, Ia. P. *Ukraïns'ke radians'ke karpatoznavstvo (bibliohrafiia prats' z etnohrafiï, fol'kloru ta narodnoho mystetsva).* Kiev: Vyd. Naukova dumka, 1972. Includes 2024 unannotated entries and an index.

0063   *Pys'mennyky radians'koho Zakarpattia.* Second edition. Uzhhorod: ZOV, 1960. Bibliography of literary works of twenty-one Soviet Subcarpathian writers.

0064   Rácz, Joseph A. "Le développement de la littérature historique carpatho-ukrainienne." *Revue d'histoire comparée,* vol. 22 (Paris, 1944), pp. 172-182.

0065   Radványi, Nikolaus. *Die Archive in der Podkarpatská Rus. Ein Beitrag zur Errichtung des Landesarchivs.* Uzhhorod, 1922.

0066   Rud', M. P. *Ukraïns'ka Radians'ka Sotsialistychna Respublika, 1917-1967: bibliohrafichni pokazhchyk literatury.* Kiev: Naukova dumka, 1969. Includes sixty-five references on Subcarpathian history.

0067   Rud', M. P. et al., eds. *Vozz'iednannia ukraïns'kykh zemel' v iedynii ukraïns'kii radians'kii derzhavi (1939-1959 rr.): bibliohrafichnyi pokazhchyk.* Kiev: ANURSR, 1959, especially pp. 48-52 and 64-70. Includes works dealing with the incorporation process and the first years of Soviet rule in Subcarpathian Rus'.

0067a Rudlovchak, Olena. "Do istoriï hazety 'Sova'." *Duklia,* vol. 18, no. 1 (Prešov, 1970), pp. 69-75.

0068   ——· "Do pytan' zhurnalistyky v ukraïntsiv Skhidnoï Slovachchyny." *Duklia,* vol. 10, no. 3 (Prešov, 1962). pp. 64-69.

0069   ——· "Pershyi pedahohichnyi chasopys: do stolittia vykhodu u svit hazety 'Uchytel'." *Shkola i zhyttia,* vol. 3, no. 10 (Prešov, 1966-1967), pp. 2-3.

0069a *Rukopisná kniha na východnom Slovensku: supis literatúry.* Prešov: SVK, 1963.

0070   Shash, Andrei. *Arkhiv privilegirovannago goroda Mukacheva 1376-1850 gg.: spravochnaia kniga po istorii, materialam i ustroistvu starago gorodskago arkhiva.* Mukachevo: Izd. goroda Mukacheva, 1927.

0071   Shlepetskii, Andrei. "Tvorcheskoe nasledie Aleksandra Pavlovicha." *Sborník Pedagogickej fakúlty Univ. P.J. Šafárika,* vol. 4, no. 2 (Prešov, 1965), pp. 78-93.

0072   Skrál, Fedor. "Tisk na Podkarpatské Rusi." *Podkarpatoruská revue,* vol. 1, nos. 2 and 3 (Bratislava, 1936), pp. 8-9 and 8.

0073   Stryps'kyi, Hiiador [Sztripszky, H]. "Egyházi schematismusaink és a helység-nevek." *Zoria-Hajnal,* vol. 3, nos. 1-4 (Uzhhorod, 1943), pp. 206-228.

0074   ——· "A hazai rutének legrégibb nyomtatványai." *Magyar könyvszemle,* vol. 19 (Budapest, 1911), pp. 117-131, 243-262.

0075 ———· *Jegyzetek a görög kultura Árpádkori nyomairól.* Budapest, 1913.

0076 Voloshyn, Avhustyn [Vološin, A.]. "Vývoj časopisectva na Podkarpatské Rusi." *Duch novin,* vol. 1, nos. 3, 4 and 5 (Prague, 1928), pp. 52-55, 79-82, and 111-114. Published first in his *Spomynŷ* (ref. 0705).

0077 Voronivs'ka, O. "Suchasna ukraïns'ka presa na Zakarpats'kii Ukraïni." *Zakhidna Ukraïna,* no. 4-5 (Kiev, 1931), pp. 109-115.

0078 *Vozz'iednannia ukraïns'kykh zemel' v iedynii Ukraïns'kii radians'kii der-zhavi (1939-1959 rr.): bibliohrafichnyi pokazhchyk.* Kiev: Vyd. ANURSR, 1959.

0079 Weingart, Miloš [M.W.]. "Zpráva o karpatoruských knihovnách a rukopi-sech v Prešově, Užhorodě a Mukačevě." *Časopis musea Království českého,* vol. 96 (Prague, 1922), pp. 273-278.

0080 Zadorozhnyi, V. Ie. "Zakarpattia v rosiis'kii publitsystytsi pershoï polovyny XIX st." *Kul'tura i pobut naselennia ukraïns'kykh Karpat.* Edited by I. M. Hranchak et al. Uzhhorod: UDU, 1973, pp. 97-105.

0081 Zapletal, Florian. *Kralová bibliografie Podkarpatské Rusi.* Olomouc, 1925, Critique with corrections and additions on the Král bibliographies (ref. 0028).

0082 Zhyvotko, Arkadii. Ohliad rus'koî lyteraturŷ dlia dîtei Pôdkarpatskoî Rusy rr. 1918-1926." *Podkarpatska Rus',* vol. 3 (Uzhhorod, 1926), pp. 161-166, 202-204, and 217-220; and vol. 4 (1927), pp. 12-15, 40-42, 89-91, and 119-120.

0083 ———· *Presa Karpats'koï Ukraïny.* Prague: Vyd. Iuriia Tyshchenka, 1940. Also in *Desiat' rokiv Ukraïns'koho istorychnoho kabinetu (1930-1940).* Inventáře Archiva Ministerstva vnitra v Praze, řada C, svaz. I. Prague, 1940, pp. 51-70. Lists 204 newspapers and journals from the region, with frequency of publication and editors.

0084 ———· "Presa Pidkarpats'koï Rusy." *Uchytel's'kyi holos,* vol. 5 (Uzh-horod, 1934), pp. 138-139 and 153-155.

0085 Zhatkovych, Iurii [Zsatkovics, Kálmán]. "A magyarországi oroszok tör-ténetírásának történelme." *Századok,* vol. 24 (Budapest, 1890), pp. 568-573 and 644-660.

0086 Zilynskyj, Orest, ed. *Sto padesát let česko-ukrajinských literárních styků 1814-1964: vědecko-bibliografický sborník.* Prague: Svět Sovětů for the Státní knihovna ČSR (Slovanská knihovna), 1968. Includes numerous items and several sections exclusively devoted to Subcarpathian Rus'.

Zsatkovics, Kálmán—*see* Zhatkovych, Iurii

B. Statistics

This section includes published collections of statistics. The most comprehensive are those based on the censuses of 1900, 1910, 1920, and 1930.

0087 *Annuaire statistique de la République tchécoslovaque.* 5 vols. Prague: Office de statistique, 1934-1938.

0088 *Československá statistika,* 180 vols. Prague: Státní úřad statistický, 1922-1949. Of the 17 series, the most pertinent are: (1) Elections; (2) Education;

(6) Population census; (7) Public finance; (12) Agriculture; (14) Movement of the population.

0089 *Lexikon obci Slovenskej Republiky.* Bratislava: Štatný štatistický úrad, 1942.

0090 *Magyar statisztikai évkönyv,* új folyam. Vols. 1-26: 1893-1918. Series continued in French as *Annuaire statistique hongrois,* nouvelle série. Vols. 24-26: 1916-1918 and Vols. 48-49: 1940-1941. Budapest, 1894-1943.

0091 *Magyar statisztikai közlemények,* új sor., vol. 1, pt. 1: *A magyar korona országaiban az 1891. év. elején végrehajtott népszámlálás eredményei.* Budapest, 1893. Vols. 1, 2, 5, 9, 12-16, 18, 27: *A magyar korona országainak 1900 évi népszámlálása.* Budapest, 1902-1909. Vols. 42, 47, 52, 56, 61, 64: *A magyar szent korona országainak 1910 évi népszámlálása.* Budapest, 1912-1920. Vol. 114: *Az 1930 évi népszámlálás,* pt. 6: *Az 1935, 1938 és 1939 évi népösszeírások végeredményei,* sect. B: *A visszacsatolt felvidéki és a visszatért Kárpátaljai terület.* Budapest, 1941. Includes detailed village-by-village statistics on language, religion, literacy, age-cohorts, and other matters.

0092 *Manuel statistique de la République tchécoslovaque,* 4 vols. Prague: L'Office de statistique d'état, 1920-1932.

0093 *Narodne hospodarstvo radians'koho Zakarpattia: statystychnyi zbirnyk.* Uzhhorod: Karpaty, 1969.

0094 *Narodne hospodarstvo Zakarpats'koï oblasti: statystychnyi zbirnyk.* Uzhhorod: ZOV, 1957.

0095 *Narodne hospodarstvo Zakarpats'koï oblasti v 1963 rotsi: korotkyi statystychnyi zbirnyk.* L'viv: Derzhstatvydav, 1964.

0096 *Néhány statisztika adat Kárpátalja viszonyairól.* Košice, 1939.

0097 *Radians'ke Zakarpattia v tsyfrakh: statystychnyi zbirnyk.* Uzhhorod: ZOV, 1960.

0098 *Sčítání lidu, domů a bytů v Československé Socialistické Republice k 1. březnu 1961,* Díl I: *Demografické charakteristiky obyvatelstva.* Prague: Ústřední komise lidové kontroly a statistiky, 1965.

0099 *Školství na Podkarpatské Rusi v přítomnosti.* Prague: Státní nakladatelství, 1933.

0100 *Statistický lexikon obcí v republice československé,* vol. 3: *Slovensko;* vol. 4: *Podkarpatská Rus.* Prague: Státní úřad statistický, 1927-1928.

0101 *Štatistický lexikon obcí v Republike Československej,* vol. 3: *Krajina Slovenská.* Prague: Ministerstvo vnutra a Štatný Úrad štatistický, 1936.

0102 *Statistický lexikon obcí v Republice československé,* vol. 4: *Země Podkarpatoruská.* Prague: Ministerstvo vnitra a Statní úřad statistický, 1937.

0103 "Statistika o dieiatel'nosti kul'turnykh i prosvietitel'nykh organizatsii." *Karpatskii sviet,* vol. 3, no. 5-6 (Uzhhorod, 1930), pp. 995-1000.

0104 *Statistická ročenka ČSSR,* 20 vols. Prague: Státní nakladatelství technické literatury, 1957-1976.

0105 Stojan, František, ed. *Representační sborník veškerého školství na Podkarpatské Rusi.* Uzhhorod, 1938.

0106 Thirring, Lajos. "A visszatért Kárpátáljai területen végrehajtott népösszeírás előzetes eredményei." *Magyar statisztikai szemle,* vol. 17, no. 8 (Budapest, 1939), pp. 939-960.

0107 Thirring, Lajos; Barsy, Gyula; and Szabó, Béla. "A Ruténföld statisztikája." *Magyar statisztikai szemle,* vol. 17, no. 3 (Budapest, 1939), pp. 196-205.

0108   Tomashivs'kyi, Stepan. "Etnografichna karta Uhors'koï Rusy." *Stat'i po slavianoviedieniiu,* vol. 3. Edited by Vladimir I. Lamanskii. St. Petersburg: Izd. vtorago otdieleniia Imperatorskoi akademii nauk, 1910, pp. 178-269. Detailed and revised analysis of the census of 1900 with proposed actual number of Rusyns; includes detailed large-scale map.

0109   *Volby do Národního Shromáždění na Podkarpatské Rusi v roce 1925.* Uzhhorod: Civilní sprava Podkarpatské Rusi, 1925.

0110   *Zprávy státního úřadu statistického republiky československé.* 19 vols. Prague, 1920-1938.

C. Indexes, gazetteers, maps

0111   *Atlas östlisches Mitteleuropa.* Bielefeld, Berlin, and Hanover: Velhagen and Klasing, 1959.

0112   Bezděk, Bohuslav. *Menoslov obcí na Slovensku.* Bratislava, 1920.

0113   Chromec, Břetislav. *Místopisný slovník československé republiky.* Prague, 1929. Second revised edition: Prague: Československý kompas, 1935.

0114   Dzendzelivs'kyi, Iosyf O. *Linhvistychnyi atlas ukraïns'kykh narodnykh hovoriv Zakarpats'koï Oblasti URSR (Leksyka). Naukovi zapysky UDU,* vols. 34 and 42. Uzhhorod, 1958-1960.

0115   Gregor, František. *Podrobná mapa Podkarpatské Rusi* (1:225,000). Mukachevo, Uzhhorod, and Berehovo: Novotný a Bartošek, 1936.

0116   K.u.k.   militär-geographisches   Institut.   *Österreich-Ungarn*   (1:75,000). Sheets: zone 8—colonne 22-24; zone 9—colonne 23-28; zone 10—colonne 23-29; zone 11—colonne 26-30; zone 12—colonne 26-31; zone 13—colonne 27-31. Vienna [n.d.]. Revised edition of these Austro-Hungarian sheets made by the Czechoslovak Vojenský zeměpisný ústav. (1:25,000). Prague, 1927-31 and (1:75,000). Prague, 1921-1938. Sheets: 4264-4268; 4365-4370; 4465-4471; 4568-4572; 4668-4673; 4769-4773; 4870-4873. Revised edition of the Czechoslovak sheets made by the German General Stab des Heeres, Chef des Kriegskarten und Vermessungswesen. Series Ungarn und Slowakei (1:75,000). [Vienna], 1940-1944. Revised edition of the Czechoslovak sheets made by the British Geographical Section, General Staff, War Office. Series no. 4060 (1:75,000). [London], 1941. Revised edition of the Czechoslovak sheets made by the Magyar Királyi Honvéd Térképészeti Intézet. (1:50,000). Budapest, 1942-1944. Revised edition of the Hungarian sheets made by the German General Stab des Heeres, Chef des Kriegskarten und Vermessungswesen. Series Ungarn (1:50,000). [Vienna], 1943-1944.

0116a   K. u. k. militär-geographisches Institut. *Österreich-Ungarn* (1:200,000). Sheets: 49°/39°-42°; 48°/40°-42°. Vienna, 1889. Revised edition made by the German OKH/General Stab des Heeres, Chef des Kriegskarten und Vermessungswesen. Series: Südost-Europa (1:200,000). [Vienna], 1941-1944.

0117   *Kárpátalja-Podkarpatiia* (1:200,000). Budapest: M. Kir. Honvéd térképészeti intézet, 194?.

0118 Krištůfek, Josef. *Distanční mapa Podkarpatské Rusi* (1:200,000). Uzhhorod, 1921.

0119 "Mapa Podkarpatské Rusi a východního Slovenska" (1:750,000). In I. Pan'kevych, *Ukraïns'ki hovory* (ref. 1878).

0120 Petrov, Aleksei L. *Karpatorusskiia mezhevyia nazvaniia iz poloviny XIX i iz nachala XX v.* Prague: České akademie věd a umění, 1929.

0121 ———· *Národopisná mapa Uher podle úředního Lexikonu osad z roku 1773.* Prague, 1924.

0122 ———· *Neznámý rukopisný materiál pro historickou demografii Slovenska a Podkarpatské Rusi z r. 1864-65: Fr. Pesty, 'Helység névtára—Seznam osad Uher'.* In *Věstník Královské české společností nauk,* třída I. Prague, 1926.

0123 ———· *Prediely ugrorusskoi riechi v 1773 g. po offitsial'nym dannym: karty. Materialy dlia istorii ugorskoi Rusi,* vol. 6, pt. 2. In *Sbornik ORISIAN,* vol. 86. St. Petersburg, 1909.

0124 ———·*Sborník Fr. Pestyho 'Helység névtára—Seznam osad v Uhrách' z r. 1864-65, jako pramen historicko-demografických údajů o slovenských a karpatoruských osadách.* Prague, 1927.

0125 *Štanglerova mapa Podkarpatské Rusi* (1:360,000). Košice, 1925.

0126 Tomashivs'kyi, Stefan. "Etnografichna karta Uhors'koï Rusy" (1:300,000). In S. Tomashivs'kyi (ref. 0108).

0127 United States Army Map Service, Corps of Engineers. Series M501 (1:250,000). Sheets: NM34-7, NM34-8, NM34-11, NM34-12, NL34-3. Series N501 (1:250,000). Sheets: NM34-9, NM34-10, NL35-1. Washington, D.C. [n.d.].

0128 Vojenský zeměpisný ústav v Praze. "Přehledná mapa Země podkarpato-ruské" (1:500,000). In *Technická práce v zemi podkarpatoruské* (ref. 1794).

0129 *Východoslovenský kraj* (1:200,000). Second edition. Bratislava: Ústredná správa geodézie a kartografie, 1964.

0130 *Zakarpatskaia oblast'* (1:600,000). Moscow: Glavnoe upravlenie geodezii i kartografii, 1970.

D. Handbooks, guidebooks, yearbooks

This section includes *adresars* (lists of institutions, businesses, administrative offices, cultural leaders), guidebooks, and *schematismi* (lists of churches and priests, schools, and teachers).

0131 *Adresar' Podkarpatskoi Rusy.* Compiled by M. P. Lyla and A. A. Bobul'-skyi. Uzhhorod, 1942.

0132 *Adresar Podkarpatskoi Rusy—Adresář Podkarpatské Rusi.* chast I: Hl. horod Uzhhorod. Compiled by M. P. Lyla. Uzhhorod: Iulii Feldeshii, 1924.

0133 *Dějiny Československa v datech.* Prague: Svoboda, 1968.

0134 Dolenský, Antonín, ed. *Kulturní Adresář ČSR.* Prague, 1936.

0135 Dostál, Jaroslav. *Podkarpatská Rus.* 2nd ed. Knižnice Klubu československých turistů, vol. 6. Prague, 1936.

0136   Gabriel, František. "Podkarpatská Rus." *Průvodce po československé republice*, vol. 3. Prague: Orbis, 1937, pp. 600-737.

0137   *Hof- und Staats-Handbuch der Österreichisch-Ungarischen Monarchie für 1899 and 1913*. Vienna: K.K. Hof- und Staatsdruckerei, 1899 and 1913. Comprehensive description of the structure of the Hungarian Kingdom with names of officials from highest to local administration and all clergy from parish level to hierarchy.

0138   Kroupa, Prokop. *Kroupův průvodce Podkarpatské Rusi*. Prague: KPPR, 1934.

0139   Lizak, Ivan. *Rukovodstvo dlia uchytel'stva narodnykh shkol na Podk. Rus*. Uzhhorod, 1933.

0140   *Magyarország tiszti cím- és névtára*, vols. 47-51. Budapest: Magyar Királyi állami nyomda, 1940-1944. Annual volumes which include separate sections for Subcarpathia listing all civil administrators and clergy.

0141   "Novyi skhematizm uchitelei Podkarpatskoi Rusi, 1.IX.1935." *Zemledîl'skii kalendar' na hod 1936*. Uzhhorod, 1935, pp. 56-100.

0142   *Pam'iatnyky Zakarpattia: dovidnyk-putivnyk*. Uzhhorod: Vyd. Karpaty, 1972.

0143   *Politický kalendář Podkarpatské Rusi*. Uzhhorod: 'Podkarpatské hlasy', 1936.

0144   Révay, Juljan, and Stojan, František. *Schematismus národních škol a učitelů na P.R. podle stavu ze dne 1.I.1935*. Uzhhorod: Viktoria, 1935.

0145   *Ročenka republiky československé*. 12 vols. Prague, 1923-1933. Annual that includes a section on Subcarpathian Rus' in each volume.

0146   *Sbírka průvodců "Orbis": Průvodce po československé republice*, vol. 3: *Slovensko—Podkarpatská Rus*. 2nd ed. Prague: Orbis, 1937.

0147   *Schematismus venerabilis Cleri Graeci Ritus Catholicorum Dioecesis Eperjesiensis*. Košice and Prešov, 1844-1908. Six editions published irregularly.

0148   *Schematismus venerabilis Cleri Graeci Ritus Catholicorum Dioecesis Munkacsiensis*. 25 vols. Buda, Košice, Pest, and Uzhhorod, 1824-1908. Published irregularly, part of an edition appeared in 1938.

0149   *Skhematizm-Adresar' pravoslavnago dukhovenstva i prikhodov Podkarpatskoi Rusi i Vostochnoi Slovakii*. Uzhhorod: Izd. Ivana Vislotskago, 1924.

0150   *Skhematizm inokov China Sv. Vasiliia Velikago ugorskoi oblasti na god 1870*. Uzhhorod, 1870.

0151   *Skhematyzm Hreko-Katolyts'koî dukhovenstva eparkhiî Mukachevskoî, Priashevskoî y Amerytskoî z dodatkom Kryzhevatskoi y Madiarskoî*. Uzhhorod, 1924.

0152   *Skhematyzm uchytel'stva vsîkh shkôl derzhavnŷkh, tserkovnŷkh y pryvatnŷkh Pôdkarpatskoî Rusy*. Compiled by Ivan Vyslotskyi. Mukachevo, 1925.

0153   *Sovetskoe Zakarpat'e: spravochnik*. Uzhhorod: ZOV, 1957.

0154   *Sovetskoe Zakarpat'e: spravochnik-putevoditel'*. Uzhhorod: Karpaty, 1968.

0155   *Uchytel'skii al'manakh*. Compiled by I. Mykhalko, E. Egretskii, and A. Markush. Uzhhorod, 1922-1923. Published for the academic years 1922/23 and 1923/24.

0156   Wiesner, František. *Seznam obcí, státních úřadů, ústavů a podniků země Podkarpatoruské*. Uzhhorod, 1929.

YEARBOOKS

Among useful reference aids are the annual school yearbooks, which frequently include biographies of teachers, statistics on attendance, and lists of courses taught and textbooks used. The following yearbooks are grouped according to towns where the schools were located.

Berehovo

0157 Derzhavna Real'na Gymnaziia. Yearbook published annually under the titles: *Zvîdomlenia* (1919/20-1921/22); *Uvîdomleniia* (1922/23-1927/28); and *Rôchne spravozdania* (1936/37). Compiled by Andrii Alys'kevych (1919-1922) and Mykhayl Grigashii (1923-1926). Uzhhorod and Berehovo, 1920-1937.

Khust

0158 Derzhavna Reformna Real'na Gymnaziia. Yearbook published annually under the titles: *Hodovŷi otchet* (1921/22-1922/23, 1924/25-1937/38) and *Uvîdomleniia* (1923/24). Compiled by Vasylii Sulynchak (1921-1934) and Anton Lukovych (1934-1936). Uzhhorod, 1923; Khust, 1924-1938.

Mukachevo

0159 A Munkácsi Egyházmegye Görög Szertartású Katholikus Népiskolák. Yearbook published for 1878 under the title: *Évkönyve*. Uzhhorod, 1879.

0160 Real'naia Gimnaziia. Yearbook published annually under the title: *Godovyi otchet* (1923/24-1937/38). Compiled by Nikolai Dragula. Mukachevo, 1924-1938.

0161 Derzhavna dvokliasna Torhovel'na Shkola. Yearbook published annually under the title: *Rôchne spravozdanie* (1921/22-1923/24). Mukachevo, 1922-1924.

0162 Derzhavna Torhovel'na Akademiia. Yearbook published annually under the title: *Zvît Dyrektsiî* (1925/26-1937/38). Compiled by Avhustyn Shtefan. Mukachevo, 1926-1938.

0163 Derzhavnaia Koèdukatsiinaia Uchitel'skaia Seminariia. Yearbook published annually under the title: *Godovyi otchet* (1927/28-1937/38). Mukachevo, 1928-1938.

Prešov

0164 Greko-Katolicheskaia Russkaia Real'naia Gimnaziia. Yearbook published annually under the title: *Otchet* (1936/37-1943/44). Prešov, 1937-1944.

0165 Greko-Katolicheskaia Russkaia Uchitel'skaia Seminariia. Yearbook published annually under the title: *Doklad* (1929/30-1937/38). Prešov, 1930-1938.

Uzhhorod

0166 A Királyi Katholikus Főgimnázium. Yearbook published annually under the title: *Értesítvénye* (1871/72-1913/14). Compiled by Ede Szieber (1871/72-1884/84), László Hódoly (1885/86-1899/1900), and Mihály Románecz (1900/01-1913/14). Uzhhorod, 1872-1914.

0167   Rus'ka Derzhavna Real'na Gymnaziia y iei rovnoriadnŷkh oddílov cheshsko-
       slovenskŷkh y madiarskŷkh. Yearbook published annually under the titles:
       Zvîdomlenia (1918/23-1926/27); *Zvît* (1927/28); *Rôchne spravozdanie*
       (1928/29-1933/34); *Hodychnŷi otchet* (1934/35-1939/40); and *Évkönyve*
       (1940/41). Compiled by Andrii Alys'kevych (1918/23) and Vasylii Sulyn-
       chak (1934-1941). Uzhhorod, 1923-1941.
0168   Gimnaziia Chyna OO. Vasyliian. Yearbook published for the academic year
       1937/38 under the title: *Zvidomlennia.* Uzhhorod, 1938.
0169   Derzhavna Rus'ka Torhovel'na Akademiia. Yearbook published annually
       under the title: *Zvît Dyrektsiî* (1922/23-1924/25). Compiled by Avhustyn
       Shtefan. Uzhhorod, 1923-1925.
0170   A Királyi Görög Szertatású Katholikus Éneklész-tanítóképezde. Yearbook
       published annually under the titles: *Értesítője* (1883/84; 1894/95-1917/18);
       and *Emlék Album . . . 100 éves fennállásának jubileumára* (1893/94). Com-
       piled by Gyula Drohobeczky (1883/84), Géza Kaminszky (1894-1917), and
       Avhustyn Voloshyn (1917/18). Uzhhorod, 1884-1918.
0171   Hreko-Katolytska Pivtso-Uchytel'ska Semynarii. Yearbook published annu-
       ally under the title: *Doklad o dîial'nosty* (1921/22-1937/38). Compiled by
       Avhustyn Voloshyn. Uzhhorod, 1922-1938.
0172   A Királyi Katholikus Liceum, Kántortanítóképző-Intézet és Gyakorló Népi-
       skola. Yearbook published for the academic year 1939/40 under the title
       Évkönyve. Compiled by Ernő Dunda. Uzhhorod, 1940.
0173   A Görög Katholikus Tanítóképző, polgári és elemi leányiskolák s az ezekkel
       kapcsolatos nevelőintézetek. Yearbook published annually under the title:
       Értesítője (1909/10-1917/18). Compiled by Gyula Melles. Uzhhorod,
       1910-1918.
0174   Hreko-Katolytska Uchytel'ska Semynariia Dîvchat. *Almanakh* commemo-
       rating the years 1902-1929. Uzhhorod, 1930. Yearbook published annually
       under the titles: *Zvît* (1931/32-1933/34); *Zvîdomlenia* (1934/35-1937/38);
       and *Hodychnŷi otchet—Évkönyve* (1938/39). Compiled by Heorhii Chur-
       hovych (1938/39).

II. SERIALS

A. Newspapers

The items in this section and in section B represent most of the titles that have appeared in Subcarpathian Rus' and the Prešov Region. Also listed are the leading
publications of the Bačka-Rusyns and American-Rusyns, which contain much valuable information on the homeland. Not included are the organs of trade groups,
which have little or no material pertinent to the nationality problem. For fuller
descriptions of each serial (publisher, editors, periodicity, and size, for example), see
the bibliography by Zhyvotko (ref. 0083) and the section "Periodika" in the bibliography by Lelekach and Haraida (ref. 0033).

0175   *Amierykanskii russkii vîstnyk—Amerikansky russky viestnik* (Mahoney
       City, Pa., Scranton, Pa., New York, Homestead, Pa., 1892-1952).

0176 *Biuleten' presovoï sluzhby Karpats'koï Ukraïny* (Khust, 1939).
0177 *The Carpathian* (Pittsburgh, 1941-1943).
0178 *Česko-ruský svaz* (Mukachevo, 1921).
0179 *Den'* (New York, 1922-1927).
0180 *Dnevnik* (Prague, 1931-1939).
0181 *Druzhestvennyi viestnik* (Uzhhorod, 1924-1938).
0182 *Golos russkago naroda* (Prešov, 1919).
0183 *Görög katholikus hírlap* (Budapest, 1903-1905).
0184 *Görög katholikus szemle* (Uzhhorod, 1899-1918).
0185 *Gospodar'* (Uzhhorod, 1934-1936).
0186 *Handia* (Uzhhorod, 1939-1944).
0187 *Határszéli újság* (Uzhhorod, 1924-1925).
0188 *Hazeta dlia narodnŷkh uchytelei* (Budapest, 1868-1873).
0189 *Hlas východu* (Uzhhorod, 1928-1936).
0190 *Holos zhyttia* (Uzhhorod, 1928-1938).
0191 *Jedinstvo* (Gary, Indiana, 1942-1943).
0192 *Karpat* (Uzhhorod, 1873-1886).
0193 *Kárpat* (Uzhhorod, 1919).
0194 *Kárpátalja* (Uzhhorod, 1926).
0195 *Kárpáti hiradó* (Mukachevo, 1924-1933).
0196 *Kárpáti lapok* (Uzhhorod, 1895-1903).
0197 *Kárpáti magyar hírlap* (Mukachevo, 1920-1934).
0198 *Kárpáti szinházi élet* (Uzhhorod, 1930-1933).
0199 *Kárpáti vasárnap* (Uzhhorod, 1939-1941).
0200 *Karpato-rus'kii vîstnyk* (Uzhhorod, 1918-1919).
0201 *Karpatoruský pokrok* (Uzhhorod, 1924).
0202 *Karpatorusskii golos* (Uzhhorod, 1932-1944).
0203 *Karpato-russkii vîstnyk* (Uzhhorod, 1921-1923).
0204 *Karpatorusskii zemledielets'* (Mukachevo, 1924-1926).
0205 *Karpatorusskije novosti* (New York, 1943-1945).
0206 *Karpatorusskoe slovo* (Uzhhorod, 1934-1938).
0207 *Karpato-russkoe slovo* (New York, 1935-1938).
0208 *Karpato-ukrajinská presa* (Prague, 1939).
0209 *Karpato-ukrajinská svoboda* (Prague, 1939).
0210 *Karpats'ka iskra* (Mukachevo and Prague, 1935).
0211 *Karpatska nedîlia* (Uzhhorod, 1939-1941).
0212 *Karpats'ka pravda* (Uzhhorod, 1922-1933; 1935-1938).
0213 *Karpatska Rus'* (Uzhhorod, 1921).
0214 *Karpatska Rus'* (Yonkers, 1939-present).
0215 *Karpats'ka Ukraïna* (Khust, 1939).
0216 *Karpatskaia Rus'* (Uzhhorod, 1921).
0217 *Karpats'kyi proletar* (Uzhhorod, 1935-1938).
0218 *Kelet* (Uzhhorod, 1888-1901).
0219 *Ku-Ku* (Mukachevo, 1931-1933).
0220 *Lemko* (Yonkers, N.Y., 1926-1939).
0221 *Magyar kárpát* (Uzhhorod, 1875-1876).
0222 *Molodaia Rus'* (Uzhhorod, 1938).
0223 *Munkás újság* (Uzhhorod, 1924-1925).

0224 *Narod* (Uzhhorod, 1920-1921).
0225 *Narodnaia gazeta* (Prešov, 1924-1935).
0226 *Narodnaia obrana* (Pittsburgh, 1915-1916).
0227 *Narodnia syla* (Uzhhorod, 1936-1938).
0228 *Narodnia volia* (Prague and Velykyi Bychkiv, 1938).
0229 *Narodnoe russkoe slovo* (Mukachevo, 1929-1938).
0230 *Nase otecsesztvo* (Prešov, 1916-1919).
0231 *Nash avangard* (Prague, 1938).
0232 *Nash karpatorusskii golos* (Uzhhorod, 1934-1935).
0233 *Nash put'* (Uzhhorod, 1935-1938).
0234 *Nashe viis'ko v SRSR* (Buzuluk, 1943-1944).
0235 *Natsiia* (Rakhiv and Khust, 1939).
0236 *Nastup* (Uzhhorod, Khust, and Prague, 1938-1944).
0237 *Nedîlia* (Budapest, 1898-1919).
0238 *Nedîlia* (Uzhhorod, 1935-1938).
0239 *Nedîlia* (Uzhhorod, 1941-1944).
0240 *Nova svoboda* (Uzhhorod and Khust, 1938-1939).
0241 *Nove zhyttia* (Prešov, 1952-present).
0242 *Novoje vremja* (Uzhhorod, 1925-1933).
0243 *Novŷi svît* (Uzhhorod, 1871-1872).
0244 *Podkarpatská Rus* (Uzhhorod, 1921).
0245 *Podkarpatská Rus* (Uzhhorod, 1925-1926).
0246 *Podkarpatskaia Rus'* (Mukachevo, 1925-1936).
0247 *Podkarpatské hlasy* (Uzhhorod, 1925-1938).
0248 *Podkarpatské listy* (Uzhhorod, 1921-1922).
0249 *Podkarpatské noviny* (Berehovo, 1924).
0250 *Postup* (Prague, 1931-1933).
0251 *Prashevskaia Rus'* (Prešov, 1938-1939).
0252 *Pratsiuiucha molod'* (Uzhhorod, 1926-1936).
0253 *Pravda* (Uzhhorod, 1920-1922).
0254 *Pravda* (Uzhhorod, 1921).
0255 *Pravoslavnyi karpatorusskii viestnik* (Uzhhorod, 1935-1938).
0256 *Přehled z Karpatské Ukrajiny* (Khust, 1939).
0257 *Prosvîta—Prosvita* (McKeesport, Pa., 1917-present).
0258 *Robitnyche-selians'ka pravda* (Uzhhorod, 1928-1929).
0259 *Rodina* (Cleveland, 1927-1939).
0260 *Rus'* (Prešov, 1921-1923).
0261 *Rusin* (Mukachevo, 1938-1939).
0262 *Rusin* (New York, 1952-1960).
0263 *Rusin—The Ruthenian* (Philadelphia, Pa., Allegheny, Pa., and Pittsburgh, Pa., 1910-1916).
0264 *Rus'ka Krayna* (Uzhhorod, 1919).
0265 *Rus'ka nyva* (Uzhhorod, 1920-1924).
0266 *Rus'ka pravda* (Mukachevo, 1919).
0267 *Rus'ko-Kraïns'ka pravda* (Budapest and Mukachevo, 1919).
0268 *Rusky novynky* (Ruski Krstur, 1929-1941).
0269 *Russkaia narodnaia gazeta* (Prešov, 1937-1938).

0270 *Russkaia pravda* (Uzhhorod, 1938-1940).
0271 *Russkaia zaria* (Novi Sad, 1934-1940).
0272 *Russkaia zemlia* (Uzhhorod, 1919-1938).
0273 *Russkii narodnyi golos* (Uzhhorod, 1934-1938).
0274 *Russkii pravoslavnyi viestnik* (Uzhhorod, 1921-1922).
0275 *Russkii vîstnyk* (Uzhhorod, 1924-1939).
0276 *Russkii vîstnyk—Russian Messenger* (Pittsburgh, 1916-present).
0277 *Russkii zemledielets'* (Košice, 1928-1937).
0278 *Russkoe slovo* (Košice, 1919-1920)—supplement to *Slovenský východ.*
0279 *Russkoe slovo* (Prešov, 1924-1938).
0280 *Russkoe slovo* (Uzhhorod, 1940-1944).
0281 *Rusyn* (Uzhhorod, 1920-1921).
0282 *Rusyn* (Uzhhorod, 1923).
0283 *Rusyn* (Rakhiv, 1938).
0284 *Ruszinszkói népszava* (Uzhhorod and Berehovo, 1921-1925).
0285 *Selo* (Uzhhorod, 1920-1924).
0286 *Slovan* (Uzhhorod, 1923).
0287 *Slovo naroda* (Prešov, 1931-1932).
0288 *Sova* (Uzhhorod, 1871).
0289 *Sova* (Uzhhorod, 1923).
0290 *Svît* (Uzhhorod, 1867-1871).
0291 *Svoboda* (Uzhhorod, 1922-1938).
0292 *Svoboda—Liberty* (New York, 1944).
0293 *Svobodnoe slovo* (Mukachevo and Uzhhorod, 1931-1935).
0294 *Tisa* (Sevliush, 1936-1938).
0295 *Tserkovnaia gazeta* (Buda, 1856-1858).
0296 *Tserkovnaia pravda* (Mukachevo and Khust, 1925-1927).
0297 *Tserkovnyi viestnik dlia Rusinov avstriiskoi derzhavy* (Buda, 1858).
0298 *Ukraïns'ke slovo* (Uzhhorod, 1932-1938).
0299 *Úřední noviny* (Uzhhorod, 1919-1938).
0300 *Uriadova hazeta* (Uzhhorod, 1920-1938).
0301 *Uriadovŷi vîstnyk* (Uzhhorod, 1921-1938).
0302 *Užhorodské noviny* (Uzhhorod, 1920).
0303 *Visnyk Narodnoï Rady Zakarpats'koi Ukraïny* (Uzhhorod, 1944-1945).
0304 *Vostok—The East* (Perth Amboy, N.J., 1920-1950).
0305 *Vpered* (Uzhhorod, 1922-1938).
0305a *Zakarpats'ka pravda* (Uzhhorod, 1944-present).
0305b *Zakarpats'ka Ukraïna* (Uzhhorod, 1944-1945).
0306 *Zaria* (Čirč, 1937).
0307 *Zemlediel'skaia politika* (Uzhhorod, 1927-1938).
0308 *Zemlia i volia* (Uzhhorod, 1934-1938).
0309 *Zorja* (Uzhhorod, 1920-1931).

B. Journals

0310 *Al'manakh vozrozhdenstsev* (Prague, 1933, 1936).
0311 *Blahovîstnyk* (Uzhhorod and Khust, 1921-1944).
0312 *Blahovîstnyk* (Košice and Bratislava, 1965-present).

0313   *Carpatica* (Prague, 1936-1940).
0314   *Do peremohy* (Uzhhorod, 1935-1936).
0315   *Dobrŷi pastŷr'* (Uzhhorod, 1932-1942).
0316   *Duklia* (Prešov, 1953-present).
0317   *Dushpastŷr'* (Uzhhorod, 1924-1941).
0318   *Felvidéki sion* (Uzhhorod, 1889-1891).
0219   *Görög katholikus népiskola* (Uzhhorod, 1913).
0320   *Holos molodi* (Uzhhorod, 1938).
0321   *Hoverlia* (Khust, 1939).
0322   *Iunoshestvo* (Mukachevo, 1927-1938).
0323   *Iunyi drug* (Uzhhorod, 1929-1930).
0324   *Karpats'ka molod'* (Velyka Kopania, 1936-1937).
0325   *Karpats'ka sich* (Toronto, 1950-1955).
0326   *Karpatskii krai* (Uzhhorod, 1924-1925).
0327   *Karpatskii sviet* (Uzhhorod, 1928-1938).
0328   *Karpaty* (Uzhhorod, 1958-1959).
0329   *Kul'tura* (Mukachevo, 1921).
0330   *Kvas* (Mukachevo, 1929).
0331   *Lelia* (Uzhhorod, 1926).
0332   *Lipa* (Mukachevo, 1921-1928).
0333   *Lyteraturna nedîlia* (Uzhhorod, 1941-1944).
0334   *Magyar tanítójelölt* (Uzhhorod, 1908).
0335   *Molodaia Rus'* (Prague, 1930-1931).
0336   *Molode zhyttia* (Uzhhorod, 1938).
0337   *Most mezi východem a západem* (Khust, 1936-1938).
0338   *Myssiinŷi vîstnyk* (Uzhhorod, 1931-1938).
0339   *Narodna shkola* (Uzhhorod, 1939-1944).
0340   *Narodnaia shkola* (Mukachevo, 1921-1938).
0341   *Nash rodnŷi krai* (Uzhhorod, 1923-1939).
0342   *Nasha shkola* (Mukachevo, 1935-1937).
0343   *Nasha zemlia* (Uzhhorod, 1927-1928).
0344   *Nashi stremleniia* (Mukachevo, 1935-1936).
0345   *Nauka* (Uzhhorod, 1897-1922).
0346   *Naukovi zapysky UDU* (Uzhhorod, 1947-present).
0347   *Naukovyi zbirnyk MUKS* (Bratislava, Prešov, and Svidník, 1965-present).
0348   *Naukovŷi zbornyk TP* (Uzhhorod, 1922-1938).
0349   *Nedîlia Rusyna* (Uzhhorod, 1923).
0350   *Nova dumka* (Vukovar, 1971-present).
0351   *Nova stsena* (Khust, 1939).
0352   *Nové obzory* (Prešov, 1959-present).
0353   *Ouchytel'* (Uzhhorod, 1867).
0354   *Pchôlka* (Uzhhorod, 1922-1932).
0355   *Podkarpatska Rus'* (Uzhhorod, 1924-1936).
0356   *Podkarpatskii student* (Prague, 1922).
0357   *Podkarpatoruská revue* (Bratislava, 1936-1938).
0358   *Plastun—Junák—Czerkész* (Uzhhorod, 1923-1938).
0359   *Pravo* (Uzhhorod, 1937).
0360   *Pravoslavnaia Karpatskaia Rus'* (Ladimirová, 1928-1934).

0361 *Pravoslavnaia Rus'* (Ladimirová and Jordanville, N.Y., 1935-present).
0362 *Proboiem* (Prague, 1934-1944).
0363 *Prosvîta* (Uzhhorod, 1925).
0364 *Radians'ke Zakarpattia* (Uzhhorod, 1951-1957).
0365 *Ridne slovo* (Ruski Krstur, 1933-1941).
0366 *Rus'ka molodezh* (Uzhhorod, 1942-1944).
0367 *Russkaia molodezh'* (Prešov, 1920-1921).
0368 *Russkaia shkola* (Prešov, 1926-1932).
0369 *Russkii skaut* (Uzhhorod, 1935).
0370 *Samoupravlenie—Samoupráva—Önkormányzat* (Uzhhorod, 1931-1935).
0371 *Shvetlosts* (Novi Sad, 1952-1954, 1966-present).
0372 *Svitlo* (Mukachevo, 1933).
0373 *Svobodnoe slovo* (Newark, 1959-present).
0374 *Tysa* (Munich, 1956-?).
0375 *Uchytel'* (Uzhhorod, 1920-1938).
0376 *Uchytel's'kyi holos* (Mukachevo, 1930-1938).
0377 *Vînochok* (Uzhhorod, 1920-1924).
0378 *Visnyk Karpats'koho soiuza* (New York, 1970-present).
0379 *Visti Etnografichnoho tovarystva Pidk. Rusy* (Mukachevo, 1935-1936).
0380 *Vîstnyk posviashchennoie Rusynov avstriîskoî derzhavŷ* (Vienna, 1850-
      1866).
0381 *Vistnyk mukachivs'koï eparkhiï v Chekho-Slovats'kii republytsi* (Khust,
      1939).
0382 *Vîstnyk narodnŷkh uchytelev* (Budapest, 1942-1944).
0383 *Vîstnyk Sokol'skoî zhupŷ Podkarpatskoî Rusy—Věstnik Sokolské župy Pod-
      karpatské Rusi* (Uzhhorod, 1923-1924).
0384 *Vîstnyk uchytel'stva horozhanskŷkh shkôl Podkarpats'koî Rusy* (Muka-
      chevo, 1932).
0385 *Zapovit sv. Kyryla i Mefodiia* (Prešov, 1958-present).
0386 *Zapysky naukovoho tovarystva KSUT* (Prešov, 1972-present).
0387 *Zaria* (Uzhhorod, 1938).
0388 *Zemskii pravytel'stvennŷi vîstnyk dlia korolevstva Ouhorshchynŷ* (Buda,
      1850-1859).
0389 *Zemskii vîstnyk* (Zemský veštník) dlia Podkarpatskoi Rusy (Uzhhorod, 1927-
      1938).
0390 *Zhivaia mysl'* (Prague, 1932-1936).
0391 *Zoria—Hajnal* (Uzhhorod, 1941-1943).

C. Almanacs

The almanacs, or *kalendars,* are an important source of information on the national
movement and a mechanism used by the intelligentsia to reach large numbers of
people. Besides data on the calendar, weather, and practical information, each issue
usually includes historical studies revealing popular ideals and conceptions, as well
as biographies of leading national figures. The entries are divided into two groups:
first, those almanacs published annually by organizations; second, individual titles.

ORGANIZATIONS

0392 Aktsiinoe Obshchestvo (later Tovarystvo) Unio.

Almanac published annually under the titles: *Tserkovnŷi kalendar'* (1903-1918); *Kalendar'* (1919-1927); *Iubyleinŷi yliustrovanŷi kalendar'* (1928); *Narodnŷi yliustrovanŷi kalendar'* (1929-1933). Compiled by Avhustyn Voloshyn (1902-1917, 1919-1924); Marko Trepet (1928); Viktor Zheltvai (1918). Uzhhorod, 1902-1932.

0393 Obshchestvo Handia.

Almanac published annually under the title: *Kalendar'* (1940-1944). Compiled by Iulii Zoltan (1940); Evgenii Gabriel (1941-1944). Budapest, 1939-1943.

0394 Obshchestvo imeni Aleksandra Dukhnovicha.

Almanac published annually under the title: *Russkii narodnyi kalendar'* (1928-1937, 1941). Compiled by Stepan A. Fentsik (1928-1934). Uzhhorod, 1927-1940.

0395 Obshchestvo sv. Vasiliia Velikago.

Almanac published annually under the titles: *Mîsiatsoslov* (1867-1889); *Krestnŷi mîsiatsoslov* (1890-1893); *Tserkovnŷi mîsiatsoslov* (1894-1902). Compiled by Iulii Drohobets'kyi (1893); Dymytrii Gebei (1894-1895); Iulii Chuchka (1897-1901); Avhustyn Voloshyn (1901-1902). Uzhhorod, 1866-1901.

0396 Organizacija Greko Kaftoličeskich Karpatorusskich Spomahajuščich Bratstv 'Svobody'.

Almanac published annually under the title: *Kalendar' 'Svobody'* (1924-1929, 1933-1941). Compiled by Basil Izak (1924); Orestes Koman (1926); Joann Petach (1927-1935); Georgij Bezinec (1936); Stephen Banitsky (1937-1938); Michael Logoda (1939); John Dickun (1940); Emery P. Konick (1941). Perth Amboy, N.J., 1924-1941.

0397 Podkarpatskoe Obshchestvo Nauk.

Almanac published annually under the title: *Velykyi sel'sko-hospodarskyi kalendar'* (1942-1944). Compiled by Ivan Haraida. Uzhhorod, 1941-1943.

0398 Sojedinenije Greko-Kaftoličeskich Russkich Bratstv.

Almanac published annually under the title: *Amerykanskii russkii mîsiatsoslov—Kalendar Sojedinenija* (1896-present). Compiled by Pavel Žatkovič (1896-1914); Iurion Thegza; Stefan Varzaly (1930-1937); Michael Roman (1938-1976). New York; Homestead, Pa.; Munhall, Pa., 1896-present.

0399 Sokol'skoje otd. Sojedinenija Greko-Kaftoličeskich Russkich Bratstv.

Almanac published annually under the title: *Mîsiatsoslov-Kalendar'* (1919-1936). Compiled by Peter Maczkov. Homestead, Pa., 1919-1936.

0400 Tovarystvo 'Prosvita'.

Almanac published annually under the titles: *Narodnŷi yliustrovanŷi kalendar'* (1923, 1928-1933); *Hospodarskii rodynnŷi kalendar'* (1924-1927); *Kalendar' 'Prosvîta'* (1934-1938). Uzhhorod, 1922-1937.

0401 Uchytel's'ka Hromada.

Almanac published annually under the title: *Kalendar'* (1934/35-1937/38). Compiled by Frants Ahii. Mukachevo, 1934-1937.

INDIVIDUAL TITLES

0402 *Amerykanskii russkii kalendar' na 1908 hod.* Compiled by Emylii A. Kubek. Uzhhorod, 1907.

0403 *Hospodarskii kalendar' na 1942 hod.* Compiled by H. P. Dolmatovskii. Uzhhorod, 1941.

0404 *Hutsul'skii kalendar' na 1942 hod.* Compiled and published by Edmond Zhegor. Velykyi Bochkov, 1941.

0405 *Iubileinyi gospodarskii kalendar' na 1929 god.* Compiled by Antonii Sedlachek. Mukachevo: 'Zemlediel'skaia politika', 1929.

0406 *Kalendar'* (1937-1938). Uzhhorod: Russkaia natsional'no-avtonomnaia partiia, 1936-1937.

0407 *Kalendar' 'Blahovîstnyka'* (1927-1944). Compiled by M. Stankanynets' (1933); I. Satmarii (1934); Iov Ham (1941); Vartolomei Dudash (1942). Uzhhorod, 1927-1944.

0408 *Kalendar'—Ku-Ku na god 1933.* Mukachevo, 1932.

0409 *Kalendar' 'Myssiinoho vîstnyka'* (1935-1944). Compiled by Aleksander Il'nyts'kii. Uzhhorod, 1934-1943.

0410 *Kal'endar na rok 1936.* Compiled by Andrej Brodij. Uzhhorod, 1935.

0411 *Kalendar' 'Pravdy'; Robitnycho-selianskyi kalendar' 'Karpats'koï pravdy'* (1921, 1923, 1925, 1927, 1928, 1932, 1933, 1938). Compiled by Ivan Mondok [Ivan Il'kiv] (1921-1928); Oleksa Borkaniuk (1932-1933); Mykola Klympotiuk (1938). Vienna and Uzhhorod: Komunistychna partiia Podk. Rusy, 1920-1937.

0412 *Kalendar 'Pryiatel' shkoliara'* (1925-1926). Compiled by Leonyd Bachyns'kyi and Pavel Kukuruza. Uzhhorod, 1924-1925.

0413 *Kalendar' robitnykiv i selian na rik 1938.* Uzhhorod: Robitnycha Akademiia na Pidk. Rusy, 1937.

0414 *Kalendar 'Vperedu' na rok 1923.* Uzhhorod: Podkarpats'ka rus'ka sotsiial-demokratychna partiia, 1922.

0415 *Kalendar 'Zemli i voli' na rik 1936.* Uzhhorod, 1935.

0416 *Karmannyi kalendar' na 1939-40 uchebnyi god.* Uzhhorod, 1939.

0417 *Karpatorusskii kalendar' 'Lemko'* (1922-1923). Compiled by Dmitrii Vislotskii. Uzhhorod, 1921-1922.

0418 *Karpatorusskij narodnyj kalendar'* (1944-1946). Perth Amboy, N.J.: Vestal Publishing Co., 1944-1946.

0419 *Krestnŷi kalendar'* (1909-1915). Compiled by Ioann Kizak. Uzhhorod, 1908-1914.

0420 *Kyshen'kovyi kalendaryk Kolos na 1938-39 shkil'nyi rik.* Uzhhorod, 1938.

0421 *Mîsiatsoslov dlia russkykh Uhorskiia krainŷ 1864-1866.* Compiled by Aleksander Gomichkov (1864-1865); Anatolii Kralitskii and Viktor Kimak (1866). Uzhhorod, 1863-1865.

0422 *Mîsiatsoslov dlia uhorskykh rusynov na hod 1854.* Compiled by Aleksander Dukhnovych. Uzhhorod, 1854.

0423 *Mîsiatsoslov hospodarskii L'vovskii na hod . . . 1857.* Compiled by Aleksander Dukhnovych. L'viv, 1856.

0424 *Narodni kalendárj vszych szvjatěch na 1895-i rok.* Compiled by Joszif Fesztory. Uzhhorod, 1894.

0425   *Narodnŷi podkarpatorusskii kalendar'* (1917-1918). Uzhhorod: Iulii Felde-
        shii, 1916-1917.
0426   *Nash kalendar na 1941 rik.* Compiled by Vasylii Potushniak. Sevliush, 1940.
0427   *Obrazkovŷi kalendar' 'Nedîlia'* (1908-1918). Compiled by Mykhail Vrabel'.
        Budapest, 1907-14.
0428   *Podkarpatorusskii zemledîl'skii kalendar'* (1925, 1926, 1934-1944). Com-
        piled by Antonii Bobul'skii (1925); Ivan Brodii (1926); Mikhail Demko
        (1934-1944). Uzhhorod: Autonomnŷi zemledîl'skii soiuz, 1924-1944.
0429   *Podkarpatskii kalendar'* (1897, 1898, 1900-1906). Uzhhorod: Vartolomei
        Ieger, 1896-1905.
0430   *Podkarpatszkij kalendar 'Nase Otecsesztvo' na hod 1917.* Compiled by
        Ioann Kizak. Prešov, 1916.
0431   *Pozdravlenie rusynov na novŷi hod 1850.* Compiled by Aleksander Dukhno-
        vych. Przemyśl, 1850.
0432   *Pravoslavnyi russkii kalendar' na 1936 god.* Uzhhorod, 1935.
0433   *Russkii kalendar' na 1942 god.* Compiled by Ernest Malinich. Uzhhorod,
        1941.
0434   *Russkii zemledîl'skii kalendar'* (1922-1923). Compiled by Iosif Kaminskii.
        Uzhhorod: Podkarpatskii zemledîl'skii soiuz, 1921-1923.
0435   *Sotacki kalendar na rok 1938.* Compiled by Andrei Brodii. Uzhhorod, 1938.
0436   *Uchenicheskii kalendar' na 1928-29.* Uzhhorod: O-vo Shkol'naia pomoshch',
        1928.
0437   *Velikii zabavnyi i gospodarskii kalendar' na 1930 god.* Compiled by Antonii
        Sedlachek. Mukachevo, 1930.
0438   *Velykyi zabavnŷi y hospodarskii kalendar' na 1938 hod.* Uzhhorod: 'No-
        vina', 1937.
0439   *Vseobshchii kalendar' na 1941 god.* Compiled by G. P. Dolmatovskii. Uzh-
        horod, 1940.
0440   *Vseobshchii ugrorusskii kalendar' na 1940 god.* Compiled by G. P. Dolma-
        tovskii. Uzhhorod, 1939.

D. Minutes and proceedings

In this section are listed the published chronicles, minutes (protocols), and reports
issued by national organizations.

CZECHOSLOVAK GOVERNMENT MINISTRY OF EDUCATION, PRAGUE

0441   "Protokol iz iazykovoï konferentsiï v Prazi, 17.III.1931, pid provodom
        ministra shkil'nytstva Dra Ivana Derera u spravi upravyl'nennia iazyko-
        vykh vidnosyn v shkil'nytstvi na Pidk. Rusy." *Podkarpatska Rus',* vol. 7,
        nos. 2-3 (Uzhhorod, 1931), pp. 56-61.

GALITSKO-RUSSKOE BLAGOTVORITEL'NOE OBSHCHESTVO, ST. PETERSBURG

0442   *Otchet o dieiatel'nosti za 1912 god.* St. Petersburg, 1913.
0443   *Otchet o dieiatel'nosti za 1913-1914 god.* St. Petersburg, 1914.

KONGRESS DLIA ORGANIZATSII AVTONOMII KATOLICHESKOI TSERKVI VENGRII, BUDAPEST.

0444 "Otchet o vtorom periodie zasiedanii Kongressa v otnoshenii ko vsiem ugor-skim greko-katolikam i osobenno v otnoshenii k ugorskim-russkim." Compiled by Konstantin Kustodiev. *Pravoslavnoe obozrienie,* nos. 3 and 4 (Moscow, 1872), pp. 450-476 and 624-650. Excerpts in English by Peter I. Zeedick. *Back in Eighteen Seventy-One.* Homestead, Pa.: ARV, 1933.

NARODNYJ KONGRESS AMERIKANSKICH RUSINOV, HOMESTEAD, PA.

0445 *Protocol-Zapisnica iz zasidanij Narodnoho Kongressa Amerikanskich Rusi-nov, pod ochranoju i rukovodstvom Amerikanskoj Narodnoj Rady Uhro Rusinov, poderžannoho v Homestead, Pa., dna 15-16-ho Septembra, 1919-ho roka.* Homestead, Pa., 1919.

OBSHCHESTVO IMENI ALEKSANDRA DUKHNOVICHA, UZHHOROD

Chronicles

0446 "Dieiatel'nost' OIAD." For 1926. *Russkii narodnyi kalendar' OIAD na god 1927.* Compiled by I. Kaminskii. Uzhhorod, 1926, pp. 43-49. For 1926-1927. *Russkii narodnyi kalendar' na god 1928.* Compiled by S. A. Fentsik. Izdanie OIAD, No. 31. Uzhhorod, 1927, pp. 47-63. For 1929-1930. Com-piled by S. A. Fentsik. *Karpatskii sviet,* vol. 3, nos. 5-6 (Uzhhorod, 1930), pp. 988-1002. Issued separately in Izdanie OIAD, no. 77. Uzhhorod, 1929. For 1930-1931. Compiled by S. A. Fentsik. *Karpatskii sviet,* vol. 4, nos. 5-7 (Uzhhorod, 1931), pp. 1168-1175. Issued separately in Izdanie OIAD, no. 104. Uzhhorod, 1932. For 1931-1932. Compiled by S. A. Fentsik. Iz-danie OIAD, no. 108. Uzhhorod, 1932. For 1933. Compiled by S. A. Fen-tsik. *Karpatskii sviet,* vol. 6, nos. 1-2 (Uzhhorod, 1933), pp. 1365-1367. For 1935-1936. *Russkii narodnyi kalendar' na god 1937.* Compiled by S. A. Fentsik. Izdanie OIAD, no. 115. Uzhhorod, 1936, pp. 59-67. For 1937. Compiled by S. A. Fentsik. *Karpatskii sviet,* vol. 7, no. 1 (Uzhhorod, 1938).

0447 Shovsh, I. D. "Dieiatel'nost' chital'ni imeni A. V. Dukhnovicha v Svalia-vie." *Karpatorusskiia dostizheniia.* Edited by A. V. Popov. Mukachevo, 1930, pp. 159-168.

0448 "Khronika kul'turnoi dieiatel'nosti O-va im. Aleksandra Dukhnovicha." Printed on the last pages of each issue of *Karpatskii sviet,* vols. 1-7 (Uzh-horod, 1928-1938).

Minutes (Protocols)

0449 "Protokoly OIAD." For "27.XII.1923, v Uzhgorodie." *Karpatskii krai,* vol. 1, nos. 3-4 (1923-1924), pp. 35-39. For "Chetvertoe obshchee so-branie, 27.VI.1927, v Priashevie." *Karpatskii sviet,* vol. 1, no. 5 (Uzh-horod, 1928), pp. 101-107. For "Godichnoe obshchee sobranie, 4.VI.1928, v Mukachevie." *Karpatskii sviet,* vol. 2, nos. 5-6 (Uzhhorod, 1929), pp. 606-621. For "Sed'moe obshchee sobranie, 2.VI.1929, v Uzhgorodie." *Karpatskii sviet,* vol. 3, nos. 5-6 (Uzhhorod, 1930), pp. 972-987. For

"Vos'moe obshchee sobranie, 1.VI.1930, v Uzhgorodie." *Karpatskii sviet,* vol. 4, nos. 5-7 (Uzhhorod, 1931), pp. 1149-1167. For "Deviatoe godichnoe obshchee sobranie, 7.VI.1931, v Mukachevie." *Karpatskii sviet,* vol. 5, no. 6 (Uzhhorod, 1932), pp. 1315-1347. Reprinted in Izdanie OIAD, no. 108. Uzhhorod, 1932, pp. 3-35. For "Desiatoe godichnoe sobranie, 5.VI. 1932, v Khustie." *Karpatskii sviet,* vol. 6, nos 1-2 (Uzhhorod, 1933), pp. 1357-1365.

Reports

0450 Fentsik, Stepan. "Doklad sekretaria-dieloproizvoditelia obshchemu sobraniiu, 27.VI.1926, v Mukachevie." *Russkii narodnyi kalendar' OIAD na god 1927.* Uzhhorod, 1926. pp. 49-75.

0451 ———· "Doklad sekretaria-dieloproizvoditelia OIAD na iubileinom kongressie OIAD, 2.VI.1929, v Uzhgorodie." *Karpatskii sviet,* vol. 2, nos. 5-6 (Uzhhorod, 1929), pp. 622-632.

0452 ———· "Doklad sekretaria-dieloproizvoditelia na desiatom obshchem sobranii OIAD, 5.VI.1932, v Khustie." *Karpatskii sviet,* vol. 5, no. 6 (Uzhhorod, 1932), pp. 1348-1351.

PEDAGOGICHESKE TOVARYSTVO PODKARPATSKOI RUSY, UZHHOROD

Chronicles

0453 "Dîial'nost' Pedagogychnoho Tovarystva od 8.V.1926 do 6.X.1929." *Podkarpatska Rus',* vol. 5, no. 7 (Uzhhorod, 1928), pp. 138-143.

0454 "Spravozdania o diial'nosti Pedagogychnoho T-va Podk. Rusy do kontsia ianuara 1926." *Podkarpatska Rus',* vol. 3, no. 2 (Uzhhorod, 1926).

Minutes (Protocols)

0455 "Protokoly z'îzd." For 9 May 1926. *Podkarpatska Rus',* vol. 3, no. 6 (Uzhhorod, 1926), pp. 145-152. For 6 October 1928. *Podkarpatska Rus',* vol. 5, no. 8-9 (Uzhhorod, 1928), pp. 169-174.

PODKARPATORUSSKII NARODOPROSVIETITEL'NYI SOIUZ, UZHHOROD

0456 *Doklad o dieiatel'nosti Kraevago narodoprosvietitel'nago soiuza na 1929 god.* Edited by Pavel Fedor. Uzhhorod, 1930.

PODKARPATSKOE OBSHCHESTVO NAUK, UZHHOROD

0457 "Protokoly." For 26 January 1941. *Zoria-Hajnal,* vol. 1, nos. 1-2 (Uzhhorod, 1941), pp. 180-184. For 25 May 1941. *Zoria-Hajnal,* vol. 1, nos. 1-2 (Uzhhorod, 1941), pp. 184-186.

TSENTRAL'NAIA RUSSKAIA NARODNAIA RADA, UZHHOROD

0458 *Protokoly obshchago sobraniia podkarpatskikh russkikh rad i pervykh 5-ti zasiedanii Tsentral'noi russkoi narodnoi rady.* Uzhhorod, 1919. Reprinted in Latin script in: *Karpatorusskije novosti,* vol. 2, no. 7 (New York, 1944), pp. 3-6. Fifth session reprinted in Z. Peška and J. Markov, eds., "Příspěvek k ústavním dějinám Podkarpatské Rusi." *Bratislava,* vol. 4 (Bratislava, 1930), pp. 419-422.

TOVARYSTVO 'PROSVITA,' UZHHOROD

0459 *Zvît yz dîial'nosty tovarystva "Prosvîta" Podkarpatskoî Rusy za chas od 9. maia 1920. do 31. maia 1921.* Uzhhorod: Vŷd. TP, 1921.

TOVARYSTVO UCHYTELÎV HOROZHAN'SKYKH SHKÔL, UZHHOROD

0460 "Protokoly." Appear in almost every issue of *Podkarpatska Rus'* (Uzhhorod, 1924-1936).

UCHITEL'SKOE TOVARISHCHESTVO, UZHHOROD

0461 "Otchet o dieiatel'nosti 'Iazykovoi komissii,' 2.II.1928." *Karpatskii sviet,* vol. 1, no. 5 (Uzhhorod, 1928), pp. 124-128.

III. PRIMARY SOURCES

A. Archives and manuscripts

In this section are listed those archives in which the author was permitted to work. Individual fonds containing material pertaining to the nationality problem in Subcarpathian Rus' are indicated; in some cases, specific examples of items or general descriptions are provided.

ARCHÍV NÁRODNÍHO MUSEA, PRAGUE

0462 Fond Brandejs. Papers of Jan Brandejs, Head of the Department of Agriculture in Uzhhorod, 1924-1934. "Dějiny Mad'arska po roce 1918" (handwritten), 135 p. "Dějiny Podkarpatské Rusi" (handwritten), 851 p. "Spominy" (handwritten), 1012 p.

0463 Fond Korespondence Kramáře. Letters of Karel Kramář, First Prime Minister of Czechoslovakia, 1918-1919. Includes correspondence with Subcarpathian Russophiles, especially A. Beskid.

0464 Fond Dr. Starý. Papers of Dr. Alois Starý, Advisor to the Prime Minister's Cabinet for Subcarpathian Affairs, 1921-1930. Includes copies of official correspondence concerning the region, as well as a comprehensive collection of newspaper articles (arranged according to subject) from the Czech press dealing with Subcarpathian Rus' (1920-1930). "Memorandum o Podkarpatské Rusi." "Podkarpatská Rus, 1921." "Podkarpatská Rus s hlediska menšinových otázek." Růžička, Otokar, "Politické proudy v Přikarpatské Rusi." Prague, 12. XI. 1919.

ARKHIV UKRAÏNS'KOHO MUZEIU, SVIDNÍK, CZECHOSLOVAKIA

0465   Historical Archives. Includes copies of several manifestos issued by Subcar-
       pathian national councils.
0466   Literary Archives. Includes unpublished works and correspondence by na-
       tional leaders such as A. Dobrianskii, A. Dukhnovych, A. Kralitskii, A.
       Pavlovych, and Iu. Stavrovskii-Popradov. Also includes the collection of
       rare Subcarpathian newspapers (1919 to 1938) from the library of the
       Czech scholar F. Tichý.

ŠTÁTNÝ ARCHÍV, PREŠOV

0467   Fond Grécko-katolícke biskupstva. Official papers of the Prešov diocese,
       which include documentation on Rusyn Affairs in the Prešov Region and
       on the liquidation of the diocese in 1950. "Memorandum o Podkarpatské
       Rusi."

ŠTÁTNÝ SLOVENSKÝ ÚSTREDNÝ ARCHÍV, BRATISLAVA

0468   Fond Ministerstvo plnou mocou pre správu Slovenska. Includes official cor-
       respondence of the Slovak administration, which was concerned with Sub-
       carpathian Rus', especially the boundary issue. "Memorandum karpato-
       russkago naroda, prinadlezhashchago dovremenno k Slovakii, napravlen k
       vp. derzhavnym delegatam Soiuza Narodov."
0469   Fond Ministerstvo Vnutra. Includes material on Rusyn developments in the
       Prešov Region (1918-1939).
0470   Fond Prezidium Krajinského úradu.
       "Illegal'nyi Komitet, pratsuiiuchyi za prykliuchenniam Karpats'koï U-
       kraïny do Soiuzu RSR v Bratislavi: Memorandum."

B. Government publications, legal sources, parliamentary speeches

Included in this section are memoranda prepared by governments that ruled Subcarpathian Rus'; statements by officials who held positions in the government; collections and individual parliamentary speeches and publications; general collections of
documents that include materials dealing with the region; collections of legal documents regarding church, diplomatic, and administrative history.

0471   Baran, Alexander, ed. *De Processibus Canonicis Ecclesiae Catholicae Uc-
       rainorum in Transcarpathia ab 1771 usque 1853*. In *Monumenta Ucrainae
       Historica*, vol. 13. Rome: Editiones Universitatis Catholicae Ucrainorum
       S. Clementis Papae, 1974.
0472   Beneš, Edvard. *Řeč o problému podkarpatoruském a jeho vztahu k česko-
       slovenské republice*. Prague: Orbis, 1934. Published also in French, Rus-
       sian, and Ukrainian translations.
0473   Beskid, Antonii G. "Posliednii memorandum." *Kalendar' ARSS na hod
       1934*. Homestead, Pa., 1934, pp. 70-72.

0474   *Boj o směr vývoje československého státu.* 2 vols. Edited by A. Kocman et al.
       Prague: Československá akademie věd, 1965-1969.
0475   Borkaniuk, Oleksa. *Za povnu avtonomiiu, za hospodars'ke, sotsiial'ne i kul'-
       turne pidnesennia Pidkarpattia: promova v parlamenti, 17.VI.1937.* Muka-
       chevo, 1937.
0476   Csáky, Stephen. "The Diplomatic Measures Leading to the Re-incorporation
       of Ruthenia: Statement of the Hungarian Foreign Minister Before the For-
       eign Affairs Committee of the Hungarian Parliament [23.III.1939]."
       Danubian Review, vol. 6, no. 11 (Budapest, 1939), pp. 6-13.
0477   Czechoslovak Government. *Development of Carpathian Ruthenia Since First
       Incorporated in Czechoslovakia.* Information Bulletin, no. 10. Prague,
       1934.
0478   ———· *Mémorandum du gouvernement tchécoslovaque sur la Russie carpa-
       thique.* Geneva, 1922.
0479   ———· *Mémorandum du gouvernement tchécoslovaque sur le 'Territoire
       autonome des ruthènes au sud des Carpathes'.* [N.p., n.d.]
0480   ———· *Mémoire No. 6: Problem of the Ruthenians of Hungary.* Paris:
       Czechoslovak Delegation to the Paris Peace Conference, 1919. French
       translation reprinted in: *La Paix de Versailles,* vol. 9: *Questions terri-
       toriales,* pt. 1. Paris: Les éditions internationales, 1939, pp. 95-100.
0481   ———· *La Russie subcarpathique au point de vue de la question des na-
       tionalités.* Prague, 1922.
0482   ———· *Sbírka zákonů a nařízení státu československého.* Prague: Státni tis-
       kárna, 1920-1938.
0483   Czechoslovak Government. *Národní shromáždění. Těsnopisecké správy o
       schůzích Národního shromáždění.* 14 vols. Prague, 1919-1920.
0484   ———· *Těsnopisecké zprávy o schůzích poslanecké sněmovny.* 45 vols.
       Prague, 1920-1938.
0485   ———· *Těsnopisecké zprávy o schůzích Senátu.* 29 vols. Prague, 1920-1937.
0486   ———· *Tisky k těsnopiseckým zprávám o schůzích poslanecké sněmovny.* 67
       vols. Prague, 1920-1938.
0487   ———· *Tisky k těsnopiseckým zprávám o schůzích Senátu.* 32 vols. Prague,
       1920-1938.
0488   ———· *Zápisy o schůzích poslanecké sněmovny.* 10 vols. Prague, 1920-1939.
0489   ———· *Zápisy o schůzích Senátu.* 13 vols. Prague, 1920-1938.
0490   Czechoslovak Ministry of Foreign Affairs [Ministre des affaires étrangères de
       la république tchécoslovaque]. *Mémoire concernant la Russie subcarpa-
       thique: territoire ruthène au sud des Carpathes.* Prague, 1921.
0491   ———· *Traité entre les principales puissances alliées et associées et la Tchéco-
       slovaquie.* Paris, 1919.
0492   *Dieiatel'nost' predstavitelei Avtonomnago zemlediel'skago soiuza dep. An-
       dreia Brodiia, dep. d-ra Ivana P'eshchaka i sen. Iuliia Fel'deshiia: riechi
       i interpellatsii.* Uzhhorod, 1938.
0493   *Diplomáciai iratok Magyarország külpolitikájához 1936-1945.* 4 vols. Edited
       by László Zsigmond. Budapest: Akadémiai kiadó, 1962-1970. Especially
       vol. 2: *A müncheni egyezmény létrejötte és Magyarország külpolitikája,*

1936-1938. Edited by Magda Ádám. Budapest, 1965; and vol. 3: *Magyarország külpolitikája 1938-1939*. Edited by Magda Ádám. Budapest, 1970.

0494   *Documents on German Foreign Policy, 1918-1945*. Series D, vol. 4: *The Aftermath of Munich, October, 1938-March, 1939*; and vol. 6: *The Last Months of Peace, March-August, 1939*. Washington, D.C.: U. S. Government Printing Office, 1951-1956.

0495   *Dokumenty rozpovidaiut'*. Edited by D. M. Bukovych and A. I. Haidosh. Uzhhorod: Vyd. 'Karpaty', 1971. Collection of documents dealing with the history of the Greek Catholic Church.

0496   Fentsik, Stepan. *Interpelliatsii*. Uzhhorod, 1936.

0497   Hadzhega, Vasylii. "Kanonychna vyzytatsiia [biskupa Dekamilysa] v Spishu r. 1701." *Podkarpatska Rus'*, vol. 11, nos. 1-10 (Uzhhorod, 1934), pp. 1-13.

0498   Hodinka, Antal, ed. *A munkácsi görög-szertartásu püspökség okmánytára*, vol. 1: *1458-1715*. Uzhhorod, 1911.

0499   Kemény, Gábor G., ed. *Iratok a nemzetiségi kérdés történetéhez Magyarországon a dualizmus korában*. 5 vols.: 1867-1913. Budapest: Tankönyvkiadó, 1952-1971. Includes more than a hundred documents pertaining specifically to Rusyns. A sixth volume is in preparation.

0500   Kozma, Miklós. *Beszédek, cikkek, előadások, nyilatkozatok*, vol. 5: 1940-1941. Budapest: Tarr László, 1942.

0501   ———· (Kozma, Nykola). *Rîch' regentskoho komyssaria proyznesena dnia 16-ho marta 1941 hoda k chlenam Soiuza ymeny Bercheniia*. Published simultaneously in Hungarian. Uzhhorod, 1941.

0502   "K podpisaniju dohovora meždu Sovitskim Sojuzom i Čechoslovackoj respublikoj." *Karpatorusskij narodnyj kalendar' na hod 1946*. Perth Amboy, N.J., 1946, pp. 116-120.

0503   Lacko, Michael. "Documenta spectanta regimen episcopi Mukačevensis Michaelis Manuelis Olšavsky, 1743-1767." *Orientalia Christiana Periodica*, vol. 25 (Rome, 1959), pp. 53-90.

0504   *Minority Grievances in Russinsko*. Publications of the Hungarian Frontier Readjustment League, no. 4. Budapest, 1928.

0505   Nemec, František, and Moudry, Vasyl. *The Soviet Seizure of Subcarpathian Ruthenia*. Toronto: Wm. B. Anderson, 1955.

0506   Pan'kevych, Ivan. "Naidavnisha hramota podkarpatorus'ka." *Podkarpatska Rus'*, vol. 2, no. 7 (Uzhhorod, 1925), pp. 114-115.

0507   Pan'kevych, Ivan, and Kynakh, Hlîb. " 'Kratkoie lîtosloviie' mukachevs'-koho monastŷria o Koriatovychovy." *Podkarpatska Rus'*, vol. 7, nos. 4-5 (Uzhhorod, 1930), pp. 97-99.

0508   *Persha promova tov. posla inzh. Ia. Nechasa v spravakh Podkarpatskoi Rusy*. Uzhhorod: Sotsyial-demokratychnaia partyia, 1924.

0509   Petrov, Aleksei L., ed. "O podlozhnosti gramoty Feodora Koriatovicha 1360 g." *Materialy dlia istorii ugorskoi Rusi*. vol. 3. In *Stat'i po slavianoviedieniiu*, vol. 2. Edited by Vladimir I. Lamanskii. St. Petersburg, 1906. pp. 270-299. Second revised edition in Petrov's *Drevnieishiia gramoty* (ref. 1921), pp. 179-215.

0510 ———· *Pervyi pechatnyi pamiatnik ugrorusskago nariechiia: Urbar i inye sviazannye s krest'ianskoi Marii Terezy reformoi dokumenty. Materialy dlia istorii Ugorskoi Rusi,* vol. 5. In *Sbornik ORISIAN,* vol. 84, no. 2. St. Petersburg, 1908.

0511 Petrovay, György, ed. "Oklevelek Máramaros vármegye történetéhez." *Történelmi tár,* vol. 10 (Budapest, 1909), pp. 1-27.

0512 *Pid Praporom Velykoho Zhovtnia: borot'ba trudiashchykh Zakarpattia za Radians'ku vladu v 1919 r.: zbirnyk dokumentiv.* Uzhhorod: ZOV, 1959.

0513 *Polum'iane slovo: statti ta promovy komunistychnykh diiachiv Zakarpattia.* Uzhhorod: ZOV, 1957.

0514 Revai, Iuliian. *Interpelatsiï i zapyty—Uchebnykovyi plebystsyt.* Uzhhorod, 1938.

0515 Regents'kyi komyssariiat Podkarpatskoi terrytoriï. *Za narod Podkarpatia: chto stalosia dosy na Podkarpatiu? Odnorochna robota madiarskoho pravytel'stva.* Uzhhorod, 1940. Published simultaneously in Hungarian translation.

0516 Royal Hungarian Ministry of Foreign Affairs. *The Hungarian Peace Negotiations: An Account of the Work of the Hungarian Peace Delegation at Neuilly s/S from January to March, 1920.* 3 vols. Budapest: Victor Hornyanszky, 1920-1922. See especially vol. 1: "Concerning the Ruthenian Question," pp. 458-493; and vol. 3, A: "Statistical Data Regarding the Ruthenian Highlands," pp. 357-409.

0517 ———· *Papers and Documents Relating to the Foreign Relations of Hungary,* vol. 1. Budapest, 1939.

0518 *Shliakhom Zhovtnia: promovy ta interpeliatsiï deputativ-komunistiv u chekhoslovats'komu parlamenti pro Zakarpats'ku Ukraïnu (1921-1938 rr.).* Uzhhorod: ZOV, 1959.

0519 *Shliakhom Zhovtnia: zbirnyk dokumentiv.* 6 vols. Uzhhorod: ZOV, 1957-67.

0520 Svîtlyk, Petro. "Obîzhnyk maramoroshskôho vykariia z roku 1814." *Podkarpatska Rus',* vol. 5, nos. 8-9 (Uzhhorod, 1928), pp. 193-197.

0521 *Taiemne staie iavnym (Dokumenty pro antynarodnu diialnist' tserkovnykiv na Zakarpatti v period okupatsiï).* Uzhhorod: ZOV, 1961.

0522 Tsurkanovich, Ilarion. *Riech' senatora proiznesennaia im 16-go dekabria 1930 g. v Senatie Narodnago Sobraniia po sluchaiu biudzhetnoi debaty.* Uzhhorod: Karpatorusskaia trudovaia partiia, 1930.

0523 ———· *Riech' senatora proiznesennaia im 18-go dekabria 1931 g. v Senatie Narodnago sobraniia po sluchaiu biudzhetnoi debaty.* Uzhhorod: Izd. Karpatorusskoi trudovoi partii, 1931.

0524 "Ukaz pravytel'stva Uhorskî Narodnî Republyky chysla 928/1919 v dîlî orhanyzatsiî Rus'kaho pravytel'stvennaho sovîtu (Budapest, 5.II.1919)." *Karpato-rus'kyi vîstnyk* (Uzhhorod), February 3, 1919.

0525 Žatkovič, Gregory I. *Otkrytie-Exposé byvšeho gubernatora Podkarpatskoj Rusi, o Podkarpatskoj Rusi.* 2nd ed. Homestead Pa.: Rusin Information Bureau, 1921.

0526 ———· *Spravoizdanije Predsidatel'a Direktoriuma Autonomičnoj Rusinii, na Pervyj Narodnyj Kongress.* Homestead Pa.: ARV, 1919.

C. Memoranda

Included in this section are memoranda issued by national councils, organizations, and individuals; statements and programs of political parties; and legal proposals for autonomy.

0527 Antalovskii, Stepan V. *Vozzvaniie Tsentral'nago soiuza podkarpatorusskikh studentov v Uzhgorodie.* Uzhhorod: Tsentral'na kantselaryia oboronŷ vîry, 1935.

0528 Beskid, Anthony and Dimitry Sobin. *The Origin of the Lems, Slavs of Danubian Provenance: Memorandum to the Peace Conference concerning their national claims.* [N.d., n.p.].

0529 "Bor'ba za avtonomiiu i russkost' pravoslavnoi tserkvi v Karpatskoi Rusi [1930]." *Svobodnoe slovo Karpatskoi Rusi,* vol. 6, nos. 11-12 (Newark, N.J., 1964), pp. 3-7.

0530 Brashchaiko, Iulii, and Revai, Fedir. "Memorandum tov. Prosvîta v Uzhhorodî o iazykovôm sporî." *Podkarpatska Rus',* vol. 8, no. 4 (Uzhhorod, 1931), pp. 81-85.

0531 Brodii, Andrei. *Prykaz No. 2 dlia chlenov Avtonomnaho zemledîl'skaho soiuza.* Uzhhorod, 1935.

0532 ———· *Tsyrkuliar Avtonomnaho zemledîl'skaho soiuza.* Uzhhorod, 1935.

0533 *Declaration and Memorandum of the Russian National Council of Carpatho-Russia in Lvov, of the League for the Liberation of Carpatho-Russia in America, and of the League for the Liberation of Carpatho-Russia in Canada.* Washington, D.C., 1919.

0534 "Deklaratsiia kul'turnykh i natsional'nykh prav karpatorusskago naroda." *Karpatskii sviet,* vol. 4, nos. 5-7 (Uzhhorod, 1931), pp. 1207-1212. Also published separately: Uzhhorod, 1931.

0535 Demko, Mikhail. *Rabotnik i rabota v avtonomnoi Podkarpatskoi Rusi: Proekt k programmie AZS.* Mukachevo: Izd. Zemlediel'skago Kalendaria, 1938.

0536 Dobrianskii, Adol'f. *Proekt politicheskoi programmy dlia Rusi avstriiskoi.* L'viv, 1871.

0537 ———· *Programm zur Durchführung der nationalen Autonomie in Oester-reich (von einem Slaven).* Vienna, 1885. First published in *Parlamentär* no. 8 (Vienna, 1885).

0538 ——— [Dobrzansky, Adolf]. *Rede des ungarischen Landtags-Abgeordneten.* Vienna, 1861.

0539 Földesi, Gyula. *Az autonóm Kárpátoroszország államjogi vázlata.* Uzhhorod: Földesi Gyula könyvnyomdaja, 1927.

0540 Franko, Ivan and Hnatiuk, Volodymyr. "I my v Ievropi: protest halyts'kykh rusyniv proty madiars'koho tysiachylitia." *Zhytie i slovo,* vol. 5, no. 1 (L'viv, 1896), pp. 1-9. Translated into Vojvodinian Rusyn by Volodymyr Nota. *Nova dumka,* vol. 6, no. 13 (Vukovar, 1977), pp. 130-133.

0541 Gerovskii, Aleksei. "Obrashchenie ko vsem chlenam Ligi Natsii po voprosu ob avtonomii Karpatskoi Rusi [20.IX.1929]." *Svobodnoe slovo Karpatskoi Rusi,* vol. 3, nos. 9-10 (Newark, N.J., 1961), pp. 12-14.

0542 *Gdie mogut i dolzhny byt' russkiia shkoly po ofitsial'noi statistikie na Slovakii.* Prešov: Russkaia narodnaia partiia, 1934.

0543 *General Account of the Second Convocation of the Antonomous Congress of the Hungarian-Catholic Church* [1871]. Translated by Peter I. Zeedick as *Back in Eighteen Seventy-One*. Homestead, Pa.: ARV, 1933.

0544 Heleban, Mykhailo. *Se to! Se nam treba!! Se my khocheme!!!*. Uzhhorod: Partiia nevdovolenŷkh tuteshnikov, 1933. Second edition: Uzhhorod, 1934.

0545 [Hodinka, A. and J. Illés-Illyasevics]. *Informations relatives à l'organisation du territoires des Ruthènes au sud des Carpathes, présentées par les Ruthènes émigrés, au secretariat général de la Société des Nations.* Budapest, 1922.

0546 *Information Regarding the Administration of the Ruthene Territory South of the Carpathians Placed at the Disposal of the Secreatary-General of the League of Nations by the Emigrant Ruthenians.* [N.p., n.d.]

0547 Kaminskii, Iosif. "Deklaratsiia kul'turnykh i natsional'nykh prav karpato-russkago naroda." *Karpatskii sviet,* vol. 4, nos. 5-7 (Uzhhorod, 1931), pp. 1207-1212.

0548 ———· *Zakonoproekt ob avtonomii Podkarpatskoi Rusi.* Uzhhorod: Avtonomnyi zemlediel'skii soiuz, 1931.

0549 ———· *Zakonoproekt Tsentral'noi Russkoi Narodnoi Rady o Konstitutsii avtonomnoi Podkarpatskoi Rusi.* Uzhhorod, 1937.

0550 *Karpatorusskaia trudovaia partiia, eia tsiel', programma i organizatsiia.* Prešov: Izd. Komiteta po organizatsii K.T.P., 1920.

0551 *Komunikat presovoho viddilu Het'mans'koï upravy.* Berlin, June 5, 1939.

0552 Kurtyak, Ivan. *Petition des Ruthènes en Tchécoslovaquie concernant l'autonomie de la Russie subcarpathique.* Uzhhorod, 1928.

0553 Kutkafalvy, Nikoláj. *Brátyá Ruszinö!* Budapest, 1920.

0554 ———· *A Génuai konferenciához!* Budapest, 1922.

0555 ———· *Új proklamació a Magyarországi ruthén néphez.* Budapest, 1920. Published also in Rusyn.

0556 *Memorandum in behalf of Podkarpatskaja Rus.* Pittsburgh: Greek Catholic Diocese, 1945.

0557 *Memorandum o iazykovom sporie glubokochtimomu gospodinu prezidentu respubliki, gospodinu predsiedateliu Sovieta ministrov, gospodinu ministru Zagranichnykh diel Chekhoslovatskoi respubliki.* Uzhhorod: OIAD, 1935.

0558 "Memorandum tov. Prosvîta v Uzhhorodî o iazŷkovom sporî." *Podkarpatska Rus',* vol. 8, no. 4 (Uzhhorod, 1931), pp. 81-85.

0559 *Mémoire concernant la Russie subcarpathique (Territoire ruthène au sud des Carpathes).* Geneva, 1921.

0560 Movchak, Ivan. *Lyst do moykh bratov rusynov khliborobov.* Uzhhorod, 1924.

0561 *Manifest do ukraïns'koho narodu Pidkarpattia.* Uzhhorod, October 17, 1937.

0562 *Manifest III zîzdu 'Obiednannia trudiashchoho selianstva'.* Uzhhorod, 1934.

0563 Markoff, Dmitrij. *Mémoire sur les aspirations nationales des Petits-Russiens de l'ancien empire austro-hongrois.* Paris, 1919.

0564 *Memorandum Russkago kongressa v Amerikie, sozvannago 'Soiuzom osvobozhdeniia Prikarpatskoi Rusi'.* New York, [1917]. Also in French translation: New York [1917]. Original reprinted in Z. Peška and J. Markov, eds. "K ústavním dějinám Podkarpatské Rusi." *Bratislava, vol.* 5 (Bratislava, 1931), pp. 511-522.

0565   Parti politique ruthène de la Hongrie. *Aide-mémoire adressé aux puissances alliées et associées.* Vienna, 1919. Published in English translation in the *Hungarian Peace Negotiations* (ref. 0516), vol. 1, pp. 483-489.

0566   Pedagogychne Tovarystvo Podkarpatskoi Rusy. "Iazŷkova anketa." *Podkarpatska Rus',* vol. 6, no. 4 (Uzhhorod, 1929), pp. 94-98.

0567   Peška, Zdeněk and Josef Markov. "Příspěvek k ústavním dějinám Podkarpatské Rusi." *Bratislava,* vol. 4 (Bratislava, 1930), pp. 419-422; and vol. 5 (1931), pp. 511-535. Includes twelve documents, mostly memoranda of Rusyn national councils in Europe and the United States from 1918-1919.

0568   *Programma Russkago narodnago soedineniia.* Mukachevo, 1931.

0569   *Programma Russkoi Natsional'no-avtonomnoi partii.* Uzhhorod, 1935.

0570   *Proklamatsiia do uhro-rus'koho naroda—Diiatel'nost' Uhro-rus'koi poly-tychnoi partiy—Rozpravleniie Uhro-rus'koi polytychnoi partiy s myrovu konferentsiiu—Memorandum do antanta, shto Uhro-rusynŷ ne khotiat odorvatysia ot Uhorshchynŷ.* Uzhhorod, 1919. Published simultaneously in Latin-Hungarian Rusyn alphabet.

0571   *Protest.* Pittsburgh: Greek Catholic Diocese, 1945.

0572   "Rezoliutsiia desiatago obshchago sobraniia OIAD, 5.VI.1932, v Khustie." *Karpatskii sviet,* vol. 5, no. 6 (Uzhhorod, 1932), pp. 1351-1352.

0573   "Rezoliutsiia d-ra Stepana A. Fentsika, edinoglasno priniataia godichnym sobraniem OIAD, 27.VI.1927, v Priashevie." *Russkii narodnyi kalendar' na god 1928.* Izdanie OIAD, no. 31. Uzhhorod, 1927, pp. 75-77.

0574   "Rezoliutsiia II-go godichnago obshchago sobraniia OIAD, 11.VI.1933, v Priashevie." *Karpatskii sviet,* vol. 6, no. 1-2 (Uzhhorod, 1933), pp. 1367-1369.

0575   *Rezoliutsiia s"iezda Tsentral'noi Russkoi Narodnoi Rady v Uzhgorodie . . . 8 maia 1934 goda.* Uzhhorod, 1934.

0576   "Rezoliutsiia vos'mogo obshchago sobraniia OIAD, 1.VI.1930, i memoran-dum sovietu ministrov Chekhoslovatskoi respubliki v Pragie." *Karpatskii sviet,* vo. 3, no. 5-6 (Uzhhorod, 1930), pp. 1003-1005.

0577   "Rezolutsiî predlozheniî na zahal'nôm z'îzdî Pedagogychnoho Tovarystva, 6. X.1928." *Podkarpatska Rus',* vol. 5, no. 8-9 (Uzhhorod, 1928), pp. 174-178.

0578   "Rezoliutsiî III. richnykh zahal'nykh zborîv Pedagogichnoho tovarystva, 3.V.1931, v Uzhhorodî." *Podkarpatska Rus',* vol. 8, no. 5-6 (Uzhhorod, 1931), pp. 128-131.

0579   [Riskó, Jenő]. *Mémorandum des ruthènes de Hongrie aux puissances alliées et associées.* Budapest, 1920. Texts in French, English, Italian, and German.

0580   ———· *Notice du parti ruthène de Hongrie présentée à la Société des Nations, aux puissances étrangères et à la Commission de délimitation.* Budapest, 1921. Text in French and English. Italian-German edition published separately.

0581 ———· *A Ruszka-Krajnai önkormányzati párt programmja tervezete.* Budapest, 1919.

0582 *La Russie Carpathique: les raisons de sa réunion à la Russie.* Paris, 1919.

0583 *Shcho take SPS, iak maie pratsiuvaty.* Pryloha'Holosu Zhyttia', no. 3. Uzhhorod, 1932.

0584 Shpak, Ivan. *Tsykuliar Avtonomnaho zemledil'skaho soiuza.* Uzhhorod, 1935.

0585 *La situation des minorités en Slovaquie et en Russie-Subcarpathique: Mémoire à la Société des Nations.* Berlin: Carl Heymanns Verlag, 1923.

0586 Sobin, Dimitrij. *Protêt contre le partage de la contrée russe des Carpathes: Appel à la justice du Congrès de la Paix à Paris.* Prague: Conseil national des Russes des Carpathes, 1919.

0587 Société des Nations. *Le territoire autonome des ruthènes au sud des Carpathes. Lettre des représentants du parti politique des ruthènes de Hongrie. Lettre de la légation tchécoslovaque à Berne.* Geneva, 1921. Text in French and English.

0588 Sova, Petr. *Zakonoproekt ob avtonomii Podkarpatskoi Rusi sostavlen komissiei Respublikanskoi zemlediel'cheskoi partii.* Uzhhorod, 1938.

0589 Stéfán, Ágoston. *Ruszka-Krajna népbiztosának előterjesztése a Magyarországi tanácsok országos gyülésének Budapesten.* Budapest, 1919.

0590 *Supplique: les Russes des Karpathes délaissés, et dignes de protection.* Marbourg, 1919?

0591 Svîtlyk, Petro. "Odyn z dokumentôv pershoî vesnŷ narodôv (memorandum rusynôv do gubernatora Uhorshchynŷ generala Hainaua v r. 1848 v spravî potreb natsional'nŷkh i ekonomychnŷkh)." *Podkarpatska Rus',* vol. 5, no. 7 (Uzhhorod, 1928), pp. 150-152.

0592 *Tajemnická zpráva k III. Zemskému Sjezdu Československé strany socialistické na Podk. Rusi.* Uzhhorod, 1925.

0593 *Vse dlia peremohy komunistychnoi partii!* Mukachevo: Pavlo Terek, 1935.

0594 "Vyslanstva Rusyniv Uhors'kykh u Vidni 1849 r." Compiled by Mykola Rusynko. *Naukovyi zbirnyk MUKS,* vol. 6, pt. 1 (Bratislava, Prešov, and Svidník, 1972), pp. 63-95.

0595 Yuhasz, Michael, Sr. *Petition concerning the Educational Complaints of the Autonomous Carpatho-Russian Territory south of the Carpathian Mountains . . . presented to the League of Nations.* Homestead, Pa.: ARV, 1932.

0596 ———· *Wilson's Principles in Czechoslovak Practice: The Situation of the Carpatho-Russian People under the Czech Yoke.* Homestead, Pa.: ARV, 1929.

0597 *Zakonoproekt Tsentral'noi Russkoi Narodnoi Rady o konstitutsii avtonomnoi Podkarpatskoi Rus—Proekt zakona Tsentral'noï Rus'koï Narodn'oï Rady pro konstytutsiiu avtonomnoï Pidkarpats'koï Rusy.* Uzhhorod, 1937.

D. Statutes

0598 Fentsik, Stepan A. *Rukovodstvo k organizatsii Russkikh narodnykh chitalen' OIAD.* Izdanie OIAD, no. 72. Uzhhorod, 1929. Also in *Karpatskii sviet,* vol. 11, no. 10 (Uzhhorod, 1929), pp. 743-753.

0599   *Kto toto Edinstvo pôdkarpats'kŷkh bratôv y shcho khoche.* Uzhhorod, 1938.

0600   *Proekt Russkago natsional'nago fonda pri OIAD.* Uzhhorod, 1935.

0601   *Statut Pedagogychnoho tovarystva Podkarpatskoî Rusy.* Uzhhorod, 1926.

0602   *Statut Tovarystva 'Prosvîta' Podkarpatskoî Rusy.* Uzhhorod: Unio, 1920.

0603   *Statut Tovarystva 'Prosvîta' v Uzhhorodî.* Uzhhorod, 1924.

0604   *Statut 'Uchytel'skoho tovarystva Podkarpatskoî Rusy v Uzhhorodî.* Uzhhorod, 1920.

0605   *Statuty Podkarpatskoho obshchestva nauk.* Uzhhorod: Vyd. PON, 1941.

0606   *Ustav Russkago Kul'turno-prosvietitel'nago obshchestva imeni Aleksandra Dukhnovicha.* Uzhhorod, 1923.

0607   *Ustav Russkago kul'turno-prosvietitel'nago obshchestva imeni Aleksandra V. Dukhnovicha v Uzhgorodie: Tsentral'noe obshchestvo.* Uzhhorod, 1924 and 1930. *Chital'nia.* Uzhhorod, 1924 and 1930.

0608   *Ustav Russkago natsional'nago fonda.* Uzhhorod, 1935.

E. Personal memoirs, correspondence, speeches

This section includes not only writings by Subcarpathians, but also materials by government officials whose decisions had a direct impact on the region and reports by observers who spent some time in the area.

0609   Alys'kevych, Aleksii. "O potrebakh rus'koho naroda na poly serednoho shkôl'nytstva: referat." *Podkarpatska Rus',* vol. 8, no. 5-6 (Uzhhorod, 1931), pp. 90-95.

0610   Aristov, Fedor F. "Pis'mo iz Moskvy, 25.XII.1928." *Karpatskii sviet,* vol. 2, no. 2-3 (Uzhhorod, 1929), pp. 474-478.

0611   Bachinskii, Edmund. *Sovremennoe politicheskoe i èkonomicheskoe polozhenie: riech' na kraevom s"iezdie doviernikov Respublikanskoi zemlediel'skoi partii, 19.IV.1936 v Beregovie.* Uzhhorod, 1936.

0612   Bachyns'kyi, Andrii F. "Mukachivs'kyi iepyskop ta ioho poslannia." Compiled by Andrii Shlepets'kyi. *Naukovyi zbirnyk MUKS,* vol. 3 (Bratislava, Prešov, and Svidník, 1967), pp. 223-241.

0613   Bezruchko, Lev. *Z pisneiu po svitakh i ridnykh zakutkakh: zamitky i spomyny uchasnyka kontsertovoï podorozhi U.R. Kapeli po Evropi ta chlena b. T-va. 'Kobzar' na Zakarpatti.* New York, 1951.

0614   Birchak, Volodymyr. *Karpats'ka Ukraïna: spomyny i perezhyvannia.* Prague: "Natsiia v Pochodi," 1940.

0615   Bobrinskii, Vladimir A. *Prazhskii s"iezd: Chekhiia i Prikarpatskaia Rus'.* St. Petersburg: Sviet, 1909.

0616   Borkaniuk, Oleksa. *Kul'tura nalezhyt' narodovi: promova na z'ïzdu Prosvity v Uzhhorodi, 17.X.1937.* Mukachevo: Iulii Hadzhega, 1937.

0617   Bradach, Ioann. "Pastŷrskyi lyst a nauchovaniu dîtei yz roka 1762." Compiled by Vasylii Hadzhega. *Podkarpatska Rus',* vol. 4, no. 6 (Uzhhorod, 1927), pp. 136-139.

0618   Chegil', Stepan M. *10 dokladov po radio: sbornik populiarno-nauchnykh dokladov, prochitannykh v ramkakh karpatorusskoi peredachi radiostan-*

tsii v Koshitsiakh. Uzhhorod, 1936.

Cibere, Pavel, *see* Tsibere, Pavel

0619 Demko, Mikhail. "Radio-riech' proiznes dnia 20.XI.1938 v Budopeshtskom radio." *Zemledîl'skii kalendar' na hod 1939.* Uzhhorod, 1938. pp. 75-79.

0620 Didytskyî, Bohdan. "Lystŷ do A. Kralytskoho: materialŷ do ystoriy znosyn Podkarpatskoî Rusy z Halychynoiu v XIX v." *Naukovyi zbôrnyk TP,* vol. 2 (Uzhhorod, 1923), pp. 113-121; and vol. 4 (1925), pp. 195-200.

0621 Dobrianskii, Adol'f. "Iz perepiski (pis'ma k O. A. Markovu)." Compiled by Osip O. Markov. *Karpatorusskii sbornik.* Uzhhorod: PNS, 1930. pp. 230-249.

0622 ———· *Patrioticheskiia pis'ma.* L'viv: Slovo, 1873.

0623 ——— [A.D.]. "Pis'mo iz Prasheva." *Viestnik iugo-zapadnoi Rossii,* vol. 2 (Kiev, 1862), pp. 140-142.

0624 Dragula, N. I. "Nemnogo vospominanii iz nedalekago proshlago." *Karpatorusskiia dostizheniia.* Edited by Aleksander V. Popov. Mukachevo, 1930. pp. 122-144.

0625 Drahomanov, Mykhailo. *Avstro-rus'ki spomyny: 1867-77.* L'viv, 1889-92. Reprinted in his *Literaturno-publitsystychni pratsi,* vol. 2. Kiev: Naukova dumka, 1970, pp. 151-288.

0626 ———· *Spravy Uhorskoi Rusy.* L'viv, 1895.

0627 ———· "Vidpovid' M. Drahomanova na iubilieini pryvitannia 16.XII. 1894." *Vybrani tvory,* vol. 1. Prague: Ukraïns'kyi sotsiolohichnyi instytut, 1937, pp. 89-92.

0628 Dukhnovych, Aleksander. *Avtobiografiia.* Uzhhorod: Vyd. TP, 1928.

0629 ———· "Kratkaia byohrafyia Aleksandra Dukhnovycha, kanonyka priashevskaho ym samŷm napysannaia." Reprinted in *Duklia,* vol. 11, no. 3 (Prešov, 1963), pp. 82-85.

0630 ———· "Lysty." *Oleksandr Dukhnovych: zbirnyk materialiv.* Edited by M. Rychalka et al. Prešov: KSUT, 1965. Pp. 385-398.

0631 ———· *Pis'ma k Ia. Golovats'komu.* Compiled by Mikhail Demko. Mukachevo: Kulturnoe otd. O-vo 'Karpatorusskii Orel', 1927.

0632 Egan, Edmund. *Ekonomichne polozhenie rus'kykh selian v Uhorshchyni.* L'viv, 1901. Also in Czech and Ukrainian parallel translation: *Hospodářský stav rusínských venkovanů v Uhrách.* Prague: Ústřední jednoty hospodářských družstev, 1922.

0633 Fedorovich, Aleksander. "Korrespondentsiia iz Uzhgoroda (ob otkrytii literaturnago Obshchestva sv. Vasiliia V.)." *Naukovyi sbornik GRM,* vol. 2, nos. 1-4 (L'viv, 1866), pp. 360-362.

0634 Feierabend, Ladislav K. *Soumrak československé demokracie.* Washington, D. C., 1967.

0635 ———· *Ve vládách Druhé republiky.* New York: Universum Press Co., 1961.

0636 Fierlinger, Zdeněk. *Od Mníchova po Košice: Svědectví a dokumenty, 1939-1945.* Prague: Prace, 1946.

0637 Fentsik, Stepan. *Dielo o pokushenii na E. I. Sabova.* Izdanie OIAD, no. 99. Uzhhorod, 1930.

0638 ———· (Fencik). *Greetings from the Old Country to all of the American Russian People.* N.p., 1935. Reprinted in *Kalendar' OS na hod 1936.* Perth

Amboy, N.J., 1936. pp. 107-112.

0639 ———· *Moia poiezdka v Bolgariiu na V. s''iezd russkikh uchenykh: karpato-rossy i rossiiane.* Izdanie OIAD, no. 98. Uzhhorod, 1930.

0640 ———· *Russkim skautam na Podkarpatskoi Rusi.* Izdanie OIAD, no. 75. Uzhhorod, 1930.

0641 ———· *Uzhgorod—Amerika: putevyia zamietki 13.X.1934-19.V.1935.* Uzhhorod: 'Nash put', 1935.

0642 Gadzhega, Iulii [Rusak, Iulii]. *Vospominaniia.* Uzhhorod: Aktsiinoe tovaristvo Lam, 1938.

0643 Galagan, Mykola. "My Last Days in Carpatho-Ukraine." *The Trident,* vol. 3, nos. 7-8, 9 and 10 (New York, 1939), pp. 18-31, 32-40 and 33-40.

0644 Gerovskii, Aleksei [Gerovskij, Aleksij]. *Karpatskaja Rus' v češskom jarmi.* N.p., 1939. Reprinted in *Karpatorusskij narodnyj kalendar' na hod 1944.* Perth Amboy, N.J., 1944, pp. 104-118.

0645 Grendzha-Dons'kyi, Vasyl'. "Moï spohady." Unpublished memoirs. Bratislava, 1966.

0646 Hnatiuk, Volodymyr. "Lysty do Ivana Pan'kevycha (1920-1926)." Compiled by Mykola Mushynka. *Naukovyi zbirnyk MUKS,* vol. 3 (Bratislava, Prešov, and Svidník, 1967), pp. 157-214.

0647 Holovats'kyi, Iakiv [J. F. H.]. "Cesta po halické a uherské Rusi." *Časopis českého museum,* vol. 15, nos. 2, 3, 4 (Prague, 1841), pp. 183-223, 302-317, 423-437; vol. 16, no. 1 (1842), pp. 42-62.

0648 Hrabar, Konstantin. "Rozhovor." *Podkarpatoruská revue,* vol. 1, no. 1 (Bratislava, 1936), pp. 3-6.

0649 Iatsko, Pavlo. "Spomyny pro pershi zbory 'Prosvity'." *Z nahody desiat'-litn'oho iuvileiu isnovannia tovarystva Prosvîta na Pidkarpats'kii Rusy: 29.IV.1920—29.VI.1930.* Vŷd. TP, no. 152. Uzhhorod, 1930, pp. 3-8.

0649a Iefremiv, Serhii. "Boi 14-15 bereznia na Karpats'kii Ukraïni." *Za derzhavnist': materialy do istoriï viis'ka ukraïns'koho,* vol. 11. Toronto: Ukraïns'kyi voienno-istorychnyi instytut, 1966, pp. 128-165.

Ivanov, E., see Sabov, Evmenii

0650 "Iz epokhi vozrozhdeniia Ugorskoi Rusi." Compiled by Vladimir A. Frantsev. *Nauchno-literaturnyi sbornik GRM,* vol. 1, no. 1 (L'viv, 1902), pp. 1-12. Published separately: L'viv: Izd. GRM, 1902. Reprinted as *K voprosu o literaturnom iazykie Podkarpatskoi Rusi.* Izd. OIAD, no. 2. Uzhhorod, 1924. Correspondence of A. Dukhnovych with P. I. Ianovych, A. F. Kralitskii, and A. I. Petrashevich.

0651 *Karpats'ka Ukraïna v borot'bi.* Vienna: Ukraïns'ka presova sluzhba, 1939.

0652 Kaminskii, Iosif V. "Vospominaniia," *Karpatorusskii golos,* vol. 2, nos. 9-107 (Uzhhorod, 1933).

0653 Kennan, George F. *From Prague after Munich: Diplomatic Papers, 1938-1940.* Princeton, N.J.: Princeton University Press, 1968.

0654 Klofáč, Václav. "Můj pohled na Podkarpatskou Rus." *Podkarpatská Rus.* Edited by Jaroslav Zatloukal. Bratislava: KPPR, 1936, pp. 90-93.

0655 Kmitsikevych, Iaroslav. "1919-i rik na Zakarpatti (spohad)." *Naukovyi zbirnyk MUKS,* vol. 4, pt. 1 (Bratislava, Prešov, and Svidník, 1969), pp. 381-384.

0656 Kohanik, Peter G. *Belgium of the East: An Interview with Dr. Dmitri A.*

Markoff. Wilkes-Barre, Pa., 1920.

0657 Kucharský, O. Letter dated March 19, 1828. *Časopis společnosti wlasten-ského Muzeum,* vol. 2, pt. 2. (Prague, 1828), pp. 127-131.

0658 Lazho, Iurko. *Russkomu narodu na Slovensku.* Vyšný Svidník, 1924.

0659 Machik, Konstantin. "Kak ostalsia ia russkim?" *Russkii narodnyi kalendar' OIAD na god 1928.* Izdanie OIAD, no. 31. Uzhhorod, 1927, pp. 83-85.

0660 Marina, Julius. "Memoirs." *Byzantine Catholic World,* vol. 20, nos. 38-49 (Pittsburgh, Pa., 1975); vol. 21, nos. 1-49 (1976); and vol. 22, nos. 1-4 (1977).

0661 Masaryk, Tomáš G. *Světová revoluce za války a ve válce, 1914-1918.* Prague, 1925. Fourth edition: Prague: Čin, 1938. English abridged translation: *The Making of a State: Memories and Observations, 1914-1918.* New York: Frederick A. Stokes, 1927.

Meteor, Uriil, *see* Sil'vai, Ivan

0662 Miller, David Hunter, *My Diary at the Peace Conference,* vols. 4, 13, 14, 16, 17. New York, 1924.

0663 Ol'shavs'kyi, Mykhail M. *Perepyska epyskopa nashoho z tohdashnymy yhu-menamy: Hedeonom Pazynom y Ioanykiom Skrypkom.* Compiled by Antonii Romanuv [Antal Hodinka]. Zhovkva, 1934.

0664 Pan'kevych, Ivan. "Lystuvannia z Filaretom Kolessoiu." Compiled by V. Hoshovs'kyi. *Naukovyi zbirnyk MUKS,* vol. 4, pt. 1 (Bratislava, Prešov, and Svidník, 1967), pp. 107-147.

0665 ———· "Lysty do Volodymyra Hnatiuka 1910-1926." Compiled by Mykola Mushynka. *Naukovyi zbirnyk MUKS,* vol. 4, pt. 1 (Bratislava, Prešov, and Svidník, 1969), pp. 62-106.

0666 ———· "Mii zhyttiepys." *Naukovyi zbirnyk MUKS,* vol. 4, pt. 1 (Bratislava, Prešov, and Svidník, 1969), pp. 17-43.

0667 Perényi, Eleanor. *More Was Lost.* Boston: Little, Brown and Co., 1964.

0668 Petrov, Aleksei L. [K.M.]. "Iz Budapeshta." *Slavianskoe obozrienie,* vol. 1, no. 1 (St. Petersburg, 1892), pp. 567-572. Reprinted in Petrov, *Mad'iar-skaia gegemoniia* (ref. 1926), pp. 5-11.

0669 ———· [Zh. Z. I.]. "Iz Koshits' (Ugriia)." *Slavianskoe obozrienie,* vol. 1, no. 2 (St. Petersburg, 1892), pp. 160-172. Reprinted in Petrov, *Mad'iar-skaia gegemoniia* (ref. 1926), pp. 11-24.

0670 Rakovskii, Ivan. "Do znaidenoho dokumentu Rakovs'koho." Compiled by Stepan V. Dobosh. *Duklia,* vol. 13, no. 3 (Prešov, 1965), pp. 97-100.

0671 ———· "Pis'ma iz Vengerskoi Rusi." *Viestnik iugo-zapadnoi i zapadnoi Rossii,* vol. 1 (Kiev, 1862), pp. 212-217; vol. 2 (1862), pp. 134-140, 167-171, and 235-238.

0672 Rohach, Ivan. *Khochemo ziednannia syly narodu.* Uzhhorod: 'Svoboda', 1938.

0673 Revai, Iuliian. *V borot'bi za pravdu: promova I. R. na Vseprosvitians'komu zïzdi v Uzhhorodi, dnia 17.X.1937.* Uzhhorod: Uchytel's'ka Hromada, 1938.

0674 Roikovich, Feodor. "Nashe stremlenie na otkrytie Gr. Kat. Russkoi gimnazii v Priashevie." *Kalendar' OS na hod 1938.* Perth Amboy, N.J., 1939, pp. 81-85.

Rusak, Iulii, *see* Gadzhega, Iulii.

0675 Sabov, Evmenii I. "Gimnazistom." *Karpatskii sviet,* vol. 2, no. 5-6 (Uzhhorod, 1929), pp. 579-583. Reprinted in Latin script: *Kalendar' OS na hod 1940.* Perth Amboy, 1940, pp. 110-113.

0676 ——— [Ivanov, E.]. "Iz moikh zapisok." *Karpatorusskii golos,* nos. 54-55, 153-154 (Uzhhorod, 1933).

0677 ———· "Riech' predsiedatelia karpatorusskago OIAD, 27.XII.1923, v Uzhgorodie." *Karpatskii krai,* vol. 1, no. 3-4 (Mukachevo, 1923-1924), pp. 41-49.

0678 ———· "Riech' predsiedatelia OIAD na obshchem sobranii OIAD, 27.VI. 1927 v Priashevie." *Russkii narodnyi kalendar' OIAD na god 1928.* Izdanie OIAD, no. 31. Uzhhorod, 1927, pp. 63-75.

0679 ———· "Vospominaniia." *Russkii narodnyi kalendar' OIAD na god 1927.* Uzhhorod, 1926, pp. 95-104. Reprinted in *Kalendar' OS na hod 1929.* Perth Amboy, N.J., 1929, pp. 148-156.

0680 ———· "Vospominaniia v Uzhgorodskoi gimnazii." *Kalendar' Sobraniia Hr. Kat. tserkovnykh bratstv na hod 1928.* McKeesport, Pa. 1928, pp. 85-94.

0681 Sabov, George. "Jak Čechi vitali karpatorussku 'delegaciju' [1929]." *Jubilee Almanac of the GKS.* Munhall, Pa., 1967, pp. 248-250.

0682 Sarich, Mikhail. *Bratskii prîviet brat'iam i sestram karpatorussam, zhivushchim v predielakh karpatskikh gor i v Amerikie.* St. Petersburg, 1893.

0683 *Shliakh do voli: zbirnyk spohadiv i dokumentiv pro natsional'no-vyzvol'nu borot'bu ukraïns'koho naselennia Chekhoslovachchyny proty fashyzmu v 1939-1945 rr.* In *Naukovyi zbirnyk MUKS,* vol. 2 (Bratislava, Prešov, and Svidník, 1966).

0684 Shtefan, Avhustyn. *Za pravdu i voliu: spomyny i deshcho z istoriï Karpats'-koï Ukraïny,* vol. 1. Toronto: 'Proboiem,' 1973.

0685 Sil'vai, Ivan A. [Uriil Meteor]. "Avtobiografiia." Excerpts compiled by A. V. Popov: *Karpatskii krai,* vol. 1, nos. 3-4, 5-6, 8, 8-9, 10, and 11-12 (Mukachevo, 1923-1924), pp. 11-16, 2-10, 11-15, 8-13, 20-23, and 39-41. Complete version: *Avtobiografiia.* Uzhhorod: Izd. 'Pis'mena', 1938. Reprinted in Sil'vai's *Izbrannye proizvedeniia* (ref. 0868), pp. 77-162.

0686 ——— [N.N.]. "O sovremennom polozhenii russkikh v Ugrii." *Slavianskii sbornik,* vol. 1 (St. Petersburg, 1875), pp. 44-54. Reprinted in Sil'vai's *Izbrannye proizvedeniia* (ref. 0868), pp. 343-351.

0687 ——— [Meteor, Uriil]. "Polozhenie ugorskikh russkikh pod upravleniem Stefana Pankovicha, episkopa Mukachevskago." *Slavianskii sbornik,* vol. 1 (St. Petersburg, 1875), pp. 55-88. Reprinted in Sil'vai's *Izbrannye proizvedeniia* (ref. 0868), pp. 352-389.

0688 Sinevirsky, Nicola. *Smersh.* New York: Henry Holt and Co., 1950.

0689 Skotzko, Eugene. "Mecca to Carpatho-Ukraine." *The Trident,* vol. 3, no. 3 (New York, 1939), pp. 6-22.

0690 Sreznevskii, Izmail I. Letters from Subcarpathian Rus', 1842. In P. Bogatyrev. "Podkarpatská Rus před 100 lety." *Podkarpatoruská revue,* vol. 2, no. 6 (Bratislava, 1937), pp. 63-64.

0691 Svientsitskii, Ilarion S., ed. *Materialy po istorii vozrozhdeniia Karpatskoi Rusi.* 2 vols. Vol. 1: *Snosheniia Karpatskoi Rusi s Rossiei v 1-oi polovinie XIX-ago vieka.* L'viv, 1905. Vol. 2: *Karpatorusskoe slavianofil'stvo* and

Ugrorusskoe dvizhenie perioda vozrozhdeniia. Nauchno-literaturnyi sbornik GRM, vol. 6, nos. 3-4. L'viv, 1909. Includes unpublished and previously published articles, correspondance, etc., of Orlai, Venelin, Berezhanin, Lodii, Dobrianskii, Luchkai, and Dukhnovych, as well as writings of Keppen, Pogodin, Sreznevskii, and others on Subcarpathian Rus'.

0692 Svoboda, Ludvík. *Z Buzuluku do Prahy.* Prague, 1961.

0693 Teodorovych, Mykola. "Materialy do ystoriï kul'turnoho zhyttia Podkarpatskoï Rusy v druhii pol. XVIII i poch. XIX v.v.: avtobiografiia sviashch. Mykola Teodorovycha (1755-1820)." Edited by Mykola Kelekach. *Podkarpatska Rus'*, vol. 11, no. 1-10 (Uzhhorod, 1934), pp. 13-31.

0694 Tershakovets', Mykhailo, ed. "Do istoriï moskofil'stva v Uhors'kii Rusy." *Ukraïns'ko-rus'kyi arkhiv NTSh*, vol. 3 (L'viv, 1907), pp. 267-285. Six documents from the years 1839-1846 dealing with Russophilism in Subcarpathia.

0695 Toth, Alexis. *Kde treba iskati pravdu?* New York, 1890.

0696 Tsibere, Pavel [Cibere, Pavel]. "Reč proiznesennaja v čechoslovackom hosudarstvennom soviti v Londoňi." *Karpatorusskij narodnyj kalendar' na hod 1944.* Perth Amboy, N.J., 1944, pp. 45-49.

0697 Vash, I. M. *Doroha do mety [spohady].* Uzhhorod: ZOV, 1963.

0698 Vîzover, Anton. "Iasînia v 1848-1849 rotsî (yz spomynôv starshykh)." *Podkarpatska Rus'*, vol. 5, no. 7 (Uzhhorod, 1928), pp. 146-150.

0699 Voloshyn, Avhustyn. "Besida na anketi o shkil'nii reformi, 11.IV.1929, v Prazi." *Podkarpatska Rus'*, vol. 6, no. 8-9 (Uzhhorod, 1929), pp. 171-178.

0700 ———. "Besîda posla y presîdatelia PTPR pry otvoreniu III. zahal'noho z'îzdu." *Podkarpatska Rus'*, vol. 5, no. 8-9 (Uzhhorod, 1928), pp. 178-180.

0701 ———. "Besîda predsîdatelia Pedagogychnoho T-stva na II. zahal'nom z'îzdî, 8.V.1926." *Podkarpatska Rus'*, vol. 3, no. 6 (Uzhhorod, 1926), pp. 129-132.

0702 ———. *Bratskoe slovo ko vîrnŷm sŷnam hreko-katolytskoî tserkvŷ.* Uzhhorod, Unio, 1922.

0703 ———. *Dvî polŷtychnî rozmovŷ.* Knyzhky 'Rusyna', no. 3 Uzhhorod, 1923.

0704 ———. *Prymitky na 'Memorandum' publykovanyi v 'Russkim narodnim golosi', 18.XII.1937.* Uzhhorod: Uchytel's'ka Hromada, 1938.

0705 ———. *Spomynŷ.* Knyzhky 'Rusyna', no. 10. Uzhhorod, 1923. Section 1 republished as "Spomynŷ." *Iuvyleinŷi yliustrovanŷi kalendar' 'Unio' na rok 1928.* Uzhhorod, 1927, pp. 41-48. Section 4 translated into Czech: "Vývoj časopisectva na Podkarpatské Rusi." *Duch novin*, vol. 1, nos. 3, 4, 5 (Prague, 1928), pp. 52-55, 79-82, 111-114. Second revised edition: *Spomyny: relihiino-natsional'na borot'ba karpats'kykh rusyniv-ukraïntsiv proty madiars'koho shovinizmu.* Philadelphia: 'Karpats'kyi holos', 1959.

0706 *Vtoryi Viedenskii protsess russkago naroda byvshoi Avstro-Vengrii v 1916 godu: obvinitel'nyi akt.* Philadelphia: 'Pravda', 1924.

0707 Winch, Michael. *Republic for a Day: An Eye-Witness Account of the Carpatho-Ukraine Incident.* London: Robert Hale, Ltd., 1939.

0707a *Zarubezhnye slaviane i Rossiia: dokumenty arkhiva M. F. Raevskogo 40-80 gody XIX veka.* Edited by V. Matula and I. V. Churkina. Moscow: Nauka, 1975. Includes correspondance of A. Dobrianskii, A. Dukhnovych, I. Rakovskii, and I. Rubii to M. Raevskii, chaplain to the Russian Embassy in Vienna and supporter of Slavic national movements in the Hapsburg Empire.

F. Contemporary reports, descriptive accounts

0708   Andrault, Robert. *À l'ombre des Carpathes: dans les régions carpathiques à la veille de la guerre.* Paris: J. Susse, 1946.

0709   Baerlein, Henry. *In Czechoslovakia's Hinterland.* London: Hutchinson and Co., 1938.

0710   ——· *Over the Hills of Ruthenia.* London: Leonard Parsons, 1923.

0711   ——· "The Restoration of Ruthenia." *Central European Observer,* vol. 16 (Prague, 1938), pp. 102-104.

0712   ——· "Ruthenia Today and Tomorrow." *Fortnightly,* n.s., vol. 106, no. 866 (London, 1939), pp. 172-176.

0713   ——· *Sunrise on Ruthenia.* London: The New Europe Publishing Co., 1944.

0714   Bartha, Miklós. *Kazár földön.* Cluj [Kolozsvár], 1901. Also in Czech translation: *V zemi Chazarů.* Mukachevo: Novotný a Bartošek, 1927.

0715   Bel, Matej. *'Tractatus de re rustica Hungarorum' a 'Notitia Hungariae novae' (1735-1742).* Compiled by A.L. Petrov. In *Věstník Kralovské české společnosti nauk,* třida 1 (Prague, 1924). Published separately: Prague, 1925. Sections on counties inhabited by Rusyns reprinted in Biblioteka 'Zapysok ChSVV', no. 6. Zhovkva, 1929, pp. 14-23.

0716   Bileckij, Michael. "Ruthenia Liberated." *Central European Observer,* vol. 21 (London, 1944), pp. 341-343.

0717   Brtníková-Petříkova, A. *Mezi Huculy.* Prague: Merkur, 1935.

0718   Budilovich, Anton S. "Putevyia zamietki o dolinie sredniago i nizhniago Dunaia." *Zhurnal MNP,* vol. 176, no. 4 (St. Petersburg, 1874), especially pp. 159-164.

0719   Caldwell, Erskine. *North of the Danube.* New York: Viking Press, 1939. Especially pp. 9-40.

0720   Chyrs'kyi, M. "Zakarpattia v ochakh mandrivnyka." *Samostiina dumka,* vol. 5, nos. 5-6 and 7-8 (Chernivtsi, 1935), pp. 365-377 and 494-506.

0721   Czech, Jan. *Death Stalks the Forest.* London: The New Europe Publishing Co., 1944.

0722   Cvrk, Otto. *Co za nás uděla SSSR v zemi pod poloninskými Karpaty.* Chocen, 1946.

0723   Dami, Aldo. "Ce que j'ai vu en Subcarpathie." *Nouvelle revue de Hongrie,* vol. 72 (Budapest, 1940), pp. 345-351.

0724   Druce, Gerald. "Subcarpathian Russia or Ruthenia." In his *In the Heart of Europe: Life in Czechoslovakia.* London: George Allen and Unwin, 1936, pp. 195-207.

0725   Dudykevych, Iosef. *Na marginesi bidy Pidkarpatskoï Rusy: sposterezhennia i zamitky.* Vyd. "Ukraïns'koho slova," pt. 2. Uzhhorod, 1937.

0726   Elwell-Sutton, A.S. "Sub-Carpathian Ruthenia." *Contemporary Review,* vol. 154 (London, 1938), pp. 716-723.

0727   Fejéváry, Károly. "Commentatio de moribus et ritibus Ruthenorum." (1776-

94). Compiled by A.L. Petrov. Biblioteka 'Zapysok ChSVV', no. 6. Zhovkva, 1929, pp. 6-14.

0727a Grendzha-Dons'kyi, Vasyl'. "Po Pidkarpattiu: Kraïna temriavy, nuzhdy, holodu i . . . chekhizatsii" and "Nuzhda, holod, temnota, rozpuka i . . . chekhizatsiia." *Nasha zemlia*, vol. 1, no. 8 (Uzhhorod, 1927), pp. 1-5, and vol. 2, no. 7 (1928), pp. 1-10. Reprinted in slightly abridged form in his *Shliakhom ternovym: vybrani tvory*. Bratislava and Prešov: SPVVUL, 1964, pp. 340-365.

0728 Griffis, Joan. "Podkarpatská Rus." *Fortnightly*, n.s., vol. 148, no. 851 (London, 1937), pp. 563-572.

0729 Hanák, J.S. *Jed'te s námi na Podkarpatskou Rus*. Vlastivědné knížky, no. 1. Prague, 1937.

0730 Hansa, Karel. *Stero črt a obrázků z Podkarpatské Rusi*. Prague, 1935.

0731 Heisler, J. and Mellon, J. *Under the Carpathians, Home of a Forgotten People*. London: L. Drummond, 1946.

0732 Holly, Eugen. *Im Lande der Kabbalisten, der Religionskämpfe und des Hungers. Quer durch Karpathorussland*. Pressburg: Verlag Grenzbote, 1927.

0733 Káňa, Vašek. *Zakarpatsko: Reportáž ze života ukrajinského proletariatu v Československu*. Prague: Karel Borecký, 1932. Also published in German translation: *Karpathenland*. Prague: Heinrich Tejml, 1932.

0734 Kravchuk, Petro. *Nezabutni zustrichi: dorozhni zamitky*. Toronto, 1970.

0735 Krúdy, Gyula. *Havasi kürt: Ruszin-Krajna kistükre*. Budapest: Ruszka-krajna népbiztosság kiadása, 1919.

0736 *Lehenda pro holod*. Uzhhorod: Vyd. Karpaty, 1969. Includes twenty descriptions of the area by foreigners like Erskine Caldwell, Karel Čapek, Béla Illés, Stanislav Neumann, and Ivan Olbracht.

0737 McBride, Robert Medill. "The Little Land of the Ruthenes." In his *Romantic Czechoslovakia*. New York: Robert M. McBride, 1930, pp. 172-202.

0738 Malkus, Jára. *Cesta pana ministra zbytečných záležitostí na zapřenou do Užhorodu*. Uzhhorod: J. Veteśník, 1924.

0739 Marunchak, Mykhailo. *Ukraïntsi v Rumunii, Chekho-Slovachchyni, Pol'-shchi, Iugoslaviï*. Winnipeg, 1969. Especially pp. 13-32.

0740 Massalky, Prince Nicholas. "A Foreigner Sees Supcarpathia." *The Hungarian Quarterly*, vol. 3, no. 3 (Budapest, 1940), pp. 434-448.

0741 Mellon, J. E. "The Bridge Between East and West." In *Czechoslovakia: Land of Dream and Enterprise*. London: Czechoslovak Ministry of Foreign Affairs, Department of Information, 1944, pp. 158-170.

0742 Mondy, Miklós. *Beszélnek a Kárpátok*. Rožňava: Sájo-Vidék, 1937.

0743 Mothersole, Jessie. *Czechoslovakia: the Land of an Unconquerable Ideal*. New York: Dodd, Mead, 1926. Especially pp. 183-200.

0744 Moss, Geoffrey, *Standing Up to Hitler*. London: Michael Joseph, 1939.

0745 *Narodzhene novym chasom*. Uzhhorod: Karpaty, 1974.

0746 Neumann, Stanislav K. *Československá cesta: deník cesty kolem republiky od 28. dubna do 28. října 1933*. 2 vols. Prague: Fr. Borový, 1934-1935. Reprinted in his *Sebrané spisy*, vol. 15. Prague: Československý spisovatel, 1955.

0747 ———· *Enciány s Popa Ivana*. Prague: Fr. Borový, 1933. Reprinted in his

      Sebrané spisy, vol. 14. Prague: Československý spisovatel, 1954.

0748 Okhrymovych, Volodymyr. *Vrazhinnia z Uhors'koï Rusy.* L'viv, 1895. First published in *Narod* (L'viv, 1895) and *Dîlo* (L'viv, 1895), nos. 109, 111-112.

0749 Oláh, György. *Jajkiáltás a Ruténföldröl.* Budapest: A magyar nemzeti szövetség kiadása, 1928.

0750 Olbracht, Ivan [Zeman, Kamil]. *Hory a staletí: kniha reportáží z Podkarpatska.* Prague: Melantrich, 1935. Reprinted in his *Spisy,* vol. 9. Prague: Československý spisovatel, 1956; and in his *Zakarpatská trilogie.* Prague: Melantrich, 1972.

0750a ────· *Země bez jména: reportáže z Podkarpatska.* Prague: O. Girgal, 1932. Reprinted in his *Hory a staletí* (ref. 0750).

0751 Oulié, Marthe. "À travers la Russie subcarpathique." *Revue de Paris,* vol. 40, no. 16 (Paris, 1933), pp. 900-914.

0752 Pataky, Mária. *Rákóczi földje.* Budapest: Officina, 1939. Also in German translation: *Karpatenland: Rákóczis Heimat.* Budapest, 1939.

0753 Péchy-Horváth, Rezső. *Kárpátalja a fenyveszúgás országa.* Budapest, 1942.

0754 Petrushevych, I. "Vrazhînia z Uhorskoï Rusy." *Literaturno-naukovyi vistnyk,* no. 1 (L'viv, 1899), pp. 52-61.

0755 Phillimore, Lion. *In the Carpathians.* London: Constable and Co., 1912.

0756 Rebet, Dariia. "Priashivshchyna na perekhresnykh shliakhakh." *Suchasnist',* vol. 9, no. 8 (Munich, 1969), pp. 93-110.

0757 Rossmann, Alexander. "A Journey in Ruthenia." *Contemporary Review,* vol. 136, no. 767 (London, 1929), pp. 638-644.

0758 "Ruthenen in Ungarn." *Donaueuropa,* vol. 1, nos. 2 and 3 (Budapest, 1941), pp. 117-118 and 199-201.

0759 Safanow, W. *In der Transkarpaten-Ukraine.* Berlin: SWA Vlg., 1948.

0760 Stona, Maria. *Eine Fahrt nach Karpathorussland.* Troppau: Adolf Dreschler, 1936.

0761 Schacher, Gerhard. "Ruthenia's Way to Autonomy." *The Contemporary Review,* vol. 153 (London, 1938), pp. 80-86.

0762 Stark, Jean. "La reconstruction de la Subcarpathie." *Nouvelle revue de Hongrie,* vol. 62 (Budapest, 1940), pp. 352-358.

0763 Street, C. J. C. *East of Prague.* London: Geoffrey Bles, 1924. Especially pp. 160-284.

0764 Szirmay, A. *Notitia topographica, politica incl. comitatus Zempleniensis* (1797). [Excerpts on Rusyns in Zemplén County] Compiled by A. L. Petrov. Biblioteka 'Zapysok ChSVV', no. 6. Zhovkva, 1929, pp. 23-27.

0765 Tarján, Ödön. "Ruthenia after the carrying into Effect of the Munich Agreement." *Danubian Review,* vol. 6, no. 7 (Budapest, 1939), pp. 10-17.

0766 V. T. "Sprava Zakarpattia (z pryvodu odnoho interv'iu iz Antoninom Rozsypaloɱ)." *Samostiina dumka,* vol. 5, no. 1 (Chernivtsi, 1935), pp. 57-61.

0767 Vortigern. "The End of Carpathian Ukraine." *Nineteenth Century and After,* vol. 125, no. 747 (London, 1939), pp. 542-545.

0767a Zatloukal, Jaroslav. *Zrazená země.* Bratislava: Podkarpatoruské nakladatelství, 1938.

0768 *Zdobutky braterstva.* Uzhhorod: Karpaty, 1967.

G. Dictionaries, grammars, and readers

The dictionaries of Subcarpthian origin are entered in the first subsection; the grammars, primers, and readers in the second subsection. Only those readers published before 1919 are included, since bibliographical references to them are difficult to obtain. The number of readers increased substantially, especially between 1920 and 1943; references to these can be found in the *Bibliografický katalog* (ref. 0004) and in the supplement to the Lelekach-Haraida bibliography (ref. 0033).

DICTIONARIES

0769   Beskid, Nikolai A. *Slovar' madiarsko-russkii,* pt. 1. Prešov, 1919.

0770   Bokshai, Emyliian; Revai, Iuliian; and Brashchaiko, Mykhailo. *Magyar-ruszin szótár—Madiars'ko-rus'kyi slovar'.* Vydania PTPR, no. 32. Uzhhorod, 1928.

0771   Chopei, Vasylii, *Rus'ko madiarskyi slovar'—Rutén-magyar szótár.* Budapest: A magyar királyi egyetemi könyvnyomdában, 1883.

0772   Gortgii, Stefan, and Ivashkov, Georgii Iv. *Mad'iarsko-russkii iuridicheskii slovar'.* Mukachevo, 1922.

0773   Kochysh, Mykola M. *Priručni terminološki rečnik srpskokhrvatsko-rusinsko-ukrajinski.* Novi Sad: 'Ruske Slovo,' 1972.

0774   Machik, Konstantin, and Emel'ianov, A. *Madiarsko-russkii iuridicheskii terminologicheskii slovar'—Magyar-orosz jogi müszótár.* Košice, n.d.

0775   *Magyarorosz, szlovák és román postai szakkifejezések.* Budapest: A magyar királyi postavezérigazgatóság, 1940.

0776   Markush, Aleksander; Fotul, Ivan; and Revai, Iulii. *Rus'ko-madiarska termynologiia dlia shkol'noho y pryvatnoho uzhyvania,* pt. 1. Uzhhorod, 1923.

0777   Mitrak, Aleksander. *Madiarsko-russkii slovar'—magyar-orosz szótár.* Uzhhorod, 1922.

0778   Mitrak, Aleksander. *Russko-mad'iarskii slovar'—orosz-magyar szótar.* Uzhhorod, 1881.

0779   Toronskii, Emylii. *Madiarsko-rus'kii pravnychii termynolohychnŷi slovar'.* Vŷd. TP, Lyteraturno-naukovŷi oddîl., no. 18. Uzhhorod, 1925-27.

GRAMMARS, PRIMERS, AND READERS

0780   Ahii, Frants. *Zhyva mova, ch.I: Hramatyka, pravopys, styl.* Uzhhorod, 1936.

0781   Bradach, Ivan. *Bukvar' ili rukovodie khoteshtym uchitise pismeny ruskoslavenskimi knig.* Vienna: J. Kurzbeck, 1770.

0782   *Bukvar iazŷka Slavens'ka.* Trnava, 1699. Reprinted in Mykhailo Mol'nar. *Slovaky i ukraïntsi.* Bratislava and Prešov: SPVVUL, 1965, pp. 119-158.

0783   Chopei, Laslov. *Chytanka dlia narodnŷkh shkol,* vol. 1. Budapest, 1889. Based on the Magyar primer by Pál Gencze.

0784   ———· *Rus'ka azbuka y pervonachal'naia chytanka dlia kliasa naròdnŷkh shkòl.* Budapest, 1881.

0785 ———· *Rus'ka chytanka dîlia druhoi klasŷ naròdnŷkh shkòl.* Budapest, 1894.

0786 Chosin, Iosif. M. *Russko-slavianskaia azbuka i pervonachal'naia kniga dlia chteniia.* Budapest, 1880. Based on a Magyar primer by Pál Gencze.

0787 Dobosh, Ivan, and Fedor, Pavel. *Karpatorusskii bukvar'.* Uzhhorod: Izdanie UTPR, 1925. Second edition: Uzhhorod, 1927. Third revised edition: Uzhhorod, 1930. Fourth edition: Uzhhorod, 1937.

0788 Dukhnovych, Aleksander. *Bukvar'.* Przemyśl, 1850.

0789 ———· *Knyzhytsia chytalnaia dlia nachynaiushchykh.* Buda, 1847. Second revised ed.: Buda, 1850. Third revised ed.: Buda, 1852.

0790 ———· *Sokrashchennaia grammatika pis'mennago ruskago iazyka.* Buda, 1853.

0791 Egretskii, E.; Gulianych, M.; and Markush, A. *Podkarpatorus'kii bukvar'.* Uzhhorod, 1923.

0792 Fentsik, Evgenii. *Pervonachal'nyia sviedieniia iz grammatiki i arifmetiki v pol'zu uchashchikhsia.* Uzhhorod, 1901.

0793 Fogarashii, Ivan. *Rus'ko ugorska ili malorus'ka grammatika—Orosz magyar grammatika—Rutheno Ungarica Grammatika.* Vienna, 1833.

0794 Gáspár, János [Gashpar, Ivan]. *Ruskaia kniga dlia chteniia.* Translated by Evmenii Fentsik. Budapest, 1870.

0795 Gyalui, György Boér. *Rutén nyelvtan.* Budapest: Szerző kiadása, 1939.

0796 Haraida, Ivan. *Hrammatyka rus'koho iazŷka.* Vŷdania PON, no. 1. Uzhhorod, 1941.

      Iador, *see* Stryps'kyi, Iador

0797 Kochysh, Mykola M. *Pravopys ruskoho iazyka.* Novi Sad, 1971.

0798 Kostel'nyk, Havryil [Kostel'nik, Gabor]. *Hramatyka bachvan'sko-ruskei beshedy.* Srmski Karlovec, 1923. Reprinted in his *Proza.* Novi Sad: 'Ruske slovo', 1975, pp. 207-312.

0799 Kotsak, Arsenii. *Grammatika russkaia ili pachi rekshi slavenskaia.* Imstych, 1788.

0800 Kyzak, Ioann. *Bukvar' dlia narodnykh shkol eparkhiy Priashevskoi.* Prešov, 1919. Reprinted 1921, 1928, 1936.

0801 ———· *Rukovodstvo k fonomymycheskomu bukvariu.* Prešov, 1920.

0802 Luchkai, Mykhail [Lutskay, Michael]. *Grammatica Slavo-Ruthena: seu Vetero-Slavicae et actu in montibus Carpathicis Parvo-Russicae, ceu dialecti vigentis linguae.* Buda, 1830.

0803 *Magyarorosz nyelvgyakorló könyv.* Uzhhorod: A Kárpátaljai terület kormányzói biztosi hivatal tanügyi osztálya, 1939.

0804 Markush, Aleksander; Bochek; and Shutka. *Rodne slovo: uchebnyk rus'koho iazŷka dlia narodnŷkh shkôl,* 2 pts. Uzhhorod, 1923.

0805 Markush, Aleksander, and Nod', Aleksander. *Rus'ka besîda: uchebnyk rus'koho iazŷka dlia narodnŷkh shkol madiars'kykh,* pt. 1, Vyd. PTPR, no. 31. Uzhhorod, 1928.

0806 Markush, Aleksander, and Revai, Iuliian. *Bukvar': Chytaite i pishet'.* Prague: Derzhavne vyd., 1931. Second edition: Prague, 1937.

0807 Maryna, Iulii et al. eds. *Hrammatyka uhrorusskoho iazŷka dlia serednykh uchebnŷkh zavedenii.* Uzhhorod: Izdanie RK, 1940.

0808 Máthé, Kálmán, and Volossynovich, Dezső. *Magyar-ruszin nyelvkönyv és kisszótár a magyar királyi honvédség és leventeoktatók részére.* Uzhhorod: A magyar királyi honvédelmi minisztérium, 1940.

0809 Nevrli, Iaroslav. *Hramatyka i pravopys ukraïns'koï movy.* 2 pts. Uzhhorod: Ivan Roman and Fedor Revai, 1937-1938.

0810 *Novŷi bukvar'.* Prešov, 1920.

0811 Pan'kevych, Ivan. *Hramatyka rus'koho iazyka dlia molodshykh klas shkôl serednykh i horozhans'kykh.* Prague and Bratislava: Derzhavne vŷd., 1922. Second revised edition: Prague, 1927. Third revised edition: Prague, 1936.

0812 Polivka, Ivan. *Uchebnaia kniga real'nykh nauk dlia podkarpatskikh ugrorusskikh narodnykh shkol.* 6 pts. Prešov, 1896.

0813 Rakovskii, Ioann [Rakovszky, János]. *Orosz nyelvtan.* Budapest: A Magyar kir. egyetem nyomdájában, 1867.

0814 *Russkaia pervaia chytanka dlia shkol narodnŷkh v Uhorshchynî.* Budapest, 1867.

0815 Sabov, Evmenii I. [Szabó, Eumén]. *Orosz nyelvtan és olvasókönyv—Russkaia hrammatyka y chytanka.* Uzhhorod, 1890.

0816 Sabov, Evmenii I., et al., eds. *Grammatika russkago iazyka dlia srednikh uchebnykh zavedenii Podkarpatskoi Rusi.* Izdanie OIAD, no. 1. Uzhhorod, 1924.

0817 Sabov, Kirill A. *Grammatika pis'mennago russkago iazyka.* Uzhhorod, 1865.

0818 ———· *Kratkii sbornik izbrannykh sochinenii v prozie i stikhakh dlia uprazhneniia v russkom iazykie.* Uzhhorod, 1868.

0819 Sedlak, Aleksander. *Grammatika russkago iazyka dlia narodnykh shkol eparkhii Priashevskoi.* Prešov, 1920.

0820 Stryps'kyi Hiiador [Iador]. *Chytanka dlia doroslykh.* Rus'ko-Krains'ka biblioteka, no. 1. Mukachevo, 1919.

Szabó, Eumén *see* Sabov, Evmenii

0821 Szémán, István. *Rutén olvasókönyv.* Prešov, 1917.

0822 Tyblevich, Lev. *Golovnyia pravila russkago pravopisaniia, sobrannyia dlia pishushchikh po malorusski.* Uzhhorod, 1920.

0823 Vasilenkov, M. Iv. *Nasha riech': metodicheskaia grammatika dlia russkikh narodnykh shkol Podkarpatskoi Rusi, pt. 1: dlia II. i III. shkol'nykh godov.* Mukachevo: Izd. UTPR, 1925.

0824 Voloshyn, Avhustyn. *Azbuka uhro-rus'koho y tserkovno-slavianskoho chteniia.* Uzhhorod, 1904. Second, third, fourth, fifth, sixth, and seventh editions: Uzhhorod, 19??, 1913, 19??, 19??, 1921, 1924. Reprint: Pittsburgh, Pa., 1917 and 1975.

0825 ———· [Volosin, Agoston]. *Azbuka uhro rusz'koho jazöka.* Uzhhorod, 1916.

0826 ———· *Azbuka y perva chytanka dlia pervoho klassa narodnŷkh shkol na rus'kom iazŷtsî.* Budapest, 1905. Second edition: 1913. Based on the Magyar text of Pál Gencze.

0827 ———· *Chitanka dlia ugrorusskoi molodezhi.* Uzhhorod, 1902?

0828 ——— [Volosin, Agoston]. *Gyakorlati kisorosz (ruszin) nyelvtan.* Uzhhorod, 1907. Reprint: Uzhhorod: Unio, 1920.

0829 ———· *Metodicheskaia grammatika ugro-russkago literaturnago iazyka dlia narodnykh shkol.* Uzhhorod: Izd. OSVV, 1899. Second edition: Uzhhorod, 1919. Third revised edition: *Metodychna hramatyka karpato-rus'koho iazŷka dlia nyzshykh klas narodnŷkh shkôl.* Uzhhorod, 1923. Fourth, fifth, and sixth editions: Uzhhorod, 1924, 1926, 1930.

0830 ———· *Nauka stylyzatsiy dlia IV, V y VI klas narodnŷkh shkol.* Uzhhorod, 1923.

0831 ———· *Praktychna hramatyka rus'koho iazŷka dlia narodnŷkh horozhan-skykh y serednykh shkol.* 2 pts. Uzhhorod: Unio, 1926-1927. Second edition: Uzhhorod, 1928.

0832 Vrabel', Mykhail A. *Bukvar'.* Uzhhorod: Izd. OSVV, 1898.

H. Literary works (anthologies and collected works)

Under this rubric are included only anthologies containing works by several authors and collected works representing individual authors. For individual literary works, see the bibliographies by Lelekach and Haraida (ref. 0032) and Magocsi and Mayo (ref. 0039); for works by Soviet Transcarpathian authors, see the bibliographies in *Pys'mennyky* (ref. 0063), *Ukraïns'ki pys'mennyky* (ref. 0907), and *Vyshnevs'kyi* (ref. 2245); for works by Prešov Region authors, see the bibliographies in Pazhur (ref. 0053) and Zilyns'kyi (ref. 2277); for works by Vojvodinian-Bačka authors, see Latiak (ref. 0030).

0833 Andrella, Mykhail. *Dukhovno-polemicheskiia sochineniia Iereia Mikhaila Orosvigovskago Andrelly protiv katolichestva i unii: Teksty.* Edited by Aleksei L. Petrov. *Materialy dlia istorii ugorskoi Rusi,* vol. 9. Prague: Nákladem Královské české společnosti nauk, 1932.

0834 Bacha, Iurii A., and Rudlovchak, Olena M., eds. *Khrestomatiia novoï zakarpats'koï ukraïns'koï literatury: druha polovyna XIX storichchia.* Bratislava: SPV, 1964.

0835 Badan, Oleksander, ed. *Gruni-stepam . . .: Al'manakh suchasnykh pys'-mennykiv Zakarpats'koï Ukraïny.* Kharkiv: Derzhavne vyd. Ukraïny, 1930.

0836 Baleha, Iurii, ed. *Vishchyi vohon': zbirnyk poeziï 1939-1944 rr.* Uzhhorod: Karpaty, 1974.

0837 Barabolia, Marko. *Tuteshniats'ka guberniia: satyry.* Compiled by My-khailo Mol'nar. Bratislava and Prešov: SPVVUL, 1970.

Bilen'kyi, Iador *see* Stryps'kyi, Hiiador

0838 Bonkáló, Sándor [Rakhivs'kyi, O.]. *Vyimky yz uhors'ho-rus'koho pys'men-stva XVII-XVIII vv.* Budapest: Rus'ko-Krayns'kyi respublychnyi sovit, 1919.

0839 Dukhnovych, Aleksander, ed. *Pozdravlenie Rusynov na hod 1851.* Vienna: Lyteraturnoe zavedenie Priashevskoe, 1850.

0840 ———· *Pozdravlenie Rusynov na hod 1852.* Buda: Lyteraturnoe zavedenie Priashevskoe, 1852.

0841 Dukhnovych, Oleksandr. *Tvory.* 2 vols. Bratislava and Prešov: SPVVUL, 1967-1968.

0842 ———· *Vybrane.* Compiled by Iurii Bacha. Bratislava and Prešov: SPVVUL, 1963.

0843 Grabar', Oleg, ed. *Poèziia Zakarpat'ia 1939-1944*. Bratislava: SVKL, 1957.
0844 Grendzha-Dons'kyi, Vasyl'. *Shliakhom ternovym: vybrani tvory*. Compiled by Mykhailo Mol'nar. Bratislava and Prešov: SPVVUL, 1964.
0845 Haraida, János. *Ruszin elbeszélők*. Szláv irók, no. 1. Uzhhorod: PON, 1943.
0846 Hartl, Antonín, ed. *Pozdravení Rusínů: výbor z literatury podkarpatoruské 1920-1935*. Bratislava: Podkarpatoruské nakladatelství, 1936.
0847 ———· *V Karpatech svíta: výbor z karpato-ukrajinské poesie XIX. a XX. století*. Prague, 1939. Typescript in the Slovanská knihovna, Prague.
0848 Iavorskii, Iul'ian. *Materialy dlia istorii starinnoi piesennoi literatury v Podkarpatskoi Rusi*. KSVSPR, no. 8. Prague: Orbis, 1934.
0849 ———· *Novyia rukopisnyia nakhodki v oblasti starinnoi karpatorusskoi pis'mennosti XVI-XVIII viekov*. KSVSPR, no. 2. Prague: Orbis, 1931.
0850 Kercha, Georgii I. [GIK], ed. *Budet den': sbornik Khustskoi literaturnoi shkoly*. Khust, 1941.
0851 ———· *Dvenadtsat': sbornik molodykh ugrorusskikh poètov*. Uzhhorod: Izd. 'Russkoi pravdy', 1940.
0852 ———· *Zhivaia struia stikhi i proza: sbornik Mukachevskoi literaturnoi shkoly*. Mukachevo, 1940.
0853 Kochysh, Mykola; Latiak, Diura; and Papharhai, Diura, eds. *Tam kolo Dunaiu: zbirnyk opovidan'*. Uzhhorod: Karpaty, 1976.
0854 Kostel'nyk, Havryil. *Pozberany dila*, 2 vols. Vol. 1: *Poezyia*. Vol. 2: *Proza na bachvansko-srymskym ruskym lyteraturnym iazyku*. Compiled by Diura Papharhai. Novi Sad: 'Ruske slovo', 1970-1975.
0855 Lazoryk, Fedir, ed. *Molodi holosy: literaturnyi al'manakh*. Bratislava and Prešov: SVKL, 1956.
0856 *Literaturnyi al'manakh*. Uzhhorod: Russkoe slovo, 1943.
0857 Lelekach, Nykolai, and Hryha, Mykhayl, eds. *Výbor yz staroho rus'koho pys'menstva Podkarpatia*. Uzhhorod: PON, 1944.
0858 Matsyns'kyi, Ivan, ed. *Rozmova storich*. Bratislava and Prešov: SPVVUL, 1965.
0859 Mol'nar, Mykhailo, ed. *Lastivka z Priashivshchyny: z narodnoï ta literaturnoï tvorchosti ukraïntsiv Chekhoslovachchyny*. Kiev: Radians'kyi pys'mennyk, 1960.
0860 Mykytas', Vasyl' and Rudlovchak, Olena, eds. *Poety Zakarpattia: antolohiia zakarpatoukraïns'koï poeziï (XVI st. - 1945 r.)*. Bratislava and Prešov: SPVVUL, 1965.
0861 *Nakanunie: sbornik stikhov i prozy Uzhgorodskoi literaturnoi shkoly*. Uzhhorod, 1941.
0862 Pavlovich, Aleksandr. *Izbrannye proizvedeniia*. Compiled by Ivan S. Shlepetskii. Prešov: KSUT, 1955.
0863 ———· *Vînets' stykhotvorenii*. Compiled by Ivan Polivka. Uzhhorod, 1920.
0864 *Poeziy Aleksandra Dukhnovycha*. Compiled by František Tichý. Lyteraturno-naukovŷi oddîl TP, no. 3. Uzhhorod, 1922.
0865 Pop, Vasilii, ed. *Zakarpatskie novelly: sbornik*. Moscow: Sovetskii pisatel', 1959.
0866 *Pryhorshchi vesny: zbirka poeziï*. Bratislava and Prešov: SPVVUL, 1966.

0867 Sabov, Evmenii, ed. *Khristomatiia tserkovno-slavianskikh i ugro-russkikh literaturnykh pamiatnikov.* Uzhhorod: Knigopechatnyi Fond Eparkhii Mukachevskoi, 1893.
0868 Silvai, Ivan A. *Izbrannye proizvedeniia.* Compiled by Vasilii Zozuliak. Bratislava: SVKL, 1957.
0869 *Shagi.* Mukachevo, 1941.
0870 Stryps'kyi, Hiiador [Bilen'kyi, Iador]. "Uhro-rus'ki litopysni zapysky." *Zapysky NTSh,* vol. 104 (L'viv, 1911), pp. 73-82.
0871 *Trembîta: Lyteraturnŷi al'manakh.* Vŷd. TP, no. 65. Uzhhorod, 1926.
0872 *V sim'i iedynii: zbirnyk khudozhnykh tvoriv ta publitsystychno-krytychnykh statei.* Uzhhorod: Knyzhkovo-zhurnal'ne vyd., 1954.
0873 *Vchora i s'ohodni: zbirnyk opovidan'.* Prešov: KSUT, 1953.
0874 Voron, A., and Khrapek, M., eds. *Al'manakh pidkarpats'kykh ukraïns'kykh pys'mennykiv.* Sevliush, 1936.
0875 *Vos'mero: poeziï molodykh avtoriv.* Bratislava and Prešov: SPVVUL, 1963.

I. Oral history

One of the advantages of working on a historical problem that developed during the twentieth century is that it is possible to speak with individuals who either participated in or observed the events. The author has had the privilege of speaking with numerous persons who lived in, were educated in, worked in, or visited Subcarpathian Rus' and the Prešov Region under several regimes during this century. Below are listed only those who played a leading role in the political and cultural life of the region.

0876 Bokshai, Rev. Emyliian. Editor of *Nedîlia,* 1935-38.
0877 Dunda, Rev. Ernest. Director of the Uzhhorod Greek-Catholic Male Teacher's College, 1938-1944.
0878 Grendzha-Dons'kyi Vasyl'. Writer, editor of *Rusyn,* 1923; *Nasha zemlia,* 1927-1928; *Nova svoboda,* 1938-39.
0879 Hryts'-Duda, Ivan. Director of the Nova Stsena Theater, Khust, 1936-1939.
0880 Kokhannyi-Goral'chuk, Kirill. Head of the Department of National Culture, Uzhhorod, 1920-1930.
0881 Kryl, Rudolf. Assistant editor of *Podkarpatské hlasy,* 1920s, Subcarpathian Forestry Service, 1930s.
0882 Marina, Rev. Julius. Subcarpathian Advisor to the Hungarian Military, 1938-1939, Head of the Department of Religion and Culture, 1939-1944.
0883 Parkanyi, Ivan. Secretary for Subcarpathian Affairs, Office of the President of the Czechoslovak Republic, 1924-1939.
0884 Revai, Iuliian. School Inspector, Deputy to National Parliament, 1935-1938, Minister of Carpatho-Ukraine, 1938-1939.
0885 Shtefan, Avhustyn. Director of the State Commercial Academy, Mukachevo, 1922-1938, Head of Ministry of Religion and Education, 1938-1939.

IV. BIOGRAPHICAL MATERIALS

A. Biographical dictionaries

It is extremely difficult to find comprehensive biographical information on leaders from a provincial area like Subcarpathian Rus', and especially to obtain the sociological data that form the basis for the entries in Appendix 2. Very often, biographical information had to be gathered from still-living fellow activists, friends, or surviving family members.

Certain published sources are useful. This section lists biographical dictionaries, only one of which deals exclusively with Subcarpathian figures (ref. 0898). The other biographical dictionaries are of a more general nature, although they include several entries on Subcarpathians. The most compehensive in this regard is the work by Szinnyei (ref. 0894), although this only covers the nineteenth century. For the most part, the other dictionaries only include those Subcarpathians who were of a particular national or political orientation: Czechophiles (refs. 0886, 0901, 0903); Magyarones (refs. 0891, 0892, 0895-0897); pro-Communists (refs. 0888, 0902, 0907); or non-Communist Ukrainophiles (refs. 0890, 0905). It is most difficult to find information on the local Russophiles, although refs. 0889 and 0901 are somewhat helpful in this regard.

0886   *Album representantů všech oborů veřejného života československého.* Compiled by František Sekanin. Prague: Umělecké nakladatelství Josef Zeidiblich, 1927.

0887   Aristov, Fedor F. *Karpato-russkie pisateli: izsliedovanie po neizdannym istochnikam,* vol. 1. Moscow: Izd. Galitsko-russkago obshchestva v Petrogradie, 1916. Second revised edition. Trumbull, Conn., 1977.

0888   *Bortsi za velyku spravu: aktyvni diiachi revoluitsiinoho rukhu na Zakarpatti: bio-bibliohrafichnyi pokazhchyk.* Uzhhorod: Karpaty, 1967.

0889   *Československé práce o jazyce, dějinách a kultuře slovanských národů od r. 1760: biograficko-bibliografický slovník.* Compiled by Milan Kudělka, Zdeněk Šimecek, et al. Prague: Státní pedagogické nakladatelství, 1972.

0890   *Entsyklopediia ukraïnoznavstva: slovnykova chastyna.* 7 vols. Edited by Mykola Hlobenko and Volodymyr Kubiiovych. Paris and New York: Vyd. 'Molode zhyttia' for the NTSh, 1955-1973.

0891   *Keresztény magyar közéleti almanach.* 2 vols. Compiled by Jenő Hortobágyi. Budapest, 1940.

0892   *Ki-kicsoda?: kortársak lexikona.* Budapest: Béta irodalmi részvénytársaság, 1938.

0893   Lehoczky, Tivadar. "Beregmegyei irók és müvészek." *Beregvármegye monographiája,* vol. 2. Uzhhorod: Pollacsek Miksa, 1881, pp. 129-165.

0894   *Magyar írók élete és munkái,* 14 vols. Compiled by József Szinnyei. Budapest: Hornyanszky, 1891-1914.

0895   *Magyar írók élete és munkái,* új sor. 6 vols. Compiled by Pál Gulyás. Budapest, 1939-1944. Intended to continue the Szinnyei dictionary, this work unfortunately stopped at the letter "D".

0896 *A magyar legujabb kor lexikona.* Compiled by Emil M. Kerkapoly. Budapest, 1930.

0897 *Magyar politikai lexikon, 1914-1929.* Edited by Lázsló Boros. Budapest: Europa irodalmi és nyomdai rt., 1929.

0898 Matsyns'kyi, Ivan. "Slovnyk istorychnoho zhyttia zakarpats'kykh ukraïntsiv." *Duklia,* vol. 15, no. 1—vol. 19, no. 1 (Prešov, 1967-1971).

0899 *Národní shromáždění republiky československé v prvím desítiletí.* Prague, 1928.

0900 Nedzel'skii Evgenii. "Priashevshchina v literaturnykh obraztsakh." *Priashevshchina: istoriko-literaturnyi sbornik.* Edited by Ivan S. Shlepetskii. Prague: Khutor, 1948, pp. 164-238.

0901 *Ottův slovník naučný—nové doby: Dodatky k velikému Ottovu slovníku naučnému.* 6 vols. Prague: J. Otto společnost, 1930-1943.

0902 *Politychni ta kul'turni iuvilei 1974* [and] *1975.* Compiled by Mykhailo Shkurla. Prešov: TsKKSUT, 1973-74.

0903 *Reprezentačný lexikon Slovenska a Podkarpatské Rusi.* Bratislava: Akademia, 1936.

0904 Roman, Michael. *Short Biographies of Famous Carpatho-Russians.* Munhall, Pa., 1962. Three biographies published previously in *The American Slav,* vol. 1, nos. 3, 9, 10 (Pittsburgh, 1939), pp. 13, 7-8, and 12-13.

0905 Romanenchuk, Bohdan. *Azbukovnyk: korotka entsykopediia ukraïns'koï literatury,* 2 vols.: A to H. Philadelphia: Kiev, 1966-1973.

0906 Shlepets'kyi, Andrii. *Nashi budyteli.* 3 vols. Prešov: TsKKSUT, 1968.

0907 *Ukraïns'ki pys'mennyky: bio-bibliohrafichnyi slovnyk.* 5 vols. Edited by O. Bilets'kyi et al. Kiev: Derzhavne vyd. khudozhn'oï literatury i 'Dnipro', 1960-1965.

0908 Yurcisin, John. "The Patrons of the A.R.S." *Kalendar' velikoho i Sokol'-skoho Otd'ilenija GKS na hod 1941.* Homestead, Pa., 1941, pp. 98-112.

B. Individual studies

0909 A. I. "50-lietniaia godovshchina o. Aleksandra Il'nitskago." *Zemledîl'skii kalendar' na hod 1939.* Uzhhorod, 1938. pp. 50-53.

0910 "Adolf Ivanovič Dobriansky." *Slavische Blätter,* vol. 1, no. 3 (Vienna, 1865), pp. 150-153.

0911 "Aleksander Vasiljevič Duchnovič." *Slavische Blätter,* vol. 1, no. 4 (Vienna, 1865), pp. 211-213.

0912 "Aleksei Iulianovich Gerovskii." *Svobodnoe slovo Karpatskoi Rusi,* vol. 7, nos. 9-10 and 11-12 (Newark, N.J., 1965), pp. 5-8 and 6-9; and vol. 8, no. 3-4 (1966), pp. 5-7.

0913 Aristov, Fedor F. "Adol'f Ivanovich Dobrianskii-Sachurov." *Russkii arkhiv,* vol. 51, nos. 3 and 4-5 (Moscow, 1913), pp. 377-411 and 665-706.

0914 ———· "Adol'f Ivanonovich Dobrianskii." *Karpatskii sviet,* vol. 4, nos. 1-2, 3-4, 5-6-7, and 8-9-10 (Uzhhorod, 1931), pp. 1132-1144, 1190-1192, 1225-1230, and 1240-1245; and vol. 5, nos. 1-2-3 and 4 (Uzhhorod, 1932), pp. 1267-1277 and 1302-1309.

0915 ———· "Aleksandr Vasil'evich Dukhnovich." *Russkii arkhiv,* vol. 51, no. 2 (Moscow, 1913), pp. 277-292.

0916 ———· *Aleksandr Vasil'evich Dukhnovich.* Izdanie OIAD, no. 55. Also in *Karpatskii sviet,* vol. 2, nos. 2-3 and 4 (Uzhhorod, 1929), pp. 451-463 and 501-510. Third revised biography, first published in Aristov's *Karpatorusskie pisateli* (ref. 0887).

0917 ———· "Anatolii Fedorovich Kralitskii." *Karpatorusskii sbornik.* Uzhhorod: Izd. PNS, 1930, pp. 69-78.

0918 Aristova, T. F., and Vavrik, V. R. "F. F. Aristov, 1888-1932 gg." *Kratkie soobshcheniia,* vol. 27. Moscow: Institut slavianovedeniia, Akademiia nauk SSSR, 1959, pp. 87-93.

0919 ———· "Zametki o professore F.F. Aristove." *Duklia,* vol. 7, no. 1 (Prešov, 1959), pp. 101-108.

0920 Baitsura, Tamara. *Iurii Ivanovych Venelin.* Bratislava and Prešov: SPVVUL, 1968.

0921 ———· *Mykhailo Andriiovych Baludians'kyi.* Prešov: TsK KSUT, 1969.

0922 ———· "Vasyl' Kukol'nyk i ioho mistse v rozvytku osvity v Rosii." *Duklia,* vol. 17, no. 5 (Prešov, 1969), pp. 55-59.

0923 Balogh-Beéry, László. "Nykolai Kozma—Kozma Miklós (1884-1941): nekrolog." *Zoria—Hajnal,* vol. 2, nos. 1-2 (Uzhhorod, 1942), pp. 194-199.

0924 Beskid, Nikolai A. *Iulii I. Stavrovskii-Popradov.* Izdanie OIAD, no. 50. Uzhhorod, 1929.

0925 ———· *Iz minuvshaho odnoj krest'anskoj semji.* Homestead, Pa., n.d.

0926 Bezsonov, P. "Iurii I. Venelin." *Zhurnal MNP,* vol. 221, no. 5 (St. Petersburg, 1882), pp. 159-206.

0927 Birchak, Volodymyr. *Avhustyn Voloshyn: ieho zhytia y diial'nôst'.* Vŷd. TP, no. 43. Uzhhorod, 1924.

0927a ———· "Avtor pro sebe." In his *Proty zakonu: povist'.* Ukraïns'ka biblioteka, no. 45. L'viv: Ivan Tyktor, 1936, pp. 5-8.

0928 ———· "Ukraïns'kyi filosof Vasyl' Dovhovych." *Iubileinyi zbirnyk na poshanu akademyka Mykhaila S. Hrushevs'koho,* vol. 2. *Zbirnyk istorychnoho-filohohichnoho viddilu Ukraïns'koï Akademiï Nauk,* vol. 76 (Kiev, 1928), pp. 455-460.

0929 ———· "Vasyl' Dovhovych-Dovhanych." *Mîsiatsoslov na 1922 hod.* Uzhhorod, 1921, pp. 68-74.

0930 Demko, Mikhail. "Andrei Brodii." *Zemledîl'skii kalendar' na hod 1939.* Uzhhorod, 1938, pp. 81-84.

0931 ———· "35-lietnii iubilei zhurnalisticheskoi dieiatel'nosti d-ra Iosifa Kaminskago." *Zemledîl'skii kalendar' na hod 1936.* Uzhhorod, 1935, pp. 40-43.

0932 "Direktor Andrii Alys'kevych z nahodŷ ieho 35 lîtn'oî uchytel'skoî dîiatel'nosty." *Podkarpatska Rus',* vol. 5, no. 1-2 (Uzhhorod, 1928), pp. 6-8.

0933 Dobosh, Stepan. *Adol'f Ivanovich Dobrianskii: ocherk zhizni i dieiatel'nosti.* Bratislava: SVKL, 1956.

0934 ———· *Iulii Ivanovich Stavrovskii-Popradov: ocherk zhizni i tvorchestva.* Bratislava and Prešov: SPVVUL, 1975.

0934a Dovhanych, O., and Khlanta, O. *Ivan Ivanovych Turianytsia.* Uzhhorod: Karpaty, 1972.

0935 "Doktor Stepan Andreevich Fentsik: deputat parlamenta." *Kalendar' OS na hod 1937*. Perth Amboy, 1937, pp. 139-141.

0936 "D-r Iosif Viktorovich Kaminskii." *Karpatskii sviet,* vol. 3, no. 7-8 (Uzhhorod, 1930), pp. 1034-1036.

0937 *Dr. Simeon Andrushevich Sabov.* Izdanie OIAD, no. 53. Uzhhorod, 1929.

0938 "Dr. Stefan Andrejevič Fencik." *Kalendar' OS na hod 1936*. Perth Amboy, N.J., 1936, pp. 100-101.

0939 "Evmenii Ivanovich Sabov." *Russkii narodnyi kalendar' OIAD na god 1927*. Uzhhorod, 1926, pp. 85-94.

0940 *Evmenii Ivanovich Sabov: kritiko-biograficheskii ocherk zhizni i dieiatel'-nosti.* Izdanie OIAD, no. 60. Uzhhorod, 1929.

0941 "Evmenii Sabov i ego trudy na pol'zu russkago prosvieshcheniia na Karpatskoi Rusi." *Kalendar' OS na hod 1936*. Perth Amboy, N.J., 1936, pp. 134-137.

0942 Fatieev, A. N. "Akademicheskaia i gosudarstvennaia dieiatel'nost' M. A. Balug'ianskago (Baludianskago) v Rossii." *Karpatorusskii sbornik.* Uzhhorod: Izd. PNS, 1930, pp. 146-208. Also in Izdanie OIAD, no. 76. Uzhhorod, 1931.

0943 Fedor, Pavel S. "A. I. Dobrianskii." *Karpatskii sviet,* vol. 2, no. 7-8-9 (Uzhhorod, 1929), pp. 648-651.

0944 ———· "Fedor Fedorovich Aristov: k 25-lietiiu ego nauchno-literaturnoi dieiatel'nosti." *Karpatskii sviet,* vol. 4, nos. 1-2, 3-4, and 5-6-7 (Uzhhorod, 1931), pp. 1117-1131, 1183-1190, and 1221-1224. Also issued separately in Izdanie OIAD, no. 86. Uzhhorod, 1931.

0945 ———· *Kratkii ocherk dieiatel'nosti A. I. Dobrianskago.* Izdanie OIAD, no. 20. Uzhhorod, 1926.

0946 Fentsik, Stepan A. "Karpatorossy i rossiiane (k istorii kul'turno-natsional'-nykh vzaimnootnoshenii)." *Karpatskii sviet,* vol. 3, no. 7-8 (Uzhhorod, 1930), pp. 1039-1051. Also issued separately in Izdanie OIAD, no. 98. Uzhhorod, 1930. Reprinted in Latin script in *Kalendar' OS na hod 1939*. Perth Amboy, N.J., 1939, pp. 71-80.

0947 ———· and Sabov, Evmenii. *A.A. Mitrak: k otkrytiiu ego pamiatnika v Mukachevie 7.VI.1931 g.* Izdanie OIAD, no. 103. Uzhhorod, 1931. Speech of Sabov reprinted in *Kalendar' Amerikanskaho Russkaho Sokola Sojedinenija na hod 1932*. Homestead, Pa., 1932, pp. 67-75.

0948 Florovskii, Anton V. "Karpatoross I. A. Zeikan—nastavnik imperatora Petra II-go." *Karpatorusskii sbornik.* Uzhhorod: Izd. PNS, 1930, pp. 112-122.

0949 ———· "A. Zeikan—pedagog iz Zakarpat'ia: stranitsa iz istorii russko-zakarpatskikh kul'turnykh sviazei pri Petre Velikom." *Russkaia literatura XVIII veka i slavianskie literatury.* Moscow: Akademiia nauk SSSR, 1963, pp. 105-122.

0950 Franko, Ivan. "Zrazok uhrorus'koho madiaro- i moskofil'stva z poch. XIX st.: Tarkovych Hryhorii." *Zhytie i slovo,* vol. 3, no. 3, (L'viv, 1895), pp. 461-466.

0951 "Georgii Gennadii Bizantsii, episkop mukachevskii." *Listok,* vol. 6, nos. 18-21 (Uzhhorod, 1890).

0952 "Georgii Iul'ianovich Gerovskii (1866-1959)." *Svobodnoe slovo Karpatskoi*

Rusi, vol. 14, no. 11-12 (Newark, N.J., 1972), p. 1.

0953 Gerovskii, Aleksei. "Kratkaia avtobiografiia." *Svobodnoe slovo Karpatskoi Rusi,* vol. 14, no. 5-6 (Newark, N.J., 1972), pp. 2-3.

0954 Gerovskii, Georgii I. "Baludianskii i ego deiatel'nost' v Rossii." *Svobodnoe slovo Karpatskoi Rusi,* vol. 11, no. 1-2 (Newark, N.J., 1969), pp. 1-3.

0955 Grot, K. Ia. "Pamiati Adol'fa Ivanovicha Dobrianskago." *Izviestiia S.-Peterburgskago slavianskago blagotvoritel'nago o-va* (St. Petersburg, 1902), pp. 1-7.

0956 Gulanich, G. "Velikij karpatorusskij tružennik—blaž. pamj. o. Andrej V. Popovič." *Kalendar' GKS na hod 1951.* Munhall, Pa., 1951, pp. 49-52.

0957 Hadzhega, Vasylii. "Ioan Fogarashii," *Podkarpatska Rus',* vol. 5, no. 10 (Uzhhorod, 1928), pp. 207-224.

0958 ———. "Konstantyn Matezonskyi, pershyi khordyrygent hr.-kat. tserkvy v Uzhhorodî," *Podkarpatska Rus',* vol. 6, nos. 1 and 2 (Uzhhorod, 1929), pp. 1-7 and 29-36.

0959 ———. "Mykhayl Luchkai, zhytiepys y tvorŷ." *Naukovŷi zbornyk TP,* vol. 6 (Uzhhorod, 1929), pp. 1-128.

0960 Haraida, Ivan. "Aleksander Stoika—Sztojka Sándor." *Zoria—Hajnal,* vol. 2, nos. 1-2 (Uzhhorod, 1942), pp. 204-209.

0961 Hnatiuk, Volodymyr [V.]. "Iurii Zhatkovych." *Literaturno-naukovyi vistnyk,* vol. 28 (L'viv, 1904), pp. 206-207. Also in *Kalendar' 'Unio' na 1921 hod.* Uzhhorod, 1920, pp. 44-47.

0962 ———. "Kil'ka prychynkiv do biografiï Iuriia Hutsy (Venelina)." *Zapysky NTSh,* vol. 47 (L'viv, 1902), pp. 4-6.

0963 ———. "Rokovyny urodyn Iuriia Hutsy (Venelina)." *Literaturno-naukovyi vistnyk,* no. 5 (L'viv, 1902), pp. 21-22.

0964 Hoholiuk, Vyktor K. *Narodnyi heroi Oleksa Borkaniuk.* Kiev: Vyd. politychnoï literatury Ukraïny, 1968.

0965 Hranchak, Ivan M. *Oleksa Borkaniuk: polum'ianyi borets' za vyzvolennia trudiashchykh Zakarpattia.* Kiev: Derzhavne vyd. politychnoï literatury, 1956.

0966 Iavorskii, Iul'ian A. "P. D. Lodii v izobrazhenii pol'skago romanista." *Karpatskii sviet,* vol. 3, no. 5-6 (Uzhhorod, 1930), pp. 1017-1021. Issued separately in Izdanie OIAD, no. 83. Uzhhorod, 1930.

0967 Iatsko, Pavlo. "Iurii Hutsa-Venelyn." *Narodnŷi yliustrovanŷi kaliendar' TP na hod 1929.* Uzhhorod, 1928, pp. 113-115.

0968 "Ilarion Tsurkanovich." *Vtoryi Viedenskii protsess russkago naroda byvshoi Avstro-Vengrii v 1916 godu: obvinitel'nyi akt.* Philadelphia: 'Pravda', 1924, pp. 92-94.

0969 Il'nyts'kyi, Aleksander. "Pavel' Vyl'helm Tomchanii—Tomcsányi Vilmos Pál." *Zoria—Hajnal,* vol. 2, no. 1-2 (Uzhhorod, 1942), pp. 200-203.

0970 "Ioann Pastelii, episkop Mukachevskii." *Listok,* vol. 7, no. 7 (Uzhhorod, 1891).

0971 "Ioann Rakovskii, narodnyi dieiatel' v Ugorskoi Rusi." *Drevniaia i novaia Rossiia,* vol. 18 (St. Petersburg, 1888), pp. 238-244.

0972 "Iosif de Kamelis, episkop mukachevskii." *Listok,* vol. 6, nos. 6 and 8 (Uzhhorod, 1890).

0973 "István Pankovics (1820-1874)." *Felvidéki sion,* vol. 2, no. 24 (Uzhhorod,

1890), pp. 188-189.
0974 "Iulii Firtsak, gr. kaf. episkop eparkhii mukachevskoi." *Listok,* vol. 7, no. 13 (Uzhhorod, 1891).
0975 "Ivan Andreevich Polivka." *Karpatskii sviet,* vol. 3 no. 7-8 (Uzhhorod, 1930), pp. 1033-1034.
0976 Ivanchov, Antonii. "Mikhail Demko." *Zemledîl'skii kalendar' na hod 1939.* Uzhhorod, 1938, pp. 97-100.
0977 J.E. *Pavel Gojdič, ČSVV, jepiskop Prjaševskij: k jeho dvadcat'ročnomu jubileju so dňa jep. posvjaščenija (1927-1947).* Prešov, 1947.
0978 "Julij Ivanovich Stavrovskij Popradov." *Kalendar' OS na hod 1934.* Perth Amboy, N.J., 1934, pp. 134-138.
0979 Khanat, Irinei I. "Koe-chto iz studencheskoi zhizni Evmeniia Iv. Sabova." *Karpatskii sviet,* vol. 2, no. 5-6 (Uzhhorod, 1929), pp. 596-598. Reprinted in Latin script: *Kalendar' OS na hod 1940.* Perth Amboy, N.J., 1940, pp. 122-124.
0980 Kontratovich, Irinei. "Vospominaniia ob A. L. Petrovie." *Karpatskii sviet,* vol. 5, no. 1-2-3 (Uzhhorod, 1932), pp. 1250-1253.
0981 Korzh, Bohdan. "Mykhailu Tomchaniiu—60 rokiv." *Duklia,* vol. 22, no. 3 (Prešov, 1974), pp. 52-55.
0982 Kosachevskaia, Evdokiia M. *Mikhail Andreevich Balug'ianskii i Peterburgskii universitet pervoi chetverti XIX veka.* Leningrad: Izd. Leningradskogo universiteta, 1971.
0983 Kostiuk, Iurii. "Dyryhent dyryhentiv (do 80-richchia Oleksy Prykhod'ka." *Duklia,* vol. 15, no. 5 (Prešov, 1967), pp. 73-76.
0984 Kovach, Fedir. "Oleksandr I. Pavlovych: 1819-1969." *Duklia,* vol. 17, no. 5 (Prešov, 1969), pp. 40-47.
0985 ———· "Oleksandr Ivanovych Pavlovych," *Shvetlosts,* vol. 7, no. 2 (Novi Sad, 1969), pp. 81-93.
0986 Kralitskii, Anatolii. "Aleksandr Vasil'ev Dukhnovich, Kryloshanin Priashevskii." *Mîsiatsoslov na hod 1866 dlia russkykh uhorskiia kraynŷ.* Uzhhorod, 1865, pp. 47-50; and *Vremennik Instituta Stavropigiiskago s miesiatseslovom na god prostyi 1871.* L'viv, 1870, pp. 117-121.
0987 ———· "Arsenii Kotsak, doktor sv. bogosloviia." *Naukovyi sbornik GRM,* vol. 2, nos. 1-4 (L'viv, 1866), pp. 66-67.
0988 ———· "Ioannikii Bazilovich protoigumen." *Listok,* vol. 6, no. 9 (Uzhhorod, 1890).
0989 Kynakh, Hlib. "Arsenii Kotsak." *Zapysky ChSVV,* vol. 2, no. 3-4 (Zhovkva, 1927), pp. 336-353.
0990 Lelekach, Nykolai. "Zeikanî: do ystorîî famyliî Zeikan'." *Zoria—Hajnal,* vol. 2, no. 1-2 (Uzhhorod, 1942), pp. 35-42.
0991 Lintur, Petr. *A. A. Mitrak: ocherk zhizni i dieiatel'nosti i izbrannyia proizvedeniia.* Russkaia narodnaia biblioteka, no. 10. Uzhhorod: RNG, 1937.
0992 ———· "Andrej Patrus." *Kalendar' OS na hod 1939.* Perth Amboy, N.J., 1939. pp. 81-90.
0993 ———· "I.A. Sil'vaj (Uriil Meteor)—100 l'it so dna roždenija." *Kalendar' velikoho i Sokol'skoho otd'ilenija Sojedinenija.* Homestead, Pa., 1939, pp. 49-52.

0994 Markov, Dmitrii. "Adol'f Ivanovich Dobrianskii." *Karpatskii krai,* vol. 1, nos. 1 and 2 (Mukachevo, 1923), pp. 25-32 and 2-8.
0995 Markov, Osip. "A. I. Dobrianskii." *Sbornik Kolos'e iz galits'ko russkoi nivy.* L'viv, 1902, pp. 89-91.
0996 Markush, Aleksander. *Pamiaty bat'ka Dukhnovycha* (1803-1928). Uzhhorod, 1929.
0997 Mol'nar Mykhailo. "Marko Barabolia," *Duklia,* vol. 18, no. 1 (Prešov, 1970), pp. 61-65.
0998 ———· "Vasyl' Grendzha-Dons'kyi," *Naukovyi zbirnyk MUKS,* vol. 4, pt. 1 (Bratislava, Prešov and Svidník, 1967), pp. 370-378.
0999 Mondok, I. Y. "Pamiat' Ioanna Churhovycha." *Mîsiatsoslov na 1865 hod.* Uzhhorod, 1864, pp. 82-102.
1000 Mosoriak, Iosyf. "Pro sim'iu Nevyts'kykh." *Druzhno vpered,* vol. 19, no. 5 (Prešov, 1969), pp. 13 and 23.
1001 Mushynka, Mykola. "Doslidnyk kul'tury zakarpats'kykh ukraïntsiv" [F. Zapletal]. *Duklia,* vol. 18, no. 1 (Prešov, 1970), pp. 56-60.
1002 ———· "Frantishek Tikhyi 80," *Naukovyi zbirnyk MUKS,* vol. 3 (Bratislava and Prešov, 1967), pp. 109-111.
1003 ———· "Frantyshek Tikhyi—80 richnyi." *Duklia,* vol. 14, no. 3 (Prešov, 1966), pp. 51-53.
1004 ———· "Hromads'ka ta naukova diial'nist' Ivana Pan'kevycha na Zakarpatti v 20-kh rokakh." *Zhovten' i ukraïns'ka kul'tura.* Prešov: KSUT, 1968, pp. 183-198.
1005 ———· "Kornylo Zaklyns'kyi." *Duklia,* vol. 14, no. 4 (Prešov, 1966), pp. 77-78.
1006 ———· "Nevtomnyi doslidnyk zakarpatoukraïns'koï kul'tury: Frantishek Tikhyi," *Duklia,* vol. 16, no. 4 (Prešov, 1968), pp. 343-344.
1007 ———· "Pro zhyttia i tvorchist' Ivana Pan'kevycha." *Duklia,* vol. 10, no. 3 (Prešov, 1962), pp. 71-74.
1008 ———· *Volodymyr Hnatiuk: pershyi doslidnyk zhyttia i narodnoï kul'tury rusyniv-ukraïntsiv Iugoslavii.* Novi Sad: 'Ruske Slovo,' 1967.
1009 Mustianovych, Em. "Iubylei lyteraturnoi dîiatel'nosty o. Iu. Zhatkovycha." *Mîsiatsoslov na hod 1907.* Uzhhorod, 1906, pp. 62-66.
1010 Mykytas', Vasyl'. *F.M. Potushniak.* Uzhhorod: ZOV, 1961.
1011 ———· *O.V. Duknovych: literaturno-krytychnyi narys.* Uzhhorod: ZOV, 1959.
1012 ———· "Oleksandr Mytrak: do 50-richchia z dnia smerti." *Duklia,* vol. 11, no. 1 (Prešov, 1963), pp. 56-58.
1012a ———· "Prosvitytel', pedahoh, pys'mennyk: do 100-richchia z dnia smerti Oleksandra Dukhnovycha." *Zhovten',* vol. 26, no. 3 (L'viv, 1965), pp. 131-135.
1013 ———· *Ukraïns'kyi pys'mennyk-polemist Mykhailo Andrella.* Uzhhorod: UDU, 1960.
1014 Myshanych, Oleksa. "V borot'bi za voliu: do 65-richchia z dnia narodzhennia V. Grendzhi-Dons'koho." *Duklia,* vol. 10, no. 2 (Prešov, 1962), pp. 22-24.
1015 Naumenko, Fedir. "Ivan Havrylovych Kolomiiets'—istoryk ukraïns'koho

Zakarpattia.'' *Zhovten' i ukraïns'ka kul'tura.* Prešov: KSUT, 1968, pp. 96-103.

1015a ———· *Osnovy pedahohiky O.V. Dukhnovycha.* L'viv: LU-L'vivs'ke Naukove Pedahohichne Tovarystvo, 1964.

1016 Nedziel'skii, Evgenii. "A.I. Dobrianskii: k 30-lietiiu so dnia smerti." *Zoria,* vol. 11, no. 8-10 (Uzhhorod, 1931), pp. 30-42.

1017 ———· [Sredin]. "A. I. Dobrianskii." *Tsentral'naia Evropa,* vol. 1, no. 23 (Prague, 1928).

1018 ———· "Aleksander V. Dukhnovich." *Vremennik Stavropigiiskago instituta na 1929 g.* L'viv, 1928, pp. 21-26.

1019 "O. Anatolij Kralickij." *Kalendar' OS na hod 1935.* Perth Amboy, N.J., 1935, pp. 74-75.

1020 "O. Ioann Feodorovich Kizak (1856-1929)." *Karpatskii sviet,* vol. 2, no. 7-8-9 (Uzhhorod, 1929), pp. 636-637.

1021 "O. Irinei Iosifovich Legeza (1861-1929)." *Karpatskii sviet,* vol. 2, no. 7-8-9 (Uzhhorod, 1929), pp. 638-639.

1022 "O. Joann Uriil Silvaj." *Kalendar' OS na hod 1934.* Perth Amboy, N.J., 1934, pp. 140-150.

1023 "O. Viktor Iosifovich Kaminskii (1854-1929)." *Karpatskii sviet,* vol. 2, no. 7-8-9 (Uzhhorod, 1929), pp. 633-635.

1024 "Otec Ivannikij Bazilovič." *Kalendar' OS na hod 1935.* Perth Amboy, N.J., 1935, pp. 84-85.

1025 Pahyria, Vasyl'. "Luka Dem'ian." *Duklia,* vol. 6, no. 5 (Prešov, 1968), p. 443.

1026 Pan'kevych, Ivan. "Dr. Vasyl' Hadzhega i pershi pochatky orhanizatsiï naukovoho rukhu na Pidkarpatskoï Rusi." *Naukovyi zbirnyk TP,* vols. 13-14 (Uzhhorod, 1938), pp. 10-13.

1027 ———· "Kil'ka novykh dat do zhyttiepysu Mykhaila Feodula Orosvegov-s'koho-Andrella." *Podkarpatska Rus',* vol. 8, no. 7 (Uzhhorod, 1931), pp. 162-164.

1028 ———· "Professor Aleksîi Petrov sîmdesiat' lîtnŷi." *Podkarpatska Rus',* vol. 6, no. 4 (Uzhhorod, 1929), pp. 73-79.

1029 Papharhai, Diura. "Zaobydzeny drahokazy Mykhaila Vrabelia." *Shvetlosts,* vol. 6, no. 2 (Novi Sad, 1968), pp. 81-88.

1030 Pekar, Atanasii. "Anatolii Kralyts'kyi, ChSVV—iak istoryk." *Analecta OSBM,* sect. 2, vol. 9 (Rome, 1974), pp. 276-292.

1031 ———· "Bishop Peter Gebey—Champion of the Holy Union (1864-1964)." *Analecta OSBM,* ser. 2, sect. 2, vol. 4, no. 1-2 (Rome, 1963), pp. 294-326.

1032 ———· *Vladyka-muchenyk Teodor Iurii Romzha.* Slovo Dobroho pastyria, no. 121. New York: Vyd. O.O. Vasyliian, 1962.

1033 Perényi, József. "Emlékezés Hodinka Antalról, 1864-1946." *Századok,* vol. 99, no. 6 (Budapest, 1965), pp. 1403-1405.

1034 Perfets'kyi, Evhenii. "K biohrafiï Ioanykiia Bazylovycha." *Nashe mynule,* no. 1-2 (Kiev, 1919).

1035 ———· "Pershyi istoryk Uhors'koï Ukraïny—Ioanykii Bazylovych (z 100-ykh rokovyn z dnia smerty)." *Nashe mynule,* no. 9 (Kiev, 1918), pp. 157-158.

1036 "Petro Gebei, epyskop Mukachevskyi." *Narodnŷi kalendar 'Unio' na rok 1932.* Uzhhorod, 1931, pp. 42-44.

1037 "50-lietnii iubilei dep. Iuliia Fel'deshiia." *Zemledîl'skii kalendar' na hod 1939.* Uzhhorod, 1938, pp. 93-94.

1038 Pôdhorianka, Mariika. *Aleksandru Dukhnovychevi, buditelovi Pôdkarpatskoî Rusy.* Dîtocha byblioteka 'Pcholka', no. 30. Uzhhorod, 1928.

1039 Popov, Aleksander V. *A. I. Dobrianskii, ego zhizn' i dieiatel'nost'.* Mukachevo: Izd. Okruzhnago narodoprosvietitel'skago sovieta Svaliavskago okruga, 1928.

1040 ———· *A. V. Dukhnovich.* Mukachevo, 1929

1041 ———· *Biografiia Iuliia Ivanovicha Stavrovskago Popradova.* Mukachevo: Izd. Filialki OIAD, 1925.

1042 ———· *Evmenii Ivanovich Sabov: kritiko-biograficheskii ocherk zhizni i dieiatel'nosti.* Izdanie OIAD, no. 60. Uzhhorod, 1929.

1043 ———· [V -v, A.]. "Iulii Ivanovich Stavrovskii-Popradov." *Karpatskii krai,* vol. 1, no. 1 (Mukachevo, 1923), pp. 17-24.

1044 ———· *Ivan Antonovich Sil'vai i Ivan Ivanovich Rakovskii: kritiko-biograficheskii ocherk.* Mukachevo: Izd. Narodoprosvietitel'noi rady Nizhne-Verechanskago okruga, 1929.

1045 Popp, Stepan. "Ivan A. Zeikan', naibol'shii karpatorusskii pedagog." *Zemledîl'skii kalendar' na hod 1936.* Uzhhorod, 1935, pp. 43-45.

1046 "Prelat-protoierei Kapytulŷ Mukachevskoi Mons. dr Vasylii Hadzhega upokoylsia." *Dushpastyr',* vol. 15 (Uzhhorod, 1938), pp. 89-90.

1047 Roman, Michael. "50-ti l'itije smerti o. Ivana A. Sil'vaj." *Kalendar' GKS na hod 1954.* Munhall, Pa., 1951, pp. 55-56.

1048 Roman, Mykhailo. "Iuvelei druha zakarpats'koho narodu." *Duklia,* vol. 20, no. 1 (Prešov, 1972), pp. 36-38.

1049 Rosokha, Stepan. "O. Avhustyn Voloshyn iak pedagog i uchytel'." *Nasha dumka,* vol. 2, no. 9 (Munich, 1948).

1050 Rudlovchak, Olena. "Oleksandr Dukhnovych: zhyttia i diial'nist'." Oleksandr Dukhnovych, *Tvory,* vol. 1. Bratislava and Prešov: SPVVUL, 1968, pp. 15-168.

1051 Rychalka, Mykhailo. *O. V. Dukhnovych: pedahoh i osvitnii diiach.* Bratislava: SVKL, 1959.

1052 S.P., "Velikij syn Prjašivčiny—Adol'f Dobrjansjkij." *Blahovistnyk,* vol. 7, nos. 10, 11, 12 (Prešov, 1971); and vol. 8, nos. 1, 2 (1972).

1053 Sato, V. "S. K. Neiman i Zakarpat'e." *Duklia,* vol. 7, no. 2 (Prešov, 1960), pp. 76-77.

1054 Sheregii, Iurii A. "Bard Zakarpats'koï Ukraïny: 70 rokiv narodzhennia Vasylia Grendzhy-Dons'koho," *Shvetlosts,* vol. 5, no. 2 (Novi Sad, 1967), pp. 141-143.

1055 ———· "Bat'ko zakarpatoukraïns'kykh khoriv: 80-richchia Oleksy Prykhod'ka." *Shvetlosts,* vol. 5, no. 4 (Novi Sad, 1967), pp. 306-308.

1056 Shima, P. "G. Iu. Gerovskii." *Duklia,* vol. 7, no. 2 (Prešov, 1959), pp. 65-66.

1057 Shlepetskii, Ivan. "Ivan Andreevich Polivka." *Duklia,* vol. 7, no. 1 (Prešov, 1959), pp. 98-100.

1058 ———· "Vera Ivanovna Fedelesh." *Svobodnoe slovo Karpatskoi Rusi,* vol.

9, nos. 3-4 (Newark, N.J., 1967), p. 18.

1059   Shternberh, Ia. I. "Novi materialy pro Ivana Zeikana." *Tezy dopovidei ta povidomlennia.* Seriia istorychna, vol. 3. Uzhhorod: UDU, 1959, pp. 49-54.

Sredin *see* Nedzielskii, Evgenii

1060   Stefan, Augustine [Shtefan, Avhustyn]. "Biohrafiia o. Avhustyna Voloshyna." *Visnyk Karpats'koho soiuzu,* vol. 2, no. 2-3 (New York, 1971), pp. 2-7.

1060a   ———· "President Msgr. Augustine Voloshyn." *America* (Philadelphia), August 27 and September 3, 10, 17, 1970.

1061   ———· "Vasyl' Grendzha-Dons'kyi." *Ameryka,* nos. 2, 3, 4 (Philadelphia), January 4, 10, 11, 1975.

1062   Stercho, Petro. "Adolf Dobrians'kyi: borets' za pravo samovyznachennia narodiv." *Samostiina Ukraïna,* vol. 20, no. 8 (Chicago, 1967), pp. 4-10.

1063   ———· "Bat'ko karpato-ukraïns'koho vidrodzhennia." *Samostiina Ukraïna,* vol. 18, nos. 7 and 8 (Chicago, 1965).

1064   Stetsiura, I. *Mykola Ivanovych Sydoriak.* Uzhhorod: Vyd. 'Karpaty', 1971.

1065   Symulyk, M. "Polum'ianyi borets' Zakarpattia—Dmytro Vakarov." *Duklia,* vol. 23, no. 2 (Prešov, 1975), pp. 47-56.

1066   Tardy, Lajos. *Balugyánszky Mihály.* Budapest: Akadémiai kiadó, 1954.

1067   Tichý, František. "Anatolij Kralickij (příspěvky k studiu jeho života i díla)." *Carpatica,* vol. 1, řada A (Prague, 1936), pp. 353-371.

1068   ———· [Tykhii, Frantsysk]. "Aleksander Pavlovych: do 25 lîtnŷkh rokovyn eho smerty)." *Podkarpatska Rus',* vol. 2 (Uzhhorod, 1925), pp. 153-154.

1069   ———· [Tykhii, Frantsysk]. "Ioannikii Bazylovych—pervŷi dîepysets' Podkarpatskoi Rusy." *Mîsiatsoslov na 1922 hod.* Uzhhorod: Unio, 1921. pp. 42-50.

1070   ———· "Michail Lučkaj." *Slovanský sborník věnovaný Františku Pastrnkovi k sedmdesátým narozeninám.* Edited by Miloš Weingart. Prague, 1923, pp. 215-220.

1071   Toldy, F. "Dóhovics Bazil emlékezete." *Toldy F. irodalmi beszédei,* vol. 1. Pest, 1872, pp. 267-270.

1072   Torysyn. "Yryna Nevytska, ieî 25-rôchna lyteraturna dîial'nôst'." *Podkarpatska Rus',* vol. 7, no. 6 (Uzhhorod, 1928), pp. 105-107.

1073   Vaida, Mykola. "Monsinior d-r Avhustyn Voloshyn." *Kalendar Provydinnia na 1959 rik.* Philadelphia, 1959, pp. 89-93.

1074   ———· *Velykyi probudytel' Zakarpattia: V pamiat' 150 litn'oho iuvileiu narodzhenniia o. Aleksandra Dukhnovycha.* Philadelphia: 'Karpats'kyi Holos', 1953.

1075   Várdy, Béla. "Antal Hodinka." *Magyar történelmi szemle,* vol. 3, no. 2 (Buenos Aires, 1972), pp. 266-274.

1076   Vergun, Dmitrii N. *A. E. Fentsik i ego miesto v russkoi literature.* Izdanie OIAD, no. 22. Uzhhorod, 1926.

1077   Volenszky, Nestor. "Dóhovics Bazil (1783-1849)." *Felvidéki sion,* vol. 1 (Uzhhorod, 1889), pp. 10-13.

1078   Voloshyn, Avhustyn. "Prelat-protoierei Dr. Vasyl' Hadzhega." *Naukovyi zbirnyk TP,* vol. 13-14 (Uzhhorod, 1938), pp. 5-9.

1079 Vozniak, Mykhailo, "Do kharakterystyky Petra Lodiia." *Zapysky NTSh,* vol. 113 (L'viv, 1913), pp. 148-155.

1080 "Vysokopr. o. Ioakym Khoma: protoyhumen chyna Vasyliia Velykoho." *Narodnŷi kalendar 'Unio' na rok 1932.* Uzhhorod, 1931, pp. 45-46.

1081 "Yvan Myhalka." *Mîsiatsoslov 'Unio' na 1926 hod.* Uzhhorod, 1925, pp. 66-68.

1082 Zaklyns'kyi, Kornii. "Deshcho pro Mykhaila Vrabelia (1866-1923)." *Naukovyi zbirnyk MUKS,* vol. 3 (Bratislava, Prešov, and Svidník, 1967), pp. 293-302.

1083 ———· "Iz mynuloho Zakarpatskoï Ukraïny (obvynuvachennia pys'mennyka Dovhovycha)." *Slavia,* vol. 29, no. 1 (Prague, 1960), pp. 126-128.

1084 Zhatkovych, Iurii Kalman [Zsatkovics, Kálmán]. "Bradács János Munkácsegyházmegyei püspök." *Szent kereszt naptár az 1895 évre.* Uzhhorod, 1894, pp. 98-100.

1085 ———· [Zsatkovics, Kálmán]. "De Kamellis József, Munkácsegyházmegyei vikárius." *Keresztes naptár az 1893 évre.* Uzhhorod, 1892, pp. 96-100.

1086 ———· "Ioann Iosyf de Kamellys, epyskop Mukachevskii y apostol'skii vykarii." *Mîsiatsoslov na 1893 hod.* Uzhhorod, 1892, p. iii.

1087 ———· "Mikhail Manuil Olshavskii, episkop Mukachevskoi i apostol'skoi vikarii." *Listok,* vol. 7, no. 1-6 (Uzhhorod, 1891). Reprinted in *Krestnyi Mîsiatsoslov na 1894 hod.* Uzhhorod, 1894.

1088 "Zhizneopisanie Mikhaila Aleksandrovicha Baludianskago." *Semeinaia biblioteka,* vol. 1 (L'viv, 1855), pp. 317-321.

1089 Zoder, Jindra. *Rodem a životem Konstantina Hrabara.* Uzhhorod, 1935.

1090 Zubrytskii, Dionyzii. "Aleksander Pavlovych (1819-1900)." *Mîsiatsoslov 'Unio' na 1926 hod.* Uzhhorod, 1925, pp. 54-57.

1091 ———· *Aleksander Pavlovych: opysanie ieho zhytia y kharakterystyka eho poeziî.* Uzhhorod, 1925.

1092 ———· *Nash Aleksander Dukhnovych.* Prešov, 1923.

V. SECONDARY SOURCES

The following section contains a wide variety of secondary sources of a scholarly, propagandistic, and even impressionistic nature. Annotations are given for collected works, with cross references to authors whose articles are given full citation elsewhere in the bibliography. In a few instances, annotations are given when the content of an entry is unclear from the title alone.

1093 Ádám, Magda. "Zaharbannia Zakarpattia Khortysts'koiu Uhorshchynoiu v 1938-1939 rr." *Ukraïns'ko-uhors'ki istorychni zviazky.* (Kiev: Naukova dumka, 1964). pp. 78-109.

1094 Adamczyk, Th. "Das Erwachen des Nationalbewusstseins in der Karpatenukraine." *Osteuropa,* vol. 14, no. 5 (Berlin, 1939), pp. 325-332.

1095 Ajtay, Endre, ed. *A magyar katona századunk legszebb magyar csatái.* 2nd ed. Budapest: Jozsef David, 1943.

1096 Andrashko, Ivan. "Ne razbivaite naroda." *Zhivaia mysl',* no. 4 (Prague, 1934), pp. 11-16.

1097   ———· "Privideniia chekhizatsii." *Zhivaia mysl'*, nos. 11-12 (Prague, 1935), pp. 10-13.
1098   Andrusiak, Mykola. "Istoriia Karpats'koï Ukraïny." *Karpats'ka Ukraïna.* L'viv: UVI, 1939, pp. 88-101.
1099   Anonymous. "Golos iz Ugorskoi Rusi." *Russkaia mysl'*, vol. 1, no. 3 (Moscow, 1880), pp. 1-13.
1100   Antalovskii, Stepan (Antalovskij, Š.). "Karpatoruské studenstvo." *Podkarpatská Rus.* Edited by J. Zatloukal. Bratislava: KPPR, 1936, pp. 102-107.
1101   Antonovyč, Marko. "Die staatsrechtliche Entwicklung und der Zustand der Karpaten-Ukraine." *Ukrainische Kulturberichte,* no. 39-44 (Berlin, 1939).
1102   Anuchin, V. A. *Geografiia sovetskogo Zakarpat'ia.* Moscow: Gosudarstvennoe izd. geograficheskoi literatury, 1956.
1103   Anuchin, V. A., and Spiridonov, A. I. *Zakarpatskaia oblast': nauchnopopuliarnoe geograficheskoe opisanie.* Moscow: OGIZ, 1947.
1104   Aradi, Victor. *A rutén skizmapör.* Nemzetiségi aktualitások könyvtára, vol. 1. Budapest, 1914.
1105   ———· "Tanulmányok a nemzetiségi kérdés köréböl (A ruthén skizma; Pásztory Árkád; A hajdudorogi püspökség; Visói Papp Simon)." *Huszadik század,* vol. 28 (Budapest, 1913), pp. 263-276, 378-391.
1106   Aristov, Fedor F. " 'Istinnaia Istoriia Karpato-Russov' A. V. Dukhnovicha: znachenie A. V. Dukhnovicha kak ugro-russkago istorika." *Russkii arkhiv,* vol. 52, no. 5 (Moscow, 1914), pp. 143-155.
1107   ———· "Ugro-russkaia literatura." *Slavianskoe ob"edinenie, no. 5-6 (Moscow,* 1915), pp. 101-104.
1108   Árky, Ákos. *Ruszinszkó küzdelme az autonómiáért 1918-1927.* Budapest: A 'Studium' kiadása, 1928.
1109   ———· *A Ruszinszkói magyarság és Ruszinszkó autonomiája.* Budapest, 1928.
1110   Arsenii, Igumen. "Russkie v Vengrii," *Zhurnal MNP,* vol. 138 (St. Petersburg, 1868), pp. 699-716.
1111   Ashkinazi, Z. G. *Pravoslavnoe dvizhenie v Podkarpatskoi Rusi.* Uzhhorod: Izd. 'Russkaia Zemlia,' 1926.
1113   Bacha, Iurii. "Do pytannia literaturnoho rukhu Uhors'koï Rusi seredyny XIX st." *Duklia,* vol. 7, nos. 2 and 3 (Prešov, 1959), pp. 70-78 and 93-102.
1114   ———· *Literaturnyi rukh na Zakarpatti seredyny XIX stolittia.* Bratislava-Prešov: SPVVUL, 1961.
1115   ———· "Uchast' zakarpats'kykh ukraïntsiv u dyskusiï pro shliakhy rozvytku literatury v zakhidkykh zemliakh Ukraïny v kintsi 40-kh i na pochatku 50-kh rr. XIX stolittia." *Sbornik FFUPJŠ,* vol. 1 (Bratislava, 1960), pp. 48-64.
1116   Bacha, Iurii and Ivan'o, Ivan. "I. Ia. Franko v borot'bi za rozvytok literatury na Zakarpatti." *Dulkia,* vol. 7, no. 2 (Prešov, 1959), pp. 120-131.
1117   Bacha, Iurii, et al. "Umovy rozvytku ukraïns'koï kul'tury v ChSSR pislia 1945 roku." *Zhovten' i ukraïns'ka kul'tura.* Prešov: KSUT, 1968, pp. 473-483.
1118   Bacha, Iurii; Kovach, Andrii; and Shtets', Mykola. *Chomu, koly i iak: vidpovidi na osnovni pytannia z zhyttia ukraïntsiv Chekhoslovachchyny.* Naukovo-populiarna biblioteka TsK KSUT, no. 1. Prešov, 1967.

1119 Bachinskii, Edmund S., ed. *Podkarpatskaia Rus' za gody 1919-1936.* Uzhhorod: RNG, 1936. A series of fifty-one articles revealing the achievements made under the Czechoslovak regime. Includes contributions by S. Chegil', A. Dekhterev, S. Fedor, Iu. Gadzhega, I. Kaminskii, V. Klima, K. Kokhannyi, L. Kreze, E. Nedziel'skii, P. Sova, and I. Zhidovskii.

1120 Bachur, George. "The Tragedy of Carpatho-Ukraine." *The Trident,* vol. 5, nos. 2 and 3 (New York, 1941), pp. 11-16 and 22-28.

1121 Bacsinszky, Tivadar. *Orosz-ruszin kapcsolatok a XIX. század közepén.* Irodalmi és tudományos könyvtár, no. 7. Uzhhorod, 1942.

1122 ——— · "A ruszin nemzeti öntudat útjai." *Zoria—Hajnal,* vol. 3, no. 1-4 (Uzhhorod, 1943), pp. 177-200.

1123 Badan, Oleksandr. "Klasy ta partiï na Zakarpats'kii Ukraïni." *Prapor marksyzmu,* vol. 2, no. 3 (Kharkiv, 1928), pp. 208-233.

1124 ——— · "Natsional'ne pytannia na Zakarpats'kii Ukraïni," *Chervonyi shliakh,* vol. 6, no. 1 (Kharkiv, 1928), pp. 130-150.

1125 ——— · *Zakarpats'ka Ukraïna: sotsial'no-ekonomichnyi narys.* Kharkiv, 1929.

1126 Baitsura, Ivan [Bajcura, Ivan]. "KSČ a ukrajinská otázka." *Z mynuloho i suchasnoho ukraïntsiv Chekhoslovachchyny.* Pedahohichnyi zbirnyk, no. 3. Bratislava: SPV, 1973.

1127 ——— · "Rozvytok polityko-pravovoho rozv'iazannia ukraïns'koho pytannia v Chekhoslovachchyni." *15 rokiv na sluzhbi narodu.* Edited by Iu. Mulychak. Prešov: KSUT, 1966, pp. 27-53.

1128 ——— · [Bajcura, Ivan]. *Ukrajinská otázka v ČSSR.* Košice: Východoslovenské vyd., 1967.

1129 ——— · "UNRP i natsional'ne pytannia." *Duklia,* vol. 12, no. 2 (Prešov, 1964), pp. 81-88.

1130 Baitsura, Tamara. *Zakarpatoukrainskaia intelligentsiia v Rossii v pervoi polovine XIX veka.* Bratislava and Prešov: SPVVUL, 1917.

1131 Bajcsy-Zsilinszky, Endre. "Subcarpathia's re-incorporation creates common Polish-Hungarian Frontier." *Danubian Review,* vol. 6, no. 11 (Budapest, 1939), pp. 14-16.

Bajcura, Ivan, *see* Baitsura, Ivan

1132 Bakhtin, Nikolai N. *Ugorskaia Rus'.* Petrograd, 1915.

1133 Balás, Vilmos. "Az Erdős Kárpátok és a Nagy-Alföld, ruszinok és magyarok." *Zoria—Hajnal,* vol. 2, no. 1-2 (Uzhhorod, 1942), pp. 108-129.

Baleczky, Emil, *see* Baletskii, Emel'ian

1134 Baleha, Iurii. *Khudozhni vidkryttia chy pravda faktu?* Uzhhorod: Karpaty, 1969.

1135 ——— · *Literatura Zakarpattia 20—30-ykh rokiv XX stolittia.* Kiev: Radians'kyi pys'mennyk, 1962.

1136 ——— · "Poeziia oporu i borot'by." *Vishchyi vohon': zbirnyk poeziï 1939-1944 rr.* Uzhhorod: Karpaty, 1974, pp. 285-299.

1137 Baletskii, Emel'ian [E.-yi]. "Evmenii Sabov y nasha diialektolohiia." *Lyteraturna nedîlia,* vol. 2 (Uzhhorod, 1942), pp. 89-92.

1138 ——— · "Iazyk hrammatyky E. Sabova z 1890-ho roku." *Zoria—Hajnal,* vol. 2, no. 3-4 (Uzhhorod, 1942), pp. 336-350.

1139 ——— [Baleczky, Emil]. *Szabó Eumén orosz nyelvtanának hangtana.* Irodálmi és tudományos könyvtár, no. 28. Budapest: PON, 1943.

1140 Ballreich, Hans. *Karpathenrussland: Ein Kapital tschechischen Nationalitätenrechts und tschechischer Nationalitätenpolitik*. Heidelberg: Carl Winter, 1938.

1141 Balogh-Beéry, László [Bereghy, Albert]. *Hogyan szakadt el a Ruthénföld?* Budapest, 1927.

1142 ────· *A magyar-lengyel közös határ és a ruthén terület*. Magyar-lengyel közlemények, no. 2. Budapest: A Magyar Egyetemi és Főiskolai. Hallgatók Lengyelbarát Egyesülete kiadása, 1936.

1143 ────· *Problemy Rusi Podkarpackiej*. Warsaw, 1939.

1144 ────· "A ruszinság rokonsági kapcsolatai." *Zoria—Hajnal,* vol. 2, nos. 1-2 (Uzhhorod, 1942), pp. 98-107.

1145 ────· *A ruthén autonómia*. A kisebbségi intézet kiadványai, no. 4. Pécs, 1937.

1146 ────· *A ruthén autonómia (Targ Henrik lengyel fordítása)*. Warsaw, 1939.

1147 ──── [Bereghy, Albert]. *Ruthén kérdés és az integritás*. Budapest, 1933.

1148 Balogh, Pál. *A népfajok Magyarországon*. Budapest: A M. Kir. vallás ésközoktatásügyi Ministerium, 1902.

1149 Baran, Alexander. *Eparchia Maramorosiensis eiusque Unio*. Analecta OSBM, 2nd ser., sect. 1, vol. 13. Rome, 1962.

1150 ────· *Iepyskop Andrei Bachyns'kyi i tserkovne vidrodzhennia na Zakarpatti*. Biblioteca Logos, vol. 33. Yorkton, Saskatchewan, 1963.

1151 ────· "Kozaky na Zakarpatti v 1619-im rotsi." *Ukraïns'kyi istoryk,* vol. 7, no. 1-3 (New York and Munich, 1970), pp. 76-81.

1152 ────· "Podil Mukachivs'koï Eparkhii v XIX storichchi." *Analecta OSBM,* 2nd ser., sect. 2, vol. 4. Rome, 1963, pp. 534-569.

1153 ────· "Tserkva na Zakarpatti v rr. 1665-1691." *Bohosloviia,* vol. 32 (Rome, 1968), pp. 77-145.

1154 Bartoš, Miroslav. "Masaryk a Podkarpatská Rus." *Podkarpatská Rus.* Edited by J. Zatloukal. Bratislava: KPPR, 1936, pp. 93-95.

1155 Barvins'kyi, B. *Nazva 'Ukraïna' na Zakarpatti*. Onomastica, no. 4. Winnipeg: Ukrainian Free Academy of Sciences, 1952.

1156 Basilovits, Joannicio. *Brevis notitia Fundationis Theodori Koriathovits, olim Ducis de Munkacs, pro Religiosis Ruthenis Ordinis Sancti Basilii Magni, in monte Csernek ad Munkacs: Anno MCCCLX*. 3 vols., 6 pts. Košice, 1799-1805.

1157 Batytskii, A. G. *Ugorskaia Rus'*. Przemyśl: Biblioteka 'Russkoi Zemli,' 1912.

1158 Bazhenova, Nina P. *Narys istoriï revoliutsiino-vyzvol'noho rukhu trudiashchykh Zakarpattia v 1917-1923 rr*. Uzhhorod: UDU, 1962.

1159 Bazylevych, F. "Vôsîm lît pratsî rus'koho teatru TP." *Narodnŷi yliustrovanŷi kaliendar' TP na hod 1929*. Uzhhorod, 1928, pp. 126-132.

1160 Belcredi-Gobbi, M. A. "La Russia subcarpatica." *La vie del mondo,* vol. 40 (Milan, 1935).

1161 ────· "La Ruthenia (Ex-Russia Subcarpatica)." *La vie del mondo,* vol. 45 (Milan, 1939), pp. 482-503.

1162 Belikovskij, Konstantin. "Kraj russkij—kraj nevidomyj." *Kalendar' OS na hod 1933*. Perth Amboy, N.J., 1933, pp. 119-121.

1163 Beneš, Edvard. "Podkarpatská Rus s hlediska zahraničně-politického."

Podkarpatská Rus. Edited by J. Zatloukal. Bratislava: KPPR, 1936, pp. 17-19.

Bereghy, Albert, *see* Balogh-Beéry, László

1164 Beskid, Antonii. "Adol'f Ivanovich Dobrianskii kak vozhd' i obshche-stvennyi dieiatel'." *Karpatskii sviet,* vol. 2, no. 7-8-9 (Uzhhorod, 1929), pp. 639-644.

1165 Beskid, Konstantin M. *Marmaroš.* Uzhhorod, 1929.

1166 ——· *Obrázky z bývalého mad'arského ráje: Monstrosní proces v Mar-marošské Sihoti.* Khust and Mukachevo: Novotný a Bartošek, 1926.

1167 Beskid, Nikolai A. *A. V. Dukhnovich i ego poèziia.* Izdanie OIAD, no. 74. Uzhhorod, 1930.

1168 ——· *Dukhnovichi.* Homestead, Pa.: Izd. ARV, 1934.

1169 ——· *Karpatorusskaia drevnost'.* Izdanie OIAD, no. 43. Uzhhorod, 1928.

1170 ——· *Karpatorusskaja pravda.* Homestead, Pa.: Izd. ARV, 1933.

1171 ——· *Karpatskaia Rus'.* Prešov, 1920.

1172 ——· "Priashevskaia eparkhiia." *Kalendar' Sojedinenija na 1933 hod.* Homestead, Pa., 1933, pp. 67-103.

1173 Bezdomý, Lev. "Karpatoruská literatura v přítomnosti." *Podkarpatoruská revue,* vol. 3, no. 4 (Bratislava, 1938), pp. 41-43.

1174 Bianchi, Gustav, ed. *Publikace pro zem Podkarpatská Rus.* Banská Bystrica: Slovan, 1932. A collection of twenty-nine short articles stressing the economic and social advances made in the region under Czechoslovak rule. Includes studies by P. Fedor, S. Fentsik, and F. Gabriel.

1175 Bidermann, Hermann J. *Die ungarischen Ruthenen, ihr Wohngebiet, ihr Er-werb, und ihre Geschichte.* 2 vols. Innsbruck: Wagner'schen Universitäts-Buchhandlung, 1862-1867.

1176 ——· *Russische Umtriebe in Ungarn.* Innsbruck: Vlg. der Wagner'schen Universitäts Buchhandlung, 1867.

1176a Bidzilia, Vasyl' I. *Istoriia kul'tury Zakarpattia na rubezhi nashoï ery.* Kiev: Naukova dumka, 1971.

1177 Bielousov, Vasyl'. *Dzherelo nezdolannosti.* Uzhhorod: ZOV, 1961.

1178 ——· *Iednannia.* Uzhhorod: Karpaty, 1966.

1179 ——· *Na shliakhu do peremohy: z istoriï komunistychnoï orhanizatsiï Zakarpats'koï Ukraïny 1929-1938 rr.* Uzhhorod: ZOV, 1958.

1180 ——· "Zakarpats'ka oblast'." *Radians'ka entsyklopediia istoriï Ukraïny.* vol. 2. Edited by A. D. Skaba et al. Kiev: ANURSR, 1970, pp. 165-169.

1181 Bielousov, Vasyl', et al. eds. *Zakarpats'ka oblast'.* Istoriia mist i sil Ukraïns'koï RSR. Kiev: ANURSR, 1969. The first Soviet encyclopedic guide to the province, with a general historical survey and similar studies for each of the regions and major cities and towns.

1182 Birchak, Volodymyr [Birčak, Vladimir]. "Dnešní stav podkarpatské litera-tury." *Podkarpatská Rus.* Edited by J. Zatloukal. Bratislava: KPPR, 1936, pp. 193-202.

1183 ——· "Literaturna tvorchist' Zakarpattia v r. 1919-1929." *Novi shliakhy,* vol. 1 (L'viv, 1929), pp. 91-96.

1184 ——· *Lyteraturnî stremlìnia Podkarpats'koî Rusy.* Výd. TP, oddîl lyt.-nauk., no. 2. Uzhhorod, 1921. Second edition: Výd. PTPR, no. 45, Uzh-horod, 1937.

1185 ——· "Ohliad literatury Pidkarpatskoï Rusy po perevoroti." *Podkarpat-*

ska Rus', vol. 12-13 (Uzhhorod, 1935-1936), pp. 14-40.

1186 ———· *Perehliad literatury Pidkarpats'koï Rusy po perevoroti.* Uzhhorod: PTPR, 1937.

1187 Bitsilli, P. M. *Problema russko-ukrainskikh otnoshenii v svietie istorii.* Prague: Izd. Obshchestva 'Edinstvo,' 1930.

1188 "Bobrinskij gróf és a magyarországi ruthének," *Huszadik század,* vol. 30 (Budapest, 1914), pp. 98-100.

1189 Bochkovs'kyi, Ol'gerd I. [Gozdawa, O.]. *Uherská Ukrajina.* Prague and Kiev: Čas, 1919.

1190 Bokšaj, Osyp. "Malířství na Podkarpatské Rusi." *Podkarpatská Rus.* Edited by J. Zatloukal. Bratislava: KPPR, 1936, pp. 214-217.

1191 Boldyzhar, Mykhailo M. "Antyklerykal'na diial'nist' Zakarpats'koï kraiovoï orhanizatsiï Komunistychnoï partiï Chekhoslovachchyny (1921-1939 rr.)." *Duklia,* vol. 24, no. 1 (Prešov, 1976), pp. 62-67.

1192 ———· *Torzhestvo lenins'kykh pryntsypiv ateistychnoho vykhovannia trudiashchykh na Zakarpatti.* Uzhhorod: UDU, 1974.

1193 Boldyzhar, Mykhailo M., et al. "Deiaki pytannia borot'by z relihiinymy perezhytkamy." *Velykyi zhovten' i rozkvit vozz'iednanoho Zakarpattia.* Uzhhorod: Vyd. Karpaty, 1970, pp. 420-433.

1194 Bölöny, József. *A kárpátaljai vajdaságról és annak önkormányzatáról szóló törvényjavaslat bírálata.* Magyar közigazgatás könyvtára, no. 12. Budapest, 1940.

1195 Bondar, Andrii D. "Iz istorii shkoly v Zakarpatskoi Ukraine do vossoedineniia ee s Sovetskoi Ukrainoi." *Sovetskaia pedagogika,* vol. 18, no. 3 (Moscow, 1954), pp. 96-110. Also in *Duklia,* vol. 2, nos. 3-4 (Prešov, 1954), pp. 150-169.

1196 ———· "O. Dukhnovych i rozvytok narodnoho shkil'nytstva na Zakarpatti." *Oleksandr Dukhnovych: zbirnyk materialiv.* Edited by M. Rychalka. Prešov: KSUT, 1965, pp. 224-236.

1197 Bonkáló, Sándor. *A kárpátalji rutén irodalom és művelődes.* Felvidéki tudományos társaság kiadványai, 1 sor., no. 2. Pécs: Dunántúl Pécsi egyetemi könyvkiadó és nyomda, 1935.

1198 ———· "Kárpátorosz, nagyorosz, orosz, ruszin, rutén, uhrorusz, ukrán." *Láthatár,* vol. 7, no. 7 (Budapest, 1939), pp. 292-295.

1199 ———· *A magyar rutének.* Budapest: Ferdinand Pfeifer, 1920.

1199a ———· "Az orosz és a rutén irodalmi nyelv kérdéséhez." *Nyelvtudomány,* vol. 5 (Budapest, 1915), pp. 80-110.

1200 ———· "Rus'kyi lyteraturnŷi iazŷk—A ruszin irodalmi nyelv." *Zoria—Hajnal,* vol. 1, no. 1-2 (Uzhhorod, 1941), pp. 54-71.

1201 ———· *A Rutének (Ruszinok).* Budapest: Franklin-Társulat, 1940.

1202 ———· "Die ungarländischen Ruthenen." *Ungarische Jahrbücher,* vol. 1 (Berlin, 1922), pp. 215-232, 313-341.

1203 Borkaniuk, Oleksa. *Chym ie dlia nas Radians'kyi Soiuz.* Bratislava: Fedor Zupka, 1938.

1204 *Borot'ba uhors'koho narodu za sotsializm: materialy respublikans'koï naukovoï sesiï, prysviachenoï 50-richchiu proholoshennia Uhors'koï Radians'koï Respubliky 1919 roku.* Uzhhorod: ANURSR-UDU, 1970.

1205 Borshavs'kyi, S. *Chorne pavutynnia.* Uzhhorod: ZOV, 1960.

1205a Borshchak, Illia. *Zakarpats'ka Ukraïna v mizhnarodnii hri.* L'viv, 1938.
Borzhava, Iurii, *see* Sabol, Sebastiian
1206 Bourgeois, Charles. "Les Gréco-catholiques en Russie-Subcarpathique," *Nouvelle revue théologique,* vol. 57, no. 7 (Tournai and Louvain, 1930), pp. 566-584.
1207 Boysak, Basil. *Echumenism and Manuel Michael Olshavsky.* Theologia Montis Regii, vol. 49. Montreal: Faculty of Theology, University of Montreal, 1967.
1208 ———· *The Fate of the Holy-Union in Carpatho-Ukraine.* Toronto and New York, 1963.
1209 Braham, Randolph L. "The Destruction of the Jews of Carpatho-Ruthenia." *Hungarian Jewish Studies.* New York: World Federation of Hungarian Jews, 1966, pp. 223-235.
1210 Brandejs, Jan. "Ce que le gouvernement tchécoslovaque avait accompli au point de vue agricole dans la Russie subcarpathique." *L'Est Européen agricole,* vol. 5 (Paris, 1935), 44 pp.
1211 ———· "Vývoj politických poměrů na Podkarpatské Rusi v období 1918-1935. *Podkarpatská Rus.* Edited by J. Zatloukal. Bratislava: KPPR, 1936, pp. 72-88.
1212 Braneshevych, Branyslav. "Rusnatsy u Voivodyny od 1849. roku po koniets 80-tykh rokokh XIX stolïtyia." *Shvetlosts,* vol. 10, no. 3 (Novi Sad, 1974), pp. 240-250.
1213 Brashchaiko, Mykhailo. *Ches'ko-rus'ki vzaemynŷ.* Knyshky 'Rusyna,' no. 4. Uzhhorod, 1923.
1214 ———· "Politychna sytuatsiia Pidkarpats'koi Rusy 25 rokiv tomu nazad i teper'." *Iuvlyleinŷi yliustrovanŷi kalendar' 'Unio' na rok 1928.* Uzhhorod, 1927, pp. 139-146.
1215 British Foreign Office. *Hungarian Ruthenia.* London: H. M. Stationery Office, 1920.
1216 Brodii, Andrei [Bródy, András]. *Az országos központi nemzeti tanács törvényjavaslata az autonom Podkárpátszká Rusz alkotmányáról.* Uzhhorod, 1936.
1217 ——— [Brodi, Andreas]. "Der Panslawismus und die Russinen des Karpatenlandes." *Südostdeutsche Rundschau,* vol. 2, no. 6 (Budapest, 1943), pp. 443-451.
1218 ———· "Korotka ystoriia piat'litnoi bor'by karpatorusskaho naroda za avtonomiiu." *Karpato-russkii zemledil'skii kalendar' na 1925 hod.* Uzhhorod, 1924. pp. 49-81.
1219 Budilovich, Anton S. "K voprosu o plemennykh otnosheniiakh v Ugorskoi Rusi." *Zhivaia starina,* vol. 13, no. 3 (St. Petersburg, 1903), pp. 265-275.
1220 ———· *Ob osnovnykh vozrieniiakh A. I. Dobrianskago.* St. Petersburg, 1901.
1221 Bukovskii, Ivan S. "Iz istorii iazykovogo khaosa karpatorosov." *Kalendar' OS na hod 1936.* Perth Amboy, 1936, pp. 179-182.
1222 Bukovych, D. *Pavutynnia omany [antynarodna diial'nist' uniats'koï tserkvy na Zakarpatti].* Uzhhorod: Karpaty, 1974.
1223 Bulla, Béla. "A Ruténföld." *Magyar szemle,* vol. 35, no. 4 (Budapest, 1939), pp. 297-303.

1224 Bunhanych, Petro P. "Movnyi riznovyd virshovanoï tvorchosti O. V. Dukhnovycha ta suchasni iomu zasoby movnoho spilkuvannia." *Oleksandr Dukhnovych: zbirnyk materialiv.* Edited by M. Rychalka. Prešov: KSUT, 1965, pp. 170-183.

1225 But, I. "Zakarpattia i evoliutsiia moskvofil'stva." *Vistnyk,* vol. 7, no. 1 (L'viv, 1939), pp. 60-63.

1226 Chaloupecký, Václav. "Dvě studie k dějinam Podkarpatska: l. Sůl z Bulharska (892). 2. Kdy bylo Horní Potisí připojeno k Uhrám." *Sborník filosofické fakulty university Komenského,* vol. 3, no. 30 (Bratislava, 1925), pp. 133-186.

1227 Charvát, V. "Konec Karpatské Ukrajiny." *Slovanský přehled,* vol. 31 (Prague, 1939), pp. 60-62, 116-117.

1228 Chegil', Stepan M. "Narodoprosvietitel'naia robota na Podkarpatskoi Rusi." *Podkarpatskaia Rus' za gody 1919-1936.* Edited by E. Bachinskii. Uzhhorod: RNG, 1936, pp. 113-120.

1229 Chmelař, Josef. "Podkarpatská Rus a Společnost národů." *Zahraničná politika,* vol. 1 (Prague, 1922), pp. 469-472.

1230 ———· "Politické pomery v Podkarpatské Rusi." *Podkarpatská Rus.* Edited by J. Chmelař et al. Prague: Orbis, 1923, pp. 184-192.

1231 Chmelař, Josef; Klíma, Stanislav; Nečas, Jaromír; eds. *Podkarpatská Rus: obraz poměrů přírodních, hospodářských, politických, církevních, jazykových a osvětových.* Prague: Orbis, 1923. Translated into Rusyn by Aleksander Fedinets' et al.: New York: 'Den', 1924. The first Czech-language general anthology, with nineteen articles on various aspects of the Subcarpathian Rus', includes works by J. Chmelař, K. Kadlec, M. Mejgeš, I. Pan'kevych, E. Perfets'kyi, J. Pešek, E. Sabov, F. Tichý, and A. Voloshyn.

1232 Chokerlii, V. "Za pravil'noe osveshchenie deiatel'nosti Dobrianskogo." *Duklia,* vol. 5, no. 4 (Prešov, 1957), pp. 98-101.

1233 Chorniak, Ostap. "V 30-littia derzhavnotvorchoho chynu ukraïns'koho Zakarpattia." unpublished typescript.

1234 Chuma, Andrii. "Iz istorii ukrainskikh shkol Zakarpat'ia i vostochnoi Slovakii: razvitie ukraïnskikh shkol v XIX veke." *Duklia,* vol. 7, nos. 1 and 2 (Prešov, 1959), pp. 42-52 and 79-91.

1235 ———· and Bondar, Andrii. *Ukraïns'ka shkola na Zakarpatti ta skhidnii Slovachchyni (istorychnyi narys),* pt. 1. Naukovo-populiarna biblioteka TsKKSUT. Prešov, 1967.

1235a Chumak, T.M. "Svoeobrazie literaturnogo protsessa v Zakarpat'e v seredine XIX veka i printsipy ego izucheniia." *Nekotorye teoreticheskie problemy russkoi literatury: nauchno-tematicheskii sbornik.* Uzhhorod: UDU, 1969, pp. 131-165.

1236 Cintulů, V. "Z národnostního rozhraní ruskoslovenského v Uhrách." *Sborník České společností zeměvědné,* vol. 12 (Prague, 1906), pp. 238-243.

1237 Coleman, Arthur P. and Bezinec, George B. "The Rise of Carpatho-Russian Culture." *Central European Observer,* vol. 16, nos. 17, 18, 19 and 20 (Prague, 1938), pp. 262-264, 280, 295-296, 311-313 and 327-328.

1238 Čollák, Ladislav. "Položenie slovenských grécko-katolikov." *Slovenská liga,* vol. 12 (Bratislava, 1935), pp. 85-97.

1239 Cornisch, Vaughan. "The World's New Boundaries and their Historic Origins: IV. The Ruthenian Borderland." *Empire Review* (London, 1927), pp. 209-213.

1240 Csáky, Étienne de. *La question ruthène.* Questions de l'Europe orientale, no. 7. Budapest: Ferd. Pfeiffer, 1920. Reprinted in *Seeds of Conflict,* series 1: *Irredentist and Nationalist Questions in Central Europe, 1913-1939: Hungary,* vol. 1. Nendeln, Liechtenstein: Kraus, 1973.

1241 *A Csallóköztől Kárpátaljáig. A visszatért magyar föld.* Budapest: Idegenforgalmi ujságirók egyesülete, 1939.

1242 Csikós, Gyula. *Kárpátoroszország a statisztika tükrében.* Budapest, 1939.

1243 Csomár, Zoltán. *Husz év Ungvár történetéböl 1918-1938.* A Magyar társaság könyvei, no. 1. Budapest, 1939.

Curkanovič, Harion J., *see* Tsurkanovich, Ilarion

1244 Cziple, Sándor. *A mármarosi püspökség kérdése.* Budapest, 1910.

1245 Dami, Aldo. *La Ruthénie subcarpatique.* Geneva and Annemasse: Les éditions du Mont-Blanc, 1944.

1246 ———· *Les nouveaux martyrs: destin des minorités.* Paris: Fernand Sorlot, 1930.

1247 Danilák, Michal. [Danylak, Mikhal]. *Halyts'ki, bukovyns'ki, zakarpats'ki ukraïntsi v revoliutsiï 1848-1849 rokiv.* Bratislava and Prešov: SPVVUL, 1972.

1248 ———· "Styky haličských a zakarpatských Ukrajincov v 2. polovici XIX storočia." *Zhovten' i ukraïns'ka kul'tura.* Prešov: KSUT, 1968, pp. 35-48.

1249 Danko, Joseph. "Plebiscite of Carpatho-Ruthenians in the United States Recommending Union of Carpatho-Ruthenia with the Czechoslovak Republic." *The Annals of the Ukrainian Academy of Arts and Sciences,* vol. 11, no. 1-2 (New York, 1964-1968), pp. 184-207.

1249a Danko, M. "Comment l'Ukraine subcarpathique lutte pour son émancipation." *Voix des peuples,* vol. 5, no. 3 (Geneva, 1938), pp. 187-192.

1250 Darás, Gábor. "A félszázados ruszin nacionalizmus." *Magyar szemle,* vol. 34, no. 3 (Budapest, 1938), pp. 254-261.

1251 ———· "Les Karpatorusses: leur chemin vers la conscience et l'unité nationale." *Nouvelle Revue de Hongrie,* vol. 59, no. 12 (Budapest, 1938), pp. 587-595.

1252 ———· *Mit kell tudnia minden magyarnak a ruténekről?* Budapest: A Magyar nemzeti szövetség kiadása, 1938.

1253 ———· *A Ruténföld elszakításának előzményei (1890-1920).* Ujpest: Vörösmarty irodalmi társaság, 1936.

1254 ———· *A ruthén kérdés tegnap és ma.* Budapest, 1938.

1255 ———· "Az ukrán eszme és a rutének." *Külügyi szemle,* vol. 17, no. 1 (Budapest, 1940).

1256 David, Klement. *Vlastivěda Slovenska a Podkarpatské Rusi pro mládež v českých školach.* Zábřeh, 192?.

1257 Davidovich, S. "Carpatho-Ukraine." *Contemporary Russia,* vol. 2, no. 4 (London, 1938), pp. 421-426.

1258 Décsy, Antal. *Az magyar oroszokrúl való igen rövid elmélkedés.* Košice: Füskúti Landerer Ferentz, 1797.

1259 Dekhterev, Aleksei. "Kak nachalos' vosstanovlenie pravoslaviia na Zakarpatskoi Rusi [1936]." *Svobodnoe slovo Karpatskoi Rusi,* vol. 4, nos. 5-6 and 7-12 (Newark, N.J., 1962), pp. 3-5 and 3-6.

1260 ——· "Pravoslavie na Podkarpatskoi Rusi." *Podkarpatskaia Rus' za gody 1919-1936.* Edited by E. Bachinskii. Uzhhorod: RNG, 1936, pp. 97-100.

1261 Demko, Mykhayl. "Podkarpatskii Zemledîl'skii Soiuz." *Russkii zemledîl'-skii kalendar' na hod 1922* (Uzhhorod: Izd. 'Podkarpatskoho Zemledîl'-skoho Soiuza,' 1922), pp. 130-148.

1262 Deshko, Andrei N. "O Karpatskoi Rusi." *Kievlianin,* vol. 3 (Moscow, 1850), pp. 19-31. Reprinted in *Semeinaia biblioteka,* vol. 1, no. 2 (L'viv, 1855), pp. 210-224.

1263 Devollan, Grigorii. "Ugorskaia Rus'." *Russkii arkhiv,* vol. 16, no. 1 (Moscow, 1878), pp. 235-250. Published separately: Moscow, 1878.

1264 Dezső, László [Dezhe, L.]. *Ocherki po istorii zakarpatskikh govorov.* Budapest: Akadémiai kiadó, 1967.

1265 Dobosh, Stepan. "Ideia slov'ians'koho iednannia v tvorchosti Stavrovs'koho-Popradova." *Zhovten' i ukraïns'ka kul'tura.* Prešov: KSUT, 1968, pp. 86-95.

1266 Dobrianskii, Adol'f [Iv. -tsch, A.]. *Nomenclation der oesterreichisch-ungarischen Russen.* Vienna: Hugo Hoffman, 1885. First published in *Parlamentär,* no. 7 (Vienna, 1885).

1267 ——· *O sovremennom religiozno-politicheskom polozhenii Avstro-Ugorskoi Rusi.* Moscow, 1885.

1268 —— [A.I.D.]. "O zapadnykh granitsakh Podkarpatskoi Rusi, so vremen sv. Vladimira." *Zhurnal MNP,* vol. 208 (St. Petersburg, 1880), pp. 134-159.

1269 ——· *Vzgliad na vopros ob obshcheslavianskom iazykie.* Warsaw, 1888.

1270 Dobrovský, Jozef. "Russniaken in der Marmarosch." *Vaterländische Blätter,* no. 45. (Vienna, 1812).

1271 Dobrylovs'kyi, Mykola. *Karpats'ka Ukraïna.* Poděbrady: Ukraïns'kyi tekhnichno-hospodars'kyi instytut, 1939.

1272 Domokos, László. *Ruszka-Krajna a népek ítélőszéke elött.* Budapest, 1919.

1273 Dontsov, Dmytro. "Berezen' 1939." *Vistnyk,* vol. 7, no. 4 (L'viv, 1939), pp. 298-305.

1274 Doroshenko, Dmytro. *Uhors'ka Ukraïna.* Informatsiina ukraïns'ka seriia, no. 1. Prague and Kiev: Vsesvit, 1919.

1275 Drahný, Václav and Drahný, František, *Podkarpatská Rus, její přirodní a zemědělské poměry.* Publikace Ministerstva zemědělství, no. 15. Prague, 1921.

1276 Drahomanov, Mykhailo. "Les paysans russo-oukrainiens sous les liberaux hongrois." *Le travailleur,* vol. 1, no. 4 (Paris, 1877). Published in Italian translation: *Revista internationale del socialismo,* no. 1 (Rome, 1880).

1277 Dudáš, Andrej. *Rusínska otázka a jej úzadie.* Buenos Aires: Zahraničná matica slovenská, 1971.

1278 Duknovych, Aleksander. "Istinnaia istoriia Karpato Rossov ili Ugorskikh Rusinov" (1853). Translated into Russian by F. F. Aristov. *Russkii arkhiv,* vol. 52, no. 4-5 (Moscow, 1914), pp. 529-559. Reprinted in O. V.

Dukhnovych. *Tvory,* vol. 2. Bratislava and Prešov: SPVVUL, 1967, pp. 531-566.

1279 ———· *Istoriia Priashevskoi eparkhii* (1846). Translated into Russian by K. Kustodiev: St. Petersburg, 1877. Reprinted in: O. Dukhnovych. *Tvory,* vol. 2 (Bratislava and Prešov: SPVVUL, 1967), pp. 451-528. Translated into English by A. Pekar: *History of the Eparchy of Prjašev.* Analecta OSBM, ser. 2, sect. 1, vol. 25. Second edition. Rome, 1971.

1280 ———· "O narodakh krainianskykh yly karpatorossakh" (1848), *Karpaty,* no. 1 (Uzhhorod, 1958), pp. 121-123. Also in: *Duklia,* vol. 6, no. 4 (Prešov, 1958), pp. 95-98.

1281 *Dukhnovych y Dukhnovychovtsî: prysviata dnevy 'Russkoi Kul'turŷ' v Uzhhorodî.* Uzhhorod, 1929.

1282 Dulichenko, Aleksander D. "Stanovlenie i razvitie rusinskogo literaturnogo iazyka v Iugoslavii." *Sovetskoe slavianovedenie,* vol. 8, no. 3 (Moscow, 1972), pp. 38-50.

1283 ———· "Z ystoryi formuvania ruskoho lyteraturnoho iazyka." *Nova dumka,* vol. 2, no. 4 (Vukovar, 1973), pp. 46-47.

1284 Dulishkovich, Ioann. *Istoricheskiia cherty Ugro-Russkikh.* 3 Vols. Uzhhorod 1874-1877.

1285 Dushnyk, Walter. "The Epopea of Carpatho-Ukraine." *The Trident,* vol. 3, no. 4-5 (New York, 1939), pp. 1-7.

1286 Dutsar, Andrii. "Iz istoriï priashivs'kykh ukraïns'kykh (rusyns'kykh) serednikh shkil ta hurtozhytkiv." *Duklia,* vol. 13, no. 3 (Prešov, 1965), pp. 100-104.

1287 Dvorský, Viktor. "Země Podkarpatská Rus." *Osm přednášek o Podkarpatské Rusi.* Edited by D. Vergun. Prague, 1925, pp. 5-10.

1288 Dzendzelivs'kyi, Iosyf O. "Spivrobitnytstvo V. Hnatiuka z Iu. Stavrovs'kym u 1896-1899 rr." *Zapysky Naukovoho tovarystva KSUT,* vol. 1, no. 1 (Prešov, 1972), pp. 43-64.

1289 Egan, Imre. *Milyen legyen a ruszin autonómia?* Uzhhorod: Husvét havában, 1939.

1290 "Eine Karpatenlandschaft sucht einen Namen: kulturgeschichtliche Glossen zur 600-jährigen (1352-1952) Geschichte der Ruthenen in den Nordost-Karpaten." *Südost-Stimmen,* vol. 2, no. 1 (Stuttgart, 1952), pp. 1-6.

1291 *Emlékkönyv a görög szertatású katholikus magyarok zarándoklatáról.* Budapest, 1914.

1292 Evseev, I. F. *Narodnye komitety Zakarpatskoi Ukrainy—organy gosudarstvennoi vlasti (1944-1945).* Moscow: Gosudarstvennoe izd. iuridicheskoi literatury, 1954. Published in Czech translation: *Z dějin Zakarpatské Ukrajiny.* Prague: Státní nákladelství politické literatury, 1956.

1293 Fall, Andrew. "The Economic Re-construction of Subcarpathia." *Danubian Review,* vol. 7, no. 5 (Budapest, 1939), pp. 20-24.

1294 ———· "The Future of Ruthenia and the Right of Self-Determination." *Danubian Review,* vol. 6 (Budapest, 1938), pp. 5-29.

1295 Fano, Štefan. "Pol'sko a Zakarpatská Ukrajina v prvej polovici tridsiatych rokov." *Slovanské študie,* vol. 14: *História* (Bratislava, 1973), pp. 85-106.

1296 Fano, Štefan. "Protičeskoslovenské ostrie pol'sko-mad'arského zbližovania v rokoch 1934-1936." *Slovanský přehled,* vol. 56, no. 5 (Prague, 1970), pp. 342-347.

1297 ———· "Zakarpatská Ukrajina v politických kalkuláciách susedných štatov v období od Mníchova po marec 1939." *Slovanské študie,* vol. 11: *História* (Bratislava, 1971), pp. 61-79.

1298 ———· "Zakarpatská Ukrajina v politike súsedov a fašistických mocností 1933-1939." Habilitation thesis. Bratislava: Ústav dejín európskych socialistických krajín SAV, 1971.

1299 Fedelesh, Viera I. *Uchebnik istorii Podkarpatskoi Rusi.* Mukachevo, 1922.

1300 ———· *Uchebnyk ystoriy Podkarpatskoi Rusy ot naidavnîishykh chasov do dneshnykh dnei y Chekhoslovakiy do XIV vîka.* 2nd ed. Uzhhorod: Unio, 1924.

1301 Fedor, Pavel S. "Krátký nástin školství na Podkarpatské Rusi." *Publikace pro zem Podkarpatská Rus.* Edited by G. Bianchi. Banská Bystrica: Slovan, 1932, pp. 65-69.

1302 ———· "Natsional'naia stoikost' karpatorusskago naroda." *Russkii narodnyi kalendar' na god 1937.* Izdanie OIAD, no. 115. Uzhhorod, 1936, pp. 89-90.

1303 ———· *Ocherki karpatorusskoi literatury so vtoroi poloviny XIX stolietia.* Izdanie OIAD, no. 56. Uzhhorod, 1929.

1304 ———· "Teatral'noe dielo na Podkarpatskoi Rusi." *Podkarpatskaia Rus' za gody 1919-1936.* Edited by E. Bachinskii. Uzhhorod: RNG, 1936, pp. 141-143.

1305 Feerchak, Petr. "Natsional'noe dvizhenie ugro-rossov." *Galitskaia Rus',* nos. 33-42 (L'viv, 1891).

1306 ———· "Natsional'noe dvizhenie v Ugorskoi Rusi." *Galitsko-russkii viestnik,* vol. 1, no. 1 (St. Petersburg, 1894), pp. 49-62.

1307 ———· *Ocherk literaturnago dvizheniia ugorskikh russkikh.* Odessa, 1888.

1308 Fejér, György. "A' Magyar országi Ruthenok' eredetéről." *Tudományos gyűjtemény,* vol. 23, no. 7 (Pest, 1839), pp. 1-25.

1309 Fel'baba, Iosyf, ed. *25—Ukraïns'komu natsional'nomu teatru.* Bratislava and Prešov: SPVVUL, 1971.

1310 Fentsik, Evgenii. "Nachalo nashei pis'mennosti." *Listok,* vol. 1, no. 6 (Uzhhorod, 1885), pp. 85-86.

1311 ———· "Ocherk ugro-russkoi pis'mennosti." *Listok,* published serially in almost every issue from vol. 8, no. 5 (Uzhhorod, 1892) through vol. 10, no. 23 (1894); and in vol. 12, no. 1 (1896).

1312 ———· [E.F.]. "Rufeny." *Listok,* vol. 2, no. 3 (Uzhhorod, 1886). Reprinted in *Karpatskii krai,* vol. 1, no. 10 (Mukachevo, 1924), pp. 18-20; and in *Kalendar' OS na hod 1935.* Perth Amboy, N.J., 1935, pp. 136-137.

1313 ———· *Sobranie sochinenii,* vol. 2: *Stat'i.* Izdanie OIAD, no. 79. Uzhhorod, 1932.

1314 Fentsik, Stepan A. *Chekhoslovaki i karpatorossy (1919-1929).* Izdanie OIAD, no. 66. Uzhhorod, 1929.

1315 ———· (Fenczik, István). *A Kárpátaljai autonómia és a kisebbségi kérdés.* A kisebbségi intézet kiadványai, no. 12. Kecskemét, 1941.

1316 ———· "Lidová výchova na Podkarpatské Rusi." *Publikace pro zem Podkarpatská Rus.* Edited by G. Bianchi. Banská Bystrica: Slovan, 1932, pp. 69-72.

1317 ———· *Nash natsional'nyi gimn.* Izdanie OIAD, no. 26. Uzhhorod, 1926. Reprinted in *Russkii narodnyi kalendar' OIAD na god 1927.* Uzhhorod, 1926, pp. 147-151. Also in *Kalendar' OS na hod 1940.* Perth Amboy, N.J., 1940, pp. 126-129.

1318 ———· "Russkoe kul'turno-prosvietitel'noe obshchestvo imeni Aleksandra V. Dukhnovicha v Uzhhorodie na Podkarpatskoi Rusi." *Karpatorusskiia dostizheniia.* Edited by A. V. Popov. Mukachevo, 1930, pp. 89-116.

1319 ———· [Fenczik, István]. "Ruszinszkó autonómiája a nemzetközi és csehszlovák alkotmányjog szempontjából." *Miskolci jogászélet* (Miskolc, 1934), pp. 3-6.

1320 ———· [Fenczik, Jenő]. "A ruthén kérdés." *Kisebbségi körlevél,* vol. 4 (Pécs, 1942), pp. 265-277.

1321 ———· ed. *T.G. Masarik: iubileinyi sbornik po povodu vos'midesiatilietiia so dnia ego rozhdeniia.* Izdanie PON, no. 2. Uzhhorod, 1930.

1322 Fiedler, Josef. "Beiträge zur Geschichte der Union der Ruthenen in Nord-Ungarn und der Immunität des Clerus desselben." *Sitzungsberichte der kaiserlischer Akademie der Wissenschaften.* Philosophische-historische Classe, vol. 39, no. 4 (Vienna, 1862), pp. 481-524.

1323 Filevich, Ivan. "Ocherk karpatskoi territorii i naseleniia." *Zhurnal MNP,* vol. 298, nos. 4 and 5 (St. Petersburg, 1895), pp. 361-385 and 157-218.

1324 Flachbarth, Ernő. *Ruszinszkó autonómiája a nemzetközi jog és a csehszlovák alkotmányjog szempontjából.* Miskolci jogászélet könyvtára, új sor., no. 6. Miskolc, 1934.

1325 ———· [Observator]. "The Ruthenians' Struggle for Autonomy." *Danubian Review,* vol. 6, nos. 3-4 (Budapest, 1938), pp. 5-29.

1326 ———· "Die Völker und staatsrechtliche Lage Karpathorusslands." *Nation und Staat,* vol. 2 (Vienna, 1928), pp. 228-235.

1327 Florinskii, T.D. *Zarubezhnaia Rus' i eia gor'kaia dolia.* Kiev, 1900.

1328 Florovskii, Anton V. "Russo-Austrian Conflicts in the Early Eighteenth Century." *Slavonic and East European Review,* vol. 47 (London, 1969), pp. 94-119.

1329 ———· *Zamietki I. S. Orlaia o Karpatskoi Rusi.* Izdanie OIAD, no. 47. Uzhhorod, 1928. Also in *Karpatskii sviet,* vol. 1, no. 9 (Uzhhorod, 1928), pp. 332-338.

1330 Földesi, Gyula. *Az autonom kárpátoroszország államjogi vázlata.* Uzhhorod, 1927.

1331 Fomin. "Soveršilosja . . . " *Karpatorusskij narodnyj kalendar' na hod 1946.* Perth Amboy, N.J., 1946, pp. 36-41. On the incorporation of Subcarpathian Rus' into the Soviet Union and the reaction of American immigrants.

1332 Franko, Ivan. "Karpato-rus'ke psy'menstvo XVII-XVIII vv." *Zapysky NTSh,* vol. 37-38 (L'viv, 1900), pp. 1-162. Introductory essay reprinted in Ivan Franko, *Tvory,* vol. 16. Kiev, 1955; and in *Khrestomatiia materializ z istorii ukraïns'koï literaturnoï movy,* pt. 1. Edited by P.D. Tymoshenko. Kiev: 'Radians'ka shkola', 1959, pp. 118-135.

1333 ———· "Studii na poli karpatorus'koho pys'menstva XVIII vv." *Zapysky NTSh,* vol. 41 (L'viv, 1901), pp. 1-50.

1334 Frantsev, Vladimir A. "Iz istorii bor'by za russkii literaturnyi iazyk v Podkarpatskoi Rusi v polovinie XIX st." *Karpatorusskii sbornik.* Uzhhorod: PNS, 1930, pp. 1-49. Published separately: Prague: Edinstvo, 1931.

1335   ———· *K voprosu o literaturnom iazykie Podkarpatskoi Rusi.* Izdanie
        OIAD, vol. 2. Uzhhorod, 1924.
1336   ———·*Russkii iezuit I.M. Martynov, sotrudnik 'Tserkovnoi gazety' i 'Tser-
        kovnago viestnika' o. Ioanna Rakovskago.* Izdanie OIAD, no. 90. Uzh-
        horod, 1930.
1337   ——— [Putnik]. "Sovremennoe sostoianie Ugorskoi Rusi." *Russkii viestnik,*
        vol. 2 (Moscow, 1900), pp. 629-655.
1338   Frey, André. "La Ruthénie." *Nouvelle Revue de Hongrie,* vol. 59 (Buda-
        pest, 1938), pp. 426-433.
1339   G. J. K. "Karpatouské národní divadlo v Užhorodě." *Podkarpatoruská
        revue,* vol. 3, no. 4 (Bratislava, 1938), pp. 43-44.
1340   Gabriel, František. "Dodatky do ystorií pohranychnỳkh odnosyn pôdkar-
        patorus'kykh u XVIII stolîtia: arkhyvna studiia." *Podkarpatska Rus',*
        vol. 9, no. 9-10 (Uzhhorod, 1932), pp. 163-177.
1341   ———· "Historický nástin." *Technická práce v zemi podkarpatoruské 1919-
        1933.* Edited by J. Musil. Uzhhorod: Odbor Spolku československých in-
        ženýrů, 1933, pp. 253-257.
1342   ———· "Hospodars'ke polozhenia Pôdkarpatskoî Rusy na pochatku XVIII.
        stolîtia." *Podkarpatska Rus',* vol. 9, no. 1-10 (Uzhhorod, 1933), pp. 2-27.
1343   ———· "Materialy k istorii kriepostnichestva na Podkarpatskoi Rusi."
        Narodnyi sbornik Sabova. Uzhhorod, 1934, pp. 46-56.
1344   ———· "Otázka Zemského divadla podkarpatoruského." *Podkarpatoruská
        revue,* vol. 1, no. 2 (Bratislava, 1936), pp. 6-8.
1345   ———· "Poddanské poměry na užhorodském panství ke koncí XVIII sto-
        leti." *Naukovŷi zbornyk TP,* vol. 10 (Uzhhorod, 1934), pp. 153-184.
1346   ———· "Pohyb obyvatelstva v bývalé užské župě v první polovici 18. sto-
        leti." *Naukovŷi zbornyk TP,* vol. 11 (Uzhhorod, 1935), pp. 185-231.
1347   ———· "Přehled dějin Zakarpatské Ukrajiny." *Pověsti ze Zakarpatské
        Ukrajiny.* Edited by Jan Dušánek and F. Gabriel. Prague: Nová osvěta,
        1946, pp. 171-187.
1348   ———· "Selský stav v užhorodském komorním panství na sklonku XVIII
        století." *Sborník Zemské musejní společnosti v Užhorodě.* Uzhhorod,
        1932, pp. 33-57.
1349   ———· "Užhorod po valce Thökölyovské." *Časopis pro dějiny venkova,*
        vol. 22, no. 1 (Prague, 1935).
1350   ———· "Uzhhorods'ka kameral'na domyniia v 90. r. XVIII st." *Podkar-
        patska Rus',* vol. 9, nos. 1-3, 4-6, and 7-8 (Uzhhorod, 1932), pp. 1-10, 49-
        56, and 101-110.
1351   ———· "Vývoj kolonisace drugetovského panství užhorodského." *Nau-
        kovŷi zbornyk TP,* vol. 9 (Uzhhorod, 1932), pp. 135-155.
1352   ———· "Die wirtschaftliche Lage Karpathorussland vom 16. bis 18. Jahr-
        hundert." *Prager Rundschau,* vol. 5, no. 2 (Prague, 1935).
1353   ———· "Zhytia v borbôl's'kôm (tsyriul'nyts'kôm) uzhhorods'kôm tsekhu."
        Podkarpatska Rus', vol. 11, no. 1-10 (Uzhhorod, 1934), pp. 38-47.
1354   ———· "Z minulosti města Užhorodu." *Publikace pro zem Podkarpatská
        Rus.* Edited by G. Bianchi. Banská Bystrica: Slovan, 1932, pp. 10-16.
1355   Gadzhega, Iulii. *Dva istoricheskikh voprosa: starozhili-li karpatorossy i o*

nachalakh khristianskoi religii na Podkarpatskoi Rusi. Izdanie OIAD, no. 42. Uzhhorod, 1928.

1356 ———· "Grekokatolicheskaia tserkov' na Podkarpatskoi Rusi." *Podkarpatskaia Rus' za gody 1919-1936.* Edited by E. Bachinskii. Uzhhorod: RNG, 1936, pp. 93-96.

1357 ———· *Istoriia Obshchestva sv. Vasiliia Velikago i riech' ko dniu 60-letiia ot ego uchrezhdeniia.* Izdanie OIAD, vol. 15. Uzhhorod, 1925.

1358 ———· *Istoriia Uzhgorodskoi Bogoslovskoi Seminarii v eia glavnykh chertakh.* Izdanie OIAD, no. 35. Uzhhorod, 1928.

1359 ———· *Kratkii obzor nauchnoi dieiatel'nosti Iuriia Ivanovicha Venelina (Gutsy).* Izdanie OIAD, no. 29. Uzhhorod, 1927.

1360 ——— [Rusak, Iulii P.]. "Mukachevskaia eparkhiia i eia bor'ba za prava russkago iazyka i narodnosti vo vremia episkopstva Vasiliia Popovicha." *Karpatorusskii sbornik.* Uzhhorod: PNS, 1930, pp. 50-67.

1361 ——— [Rusak, Iulii]. *Ocherki kul'turnoi istorii Podkarpatskoi Rusi.* Uzhhorod, 1927.

1362 ———· *Stat'i po voprosam 'pravoslaviia', narodnosti i katolichestva.* Uzhhorod: 'Unio', 1921.

1363 Gagatko, Andrei M. *Po sluchaiu iubileinykh torzhestv v Podkarpatskoi Rusi.* Uzhhorod: Russkaia zemlia, 1924.

1364 Garennie, Dalmay de la. "La Ruthénie tchécoslovaque: Russie subcarpathique." *Annales de géographie,* vol. 33 (Paris, 1924), pp. 443-456.

1365 Gaujal, Báró. "A magyarországi ruthénokról." *Tudománytár,* uj folyam, vol. 5 (Buda, 1839).

1366 Gerando, Ferdinand. *Le complot rouge en Ruthénie.* Paris: Jouve et Co., 1930.

1367 Gergely, Ernő. "A proletárforradalom és a tanácshatalom Kárpátalján és Nyugat-Magyarországon." *Jogtudományi közlöny,* vol. 18 (Budapest, 1963), pp. 541-552.

1368 Gerovskii, Aleksei. "Bor'ba cheshskogo pravitel'stva s russkim iazykom." *Svobodnoe slovo Karpatskoi Rusi,* vol. 14, no. 5-6 (Newark, N.J., 1972), pp. 11-16.

1369 ———· "Chekhoslovatskii 'Liberalizm'." *Svobodnoe slovo Karpatskoi Rusi,* vol. 10, no. 9-10 (Newark, 1968), pp. 2-5.

1370 ———· "Cheshskaia politika i pravoslavnaia tserkov' na Karpatskoi Rusi." *Svobodnoe slovo Karpatskoi Rusi,* vol. 5, no. 1-6 (Newark, N.J., 1963), pp. 18-21.

1371 ———· "Iza i Sigotskii protsess." *Svobodnoe slovo Karpatskoi Rusi,* vol. 3, nos. 9-10 and 11-12 (Newark, N.J., 1961), pp. 4-8, 3-5.

1372 ——— [Gerovskij, Aleksij]. "Jak upravl'ali mad'ary v Karpatskoj Rusi." *Karpatorusskij narodnyj kalendar' na hod 1945.* Perth Amboy, N.J., 1945, pp. 133-140.

1373 ———· "Kak Karpatskaia Rus' byla prisoedinena k Chekhoslovakii." *Svobodnoe slovo Karpatskoi Rusi,* vol. 7, no. 7-8 (Newark, N.J., 1965), pp. 1-8.

1374 ———· "Pravoslavnaia tserkov' pod chekhami." *Svobodnoe slovo Karpatskoi Rusi,* vol. 6, no. 1-6 (Newark, N.J., 1964), pp. 18-21.

1375 ———· "Russkie rubli dlia Karpatskoi Rusi." *Svobodnoe slovo Karpatskoi Rusi,* vol. 4, no. 1-2 (Newark, N.J., 1962), pp. 9-10.

1376 ———· "Shkoly Karpatskoi Rusi pod chekhoslovatskim iarmom." *Svobodnoe slovo Karpatskoi Rusi,* vol. 7, no. 1-2 (Newark, N.J., 1964), pp. 2-5.

1377 ——— [Gerovskij, Aleksij]. "Sud̆ba Karpatskoj Rusi." *Karpatorusskij narodnyj kalendar' na hod 1946.* Perth Amboy, N.J., 1946, pp. 139-146.

1378 ———· "Uniia v Karpatskoi Rusi." *Svobodnoe slovo Karpatskoi Rusi,* vol. 5, no. 7-12 (Newark, N.J., 1963), pp. 4-11; vol. 6, no. 1-6 (1964), pp. 14-18.

1379 Gerovskii, Georgii. *Grammatika Pan'kevicha: razbor eia, na osnovanii dannykh nauki o iazykie, po retsenzii Professora Georgiia Gerovskago.* Uzhhorod: 'Svobodnoe slovo', 1930.

1380 ———· "Istoricheskie svodki: (1) Vremia zaseleniia iuzhnykh sklonov karpatskikh gor nashim narodom; (2) Proiskhozhdenie predkov nashego naroda." *Duklia,* vol. 7, no. 1 (Prešov, 1959), pp. 53-58.

1381 ———· "Istoricheskoe proshloe Priashevshchiny." *Priashevshchina.* Edited by I. S. Shlepetskii. Prague: Khutor, 1948, pp. 57-93.

1382 ———· *Istoriia ugro-russkoi literatury v izobrazhenii Volodimira Birchaka.* Uzhhorod, 1943.

1383 ——— [Gerovskij, Georgij]. "Jazyk Podkarpatské Rusi." *Československá vlastivĕda,* vol. 3. Prague: Sfinx, 1934, pp. 460-517.

1384 ———· "K voprosu o znachenii nazvaniia Rusnak." *Duklia,* vol. 6, no. 3 (Prešov, 1958), pp. 47-52. Reprinted in *Svobodnoe slovo Karpatskoi Rusi,* vol. 13, no. 5-6 (Newark, N.J., 1971), pp. 2-5.

1384a ———· "Karpatskoe nazvanie Rusnak i iego zapadnoslavianskie sootvetstviia." *Československá rusistika,* vol. 2 (Prague, 1957), pp. 429-442.

1385 ———· "Kniaz' Fedor Koriatovich." *Svobodnoe slovo Karpatskoi Rusi,* vol. 13, no. 11-12 (Newark, N.J., 1971), pp. 2-4.

1386 ——— [Gerovskij, Georgij]. " 'Mluvnice ruského jazyka' Ivana Paňkeviče." *Slavia,* vol. 6 (Prague, 1927), pp. 133-142.

1387 ———· "Narodnaia rech' Priashevshchiny." *Priashevshchina.* Edited by I. S. Shlepetskii. Prague: Khutor, 1948, pp. 94-144.

1388 ———· "Russkii iazyk v tserkovno-slaviansko-russkoi grammatikie M. Popa-Luchkaia." *Karpatorusskii sbornik.* Uzhhorod: Izd. PNS, 1930, pp. 259-311.

1389 Gerovskii, Georgii, and Krainianitsa, V. Iu., eds. *Razbor grammatiki ugrorusskogo iazyka.* Second edition. Uzhhorod, 1941.

1390 Giusti, Wolfgang. "La Russia subcarpatica e la sua letteratura." *Revista di letterature slave,* vol. 1, no. 1-2 (Rome, 1926), pp. 115-138.

1391 Gogolák, Lajos. "Ruszinszkó a cseh politikában." *Magyar szemle,* vol. 26, no. 2 (Budapest, 1936), pp. 159-168.

1392 Gojdics, Method. "Le territoire autonome ruthène." *Revue de l'Europe orientale,* vol. 1 (Rome, 1919), pp. 45-56.

1393 "Golos iz Ugorskoi Rusi." *Russkaia mysl',* vol. 1, no. 3 (Moscow, 1880), pp. 1-24.

Golovatskii, Iakov F., see Holovats'kyi, Iakiv F.

1394 Gomichkov, Vladimir. "Nashi v Budapeshtie." *Zemlediel'skii kalendar' na vysokonosnyi god 1936.* Uzhhorod, 1935; pp. 106-109.

1395 Gower, Sir Robert. *The Hungarian Minorities in the Succession States.* London: Grant Richards, 1937.

1396 ———· *Treaty-Revision and the Hungarian Frontiers.* London: Grayson and Grayson, 1937.

Gozdawa, O., *see* Bochkovs'kyi, Ol'gerd I.

1397 Grabar', Oleg. *Poèziia Zakarpat'ia, 1939-1944.* Bratislava: SVKL, 1957.

Grabets', Miroslav, *see* Hrabets', Miroslav

1398 Grechko, Andrei A. *Cherez Karpaty.* Moscow: Voennoe izd. Ministerstva oborony SSSR, 1970.

1399 Grigássy, Gyula. *A magyar görögkatholikusok legujabb tőrténete.* Uzhhorod, 1913.

1400 Gulovich, Stephen C. "The Rusin Exarchate in the United States." *The Eastern Churches Quarterly,* vol. 6 (London, 1946), pp. 477-479.

1401 Gulya, Károly. *A magyarországi rutén kérdés 1910-1914 között.* Acta Historica, vol. 31. Szeged, 1968.

1402 Gumetskii, L. K. "Kratkaia istoriia o-va karpatorusskikh studentov 'Vozrozhdenie' i ego dieiatel'nost' v nastoiashchee vremia." *Karpatorusskiia dostizheniia.* Mukachevo, 1930, pp. 145-158.

1403 Gumetskii, I. I. *Znachenie russkago Prikarpat'ia dlia Rossii.* St. Petersburg, 1914.

1404 Günther, Friedrich. "Der Weg zur autonomen Karpathen-Ukraine." *Osteuropa,* vol. 14, no. 4 (Berlin, 1939), pp. 301-305.

Gus'nai, Igor I., *see* Hus'nai, Ihor I.

1405 Hadzhega, Vasylii. "Deiaki zamitky do pytannia: tsy pidkarpats'ki rusyny avtokhtony na Pidkarpats'ki Rusy?" *Al'manakh Soiuzu pidkarpats'kykh rus'kykh studentiv u Prazi 1920-21—1930-31.* Prague, 1931, pp. 36-40.

1406 ———· "Dodatky k istoriî rusynôv y rus'kykh tserkvei: studiî ystorychnoarkhyvnî." Series of studies on individual counties. "Maramarosh." *Naukovŷi zbôrnyk TP,* vol. 1 (Uzhhorod, 1922), pp. 140-228. "Uzh." Ibid., vol. 2 (1923), pp. 1-64 and vol. 3 (1924), pp. 155-239. "Ugocha." Ibid., vol. 4 (1925), pp. 117-176 and vol. 5 (1927), pp. 1-62. "Zemplyn." Ibid., vol. 7-8 (1931), pp. 1-167; vol. 9 (1932), pp. 1-67; vol. 10 (1934), pp. 17-120; vol. 11 (1935), pp. 17-182; and vol. 12 (1937), pp. 37-83.

1407 ———· "Kniaz Fedor Koriatovych i Maramarosh." *Podkarpatska Rus',* vol. 7, nos. 1-2, 3, 4-5, 6, 7-8, and 9-10 (Uzhhorod, 1930), pp. 1-3, 40-46, 76-88, 108-120, 134-152, 179-193; and vol. 8, nos. 1-2, 2-3, 4, 5-6, 7, and 8 (Uzhhorod, 1931), pp. 13-19, 38-46, 68-75, 99-113, 141-148, and 169-175.

1408 ———· "Nazva Uzhhoroda." *Narodnŷi kalendar 'Unio' na rok 1932.* Uzhhorod, 1931, pp. 61-66.

1409 ———· "Nashî kul'turnî y tserkovnî spravŷ na epyskopskykh naradakh r. 1773. u Vîdny." *Podkarpatska Rus',* vol. 3, nos. 5, 7-8, 9, and 10 (Uzhhorod, 1926), pp. 105-108, 167-170, 199-201, and 213-215.

1410 ———· "O pereseleniu kniazia Fedora Koriatovycha do Madiarshchyny." *Podkarpatska Rus',* vol. 6, no. 7 (Uzhhorod, 1929), pp. 153-157.

1411 ———· "O pervŷkh pochatkakh narodn'oho shkôl'nytstva na Pôdkarpatskôi Rusy." *Podkarpatska Rus',* vol. 4, nos. 1, 2, 3, 4, and 5 (Uzhhorod, 1927), pp. 8-10, 29-33, 55-57, 82-86, and 110-114.

1412 ———· "Persha sproba istoriĭ hreko-katolycheskoĭ mukachevskoĭ eparkhiĭ,"
Naukovŷi zbornyk TP, vol. 3 (Uzhhorod, 1924), pp. 1-27.
1413 ———· [Hadžega, Vasil]. "Přehled církevních dějin na Podkarpatské Rusi."
Podkarpatská Rus. Edited by J. Zatloukal. Bratislava: KPPR, 1936. pp.
270-278.
1414 ———· "Rolia Aktsiinoho tovarystva 'Unio' v dukhovnom rozvytku nashoho rus'koho naroda." *Iuvyleinŷi yliustrovanŷi kalendar' 'Unio' na rok
1928.* Uzhhorod, 1927, pp. 57-61.
1415 ———· "Vplŷv reformatsiĭ na podkarpatskykh rusynov." *Zoria—Hajnal,*
vol. 3, no. 1-4 (Uzhhorod, 1943), pp. 5-50.
1416 ———· "Vŷtiahy yz lîtopysa Anonyma." *Podkarpatska Rus',* vol. 6, no. 3,
4, 5, 6, 7, 8-9, and 10 (Uzhhorod, 1929), pp. 54-61, 79-85, 111-113, 140-
143, 174-176, 178-184, and 207-215.
1417 ———· "Ystoriia katedral'noĭ kapytuly hreko-katolytskoĭ eparkhiĭ mukachevskoĭ." *Podkarpatska Rus',* vol. 4, no. 7, 8, 9, and 10 (Uzhhorod,
1927), pp. 160-163, 182-186, 211-214, and 231-235.
1418 Halaga, Ondrej R. *Slovanské osídlenie Potisia a východoslovenskí grécko-
katolíci.* Košice: Východoslovenský kultúrny spolok "Svojina," 1947.
1419 Halas, K.I. et al. "Dosiahennia ukraïns'koho ta slov'ians'koho movoznavstva na Zakarpatti za roky radians'koï vlady." *Velykyi Zhovten' i rozkvit
vozz'iednanoho Zakarpattia.* Uzhhorod: Karpaty, 1970, pp. 530-552.
1420 Hanak, Walter K. *The Subcarpathian Ruthenian Question: 1918-1945.* Munhall, Pa.: Bishop Takach Carpatho-Russian Historical Society, 1962.
1421 Hanchyn, V. Iu. "Miunkhens'ka zmova i Zakarpattia." *Velykyi Zhovten' i
rozkvit vozz'iednanoho Zakarpattia.* Uzhhorod: Karpaty, 1970, pp. 222-
235.
1421a ———· "Stanovyshche Zakarpattia v skladi burzhuaznoï Chekhoslovachchyny (1919-1920 rr.)." *Ukraïns'kyi istorychnyi zhurnal,* vol. 12, no. 10
(Kiev, 1968), pp. 83-87.
1422 Hanulya, Joseph. *Rusin Literature.* Cleveland, 1941.
1423 Hapak, Pavlo. "Za pravyl'ne vysvitlennia diial'nosti A. I. Dobrians'koho."
Duklia, vol. 7, no. 1 (Prešov, 1959), pp. 72-84.
1424 Hapak, Stepan. *Obrazotvorche mystetstvo ukraïntsiv Chekhoslovachchyny.*
Bratislava and Prešov: SPVVUL, 1975.
1425 ———· "Ukraïns'ke obrazotvorche mystetstvo v pershii Chekhoslovachchyni." *Zhovten' i ukraïns'ka kul'tura.* Prešov: KSUT, 1968, pp. 566-599.
1426 Haraksim, L'udovít. "Do pytannia tak zvanoho natsional'noho rukhu sered
ukraïntsiv buvshoï Uhorshchyny do revoliutsii 1848 roku." *Duklia,* vol. 8,
no. 3 (Prešov, 1960), pp. 85-91.
1427 ———· "K problematike obrodenia Ukrajincov východného Slovenska a
Zakarpatska." *Oleksandr Dukhnovych: zbirnyk materialiv.* Edited by M.
Rychalka. Prešov: KSUT, 1965, pp. 17-29.
1428 ———· *K sociálnym a kúlturnym dejinám Ukrajincov na Slovensku do roku
1867.* Bratislava : SAV, 1961.
1429 ———· "Die Russinen und der Ausgleich." *Die österreichisch-ungarische
Ausgleich 1867.* Bratislava: Historický ústav, SAV, 1971, pp. 746-763.
1430 Harcsár, Nicolas. "La Societé savante de Subcarpathie de Ungvár." *Revue
d'histoire comparée: études hongroises,* vol. 21 (Paris, 1943), pp. 624-626.

1431   Hartl, Antonín. "Deset let podkarpatského písemnictví." *Slovanský přehled,* vol. 22, no. 3, 4, 5, 6, and 7 (Prague, 1930), pp. 183-199, 272-280, 319-333, 425-435, and 487-504. Published separately under the title: *Literární obrození podkarpatských rusínů v letech 1920-1930.* Prague, 1930.

1432   ———· "Deux problèmes de la Russie subcarpathique." *Le Monde slave,* vol. 13, no. 2 (Paris, 1936), pp. 93-102.

1433   ———· "Das heutige literarische Schaffen in Karpathorussland." *Prager Rundschau,* vol. 7 (Prague, 1937), pp. 39-46.

1434   ———· "Jazyk a písemnictví na Podk. Rusi." *Nové Čechy,* vol. 6, no. 2 (Prague, 1923), pp. 1-5, 62-69.

1435   ———· "K jazykovým sporům na Podkarpatské Rusi." *Slovo a slovesnost,* vol. 4 (Prague, 1938), pp. 160-173.

1436   ———· *Kulturní život osvobozené Podkarpatské Rusi.* Letáky 'Nové Svobody', no. 2. Prague: Nákladem Grafického, knihařského a nakladatelského družstva, 1924.

1437   ———· "Literatura podkarpatských rusínů v XX. století." *Encyklopedia XX století,* vol. 7, pp. 119-122.

1438   ———· *Die literarische Renaissance der Karpathoruthenen.* Prague: Orbis, 1932.

1439   ———· *Osnovŷ rus'koî narodnoî y kul'turnoî polytyky.* Knyzhky 'Rusyna,' no. 5. Uzhhorod, 1923.

1440   ———· "Pisemnictvi Podkarpatských Rusínů." *Československá vlastivěda,* vol. 7. Prague: "Sfinx" Bohemil Janda, 1933, pp. 273-290.

1441   ———· "Pisemnictví podkarpatských Rusinů v XX. století." *Poznání,* vol. 2, no. 6 (Prague, 1937), pp. 95-102.

1442   ———· *Podkarpatští Rusíni a my.* Prague, 1930.

1443   ———· "Podkarpatoruští Rusíni za války a za převratu." *Slovanský přehled,* vol. 17 (Prague, 1925), pp. 55-57, 138-142.

1444   ———· "Právní stránka jazykové otázky Podkarpatské Rusi." *Slovanský přehled,* vol. 18 (Prague, 1926), pp. 281-284.

1445   ———· "Přehled literárního hnutí na Podkarpatské Rusi." *Podkarpatská Rus.* Edited by J. Zatloukal. Bratislava: KPPR, 1936, pp. 181-187.

1446   ———· "Soudobá podkarpatská literatura." *Národnostní obzor,* vol. 1, no. 1 (Prague, 1930), pp. 56-58.

1447   ———· "Z politického života v Podkarpatské Rusi." *Slovanský přehled,* vol. 17 (Prague, 1925), pp. 296-299, 436-437, 635.

1448   Hassinger, Hugo. "Die karpathorussische Frage." In his *Die Tschechoslowakei: ein geographisches, politisches and wirtschaftliches Handbuch.* Vienna-Leipzig-Munich: Rikola, 1925, pp. 490-503.

1449   Hatalák, Petr. "Carpathian Russians and the Czechoslovaks." *The Bohemian Review,* vol. 2, no. 5 (Chicago, 1918), pp. 70-72.

1450   ———· *Jak vznikla myšlenka připojiti Podkarpatskou Rus k Československu.* Uzhhorod, 1935.

1451   Hens'ors'kyi, A. I. "Do pokhodzhennia zakarpats'kykh rusyniv." *Ukraïns'kyi istorychnyi zhurnal,* vol. 12, no. 10 (Kiev, 1968), pp. 77-82.

1452   Hexner, Erwin. *Das Dienstvertragsrecht in Karpathorussland: mit einer systematischen Einfuhrüng und Erlauterungen.* Brno: R. M. Rohrer, 1925.

1453   Hladik, V.P. "Istoričny danny o Prikarpatskoj i Karpatskoj Rusi." *Karpato-*

russkij narodnyj kalendar' na hod 1945. Perth Amboy, N.J., 1945, pp. 88-93.

1454 Hnatiuk, Volodymyr. "Chy zakarpats'ki ukraïntsi avtokhtony?" *Literaturno-naukovyi vistnyk,* vol. 76, no. 3 (L'viv, 1922), pp. 269-276.

1455 ———· "Hungarico-Ruthenica." *Zapysky NTSh,* vol. 28, no. 2 (L'viv, 1899), pp. 29-38.

1456 ———· "Madiars'ka svoboda." *Literaturno-naukovyi vistnyk,* vol. 2 (L'viv, 1905), pp. 143-154.

1457 ———· *Natsional'ne vidrodzhennie avstro-uhors'kykh ukraïntsiv (1772-1880 rr.).* Vienna: Soiuz vyzvolennia Ukraïny, 1916.

1458 ———· "Prychynok do istoriï znosyn halyts'kykh i uhors'kykh rusyniv." *Literaturno-naukovyi vistnyk,* vol. 7, no. 10 (L'viv, 1899), pp. 162-178.

1459 ———· "Rusyny Priashivs'koï eparkhiï i ïkh hovory." *Zapysky NTSh,* vol. 35 (L'viv, 1900), pp. 1-70.

1460 ———· "Rusíni v Uhrách." *Slovanský přehled,* nos. 5 and 9 (Prague, 1898), pp. 216-220 and 418-427.

1461 ———· "Slovaky chy Rusyny?: prychynok do vyiasnenia sporu pro natsional'nist' zakhidnykh rusyniv." *Zapysky NTSh,* vol. 42, no. 4 (L'viv, 1901), pp. 1-81.

1462 ———· "Uhrorus'ka mizeriia." *Zhytie i slovo,* vol. 6, no. 1 (L'viv, 1897), pp. 46-62.

1463 ———· "Uhro-rus'ki novyny." *Zhytie i slovo,* vol. 6 (L'viv, 1897), pp. 124-130.

1464 ———· "V spravi literaturnoï movy pidkarpats'kykh rusyniv." *Naukovyi zbirnyk MUKS,* vol. 3 (Bratislava, Prešov, and Svidník, 1967), pp. 19-25.

1465 Hopko, Vasilij. *Greko-Katholičeskaja cerkov 1646-1946.* Prešov: Izd. 'Petra', 1946.

1466 Hodinka, Antal. *Adalékok az Ungvári vár és tartománya és Ungvár városának történetéhez.* Uzhhorod, 1917.

1467 ———· *Gens fidelissima.* Felvidéki tudományos társaság kiadványai, 1 sor., no. 4. Budapest, 1937.

1468 ———· *Gens fidelissima: II. Rákóczi F. beregmegyei rutén jobbágyai az 1704-1711-i szabadságharczban.* Uzhhorod: 'Unio,' 1915.

1469 ———· "Gramotnost' i uchennost' nashikh sviashchennikov do episkopa A. Bachinskago." *Zemledîl'skii kalendar' na hod 1936.* Uzhhorod, 1935, pp. 119-122.

1470 ———· [Hodynka, Antonii]. "Iak zhyly davno nashy rusynŷ?" *Zemledîl'-skii kalendar' na 1935.* Uzhhorod, 1934, pp. 47-54.

1471 ———· "Jelentése ruténeink úniójáról." *Akadémiai értesítő,* vol. 7, no. 9 (81) (Budapest, 1896), pp. 497-499.

1472 ———· *A munkácsi görög-katholikus püspökség története.* Budapest: MTA, 1910.

1473 ——— [Hodynka, Antonii]. "Nashî kleryky v Tyrnavî ot 1722 do 1760 roku." *Zoria—Hajnal,* vol. 1, no. 1-2 (Uzhhorod, 1941), pp. 18-31.

1474 ———· *II. Rákoczi Ferenc fejedelem és a gens fidelissima.* Pécs, 1937.

1475 ———· "Die Ruthenen." *Die österreichisch-ungarische Monarchie in Wort und Bild,* vol. 5 Ungarn, pt. 2. Vienna: K.K. Hof- und Staatsdruckerei, 1900, pp. 401-418.

1476 ——— · [Hodynka, Antonii]. "Sobor nashoi diotseziî poderzhanŷi v dniakh 11-12 marta 1726 roka v Eheri (Eger)." *Lyteraturna nedîlia,* vol. 4, no. 8 (Uzhhorod, 1944), pp. 90-94.

1477 ——— · [Sokyrnyts'kii Syrokhman]. *Uttiuznyna, gazduvstvo y proshlost' iuzhnokarpats'kykh rusynov.* Budapest, 1922. Published also in Hungarian: *A kárpátalji rutének lakóhelye gazdasaguk és multjuk.* Budapest, 1923; and in French: "L'habitat, l'économie, et le passé du peuple ruthène," *Revue des études hongroises et finno-ougriènnes,* vol. 2 (Paris, 1924), pp. 244-275.

1478 Hodnett, Grey, and Potichnyj, Peter J. *The Ukraine and the Czechoslovak Crisis.* Australian National University, Department of Political Science, Occasional Paper no. 6. Canberra, 1970.

1479 Hodža, Milan. "U karpatských rusov." *Články, reči, štúdie,* vol. 3. Prague: Novina, 1931, pp. 289-322. Translated into Russian: *U Karpatskikh russkikh: stat'i 1898-1914 g.* Compiled by E. Bachinskii. Russkaia narodnaia biblioteka, no. 9. Uzhhorod: RNG, 1936.

1480 Hoensch, Jörg K. *Der ungarische Revisionismus und die Zerschlagung der Tschechoslowakei.* Tübingen Studien für Geschichte und Politik, No. 23. Tübingen: J. C. B. Mohr, 1967.

1481 Hoffmann, Ottó. *A rutén kérdés.* Pécs, 1918.

1482 Hokky, Charles J. *Ruthenia, Spearhead Toward the West.* Gainesville, Florida: Danubian Research and Information Center, 1966.

1483 Holovats'kyi, Iakiv [Golovatskii, Iakov]. "Karpatskaia Rus': geografichesko-statisticheskie i istorichesko-ètnograficheskie ocherki." *Slavianskii sbornik,* vol. 1 (St. Petersburg, 1875), pp. 1-30; vol. 2 (1877), pp. 55-84. Reprinted in his *Narodnyia piesni Galitskoi i Ugorskoi Rusi,* vol. 3, pt. 2. Moscow: Imperatorskoe obshchestvo istorii i drevnosti rossiskikh, 1878, pp. 557-615.

1484 ——— · [Golovatskii, Iakov]. "Karpatskaia Rus': istoriko-ètnograficheskii ocherk." *Zhurnal MNP,* vol. 179, no. 2 (St. Petersburg, 1875), pp. 349-396. Reprinted in his *Narodnyia piesni Galitskoi i Ugorskoi Rusi,* vol. 3, pt. 2. Moscow: Imperatorskoe obshchestvo istorii i drevnosti rossiiskikh, 1878, pp. 616-670.

1485 ——— · [J. F. H.]. "O halické a uherské Rusi." *Časopis českého museum,* vol. 17, no. 1 (Prague, 1843), pp. 12-52.

1486 Honcharenko, O. "Stan shkil'nytstva na Zakarpatti (v 70-90 rr. XIX—na pochatku XX st.)." *Duklia,* vol. 11, no. 2 (Prešov, 1963), pp. 76-82.

1487 Hora, Alois. *Karpatská Rus a hranice našeho státu.* Propagační knihovna, no. 3. Prague: Československý cizinecký úřad, 1919.

1488 ——— · *Organisace státní správy Podkarpatské Rusi.* Propagační knihovna československ. cizeneckého úřadu, no. 10. Prague, 1919.

1489 ——— · *Podkarpatská Rus: přehled poměrů karpatoruských.* Propagační knihovna, no. 7. Prague: Československý cizinecký úřad, 1919.

1490 ——— · *Uherská Rus za války a v míru.* Propagační knihovna, no. 1. Prague: Ceskoslovenský cizinecký úřad, 1919.

1491 Horbach, Oleksa. "Literaturna mova bachvans'ko-srims'kykh ('rusyniv')." *Zapysky NTSh,* vol. 169 (New York, and Paris, 1962), pp. 265-282.

1492 ——— · "Ukrainians Abroad: in Yugoslavia." *Ukraine: A Concise Encyclo-*

pedia, vol. 2. Toronto: University of Toronto Press for the Ukrainian National Association, 1971, pp. 1248-1253.

1492a Hordyns'kyi, Sviatoslav. "Suchasna zakarpats'ka poeziia." *S'ohochasne i mynule,* vol. 1, no. 2 (L'viv, 1939), pp. 23-32.

1493 Horniak, Nikolai A. "Karpatorusskiia nariechiia i russkii iazyk." *Kalendar' ARSS na hod 1934.* Homestead, Pa., 1934, pp. 72-74.

1494 —— [Hornjak, Nikolaj A.]. "Molodaja posl'ivojennaja literatura karpatorossov i ich kul'turno-političeskoje položenije." *Kalendar' OS na hod 1937.* Perth Amboy, 1937, pp. 142-156.

1495 Hoshovs'kyi, Volodymyr. "Pochatky khorovoho spivu na Zakarpatti." *Naukovyi zbirnyk MUKS,* vol. 6, pt. 1. (Bratislava, Prešov, and Svidník, 1972), pp. 97-104.

1496 Hostička, Vladimír. "Národní obrození haličských Ukrajinců a O. Duchnovyč." *Oleksandr Dukhnovych: zbirnyk materialiv.* Edited by M. Rychalka. Prešov: KSUT, 1965, pp. 83-92.

1497 *Hovoryt' Priashiv . . . 30 rokiv ukraïns'koho radiomovlennia v Chekhoslovachchyni.* Naukovo-populiarna biblioteka TsK KSUT, no. 3. Prešov, 1968.

1498 Hrabets', Miroslav [Grabets', M.]. *K istorii Marmaroshskago protsessa: dielo 94-kh.* Uzhhorod: Izd. Karpatorusskoi trudovoi partii, 1934.

1499 —— [Hrabec, Miroslav]. "Marmarošský proces a jeho podstata." *Podkarpatská Rus.* Edited by J. Zatloukal. Bratislava: KPPR, 1936. pp. 57-60.

1500 Hrabovets'kyi, Volodymyr. *Antyfeodal'na borot'ba karpats'koho opryshkivstva XVI-XIX st.* L'viv: Vyd. LU, 1966.

1501 Hranchak, Ivan M., ed. *Doslidzhennia starodavn'oï istoriï Zakarpattia.* Uzhhorod: UDU, 1972.

1502 Hranchak, Ivan M., et al., eds. *Kul'tura i pobut naselennia ukraïns'kykh Karpat.* Uzhhorod: UDU, 1973. A collection of fifty-two articles from a scholarly conference which revealed the results of recent Soviet scholarship on various aspects of Subcarpathian Rus'. Includes contributions by S. Bilak, D. Danyliuk, I. Kashula, V. Lohoida, O. Mazurok, V. Pal'ok, and V. Zadorozhnyi.

1503 Hranchak, Ivan M., et al. *Vesna vidrodzhenoho kraiu.* Uzhhorod: Karpaty, 1974.

1504 Hranchak, Ivan M., and Mishchenko, Serhii. "Onovlena zemlia." *Vesna vidrodzhenoho kraiu.* Uzhhorod: Karpaty, 1974, pp. 117-176.

1505 Hranchak, Ivan M., and Pal'ok, Vasyl'. *Misto nad Uzhem.* Uzhhorod: Karpaty, 1973.

1506 Hryvna, Vasyl'. "Vplyv Zhovtnia na natsional'no-vyzvol'nyi rukh ukraïntsiv Chekhoslovachchyny." *Zhovten' i ukraïns'ka kul'tura.* Prešov: KSUT, 1968, pp. 121-131.

1507 Húsek, Jan. *Národopisná hranice mezi Slováky a Karpatorusy.* Knižnica 'Prúdov', no. 2. Bratislava, 1925.

1508 ——. "O národnom povedomí na východnom Slovensku." *Prúdy,* vol. 8 (Bratislava, 1924), pp. 559-564.

1509 ——. "O národnom povedomı podkarpatských Rusov," *Prúdy,* vol. 9 (Bratislava, 1925), pp. 89-101.

1510 ——. "Rodí se podkarpatoruský národ?." *Podkarpatoruská revue,* vol. 1, no. 7-8 (Bratislava, 1936), pp. 6-8.

1511 Hus'nai, Ihor I. [Gus'nai, I.]. *Iazykovyi vopros v Podkarpatskoi Rusi.* Prešov, 1921.

1512 Iasko, Mykola. "Narodnopoetychna tvorchist' Zakarpattia pro borot'bu z fashysts'kymy zaharbnykamy (1939-1944 r.)." *Karpaty,* vol. 11, no. 3 (Uzhhorod, 1958), pp. 74-80.

1513 Iatsko, Pavlo. "Mynuvshyna 'bîloho' makovytskoho zamku." *Podkarpatska Rus',* vol. 4, no. 9 (Uzhhorod, 1927), pp. 201-205.

1514 ———· "Unyversytet Podkarpatskykh Rusynôv v Uzhhorodî." *Podkarpatska Rus',* vol. 4, no. 6 (Uzhhorod, 1927), pp. 129-131.

1515 ———· "Volodymyr, korol' Bolhariî y rus'koho Pôdkarpatia v 892 r." *Podkarpatska Rus',* vol. 4, no. 7 (Uzhhorod, 1927), pp. 153-159.

1516 Iavdyk, L. *Istoriia Ugorskoi Rusi.* Warsaw, 1904.

1517 Iavorskii, Iul'ian A. 'Literaturnye otgoloski 'rus'ko-krainskago' perioda v Zakarpatskoi Rusi 1919 goda." *Karpatorusskii sbornik* (Uzhhorod, 1930), pp. 79-87.

1517a ———· "Znachenie i miesto Zakarpat'ia v obshchei skhemie russkoi pis'-mennosti." *Sborník prací I. sjezdu slovanských filologů v Praze 1929,* vol. 2 (Prague: Orbis, 1931), pp. 74-89.

1517b Iedlins'ka, U. Ia. "Z istoriï borot'by za iedynu literaturnu movu na Zakarpatti 1919-1938 rr." *Filolohichnyi zbirnyk.* Kiev: Vyd. ANURSR, 1958.

1518 Iedynak, Andrii. "Pro natsional'ne ta kul'turne stanovyshche ukraïntsiv v Avstriis'kii monarkhiï v 30-40-kh rokakh XIX stolittia." *Duklia,* vol. 18, no. 5 (Prešov, 1970), pp. 44-50.

1519 Ihnat, A. M. "Stan osvity na Zakarpatti v 20-30 kh rr. XX st." *Velykyi Zhovten' i rozkvit vozz'iednanoho Zakarpattia.* Uzhhorod: Karpaty, 1970, pp. 212-221.

1520 ———· "Uspikhy kul'turno-osvitn'oï roboty v Zakarpats'kii oblasti za roky radians'koï vlady." *Naukovi zapysky,* vol. 9 (Uzhhorod, 1954) pp. 369-397.

1520a Il'ko, Vasyl' I. *Zakarpats'ke selo na pochatku XX st.: 1900-1919 rr.* L'viv: LU, 1973.

1521 Illes-Illyasevics, Joseph. "The Autonomy of Ruthenia and the Czechoslovak Minority Questions." *Danubian Review,* vol. 6, no. 2 (Budapest, 1938), pp. 11-17.

1522 ———· "Un peuple libéré—et anéanti." *Revue de Hongrie,* vol. 24 (Budapest, 1921), pp. 12-21.

1523 ———· *A ruszinszkói kérdés.* Az országos nemzeti klub kiadványai, no. 26. Budapest: Király magyar egyetemi nyomda, 1939.

1524 Il'nyts'kyi, Aleksander. "Kartiny o russko-mad'iarskom bratstvie." *Zemlediel'skii kalendar' na god 1939* (Uzhhorod, 1938), pp. 40-43.

1525 ———· "Madiarskoe pravytel'stvo y narodnŷi iazŷk Podkarpatskykh rusynov." Pryloha, *Menshynovŷi obîzhnyk,* vol. 7, no. 2 (Pécs, 1943).

1526 ———· [Ilniczky, Sándor]. "Magyar és ruszin kulturális kapcsolatok." *Láthatár,* vol. 8 (Budapest, 1940), pp. 49-50.

1527 ——— [Ilniczky, Sándor]. "A magyarországi ruthének." *Láthatár,* vol. 10, no. 10 (Budapest, 1942), pp. 257-260.

1528 ——— [Ilniczky, Sándor]. "Ruszinok és magyarok." *Magyar szemle,* vol. 37, no. 2 (Budapest, 1939), pp. 105-113.

1529 ———· "Novorochna prohrama rusynov." *Kalendar' 'Handia' na 1941 hod.* Budapest, 1940, pp. 18-26.

1530 ———· [A.S.I.]. "Razvitie ukrainskoi ideologii na Podkarpatskoi Rusi." *Zemledîl'skii kalendar' na hod 1939.* Uzhhorod, 1938, pp. 90-92.

1531 ——— [Ilnický, Alexander]. "Řeckokatolická církev na Podkarpatské Rusi." *Podkarpatská Rus.* Edited by J. Zatloukal. Bratislava: KPPR, 1936, pp. 278-280.

1532 ———· "Usloviia madiarsko-rus'koi bratskoi spolurobotŷ." *Kalendar' 'Handia' na 1941 hod.* Budapest, 1940, pp. 22-24.

1533 Il'nyts'kyi, Iurii V. *Vikhy zvytiazhoho postupu.* Uzhhorod: Karpaty, 1975.

1534 ———· *20 radians'kykh rokiv.* Uzhhorod: Karpaty, 1965.

1535 Inostrancev, M. A. "Paskevičovo uherské tažení r. 1849 a jeho ohlas v Podkarpatské Rusi." *Vojensko-historický sborník,* vol. 2, no. 1 (Prague, 1933), pp. 33-68.

1536 *Istoriia Podkarpatskoî lyteratury.* Uzhhorod: Izd. RK, 1942.

1537 "Istorija Greko-Kaft. Sojedinenija." *Zoloto-jubilejnyj kalendar' GKS na hod 1942.* Homestead, Pa., 1942, pp. 39-74.

1538 "Istorija Mukačevskoj jeparchii." *Zoloto-jubilejnyj kalendar' GKS na hod 1942.* Homestead, Pa., 1942, pp. 212-232.

1539 "Istorija Prjaševskoj jeparchii." *Zoloto-jubilejnyj kalendar' GKS na hod 1942.* Homestead, Pa., 1942, pp. 233-242.

1540 "Iz istorii gr.-kat. russkoi gimnazii v Preshovie." *VIII. godovyi otchet Gr.-kat. russkoi gimnazii v Preshovie za uchebnyi god 1943-1944.* Prešov, 1944, pp. 53-63.

1541 Ïzhak. *Ukraïnets' chy russkii?.* Mukachevo, 1938.

Izoryn, A., *see* Nedziel'skii, Evgenii

1542 Jary, Riko. "Podkarpatska Rus." *The Ukrainian Question: a Peace Problem.* Geneva: Publicity Department of the Executive of Ukrainian Nationalists, 1928, pp. 36-39.

1543 Jászi, Oscar. "The Problem of Sub-Carpathian Ruthenia." *Czechoslovakia.* Edited by Robert J. Kerner. Berkeley and Los Angeles: University of California Press, 1940, pp. 193-215.

1544 "Jazykový spor na Podkarpatské Rusi." *Slovanský přehled,* vol. 15 (Prague, 1933), pp. 427-429.

1545 Jelačíc, Aleksije. *Most male antante (Karpatska Rusija).* Biblioteka narodnog univerziteta, no. 6. Šabac, 1935.

1546 Jirasek, Josef. "A. V. Duchnovič jako básník a dramatik." *Podkarpatská Rus.* Edited by J. Zatloukal. Bratislava: KPPR, 1936, pp. 203-207.

1547 Jócsik, Lajos. "A Ruténekről." *Az ország útja* (Budapest, 1939), pp. 628-639.

1548 K.Z. "Natsional'ne výkhovanie." *Podkarpatska Rus',* vol. 7, no. 3 (Uzhhorod, 1930), pp. 56-61.

1549 Kachaniuk, S. "Z istorychnoho mynuloho Zakarpats'koï Ukraïny." *Zakhidna Ukraïna,* no. 4-5 (Kiev, 1931), pp. 70-75.

1550 Kachii, Iurii. "Zv'iazky naselennia Zakarpattia z rosiis'kym viis'kom v roky pershoï svitovoï viiny." *Arkhivy Ukraïny,* vol. 19, no. 6 (Kiev, 1965), pp. 41-47.

1551 Kačur, Iliya. *Stručný prehl'ad histórie pravoslavnej cirkvi v bývalom*

Uhorsku a v Československu. Prešov: Pravoslávna bohoslovecká fakúlta, n.d.

1552 Kadlec, Karel. "O právní povaze poměru Podkarpatské Rusi k republice Československé." *Podkarpatská Rus.* Edited by J. Chmelař et al. Prague: Orbis, 1923, pp. 9-16.

1553 ———· *Podkarpatská Rus.* Mírové smlouvy kongressu Pařížského a stát československý, no. 6. Prague: Státovědecká společnost, 1920.

1554 ———· "Les Russes au sud des Carpathes citoyens de la République tchécoslovaque." *La Nation tchéque,* vol. 4 (Paris, 1919), pp. 804-814.

1555 Kaigl, Ladislav. "Umění na Podkarpatské Rusi." *Podkarpatská Rus.* Edited by J. Zatloukal. Bratislava: KPPR, 1936, pp. 209-214.

1556 Kaminskii, Iosif V. "Avtonomiia karpatorusskago naroda v Mad'iarii." *Zemlediel'skii kalendar' na god 1939* (Uzhhorod, 1938), pp. 43-47.

1557 ———· *Dodatki k istorii O-va Vasiliia Velikago v 1895-1902 rokakh.* Uzhhorod, 1937.

1558 ———· *Istoriia Tsentral'noi Russkoi Narodnoi Rady.* Uzhhorod, 1927.

1559 ———· "Nasha avtonomiia (samouprava)." *Russkii zemledîl'skii kalendar'* (Uzhhorod, 1922), pp. 69-76.

1560 ———· *Natsional'noe samosoznanie nashego naroda.* Izdanie OIAD, vol. 13. Uzhhorod, 1925.

1561 ———· "Posly i senatory karpatorusskago naroda v 1862-1919 godakh." *Zemledîl'skii kalendar' na 1937 hod.* Uzhhorod, 1936, pp. 66-77.

1562 ———· "T. G. Masarik i Podkarpatskaia Rus'." *Karpatskii sviet,* vol. 3, nos. 1-2 (Uzhhorod, 1930), pp. 776-781. Reprinted in *T. G. Masarik: iubileinyi sbornik.* Edited by S. A. Fentsik. Uzhhorod: PNS, 1930.

1563 ———· "Tsentral'naia Russkaia Narodnaia Rada." *Zemledîl'skii kalendar' na 1935 hod.* Uzhhorod, 1934, pp. 38-44.

1564 Kamins'kyi, V'iacheslav. "Uhors'ka Ukraïna v etnohrafichnykh pratsiakh akad. Volodymyra Hnatiuka." *Zapysky istorychno-filolohichnoho viddilu vseukraïns'koï AN,* vol. 25 (Kiev, 1929), pp. 148-174.

1565 Kapishovs'kyi, Vasyl'. "Ekonomichni peredumovy rozvytku ukraïns'koï kul'tury v ChSSR." *Zhovten' i ukraïns'ka kul'tura.* Prešov: KSUT, 1968, pp. 484-497.

1566 ———· "Nashe zhyttia v mynulomu i suchasnomu." *15 rokiv na sluzhbi narodu.* Edited by Iu. Mulychak. Prešov: KSUT, 1966, pp. 5-26.

1567 ——— [Kapishovskii, Vasilii]. "Shkol'noe delo na Priashevshchine." *Priashevshchina.* Edited by I. S. Shlepetskii. Prague: Khutor, 1948, pp. 273-283.

1568 Karácsonyi, János. *A görögkatholikus magyarok eredete.* Budapest: Stephaneum, 1924.

1569 Karpatoross. "The Fate of Carpathian Ruthenia." *Central European Observer,* vol. 17 (London, 1940), pp. 116-118. Also in the French edition: "Le douloureux destin de la Russie subcarpathique." *L'Europe centrale,* vol. 15, no. 8 (Paris, 1940), pp. 7-8.

1570 *Karpatorusskii sbornik: Podkarpatskaia Rus' v chest' prezidenta T.G. Masarika 1850-1930.* Uzhhorod: Izd. PNS, 1930. A collection of fifteen substantial studies by Russophile scholars including F. Aristov, A. Fatieev,

A. Florovskii, V. Frantsev, G. Gerovskii, Iu. Iavorskii, I. Kontratovych, O. Markov, I. Panas, A. Petrov, and Iu. Rusak.

1571 *Karpats'ka Ukraïna.* L'viv: UVI, 1939. Comprehensive survey of the geography, history, and culture of the region in twelve articles by Galician Ukrainian authors presenting the Ukrainophile viewpoint. Includes studies by M. Andrusiak, V. Kubiiovych, Ie. Pelens'kyi, and V. Sïmovych.

1572 Karpatskij, Ivan. *Piznajte pravdu.* New York: Komitet oborony Karpatskoji Ukrajiny, 1939.

1573 Karskyj, M. "Karpatho-Ukraine." *Nation und Staat,* vol. 1 (Vienna, 1927-1928), pp. 874-876.

1574 Kashula, Ivan I. "O.V. Dukhnovych i vyvchennia ioho spadshchyny." *Velykyi Zhovten' i rozkvit vozz'iednanoho Zakarpattia.* Uzhhorod: Karpaty, 1970, pp. 523-529.

1575 ———· "Pytannia kul'tury i pobutu v suspil'no-filosofs'kii dumtsi na Zakarpatti seredyny XIX st." *Kul'tura i pobut naselennia ukraïns'kykh Karpat.* Edited by I. M. Hranchak et al. Uzhhorod: UDU, 1973, pp. 126-130.

1576 Kazanskii, P. E. *Prisoedinenie Galichiny, Bukoviny i Ugorskoi Rusi.* Odessa, 1914.

1577 Kemény, Gábor. *Ez a föld Magyarország!* A kisebbségi intézet kiadványai, vol. 13. Kecskemét, 1941.

1578 ———· [Kemen', Havriyl]. "Madiarsko-rus'kî dukhovnî vzaemynŷ." *Menshynovŷi obîzhnyk,* vol. 7, no. 5 (Pécs, 1943), pp. 1-16.

1579 ———· "Ungarn und die ruthenische Kulturgeschichte." *Donaueuropa,* vol. 3 (Budapest, 1943), pp. 597-610.

1580 ———· *Verhovina feltámad: A ruszin sors könyve.* Budapest: Mefhosz könyvkiadó, 1939.

1581 Kerechanyn, V. M. "Rol' kul'turno-osvitnikh ustanov Zakarpats'koï oblasti v komunistychnomu vykhovanni trudiashchykh." *Velykyi Zhovten' i rozkvit vozz'iednanoho Zakarpattia.* Uzhhorod: Karpaty, 1970, pp. 478-489.

1582 Khainas, Vasyl' V. "Borot'ba trudiashchykh Zakarpats'koï Ukraïny za vozz'iednannia z Radians'koiu Ukraïnoiu (1944-1945 rr.)." *Velykyi Zhovten' i rozkvit vozz'iednanoho Zakarpattia.* Uzhhorod: Karpaty, 1970, pp. 252-262.

1583 ———· *Roky velykykh podiï: borot'ba trudiashchykh Zakarpattia pid kerivnytstvom komunistychnoï partiï za vozz'iednannia z Radians'koiu Ukraïnoiu (1944-1945 rr.).* Uzhhorod: ZOV, 1959.

1584 ———· *Zdiisnennia mriï: z istoriï Zakarpats'koï komunistychnoï orhanizatsiï 1938-1945 rokiv.* Uzhhorod: Karpaty, 1964.

1585 Khalus, Petro I. "Miunkhen i Zakarpattia." *Duklia,* vol. 6, no. 3 (Prešov, 1958), pp. 53-62.

1586 ———· *V boiakh za voliu: borot'ba trudiashchykh Zakarpattia proty inozemnykh ponevoliuvachiv za vozz'iednannia z Radians'koiu Ukraïnoiu (1939-1944 rr.).* Uzhhorod: ZOV, 1959.

1586a Khichii, O. F. "Z istoriï shkil'nytstva v Zakarpatti z XVIII stolittia do vozz'iednannia ioho z Radians'koiu Ukraïnoiu." *Naukovi zapysky UDU,* vol. 29 (Uzhhorod, 1957).

1587 Khlanta, O.V. *Ïkh vely komunisty: z istoriï zakarpats'koï komunistychnoï orhanizatsiï 1924-1929 rokiv.* Uzhhorod: ZOV, 1962.

1588 ———· "Komunisty Zakarpattia—orhanizatory i kerivnyky klasovoï borot'by trudiashchych v period tymchasovoï vidnosnoï stabilizatsiï kapitalizmu (1924-1929 rr.)." *Naukovi zapysky UDU,* vol. 50 (Uzhhorod, 1963), pp. 22-40.

1589 ———· "Z istoriï kolonial'noï polityky ches'koï burzhuaziï na Zakarpatti v 20-kh rokakh XX st." *Naukovi zapysky UDU,* vol. 36 (Uzhhorod, 1958), pp. 90-104.

1590 Khoma, Vasyl'. "Umovy rozvytku ukraïns'koi literatury Skhidnoï Slovachchyny pislia 1945 roku." *Zhovten' i ukraïns'ka kul'tura.* Prešov: KSUT, 1968, pp. 536-548.

1590a Khraplyvyi, Evhen. *Karpats'ka Ukraïna v chyslakh.* L'viv, 1938.

1591 Klíma, Stanislav. "Ruskoslovenské hranice na východě Slovenská." *Slovánský přehled,* vol. 9 (Prague, 1907), pp. 60-63, 112-121.

1592 Klíma, Viktor. "Shkol'noe dielo i prosvieshchenie na Podkarpatskoi Rusi." *Podkarpatskaia Rus' za gody 1919-1936.* Edited by E. Bachinskii. Uzhhorod: RNG, 1936, pp. 101-105.

1593 Klochurak, Stepan. "Do hromads'koï diial'nosti d-ra I. Pan'kevycha v Zakarpats'kii Ukraïni." *Naukovyi zbirnyk MUKS,* vol. 4, pt. 1 (Bratislava, Prešov, and Svidník, 1967), pp. 259-262.

1594 Klympotiuk, Mykhailo. *Iunist' v borot'bi.* Uzhhorod: ZOV, 1959.

1595 ———· *Pidstupy amerykans'kykh imperialistiv na Zakarpatti.* Uzhhorod, 1952.

1596 Kočí, Bohumil. *Podkarpatská Rus: její poměry hospodářské, kulturní a politické.* Prague: Čas, 1922.

1597 Kokhanik, Petr. *Nachalo istorii Amerikanskoi Rusi.* Second edition. Trumbull, Conn.: Peter S. Hardy, 1970.

1598 Kokhannyi-Goral'chuk, Kirill V. *Iskry: synam Podkarpatskoi Rusi.* Uzhhorod, 1922.

1599 ———· "Kul'turnyia dostizheniia na Podk. Rusi." *Karpatorusskiia dostizheniia.* Edited by A. V. Popov. Mukachevo, 1930, pp. 81-88.

1600 ———· *Kul'turna pratsa vnî shkoly.* Uzhhorod, 1922.

1601 ——— [Kochannyj, Cyril]. *O Podkarpatské Rusi.* Občanská knihovna, no. 83. Prague: Péčí min. školství a narodní osvěty, 1929.

1602 ——— [Kochannyj-Goralčuk, K.]. *Podkarpatská Rus v minulostí a přitomnosti.* Prague: Státní nakladatelství, 1931.

1603 ———· "Vnieshkol'nyia dostizheniia." *Podkarpatskaia Rus' za gody 1919-1936.* Edited by E. Bachinskii. Uzhhorod: RNG, 1936, pp. 109-112.

1604 Kol'esar, Iuliian D. *Istoriia ruskoho narodnoho mena.* Montreal, 1973.

1605 Kolessa, Oleksander. "Prychynky do istoriï uhors'ko-rus'koï movy i literatury." *Zapysky NTSh,* vol. 35-36 (L'viv, 1900).

1606 Kołodziejczyk, Edmund. "Ruś węgierska." *Świat słowiański,* vol. 1 (Cracow, 1911), pp. 106-115.

1607 Kolomiets, Ivan G. *Ocherki po istorii Zakarpat'ia,* pt. 1. Trudy Tomskogo gosudarstvennogo universiteta im. V.V. Kuibysheva: Sbornik rabot po voprosam istorii. Seriia istoricheskaia, vol. 121, no. 2 (Tomsk, 1953). Reprinted in Prešov: KSUT, 1955. Part 2: *Sotsial'no-èkonomicheskie otnosheniia, natsional'no-politicheskoe i kul'turnoe dvizhenie v Zakarpat'e v XIX veke.* Tomsk: Izd. Tomskogo universiteta, 1959.

1608 ——· *Sotsial'no-èkonomicheskie otnosheniia i obshchestvennoe dvizhenie v Zakarpat'e vo vtoroi polovine XIX stoletiia.* 2 vols. Tomsk: Izd. Tomskogo universiteta, 1962.

1609 *Kolomŷika: zbôrnyk prysviachenyi I. zîzdu Rus'kykh Natsional'nŷkh Khorov Podkarpatskoi Rusy.* Uzhhorod, 1926.

1610 Komanitskii, P. F. "OKS 'Vozrozhdenie' i studencheskie organizatsii." *Priashevshchina.* Edited by I.S. Shlepetskii. Prague: Khutor, 1948, pp. 301-307.

1611 Komenar. *Rusyn chy ukraïnets'?.* Uzhhorod, 1937.

1612 Kompaniiets', Ivan I. "Zakarpats'ka Ukraïna." *Radians'ka entsyklopediia istoriï Ukraïny,* vol. 2. Edited by A. D. Skaba et al. Kiev: ANURSR, 1970, pp. 170-173.

1613 Kontratovych, Irynei M. [Kontratovics, Irén]. "Az amerikai ruszinok." *Magyar szemle,* vol. 42, no. 1 (Budapest, 1942), pp. 21-24.

1614 ——· "Bor'ba za rus'kii iazŷk v Uzhhorodskôi gymnaziy." *Podkarpatska Rus',* vol. 4, no. 6 (Uzhhorod, 1927), pp. 132-136.

1615 ——· "Dodatky k ystoriï shkôl'nytstva Pôdkarpatskoî Rusy." *Podkarpatska Rus',* vol. 1, no. 2 (Uzhhorod, 1923), pp. 33-37.

1616 ——· "Iak postavyv zhebrakamy vîden'skii tsysarskii dvor predkov nashykh uhorskykh rusynov?" *Russkii zemledîl'skii kalendar' na 1923 hod.* Uzhhorod, 1922, pp. 55-68.

1617 ——· "Iz drevnoi zhizni podkarpatorusskago naroda." *Kalendar Sojedinenija na hod 1936.* Homestead, Pa., 1936, pp. 71-76.

1618 ——· *K istorii starodavniago Uzhgoroda i Podkarpatskoi Rusi do XIV vieka.* Izdanie OIAD, no. 39. Uzhhorod, 1928.

1619 ——· "Kniaz' Fedor Koriiatovych y Mukachevskii monastŷr'." *Podkarpatska Rus',* vol. 1, no. 1 (Uzhhorod, 1923), pp. 30-32.

1620 ——· "Korotka ystoriia Obshchestva sv. Vasyliia Velykoho." *Iuvyleinŷi yliustrovanŷi kalendar' 'Unio' na rok 1928.* Uzhhorod, 1927, pp. 41-48.

1621 —— [Kontratovich, I. M.] "Ocherki iz istorii Mukachevskoi eparkhii: episkopy Ol'shavskie i ikh dieiatel'nost' v bor'bie za tserkovnuiu uniiu i za kanonizatsiiu Mukachevskoi eparkhii." *Karpatorusskii sbornik.* Uzhhorod: Izd. PNS, 1930, pp. 91-111. Published separately: Uzhhorod, 1931; and in English translation by George Parvensky: "The Olšavsky Bishops and Their Activity." *Slovak Studies,* vol. 3 (Rome, 1963), pp. 179-198.

1622 ——· *Ystoriia Podkarpatskoî Rusy dlia naroda.* Vŷd. TP, nos. 35-37. Uzhhorod, 1930.

1623 Kopans'kyi, Mykola. *Iak pobidyv narodovets'kyi rukh v Staromu Kraiu na b. Pidkarpats'kii Rusy.* Bridgeport, Conn.: Nash Uzhhorod, 1950.

1624 Kopystians'ka, N. Kh. "Tvory Ivana Ol'brakhta pro Zakarpats'ku Ukraïnu." *Duklia,* vol. 6, no. 1 (Prešov, 1958), pp. 51-60.

1625 Korol', Ivan. "Dopomoha komunistiv Chekhoslovachchyny v orhanizatsiinomu zmitsnenni zakarpats'koï kraiovoï orhanizatsiï." *Duklia,* vol. 19, no. 2 (Prešov, 1971), pp. 47-52.

1626 "Korotka istorija eparchii Mukačevskoji," *Kalendar' OS na hod 1933.* Perth Amboy, N.J., 1933, pp. 69-77.

1627 Koržinský, K. *Původ a vývoj hnutí ukrajinského.* Moravská Ostrava, 1919.

1628 Kostelnyk, Vlado. "Hornitsa pred doselien'om Rusnatsokh do Bachky y Srymu." *Nova dumka,* vol. 3, no. 7 (Vukovar, 1974), pp. 131-153; no. 8, pp. 91-105; vol. 4, no. 9 (1975), pp. 96-111; no. 10, pp. 73-91; vol. 5, no. 11 (1976), pp. 100-110.

1629 Kovach, Andrii. "Natsional'na polityka Slovatskoï Respubliky po vidnoshenniu do rusyniv-ukraïntsiv (1938-1945)." *Zhovten' i ukraïns'ka kul'-tura.* Prešov: KSUT, 1968, pp. 132-144.

1630 ———· "Stanovyshche zakarpats'kykh ukraïntsiv (rusyniv) i zanepad pershoï ChSR," *Naukovyi zbirnyk MUKS,* vol. 6, pt. 1 (Bratislava, Prešov, and Svidník, 1972), pp. 7-38.

1631 ———· "Ukraïntsi Priashivshchyny i deiaki pytannia kul'turnoï polityky Slovats'koï Respubliky." *Naukovyi zbirnyk MUKS,* vol. 4, pt. 1 (Bratislava, Prešov, and Svidník, 1969), pp. 401-412.

1632 ———· "Ukraïntsi Priashivshchyny v riadakh Chervonoï Armiï." *Naukovyi zbirnyk MUKS,* vol. 2 (Bratislava, Prešov, and Svidník, 1966), pp. 315-348.

1633 ———· "Ukraïntsi skhidnoï Slovachchyny naperedodni slovats'koho narodnoho povstannia." *Z mynuloho i suchasnoho ukraïntsiv Chekhoslovachchyny.* Pedahohichnyi zbirnyk, no. 3. Bratislava: SPV, 1973, pp. 196-216.

1634 ———· "Vyzvolennia Priashivshchyny (1944-1945 rr.)." *Naukovyi zbirnyk MUKS,* vol. 2 (Bratislava, Prešov, and Svidník, 1966), pp. 413-424.

1635 Kovach, Fedir. "Amators'kyi narodnyi teatr na Priashivshchyni." *15 rokiv na sluzhbi narodu.* Edited by Iu. Mulychak. Prešov: KSUT, 1966, pp. 78-96.

1636 ———· *Deiaki problemy rozvytku ukraïns'koï literatury v Chekhoslovachchyni (pisliavoiennyi period).* Naukova-populiarna biblioteka KSUT, no. 6. Prešov, 1973.

1637 Kovács, Endre. "Zakarpattia naperedodni burzhuaznoï revoliutsiï 1848 r." *Ukraïns'ko-uhors'ki istorychni zv'iazky.* Kiev: Naukova dumka, 1964, pp. 229-240.

1638 Koval', M. F. "Oleksandr Dukhnovych i iednist' slov'ians'kykh narodiv." *Oleksandr Dukhnovych: zbirnyk materialiv.* Edited by M. Rychalka. Prešov: KSUT, 1965.

1639 Koval', M. F., and Rychalka, Mykhailo I. "Dukhnovych iak osvitnii diiach." *Oleksandr Dukhnovych: zbirnyk materialiv.* Edited by M. Rychalka. Prešov: KSUT, 1965, pp. 213-223.

1640 Kozauer, Nikolaus J. "The Carpatho-Ukraine between the Two World Wars." Ph.D. dissertation, Rutgers University, 1964.

1641 Kozma, Nicholas. "Le problème ruthène." *Nouvelle revue de Hongrie,* vol. 61, no. 7 (Budapest, 1939), pp. 3-14.

1642 Kózmiński, Maciej. *Polska i Węgry przed drugą wojną światową.* Warsaw: Wy-wo Polskiej Akademii Nauk, 1970.

1643 Král, Jiří. "Osídlení Karpatské Rusi: historický přehled." *Sborník československé společnosti zeměpisné,* vol. 29 (Prague, 1923), pp. 65-83. Abridged translation in Rusyn: "Ystoriia kolonyzatsiï Pôdkarpatskoî

Rusy." *Podkarpatska Rus'*, vol. 1, nos. 2 and 3 (Uzhhorod, 1923), pp. 37-43 and 68-72.

1644 ———· *Podkarpatská Rus*. Prague, 1924.

1645 Kralitskii, Anatolii. "Daty k istorii ugorskikh rusinov po zherelam Bazilovicha i Baludianskago." *Galichanin*, bk. 1, nos. 3-4 (L'viv, 1863), pp. 181-190.

1646 ———· "Istoricheskoe opisanie monastyrei china Sv. Vasiliia Velikago v Ugorshchinie." *Mîsiatsoslov na hod 1865 dlia russkykh uhorskiia kraynŷ*. Uzhhorod, 1864, pp. 49-54.

1647 ——— [A.K.]. "Istoricheskoe opisanie monastyrei sv. Vasiliia Velikago v Ugorshchinie: Monastyr' Mukachevskii na Gorie Chernetskoi." *Mîsiatsoslov na hod 1866 dlia russkykh uhorskiia kraynŷ*. Uzhhorod, 1865, pp. 33-35.

1648 ———· "Korotkii opis Monastyria Mariia-Povchanskogo china Sv. V. Velikago v Ugrii." *Galichanin*, bk. 1, no. 2 (L'viv, 1863), pp. 150-153.

1649 ——— [A.K.]. "Monastyr' Bereznitskii." *Listok*, vol. 6, no. 8 (Uzhhorod, 1890).

1650 ——— [A.K.]. "Monastyr' Mariia-Povchanskii." *Listok,* vol. 6, no. 3 (Uzhhorod, 1890).

1651 ———· "Monastyr' Sv. o. Nikolaia na Gorie Chernetskoi vozlie Mukacheva." *Vremennik Stavropigiiskago instituta na 1891 god*. L'viv, 1890, pp. 156-158.

1652 ———· "O sovremennom polozhenii russkikh v Ugrii." *Slavianskii sbornik,* vol. 1 (St. Petersburg, 1875), pp. 44-45.

1653 Kreze, Leonid A. "O knizhnom prosvieshchenii na Podkarpatskoi Rusi." *Podkarpatskaia Rus' za gody 1919-1936*. Edited by E. Bachinskii. Uzhhorod: RNG, 1936, pp. 121-124.

1654 Krhoun, Měčislav. "Jaroslav Zatloukal a Zakarpatská Ukrajina." *Zhovten' i ukraïns'ka kul'tura*. Prešov: KSUT, 1968, pp. 248-253.

1655 Krofta, Kamil. "Čechoslováci a Podkarpatská Rus." *Podkarpatská Rus.* Edited by J. Zatloukal. Bratislava: KPPR, 1936, pp. 19-29.

1656 ———· *Podkarpatská Rus a Československo*. Knihova svazu národního osvobození, no. 98. Prague, 1935. Also in Russian translation: Prague: Orbis, 1935. Expanded version in his *Byli jsme za Rakouska: úvahy historické a politické*. Prague: Orbis, 1936, pp. 113-141.

1657 ———· "Ruthenes, Czechs, and Slovaks." *Slavonic and East European Review*, vol. 13 (London, 1935), pp. 362-371, 611-626.

1658 Krupnyckyj, B. "Ein kurzer überblick über die Entwicklung der Karpaten-Ukraine." *Nation und Staat*, vol. 12 (Vienna, 1938-1939), pp. 73-74.

1659 Krushel'nyts'kyi, Antin. "Natsional'ne pytannia v shkil'nytstvi na Prykarpatti." *Nova hromada*, nos. 3-4 (Vienna, 1923), pp. 51-71.

1660 "Kruzhok po izucheniiu Podkarpatskoi Rusi pri Russkom narodnom universitetie v Pragie v 1931-32 uch. godu." *Zhivaia mysl'*, no. 2-3 (Prague, 1933), pp. 22-25.

1661 Krylatyi, Iurii. "Zakarpattia 30 rokiv tomu." *Duklia*, vol. 17, no. 5 (Prešov, 1969), pp. 74-77.

1662 Krypinskii, Iosif. "Avtonomiia Podkarpatskoi Rusi." *Vosem' lektsii o Podkarpatskoi Rusi*. Edited by D. Vergun. Prague, 1925, pp. 11-31.

1663 Kryvda-Sokolenko, Petro. " 'Ukraynyzatsiia' Podkarpatskoi Rusy." *Karpatorusskii kalendar' 'Lemko' 1923* (Uzhhorod, 1922), pp. 109-123.
1664 Kubiiovych, Volodymyr. "Liudnist'." *Karpats'ka Ukraïna.* L'viv: UVI, 1939, pp. 37-49. Revised version: *Entsyklopediia ukraïnoznavstva: slovnykova chastyna,* vol. 2. Paris and New York: Vyd. Molode zhyttia, for the NTSh, 1955-1957, pp. 723-726.
1665 ――― [Kubijovič, Vladimir]. *Rozšíření kultur a obyvatelstva v severních Karpatech.* Bratislava, 1932.
1666 Kubinyi, Julius. *The History of Prjašiv Eparchy.* Editiones Universites Catholicae Ucrainorum S. Clementis Papae, vol. 32. Rome, 1970.
1667 Kudryk, A. *Vid Popradu po Tysu.* L'viv: Prosvita, 1939.
1668 Kundrat, Iurii. "Chekhoslovats'ka viis'kova presa v SRSR." *Duklia,* vol. 23, no. 3 (Prešov, 1975), pp. 55-63.
1669 Kupchanko, Hryhorii. *Nasha rodyna.* Vienna, 1897.
1670 ――― *Uhorska Rus' y ei russky zhytely.* Vienna, 1897.
1671 "Kurtyák Iván közmüvelödési egyesület." *Láthatár,* vol. 9 (Budapest, 1941), pp. 286-287.
1672 Kuschnir, Wladimir. "Die Ruthenen in Ungarn." *Ruthenische revue,* vol. 2, no. 14 (Vienna, 1904), pp. 320-327.
1673 ――― "Die Ruthenen in Ungarn." *Ukrainische Rundschau,* vol. 9 (Vienna, 1911), pp. 17-21.
1674 Kushchyns'kyi, Antin. "Zi slavnykh dniv Karpats'koï Ukraïny." *Samostiina Ukraïna,* vol. 14, no. 4 (Chicago, 1961), pp. 8-11.
1675 Kustodiev, Konstantin. "Iz istorii razocharovaniia avstriiskikh slavian: posol'stvo ugorskikh russkikh v Vienie v 1849 godu." *Russkii viestnik,* vol. 98, no. 4 (Moscow, 1872), pp. 377-407.
1676 ――― "Kongress katolikov Vengrii i Ugorskie-Russke." *Pravoslavnoe obozrenie,* nos. 3, 4, 5, 10, and 12 (Moscow, 1871); nos. 3 and 4 (1872).
1677 ――― "Tserkov' ugorskikh russkikh i serbov v ikh vzaimootnoshenii." *Pravoslavnoe obozrienie,* nos. 5 and 6 (Moscow, 1873), pp. 1012-1034 and 1012-1034.
1678 Kutsenko, K. O. "Kommunisty Zakarpat'ia―organizatory bor'by trudiashchikhsia protiv fashistskikh zakhvatchikov: 1939-1944 rr." *Voprosy istorii KPSS perioda Velikoi Otechestvennoi voiny.* Kiev, 1961, pp. 270-277.
1679 ――― "Zakarpattia v roky fashysts'koï okupatsiï ta vyzvolennia ioho Radians'koiu Armiieiu." *Naukovi zapysky UDU,* vol. 30 (Uzhhorod, 1957), pp. 123-139.
1680 Kutsera, O. *Pidkarpats'ka Ukraïna.* Poděbrady: Vyd. Tovarystva pry P.H.A., 1922.
1681 Kuziela, Zenon. "Karpaten-Ukraine." *Ukrainische Kulturberichte,* nos. 39-44 (Berlin, 1939).
1682 Kyryliuk, Ievhen P. "Ivan Franko i ukraïns'ka literatura na Zakarpatti." *Oleksandr Dukhnovych: zbirnyk materialiv.* Edited by M. Rychalka. Prešov: KSUT, 1965, pp. 42-53.
1683 L. "Die Karpathen-Ukraine." *Nation und Staat,* vol. 12 (Vienna, 1938-39), pp. 75-80.
1684 Laborchan. "Istoricheskie otryvki, kasaiushchiesia Ugorskoi Rusi." *Mî-*

siatseslov na 1869 hod. Uzhhorod: OSVV, 1868.

1685 Lacko, Michael. "A Brief Survey of the History of the Slovak Catholics of the Byzantine Slavonic Rite." *Slovak Studies,* vol. 3: *Cyrillo-Methodiana,* no. 1 (Cleveland and Rome, 1963), pp. 199-224.

1686 ——· "The Forced Liquidation of the Union of Užhorod." *Slovak Studies,* vol. 1: *Historica,* no. 1 (Rome, 1961), pp. 145-185.

1687 ——· "The Pastoral Activity of Manuel Michael Olšavsky, Bishop of Mukačevo." *Orientalia Christiana Periodica,* vol. 27 (Rome, 1961), pp. 150-161.

1688 ——· "The Re-establishment of the Greek-Catholic Church in Czechoslovakia." *Slovak Studies,* vol. 11: *Historica,* no. 8 (Cleveland and Rome, 1971), pp. 159-189.

1689 ——· *Synodus episcoporum ritus byzantini catholicorum ex antiqua Hungaria, Vindobonae anno 1773 celebrata.* Orientalia Christiana Analecta, no. 199. Rome, 1975.

1690 ——· *Unio Užhorodensis Ruthenorum Carpathicorum cum Ecclesia Catholica.* Orientalia Christiana Analecta, no. 143. Rome, 1955.

1691 ——· "The Union of Užhorod." *Slovak Studies,* vol. 6: *Historica,* no. 4 (Cleveland and Rome, 1966), pp. 7-190. Published separately: Cleveland and Rome: Slovak Institute, 1968. Second edition: 1976.

1692 ——· "Die Užhoroder Union." *Ostkirchliche Studien,* vol. 8, no. 1 (Würzburg, 1959), pp. 3-30.

1693 Lakyza, Ivan. *Zakarpats'ka Ukraïna.* Kharkiv: Knyhospilka, 1930.

1694 Lapica, Michael. "The Rise of Carpatho-Ukraine." *The Trident,* vol. 3, nos. 1-2 (New York, 1939), pp. 7-21.

1695 Lapica, Michael, and Lacyk, Roman. "Republic for a Day." *The Trident,* vol. 3 nos. 4-5 (New York, 1939), pp. 8-27.

1696 Lazar, Ie. "Do pytannia pro slovats'ko-ukraïns'ki literaturni vidnosyny v XIX stolitti." *Z istoriï chekhoslovats'ko-ukraïns'kykh zv'iazkiv.* Bratislava: SVKL, 1959, pp. 370-388.

1697 Lebl, Arpad. "Poviazanosts sotsyialnoho y natsyonalnoho pytania pry Rusnakokh 1887-1918," *Shvetlosts,* vol. 12, no. 4 (Novi Sad, 1974), pp. 341-355.

1698 Lehoczky, Tivadar. *Beregmegye és a Munkácsi vár 1848-1849-ben.* Mukachevo, 1899.

1699 ——· *A beregmegyei görögszertartású katholikus lelkészségek története a XIX. század végéig.* Mukachevo, 1904.

1700 ——· *Beregvármegye monográfiája.* 3 vols. Uzhhorod, 1881-1883.

1701 ——· "Korjatovics Tódor hg. és az 1490-iki pöre." *Századok,* vol. 27 (Budapest, 1893).

1702 ——· *Munkács város új monografiája.* Mukachevo: Grünstein Mór kiadása, 1907.

1703 ——· *A munkácsi vár rövid története.* Mukachevo, 1912.

1704 Lelekach, Mykola. "Ideinyi rozvii pidkarpats'koï literatury." *Proboiem,* vol. 1, nos. 2-3, 4, and 5 (Prague, 1934), pp. 11-13, 46-48, and ?

1705 ——· "Kul'turni zv'iazky Zakarpattia z Ukraïnoiu i Rossiieiu v XVII-XVIII st." *Naukovi zapysky UDU,* vol. 9 (Uzhhorod, 1954), pp. 141-164.

1705a ———· "Munkachevska bohoslovska shkola (1744-1776)." *Lyteraturna nedîlia*, vol. 3 (Uzhhorod, 1943), pp. 237-240.

1706 ———· "Novi prychynky do politychnoï diial'nosty Adol'fa Dobrians'koho." *Naukovyi zbirnyk TP*, vol. 13-14 (Uzhhorod, 1938), pp. 160-166.

1707 ———· "Persha rus'ka rukopysna chytanka [Nykolaia Teodorovycha od 1801 roku]." *Lyteraturna nedîlia*, vol. 3 (Uzhhorod, 1943), pp. 162-164.

1708 ———· "Podkarpatskoe pys'menstvo na pochatku XX vîka." *Zoria-Hajnal*, vol. 3, no. 1-4 (Uzhhorod, 1943), pp. 229-257.

1709 ———· "Pro prynalezhnist' Zakarpattia do Kyivs'koï Rusi v X-XI st." *Naukovi zapysky UDU*, vol. 2 (Uzhhorod, 1949), pp. 28-39.

1710 ———· "Rus'ka shliakhta Uzhhorods'koï Kraïni na Pidk. Rusy." *Podkarpatska Rus'*, vol. 12-13 (Uzhhorod, 1935-1936), pp. 6-13.

1711 Lengyel, Constantin Mihály. *Ruthénekről: sztavna község multja és jelene.* Uzhhorod: B. Jäger, 1898.

1712 Levyts'kyi, Volodymyr. *Hitler, Chekhy i Karpats'ka Ukraïna.* Scranton, Pa.: 'Narodna Volia', 1939.

1713 Lewandowski, Krzysztof. *Sprawa ukraińska w polityce zagranicznej Czechosłowacji w latach 1918-1932.* Wrocław-Warsaw: Polska akademia nauk, 1974.

1714 Linek, Josef. *Podkarpatská Rus: úvahy a poznámky.* Třebechovice pod Orebem: Nákladem 'Věstníku lidovýchovy a samosprávy', 1922.

1715 Lintur, Petro V. "Traditsii russkogo klassitsizma v literature Zakarpat'ia XIX v." *Russkaia literatura XVIII veka i slavianskie literatury.* Moscow-Leningrad: Akademiia nauk SSSR, 1963, pp. 123-136.

1716 ———· "Traditsii russkogo sentimentalizma v tvorchestve A.V. Dukhnovicha." *Voprosy russkoi literatury*, no. 2 (5). L'viv: Izd. LU, 1967, pp. 82-87.

1717 Liprandi, A. P. "Zabytyi ugolok Russkoi zemli (Ugorskaia Rus')." *Russkaia besieda*, vol. 2, no. 4. (St. Petersburg, 1896), pp. 74-94.

1718 Lisovyi, Pavlo. *Blyz'kyi i dorohyi.* Uzhhorod: ZOV, 1961.

1719 ———· *Cherez Beskydy: literaturna besida.* Uzhhorod, 1972.

1720 ———· "Poeziia borot'by." *Duklia*, vol. 15, no. 3 (Prešov, 1967), pp. 61-69.

1721 ———· "Vplyv idei Zhovtnia na rozvytok prohresyvnoï literatury Zakarpattia v 20-kh—v pershii polovyni 40-kh rokiv." *Zhovten' i ukraïns'ka kul'tura.* Prešov: KSUT, 1968, pp. 392-421.

1722 ———· "Z istoriï revoliutsiino-vyzvol'noï borot'by trudiashchykh Zakarpattia v roky svitovoï ekonomichnoï kryzy (1929-1933)." *Zapysky Naukovoho tovarystva KSUT*, no. 3 (Prešov, 1975), pp. 111-120.

1723 Lisovyi, Pavlo, and Babydorych, Mykhailo. *Trybuna trudiashchykh: do 50-richchia hazety 'Zakarpats'ka pravda'.* Uzhhorod: Karpaty, 1970.

1724 Liubymov, Volodymyr. "Rozvytok muzychnoï ta khorovoï kul'tury." *15 rokiv na sluzhbi narodu.* Edited by Iu. Mulychak. Prešov: KSUT, 1966, pp. 55-77.

1725 Lizanets', Pavlo M. *Magyar-ukrán nyelvi kapcsolatok (A kárpátontúli ukrán nyelvjárások anyaga alapján).* Uzhhorod: UDU, 1970.

1726 Lohoida, V. M. "Hromadians'ki sviata radians'koho Zakarpattia i podolannia relihiinykh perezhytkiv." *Kul'tura i pobut naselennia ukraïns'kykh Karpat.* Uzhhorod: UDU, 1973, pp. 60-65.

1727   Luchkai, Mykhail [Lutskay, Michael]. "Historia Carpatho-Ruthenorum in Hungarica Sacra et civilis. Ex probatissimis Autoribus, Diplomatibus Regiis, et Documentis Archivi Diocesis Munkats." 6 vols. Manuscript in the University Library, Uzhhorod.

1728   Lukács, György. "A rutén probléma." *Magyar külpolitika* (Budapest, 1939), pp. 9-10.

1729   Lukovich, Antonii. "Natsional'naia i iazykovaia prinadlezhnost' russkago naseleniia Podk. Rusi." *Karpatskii sviet,* vol. 1, nos. 9 and 10 (Uzhhorod, 1928), pp. 327-331, 349-354; and vol. 2, no. 1 (1929), pp. 397-403.

1730   Lukevich, Antonii, and Dušanek, Jan. *Chust v Marmaroši: náčrt dějin hradu a župy.* Khust: Okresni výbor a městský úřad, 1937.

1731   Lukych, Vasyl'. *Uhors'ka Rus', iey rozvôi y teperîshnii stan.* L'viv, 1887.

Lutskay, Michael, *see* Luchkai, Mykhail

1732   Lyshak, P. *Rishenyi iazykovoho voprosu.* Tiachiv-Uzhhorod: Vyd. filii TP v Tiachovi, 1935.

1733   Macartney, Carlisle A. "Ruthenia." *Hungary and Her Successors: The Treaty of Trianon and its Consequences, 1919-1937.* London: Oxford University Press, 1937.

1734   Máchal, Jan. "Podkarpatští rusové a slovanské obrození." *Slovanský sborník věnovaný prof. Františku Pastrnkovi.* Edited by Miloš Weingart. Prague: Klub moderních filologů, 1923, pp. 208-214.

1735   Maču, Pavel. "National Assimilation: The Case of the Rusyn-Ukrainians of Czechoslovakia." *East-Central Europe,* vol. 2, no. 2 (Pittsburgh, 1975), pp. 101-131.

1736   ———· "The Present State of National Consciousness among the Rusyns of Czechoslovakia." *Europa ethnica,* vol. 31, no. 3 (Vienna, 1974), pp. 98-111. Republished in shortened form: "The Rusyns of Czechoslovakia." *The Cornish Banner,* vol. 1, no. 2 (Trelispen, Cornwall, 1975), pp. 4-6.

1737   Magocsi, Paul R. "The Development of National Consciousness in Subcarpathian Rus', 1918-1945." Doctoral dissertation. Princeton University, 1972.

1738   ———· "Moï vrazhennia z podorozhi po Iugoslavii." *Nova dumka,* vol. 3, no. 8 (Vukovar, 1974), pp. 116-118.

1739   ———· "The Political Activity of Rusyn-American Immigrants in 1918." *East European Quarterly,* vol. 10, no. 3 (Boulder, Colo., 1976), pp. 347-365. Reprinted in Harvard Ukrainian Research Institute Offprint Series, no. 13. Cambridge, Mass. [1976].

1740   ———· "The Role of Education in the Formation of a National Consciousness." *East European Quarterly,* vol. 7, no. 2 (Boulder, Colo., 1973), pp. 159-165.

1741   ———· "The Problem of National Affiliation among the Rusyns (Ruthenians) of Yugoslavia." *Europa Ethnica,* vol. 34, no. 1 (Vienna, 1977), pp. 5-8.

1742   ———· "The Subcarpathian Decision to unite with Czechoslovakia." *Slavic Review,* vol. 34, no. 1 (Seattle, Wash., 1975), pp. 360-381. Reprinted in

Harvard Ukrainian Research Institute Offprint Series, no. 3. Cambridge, Mass. [1975].

Maier, Mariia, *see* Mayer, Mária

1743 Makara, M.P., and I.M. Chavarha. "Osushchestvlenie Leninskoi natsional'-noi politiki na Zakarpat'e." *Kul'tura i pobut naselennia ukraïns'kykh Karpat.* Uzhhorod: UDU, 1973, pp. 3-9.

1744 Makara, M. P.; Khainas, V. V.; and Chavarha, I. M. *Torzhestvo lenins'-koï natsional'noï polityky na Zakarpatti: navchal'nyi posibnyk.* Uzhhorod: UDU, 1974.

1745 Mamatey, Victor S. "The Slovaks and Carpatho-Ruthenians." *The Immigrants' Influence on Wilson's Peace Policies.* Edited by Joseph P. O'Grady. Lexington, Ky.: University of Kentucky Press, 1967, pp. 224-249.

1746 Manning, Clarence A. "The Linguistic Question in Carpatho-Ukraine." *The Ukrainian Quarterly,* vol. 10, no. 3 (New York, 1954), pp. 247-251.

1747 Markus, Vasyl. "Carpatho-Ukraine under Hungarian Occupation (1939-1944)." *The Ukrainian Quarterly,* vol. 10, no. 3 (New York, 1945), pp. 252-256.

1748 ———· *L'incorporation de l'Ukraine subcarpathique à l'Ukraine soviétique, 1944-1945.* Louvain: Centre d'études ukrainiens en Belgique, 1956.

1749 ———· "Madiars'ka okupatsiia Karpats'koï Ukraïny v 1939-1944 rr." *Vistnyk,* vol. 6, no. 2 (New York, 1952), pp. 15-22.

1750 ———· "Nyshchennia hreko-katolyts'koï tserkvy v Mukachivs'kii Ieparkhiï v 1945-50 rr." *Zapysky NTSh,* vol. 169 (Paris and New York, 1962), pp. 386-405.

1751 ———· "Transcarpathia [During World War II]." *Ukraine: A Concise Encyclopedia,* vol. 1. Toronto: University of Toronto Press for the Ukrainian National Association, 1963, pp. 891-892.

1752 ———· "Zakarpattia." *Entsyklopediia ukraïnoznavstva: slovnykova chastyna,* vol. 2, Paris and New York: Vyd. Molode zhyttia for the NTSh, 1955-1957, pp. 720-723.

1753 Markush, Aleksander. *Shkolnŷ voprosŷ.* Uzhhorod: Izd. Podkarpatskoho zemledîls'koho soiuza, 1922.

1754 Martel, René. "Le nom d' 'ukrainien' en Russie subcarpathique." *Le monde Slave,* vol. 14, no. 1 (Paris, 1937), pp. 560-569.

1755 ———· "La politique slave de la Russie d'avant-guerre." *Affaires étrangères,* vol. 6, no. 10 (Paris, 1936), pp. 623-634; and vol. 7, no. 1 (1937), pp. 58-64.

1756 ———· *La Ruthénie subcarpathique.* Paris: Paul Hartmann, 1935.

1757 Martynovych, B. "Spîv y natsional'nî khorŷ na Pôdkarpatskôi Rusy." *Kalendar 'Prosvîtŷ' 1929* (Uzhhorod, 1928), pp. 137-144.

1758 Matisov, O. "Dvizhenie narodnoi zhizni v Ugorskoi Rusi." *Besieda,* vol. 1, no. 6-7 (Moscow, 1871), pp. 225-246.

1759 Matoušek, Karel. *Podkarpatská Rus.* Země a lidé, no. 55. Prague: Nákladem České grafické unie, 1924.

1760 Matsyns'kyi, Ivan. *Rozmova storich.* Bratislava and Prešov: SPVVUL, 1965.

1761 ———· "Skhidna Slovachchyna v zakarpatoukraïns'komu kul'turnomu
      zhytti." *Duklia,* vol. 16, nos. 1, 2, and 3 (Prešov, 1968), pp. 1-7, 129-139,
      and 195-204.
1762 Mayer, Mária. "Beiträge zur Geschichte der Ruthenen (Karpatoukrainer) um
      die Jahrhundertwende." *Acta Historica Academiae Scientiarium Hun-
      garicae,* vol. 19, no. 1-2 (Budapest, 1973), pp. 115-150.
1763 ———· "A XIX. századvégi kárpátukrán agrárnépesség társadalmi szerke-
      zetének statisztikai ábrázolása." *Történelmi szemle,* vol. 4, no. 3 (Buda-
      pest, 1961), pp. 330-346.
1764 ———· "A Ruszinok (Kárpátukránok) és az 1865. évi képviselövá-
      lasztás." *Századok,* vol. 108, no. 4-5 (Budapest, 1974), pp. 1142-1175.
1765 ———· [Maier, M.]. "Stanovyshche trudiashchykh Zakarpattia v roky per-
      shoï svitovoï viiny." *Ukraïns'ko-uhors'ki istorychni zv'iazky.* Kiev:
      ANURSR, 1964, pp. 217-228.
1766 ——— [Maier, Mariia]. "Zakarpats'ki ukraïntsi na perelomi stolit'." *Zhov-
      ten' i ukraïns'ka kul'tura.* Prešov: KSUT, 1968, pp. 49-73.
1767 Mazurok, O. S. "Z istoriï kul'turnykh vzaiemyn Zakarpattia z inshymy
      ukraïns'kymy zemliamy ta Rosiieiu v druhii polovyni XIX—pochatku XX
      st." *Kul'tura i pobut naselennia ukraïns'kykh Karpat.* Edited by I. M.
      Hranchak et al. Uzhhorod: UDU, 1973, pp. 85-91.
1768 Mejgeš, Michail. "Pravoslavné hnutí v Podkarpatské Rusi." *Podkarpatská
      Rus.* Edited by J. Chmelař et al. Prague: Orbis, 1923, pp. 113-116.
1769 Mel'nikova, Irina N. "Iz istorii revoliutsionnogo dvizheniia na Zakarpat-
      skoi Ukraine v 1921-1924 gg." *Uchenye zapiski Instituta slavianovedeniia,*
      vol. 6 (Moscow, 1952), pp. 5-59.
1770 ———· "Kak byla vkliuchena Zakarpatskaia Ukraina v sostav Chekhoslo-
      vakii v 1919 g." *Uchenye zapiski Instituta slavianovedeniia,* vol. 3 (Mos-
      cow, 1951), pp. 104-135.
1771 ———· "Ustanovlenie diktatury cheshskoi imperialisticheskoi burzhuazii v
      Zakarpatskoi Ukraine v 1919-1920 gg." *Uchenye zapiski Instituta slavia-
      novedeniia,* vol. 4 (Moscow, 1951), pp. 84-114. Published in Czech transla-
      tion: *Sovetská věda: Historie,* vol. 3 (Prague, 1953), pp. 69-94.
1772 ———· "Zakarpatskaia Ukraina v revoliutsii 1848 goda." *Voprosy istorii,*
      vol. 4, no. 8 (Moscow, 1948), pp. 70-86. Revised version in *Uchenye zapiski
      Instituta slavianovedeniia,* vol. 1 (Moscow and Leningrad, 1949), pp.
      241-292. Reprinted in Prešov: KSUT, 1952. Translated into Slovak by V.
      Matula: "Zakarpatská Ukrajina v revolúcii r. 1848." *Historický sborník
      SAV,* vol. 10 (Bratislava, 1952), pp. 116-183.
1773 Mel'nyk, Vasyl'. *Istoriia Zakarpattia v usnykh narodnykh perekazakh ta
      istorychnykh pisniakh.* L'viv: Vyd. LU, 1970.
1774 Mészáros, Károly. *A magyarországi oroszok története.* Budapest, 1850.
1775 ———· *Ungvár története a legrégibb időktől máig.* Pest: Rath Mor, 1861.
1776 Mishchenko, Serhii O., et al. *Shliakhom do shchastia: narysy istoriï Zakar-
      pattia.* Uzhhorod: Karpaty, 1973.
1777 Miskolczy, Ágoston. "A mármarosi skizma-per 1913-1914-ben." *Magyar
      szemle,* vol. 2, no. 4 (Budapest, 1928), pp. 402-408; vol. 3, nos. 1, 2, 3, and

4 (1928), pp. 92-96, 186-192, 285-288, and 391-392; and vol. 4, nos. 1 and 3 (1928), 92-96 and 311-316.

1778 Mitrak, Aleksander. "Russkii narod." *Mîsiatsoslov na hod 1865 dlia russkykh uhorskiia krayn̂ŷ.* Uzhhorod, 1865, pp. 50-54.

1779 Mogilianskii, N. "Podkarpatskaia Rus' i natsional'nyi vopros." *Karpatskii sviet,* vol. 1, no. 6 (Uzhhorod, 1928), pp. 155-158.

1780 Mogil'nitskii, V. K. "Karpatorusskoe studenchestvo." *Karpatskii sviet,* vol. 1, nos. 4 and 5 (Uzhhorod, 1928), pp. 81-83 and 129-131.

1781 Molnar, Andreas. "Das Ergebnis der Volkszählung von 1930 in der Slowakei und in Karpathoruthenien." *Nation und Staat,* vol. 7, no. 7 (Vienna, 1934), pp. 429-441.

1782 Mol'nar Mykhailo. *Slovaky i ukraïntsi: prychynky do slovats'ko-ukraïns'kykh literaturnykh vzaiemyn.* Bratislava and Prešov: SAV and SPVVUL, 1965.

1783 ——— [Molnár, Michal]. "Štúrovci a Zakarpatská Ukrajina." *L'udovit Štúr: Život a dielo, 1815-1856.* Bratislava: SAV, 1956, pp. 489-494.

1784 ———· "Ukraïnistychni zatsikavlennia Zdeṇieka Neiedloho." *Duklia,* vol. 21, no. 5 (Prešov, 1973), pp. 60-68.

1785 "Monastyr' china sv. Vasiliia v M. Bereznom." *Mîsiatsoslov na 1891 hod.* Uzhhorod, 1890, pp. 105-112.

1786 Mondok, Ivan. "Shliakhy ches'koho imperiializmu na Zakarpats'kii U-kraïni." *Zakhidna Ukraïna,* no. 4-5 (Kiev, 1931), pp. 75-79.

1787 Moricz, Béla. *Kárpátalja hősei.* Budapest: Vitézi Rend Zrinyi csoportja, 1939.

1788 Mosca, Rodolfo. *La Ruthénia ciscarpatica della collonizazzione a l'autonomia.* Milan, 1929.

1789 Mousset, Jean. "Le problème juif en Russie subcarpathique," *Affaires étrangères,* vol. 8, no. 8 (Paris, 1938), pp. 501-572.

1790 ———· *Les villes de la Russie subcarpatique (1919-1938).* Travaux publiés par l'Institut d'études slaves, vol. 18. Paris: Librarie Droz, 1938.

1791 Mráz, Andrej. "Volanie Podkarpatskej Rusi." *Slovanské pohl'ady,* vol. 53, no. 10 (Turčiansky Sv. Martin, 1937), pp. 566-576. Reprinted in Mykhailo Mol'nar. *Slovaky i ukraïntsi.* Bratislava and Prešov: SAV and SPVVUL, 1965, pp. 365-377.

1792 Mulychak, Iurii, ed. *15 rokiv na sluzhbi narodu: zbirnyk statei ta fotodokumentiv z nahody 15-richchia diial'nosti KSUT.* Prešov: KSUT ta Osvitn'oho instytutu v Bratislavi, 1966. Collection of nine articles on the Prešov Region. Includes studies by I. Baitsura, V. Kapishovs'kyi, F. Kovach, and V. Liubymov.

1793 Mushynka, Mykola. *Sribna rosa: z repertuaru narodnoï spivachky Antsi Iabur iz Stashchyna.* Naukovo-populiarna biblioteka Tsk KSUT, no. 4. Prešov, 1970.

1794 Musil, Jaromír, ed. *Technická práce v zemi podkarpatoruské 1919-1933.* Uzhhorod: Odbor Spolku československých inženýrů, 1933. A collection of thirty-seven articles by Czech specialists who describe the advances made in communications, construction, agriculture, and use of natural resources. Includes contributions by F. Gabriel and J. Pešina.

1795 Mykytas', Vasyl' L. *Davnia literatura Zakarpattia: narysy literatury Zakarpattia doby feodalizmu.* L'viv:Vyd. LU, 1968.

1796 ———· *Haluzka mohutn'oho dereva: literaturnyi narys.* Uzhhorod: Karpaty, 1971.

1797 ———· *Literaturnyi rukh na Zakarpatti druhoï polovyny XIX st.* Uzhhorod: UDU, 1965.

1798 Myshanych, Oleksa. "Davni zv'iazky." *Duklia,* vol. 11, no. 1 (Prešov, 1963), pp. 78-82. On literary ties between Rusyns, Czechs, and Slovaks before the eighteenth century.

1799 ———· *Literatura Zakarpattia XVII-XVIII stolit'.* Kiev: 'Naukova dumka', 1964.

1800 ———· "Pysmenstvo rusynokh Zakarpatia na narodnei beshedy uzh od kontsa XIV stolityia." *Nova dumka,* vol. 3, no. 7 (Vukovar, 1974), pp. 105-115.

1800a ———· "Z lyteraturnoho zhyttia Zakarpattia XVII-XVIII stolit'." *Radians'ke literaturoznavstvo,* vol. 5, no. 6 (Kiev, 1961), pp. 63-72.

1801 ———· "Z ystoryi shkolskei prosvyty y drukovania knizhokh na Zakarpat'iu u XVII y XVIII stolityiu." *Nova dumka,* vol. 5, no. 11 (Vukovar, 1976), pp. 80-86.

1802 Myshuha, Luka. "Pidkarpats'ka Rus'." *Kaliendar' Ukraïns'koho narodnoho soiuza na 1922 r.* New York, 1921. pp. 108-114.

1803 ———· *Pidkarpats'ka Rus': suchasnyi stan.* Vienna, 1921.

1804 Mytsiuk, Oleksander. "Do tereziians'ko-rus'koho urbaru dlia kolyshn'oï Uhors'koï Rusy." *Podkarpatska Rus',* vol. 11, no. 1-10 (Uzhhorod, 1934), pp. 65-66.

1804a ———· "Madiaryzatsiia zakarpats'kykh ukraïntsiv za dualizmu." *S'ohochasne i mynule,* vol. 1, no. 1 (L'viv, 1939). pp. 16-23.

1805 ———· *Narysy z sotsiial'no-hospodarskoï istoriï, b. uhors'koï, nyni Pidkarpats'koï Rusy.* 2 vols. Uzhhorod-Prague, 1936-38.

1806 ——— [Mycjuk, Oleksander]. "Die Podkarpatská Rus im Mittelalter: die Grundzüge ihrer sozialökonomischen Entwicklung." *Prager Rundschau,* vol. 6, (Prague, 1936), pp. 345-354.

1807 ———· "Z emihratsiï uhro-rusyniv pered svitovoiu viinoiu." *Naukovyi zbirnyk TP,* vol. 13-14 (Uzhhorod, 1937-1938), pp. 21-32.

1808 Nagy, Vilmos. "Kárpátalja új fejlődés előtt." *Magyar szemle,* vol. 42, no. 5 (Budapest, 1942), pp. 250-253.

1809 Narizhnyi, Symon. *Ukraïns'ka emigratsiia: kul'turna pratsia ukraïns'koï emigratsiï mizh dvoma svitovymy viinamy.* Studiï Muzeiu vyzvol'noï borot'by Ukraïny, vol. 1. Prague, 1942.

1810 *Narodynyi katikhiz.* Izdanie OIAD, no. 19. Uzhhorod, 1926.

1811 *Narysy istoriï Zakarpats'koï oblasnoï partiinoï orhanizatsiï,* vol. 1: (*1918-1945rr.*). Uzhhorod: Vyd. Karpaty, 1968.

1812 *Nashi shkoly v pershom desiatilietiiu cheskoslovatskoi republiki 1918-1928.* Prague: Ministerstvo shkol'stva i narodnogo prosvieshcheniia, 1928.

1813 *Nashi zarubezhnye brat'ia v bor'bie za narodnost': Ugorshchina (Ugorskaia Rus').* Otechestvennaia biblioteka, no. 11. St. Petersburg: Izd. Vserossiiskago natsional'nago kluba, 1911.

1814 Nečas, Jaromír. *Uherská Rus a česká žurnalistika: neuzavírejte kruh našich nepřátel.* Uzhhorod, 1919.

1815 ———· *Východoevropská tragedie a Ukrajina.* Prague: Všesvit, 1919.

1816 Nedziel'skii, Evgenii [Nedzel's'kyi, Ievhenii]. "Dekil'ka zauvazhen' pro Zakarpattia." *Z ust narodu.* Prešov: Vyd. KSUT, 1955, pp. 3-43.

1817 ———· "Desiat' liet karpatorusskoi literatury." *Karpatorusskiia dostizheniia.* Edited by A. V. Popov. Mukachevo, 1930, pp. 117-121.

1818 ——— [Nedzelskij, E.]. "Desat' rokov podkarpatoruskej literatury." *Slovenské pohl'ady,* vol. 45 (Turčiansky Sv. Martin, 1929), pp. 503-506.

1819 ———· "Karpatoruská literatúra po prevrate." *Slovenské pohl'ady,* vol. 53, no. 10 (Turčiansky Sv. Martin, 1937), pp. 538-541.

1820 ———· "Literatura i izdatel'skaia dieiatel'nost' na Podkarpatskoi Rusi poslie perevorota." *Podkarpatskaia Rus' za gody 1919-1936.* Edited by E. Bachinskii. Uzhhorod: RNG, 1936, pp. 131-136.

1821 ——— [Nedzielskij, Jevgenij]. "Nová karpatoruská beletrie." *Podkarpatská Rus.* Edited by J. Zatloukal. Bratislava: KPPR, 1936, pp. 187-192.

1822 ———· *Ocherk karpatorusskoi literatury.* Uzhhorod: PNS, 1932. Chapters 1 and 2 reprinted in Latin script: *Kalendar' OS na hod 1938.* Perth Amboy, N.J., 1938, pp. 102-122.

1823 ———· "O karpatorusskoi poèzii." *Tsentral'naia Evropa,* vol. 1 (Prague, 1928).

1824 ———· "Sovremennaia karpatorusskaia literatura." *Tsentral'naia Evropa,* vol. 4, no. 4 (Prague, 1931), pp. 201-212.

1825 ——— [Nedzielskij, Evgenij]. "Spolek Alexandra V. Duchnoviče." *Podkarpatská Rus.* Edited by J. Zatloukal. Bratislava: KPPR, 1936, p. 298.

1826 ——— [Izoryn, A.]. "Suchasnî rus'kî khudozhnyky." *Zoria—Hajnal,* vol. 2, nos. 3-4 (Uzhhorod, 1942), pp. 390-395.

1827 ———· *Ugro-russkii teatr.* Uzhhorod, 1941.

1828 Nejedlý, Zdeněk [Needli, Z]. "Istoriia Zakarpatskoi Rusi do XIV stoletiia." *Izvestiia Akademii Nauk SSSR. Seriia istorii i filosofii,* vol. 2, no. 4 (Moscow, 1945), pp. 201-220.

1829 Nemec, František, and Vladimir Moudry. *The Soviet Seizure of Subcarpathian Ruthenia.* Toronto: Wm. B. Anderson, 1955.

1830 Netochaiev, Vasyl' I. "Kolonial'na polityka uhors'koho burzhuaznoho uriadu na Zakarpatti v kintsi XIX i na pochatku XX st." *Naukovi zapysky UDU,* vol. 36 (Uzhhorod, 1958), pp. 30-54.

1831 ———· "Zakarpattia naperedodni pershoï svitovoï viiny 1908-1914 rr." *Naukovi zapysky UDU,* vol. 29 (Uzhhorod, 1957), pp. 91-136.

1832 ———· "Zakarpattia v roky pershoï svitovoï imperialistychnoï viiny (1914-1917)." *Dopovidi ta povidomlennia.* Seriia istoryko-filolohichna, vol. 1. Uzhhorod: UDU, 1957, pp. 26-29.

1833 Netochaiev, Vasyl' I., and Lelekach, Mykhailo. "Vplyv Velykoï Zhovtnevoï sotsialistychnoï revoliutsiï na Zakarpattia i rozhortannia borot'by trudiashchych za vozz'iednannia z usim ukraïns'kym narodom v 1918-1919 rr." *Naukovi zapysky UDU,* vol. 30 (Uzhhorod, 1957), pp. 45-66.

1834 Netochaiev, Vasyl' I., and Lelekach, Mykhailo. "Z istoriï borot'by za vladu Rad i proty interventsiï SShA i Antanty na Zakarpatti v 1918-1919 rr."

Naukovi zapysky UDU, vol. 9 (Uzhhorod, 1954).

1835 "The New Republic of Rusinia, Mostly Made in America." *Literary Digest,*
      vol. 69, no. 13 (New York, 1921), pp. 41-43.

1836 *Nezhasnyi iunosti vohon'.* Uzhhorod: Karpaty, 1968.

1837 Niederle, Lubor. "Ještě k sporu o rusko-slovenskou hranicí v Uhrách."
      Slovánský přehled, vol. 6 (Prague, 1904), pp. 258-261.

1838 ———· "K sporu o rusko-slovenské rozhraní v Uhrách." *Slovanský při-*
      hled, vol. 5 (Prague, 1903), pp. 345-349.

1839 ———· "Nová data k východní slovenské hranici v Uhrách." *Národopisný*
      věstník českoslovanský, vol. 2 (Prague, 1907), pp. 1-3.

1840 ———· "Počátky Karpatské Rusi." *Národopisný věstník československý,*
      vol. 15, pt. 2 (Prague, 1922), pp. 22-31.

1841 ———· "Počátky slovanského osídlení na Podkarpatské Rusi." *Národo-*
      pisný věstník československý, vol. 24 (Prague, 1931), pp. 39-41.

1842 ———· "Uherští rusíni ve světle maďarské statistiky." *Slovanský přehled,*
      vol. 6 (Prague, 1904), pp. 460-462.

1842a Nikolaienko, Z. H. "Borot'ba navkolo movnykh pytan' na Zakarpatti v
      20—30-kh rokakh XX st." *Ukraïns'ka mova v shkoli,* vol. 9, no. 5 (Kiev,
      1959), pp. 25-29.

1843 Novotný, Emil. "Zánik Karpatskej Ukrajiny." *Slovenské vojsko,* vol. 1,
      nos. 6, 8, and 9 (Bratislava, 1940), pp. 68-88, 130-133, and 151-152.

1844 Nowak, Robert, *Der Künstliche Staat: Ostprobleme der Tschecho-Slowakei.*
      Oldenburg: G. Stalling, 1938.

1845 ———· "Von der Karpatenukraine zum Karpatenland." *Zeitschfrift für*
      Geopolitik, vol. 16, no. 5 (Heidelberg, Berlin and Magdeburg, 1939), pp.
      313-322.

1845a ———· "Die Zukunft der Karpatenukraine." *Zeitschrift für Geopolitik,*
      vol. 15, no. 11 (Heidelberg, Berlin and Magdeburg, 1938), pp. 889-899.

1846 Observator. "Shkil'nytstvo na Pidkarpats'kii Ukraïni." *Literaturno-*
      naukovyi vistnyk, vol. 79, no. 1 (L'viv, 1923), pp. 79-84.

1847 Ochevidets. *Ugorshchina (Ugorskaia Rus').* St. Petersburg, 1911.

1848 Ohonovs'kyi, Volodymyr. "Chyslo ukraïntsiv u mezhakh teperishn'oï
      Slovachchyny." *S'ohochasne i mynule,* vol. 1, no. 2 (L'viv, 1939), pp. 59-
      68.

1849 Onats'kyi, Ievhen. "Karpats'ka Ukraïna." *Kalendar' Vidrodzhennia na*
      1952 rik. Buenos Aires, 1951, pp. 33-73.

1850 "L'ordre nouveau en Subcarpathie." *Nouvelle revue de Hongrie,* vol. 61
      (Budapest, 1939), pp. 160-165.

1851 Orlai, Ivan. "Istoriia o Karpato-Rossakh, ili o pereselenii Rossian v Karpat-
      skiia gory i prikliucheniiakh s nimi sluchivshikhsia." *Sievernyi viestnik,*
      vol. 1, pts. 1 and 3 (St. Petersburg, 1804), pp. 158-172, 261-276, and 267-
      294. Reprinted in Ilarion S. Svientsitsskii, ed. *Materialy po istorii vozrozh-*
      deniia Karpatskoi Rusi, vol. 1 L'viv, 1905, pp. 56-83.

1852 Orshan-Tschemerynsky, Jaroslav. *Karpathen-Ukraine.* New York: Ukrai-
      nian Press Service, 1938.

      Ortoskop, *see* Tvorydlo, Mykhailo

1853 Ortutay, Tivadar, *Cseh világ a Kárpátokban.* Uzhhorod, 1941.

1854 Ostapchuk, Iatsko. "Uhors'ka Ukraïna, ïï stan i zavdannia ches'koï poli- tyky." *Kalendar Vperedu* (L'viv, 1920), pp. 120-123.
1855 Ostrovs'kyi, Hryhorii. *Obrazotvorche mystetstvo Zakarpattia*. Kiev: 'Mys- tetstvo', 1974.
1856 *Otzyvy po voprosu karpatorussko-slovatskikh otnoshenii*. Prešov: Fedor Roikovich, 1936.
1857 P. "Nash natsional'nyi muzei." *Podkarpatska Rus'*, vol. 5, nos. 4 and 5 (Uzhhorod, 1928), pp. 78-81 and 129-130.
1858 ———· "Pôdk. Rusynŷ na kul'turnôi mysiî u Rusynôv halytskykh pry kôntsy XVIII y pochatkom XIX st." *Podkarpatska Rus'*, vol. 4, nos. 9- 10 (Uzhhorod, 1927), pp. 205-211 and 228-231.
1859 Pachovs'kyi, Vasyl'. *Chto to Prosvîta?* Vŷd. TP, no. 1. Uzhhorod, 1920.
1860 ———· *Sribna zemlia: tysiacholittia Karpats'koï Ukraïny*. Vyd. Kooperatyvy 'Druzhyna', no. 6. L'viv, 1938. Second edition: New York: Howerla, 1959.
1861 *Istoriia Podkarpatskoî Rusy*. Vŷd. TP, no. 4-7. Uzhhorod, 1921. Revised edition: *Istoriia Zakarpattia*. Munich: Bdzhilka, 1946.
1862 Panas, E. O. *K voprosu o russkom natsional'nom imeni*. Uzhhorod, 1934.
1863 Panas, Ivan O. "Karpatorusskie otzvuki russkago pokhoda v Vengriiu 1849 goda." *Karpatorusskii sbornik*. Uzhhorod: PNS, 1930, pp. 209-229.
1864 Paneth, Philip. *Umbruch im Osten: ein Tatsachenbericht aus Karpatoruss- land*. Vienna: Renaissance Vlg, 1937.
1865 Panin, P. "Narodnye buditeli Zakarpatskoi Rusi posle 1848 g." *Svobodnoe slovo Karpatskoi Rusi*, vol. 11, no. 3-4 (Newark, N.J., 1969), pp. 2-5.
1866 Pan'kevych, Ivan. "Do ystoriî obsadzhenia epyskopstva mukachevskoho po smerty Povchiia r. 1832." *Podkarpatska Rus'*, vol. 6, no. 3 (Uzhhorod, 1929), pp. 62-64.
1867 ———· "Ivan Franko i Zakarpattia." *Literaturno-naukovyi vistnyk*, vol. 90, no. 7-8 (L'viv, 1926), pp. 292-294.
1868 ———· "Khto buv Ivan Berezhanyn—Mykhailo Luchkai chy Ivan Foga- rashii?," *Naukovŷi zbornyk TP*, vols. 7-8 (Uzhhorod, 1931), pp. 168-188.
1869 ———· "Kniaz' Fedor Koriiatovych v usnôi narodnôi tradytsiy." *Podkar- patska Rus'*, vol. 7, no. 3 (Uzhhorod, 1930), pp. 47-52.
1870 ——— [Paňkevič, I.]. "Jazyková otázka v Podkarpatské Rusi." *Podkar- patská Rus*. Edited by J. Chmelař et al. Prague: Orbis, 1923, pp. 130-150.
1871 ———· "Mykhayl Orosvehovskii chy Mykayl Feodul?" *Naukovŷi zbornyk TP*, vol 4 (Uzhhorod, 1925), pp. 5-16.
1872 ———· *Narys istoriî ukraïns'kykh zakarpats'kykh hovoriv: Fonetyka*. Acta Universitatis Carolinae—Philologica, vol. 1, Prague, 1958.
1873 ———· "Odpovîd' na anonymnu broshuru 'Grammatika Pan'kevicha, raz- bor eia'." *Podkarpatska Rus'*, vol. 7, nos. 7-8 and 9-10 (Uzhhorod, 1930), pp. 170-174 and 200-208.
1874 ———· [Paňkevič, Ivan]. "Prešovskí Ukrajinci a Ukrajina v minulosti." *Věčná družba*. Prague, 1955, pp. 237-250.
1875 ———· "Shcho chytaly dîty nashykh pradîdov v shkolakh v druhôi polo- vytsî XVIII stolîtia." *Podkarpatska Rus'*, vol. 2 (Uzhhorod, 1925), pp. 117-118.
1876 ———· "Slavenorus'ka hramatyka Arseniia Kotsaka druhoï polovynŷ XVIII

vîka." *Naukovŷi zbornyk TP,* vol. 5 (Uzhhorod, 1927), pp. 232-259.

1877 ——— [Paňkevič, Ivan]. "Spolek 'Prosvita' v Užhorodě," *Podkarpatská Rus.* Edited by J. Zatloukal. Bratislava: KPPR, 1936, pp. 299-300.

1878 ———· *Ukraïns'ki hovory Pidkarpats'koï Rusy i sumezhnykh oblastei.* KSVSPR, no. 9. Prague: Orbis, 1938.

1878a ———· "Zakarpats'kyi dialektnyi variant ukraïns'koï literaturnoï movy *XVII-XVIII* vv." *Slavia,* vol. 27, no. 2 (Prague, 1958), pp 171-181.

1879 Pantschenko-Jurewicz, W. von. "Die Karpathen-Ukraine." *Die Tat,* vol. 30, no. 10 (Jena, 1939), pp. 649-660.

1880 Papp, György. *Adalékok de Camillis József munkácsi püspök műkődéséhez.* Miskolc: Ludvig István könyvnyomdája, 1941.

1881 ———· *A munkácsi püspökség eredete.* Miskolc: A Szemisz tudományos és irodalmi osztálya, 1940.

1882 Paris, Frigyes. *Tájékoztató a ruthén actiónál való műkődésem felől.* Budapest, 1904.

1883 Pataky, Mária. "A magyar-ruszin kulturális együttműködés." *Láthatár,* vol. 7, no. 7 (Budapest, 1939), pp. 289-292.

1884 Patrus, Andrei. "Položenije Karpatskoj Rusi (pered razdilenijem)," *Kalendar' OS na hod 1939.* Perth Amboy, N.J., 1939, pp. 27-37.

1885 Pavlovich, Nikolai. *Russkaia kul'tura i Podkarpatskaia Rus'.* Izdanie OIAD, no. 23, Uzhhorod, 1926. Reprinted in Latin script: *Kalendar' OS na hod 1940.* Perth Amboy, N.J., pp. 86-97.

1886 Pazhur, Stepan [Pažur, Štefan]. "O vývoji národnostých pomerov na východnom Slovensku v jesenných mesiacoch roku 1938." *Nové obzory,* vol. 10 (Prešov, 1968), pp. 13-25.

1887 Pazhur, Stepan, and Horkovych, Vasyl'. "Do pytan' uchasti ukraïns'koho naselennia Skhidnoï Slovachchyny v natsional'no-vyzvol'nii borot'bi v 1939-1944 rokakh." *Naukovyi zbirnyk MUKS,* vol. 2 (Bratislava, Prešov, and Svidník, 1966), pp. 11-35.

1888 Pekar, Athanasius B. "Basilian Reform in Transcarpathia." *Analecta OSBM,* vol. 7 (Rome, 1971), pp. 143-226.

1889 ———· *De erectione canonica eparchiae Mukačoviensis (anno 1771).* Analecta OSBM, ser. 2, sect. 1, vol. 3. Rome 1956.

1890 ———· *Historic Background of the Eparchy of Prjashev.* Pittsburgh, Pa.: Byzantine Seminary Press, 1968.

1891 ———· *Narysy istoriï tserkvy Zakarpattia,* vol. 1. Analecta OSBM, ser. 2, sect. 1. Rome, 1967.

1892 ———· *Our Past and Present: Historical Outlines of the Byzantine Ruthenian Metropolitan Province.* Pittsburgh, Pa.: Byzantine Seminary Press, 1974.

1893 ———· "Restoration of the Greek Catholic Church in Czecholslovakia." *The Ukrainian Quarterly,* vol. 39, no. 3 (New York, 1973), pp. 282-296.

1894 Pelens'kyi, Ievhenii Iu. "Pys'menstvo." *Karpats'ka Ukraïna.* L'viv: UVI, 1939, pp. 108-121.

1895 ———· "Shkil'nytstvo i kul'turno-osvitnie zhyttia." *Karpats'ka Ukraïna.* L'viv: UVI, 1939, pp. 122-137.

1896 Peniak, S. I. "Do pytannia pro chas zaselennia skhidnymy slov'ianamy verkhn'oho Potyssia." *Velykyi Zhovten' i rozkvit vozz'iednanoho Zakar-pattia.* Uzhhorod: Karpaty, 1970, pp. 73-85.

1897 ———· "Vostochny slavianie u verkhnïm Potysiu u pershei polovky i ty-siachlityia n.e." *Nova dumka,* vol. 2, no. 4 (Vukovar, 1973), pp. 101-105.

1898 Perényi, József [Pereni, I]. *Iz istorii zakarpatskikh ukraintsev: 1849-1914.* Studia Historica Academiae Scientiarum Hungaricae, vol. 14. Budapest, 1957.

1899 ———· "A karpátalji ukránok egyházi uniójának kezdete a XVII. század közepén." *A magyar tudományos akademia, nyelv- és irodalomtudományi osztályának közleményei,* vol. 12, no. 1-4 (Budapest, 1958), pp. 179-198.

1900 Perfets'kyi, Evhenii [Perfeckij, Eugen]. "Boj za náboženskú a národnostnú samostatnost' cirkve v Podkarpatskej Rusi." *Prúdy,* vol. 8 (Bratislava, 1924), pp. 147-153.

1901 ———· [Perfeckij, E.]. "Brief Sketch of Russinian History." *Czechoslovak Review,* vol. 8, no. 5 (Chicago, 1924), pp. 129-131.

1902 ——— [Perfecký, Eugen]. "Hlavné vývojové stupne v cirkevných dejinách Podkarpatskej Rusi." *Prúdy,* vol. 8 (Bratislava, 1924), pp. 2-11.

1903 ——— [Perfeckij, Eugen]. "Podkarpatské a haličskoruské tradice o králi Matyášovi Corvinovi." *Sborník filosofické fakulty university Komen-ského,* vol. 4, no. 42 (Bratislava, 1926), pp. 219-278.

1904 ——— [Perfeckij, E.]. "Přehled dějin Podkarpatské Rusi." *Podkarpatská Rus.* Edited by J. Chmelař et al. Prague: Orbis, 1923, pp. 88-93.

1905 ——— [Perfetskii, E.]. "Religioznoe dvizhenie v XVI-om i nachale XVII-ogo vieka v Ugorskoi Rusi." *Izviestiia ORISIAN,* vol. 20, no. 1 (Petro-grad, 1915), pp. 24-77.

1906 ——— [Perfeckij, Eugen]. *Sociálně-hospodářské poměry Podkarpatské Rusi ve století XIII-XV.* Bratislava, 1924.

1907 ———· "Uhors'ka Rus'-Ukraïna v pershii polovyni XVII-ho viku." *U-kraïna,* vols. 3-4 (Kiev, 1917).

1908 ———· "Vasylii Tarasovych, epyskop Mukachevs'kyi: do istoriï pochatkiv tserkovnoï Uniï v Pidkarpattiu." *Naukovŷi zbornyk TP,* vol. 2 (Uzh-horod, 1923), pp. 84-92.

1909 ———· [Perfeckij, E.]. "Východní církev Podkarpatské Rusi v nejstarší době." *Podkarpatská Rus.* Edited by J. Chmelař et al. Prague: Orbis, 1923, pp. 94-98.

1910 Perfets'kyi, Evhenii [Perfeckij, E.], Matoušek, K., and Vergun, D. "Pod-karpatská Rus." *Masarykův slovník naučný,* vol. 5. Prague: Nakladem československého Kompasu, 1931, pp. 777-782.

1911 Pešek, Josef. *Kulturní poměry a osvětová práce v Podkarpatské Rusi.* Uzh-horod: Ždímal a Vetešník, 1921.

1912 ———· "Školstvi v Podkarpatské Rusi." *Podkarpatská Rus.* Edited by J. Chmelař et al. Prague: Orbis, 1923, pp. 161-170.

1913 Pešina, Josef. "Národní školství na Podkarpatské Rusi." *Podkarpatská Rus.* Edited by J. Zatloukal. Bratislava: KPPR, 1936, pp. 259-266.

1914 ——— [Peshina, Iosif]. "Shkol'noie dielo na P. Rusi v 1919-1929 godakh." *Karpatorusskiia dostizheniia.* Edited by A.V. Popov. Mukachevo, 1930, pp. 41-53.

1915 ———· "Školství národní a střední." *Technická práce v zemi podkarpatoruské 1919-1933.* Edited by J. Musil. Uzhhorod: Odbor Spolku československých inženýrů, 1933, pp. 259-267.

1916 Peška, Zdeněk. *Nové zřízení Podkarpatské Rusi.* Národnostní otázky, no. 13. Prague: Orbis, 1938.

1917 ———· "Podkarpatská Rus." *Slovník veřejného práva československého,* vol. 3 (Brno: Polygrafia, 1934), pp. 107-115.

1918 ———· "Le statut de la Russie subcarpathique." *Bulletin de droit tchécoslovaque,* vol. 3, no.1 (Prague, 1930-32), pp. 26-36.

1919 ———· "Ústava Podkarpatské Rusi: k desetiletí připojení Podkarpatské Rusi k Československé republice." *Učené Společnosti Šafaříkovy,* vol. 3, no. 2 (Bratislava, 1929), pp. 327-334.

1920 Petrigalla, Petr I. "Mukachevo v techenie 10 liet respubliki." *Karpatorusskiia dostizheniia.* Edited by A.V. Popov. Mukachevo, 1930, pp. 293-301.

1921 Petrov, Aleksei L. *Drevnieishiia gramoty po istorii karpato-russkoi tserkvi i ierarkhii, 1391-1498 g.* KSVSPR, no. 1. Prague: Orbis. 1930.

1922 ———· "K istorii 'russkikh intrig' v Ugrii v XVIII viekie." *Karpatorusskii sbornik.* Uzhhorod: PNS, 1930, pp. 123-136.

1923 ———· *K voprosu o slovensko-russkoi ètnograficheskoi granitsie.* Deshevaia biblioteka, no. 10. Uzhhorod, 1923. Published in Czech: "K otázce slovensko-ruské etnografické hranice." *Česká revue,* vol. 16 (Prague, 1923), pp. 115-119, 234-243.

1924 ———· "Kanonicheskaia vizitatsiia 1750-1767 gg. v varmediakh Zemplinskoi, Sharishskoi, Shpishskoi i Abauiskoi." *Naukovŷi zbornyk TP,* vol 3 (Uzhhorod, 1924), pp. 104-135.

1925 ———· "Kogda voznikli russkiia poseleniia na ugorskoi 'Dol'nei zemlie'?" *Izviestiia ORISIAN,* vol. 16, no. 1 (St. Petersburg, 1911), pp. 8-27. Revised and republished in his *Prediely ugrorusskoi riechi v 1773 g. po offitsial'nym dannym* (ref. 1929), pp. 150-181; and in Czech translation: "Kdy vznikly ruské osady na uherské Dolni zemi a vůbec za Karpaty?" *Český časopis historický,* vol. 29 (Prague, 1923), pp. 411-442.

1926 ———· *Mad'iarskaia gegemoniia v Ugrii (Vengrii) i Ugorskaia Rus'.* St. Petersburg, 1915.

1927 ———· "Národnostní hranice Slováků a Karpatorusů mezi sebou a s Mad'ary v XVIII st. podle současných archivních údajů." *Česká revue,* vol. 17 (Prague, 1924), pp. 82-89.

1928 ———· *Ob ètnograficheskoi granitsie russkago naroda v Austro-Ugrii: O somnitel'noi "Vengerskoi" natsii i o nedielimosti Ugrii.* St. Petersburg, 1915.

1929 ———· *Prediely ugrorusskoi riechi v 1773 g. po offitsial'nym dannym: izsliedovanie i karty. Materialy dlia istorii ugorskoi Rusi,* vol. 6, pt. 1. Zapiski IFFISPU, vol. 105. St. Petersburg, 1911.

1930 ———· "Staraia viera i uniia v XVII-XVIII vv." *Materialy dlia istorii ugorskoi Rusi,* vols. 1-2. In *Novyi sbornik statei po slavianoviedieniiu.* Edited by Vladimir I. Lamanskii. St. Petersburg, 1905, pp. 183-257; and *Sbornik statei posviashchennykh pochitateliami V. I. Lamanskomu,* pt. 2. St. Petersburg, 1908, pp. 941-1028.

1931 ——— · *Stat'i ob ugorskoi Rusi. Materialy dlia istorii Ugorskoi Rusi,* vol. 4. Zapiski IFFISPU, vol. 81. St. Petersburg, 1906.

1932 ——— · "Zamietki po Ugorskoi Rusi." *Zhurnal MNP,* vol. 279, no. 2 (St. Petersburg, 1892), pp. 439-458. Reprinted in his *Stat'i ob ugorskoi Rusi* (ref. 1931), pp. 1-18.

1933 Petruščak, Ivan. *Karpatští Ukrajinci a Slované.* London: Československý výbor pro slovanskou vzájemnost, 1944.

1934 Podešt, Jan. "Styky podkarpatorusko-rumunské." *Podkarpatská Rus.* Edited by J. Zatloukal. Bratislava: KPPR, 1936, pp. 99-102.

1935 *Podkarpatskaia Rus' protiv revizionizma.* Uzhhorod: Izd. redaktsii 'Russkoi zemli', 1933.

1936 "Podkarpatská Rus." *Slovanský přehled,* vols. 17-18, 22-31 (Prague, 1925-1939). A series of thirty articles and reports on the language question, religion, statistics, economic situation, and political developments by A. Hartl, A. Raušer, and V. Charvát.

1937 "Podkarpatští Rusini v Americe před válkou a za války." *Naše revoluce,* vol. 4 (Prague, 1926-1927), pp. 267-279.

1937a Pogorielov, Valerii A. *Karpatorusskie ètiudy.* Spisy Filozofickej fakulty Slovenskej univerzity, no. 29. Bratislava, 1939.

1938 ——— · *Mikhail Luchkai i ego 'Grammatica slavo-ruthena'.* Izdanie OIAD, no. 82. Uzhhorod, 1930. Reprinted in *Karpatskii sviet,* vol. 3, no. 5-6 (Uzhhorod, 1930), pp. 1022-1032. Published separately in Izdanie OIAD, no. 82. Uzhhorod, 1930.

1939 Polla, B. "Návrhy stanov slovensko-rusínskeho Tatrína a Matice slovanských národov v Uhorsku." *Historické štúdie,* vol. 6 (Bratislava, 1960), pp. 321-335.

1940 Ponomarev, V. P. *Avstro-Vengriia i eia slavianskie narody.* Baku, 1915.

1941 Pop, Ivan. "Zakarpats'ka Ukraïna v ievropeis'kii kryzi 1938-1939rr." *Duklia,* vol. 15, no. 1 (Prešov, 1967), pp. 62-66.

1942 Pop, Vasyl' S. "Obraz V.I. Lenina v tvorchosti pys'mennykiv Zakarpattia." *Kul'tura i pobut naselennia ukraïns'kykh Karpat.* Edited by I. M. Hranchak et al. Uzhhorod: UDU, 1973, pp. 10-18.

1943 ——— · "Podykh chasu: notatky pro doradians'kyi period tvorchosti Iu. Goidy." *Karpaty,* vol. 12 (Uzhhorod, 1958), pp. 144-151.

1944 ——— · "Rozvytok novely na Zakarpatti pislia Velykoï Vitchyznianoï viiny." *Duklia,* vol. 14, no. 6 (Prešov, 1966), pp. 49-55.

1945 Popov, Aleksander V., ed. *Karpatorusskiia dostizheniia.* Mukachevo, 1930. An anthology of thirty articles by Russophile authors who praise the achievements made in Subcarpathian Rus' during the first decade of Czechoslovak rule. Includes studies by N. Dragula, S. Fentsik, A. Gumetskii, K. Kokhannyi-Goral'chuk, E. Nedziel'skii, J. Pešina, A. Popov, and I. Shovt.

1946 ——— · "Kul'turnyia dostizheniia za 10 liet." *Karpatorusskiia dostizheniia.* Edited by A. V. Popov. Mukachevo, 1930, pp. 67-80.

1947 ——— · "Politicheskoe razvitie za 10 liet." *Karpatorusskiia dostizheniia.* Edited by A. V. Popov. Mukachevo, 1930, pp. 287-292.

1948 ——— · "Shkol'noe dielo na Podk. Rusi v 1919-1929 godakh." *Karpatorus-*

skiia dostizheniia. Edited by A. V. Popov. Mukachevo, 1930, pp. 41-53.

1949 Popov, Nil. "Izbienie russkikh v konstitutsionnoi Vengrii i postanovleniia mukachevskago s"iezda." *Viestnik Zapadnoi Rossii,* vol. 6 (Vilna, 1866), pp. 361-366.

1950 ———· "Russkii pisatel' v Vengrii, A. V. Dukhnovich." *Besiedy v Obshchestvie liubitelei rossiiskoi slovesnosti,* vol. 3 (Moscow, 1871), pp. 50-61.

1951 Popovych, A. V. "Rol' radians'koho kinomystetstva v politychnomu vykhovanni trudiashchykh Zakarpattia." *Velykyi Zhovten' i rozkvit vozz'-iednanoho Zakarpattia.* Uzhhorod: Karpaty, 1970, pp. 490-494.

1952 Popradov, P. "Podkarpatoruské pravoslaví." *Podkarpatská Rus.* Edited by J. Zatloukal. Bratislava: KPPR, 1936, pp. 280-283.

1953 Potemra, Ladislav A. "Ruthenians in Slovakia and the Greek Catholic Diocese of Prešov." *Slovak Studies,* vol. 1: *Historica,* no. 1. Rome, 1961, pp. 199-220.

1953a Potushniak, Fedir M. *Arkheolohichni znakhidky bronzovoho ta zaliznoho viku na Zakarpatti.* Uzhhorod: UDU, 1958.

1954 ———· "Korotkŷi narys fylozofiî Podkarpatia." *Lyteraturna nedîlia,* vol. 3 (Uzhhorod, 1943), pp. 17-20, 32-34, 43-47, 54-56, and 68-70.

1955 *Poznai sebia: besieda o nashem iazykie.* Narodnaia biblioteka, no. 5. Izdanie OIAD, no. 9. Uzhhorod, 1925.

1956 Pritsak, Omeljan. "Khto taki avtokhtony Karpats'koï Ukraïny." *Nova zoria,* no. 1 (L'viv, 1939), pp. 15-16.

1957 ———· "Khust." *Nova zoria,* no. 15 (L'viv, 1939), pp. 6-7.

1958 ———· "Mukachevo." *Nova zoria,* no. 23 (L'viv, 1939), pp. 6-7.

1959 Prochazka, Theodore. "Some Aspects of Carpatho-Ukrainian History in Post-Munich Czechoslovakia." *Czechoslovakia Past and Present.* The Hague: Mouton, 1968, pp. 107-114.

1960 Punyko, Alexander. *Bishop Theodore G. Romzha and the Soviet Occupation 1944-1947.* New York: Basilian Fathers Publication, 1967.

Putnik, *see* Frantsev, Vladimir

1961 Pysh, Simeon. *A Short History of Carpatho-Russia* [1938]. Translated by Andrew J. Yurkovsky. N. p., 1973.

1962 *Pytannia rozvytku narodnoho hospodarstva radians'koho Zakarpattia. Naukovi zapysky UDU,* vol. 44 (Uzhhorod, 1961).

1963 R. N. "Holhota Uniï v Karpats'kii Ukraïny: trylitnia diial'nist' ostann'oho iepyskopa dr. Teodora Romzhi." *Zhyttia i slovo,* no. 3-4 (Waterford, Ontario, 1948-1949), pp. 327-348.

1964 Rácz, József. "Kelet és nyugat a ruszin egyházi müvészetben." *Zoria— Hajnal,* vol. 2, nos. 1-2 (Uzhhorod, 1942), pp. 43-57.

1965 ———· "A legújabb ruszin irodalom." *Kisebbségi körlevél,* vol. 7, no. 4 (Pécs, 1934), pp. 219-234. Revised version published separately: Kecskemét: A szerző kiadása, 1943.

1966 ———· "A ruszin festőmüvészet." *Láthatár,* vol. 10 (Budapest, 1942), pp. 61-62.

1967 ———· "A ruszin kulturválság." *Láthatár,* vol. 9 (Budapest, 1941), pp. 306-310.

1968 ———· "A ruszin nemzeti színház fejlődése." *Láthatár,* vol. 10 (Budapest, 1942), pp. 17-19.

1969 Radost, St. "Ruś Podkarpacka." *Nasza przyszłośč* (Warsaw, 1932), pp. 14-23.

1970 Rath, Ignác, "Náboženské dějiny Podkarpatské Rusi do r. 1498." *Sborník historického kroužku,* vol. 34, no. 1 (Prague, 1933). pp. 1-10. Also separately: Prague, 1933.

1971 Raušer, Alois. "President dr. Eduard Beneš a Podkarpatská Rus." *Podkarpatoruská revue,* vol. 1, no. 1 (Bratislava, 1936), pp. 6-8.

1972 ———· "Připojení Podkarpatské Rusi k Československé republice." *Podkarpatská Rus.* Edited by J. Zatloukal. Bratislava: KPPR, 1936, pp. 60-72.

1973 Rédei, József. "A rutének vallásos tömegmozgalmi." *Huszadik század,* vol. 30 (Budapest, 1914), pp. 470-473.

1974 Reikhert, L. *Khto toto iedynstvo pôdkarpats'kykh bratôv i shcho khoche.* Uzhhorod, 1936.

1975 Reshetar, John. "Carpatho-Ruthenia" and "Carpatho-Ukraine." *Slavonic Encyclopedia.* Edited by Joseph S. Rouček. New York: Philosophical Library, 1949, pp. 132-136.

1976 "Le retour de la Subkarpathie." *Journal de la Société hongroise de statistique,* vol. 4 (Budapest, 1939), pp. 101-103.

1977 Revay, Julian. "The March to Liberation of Carpatho-Ukraine," *The Ukrainian Quarterly,* vol. 10, no. 3 (New York, 1954), pp. 227-234.

1978 Reychman, Jan. "Granica etnograficzna słowacko-ruska." *Sprawy narodowościowe,* vol. 13 (Warsaw, 1939).

1979 Richard, D. *Podkarpatská Rus jindy a nyní: politické a narodohospodářské náčrtky.* Mukachevo: Karpatia, 1927.

1980 Roikovich, F. "Gr. kaf. Alumnei, Obshchestva sv. Ioanna Krestitelia v Preshovie." *VIII. godovoi otchet Gr.-kat russkoi gimnazii v Preshovie za uchebnyi god 1943-1944.* Prešov, 1944, pp. 33-47.

1981 Románecz, Aladár. *A ruthén kérdés megoldása.* Bereg and Ilosva, 1914.

1982 ———· *A Ruténekről.* Budapest, 1901.

1983 ———· *Tizenöt év a munkácsi egyházmegye történetéböl.* Sighet, 1905.

1984 Rosokha, Stepan. "The First Diet of Carpatho-Ukraine." *The Trident,* vol. 3, no. 9-10 (New York, 1939), pp. 21-32.

1985 ———· "Karpats'ka Sich." *Istoriia ukraïns'koho viis'ka.* Second edition: Winnipeg: Kliub priateliv ukraïns'koï knyzhky, 1953, pp. 593-603.

1986 ———· "OUN v rozbudovi Karpats'koï Ukraïny." *Za samostiinist',* vol. 3, nos. 3-4 (Munich, 1948), pp. 1-7.

1987 ———· *Soim Karpats'koï Ukraïny.* Winnipeg: Kul'tura i osvita, 1949.

1988 Rostots'kyi, Osyp. "Zakarpattia." *Rozbudova natsiï,* vol. 4, nos. 3-4 and 5-6 (Prague, 1931), pp. 79-84 and 137-141.

1988a Rot, Aleksander. "Iosif Dobrovskii o iazyke zakarpatskikh ukraintsev." *Naukovi zapysky UDU,* vol. 9 (Uzhhorod, 1954), pp. 254-260.

1989 ———· "Pro kul'turni zv'iazky chekhiv i slovakiv iz zakarpats'kymy ukraintsiamy." *Z istoriï chekhoslovats'ko-ukraïns'kykh zv'iazkiv.* Bratislava: SVKL, 1959, pp. 307-342.

1990 Rotman, Mykola. *Fáklyavivők: a Munkás újság rövid története.* Uzhhorod:

Kárpáti könyvkiadó, 1972.

1991   ———· *Naperedodni Druhoï Svitovoï: z istoriï zakarpats'koï komunistych-noï orhanizatsiï 1933-1938 rokiv*. Uzhhorod: Karpaty, 1964.

1992   ———· "Z istoriï komunistychnoho pidpillia na Zakarpatti v 1938-1940rr." *Naukovi zapysky UDU*, vol. 50 (Uzhhorod, 1962), pp. 61-67.

1993   Rozsypal, Antonín. "Budoucnost Podkarpatské Rusi a jejich národů." *Podkarpatská Rus*. Edited by J. Zatloukal. Bratislava: KPPR, 1936, pp. 29-32.

1994   Rudlovchak, Olena. "Do pytan' istoriï zv'iazkiv ukraïntsiv Skhidnoï Slovachchyny z Rosiieiu u XIX stolitti." *Duklia*, vol. 21, no. 6 (Prešov, 1973), pp. 66-72. On the relations of Prešov Region national leader, Iosyf Rubii (1838-1919), with Russia.

1995   ——— [Rudlovčáková, Helena]. "K otázkam vzájomných kultúrnych stykov Slovákov a zakarpatských Ukrajincov v polovici minulého storočia." *Sbornik Ševčenkovský FFUPJŠ*, vol. 5 (Bratislava, 1965), pp. 149-165.

1996   ——— [Rudlovčáková, Helena]. "Na podorozhakh z Ia. Holovats'kym." *Duklia*, vol. 12, no. 4 (Prešov, 1964), pp. 79-83.

1997   ———· "Literaturni stremlinnia ukraïntsiv Skhidnoi Slovachchyny u 20-30-kh rokakh nashoho stolittia." *Zhovten' i ukraïns'ka kul'tura*. Prešov: KSUT, 1968, pp. 145-172.

1998   ———· "Priashivs'ka literaturna spilka Dukhnovycha i literaturni problemy." *Duklia*, vol. 13, nos. 1, 2, 3, and 4 (Prešov, 1965), pp. 88-93, 56-66, 79-88, and 76-87.

1999   ———· "Tvorchyi shliakh Dukhnovycha." *Oleksandr Dukhnovych: zbirnyk materialiv*. Edited by M. Rychalka. Prešov: KSUT, 1965, pp. 115-150.

2000   ———· "Za zavisoiu mynuloho: materialy do vzaiemyn Zakarpattia z Rosiieiu." *Duklia*, vol. 18, nos. 3 and 4 (Prešov, 1970), pp. 60-67 and 59-68.

2001   Rudlovchak, Olena, and Hyriak, Mykhailo, eds. *Z mynuloho i suchasnoho ukraïntsiv Chekhoslovachchyny*. Pedahohichnyi zbirnyk, no. 3. Bratislava: SPV, 1973. A collection of fifteen articles from several disciplines, including studies by I. Baitsura, A. Kovach, and I. Vanat.

2002   Rudlovchak, Olena, and Shtets', Mykola. "Surmach vidrodzhennia: do 180-richchia z dnia narodzhennia Mykhaila Luchkaia." *Duklia*, vol. 17, no. 6 (Prešov, 1969), pp. 63-66.

2003   Rudnytsky, Ivan L. [Lysiak-Rudnyts'kyi, I.]. "Zakarpattia." *Entsyklopediia ukraïnoznavstva: slovnykova chastyna*, vol. 2. (Paris and New York: Molode zhyttia for NTSh, 1955-1957), pp. 716-720. Shorter version: "Transcarpathia (Carpatho-Ukraine)." *Ukraine: A Concise Encyclopaedia*, vol. 1. Toronto: University of Toronto Press for Ukrainian National Association, 1963, pp. 710-714.

2004   Ruman, Ján. *Otázka slovensko-rusínskeho pomeru na východnom Slovensku*. Košice: Slovenská liga, 1935.

Rusak, Iulii, *see* Gadzhega, Iulii

Rusinsky, Beloň, *see* Stryps'kyi, Hiiador

2005   "Die Russen (Karpathorussland)." *Die Nationalitäten in den Staaten Europas*. Edited by Ewald Ammende. Vienna and Leipzig: Wilhelm Braumüller, 1931, p. 282-295.

2006   Russkij. " 'Rusin' (Ruthenian)," *Kalendar' GKS na hod 1943*. Homestead,

Pa., 1943, pp. 81-84.

2007 "Ruszin-orosz-ukrán kérdés." *Magyar kisebbség,* vol. 20 (Lugos, Rumania, 1941), pp. 3-4, 66-67.

2008 *Ruszka-Krajna politikai jelentösége.* Az Orsz. Néptanulmányi Egyesület kiadványai, no. 2. Budapest, 1919.

2009 Ruttkay, László. "Az ukrán mozgalom és a Ruténföld." *Magyar szemle,* vol. 11, no. 4 (Budapest, 1931), pp. 366-376.

2010 Rychalka, Mykhailo, ed. *Oleksandr Dukhnovych: zbirnyk materialiv naukovoï konferentsiï, prysviachenoï 100-richchiu z dnia smerti (1865-1965).* Prešov: KSUT, 1965. Collection of twenty papers, nine commentaries, and other documentary material. Includes contributions by A. D. Bondar, P. P. Bunhanych, L. Haraksim, V. Hostička, M. F. Koval', Ie. P. Kyryliuk, V. L. Mykytas', O. M. Rudlovchak, A. S. Shlepets'kyi, and M. M. Shtets'.

2011 Sabol, Sevastiian [Borzhava, Iurii]. *Vid Uhors'koï Rusy do Karpats'koï Ukraïny.* Philadelphia, Pa.: Vyd. 'Karpats'kyi holos', 1956.

2012 Sabov, Evgenii. "Literární jazyk Podkarpatské Rusi." *Podkarpatská Rus.* Edited by J. Chmelař et al. Prague: Orbis, 1923, pp. 125-129.

2013 ———· *Russkii literaturnyi iazyk Podkarpatskoi Rusi i novaia grammatika russkago iazyka.* Izdanie OIAD, no. 7. Uzhhorod, 1925. Reprinted in *Kalendar Sojedinenija na hod 1936.* Homestead, Pa., 1936, pp. 48-54.

2014 ——— [Szabó, Eugen]. "Rután intelligencia." *Magyar kultúra,* vol. 3, no. 8 (Budapest, 1915), pp. 356-361.

2015 Sabov, Georgij. "Karpatorusskij Sojuz v Ameriki." *Kalendar' OS na hod 1936* (Perth Amboy, N.J., 1935), pp. 62-64.

2016 Salisnjak, Nikolay. "The Problem of Carpathian Ukraine." *Contemporary Russia,* vol. 2, no. 3 (London, 1938), pp. 317-330.

Sas, Andor, *see* Shash, Andrei

2017 Sasinek, V. "Uhorskí rusi." *Slovenské pohl'ady,* vol. 26, no. 11 (Turčiansky Sv. Martin, 1906), pp. 636-646.

2018 *Sbornik statei posviashchennykh pamiati A.I. Dobrianskago po povodu otkrytiia ego pamiatnika v Uzhgorodie, 17.XI.1929.* Izdanie OIAD, no. 70. Uzhhorod, 1929.

2019 Scrimali, Antonio. *La regione autonoma della Rutenia dopo il trattato di San Germano.* Palermo, 1938.

2020 ———· *La Ruthénie subcarpathique et l'État tchécoslovaque.* Paris: La technique du livre, 1938.

2021 Seheda, T. S. "Spilka molodi Zakarpats'koï Ukraïny v borot'bi za vozziednannia Zakarpattia z Radians'koho Ukraïnoiu (lystopad 1944—cherven' 1945 rr.)," *Velykyi Zhovten' i rozkvit vozz'iednanoho Zakarpattia.* Uzhhorod: Karpaty, 1970, pp. 270-282.

2022 Semerad, Jan. "Natsional'nye i iazykovye spory v Podkarpatskoi Rusi." *Vosem' lektsii o Podkarpatskoi Rusi.* Edited by D. Vergun. Prague, 1925, pp. 33-47.

2023 Shandor, Vincent. "Annexation of Carpatho-Ukraine to the Ukrainian SSR." *The Ukrainian Quarterly,* vol. 13, no. 3 (New York, 1957), pp. 243-254.

2023a ———· "Carpatho-Ukraine: Important Part of the Ukrainian State." *The*

Ukrainian Quarterly, vol. 25, no. 4 (New York, 1969), pp. 337-349.

2024 ———· "Carpatho-Ukraine in the International Bargaining of 1918-1939." *The Ukrainian Quarterly,* vol. 10, no. 3 (New York, 1954), pp. 235-246.

2025 ———· "Karpats'ka Ukraïna—zfederovana derzhava." *Zapysky NTSh,* vol. 177 (New York, 1968), pp. 319-339.

2025a ———· "U trydtsiatylittia Karpats'koï Ukraïny." *Suchasnist',* vol. 9, no. 4 (Munich, 1969), pp. 98-105.

2026 Sharanevich, Isidor. "Starinnyi puti rusko-ugorskii cherez Karpaty i rusko-pol'skii cherez Sian i Vislu." *Literaturnyi sbornik GRM,* vol. 1, nos. 1-4 (L'viv, 1869), pp. 46-139.

2027 Shash, Andrii. "Deshcho yz torhovel'no-hospodarskoî ystoriî panstva Mukachevsko-Chynadîievskoho u XVIII st." *Podkarpatska Rus',* vol. 9, no. 9-10 (Uzhhorod, 1932), pp. 145-150; and vol. 10, no. 1-10 (1933), pp. 28-34.

2028 ———· *Iz proshlago goroda Mukacheva.* Mukachevo, 1928. Texts also in Czech and Hungarian.

2029 ——— [Sas, Andor]. *Egy kárpáti latifundium a hűbéri világ alkonyán.* Bratislava: Csehszlovákiai magyar könyvkiadó, 1955.

2030 Shelepets', Iosyf. "Problemy i zavdannia doslidzhennia starykh pysemnykh pam'iatok ukraïns'kykh hovirok Skhidnoï Slovachchyny i Zakarpattia." *Naukovyi zbirnyk MUKS,* vol. 1 (Bratislava, Prešov, and Svidník, 1965), pp. 251-258.

2031 ———· "Sens istoriï kul'tury pivdennokarpats'kykh ukraintsiv." *Zhovten' i ukrains'ka kul'tura.* Prešov: KSUT, 1968, pp. 84-85.

2032 Shelukhyn, S. "Nazva Pidkarpattia Ukraïnoiu." *Al'manakh Soiuzu pidkarpats'kykh rus'kykh studentiv u Prazi 1920-21—1930-31.* Prague, 1931, pp. 40-52.

2033 Sherehii, Iurii. "P'iatdesiatyrichchia ukraïns'koho teatru na Zakarpatti." *Nove zhyttia,* nos. 3, 4, 5, 6, 7, 8 (Prešov, 1971).

2034 Shereghy, Vasil. "Istorija Mukačevskej Eparchii." *The Queen of Heaven,* vol. 24 (Uniontown, Pa., 1950), pp. 5-11.

2035 ———· "Odyn rok uspishnoi pratsi Podkarpats'koho Obshchestva Nauk," *Lyteraturna nedîlia,* vol. 3 (Uzhhorod, 1943), pp. 142-144.

2036 Shereghy, Vasilij, and Pekar, Vasilij. *Vospitanije Podkarpato-ruskoho svjaščenstva—The Training of Carpatho-Ruthenian Clergy.* Pittsburgh, 1951.

2037 Shevchenko, F. P. "Mistse Zakarpattia v zahal'noukraïns'komu istorychnomu protsesi." *Velykyi Zhovten' i rozkvit vozz'iednanoho Zakarpattia.* Uzhhorod: Karpaty, 1970, pp. 43-54.

2038 Shkirpan, Natal'ia R. "Dukhnovich i natsional'noe vozrozhdenie v Podkarpatskoi Rusi." *Karpatskii sviet,* vol. 1, no. 6 (Uzhhorod, 1928), pp. 159-164.

2039 ———· *Rukopis': zapiski po istorii Podkarpatskoi Rusi.* Mukachevo, 192?

2040 Shlepetskii, Andrei. "Istoricheskoe proshloe Makovitsy i A. I. Pavlovich." *Naukovyi zbirnyk MUKS,* vol. 1 (Bratislava, Prešov, and Svidník, 1965), pp. 77-95.

2041 ———· "O. V. Dukhnovych to ioho suchasnyky." *Oleksandr Dukhnovych: zbirnyk materialiv.* Edited by M. Rychalka. Prešov: KSUT, 1965, pp. 192-205.

2042 ———· "Tvorcheskoe nasledie Aleksandra Pavlovicha." *Sborník pedago-gickej fakúlty university P. J. Šafárika v Prešove,* vol. 4, no. 2 (Bratislava, 1965), pp. 41-93.

2043 ———· *Zakarpats'ki budyteli ta nasha suchasnist'.* Prešov: KSUT, 1957.

2044 Shlepetskii, Ivan. "Karpatoross, karpatorusskii." *Svobodnoe slovo Karpat-skoi Rusi,* vol. 9, no. 3-4 (Newark, N.J., 1967), pp. 19-20.

2045 ———· "Studenchestvo i Karpatskaia Rus'." *Kalendar' OS na hod 1936.* Perth Amboy, N.J., 1936, pp. 146-147.

2046 ———· "Vozrozhdenie karpatorusskago studenchestva." *Al'manakh Voz-rozhdentsev* (Prague, 1936), pp. 71-75.

2047 ———, ed. *Priashevshchina: istoriko-literaturnyi sbornik.* Prague: Khutor, 1948. A collection of thirty articles expressing the Russophile viewpoint including items by G. Gerovskii, V. Kapishovskii, and E. Nedzel'skii.

2048 Shman'ko, Heorhii I. *Mitsna iak krytsia.* Uzhhorod: Karpaty, 1975.

Shtefan, Auhustyn, *see* Stefan, Augustin

2049 Shtets', Mykola. "Borot'ba za literaturnu movu ukraïnts'iv Skhidnoï Slo-vachchyny v 1919-1945 rr." *Zhovten' i ukraïns'ka kul'tura.* Prešov, KSUT, 1968, pp. 284-292.

2050 ———· *Literaturna mova ukraïntsiv Zakarpattia i Skhidnoï Slovachchyny pislia 1918.* Pedahohichnyi zbirnyk, no. 1. Bratislava: SPV, 1969.

2051 ———· "Mova 'Bukvaria' ta inshykh posibnykiv O. V. Dukhnovycha." *Oleksandr Dukhnovych: zbirnyk materialiv.* Edited by M. Rychalka. Prešov: KSUT, 1965, pp. 184-191.

2052 ———· "Rozvytok ukraïns'koho pravopysu na Zakarpatti i v Skhidnii Slo-vachchyni." *Naukovyi zbirnyk MUKS,* vol. 4, pt. 1 (Prešov, 1969), pp. 279-292.

2053 ———· "Z istoriï borot'by za literaturnu movu v Skhidnii Slovachchyni." *Naukovyi zbirnyk MUKS,* vol. 1 (Bratislava, Prešov, and Svidník, 1965), pp. 259-278.

2054 Shul'ha, Illia H. "Rozvytok kul'tury radians'koho Zakarpattia." *Velykyi Zhovten' i rozkvit vozz'iednanoho Zakarpattia.* Uzhhorod: Vyd. Karpaty, 1970, pp. 463-477.

2055 ———· *Sotsial'no-ekonomichne stanovyshche Zakarpattia v druhii polovyni XVIII st.* Uzhhorod: UDU, 1962.

2056 ———· *Sotsial'no-ekonomichni vidnosyny i klasova borot'ba na Zakarpatti v kintsi XVIII-pershii polovyni XIX st.* L'viv: Vyd. LU, 1965.

2057 Sil'vai, Ivan [N.N.]. "Slovaki i russkie v statistikie Vengrii." *Slavianskii sbornik,* vol. 1 (St. Petersburg, 1875), pp. 621-623.

2058 Simpson, G.W. "The Fate of Carpatho-Ukraine." *The Trident,* vol. 3, no. 6 (New York, 1939), pp. 21-25.

2059 Simonffy, Aladar. *Zweienhalb Jahre Karpathenland: Ungarns Aufbauwerk im Karpathenlande.* Budapest, 1941.

2060 Simovych, Vasyl'. "Grammatica Slavo-Ruthena M. Luchkaia." *Naukovŷi zbornyk TP,* vol. 7-8 (Uzhhorod, 1930-31), pp. 217-306.

2061 ———· "Mova." *Karpats'ka Ukraïna.* L'viv: UVI, 1939, pp. 102-107.

2062 Šip, František, "Naše finanční pomoc při vzniku karpatoruských vojsk na Sibiři," *Naše revoluce,* vol. 3 (Prague, 1925-1926), pp. 388-391.

2063 Sirko, P. S. "Zakarpattsi v Chekhoslovats'kii viis'kovii chastyni v SRSR u period Velykoï vitchyznianoï viiny." *Velykyi Zhovten' i rozkvit vozz'ied-nanoho Zakarpattia.* Uzhhorod: Karpaty, 1970, pp. 236-244.

2064 Skácelik, F. "Memento z Podkarpatské Rusi." *Lumír,* vol. 50 (Prague, 1923), pp. 366-372.

2065 ———· "Podkarpatská Rus nedávno a dnes." *Lumír,* vol. 52 (Prague, 1925), pp. 527-530.

2066 Škultéty, Jozéf. "O hraníci medzi rusmi a slovákmi v Uhorsku." *Slovenské pohl'ady,* vol. 16, no. 2 (Turčiansky Sv. Martin, 1896), pp. 125-126.

2067 Skrypnyk, Mykola. "Natsional'ne vidrodzhennia v suchasnykh kapitalis-tychnykh derzhavakh na prykladi Zakarpats'koï Ukraïny." *Prapor mark-syzmu,* vol. 2, no. 1 (Kharkiv, 1928), pp. 208-231.

2068 Skýpala, Otakar. *Dnešní Podkarpatská Rus.* Prague: Cesta, 1937.

2069 Slánský, Rudolf. "O novou československou politiku na Karpatské Ukra-jině." *Za nové Československo: sborník článků projevů a dokumentů.* Knižnice 'Československých listů', no. 11. Moscow, 1944, pp. 77-83.

2070 Slivka, John. *Correct Nomenclature: Greek Rite or Byzantine Rite, Rusin or Ruthenian, Rusin or Slovak.* Brooklyn, N.Y., 1973.

2071 ———· *The History of the Greek Rite Catholics in Pannonia, Hungary, Czechoslovakia and Podkarpatska Rus' 1863-1949.* N.p., 1974.

2072 *Slovensko-ukrajinské literárne vzt'ahy.* Bratislava: SPN, 1975.

2073 Slyvka, Iurii. *Pidstupy mizhnarodnoï reaktsiï na Zakarpatti v 1938-1939rr.* L'viv: Vyd. LU, 1966.

2074 ———· *Revoliutsiino-vyzvol'na borot'ba na Zakarpatti v 1929-1937 rr.* Kiev: ANURSR, 1960.

2075 Smiian, Petro K. "Poshyrennia lenins'kykh idei na Zakarpatti." *Zhovten',* vol. 30, no. 8 (L'viv, 1970), pp. 110-114.

2076 ———· *Revoliutsiinyi ta natsional'no-vyzvol'nyi rukh na Zakarpatti kin-tsia XIX—pochatku XX st.* L'viv: Vyd. LU, 1968.

2077 ———· *Zhovtneva revoliutsiia i Zakarpattia: 1917-1919 rr.* L'viv: Vyd. LU, 1972.

2077a Smishko, Markian Iu. *Karpats'ki kurhany pershoï polovyny pershoho tysiacholittia nashoï ery.* Kiev: ANURSR, 1960.

2078 Sobolevskii, A. "Kak davno Russkie zhivut v Karpatakh i za Karpatami." *Zhivaia starina,* vol. 4, no. 3-4 (Petrograd, 1894), pp. 524-526.

2079 *Socialistickou cestou k národnostnej rovnoprávnosti: zborník štúdií o roz-voji ukrajinskej národnosti v ČSSR.* Bratislava: Pravda, 1975.

2080 Sokolovych, Iurko. "Narodnŷi Dôm-kul'turna palata Rusynôv." *Kalendar 'Prosvîty' 1929.* Uzhhorod, 1928, pp. 66-69.

2081 Sole, Aryeh. "Modern Hebrew Education in Subcarpathian Ruthenia." *The Jews of Czechoslovakia,* vol. 2. Philadelphia and New York: Jewish Pub-lication Society and Society for the History of Czechoslovak Jews, 1971, pp. 401-439.

2082 ———· "The Jews of Subcarpathian Ruthenia: 1918-1938." *The Jews of Czechoslovakia,* vol. 1. Philadelphia and New York: Jewish Publication Society of America, 1968, pp. 125-154.

2083 Sova, Petr P. "Podkarpatskaia Rus' i russkii iazyk." *Russkii narodnyi kalendar' na god 1937.* Izd. OIAD, vol. 115. Uzhhorod, 1936, pp. 68-83.

2084 ———· *Proshloe Uzhgoroda.* Uzhhorod, 1937.

2085 ———· "Razvitie podkarpatorusskago obshchinnago i oblastnago samou-pravleniia." *Podkarpatskaia Rus' za gody 1919-1936.* Edited by E. Bachinskii. Uzhhorod: RNG, 1936, pp. 68-70.

2086 ———· "Spolek 'Školnaja pomošč' v Uzhorodě." *Podkarpatská Rus.* Edited by J. Zatloukal. Bratislava: KPPR, 1936, p. 300.

2087 ———· [Szova-Gmitrov, Peter]. "Ungvár multja." *Zoria—Hajnal,* vol. 3, no. 1-4 (Uzhhorod, 1943), pp. 51-118.

2088 ———· "Uzhgorod—gorod budushchago." *Podkarpatskaia Rus' za gody 1919-1936.* Edited by E. Bachinskii. Uzhhorod: RNG, 1936, pp. 147-151.

2089 Sozans'kyi, Ivan. "Poetychna tvorchist' Oleksandra Dukhnovycha." *Zapysky NTSh,* vol. 86 (L'viv, 1908), pp. 1-123.

2090 Spanovskii, Ia. *Russkii narod v Karpatakh.* Kiev, 1915.

2091 Spivak, Borys I. "Do pytannia pro uchast' trudiashchykh Zakarpattia u zakhysti Uhors'koï Radians'koï Respubliky u 1919 rotsi." *Dopovidi ta povidomlennia.* Seriia istorychna, no. 4. Uzhhorod: UDU, 1960, pp. 60-77.

2092 ———· *Narysy istoriï revolutsiinoï borot'by trudiashchykh Zakarpattia v 1930-1945 rokakh.* L'viv: Vyd. LU, 1963.

2092a ———· "Pid praporom Velykoho Zhovtnia: narysy pro revoliutsiinu borot'bu trudiashchykh Zakarpats'koï Ukraïny." *Duklia,* vol. 6, nos. 3 and 4 (Prešov, 1958), pp. 63-73 and 63-69.

2093 ———· *Storinky istoriï.* Uzhhorod: ZOV, 1962.

2094 ———· *U polum'i revoliutsiinykh boïv: do istoriï vynyknennia i diial'nosti pershykh komunistychnykh orhanizatsii na Zakarpats'kii Ukraïni.* Uzhhorod: ZOV, 1959.

2095 Spivak, Borys, and Troian, Mykhailo V. *40 nezabutnikh dniv: z istoriï borot'by za vladu Rad na Zakarpatti v 1919 rotsi.* Uzhhorod: Karpaty, 1967.

2096 Sreznevskii, Ivan. "Rus' Ugorskaia: otryvok iz opyta geografii russkago iazyka." *Viestnik Imperatorskago russkago geograficheskago obshchestva,* vol. 1, no. 1-2 (St. Petersburg, 1852), pp. 1-28.

2097 St., Gy. "A magyarországi oroszok." *Hazánk és külföld,* vol. 4 (Budapest, 1869), pp. 5-?

2098 Sta-. "Vzniká už národ podkarpatských Rusínů?" *Přítomnost,* vol. 9, no. 10 (Prague, 1932), p. 148.

2099 Staurovsky, M. M. "My russkije—Russians." *Kalendar' ARSS na hod 1932.* Homestead, Pa., 1932, pp. 36-42.

2100 Stavrovs'kyi, Omel'ian. *Slovats'ko-pol's'ko-ukraïns'ke prykordonnia do 18-ho stolittia.* Bratislava and Prešov: SPVVUL, 1967.

2101 Stefan, Augustin. *From Carpatho-Ruthenia to Carpatho-Ukraine.* New York: Carpathian Star Publishing Co., 1954.

2102 ———· "Contacts between Carpatho-Ukraine and L'viv." *L'viv: a Symposium on its 700th Anniversary.* Edited by V. Mudry. New York: Shevchenko Scientific Society, 1962, pp. 272-279.

2103 ———· *Karpats'kyi Berezen'.* Bridgeport, Conn.: Nash Uzhhorod, 1950.

2104 ———· "Khust, 1919-1939." *Al'manakh Homonu Ukraïny na rik 1959.* Toronto, 1959, pp. 81-87.

2105 ———· [Shtefan, Avhustyn]. "Kol'ory-herby i prapory Zakarpattia." *Al'manakh Provydinnia na rik 1971* (Philadelphia, Pa., 1970), pp. 156-161.

2106 ———· "Myths About Carpatho-Ukraine." *The Ukrainian Quarterly,* vol.

10, no. 3 (New York, 1954), pp. 219-226.

2107 ———· "Transcarpathia (Carpatho-Ukraine)." *Ukraine: A Concise Encyclopedia,* vol. 1. Toronto: University of Toronto Press for the Ukrainian National Association, 1963, pp. 850-856.

2108 ———· [Shtefan, Avhustyn]. *Ukraïns'ke viisko v Zakarpatti.* Toronto and New York: 'Visti Kombatant,' 1969.

2109 Štefánek, A. "Marmarošsky process a zahraničná politika našej monarchie." *Prúdy,* vol. 5, no. 6 (Ružomberok, 1914), pp. 241-258.

2110 Stepanovich, A. "Religiia i ukrainizm na Podkarpatskoi Rusi." *Zemledil'skii kalendar' na hod 1939.* Uzhhorod, 1938, pp. 84-88.

2111 Stepovyi, Iurko. *Sribna zemlia v ohni i v buri revoliutsiï.* OUN, 1947.

2112 Stercho, Peter G. *Diplomacy of Double Morality: Europe's Crossroads in Carpatho-Ukraine, 1919-1939.* New York: Carpathian Research Center, 1971.

2113 ———· "Dopomoha ODVU Karpats'kii Ukraïni." *Samostiina Ukraïna,* vol. 8, nos. 4 and 5 (Chicago, 1955), pp. 6-10 and 11-14.

2114 ———· "Heroichnyi zmah sribnoï zemli do voli." *Al'manakh 'Provydinnia' na rik 1969.* Philadelphia, 1969, pp. 85-106.

2115 ———· *Karpato-ukraïns'ka derzhava: do istoriï vyzvol'noï borot'by karpats'kykh ukraïntsiv v 1919-1939 rokakh.* Toronto: NTSh, 1965.

2116 ———· "Natsional'ne vidrodzhennia Karpats'koï Ukraïny." *Orhanizatsiia Ukraïns'kykh natsionalistiv: 1929-1954.* Paris: Persha ukraïns'ka drukarnia u Frantsiï, 1955, pp. 187-212.

2117 ———· "Masaryk i Karpats'ka Ukraïna." *Samostiina Ukraïna,* vol. 14, nos. 3 and 4 (Chicago, 1961), pp. 14-17 and 17-20.

2118 ———· "Rolia Karpats'koï Ukraïny v zaktualizuvanni vseukraïns'koho pytannia v mizhnarodnii politytsi 1938-1939 rr." *Samostiina Ukraïna,* vol. 11, nos. 7, 8, and 9 (Chicago, 1958), pp. 4-8, 8-10, and 18-20.

2119 ———· "Slovats'ko-ukraïns'ki vzaiemovidnosyny, 1938-1939." *Suchasnist',* vol. 5, no. 9 (Munich, 1965), pp. 85-101.

2120 ———· *Uriadova koordynatsiia operatsii madiars'kykh i pol's'kykh terorystiv u Karpats'kii Ukraïni v 1938-1939 rr.* Philadelphia: 'Amerika', 1971.

2121 Steuer, Lajos. "A csehek Ruszinszkói politikája." *Magyar szemle,* vol. 6, no. 4 (Budapest, 1929), pp. 367-369.

2122 Stransky, Hugo. "The Religious Life [of Jews] in Slovakia and Subcarpathian Ruthenia." *The Jews of Czechoslovakia,* vol. 2. Philadelphia and New York: Jewish Publication Society and Society for the History of Czechoslovak Jews, 1971, pp. 347-392.

2123 Stripskii, Konstantin. "Iazyk literaturnoi traditsii Podkarpatskoi Rusi." *Karpatskii sviet,* vol. 3, no. 9-10 (Uzhhorod, 1930), pp. 1083-1093. Also issued separately in Izdanie OIAD, no. 102. Uzhhorod, 1930. Reprinted in *Kalendar' ARSS na hod 1932.* Homestead, Pa., 1932, pp. 76-96; and in *Kalendar' OS na hod 1934,* pp. 73-83.

2124 Stryps'kyi, Hiiador. "Epyskop Mykh. Ol'shavskyi o relyhiinom polozheniu svoei dyotseziî." *Lyteraturna nedîlia,* vol. 4, no. 10 (Uzhhorod, 1944), pp. 117-119.

2125 ———· [Sztripszki, Hiador]. "Era Olšavickich v našej istorii." *Kalendar' GKS na hod 1932.* Homestead, Pa., 1932, pp. 70-79. Republished in English translation by George M. Parvenski: "The Era of the Olsavski Bishops in Our History." *Jubilee Almanac of the GKS.* Munhall, Pa., 1967, pp. 162-175.

2126 ———— [Strypskii, Iador H.]. *Hdî dokumentŷ starshei ystoriy Podkarpatskoi Rusy? O mezhevŷkh nazvaniiakh.* Uzhhorod, 1924.

2127 ———— [Th. Beregiensis]. "Iak narod dîlyt' sebe." *Lyteraturna nedîlia,* vol. 2 (Uzhhorod, 1942), pp. 185-189.

2128 ————· "Pochatky drukarstva na Podkarpatiu." *Zoria—Hajnal,* vol. 2, no. 3-4 (Uzhhorod, 1942), pp. 261-289.

2129 ———— [Bilen'kyi]. *Starsha rus'ka pys'mennost' na Uhorshchynî.* Uzhhorod: Aktsiine ob-vo Unio, 1907.

2130 ———— [Rusínsky, Beloň]. "Trnavská univerzita v službe unionistickej idey." *Pamiatka Trnavskej university 1635-1777.* Trnava, 1935, pp. 243-257.

2131 ————· "Vîden'skyi Bukvar' r. 1770." *Lyteraturna nedîlia,* vol. 3 (Uzhhorod, 1943), pp. 274-276.

2132 ————· [Sztripszky, Hiador]. "Volt-e könyvsajtó a máramarosi Körtvélyesen." *Zoria—Hajnal,* vol. 2, no. 1-2 (Uzhhorod, 1942), pp. 5-34.

2133 ————· "Z starshoï pys'mennosty Uhors'koï Rusy." *Zapysky NTSh,* vol. 117-118 (L'viv, 1913), pp. 179-195.

2134 ————· "Zabludîlym sŷnam Podkarpatia." *Lyteraturnia nedîlia,* vol. 1, no. 14 (Uzhhorod, 1941), pp. 117-121.

2135 Studyns'kyi, Kyrylo. "Aleksander Dukhnovych i Halychyna." *Naukovŷi zbornyk TP,* vol. 3 (Uzhhorod, 1924), pp. 28-103.

2136 Šuhaj, Janko. *Carpathian Ruthenia on the Warpath.* London: New Europe Publishing Co., 1944.

2137 Suk, V. "Podkarpatoruští Rusíni před stodvacetı lety (s poznámkami Josefa Dobrovského)." *Podkarpatoruská revue,* vol. 1, no. 6 (Bratislava, 1936), pp. 1-4.

2138 Suprun, Dmytro. *Spokonvichna mriia zbulasia: komunisty Zakarpattia na choli borot'by trudiashchykh za vozz'iednannia z Radians'koiu Ukraïnoiu ta zdiisnennia sotsialistychnykh peretvoren' v oblasti.* Kiev: Vyd. Politychnoï literatury Ukraïny, 1969.

2139 Suško, Ladislav. "Nemecká politika voči Slovensku a Zakarpatskej Ukrajine v období od septembrovej krizy 1938 do rozbitia Československa v marci 1939." *Československý časopis historický,* vol. 21, no. 2 (Prague, 1973), pp. 161-197.

2140 "Rokovania o autónomii Zakarpatskej Ukrajiny od roku 1936 do leta 1938." *Nové obzory,* vol. 15 (Prešov, 1973), pp. 33-59.

2141 Svientsyts'kyi, Ilarion S. "Karpato-rus'ke rusofil'stvo." *Literaturno-naukovyi vistnyk* (L'viv, 1918), pp. 134-140.

2141a ————· "Kul'turno-natsional'nyi rukh na Zakarpatti i v Halychyni v XVIII-XIX v." *S'ohochasne i mynule,* vol. 1, no. 1 (L'viv, 1939), pp. 30-37.

2142 ———— [Svientsitskii, I. S.]. "Obzor snoshenii Karpatskoi Rusi s Rossiei v l-uiu pol. XIX v." *Izvestiia ORISIAN,* vol. 11, bk. 3 (St. Petersburg, 1906), pp. 259-367.

2143 Svistun, Filip I. "Vengerskaia Rus'." *Iliustrovannyi russko-amerikanskii kalendar' na 1913. god.* Olyphant, Pa. 1912, pp. 85-103.

2144 Sv-skii, M. "A. I. Dobrianskii i eho bor'ba za avtonomiiu Podkarpatskoi Rusy." *Zemledîl'skii kalendar' na hod 1935.* Uzhhorod, 1934, pp. 59-66.

Szabó, Eugen, *see* Sabov, Evgenii

2145 Szabó, István. "A rutén föld." *Magyar szemle,* vol. 34, no. 4 (Budapest, 1938), pp. 376-379.

2146 ———· *Ugocsa megye.* Magyarság és nemzetiség tanulmányok a magyar népiségtörténet köréböl, vol. 1. Budapest: MTA, 1937.

2147 Szabó, Jenő. *A görög-katholikus Magyarország utolsó kálvária útja.* Budapest, 1913.

2148 ———· *A magyarországi görög-katholikusok nyelvi statisztikája és az óhitű magyarság veszedelme.* Budapest, 19??.

2149 Szabó, Oreszt. *A magyar oroszokról (ruthenek).* Nemzetiségi ismertető könyvtár, vol. 1. Budapest, 1913, chapters 1-3. Translated into Vojvodinian Rusyn by Simeon Sakach: "O uhrorusokh (rutenokh)." *Nova dumka,* vol. 5, no. 12 (Vukovar, 1976), pp. 97-108.

Szova-Gmitrov, Peter, *see* Sova, Peter P.

Sztripszky, Hiador, *see* Stryps'kyi, Hiiador

2150 Tajták, Ladislav. *Národnodemokratická revolúcia na východnom Slovensku v roku 1918.* Acta Facultatis Philosophicae Universitatis Šafarikanea, Monograph no. 6. Bratislava, 1972.

2151 ———· [Taitak, V.]. "Pereselennia ukraïntsiv Skhidnoï Slovachchyny do 1913 r." *Duklia,* vol. 9, no. 4 (Prešov, 1961), pp. 97-103.

2152 Tan'chak, K. *Mizh Madiarshchynoiu, Pol'shcheiu i Chekhoslovachchynoiu.* Uzhhorod, 1936.

2153 Tarján, Ödön, and Fall, A. *Hungarians, Slovaks and Ruthenians in the Danubian Valley.* Budapest, 1938.

2154 Terletskii, Vladimir. *Ugorskaia Rus' i vozrozhdenie soznaniia narodnosti mezhdu russkimi v Vengrii.* Kiev, 1874.

2155 Tichý, František. "Bohuš Nosák a Podkarpatské Rusıni." *Sborník Matice Slovenskej,* vol. 5, no. 1-2 (Turčiansky Sv. Martin, 1927), pp. 1-11.

2156 ———· "Dejiny podkarpatsko-ruského literárného spolku prešovského." *Slovenské pohl'ady,* vol. 40 (Turčiansky Sv. Martin, 1924), pp. 468-471.

2157 ———· "Drobné příspěvky k studiu literární kultury Podkarpatské Rusi." *Sborník věnovaný Jaroslavu Bidlovi.* Prague, 1928, pp. 372-375.

2158 ———· "Fr. L. Rieger či A. I. Dobrjanskij?" *Naša doba,* vol. 28 (Prague, 1921), pp. 325-333.

2159 ———· "Iz slovats'ko-ukraïns'kykh zv'iazkiv u p'iatdesiatykh i shistdesiatykh rokakh mynuloho stolittia." *Z istoriï chekhoslovats'ko-ukraïns'kykh zv'iazkiv.* Bratislava: SVKL, 1959, pp. 588-593.

2160 ———· "Josef Dobrovský a Podkarpatská Rus." *Josef Dobrovský: sborník statí k stému výročí smrti.* Prague, 1929, pp. 332-343.

2161 ———· "Náboženský a církevní problém Podkarpatské Rusi." *Kalích,* vol. 2 (Prague, 1922), pp. 114-123.

2162 ———· "Písemnictví na Podkarpatské Rusi." *Podkarpatská Rus.* Edited by J. Chmelař et al. Prague: Orbis, 1923, pp. 151-160.

2163 ———· "Podkarpatoruské písemnictví v dvojím zrcadle." *Slovanský přehled,* vol. 18 (Prague, 1926), pp. 340-350.

2164 ———· "Prvá vlna západnictví v písemnictví podkarpatském." *Sborník prací věnovaných profesoru dru. Janu Máchalu 1855-1925*. Prague: Klub moderních filologů, 1925, pp. 268-276.

2165 ———· "Prvý podkarpatoruský umělecký projev literární." *Naukovyi zbirnyk TP*, vols. 13-14 (Uzhhorod, 1938), pp. 14-20.

2166 ———· "Styky větve podkarpatoruské s československou v době literárního romantismu." *Atheneum*, vol. 1, no. 1 (Prague, 1922), pp. 64-69.

2167 ———· *Vývoj současného spisovného jazyka na Podkarpatské Rusi*. KSVSPR, vol. 11. Prague: Orbis, 1938.

2168 ———, et al. "Podkarpatská Rus." *Ottův slovník naučný: nové doby*, vol. 4 pt. 2. Prague, 1937, pp. 1156-1167.

2169 Tilkovszky, Loránt. "A csehszlovák földreform magyar reviziója az első bécsi döntéssel átcsatolt területen (1938-1945)," *Különlenyomat az agrártörténeti szemle*, no. 1-2 (Budapest, 1964), pp. 113-142.

2170 ———· *Revizió és nemzetiségpolitika Magyarországon 1938-1941*. Budapest: Akadémiai kiadó, 1967.

2171 Tkachenko, L. O. "Dynamika etnichnoho skladu naselennia Zakarpattia." *Narodna tvorchist' ta etnohrafiia*, vol. 50, no. 1 (Kiev, 1974), pp. 65-68.

2172 Tokar, H.S. "Rozrobka pytan' rosiis'koho movoznavstva na Zakarpatti za roky radians'koï vlady." *Velykyi Zhovten' i rozkvit vozz'iednanoho Zakarpattia*. Uzhhorod: Karpaty, 1970, pp. 558-576.

2173 Tomashivs'kyi, Stepan [Tomashevskii, S.]. "Ugorskaia Rus'." *Ukrainskii narod v ego proshlom i nastoiashchem*, vol. 2. Petrograd, 1916, pp. 412-426.

2174 ———· "Uhors'ki rusyny v svitli uriadovoï uhors'koï statystyky." *Zapysky NTSh*, vol. 61 (L'viv, 1903), pp. 1-46.

2175 Török, Péter. *Délibáb a Verchovinán*. Nyiregyháza, 1929.

2176 "Törvényjavaslat a Kárpátaljai vajdaságról és annak önkormányzatáról." *Kisebbségi körlevel*, vol. 2 (Pécs, 1940), pp. 37-47.

2177 *Tradytsyina kultura iugoslavianskykh Rusynokh*. Novi Sad: 'Ruske Slovo,' 1971.

2178 "Tragediia sribnoï zemli." *Vistnyk*, vol. 7, no. 4 (L'viv, 1939), pp. 296-298.

2179 *The Tragedy of the Greek Catholic Church in Czechoslovakia*. New York: Carpathian Alliance, 1971.

2180 Troian, Mykhailo V. "Borot'ba trudiashchykh Mukachivshchyny za Radians'ku vladu v 1918-1919 rr." *Naukovi zapysky UDU*, vol. 30 (Uzhhorod, 1957), pp. 67-84.

2181 ———· *Uhors'ka komuna 1919 r.*. L'viv: LU, 1970.

2182 ———· "Ustanovlennia Radians'koï vlady na Zakarpatti ta borot'ba za ïï zmitsnennia v 1919 r." *Naukovi zapysky UDU*, vol. 46 (Uzhhorod, 1958), pp. 55-70.

2183 ———· "Vplyv velykoï zhovtnevoï sotsialistychnoï revoliutsiï na rozhortannia revoliutsiinoho rukhu v Zakarpatti (1917-1919 rr.)." *Velykyi Zhovten' i rozkvit vozz'iednanoho Zakarpattia*. Uzhhorod: Karpaty, 1970, pp. 110-127.

2184 Troitskii, S. *Kak zhivut i stradaiut pravoslavnye uniaty v Avstro-Vengrii*. St. Petersburg, 1914.

2185 Tsurkanovich, Ilarion [Curkanovič, Harion J.]. *Ideové směrnice karpato-*

ruských politických stran. Cyklus přednášek 'O ideologii československých politikých stran,' no. 10. Prague: Ústřední svaz československého studenstva, 1931.

2186 Turianitsa, Mikhail. "Avantiura galitskikh samostiinikov na Zakarpatskoi Rusi." *Svobodnoe slovo Karpatskoi Rusi,* vol. 1, nos. 1-2, 3-4, 5-6, and 7-8 (Newark, N.J., 1959), pp. 20-26, 27-29, 13-15, and 4-8.

2187 ———· "Tragediia molodezhi Zakarpatskoi Rusi." *Svobodnoe slovo Karpatskoi Rusi,* vol. 1, nos. 5-6, 7-8, and 9-10 (Newark, N.J., 1959), pp. 22-26, 10-13, and 2-4.

2188 Tvorydlo, Mykhailo [Ortoskop]. *Derzhavni zmahannia Prykarpats'koï Ukraïny.* Vienna: Vyd. Nova hromada, 1924.

2189 Udovychenko, Hryhorii. "Styl' i mova opovidan' M. Tomchaniia." *Karpaty,* vol. 11, no. 3 (Uzhhorod, 1958), pp. 65-68.

2190 Ugroruss. "Latinizatsiia i mad'iarizatsiia russkikh v Vengrii." *Russkoe obozrienie,* vol. 4 (Moscow, 1893), pp. 634-656.

2191 "Uhorskaia Rus'." *Ungvarskii russkii kalendar' sv. Mariy Povchanskoi na 1917 hod.* Máriapócs, 1917, pp. 67-91.

2192 Unbegaun, Boris. *L'origine du nom des ruthènes.* Onomastica, no. 5. Winnipeg: Académie ukrainiènne libre des sciences, 1953. Reprinted in his *Selected Papers on Russian and Slavonic Philology.* Oxford: Clarendon Press, 1969, pp. 128-135.

2193 Uram, Pavlo. "Rozvytok ukraïns'koho shkil'nytstva v 1948-1953 rr." *Zhovten' i ukraïns'ka kul'tura.* Prešov: KSUT, 1968, pp. 523-535.

2194 Usenko, Vasyl' V. *Vplyv Velykoï Zhovtnevoï sotsialistychnoï revoliutsiï na rozvytok revoliutsiinoho rukhu v Zakarpatti v 1917-1919 rr.* Kiev: ANURSR, 1955.

2195 *V pamiat Aleksandra Dukhnovycha 1803-1923.* Knyzhky Rusyna, no. 8. Uzhhorod, 1923.

2196 V. O. "Ob unii vengerskikh rusinov." *Russkaia besieda,* vol. 4 (Moscow, 1859), pp. 1-50.

2197 Vaida, Mykola. "Pered vidznachenniam 50-richchia Plastu na Zakarpatti (1921-1951)." *Visnyk Karpats'koho soiuzu,* vol. 2, nos. 2-3 (New York, 1971), pp. 10-11.

2198 Valičová, Božena. *Z bratrské země: kapitoly z Podkarpatské Rusi z let 1922-1931.* Kolín, 1932.

2199 Vanat, Ivan. "Do deiakykh pytan' zakordonnoï vyzvol'noï borot'by zakarpats'kykh ukraïntsiv pid chas druhoï svitovoï viiny." *Zhovten' i ukraïns'ka kul'tura.* Prešov: KSUT, 1968, pp. 351-369.

2200 ———· "Do kul'turno-natsional'nykh problem ukraïntsiv Priashivshchyny v period domiunkhens'koï respubliky." *Druzhno vpered,* vol. 17, no. 6 (Prešov, 1967), pp. 18-19.

2201 ———· "Do pytannia vzhyvannia terminiv 'Zakarpattia' ta 'Priashivshchyna'." *Zhovten' i ukraïns'ka kul'tura.* Prešov: KSUT, 1968, pp. 602-603.

2202 ———· "K niekotorým otázkam zahraničného odboja zakarpatských Ukrajincov počas druhej svetovej vojny." *Zhovten' i ukraïns'ka kul'tura.* Prešov: KSUT, 1968, pp. 351-369.

2203 ———· "Shkil'ne pytannia na Priashivshchyni pid chas domiunkhens'koï respubliky." *Duklia,* vol. 14, nos. 5 and 6 (Prešov, 1966), pp. 60-68 and 59-64.

2204 ———· "Ukrajinská otázka na Slovensku v rokoch 1918-1929." Doctoral dissertation, University of Bratislava, 1968.

2205 ———· "Zakarpats'ki ukraintsi v chekhoslovats'komu viis'ku v SRSR." *Duklia,* vol. 12, no. 3 (Prešov, 1964), pp. 47-50.

2206 ———· "Zakarpats'ki ukraïntsi v chekhoslovats'komu viis'ku v SRSR." *Shliakh do voli, Naukovyi zbirnyk MUKS,* vol. 2 (Bratislava, Prešov, and Svidník, 1966), pp. 183-201.

2207 Váradi-Sternberg, János. *Utak, találkozások, emberek: írások az orosz-magyar és ukrán-magyar kapcsolatokról.* Uzhhorod and Budapest: Kárpáti és Gondolat, 1974.

2208 Várady, Gábor. *A magyarországi oroszokról.* Sighet: A Máramarosi részvénynyomda, 1895.

2209 Varkhola, Vasyl'. "Ukraïns'ki radioperedachi." *Duklia,* vol. 17, no. 4 (Prešov, 1969), pp. 3-6.

2210 Vasica, J. "Katolická církev u podkarpatských rusínů." *Rodinná katolická čítanka.* Nový Jičín, 1922, pp. 71-85.

2211 ———· "Na Podkarpatské Rusi." *Apoštolát sv. Cyrila a Metoděje,* vol. 17 (Olomouc, 1926), pp. 41-47, 148-157.

2212 ———· "O Podkarpatské Rusi." *Časopis Vlastenecké musejní společností v Olomouci,* vol. 39 (Olomouc, 1928), pp. 164-171.

2213 ———· "Vývoj písemnictví na Podkarpatské Rusi." *Časopis Vlasteneckého spolku musejního v Olomouci,* vol. 34 (Olomouc, 1923), pp. 57-72.

2214 Vasilenko, Mikhail I. "Uchitel'skoe Tovarishchestvo Podkarpatskoi Rusi." *Russkii narodnyi kalendar' na god 1937.* Izdanie OIAD, no. 115. Uzhhorod, 1936, pp. 89-90.

2215 Vasil'ev, A. F. *Zarubezhnaia Rus'.* Petrograd, 1915.

2216 Vasilevskii, L. [Plokhotskii]. "Vengerskie 'rusnaki' i ikh sud'ba." *Russkoe bogatstvo,* no. 3 (St. Petersburg, 1914), pp. 362-385.

2217 Vavrik, Vasilii R. *Karpatorossy v Kornilovskom pokhodie i Dobrovol'-cheskoi Armii.* L'viv, 1923.

2218 *Velykyi Zhovten' i rozkvit vozz'iednanoho Zakarpattia.* Uzhhorod: Karpaty, 1970. A collection of fifty-one papers from a conference held in Uzhhorod on June 29-July 2, 1967 that was dedicated to the fiftieth aniversary of the Bolshevik Revolution. Includes studies by M. Boldyzhar, V. Hanchyn, A. Ihnat, I. Kashula, V. Kerechanyn, V. Khainas, P. Lisovyi, S. Peniak, A. Popovych, T. Seheda, F. Shevchenko, I. Shul'ha, P. Sirko, and M. Troian.

2219 Venelin, Iurii I. "Nieskol'ko slov o Rossiianakh Vengerskikh, i takzhe odno slovtso istoricheskoe o Pravoslavnoi Greko-Vostochnoi Tserkvi v Vengrii." *Materialy po istorii vozrozhdeniia Karpatskoi Rusi,* vol. 1. Edited by I.S. Svientsitskii. L'viv, 1905, pp. 93-96.

2220 "Die verfassungsrechtliche Stellung der Karpaten-Ukraine." *Nation und Staat,* vol. 12 (Vienna, 1938-1939), pp. 397-412.

2221 Vergun, Dmitrii N. "Karpatorusskaia literatura: kratkii ocherk." *Vosem' lektsii o Podkarpatskoi Rusi.* Edited by D. N. Vergun. Prague, 1925, pp. 47-60. Published separately: Prague, 1925.

2222 ——· "Opatření rakouského ministra Alexandra Bacha k ochromení karpatského obrození r. 1849-50." *Zapiski nauchno-izsliedovatel'skago ob"edineniia Russkago svobodnago universiteta,* vol. 8 (Prague, 1938), pp. 227-240.

2223 ——, ed. *Vosem' lektsii o Podkarpatskoi Rusi.* Prague: Izd. Cheshskoi shkoly politicheskikh uchenii, 1925. Also in Czech: *Osm přednášek o Podkarpatské Rusi.* Prague, 1925. A collection of eight lectures originally given at Charles University between November 1924 and March 1925. The lectures analyze political and cultural problems and include contributions by V. Dvorský, K. Kadlec, I. Krypinskii, I. Semerad, and D. Vergun.

2224 Vernadskii, Georgii. "Ugorskaia Rus' i eia vozrozhdenie v seredinie XIX vieka." *Golos minuvshago,* vol. 3, no. 3 (Moscow, 1915), pp. 5-17.

2225 Vico, Fedor. "Ohlas maďarskej republiky rád v ukrajinských obciach Zakarpatska." *Nové obzory,* vol. 1 (Prešov, 1959), pp. 47-51.

2226 Vilinskii, Valerii S. *Korni edinstva russkoi kul'tury.* Izdanie OIAD, no. 37. Uzhhorod, 1928.

2227 Vodovozov, N. V. "Russkie pisateli v Chekhoslovakii." *Russkaia literatura i narodnoe tvorchestvo.* Edited by A. I. Reviakin. Uchenye zapiski Moskovskogo gosudarstvennogo pedagogicheskogo instituta, vol. 178. Moscow, 1962, pp. 186-218.

2228 Vojtěch, Lev. *Brána na východ (Karpatská Rus).* Prague: Československá socialně demokratická strana, 1920.

2229 Volkonskii, Aleksander M. "'V chem glavnaia opasnost'? Maloruss ili ukrainets?" *Karpatskii sviet,* vol. 2, no. 4 (Uzhhorod, 1929), pp. 493-500. Also in Izdanie OIAD, no. 69 (Uzhhorod, 1929).

2230 Voloshchuk, Illia. "Politychni vidnosyny v chekhoslovats'komu viis'ku v SRSR." *Shliakh do voli. Naukovyi zbirnyk,* vol. 2 (Bratislava, Prešov, and Svidník, 1966), pp. 214-220.

2231 ——· *Sovremennaia ukrainskaia literatura v Chekhoslovakii.* Bratislava: SVKL, 1957.

2232 ——· "Zakarpats'ki ukraïntsi v chekhoslovats'komu viis'ku v SRSR." *Duklia,* vol. 23, no. 3 (Prešov, 1975), pp. 64-67.

2233 Voloshyn, Avhustyn [Vološin, Augustin]. "Carpathian Ruthenia." *The Slavonic and East European Review,* vol. 13 (London, 1935), pp. 372-378.

2234 ——· "Demokratychna shkôl'na systema (Do pŷtania novelyzatsiî shk. zakonôv)." *Podkarpatska Rus',* vol. 5, no. 8-9 (Uzhhorod, 1928), pp. 181-186.

2235 ——· [Vološin, Augustin]. "Napady madarsjkych kommunistiv v 1919." *Vpad maďarských bol'ševikov na Slovensko v roku 1919.* Edited by J. Zimák. Bratislava: 1938, pp. 237-240.

2236 ——· "Oborona kyrylyky: iak oboronialysia pidkarp. rusyny proty ostann'oho ataku madiaryzatsiî pered perevorotom?" *Naukovyi zbirnyk TP,* vol. 12 (Uzhhorod, 1937), pp. 87-117.

2237 ——· *O pys'mennom iazŷtsî podkarpatskykh rusynov.* Vŷd. TP, Lyt. nauk. oddîl, no. 1. Uzhhorod, 1921.

2238 ———· Počátky národního probuzení na Podkarpatské Rusi.'' *Podkarpatská Rus.* Edited by J. Zatloukal. Bratislava: KPPR, 1936, pp. 53-56.

2239 ———· ''Řecko-katolická církev v Podkarpatské Rusi.'' *Podkarpatská Rus.* Edited by J. Chmelař et al. Prague: Orbis, 1923, pp. 99-112.

2240 ———· ''Relihiini vidnosyny na Pidk. Rusy.'' *Acta Conventus Pragensis pro Studiis Orientalibus anno 1929 celebrati,* Olomouc, 1930, pp. 218-222.

2241 ———· ''Zaisnovannia i rozvytok t-va Prosvita.'' *Narodnyi kalendar TP na rik 1939.* Uzhhorod, 1938, pp. 70-72.

2242 Voskresenskii, G. A. *Pravoslavnye slaviane v Avstro-Vengrii.* St. Petersburg, 1914.

2243 Vozniak, M. *Nash rodnŷi iazyk.* Knyzhky Rusyna, no. 15. Uzhhorod, 1923.

2244 Vyshnevs'kyi, Ivan. ''Ivan Franko i Zakarpattia.'' *Zhovten',* vol. 12, no. 12 (L'viv, 1962), pp. 131-134.

2245 ———· *Tradytsiï ta suchasnist'.* L'viv: Knyzhkovo-zhurnal'ne vyd., 1963.

2246 ———· *Zakarpats'ki novelisty.* L'viv: Vyd. LU, 1960.

2247 Wanklyn, Harriet. ''Sub-Carpathian Russia.'' In her *Czechoslovakia.* New York: Frederick A. Praeger, 1954, pp. 407-429.

2248 Warzeski, Walter C. *Byzantine Rite Rusins in Carpatho-Ruthenia and America.* Pittsburgh: Byzantine Seminary Press, 1971.

2249 Weidhass, Hermann. ''Karpatenrussland.'' *Osteuropa,* vol. 10, no. 8 (Berlin, 1935), pp. 482-492.

2250 Winter, Eduard. ''Die Kämpfe der Ukrainer Oberungarn um eine nationale Hierarchie im Theresianischen Zeitalter.'' *Kyrios,* vol. 11 (Königsberg, 1939-1940), pp. 129-141.

2251 *Z nahody desiat'litn'oho iuvileiu istnovannia tovarystva Prosvita na Pidkarpats'kii Rusy: 29. IV. 1920—29.VI.1930.* Vyd. TP, no. 152. Uzhhorod, 1930.

2252 ''Zakarpats'ka Ukraïna.'' *Ukraïns'ka radians'ka entsyklopedia,* vol. 5. Kiev: ANURSR, 1961.

2253 Zakarpatskii, D. G. ''Pravoslavnoe Mukachevskoe episkopstvo do zakliucheniia Uzhgorodskoi unii.'' *Ezhegodnik Pravoslavnoi tserkvi v Chekhoslovakii* (Prague, 1968), pp. 7-20.

2254 Zaklyns'kyi, Kornylo. ''Narys istoriï Krasnobrids'koho monastyria.'' *Naukovyi zbirnyk MUKS,* vol. 1 (Bratislava, Prešov, and Svidník, 1965), pp. 43-57.

2255 ———· *Narodnî opovîdannia pro davnynu.* Košice, 1925.

2256 Zapletal, Florian, *A. I. Dobrjanský a naši Rusíni r. 1849-51.* Prague, 1927.

2257 ———· ''Podkarpatská Rus části Veliké Moravy?'' *Časopis Vlasteneckého spolku musejního v Olomouci,* vol. 37 (Olomouc, 1926), pp. 120-121.

2258 ———· *Rusíni a naši buditelé.* Prague: Kolokol, 1921.

2259 *Za ridne slovo: polemika z rusofilamy.* Mukachevo: Uchytel's'ka hromada, 1937.

2260 Žatkovič, Gregor. ''La Podcarpatho-Russie.'' *Le Correspondant,* no. 279 (Paris, 1920), pp. 645-664.

2261 Zatloukal, Jaroslav, ed. *Podkarpatská Rus: sborník hospodářského, kulturního a politického poznání Podkarpatské Rusi.* Bratislava: KPPR, 1936. The most comprehensive one-volume study of the area, with sixty-seven articles on all aspects; includes contributions by S. Antalovskij, M. Bartoš, E. Beneš, V. Birchak, I. Bokshai, J. Brandejs, F. Gabriel, V. Hadzhega, A. Hartl, M. Hrabets', A. Il'nyts'kyi, J. Jirásek, L. Kaigl, V. Klofáč, K. Krofta, E. Nedziel'skii, I. Pan'kevych, J. Pešina, P. Popradov, A. Raušer, A. Rozsypal, P. Sova, and A. Voloshyn.

2262 Zawadowski, Zygmunt. *Ruś Podkarpacka i jej stanowisko prawnopolityczne.* Warsaw: Zakłady graficzne Straszewiczów, 1931.

2263 Zeedick, Peter I. "Korotkij očerk istoriji našeho naroda." *Zoloto-jubilejnyj kalendar' GKS na hod 1942.* Homestead, Pa., 1942, pp. 259-296.

2264 Žeguc, Ivan. *Die nationalpolitischen Bestrebungen der Karpato-Ruthenen 1848-1914.* Veröffentlichungen des Osteuropa-Institutes München, vol. 28. Wiesbaden: Otto Harrassowitz, 1965.

2265 Zerkal', Sava. *Natsional'ni i relihiini vidnosyny na Zakarpatti.* New York: Ukraïns'ka Hromada im. Shapovala, 1956.

2266 ———· *Ukraïns'ka zemlia i narid za Karpatamy,* vol. 1. Biblioteka 'Ukraïns'koho hromads'koho slova', no. 14. Paris and New York, 1976.

2267 Zhatkovych, Iurii [Zsatkovics, Kálmán]. "Az egri befolyás és az ez ellen vivott harcz a munkácsi görög szertartású egyházmegye történelmében." *Századok,* vol. 18 (Budapest, 1884), pp. 680-696, 766-786, and 839-877. Translated by P.I. Zeedick and A.M. Smor: *Jagerskoje vl'ijanije: bor'ba protiv toho v istorii mukačevskoj grečeskoho obrjada diocezii.* Homestead, Pa., 193?

2268 ———· "Episkopy Maramoroshkie." *Listok,* vol. 7, nos. 14-22 (Uzhhorod, 1891).

2269 ———· "Narys istoriï Hrushivs'koho monastyria na Uhors'kii Rusy." *Naukovyi zbirnyk prysviachenyi M. Hrushevs'komu.* L'viv, 1906, pp. 155-157.

2270 ———· [Zsatkovics, Kálmán]. "A magyaroroszági oroszok történetirásának történelme." *Századok,* vol. 24 (Budapest, 1890), pp. 568-573 and 644-660.

2271 ———· "Nîskol'ko slov o russkykh, zhyvuchykh v Uhorshchynî: istorycheskii ocherk." *Mîsiatsoslov na hod 1890.* Uzhhorod, 1889, pp. 68-76.

2272 Zhidovskii, Ivan. *Iazykovyia prava avtonomnoi Podkarpatskoi Rusi.* Prešov, 1930.

2273 ———· "Priashevskaia Rus' v bor'bie za svoi prava." *Podkarpatskaia Rus' za gody 1919-1936.* Edited by E. Bachinskii. Uzhhorod: RNG, 1936, pp. 87-91.

2274 ——— [Židovský, Ivan]. *Ruská otázka v Československu: věci Podk. Rusi.* Prešov and Uzhhorod: Ruská narodná strana, 1933.

2275 *Zhovten' i ukraïns'ka kul'tura: zbirnyk materialiv z mizhnarodnoho sympoziumu.* Prešov: KSUT, 1968. A collection of forty-three longer and twelve shorter papers delivered at a conference held in Prešov on December 6-8, 1967. Includes studies by Iu. Bacha, M. Danilák, S. Dobosh, S. Hapak, V. Hryvna, V. Kapishovs'kyi, V. Khoma, A. Kovach, M. Krhoun, P. Lisovyi, M. Mayer, M. Mushynka, F. Naumenko, O. Rudlovchak, I. Shelepets', M. Shtets', P. Uram, and I. Vanat.

Židovský, Ivan, *see* Zhidovskii, Ivan

2276 Zilyns'kyi, Ivan. "Mova zakarpats'kykh ukraïntsiv." *S'ohochasne i mynule,* vol. 1, no. 2 (L'viv, 1939), pp. 33-40. Also published separately: L'viv, 1939.

2277 Zilyns'kyi Orest, ed. *Literatura chekhoslovats'kykh ukraïntsiv 1945-1967: problemy i perspektyvy.* Bratislava and Prešov: SPVVUL, 1968.

2278 "Značenije Alexandra V. Duchnoviča v karpatorusskoj obščestvennoj žizni." *Kalendar' OS na hod 1936.* Perth Amboy, N.J., 1936, pp. 40-49.

2279 Zorkii, N. *Spor o iazykie v Podkarpatskoi Rusi i cheshskaia Akademiia Nauk.* Uzhhorod, 1926.

Zsatkovics, Kálmán, *see* Zhatkovych, Iurii

Index

(Italicized page numbers refer to information to be found in the Bibliography)

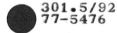